THE NEW
AMERICAN
COMMENTARY

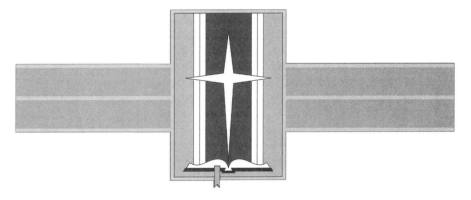

An Exegetical and Theological
Exposition of Holy Scripture

THE NEW
AMERICAN
COMMENTARY

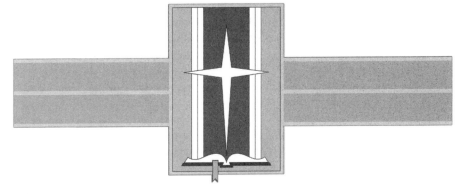

Volume
15B

ISAIAH 40-66

Gary V. Smith

PUBLISHING GROUP

Nashville, Tennessee

© Copyright 2009 • B&H Publishing Group
All rights reserved.
ISBN 978–0–8054–0144–8
Dewey Decimal Classification: 224.1
Subject Heading: BIBLE. O.T. ISAIAH
Printed in the United States of America
4 5 6 7 8 9 10   •   21 20 19 18 17
LB

Dedicated to

My son and daughter-in-law
Todd and Angela Smith
and our grandchildren
Charles and Bennett

"As a mother comforts her child,
so I will comfort you;
and you will be comforted over Jerusalem.
When you see this, your heart will rejoice
and you will flourish like the grass;
and the hand of the Lord will be made known to his servants."
(Isa 66:13–14)

Editors' Preface

God's Word does not change. God's world, however, changes in every generation. These changes, in addition to new findings by scholars and a new variety of challenges to the gospel message, call for the church in each generation to interpret and apply God's Word for God's people. Thus, THE NEW AMERICAN COMMENTARY is introduced to bridge the twentieth and twenty-first centuries. This new series has been designed primarily to enable pastors, teachers, and students to read the Bible with clarity and proclaim it with power.

In one sense THE NEW AMERICAN COMMENTARY is not new, for it represents the continuation of a heritage rich in biblical and theological exposition. The title of this forty-volume set points to the continuity of this series with an important commentary project published at the end of the nineteenth century called AN AMERICAN COMMENTARY, edited by Alvah Hovey. The older series included, among other significant contributions, the outstanding volume on Matthew by John A. Broadus, from whom the publisher of the new series, Broadman Press, partly derives its name. The former series was authored and edited by scholars committed to the infallibility of Scripture, making it a solid foundation for the present project. In line with this heritage, all NAC authors affirm the divine inspiration, inerrancy, complete truthfulness, and full authority of the Bible. The perspective of the NAC is unapologetically confessional and rooted in the evangelical tradition.

Since a commentary is a fundamental tool for the expositor or teacher who seeks to interpret and apply Scripture in the church or classroom, the NAC focuses on communicating the theological structure and content of each biblical book. The writers seek to illuminate both the historical meaning and contemporary significance of Holy Scripture.

In its attempt to make a unique contribution to the Christian community, the NAC focuses on two concerns. First, the commentary emphasizes how each section of a book fits together so that the reader becomes aware of the theological unity of each book and of Scripture as a whole. The writers, however, remain aware of the Bible's inherently rich variety. Second, the NAC is produced with the conviction that the Bible primarily belongs to the church. We believe that scholarship and the academy provide an indispensable foundation for biblical understanding and the service of Christ, but the editors and authors of this series have attempted to communicate the findings of their research in a manner that will build up the whole body of Christ. Thus, the commentary concentrates on theological exegesis while providing practical, applicable exposition.

THE NEW AMERICAN COMMENTARY's theological focus enable the reader to see the parts as well as the whole of Scripture. The biblical books vary in content, context, literary type, and style. In addition to this rich variety, the editors and authors recognize that the doctrinal emphasis and use of the biblical books differs in various places, contexts, and cultures among God's people. These factors, as well as other concerns, have led the editors to give freedom to the writers to wrestle with the issues raised by the scholarly community surrounding each book and to determine the appropriate shape and length of the introductory materials. Moreover, each writer has developed the structure of the commentary in a way best suited for expounding the basic structure and the meaning of the biblical books for our day. Generally, discussions relating to contemporary scholarship and technical points of grammar and syntax appear in the footnotes and not in the text of the commentary. This format allows pastors and interested laypersons, scholars and teachers, and serious college and seminary students to profit from the commentary at various levels. This approach has been employed because we believe that all Christians have the privilege and responsibility to read and seek to understand the Bible for themselves.

Consistent with the desire to produce a readable, up-to-date commentary, the editors selected the New International Version as the standard translation for the commentary series. The selection was made primarily because of the NIV's faithfulness to the original languages and its beautiful and readable style. The authors, however, have been given the liberty to differ at places from the NIV as they develop their own translations from the Greek and Hebrew texts.

The NAC reflects the vision and leadership of those who provide oversight for Broadman Press, who in 1987 called for a new commentary series that would evidence a commitment to the inerrancy of Scripture and a faithfulness to the classic Christian tradition. While the commentary adopts an "American" name, it should be noted some writers represent countries outside the United States, giving the commentary an international perspective. The diverse group of writers includes scholars, teachers, and administrators from almost twenty different colleges and seminaries, as well as pastors, missionaries, and a layperson.

The editors and writers hope that THE NEW AMERICAN COMMENTARY will be helpful and instructive for pastors and teachers, scholars and students, for men and women in the churches who study and teach God's Word in various settings. We trust that for editors, authors, and readers alike, the commentary will be used to build up the church, encourage obedience, and bring renewal to God's people. Above all, we pray that the NAC will bring glory and honor to our Lord who has graciously redeemed us and faithfully revealed himself to us in his Holy Word.

SOLI DEO GLORIA
The Editors

Author's Preface

The message of chapters 40–66 is above all else a word of comfort and good news. It offers hope for both the person who is weary because of the trials of life and for the person who may think that God has forgotten about them. These oracles of salvation offer God's strength because God is near to help and able to deliver his people from danger. Although God may seem to be far away at times, he never forgets his children and always is attentive to hear and answer their prayers. He is a God who is powerful because he has a strong arm and can overcome any obstacle. The major political and economic problems of this world amount to nothing in his eyes because he is able to direct the course of history. Thus the challenge is for every believer to gain an authentic understanding of just how great God really is. He is the Creator of the heavens and the earth, the one who knows the name of every star, the one who controls the rise and fall of nations and their leaders, the compassionate Redeemer of his people, the Holy one, and the King of this universe. Once a person begins to catch Isaiah's vision of God's incomparable power and his wonderful plans for this world, he can begin to rest in the knowledge that God can give each person who trusts in him the ability to overcome every threat and victoriously endure every challenge.

The prophesies in chaps. 40–66 do not predict that there will be no problems; in fact, the lives of the Israelites addressed in these oracles were full of problems. Some fell into sin and worshipped pagan gods, some were rebellious and stubborn so that they did not follow God's directions. Others prayed at pagan high places and offered useless sacrifices that did not honor God. Sin always causes a separation from God and usually results in some much needed divine discipline. But God has revealed in these prophecies the good news that his chosen Servant will bring into existence a new world of justice for all people in every nation and make possible a new covenant relationship with God. This Servant will suffer for the sins of others, bear the guilt for their sins, and take on himself the punishment that these sinners deserved. This Servant will be exalted for his work and will exalt all those who confess their sins and follow the path of the suffering Servant. Another part of this good news is found in a series of salvation proclamations about God's preparation of a glorious city in Zion where he will dwell in all his glory. He will bring all his servants to this wonderful place so that they can glorify God for the rest of eternity. People from all the nations of the earth will flock to Zion to join the millions of others praising God and glorifying his name. This will be a wonderful time when all the people on earth will be holy; there will be no sorrow or shame, and there will be peace in all the earth.

If this sounds like an inviting place to be, then it would be wise to spend some time reading the book of Isaiah to hear about all the details that are explained in these prophecies. These prophetic words were written to inform and to persuade people to join the millions who will be enjoying the most fulfilling experience that will be greater than anything they have ever imagined. Once people understand how great God is and what he plans to do for his people, many will want to confess their sins and be forgiven. Then they can confidently know that they will one day live in that holy city with God because their future destiny is secure.

Although God's marvelous thoughts and ways are far above and beyond any of our thoughts, God has given a glimpse into some of his thoughts in the prophecies in the book of Isaiah. It is a breathtaking story with unbelievably tragic failures by the enemies of God, but it also has a fantastic ending for those who love and serve God. The heights of God's wrath are illustrated as he tramples the wicked in his anger, but his tender love is illustrated by comparing him to a shepherd who gently carries his lambs to safety. These oracles record the preaching of a prophet who might be called an Old Testament evangelist. He gives his audience two choices, either glorify God and enjoy life in his presence forever or reject him and end up in that other terrible place where the fire never goes out and the worm never dies.

In the preface to volume one, which deals with Isaiah 1-39, I compared the writing of this commentary to the challenges of climbing Mount Everest. At that time I thought I knew the terrain of the mountain and many of the dangers of the trek, but as I have climbed to even higher peaks in chaps. 40-66, I realized again just how difficult this journey is. There are so many contradictory opinions on which path to take and so many different interpretations of the evidence within these prophecies that a person sometimes wonders which way to turn. To be safe it is sometimes easier to follow the path of great men who have blazed the trail through Isaiah in the past, but there are from time to time opportunities to blaze some new trails where few have ventured. I have learned much from the mistakes and the wisdom of past travelers through Isaiah, especially the great Dutch commentator J. L. Koole, but I have tried also to lay down some new trails for readers to examine, evaluate, and follow. Some will no doubt be rightly skeptical of these new trails and want to keep to the security of the old paths, but I invite all who read this commentary to expand their imagination about what these prophecies might be saying. I pray that some will offer additional evidence to enhance the perspective of these new paths and that some will correct ideas where mistakes were made so that the truth that God was sharing through this prophet will ultimately cause the light of God's word to shine more brightly to a world that needs to hear some good news for a change.

Although writing a commentary on Isaiah is a great challenge, it is not wisely done alone. The words of explanation are mine, but I gladly acknowledge the contributions of former teachers, fellow faculty members at Union University, and the outstanding commentaries that are available for our generation to study. I thank God for these people and the works that have shaped my approach to the Hebrew text and its interpretation. I also owe a great debt to those at B&H Publishers who have reviewed, edited, and improved the way things are said. I want to express a special word of thanks to E. Ray Clendenen and his staff for their care and faithfulness in publishing this study. I want to thank my wife Susan for her support all these years and for her careful reading of the manuscript to help remove as many errors as possible.

I am dedicating this volume to our son Todd and his family. Every believing parent prays that God will provide healthy and normal children who will grow up to love God and be his servants. One can only thank God for his grace in guiding them through life, for helping them to find a godly partner to marry, and for blessing them with children. My prayer is that my children and grandchildren will know the great joy of being God's servants. May all glory go to God for the great things that he will do.

Gary V. Smith
Union University
Jackson, TN

Abbreviations

Bible Books

Gen	Isa	Luke
Exod	Jer	John
Lev	Lam	Acts
Num	Ezek	Rom
Deut	Dan	1, 2 Cor
Josh	Hos	Gal
Judg	Joel	Eph
Ruth	Amos	Phil
1, 2 Sam	Obad	Col
1, 2 Kgs	Jonah	1, 2 Thess
1, 2 Chr	Mic	1, 2 Tim
Ezra	Nah	Titus
Neh	Hab	Phlm
Esth	Zeph	Heb
Job	Hag	Jas
Ps (pl. Pss)	Zech	1, 2 Pet
Prov	Mal	1, 2, 3 John
Eccl	Matt	Jude
Song	Mark	Rev

Commonly Used Sources

AASOR	Annual of the American Schools of Oriental Research
AB	Anchor Bible
ABD	*Anchor Bible Dictionary,* ed. D. N. Freedman, 6 vols., 1992
ABW	*Archaeology and the Biblical World*
AC	An American Commentary, ed. A. Hovey
AcOr	*Acta orientalia*
AEL	*Ancient Egyptian Literature,* M. Lichtheim, 3 vols., 1971–1980
AJSL	*American Journal of Semitic Languages and Literature*
Akk	Akkadian
ALUOS	*Annual of Leeds University Oriental Society*
AnBib	Analecta Biblica
ANEP	*Ancient Near East in Pictures Relating to the Old Testament,* ed. J. B. Pritchard
ANET	*Ancient Near Eastern Texts,* ed. J. B. Pritchard, 1969
ANETS	Ancient Near Eastern Texts and Studies
AOAT	Alter Orient und Altes Testament
AOTS	*Archaeology and Old Testament Study,* ed. D. W. Thomas, 1967

ArOr	Archiv orientální
ASTI	*Annual of the Swedish Theological Institute*
ATANT	Abhandlungen zur Theologie des Alten und Neuen Testaments
ATD	Das Alte Testament Deutsch
ATR	*Anglican Theological Review*
Aug	*Augustinianum*
AusBR	*Australian Biblical Review*
BA	*Biblical Archaeologist*
BAR	*Biblical Archaeology Review*
BASOR	*Bulletin of the American Schools of Oriental Research*
BBR	*Bulletin for Biblical Research*
BDAG	W. Bauer, F. W. Danker, W. F. Arndt, and F. W. Gingrich, *Greek-English Lexicon of the New Testament,* 1999
BDB	F. Brown, S. R. Driver, and C. A. Briggs, *Hebrew and English Lexicon of the Old Testament,* 1907
BETL	Bibliotheca ephemeridum theologicarum lovaniensium
BFCT	Beiträge zur Förderung christlicher Theologie
BFT	Biblical Foundations in Theology
BHS	*Biblia Hebraica Stuttgartensia,* ed. K. Elliger and W. Rudolph, 1983
Bib	*Biblica*
BJRL	*Bulletin of the John Rylands University Library of Manchester*
BKAT	Biblischer Kommentar: Altes Testament
BO	*Bibliotheca orientalis*
BRev	*Bible Review*
BSac	*Bibliotheca Sacra*
BSC	Bible Study Commentary
BST	The Bible Speaks Today
BT	*Bible Translator*
BTB	*Biblical Theology Bulletin*
BurH	*Buried History*
BV	*Biblical Viewpoint*
BWANT	Beiträge zur Wissenschaft vom Alten und Neuen Testament
BZ	*Biblische Zeitschrift*
BZAW	Beihefte zur ZAW
CAD	*The Assyrian Dictionary of the Oriental Institute of the University of Chicago,* ed. I. Gelb, et al., 1956–
CAH	Cambridge Ancient History
CBSC	Cambridge Bible for Schools and Colleges
CBC	Cambridge Bible Commentary
CBQ	*Catholic Biblical Quarterly*
CC	Continental Commentaries
CHAL	*Concise Hebrew and Aramaic Lexicon,* ed. W. L. Holladay, 1971

IDB	*Interpreter's Dictionary of the Bible,* ed. G. A. Buttrick et al., 4 vols. 1962
IDBSup	*IDB Supplementary Volume,* ed. K. Crim, 1976
IEJ	*Israel Exploration Journal*
IES	Israel Exploration Society
Int	*Interpretation*
IOS	Israel Oriental Society
ISBE	*International Standard Bible Encyclopedia,* rev. ed. G. W. Bromiley, 4 vols., 1979–1988
IJT	*Indian Journal of Theology*
ITC	International Theological Commentary
JANES	*Journal of Ancient Near Eastern Society*
JAOS	*Journal of the American Oriental Society*
JBL	*Journal of Biblical Literature*
JBR	*Journal of Bible and Religion*
JCS	*Journal of Cuneiform Studies*
JEA	*Journal of Egyptian Archaeology*
JETS	*Journal of the Evangelical Theological Society*
JJS	*Journal of Jewish Studies*
JNES	*Journal of Near Eastern Studies*
JNSL	*Journal of Northwest Semitic Languages*
JPOS	*Journal of Palestine Oriental Society*
JQR	*Jewish Quarterly Review*
JSJ	*Journal for the Study of Judaism in the Persian, Hellenistic, and Roman Period*
JSNT	*Journal for the Study of the New Testament*
JSOR	*Journal of the Society for Oriental Research*
JSOT	*Journal for the Study of the Old Testament*
JSOTSup	JSOT—Supplement Series
JSPSup	*Journal for the Study of the Pseudepigrapha Supplement Series*
JSS	*Journal of Semitic Studies*
JTS	*Journal of Theological Studies*
JTSNS	*Journal of Theological Studies, New Series*
KAT	Kommentar zum Alten Testament
KB	Koehler and W. Baumgartner, *Lexicon in Veteris Testamenti libros,* ed. E. Vogt, 1971
KTU	*Die keilalphabetischen Texte aus Ugarit.* Ed. M. Dietrich, O. Loretz, and J. Sanmartin. Münter, 1995.
LCC	Library of Christian Classics
LLAVT	*Lexicon Linguae Aramaicae Veteris Testamenti,* ed. E. Vogt. Pontificium Institutum Biblicum, 1971
LTQ	*Lexington Theological Quarterly*
LQ	*Lutheran Quarterly*

MT	Masoretic Text
NAC	New American Commentary
NCBC	New Century Bible Commentary
NEASB	*Near East Archaeological Society Bulletin*
NIB	New Interpreter's Bible. 12 vols. Abingdon, 1994–1998
NIBC	New International Biblical Commentary
NICOT	New International Commentary on the Old Testament
NIVAC	NIV Application Commentary
NJPS	*Tanakh: The Holy Scriptures: The New JPS Translation according to the Traditional Hebrew Text*
NKZ	*Neue kirchliche Zeitschrift*
NovT	*Novum Testamentum*
NovTSup	Novum Testamentum Supplements
NTS	*New Testament Studies*
Or	*Orientalia*
OTE	*Old Testament Essays*
OTG	Old Testament Guides
OTL	Old Testament Library
OTS	*Old Testament Studies*
OTWSA	*Ou-Testamentiese Werkgemeenskap in Suid-Afrika*
PaVi	*Parole di Vita*
PCB	*Peake's Commentary on the Bible,* ed. M. Black and H. H. Rowley
PEQ	*Palestine Exploration Quarterly*
POT	De Prediking van het Oude Testament
POTT	*Peoples of Old Testament Times,* ed. D. J. Wiseman
QD	Quaestiones disputatae
RA	*Revue d'assyriologie et d'archéologie orientale*
RB	*Revue biblique*
ResQ	*Restoration Quarterly*
RevExp	*Review and Expositor*
RivB	*Revista biblica italiana*
RSR	*Recherches de science religieuse*
RTR	*Reformed Theological Review*
SANE	Sources from the Ancient Near East
SBJT	*Southern Baptist Journal of Theology*
SBLDS	Society of Biblical Literature Dissertation Series
SBLSCS	Society of Biblical Literature Septuagint and Cognate Studies
SBT	Studies in Biblical Theology
ScrB	*Scripture Bulletin*
SEAJT	South East Asia Journal of Theology
SJOT	*Scandinavian Journal of Theology*
SJT	*Scottish Journal of Theology*
SP	Samaritan Pentateuch

SR	Studies in Religion/Sciences religieuses
ST	*Studia theologica*
SthU	*Schweizerische theologische Umschau*
STJD	Studies on the Texts of the Desert of Judah
SwJT	*Southwestern Journal of Theology*
Syr	Syriac
TANE	*The Ancient Near East: An Anthology of Texts and Pictures,* ed. J. B. Pritchard. Princeton University Press, 1958
TB	Theologische Bücherei: Neudrucke und Berichte aus dem 20. Jahrhaudert
TDNT	*Theological Dictionary of the New Testament,* ed. G. Kittel and G. Friedrich. Trans. G. W. Bromiley. 10 vols. Eerdmans, 1964–1976
TDOT	*Theological Dictionary of the Old Testament,* ed. G. J. Botterweck and H. Ringgren, 8 vols., 1974–2006
Tg	Targum
TJ	*Trinity Journal*
TLOT	*Theological Lexicon of the Old Testament,* ed. E. Jenni and C. Westermann. Trans. M. E. Biddle. 3 vols. Hendrickson, 1997
TLZ	*Theologische Literaturzeitung*
TMSJ	*The Master's Seminary Journal*
TOTC	Tyndale Old Testament Commentaries
TS	*Theological Studies*
TWAT	*Theologisches Wörterbuch zum Alten Testament,* ed. G. J. Botterweck and H. Ringgren
TWOT	*Theological Wordbook of the Old Testament,* ed. R. L. Harris, G. L. Archer Jr., B. K. Waltke. 2 vols. Moody, 1980
TynBul	*Tyndale Bulletin*
TZ	*Theologische Zeitung*
UF	*Ugarit-Forschungen*
Vg	Vulgate
VT	*Vetus Testamentum*
VTSup	Vetus Testamentum, Supplements
WBC	Word Biblical Commentaries
WEC	Wycliffe Exegetical Commentary
WTJ	*Westminster Theological Journal*
WMANT	Wissenschaftliche Monographien zum Alten und Neuen Testament
ZABR	*Zeitschrift für altorientalische und biblische Rechtsgeschichte*
ZAW	*Zeitschrift für die alttestamentliche Wissenschaft*
ZDMG	*Zeitschrift der deutschen morgenländischen Gesellschaft*
ZDPV	*Zeitschrift des deutschen Palätina-Vereing*
ZKT	*Zeitschrift für katholische Theologie*

OTHER ABBREVIATIONS

Cf. confer, compare, see
fem. feminine
Hb. Hebrew
lit. literal(ly)
LXX Septuagint
masc. masculine
ms(s) manuscript(s)
pers. person (1st, 2nd, or 3rd)
pl. plural
sg. singular
v(v). verse(s)

Contents

Isaiah 40–66

———————————————   **INTRODUCTION**   ———————————————
1. Introduction

As C. R. Seitz has already recognized in his "Introduction" to Isaiah 40–66, it is quite odd to have another "Introduction" added in the middle of a commentary on a book of the Bible.[1] Most novels, history books, and textbooks do not have a second introduction inserted about halfway through the book. This is not usually done with other biblical books, so why is it done here? Some might excuse another introduction at this point because most other commentary series have a second introduction before chap. 40 and even a third introduction before chap. 56–66 (they view these as separate books by different authors), but if this material was originally written and canonized as one book, surely the most logical thing to do would be to develop one introduction at the beginning of Isaiah.

In light of this problem, the "Introduction" that is found here should properly be seen as a continuation or supplement to the introductory material preceding the exegesis of chaps. 1–39.[2] This continuation of the introductory material will not address the same issues that were discussed in volume 1, but will focus only on the different approaches to interpreting chaps. 40–66, questions about the setting of these chapters, the structure of the material, the theology, and several key interpretive issues that are unique to chaps. 40–66. There are three practical reasons for separating these issues from the initial introduction before chaps. 1–39. First, the length of the book of Isaiah is enormous, and the material varies considerably; thus it is logistically difficult and methodologically problematic to deal with all these issues at one time. Even if all the introductory issues were put in one place, it would be necessary to deal with the various unique issues of these chapters in a separate section of that initial introduction. Second, those who are investigating the book of Isaiah need to know about the different methods of interpreting chaps. 40–66 when they are ready to start studying chap. 40–66. Third, putting these issues here in this volume makes them readily available for consultation by those who are beginning to wrestle with these chapters.[3]

2. The Larger Structural Organization of 40–66

It is widely believed that the larger structural markers within chaps. 40–66 demonstrate that there is a literary organization of these chapters into two main groups: chaps. 40–55 and chaps. 56–66. Although some believe this grouping

---

[1] C. R. Seitz, "The Book of Isaiah 40–66," *NIB* 6:309–14.

[2] G. V. Smith, *Isaiah 1–39*, NAC (Nashville: B&H, 2007), 21–87. It covered the historical and religious background, the life and role of the prophet, the Masoretic, Greek, Aramaic, and Qumran textual witness, composition, and theology of chaps. 1–39.

[3] It would be cumbersome to have to refer back to volume 1 while one is working on material covered in volume 2. Since new issues arise that are unrelated to 1–39, now is the time to address them.

of chapters begins at chap. 34[4] and a few others suggest a different ending point other than chap. 55,[5] most commentators conclude that chap. 40 starts a new section and chap. 55 ends this literary unit. This division of the text is partially based on the fact that the narrative about Sennacherib's attack on Jerusalem ends the last section of chap. 1–39. R. Melugin believes this literary unit extends from chap. 40 through 55 because 40:1–11 appears to be a prologue and chap. 55:6–13 is written like an epilogue.[6] Both passages deal with some of the same motifs, thus creating an *inclusio*. One of those motifs is the idea that the word of the Lord will stand forever (40:8), which is similar to the conclusion that when God's word goes forth it accomplishes what God desires (55:11). The call to seek God and repent in 55:6–7 is also what one might expect in a concluding chapter that calls people to action or to make a decision to follow God. In addition, chap. 56 appears to introduce a new literary unit with its discussion of the need for the foreigner and eunuch to act justly, hold fast to the covenant, and keep the Sabbath. Since several other literary units end with a hymn (12:1–6; 42:10–13; 44:23), the final hymn in 55:12–13 is an additional sign that chap. 55 functions as a conclusion to the preceding group of chapters. This leaves chaps. 56–66 as the final literary unit in the book of Isaiah. Since these two groups of chapters have many unique problems and commentators interpret them quite differently, they will be discussed separately.

---

[4] J. D. W. Watts, *Isaiah 34–66*, WBC (Waco: Word, 1987), 7, and R. K. Harrison, *Introduction to the Old Testament* (Grand Rapids: Eerdmans, 1969), 788, thought this long section of new speeches actually began at chap. 34 (not 40), and Harrison used this division of the text to support a parallel structure in both halves of the book. Harrison drew his analysis from ideas in W. Brownlee, *The Meaning of the Dead Sea Scrolls for the Bible* (Oxford: Oxford University, 1964), 247–59. This division between chaps. 33 and 34 is problematic because chaps. 34–35 seem to be a conclusion to 28–33 and because chap. 40 makes a much clearer and stronger breaking point.

[5] R. H. O'Connell, *Concentricity and Continuity: The Literary Structure of Isaiah* (Sheffield: Academic Press,1994), 151–215, understood chaps. 40–54 as exonerating God of false charges by the exiles in covenant disputes, thus chap. 55 moves on to the next step of reconciliation so chaps. 55–66 is the last section of Isaiah. He uses the change in "designated addresses" (Jerusalem/Zion or Jacob/Israel), divine epithets, and a change of tone (consolation or disputation) to determine his outline. M. A. Sweeney, *Isaiah 1–39 with an Introduction to the Prophetic Literature*, FOTL (Grand Rapids: Eerdmans, 1996), 40,47, makes chaps. 34–54 a unit distinguished from 55–66 because (a) 55:1 begins with "come," which distinguished it from what proceeds; (b) 55 and 56 address a masculine plural audience while 54 addresses a feminine singular (Zion); and (c) adherence to the covenant is a theme in 1:8; 55:1–5; 56:4–5; 59:21. L. J. Liebreich, "The Compilation of the Book of Isaiah," *JQR* 46 (1956): 259–77, made chaps. 50–66 the final group of chapters in Isaiah based on the use of the terms עֶבֶד "servant" and נחם "compassion" as well as a group of twelve words that appear in both chaps. 50 and 66. Seitz, "Isaiah 40–66," 6:471–74, considers this section to be dealing with the vindication of God's servants. Because of the close association of ideas in chaps. 55–56 (servants, banquets, persuasive form of speech), he includes chaps. 54–55 with chaps. 56–66.

[6] R. Melugin, *The Formation of Isaiah 40–55*, BZAW (Berlin: de Gruyter, 1976), 78, accepts this position based on the work of E. Hessler, *Gott der Schöpfer: Ein Beitrag zur Komposition und Theologie Deuterojesajas* (1961) or her "Die Struktur der Bilder bei Deuterojesaja," *EvT* 25 (1965): 349–69.

3. Compositional Issues Related to 40–55

The various methodological approaches to understanding the composition of portions of Isaiah (several sources, a prophetic school, redactional editing, rhetorical argumentation, and canonical formation) were introduced in my introduction to chaps. 1–39,[7] but there is a need to describe how these approaches uniquely deal with the literature in chaps. 40–55 so that each methodology can be evaluated. The reader needs to be aware of the strengths and weaknesses of the approaches used by the commentaries they might consult. This survey is not an exhaustive introduction to each methodology but a summary of a few of the key compositional issues that interpreters of chaps. 40–55 have addressed over the years. Primary attention is given to the present state of discussion in more recent commentaries; this is not an historical account of how each approach arose and developed.

(1) Early Perspectives

The high regard that later Hebrew authors had for the prophecies within the book of Isaiah is evidenced by the frequent allusions to what the prophet said. For example, (a) the phrase "I am, and there is no God besides me" in Zeph 2:15 seems to be based on the common use of this phrase in Isaiah (45:5,6,18,21; 47:8); (b) Mal 3:1 picks up the idea of one who will come to "clear a way before the Lord" from Isa 40:3 and develops this idea even further; (c) Jer 31:35 refers to God stirring up the sea and making its waves roar, similar to Isa 51:15; and (d) there are several allusions in Nahum that seem to come from Isaiah 40–66.[8] None of these authors indicate that they are quoting from the book of Isaiah and some modern scholars have questioned who is quoting whom.[9] Nevertheless, when one looks at the number of times later prophets allude to or quote from the book of Isaiah, it is clear that these messages had a powerful impact on the theological thinking of later biblical and nonbiblical writers.

The value and high esteem for the book of Isaiah is very evident from the number of manuscripts that were found in the caves in the general vicinity of the Dead Sea.[10] These excavations resulted in the discovery of numerous Isaiah scrolls (probably 21) and many small fragments that contain only a

---

[7] Smith, *Isaiah 1–39*, 55–68.

[8] The "overflowing flood" in Nah 1:8 is similar to the same phrase in Isa 8:7–8; the reference to the "feet of him who brings good news, who announces peace" in Nah 1:15 is similar to Isa 52:7; 40:9. C. Armerding, "Nahum," *EBC* (Grand Rapids: Zondervan, 1985), 7:454–55 illustrates the close relationship between Isaiah 51–52 and Nahum. A similar comparison is found in K. L. Barker and W. Bailey, *Micah, Nahum, Habakkuk, Zephaniah*, NAC (Nashville: B&H, 1998), 146–47.

[9] The one quoting is often determined by external factors found in the superscription or other historical factors. If the quote is identical in both documents, or even if it is different, it is not easy to determine which document was the original source.

[10] M. Burrrows, *The Dead Sea Scrolls* (New York: Viking, 1955) has a fairly complete description of the discovery (even a picture of the Bedouin, Muhammad adh-Dhib), the strange journey

few words or verses from Isaiah. These are among the more important longer documents:[11]

1. 1QIs[a], known as the "Great Isaiah Scroll," dates to around 200–150 BC. It contains most of the 66 chapters in Isaiah.
2. 1QIs[b] contains portions of 7:22–66:24 (though many chapters are only partially preserved) that comes from the Herodian period. Within chaps. 40–66 it specifically includes 40:2–3; 41:3–23; 43:1–13,23–27; 44:21–28; 45:1–13; 46:3–13; 47:1–14; 48:17–22; 49:1–15; 50:7–11; 51:1–10; 52:7–15; 53:1–13; 55:2–13; 56:1–12; 57:1–4,17–21; 58:1–14; 59:1–8,20–21; 60:1–22; 61:1–12; 63:1–19; 64:1,6–8; 65:17–25; 66:1–24.
3. 4QIs[b] includes chaps. 1–3, 5, 9, 11–13, 17–22, 24, 26, 35–37; plus within chaps. 40–66 it contains 40:1–4,22–26; 41:8–11; 42:2–7,9–12; 43:12–15; 44:19–28; 45:20–25; 46:1–3; 48:6–8; 49:21–23; 51:1–2,14–16; 52:2,7; 53:11–12; 61:1–3; 64:5–65:1; 66:24. It can be dated around 35 BC.
4. 4QIs[c] is an Herodian text that has some Paleo-Hebrew script (for the name of God) and includes chaps. 9–12, 14, 22–26, 28, 30, 33, and specifically 44:3–7,23; 45:1–4,6–8; 46:8–13; 48:10–15,17–19; 49:22; 51:8–16; 52:10–15; 53:1–3,6–8; 54:3–5,7–17; 55:1–7; 66:20–24.
5. 4QIs[d] includes portions from chaps. 45:20; 46:10–13; 47:1–6,8–9; 48:8–22; 49:1–15; 52:4–7; 53:8–12; 54:1–11; 57:9–58:3,5–7.

In addition to these early biblical manuscripts, numerous nonbiblical documents that describe the life, culture, and beliefs of the Qumran community contain quotations of verses from Isaiah 40–66 to justify their theology and their way of life. For example, within the Sectarian Laws in 4Q265, fragment 1, is the statement, "it is written in the b[ook,] of Isaiah the prophet . . . shout you who have not been in labor, for the children of your desolation will be more" from Isa 54:1–2.[12] The Damascus Document, column 6, claims that the "rod" in Num 21:18 refers to the interpreter of the law and it justifies this interpretation by stating that "Isaiah said, 'he brings out a tool for his work'"[13] from Isa 54:16. 4Q176 *tanḥumîm* quotes from 40:1–5; 41:8–9; 43:1–6; 49:7,13–17;

of the scrolls through various hands, and the later systematic excavation of several other caves for additional written material.

[11] Lists of Qumran texts can be found in E. Ulrich, "An Index to the Isaiah Manuscripts from the Judean Desert," in *Writing and Reading the Scroll of Isaiah: Studies of an Interpretive Tradition*, ed. C. C. Broyles and C. A. Evans (Leiden: Brill, 1997), 2:477–80, and P. W. Flint, "The Isaiah Scrolls from the Judean Desert," in *Writing and Reading the Scroll of Isaiah*, 2:481–89. The official publication of these texts with notes and analysis is available in the series Discoveries in the Judean Desert (*DJD*) (Oxford: Clarendon, 1952). E.g., the Isaiah texts from cave 4 were published by E. Ulrich, et al., *Qumran Cave 4, X: The Prophets* in *DJD*, 15 (Oxford: Clarendon, 1997).

[12] M. Wise, M. Abegg, E. Cook, eds., *A New Translation of the Dead Sea Scrolls* (San Francisco: Harper Collins, 2005), 358.

[13] Ibid., 57.

51:22–23; 52:1–3; and 54:4–10. These few examples show how highly these people regarded the writing of the prophet Isaiah, but they do not provide much information about key issues related to the actual composition of the book of Isaiah.

Josephus (around AD 75) speaks about the writing of the prophecies in the book of Isaiah. After he describes Isaiah's interaction with Hezekiah about Sennacherib's failed attack (chaps. 36–37 and 38–39), he indicates that Isaiah "out of the assurance that he had never written what was false, wrote down all his prophecies and left them behind him in books."[14] This statement affirms his beliefs about the authorship and the authority of the messages within the book of Isaiah. It does not describe how many books Isaiah wrote, what the title of each book was, what topics were covered in each of them; and it says nothing specific about the manner in which he composed these books.

The New Testament writers frequently quote verses from the book of Isaiah and some of these are connected directly to the prophet Isaiah. The following quotes have an introduction that attributes the quoted material to Isaiah:

40:3–5	Matt 3:3; Mark 1:2–3; Luke 3:4–6; John 1:23
42:1–4	Matt 12:18–21
53:1	John 12:38; Rom 10:16
53:4	Matt 8:17
53:6–8	Acts 8:28,32–33
61:1–2	Luke 4:17–19
65:1–2	Rom 10:20–21

Some of the introductions to these quotations merely claim that the man "Isaiah said" what is quoted (Rom 10:20–21; 15:12), although Luke 3:4 refers to what "is written in the book of the words of Isaiah." These quotations indicate that at that time early Christians viewed these words as the authoritative words spoken by the prophet Isaiah. Of course, there are numerous other quotations from the book of Isaiah that are found in the New Testament that do not specifically mention that they are quotations from the prophet Isaiah or from the book of Isaiah.[15]

Many early Christian writings quote or allude to the book of Isaiah to justify some conclusion. The "General Epistle of Barnabas" was written shortly after the Roman conquest of Jerusalem in AD 70. It admonishes Gentile Christians not to be led astray by those who were teaching that Christians must follow the Old Testament laws. It claims that even the ancient Hebrews perceived these physical requirements (circumcision, sacrifices, food laws, etc.) were really meant to be spiritual ways to mortify the passions of the flesh and to encour-

---

[14] Josephus, *Antiquities*, X.ii.
[15] Luke 19:46 uses Isa 56:7; Acts 8:32–33 quotes Isa 53:7–8; Acts 13:47 quotes Isa 49:6; Rom 11:26–27 quotes Isa 59:20–21.

age the sanctification of the body.[16] In making his case, this author repeatedly refers to passages throughout Isaiah, quoting extensive portions to prove his point.[17] There is no question about the authority, unity, or practical wisdom of Isaiah's writings. This was the general attitude toward the book of Isaiah throughout the Early Church period. It does not matter if one looks at the allegorical use of Isaiah in Irenaeus's (AD 130–200) *Demonstrations of Apostolic Preaching* or the nonallegorical study of Isaiah by Theodoret of Cyrus (AD 393–460);[18] all were focused on explaining what the text meant and how it related to their own Christian faith.

In *Baba Bathra 15a* the Talmud expresses the opinion that "Hezekiah and his company wrote Isaiah, Proverbs, the Song of Solomon, and Ecclesiastes," but it is hard to know what it meant by the statement that they "wrote" these books. Certainly one would not expect them to claim that Hezekiah's scribes were inspired prophets or that they wrote what the text attributes to Solomon and Isaiah. This idea may have originated from Prov 25:1, where it says that the "men of Hezekiah" copied or compiled the proverbs of Solomon. Of course the historical basis and the veracity of this opinion is unknown, so it is difficult to judge its historical value. Many years later the great Jewish exegete Ibn Ezra (AD 1092–1167) refers to the heretical views of Moses ben Samuel Ibn Geketilla who questioned if Isaiah wrote the second half of the book of Isaiah, but it does not appear that Ibn Ezra followed this opinion.[19] In spite of a few questions like these, up until the rise of the critical approaches in the eighteenth century, most people thought that Isaiah was the one who wrote down his prophecies, so there was little talk about the place, the time, or the actual process of composition.

The great reformer J. Calvin notes that 40:1 introduces a new subject that relates to a future time (the time of the captivity in Babylon, the deliverance, and the reign of Christ) after the death of the prophet. When he came to chap. 56 apparently he did not see a major break in the flow of thought between chaps. 55 and 56. He rejected the allegorical method of exegesis that was so popular in his day because he believed that an historical approach that was built on a

---

[16] J. Quasten, *Patrology: Vol. 1: The Beginnings of the Patristic Literature* (Westminster, Maryland: Newman Press, 1951), 85–91.

[17] In 17 short chapters he refers to Isa 1:6–9,11–14; 3:9; 5:21; 8:14; 16:1–2; 28:16; 33:13, 16–17; 40:3,12; 42:6; 43:18–19; 45:1–2; 46:1; 49:6,17; 53:5–7; 58:4–10.

[18] B. S. Childs, *The Struggle to Understand Isaiah as Christian Scripture* (Grand Rapids: Eerdmans, 2004), 45–55 on Irenaeus, 62–74 on Origin, and 130–47 on Theodoret of Cyrus. He provides brief information about each person's life, hermeneutical approach, and a survey of their understanding of Isaiah.

[19] R. B. Dillard and T. Longman III, *An Introduction to the Old Testament* (Grand Rapids: Zondervan, 1994), 268–69, draw attention to these statements made by Ibn Ezra in his commentary on Isaiah at 40:1; 42:10; 45:4–5; and 49:4. They conclude that he believed that the book of Isaiah was the product of a single author.

good understanding of the grammar would provide the best understanding of the original author's meaning.[20]

(2) More Recent Scholarly Approaches

Critical questions about the composition of the book of Isaiah began in earnest when J. C. Döderlein published a Latin translation of Isaiah with notes in 1775.[21] He concluded that the prophet Isaiah did not write chaps. 40–66; instead, an exilic prophet who knew about Cyrus and the fall of Babylon wrote them. J. G. Eichhorn thought that the oracles in Isaiah were in chronological order and that later exilic and postexilic oracles were added to this collection as appendices. He identified these later writings based on messages that indicate a Babylonian setting and different Hebrew forms of expression. He noted that Isaiah's oracles were focused on moral themes, while later writings refer to the exile, the coming of Cyrus, and the fall of Babylon.[22]

M. A. Sweeney has traced the development of these critical views that led to B. Duhm's commentary. Based on five principles, W. Gesenius's 1821 commentary on Isaiah attributed the second half of the book of Isaiah to an exilic author he calls "Pseudo-Jesaia" who lived in Babylon.[23] F. Hitzig's 1833 commentary on Isaiah attributed chaps. 40–66 to an author who wrote at the conclusion of the exile,[24] while H. G. A. Ewald's 1840 book on the prophets claims that a whole series of oracles (chaps. 13–14; 21; 40–48; 49–66) were added to the writings of Isaiah by a less-gifted anonymous writer sometime after the fall of Babylon.[25] A. Dillmann's 1890 commentary on Isaiah hailed Isaiah as a great hero of the faith who proclaimed God's majesty. He breaks the

---

[20] Childs, *The Struggle to Understand Isaiah as Christian Scripture*, 207–29 has a thorough discussion of Calvin's hermeneutical methods and his writings on Isaiah. For an overview of his commentaries on the Old Testament see T. H. L. Parker, *Calvin's Old Testament Commentaries* (Edinburgh: T&T Clark, 1986).

[21] J. C. Döderlein, *Esaias/ex recensione textus Hebraei ad fidem codicum manuscriptorum et versionum antiquarum Latine vertit notasque varii argumenti subiecit Ioannes Christophorus Doederlein* (Norimbergae et Altdorfi: Apud Georg. Petr. Monath, 1789).

[22] J. G. Eichhorn, *Einleitung in das Alte Testament*, 3 vols. (Göttingen: Rosenbusch, 1780–1783). M.A. Sweeney, "On the Road to Duhm: Isaiah in Nineteenth-Century Critical Scholarship," *SBL 2002 Seminar Papers* (Atlanta: SBL, 2002), 191–211, contains an excellent description of these early critical studies which are summarized here.

[23] W. Gesenius, *Philologisch-kritischer und historischer Commentar über den Jesaia* (Leipzig: Vogel, 1921), thought that a "Pseudo-Isaiah" wrote 40–66 from Babylon in exilic times because (a) historical reference points to a time after Isaiah (Jerusalem is in ruins), (b) these chapters refer to Babylon and Cyrus, (c) the oracles look forward to a return from exile, (d) the language is different from Isaiah, and (e) these oracles were attributed to Isaiah so that he could be seen as the one who foretold the judgment of Judah.

[24] F. Hitzig, *Der Prophet Jesaja* (Heidelberg: Winter, 1933), concludes that chaps. 40–66 were written by an exilic author who was heavily influenced by the Psalms.

[25] H. G. A. Ewald, *Die Propheten des Alten Bundes* (Göttingen: Vandenhoeck and Ruprecht, 1840), believed that later anonymous oracles from the era of the fall of Babylon, Cyrus, and the restoration of the nation in 40–66 were added to Isaiah's writings.

oracles within Isaiah into a series of collections (1–12; 13–23; 24–27; 28–33) but assigned most of chaps. 40–66 to an anonymous exilic prophet who depended on the vocabulary of 1–39 when he wrote just before the fall of Babylon. Chapters 63–66 were a later appendix that describes the postexilic return of the people to their land.[26] Because of these developments before the time of Duhm, Sweeney concludes that Duhm's 1892 epic work on Isaiah was based on a fairly firm consensus of critical scholarship at that time.

Duhm not only argued that parts of Isaiah were composed at a later time; he separated chaps. 56–66 from 40–55 and attributed 56–66 to a "Third-Isaiah" figure in the postexilic era of Ezra and Nehemiah, long after the exiles returned to Jerusalem. He thought that a prophet in Lebanon wrote chaps. 40–55 around 540 BC while another prophet composed chaps. 56–66 in Jerusalem during the time of Ezra and Nehemiah (450 BC). Duhm concluded that later insertions were added to these writings all the way down to the Hasmonean period (first century BC).[27] He did not think that the servant poems fit into the contexts where they were placed; therefore, he attributed the servant passages to a different author living around 500–450 BC. Although each present-day scholar has his own unique variation of these issues, Duhm's basic approach to chaps. 40–66 is still being followed in many critical commentaries today.

S. R. Driver presents this theory in what might be called its classical form in 1897. His approach is based on the "analogy of prophecy," which states that most prophets lived in the era that they describe and preach to the people in that setting. Prophets do not abandon their historical setting but speak about it and to it. He believes there is no prophecy of an exile in chaps. 40–66; it is presupposed as a thing of the past. Thus the future predictions are about the release from exile. He contends that it is completely contrary to the nature of prophecy for a prophet to speak to a future people and abandon his contemporaries.[28] This is not a complete denial of prophetic ability but a limitation of it to a very narrow period of time. He provided three arguments to support his understanding of 40–66.

1. The internal evidence shows that Jerusalem is ruined and deserted (44:26b; 58:12; 61:4; 63:18; 64:10), the Hebrew people are suffering under the Chaldeans (42:22,25; 47:6; 52:5), and a return from exile is very imminent (40:2; 46:13; 48:20). Thus in these chapters the prophet was speaking to those people who were living in the Babylonian exile.

---

[26] A. Dillmann, *Der Prophet Jesaia*, HKAT 5 (Leipzig: Hirzel, 1890), found in the book of Isaiah prophecies from a number of different prophets. Chapters 40–66 come from an exilic prophet shortly before the fall of Babylon.

[27] B. Duhm, *Das Buch Jesaja*, *Handkommentar zum Alten Testament* (Göttingen: Vandenhoeck and Ruprecht, 1892).

[28] S. R. Driver, *An Introduction to the Literature of the Old Testament* (Cleveland: World Publishing, 1956), 237.

2. The literary style and subject matter of chaps. 40–66 is different from 1–39. Driver presents a list of words that appear only (or primarily) in chaps. 40–66 and a few stylistic characteristics (e.g. the duplication of words). These factors support his conclusion that the author of chaps. 1–39 did not write 40–66.

3. The theology of chaps. 40–66 presents a distinctive emphasis by a different prophet. For example, chaps. 1–39 describe God's majesty, while 40–66 emphasize his infinitude.[29]

Since the time of Driver several criticisms of this approach have appeared, and less value is now given to small stylistic changes or the introduction of a new topic (point 2). Although most would find some changes in the theology of chap. 40–66, much more attention is being given to the common theological themes that can be traced throughout all sections of the book (point 3). Thus the historical evidence for a change in the location and setting of the prophet and his audience in chaps. 40–55 and 56–66 seems to be the lasting legacy of this approach (point 1). Although some still find much to be valued in this traditional critical method of analyzing Isaiah based on the analogy of prophecy, new ways of understanding chaps. 40–55 have developed in the intervening years. So a brief survey of some of the main alternative methodologies will help inform the reader about the nature of the present debate concerning the composition of chaps. 40–55.

DRAMATIC.   The two-volume commentary on the whole book of Isaiah by J. D. W. Watts[30] and Klaus Baltzer's one-volume commentary on chaps. 40–55 employ a dramatic interpretation of the book of Isaiah; thus, they have a focus that is quite different from the assumptions and methodologies of S. R. Driver. Watts takes a "reader-oriented approach" to understanding the messages in Isaiah. He identifies 12 long acts within the vision of Isaiah (acts VII–XII are found in chaps. 40–66),[31] with several scenes within each act, and a few episodes within each scene. Watts attempts to assign each verse of the text to a speaker in the drama (God, the heavens, the earth, a herald, a messenger, a chorus, Cyrus, Darius, or Tattenai). He dates the completion of the book to 435 BC and the authorship to one of the persecuted people mentioned in 66:3–5.[32] This unknown author identified with the historical prophet Isaiah (chaps. 1–39), with the suffering of the persecuted servant of the Lord (chaps. 42–53), and with the final group of servants in 54:17; 65:9–16, so he used older traditions about these people from earlier times to present this grand vision of God's strategy for the world. Watts does not employ the common critical concepts of

---

[29] Ibid., 236–43.

[30] J. D. W. Watts, *Isaiah 1–33*, WBC 24 (Waco: Word, 1985) and *Isaiah 34–66*.

[31] The demarcation of some of these acts is quite unusual. For example it is very odd to have an act break after chap. 14 (instead of after 12), to break after chap. 22 (instead of after 23), and after chap. 61.

[32] Watts, *Isaiah 1–33*, xxxi.

a first, second, and third Isaiah, but deals with the whole book more as a grand unified vision. This vision for Zion and the rest of the world addresses the people of Jerusalem who were struggling with the influence of syncretistic tendencies and the fragmentation of their community into separate parties (people of the land, exiles, priests, the governor). Watts attempts to correlate each chapter with some historical period, but this leads to some very unusual conclusions. For example, the servant in chap. 42 is actually the Persian king Cyrus, the servant in chaps. 49, 52–53 refers to the Persian king Darius, the servant in chap. 50 is Zerubbabel, and the Anointed One in 61:1–3 is the Persian king Artaxerxes.[33] This unified conception of the book as one unified vision is very helpful because it tends to reduce the excessive fragmentation of the diverse messages in the book of Isaiah by connecting them with a central idea: God's strategy for establishing his plans for the world. Nevertheless, his classification of these speeches as a series of dramas and his identification of the characters who speak within these dramas are very suspect. In addition, few would accept his identification of certain acts or speeches with the specific historical periods he identifies, nor would they identify the persecuted servant with the historical figures he proposes. There is very little indication that chaps. 40–66 are describing a drama that was presented by a cast of characters.

The work of K. Baltzer is based on the traditional critical conclusion that the book of Isaiah should be divided into three unique sections, though he believes that the emphasis on Zion/Jerusalem acts as a unifying factor that draws these three unique parts together.[34] Baltzer recognizes the possibility of later redactional additions to the text, but he believes they were relatively minor.[35] He identifies various form-critical genres but is much more interested in how these shorter messages were put together into the larger literary units and how they function within the drama. The fundamental thesis of the commentary is that "DtIs's work is a liturgical drama"[36] that was performed with people acting in multiple scenes with an audience listening in a worship setting. Baltzer points to similar ancient dramas in the Babylonian New Years *(akitu)* festival, the coronation of the Egyptian Middle Kingdom ruler Sesostris I (1972–1928 BC), and the drama of a struggle between the gods Horus and Seth (713–698 BC).[37] Baltzer admits that the drama in Isaiah is "strikingly different from the Attic texts,"[38] but he is still able to infer several actors plus a chorus who performed

---

[33] Watts, *Isaiah 34–66*, 114, 119, 187, 222–25, 302.

[34] K. Baltzer, *Deutero-Isaiah* (Minneapolis: Fortress, 2001), 1, divides the prophetic speeches into Isaiah I (1–39), Isaiah II (40–55), and Isaiah III (56–66). This issue receives little attention, but is based on (a) different historical periods, (b) reference to the name of Cyrus, (c) different style and genres, and (d) differences in theology. Later he does admit that he "no longer considers the sequence Deutero-Isaiah (40–55) –Trito-Isaiah (56–66) to be self-evident."

[35] Ibid., 5.

[36] Ibid., 7.

[37] Ibid., 7–13.

[38] Ibid., 14.

this play at the seven-day pilgrimage festival of Passover on the southeast slope of Jerusalem in the time of Nehemiah (450–400 BC).[39] This drama had six acts (chap. 40 was the prologue and 55 was the epilogue), with three scenes per act, and each act ended with a hymn (except one, 53:12). The dramatic action includes processions of people (45:14–17), throne scenes (44:24–45:25), law-court scenes (41:1–5a;21–29), a battle scene (43:11–16; 51:9–11), an artisan scene (44:9–20), a marriage scene (54:14–17), and musical acts with dance, mime, and singing.[40] Some acts take place on earth, others in the underworld, and several happen in heaven. Baltzer does view chaps. 40–55 as a homogeneous literary unit; that is, it is one unified drama. Baltzer connects the "Servant of God" with Moses because the Servant and Moses both functioned as teachers appointed to "bring out" the people, were sent by God, and were put in a grave (Deut 34; Isa 53). But one wonders about his conclusion. Did Moses bring justice to the nations (42:1–4)? Was he beaten and killed by persecutors (53:1–9)? Did he pay the penalty for other people's sins (53:4–9)? Was he a covenant to the nations (49:6)?

A major criticism of Watts and Baltzer is that the speeches by Isaiah lack theatrical directions or named actors, so the basic methodology is primarily a series of imaginative recreations of what might have happened if this was used as a drama. The whole underpinning of this hypothesis about the existence of ancient dramas is rather precarious, for the Babylonian New Year festival was not a drama conducted in public before an audience; it was a private royal ritual of the king. Although rituals have people acting in certain predictable ways, it is a gross misrepresentation to describe the coronation of a king as a drama. One of the positive aspects of this approach is that it enables these authors to view chaps. 40–55 as a unified whole.

TRADITIONAL.   J. N. Oswalt's two commentaries on Isaiah do not follow the traditional critical division of Isaiah into three separate authors (stylistic and theological difference are not that great), and a strong part of his logic is his rejection of the critical conclusion that "predictive prophecy is impossible."[41] Although many critical scholars would object to Oswalt's characterization of their perspective and say that they do believe in certain types of prophecy, it is true that most critical works follow the understanding of prophecy that prophets primarily gave speeches to and about the people in their own setting. Oswalt does allow for some editorial work by Isaiah or one of his followers to arrange and add transitional statements when producing the final form of his book.[42] Oswalt agrees with critical interpretations when he interprets the setting of the audience in chaps. 40–55 to be in exile and the setting

---

[39] Ibid., 22–23.

[40] Ibid., 15–18.

[41] J. N. Oswalt, *The Book of Isaiah 40–66*, NICOT (Grand Rapids: Eerdmans, 1998), 3 and *Isaiah*, NIVAC (Grand Rapids: Zondervan, 2003), 33–41.

[42] J. N. Oswalt, *The Book of Isaiah 1–39*, NICOT (Grand Rapids: Eerdmans, 1986), 26.

of the audience in chaps. 56–66 to be in the postexilic period. Oswalt rejects redactional theories and only mentions in passing form-critical observations about the genre of various oracles.

Oswalt finds very few historical references in chaps. 40–66, a view that is somewhat similar to B. S. Childs's perspective that the historical setting of chaps. 40–66 was consciously suppressed. Oswalt strongly supports those studies that point to a theological unity to Isaiah (Brueggemann, Childs, Clements, Rendtorff),[43] though he recognizes that these authors do not think theological unity implies authorial unity. Oswalt maintains that the theology of 40–66 teaches that God knows and plans the future; therefore, these prophecies must be the supernatural revelation of what God plans to do in the future and not a discussion of what God was doing at the present time around 540 BC.[44] Oswalt finds servanthood at the center of Isaiah's theology, and he believes the "fundamental point that chs. 40–55 addresses is the possibility of restoration . . . First, ability: *can* God restore? Second, intention: does he *want* to restore?"[45] Finally, it is noteworthy that Oswalt views many of the short hymnic passages within chaps. 40–55 as introductions to a new section rather than the conclusion to the preceding messages (42:10–13; 44:23, etc.).[46]

When one comes to chaps. 56–66, Oswalt rejects P. Hanson's sociological analysis suggesting that these chapters describe a conflict between two priestly groups. Instead, these chapters explain the necessity of living righteously, the key mark of a servant of God. "Chs. 56–66 are a synthesis of what seems to be the conflicting points of view in chaps. 7–39 and 40–55."[47] The first section (chaps. 7–39) calls people to righteous living or else God will judge them, while the second (40–55) emphasizes God's grace that his chosen people can freely receive. Oswalt believes these opposing emphases are synthesized in chaps. 56–66.

J. A. Motyer's one-volume work on Isaiah defends the unity of Isaiah and the Isaianic authorship of the whole. Isaiah provided the unifying influence from the beginning of the production of this book rather than a group of later disciples at the end of the process. His aim is to explain the meaning of the text, so he places a good deal of emphasis on rhetorical factors that emphasize five unifying motifs in Isaiah. These are (a) the messianic hope; (b) the city; (c) the Holy One of Israel; (d) history and faith; and (e) literary and structural features.[48] Motyer views all the messages in Isaiah as the written condensations of what the prophet preached, but he does not believe that the variations in style are so diverse that they require one to assume a different person wrote

---

[43] Oswalt, *Isaiah 40–66*, 4.
[44] Ibid., 5.
[45] Ibid., 8.
[46] Ibid., 120, 189,
[47] Ibid., 452–53.
[48] J. A. Motyer, *Isaiah* (Downers Grove: InterVarsity, 1993), 13–23.

each different type of oracle. The structure he finds "is based on a concentrated 'structurist' study" which reveals several extended doublets.[49] He also finds the "arch/trajectory structure" (chiastic structure) and the use of the *inclusio* to mark the beginning and end of speeches. At times this leads to some unusual structural divisions of the text, plus some chiastic organizational features that appear somewhat forced.[50] His explanations of verses and words are rather brief with relatively little discussion of contrary points of view. He finds no evidence of a Babylonian background in chaps. 40–55, so he opts for a Palestinian setting for it and for chaps. 56–66.[51] Although chaps. 46–47 are about Babylon, he does not believe their setting is Babylonian because the suffering of God's people in these chapters does not conform to what happened in the Babylonian exile. The reportage in these chapters is filled with stereotypical phrases that do not sound like eyewitness reporting.[52] He does not interact much with form-critical or redactional theories. Motyer believes chaps. 56–66 condemn preexilic Canaanite cults (not a postexilic problem), and he does not accept P. Hanson's sociological analysis of these conflicts as being a struggle for power between two different priestly groups.

Neither of these studies makes much use of critical methodologies, but a more informed use of form-critical results in the past fifty years would have enabled them to advance their understanding of the implications of the prophetic use of various literary forms to express these messages of hope and condemnation. Although Motyer's briefness is a refreshing change from the long-winded discussion in some commentaries, his interaction with problems and even his own explanation of the text is sometimes so brief that one does not always know why he came to certain conclusions. Oswalt presents a number of variant textual readings and a fuller explanation of the text, but his discussion sometime gets bogged down defending theological issues. Both present viable traditional understandings of the message of the book of Isaiah that need to be heard.

RHETORICAL.   J. Muilenburg's rhetorical approach to chaps. 40–66 recognizes the existence of a Second and Third Isaiah, but his main focus is turned away from issues of redactional additions to observing the style and the rhetorical beauty of the poetry, as well as the unity that can be found within these speeches.[53] He disagrees with form-critical tendencies to break these chap-

---

[49] Ibid., 24. The doublets he finds include 7:1–9:6 on Judah and 9:7–11:16 on Israel; 42:18–43:21 and 43:22–44:23, as well as a parallelism between Cyrus and the Servant.

[50] Ibid., 6–7, puts chaps. 38–55 into one large unit, which he divides into only four large subsections. Chiastic features are found on pp. 461, 468, 469, 478, 490, 493, 516, 522.

[51] Ibid., 27.

[52] Ibid., 28.

[53] J. Muilenburg, "Isaiah 40–66," *IB* 5:383–84, believes that "it is likely that they are the work of followers of the prophet" just a few years after the prophet. J. Muilenburg, "Form Criticism and Beyond," *JBL* 88 (1969): 1–18, presents his programmatic approach to interpretation in this article.

ters up into innumerable small oracles based on the use of different genres. He rejects H. Gressmann's identification of 49 independent poems in chaps. 40–66 and J. Begrich's discovery of 70 poems; instead, Muilenburg puts different poems together based on catchwords and other rhetorical mechanisms that point to the unity of longer speeches. Among the rhetorical features he identifies are the repeated use of hymns, poetic parallelism, assonance, the use of "behold" *(hēn)*, interrogatives, a dialogical style, the use of quotations, exclamations, imperatives, and the repetition of key words (like "fear not" or "I am the Lord").[54] Muilenburg found several triadic organizations of material and ends up dividing chaps. 40–48 into fifteen units, 49–55 into seven units, and 56–66 into thirteen units.[55] Although Muilenburg's work began to turn the tide against the excessive division of the text of Isaiah by form critics, some would suggest that he could have found much greater unity by joining many of his small units into larger segments. When Muilenburg turned to study chaps. 56–66 he found much less evidence of coherence.[56]

Muilenburg placed Second Isaiah in Babylon because he thought the prophet had firsthand knowledge of conditions in Babylon (44:24–25; 47:12–13) and that his writings have some affinities with Babylonian literature.[57] He believes this prophet was one of the greatest prophets because of his unusual skill in writing and his presentation of his material in a dramatic and emotional manner. Finally, Muilenburg claims that "the thought of Second Isaiah is eschatological, and the primary matrix of all the poems is eschatological."[58] This sharply distinguishes his interpretation from other critical studies that claim that many of these poems were addressed to the exilic situation in Babylon. Thus he believes that the themes of redemption, creation, and history should be understood primarily in light of God's great plan to redeem his people so that they can live in his new creation in the age to come. This is the new event that the prophet announces (it is not Cyrus's defeat of Babylon); God will one day come in all his glory to transform nature, establish justice, and bring people from many nations into his kingdom. This eschatological perspective is an important insight that has a major impact on how one conceives of the role of the prophet (a prophet did not always address the immediate situation of the people he was speaking to), the setting of the prophet (eschatological prophecies often do not help locate the setting of the prophet), and the theology of his message (the new things he predicted are about eschatological, not present exilic, events).

---

[54] Muilenburg, "Isaiah 40–66," 5:386–89.

[55] Ibid., 5:415–19. Many of these divisions are suspect, which throws Muilenburg's whole methodology into question.

[56] Ibid., 5:414, he says that "chs. 56–66 do not have the dominating coherence of Second Isaiah's eschatological poems."

[57] Ibid., 5:397.

[58] Ibid., 5:399.

G. T. Polan uses a similar rhetorical methodology in his detailed interpretation of chaps. 56–59.[59] A somewhat similar approach was employed by P. D. Quinn-Miscal who treats the whole book of Isaiah as a literary unit, although he is less historical in his analysis and does not present a verse-by-verse commentary on each chapter[60] Miscal understands Isaiah to be a grand poetic vision, so his goal is to uncover the richness of themes that were imaginatively presented in intricate and complex poetic discourse. Y. Gitay's persuasive approach to rhetorical arguments provides another way of using rhetoric to analyze the logic of the speeches in chaps. 40–48.[61]

REDACTIONAL. Those who propose one or more redactions of chaps. 40–55 naturally raise serious questions about the unity of these prophetic messages because in each new redactional process different people from different eras were addressing new issues and inserting their new ideas into the text. For example, H. J. Hermission suggested that the complex development of chaps. 40–55 involved (a) an original collection of oracles written sometime around 539 BC that included the servant poems, (b) a *qarob* ("near") layer of texts that were inconsistent with these earlier oracles because they stressed the nearness of God (46:8,12–13; 48:17–19; 51:1–2,4–8; 54:11–17), and (c) an anti-idolatry redaction (44:9–20; 46:5–7).[62] R. G. Kratz argues for as many as five redactional layers, including (a) the early foundation layer (much of 40–48) from sometime near the beginning of Cyrus's reign; (b) the Zion expansion, which is primarily in chaps. 49–54, developed near the end of Cyrus's reign; (c) the Cyrus supplement from the time of Darius I; (d) an idol layer in chaps. 40–46 from the end of Darius's reign; (e) a servant-Israel redaction from the fifth century; and (f) other later small additions.[63] This is initially based on two presentations of Cyrus (first, as the one who defeats Babylon and second, as a light to the nation). J. van Oorschot's redactional study identifies a basic layer of texts with judgment speeches, plus disputations (40:12–31) and salvation oracles (41–44), which focus on God's plan to bring the Israelites back from exile (the new exodus). A second layer of Zion texts (40:1–11; 44:23; 49:14–21; 51:9–19; 52:1–2,7–10) were centered around the restoration

---

[59] G. J. Polan, *In the Way of Justice toward Salvation: A Rhetorical Analysis of Isaiah 56–59* (Frankfort: Lang, 1985) uses a methodology directly dependent on Muilenburg.

[60] P. D. Quinn-Miscal, *Reading Isaiah: Poetry and Vision* (Louisville: WJK, 2001).

[61] Y. Gitay, *Prophecy and Persuasion: A Study of Isaiah 40–48*, FTL 14 (Bonn: Linguistica Biblica, 1981) uses Greek rhetorical terminology, which is somewhat anachronistic for the study of Isaiah.

[62] H. J. Hermission, "Einheit und Komplexitat Deuterojesajas: Probleme der Redaktionsgeschichte von Jes 40–55," in *The Book of Isaiah,* ed. J. Vermeylen, BETL 81 (Leuven: University Press, 1989), 287–312. H. G. M. Williamson, *The Book Called Isaiah* (Oxford: Clarendon, 1994), 24–27, who finds only one editor in chaps. 40–55, has already raised some serious problems with this analysis because he does not believe that the *qarob* redaction is incompatible with the earlier writings of Second Isaiah (49:1–6 helps bridge this gap).

[63] R. G. Kratz, *Kyros im Deuterojesaja-Buch: redaktionsgeschichtliche Untersuchungen zu Entstehung und Theologie von Jes 40–55,* FAT 1 (Tübingen: Mohr-Siebeck, 1991).

of Zion. A third redaction focused on the "servant of the Lord" (42:1–4; 49:1–6; 52:13–53:12), and the fourth redactional layer emphasized the nearness of God's salvation (46:12–13; 51:4–5; 55:6–8). A fifth layer involved later Zion texts (45:25–26a; 49:24–26; 51:1–2,7–8,12–15,20–23; 54:1–55:5,10–11) that describe God's future blessings on Zion, including a new covenant. A sixth redactional layer emphasized Israel's disobedience, and a seventh the manufacture and worship of idols.[64] Finally, the redactional study of R. P. Merendino on chaps. 40–48 proposed that there were five small original independent units that were authentic to Deutero-Isaiah. Each is characterized by strong self-affirmations by God ("I am Yahweh; the First and the Last") in 44:24–48:22. Later redactional additions gave this core a more universalistic tone, then another layer about the making of idols was added to this material.[65]

Such theories seem unusually subjective in their subdivision of themes and symbols to completely separate authors, for it would appear to be quite normal for the average prophet to be able to address a large number of themes and express himself in diverse syntactical and symbolic ways. To limit an author/redactor to one narrow line of thought and only one means of expression seems quite rigid and unrealistic, for normal people and especially a gifted poet will be skilled in presenting a multitude of arguments in a variety of ways, depending on the audience he is addressing. Jeremiah lived in Jerusalem, but he knew about and addressed a letter to the exiles (Jer 29); and Ezekiel's presence in exile did not prevent him from discussing events in Jerusalem. These examples suggest that one cannot limit a prophet's oracles to the issues of the people right in front of him and that references to different audiences or new themes do not automatically imply a change of authors. Although it is certainly possible to imagine that there might be some small additions to this book by a disciple of the prophet, there does not seem to be a lot of explicit evidence of multiple redactional layers being reworked in chaps. 40–55.

CANONICAL. B. S. Childs's commentary on the whole book of Isaiah is a good example of a canonical approach. Childs indicates that he wants to present "a fresh interpretive model that does not get lost in methodological debates, and that proves to be illuminating in rendering a rich and coherent interpretation of the text as sacred scripture for the church and synagogue."[66] He is especially concerned about the unity of the canonical form of the book, but he hesitates to call this a canonical approach. He agrees with the critical view that the book has three distinct parts, although he does not accept the idea that a separate prophet called Trito-Isaiah wrote the literature in chaps. 56–66.[67]

---

[64] J. van Oorschot, *Von Babel zum Zion: Eine literarkritische und redaktionsgeschichtliche Untersuchung*, BZAW (Berlin: de Gruyter, 1993).

[65] R. P. Merendino, *Der Erste und der Letzte: Eine Untersuchung von Jes 40–48*, VTSup 31 (Leiden: Brill, 1981).

[66] B. S. Childs, *Isaiah*, OTL (Louisville: Westminster John Knox, 2001), 7.

[67] Ibid., 444.

He recognizes in principle the multilayered nature of the redactional process, but he does not find any unity or canonical authority in these successive layers and does not believe it is possible to reconstruct the "precise stages in the compositional history of the book of Isaiah."[68] Childs's "aim is not to reconstruct an allegedly original oracle of the prophet that can be distinguished from later accretions within the final form."[69] Childs places great emphasis on the intertextual reuse of common themes to identify the unified nature of the text (following Beuken) and provides some synchronic and diachronic analysis.[70]

Childs accepts the common critical reasons for identifying chaps. 40–55 as a separate later work written in the exile.[71] He believes the strongest argument for this position is that the work of Cyrus is not presented as a future prediction but as an accomplished fact.[72] He views the multigenre messages in chaps. 40–55 as a literary composition, not a record of the oral preaching of a prophet. Childs does not spend much time describing his hermeneutical methodology, but he does reject the hypothetically reconstructed redactional and form-critical approaches that atomize the text into innumerable short units based on the appearance of different genres or a different theme.[73]

Childs rejects the view that the Servant poems are secondary additions; instead, they should be interpreted in light of their surrounding literary context.[74] Thus Israel's complaint that God was not just (40:27) is answered by revealing that God's chosen and anointed servant will bring forth justice to all nations (42:1–4). In 42:1–6 the servant will in some way embody a covenantal relationship with the nations, but it is still a mystery how Israel might be this servant.[75] According to Childs, this unidentified servant individual (he is not the prophet Isaiah) remains a mystery in Isaiah.[76]

Childs's commentary on most individual verses is very brief and cursory. He often renders judgments on various approaches or interpretations without explaining why he has a different interpretation. At times Childs ignores historical data to his own detriment,[77] for further investigation of historical problems

---

[68] Ibid., xiii.

[69] Ibid., 63.

[70] Ibid., 2–5.

[71] Ibid., 289–91: (a) The historical setting is an exilic period; (b) there are differences of language, style, and concepts; (c) to suggest that an eighth-century prophet spoke to people 150 years later has no parallel in the rest of the Old Testament.

[72] Ibid., 291.

[73] Ibid., 306.

[74] Ibid., 323.

[75] Ibid., 325–26.

[76] Ibid., 420–22.

[77] For example, Childs admits that scholars have noticed that the violent fall of Babylon described in chap. 46 does not match Cyrus's conquest in 539 BC, yet he ignores this problem. He also refuses to discuss the historical issues surrounding God's giving of Egypt, Cush, and Seba to an unnamed king (43:3), assuming this was Cyrus even though it is well known that these countries were not conquered until 17 years after the death of Cyrus.

could lead to a deeper appreciation of the setting of the prophet's audience and the need for the words of hope provided by the prophet. Childs wisely questions some modern interpretations. For example: (a) he understands that the proclamations of salvation are predicting changes that will happen in an eschatological era (41:17–20; 51:7–12) and is not describing idealistic prophecies about the postexilic era, (b) he admits that some messages that are assigned to an exilic setting do not actually have anything within them that can enable one to connect them to the exile,[78] and (c) he believes chaps. 56–66 function to consciously unite the themes in chaps. 1–39 and 40–55. Thus Childs helpfully challenges several common critical interpretations and begins to balance the scales of opinion by focusing on some synchronic issues that unite the messages of Isaiah.

CONCLUSION. Every reader of Isaiah comes to the text with some assumptions and uses some methodology in interpreting the messages presented in chaps. 40–55. Each of the methodologies presented above has strengths and weaknesses. No one approach has the golden key that unlocks all the treasure house of wisdom that will solve every mystery in understanding chaps. 40–55. There are rhetorical markers in the text that help the interpreter to organize and understand the flow of each message, but anyone using the rhetorical approach also needs to take into consideration the results of the form-critical investigation of the genre of each oracle. Certainly one must have a focus on the final canonical form of the literature that has come down through the ages, but this does not mean the interpreter should totally ignore the possibility that some oracles were edited in various ways (the selection process, the ordering of these oracles, and the use of a hymn as a conclusion) as they were put into their final form. No one should simply ignore the wisdom of the traditional interpretations of our forefathers when reading chaps. 40–55, but one should never allow the traditional interpretation of a verse to prevent the possibility of understanding a verse in a new way if the preponderance of evidence points in a new direction. A good dose of common sense, a careful comparison and evaluation of the results of each methodology, and the guidance of the Holy Spirit will usually lead one to understand the main theological message that each oracle is communicating.

(3) Some Key Issues in the Debate

Isaiah 40–55 is a rich resource of hope and theological reflection that presents a general outline of God's present and future plans for his people, as well as for all the foreign nations of this world. The interpretation of God's message through this prophet is complicated by the fact that there are several basic issues of interpretation where there is still little agreement among Old Testament commentators. First, the exact location and circumstances of the prophet and his audience tend to be somewhat hidden because the poetic messages are not

---

[78] Ibid., 308, recognizes that there is nothing in 40:12–31 that indicates and exilic setting.

inextricably tied to (a) a narrative framework about named Israelite kings or to (b) many clearly identifiable historical events. In those few places where historical events are hinted at, it is not always easy to know how the author was temporally located in relationship to those events. The statement that "this is a people plundered and looted, all of them are trapped in pits or hidden in prisons" (42:22) could be understood from the perspective that the prophet was in exile and was referring to the oppressive Babylonian treatment of the Israelite captives. But in fact the text does not say who did this to the Israelites, nor does it identify where the people were presently living. Although some believe that this text describes the conditions of the Babylonian exiles, there is no comparable text from other books written about the exilic period that says the Babylonians actually put the exiles in prisons or that people were hiding in pits while they were in exile 70 years. One of the keys to resolving the meaning of these confusing passages is to identify the geographical location of the audience the prophet was speaking to. Two primary choices are available: (a) the audience was in Judah, or (b) the audience was in Babylonian exile.

Second, the literary construction and ordering of the short oracles in chaps. 40–55 can be quite puzzling because many different short prophetic genres were placed next to one another in a somewhat confusing way. Consequently, it is hard to know exactly how to deal with these brief oracles. Are these just a hodgepodge of short messages that need to be dealt with individually, or do several of these separate genres somehow fit together to form longer cohesive units? A clearer understanding of these structural issues would provide a clearer exegetical basis for understanding some of the theological issues raised in these messages and the overall structural organization of these chapters.

Third, there is some confusion about the past, present, near future, or distant future references in many prophetic statements. It is not always clear whether a passage refers to a present Assyrian crisis, a Babylonian crisis, problems while in exile, issues in Judah after the return of over 50,000 from exile (Ezra 1–2), or an eschatological event. Neither is it sometimes clear whether the perfect verb in some of these messages actually refers to past events or future events (taking the perfect verb as a prophetic perfect of certainty).[79]

GEOGRAPHICAL SETTING. The audience's setting is not clearly described in each message in chaps. 40–55, so most of the time it has to be implied from a limited amount of circumstantial evidence, hints in surrounding texts, and ambiguous statements that are sometimes open to multiple interpretations. Many critical commentaries suggest that an exilic prophet ("Deutero-Isaiah") wrote chaps. 40–55 to the people who were geographically located in

---

[79] GKC §106n refers to the perfect of certainty when an author wishes "to express facts which are undoubtedly imminent, and therefore in the imagination of the speaker, already accomplished." The prophetic perfect is used in situations when the "prophet so transports himself in imagination into the future that he describes the future event as if it had been already seen or heard."

Babylonian exile, somewhere around 550–540 BC.[80] In contrast, many traditional conservative commentators hypothesize that the prophet Isaiah wrote these words during the final days of Hezekiah (around or after the 701 BC events) and prophetically applied them to a future audience who would eventually be geographically located in Babylonian exile (39:6–7).[81] The disagreement between these two conclusions is over authorship; it is usually not about the geographic location of the audience.[82] Since the issue at hand is the question of the geographical location of the audience, the issue of authorship should be set aside as largely immaterial to answer the present question.

Most critical and many traditional conservative commentators agree with the idea that the audience in chaps. 40–55 was living in Babylonian exile.[83] But is there enough evidence to support this exilic interpretation as the location of the audience? It may be surprising to modern students of the book of Isaiah, that several early scholars did not place the author and the audience in chaps. 40–55 in Babylon. B. Duhm located the prophet in Phoenicia while H. Ewald put him in Egypt.[84] Later interpreters favored a Babylonian geographical location because of (a) the complaints of the exiles (40:27; 45:9–10); (b) information about Babylonian life, religion, and conditions (43:14; 46:1–47:15; 49:24); (c) knowledge of Cyrus, the Persian king who defeated Babylon in 539 BC (44:28; 45:1); and (d) the use of a first person style of writing found in the hymns of Ishtar and Royal Babylonian inscriptions.[85] In addition, some pointed to verses where Jerusalem was pictured as a city in ruins (44:26), as a widow that has lost her children (49:15; 52:1–3; 54:1–3), and the people were under Babylon's yoke or in prison (47:6; 49:9; 51:23).[86]

There are fundamental problems that make this method of interpreting these texts problematic, and much of the evidence for a Babylonian geographical location is open to alternative interpretations. For example: (a) 40:12–31 does not say that the people are in exile, so the so-called complaints of the exiles

---

[80] R. E. Clements, "Beyond Tradition-History: Deutero-Isaianic Development in First Isaiah's Themes," *JSOT* 31 (1985): 95–113, finds the sixth-century Babylonian background to 40–55 explicit.

[81] R. B. Chisholm, *Handbook on the Prophets* (Grand Rapids: Baker, 2002), 92, believes that "Isaiah assumes the perspective of the future exiles . . . he projects himself into the future and speaks to the exiles as if actually present with them in captivity."

[82] Ibid., 27, places the prophet and the audience in Israel.

[83] The critical commentary by R. N. Whybray, *Isaiah 40–66*, NCB (London: Marshall, Morgan, and Scott, 1975), 40–70, relates these chapters to an exilic setting, while the traditional conservative commentary by Oswalt, *Isaiah 40–66*, 45–105 relates the verses in chaps. 40–41 to an exilic setting.

[84] B. Duhm, *Das Buch Jesaja* (Göttingen: Vandenhoeck and Ruprecht, 1902), 336, and H. Ewald, *Die Jüngsten Propheten des Alten Bundes* (Göttingen: Vandenhoeck and Ruprecht, 1868), 30, both use the reference to סִינִים in 49:12 as their clue, but they found this site in different countries.

[85] E. Sellin and G. Fohrer, *Introduction to the Old Testament,* trans. D. E. Green (Nashville: Abingdon, 1968), 376, is a representative of this approach.

[86] J. Skinner, *The Book of the Prophet Isaiah: Chapters XL-LXVI*, CBSC (Cambridge: Cambridge University Press, 1929), xxxiii-xxxiv.

in 40:27[87] could have arisen for any number of reasons and from almost any geographical location. There simply is no objective evidence that these people were in Babylon. (b) Since Judah and other nations had trade and political relationships with Babylon, it is most likely that people throughout the ancient Near Eastern world had general information about Babylonian life and their religious practices; thus prophecies about the future defeat of Babylon (43:14; 46:1–47:15) do not require the conclusion that the audience was living in Babylon (any more than chaps. 13–14 require the audience to be living in Babylon). Although Isaiah spoke in detail about Egyptian life, religion, and culture in chaps. 19 and 30–31, commentators do not put the author and his audience in Egypt. (c) The use of a first person style of writing is common in the Bible, especially in Psalms and the prophets, so direct dependence on Babylonian hymns to Ishtar and Royal inscriptions is quite unlikely. (d) Jerusalem is pictured as a city in ruins, but it was repeatedly in ruins throughout the history of the nation, so how is one able to identify this as ruins caused specifically by the Babylonian army? The ruins of Judah and Jerusalem in chaps. 40–55 are usually not connected to any specific war or army, so most assume a Babylonian conquest without any evidence. (e) Prophecies about what will happen in the future to Babylon, to the exiles, to those who return from exile, and the eternal kingdom of God do not require the audience to be in any one setting, for these prophecies could be given anywhere. The content of a future prophecy does not determine the present location of the audience. Ezekiel could talk about what was happening in Jerusalem in 8:1–18, but his audience was in exile, not in Jerusalem. Later he could talk about the eschatological situation in Jerusalem (chaps. 40–48), but he was still talking to an audience in exile.

There are also difficulties with placing the audience in chaps. 40–55 in exile. (a) The description of Hebrew people making and worshipping pagan wooden idols was not a major problem addressed by other exilic and postexilic prophets. Since the prophetic books of Ezekiel, Daniel, Haggai, and Zechariah, and the historical books of Ezra and Nehemiah did not condemn the exiles or the postexilic community for making or worshipping idols, it is more likely that these chapters are addressing issues in another time and place when the worship of idols was a problem for the audience. (b) The oppressive trials of life (42:22–25) and wars (41:11–12) were not issues raised as major problems by other exilic or postexilic authors who were known to live in the Babylonian exile or who wrote to or about those in exile (Jeremiah, Ezekiel, Daniel, and Ezra). (c) Several of the prophecies in chaps. 40–55 about a glorious return of the people and the dramatic restoration in the land of Judah do not match what actually happened to the people when they left Babylon (as described in the accounts of Haggai, Zechariah,

---

[87] According to Whybray, *Isaiah 40–66*, 58, "My way is hidden from the LORD" does not mean that "God is unable to see the fate (way) of the exiles. . . . Israel's right (*mišpāṭ*) is the right that the exiles are claiming."

Ezra, Nehemiah).[88] Was Isaiah a false prophet with rose-tinted glasses? Was he prone to overinflated, grand rhetorical exaggeration, or is there another way of interpreting what he said? Possibly he was not speaking to exiles about their return from exile in Babylon in some of these messages of hope. Many of these passages appear to be eschatological promises that would be welcomed by any audience, but they do not imply that the audience was in exile.

Some interpreters have sensed the weaknesses of the evidence for a Babylonian setting for all of chaps. 40–66 and have suggested that the so-called "Trito-Isaiah" wrote chaps. 56–66 in Palestine after the people returned from Babylonian exile.[89] E. Sellin found a "general Palestinian point of view" in chaps. 56–66 and maintained that the later chapters "presuppose throughout the existence of the new Temple, which was dedicated in 515 BC."[90] The Sabbath was being celebrated in God's house (56:1–8), Jerusalem and its gates were standing (62:1–9), and Zion has brought forth sons and is joyful (66:7–13). Doubts about the Babylonian setting were extended to chaps. 49–55 when M. Haran found a Palestinian setting for chaps. 49–66.[91] He argued that these messages were primarily addressed to people in Judah (49:14–26; 51:17–23; 54), contained descriptions of people living in Jerusalem (49:18–22; 51:1–3; 50:4–9), rebuked people for sinfulness (50:10–11; 51:12–13; 55:2–3,6–7), and instructed them to "go out from there" (52:11), which implies that the author was not "there in Babylon" but lived somewhere else.

Some scholars are now questioning if the audience was in Babylonian exile in any of chaps. 40–55. C. Seitz suggests that "Judah is the most likely provenance" of the writer of 40–55.[92] J. D. Smart also found nothing that demands the prophet wrote in Babylon; instead, it appears that he may be countering idol worship in Judah and was looking forward to an eschatological restoration of people from the four corners of the earth.[93] H. C. Spykerboer states that "the coherence of 40:12–55:5 as demonstrated in our study must also lead to the conclusion that the

[88] R. P. Carroll, "Second Isaiah and the Failure of Prophecy," *ST* 32 (1978): 119–31, highlights this conflict in expectations, for there never was a glorious return of so many exiles that the land was crowded. Nor did the land all of a sudden turn into a wet and fertile land of plenty; nor did the nations bow to Yahweh and worship him with the Hebrews in Jerusalem; and the salvation and protection of God did not last forever.

[89] C. Westermann, *Isaiah 40–66*, OTL (Philadelphia: Westminster, 1977), 296, puts "Trito-Isaiah" at 537–521 BC in Jerusalem, dating 60:13 before 521 BC because it indicates that the temple was not rebuilt yet.

[90] Sellin and Fohrer, *Introduction to the Old Testament,* 384.

[91] M. Haran, "The Literary Structure and Chronological Framework of the Prophecies in Isa 40–48," *Congress Volume Bonn 1962,* VTSup (Leiden: Brill, 1963), 150–55.

[92] C. Seitz, "The Divine Council: Temporal Transition and New Prophecy in the Book of Isaiah," *CBQ* 109 (1990): 230, n. 5, bases this on the relationship of chaps. 40–66 with Lamentations, Zechariah 1–8, and numerous Psalms.

[93] J. D. Smart, *History and Theology in Second Isaiah: A Commentary on Isaiah 35, 40–66* (Philadelphia: Westminster, 1965), 20–33, admits that no one knows the location of the prophet for certain but argues against a Babylonian location.

whole work is meant for the same group of people, i.c. primarily for the Israelites in Jerusalem."[94] Long ago J. H. Maynard saw that these chapters, (a) seemed to show relatively little knowledge about Babylonian culture; (b) mentioned trees that grew in Palestine rather than Babylon; (c) described making idols out of trees not available in Babylon and never referring to the popular Babylonian palm tree; (d) talked about enemies coming from the north and east, a sign that the people were in Judah; (e) conceived of Ur as the "ends of the earth" in 41:9, an unlikely statement if the people were living next door in Babylon; (f) spoke about people being taken "from here" (meaning Jerusalem) in 52:5; and (g) described those exiled by Assyria.[95] H. M. Barstad argues for a setting in Judah, concluding that there was little Akkadian linguistic influence on Isaiah's writing and little evidence to support a Babylonian background for 40–55.[96] J. Motyer maintains that chaps. 40–55 are Babylonian in orientation but not in setting.[97] After connecting several phrases from Lamentations to passages in Isaiah 40–55, L. S. Tiemeyer concludes that these interlinking connections argue for the conclusion that chaps. 40–55 have a Judahite perspective and that this prophet is attempting "to convince the people of Judah that a return of their exilic brothers and sisters would be in their interest."[98]

These studies present convincing evidence that the audience that first heard these messages was not living in Babylon but rather in Judah. This conclusion would alleviate some of the problems mentioned above and significantly change the interpretation of many of the messages found in chaps. 40–55. There are several reasons why the evidence in chaps. 40–55 fits a geographic location of an audience in Judah.

---

[94] H. C. Spykerboer, *The Structure and Composition of Deutero-Isaiah with Special Reference to the Polemics against Idolatry* (Meppel: Krips, 1976), 187. He interprets many of the references to the new things, the restoration of nature, water in the desert, and the restoration of Zion as references to what will eventually happen when the Lord comes. He theorized that the prophet Deutero-Isaiah was in exile writing to the people in Jerusalem to comfort them.

[95] J. H. Maynard, "The Home of Deutero-Isaiah," *JBL* 36 (1917): 213–24, also mentions that the geographical countries the prophet mentions are those of Lebanon (40:16), Sela (42:11), Egypt and Ethiopia (43:2)—places around Judah, not Babylon. These and other similar arguments were also made by M. Buttenwieser, "Where Did Deutero-Isaiah Live?" *JBL* 38 (1919): 94–112.

[96] H. M. Barstad, "On the So-Called Babylonian Literary Influence in Second Isaiah," *JSOT* 2 (1987): 90–110 and his *The Babylonian Captivity of the Book of Isaiah: "Exilic" Judah and the Provenance of Isaiah 40–55* (Oslo: Novus, 1997), 64–65.

[97] Motyer, *Isaiah*, 28, finds that the circumstances of the people "bear no relation to what we know of the actual experience of those who were transported to Babylon (cf. Jer 29; Ezk)."

[98] L. S. Tiemeyer, "Geography and Textual Allusions: Isaiah xl–lv and Lamentations as Judahite Texts," *VT* 57 (1007): 367–85, makes these comparisons: (a) "comfort" in 40:1; 49:13; 51:12 with Lam 1:2,9,16–17,21; 2:13; (b) "being abandoned, forgotten" in 49:14 with Lam 5:20; (c) Zion is a mother and her children in 49:17–23 with Lam 2:11–22; 4:1–10; and (d) Jerusalem's starving and dying children in 51:17–23 and Lamentations 2 and 4. Although agreeing with some of this evidence, this commentary takes several of these texts as referring to the eschatological setting of the nations in Jerusalem. Those examples do not say much about the prophet's present audience or location, but we agree that these texts do not support an exilic interpretation of chaps. 40–55.

(a) The people living in Judah did worship idols made of wood (40:18–20; 44:9–20) and did offer worthless sacrifices (1:10–15; 2:8; 10:11; 43:22–24). The prophets in Judah repeatedly condemned the nation for these kinds of sins (Mic 5:13; Jer 10:1–16; Ezek 8:5–18). The exilic prophets Daniel and Ezekiel did not condemn the exiles for making and worshipping pagan idols. Placing the audience in Jerusalem makes sense of the prophet's condemnation of the making and worshipping of idols.

(b) Several of the prophecies that are often connected to the return to Jerusalem and the restoration in the land of Judah in chaps. 40–55 do not match what actually happened to the people after the return to Judah according to the records in Haggai, Zechariah, Ezra, and Nehemiah. If these positive statements about a glorious restoration of Zion in chaps. 40–55 were about the future of those in exile, they were misleading at best, if not outright falsehoods. But if these proclamations of salvation are understood as eschatological prophecies to be fulfilled in the distant future, this would alleviate the claims that Isaiah was a false prophet. In addition, if these proclamations of salvation are viewed as eschatological, this would naturally eliminate much of the evidence that is typically used to support an exilic setting for those oracles. In this understanding, the physical transformation of nature and the spiritual revival of the people in 44:1–5 are an ideal eschatological hope, not a promise of immediate restoration to an audience that is presently dwelling in exile. This does not mean that one can simply eliminate (like C. C. Torrey) or eschatologically reinterpret all references to Babylon or reinterpret references to the Persian King Cyrus (43:14; 44:28; 45:1; 46–47; 48:20). It simply means that one must carefully decipher how the prophet skillfully used eschatological themes to support his message of hope for his audience. These adjustments would alleviate the charges that this inspired prophet provided grossly exaggerated claims that were never fulfilled. This would also remove the need to interpret chaps. 55–66 as an attempt to reinterpret and spiritualize the failed promises of chaps. 40–55 (Zimmerli). Understanding these proclamations of salvation as eschatological does not prove the audience was in Jerusalem, for proclamations of salvation seldom give any hint about the location of the prophet's present audience. This understanding of these oracles does remove evidence that is often used to suggest a location in exile.

(c) The prophet did speak about a future judgment for his people in Babylon (39:7), that Jerusalem would one day be destroyed (43:28), that Babylon would eventually be destroyed (43:4; 46–47; 48:14), that people would return from Babylon (48:20), and that God would gather them back to their land. But since very few of these prophecies were overtly connected to historical events (only a few refer to Babylon), it is not always easy to distinguish between past and future events, Assyrian and Babylonian wars, or near or eschatological fulfillments. Consequently, the interpreter should be careful not to immediately harmonize everything in these chapters to one setting (the Babylonian exile) or assume that these chapters are all in some sort of chronological order. Each passage must be based on the evidence presented, and due consideration must be given to the possibility that a passage may be eschatological, or it may refer to situations related to the Assyrian conquest of Jerusalem in chaps. 36–39 or to events in the time of Cyrus. Most important, one must also be prepared to conclude that many oracles do not have enough information in them to indicate when or to whom they were spoken.

The perspective one has on the geographic location of the audience will have a significant effect on the interpretation of chaps. 40–55. Since the historical acts of divine punishment on Judah in chaps. 40–55 are not connected to any specific historical king (42:22,24–25; 48:10; 52:4–5; 54:4,7–8), it is hypothetically possible to connect God's dealings with his people to either an Assyrian, Babylonian, or Persian time frame. In 52:4–5 the prophet refers to the past oppression of the nation in Egypt and a more recent exiling of people by an Assyrian king. This Assyrian context of the people in Judah cannot be ignored in the interpretation of chaps. 40–55, even though a hypothetical Babylonian setting for 52:5 is implied or assumed by some. Each text must be investigated for the evidence it presents, rather than imposing on all texts one setting by harmonizing them all to an exilic setting.

GENRE.   The prophetic messages in chaps. 40–55 are patterned after numerous literary forms of speech. Some of the key literary forms are: (a) disputation speech, (b) salvation oracle, (c) proclamation of salvation, (d) trial speech, (e) servant poem, and (f) hymn. The form-critical understanding of these different genres will play a major role in how one interprets each oracle and how one organizes these different oracles into longer unified speeches. Each of these different genres will be introduced later as they appear in the text of Isaiah.

Two main issues are raised by the use of these literary forms in chaps. 40–55. First, when a series of these different genres is put together in a chapter, are the distinct forms of speech to be treated individually as if each one was a short independent speech that has nothing to do with the one following it, or should they be connected to each other in some way to form a longer multifaceted speech? Were these different form-critical genres editorially collected together as a hodgepodge of unconnected short sayings, or were they purposely strung together to form a complex unified longer message? A second issue that needs to be addressed is, Do these different genres keep their distinct literary and cultural flavor when they are joined to different forms of speech, or do they lose some of their original cultural meaning by their use in these complex messages?

When a reader comes to a new form of speech, it is rather natural to assume that a new rhetorical unit is being introduced, but is that always so?[99] The

---

[99] Melugin, *The Formation of Isaiah 40–55*, 1–2, agrees that this applies in the early prophets but not in Isaiah 40–55. H. Gressmann, "Die Literarische Analyse Deuterojesajas," *ZAW* 34

regularly structured war oracles against the nations in Amos 1:3–2:16 end at the conclusion of chap. 2 when that form of literature stops. Similarly, the introduction of a dirge in Amos 5:1 or a woe oracle in 6:1 marks the beginning of new literary forms and new oracles. On the other hand, the prophet Amos does introduce a short hymn (4:13) as the conclusion to 4:6–13, without starting a totally new message.[100]

Many years ago H. Gressmann treated each short speech in chaps. 40–55 separately as a self-contained unit representing one genre,[101] and in some ways C. Westermann continued that general emphasis on the unique contribution of each short paragraph that represents a different genre. J. Muilenburg's rhetorical approach to chaps. 40–55 argued that although this prophet drew from several different literary genres in each message, he did not isolate each into a separate unrelated speech. The prophet somewhat modified each literary form when editing them together in order to construct longer cohesive units of thought.[102] Studies by R. Melugin do not completely share J. Muilenburg's opinion about the limited value of a form-critical analysis of each unit, though Melugin agrees that the prophecies in chaps. 40–55 have uniquely joined several literary forms together into longer structural units.[103] Melugin attempts to develop a balance between the distinctive uniqueness of each genre and the prophet's creative ability to invent new longer literary messages that contain a combination of different influences that no longer follow the traditional parameters of individual genres. This struggle between the original use of unique forms of speech and their present creative function in the complex messages of Isaiah requires the interpreter to appreciate both the traditional use of each genre, but also to be open to the prophetic modification of each form of speech so that it can function in a new way. Any attempt to find unity within these diverse genres in a single message involves some subjective judgments, yet rhetorical features like the repetition of vocabulary can provide objective evidence of this unifying effort. Maintaining this balance between an appreciation of the original form as well as openness to the creative prophetic modification of these forms eliminates the need for complex redactional theories that attribute different elements to different stages of the development of the text. The real problem therefore is not in identifying the various literary forms of speech (although not all agree on this matter), but in discovering how these

---

(1914): 254–97, followed this approach, and the recent work of A. Schoors, *I Am God Your Savior: A Form-critical Study of the Main Genres of Is XL–LV* (Leiden: Brill, 1973), 15, 52, 297, treats the genres in isolation and finds no structural connection between them.

[100] G. V. Smith, *Amos* (Fearn: Christian Focus, 1998), 59–65, 205–15, 259–65, provides a discussion of each unit and the characteristics of each genre of literature.

[101] Gressmann, "Die Literarische Analyse Deuterojesajas," *ZAW* 34 (1914): 254–97, thought someone had created an anthology of numerous short saying by the prophet but made no attempt to put them together into longer speeches.

[102] Muilenburg, "Isaiah: Chaps. 40–66," 5:381–90.

[103] Melugin, *Formation of Isaiah 40–55*, 77–89.

were structurally put together and how they function together. In the commentary below, there will be an introduction to each section of the text that will present a possible way of dealing with the unifying factors in each literary unit from a rhetorical, genre, and theological perspective.

An interrelated interpretive issue is the relationship of the servant poems (a unique genre) to their literary context. Because of different conclusions on this issue, commentators offer widely divergent outlines of the structure of these chapters. There is a need for an explanation of how this particular genre fits together with the surrounding passages to create some sort of unified whole. This is a complex issue that is dealt with in the exegesis of each servant poem (42:1–13; 49:1–13; 50:4–11; 52:13–53:12) by connecting vocabulary in the surrounding chapters to the vocabulary used in the servant poem. For example, it will be argued that 42:1–13 is connected to its literary context in several ways (a) God will bring "justice" (*mišpāṭ* in 42:1,3,4) to his people who think that they were not being dealt with justly (40:27) and to the nations who need to be treated with justice (41:1). (b) This servant poem contrasts the former and new things (42:9), similar to the past and future events mentioned in 41:22,26. (c) In earlier oracles God acted in past and future history to prove that he is God and not the idols (40:18–20; 41:21–19), and this idea appears again in 42:8. (d) The nations and islands by the sea that are nothing in 40:15,17 will receive hope and the promise of justice in 42:1,4 so that they, too, can proclaim God's praise (42:10–13). (e) Finally, just as God promised to "uphold" his fearful, oppressed people in 41:10, so he will "uphold" his servant in 42:1. These common themes suggest that one should not remove this message from the surrounding literary context of chap. 41[104] and should not view it as a later secondary editorial insertion that does not fit in this context.[105] It seems most logical to favor the outline that is based on various linguistic signs that signal the structural organization of the whole and observes the internal development of ideas within and across different literary units. Thus it will be argued in each situation that the unique "servant poems" should not be seen as later redactional additions to the text of Isaiah.

TIME. It is sometimes difficult to know if a specific message is referring to events and ideas that relate to the present time of the prophet and his audience, to a near future prophetic event that is about to happen in a few years, or if he is talking about a distant future eschatological idea that will not happen for many

---

[104] Spykerboer, *The Structure and Composition of Deutero-Isaiah*, 80–81, suggests that the use of הן as the first word in 42:1 is "a suitable way of introducing an important statement, which however does not stand on its own, but follows from what has been said in the preceding line(s)." He notes that הן functions to introduce a strong contrast in 40:19 and that 41:24 and 29 use this particle to introduce the conclusion that the idol gods are nothing. Thus he concludes that הן does not introduce totally new paragraphs.

[105] C. R. Seitz, "'You are my Servant, You are the Israel in whom I will be Glorified:' The Servant Songs and the Effect of Literary Context in Isaiah," *CTJ* 39 (2004): 117–34, addresses this issue.

years. Consequently, it is not always clear if a passage refers to something that is happening in the present Assyrian or Babylonian crisis, or if a message is referring to a problem associated with people who were living in the Babylonian exile, or if the prophet is talking about issues associated with life in Judah after the return of the Hebrew people from exile. These problems are sometimes connected to the interpretation of the perfect verb (cf. 40:2; 65:10–11) or textual critical issues (cf. 43:28), for the perfect form of the verb can syntactically function to represent action in the past or to action within a future time frame (taking the perfect verb as a prophetic perfect of certainty).[106]

While some authors make almost all prophecies applicable to the immediate time frame of the prophet, others distinguish between themes (the appearing of the glory of God) and literary genres (the proclamation of salvation) that primarily address eschatological themes and events. In order to be able to distinguish between different salvation messages about God's future plans for Zion, it is necessary to understand adequately the audience's expectation for the future. If one interprets all salvation messages to refer to the what will happen in the near future after the exile, it appears that most of the rosy prophecies of chaps. 40–55 failed to materialize in the depressing postexilic era. R. Carroll concludes that some of these optimistic prophecies gave a false impression of unparalleled revival and restoration that did not happen after the return from exile. Therefore there was a need in the postexilic period for a new reapplication of these failed prophecies in light of the depressing situation of the nation after the exile. But others question if such a conclusion is necessary, an appropriate way of dealing with an inspired prophetic text, or the only option available to the interpreter. Can a different interpretation of these prophecies alleviate the distasteful conclusion that Isaiah gave false prophecies in chaps. 40–55 and thus prevent an inevitable undermining of the authority of the salvation messages in this book? A conclusion suggesting that Isaiah's prophecies were not true runs contrary to the theological argument that Isaiah's God knows, can predict, and is able to fulfill what he predicts. If God's description of what will happen in the future was false, this seriously undermines the message of the whole book of Isaiah. If some of these messages (especially the proclamations of salvation) are understood as eschatological prophecies related to the distant future (the perspective of Muilenburg), then the fact that these prophecies were not fulfilled in the postexilic era is immaterial, for they refer to another era, not the postexilic period. This will also alleviate the need to understand chaps. 56–66 as a spiritualization and reapplication of the failed prophecies of chaps. 40–55.

(4) Structure

If the genres of literature are to be joined together to form longer units of speech, the interpreter must identify any structural signs that mark the beginning

---

[106] GKC §106n.

and the end of this long literary unit; identify any patterns of structure within smaller literary units; and identify the flow of thought or logical progression that exists between the main segments in chaps. 40–55. Although it is impossible to discover the thought process that the author had in his own mind when structuring these prophecies, one can observe certain linguistic markers that reveal some information about the structuring mechanisms used to provide organization to these chapters. The structuring mechanisms found in this study include the use of the hymns, repeated words or themes, an *inclusio*, and the practice of alternating between two different forms of speech.

First, the interpreter must identify the limits of the main literary sections. At the beginning of this introduction it was argued that the larger structural organization of chaps. 40–66 can be divided into two literary units: chaps. 40–55 and chaps. 56–66. Most interpreters view the introduction of poetic words of comfort in 40:1 as a signal that the prophet was beginning a new series of speeches different from the historical narratives of chaps. 36–39. Chapters 40–48 and 49–55 are frequently grouped together because the earlier chapters are addressed to Jacob/Israel whereas the later chapters are addressed to Zion/Jerusalem. In addition, many of the themes in 40–48 (condemnation of idols, war against Israel, reference to Babylon, God is the first and the last) are not found in chaps. 49–55. Nevertheless, chap. 48 does not mark the end of a major literary unit; it is merely the end of one of the smaller segments within 40–55. When one moves past these general thematic differences between 40–48 and 49–55, there is little consistent agreement between commentators about how to organize the material in 40–55 into smaller segments.[107]

It is difficult to follow a natural thematic flow of thought to a conclusion that marks the end of each of the smaller segments of thought in chaps. 40–55. It appears that the main structuring device that was used to mark the end of these smaller literary segments within chaps. 40–55 was the hymn, a literary genre that earlier marked the end of chaps. 2–12.[108] Thus it is not surprising to find that 55:12–13 ends this long section with a hymn of praise. Hymns also mark the end of each of the main messages after the introduction.

---

[107] A. Laato, "The Composition of Isaiah 40–55," *JBL* 109 (1990): 207–28, finds a five-cycle chiastic macrostructure (A – B – A′ – B′ – A″) in which the A cycles have a chiastic arrangement and the B cycles have a parallel arrangement (consult the diagram on his pp. 212–13). This hypothetical reconstruction is not very convincing, for the calling of the servant to bring forth justice in 42:1–4 is not really parallel to the questions and encouraging reassurance found in 40:27–31. It also does not appear that 40:12–26 and 42:5–9 are two matching pairs in a chiasm. In the fifth cycles the description of the ministry of the servant in 49:1–13 does not seem to be a chiastic match for 52:7–10. He concludes that 40:1–2 is a prologue and 52:13–53:12 is an epilogue, thus chaps. 54–55 do not actually belong to this structural unit. This approach totally ignores the role of the hymns to mark the end of literary units.

[108] E. Hessler, "Die Struktur der Bilder bei Deuterojesaja," *EvT* 25 (1965): 349–69, noticed this feature and pointed out the structural importance of these hymns.

These textually marked units will form the skeleton for the structural outline of chaps. 40–55; as each segment is considered in the commentary below, it will be outlined into several smaller paragraphs. Based on the thematic emphasis within the segments marked out above, it is possible to group some of these sections together.

For example, it is possible to divide chaps. 40–48 into 40:12–44:23 and 44:24–48:22 based on the main themes they treat. The first group begins with assurances of God's power to strengthen his people in times of trials and weakness (40:12–42:13). The people of Israel do not need to fear other more powerful nations or the idol-gods of these nations, for God knows the future and will bring justice and salvation to all. In 42:14–44:23 God accuses his blind servants of being sinful and therefore deserving punishment, but the blind must trust God, not the idols, for he will forgive them and transform their world. Why would anyone be so deceived that they would trust a piece of wood? These messages to Jacob/Israel have a simple structure:

| God's power will bring strength and justice | 40:12–42:13 |
| God will punish, forgive, and restore his blind people | 42:14–44:23 |

The second grouping of 44:24–48:22 deals with God's deliverance of his people and the rebuilding of his temple through the work of the great king Koresh. Eventually there will be a day when all nations will come and bow before God. Before that happens, God will destroy sinful Babylon and stubborn Judah. These messages include

| God will restore Jerusalem, then offer salvation to all | 44:24–45:25 |
| God will humble sinful Babylon and Judah | 46:1–48:22 |

The next general group of messages in chaps. 49–55 address Zion/Jerusalem, suggesting a greater change of emphasis within these chapters. These new messages are set apart from chaps. 40–48 by the omission of previous themes. For example, the messages in chaps. 49–55 do not address (a) the coming of a

---

great conqueror of the nations, Israel's fear, and her wars, (b) the defeat of the Daughter of Babylon and her gods, (c) the uselessness of constructing and trusting idols made of wood, (d) themes like the former things and the later things, (e) descriptions of God as the first and the last, and (f) references to Jacob/Israel.[110] These were very important issues that were central to the messages in 40–48, but chaps. 49–55 focus much more attention on the character, role, and difficult ministry of the "servant of the Lord" (49:1–13; 50:4–11) and include a long discussion of the suffering and victory of this individual (52:13–53:12). Alternating between and after the three servant poems are eschatological proclamations of salvation that give new hope to the Daughter of Zion/Jerusalem (49:14–50:3; 51:1–52:10; 54:1–17). This creates the structure:

Servant poem	49:1–13
Salvation for Zion	49:14–50:3
Servant poem	50:4–11
Salvation for Zion	51:1–52:12
Servant poem	52:13–53:12
Salvation for Zion	54:1–17
Conclusion	55:1–13

This emphasis on the positive eschatological hope of Zion/Jerusalem replaces the earlier discussion of the rebellion and blindness of Jacob/Israel in chaps. 40–48. This Daughter of Zion should not be hopeless, for she will no longer suffer ruin, oppression, and widowhood. God's anger against her is past, her enemies will be defeated, and Mother Zion will have many children (49:17–25; 54:1–17). It is difficult to know what caused these changes in emphasis and themes, but it appears that most of chaps. 40–48 address present or near-future problems while chaps. 49–55 mainly address eschatological themes of the distant future. It would not be odd to have similar thematic material gathered together in one place in chaps. 40–48 and then another group of similar messages gathered together in an alternating pattern in chaps. 49–55.

The flow of thought within the segments of this outline depends on how one evaluates and highlights the themes emphasized in each paragraph; consequently, the flow of thought in various outlines can look quite different from one commentary to the next. The content of the first paragraph suggests that the prophet began by announcing the eschatological coming of the Lord to shepherd his sheep (40:1–11). Although the prophet's audience in Jerusalem had many fears, God announced that he is stronger than any nation or any pagan god, has control over the history and power of each nation, and will eventually establish justice on the earth through His Servant (40:12–42:13). Many of

---

[110] C. Stuhlmueller, "Deutero-Isaiah: Major Transitions in the Prophet's Theology and in Contemporary Scholarship," *CBQ* 42 (1980): 1–29, and specifically his discussion of the chart of differences between 40–48 and 49–55 on pp. 5–9. P. Wilcox, "The Servant Songs in Deutero-Isaiah," *JSOT* 42 (1988): 79–102, also lists some of these same characteristics for 40–48 and 49–55.

God's people had acted sinfully like his blind servant; therefore, they had great fear because they were facing a military crisis of divine judgment. Nevertheless, God promises to be with them, forgive their sins, and eventually restore them to their land (42:14–44:23). At some point God will rebuild Jerusalem through Koresh, after Babylon and her gods are destroyed. Then many nations will bow and glorify God (44:24–48:22). God's special Servant will play a central role in bringing God's people and the nations to trust and glorify God (49:1–13). Though briefly forsaken, if Zion will follow God, like his Servant, God's strong arm will bring salvation and restoration (50:1–52:12). Since the Servant will suffer for the sins of many, compassion and joy are possible, but Judah needs to repent of her sins (53:13–55:13). The message of comfort is clear; the sovereign God of history will restore his people and the nation by removing the guilt of their sins and destroying their enemies.

4. Compositional Issues Related to Chapters 56–66

Since chaps. 56–66 are a separate literary unit and are frequently attributed to a later prophet (often called "Trito-Isaiah"), it is necessary to address the specific issues that are connected to interpreting these chapters. It is important to understand the issues that led to the formulation of this hypothesis, trace the arguments for and against this approach to understanding these chapters, and consider carefully the implications of accepting or rejecting this theory. This process of evaluation will enable the reader to interact with the conclusions of various commentators that hypothesize a Trito-Isaiah who lived in the post-exilic era around the time of Ezra and Nehemiah.

When a person initially starts reading chaps. 56–66, it may appear to be introducing a new theological perspective because it deals with the new themes of Sabbath keeping, allowing foreigners into the temple, and observing a fast that honors God. These are not common themes in the preceding chapters. But the more one reads and examines the messages in this new literary section, the more one realizes how close these messages are to the themes within the theology of the rest of the book of Isaiah. In fact, there are numerous quotations, restatements, or allusions to ideas treated earlier in chaps. 1–55. The Sabbath and fasting may be new topics, but in reality they are just another way to talk about how one can demonstrate true righteousness, just relationships, and trust in God. The underlying theology of these messages still relates to God's judgment of human sinfulness, his promises to bring salvation to all people, and the need for people to act justly and maintain their covenant relationship with God. They do not sound that different from the essential thrust of the earlier messages in the book of Isaiah. Therefore it is important to weigh very carefully the evidence for suggesting that chaps. 56–66 were written at a different time by a different author and addressed to a different audience.

Although the literary evidence suggests that the unit beginning in chap. 40 ends in 55, thus making 56–66 the final section of chapters in this book, it is doubtful that these messages are so unique that they must be placed in a completely different setting, at a different date, and by a different author(s). Early precritical studies of the book of Isaiah, like the commentary by J. Calvin, do not mention any problems of consistency between chaps. 56–66 and the theology of the preceding chapters.[111]

(1) Are Chapters 56–66 a Separate Book?

Critical commentators since the time of B. Duhm[112] (1892) have usually identified chaps. 56–66 as a separate book by a prophet called Trito-Isaiah from Jerusalem (not from Babylon) in the postexilic era (not from the Babylonian exile). Duhm distinguished this book from the earlier chapters in Isaiah partially because the subject matter (sacrifices and Sabbath) and the setting seemed to be somewhat different. He thought this section was written shortly before the time of Nehemiah with later redactional processes adding a few verses down to the Hasmonean period (78–69 BC). He related the internal disagreements within the community over the temple in Jerusalem (66:1) to the Samarians' opposition described in Ezra 4:1–5. Some commentators agreed with Duhm's position on the unity of chaps. 56–66 (K. Elliger) and his dating of the material, but many later studies have tended to identify various dates for different chapters and multiple authors or redactors within chaps. 56–66.[113]

Although Duhm's theory quickly spread and was widely accepted by many critical scholars, not everyone thought that chaps. 56–66 were a separate book written by someone different from the author of 40–55. C. C. Torrey examined and rejected the dominant critical hypotheses of his day concerning Trito-

---

[111] J. Calvin, "Commentary on the Prophet Isaiah," *Calvin's Commentaries*, VIII (Grand Rapids: Baker, 2003), 175ff, on 56:1 says, "This is a remarkable passage, in which the Prophet shews (*sic*) what God demands from us." But he has no problem integrating chaps. 56–66 into the flow of the book's argument. Childs, *The Struggle to Understand Isaiah as Christian Scripture*, 207–29, deals with Calvin's exegetical methodology and gives general comments on his commentary on Isaiah.

[112] B. Duhm, *Das Buch Jesaia*, 4th ed. (Göttingen: Vandenhoeck & Ruprecht, 1922, [1892]). He believed that Isaiah did not receive its final form until the Hasmonean period (70 BC). A. Rofé, "How Is the Word Fulfilled? Isaiah 55:6–11," in *Canon, Theology, and Old Testament Interpretation: Essays in Honor of B. S. Childs*, ed. G. M. Tucker, D. L. Petersen, R. R. Wilson (Philadelphia: Fortress, 1988), 246–62, indicates that A. Kuenen suggested this before Duhm.

[113] B. Schramm, *The Opponents of Third Isaiah*, JSOT Sup 193 (Sheffield: Sheffield Academic Press, 1995), 16–20, provides a chart of seven different approaches (Elliger, Volz, Fohrer, Soggin, Westermann, Pauritsch, and Hanson) that identify multiple authors and the multiple different dates when various verses were written. P. D. Hanson, *The Dawn of Apocalyptic: The Historical and Sociological Roots of Jewish Apocalyptic Eschatology* (Philadelphia: Fortress, 1975), 32–40, gives a survey of past studies of chaps. 56–66. K. Elliger, *Die Einheit Tritojesaia*, BWANT 45 (Stuttgart: Kohlhammer, 1928) hypothesizes that most of the book was written by a disciple of Isaiah between 538 and 500 BC.

Isaiah, partially because he did not believe the author of chaps. 40–55 was in Babylon[114] (thus there was no change in setting when one comes to chaps. 56–66) and because he thought that many of the promises of hope in chaps. 40–66 referred to the distant future, not the postexilic era. Torrey does makes the very questionable claim that the verses about Cyrus and Babylon were added to the text of Isaiah by someone who was trying to make Isaiah's prophecies fit the theological and historical framework of Chronicles; thus, he attempted to understand the book of Isaiah without these passages. Since there is no real basis for dismissing the verses about Cyrus and Babylon, Torrey's views are usually considered somewhat extreme, so his perspective has not gained acceptance; in fact, many commentators largely ignore his contributions.[115] Much more attention is now being given to the several possible redactions of Isaiah 56–66.

(2) Redactional Theories

C. Westermann's analysis of the growth of chaps. 56–66 has had a major impact on the discussion of the redaction and composition of these chapters. He proposed several distinct compositional stages with their own distinctive approaches to key theological themes in order to justify his interpretation of the literary production of chaps. 56–66.

1. Stage one was when the nucleus of the message of salvation in chaps. 60–62 was written. It includes an unqualified offer of salvation very similar to what is found in earlier chapters of Isaiah (plus other salvation oracles in 57:14–20; 65:16b–25; 66:6–16, and possibly 58:1–12). The foreign nations will bring back Israelites and serve them, thus they have a part in the salvation God will establish in Zion. Westermann views this salvation as unconditional. Within this material the first person voice of the prophet Trito-Isaiah is heard in 61:1–3, a disciple of Deutero-Isaiah. He dates these chapters to the era of Haggai and Zechariah (around 520–515 BC).[116] These chapters were set within the framework of two preexilic community laments in chaps. 59 and 63:7–64:11 (63:7–64:11

---

[114] C. C. Torrey, *The Second Isaiah* (New York: Scribner's Sons, 1928), 20–21, illegitimately dropped five references to Cyrus and Babylon (43:14; 44:28; 45:1; 48:14,20) because he thought they were later interpolations along with 52:2–6, thus he was able to remove almost all hints of Babylon. He dates 40–66 to about 400 BC. Smart, *History and Theology in Second Isaiah*, 229–31, accepted many of ideas from Torrey against the idea of a Third Isaiah. Smart dropped the legalistic passages about the Sabbath (56:1–7; 58:13–14) as latter additions by an orthodox legalist. Both Torrey and Smart thought that the same author who wrote 40–55 also wrote 56–66 in Jerusalem. He dated the author of 40–66 around 540 BC.

[115] Schramm, *The Opponents of Third Isaiah*, 21–29, is one of the few who take the time to outline and evaluate Torrey's hypothesis.

[116] Westermann, *Isaiah 40–66*, 296 believes that chaps. 60–62 "show from first to last a provenance from, or harkening back to, that of Deutero-Isaiah."

was a lament spoken shortly after the fall of Jerusalem in 587 BC).[117] This material shows no serious division of the Hebrew community between the righteous and those who rebelled against God.

2. A second stage involved the addition of several independent messages (mostly preexilic prophetic judgment oracles that were reapplied to a postexilic setting) referring to the conflict between the righteous believers and the wicked transgressors (56:9–57:13; 57:21; 59:2–8; 65:1–16a; 66:3,5,17). These messages contrast the worship and the destiny of these two groups.

3. The third stage in the process of developing chaps. 56–66 involved the addition of harsh judgments on foreign nations (60:12; 63:1–6; 66:6,15–16,20,22–23) that are quite different from the positive attitude toward the foreign nations that is found in earlier chapters in Isaiah and in 60–62. This stage also included some apocalyptic additions in 60:19–20; 65:17,26; 66:20,22–24.

4. A fourth stage involved the addition of short messages at the beginning and end of this series of messages (56:1–8; 66:18–19,21) that invite Gentiles into the community on equal terms with the Hebrews.[118]

Westermann suggests that these messages were primarily intended to encourage those who were greatly disillusioned because the grand promises made about the city of Jerusalem in earlier chapters of Isaiah (chaps. 40–55) were not being fulfilled in the postexilic era. This hypothetical reconstruction of the gradual development of chaps. 56–66 was based on the questionable hypothesis that each different topic requires a separate author and a later stage in the development process, even though many of the topics in each of these stages have already received some treatment in earlier chapters of the book of Isaiah. P. D. Hanson justifiably criticized Westermann's approach as being too rigid in attributing only one narrow theme to each of the different stages, thus ignoring the complexity of the community's situation and their broad theological background.[119]

More recent studies by J. Vermeylen and S. Sekine have produced even more complicated redactional theories that suggest that multiple redactors used preexilic, exilic, and postexilic texts that they adapted, expanded, or reapplied to address the contemporary situation of the Hebrew people during the time

---

[117] Ibid., 300–3, 386. His approach assumes that this author primarily wrote about one theme (salvation), so he concludes the laments are related to a worship setting that is unconnected to Trito-Isaiah's salvation messages (the judgment oracles also are different from Trito-Isaiah's salvation message).

[118] Ibid., 307, summarizes his analysis of the way these chapters were formed by repeated redactions and additions.

[119] Hanson, *The Dawn of Apocalyptic*, 40, n. 24 also criticizes most discussions of chaps. 56–66 for their "preoccupation with the problem of authorship." He considers these chapters to be an "anonymous collection."

of Nehemiah down to the third century BC.[120] These studies tend to emphasize how very different ideas (sometimes even contradictory) were brought together, demonstrating how fragmented these chapters really are (especially 56–59 and 63–66). The thorough and well-argued study of P. A. Smith has moved the pendulum back to a less complicated and a more believable conclusion that there were only two author/redactors, TI (Trito-Isaiah) who wrote 60:1–63:6 and TI_2 who wrote 56:1–8; 56:9–57:21; 58:1–59:20; 65:1–66:17. His primary criteria for identifying these two redactors were their distinctive vocabulary and ideology.[121] His analysis provides many significant insights into each literary unit, but one could suggest that several of the distinctive differences he identifies (the use of rhetorical questions, distinct vocabulary) are largely attributable to the differences in the topics under discussion rather than the differences between two different authors. Most of the redactional studies, with the exception of P. A. Smith, have produced highly fragmented readings of these chapters that overstress the differences between ideas that are not inherently contradictory.[122] Since an author/redactor is multidimensional and can weigh both sides of contradictory ideas in different ways, the results of some of these studies are quite subjective. They fail to appreciate the coherence of the literary structures within these chapters and their common dependence on earlier messages in the book of Isaiah.

(3) Sociological Reconstructions

In contrast to the different redactional approaches to chaps. 56–66, P. D. Hanson understood chaps. 56–66 as a collection of anonymous oracles that have "adhesive ingredients" that "betray a sort of a unity" around basic themes defined by a similar community situation, but he largely ignores the authorship/redaction debate. He adopts what he calls a "contextual-typological method" of analyzing the poetic structures, meter, and genres (the rise of apocalyptic and the salvation-judgment oracle), which includes a sociological analysis of the conflict found in chaps. 56–66. He uses this information to understand the growth of ideas from earlier chapters, the breakdown of classical prosaic forms and genres, and the evidence for a new crisis situation where different social groups (prophetic visionaries and noneschatological Zadokite hierocrats) were struggling

---

[120] J. Vermeylen, *Du Prophète Isaïe à l'apocalyptique. Isaïe I–XXXV, miroir d'un demi-millénaire d'expérience religieuse en Isräel*, 2 vols. (Paris: Gabalda, 1977–78), tries to make chaps. 56–66 fit his analysis of 1:1–2:5, but this requires the omission of 63:7–64:11 and 65:16–66:14, so his hypothesis is quite unpersuasive. His hypothesis of redaction finds seven stages or layers of tradition joined together from the sixth to the third century BC. S. Sekine, *Die Tritojesajanische Sammlung (Jes 56–66) redaktionsgeschichtliche untersucht*, BZAW 175 (Berlin: de Gruyter, 1989).

[121] P. A. Smith, *Rhetoric and Redaction in Trito-Isaiah: The Structure, Growth, and Authorship of Isaiah 56–66*, VTSup 62 (Leiden: Brill, 1995), 173–86.

[122] The eschatological promises in 60–62 are by their very definition going to be different from laments or ethical exhortations which are not eschatological because the setting, genre, and topics are different.

against one another for control of the temple in Jerusalem.[123] He concludes that the Zadokite priests who agreed with Ezekiel's program of temple restoration in Ezek 40–48 had control of the temple and its syncretistic services. They wanted to maintain their authority, while their opponents who followed Second-Isaiah and the restoration program of chaps. 60–62 felt rejected and powerless. This led the disillusioned visionaries toward an apocalyptic solution where God would come to his temple and restore true worship after judging the unrighteous. He identifies chaps. 56–66 as a distinct group of texts because the traditional bi- and tricolon structure of earlier prophecy has given way to what he calls longer more "baroque prosodic units."[124] By identifying 66:1–16 with the construction of the temple at the time of Haggai and Zechariah, he pinpoints an absolute date (520–515 BC) for the writing of this message and consequently he attempts to give a general chronological order to all the other oracles. In spite of this innovative way of analyzing chaps. 56–66, J. L. Kugel largely dismissed Hanson's syllable counting method of understanding poetry; thus, he seriously undermined the poetic evidence supporting part of Hanson's thesis.[125] B. Schramm thoroughly critiqued Hanson's sometimes circular reasoning and identified several areas where his interpretations of specific verses are problematic.[126] B. S. Childs also rejected Hanson's speculative sociological reconstruction of two postexilic warring parties (visionaries and hierocrats) in chaps. 56–66.[127] Many would agree that a great deal of Hanson's reconstruction is read into material; for example, Hanson understands the references to Abraham our father in 63:16 as a claim by the rejected visionaries that they have a relationship to the patriarch Abraham.

---

[123] Hanson, *The Dawn of Apocalyptic*, 29, 41–44, tends to ignore the issue of authorship. E. Achtemeier, *The Community and Message of Isaiah 56–66* (Minneapolis: Augsburg, 1982), follows Hanson's analysis of chaps. 56–66.

[124] Hanson, *The Dawn of Apocalyptic*, 46–61, tries to date oracles on the basis of this criteria, thus 60–62 are quite similar to the bicolons in 40–55. Chapters 60–62 also have many thematic connections with 40–55, plus it views God's salvation, past history, and restoration similar to 40–55. These factors enable him to date 53:9–57:13 as the latest dated material.

[125] J. L. Kugel, *The Idea of Biblical Poetry* (Baltimore: Johns Hopkins University, 1981), 107–17, rejects the value of syllable counting in poetry, thus undermining one of Hanson's key controls for understanding the chronology of chaps. 56–66.

[126] Schramm, *The Opponents of Third Isaiah*, 88–89, claims that Hanson uses his presuppositions about the priesthood in chap. 3 to support his exegesis of chaps. 56–66 in chap. 2, then he uses those conclusions to justify his exposition of priesthood in chap. 3. On pp. 108–11 she points out numerous inconsistencies (most view 56–66 as a development of 40–55, so how could this material be against exilic priests from Babylon?) and some very unlikely aspects of his interpretation (the Zadokite priest are the ones who have accepted Canaanite worship practices). H. G. M. Williamson, "Isaiah 63,7–64,11. Exilic Laments or Postexilic Protest?" *ZAW* 102 (1990): 48–58, critically examines the arguments put forward by Hanson. He rejects Hanson's circular reasoning, his connections between chaps. 40–55 and 63:7–64:11, his interpretation of 63:16 as an indication of inner-community conflict, and then suggests that 63:7–64:11 is a liturgical text from the Palestinian community during the time of the exile (similar to Ps 106 and Neh 9). J. Goldingay, *Isaiah*. NIBC (Peabody: Hendrickson, 2001), 318, also rejects Hanson's reconstruction of this situation.

[127] Childs, *Isaiah*, 444.

Their argument was to counter the Zadokites who claimed the names Abraham and Israel for themselves. This interpretation is highly questionable, for there is no other independent evidence to confirm that the name Abraham was ever used to identify a specific priestly group in Judah. Although chap. 58 is not aimed at one group, Hanson reinterprets the criticism of those fasting as part of a polemic against the Zadokite priest who professed to be close to God but were really unworthy. There are numerous anomalies that do not make much sense in Hanson's broader interpretation of the rise of apocalyptic, for example his negative view of the hopes of the prophets Haggai and Zechariah. In addition, if the priestly ideas in Zechariah 1–8 were united in one book with the apocalyptic material in Zechariah 9–14, could these two approaches really be mortal enemies of one another at the time Third Isaiah was written? If these two approaches are as contradictory as Hanson claims, why were they both placed in the same book (Zechariah)?[128]

J. Blenkinsopp hypothesizes that chaps. 56–66 once had a superscription just like 1:1, but it was editorially removed when these messages were added to the book of Isaiah.[129] Although he finds some themes that are common within both chaps. 40–55 and 56–66 (comfort, the coming of God, the glory of God, justice, and the servant/servants) and chaps. 1–39 (the condemnation of Edom in chaps. 34 and 63), two of the distinct ideas in 56–66 are that God's offer of salvation is contingent on the removal of all moral obstacles, and that not all the people of Israel are God's people. Blenkinsopp also finds a strong influence from deuteronomic language and theology.[130] He hypothesizes that there is a connection between the "tremblers at God's word" in 66:2,5 and the persecuted "tremblers at God's word" in Ezra 9:4; 10:3. The idolatrous temple priests who were in power in Jerusalem excluded the righteous from holding land; thus, he finds both theological and sociological factors impacting the life and literature in chaps. 56–66.[131] Within chaps. 56–66 Blenkinsopp was able to find "faint imprints of prophetic and scribal activity carried on over several generations by a movement or school owing allegiance to the prophetic leader and teacher responsible for the core of 40–55."[132] The audience for this book was the disillusioned and disoriented people of Judah who endured rampant

---

[128] R. J. Coggins, *Haggai, Zechariah and Malachi* (Sheffield: JSOT Press, 1987), 59, argues that these two approaches are not alien to one another, and he rejects his negative attitude toward these books. R. P. Carroll, "Twilight of Prophecy or Dawn of Apocalyptic?" *JSOT* 14 (1979): 3–35, criticizes Hanson for his "obsessive polarization" of these two groups for prophecy and cult were not inherent enemies.

[129] J. Blenkinsopp, *Isaiah 56–66*, AB (New York: Doubleday, 2003), 29, suggests this to support his contention that 56–66 was a distinct book, but there is absolutely no textual evidence for this hypothesis, so it is a worthless suggestion.

[130] Ibid., pp. 32–36 deal with similar themes, while p. 37 refers to deuteronomistic influences.

[131] Ibid., 51–54, thinks Isaiah 56–66 and Ezra 9–10 address the same issues from different perspectives. In Ezra 9–10 the tremblers and Ezra are able to dictate policy while either before or after Ezra's reform they were shunned.

[132] Ibid., 65.

injustices over several years, so these messages were an "ongoing writing" that underwent "development, modification, reinterpretation, and reconfiguration to meet the demands of new situations."[133] The evidence for some of these conclusions is minimal or nonexistent,[134] so it is significant that Blenkinsopp does not focus his exegesis on a redactional analysis of the "modifications" and "reconfiguration" of each verse.

(4) Balancing Continuity and Discontinuity

Although many critical commentators refer to a distinctive prophetic person called "Third Isaiah," others focus much more attention on the interconnections that chaps. 56–66 have with 1–55, rather than just highlighting areas of discontinuity. A few find so much continuity with chaps. 1–55 that they do not even hypothesize a Third Isaiah prophet, but only the presence of a new literary unit that could be referred to as the third section of the book of Isaiah.

J. Muilenburg used the insights of rhetorical criticism to identify the literary characteristics that are found in biblical texts in order to discover their structure, stylistic features, repetitions, and their use of rhetorical devices. He observed that the language and style of chaps. 40–55 and 56–66 are very close, thus the "weightiest arguments against the literary integrity of 40–66 is the difference in historical situations which they appear to presuppose."[135] He recognizes in chaps. 56–66 a different author from chaps. 40–66 because 56–66 include different topics like the Sabbath, fasting, fractional strife, a different eschatological outlook, less literary independence, and a different setting.[136] He concludes that these messages represent the religious life in Judah after 538 BC. But when he comes to 56:1 in his commentary he states that "we have not a radical break with the past, but a development. . . . The poem as a whole is akin to Second Isaiah. . . .Yet there are striking differences."[137] He views this new writer as a disciple of Second Isaiah. Within his exegetical notes he does identify a few later additions (59:21; 62:12; 66:17–24), but he spends far more time and effort demonstrating the close relationship and dependence these verses have with earlier traditions in the book of Isaiah. Thus he finds many areas of continuity as well as a few signs of discontinuity.

B. S. Childs claims that chaps. 56–66 were deliberately dehistoricized so that they could be read as the eschatological fulfillment of the prophecies of

---

[133] Ibid., 77.

[134] There is (a) absolutely no evidence for his suggestion that 56:1 originally had a separate superscription that was later omitted; (b) little evidence that one group was not allowing another group to own land; and (c) little hard evidence that proves that these messages went through a long process of "development, modification, reinterpretation, and reconfiguration."

[135] Muilenburg, "Isaiah 40–66," 5:383.

[136] Ibid., 5:384.

[137] Ibid., 5:653. He finds a difference in passion and fervor and a much stronger emphasis on cult, law, temple, and prayer.

chaps. 1–55. Thus one should not use a different historical setting as the main issue that makes 56–66 unique. He "strongly supports the recent move (cf. Beuken, Rendtorff, Steck) to interpret chaps. 56–66 as part of a larger literary collection rather than to assume its function as an independent corpus."[138] His canonical approach causes him to reject the extremes of some redactional treatments and pay far more attention to the close interdependency between chaps. 1–55 and 56–66. He does not view these allusions to earlier texts as an attempt to correct or remold earlier messages; instead, he believes these allusions draw on the authoritative status of earlier texts to support what is being said in chaps. 56–66.[139] He rejects Hanson's sociological reading and prefers to focus on the role of intertextuality, a phenomenon that signals the continuity with past messages in 1–39 as well as 40–55. Childs concludes that the role of these chapters is "to unite the major themes of both First and Second Isaiah into one literary composition."[140] Thus he rejects the common hypothesis that Third Isaiah reinterprets the unfulfilled hopes of salvation in Second Isaiah.

C. R. Seitz follows some of Child's conclusions, though he states them in such a way as to offer his own nuanced understanding. He recognizes that the messages in chaps. 40–66 do not emphasize the social location of this audience. He concludes that all of 40–66 has a Jerusalemite orientation,[141] thus one cannot use a change of historical location as a means of dividing chaps. 40–55 from 56–66. Seitz also breaks with the traditional division of the final unit by identifying chaps. 54–66 (not 56–66) as the final literary unit in the book. Although many commentators focus a great deal of attention on the destruction of the temple and its rebuilding, Seitz can find no place in chaps. 40–66 where the text reports the destruction of the temple or its rebuilding. He finds any attempt to date or propose an historical setting based on temple information to be highly speculative. He concludes that the focus is much less on the status of the temple and much more on God's judgment of Israel, the nations, and the whole world. Emphasis is given to the eventual revelation of his glorious salvation to the redeemed from Zion and from all over the world.[142] Seitz believes chaps. 40–66 "are concerned with God's vindication of the servant, as promised in 52:13–53:12"[143] and his seed, the "servants" of 56–66. His exegetical comments emphasize the continuity between the theology of 40–53 and 54–66

[138] Childs, *Isaiah*, 441, though he does recognize a difference in style, historical background, and theological emphasis in chaps. 56–66.

[139] Ibid., 442. He does not agree with W. Zimmerli, "Zur Sprache Tritojesajas," *SthU* 20 (1950): 110–22, who thought that Third Isaiah was frequently adjusting the message of Second Isaiah to a new situation by spiritualizing what was previously said.

[140] Childs, *Isaiah*, 447.

[141] Seitz, "Isaiah 40–66," 6:316 also notes that Duhm also had this view.

[142] C. R. Seitz, "Isaiah, Book of (Third Isaiah)," *ABD* (New York: Doubleday, 1992), 3:503, states that "the fall of the temple and its restoration, as such, are not meaningful literary, historical, or theological indexes in Isaiah."

[143] Seitz, "Isaiah 40–66," 6:471.

based on similar themes as well as direct allusions or quotations of earlier messages. The conflict between different groups in 56–66 is not viewed as anything new, for similar conflicts are evident in 40–55 (42:18–20; 43:22–24; 44:25; 45:9–13; 50:4–9).[144]

J. Oswalt concludes that chaps. 56–66 were written to address a situation after the return from exile, but he finds relatively little historical evidence within these chapters. Chapters 56–66 address the "necessity of living out God's righteousness and the inability or failure of people to do so."[145] There is some level of discontinuity though, for he interprets the audience to be made up of people who have returned from the exile.[146] In these messages the prophet identifies the characteristics that are found in God's elect, the marks of the servant of the Lord. It is possible to display these characteristics because God's grace enables a person to be delivered from the effects of sin and live a holy life. Oswalt also states that these chapters "were written to show how the theology of 40–55 fits into that of chapters 1–39."[147] Thus part of the purpose was to demonstrate a certain level of continuity throughout the book of Isaiah. He rejects Hanson's sociological reconstruction and other redactional approaches that divide these chapters into ever-smaller editorial additions.[148] The key themes in these chapters are: (a) God's grace is available to all; (b) God has a universal mission for his people; (c) Israel's ethical performance did not match up to God's promises; and (d) God gives people the grace to live righteous lives. These are themes that are treated again and again in prophetic messages throughout this book.

This survey highlights a few of the methods and conclusions of several important works on Isaiah. The commentary below will depend on the canonical Masoretic text of chaps. 56–66 and will not wade into the task of identifying anything but the most obvious editorial additions (57:21; 59:21) that were probably made when these oracles were put into writing. Although sociological differences existed between people in Israel, P. Hanson's methodology presents an understanding of the conflict that is not borne out by the exegesis of many of his key passages. Although there is tension between the different groups (the wicked and the righteous) mentioned in chaps. 56–66, there is relatively little conflict between the theological principles expressed in 40–55 and 56–66. Chapters 56–66 are not foreign to the theology of Isaiah 1–55; they continue to offer God's servants eschatological hope and the ethical guidance

---

[144] Seitz, "Isaiah," *ABD*, 3:506, also identifies the first person voice in 42; 49; 50, and 61 making another interconnection that illustrates his sense of continuity.

[145] Oswalt, *Isaiah 40–66*, 452, couples with this theme "the question of what qualifies a person to be among God's elect." Seitz, "Isaiah, Book of (Third Isaiah)," *ABD*, 3:452, calls this the "central idea" in 56–66.

[146] Oswalt, *Isaiah 40–66*, 11, pinpoints some time in the years after 538 BC.

[147] Ibid., 11.

[148] Ibid., 456, n. 33.

that is necessary for people to hold fast to their commitments in a world where many have forsaken God's ways.

5. The Relationship between 40–55 and 56–66

One of the significant reasons why some commentators separate these chapters (often called Trito-Isaiah) from chaps. 40–55 is that sometimes when they quote or allude to ideas in chaps. 40–55 (and 1–39), the tone, style, or perspective changes, thus betraying a different prophet in a different setting promoting a slightly different message.[149] But such arguments can be slippery and quite subjective. It would not be hard to imagine that even on the very same day a prophet would likely modify or change his tone and style if he were addressing humble believers who agreed with the prophet on one occasion and an unjust and syncretistic Israelite that needed to repent on another occasion. In fact, it would be possible for a prophet to change his tone and style when addressing the same group a week later because circumstances have changed.[150] It is sometimes suggested that in chaps. 40–55 Isaiah looked forward to God's saving act of returning the people from exile, while in chaps. 56–66 the people had already returned from exile and were disillusioned. Some believe that their earlier optimism has now turned into pessimism because of unfulfilled expectations, but is this the case?

In contrast to this evaluation, this commentary will not interpret most of chaps. 56–66 as overly pessimistic, for 56:1–8; 60–62; 63:7–14; 65:17–25; 66:18–24 are full of the optimistic promises of what God will do in the future. A brief review of the book of Isaiah will show that there were several criticisms of the audience in 1–39; 40–48,[151] as well as in 56–66, so criticism of the wicked (Hebrew or Gentile) is not something new to these chapters. There are also numerous examples of the prophet looking forward to God's eschatological salvation in 40–55 (40:1–11; 41:17–20; 44:1–5; 51:1–16; 52:1–10;

---

[149] G. I. Emmerson, *Isaiah 56–66* (London: T&T Clark, 1992), 40–50, deals with these issues and concludes that the differences are significant enough to prove the existence of Third Isaiah. For example, she claims that the judgment oracles in 56–66 are more like the preexilic oracles of judgment in 1–39 than they are to anything found in chaps. 40–55.

[150] A parent or any person in authority will change his tone and style when talking to different people. A parent may have one tone and style in the morning, but if the child comes home that night and announces that he was at fault for causing an automobile accident, the tone will probably change significantly.

[151] (a) In 40:11–31 the prophet is critical of those who fear the nations and idols, thinking that God is hidden from them, but he uses a positive approach to assure them of God's care. (b In 42:18–25 the audience is criticized for being blind and not listening to or obeying God's laws. (c) In 43:22–28 the nation is accused of not honoring God when they brought their offering, being burdened with sin, and having rebelled. (d) 44:6–20 unveils the misunderstanding of those who worshipped idols. (e) 45:9–13 condemns those who question and quarrel with the actions of their Maker. (f) In 48:1–11 Israel was not righteous but stubborn and treacherous, in need of refining and testing.

54:1–17); thus, messages of divine salvation and optimism exist throughout 1–39; 40–55; and 56–66. In addition, when a pessimistic view of the present or the future is found in chaps. 56–66 it is often due to a specific set of sinful acts. Nevertheless, there is very little information that would identify the date and location of the sinful audience in 56–66.

Everyone can identify some differences between chaps. 40–55 and 56–66, including the emphasis on the singular servant in chaps. 40–55 and the plural servants in 56–66. Although differences surely do exist, it is highly questionable to suggest that (a) there is enough difference between the question in 50:2 "Was my arm too short to ransom you?" and the statement in 59:1 "My arm is not too short to save" to prove that 59:1 was communicating a different message by a different person. (b) Although one passage mentions chains and the others do not, is there really a major difference between the report that the wealth of the Gentile nations will come to Jerusalem in 45:14 or 49:22 and the similar report in 60:4–6,14? (c) It is true that the Gentiles are dealt with quite harshly in some earlier passage (chaps. 12–23; 34; 46–47), but 60:12; 63:1–6; 66:15–17 are just as harsh, though the punishment is not described in as much detail. These and similar passages (54:1–3 and 66:6–7) are sufficiently similar in content and intention to be from the same mind; they do not contradict one another.

G. Emmerson argues that the unique aspects within chaps. 56–66 contrast so much with 40–55 that one must assume a different author ("Trito Isaiah") is writing. But in examining her evidence it appears that both 46:13 and 56:1 announce that God's salvation will not be delayed. She argues that the stylistic difference between the direct address, "I will grant salvation to Zion," in 46:13a is significantly different from the intransitive and passive statements in 56:1, "my salvation is close at hand and my righteousness will soon be revealed," to indicate different authors. But certainly any author can express the same truth in one message in an active voice and in another message using a passive verb. In fact, in 46:13b the author uses the passive in the preceding parallel clause, "my salvation will not be delayed."

In a second example Emmerson compares 40:9–10 and 62:11 because both refer to God coming and bringing his recompense with him. Emmerson finds that 40:9–10 is direct, sudden, and a dramatic, immanent intervention by God, while 62:11 is less direct and refers to more of a transformation.[152] Yet what does 62:11 refer to other than the dramatic and sudden coming of God in 60:1–3? Chapter 62 does talk about the transformation of this world, but how can one read 40:9–11 without concluding that there will be a great transforma-

---

[152] Emmerson, *Isaiah 56–66*, 44–49, presents several other examples such as 40:3 and 57:14; 49:18a and 60:4a; 52:12 and 58:8; 55:5 and 60:9; 62:10. She also lists some passages where it appears that Third Isaiah misunderstood Second Isaiah, e.g., the reference to various trees in the desert area in 41:19 and these same trees in the temple area in 60:13. She does not view this as a misunderstanding "but a new and significant slant given to a familiar saying." The key question is, whether this shift is one that is so great that Second Isaiah could not have expressed it.

tion of Zion in that final day. Even if one concedes that 62:11 somewhat softens 40:9–11 as some claim, the difference is hardly enough to require these two passages to be written by two different authors.

In light of the weaknesses of some of these arguments, new voices have arisen that question various aspects of the "Trito-Isaiah" hypothesis. Among these newer contributions, the insights of B. S. Childs are helpful, for he rejects the typical explanation that chaps. 56–66 abandon the hopes of earlier messages in Isaiah.[153] Childs also rejects the notion that "Trito-Isaiah" is a prophetic person.[154] Thus chaps. 56–66 are just a continuation of thoughts, similar to what is found in 40–55.

W. A. M. Beuken illustrated the continuity with earlier chapters in the book of Isaiah by connecting the reference to the "seed, offspring" of the Servant in 53:10 with the plural "servants" in 54:17, who become one of the main topics in chaps. 56–66.[155] These servants are the "righteous" (45:25; 48:18) who faithfully do what is just, serve the Lord (56:1,6; 57:1; 59:21; 61:3), and do not follow the ways of wicked idolaters (57:3–21). God will eventually vindicate his servants (63:17; 65:8–16) when he establishes them in the new heavens and the new earth (65:17–25). R. E. Clements takes the theme of "a light to the nations" and illustrates how this theme operates in early chapters (2:5; 9:2; 10:17), the middle section of the book (42:6–7,16; 49:6; 50:10–11), as well as this final series of chapters (60:1–3).[156] W. A. M. Beuken also finds chaps. 56–66 unifying 1–39 and 40–55 by means of its focus on mount Zion, the "Holy Mountain" (2:2; 4:5; 11:9; 25:6; 37:32; 40:9), which is the "nodal point in the artistic ordering of the book of Isaiah."[157]

In contrast to those who make numerous divisions among different sources that were redacted over a long period of time, J. Muilenburg recognizes the "integrity of chapters 40–66" because "the language and style are frequently similar, and there are numerous resemblances in thought."[158] Although Muilenburg

---

[153] Childs, *Isaiah*, 447.

[154] It seems that most just assume the prophetic figure "Trito-Isaiah," but Emmerson, *Isaiah 56–66*, 71–78, believes that the prophet was addressed in 58:1 and 59:21, and the prophet speaks in 61:1–3. The exegetical consideration of 59:21 and 61:1–3 below will suggest a different conclusion.

[155] W. A. M. Beuken, "The Main Theme of Trito-Isaiah: 'the Servants of Yhwh,'" *JSOT* 47 (1990): 67–87.

[156] R. E. Clements, "A Light to the Nations: A Central Theme of the Book of Isaiah," in *Forming Prophetic Literature: Essays on Isaiah and the Twelve in Honor of John D. W. Watts*, ed. J. W. Watts and P. R. House (Sheffield: Sheffield Academic Press, 1996), 57–69.

[157] W. A. M. Beuken, "Isa 56:9–57:13: An Example of the Isaianic Legacy of Trito-Isaiah," in *Tradition and Reinterpretation in Jewish and Early Christian Literature: Festschrift fur J. C. H. Labram*, ed. J. W. van Henten, et al. (Leiden: Brill, 1986), 51.

[158] Muilenburg, "Isaiah 40–66," 5:383. He lists others who maintain the unity of 40–66, including C. C. Torrey, E. König, L. Glahn, A. Töpelmann, L. Finkelstein, and F. James. Later on pp. 653–64 he expresses the opinion that chaps. 56–66 are "not a radical break with the past" but "there are striking differences" because of a change of mood and a strong emphasis on the cult.

recognizes Trito-Isaiah and some differences in chaps. 56–66, he hypothesizes a noticeable level of unity because Isaiah's disciples carried on his thoughts. Childs focused attention on the canonical formation of the book of Isaiah by de-emphasizing the historical background differences between these sections and by emphasizing the theological relationship and function of each section within the book. Thus he concludes, "It is erroneous to treat First Isaiah as mainly preexilic oracles of the eighth-century prophet to which a bloc of exilic and postexilic material was later attached."[159] Instead, he finds all parts of the book theologically interconnected and does not find conflict between the ideas in 40–55 and 56–66. R. E. Clements observed that the theme of Israel's blindness (6:9–10; 32:1–8; 32:3; 35:5; 42:18–20; 43:8) is found in many places within the book of Isaiah, suggesting some level of theological interconnectedness. Thus he concludes that chaps. 56–66 "were intended to be understood, not as a fresh and entirely self-contained declaration from Yahweh to the postexilic community, but rather as a carrying-forward of the divine word" from chaps. 40–55.[160] In addition, G. I. Davies found a plethora of negative and positive references to the destiny of the nations throughout Isaiah, R. Lack identified righteousness and justice as the "symbolic system" of the whole book, and W. J. Dumbrell found the master unifying theme of Isaiah to be God's devotion to the city of Jerusalem.[161]

This emphasis on continuity naturally raises the question of whether it is any longer necessary to talk about this hypothetical person "Trito-Isaiah" or a section of the book called "Trito-Isaiah." After a careful consideration of several key themes, H. G. M. Williamson concludes that, "there is little that is new in what we have seen of these chapters beyond the bare fact of the extension of the promise."[162] After reviewing K. Pauritsch's study of Isaiah 56–66, A. Murtonen compares the frequency of words in chaps. 56–66 with selected earlier chapters in the book and concludes that "the result is fully compatible with

---

[159] B. S. Childs, *Introduction of the Old Testament as Scripture* (Philadelphia: Fortress, 1979), 330.

[160] R. E. Clements, "The Unity of the Book of Isaiah," *Int* 36 (1982): 117–29, rejected the idea that a unity of themes implied a unity of authorship. W. Brueggemann, "Unity and Dynamics in Isaiah," *JSOT* 29 (1984): 89–107, uses a sociological model to illustrate the dynamic cohesiveness of and interrelatedness of the various sections of Isaiah. He suggests that chaps. 1–39 critique the false ideology of the people, 40–55 are a public embrace of the pain which leads to hope, and 56–66 are a release of social imagination.

[161] G. I. Davies, "The Destiny of the Nations," in *The Book of Isaiah: Le Livre D'Isaïe*, ed. J. Vermeylen (Leuven: Peeters, 1989), 93–120; R. Lack, *La Symbolique du d'Isaïe* (Rome: Pontifical Biblical Institute, 1973); W. J. Dumbrell, "The Purpose of the Book of Isaiah," *TynBul* 36 (1985): 111–28. R. Rendtorff, "The Book of Isaiah: A Complex Unity. Synchronic and Diachronic Reading," in *New Visions of Isaiah*, ed. R. F. Melugin and M. A. Sweeney, JSOTSup 214 (Sheffield: Sheffield Academic Press, 1996), 32–48, discusses various approaches to the issue of unity noting significant differences in methodology and results.

[162] Williamson, *Variations on a Theme*, 174, though this does not lead him to the conclusion that 40–66 should all be united as one literary unit.

the assumption of a single author for all the chapters involved, i.e., the identity of 'Third' and 'Second' Isaiah."[163] Similarly, M. Haran found no significant break in chaps. 55–56 and attributes chaps. 56–66 to "Deutero-Isaiah."[164]

W. L. Holladay believes that if one "subtracts a few redactional additions from chapters 56–66 one hears in the remainder the same individual that is heard in chapters 40–55. . . . This is to say, I reject the hypothesis of a Trito-Isaiah."[165] In addition, C. R. Seitz suggests that "chapters 40–55 treat different *aspects* of the restoration of Zion than do chapters 56–66, . . . the sharp distinction drawn between these sections on historical grounds falls away. The distinction becomes thematic and theological." In fact, W. A. M. Beuken finds such a little break between 55 and what follows that he concludes that chaps. 56–57 are actually a commentary on chap. 55.[166]

What can one take from these studies to aid one in the analysis and synthesis of the message of 56–66? First, those interlinking connections with earlier themes in Isaiah should play a significant role in providing background for the theological messages in chaps. 56–66 because they enable one to judge the level of continuity/discontinuity with the past. Second, since 61:1–3 is related to earlier servant passages (chaps. 42 and 49), one should not conclude that a new prophetic figure ("Trito-Isaiah") is introduced in 61:1–3. Third, the canonical form that preserved chaps. 56–66 together indicates that these chapters are a literary unit and their structure suggests a purposeful organization; thus, they should be interpreted as a united presentation of diverse genres that deal with the destiny of God's servants in their future setting in Zion. Fourth, the conflicts and different destinies of the righteous and wicked are not new thoughts introduced in chaps. 56–66, for the differences between these groups are inherent in many chapters throughout Isaiah, beginning with chap. 1.[167] Fifth, there is very little evidence to justify the hypothesis that there was a prophet who might be called "Trito-Isaiah." The literary distinctions between the content and style of chaps. 40–55 and 56–66 is not sufficient to identify them as separate books written by different authors. Sixth, although some suggest that the place where the audience in chaps. 56–66 is located is in Jerusalem, in most cases this is actually the location of future eschatological events where all God's servants (from Israel and the nations) will gather (60:1–63:6; 66:18–24). This future setting has little to do with the present location of the prophet and his immediate audience.

---

[163] A. Murtonen, "Third Isaiah—Yes or No?" *Abr-Nahrain* 19 (1980–1981): 20–41.

[164] M. Haran, "The Literary Structure and Chronological Framework of the Prophecies in Isa XL-XLVIII," *Congress Volume, Bonn 1962* (Leiden: Brill, 1963): 127–55.

[165] W. L. Holladay, "Was Trito-Isaiah Deutero-Isaiah After All?" in *Writing and Reading the Scroll of Isaiah*, 2:193–217, notes that both sections have double imperatives and similar expansion techniques.

[166] Beuken, "Isa 56:9–57:13: An Example of the Isaianic Legacy of Trito-Isaiah," 48–64.

[167] Seitz, "Isaiah 40–66," 6:47, mentions this conflict in 50:10–11, in the oracles about the servant, but one could also point to conflict of perspectives between groups in chaps. 1; 3; 7–8; 9:8–21; 22; 28–31; 40:12–31; 42:18–25; 43:22–28; 45:9–11; 48:1–11.

Seventh, all the messages in chaps. 56–66 are eschatologically oriented, describing what people of all ages need to do if they want to enjoy the riches of God's glorious new kingdom and what they must avoid so they will not have to suffer under the wrath of God's judgment. This information identifies who will and will not enter God's glorious kingdom in the future.

6. Theology of 40–66

When describing the theology of chaps. 1–39, several factors were identified that present problems to the task of formulating a succinct theology of any section of Isaiah. On the one hand, the theology of any one oracle is limited to the problems being addressed to the people in that historical setting. Thus the divine revelation the prophet received about a particular situation specifically applies to the people at that time and its emphasis may be somewhat diverse from the theological point being made in another chapter which arises out of a different set of circumstances. This problem could be somewhat minimized by limiting the discussion of the theological emphasis of Isaiah's message to each historical era or each group of chapters in a smaller literary unit. Thus one could develop a theology of literary units including chaps. 40–44 or 60–62 or an essay on the theology of the eschatological era. Hypothetically, an overview that integrates the different themes within each literary unit or on each topic should be able to draw together the main themes and emphases throughout these messages, ending up with a theology of the chaps. 40–66.

A second difficulty that confronts any theological effort in the book of Isaiah relates to issues of authorship, redaction, and the date of each redactional addition. If one holds that all eschatological messages of hope were much later redactional additions to the book of Isaiah, one has to face the issue that the prophet's theology was quite different from what is presented in the final form of the book. Consequently, one must decide what passages belonged to each redactional layer as well as the methodological question of whether one should speak of the theology of the Assyrian (or Josiah) redaction, the idol redaction, and the foreign nation redaction or if one can legitimately speak of the theology of the present canonical book of Isaiah. A more canonical approach will pay more attention to the final form of the completed manuscript of 40–66. Since the identification of redactional layers and their theological purposes are more elusive and since that approach is based on many more subjective decisions; it seems wiser to use a more canonical approach that does not address the theology of each of these different redactional layers. This will allow the interpreter to develop a more holistic approach that synthesizes the theology of Isaiah 40–66.

A third tension involves the process of integrating and reducing a hundred different specific theological comments into a few broad central statements that make up the core from which the specific messages derive their foundation. Because of this difficulty some have abandoned any pursuit of a unifying core and instead are content to comment on the prophet's view of the standard systematic topics of God, man, sin, judgment, and redemption.[168] Or, in order to avoid harmonization and the charge of reductionism, some address one of the theological themes that runs through many of the prophetic messages (like the Servant or God's plan for the nations)[169] and do not attempt to put the theology of the book together in some sort of unified perspective. For example, R. E. Clements takes the theme of "a light to the nations" and illustrates how this theme operates in early chapters (2:5; 9:2; 10:17), the middle section of the book (42:6–7,16; 49:6; 50:10–11), as well as this final series of chapters (60:1–3).[170] W. A. M. Beuken also finds chaps. 56–66 unifying 1–39 and 40–55 by means of its focus on mount Zion, the "Holy Mountain" (2:2; 4:5; 11:9; 25:6; 37:32; 40:9; 56:7; 57:13; 65:11; 66:20), which is the "nodal point in the artistic ordering of the book of Isaiah."[171] These are very helpful studies, but they do not present a full theology of all the messages in 40–66. In spite of the dangers involved with a holistic approach, a more focused articulation of the theological core is worthwhile in order to understand both the foundation of the prophet's thinking and the central thrust of his ministry. The repeated interlinking of vocabulary and ideas from earlier messages within the framework of later oracles argues for a theological interdependence and a broad consistency of core convictions that do not dramatically change from oracle to oracle.[172] J. J. M. Roberts maintains that "it should be possible, therefore, to delineate the central core of Isaianic theology, while not ignoring the different accents placed on that core in the different stages of the book."[173]

(1) Finding Some Unity within the Diversity

Within the commentary itself there are many discussions of the primary theological issues that are addressed in each specific message. There one will see the contrast between Isaiah's distinctive theological approach and the contrasting theology of his audience or the theological beliefs of Israel's enemy the Babylonians (chaps. 46–47). The theological discussion of each oracle is necessarily somewhat limited by the needs of the audience and somewhat imbalanced by its focus on responding to the specific needs at that time. None of

---

[168] Oswalt, *Isaiah 1–39*, 31–41, takes this option, but he also seems to find "servanthood" as a broad unifying theme throughout Isaiah's messages.

[169] Clements, "The Unity of the Book of Isaiah,' 117–29.

[170] Clements, "A Light to the Nations: A Central Theme of the Book of Isaiah," 57–69.

[171] Beuken, "Isa 56:9–57:13: An Example of the Isaianic Legacy of Trito-Isaiah," 51.

[172] C. R. Seitz, "Isaiah 1–66: Making Sense of the Whole," in *Reading and Preaching the Book of Isaiah* (Philadelphia: Fortress, 1988), 105–26. R. J. Marshall. "The Unity of Isaiah 1–12," *LQ* 14 (1962): 21–38.

[173] J. J. M. Roberts, "Isaiah in Old Testament Theology," *Int* 36 (1982): 131, finds many inner consistencies within the theology of Isaiah.

these oracles present anything like a well-organized systematically arranged theology of all the prophet's beliefs. Yet in the midst of all the diversity of people in his audiences, different theological opinions, different practical and theological problems, certain fundamental convictions about God and his relationship to different groups of people emerge within these messages. By finding the underlying theological factors that support many of his specific messages that are temporally and topically related to specific individuals in their ancient historical context, one can attempt to synthesize a broadly stated core perspective that integrates and interrelates the main themes and main emphases within all his messages. When surveying these messages it is important to notice how various ideas are interrelated to one another so that one can identify the broad categories that enable one to interconnect these ideas together into some sort of Isaianic perspective.

GOD AND THE GODS. It becomes very apparent, even in chap. 40, that one of the unifying theological aspects within chaps. 40–66 relates to the identity of who is God, the characteristics of God as opposed to the idols, and what God has done and will do. In the ancient Near East "supernatural powers" were seen as the living powers that controlled all parts of nature; thus, in many ancient Near Eastern myths the many "divine powers" (gods)[174] are often found fighting one another for control of various part of the heavens and the earth. But the God of Israel was not part of nature, was not identified with any natural activity, and cannot even be remotely comparable to any of these "supernatural powers" (40:18–20,25) nor the idols of wood that represented these gods. Because there were some Israelites who seemed to be confused about the identity of God, considerable time is spent, particularly in chaps. 40–44 and 46–47 separating the identity and functions of Israel's God from other gods ("supernatural powers"). In later chapters these identifying functions enable the prophet to assure his audience that their God will do what he has said he will do because of who he is (55:10–11).

God's acts define who he is, so one can express a theological idea by describing the activity he does or by giving a title to him based on what he has done. The God of Israel "creates" so he deserves the title, the "Creator" of the heavens and the earth (40:12–13,21,26,28; 42:5; 45:18; 48:13; 66:2). Although he is not identified with any part of the created world like the ancient

---

[174] The term "supernatural powers" is employed to communicate to the modern reader that the Israelites had taken on the ancient Near Eastern idea that these idols represented real divine beings that had power to control their world. Although many today think of these gods as just pieces of wood (and that point is made in these chapters as well), there is every reason to believe that real and powerful demonic forces were at work behind many of these gods. Thus the term "supernatural powers" is more consistent with their thinking and consistent with Daniel's description of Michael the archangel's experience of fighting against the prince of the Persian kingdom who resisted Michael for 21 days (Dan 10:12–13). These might well be interrelated to the "principalities and spiritual powers" that Paul refers to in Eph 6:10–12.

Near Eastern gods,[175] he formed the entire created world and controls every part of it. He is also the Creator of mankind (45:12), the Creator of the nation of Israel (43:1,7,15), and someday in the future he will create a new heaven and a new earth (65:17; 66:22). Another identifying title is "everlasting God" or "the First and the Last" (40:28; 41:4; 44:6; 48:12). God is not a child of another god who has come into existence recently, and he will not die like some of the gods in ancient Near Eastern mythology.[176] A third title attributed to God is "your Redeemer" (41:14), a concept that derives from God acting as a family member who pays a debt to free another family member from an obligation, some enslavement, or a punishment. This title, which is somewhat similar to "Savior," is used in contexts where people need encouragement that God's redemptive power will deliver them in times of war (41:14; 49:26) or from trials of oppression (43:1,14; 49:7; 52:3; 63:16). As Redeemer he assures, comforts, or challenges people to trust him (44:6; 48:17; 51:10; 54:5), and he calls people to repent (44:22). At other times he confirms his intention to destroy Israel's enemies (47:4), and then he assures people of his plans to restore the nation (54:8; 60:16). A fourth title is "the Holy One," a favorite Isaianic concept that was derived from the prophet's call experience (6:3). When Isaiah refers to God as the Holy One, he means that he is completely separate and different from everything that was created, from everything that is sinful, and is uniquely glorious in his splendor and majesty.[177] H. Wildberger conceives of this holiness as a "dynamic reality, not a static quality,"[178] but it might be better to view holiness as an inner distinctive of God's essence that is manifested in the amazing splendor and majesty of his glory. Holiness sets God apart as an almighty divine power; thus, it is not surprising that those texts that emphasize God's distinctive redemptive power over various earthly factors legitimate his abilities to accomplish his will by referring to his holiness (41:14; 43:3,14; 47:4; 49:7). God's name as the Holy One is also associated with God's marvelous eschatological deliverance and transformation of this world into a holy place where God dwells in Zion with his holy people (41:16,20; 54:5; 60:9,14). These and other titles (the God of Israel, Yahweh, Lord of Hosts, Father, King) give one insight into the exalted nature of God and the relationship God has with this world. These titles indicate that the God of Israel is not comparable to any of the other "supernatural powers." Even though some of the gods of the

---

[175] In Egypt the king of the gods was Ra who was the sun god; in Babylon Shemesh was the sun god, and Utu was the Sumerian sun god.

[176] In the Baal Epic the god Baal (the god of fertility) is killed and defeated by the god Mot (the god of death and drought) when the spring rains end and drought takes control of the weather.

[177] H. Ringgren, *The Prophetic Conception of the Holiness of God* (Uppsala: Lundequistska, 1948).

[178] H. Wildberger, *Isaiah 1–12*, CC, trans. T. H. Trapp (Philadelphia: Fortress Press, 1991), 266, seems to deny this is a "quality" of God, but if he acts and relates to people as a holy God then it seems one can conclude that this is a character quality.

nations may even have somewhat similar titles (lord, king, creator, holy), they are virtually nothing when set next to the God of Israel.

God's actions correlate to his titles, and the prophecies of Isaiah refer primarily to the past and future acts of God. In the past he created the heavens and the earth (42:5), chose and creates a people for himself (43:1,7), and later allowed his people to live under the power of Egypt and Assyria (52:3–4). At times he protected them and guided his people through his servant Moses and through the power of his Holy Spirit (63:8–14), and at other times he allowed his people to be plundered (42:24–25). But in the future God will strengthen his people (41:10) and defeat those who war against them (41:11–12), so that none will be able to find their enemies (41:12–16). At some point in the distant future God will transform nature and make the dry places fertile (41:17–20), send his chosen Servant to establish justice on the earth, restore his people, and have this Servant function as a light to the nations (42:1–13). Eventually God will gather his people, reign as King among them, and make an everlasting covenant of peace with them (51:1–6; 52:7–10; 54:1–17). God's glory will come and he will dwell in Zion, then many people from distant nations will come to worship him in Zion (45:22–25; 60:1–12; 66:18–23). Those who refuse to serve God will be destroyed (60:12; 63:1–6; 66:15–17,23), but God will create a new heaven and a new earth where he will dwell with his holy people forever (65:17; 66:22). This brief survey of the titles of God and his action in this world reveal that God is at the center of all theological discourse in chaps. 40–66.

ISRAEL AND THE NATIONS.   A second central pivotal concept in the theology of chaps. 40–66 is located by noticing who God interacts with as Creator, Redeemer, Holy One, King, and Savior. The "who" that God speaks to, works with, saves, and punishes includes both his own people of Jerusalem/Zion/Jacob/Israel and the people in other nations throughout the world.[179] This is identical to the conclusion derived when examining the theology of chaps. 1–39,[180] but one difference is that in 1–39 the prophet Isaiah addressed individual officials (Ahaz in chap. 7; Rabshakeh in 36; and Hezekiah in 39); but there are no similar narrative conversations in 40–66.[181] The only individual addressed is the Servant in chaps. 42:1–13; 49:1–13; 50:4–11; 52:13–53:12, but even these chapters are spoken to the Israelites so that they would know about God's plans to bring justice and salvation to all the nations on the earth. Even the messages that relate to the foreigner and eunuch (56:1–8) do not seem to be directly addressed to those individuals; instead, these passages are addressed to the Israelites to instruct them about how they are to treat these

---

[179] Davies, "The Destiny of the Nations in the Book of Isaiah," 93–120, looks at the importance of the nations throughout the book of Isaiah.

[180] Smith, *Isaiah 1–39*, 77–87.

[181] Isaiah 45:1–5 appears to address Cyrus directly, but this seems to be spoken to the Israelites so that they would know God's plans. There is no indication that this oracle was spoken directly to Cyrus.

people when they come to worship God. In 40:1–11 the prophet is charged to speak kindly to Jerusalem (40:1) and to bring good news to Zion (40:9), while 40:27–31 contains exhortations that respond to the complaints of Jacob. Isaiah 41:18–19 addresses God's blind servant, the people of Jacob who were plundered and suffering under a military attack. Isaiah 44:1–5 encourages Jacob, my servant, to not be afraid because God has chosen them to be his people. Jacob functions as God's witness to the nations (43:10), but they were stubborn (48:4), rebellious (48:8), and did not pay attention to God's instructions (48:18). Some of these people were involved with pagan worship (57:3–13; 65:3–7; 66:3–4,15–17) while others are the righteous servants of God (57:1–2; 65:9–16).

There is much less attention to specific nations when chaps. 40–66 are compared to 1–39 (especially in 13–23; 30–31; 36–39), although there are repeated references to people in the nations and distant islands of the sea (40:15; 41:1; 42:7,12; 49:1). One discovers that Egypt, Cush, and Sheba will be given as a ransom for Israel (43:3; 45:14), and Assyria and Egypt oppressed Israel (52:4). In the final evangelistic push to tell the good news to all the nations, messengers will be sent to Tarshish, Libya, Lydia, Tubal, Greece, and other distant islands of the seas (66:19). The nation of Edom (63:1) serves as a symbol of the nations that are the enemies of God. These will be destroyed in God's wrath (63:1–6). Babylon, which claimed for itself a sort of divine status (47:7–8), is another major enemy that God will defeat (43:14; 47:1–15), and her chief gods Bel and Nebo will be humiliated (46:1–13). Other messages relate God's plans for the nations or to all men in general. Although the Hebrews feared the military power of the nations, in God's eyes they were actually nothing (40:15,17). The people who reject God will be destroyed (63: 3,6; 60:12; 66:16), but those nations or peoples that bow down before God will enjoy life with God (45:22–25; 49:6b,7b; 52:13; 55:4–5) and join others who worship God in Zion (56:1–7; 60:1–11; 66:18–23). Thus the main issue that determines the destiny of individual people and nations is not what ethnic or national group they belong to but their relationship to God.

THE CREATED WORLD. The third fundamental theological factor that is repeatedly intertwined with messages about people on earth is the world that God created (40:12–13,21,26,28; 42:5; 45:18; 48:13; 51:13,16; 66:2). God stretched out the heavens in his power, and he sits enthroned as King of this world (40:22; 45:12). He is able to measure the waters in the oceans in the palm of his hand and the distance between the stars by stretching out his fingers (40:12). He knows the names of all the stars and makes sure that none of them go missing (40:26). Since God's people Israel and the people in the foreign nations live on the land that God made and owns, he is able to control these nations (40:23–24) and he determines who controls what land (41:2–3,11–12). He did this in the past when the children of Israel passed unharmed through the waters of the Red Sea (43:16; 63:11–12). The angel of God's presence saved his people, and he shepherded and guided them through the dry Sinai wilderness (63:10–11). In eschatological passages, God describes how he will transform dry land by sending abundant water (41:17–18; 42:15; 43:19–20; 44:3) and causing many trees to grow (41:19; 44:4). Eventually he will create a new heavens and a new earth (65:17; 66:22). The city of Jerusalem will be transformed by the presence of the glory of God (60:1–3; 61:4), and it will get new names (60:14; 62:4).

The theology of chaps. 40–66 deals with God's relationship and interaction with the people on earth in the world he created. A succinct yet broad summary of all that was found in 1–39 was "God controls/rules everything,"[182] and that is true in chaps. 40–66 as well. But this statement is so broad that it misses the unique flavor or thrust that is distinctive of chaps. 40–66. "Trusting the Holy One who rules the world" was viewed as a more specific way of representing the core theology of chaps. 1–39, but chaps. 40–66 do not have the exact same emphasis.

(2) Glorify the Holy Redeemer Who Transforms the World

This formulation of the theological message of chaps. 40–66 describes God's relationships to the world he created. At its core this theological statement is still very much related to the concept of trusting God who rules the earth (the theme of chaps. 1–39), but in chaps. 40–66 this act of trust is expressed in: (a) the recognition, honor, and glorification of the God instead of the idol-gods; (b) singing and glorifying God the Redeemer for his transformation of justice, salvation, and removal of guilt through the Servant; (c) all righteous and holy people glorifying God in his transformed Holy Mountain when he recreates the new heavens, the earth, a holy and redeemed people, and a new world of nature, and (d) the destruction of everything that refuses to bring glory to God.

GLORIFY GOD, NOT THE IDOLS. Numerous oracles deal with the characteristic of "supernatural beings" (the gods) so that the audience would know which divine power was worthy of worship and praise. The supernatural beings of the ancient Near Eastern world made various claims in their traditional mythology so it was important for people to know which one of these gods (or which God) was the most powerful, most knowledgeable about the past and the future, and most splendorous and worthy of trust and worship. Isaiah 40:12–27 claims that the God of Israel is so grand that he can measure the distance between the stars by just stretching out his fingers and can weigh the vast mountains of the world on his scale (40:12). No known power in heaven or the earth is comparable to him, for the kings and nations of the earth are like grasshoppers and are in effect nothing in comparison to God's power (40:15,17,22–24). The idol gods are really just pieces of wood (40:18–20; 41:6–7; 44:10–20) that can do nothing or say nothing (41:22–24,29; 44:9), but the God of Israel can provide strength and hope for the weary (40:29–31) and he subdues and raises up kings to do his will (41:2,25). He knows the past and future (41:26–27), plus he chooses, protects,

---

[182] Smith, *Isaiah 1–39*, 80.

and redeems his own special people (41:8–14) so that they will believe in him and witness to others of his greatness (43:7,10). There is no other Savior like God (43:11–13), for he saved/redeemed his people in the past when they came out of Egypt (43:15–17) and will do new things that will bring greater praise (43:19–21). God also redeemed his people by blotting out their sins (43:25; 44:22), so they should sing for joy (44:23). Babylon and the gods of Babylon may claim to be powerful and eternal (48:7–8), but they will become nothing (46:1–2,5–7; 48:1–2,5–6,9–11). Since God is the Creator, King, and Redeemer of Israel, people should trust him and give him great glory and unending praise.

GLORIFY GOD FOR HIS TRANSFORMING REDEMPTION THROUGH THE SERVANT.   A central part of God's relationship with mankind is interconnected with the work of the Servant who suffered, died, and was later exalted (53:1–12). He is the instrument God used to bring the transformation of justice (43:1–4), light and salvation to all nations (42:6; 49:6,8), and the removal of guilt of sin (53:4–12). This happened so that the people who accepted and followed his righteousness (50:10) could have a new covenant relationship with God (55:3) through the work of this messianic leader. The guilt of all sinners was laid on him, and he suffered for "us" because it was God's plan to allow him to bear the punishment for "our" sins. Later he was highly exalted (52:13,15; 53:12), he demonstrated victory over the powers that defeated him, and he shared the benefits of his victory with many people. Therefore, all who trust him, glorify and praise God the Redeemer and his Servant who provided salvation for his people (42:10–12; 49:13). Through his work it will be possible for God to transform Israel and bring salvation to all the nations (49:6). He will transform the blind by opening their eyes and free those who were captives of false beliefs (49:9; 61:1–2). This anointed one will proclaim the good news that the favorable year of the Lord has arrived (61:2).

GLORIFY GOD IN HIS TRANSFORMED HOLY MOUNTAIN.   Many of the messages (especially after chap. 48) relate to the eschatological era when God will come in all his glory to dwell at his holy place on Mount Zion. It is at this point that God establishes his kingdom in the new heavens and the new earth. This will be the time when the full measure of God's comfort will be known by his people (40:1), for the full glory of the Lord will be revealed to all mankind in Zion (40:8) and God will gently shepherd his people (40:11). Some eschatological promises only mention God's transformation of nature (41:17–20), while others refer to the pouring out of his Spirit (44:1–5). In addition, some verses describe the sudden gathering of Gentile nations and many Hebrew children (49:17–23; 54:1–4; 66:18–23), while others specifically address what will happen in God's Holy Mountain of Zion. All those who keep the covenant with God and maintain justice, no matter who they are or what ethnic group they come from, may come and worship God at his Holy Mountain (56:1–8). All the transformed people who are humble and contrite (56:14–15), plus those who fast to please God, will honor and glorify God (58:6–14). When the glory of God's presence comes to Zion, God's people from all over the world will proclaim his praise (60:1–6), honor the Lord (60:9b), and glorify God's sanctuary on his Holy Mountain (60:13). At that time Zion will be transformed and given new names (62:4), and all the people in Jerusalem will be holy and the redeemed children of the Lord (62:12). God's servant will receive a great blessing (65:13–16), will delight in the Lord (61:10–11), and will rejoice in the idyllic new heaven and new earth (65:17–25). Those who listen to what God says will glorify him (66:5) with people from nations all over the world (66:18–23).

GLORIFY GOD OR SUFFER DESTRUCTION. Unfortunately, these prophecies indicate that not everyone will recognize God as the only true God and not everyone will choose to honor him with their worship. Those who raged against God's people and attacked Jerusalem will perish and be nothing (41:11–12). A similar destiny happens to Israel itself when God hands his people over to plunderers who consume them because they had sinned (42:22–25). Babylon and her gods Bel and Nebo will be humiliated and suffer under God's vengeance because they attempted to make themselves equal to God (46:1–2; 47:1–15) and refused to recognize God's glory.

The blind watchmen of Israel, the selfish shepherds who kill the righteous, worship other gods, involve themselves in shameful activities at pagan temples, and are unjust, will suffer under God's severe wrath (see 56:10–11; 57:1–13,17; 59:3–14,18; 60:12; 65:3–5; 66:3–4,15–17). God will completely trample them under foot in his anger like one trampling out the grapes in the day of his vengeance (63:1–6). They will end up in that terrible place where the worm does not die and the fire burns forever (66:24).

Conclusion

Although the word "trust" *(bātaḥ)* was a key theme in chaps. 1–39, it is used infrequently in chaps. 40–55. Nevertheless, the reason the prophet works so hard to discredit the idol-gods in 40–44 is to get the people to recognize, trust, and glorify the incomparable God of Israel. Between the time a person initially recognizes the power and holiness of God and the consequent response of glorification, there is that moment when one decides that this is a God who can be fully trusted. Babylon "trusted" in wickedness, in false gods, and in the belief that she was god of her own future (47:10), but God destroyed Babylon because she glorified herself instead of God. The blindness of Israel was due to her "trust" in images and her blindness to God's ways (42:16–17), so Israel also had to go through a time of discipline and divine judgment. In contrast the Servant of the Lord, who went through great suffering for the sins of others, placed his complete confidence in God's vindication (50:7–8). The only hope for those who walk in darkness is for them to transform their lives, follow the way of the Lord like the Servant, fear God, obey God's instruction, and "trust" in the Lord (50:10).

Isaiah 40–66 deals more with the glorification of God, an act that demonstrates that a person fully trusts God. If the people in Israel and the nations will only reject the foolishness of worshipping idols and recognize God as incomparably more powerful, holy, and just, then they will be able to trust God completely and glorify his name with praise and exaltation. People need to recognize what the Servant has done for them so that justice can be established throughout the earth (42:1–4), so that they can have salvation and a covenant with God through the Servant (49:6), and so that they can have their guilt removed though the death of the Servant (53:1–12). If they trust God and his work through the Servant, they can enjoy the pleasures of God's great salvation. Then they will gladly praise God for all that he has done (42:10–13; 49:13). Trust naturally leads to glorification.

─────────────── *OUTLINE OF ISAIAH 40–66* ───────────────

I. The Only True God Will Restore His People (40:1–55:13)
    1. Prepare, for God is coming to shepherd his people (40:1–11)
    2. God's power removes fear; he will bring justice (40:12–42:13)
    3. God will deliver and forgive the sins of his blind servants (42:14–44:23)
    4. God will restore Jerusalem, but offers salvation to all (44:24–45:25)
    5. Trust God who humbles Babylon and offers salvation to all (46:1–48:22)
    6. God's Servant Will Bring Salvation to Israel and the Nations (49:1–13)
    7. God Has Not Forsaken Zion (49:14–52:12)
    8. Exaltation and Joy Comes When Sin Is Taken Away (52:13–55:13)
II. The Destiny of God's Servants (56:1–66:24)
    1. The Just Will Experience God's Future Salvation (56:1–59:21)
    2. God Will Bring Salvation, Transform Zion, Destroy the Wicked (60:1–63:6)
    3. Lament and Response: the Destiny of Servants and Rebels (63:7–66:24)

I. The Only True God Will Restore His People (40:1–55:13)
  1. Prepare, for God Is Coming to Shepherd His People (40:1–11)
  2. God's Power Removes Fear; He Will Bring Justice (40:12–42:13)
    (1) God's Incomparable Power Gives Strength to the Weak (40:12–31)
      There Is No Power Stronger Than God (40:12–20)
      God Is in Control of the Heavens and Earth (40:21–26)
      God Will Strengthen Those Without Hope (40:27–31)
    (2) Fear Not, God Is Stronger Than Other Nations and Gods (41:1–20)
      Who Controls History? (41:1–7)
      God Should Be the Source of Israel's Strength (41:8–16)
      God Will Transform Nature to Affirm His Blessing (41:17–20)
    (3) The Gods Are Impotent, but God Controls History (41:21–29)
      The Challenge: What Can the Gods Do? (41:21–24)
      The Challenge: What Are God's Acts? (41:25–29)
    (4) God's Servant Brings Justice and Is a Light to the Nations (42:1–13)
      God's Chosen Servant Will Establish Justice on Earth (42:1–4)
      God's Servant Will Be a Covenant and Light (42:5–9)
      Sing a Hymn of Praise to Glorify God (42:10–13)
  3. God Will Deliver and Forgive the Sins of His Blind Servants (42:14–44:23)
    (1) Fear Not, God Will Deliver His Sinful Blind Servants (42:14–43:7)
      The Blind Are Not Forsaken (42:14–17)
      The Blind Servant's Sins Result in Punishment (42:18–25)
      Fear Not, God Will Ransom and Redeem His People (43:1–7)
    (2) Fear Not, the Blind Will Be Delivered and Forgiven (43:8–44:5)
      You Are Witnesses That There Is No Other God (43:8–15)
      God's Deliverance Transforms Life (43:16–21)
      Burdensome Worship Brings Judgment (43:22–28)
      God's Servants Belong to Him (44:1–5)

I. THE ONLY TRUE GOD
WILL RESTORE HIS PEOPLE
PART ONE (40:1–48:22)

The previous section of the book of Isaiah describes Rabshakeh's threats against Jerusalem (chaps. 36–39) and God's miraculous defeat of the Assyrian troops (37:36). During these events and in the years that followed, one can imagine that a host of questions arose about the present situation in Jerusalem as well as the future state of the nation of Judah. Is God strong enough to defeat all the foreign nations and prove that their gods were nothing? Will some foreign nation actually defeat Judah some time in the future (39:6–7), and what will Judah's political status be if that happens? How will the promised defeat of Babylon, Egypt, and other nations (chaps. 13–23) affect Israel's history, now and in the future? Will God totally forsake his people (40:27), or is there no need to fear about the future? Will God ever forgive the people for their sinful rebellion and be compassionate toward them again? Are God's earlier promises about the restoration of a remnant to Zion still true (2:1–4; 4:2–6; 10:20–22; 11:1–16; 14:1–3)? Will these new events prevent or delay the exalted son of Jesse from reigning on the throne of David forever (9:1–7)?

Some of the messages in chaps. 40–55 give hints about God's answers to questions like these and provide great comfort to the Israelite audience that was facing an unclear future. God claims that he is all-powerful, the Creator of the world, the Redeemer of his people, and stronger than any nation or pagan god (40:12–31). These messages of assurance and salvation verify that God has not forgotten his people in their time of trouble but will fulfill his promises and re-store his people. God will have compassion on those he loves, and he will for-give the nation's sins. God's servant will bear the sins of the people (53:1–12) and restore them. These confirmations of God's plans were spoken to produce repentance (55:6–8) and trust in the hearts of these Israelites.

The Introduction has already dealt with the several different approaches to interpreting chaps. 40–55 as well as three key interpretive issues: (a) the geographic location of the prophet and his audience; (b) the problem of putting together numerous short oracles derived from different genres into unified lon-ger messages; and (c) the difficult task of determining if prophetic statements refer to near-term events or eschatological circumstances.[1]

Many critical commentaries suggest that an exilic prophet (called "Deutero-Isaiah") wrote chaps. 40–55 to people who were living in Babylonian exile, somewhere around 550–540 BC and just before Cyrus defeated Babylon.[2] In most cases this is an assumption or educated guess, for there is actually little historical evidence in most oracles that demonstrates that the audience was liv-ing in Babylonian exile or that these words were given at a certain date. In fact, some of the problems addressed in these oracles do not fit an exilic setting. There is no indication in the writings of the exilic prophets Ezekiel and Jeremiah, or in Ezra that (a) the worship of pagan idols was a problem for the people living in exile, (b) the Israelites were at war while they were in exile, or (c) the people offered useless sacrifices while in exile. Since the historical acts of divine pun-ishment on Judah in 42:22,24–25; 48:10; 52:4–5; 54:4,7–8 are not connected to any specific historical king, it is hypothetically possible to connect God's punishment of his people in these verses either to an Assyrian, Babylonian, or

---

[1] Consult the section of the Introduction dealing with the composition of Isa 40–55.

[2] R. E. Clements, "Beyond Tradition-History: Deutero-Isaianic Development in First Isaiah's Themes," *JSOT* 31 (1985): 95–113, finds the sixth-century Babylonian background to 40–55 ex-plicit.

Persian setting. In one text (52:4–5) the prophet refers to their past oppression by Egypt and a more recent exiling of people by an Assyrian king, but most oracles have little historical evidence that enables one to date them. Each text must be investigated for the evidence it presents, rather than harmonizing every oracle to one situation by imposing on all texts one setting.

STRUCTURE. Most commentators believe chaps. 40–55 form the larger unit. This is based on the observation that 40:1–11 introduces this section while chap. 55 sounds like a concluding call to action. This is somewhat comparable to the concluding call for thanksgiving (chap. 12), which ends chaps. 2–12. The change of focus from messages addressed to Jacob/Israel in chaps. 40–48 to messages primarily addressed to Zion/Jerusalem in 49–55, suggests an important change of emphasis within these chapters.[3]

The structuring device that is used to mark the end of the smaller literary units within chaps. 40–55 is the hymn.[4] Since 55:12–13 ends with a hymn of praise, this is a second factor which points to the conclusion that chap. 55 ends this long literary unit. Hymns also mark the end of each of the main messages in this section.

40:12–42:13	ends with a hymn in 42:10–13
42:14–44:23	ends with a hymn in 44:23
44:24–45:25	ends with a hymn in 45:24–25
46:1–48:22	ends with a hymn in 48:20–21
49:1–13	ends with a hymn in 49:13
49:14–52:12	ends with a hymn in 52:7–10
52:13–55:13	ends with a hymn in 55:12–13[5]

These textually marked units will form the skeleton for the outline of chaps. 40–55, though each section will be outlined into smaller paragraphs.

FLOW OF THOUGHT. The flow of thought within the segments of this outline depends on how one evaluates the themes emphasized in each section; consequently, the story line in various outlines can look quite different from one commentary to the next.[6] The content of the first paragraph suggests

---

[3] Cyrus, Babylon, and the making and worship of idols, which are important themes in chaps. 40–48, cease to appear as the main building blocks of chaps. 49–55. Instead, the servant theme (49; 50; 53) alternates with the restoration of Zion in chaps. 49–55.

[4] E. Hessler, "Die Struktur der Bilder bei Deuterojesaja," *EvT* 25 (1965): 349–69, noticed this feature and pointed out the structural importance of these hymns.

[5] B. S. Childs, *Isaiah*, OTL (Louisville: Westminster John Knox, 2001), 327, 344, 378, 406, 438, is an example of one who finds the hymns as significant markers of the end of a literary unit. Although at one point J. Oswalt, *Isaiah 40–66*, NICOT (Grand Rapids: Eerdmans, 1998), 366, recognizes that major segments end with hymns, he actually begins new units with the hymns in 42:10–13 and 44:23.

[6] A. Laato, "The Composition of Isaiah 40–55," *JBL* 109 (1990): 207–28, divides chaps. 40–55 into five chiastic sections (with each unit being a chiasm) ending at 42:17; 44:8; 46:2; 48:21; and 57:12. This arrangement is not convincing because only 48:21 agrees with the natural hymnic breaks, several passages serve double duty both as the conclusion to one chiasm and the beginning

that the prophet began by announcing the eschatological coming of the Lord to shepherd his sheep (40:1–11). Although the prophet's audience in Jerusalem had many fears, God announced that he was stronger than any nation or any pagan gods, controls history, and will eventually establish justice on earth through his servant (40:12–42:13). Many of God's people have acted sinfully like his blind servants; therefore, they were fearful because of their present crisis of divine judgment. Nevertheless, in the end God promises to be with them, forgive their sins, and eventually restore them to their land (42:14–44:23). God will rebuild Jerusalem through a king named Cyrus (Hb. Koresh), and at some point Babylon and her gods will be destroyed. Then many nations will bow and glorify Israel's God (44:24–48:22). God's special servant will play the central role in bringing God's people and the nations to glorify God (49:1–13). Though briefly forsaken, if Zion will follow God like his servant, God's strong arm will bring salvation and restoration (50:1–52:12). Since the servant will suffer for the sins of many (52:13–53:12), compassion, joy, and many new children will appear at some point in the future, but Judah itself needs to seek God and repent now (55:1–13). The message of comfort is clear; the sovereign God of history will restore his people and the nation by conquering sin and their enemies.

THEOLOGICAL SITUATION. The theological message of the prophet contains God's plans for his people and the nations. In order to perceive how these plans apply to Isaiah's audience, the reader needs to understand the present source of the people's fear, know why they need to repent, and have some idea about what necessitated a transformation from their present status.

The prophet describes his audience as sinful, theologically blind people (42:7,16,18–19; 43:8; 44:18; 48:4) who do not obey God's law (42:24; 48:18), are obstinate (48:4), offer useless sacrifices (43:22–24), and need their sins forgiven (43:25; 44:22). These descriptors could apply to many different periods of the nation's history. Nevertheless, the textual connections with these same concepts in chaps. 1–39 suggest that the text is describing blind people who have many of the same problems as the blind people in chaps 1–39. At the death of Uzziah Isaiah was told that his future audiences would be deaf and blind (6:9–10) and that in the future God would someday open their blind eyes (35:5). The era of spiritual blindness in chaps. 40–55 is also similar to the blindness of the leaders and people who struggled to trust God during the Assyrian attack on Judah (29:9–18). The rejection of God's word in his law in 42:23–24 is parallel to Isaiah's description of the sinfulness of the people who rejected God's words and trusted in Egypt (30:9–12). God's words were sealed up like a closed book (29:11–12), and they did not trust or obey him (30:12–13). This was an obstinate and stiff-necked generation (2 Chr 30:8;

of the next (42:14–17), 52:12–53:12 stands outside this pattern and serves as an epilogue, and chaps. 54–55 are the conclusion.

Isa 48:4) that wearied God with its useless sacrifices (1:10–15; 43:22–24). They honored God with their lips, but it was all meaningless tradition rather than true worship (29:13).

In some chapters the fearful people the prophet spoke to are described as punished for their sins (42:22,24–25; 48:10; 52:4–5; 54:4,7–8), but the historical setting of that punishment is usually not clearly defined. That the prophet was speaking in the context of a significant military conflict in 41:11–12 and 42:22–25 is indicated by references in chaps. 40–44 to a destroyer, being afflicted, exiled, bereavement, desolation, and drinking from the cup of God's wrath. These prophecies probably refer to the desolation of Judah either by: (a) Sennacherib in 701 BC or by (b) Nebuchadnezzar in 587 BC. It seems nearly impossible to relate these problems to the exilic conditions of the nation while they were in Babylon, for the exilic writers Ezekiel, Daniel, and Ezra give no indication that the Hebrew people were at war while living in Babylon.[7] But God did give his people as spoil and plunder (42:22–24) as a result of fierce battles that resulted in the burning of many towns when both Sennacherib and Nebuchadnezzar attacked the nation (42:25). But most of the terms describing these conflicts are too imprecise to fit exclusively to an Assyrian or a Babylonian historical setting. The one specific oppression that is mentioned is the Assyrian conquest in 52:4. This fits the "brief moment God left his people" and hid his face (54:7–8), and this idea matches the "little while" when the people needed to hide from God's wrath (26:20) before God punished the Assyrians (26:21–27:1).

A second helpful factor is the promise that God would make their enemies who were warring against them "as nothing," for you will not be able to find them (41:11–12). This is exactly what happened after the angel of God destroyed 185,000 Assyrian troops (37:36). These comments do not fit the Babylonian conquest of Jerusalem, for God did not forsake them for just a brief time but for 70 years (Jer 25:12), and he did not make the Babylonian army "as nothing." The admission that God hid his face for a short time may explain why some questioned God in 40:27 and why some felt forsaken in 49:14. Some Hebrews wondered what their Maker, the Potter, was doing in 45:9–10, thus making an intertextual connection to the questioning associated with God's plans to bring Ariel (Jerusalem) to its feet in 29:16 (referring to the conquest by the Assyrians). If this correctly defines the theological crisis situation implied in these texts, the "fear not" oracles that come from a military setting (41:10–13; 43:1,5) are more understandable. Since Assyria had destroyed numerous nations, plus all of Judah except Jerusalem, apparently some in Judah began to wonder if the pagan gods were not stronger than the God of Israel

---

[7] The persecution of Shadrach, Meshach, and Abednego in Daniel 3 appears to be a political test of loyalty to Nebuchadnezzar, for only key political personnel were required to be at this meeting (3:2–3). There is no indication that this event had any impact on the rest of the Jewish population in Babylon.

(36:18–20). In this reading of the theological situation, chaps. 28–31 negatively argue against the present policies and behavior of the nation of Judah, while chaps. 40–44 call for a positive trust in God during this crisis. Through these messages God encouraged the leaders of Judah not to worry about the Assyrian gods, the military power of their enemies, or their collaborators. Assyria will pass away and be as nothing (37:36; 41:11–12); later Judah will serve Babylon, but eventually Babylon will fall to Cyrus (Hb. Koresh, 44:28–45:2). In the future eschatological era God will restore his people, all of nature, and every nation will bow before him (45:22–25). God will accomplish his word; it will not fail (40:8; 55:11).

The verbal interlinking of messages through the repetition of vocabulary and themes introduced in chaps. 2–39 allows the interpreter to identify a theological connection between many of the themes in chaps. 40–55, thus bringing unity between the message in 40–55 and 2–39. For example: (a) References to the fall of Babylon in 43:14; 46:1–47:15; 48:14 do not appear in a vacuum, but need to be interrelated to earlier prophecies about the destruction of Babylon in 13:17–14:23; 21:1–10. (b) Prophecies about a future restoration of God's people in 2:2–4; 10:20–22; 11:1–16; 14:1–3; 27:2–12; 30:19–26; 33:1–24; 35:1–10 should be interrelated with the numerous expanded treatments of these ideas throughout chaps. 40–55; (c) God's plan to save many people from the foreign nations in 2:2–3; 11:10; 12:4–5; 14:1; 19:23–25 flow naturally into the similar ideas expressed in 42:6–7,10–11; 45:14–25; 49:6,8,22–26. R. Clements has identified the theme that Israel was "blind and deaf" in 6:9–10; 29:18; 35:5; 42:16–19; 43:8; 44:18 and the idea that God would send "a light to the nations" in 9:2; 10:17; 42:6–7; 49:6; 50:10–11; 60:1–3 as evidence of a redactional, theological unity within the book of Isaiah.[8] Since most messages in chaps. 40–55 lack a specific historical context, these interlinking connections provide a contextual guide for interpreting these theological ideas.

All interpreters, regardless of their methodology, should give due attention to the development of aspects of intertextual continuity and discontinuity within each theme. Those who focus almost exclusively on differences between oracles and settings run the danger of ignoring or disconnecting the theology of 40–55 from the foundation that was laid in chaps. 1–39.[9] These interlinking

---

[8] Clements, "Beyond Tradition-History: Deutero-Isaianic Development in First Isaiah's Themes," 95–113, and "A Light to the Nations: A Central Theme of the Book of Isaiah," in *Forming Prophetic Literature: Essays on Isaiah and the Twelve in Honor of John D. W. Watts*, ed. J. W. Watts and P. R. House (Sheffield: Sheffield Academic Press, 1996), 57–69.

[9] Of course the appearance of similar themes does not prove that the chaps. 40–66 were written at the same date or by the same person, for another author or a disciple could easily quote ideas from an earlier document. But if the setting is similar (as argued above), then these similarities become much more significant. Studies of the quotations of Isaiah 1–39 in later messages are investigated by R. L. Schultz, *Search for Quotations: Verbal Parallels in the Prophets* (Sheffield: Sheffield Academic Press, 1999). H. G. M. Williamson, *The Book Called Isaiah: Deutero-Isaiah's Role in Composition and Redaction* (Oxford: Clarendon, 1994), proposes that the closeness of

connections provide a much more solid resource for informing the reader about the theological issues discussed in chaps. 40–55 than some of the implied settings and assumed problems that some interpreters hypothesize based on minimal evidence.

1. Prepare, for God Is Coming to Shepherd His People (40:1–11)

¹Comfort, comfort my people,
  says your God.
²Speak tenderly to Jerusalem,
  and proclaim to her
that her hard service has been completed,
  that her sin has been paid for,
that she has received from the LORD's hand
  double for all her sins.

³A voice of one calling:
  "In the desert prepare
  the way for the LORD;
make straight in the wilderness
  a highway for our God.
⁴Every valley shall be raised up,
  every mountain and hill made low;
the rough ground shall become level,
  the rugged places a plain.
⁵And the glory of the LORD will be revealed,
  and all mankind together will see it.
          For the mouth of the LORD has spoken."

⁶A voice says, "Cry out."
  And I said, "What shall I cry?"

"All men are like grass,
  and all their glory is like the flowers of the field.
⁷The grass withers and the flowers fall,
  because the breath of the LORD blows on them.
  Surely the people are grass.
⁸The grass withers and the flowers fall,
  but the word of our God stands forever."

⁹You who bring good tidings to Zion,
  go up on a high mountain.
You who bring good tidings to Jerusalem,
  lift up your voice with a shout,
lift it up, do not be afraid;
  say to the towns of Judah,

---

themes and quotations suggest that "Deutero-Isaiah" was the author/redactor of 1–39 as well as 40–55.

"Here is your God!"
¹⁰See, the Sovereign LORD comes with power,
    and his arm rules for him.
See, his reward is with him,
    and his recompense accompanies him.
¹¹He tends his flock like a shepherd:
He gathers the lambs in his arms
and carries them close to his heart;
    he gently leads those that have young.

This message begins a new poetic literary unit that discontinues the historical narrative account of Hezekiah in chap. 39. Nevertheless, many of the themes in this new literary unit are consistent with and might be called elaborations on what the prophet has already communicated in earlier chapters. Even though this commentary does not put chaps. 34–39 with the second half of the book,[10] there are several thematic interconnections between chaps. 34–35 and what follows in chaps. 40–55. The bold call to "comfort, express compassion" for God's people (40:1) repeats the expectation introduced much earlier in chap. 12:1–2 ("you have comforted me. Surely God is my salvation"), for in both texts God's comfort is related to experiencing God as the source of the nation's salvation. Although the term "comfort" (*nāḥam*) is not used frequently in either 1–39 or in 40–55,[11] the prophet laid the foundation for understanding 40:1 by repeatedly talking in chaps. 2–35 about the numerous ways in which God's salvific acts will extend his compassion to his people. God's acts of salvation bring comfort because his people know that he has promised to defeat their enemies (7:4–9; 10:5–34; 14:24–27; 37:21–29), to establish his glorious holy kingdom (2:1–4; 4:2–6; 30:18–26; 35:1–10), to set his eternal king from the line of David on his throne (9:6–7; 11:1–6; 33:17–24), and to extend his love (*rḥm*) to his faithful followers who will dwell in their land (11:11–16; 14:1–3; 30:18; 35:1–10). This new paragraph in chap. 40 is a continuation of Isaiah's core theological beliefs, dressed carefully in new phrases that speak to the hearts of the people in his audience.

GENRE. Some commentators find fragments of a call narrative of a new prophet (often identified as "Deutero-Isaiah") in the setting of a divine council scene in heaven in 40:1–11. By comparing similar call narratives, such as the commissioning of Isaiah (6:1–8) or Micaiah ben Imlah (1 Kgs 22) with 40:1–11, some have identified the common elements of: (a) angelic heavenly beings calling out in 6:3 and 40:1–6; (b) the coming of the glory of the Lord in the

---

[10] W. Brownlee, *The Meaning of the Qumran Scrolls for the Bible* (New York: Oxford, 1964), 246–59, partially based this interpretation on similar themes and organization of the two halves of Isaiah and partially on the break in the Qumran scrolls between chaps. 33 and 34. J. D. W. Watts, *Isaiah 34–66*, WBC (Waco: Word, 1987), 1–2,7,71–74, also divides the book between chap. 33 and 34 and dates 34 to an exilic period.

[11] The root נחם is used in 1:24; 12:1; 22:4 plus in 40:1; 49:13; 51:3,12,19; 52:9; 61:2; 66:13.

future in 6:3 and 40:5; (c) a prophetic response of despair in 6:5 and 40:6; and (d) a call for forgiveness of sins in 6:7 and the accomplishment of forgiveness in 40:2.[12] Although these common themes draw attention to some similarities between 6:1–8 and 40:1–11, a deeper analysis of these points reveals several significant differences in the treatment of each of these themes. For example, there is no clear statement in chap. 40 that those calling out were angelic beings similar to the clearly identified seraphim in 6:3. The praising function of the seraphim, who said "holy, holy, holy" in 6:3, is completely different from the messenger role of the voices calling out in 40:3 and 6. In addition, if 40:5–6 are viewed as a human objection to a calling that is responded to by God in 40:7–8,[13] this would mean that the call would have to be found in 40:1–5. Yet there is no prophetic call in 40:1–5, so J. L. Koole rightly criticizes this perspective, for this interpretation is seriously weakened by the absence of any explicit "sending" or "calling" of a prophet.[14] Instead, the only explicit sending is the command that "Zion" is to declare the good news in 40:9. In addition, there is no indication that a prophet accepted a call in these verses (contrast this with 6:8), plus the so-called objections in 40:6–7 are not comparable to Isaiah's objection to God's call in 6:5 or any other call narrative.[15] It is also unknown if the speakers in 40:1–6 are heavenly voices from the divine council.[16] One can hypothesize some verbal or thematic connections with interrelated passages (6:1–8; 52:7–10; 62:1–12) without being pushed into the unlikely suggestion that this passage describes the commissioning of another prophet or the recommissioning of Isaiah to a new role.

In light of the weakness of the evidence for identifying 40:1–11 as a call narrative, it is better to approach these verses as a joyous eschatological "proclamation of salvation" (notice the similarity between 52:7–10 and 40:9–11). Instead of focusing on the unidentified speakers who are calling out, the inter-

---

[12] Williamson, *The Book Called Isaiah*, 38, identified a direct literary influence between Isaiah 6 and 40. N. Habel, "The Form and Significance of the Call Narrative," *ZAW* 77 (1965): 297–323, outlines the basic characteristics of several call narratives as (a) divine confrontation, (b) introductory words, (c) commission, (d) objection to the call, (e) reassurance by God, and (f) a sign.

[13] P. D. Hanson, *Isaiah 40–66,* IBC (Louisville: John Knox, 1995), 23, follows this interpretation of 40:6–8.

[14] J. L. Koole, *Isaiah III, Volume 1: Isaiah 40–48,* trans. A. P. Runia, HCOT (Kampen: Kok Pharos, 1997), 48, concludes that this interpretation of 40:1–11 "is based on assumptions which are still being debated."

[15] C. Seitz, "The Divine Council: Temporal Transition and New Prophecy in the Book of Isaiah," *JBL* 109 (1990): 236–37, concludes that this is just a redirection of Isaiah rather than the calling of a new prophet. Oswalt, *Isaiah 40–66,* 48, also refers to this "not as a new call of a new person, but as an expansion and adaptation of Isaiah's single original call."

[16] Koole, *Isaiah III, Volume 1: Isaiah 40–48,* 49, questions attempts to find a divine council in 40:1–6 and notes that the Targum interpreted these speakers as prophets while the Old Greek thought they were priests. Similarly, J. Goldingay and D. Payne, *Isaiah 40–55,* ICC (London: T&T Clark, 2006), 1:59, find 12 linguistic connections between chap. 28 and chap. 40, but they do not try to define the genre or setting of chap. 40:1–11 based on chap. 28.

pretation of the passage should primarily be guided by God's message of salvation in 40:1–2,5,9–11.[17] C. Westermann rightly distinguishes this "proclamation of salvation" from the "oracle of salvation," for the proclamation "speaks of events which still lie in the future."[18]

SETTING.   If the setting is not related to the call or recommissioning of a prophet, what can be said about the setting? Commentators as diverse as F. Delitzsch to C. Westermann relate the statement that "her hard service has been completed" to the idea that "Israel's physical hardship in enforced exile" has ended.[19] Later Westermann connects the road that is to be made straight in 40:3 with the highway that the Babylonian exiles would use to travel back to Jerusalem (11:11–16).[20] R. N. Whybray interprets this comfort to refer to the near-future return of the exiles to Jerusalem (40:9–11); thus his reading creates a discontinuity with the historical setting in chaps. 36–39 and ignores how close these comforting words of God are to chap. 35. In contrast to Whybray, B. Childs reads this passage in continuity with the future eschatological promises already recorded in chap. 35,[21] which suggests to him that chaps. 35 and 40 were closely connected before chaps. 36–39 were inserted to separate these two chapters. If one lets these earlier prophecies in chap. 35 inform the theological analysis of 40:1–11, it appears that the full level of comfort this passage is describing will not be experienced until sometime in the distant future when the glory of God will be revealed to all flesh (40:5) and God actually establishes his glorious kingdom (40:9–11).

Thus the present setting of the prophet and his audience is unknown. But it is known that the full revelation of God's divine glory among his people was not seen in Isaiah's day, during the exile, or in the time of the return from Babylonian exile. J. Goldingay states that "in itself, ch 40 contains no explicit pointers to the geographical or chronological setting" of the author,[22] which is

---

[17] It is possible that the text purposely omits any direct reference to the speakers to prevent the listener from preoccupation with issues that are not the main point, namely, the message.

[18] C. Westermann, *Isaiah 40–66*, OTL (Philadelphia: Westminster, 1977), 13, or note the similar discussion in A. Schoors, *I Am God Your Savior: A Form-critical Study of Is. XL–LV*, VTSup 24, (Leiden: Brill, 1973), 44–45.

[19] F. Delitzsch, "Prophecies of Isaiah," *Commentary on the Old Testament* (Grand Rapids: Eerdmans, 1969), 7:140, says, "it refers to the captivity or exile." Westermann, *Isaiah 40–66*, 35, removes all reference to war. This approach agrees with the interpretation of the Aramaic Targum.

[20] Westermann, *Isaiah 40–66*, 38–39, suggests that the way of the desert "presumes the release from Babylon," which is spoken of in 11:16; 33:8; 35:8. J. Goldingay, *The Message of Isaiah 40–55: A Literary-Theological Commentary* (London: T&T Clark, 2005), 18, claims, "Probably the highway is implicitly one for the Judeans to march on their own return to Jerusalem."

[21] R. N. Whybray, *Isaiah 40–66*, NCBC (London: Marshall, Morgan, and Scott, 1975), 51–53, finds God bringing the Babylonian exiles with him. Childs, *Isaiah*, 301, discovered five verbal connections between 35 and 40:1–11. That chaps. 36–39 were inserted between 35 and 40 is not clearly demonstrated.

[22] Goldingay, *The Message of Isaiah 40–55*, 4. It appears that the explicit reference to Jerusalem

exactly what one would expect in a proclamation of salvation. Since many of the oracles in this book are not in strict chronological order and this announcement of salvation predicts eschatological events, it is best to admit that it is impossible to date the time or setting when the prophet gave this prophecy. All one can say is that it was spoken before the glory of God appears in Zion.

STRUCTURE. This message of comfort contains repeated linguistic characteristics that divide it into several parts based on who is speaking. Initially, God himself gives instructions for someone to speak words of comfort using four imperative verbs (40:1). This is followed by three *kî* "that" clauses (40:2) which give the content of this message. In 40:3–5 an unidentified voice calls out for people to prepare the way for the appearance of the glory of God, and then in 40:6–8 another unidentified voice calls out about the frailty of humanity and the permanence of God's plans. The paragraph ends with a final instruction for Zion to proclaim God's good news to other people in Judah (40:9–11). The structure of the paragraph is divided into four parts based on the four instructions (the imperative verbs) found in this text.[23]

Proclaim comfort to Jerusalem	40:1–2
Announce the glorious coming of God	40:3–5
Be assured, people fade, but God is dependable	40:6–8
Shout, God will rule over his sheep in Zion	40:9–11

This outline simply follows the development of the different speech acts, which originate with the imperative "comfort" in v. 1, the "a voice calling" in v. 3, "a voice says" in v. 6, and the new command to those who are bringing good tidings in v. 9.

40:1–2 This new literary unit begins with two imperative verbs in which God exhorts someone to give words of divine "comfort/compassion" (*nāḥam*)[24] to God's people. The repetition of the same imperative verb ("comfort, comfort") emphasizes this idea and may imply some urgency in following God's instructions. In other passages in Isaiah (12:1; 30:18; 49:13; 51:3,12; 52:9; 61:2; 66:13) God's comfort is closely associated with a time of great joy, the restoration of the land, and the redemption of his people. These are events that mark the eschatological establishment of his kingdom on earth. This audience will receive God's comfort because "your God" (not a friend, a neighbor, or

---

in v. 2 is a hint about the location of the audience the prophet was speaking about. One can assume he was speaking to Hebrews, but the date and location are unknown.

[23] D. N. Freedman, "The Structure of Isaiah 40:1–11," in *Perspectives on Language and Texts,* ed. E. W. Conrad and E. G. Newing (Winona Lake: Eisenbrauns, 1987), 167–93, finds a chiasm with 1–2 matching 9–11, 3–4 matching 6–8, and v. 5 in the center. Only a brief glance at vv. 3–4 will demonstrate that they are quite different from vv. 6–8.

[24] N. H. Snaith, "A Note on the Hebrew Root נחם," *ExpTim* 44 (1932–33): 191–90, suggests the root means to bring about a change of attitude. H. van Dyke Parunak, "A Semantic Survey of *nhm,*" *Bib* 56 (1975): 512–32, points back to the root idea of compassion or comfort. The imperative verb functions as an exhortation in this context (GKC §110a).

some other god) has positive plans to act in compassionate ways toward those within his family ("my people").[25] This terminology connects "your God" to "my people," employing covenantal language that reflects God's relationship to his Hebrew people. One can infer from this information that something negative has happened to God's people at some earlier point because they are in need of comfort. Since no present historical event is identified in this verse, it is inappropriate to impose any specific setting on this general announcement of comfort and salvation. The means of bringing news of comfort to the people in "Jerusalem" (40:2,9, not those living in exile)[26] was through the process of sending some unidentified speakers (the command to comfort is a pl verb) who proclaim good news (40:2). Although the Targum thought some "prophets" would declare these words to Jerusalem, the Old Greek translation hypothesizes that God was instructing "priests" to speak this good news, while the Latin Vulgate suggests "my people" (consistent with 40:9) would declare these encouraging words. Since these speakers who call out are not specifically identified in the text, it is not profitable to speculate about who they are (Isaiah's disciples, or members of the divine council[27]). What is of utmost importance is that the prophet is now to communicate to his Hebrew audience that God instructed someone to speak words of comfort about Zion.[28]

The content of this message of compassion is found in three parallel subordinate clauses, each beginning with "that" (*kî*). In the NIV the first phrase announces, "that her hard service has been completed." The perfect verb (*mālĕʾâ*) usually describes completed action, but in a context of a proclamation of salvation where future events are predicted (40:5, 9–11), a past translation does not fit the context. Since God has not yet appeared in power to care for his sheep (40:9–11), this verb should be understood as a prophetic perfect that refers to things that will be fulfilled in the future;[29] thus, an English future verb would

---

[25] The noun עַמִּי "my people" is usually used of the covenant people of Israel, and 40:9–11 argues for that interpretation here. In other places it may have a broader meaning (cf. 42:6 "covenant of the people" which is parallel to "nations, Gentiles" in the next line).

[26] J. Blenkinsopp, *Isaiah 40–55*, AB (New York: Doubleday, 2000), 180–81, identifies the audience as the Babylonian exiles, even though the text refers to Jerusalem in 40:2,9.

[27] F. Cross, "The Council of Yahweh in Second Isaiah," *JNES* 12 (1953): 74–77, suggested this interpretation though Koole, *Isaiah III, Volume 1: Isaiah 40–48*, 49, rejects it in 40:1–11, partially because there was no divine council in 6:1–8. Blenkinsopp, *Isaiah 40–55*, 179–80, is not convinced that there is a divine council in this text because: (a) 40:1–8 lacks the deliberative style of 1 Kgs 22 and Job 1–2; (b) the voices singing God's praise in 6:3–4 function completely different than those sent to call out in 40:1–8; and (c) 40:6–8 are not the objections of the hearer of God's call. R. R. Wilson, "The Community of Second Isaiah," in *Reading and Preaching the Book of Isaiah* ed. C. R. Seitz (Philadelphia: Fortress, 1988), 53–70, proposes Isaiah's disciples are declaring these words of comfort.

[28] Goldingay, *Message of Isaiah 40–55*, 11, concludes that, "the effect of not identifying the comforters is again to put stress on the *fact* of comfort rather than its agents."

[29] GKC §106n refers to this prophetic perfect as a situation in which a prophet views a future event as if it had already happened; thus, a perfect verb is used. Thus מָלְאָה would be translated "will end."

be a more fitting translation. The first *kî* clause refers to "warfare" (*ṣābāʾ*), not "hard service." The verb form of the root (*ṣābāʾ*) usually means, "to go to war" (2:6; Num 31:7) or in just a few instances, "to do temple work, spiritual warfare" (Num 4:23). The noun form was used in the divine title "the LORD of Hosts," meaning the Lord of the "armies" (*ṣĕbāʾot*) of heaven. When this term is used of people, it usually describes "military service." Some commentators prefer a more general meaning related to the activity of "compulsory labor" based on Job 7:1; 14:14, but even in those cases N. C. Habel is convinced that military service is the compulsory work that this word is describing.[30] It is difficult to accept C. Westermann's interpretation that this clause announces the end of "Israel's physical hardship in enforced exile"[31] in Babylon. There are no other examples in Isaiah where *ṣābāʾ* has the meaning of forced suffering in exile (contrast 29:7,8; 31:4; 34:2), plus there is no evidence that the Israelites suffered physical hardship or hard labor in exile in the writings of Jeremiah, Ezekiel, Daniel, or Ezra (although admittedly this is an argument from silence). K. Baltzer is closer to the correct meaning when he suggests that God was announcing the end of Jerusalem's years of warfare (cf. 2:4).[32] This understanding of the future points beyond the immediate context of the prophet and the Assyrian warfare in chaps. 36–37. But this passage does not make a "universal" statement about the absolute end of all war, as in 2:4.[33] Nevertheless, the later context of God's eschatological rule over his people in 40:9–11 would lend support to this idea. When God comes to set up his kingdom and to shepherd his sheep, his powerful arm will rule all people and there will be no warfare anymore (cf. 2:4). Indeed, this is comforting news.

The second *kî* clause assures the audience that her guilt/iniquity "will be pardoned/paid for,"[34] but this clause does not say who will pay for these sins. C. Westermann suggests that Israel discharged the guilt for her sins through severe suffering in Babylonian exile,[35] but 43:25 (53:6–12; 55:7) makes it abun-

---

[30] N. C. Habel, *Job*, OTL (Philadelphia: Westminster, 1985), 157, concludes that Job was being forced to labor as a military conscript. K. Baltzer *Deutero-Isaiah* (Minneapolis: Fortress, 2001), 52, finds "the military overtone of the word here."

[31] Westermann, *Isaiah 40–66*, 35, removes all reference to war.

[32] Baltzer, *Deutero-Isaiah*, 52, keeps the military significance of צָבָא. Hanson, *Isaiah 40–66*, 20, maintains that Isaiah "unfolds a vision of the restoration of blessing in place of the chaos of warfare."

[33] In the immediate context of the wars going on in chaps. 28–39, it seems hypothetically possible to take this as an announcement that Jerusalem's war with Assyria in 701 BC is over. If the prophet proclaimed these prophetic words close to the time when the 185,000 Assyrians were struck down, this would have brought great comfort to the people in Jerusalem. Nevertheless, this message must be related to the eschatological significance of 40:9–11, not the immediate context of the prophet.

[34] Koole, *Isaiah III, Volume 1: Isaiah 40–48*, 51, translates this clause "her debt has been paid" using root II of the verb רָצָה.

[35] Westermann, *Isaiah 40–66*, 35, says this text is an "echo of glad tidings that Israel's physical hardships in enforced exile are now at an end."

dantly clear that God is the one who blots out the guilt of the transgressor when people repent of their sins. God sweeps away their sins because he is the one who redeems them (44:22) through the servant of Isaiah 52–53. Isa 1:18–20 as well as Isaiah's experience of having his own sins forgiven (6:5–7) demonstrate that only God's grace brings forgiveness of sins. Human suffering is sometimes a punishment for sin, but no salvation or merit is gained just because people justly suffer for their own iniquity. God's compassionate forgiveness of Jerusalem will be an act of divine grace that will bring comfort to his people.

The third *kî* clause must be read in the light of the contextual picture of God's compassion in the first two clauses. This raises problems with the typical approach that views God giving his people double punishment for their sins (cf. Jer 16:18; 17:18). This interpretation almost pictures God as vindictive and prone to require an excessively long or severe punishment.[36] This interpretation of these words does not sound very compassionate and would not be a message of comfort to the prophet's audience. This approach also raises questions about the justice of God's punishment (is it just to give them double punishment?), so G. von Rad proposed a more general meaning for *kiplayim* by suggesting that God will give them an "equivalent" punishment.[37] A completely different way to understand this phrase suggests that it must refer to something positive that is comforting news, just like the rest of vv. 2,5 and 9–11. J. L. Koole argues that v. 2b forms a positive climax of God's comfort by announcing that the people will receive a double[38] portion of God's grace (not a double punishment), consistent with the "double portion" of eschatological blessing that the nation will receive in 61:7. With this interpretation all three statements bring great comfort to God's people in Jerusalem.

40:3 A second unidentified voice relates a second word from the "mouth of the Lord" (40:5). Since this is the word of the Lord, it is not really that important to identify whom this anonymous speaker was, for the one speaking is only a messenger who conveys God's good news.

Since God is holy, all who meet him must be holy or they will be judged (6:1–5). Therefore, 40:3 encourages God's people to make appropriate preparation for the time when all flesh will meet God (40:5; a similar theme is in 62:10–11). The process of preparation is described using the analogy of a royal

---

[36] J. McKenzie, *Second Isaiah*, AB (Garden City: Doubleday, 1967), 17, notes that double punishment was imposed on a thief (Exod 22:4,7) and for a breach of trust (Exod 22:9). In these cases the root שׁנה "double" is used rather than כִּפְלַיִם. L. L. Walker, *Isaiah*, Cornerstone Biblical Commentary (Wheaton: Tyndale House, 2005), 166, connects the double punishment with the two different kinds of calamities that will fall on Judah in 51:19. The Aramaic Targum also interpreted this to be a double punishment.

[37] G. von Rad, "כִּפְלַיִם in Jes 40:2 = Equivalent," *ZAW* 79 (1967): 80–82, suggested that this word is an idiomatic way of saying an amount "equivalent" to something else.

[38] Koole, *Isaiah III, Volume 1: Isaiah 40–48*, 55, and E. J. Young, *The Book of Isaiah* (Grand Rapids: Eerdmans, 1965–72), 3:23, argue for a positive interpretation. The term כִּפְלַיִם refers to a doubling in Exod 26:9; 28:16; 39:9.

edict to repair the roads because a great emperor will soon approach. The audience is exhorted to "prepare the way" and "make straight" (both are imperative verbs)[39] a highway for God by leveling out the high and low sections of the road and by smoothing out the rough spots. This exhortation should not be understood literally because no one would have thought God's way could be hindered by physical obstacles.

This royal road is not the highway that was built in the city of Babylon for the religious festival when the Babylonian gods were carried in a great processional march to their temples.[40] Neither should this highway be confused with the highway that people will use to travel back to Jerusalem in an eschatological exodus experience that is mentioned in 11:11–16; 49:11–12; 62:10.[41] J. Blenkinsopp is right in declaring that "there is no mention here of preparing a route for those returning from exile in Babylon";[42] this is a highway for God. Thus there are two or more different and distinct returns to Zion. In some contexts God prepares the highway for his people to use when they return to Zion, but in other contexts (such as 40:3) the people are to make appropriate spiritual preparations[43] for God's arrival (Pss 24:3–10; 50:23; 68:1–4; Isa 42:16; 48:17–18; 55:6–9).

40:5 The announcement that people will see the glory of God does not seem to refer to people seeing the glory of God in some general way; for example, by observing his glorious deeds in history (24:15; 25:3; 41:16; 42:12) or by seeing his glory in nature (Ps 19:1–2). Instead, the good news is that all flesh will actually view with their physical eyes the majestic glory of God himself (40:5; 60:1–3). This announcement seems to require a great theophany appearance that will be universally visible, if all flesh will see it. In Exod 24:9–18 God's glory appeared before Moses and the elders and in Isa 6:1–8 the prophet Isaiah had a brief private glimpse of the glory of God, the King on his

---

[39] The imperative (פַּנּוּ and יַשְּׁרוּ) could be commands or exhortations (GKC §110a).

[40] Westermann, *Isaiah 40–66*, 38, quotes the Babylonian hymn that refers to similar images that describe the Babylonian preparation of a highway for their gods: "Make his way good, renew his road, make his path straight, hew him out a trail." But the Israelites did not have an image of God and did not carry him around on roads, so the preparation of the road cannot be taken literally.

[41] Goldingay, *Message of Isaiah 40–55*, 18, claims that, "Probably the highway is implicitly one for the Judeans to march on their own return to Jerusalem," though he later clarifies that the focus of this passage is not on the returning exiles but on God's return. J. Calvin, "Commentary on the Book of the Prophet Isaiah," *Calvin's Commentaries* (Grand Rapids: Baker, 2003), 7:204, in a similar manner says "these words relate to the hard bondage which they should undergo in Babylon," and he suggests that the command to prepare the way was addressed to Cyrus and the Persians who were to make a passage way so that the exiles could return to Judah. This completely misses the focus on God returning.

[42] Blenkinsopp, *Isaiah 40–55*, 181, does find a return of the exiles in 35:8–10, but that event should be distinguished from what is described here in chap. 40:1–11.

[43] C. R. North, *Isaiah 40–55* (London: SCM, 1959), 39, interprets as physical hindrances, not moral hindrances, but God's movement is not hindered by any kind of physical impediment.

throne. The seraphim sang of this future day when they said "the whole earth will be full of his glory" (6:3); and later prophecies celebrate how people from all over the world will fear God because of his glory, be drawn by his glorious light, and repent and come to Zion (59:19–60:3). In earlier prophecies Isaiah announced that at the end of time God's glory would be visible as a shelter around all his holy people in Zion (4:4–6). In chap. 35, the most transcendent holy power in the world will openly display his real presence to people in a marvelous way. Isaiah 40:5 develops the ideas found in 35:2,4 that "they will see the glory of the Lord, the splendor of our God." This is the day that will bring divine comfort to all people; it is a day all believers look forward to (cf. Matt 16:27; 24:30; Mark 8:38; John 17:22–24).

Since "all flesh" will see[44] God's glory at this time, the prophet must be referring to the eschatological event explained in 40:9–11. The overwhelming presence of God's "glory"[45] will be at center stage as he fulfills his promise to come to earth to reign (4:2–6). There may be many other mysterious factors about these eschatological events that people then and today do not fully understand, but one thing every person can be absolutely certain about is that "the mouth of the LORD" has promised that God's glory will appear on earth some day. This theme is picked up later at the end of chaps. 40–55 when the prophet assures the reader that God's word will accomplish its purpose (55:10–11).

40:6–8 At the start of the third subparagraph, another (or the same one) unidentified voice instructs someone to call out, but the one hearing this command does not know what words to communicate.[46] Those who view this passage as a prophetic call narrative consider these words as the prophet's lamenting objection to God's call. The prophet cannot fulfill the call of God because Judah is destroyed like the grass and those in exile are like a withered flower.[47] In this interpretation 40:8 is God's rebuttal of the prophet's hopelessness. Nevertheless, "all flesh" can hardly be a reference to several thousand Hebrew people in Babylonian exile. This approach also does not adequately deal with the fact that 40:6–7 (a) are not comparable to any other prophetic objections to God's calling, (b) there is no call of God for someone to be a prophet before v. 6; and (c) this statement does not communicate any personal resistance to

---

[44] The two prophetic prefect verbs refer to what will happen in the future (GKC §106n). Thus וְנִגְלָה should be translated "and it will be revealed" and וְרָאוּ "and they will see."

[45] The glory (כָּבוֹד) of God refers to the splendor of God's majesty that no sinful person can observe (cf. Isaiah 6).

[46] NIV and RSV have "I said," reading וָאֹמַר, which follows the reading of the Old Greek and 1QIs[a] in agreement with the next verb ("I cry"). This would mean that this is a biographical statement by the prophet Isaiah where he is asking what he should say. The MT reading is a third pers. perfect verb "he said" וְאָמַר (Targum, NASB; HCSB) which makes good sense and does not need to be changed.

[47] J. Muilenburg, "Isaiah 40–66," *IB* 5:429, views these words as "deep pessimism" about the nations present defeated situation.

speaking God's words that is comparable to the excuses in Exodus 3–5 or Jer 1:4–10.

It is far better to interpret 40:6–8 as God's words of hope and comfort that the speaker should declare to his audience in Zion, as 40:1 suggests. The good news of comfort for God's people is that like the bloom of the flower, "all people, all flesh,"[48] (v. 6 picks up this term from v. 5) is grass. This must mean that all the people who oppose God will fade and wither away just like the grass fades when God comes (40:24).[49] Just as sinful Isaiah could not stand before the glory of a holy God in 6:3–5, so in the future when God reveals his glory to "all flesh" (40:5), the sinners among them will not be able to stand in his glorious presence.[50] A similar meaning of this kind of imagery is evident in the interlinking images in 28:1–4 where the prophet described the withering of the flowering beauty of Ephraim, which was destroyed because of its pride and drunkenness.[51] Isaiah 51:12 also pictures the enemy that opposes God as weak like grass that withers. In all these examples people under the judgment of a powerful God are compared to withering flowers, so there is no need for the people of Zion to fear any enemy. This news reassures those listening that God will be victorious.

The Hebrew text does not mention the "glory" (NIV follows the Old Greek translation here)[52] of the grass or humanity that will wither and fade. Humanity's "faithfulness, dependability" (ḥasdô)[53] fades and is like the dependability of a bloom on a flower. The people who oppose God's plans will fall just like the flower petals of a rose when God comes in all his glory. In contrast to man's fading lack of dependability is the sure and totally dependable word of the

---

[48] Both verses refer to "all flesh" כָּל בָּשָׂר in v. 5 and כָּל הַבָּשָׂר in v. 6.

[49] The verbs יָבֵשׁ "withers" and נָבֵל "fades" describe what characteristically happens every year in something like a proverbial or wisdom saying; thus the perfect verbs in 40:7 should be understood as gnomic perfects (GKC §106k) and translated in the present tense. The Aramaic Targum interprets this to say "all the wicked are like grass."

[50] Whybray, *Isaiah 40–66,* 51; Hanson, *Isaiah 40–66,* 23–24, distinguishes between those who look to God for deliverance (who are saved) and those who do not (who wither in the presence of God's judgment).

[51] Both Seitz, "The Divine Council: Temporal Transition and New Prophecy in the Book of Isaiah," 236–37, and Williamson, *The Book Called Isaiah,* 78–79, make this connection between 40:6–8 and 28:1–4. Seitz also sees a connection with similar themes in 37:27.

[52] It is not necessary to emend the reading to הָדָר "honor, adornment" or חֶמְדָּה "desirable," though the similarity of these words may explain why the Old Greek translated this word "glory." The word חֶסֶד usually refers to God's steadfast covenant love for his covenant people. When referring to people in comparison to the grass, this term contrasts the grass withering and the sure word of the Lord. L. J. Kuyper, "The Meaning of חסדו in Is. 40:6," *VT* 13 (1963): 489–92, suggests the meaning "his strength" for חסדו based on 2 Kgs 20:20 and 2 Chr 32:32 and the Targum translation "strength" in 40:6.

[53] G. R. Clark, *The Word Hesed in the Hebrew Bible,* JSOTSup 157 (Sheffield: JSOT, 1993), traces the various meanings of חֶסֶד. This word emphasizes a person's enduring commitment to a social relationship and could be translated "steadfast covenant love" in cases where it refers to God's commitment to his people.

Lord (40:5,8). One should not trust other people or put any hope in them, for God's promises are man's only solid and a sure source of strength (55:10–11). The contrast is clear; flowers "fall," but God's word "will stand." What he promises will happen.

40:9–11 Now at the climax of this introductory announcement of salvation comes God's sure words describing what will stand forever. If 40:1–8 can be understood as comforting words concerning God's glorious appearing to the people of Jerusalem (40:1), then 40:9–11 are God's instructions that Zion is to "go up"[54] to a high mountain (cf. 52:7) to loudly and fearlessly proclaim a message of good news to the people who live in the cities of Judah (nothing is said about speaking to those living in exile).[55] The people who are instructed to shout are called the "messengers of good news";[56] they are the ones who will fearlessly declare the "good news" (*bāśār*) that God is coming.[57] They should have no fear of what other people might think or say. The good news is the marvelous announcement that "your God is here" (lit. "behold your God"), for the glory of God is going to be revealed for all people to see (40:5). This seems to parallel the message of those who bring good news to Zion in 25:9; 35:2, and later in 52:7. In 52:7 the text also proclaims the joyous news that "your God reigns." This is a startling development, a final fulfillment of God's prophetic plan, and a word of assurance and joy. God will not just watch over his people in some general way by watching over the course of nature; he will personally be present in power, accomplishing his will among his people.

40:10 The transforming power of God's presence is textually interlinked to earlier references in chaps. 25 and 35 which refer to the eschatological coming of God.[58] This textual interlinking informs the reader how to approach these promises. God's coming will be marked by a powerful demonstration of

---

[54] The use of three parallel imperative exhortations ("go up, lift up, lift up"), three similar sounding words (*har, hārîmi, hārîmi*), and three interjections ("behold, see" הִנֵּה) illustrate a three-fold stylistic way of writing that is often repeated in these chapters. These three imperatives, plus the imperative "say, speak" at the end of the verse express an urgency that Zion needs to tell people about God's coming.

[55] Goldingay, *Message of Isaiah 40–55*, 28, maintains that "the towns of Judah, like Zion itself, are ruined and desolate" because of the Babylonian conquest of Judah, but this reads into the text a great deal that is not stated in this oracle. There were many wars when the cities of Judah were destroyed, so it is impossible to say which war caused these ruins. In fact, 40:9 never says that the cities of Judah are ruined; that is an idea read into this text from other passages like 44:26.

[56] The NIV translation "You who bring good news to Zion" fails to understand that the word Zion is in apposition to those "who bring good news," thus suggesting that the heralds of the good news are someone other than the people of Jerusalem. In contrast, the text suggests that the people of Zion and Jerusalem will declare the good news to others.

[57] The word בְּשֹׂר refers to "news," which may be bad (1 Sam 4:17) or good (41:27; 61:1; Jer 20:15). In Psalms it refers to the news of God's great acts of salvation on behalf of his people (40:10; 96:2). This root is found seven times in Isa 40–66.

[58] Childs, *Isaiah*, 301, notes the similar terms in 35:4 and 40:9–10: (a) "say to those who fear" (35:4) and "say to the cities of Judah" (40:9); (b) "be strong" (35:4) and "with power" (40:10); (c) "fear not" (35:4) and "fear not" (40:9); (d) "behold your God" (35:4) and "behold your God"

his sovereign rule through his "arm" that sovereignly controls history.[59] One day he will reign as Lord and Master over his people and over the whole earth. His strength will assure his victory. This picture of God's power should give the audience confidence that no earthly power will be able to resist his will. These images are suggestive of a Divine Warrior whose power defeats his enemy and rescues his own people (although there is no battle in this oracle).

He will bring appropriate "works" (*śĕkārô* "his reward" NIV) and recompense (*pĕʿullātô*) with him.[60] These are probably not the material spoils of war that were granted to soldiers after a battle. These "wages, works" should also not be identified with the exiled people who are sometimes viewed as God's booty, his wages/reward for defeating the Babylonians as Whybray suggests.[61] God's "works" and recompense metaphorically describe his "salvific works" on behalf of his people. At this time he will be their "Savior" (as in 62:11), and he will share the benefits of his work of salvation with his people. Salvation is God's greatest work and his greatest gift to humanity.

40:11 The oracle ends with pictures of God as a shepherd caring for the emotional and material needs of his people. He will compassionately protect them in his powerful and loving arms. His compassionate care is illustrated in the way he tenderly holds his people and gently leads those who are weak. He is the good shepherd (Ps 23:1; Ezek 34) who will take responsibility for his sheep, especially those that are vulnerable among the flock. The metaphors of gathering, feeding, carrying, and leading represents a full-orbed presentation of the various roles of a shepherd. This picture presents the intimate positive relationship God will have with his own people.

THEOLOGICAL IMPLICATIONS. Although the exact setting of this oracle is unknown, this introductory salvation oracle continues the prophet's earlier eschatological words of hope about God's final rule of this world in 35:1–10. This is consistent with the earlier picture that God will come to Zion to protect and care for his people (2:2–4; 4:2–6). It reconfirms the nature of God's rule when his glorious presence will dwell among his people (35:2–4). It looks forward to a time when sin will be removed, his enemies will fade like grass (40:6–8), and everyone will be holy because the Lord will wash away the filth of sin (4:3–4).

Some new aspects are emphasized in this message of hope and comfort. There is a need for people to prepare for the coming of the glory of the Lord. This does not mean that people can hasten the coming of the Lord through their

---

(40:9); (e) "he will come" (35:3) and "the Lord God comes" (40:9). Several other ideas that chap. 35 envisions in the future are parallels with ideas fulfilled in 40:9–11.

[59] Earlier examples of the work of God's arm are in 30:30; 33:2; 48:14, while later references are in 50:2; 51:5,9; 52:10; 53:1.

[60] Rev 22:12 expands on the eschatological fulfillment of this verse.

[61] Whybray, *Isaiah 40–66*, 52, believes this "refers to the spoils of victory, but in this case the spoils are the rescued exiles."

own righteous deeds (fasting, prayer, humility), nor does it suggest that God's coming is conditionally based on an appropriate human response. God will come at a time that he alone determines. All that people can do is make sure that they are prepared to meet God when he comes. People do not influence the day of his coming; they can only impact the nature of their own treatment when he comes. When God comes all flesh will bow in reverence at the sight of his glory. Some will wither away like the grass while others will be gently protected in God's almighty arms. The challenge is for Isaiah's audience, and everyone who hears the prophet's words today, to prepare their hearts to meet the Lord face to face. He offers comfort, forgiveness of sins, his holy presence, protection, gentle care, and an appropriate blessing of salvation. These factors should legitimate a decision by all hearers to respond positively to God's compassionate grace.

This message persuasively argues for the prophet's audience to trust God for their future and to begin to prepare for his glorious coming. He will forgive their sins, he will appear in all his glory, he will establish his rule over the earth, and he will care for his people. God has spoken these promises (40:5); they will be fulfilled. First Peter 1:24–25[62] quotes 40:6–8 to make a similar point. Peter encourages his readers to remain firm in their faith. The Christians at that time were strangers and aliens in a pagan Roman world (1 Pet 2:11) and some were facing major persecution (1 Pet 1:6–7; 3:14,17; 4:12–14). Peter wanted his audience to know that the things of this world were perishable and they will pass away like the grass. In contrast, their faith was imperishable because it was based on the sure promises in God's eternal Word.[63]

This prophetic announcement about preparing the way for the coming of the Lord had a major impact on the life of John the Baptist. He not only saw the need to prepare himself for the day of the Lord's coming but also the need to dedicate himself to preparing others by calling them to repentance. This call to proclaim to others the good news of God's coming is a responsibility that every believer should embrace without fear. It is wonderful news of God's comfort, his removal of sins, and his coming to earth. It is the good news of the inauguration of his kingdom. The later application of these verses to the ministry of John the Baptist (Matt 3:3; 11:10; Mark 1:2–3;[64] Luke 7:27; John 1:23) was influenced by the interlinking of the ideas in 40:3–5 with the further comments

---

[62] D. A. Carson, "1 Peter," *CNTOT*, 1020–22, discusses Peter's use of Isa 40:6–8. He does not see these verses fulfilled in the return from exile, though he views the prophet addressing people in exile.

[63] L. Goppelt, *A Commentary on 1 Peter* (Grand Rapids: Eerdmans, 1993), 125–28, notes the textual change from the Hebrew, for Peter follows the Old Greek, which refers to the "glory" of the flower fading, while the Hebrew refers to the "dependability, faithfulness" (read n. 65 on this point).

[64] R. E. Watts, "Mark," *CNTOT*, 113–20, has an extensive discussion of Mark's use of Isa 40:3 and Mal 3:1, though he reads into this text far too much exodus imagery and relates 40:1–11 with the end of the exile instead of the eschatological coming of God.

in Mal 3:1,23–24. Malachi connected the messenger who helps prepare the way for the coming of God with the coming of the messianic messenger of the covenant.[65] Although Isaiah did not give as many details as Malachi, it is easy to understand how the New Testament writers would identify John the Baptist as the fulfillment of this prophecy based on the additional information provided by Malachi. John the Baptist declared the word of God in the wilderness, he prepared people for the coming of God by calling them to repent, and he was the forerunner who came before the Messiah.[66]

2. God's Power Removes Fear; He Will Bring Justice (40:12–42:13)

This complex group of oracles includes diverse, yet thematically interrelated messages about (a) God's ability to bring about justice, and (b) how God's power will show that the nations and their gods have no power. No one in Judah needed to question the justice of God's sovereign control over the political history of the nations (40:14, 27). No one in Judah needed to wonder if God's almighty power is stronger than the power of the gods of the surrounding nations (40:15,17–19).[67] If God took the nations and their gods to an imaginary court of justice (41:21), it would become clear that God can protect his chosen servants (41:9–10) and that these nations and their gods would be seen as completely impotent (41:12–13,24,29).

Eventually, God's special chosen servant "will bring forth justice" (42:1,3) and "establish justice on the earth" (42:4). His life will proclaim God's glory throughout the earth (42:8–12) and demonstrate that the power of the idols and the nations that serve them are of little significance (42:8,13). The prophet's audience should respond in faith, confidence, and joy (42:10–13), knowing that God will strengthen them (40:28–31) while defeating their enemies and the gods that their enemies depend on (41:11).

These theological truths are structured into four interrelated messages that are designed to give hope to the weak and fearful audience the prophet was ad-

---

[65] E. R. Clendenen, "Malachi," in *Haggai, Malachi*, NAC, 384–85, provides a discussion of how Malachi understood Isaiah 40:3.

[66] K. R. Snodgrass, "Streams of Tradition Emerging for Isaiah 40:1–5 and Their Adaptation in the New Testament," *JSNT* 8 (1980): 24–45, compares the Old Testament, Old Greek, the Aramaic Targum, Dead Sea Scrolls text, Apocryphal quotations of 40:1–5 in Baruch 5:7 and the Assumption of Moses 10:1–5, and Talmudic references in order to understand the fuller midrashic development that resulted in the NT application of this passage to John the Baptist. R. Beaton, "Isaiah in Matthew's Gospel," in *Isaiah in the New Testament*, ed. S. Moyise and M. J. J. Menken (London: T&T Clark, 2005), 66–67, misinterprets 40:3 to be about preparing the way for the return of the exile; thus he finds considerable discontinuity between the original prophecy and how Matthew used it.

[67] C. J. Labuschagne, *The Incomparability of Yahweh in the Old Testament* (Leiden: Brill, 1966), 1–4, concludes that the distinctiveness of Israelite religion, when compared to the other religions of the ancient Near East, is based on the distinctive theology of God. "She proclaimed that her God, Yahweh, was incomparable."

dressing. The first message (40:12–31) should persuade the listener to believe that courage and strength are possible because God is wise (40:13–14) and incomparably more powerful than the nations and their gods (40:15–26). The second oracle encourages confidence in God based on his ability to control political events (41:1–16) and transform nature (41:17–20). The third message argues in legal terminology that God controls history and that other gods are not able to control anything (41:21–29). The fourth oracle confidently promises the establishment of God's new world of justice and joy through the work of his chosen servant (42:1–13). By trusting God's promise, Israel can gain new strength (40:29–31; 42:8–10) and will give praise and glory to God (42:8,10–13).

SETTING. The exact setting of this group of messages is not explicitly stated at the beginning, for the prophet does not refer to the reign of any king in Judah, nor provide the name of any ruler of any foreign nation. The audience is made up of Hebrews who wonder what God is doing (40:27), who feel weak and helpless (40:29; 42:10,14), and who face people who are opposing and waging war against them (41:11–12). J. D. W. Watts suggested that these conditions should be read against the backdrop of the Hebrew people living in Babylonian exile.[68] This interpretation is largely based on identifying the Persian king Cyrus as the unidentified conqueror from the east who will arise and defeat many nations (41:2–3, 25),[69] but Cyrus is not mentioned in chapters 40:12–42:13. Even J. Calvin assumed that the prophet was giving hope to the exiles "because it was difficult for captives and exiles while they were at a great distance from their native country to hope for a return . . . Having been scattered throughout Chaldea and the neighboring countries, they thought that the road which led homeward was shut up against them."[70] Nevertheless, since many Assyrian, Babylonian, and Persian kings came from the east to conquer western states along the Mediterranean coast, it is important not to jump too quickly to a conclusion about which conqueror 41:2–3,25 describes.

B. Childs recognized that any approach that identifies Cyrus as the ruler who was defeating many nations in order to let the exiles go home from Babylon is weakened by the lack of any explicit reference to the Hebrew people in exile in these verses and no mention of Babylon in these chapters.[71] In many sections of the Book of Isaiah one cannot assume that all the chapters are necessarily in

[68] Watts, *Isaiah 34–66*, 94, believes the people are "now in Babylonian exile, no longer a nation and scarcely a people."

[69] McKenzie, *Second Isaiah*, 27–28, confidently concludes that "no one could be uncertain of whom he meant, although the name of Cyrus does not appear until xliv 28." Such harmonization of texts seems to inappropriately historicize this text and consequently lessen the emphasis on the unspecified sovereign plan of God which must be trusted without clear foresight about its fulfillment.

[70] J. Calvin, "Isaiah," *Calvin's Commentaries* (Grand Rapids: Eerdmans, 1948), 8:246, suggests that the person from the east was actually Abraham, not Cyrus.

[71] Childs, *Isaiah*, 308, recognizes this weakness of this view but still maintains that 40:27

chronological order or that they were all given at the same time and place (chaps. 13–23). The precariousness of the exilic hypothesis needs to be recognized, for people can feel weak and helpless for many reasons. A more serious objection to this setting is that there is no record of the Israelites fighting wars and God defeating their enemies (42:11–12) while the people were in exile. Because of multiple possible settings for this oracle, the interpreter is left in the dangerous position of having to propose an historical setting in 40:12–42:13 based on a minimal amount of historical information in these paragraphs.

Nevertheless there are a few hints in 40:12–42:13 that might provide some evidence of the setting of the audience. (a) The Hebrews are very fearful and lack the strength they need; thus God encourages them not to fear and to be strong (40:29–31; 41:10,13–14). (b) God was stirring up a ruler from the east/north who would call on God's name and subdue many rulers and nations (41:2–3,25). (c) Some enemy is raging against, opposing, and waging war against God's people, but soon that enemy will be as nothing and will not be found (41:11–12). The first factor of having fear is probably too general to date these prophecies to any specific event or time, but the second and third factors invite one to compare various possible options that might fit these circumstances.

Since there is such a strong emphasis on the nations and their gods as powerless (40:15–20,23–24; 41:24), it appears that one of the fears that the Hebrews had was derived from the threats of a stronger nation and its gods. This connection is explicitly made in 41:10–13. The opposing nation is not named, but many commentators connect the ruler who subdues many nations in 41:2–3 and 41:25 with the rise of Cyrus around 540 BC.[72] Although Cyrus was a strong ruler who did many of the things mentioned here, it is difficult to defend the suggestion that Cyrus actually called on the name of Yahweh (41:25; see comments there).

A second problem is that there is no known text that indicates that Cyrus ever made war against the Hebrews or was considered their enemy. There is no indication in history or the Bible that God judged Cyrus by reducing him to nothing (41:11–12). Cyrus simply does not match the evidence of 41:11–12 or 41:25. In addition, there is no indication in the writings of the exilic prophet Ezekiel that the Hebrew people in Babylonian captivity feared for their lives or were waging war against another nation. Jeremiah's letter (29:1–23) to the exiles makes no reference to the Hebrews fighting wars while in Babylonian exile. Thus it is difficult to find an exilic setting that will provide an adequate backdrop for these chapters.

---

reflects the despair of the exile. Goldingay, *Message of Isaiah 40–55*, 33, also relates this chapter to the "needs of the Judeans in exile in Babylon, even though Babylon is not mentioned."

[72] Watts, *Isaiah 34–66*, 102, says, "Yahweh claims to be the one who has made Cyrus's victory possible," while Whybray, *Isaiah 40–66*, 61, claims that 41:2 "describes the lightening career of Cyrus in the years preceding the fall of Babylon."

The fear of some strong military nation and its gods provides the general background for the setting of these chapters (41:10–13). Two possible military conflicts deserve consideration. First, a significant military setting where the Hebrews were opposed in a major war was at the fall of Jerusalem in 605–587 BC when God raised up Nebuchadnezzar to subdue most of the ancient Near Eastern nations, including Judah (Jer 22:3–10; 25:8–11; Ezek 5–6; Dan 1:1–3). This situation did cause the Hebrews to have great fear and this conflict would fit the military setting of 41:2–4,11,25. But the statements that God will (a) make Judah's enemies nothing, (b) help and strengthen his people, and (c) work on their behalf so that they need not fear (41:10–16), does not fit what happened at the fall of Jerusalem. God opposed his sinful people because of their wickedness and did not defeat their enemy Nebuchadnezzar. Certainly Nebuchadnezzar and his army were not reduced to nothing.

A second military setting that might qualify would be the Assyrian attack on Jerusalem in 701 BC when God raised up Sennacherib to subdue many nations and defeat Judah (22:1–13; 29:1–8). In this context God not only promised that he would punish Judah for its sins, but that "your many enemies will become like dust" (29:5) for the "voice of the Lord will shatter Assyria" (30:31–32). The Assyrians did become almost nothing when God killed 185,000 Assyrian troops in one night (37:36). Isaiah 41:11–12 fits this situation perfectly, for at that time those who opposed Judah perished and their gods were proven powerless.[73]

Based on an Assyrian military setting (found in chaps. 36–37), these messages make sense and come alive as prophetic encouragement not to fear Assyria or its gods. If the Assyrians were just outside the walls of Jerusalem, one could understand why the audience was in need of so much encouragement to trust God and not fear the strong nation that was warring against them.[74] Although Sennacherib arrogantly claimed that he and his gods had defeated all the other nations and their gods (36:18–20; 37:11–13), these oracles in 40:12–42:13 present a rhetorical argument for drawing one's strength and hope from the powerful God of Judah. From God's perspective Assyria, its army, and its gods have no power in comparison to Israel's true God who sovereignly created the world and controls its history.

(1) God's Incomparable Power Gives Strength to the Weak (40:12–31)

GENRE. The genre of 40:12–31 is sometimes connected to a disputation speech because of the Israelites complaint (in 40:27) that God was not showing

---

[73] If this interpretation is acceptable, one should also look for a possible time when Sennacherib "calls on my name" (41:25). See my comments there.

[74] Goldingay, *Message of Isaiah 40–55*, 33, admits that this section "contains no very explicit reference to its audience's identity and context," but then goes on to say that "Verses 12–31 implicitly relate more directly to the situation, fear and needs of Judeans in exile in Babylon, even though Babylon is not mentioned." In light of the historical statements (not hints or implicit suggestions) in 41:11–13 that a nation was warring against the prophet's audience, an exilic context is excluded.

proper concern for them and is not treating them justly.[75] R. F. Melugin found a wisdom influence in the rhetorical questions in 40:12–17 (compare with Job 40:25–32) and connected the complaint in 40:27 to the style of the individual lament psalms, with 40:28–31 being an expression of confidence.[76]

Although one cannot find a totally consistent structural pattern for all the disputation speeches in the prophets (or in Isaiah), they usually begin by raising an issue where there is some theological misunderstanding, and then they present a divine correction and conclude with some sort of substantiation of the correct theological answer.[77] As a whole, 40:12–31 does not follow this pattern very well, although the final paragraph (40:27–31) has some similarities to it. One is left to conclude that this literary unit does not follow the pattern of any well-known genre of literature.

Nevertheless, this message follows the regular pattern of beginning each paragraph with a series of rhetorical questions (40:12–13,18,21,25, 27–28a) that are then answered by God in order to instruct the audience. These organized questions serve several functions: (a) to structure the material into orderly subparagraphs; (b) to invite the audience to reflect on the answers to the questions and reconsider their own beliefs in light of what God was saying; and (c) to prove the absolute incomparability of God.[78] Together these factors function "to lift up, to increase strength, to bolster and rejuvenate (40:28–31)"[79] the prophet's audience. Interestingly, this positive instructional speech on the greatness of God has some parallels with the hymnic material in Psalm 33.[80]

STRUCTURE.   The structure of this message is signaled by the repetition of similar grammatical questions ("who?" *mî* in 12,13,14,18,25), interjections

---

[75] Schoors, *I Am God Your Savior,* 247–50, calls this a disputation but later admits that "vss 12–17 do not necessarily involve a dispute . . . 12–17 may also be a hymn." Westermann, *Isaiah 40–66,* 48–49, claims "only the final section, vv. 27–31, is introduced as a true disputation," while the three preceding paragraphs are modeled after descriptive hymns of praise. Hanson, *Isaiah 40–66,* 26, pictures this speech as a disputation that "addresses and argues with the doubts that impede an exiled people's embracing the message of God's imminent entry into their lives."

[76] In spite of these different influences R. F. Melugin, *The Formation of Isaiah 40–55,* BZAW (Berlin: de Gruyter, 1976), 35, 90–93, argues that 40:12–31 is a creatively composed literary unit that is unique to Isaiah.

[77] A. Graffy, *A Prophet Confronts His People: The Disputation Speech in the Prophets* (Rome: Pontifical Biblical Institute, 1984) or D. F. Murray, "The Rhetoric of Disputation: Re-examination of a Prophetic Genre," *JSOT* 38 (1987): 95–121.

[78] J. K. Kuntz, "Rhetorical Questions in Deutero-Isaiah," in *Writing and Reading the Scroll of Isaiah: Studies of an Interpretive Tradition,* ed. C. C. Broyles and C. A. Evans, VTSup 70 (Leiden: Brill, 1997), 129–35. M. Dijkstra, "Lawsuit, Debate, and Wisdom Discourse in Second Isaiah," in *Studies in the Book of Isaiah: Festschrift W. A. M. Beuken,* ed. J. van Ruiten, et al. (Leuven: University of Leuven Press, 1997), 251–71, finds the rhetorical questions in more than one genre of literature.

[79] C. Seitz, "Book of Isaiah 40–66," *NIB,* 6:342, concludes that the form "falls short of a pure disputation."

[80] Westermann, *Isaiah 40–66,* 130, and Koole, *Isaiah III, Volume 1: Isaiah 40–48,* 87, make this comparison.

("behold," *hēn* in 15,15b), rhetorical questions ("do you not know," *hălô* in 21a,21b,21c,28), and a regular thematic movement. The subparagraphs deals with (a) who God is, (b) how he views the nations, and (c) how he compares to the idols.[81] This repeated pattern naturally divides 40:12–31 into three parts.

The first subparagraph in 40:12–20

    (1) begins with a series of questions (40:12–14)
    (2) offers hope by comparing God to the nations (40:15–17)
    (3) begins with a question of comparison (40:18)
    (4) offers hope by contrasting God and idols (40:19–20)

The second subparagraph in 40:21–26

    (1) begins with a series of rhetorical questions (40:21)
    (2) offers hope by comparing God to the rulers of the nations (40:22–24)
    (3) begins with a question of comparison (40:25)
    (4) offers hope by exalting God's greatness (40:26)

The third subparagraph in 40:27–31

    (1) begins with a series of lamenting questions (40:27)
    (2) offers hope by extending God's strength to the weak (40:28–31).[82]

In light of the evidence presented in the answers to Judah's first two questions, it was no longer meaningful to make a comparison between God and the idols in the last section of this paragraph, for they are nothing. God's final answer also drops any comparison between God and the nations (40:28–31), presenting only promises of hope for those who truly trust him.

THERE IS NO POWER STRONGER THAN GOD (40:12–20)

¹²Who has measured the waters in the hollow of his hand,
    or with the breadth of his hand marked off the heavens?
Who has held the dust of the earth in a basket,
    or weighed the mountains on the scales
    and the hills in a balance?
¹³Who has understood the mind of the LORD,
    or instructed him as his counselor?

---

[81] Muilenburg, "Isaiah 40–66," 5:434, finds six strophes in this section (12,13–14,15–17, 18–20, 21–24,25–27, 28–31), which is similar to some of the divisions we find. He notes a parallelism between the fourth and sixth strophes (18–20 and 25–27), plus between the fifth and the seventh (21–24 and 28–31). His analysis differs at several points from the outline suggested below. R. H. O'Connell, *Concentricity and Continuity: The Literary Structure of Isaiah* (Sheffield: Academic Press,1994), 164–65, ignores the form-critical distinctions between 40:12–31 and 41:1–7 in order to find a unit in 40:12–41:7.

[82] Goldingay and Payne, *Isaiah 40–55*, 1:97, contain a somewhat similar structure but only take into consideration 40:12–26.

¹⁴Whom did the LORD consult to enlighten him,
    and who taught him the right way?
Who was it that taught him knowledge
    or showed him the path of understanding?

¹⁵Surely the nations are like a drop in a bucket;
    they are regarded as dust on the scales;
    he weighs the islands as though they were fine dust.
¹⁶Lebanon is not sufficient for altar fires,
    nor its animals enough for burnt offerings.
¹⁷Before him all the nations are as nothing;
    they are regarded by him as worthless
    and less than nothing.

¹⁸To whom, then, will you compare God?
    What image will you compare him to?
¹⁹As for an idol, a craftsman casts it,
    and a goldsmith overlays it with gold
    and fashions silver chains for it.
²⁰A man too poor to present such an offering
    selects wood that will not rot.
He looks for a skilled craftsman
    to set up an idol that will not topple.

The unit begins with a series of interrogative questions (*mî* "who") in 40:12,13, and 14. The second line in each verse presents another parallel question with an interrogative "who" implied. Although there is no explicit indication in these verses that identifies who was raising these questions, it is safe to assume that something was happening in that historical context that caused people in the prophet's audience to question God's wisdom, power, and greatness (possibly the war mentioned in 41:11–12). If Judah's enemies and their gods were winning military victories, this would inevitably cause some Hebrew people to wonder if God's abilities were weaker than the wisdom, power, and greatness of this enemy nation and its gods. Although the grammatical form of a question is used to raise this issue, the prophet has no doubt about the answers to these rhetorical questions (these are not negative statements of unbelief).[83] The obvious answers to the questions should cause these questions to function as reaffirmations of the audience's faith. The question format invites the listeners to remember what their traditions say about God. If these foundational truths are accepted, they have major implications for how the audience should view the strong enemy army and its gods.[84] The messengers of the Assyrian king may

---

[83] Labuschagne, *The Incomparability of Yahweh in the Old Testament*, 16–17, rejects the approach of B. Hartmann, who argues that the interrogative מִי should be treated as a negative particle (based on the interplay of מִי and אֵין in parallel accounts in 2 Sam 20:1 and 1 Kgs 12:16).

[84] This setting is implied based on the literary connection this section has with chap. 41. Read the above section on the "Setting" of 40:12–42:13.

have sounded very intimidating when he spoke outside the walls of Jerusalem about the great deeds of their army and their gods (36:1–20; 37:9–13),[85] but the prophet's assertions in this chapter counter those claims.

This paragraph is organized around four points.

Who can understand the greatness of God?	40:12–14
God views the nations as nothing	40:15–17
Can God be compared to idols?	40:18
The idols are man made	40:19–20

40:12–14 The first series of rhetorical questions inquire about God's greatness (12), his sovereign knowledge and wisdom (13), and his incomparable understanding of justice (14). These questions reflect on God's character and ability to do what a divine being should be able to do. God's ability to excel beyond everything that is imaginable argues that he is an incomparably great God.

40:12 The initial questions seek to find out who can (a) measure out the water in the oceans; (b) "mark off, measure" (*tikkēn*) the distances between the stars and planets in the heavens; (c) "contain, hold"[86] the dust of the earth in a standard measuring devise,[87] and (d) weigh out the various mountains to make sure that everything on earth balances out. The rhetorical question format would encourage the audience to think about how they might answer these questions. It is very unlikely Isaiah was raising controversial issues that no one could answer from their religious traditions. Most people in the audience would immediately agree that their great God could do these superhuman things because that is what early Hebrew traditions said. The audience could reflect on the truths that they had read in Hebrew creation texts (Gen 1; Prov 8; Job 38) and come to a legitimate conclusion.[88] Once the prophet has reestablished these fundamental truths about God, he could explain how these beliefs impacted the difficult situation the audience was facing.

These questions point not only to God's ability to do what is humanly impossible, but also to his unfathomable greatness and power. When people consider the size of the oceans, the vastness of the heavens, and height and grandeur of the mountains, they would naturally find it hard to even imagine the enormous amounts of water in an ocean that is over six miles deep, the trillions of miles

---

[85] See comments on 40:18.

[86] וְכָל is from the verb כּוּל "contain, hold" which is used in Solomon's prayer (1 Kgs 8:27) when he says, "The heavens, even the highest heaven cannot contain you." Although Jeremiah did not want to speak God's words because of the persecution he received, in the end he had to admit that "I am weary of holding it in; indeed, I cannot" (Jer 20:9).

[87] שָׁלִשׁ literally means "a third" (BDB, 1026) and probably refers to a third of an ephah (about three gallons). God knows how many of these small measures of dirt it would take to build a pile as big as the earth.

[88] Similar comparisons are found in Exod 15:11; Deut, 32:31; 1 Sam 2:2; Ps 74:14; 88:8; Jer 10:7–16.

between the distant stars in all the different galaxies, and the untold tons of rocks and soil in each individual mountain or mountain range. But the truth is that when God deals with these parts of nature, he is able measure the small amount of liquid in each body of water by simply cupping his hand and filling it with water.[89] God can measure the enormous breadth of the heavens by simply stretching out his fingers (Ps 33:6–7) to mark the distance between two stars. Indeed, God is glorious and great, far beyond human imagination. This passage does not expressly deal with God's creation of the world; it merely deals with his abilities to measure the size of the heavens, the seas, and various parts of the earth that are already in existence. Although no express comparison is made with other gods at this point (40:18–20), these initial claims will later serve as criteria whereby one can compare the God of Israel with the gods of the other nations.

40:13–14 Next the prophet addresses the issue of God's wisdom. J. Oswalt points to the essence of the implied question: "if we cannot even take the measure of the physical world, how can we take the measure of God?"[90] It is preposterous to think that anyone can "measure" (*tikkēn*) the depth and breadth of the "mind"[91] of God to understand how it works.[92] Although some of the Hebrews in Jerusalem may have questioned what God was doing in Judah at this time, would anyone in the prophet's audience be so bold as to suggest that they might be able to help God understand the mysteries of this world through their very limited human knowledge?[93] Does God need consultants, instructors, or advisors on how to govern the world according to a plan[94] that will

---

[89] בְּשָׁעֳלוֹ "with the hollow of his hand" (also in 1 Kgs 20:10; Ezek 13:19).

[90] Oswalt, *Isaiah 40–66*, 59, does not view the "spirit" as the Holy Spirit but the "mind" (including the volitional, affective, and cognitive aspects) of God.

[91] The verb תִּכֵּן means "measure" in 40:12, so it would be odd for it to have another meaning in the very next verse. The word can mean "understand" (Ezek 19:25,29; 33:17–30), but "measure" seems to be more fitting. First Corinthians 2:16 follows the Old Greek rendition, "Who has known the mind of God?" Goldingay and Payne, *Isaiah 40–45*, 101–2, follow the Aramaic Targum and translate this verb "directed" instead of "measure." The word רוּחַ means "spirit" in most cases, but in light of the emphasis on knowing in this verse, "mind" (the Old Greek also translates this as "mind") is appropriate (also in passages like Ezek 20:32; 1 Chr 28:12).

[92] W. Brueggemann, *Isaiah 40–66*, Westminster Bible Companion (Louisville: WJK, 1998), 23, interprets this as an attack on the Babylonian gods, claiming that "the gods of Babylon had too long impressed and intimidated the exiles." This inappropriately reads into the verse material about other gods from vv. 18–20, implies these gods are Babylonian gods, and inserts the idea that the Israelites were intimidated.

[93] R. N. Whybray, *The Heavenly Counselor in Isaiah xl 13–14* (Cambridge: Cambridge University Press, 1971) argues that these verses parallel other ancient Near Eastern religions which had a small group of major gods at the head of the pantheon. Other religions had gods of wisdom that could give advice (Kothar in Ugarit or Ea in Babylon). Whybray views these verses as a polemic against the Babylonian religion, for the God of Israel did not need other deities in order to know what to do.

[94] J. Jensen, "Yahweh's Plan in Isaiah and the Rest of the Old Testament," *CBQ* 48 (1986): 443–55, provides a broader picture of the biblical teaching about "his plan" (עֵצָתוֹ) by tracing this theme throughout the book of Isaiah.

allow justice to prevail (Ps 119:24)? This theme may be interlinked to Isaiah's earlier statement in 14:24–27 that claims that God has a "plan" to crush the Assyrians and his promise that he will accomplish what he has planned (28:29).[95] God is the one who teaches men knowledge and wisdom (Ps 94:10; 119:66); people cannot teach God anything. God knows how to bring about "just results" (*mišpāṭ*) on earth without man's advice or counsel. Although "just results" often refer to the forensic decisions that a judge renders at the end of a trial (50:8; 54:17) or God's righteous judgment of sinful people (Ps 96:13; 98:9), in this context the term probably has a general application to God's judgments in making right decisions in running the world (28:8–9; 40:27).[96] God's supreme abilities and wisdom should have given the prophet's audience a great deal of confidence to put their trust in him. He knows what is right; plus he has the power to establish his just plans on the earth.[97]

40:15 Both the first and third phrases in this verse are introduced by "surely, behold" (*hēn*). These introductory exclamations draw attention to what follows, typically introducing an inference or conclusion that can be drawn from what precedes (41:11,24,29). If the mountains, heavens, and seas in 40:13–14 are so small from God's perspective, surely the great nations that dominate this small planet and oppose God's people are no greater than a tiny drop of water (an exaggerated comparative hyperbole).[98] The infinitesimal size of these great nations like Assyria and Babylon is emphasized when they are compared to dust, so no one should fear their puny power. In 45:8 the noun *šaḥaq* refers to something ground to powder, resulting in a "cloud of dust," so in 40:15 the prophet is comparing a nation to a weightless speck of dust that floats in the air. This does not mean that God does not care about the nations or that the people in these nations are of no value to God. Instead, the prophet states that God "thinks of, regards" (40:15,17)[99] these strong international empires as

---

[95] God's dialogue with the wise man Job in chaps. 38–42 demonstrated that God knows far more about nature and creation than any person on this earth.

[96] B. K. Waltke, *Creation and Chaos* (Portland: Western Conservative Baptist, 1974), 63, says, "Normally this concept is applied to society; i.e., the bringing of society into the right order or arrangement. In this sense it is translated 'justice,' [but] the concept of social justice does not fit the context, but the unusual notion of constructing a building according to a plan."

[97] In Rom 11:34 the apostle Paul quotes this verse near the end of his sermon on understanding God's ways of directing the course of history in order to magnify the greatness of God. M. Seifrid, "Romans," in *CNTOT*, 678, believes 11:33–36 is a hymn which Paul composed with allusions to Isa 40:13 and 11:34. Then in 1 Cor 2:16 Paul quotes this verse when he contrasts the spiritual discernment of the mind of the believer with the mind of the unbeliever. Since the spiritual person has the Spirit of God and the "mind of Christ" dwelling in them, they have access to God's wisdom, for no natural man has instructed the mind of God.

[98] The word דְּלִי "bucket" is used one other time in Num 24:7, "Water will flow from their buckets," but מַר "drop" is only found in this text so its meaning is somewhat in doubt. The parallelism in the following lines could also suggest that this word refers to a small grain of dust in a bucket that is put on the scales to be weighed.

[99] The root חָשַׁב refers to how something is "thought of, regarded, evaluated" in comparison to the massive greatness of God.

entitics that have no real power. The island or little coastland nations (nations like Greece and Phoenicia) are even smaller[100] than the great land nations like Assyria, so they are compared to very fine dust.[101] The powerlessness of the nations and God's sovereign power over them was a point made again and again throughout chaps. 13–23; 29–34. Isaiah's audience should not fear any of these nations or their armies; they should trust in God's power, wisdom, and greatness.

40:16 Initially it appears that 40:16 interrupts the natural flow of thought between vv. 15 and 17. Instead, one should interpret both 40:15 and 16 as demonstrating the greatness of God and the smallness of everything on earth, with 40:17 serving as a conclusion. The logic of v. 17 is consistent with 40:15–16, though stated differently. Since the greatness of a nation on earth is insignificant when compared to God (40:15), the largest altar imaginable with the largest pile of firewood conceivable (the grand cedars of Lebanon, 2:13; 10:34; 33:19) and the finest animals available would not provide an adequate burnt sacrifice[102] to honor God (40:16). The prophet is not criticizing sacrificial worship (like 1:10–15) or pointing out that God is more interested in the transformation of the heart than sacrifices (Ps 51:17; Mic 6:8). The focus of this persuasive argument is on demonstrating the greatness of God.

40:17 These two comparisons within 40:15 and 16 lead to the conclusion that everything that humanity can do amounts to nothing in comparison to the greatness of God (40:17). Three degrees of diminishing amounts of nothingness are described in v. 17 as: (a) nothing (*'ayin*), (b) end of existence (*'epes*), and (c) emptiness (*tōhu*).[103] The preposition before the first negation is *kĕ* "as," giving the translation "as nothing" (a similar phrase is in 41:24 *mē'ayin*) but the second negation has *mîn* which could be interpreted as a comparative "than" ("less than nothing" NIV, NASB). These statements should not be viewed as philosophical abstractions or theoretical expressions about the existence of human life or nations, for these nations did indeed exist.[104] As a sovereign divine spirit being, God simply dwells in a different plane of reality. One of the implications of God's transcendent incomparability is that the world does not

---

[100] The word דַּק refers to something that is thin (one hair), small, or very fine.

[101] The verb יִטּוֹל is problematic because: (a) the subject "he" does not match the grammar of 40:15–16 (God is not introduced until v. 17), (b) the versions suggest a metathesis of letters (יִטְלוּ), which matches the previous verb, and (c) the root of the word could be נָטַל "lift up, weigh" or טוּל "throw away." If metathesis took place in copying, the text could read, "the islands are weighed like fine dust."

[102] The first line of 40:16 implies that the author is referring to a sacrifice (note the parallel term "burnt offering" (עוֹלָה) in the second line, but the first line only says "burning" בָּעֵר a *pi'el* infinitive construct (NIV "altar fires").

[103] These terms are textually linked to 34:10–12 where God speaks of his final defeat of all his enemies. They will be employed later in similar circumstances in 40:23; 41:11–12,24,29; thus they serve to draw chap. 40:12–31 and chap. 41 together.

[104] Oswalt, *Isaiah 40–66*, 62, also concludes that these statements do not indicate that individuals or nations have no value to God.

actually revolve around the great nations of the earth and is not determined by personal wishes, human accomplishments, or national goals. What goes on in this world is actually centered on God and his plans. Therefore, in reality these nations have no power.

Those interpreters who connect this prophecy to exilic and postexilic events have some problems understanding these glorious promises, for God did not show his power and defeat the foreign nations and their gods at that time. During and after the exile of Judah, the kingdoms of Babylon and Persia maintained their power over Israel for many years; the nations of the earth were not turned into nothing. But, if these promises are read in light of God's dramatic power over the Assyrian army at Jerusalem in 701 BC (chaps. 36–37), the interpreter does not have to wrestle with this problem.[105] In 701 BC God did show his great power over the nations and their gods by destroying 185,000 troops in the Assyrian army, thus literally making the power of Assyria and its gods as nothing. Isaiah's use of similar terminology in his prophecy about the fall of Assyria in 29:20 ("the ruthless will vanish," *'esep* "be nothing") could interlink this passage with what he said earlier.

40:18 In light of the evidence presented thus far in 40:12–17, is it possible to compare God to anything else (Exod 15:11; Ps 113:5–6)? On the one hand God is totally unique, but on the other hand all human thought about God is based on some comparative analogies (God has some "likeness" *dĕmût* to a shepherd, a king, a rock, a warrior) that are part of human experience. But no one human analogy or representation can adequately capture the fullness of the glory of this supernatural deity. So the question the prophet raises is not an argument against the use of analogies; he is inquiring about how people comprehend these analogies.

Specifically, the prophet asks how people might "arrange"[106] to compare the likeness of the power and glory of God to the lifeless idols that represent the "supernatural powers" (the gods) of the nations (44:6–20; 46:5–7).[107] No one confuses the comparative analogies of a shepherd, a rock, or a warrior with God himself. Everyone knows that each of these objects or persons has only a

---

[105] R. P. Carroll, "Second Isaiah and the Failure of Prophecy," *ST* 32 (1978): 119–31, highlights this conflict in expectations, for there never was a glorious return of so many exiles that the land was crowded, the land did not all of a sudden turn into a wet and fertile land of plenty, the nations did not bow to Yahweh and worship him with the Hebrews in Jerusalem, and the salvation and protection of God did not last forever. The power of the surrounding nations was not suddenly "nothing" after the exile.

[106] תַּעַרְכוּ means "will you arrange, set in order" suggesting the literal question, "What likeness will you arrange to set next to him?" Is it possible to take one of the idols standing in a temple and make some comparison between its likeness and God's?

[107] Analogies failed Ezekiel when he tried to describe "the appearance of the likeness of the glory of God" (1:28), but he could draw on an array of general impressions such as "an immense cloud with flashing lightning and surrounded by brilliant light. The center of the fire looked like glowing metal" (1:4). Later he refers to "what looked like a throne of sapphire and high above on the throne was a figure like that of a man . . . he looked like glowing metal" (1:26–27).

few metaphorical similarities that are comparable with God, but none of these similarities make them God. At this point the prophet wants his audience to affirm their belief in the uniqueness and superiority of their God. He is trying to persuade them that, if one is comparing God to anything else that might claim to be a supernatural power, the glory of Israel's God is fundamentally incomparable to the characteristics of anything else on earth. Although some Mesopotamian hymns claimed that their gods were incomparable,[108] which agrees with Sennacherib's perspective concerning their power in chaps. 36–37, Isaiah counters this ideology by demonstrating to his readers that none of these gods is in any way comparable to Israel's glorious God.

40:19 If someone might hypothetically think for a moment that "God" (*ʾēl* in 40:18) could be likened in some way to an "idol" (*hāppesel* in 40:19), the prophet reminds that person to pay careful attention to the characteristics of each. At every stage of construction of an idol, a human being does the work[109] of "casting" (*nāsak*), "overlaying, beating out" (*rāqaʿ*), "selecting, choosing" (*bāḥar*), and "setting up" (*kûn*) the idol-gods.[110] At this point the prophet does not even bother to convince the listener that God is superior. It is so obvious that it is beyond question. The idol-god has no shape or beauty other than what the human craftsmen can give it through their skill at carving wood, molding metals, or overlying an object with a thin layer of gold.

40:20 Humorously, the prophet describes how a "special hardwood" (not "a man too poor"[111]) that will not rot was chosen to serve as a base or pedestal. If this hardwood base rotted away and the idol fell over, it would demonstrate just how weak this god really is. After all, the impotence of the idol would be exposed if it fell over and broke (like the Philistine god Dagan in 1 Sam 5:1–4).

---

[108] Labuschagne, *The Incomparability of Yahweh in the Old Testament*, 33–63, lists various ancient Near Eastern claims about the incomparability (a means of giving lavish praise to a supreme god) of the Assyrio-Babylonian gods *Shemesh, Enlil, Ishtar,* and *Nergal* in various hymns and prayers.

[109] The "craftsman" שׁרָחָ is actually one who "works, cuts" different material. If one "works or cuts" the soil, one might call that person a farmer or one who ploughs/works the soil (28:24). In this case he is actually one who works, cuts, engraves different metals.

[110] Whybray, *Isaiah 40–66*, 55, believes 40:19–20 are interpolations added by a later commentator, which interrupt the natural flow of thought between vv. 18 and 20. On the other hand, Schoors, *I Am God Your Savior*, 253, refuses to delete vv. 19–20, but instead suggests that one should add 41:6–7 to 40:19–20. Neither reediting of the text is necessary.

[111] The word הַמְסֻכָּן is found only in this verse so the meaning of the word is in doubt. BDB, 698, connects this word to מִסְכֵּן "poor, needy" (Deut 8:9), but why would this text contrast the idol of a rich man in v. 19 with that of a poor man in v. 20? T. N. D. Mettinger, "The Elimination of a Crux? A Syntactical and Semantic Study of Isaiah xl 18–20," in *Studies in Prophecy* (VTSup 26, Leiden: Brill, 1974): 77–83, connects this word to the Ugaritic *skn* "to make, form, set up," with this participle referring to "what was made, the statue." E. Lipinski, "*skn* et *sgn* dans le sémitique occidental du nord," *UF* 5 (1973): 181–207, identifies this as a wood like ebony. H. G. M. Williamson, "Isaiah 40:20—A Case of Not Seeing the Wood for the Trees," *Bib* 67 (1986): 1–20, summarizes the various proposals and concludes that this verse describes "valuable sissoo wood," a wood mentioned in various Assyrian documents.

Ironically, the person wanting a god has to "choose" (*bāḥar*) the wood used to make the god, a clear reversal of the biblical pattern where God "chose" Israel to be his own people (41:8; 43:20; 45:4). Men make the idol, but Israel's God made humanity (Gen 1–2). The "skilled, wise" (*ḥākām*) craftsman who is needed to make the idol dramatically contrasts with the wisdom of God, the master craftsman who measures out the heavens with his hands, determines the amount of water to put in the ocean, and weighs out the rocks for each mountain (40:12–13). God fashions humanity and the wonders of this world, but it is necessary for a human metal worker, "smelter, refiner" (*ṣôrēp*) with silver, to fashion a beautiful chain to adorn the idol-god so that it will be aesthetically pleasing (40:19b).[112] These contrasts make it abundantly evident that the prophet is not talking about a comparable divine being; these gods have almost nothing in common with the God of Israel. Is it not crystal clear that the Israelite audience should fear and trust God and not the foreign nations or their gods?

GOD IS IN CONTROL OF THE HEAVENS AND EARTH (40:21–26)

²¹Do you not know?
    Have you not heard?
  Has it not been told you from the beginning?
    Have you not understood since the earth was founded?
²²He sits enthroned above the circle of the earth,
    and its people are like grasshoppers.
  He stretches out the heavens like a canopy,
    and spreads them out like a tent to live in.
²³He brings princes to naught
    and reduces the rulers of this world to nothing.
²⁴No sooner are they planted,
    no sooner are they sown,
    no sooner do they take root in the ground,
  than he blows on them and they wither,
    and a whirlwind sweeps them away like chaff.

²⁵"To whom will you compare me?
    Or who is my equal?" says the Holy One.
²⁶Lift your eyes and look to the heavens:
    Who created all these?
  He who brings out the starry host one by one,
    and calls them each by name.
  Because of his great power and mighty strength,
    not one of them is missing.

The second paragraph begins with a series of four rhetorical questions, just like 40:12–14. Later in 40:25 comes another comparative question similar to

---

[112] Note pictures of ancient Near Eastern gods with these beautification ornamentations in *ANET*, 494–96.

40:18. Closely matching the structure of the first paragraph, this paragraph discusses:

Do people not know of God's greatness?	40:21–22
God has power over the rulers of the nations	40:23–24
Can God be compared to the idols?	40:25
God made and controls the stars	40:26

40:21 The initial questions in 40:21 have the effect of making positive affirmations.[113] In reality the question "Do you not know?" actually means, "Surely, you do know." The imperfect verbs in the first two questions suggest incomplete repeated action[114] meaning something like: "Have you not continually known? Have you not repeatedly heard?" These things that the prophet was talking about were not new ideas. These facts were known from their reading of *Torah*, from hearing the priests teach the *Torah* in the temple, from the hymns they sang at festival times, and from the sermons of the prophets. Although one might take the last two lines in 40:21 as parallel to one another based on the NIV "since the earth was founded," there is no preposition in the final clause (HCSB rightly omits the preposition). Thus in the last line the prophet is asking if the Hebrew audience has no understanding of the way God laid the foundations of the earth.[115] These people needed to pay attention to what was already revealed in the *Torah* about God. This information is as old as the hills.

40:22 The prophet reaffirms more information that the audience should already know about God. The description of the work of God is presented in hymnic style (cf. Job 9:5–10; Ps 104) that describes God's greatness and power. The prophet focuses on God's heavenly dwelling place. He is the powerful deity that sits enthroned (implying his kingship) over the whole earth. The significance of the "circle[116] of the earth" is unclear (cf. Job 22:14), but there is little evidence that people at this time understood that the earth was in the form of a round ball. But their astronomical observation of the movement of the stars in regular patterns across the dome of the sky caused them to see their nightly

---

[113] The questions begin with הֲלֹא, a negative interrogative marker that introduces a question whose answer is obvious. Thus it serves to express beliefs that are well known to the hearer and unconditionally accepted. One could in effect translate this rhetorical question as equivalent to the affirmative statement "surely you know that. . . ."

[114] GKC §107b,e indicates that the imperfect verb (תֵדְעוּ and תִשְׁמָעוּ) can express continual or repeated action in past, present, or future time.

[115] The parallelism suggests the reading "from the foundations of," מוֹסְדוֹת, but this word is missing the preposition "from" (מִן). One might explain this as haplography or that the initial מִמ has assimilated into one letter. On the other hand J. Blenkinsopp, *Isaiah 40–55*, 188–90, does not imply "from" but translates the clause "Have you not grasped how the earth was founded," since that is the topic of the next verse. Seitz, "Isaiah 40–66," 343, prefers "Have you not understood the foundations of the earth."

[116] The word חוּג refers to the horizon, circle, vault, or the heavens.

movement from horizon to horizon in a half circle (Job 22:14). It would not be impossible for someone to imply the other unseen half of the circuit of the stars as an explanation of how the stars returned to their original starting point the next night, but this is not clearly stated. The circle could refer to the circle of the horizon that one can observe all around on all sides. This understanding would emphasize that God rules over everything the eye can see in every direction, even to the distant ends of the earth. But God's rule is not limited to what is visible to the naked eye, for his dwelling place is in his tent above this domed half-circle (1 Kgs 8:27). The important point to emphasize is God's kingly rule over all the earth—from one end to the other. He is so great that people are comparatively imagined as tiny insignificant grasshoppers. God's power is celebrated and his glory proclaimed by remembering the tradition that God stretched out the vast heavens like a fine cloth[117] (42:5; 44:24; 45:12; 51:13 "the canopy of the heavens"), just like a person might stretch netting over the poles of a tent.

40:23-24 If God has this kind of power and control over the universe, he is surely able to control the grasshopper kings that walk throughout the earth. God's rule over the heavens and the earth as king is the theological basis for extrapolating his control over the powerful human rulers of this world at this time. God has the power and authority to make nations (40:15–17), their strong rulers,[118] and mighty judges (the king did this) into nothing (40:23b). The discontinuity between the grandeur of the power of God Almighty and the nothingness of earthly kings would be a word of encouragement to the people of Judah who were being attacked by a strong earthly king.

In order to further undermine the power of this enemy, the author compares the rulers of this world to fragile young sprouts of seeds (40:24; Hos 2:25).[119] These kings may proudly proclaim their greatness and power, but from God's perspective these arrogant kings are no stronger than a weak tender plant. God's swift and effective judgment of the rulers of this world is expressed in three parallel "no sooner" (*'ap bal*) clauses in v. 24.[120] In God's framework of eternal time, these kings rule only a short time, so they also can be compared to something that is "no sooner" (*'ap bal*)[121] planted, something that has "scarcely, no sooner" (*'ap bal*) taken root in the soil. Because their root system is not well developed, these plants are very vulnerable to the slightest changes

---

[117] Koole, *Isaiah III, Volume 1: Isaiah 40–48*, 109, suggests that דֹּק, which is only found here, refers not to a heavy cloth from the skin of an animal but probably to a thin transparent veil.

[118] רוֹזְנִים comes from a root that means "strong" so the participle refers to the kings of this earth as the "strong ones."

[119] This type of imagery is even applied to Israel's messianic king (11:1 "a shoot out of Jesse" or 53:2 "a shoot from the dry ground") to demonstrate his lowly beginning.

[120] The term אַף is used repeatedly, often in a series of similar clauses, in 41:10,26; 44:15; 46:11.

[121] The word אַף is used 24 times in chaps. 40–48 and often in a series of parallel clauses (41:10,26; 44:15).

in the weather. These strong rulers are no different than the young plants, for they will quickly wither and suffer the common fate of useless chaff when God sends the destructive wind of his judgment on them. One wonders if there is a more specific intent in these words. This same imagery was used when God announces that he will destroy the nation that is roaring against his people. The Assyrians will be swept away like chaff: "In the evening, sudden terror! Before the morning, they are gone! This is the portion of those who loot us" (17:14). Later in 29:5 Isaiah refers to the destruction of the Assyrian army: "But your many enemies will become like fine dust, the ruthless hordes like blown chaff. Suddenly, in an instant. . . ." This interlinking vocabulary may be providing a reminder of the words of hope that the people had heard in other prophecies.

40:25–26 Now there is the question of comparison, just like the final verses of the preceding paragraph (40:18). In this question the Holy One challenges the listeners to come to a conclusion based on the evidence that is available. The question, "To whom can you compare me?"[122] asks if there is anyone who has a likeness that is in any way slightly comparable to the Holy God of Judah? It is obvious from the preceding verses that one cannot draw a comparison between a great sovereign Holy God and the strong rulers of this world. Are there any other beings "that I might be equal to?"[123] This question must be asking for a possible comparison to some other divine beings that someone might imagine to be equal to God. Although no other idols or gods are explicitly mentioned, the reference to God's creation of (*bārā᾽*), control of, naming of, and power over the "heavenly hosts" (*ṣābā᾽*) suggests an implicit rejection of any comparison between Israel's supernatural God and the ancient Near Eastern gods that were connected to various planets or stars (Amos 5:26; 2 Kgs 17:16; 21:3). God reveals that these "starry hosts" are not divine beings at all.

This question of comparison is answered by identifying the nature of the thousands of heavenly objects that one sees in the sky. When people "lift up their eyes" they can either worship the natural world that they see (cf. Deut 4:19) because they view these lights as representation of powerful gods, or they can regard them as created[124] objects controlled by the God of Israel. The answer to the question in v. 26a is found in a series of participial clauses in 26b, parallel to the use of hymnic participles in the answer in 40:22.[125] The verse

---

[122] The imperfect verb תְּדַמְּיוּנִי functions as a modal subjunctive (GKC §107m,r) to represent willed action that has the potential of taking place (corresponding to "can, might, should"); consequently it is contingent.

[123] וְאֶשְׁוֶה comes from a root that means "to be like, be equal, on the same level" and it is a first pers. verb, not a noun with an object pronoun (Goldingay, *Message of Isaiah 40–48*, 58, rightly interprets this as a first pers. verb). The *waw* before the verb could be understood as a coordinating conjunction continuing the initial question "or (who is) my equal" (NIV) or to express a result "that I should be like (him)."

[124] God is the only one who "creates" בָּרָא in the Old Testament, so the answer would be very familiar to anyone acquainted with Old Testament traditions.

[125] Koole, *Isaiah III, Volume 1: Isaiah 40–48*, 113, interprets 26b as a continuation of the ques-

never directly states that God is the one who does all the things mentioned in 26b, but the implication is that these are the deeds of the Holy One mentioned in 40:25. He is the one who causes the hosts of heaven to go out into the sky by number and name, just like a commander of a military host of soldiers calls out his troops by number and name (Job 38:31–33; Ps 147:4–5). This probably refers to the sending out of the starry hosts of heaven to shine each night rather than the original act of sending them out at the time of creation. Although there are thousands upon thousands of stars in the many galaxies of the heavens, because of God's great power, not one of them gets lost or goes missing. God made, named, controls, and cares for each one of them. C. R. Seitz observes, "God's total grasp of every star in the sky—not one missing—is meant to anticipate the concern of Jacob/Israel that somehow God has disregarded or forgotten about the way of the people."[126] If God can keep track of a million stars across the broad heavens, certainly he can keep track of every one of his chosen people.

GOD WILL STRENGTHEN THOSE WITHOUT HOPE (40:27–31)

[27]Why do you say, O Jacob,
    and complain, O Israel,
"My way is hidden from the LORD;
    my cause is disregarded by my God"?
[28]Do you not know?
    Have you not heard?
The LORD is the everlasting God,
    the Creator of the ends of the earth.
He will not grow tired or weary,
    and his understanding no one can fathom.
[29]He gives strength to the weary
    and increases the power of the weak.
[30]Even youths grow tired and weary,
    and young men stumble and fall;
[31]but those who hope in the LORD
    will renew their strength.
They will soar on wings like eagles;
    they will run and not grow weary,
    they will walk and not be faint.

The idea that Isaiah was using a disputation genre to argue about God's care for his people is usually based on the complaint in 40:27.[127] R. Melugin

tion in 26a, but the questions in 40:12–14 are followed by an answer in vv. 15–17, the questions in 40:18 are followed by an answer in vv. 19–20, and the questions in 40:21 have an answer in vv. 22–24.

[126] Seitz, "Isaiah 40–66," 344, concludes therefore that the real problem is not God's forgetfulness.

[127] Goldingay, *Message of Isaiah 40–55*, 64, finds a comparison between this structure and the

compares the complaint in 40:27 to similar protests in lament psalms and the answer in 40:28–31 to assurances of salvation in similar Psalms.[128] Although some assume that this is a complaint by those who felt abandoned while in Babylonian exile,[129] there is no reference to the exile in this passage. Based on the historical setting identified for the whole of 40:12–42:13 (in the section on Setting above), the idea of being hidden from God could refer to that brief period when God allowed the Assyrian army to attack and defeat all of Judah except Jerusalem. Isaiah 22:1–11; 26:16–20; and 29:1–4 describe the difficulty of those days. God does sometimes hide his face from his people when they fall into sin (8:17; 54:8; 59:2; 64:7; Deut 31:17; Mic 3:4; Ezek 39:23–24), so it is not surprising that people would have had this reaction at this time. In response to these fears Isaiah proclaimed words of salvation mirroring what was said in 35:3–5,10. God will be your strength, so put your hope in him.

The final paragraph includes:

A question about Judah's situation	40:27
Do people not know that God gives strength?	40:28–29
God gives hope by renewing the weary	40:30–31

40:27 The initial question inquires about the audience's rationale for the repeated statements (they "are continually saying"[130]), almost implying that they should have figured out the answer by now. This complaint is about "my God," who should be taking care of his people and insuring that they are dealt with justly. One assumes that the "way" (*derek*) that is hidden from God's eyes refers to the difficult path the people were facing at this time, but there is no explicit explanation of what troubles the people were facing or what injustice the lamenter is referring to. They probably expected, based on their covenant relationship with God, that God would deal with them mercifully, but this was not happening. These statements could be interpreted almost as accusations against God (as in a dispute), but they are actually part of a sorrowful lamenting plea that is searching for an answer (they are not accusing God of evil). They wanted God to intervene on their behalf, but so far he has done almost nothing. These lamenting questions correspond in many respects to the lament that was expressed in 26:7–27:1. When Assyria was attacking, the people of Judah "yearned for God" because they wanted to see his "judgments come

---

disputations in Jer 8:8–9; 33:23–26; Ezek 11:14–17; 37:11b–13b. A. Graffy, *A Prophet Confronts His People*, 86–91.

[128] Melugin, *Formation of Isaiah 40–55*, 35 and 92, finds the prophet uniquely transforming the disputation by borrowing material from lament psalms.

[129] Goldingay and Payne, *Isaiah 40–55*, 1:125, say, "We assume that empirically Jacob-Israel denotes Judean refugees in Babylon." Watts, *Isaiah 34–66*, 94, connects these words to a group of people that is no longer a nation in Babylonian exile, who feel that her rights are not prominent in God's plans.

[130] The imperfect verb תֹאמַר refers to action that is repeated or continual (GKC §107b,e).

upon the earth" (26:9–10) to defeat their enemy. But the prophet asks, why (*lāmmâ*) are the people of God saying these things? Do these people really think that God does not know what they are doing (their "way, path, conduct" *derek*)? Is God really unjust?

40:28 The answer to this lament follows the pattern already established in 40:21–22. First the audience is asked two rhetorical questions. The first, "Do you not know?" begins with *halô*ʾ, implying that the listeners should already know the answer to these questions. Past experience, teachings from the *Torah*, and prophetic proclamations adequately explain who God is and how he deals with his people.

Sensing that the people need to be reminded of these traditions, the prophet repeats for his audience some hymnic declarations about God (40:28b). If they recall who God is then they should be able to remember the correct answer to their questions. The answer is: (a) God is everlasting or eternal (*ʿôlām*), having no beginning or end; therefore, there is nothing in the past or the future that is outside his knowledge. (b) God is the Creator of the whole earth and everything that is in it; therefore, there is no nation or group of people on the face of the earth that is outside his knowledge or control. He is not a local divine being who has limited control over a small territory or just one part of nature. His creative power and control extends to the limits of civilization and the limitless expanse of the heavens. (c) God's power to administer the affairs of thousands of stars in the heavens and the millions of people on the earth never brings fatigue or weakens him because of exhaustion (cf. the servant in 49:4; 51:4; he would become weak to deliver the weak). Therefore, he is never worn out by a large task and nothing is too complex for him to figure out. (d) God's wisdom is unlimited and totally beyond human comprehension; therefore, there are no loose ends or uncontrollable circumstances of fate that overtax God's ability to keep track of them. These confessions of faith profess God's involvement with every time period, every space or territory in the universe, every detail of life, and his total understanding of what has, does, and will happen throughout the heaven and earth.

In response to the lament in 40:27, these affirmations in 40:29–31 maintain that the very nature of God proves that: (a) nothing has or ever will be hidden from God, and (b) no issue of justice has or ever will be overlooked by God. This means that there must be some other reason for the trials the nation was enduring. Hard times often come because people are weak and weary, because they have sinned, or because they do not understand some part of God's plans.[131] It may be confusing when God's longsuffering patience delays the establishment of justice, but the nation's present difficulties cannot be attributed to divine weakness, neglect, injustice, or misunderstanding.

---

[131] Seitz, "Isaiah 40–66," 344, points to one of Israel's problems (40:29) when he identifies the "underlying problem: Israel's exhaustion and weariness."

40:29 So how should God's people respond when they are in a difficult situation that they do not understand? The prophet offers a word of comfort and encouragement by suggesting that they can endure trials through God's help, which is available to them. God is the "one who gives"[132] them extra strength (*kōaḥ*) so that the weary ones will not grow tired or weak during this time of hardship.[133] God is not absent, unavailable, or unwilling to help. Complaining about present problems will not make them go away. The solution is to recognize that everything that happens is part of God's sovereign plan and that God freely and abundantly gives a portion of his strength to those who need it in difficult times. Through human weakness, his power and glory are displayed.

40:30–31 How does one receive a measure of God's power so that one can endure trials? First, one must come to the realization that God's strength is needed. Everyone knows that they sometimes grow weary, even young energetic overachievers burn out if they work too long or too hard.[134] The best and brightest are not immune to failure. The choicest and best-trained military recruits occasionally fail in times of war.[135]

Second, in 40:31 the means of overcoming these problems is to tap into God's "strength" (*kōaḥ*; as in v. 29) by finding hope in the Lord. Strength is available to "replace, exchange, renew" (*yaḥălîpû*)[136] those who are worn out. Third, a prerequisite for this transformational change is the placement of all expectations or hope (*qāwâ*) in the Lord. This hope is an active dependence on God that patiently awaits his timing with confident expectation. This trust in God will replace any false leaning on a person's own strength. Placing hope in God implies that a spiritual bond exists that allows people to admit their own helplessness and to commit their welfare completely into the hands of his strong power. This act of trust will enable God to replace human weakness with the powerful metaphorical soaring wings of an eagle (cf. Exod 19:4; Deut 32:11). Their weary legs will be transformed into strong legs that run fast; the fainting person will be able to walk for miles. Trust is never easy, but it is the key to unlocking God's power. Trust enables people to walk the path (41:31) that God has chosen for their lives (whether it be pleasant or unpleasant) without growing weary or wanting to quit.

---

[132] The participle נֹתֵן is durative and does not limit God's action just to the past or future; it is always available.

[133] The author uses the root "faint, weary" (יָעַף) and "tired, weak" (יָגַע) repeatedly in 28,29, 30, 31 to emphasize the contrast between God's strength and human weakness.

[134] The addition of the infinitive absolute כָּשׁוֹל "stumbling" to the finite verb "they will stumble" creates the emphatic "they will surely stumble" (GKC §113n).

[135] Goldingay, *Message of Isaiah 40–66*, 72, suggests that the prophet is referring to military men who were specially picked and trained; thus, they were the least apt to stumble (31:8; Dan 11:19).

[136] This root חָלַף "renew" will be used in the next chapter (41:1) to interconnect these messages.

THEOLOGICAL IMPLICATIONS. This prophetic message convincingly makes three main points. First, since God is the all-powerful wise Creator of the heavens and the earth, his wisdom and sovereign control of this world is unlimited and goes far beyond man's understanding. If God can mark off the distances in the heavens with his hands, can measure out the water of the oceans in the palm of his hand, and can call all the stars by name, he can do anything he decides to accomplish. His power is unfathomable; his realm of influence is unlimited; his wisdom has no limits. This means that every person can know for certain that God is able to control every aspect of this world. Even today, hope is based on a solid foundation of what God has done in the past; therefore, trusting in God for the future makes sense. When trials and doubts arise, the people of God today must return to the foundation of their faith, the character of God that is revealed in Scripture. It pictures a great God who is worthy of trust.

Second, from the divine perspective the strongest kings of the greatest nations of this earth have no power in comparison to God. These so called world emperors who claim they have sovereignty over large portions of the civilized world are really not as fearsome or powerful as they appear. In God's eyes these rulers and their nations can be compared to a drop in a bucket or a speck of dust. God sets them up and in a short time they will fall. In comparison to God's time frame, their time of rule is extremely short and their sovereignty is very limited. Therefore, every audience that hears these words should be comforted because those human forces that oppressed them have very limited power. Instead people should fear God and trust in him.

Third, the man-made idols that many people call "gods" are not in any way comparable to Israel's powerful God. They are merely characters in epic myths that attempt to make sense of the world. But that mythic worldview presents a theory about who runs the world that does not stand up to close inspection. These gods and the ancient myths are man-made by skilled craftsmen and mythmakers who bring them into existence through their imagination. In fact, upon thorough examination, these "supernatural beings" cannot even stand up by themselves. Therefore, no one should ever fear the claims of other gods or the philosophical worldview that pretends to explain how these gods control the world. No one should be deceived into thinking that these perspectives are anything other than a set of beliefs that deny the power and glory of God. No believer should be intimidated by such theories; instead, the people of God should put their hope in the powerful and glorious God of heaven and earth who will greatly strengthen all those who trust in him.

(2) Fear Not, God Is Stronger Than Other Nations and Gods (41:1–20)

The key issues of God's power and justice in 40:12–31 continue to be matters for discussion and debate in this new literary unit. This message picks up the key themes of "renewing strength" (*yahălîpû kōaḥ*) from 40:31 to legitimate more completely the claims of the previous speech.[137] Will any of the nations be able to "renew their strength" (*yaḥălîpû kōaḥ*, 41:1) by themselves or because of their gods, or must nations and individuals gain strength solely by drawing on the strength of God (40:31)? God reiterates that others may try to get "strength, courage" (from *ḥāzaq*) from other sources (41:6,7), but it is only God that "strongly holds" (from *ḥāzaq* in 41:9,13) his people in his right hand to help (41:10) and provide for them so that they do not need to fear (41:10,13,14). God has not forsaken his chosen servant Israel (41:8–10) but will destroy those who afflict them (41:11–12).[138] He will fulfill all his covenant promises, and in the end he will recreate nature and humanity (41:17–20). Although 41:1–20 is a new literary unit that uses new literary genres to communicate to the prophet's audience, the repetition of the same vocabulary demonstrates a literary continuity that ties it to the theological issues considered in 40:12–31.

GENRE.   Some believe 41:1 and 41:21 invite the nations to meet together to present evidence before God in a trial at court. J. Begrich suggested that these messages are trying to imitate the proceedings of a traditional trial by the elders in a city gate (Deut 21:19; 22:24).[139] This approach is somewhat problematic, since there are no explicit accusations against the accused, as is common in a usual court setting. In addition, the second half of the first paragraph has nothing to do with a trial setting (41:8–20). Therefore, in spite of some legal terminology in 41:1b, one must conclude that Isaiah was not attempting to present God's civil or criminal case against the nations.

It seems more appropriate to suggest that the purpose of this legal language was to convince the people of Judah (not the distant nations) that they could trust God to strengthen and care for them. This goal was accomplished by having God testify about his power before the nations. This imaginary process could present essential evidence that should persuade the Hebrew audience to accept the idea that God is more powerful than the nations and their gods. The language illustrates that one can logically test the validity of the claims made by God and the claims of the distant peoples and their gods.

Since there is no precedent for a trial like this in any secular courts, C. Westermann concluded that the prophet created a new literary genre that simply borrowed court language, while R. Melugin noted how creatively this speech borrowed from the language of disputations (the questions), the cult ("do not

---

[137] Hanson, *Isaiah 40–66*, 34, believes that "the intonations from what preceded continues to reverberate in the new chapter. . . . A second argument needed to be added to the first" and this is made clear through the interlinking of vocabulary in 40:27 about "justice, judgment" in 41:1.

[138] In my introduction to 40:12–42:13 the enemies who were oppressing God's people are identified as the Assyrians who were attacking Judah around 701 BC.

[139] J. Begrich, *Studien zu Deuterojesaja* (Münich: Kaiser, 1963), 27, based this setting primarily on the call to court rather than the structure of the message. A. Schoors, *I Am God Your Savior*, 181–88, surveys past approaches to understanding trial speeches.

fear"), and the court ("meet for judgment").[140] In reality it appears that there never was a literal trial,[141] only a verbal challenge that would help the Hebrew people consider God's claims. Thus the prophet's aim was to challenge the popular pessimistic Israelite worldviews of that day and encourage people to think in new ways (41:8–20).[142] God was trying to defeat the idea that the foreign armies and their gods control the world.

Isaiah 41:8–16 is a salvation oracle that encourages Israelites not to fear their present enemies because God will strengthen them, while the last paragraph (41:17–20) is a proclamation of salvation about the distant future. The proclamation of salvation is different from the salvation oracle in that it lacks the direct address of the salvation oracle, omits the "fear not" terminology, and focuses on God's eschatological fulfillment of his promises to transform nature. These two promises should prove to the prophet's audience that God does not intend to forsake or forget his people (40:27).

STRUCTURE.   Although the use of three distinct genres of literature in this paragraph might suggest that there is not much unity, the linking of ideas within the paragraphs argues for a unified composition. In the first paragraph God challenges the claims of the nations (41:1,5) so that his Hebrew audience can decide who is in sovereign control over political history. In the second paragraph (41:8–16) God promises his strength over those who war against Israel, so they do not need to be fearful like the nations (41:5). In the final proclamation of salvation (41:17–20) God demonstrates his power to transform nature by producing abundant fertility to prove that he alone is God. The structure of this literary unit can be divided into three paragraphs.

Who controls history?   41:1–7
God should be the source of Israel's strength   41:8–16
God will transform nature to affirm his blessings   41:17–20

SETTING.   The historical setting that forms the background for understanding these oracles is related to an unidentified conqueror from the east/north (41:2–3,25) who appears to be the leader of a nation that is making war against God's people (41:11–12). Although many critical and traditional scholars suggest that this leader is Cyrus (a few think the person in 41:2–3 was Abram),[143]

---

[140] Westermann, *Isaiah 40–66*, 63. This consideration of who is a true deity has some similarities with Elijah's contest with the Baal prophets (1 Kgs 18), though one is a narrative of events while the other is a poem with a completely different structure.

[141] Schoors, *I Am God Your Savior*, 208, follows C. Westermann who argues for a civil case related to some claim, not a criminal trial of guilt.

[142] Goldingay, *Message of Isaiah 40–55*, 81, maintains that this unit's purpose is "to dispute this claim and to demonstrate both that the nations have no case to make . . . it is the Judean community that the prophet is concerned to convince."

[143] Seitz, "Isaiah 40–66," 354, believes this text is "capable of both interpretations" (Abram and Cyrus) and finds a typological association between them. Abram's defeat of other nations relates to Gen 14. N. H. Snaith, "The Servant of the Lord in Deutero-Isaiah," in *Studies in Old*

his name is not used here. In fact, there is no historical evidence that Cyrus ever made war against the Israelites, or that he ever called on God's name. Consequently, in the introduction to 40:12–43:12 it was argued that the prophet was referring to the Assyrian king Sennacherib, who did make war against Judah in 701 BC. In light of this historical context, Isaiah is attempting to encourage his audience in Judah[144] not to buy into the Assyrian claims that they and their gods are superior to Judah and her God (36:18–20; 37:3–4,11–13). The prophet claims that Israel's God has all power and he will strengthen them (41:10–14) during this time of great trials. God will win this war and "those who wage war against you will be as nothing" (41:12 was fulfilled in 37:36).

WHO CONTROLS HISTORY? (41:1–7)

> [1]"Be silent before me, you islands!
>   Let the nations renew their strength!
>   Let them come forward and speak;
>   let us meet together at the place of judgment.
>
> [2]"Who has stirred up one from the east,
>   calling him in righteousness to his service?
>   He hands nations over to him
>   and subdues kings before him.
>   He turns them to dust with his sword,
>   to windblown chaff with his bow.
> [3]He pursues them and moves on unscathed,
>   by a path his feet have not traveled before.
> [4]Who has done this and carried it through,
>   calling forth the generations from the beginning?
>   I, the LORD—with the first of them
>   and with the last—I am he."
>
> [5]The islands have seen it and fear;
>   the ends of the earth tremble.
>   They approach and come forward;
> [6]each helps the other
>   and says to his brother, "Be strong!"
> [7]The craftsman encourages the goldsmith,
>   and he who smooths with the hammer
>   spurs on him who strikes the anvil.
>   He says of the welding, "It is good."
>   He nails down the idol so it will not topple.

Testament Prophecy, ed. H. H. Rowley (Edinburgh: T&T Clark, 1957), 187–200, rejects the view that this refers to Cyrus, but instead hypothesizes that it refers to the exiled people of Israel who will conquer their enemies. This interpretation does not fit the circumstances of Israel.

[144] J. M. Vincent, *Studien zur literarischen Eigenart und zur geistigen Heimat von Jesaja, Kap 40–55*, BET 5 (Frankfurt, 1977), 147–61, connects this fear not oracle to a military crisis that is preexilic and compares this oracle to Isaiah's "fear not" oracle to King Ahaz in 7:3–9 and a similar oracle to Hezekiah in 37:6–7.

The initial invitation calls people to gather together so that certain ideas can be evaluated to determine which claims are true. Are the nations in 40:12–31 really nothing or do they control the political history of the ancient Near East? Because of God's claims, the nations responded with fear (41:5), demonstrating that they were still putting their trust in idols (41:6–7). The paragraph includes:

A summons to meet for judgment	41:1
Interrogation: Who stirs up conquerors?	41:2–4
The response of the fearful nations	41:5–7

This section contains imperative and jussive verbs (41:1) that are followed by two questions (41:2a,4a begin with the interrogative "who" *mî*), plus the answers to these two questions (41:2b–3,4b). The last part of the paragraph (41:5–7)[145] has plural verbs in which the people in the nations turn to each other and their man-made gods for strength and comfort. The fear and lack of strength among the peoples of the nations indicates that their solution of depending on idol-gods is a hopeless approach, a conclusion that is consistent with 40:12–31.

41:1 In order to treat the theological issues of who controls history and to discover how divine justice works, God invites the parties (Hebrews and imaginary foreigners) to gather together so that he can lay out the evidence before everyone. The initial imperative calling for "silence" (*haḥărîšû*) gets the people's attention and prepares them to hear what God has to say ("listen to me" also is in 46:3; 49:1). The nations that God summons are not identified, but they include the smaller nations in the distant islands and coastlands[146] of the Mediterranean Sea and some larger nations. These nations do not function as witnesses, nor are they an imaginary jury that will decide the case;[147] instead they function as quasi participants/observers who reveal what they believe by their speech and actions. All participants should come to this meeting for the positive results of "renewing their strength,"[148] thus interlinking this

---

[145] H. C. Spykerboer, *The Structure and Composition of Deutero-Isaiah with Special Reference to the Polemics against Idolatry* (Meppel: Krips, 1976), 58–59, reviews the arguments for the inclusion or rejection of these verses about idols, but he concludes that they fit into the context of God's judgment of the nations in chap. 41.

[146] אִיִּים probably refers not just to the coastlands nations of the Mediterranean Sea but also the small nations on islands.

[147] Schoors, *I Am God Your Savior*, 209, views the nations as a jury that witnesses the contest between God and the idols. But if this is so why do they fear and tremble in 41:5? There is a close connection between the fate of a people and their gods, but people have the choice to reject their gods or trust them.

[148] The verb יַחֲלִיפוּ is connected with the following verb forms and is interpreted as a jussive in NIV, NASB "let the nations renew their strength," but hypothetically it could be a result clause that would encourage others to accept God and enjoy the benefits of his strength. Goldingay and Payne, *Isaiah 40–55*, 140, translate the jussive verbs in vv. 1 and 2 with "must get strength; must come forward," but it makes more sense to view this as an invitation like the NASB, HCSB, NIV.

argument with 40:31. There is no sign at the beginning of this discussion that God intends to condemn these foreign people; instead, he invites them (a) to recognize himself as the sovereign who controls history (41:2–4) and (b) to renew their strength by trusting in his power (41:1). They need not fear the future if they make the right decision. The invitation for the peoples from other nations to participate is found in three jussive verbs that express a desire[149] for them to "approach" (*nāgaš*) the Lord, speak their views, and then conclude the experience by "drawing near" (*qārab*) to hear the just decision of this matter. Initially the prophet's Hebrew audience appears to be onlookers, observing God challenging the claims of the foreign nations and their gods. But in reality the challenge to the nations and their gods was initiated from the beginning solely for the benefit of the prophet's Hebrew audience. It was important for the Hebrews to understand God's defense of his sovereignty so that later, when they are directly challenged to not fear in 41:8–16, they will accept God's promises and not fear the enemy that was warring against them. By comparing the worldview of the nations and what God has to offer, it is evident that no one needs to fear these nations for their gods have control of nothing.

41:2–4 God puts forward two challenging questions (2a,4a both begin with *mî* "who") and then offers two answers to these questions (2b–3, 4b). The first question focuses on "who" controls the political events that were happening at that time (the rise of the strong king). The first half of the question asks: Who "stirs up, raises up" (*'ûr*) the spirit of someone from the east to act? This stirring refers to God motivating or directing some ruler to go to war, but the name of the king is not provided.[150] Earlier Isaiah spoke of God's plan to "stir up" various kings (10:26; 13:17; 41:25; cf. Jer 50:9; 51:1,11) and of God sending the Assyrian king as his "rod" to punish people who anger God (10:5); so the idea of God motivating foreign kings to accomplish his will is not a new idea.

The second half of the question is unclear because: (a) the verb translated "calling" in the NIV could come from two different roots and the root meaning "calling" is probably not the best choice;[151] (b) the noun *ṣedeq* can mean "righteousness" or in a military context it can refer to a "victory,"[152] and

---

[149] The jussive expresses a wish, desire, or advice (GKC §109b).

[150] R. J. Coggins, "Do We Still Need Deutero-Isaiah?" *JSOT* 80 (1998): 77–92, suggests that "It would be dangerous to treat this poem as originally intended to 'refer' to Cyrus" and seems to agree with G. H. Jones, "Abraham and Cyrus: Type and Anti-type," *VT* 22 (1972): 304–19, that neither the identification of this person with Abraham or Cyrus is satisfactory. Jones tries to relate this figure to both Abraham and Cyrus, however, which is not very convincing.

[151] יִקְרָאֵהוּ comes from קָרָא, but this word had two very different meanings: "he will call him" or "it will meet him" (usually קָרָה but sometimes קָרָא). Some prefer "will call" based on the later analogies with the text in 42:6 where God speaks of the suffering servant and says, "I the LORD have called you in righteousness," but "meet" makes good sense in this context (cf. ESV).

[152] The translation "in righteousness" (NIV) adds the preposition "in" since it is an adverbial accusative. The preposition is in the text in 45:13 (בְּצֶדֶק), but it is not present in 41:2. צֶדֶק can

(c) the meaning of the idiomatic "to his feet" is unclear. When interpreting this verse, one should not view the word "righteousness" as a noun referring to "the righteous one"[153] (God or the righteous messianic king he would raise up). Although it is possible to follow the translation in the NIV, "calling him in righteousness to his service," a preferable translation might be "who meets/ encounter victory as he goes,"[154] which fits better with the next line.

The answer to the first question is presented in 40:2b–3. "He [implying God] will give" (*yittēn*) nations to such a king, and God empowers his appointed rulers to subdue others.[155] The king that God empowers is unstoppable in his progress, and so he moves on safely to conquer new territories. No monarch is mentioned by name (the Aramaic Targum mentions Abraham)[156] because the author wants to focus all the glory and attention toward God. He is the one who causes this king to be successful. With the sword and bow, God gives this king the ability to pulverize his enemies into dust that is easily blown away. He pursues an enemy, he successfully defeats them, and passes on to the next fortified city, entering and conquering new territory where his feet have never walked before (41:3).[157] These are almost stereotyped phrases about the rule of God that brings nations to nothing. This same chaff imagery was used earlier (and will appear later in 41:15) when God announced that he would destroy the nations. Interestingly 37:36 refers to God's sudden destruction of the Assyrians by saying that he would turn them into "chaff" (*qaš*), and 17:13–14 refers to the destruction of Judah's Assyrian enemy who will be "driven before the wind like chaff." Later in 29:5 Isaiah refers to the destruction of the Assyrian army when he says "but your many enemies will become like fine dust, the ruthless hordes like blown chaff, suddenly in an instant" (cf. 40:24) This interlinking vocabulary can be connected to the prophet's discussion in 41:2 to show that his work to destroy Assyria like chaff was preceded by his earlier empowerment of

---

mean something close to "victory, salvation" (46:13; 51:5), while it refers to just behavior in other places.

[153] The Greek translations of Aquila, Theodotian, and Symmachus follow this approach.

[154] לְרַגְלָיו is literally "to his feet," an idiomatic phrase that points to his walk as he marches across the country. C. R. North, *Second Isaiah: Introduction, Translation and Commentary to Chapters XL–LV* (Eugene: OR: Wipf & Stock, 2005), 93, translates the phrase, "wherever he goes" based on Gen 30:30.

[155] The verb יַרְדְּ appears to be a corrupt form. It could be an apocopated *hiphil* from רָדָה "to rule" or from רָדַד "to beat down," though 1QIs[a] has a *hiphil* יוריד from יָרַד "to cause to go down."

[156] Unfortunately, most commentaries place much more emphasis on a specific person, often a political conqueror God stirred up in the East. Calvin and Luther thought this referred to God's call of righteous Abraham from the east, others thought this refers to the righteous conquering Messiah (9:1–7; 11:1–5), but most commentators hypothesize a reference to the Persian king Cyrus because his quick military victories in 45:1–3 match what is said in 41:2–3. Nevertheless, with such limited general information, these characteristics could be applied to almost any major conqueror.

[157] G. Gerleman, "ברגליו as an Idiomatic Phrase," *JSS* 4 (1959): 59, takes this phrase to mean "instantly" or "directly," but examples like Deut 2:28 and Job 18:8 do not support this interpretation.

Assyria to turn other nations into chaff (41:2; as in 7:20; 10:6). Both aspects of his mysterious work demonstrate the completeness of God's sovereignty over the nations. No people will survive if he decrees their demise. Although the Hebrew audience knew the answer to these rhetorical questions were referring to God, the poem does not provide an explicit identification of who "he" is at this point in the poem.

Verses 2–3 build tension by implying but not revealing explicitly who empowers this unidentified conquering king (was it God or some foreign gods?). The climax comes in 41:4 where there is a clear answer to this question: "Who has done this and carried it through?" Is someone responsible for bringing all the generations of humanity into existence and directing the past course of history through its various wars? God boldly proclaims (lit.), "I, Yahweh, am the first, and with the last—I am he." This self-introduction formula claims sovereignty and divine control over history. God is the one who has "acted, worked" (pāʿal), the one who has "done, performed" (ʿāśâ) his deeds to direct the course of history from the beginning of time until the last events in history. Therefore, God can be rightly called "the first and the last,"[158] a title that will also appear in later chapters (44:6; 48:12). The two "I am" clauses in 4b answer the questions in 41:2–4a; they emphasize God's claim to sovereignty over history. This statement ("I am he" ʾănî hûʾ which is similar to the "I am" self-identification clause in Exod 3:14; 6:2–3),[159] claims that Yahweh, the God of Israel, is the one God who has the status, the longevity, and the past performance to support the suppositions made in 41:2–4a. God's past deeds leave a record that is irrefutable. This defense of God's divine character should have strengthened the confidence of the Hebrew audience that was listening to the prophet. They need not fear other nations or their gods.

41:5–7 Once the far away island and coastland nations hear what God is doing through this powerful king he is directing to defeat other nations, they respond with great fear and trembling (41:5). This contrasts with the idea that those who put their trust in God do not need to fear (in the next paragraph 41:10,13,14). All these foreign nations can do is to frantically turn to one another for mutual support and encouragement. Unfortunately, these peoples have chosen not to gain strength from Israel's God; instead, they attempt to

---

[158] H. G. M. Williamson, "The First and the Last in Isaiah," *Of Prophets' Visions and the Wisdom of the Sages: Festschrift for R.N. Whybray,* ed. D. J. A. Clines and H. McKay (Sheffield: JSOT, 1993), 95–108, connects this title to God's past judgment and future bringing of light in the future in 9:1 (8:23 in Hebrew). This passage supports the theory that God worked in history in the past and will in the future, but this title does not carry any of the negative–positive connotations found in 9:1; thus there is a legitimate question whether this title comes from that source (9:1). It is likely a much older theological tradition. Later in Rev 1:8; 21:6; 22:13 Jesus is identified as the Alpha and Omega, a phrase similar to the first and last.

[159] P. B. Harner, *Grace and Law in Second Isaiah: 'I Am the Lord',* ANETS 2 (Lewiston: Mellen, 1988), 67–141, understands the "I am Yahweh," "I am God," and "I am he" phrases as substantiating the prophet's argument.

gain "help" (*ʿāzar*) and "strength" (NIV "courage" *ḥāzaq*) from each other and their man-made gods (41:6). One worker "strengthens" (*wayĕḥazzēq*) the other and they "strengthened" (*wayĕḥazzēqhû*, NIV "nails down") the idol with pegs so that it does not fall over. They look for help from the wrong place, for true strength comes only from God (41:10,13,14).

In order to show the Israelite audience how ridiculous this worldview is, the prophet describes their deluded trust in idols made by skilled craftsmen, goldsmiths, and other workers (41:7).[160] The builders of these idols say that the results of their effort to construct this man-made god are "good" (*ṭôb*), but Gen 1:12,31 indicates that only what God created was "good." In order to show how precarious the strength of their faith in the idol was, the prophet explains that it all depends on the nail or peg that will keep the idol standing up securely on a pedestal. If that gives away the idol is in danger of falling over. Can salvation and strength come from this source? The Israelites need not fear the strong Assyrians or their gods, for the God of Israel was the one who empowered this strong king to conquer many lands, not their man-made idols.[161]

GOD SHOULD BE THE SOURCE OF ISRAEL'S STRENGTH (41:8–16)

8"But you, O Israel, my servant,
  Jacob, whom I have chosen,
  you descendants of Abraham my friend,
9I took you from the ends of the earth,
  from its farthest corners I called you.
I said, 'You are my servant';
  I have chosen you and have not rejected you.
10So do not fear, for I am with you;
  do not be dismayed, for I am your God.
I will strengthen you and help you;
  I will uphold you with my righteous right hand.

11"All who rage against you
  will surely be ashamed and disgraced;
those who oppose you
  will be as nothing and perish.
12Though you search for your enemies,
  you will not find them.

---

[160] The vocabulary in 41:7 is difficult. For example פַּעַם can mean "time" (Josh 6:3; Prov 7:12) or "foot" (Ps 57:7; Prov 29:5), but many suggest it means something like "anvil" in this one case because of the parallelism with "hammer" in the preceding line. Based on 1 Sam 26:8 פַּעַם may mean "one stroke."

[161] If this oracle was given when the nations were gathered together around Jerusalem in the form of the Assyrian army of Sennacherib in 701 BC (41:11–12) and the Assyrian army was trusting in their Assyrian gods to give it victory (36:18–20), then this oracle would serve to undermine the claims of Sennacherib and his gods.

Those who wage war against you
will be as nothing at all.
¹³For I am the LORD, your God,
who takes hold of your right hand
and says to you, Do not fear;
I will help you.
¹⁴Do not be afraid, O worm Jacob,
O little Israel,
for I myself will help you," declares the LORD,
your Redeemer, the Holy One of Israel.
¹⁵"See, I will make you into a threshing sledge,
new and sharp, with many teeth.
You will thresh the mountains and crush them,
and reduce the hills to chaff.
¹⁶You will winnow them, the wind will pick them up,
and a gale will blow them away.
But you will rejoice in the LORD
and glory in the Holy One of Israel.

This salvation oracle promises divine help and the defeat of the enemies of God's people. A salvation oracle typically: (a) begins with a direct address to the audience (but "you"), (b) promises salvation and encourages the audience not to fear, (c) gives a reason for trusting God based on his power to deliver them (the substantiation of the promise), (d) states the consequences, and (e) concludes with God's intended purpose (giving glory to God).[162] The first half of this paragraph is characterized by the repetition of the "do not fear" clause (41:10,13,14) plus repeated promises of God's help and strengthening. J. Begrich thought this kind of oracle was drawn from the context of the temple services when a priest would answer a person's complaint with positive news of God's help, but C. Westermann derived the oracle from prophetic circles, and E. W. Conrad compared the "fear not" in these salvation oracles to God's promises of victory in war oracles.[163] Since 41:11–12 indicate this was a time of war, Conrad's interpretation matches both the structure and setting of this oracle. This salvation oracle imitates God's earlier positive promises of victory in times of war.[164]

---

[162] Discussion of this oracle can be found in P. Harner, "The Salvation Oracle in Second Isaiah," *JBL* 88 (1969): 418–34, or Schoors, *I Am God Your Savior,* 47, who compares the structure of various oracles of salvation.

[163] J. Begrich, "Das priestliche Heilsorakel," *ZAW* 52 (1934): 81–92; Westermann, *Isaiah 40–66,* 68–69.

[164] E. W. Conrad, "The 'Fear not' Oracles in Second Isaiah," *VT* 34 (1984): 129–52, finds two war oracles: 41:8–13 and 41:14–14 having the structure of: (a) address, (b) assurances, (c) basis of assurance, and (d) the results. E. W. Conrad, "Second Isaiah and the Priestly Oracle of Salvation," *ZAW* 93 (1981): 234–46. These two articles compare Isaiah's salvation oracle with similar war oracles in Deut 3:2; Josh 8:1–2; 10:8; 11:6, but all of these are shorter.

Fear not, for God will strengthen you	41:8–13
Israel is God's chosen servant	8–9
Do not fear, I will strengthen you	10
Your enemies will perish	11–13
God will defeat your enemies	41:14–16
Do not fear, I will help	14
Your enemy will be crushed	15–16[165]

This paragraph can be divided into two subparagraphs based on repeated vocabulary within each: (a) 41:8–13 "you are my servant"; "I have chosen you"; "do not fear" and "I will help/strengthen you"; and (b) 41:14,16 the "Holy One of Israel." The first line of 41:8 begins "but you" (wĕ'attâ), and the last line in 41:16 begins with "but you" (wĕ'attâ). Both of these subparagraphs were addressed to Israel to give them assurance and to provide hope in what God will achieve.

41:8–9 This new paragraph turns from the distant nations to address the prophet's audience directly with an oracle of salvation in order to give the people comfort in a time of war.[166] "But you" (wĕ'attâ) contrasts the status and fate of the fearful nations who follow idols in the previous paragraph with the destiny of Israel in this new paragraph. Israel has four identifying qualifiers that define her relationship to God. The people of Israel are: my servants, the people whom I have chosen, the seed of Abraham, and my "friend" (41:8; lit. "my beloved").[167] It is possible that these descriptions move to a climax at the end, showing an ever-closer and stronger relationship between the people and God. Being a servant involves the active decision to do the will of a master, while being chosen is the status of being graciously selected by someone else (no active decision is made by the recipient). If one is chosen, it is implied that the one making the choice values the one chosen. The one chosen may not deserve and does not earn the right to be chosen, for God chooses out of pure love (Deut 7:6–7), not because one party has earned a special privilege. Being chosen to be "my servant" ('abdî) indicates both a close possessive relationship as well as a purposeful desire to employ the servant in the fulfillment of God's plans.

---

[165] O'Connell, *Concentricity and Continuity*, 168–69, uses repeated themes to form a chiastic structure within 41:8–20. This approach does point out the extensive repetition of themes, thus showing the connection between paragraphs, but it seems to suggest that the different forms of speech (genres) are relatively insignificant.

[166] C. Westermann, *Prophetic Oracles of Salvation in the Old Testament* (Louisville: WJK, 1991), 42, appropriately distinguishes this from the proclamation of salvation but relates these oracles to community laments. Although J. Begrich, "Das priestliche Heilsorakel," 81–92, connects these oracles to worship at the temple, Conrad's evidence for a war setting is much more persuasive. Goldingay and Payne, *Isaiah 40–55*, 156, follow the analysis of Conrad though they believe that the foe is more general since the name of a foe is not mentioned.

[167] James 2:23 refers to Abraham as the friend of God.

The titles Israel, Jacob, and seed of Abraham may be honorific titles connecting the audience to the genealogical and spiritual heritage of their great
spiritual forefathers. God chose Abram and the nation to be a special people
who would honor God as their Lord and serve him by maintaining their covenant relationship with him (Exod 19:4–6). The status of being a chosen servant
carries with it not just a sense of duty but also a place of privilege, protection,
and rewards because of God's promises to bless and care for his obedient servants (Deut 27–28). The use of these titles with the present generation unites
God's past call and purposes for their forefathers with his present plans for this
new generation. They are not just common people; they are still "my servants"
and "my beloved" (NIV has "my friend"), the loved people of Israel (Deut 7:6–
10; 10:15). When God refers to his people in this way, he reassures his special
chosen people; they have not been rejected or forgotten (cf. 40:27).

Verse 9 repeats some of the themes in v. 8 to emphasize the sureness of
God's relationship with his people.[168] By recalling early experiences in ancient history in 41:9, God reminds the audience that their forefathers at one
time were living at the far ends of the earth (probably referring to Abram living
in Ur), but this did not limit God's ability to act on his behalf. At that time God
"strengthened you," or "firmly grasped you"[169] (NIV "took"), an act of divine
grace that coincided with the call of Abram (Gen 11:31; Neh 9:7).[170] That
strong "seizing, strengthening" of Abram was designed to make him God's servant (Gen 26:24). God's decision was to choose this one man so that through
him God could raise up a mighty nation that would bring a blessing to all the
nations of the earth (Gen 12:3). Since God made a commitment to be the God
of "his servant" when he chose them, God has no intention of "spurning, rejecting" (*māʾas*, 41:9b) his people now (40:27; 49:14). God's love and committed
relationship with his chosen people is the cornerstone that now serves as the
basis for his dealings with his people during this time of trials and warfare. Assurances of God's love and commitment provide security and peace to all who
hear God's words.

41:10   Three practical aspects of God's salvation are highlighted: (a)
God's servants do not need to fear others, for God is with them (10a); (b) God
will strengthen and help his servants in the midst of these trials (10b); and then
in 41:11–13 (c) God will cause their enemies to be nothing. The placement of
the phrase "do not fear"[171] at the beginning (10a) and end (13b,14a) shows that

---

[168] J. T. Walsh, "Summons to Judgment: A Close Reading of Isaiah xli 1–20," *VT* 43 (1993):
351–71, takes the three things repeated in v. 9 to be in a chiastic relationship with v. 8.

[169] This word comes from חָזַק "he strengthened," the same word that appears in 41:6,7.

[170] "The ends of the earth" would be an inappropriate and odd description of Mesopotamia
if the prophet and his audience were actually living in Babylonian exile at this time as some hypothesize.

[171] אַל תִּירָא "do not fear" is a mild prohibition that uses the jussive verb (GKC §109c). The
parallel term אַל תִּשְׁתָּע "do not be dismayed" is often thought to be a *hithpael* form from שָׁעָה

it was of prime importance in this message. If a powerful enemy was attacking Judah, it is possible that they were dismayed about God's inaction (he was not defeating this enemy), and this may have caused some to wonder if God still loved them and would deliver them. This word of divine hope encouraged the removal of all thoughts of fear from the present situation. The reason why fear is unnecessary is initially found in the two motive clauses that explain that "I am with you" and "I am your God" (41:10). Both contain the personal pronoun "I" (*'ănî*) to emphasize God's personal commitment and presence. This is similar to the promise of God to be present with their forefathers (cf. Gen 15:1; 21:17; Josh 8:1). This is their own God who is still present with them and available to care for them. God will empower his people by "strengthening you, helping you, and upholding you" (41:10b).[172] This is God's firm promise to his fearful people based on his powerful and "victorious"[173] right hand that brings salvation in times of war. Because of God's power and love, people in the past and today can face the trials of life with courage, for God's promise to be with his people has not changed (Matt 28:18–20). All power still rests in his hands.

41:11–13 God's presence and strengthening will result in the defeat of Judah's enemies (41:11–12). The identification of these enemies is very important if one desires to discover the setting of the prophet and his audience, but relatively few commentators labor to discover the impact of these words. J. D. W. Watts believes these words "point to Israel's opponents in all the conflicts of the past," but the imperfect verbs in these verses most likely point to a defeat of Israel's enemies at some point in the future. It also is difficult to suggest that this is God's promise to the exiles about the imminent fall of Babylon,[174] for the prophetic books referring to the exile never refer to the Babylonians or the Persians being enraged with or at war against the Jewish people while they were in exile. A. Schoors admits that it is very difficult to fit this chapter into an exilic setting in Babylon for "it is hard to accept that Israel was at war (*milḥāmâ*) with any nation"[175] during those days. But if the text does not fit a peaceful exilic context in Babylon, then this literary unit must

---

meaning "to gaze about," implying anxiety and fear, but it probably is a *qal* form coming from a similar root (שתע) used as a semantic parallel to the Ugaritic *yr'* "to fear."

[172] These three parallel perfect, first pers. verbs (אמצתיך עזרתיך תמכתיך) should be understood as referring to God's future promises to help his people (GKC §106n refers to prophetic perfects). GKC suggest that these verbs appear in the perfect because "the prophet so transports himself in imagination into the future that he describes the future event as if it had already been seen or heard by him."

[173] NIV translates צדקי "my righteous" right hand, but this context is not about the justice of God's actions but about God's power to deliver and uphold his people in a time when enemies were at war with them; thus, "my victorious" right hand seems more appropriate, as North, *The Second Isaiah*, 97, suggests.

[174] McKenzie, *Second Isaiah*, 30, thinks it includes the fall of their neighbors the Ammonites and Edomites who took advantage of the people in Jerusalem in 587 BC.

[175] Schoors, *I Am God Your Savior*, 56–57, suggests that there was some legal problem and that

be set in a different historical setting where a major conqueror from the east defeated many nations and made war against God's chosen people (41:2–3). The most natural setting is during the Assyrian attack on Judah (701 BC) or the Babylonian attack on Jerusalem in 587 BC.

The introductory "behold" (*hēn* in 41:11, omitted in NIV) draws attention to an important announcement of divine deliverance. The enemy is "strongly enraged" (*ḥārâ* "to grow hot") against the people of God; in fact, they "opposed"[176] God's people so strongly that they "wage war"[177] (41:12b) against them. The name of the enemy is not disclosed, but further hints about the identity of the enemy and the setting are provided in the prophet's description of the destiny of their military opponent. Something will happen to "shame" (*bôš*) and "humiliate" (*kālam*; 41:11) those who make war against God's people. This will be a dramatic event, for the enemy will perish, will become " as nothing" (*kĕ'ayin*), an idea emphasized by announcing it in both 41:11 and 12 (agreeing with 40:15,17). After this dramatic defeat, those who search for them will not find Israel's enemies.[178] Since Nebuchadnezzar was not defeated or humiliated when he attacked Judah, this sounds very much like what happened when the Assyrians attacked Jerusalem during the reign of Hezekiah (22:1–14; 29:1–24; 36–37).[179] Interlinking vocabulary in earlier chapters reflects a time when the hordes of all the nations were attacking Jerusalem and when the Lord appeared in power (29:5–7), who caused the enemies to vanish (29:20), shattered the Assyrian troops (30:31; 31:4–9), and caused them to disappear (33:18–19). Sennacherib was accused of raging against God (37:28–29), but when the angel of the Lord killed 185,000 Assyrian troops in one night, he and the rest of the Assyrian army vanished and in shame returned to Nineveh (37:36–37). If this is the setting for this oracle of salvation, one can understand the source of fear in the hearts of the people of God, as well as the importance of Isaiah's promise of God's presence with them. These words brought hope that God would help his people and strengthen (NIV "uphold") their right hand (41:13, repeating promises from v. 10). Indeed, with God's personal assistance and presence, there was no need to fear. With God's helping hand the seemingly impossible

---

individuals had some personal enemies (in the time of Nabonidus), but "war" (*milḥāmâ*) is never used in this sense.

[176] "Opposed you" translates רִיבֶךָ, but this word tends to be used in legal settings when one party brings a "case, lawsuit" (רִיב) against another. J. Limburg, "The Root רִיב and the Prophetic Lawsuit Speeches," *JBL* 88 (1969): 291–304, indicates that such complaints can be derived from offenses against international treaties. Second Kings 18:7–16 indicates that Hezekiah rebelled against Sennacherib and did not pay his tribute, so this could be the legal dispute that is referred to here.

[177] At the end of v. 12 NIV translates אַנְשֵׁי מִלְחַמְתֶּךָ "men of war against you" as "those who wage war against you."

[178] 1QIsᵃ omits the phrase "you will seek for them and not find them," but this appears to be a case of scribal error.

[179] Vincent, *Studien zur literarischen Eigenart und zur geistigen Heimat von Jesaja, Kap 40–55*, 147–61, connects this to a military crisis that is preexilic.

(the defeat of an enemy) would become possible because "I am the LORD your God," the very one who is speaking (*hāʾōmēr*) these promises.

41:14 In the second subparagraph God repeats some of his earlier promises and then goes on to add new indications that their enemy will be defeated. This admonition offers additional words of hope because the "Holy One of Israel" (41:14,16) will transform his weak people into something powerful enough to crush their enemies. God's people, called Jacob, is initially described as a lowly "worm" (*tôlaʿâ*), an image of powerlessness and insignificance (cf. Ps 22:6). This derogatory picture may represent the Israelites' self-image of themselves as they faced the enormously superior forces surrounding Jerusalem.[180] They cannot be compared to a strong lion that could defeat an enemy army; they are more like a defenseless worm that is about to be crushed. The second title given to the Israelites, "O little Israel" (NIV), is a problematic translation based on the Old Greek rendering of this text.[181] The text could be read to say "men of Israel," but since that is not parallel to "O worm Jacob" some emend *mĕtê* "men of" to *rimmat* "maggot"[182] based on the parallelism of maggot and worm in 14:11 and Job 25:6. This makes good sense, but there is no textual evidence to support this hypothetical emendation.[183] Maybe the best option is to follow 1QIsᵃ and the Greek translation of Aquila who read *mĕtê* from "to die" (*mût*) and pessimistically refer to the hopelessly weak Israelites as the "dead ones of Israel." In spite of the textual difficulty, it is evident that even though God's people have a terrible self-image, they need not fear because God will help them (repeating a promise from v. 10). Yes, the Holy God, Israel's "redeemer" (*gôʾēl* cf. 43:14; 47:4; 48:17; 49:7; 54:4) will come to their aid (41:14). In the military context of war, this redemption is a military deliverance of a family covenant member. The promise is absolutely certain because the Holy God who is exalted and incomparable (40:12–31) will act on their behalf.

41:15–16 The prophet employs metaphorical language to describe the transformation that God will accomplish by turning the weak worm Israel into a crushing threshing sled that symbolically pulverizes great mountains. The threshing sled was a wooden platform with sharp stones or metal embedded on the underside. It was used in the threshing process in order to separate the grain from the stalk.[184] The mountains represent the problem Israel faces. Because

---

[180] W. Brueggemann, *Isaiah 40–66*, Westminster Bible Companion (Louisville: WJK, 1998), 34–35, thinks they perceived themselves as "lowly, ignoble, without hope."

[181] The Old Greek reading is ὀλιγοστός, "few people," implying that after God's judgment only a few people would be left (cf. Deut 4:27; 26:5).

[182] Schoors, *I Am God Your Savior*, 61, prefers this option.

[183] Koole, *Isaiah III, Volume 1, Isaiah 40–48*, 167–68, has a long discussion of various options for interpreting this word, but there is no obvious good solution to this problem.

[184] Goldingay and Payne, *Isaiah 40–55*, 173, suggest that the first word מוֹרַג was used to break up the ground for ploughing . . . The latter was used for flailing harvested corn so as to separate the wheat from the chaff." Later on p. 174 they note that Tiglath-pileser III's account of how he

of the large nation they were at war with (41:11–12) there was a large psychological obstacle (a lack of faith) that led to a defeatist attitude. The harvesting
imagery of threshing, winnowing, and having the wind blow away the chaff is
used elsewhere of God's complete defeat of his enemies (17:13; 21:10; 29:5–
8).[185] These vivid metaphors communicate a powerful message of hope and
victory over formidable problems. It is best to relate these images to the victory
God would bring over both their physical enemies (the warring army) and the
psychological enemy of feeling powerless (the worm image) that destroyed the
confidence of these Israelites.[186]

The main purpose of this salvation oracle is to offer a message of hope to
fearful people by assuring them that God will help and strengthen his people
in the midst of this trial. Their problems will be carried far away just like chaff
being scattered by the wind (41:16a). God's fulfillment of his promises will result in great rejoicing and words of praise and honor to the Holy God of Israel
(41:16b). Fear will turn to salvation and redemption from trouble will result in
thankful praise to the Holy One. Indeed, all praise goes to God Almighty.

GOD WILL TRANSFORM NATURE TO AFFIRM HIS BLESSING (41:17–20)

17"The poor and needy search for water,
    but there is none;
    their tongues are parched with thirst.
But I the LORD will answer them;
    I, the God of Israel, will not forsake them.
18I will make rivers flow on barren heights,
    and springs within the valleys.
I will turn the desert into pools of water,
    and the parched ground into springs.
19I will put in the desert
    the cedar and the acacia, the myrtle and the olive.
I will set pines in the wasteland,
    the fir and the cypress together,
20so that people may see and know,
    may consider and understand,
    that the hand of the LORD has done this,
    that the Holy One of Israel has created it.

"crushed Beth-Amukken as with a threshing sledge" fits the imagery used in this account (Amos
1:3–5).

185 E. W. Conrad, "The Community as King in Second Isaiah," in *Understanding the Word:
Essays in Honor of B. W. Andersen*, eds. J. T. Butler, E. W. Conrad, B. C. Ollenburger (Sheffield:
JSOT, 1985), 99–111, interprets these metaphors in relationship to 40:1–11 where it says that
Israel's warfare has ended. Israel is to prepare a highway for God by bringing mountains low and
heralding the good news of God's coming. The mountains are metaphorical obstacles.

186 Koole, *Isaiah III, Volume 1, Isaiah 40–48*, 165, believes that the victory God was promising
in these verses was "Not over external opposition but over inner powerlessness: fatalism, lack of
faith, disbelief. These are 'mountains' which man cannot climb."

At the end of this section is a proclamation of salvation (41:17–20).[187] It differs from the oracle of salvation in that it lacks the direct address to "you," omits the "fear not" and "strengthening" terminology, and focuses on God's future fulfillment of his promises in the eschatological era.[188] Although some view this passage as a reference to the abundance of water in the deserts when the Israelites returned from exile (a second exodus),[189] there is no discussion of a return of people or walking through the desert in these verses.[190] It is better to fit this passage in with numerous other proclamations of salvation that describe God's marvelous eschatological recreation of nature (11:6–7; 55:13; 65:17–25; Hos 2:18–22; Amos 9:13; Ezek 34:25–27). These future promises should prove to everyone that God would not forsake or ever forget his promises to his people (41:17 and 40:27). Present circumstances may not be the best, and it may seem like God will not establish his glorious newly created kingdom for his chosen people, but it is absolutely certain that it will happen some day. In faith, his people can confidently act now, based on divine assurances about what God will do in the future.

The imagery of this proclamation of salvation was drawn from the culture and experiences of droughts that frequently effected people in the land of Israel. It does not have its linguistic origin in the fertile land of Babylon where there was an abundance of water from the great Tigris and Euphrates rivers. In addition, the information included here does not reflect the species of trees that were common in an exilic Babylonian setting. This proclamation of salvation presents:

---

[187] Westermann, *Isaiah 40–66*, 79, believes the proclamation of salvation was a prophetic response to a communal lament, but it does not seem to be necessary to limit it to such a narrow context (the salvation oracle was thought to be a priestly response to an individual lament). Since this prophet uses many different genres of literature in rather unique ways, one should not limit the contextual origin or use of this literary form of speech to only one traditional approach. In discussing this literary form Whybray, *Isaiah 40–66*, 66, appropriately reminds the interpreters that, "it is necessary to bear in mind the unusual freedom with which Deutero-Isaiah treats traditional forms."

[188] Westermann, *Isaiah 40–66*, 79, and Schoors, *I Am God Your Savior*, 44, appropriately distinguish the structure of the oracle of salvation from the proclamation of salvation. Westermann's suggestion that this proclamation of salvation was given in response to a lament by the people (in 41:17a) is more speculative. There is no clear indication that the people in this paragraph are lamenting, though that could be implied based on the information that they are fearful of the attacking enemy in 41:11–12.

[189] Childs, *Isaiah,* 320, accepts this approach. The premise for this interpretation is unfounded, for the people later walked back from Babylon by following the Euphrates River (not through desert areas), so they had no need for God to supply them water for most of their trip. Blenkinsopp, *Isaiah 40–55*, 202–3, argues against an exilic interpretation and identifies the species of trees as Syria-Palestinian, not Babylonian. Koole, *Isaiah III, Volume 1, Isaiah 40–48*, 175, 177, indicates that: "At the waters of Babylon Israel did not suffer from the same droughts as in the land of their fathers." Later the comment is made that "this lack of water is more properly situated in the earlier Palestinian period than in Babylon."

[190] Whybray, *Isaiah 40–66*, 66, suggests that this oracle should be taken literally about "the homeward march of the exiles through the desert."

The weak and needy have nothing	41:17a
God's salvation will solve this problem	41:17b–19
The transformation of God's people	41:20

In this proclamation of salvation God's promises are rehearsed to "them" (not "you" as in 8–16), showing how God will transform nature by pouring out his blessings of abundant water and fertility to prove that he alone is God. God's promises are expressed in a series of "I will" clauses that should persuasively prove that God would not forsake his people (41:17 is similar to the question in 40:27).

41:17a   The poor and needy are the disenfranchised in every culture, but here they are not defined by nationality or location. One might suggest that this refers to all the people of Israel in the last paragraph who felt like worms (41:14). This oracle refers to Israelites, to all those who had no power, no wealth, cannot care for themselves, and were dependent on God for protection. This prophecy does not provide a theological reason for the lack of rain, but droughts can sometimes indicate the withdrawal of God's blessing of the rain (Jer 14; Hag 1:9–11). Thirst can be understood metaphorically as a lack of anything that is necessary for a healthy life, including spiritual necessities (55:1–2; Ps 42:2; Amos 8:11), but the imagery of the whole oracle is more about the physical transformation of nature. The act of seeking mentioned in 17a is a continuous activity,[191] but there is no explicit sign that this involved intercessory prayer to God, though it might be included.[192]

41:17b–19   The resolution of this problem will be accomplished by God's powerful intervention. He is the God of Israel; he knows their needs; he will care for them; he will answer them; he will not "forsake" (*'āzab* as in 49:15–16) them. God's miraculous provisions will involve his blessing of water (v. 18) and plants (v. 19). God will cause great rivers of water to flow abnormally out of mountains (reminiscent of what happened in the wilderness journey from Egypt in Exod 17:1–7; 21:33; Num 20:1–13). Wells in the middle of valleys will be full of water. God will cause the formerly dry desert areas of Palestine to have pools of water available for people to drink. He will cause dry arid lands suddenly to have springs producing water. This abundant production of water is a vivid sign of God's fulfillment of his great covenant promises (30:25; 44:3–5; Deut 11:14). The geographical characteristics refer to the kind of topography that is present in the land of Israel, not in Babylon or in the Arabian Desert that lies between Babylon and the land of Israel. This transformation of

---

[191] The *piel* participle מְבַקְשִׁים "seeking, searching" functions as a verb that expresses durative action (GKC §116c).

[192] Westermann, *Isaiah 40–66*, 80, and Oswalt, *Isaiah 40–66*, 95, assume that these people were seeking God with prayers, since he answered them. עָנָה means "to respond, react" and does not require an initial request. The Aramaic Targum interprets this spiritually as the faint of heart longing to be instructed.

nature is a complete reversal of what the people of Israel knew. Surely, this is
the miraculous hand of God.

In 41:19 God will cause trees to grow in what were formerly desert areas,
where next to nothing grew in the past (29:17; 32:2,15; 35:1–2,6–7). God
promises, "I will give, put" (ʾettēn implying a free act of grace) trees to refor-
est the desolate land (probably referring to the desert areas of Israel). These
trees are native to Syria-Lebanon-Palestine area, and the common palm tree
of Babylon is never mentioned. This suggests that the writer was not from that
part of the Babylonian world but from Israel. The trees represent the surprising
blessings of God's creative and restorative ability. This transformation is not
described as the reinstitution of the garden of Eden at this point (no fruit trees
are present), but later this idea rather naturally develops into that idea (51:3;
Ezek 28:13; 31:8–9).

41:20 Why will God do this? The conclusion to this oracle provides God's
motivation for accomplishing this miraculous transformation of nature. It will
happen not just to have a pretty park to enjoy or have fresh cool water to drink,
but "so that"[193] people may finally perceive the presence of the hand of God at
work in their midst. It is all too easy to excuse things as quirks of nature, but
when these unusual and unbelievable changes take place (metaphorically), no
one will be able to deny the presence of the hand of God. When these people
observe this, they will finally understand the significance of God's creative
power. This opening of their eyes (as in 29:18; 32:3–4) is a complete reversal
of the blindness of the people's eyes in the period of Isaiah (6:9–10; 42:16,18).
If the hand of God can do these miracles, if the creative power of the Holy Lord
of Israel can produce these transformations in the distant future, is he not to be
trusted by people for their present problems?

THEOLOGICAL IMPLICATIONS. These messages challenge people to
decide whom they will trust while they are in the midst of a hopeless war
against superior military forces. They can look at the power of human armies
and be intimidated and overcome with fear (41:2–3,11–12), but before they do
that they need to remember that God has promised that it will all vanish and
soon be nothing (41:12). The enemy may boast about the strength of their man-
made gods (41:5–7) and all their other man-made instruments of war, but they
will soon realize that these gods actually cannot even stand up without some
human help. When one compares, considers, and wisely evaluates the claims
of the other nations, God's power and promises are far superior. No other supernatural power or human resource can compare to his glory, so certainly it
makes sense to trust in him for today and the future.

He is God and the idols that the nations trust are simply man-made objects
of wood and expensive metal. The God of Israel is one who faithfully keeps his

---

[193] לְמַעַן "so that, in order that" introduces either a purpose or result clause (GKC §165b), and
the verbs in these clauses usually carry the subjunctive meaning of "may" (GKC §107q).

covenant promises to his people, his servants, and his chosen ones (41:8). He even reaches out to renew the strength of the distant nations that are willing to trust him (41:1). He will redeem his people by miraculously delivering them from the vastly superior forces that oppose them. Though Israel was nothing (a "worm" in 41:14) in comparison to their enemy, God promises to help and strengthen his people and defeat their foe. All of God's acts of power, whether they are military or the transformation of nature (41:18–19), are designed to bring glory to God (41:16). His people will finally recognize the hand of God at work in their lives when they see God's power miraculously bring victory out of the jaws of defeat and when God graciously transforms the desolate places into fertile lands that flow with an abundance of water. If God can do these things, is he not worthy of trust and praise even before he actually fulfills all these promises?

(3) The Gods Are Impotent, but God Controls History (41:21–29)

J. Oswalt makes 41:21–42:9 the next literary unit because he finds a parallelism between the two paragraphs that challenge the gods (41:1–7 and 41:21–29) and two matching paragraphs about the servant (41:6–20 and 42:1–9).[194] This division of the material is problematic because there is nothing parallel to the proclamation of salvation (41:17–20) in 42:1–9 and because these two paragraphs do not refer to the same servant.[195] By limiting this paragraph to 41:21–29 it is easy to conceive of the development of this speech around the idea of an imaginary trial that will evaluate the real status of the gods. But in the end this paragraph becomes more of a taunting humiliation of the idols and their worshippers because of the prophet's sarcastic questions and the idols inability to do anything.[196] Court proceedings are imagined in (a) 41:21–23 where the idols are challenged to testify; (b) 41:24 because their testimony is cross-examined and evaluated; (c) 41:25–27 where God's testimony is presented so that it can be compared to what is said about the idols; and (d) 41:28–29 when a final verdict about the idols is reached. The material in this paragraph falls into two sections:

The challenge: What can the gods do?   41:21–24
The challenge: What can God do?   41:25–29

[194] Oswalt, *Isaiah 40–66*, 99, does this even though he acknowledges that the fearful servant in 41:8–16 is very different than the servant of the Lord in 42:1–9.

[195] We argue that the hymn in 42:10–13 marks the end of a literary unit here and elsewhere in 40–55, so ending this unit at 42:9 (or 42:17 by Goldingay) ignores this literary signal consistently used by the author. Another somewhat problematic feature is that the servant in 42:1–13 is very different from the servant in 41:8–16, though hypothetically it could be argued that these are purposeful contrasts.

[196] J. W. Adams, *The Performative Nature and Function of Isaiah 40–55*, LHB/OTS 448 (London: T&T Clark, 2006), 130, recognizes that there "is not a 'real' trial."

The two conclusions, which end each of these subparagraphs (41:24 and 29), are constructed in a similar manner. Both conclusions are introduced by "behold, see" (*hēn*) clauses, and before these two concluding statements are clauses introduced by "even, indeed, in fact" (*'ap*) in 41:23b and 26b(2x).[197] Both God and the idol-gods are challenged to demonstrate their power, if they can "declare, tell" (41:22,23,26[2x] from *nāgad*) what will happen in the future. Both 41:22 and 27 refer to "the first things." This idea of comparing God to the idols continues the theme already introduced in 40:18–20,25–26; 41:5–10. The consistent conclusion throughout these texts is that Israel's God is incomparable in his power, his knowledge, his action, and his ability to reveal what will happen in the future.

Some view this oracle as an argument against Babylonian gods, but there is no mention of any location (Babylon, Assyria, or Ur), the names of any gods (Marduk, Nebo, Nanna, Bel), temples, names of the people honoring these gods, or the unique theological claims of these pagan gods. Interpreters must be careful not to impose on this passage an external limitation. Even though the text refers to the "one from the north" in 41:25, who is not identified by name (he is probably the same person mentioned in 41:2), but the text never explicitly states who this is.

THE CHALLENGE: WHAT CAN THE GODS DO? (41:21–24)

21"Present your case," says the LORD.
"Set forth your arguments," says Jacob's King.
22"Bring in [your idols] to tell us
    what is going to happen.
Tell us what the former things were,
    so that we may consider them
    and know their final outcome.
Or declare to us the things to come,
23tell us what the future holds,
    so we may know that you are gods.
Do something, whether good or bad,
    so that we will be dismayed and filled with fear.
24But you are less than nothing
    and your works are utterly worthless;
    he who chooses you is detestable.

The exact setting for this persuasive speech is unstated, but it is frequently connected to an exilic Babylonian or Persian setting because some commentators think 41:25 refers to the coming of Cyrus at the end of the exilic period (ca.

---

[197] The particle אַף appears very frequently (over 20x) in chaps. 40–48 and relatively infrequently throughout the rest of Isaiah (26:8,9,11; 33:2; 35:2). O'Connell, *Concentricity and Continuity*, 170, tries to group 41:21–29 with the servant poem in 42:1–17 and make them a unified literary piece, but 41:21–29 is presented as a trial to prove who is God, but that is not the point of 42:1–17.

540 BC).[198] But there is no evidence that Cyrus ever called on the name of the Lord; in fact, 45:4 and 5 repeat the claim that Cyrus did not know/acknowledge God, a clear sign that the author of this section did not believe 41:25 was about Cyrus. Since 41:11–12 refers to the time of war and this oracle is thematically connected to the preceding oracle about a coming conqueror (41:2–4a,25), a fitting context for this discussion of these gods could have arisen because of Sennacherib's claims that the Assyrian gods had defeated all the gods of the other nations (36:18–20). Because of these past acts of these gods on behalf of the Assyrians, Sennacherib concluded that Yahweh the God of Israel was untrustworthy and unreliable (36:7,15,18,20) and could not deliver the Israelites. Cyrus never makes any similar claims about his gods to the Israelites, so there was no threat that the Hebrews would adopt the Zoroastrian gods of Persia; therefore, there would be no need for any exilic prophet to refute any claims by Cyrus.[199] This message seems to be countering the theological claim that other gods are superior to the God of Jerusalem. By demonstrating to the people of Jerusalem (41:27) the incomparable greatness of God and the impotence of all other man-made gods, this message should persuade the people in Jerusalem to trust in Yahweh, Israel's God. The paragraph is made up of three parts:

Summons to speak	21
Present the evidence of the gods	22–23
God's evaluation of these gods	24

41:21   Who really is the divine power that controls this world? This debated issue is addressed by creatively setting the evidence for divinity before an imaginary court of ideas[200] so that the counter claims of different divine beings can be logically evaluated. It is very significant that the God of the Israelites is initially called "Jacob's King" (cf. 6:5), for this title immediately sets God in the role of judge and ruler over the history of his people.[201] Divine kingship implies unequaled power and glory, authority over a large empire (the whole

---

[198] Muilenburg, "Isaiah 40–66," 5:462, claims Cyrus came from the east and north.

[199] In fact in Ezra 1:1–4 Cyrus appears to recognize the Hebrews' right to return to Jerusalem and build the temple of the God of Jerusalem, so he was not presenting a theological threat that would have raised these strong words of protest against pagan gods in Isa 40–48. From Persian evidence it appears that the Persians were very tolerant of other religions and did not try to impose their beliefs on others; thus, 41:21–29 do not fit the Persian context of Cyrus. There was no reason to argue against his gods.

[200] Koole, *Isaiah III, Volume 1, Isaiah 40–48*, 189, believes this is a legal proceeding but claims that the use of רִיב "case, arguments" "does not mean a legal suit in a general sense . . . but the tone of v. 22f. is so defiant that it is rather the opposite party which must defend itself, and so רִיב is a protest, objection, contention, or the like." Goldingay, *Message of Isaiah 40–55*, 132, finds a court scene in these verses where God is the plaintiff and not the judge (this differs from Ps 82 where God is the judge).

[201] G. V. Smith, "The Concept of God/the gods as King in the Ancient Near East and the Bible," *TJ* 3 (1982): 18–38, illustrates the common use of the title "king" among the gods of the ancient Near East but demonstrates the unique characteristics of God's kingship.

world), and his ability to control the events that take place in every kingdom (Pss 95:3; 96:10; 97:1; 98:6). God himself exhorts some unidentified challengers (presumably the gods themselves, or their followers, based on v. 23) to come forward and present[202] the strongest argument they have to support their claims of having supernatural power.

41:22–23 The gods and their supporters are again invited to draw near[203] to declare what will happen in the future[204] so that they can prove that they are supernatural divine beings. They are challenged to declare the past as well the future "so that we may consider them."[205] If these gods can do this, then the listeners will know for certain what all the events of the past ("the former things") mean. The trial participants are not interested in just "considering" (*śîm*) or "knowing" (*yādaʿ*) a few extraneous facts; they want the gods to extend their analysis beyond that to declare the causal connection between historical events. J. Oswalt understands this to mean that the "gods are being asked to explain in such a way that these events make sense of the present,"[206] which logically follows from past prediction. C. Westermann believes the gods were being asked to interpret history, not just spit out some past facts.[207] In either case these declarations are supposed to prove whether these idols have divine powers or not (41:23).

It appears that none of these gods said anything when God asked for predictions about the future or an explanation of things in the past. The meaning of these "former/first things" (*hāʾriʾšōnôt*) in 41:22 is much debated. A. Schoors believes that this word refers to earlier historical events related to the exodus in 43:16–21, but there is no indication that it has this specific meaning in 41:22. Based on other passages where the gods are asked to "foretell" (*nāgad*) the future (42:9; 48:5), he concludes that God is not challenging these gods to

---

[202] קָרְבוּ "present" is a *piel* imperative, not a *qal* perfect, so it should be interpreted as an exhortation (GKC §110a). This is evident, based on its parallelism with the second verb, which is clearly written as an imperative form.

[203] Many commentators change this *hiphil* (יַגִּישׁוּ) into a *qal* jussive "let them bring" since in its present form it does not have an object (Baltzer, *Deutero-Isaiah*, 115). Nevertheless, not all *hiphil* verbs are transitive, so a change is not necessary.

[204] Whybray, *Isaiah 40–66*, 68, argues that the verb תִּקְרֶינָה (an imperfect verb) "should not be taken as future but in a general sense: 'what happens', i.e., 'the events of history.'" This general idea is then broken down into past and future events in the next verse. This makes common sense, but the use of the imperfect would argue that the main concern of the argument is about the ability to predict the future. The past comes up for discussion only because what was said in the past (past prophecy about the future) enables one to evaluate whether the past predictions were fulfilled accurately.

[205] This cohortative verb (נָשִׂימָה), which follows an imperative, is used "to express an intention or intended consequence" (GKC §109d). The literal phrase "that we may set it on our hearts" implies "considering" (NIV) an issue for the purpose of accepting it.

[206] Oswalt, *Isaiah 40–66*, 101; W. Brueggemann, "Unity and Dynamic in the Isaiah Tradition," *JSOT* 29 (1984): 89–107, takes the former things to be earlier words of judgment while the later things are positive statements of hope, but this approach does not fit these verses.

[207] Westermann, *Isaiah 40–66*, 85.

tell about the former things, but to state what they foretold about the former things.[208] There seems to be little basis in this text for suggesting that the "former things" refer specifically to Cyrus's initial military successes or his capture of Babylon.[209] There is no indication that this question is requesting information about any one specific past or future event, but in order to satisfy the request the gods would have to speak or demonstrate their knowledge of some distant past event and reveal what will happen in the future.

One might assume a period of embarrassing silence (after 41:23a) in which there was again no answer from the gods. This strange and awkward silence raised serious questions about the ability of these idols to predict the future. So, in a rather mocking challenge, God ridicules these gods in 41:23b: "Do something, whether good or bad" (cf. 44:7 where God does both). Do something out of the ordinary to cause people to fear[210] your power. Scare us, cast a curse, say boo, do something!

41:24 The first part of this imaginary contest between the divine powers ends with an intermediate conclusion about the idols that did not speak. This is a far more devastating condemnation than any verdict of giving false prophecy about the future. The gods are not proven untrustworthy; rather they are shown to be totally impotent and nothing. God introduces his decision with "behold, see" (*hēn*),[211] to mark his conclusion off from the earlier questioning. The interim verdict, based on the evidence so far, is that these gods are nothing; literally, "they are from nothing";[212] in fact, their deeds are "from nothing."[213] The interpretation of these statements could lead one to conclude that the prophet was saying

---

[208] Schoors, *I Am God Your Savior*, 215–16, notes that several times נָגַד means "he foretold" (Eccl 6:12; 10:14; Isa 44:7,8; 45:21; 46:10; 48:3). Koole, *Isaiah III, Volume 1, Isaiah 40–48*, 192, agrees with this approach because it makes sense "if the gods are called upon to repeat now, in this trial, what they had previously foretold."

[209] M. Haran, "The Literary Structure and Chronological Framework of the Prophecies of Is XL–XLVIII," in *Congress Volume*, VTSup 9 (1963): 127–55.

[210] The written text (כְּתִיב) and the spoken oral tradition (קְרֵא) suggest different readings of these two verbs. The written form has "that we may be alarmed" (from שָׁעָה) "and fear" (from יָרֵא NASB, NIV, RSV), while the spoken form of the text has the second verb as "see" (from רָאָה HCSB). 1QIsᵃ agrees with the spoken text. Both make good sense (and GKC §48g suggests the written form may also be from רָאָה) though the written text casts more ridicule toward the gods and is preferable since it fits the terminology of 41:10, the established response to a divine being.

[211] D. J. McCarthy, "The Uses of *wĕhinnēh* in Biblical Hebrew," *Bib* 61 (1980): 30–42, deals with the meaning and functions of this particle.

[212] The use of the preposition מִן "from" is debated. Some prefer a partitive usage (GKC §119w, fn. 2) "a part of all that is nothing" or the comparative מִן (GKC §119y, fn. 3; § 133 a) "less than nothing" which is preferred in NIV.

[213] The word מֵאָפַע is found only here in the Hebrew Bible. Elsewhere in similar contexts (40:17; 41:12) מֵאַיִן is paired with אֶפֶס (so also 1QIsᵃ), so most commentators view this unknown word מֵאָפַע as a scribal misspelling of the more familiar term. Whybray, *Isaiah 40–66*, 69, resolves this problem by suggesting a scribal error, hypothesizing that the prefixed מ is a dittography, since the preceding word ends with מ. L. Boadt, "Intentional Alliteration in Second Isaiah," *CBQ* 45 (1983): 353–63 (esp. p. 360), believes this was written this way in order to develop alliteration in this line, so he suggests the MT is the original reading. The comparative use of the preposition מִן

that the gods simply are nothing, that there was nothing to substantiate the claims of their existence. But the prophet was not a philosopher, and there is little evidence that he was trying to present ontological arguments about the nonexistence of these gods. The earlier claims that the nations were "nothing" (40:17) did not prove that nations did not exist; it merely proved that they were not an important factor to take into consideration in making a decision about whom to trust or fear. So here, God's evaluation is that the gods amount to nothing. They cannot tell the future, explain the past, and are not even able to do anything good or evil.

These evaluative conclusions have implications for the prophet's Hebrew audience. Why would they fear the divine beings the nations worship? Should they believe the Assyrians who claimed that their gods have power over all the nations and gods of the ancient Near East (36:18–20)? If they would follow the line of argumentation in 21–24 they would have to conclude that these gods have no power.

The final line in the verdict could be formulated in different ways because an "abomination" (*tôʿēbâ*) could refer to the people who follow idols or to the idols themselves. Idols are called an "abomination" (44:19; Deut 27:15; 2 Kgs 23:13), pagan cultic customs are abominable (Deut 17:1), and even pagan worshippers can take on the characteristic of being abominable (Deut 22:5). NIV makes "he who chooses you" a subject clause, while "is an abomination" is the predicate; thus because it is an abomination, you are an abomination. If this is the result of idol worship, why would anyone ever choose to follow or fear a powerless, speechless, and detestable idol?

THE CHALLENGE: WHAT ARE GOD'S ACTS? (41:25–29)

> **25"I have stirred up one from the north, and he comes—**
>   **one from the rising sun who calls on my name.**
> **He treads on rulers as if they were mortar,**
>   **as if he were a potter treading the clay.**
> **26Who told of this from the beginning, so we could know,**
>   **or beforehand, so we could say, 'He was right'?**
> **No one told of this,**
>   **no one foretold it,**
>   **no one heard any words from you.**
> **27I was the first to tell Zion, 'Look, here they are!'**
>   **I gave to Jerusalem a messenger of good tidings.**
> **28I look but there is no one—**
>   **no one among them to give counsel,**
>   **no one to give answer when I ask them.**
> **29See, they are all false!**
>   **Their deeds amount to nothing;**
>   **their images are but wind and confusion.**

---

is discussed in GKC §133a-b. Paul in 1 Cor 8:4 may base his statement about the idols being nothing from passages similar to 41:23–23.

The second half of this discussion in 41:25–29 supports the case that God is indeed a divine being who can do the things that the idols cannot do. This challenge is constructed similar to the preceding one:

Present the evidence of God   25–27
Evaluation of the idols   28
Conclusion: the gods are nothing   29

41:25 The second part of this discussion features testimony from God about his abilities. The audience will want to know if he has power over history and if he has the ability to predict the future, so that they can decide if he should be feared. To support his case, God speaks and testifies of his ability to control history by returning to the evidence recorded in 41:2–3. In the past he acted by stirring up a mighty conqueror from the north and from the east. The identity of this person remains hidden (though it appears to refer to the same conqueror mentioned in 41:11–12). The exact name of the king God used to do his will is not even important enough to record it for posterity. If that king was just outside Jerusalem's gates, the name of the king was obvious to all who heard the prophet speak.[214]

Some connect 41:2–3 and 41:25–26 with the coming of Cyrus, but it is hard to believe that Cyrus actually called on the name of Yahweh, since he was a Zoroastrian from Persia and proclaimed his allegiance to the Babylonian god Marduk in the Cyrus Cylinder (*ANET,* 315–16). Additionally, the one explicit prophecy about the Persian king Cyrus in 45:4,5 states that "you do/have not acknowledge[d] [or "known"] me," indicating that 41:25 is not about Cyrus.[215] In order to resolve this dilemma and make Cyrus fit the criteria laid out in 41:25, many commentators emend 45:4,5[216] to remove this problem so that it says God summoned/called this conqueror (rather than this conquering king called on the name of the Lord).[217] This emendation should be rejected, and it should be recognized that 45:4,5 indicates that Isaiah did not view 41:25 as a reference to the Persian king Cyrus.

In order to prove that God controls history, this conqueror needs to refer to a person involved with past events that were already accomplished so that the audience can verify that what was predicted by God actually came true. If this is a prophecy of what God will do in the future through some future conqueror like

---

[214] Watts, *Isaiah 34–66*, 118, as well as Oswalt, *Isaiah 40–66*, 103, view this as Cyrus. *Leviticus Rabbah* 9:6 connects this person to the Messiah. In 41:2–3 I suggested that this refers to the Assyrian King Sennacherib.

[215] See my comments introducing Isaiah 40:12–42:13.

[216] The Old Greek has a passive verb "they will be called by my name" while 1QIs[a] has "I will call on his name" similar to 45:3. McKenzie, *Second Isaiah*, 33–35, changes the text to "I have called him by name" because he assumes that "an overzealous scribe converted Cyrus to a worshipper of Yahweh."

[217] If a text does not say what one thinks it should say, it is inappropriate to change it so that it will say what your theory needs it to say.

Alexander the Great), it proves nothing because the audience does not know if it really will happen this way. In light of the war context of 41:11–12, it seems more likely to suppose that this conqueror refers to the king at war with Jerusalem, the Assyrian king Sennacherib. In earlier prophecies God repeatedly warned the people through the prophet Isaiah that he would bring the Assyrians to conquer Jerusalem (22:1–14; 29–33).[218] He was the one who overcame the rulers of the nations like a potter treading on the clay.

41:26 Returning back to the imagery of the cross-examination of witnesses, the text asks: Who predicted this (41:26 parallels the similar question in 41:4,22b)?[219] To ensure fairness and comparable questioning of all witnesses, it is necessary to ask: Who announced[220] that this would happen before it actually happened? Did the idols do this or did the God of Jerusalem? It would be essential to establish this fact of history "so we could know"[221] for certain who has this kind of divine power. Then people would confess, "he was right."[222] This conclusion would decide this controversy either in the favor of the gods or Yahweh the God of Israel. The question is answered both negatively (26b) and positively (27). The negative response is contained in three emphatic "even, surely, in fact" clauses (*'ap 'êyn*, similar to 41:23b). In light of the next verse that identifies God's positive role, these clauses must refer to the failures of the gods. Surely, none of them announced these things ahead of time. The strong negative emphasis is that none, nobody, not one of these gods knew the words that God was able to pronounce about these events.

---

[218] Some might question if Sennacherib called on God. Although there is no explicit answer given in any text, when Sennacherib's general Rabshakeh gave the king's challenge to the people of Jerusalem, he claimed Yahweh told Sennacherib to come and attack the land of Judah (36:10), suggesting that Sennacherib did call on the name of the Lord. It is unclear whether the king's general was being honest or just playing politics in 36:10, but he claimed that Sennacherib consulted God and that God told him to do what he was doing. Lest one dismiss this claim too quickly, the Egyptian pharaoh Neco made a similar claim of speaking with God at the time Josiah was killed at Megiddo, and the text seems to suggest that this was true (2 Chr 35:20–22). A second setting where Sennacherib was forced to recognize the power of Israel's God was when 185,000 of his troops were killed in one night (37:36). It would not be hard to imagine that the king called out to God to have mercy on him as he quickly left Jerusalem and went home. At least there is no place where the text explicitly says Sennacherib did not know God as is the case with Cyrus.

[219] Labuschagne, *The Incomparability of Yahweh in the Old Testament*, 23, states that the "rhetorical question is one of the most forceful and effective ways employed in speech for driving home some idea or conviction." This is because it invites the listener to answer the question in his mind and enter into the process of the debate. J. K. Kuntz, "The Form, Location, and Function of Rhetorical Questions in Deutero-Isaiah," in *Writing and Reading the Scroll of Isaiah*, ed. C. C. Broyles and C. A. Evans (Leiden: Brill, 1997). 121–41.

[220] With the modifying clause "from the beginning" one can conclude that the verb נַגָּד "he announced, declared" refers to a prediction of a future event, not just an explanation of an event.

[221] The cohortative וְנֵדָעָה "so that we might know" introduces the intended consequences (cf. "so we could know" in 41:22; see GKC §108d).

[222] There is only one word צַדִּיק "righteous, just, true" here. It is common for Hebrew to imply the "to be" verb, but it is unclear what the subject should be. NIV is correct to suggest, "he."

41:27 God did announce these things to his people in Zion (not those in Babylonian exile) beforehand,[223] for he revealed what would happen. God also continually gave[224] good news (40:9; 52:7)[225] to his people in Jerusalem, possibly a reference to Micah's and Isaiah's repeated predictions that God would destroy the Assyrian attackers surrounding Jerusalem (29:17–24; 30:27–33; 31:8–9; 37:22–36). This interpretation is based on several difficult textual decisions. First, it assumes, based on the content of the second line that the whole verse is describing the positive news God revealed to his people, even though a verb of speaking or telling is not included in the first line (NIV adds "to tell" to help make sense of the line). Second, it interprets the enigmatic "behold, behold them" in the second half of line 1 (NIV "Look, here they are!") as authentic and not in need of emendation.[226] The prophet's audience thus has ready access to God's prophetic predictions, but no prediction from the idol-gods.

41:28 Having proven his divine qualities and proven the powerlessness of the gods, God awaited "and repeatedly looked"[227] (NIV, "I look") for some response from the gods to defend themselves, but there was no response from among any of these supernatural beings. God could find no wise "counselors, planners" (*yāʿaṣ*) who can defend the gods by showing that they have the wisdom to plan and predict the future. The second half of the verse is sometimes constructed parallel to the first half of the verse with a negative "no one answers," preceded by a temporal or conditional clause ("when/if I ask them"). Since there is no negative term in the second clause, it cannot be parallel to the first half of the verse (as it is in NIV). The final two verbal clauses are probably result clauses in the subjunctive mood, "so that I might ask them and they

---

[223] "First" רִאשׁוֹן is sometimes made into a noun referring to God as "the First One" (Koole, *Isaiah III, Volume 1, Isaiah 40–48*, 200–201), but the question throughout this section is about the one who can announce things "first" before they happen, so that one can demonstrate divine power (41:4,22–23). The use of מָה הֵנָּה "what will happen" in 41:22 is similar to the הִנֵּה הֵנָּה "behold, these things will happen" in 41:27. Both point to the future; the second is not present as in NIV ("here they are"). D. W. Thomas, "A Note on the Hebrew Text of Isaiah XLI.27," *JTS* 18 (1967): 127–28, suggests that הנם comes from the root מָנָה which means to "appoint, ordain."

[224] The imperfect verb אֶתֵּן "I will give" (NASB) is translated as completed past action in the NIV. NASB has the future "I will give," but a past translation is not impossible ("I continually gave") to match the first half of the verse.

[225] NIV refers to a "messenger of good tidings," but the Hebrew text does not have two words here. Usually translations choose to translate either "good news" or "herald, messenger." N. J. McElney, "The Translation of Isaiah 41,27," *CBQ* (1957): 441–43, suggests reading "messenger."

[226] J. G. Janzen, "Isaiah 41:27: Reading הנה הנומה in 1QIsᵃ and הנה הנם in the Masoretic Text," *JBL* 113 (1994): 597–607, rejects the Qumran reading while A. Gelston, " 'Behold the Speaker': A Note on Isaiah 41:27," *VT* (1993): 405–8, accepts the Qumran reading and derives from the verb נם "to say, speak." Janzen concludes the Qumran reading is not different from the Masoretic (the addition of the ו merely represents the vocalization of the *kamets* under the נ. Janzen's conclusion that the "them" refers to the "flock" that returns to Jerusalem is less convincing, for in 40:9–11 the surprising thing the people were beholding was God himself.

[227] The imperfect verb וָאֵרֶא probably expresses repeated or continuous action (GKC §107e).

might return an answer."[228] This statement was intended to show the fairness of the proceedings. God gave them a chance to speak, but no one responded. It is a condemnation of the gods, for none of them could do what God can and has done.

41:29 This paragraph ends with the final conclusion (parallel to the first conclusion in 41:24, which also began with "see, behold" *hēn*). The verdict is that these idol gods are "false, nothing."[229] These gods are an illusion of power, and their deeds amount to nothing. All this talk about gods in molten images appears to be just "wind" (*rûaḥ*) and "emptiness" (*tōhû*, not "confusion" as in NIV). This means that the theology of the followers of these gods is useless, based on delusional claims, empty talk, no real deeds, and false promises. Therefore, the prophet's audience does not need to fear these gods. There is only one God who controls Israel's future.

THEOLOGICAL IMPLICATIONS. For most Westerners the issue of serving other gods is not a major problem that they confront on a regular basis; although, more and more immigrants are coming to this country bringing with them their native religions and some have idols they erect in their homes or places of worship. These words about the impotence of any man-made gods have a more direct application to these idols and their worshipers.

A bigger problem for most Westerners is the validity of each person's mental construction of God—the image of God that they have created in their minds. Some view him as a loving father, others find a strong sovereign king, while many imagine a cruel judge who wants "to get them." C. Plantinga explains this as a human desire to make God in our image: "Why else does God emerge as a racist, sexist, chauvinist, politically correct, legalist, socialist, capitalist? If we are intellectuals, God is a cosmic Phi Beta Kappa; if we are laborers, God is a union organizer (remember his son was a carpenter); if we are entrepreneurs, God is for free enterprise."[230] It is important to ask, do these mental formulations of theological beliefs match the God of Scripture, or have some people actually reconstructed an image of God that is "from nothing" but their own imagination, much like the ancient idolaters? Every person needs to examine

---

[228] Koole, *Isaiah III, Volume 1, Isaiah 40–48*, 203–4, follows this approach. GKC §165 has a discussion of the final clause. The modal use of the imperfect is discussed in §107m, and it is used to express what might or could happen. Goldingay and Payne, *Isaiah 40–55*, 1:206–207 keep the three negative clauses, although they admit that a "more straightforward reading of the last colon in v. 28 would render it " . . . so that I might ask them."

[229] The Hebrew text has אָוֶן "iniquity, delusion, false" which give an acceptable meaning (RSV; HCSB; NIV), but 1QIs[a] and the Targum have the more expected אַיִן "nothing," which is parallel to אֶפֶס "nothing" in 40:17; 41:24. In some respects the Masoretic reading is more difficult, but if one is only talking about the difference between a י and a ו (two forms that are almost identical in written handwriting) it is just as easy for the penmanship of a scribe to make one mistake as the other.

[230] C. Plantinga, *Not the Way It's Supposed to Be: A Breviary of Sin* (Grand Rapids: Eerdmans, 1995), 109.

their perception of God to make sure that it is not just an illusion that arises from one's own philosophical presuppositions, modern cultural impressions, religious tradition, or personal desires. In this portion of Scripture the prophet reminds the reader about the true identity of God.

How should one conceive of God? Look at what he has said in the past, to observe what he has done in years gone by and to notice what he has promised for the future. Does he have power over history? Did he create the heaven and the earth? Has he foretold what will happen in the future and then accomplished that very thing? The answers to these questions do not tell one everything about God, but they do indicate that he is God, that he speaks and accomplishes the things he says he will do, that he is holy, should be feared, and is trustworthy. He is not an illusion, an imaginary idea, an abomination, a magic Santa, or simply nothing. He has planned the future for this world, so it makes sense to fear him, follow him, and trust in him. He is God.

(4) God's Servant Brings Justice and Is a Light to the Nations (42:1–13)

The preceding messages deal with God's words of comfort and encouragement, which were supposed to cause the people in Jerusalem (a) to look to God for strength and deliverance and (b) to reject the idea that they needed to fear any attacking army or their gods. These nations and their gods are nothing in God's eyes (40:15–23; 41:21–24,28), for God is the one who sovereignly directs the course of history (41:2–4,10–16). The Israelites who heard these words should put their trust in the sovereign power and plan of God in their time of crisis. God will be their help now (40:28–31; 41:10–16), and eventually in the eschatological period God himself will come to Zion in power to care for his people, reward those who trust him, and transform this world (40:9–11; 41:17–20). But how will this holy God transform this world so that he can dwell among his people and rule it in power? The final message in this longer literary unit (40:12–42:13) introduces God's special servant who will help his people, bring justice to the earth, and serve as a light to all the nations of this world. This servant is not explicitly identified by name in this paragraph (later messages will provide greater clarity concerning who he is); consequently, primary attention is drawn to his essential task of establishing justice throughout the earth (42:1–4).

IDENTITY OF THE SERVANT. This paragraph does not focus on the identity of the servant. If one wants to inquire about the identity of the servant in the Book of Isaiah, the first and most fundamental question one should ask is: What did the prophet and the people in his audience understand about the identity of this servant, not what did other later Old Testament authors, New Testament writers, or the Early Church Fathers believe about this servant? Although all these views of the servant should be consistent, the primary meaning of any text is based on the grammatical-historical interpretation of what that text means in its original historical setting and literary context.[231] When attempting to answer this question, one should be aware of various possibilities based on the use of the term "servant" (*'ebed*) elsewhere in the context of the Book of Isaiah and the rest of the Old Testament.[232]

1. The nearest references to God's servant are in 41:8 and 9 where the nation of Israel is identified collectively as an individual who is called God's servant. Based on this contextual evidence the reader might initially try to identify God's people as this servant in 42:1–4 because: (a) in 41:8–10 and 42:1–4; 44:1; and 45:4 this servant and Israel are "chosen" (*bāḥar*) and "upheld" (*tāmak*) by God;[233] (b) in some passages God's servant is specifically identified as the people of Israel, who will receive the outpouring of God's Spirit, suggesting a connection between 42:1 and 44:3; and (c) God's many "servants" (65:9,13–14), who are God's chosen ones (42:1; 65:9), are the Israelites who will live in Zion in the future.[234] Although authors who hold this view have a unique series of reasons for supporting their conclusions, J. Collins concludes that the servant of the Lord is Israel because Cyrus was the "Gentile Messiah" and because chap. 53 is seldom cited in the New Testament in relationship to Jesus.[235] Although few will agree with this conclusion, H. W. Robinson used the popular concept of "corporate personality" to explain that the nation of Israel was individualized as one corporate person, the servant.[236] C. C. Torrey connected the servant songs to words sung on national days of lamentation. An editor later inserted these songs into the Book of Isaiah because the servant was

---

[231] This principle is true of everyday conversations between people today. When a wife says something to her husband, the content of the message that she spoke is based on the meaning of her words, not on the meaning that someone who overheard the conversation thought she might have meant by what she said.

[232] Many sources survey this field. H. H. Rowley, "The Servant of the Lord in Light of Three Decades of Criticism," *The Servant of the Lord* (Oxford: Blackwell, 1965), 7–20, or for a briefer summary read R. E. Clements, "Isaiah 53 and the Restoration of Israel," in *Jesus and the Suffering Servant: Isaiah 53 and Christian Origins,* ed. W. H. Bellinger and W. R. Farmer (Harrisburg: Trinity Press, 1998), 39–54, who looks at the options of the servant as collective Israel, a royal figure, the prophet, and Moses.

[233] Goldingay and Payne, *Isaiah 40–55,* 1:212, conclude that the context of chap. 41 argues that the servant is Jacob-Israel and that the role of the servant is very different from Cyrus.

[234] L. E. Wilshire, "The Servant-City: A New Interpretation of the 'Servant of the LORD' in the Servant Songs of Deutero-Isaiah," *JBL* 94 (1975): 356–67, suggests that the servant is the cultic center of Zion-Jerusalem by drawing on images of Zion-Jerusalem in Lamentations and the lamentations over the fall of Ur. He suggests Zion and the servant have a similar history (both suffered) and role (both were to offer light to others). This suggestion has many weaknesses including the difficulty of imagining that the prophet would actually think of Zion-Jerusalem as innocent of sin and suffering for the sins of others. Of course Zion never brought justice to all the nations of the earth.

[235] J. Collins, *The Scepter and the Star: The Messiahs of the Dead Sea Scrolls and Other Ancient Literature* (New York: Doubleday, 1995), 28.

[236] H. W. Robinson, *Inspiration and Revelation in the Old Testament* (Oxford: Clarendon, 1946), 71.

seen "not as the imaginary representative of Israel, the Messiah, but rather the personified nation itself, a representative of Israel."[237]

Because it is difficult to understand how faithless Israel could bring back faithless Israel, others identified this servant as a smaller group of faithful people within the nation of Israel. R. I. Watts claims that the Book of Isaiah predicts judgment for Israel but "they are not without hope for a purified remnant."[238] Because of her sin Jacob-Israel lost her office of being the servant, and the unknown servant in chaps. 52–53 makes possible a new exodus. His own people rejected this person, so this servant cannot be the nation of Israel. The role of being the servant was given to the faithful remnant, which is presented as one ideal person.[239] Similarly, J. Gray believes that the life of the servant "describes how the mission of true Israel, the saving remnant, will be achieved, by atoning suffering and here is the disclosure of the ultimate implication of the election of Israel."[240]

Although this conclusion is based on evidence from the text of Isaiah, this solution is somewhat problematic because: (a) the royal responsibilities of bringing forth justice (42:1–4) does not fit the negative picture of God's people in several of the passages where Israel is clearly identified as God's servant; (b) the blindness of the servant Israel (42:16–20; 43:8) does not match with the characteristics of the servant in 42:1–9 (he opens eyes of the blind) or the other servant songs; (c) there is no indication that God's future servants in 65:9–14 have the same role as the servant in chap. 42; (d) some servant passages have the servant conducting a ministry to Israel (49:5–6), so it is impossible for the servant to be the whole people of Israel, for then God would be introducing "the servant Israel" to themselves in 42:1–4; and (e) neither the nation of Israel, nor the righteous remnant of Israel, was innocent of sin and they did not suffer for the sins of others (53:1–12) but suffered for their own sins. Consequently, the evidence suggests that this servant was a godly Israelite individual, not the collective personification of the rebellious Israelites of that day or the righteous remnant.

2. Another possibility is to connect the servant with an important individual in the Old Testament (some suggest the prophet Isaiah or Moses, while others propose a royal figure like the Persian king Cyrus or Judah's king Jehoiakim).[241] R. N. Whybray concludes that since the servant is given the

---

[237] C. C. Torrey, *Second Isaiah: A New Interpretation* (New York: Scribner's, 1928), 34–35, 410–23.

[238] R. E. Watts, "Consolation or Confrontation: Isaiah 40–55 and the Delay of the New Exodus," *TynBul* 41 (1990): 31–59.

[239] Ibid., 55.

[240] J. Gray, *The Biblical Doctrine of the Reign of God* (Edinburgh: T&T Clark: 1979), 180.

[241] Rowley, "The Servant of the Lord in Light of Three Decades of Criticism," 7–20, describes and critiques Mowinckel's theory that the servant was the prophet himself, Sellin's idea that he was Jehoiakim, and Sellin's suggestion that he might be Moses. Other past guesses are: (a) a leprous Rabbi, (b) Uzziah, and (c) Meshullam. One can also consult the survey by C. R. North, *The Suf-*

task of bringing Israel back to Yahweh, he must be distinct from Israel. The prophet Deutero-Isaiah is the one who is called to fulfill the role of the servant. Thus he maintains that 53:1–12 refers to the prophet while 52:13–15 refers to Israel.[242] While it is true that the prophet Isaiah was called "my servant" in 20:3, Isaiah never established justice in the earth during his lifetime and he was not an innocent man who died for the sins of others. Since Moses was repeatedly called "my servant" (Josh 1:1,2,7,13,15) and he fits some of the roles of this servant, G. P. Hugenberger makes a strong case for interpreting the servant's kingly and prophetic roles in terms of a second Moses of the future. He finds a lot of second exodus terminology in chaps. 40–55, so it is appealing to connect the prophetic and leadership roles of the servant to a future Second Moses figure. Nevertheless, there is no passage that directly identifies Moses with the servant, and there is no indication that Moses ever died for the sins of the people of Israel.[243]

Those who find an emphasis on Cyrus in 41:2–3,25 and 44:24–45:5 argue that Cyrus[244] was one who established justice for God's people (42:1–4) by sending them home from Babylonian exile. Since the Bible elsewhere refers to the Babylonian king Nebuchadnezzar as "my servant" (Jer 25:9; 27:6), it would be fitting for the author of Isaiah to apply that same term to the Persian king Cyrus who was called "my shepherd" (44:28). S. Paul notes the royal role of the servant and various terms that were used of both the servant and Cyrus ("I have summoned you by name," e.g., 43:1), factors that suggest that Cyrus was the servant.[245] M. Lind also views the servant in terms of kingly characteristics and notes the similarities between the servant and Cyrus. In the end he concludes that these kingly functions are central to understanding the servant, but that Cyrus failed to be this servant.[246] The Cyrus theory is weakened by the fact that there is no direct identification of Cyrus as this servant and because

---

fering Servant in Deutero-Isaiah: An Historical and Critical Study (Oxford: Oxford University Press, 1956) or T. N. D. Mettinger, *A Farewell to the Servant Songs: A Critical Examination of an Exegetical Axiom* (Lund: Gleerup, 1983).

[242] Whybray, *Isaiah 40–66*, 169–83.

[243] G. P. Hugenberger, "The Servant of the Lord in the 'Servant Songs' of Isaiah: A Second Moses Figure," *The Lord's Anointed: Interpretation of Old Testament Messianic Texts,* eds. P. E. Satterthwaite, R. S. Hess, G. J. Wenham (Grand Rapids: Baker, 1995), 105–39. Baltzer, *Deutero-Isaiah,* 125–26, believes Moses is the servant, but his name was not recorded here in these passages because Moses agreed to have his name stricken from God's book in Exod 32:31–32.

[244] Watts, *Isaiah 34–66,* 119, suggests, "Cyrus has been chosen to be God's agent to put that verdict into effect." Blenkinsopp, *Isaiah 40–55,* 210, says, "The language in which the commissioning is described creates a strong prima facie case that the original identification of the servant was Cyrus." Some others who follow this approach are A. Laato, *The Servant of YHWH and Cyrus: A Reinterpretation of the Exilic Messianic Programme in Isaiah 40–55* (Stockholm: Almqvist and Wiksell, 1992) and R. G. Kratz, *Kyros im Deuterojesaja-Buch,* FAT 1 (Tübingen: Mohr, 1991).

[245] S. M. Paul, "Deutero-Isaiah and Cuneiform Royal Inscriptions" *JAOS* 88 (1968): 180–86.

[246] M. Lind, "Monotheism, Power, and Justice: A Study of Isaiah 40–55," *CBQ* 46 (1984): 432–46.

the references to Cyrus are found only in a few verses in chaps. 44–45 and not in chaps. 49–55, the place where most of the servant poems exist. Of course, there is no indication that the pagan ruler Cyrus ever died for the sins of others (53:1–12) or established justice in all nations.

3. Finally, in 37:35 King David was called "my/your servant" (2 Sam 7:5,8,19, 20,25–29; 1 Kgs 8:24,26) and earlier oracles in Isaiah predicted a future great Davidic king (the Messiah) who would be filled with the Spirit (11:2; 42:1), would be a great light (9:2; 42:6), and would establish everlasting justice over the earth (9:7; 42:1–4). If one compares this figure with the servant there is a good amount of continuity or overlap with the role of the servant in 42:1–4. H. G. M. Williamson concludes that, "There is considerable agreement nowadays that, whatever else is to be said about the servant in Isaiah 42:1–4, he is presented to us in royal disguise."[247] Nevertheless, some would find an inherent contradiction when one compares the role of the weak suffering and dying servant with that of a victorious reigning messianic king. Yet in spite of these theological tensions, the ancient Aramaic Targum took this approach and explicitly interpreted the servant idea in Isaiah 42 as a reference to the Messiah.[248]

In conclusion, since there are a variety of different attributes and identifying markers associated with the servant role in this book, one is naturally directed to the thesis that there are multiple "servant" figures in the Book of Isaiah, not just one person or group that fits all the passages where the word "servant" appears. There is no doubt that the nation of Israel is personified as the "blind servant" in 41:8–9, but the "servants" in 65:9–16 are a unique group of righteous Israelites who bear God's name (not the whole nation). The prophet Isaiah was God's servant in 20:3 and David was called God's servant in 37:35, but the servant in the poem in 42:1–13 does not appear to be any of these. As each new servant passage is examined, the reader must compare and contrast the characteristics of this servant with the characterizations of other servant figures within the book in order to make an appropriate identification of the servant in that context. Initially a clear picture may not emerge, but when new servant roles are introduced and more is revealed about the servant in later passages, a clearer understanding of the identity of the servant figure will emerge.

SETTING AND CONTINUITY. There are two ways of dealing with new passages that introduce new topics and that are not explicitly dated (like 42:1–

---

[247] H. G. M. Williamson, *Variations on a Theme: King, Messiah and Servant in the Book of Isaiah* (Carlisle: Paternoster, 1998), 132–34, presents the evidence for this royal interpretation. In spite of this connection, Williamson maintains (p. 140) that the servant in 42:1–4 is actually Israel because he believes that "Deutero-Isaiah consistently (and in 55:3–5 explicitly) presents Israel as a royal figure." He views Israel as taking over the status and function given to the king in earlier history.

[248] F. D. Lindsey, "Isaiah's Songs of the Servant, Part I: The Call of the Servant in Isaiah 42:1–9, *BSac* 139 (1982): 12–31, is guided by the New Testament but consistently fits the material in chap. 42 into a royal figure.

13): (a) If one can find several literary connections between this new paragraph and its surrounding material, one can suggest that the new material fits the general historical, literary, and ideological setting of the surrounding chapters. (b) If one cannot find interlinking vocabulary, historical hints, or similar theological ideas under discussion in a new prophetic message, it is more difficult to hypothesize any solid connections with the surrounding chapters and their setting.[249] Long ago, B. Duhm argued that the "servant songs" did not fit into their present literary context and proposed the idea that they were added into the Isaiah text at a later time by some later redactor.[250] If this is the case, then the surrounding chapters will provide little help in discovering the setting of this oracle and will not be that helpful in interpreting the meaning of this passage.

In contrast to this interpretive procedure, the following interlinking connections suggest that 42:1–13 should be closely tied to its present literary context. This new message continues the theme that: (a) God will bring "justice" (*mišpāṭ* in 42:1,3,4) to his people, who seem to think that they were not being dealt with justly (40:27) and to the nations who need to be treated with justice (41:1). (b) This message contrasts the former and new things (42:9), similar to the past and future events mentioned in 41:22,26. (c) In earlier oracles God's acted in past and future history to prove that he is God and not the idols (40:18–20; 41:21–19), an idea that appears again in 42:8. (d) The nations and islands by the sea that are nothing in 40:15,17, will receive hope and the promise of justice in 42:1,4 so that they, too, can proclaim God's praise (42:10–13). (e) Finally, just as God promised to "uphold" (*tmk*) his fearful oppressed people in 41:10, so he will "uphold" (*tmk*) his servant in 42:1. These common themes suggest that one should not remove this message from the surrounding literary context of chap. 41[251] and should not view it as a later secondary editorial insertion that does not fit in this context.[252] This conclusion argues for a literary interconnectedness, but this does not prove anything about the historical setting of this oracle. It would be natural to suggest that this oracle comes from

---

[249] Westermann, *Isaiah 40–66*, 92, has the perspective that the "songs represent a special strand within the book of Deutero-Isaiah, and therefore they did not come into being at the same time as their context." Nevertheless, he believes they come from Deutero-Isaiah or his disciple.

[250] B. Duhm, *Das Buch Jesaja*, HKAT (Göttingen: Vanderhoeck and Ruprecht, 1892), 311, separates these verses from their literary context, but their content demonstrates many interlinking points of contact with vocabulary and themes in 40:12–42:13.

[251] Spykerboer, *The Structure and Composition of Deutero-Isaiah*, 80–81, suggests that the use of הן as the first word in 42:1 is "a suitable way of introducing an important statement, which however does not stand on its own, but follows from what has been said in the preceding line(s)." He notes that הן functions to introduce a strong contrast in 40:19 and that 41:24 and 29 use this particle to introduce the conclusion that the idol gods are nothing. Thus he concludes that הן does not introduce totally new paragraphs.

[252] C. R. Seitz, "'You are my Servant, You are the Israel in whom I will be Glorified:' The Servant Songs and the Effect of Literary Context in Isaiah," *Calvin Theological Journal* 39 (2004): 117–34, addresses this issue.

the setting of the surrounding chapters, but there is little evidence within the oracle itself that would enable an interpreter to establish a date or setting.

Through this positive message about the servant establishing justice on the earth, God was able to raise the hopes of his audience. By giving them information concerning God's new plans for Israel and the nations, God shows that he controls the destiny of his people and this world, both now and in the future. These plans were designed to strengthen the discouraged (40:27; 41:10,13) and ultimately to bring great glory to God's name (42:10–13).

GENRE.   This is the first of four passages that are typically called "servant songs" (the others are in 49:1–6; 50:4–11; 52:13–53:12). Although there is a brief song of praise to God at the end of this servant oracle (42:10–13), the title "song" is somewhat misleading because 42:1–9 is not a song[253] but a poetic oracle that looks more like an installation, commissioning, or presentation account.[254] God presents his servant in 42:1–4 to his people, accompanied with words of divine approval, empowerment, and predictions of success. Once the servant is introduced God speaks directly to the servant (42:5–9), reassuring him of God's power and commissioning him to a task. This commissioning aspect is not present in some of the following servant poems.

The commissioning of a servant could derive from two different cultural settings in Israel. First, one might think that this servant is just one of a long list of prophetic figures that functions as God's servant.[255] The prophets Ahijah of Shiloh (1 Kgs 15:29), Elijah (2 Kgs 9:36), Jonah (2 Kgs 14:25), Isaiah (Isa 20:3), Moses (Deut 3:24; Josh 1:1–2,7,13,15; 8:31), and many other prophets (2 Kgs 9:7; 17:13,23; 21:10; 24:2) were considered God's servants. They were commissioned by God, empowered by his Spirit, boldly spoke about matters of justice, and sometimes were persecuted or killed (2 Kgs 9:7). Second, the role of bringing forth justice to the nations sounds very much like a kingly role,[256] for kings were also called God's servants. King David was known as

---

[253] Isaiah 42:1–9 does not call people to sing or praise God like many songs, and it does not use a series of imperatives and participles as many songs do.

[254] Baltzer, *Deutero-Isaiah*, 124–25, views this as an installation in the council of the heavens. Melugin, *The Formation of Isaiah 40–55*, 64–69, prefers to use "commissioning" terminology, but there seems to be little difference between these terms. W. A. M. Beuken, "*mišpāṭ*: The First Servant Song and Its Context," *VT* 22 (1972): 1–30, calls this a royal designation oracle similar to 1 Sam 9:17; 16:12–13; Zech 3:8; 6:12.

[255] Whybray, *Isaiah 40–66*, 71, believes this is a second recommissioning of the prophet Deutero-Isaiah in which God reconfirms his confidence in the prophet. He rejects the idea that this is Israel because the servant Israel is always passive, while this servant is active and aggressively establishing God's justice. Baltzer, *Deutero-Isaiah*, 125–26, concludes that the servant was the prophet Moses.

[256] Blenkinsopp, *Isaiah 40–55*, 210, believes that the prophet was talking about the commissioning of King Cyrus to be his servant. Melugin, *Formation of Isaiah 40–55*, 64–65, surveys other theories (liturgical drama of presenting a king, the commissioning of a prophet, or a free composition) about the background for this poem.

the servant of the Lord,[257] Solomon understood he was God's servant (2 Kgs 8:28–30), and the future messianic king was viewed in similar terms (9:1–7; Ps 89:3–4; Ezek 34:23–24; 37:24–25).[258] God chose these kings, empowered them with his Spirit, commissioned them to establish justice, and some suffered persecution from their political enemies.

STRUCTURE. The first section of this paragraph is held together by repeated references to the role of the servant to establish *mišpāṭ* "justice, judgment" in 42:1b,3b, 4b. The second subparagraph is introduced by a messenger formula ("This is what God, the LORD, says"), and it records the marvelous things that God has done and what he will do in the future through his chosen servant. The final section (42:10–13) contains a series of imperatives and jussive verbs that encourage people from all over the world to sing and praise God. Based on these distinct characteristics one can divide this message into three subparagraphs:

God's chosen servant will establish justice on earth   42:1–4
God's servant will be a covenant and light   42:5–9
Sing a hymn of praise to glorify God   42:10–13

GOD'S CHOSEN SERVANT WILL ESTABLISH JUSTICE ON EARTH (42:1–4)

[1]"Here is my servant, whom I uphold,
   my chosen one in whom I delight;
 I will put my Spirit on him
   and he will bring justice to the nations.
[2]He will not shout or cry out,
   or raise his voice in the streets.
[3]A bruised reed he will not break,
   and a smoldering wick he will not snuff out.
 In faithfulness he will bring forth justice;
[4]he will not falter or be discouraged
   till he establishes justice on earth.
 In his law the islands will put their hope."

On the one hand and in a more general sense all the people of Israel were supposed to function as God's faithful servants[259] who were chosen and

---

[257] 2 Sam 3:18; 7:5,8,19,25,27–29; 1 Kgs 3:6; 8:24–26; 11:32,34,36,38; 14:8; 2 Kgs 8:19; 19:34; 20:6; Ps 18:1; 36:1; 78:70; 89:4,21,40; 132:10; 144:10.

[258] Two Aramaic Targums and Matt 12:18–21 interpret this servant as the Messiah. C. L. Blomberg, "Matthew," in *CNTOT*, 42–44, maintains this is an example of double fulfillment, suggesting that Israel was this servant in OT times and that later there was a greater messianic fulfillment. I reject this double fulfillment conclusion because Israel did not fulfill the roles of this servant in 42:1–13.

[259] 2 Kgs 8:23,32; Isa 41:8; 48:20; 65:9,13,14,15; Jer 30:10; 46:27–28; Ezek 28:35; 37:25. Muilenburg, "Isaiah 40–66," 5:464, views Israel as the servant because of this identification in 41:8–9.

empowered to serve him in this world. Nevertheless, Israel as a nation failed to internalize its role or take its responsibility seriously, so it appears that this role is now being granted to another person who would faithfully function as God's true servant. Since the establishment of justice is strongly emphasized in these verses and the servant's function influenced all the nations of the earth, the kingly background of the servant stands out as the most predominant emphasis in 42:1–4.

The structure of this paragraph is:

God prepares the servant to bring justice	42:1
What the servant will not do to bring justice	42:2–3[260]
The servant will not fail to bring justice to all	42:4

42:1 The prophet's audience is unclear until 42:9. The plural pronoun "you" (*'etkem*) implies that the prophet was possibly speaking to the same general Israelite audience that was listening to 40:12–41:29.[261] God presents to them this new individual called only "my servant" (*'abdî*), and he draws their attention (*hēn* "behold, look," NIV has "here")[262] to what he has done to empower this servant to accomplish God's will. Later God will give the servant the mission to restore Israel (49:6)[263] and bring justice to all nations.

Like God's other servants (41:9–10), God will "support, grasp, or uphold" (*'etmāk*)[264] this person to empower him to accomplish God's purpose and protect him in times of trial or discouragement (42:2–4). God's strong hand of support indicates that the servant will not succeed on his own strength but will deeply depend on God's strong hand to undergird his efforts. His status as

---

[260] Seven times in these three verses one learns what will "not" (לֹא) happen.

[261] Melugin, *Formation of Isaiah 40–55*, 100, concludes that this pl. pronoun applies to the prophet's Israelite audience, while Goldingay, *Message of Isaiah 40–55*, 168, hypothesizes that the pl. pronoun "you" does not refer to the Israelites but to "the gods who were being addressed in 41.21–19."

[262] Goldingay and Payne, *Isaiah 40–55*, 1:211, suggest (following Rignell) that the repetition of הֵן "behold, look," in 42:1 connects this message with 41:29, but the two terms have different functions in the two different paragraphs. In 41:29 הֵן "behold, look" introduces a conclusion just like 41:24, but in 42:1 הֵן "behold, look" introduces a new paragraph; thus, הֵן "behold, look" in 42:1 is not structurally connected to 41:24,29.

[263] This presentation would be rather awkward if the servant was Israel and God was presenting Israel to themselves. The Old Greek inserts "Jacob" to identify "my servant" and "Israel" to identify "my chosen." This is only an interpretive addition, that reveals how one group interpreted this passage. It has little value for determining what the original text meant; these were not part of the original Hebrew text.

[264] Paul, "Deutero-Isaiah and Cuneiform Royal Inscriptions," 180–86, notes that this terminology of divine support for this servant is parallel to the support of Mesopotamian gods for the ANE kings of that day. Ps 63:8 connects this verb to God's relationship to the king (note the context of v. 11), and 45:1 has a similar idea (though it uses a different verb) to describe God's relationship to Cyrus. It would naturally be expected that God would support any servant that he chose to do his will.

"my chosen"[265] (*bĕḥîrî*—paralleling another servant in 41:8) eliminates any critique that he promoted himself to a position of importance; his status is due to the plan and purposes of God. A significant factor governing his election by God was a personal relationship of "affection, delight"[266] in the servant. Such strong words of personal approval and divine satisfaction with the servant presuppose a godly character, his willingness to fulfill God's commission, and a close walk with God. This presents a dramatic contrast with God's displeasure or lack of delight with his "blind servant" Israel (42:18–22).

God's empowerment of this servant will be through a special outpouring of the Spirit, an empowerment that was characteristic of divine appointments of prophets (Ezek 2:2; 3:24; Mic 3:8; 2 Chr 15:1; 20:14; 24:20) and kings (1 Sam 10:6,10; 16:13; Isa 11:2; 61:1). The purpose of this divine preparation was to enable this servant to cause justice to go out to the nations (42:1b). This is a primary responsibility that a political leader would carry out, but few Israelite kings lived up to this ideal. David administered justice over his people (2 Sam 8:15), although he did not always act justly toward others (his treatment of Uriah and Bathsheba in 2 Sam 11–12). Solomon asked God for special wisdom so that he could judge the people justly (2 Kgs 3:9), but later he turned away from God (1 Kgs 11). The Messiah's rule is consistently characterized by the administration of justice (9:7; 11:3–4; 32:1; Ps 72:1–5; Jer 23:5; 33:15). God's Spirit will empower this servant to proclaim and cause God's rule to extend to all the earth (lit. "justice to the nations he will cause to go out"; NIV renders "and he will bring justice to the nations"). The universal role of the servant's task indicates that this prophecy is speaking of a future fulfillment, not the temporal authority of an Israelite or foreign king (i.e., Cyrus, Josiah, or Jehoiakim). Universal justice for the nations is characteristic of earlier descriptions of the eschatological establishment of God's kingdom in 2:2–4 or the messianic promises in Ps 2:8–9; Isa 9:1–7. The term "justice" (*mišpāṭ*) appears to be a fairly straightforward concept, but interpreters have connected this term with a multitude of ideas, bridging the semantic field from: (a) the general idea of a custom, manner of behavior; (b) a place of judgment; (c) a case to be presented for judgment, (d) the sentence, decision of a case;[267] (f) ordinance, laws, rules

---

[265] Williamson, *Variations on a Theme: King, Messiah and Servant in the Book of Isaiah*, 133–34, notes that the terminology of "choosing" was not used of prophets (thus eliminating that option) but was commonly used of God's election of kings (1 Sam 10:24; 16:1–13; 2 Sam 6:21; 1 Kgs 8:16; 11:34).

[266] The verb רָצְתָה is third fem. sg. because נַפְשִׁי "my soul" is a fem. noun. The verb refers to the action of "favoring, wanting, delighting, being pleased" with someone. Goldingay and Payne, *Isaiah 40–55*, 1:211–12, prefer the translation "whom I myself accepted" instead of "in whom my soul delights." In both cases the translators rightly supply the relative pronoun "whom" (borrowed from the previous clause) in order to connect this clause to the rest of the sentence.

[267] Goldingay and Payne, *Isaiah 40–55*, 1:213, translate this "He will issue a decision to the nations," which basically agrees with the Aramaic Targum which has "my judgment." Others would connect this term with Torah, the law (2:3–4; Jer 5:4–5)

of behavior; (g) a right, privilege of law; (h) true religion; or (i) religious teaching, the rule of salvation.[268] It appears that the proclamation of just laws and just decisions is in view in vv. 1 and 3 (as in 2:3–4), while the successful establishment of his administration of justice is assured in v. 4.[269] God intends to restore justice when his kingdom is introduced (1:27; 2:2–4; 4:4; 5:16; 11:1–5; 26:9; 28:6; 30:18; 33:5), and this servant will have a key role in accomplishing this goal.

42:2–3 The prophet also indicates what the servant will not do in the process of establishing justice on earth in seven negative phrases. His method of operations will not include various aggressive or violent activities that might be expected of a king who establishes his justice by force (like Nebuchadnezzar or Cyrus). But is this verse saying he will not "cry out"[270] like the miserable crying people of Israel (40:27),[271] that he will not scream and yell about justice like some overly passionate prophets, or that he will not act like an oppressive demanding king? The general idea is that in the midst of the difficulty in establishing justice he will not give up or "cry out" (ṣāʿaq) in frustration and exasperation just because the responsibility is difficult. Instead, he will be guided by patient endurance, humility, and steadfastness in the face of opposition.

It is very unlikely that the servant's care for and refusal to reject the "bruised reed" and "smoldering wick" (42:3) refers to his acceptance of the Egyptians (called a "splintered reed" in 36:6; cf. 19:15) under God's rule as H. C. P. Kim proposes.[272] Instead, these two objects are symbolic of anybody who is broken, abused, worthless, and about to be discarded (cf. 43:17; 61:3). A bruised or crushed reed may not be of much value to some people, but the servant will

---

[268] Williamson, *Variations on a Theme: King, Messiah and Servant in the Book of Isaiah*, 135–37, reviews many of these suggestions and opts for a royal duty of defending the weak and ordering the total "well-being of the community" based on earlier ideals presented in 2:2–4 and 11:1–5.

[269] W. A. M. Beuken, *"mišpāṭ: The First Servant Song and Its Context,"* 1–30, believes this poem fits into the immediate literary context which helps one define what "justice" means. He concludes that in vv. 1 and 3 justice is "more of a situation, a state of being, to be realized than a decision to be proclaimed . . . an event to be realized, a process and its execution resulting in relations of righteousness, the background obviously being this; that the present situation is devoid of justice."

[270] Koole, *Isaiah III, Volume 1, Isaiah 40–48,* 220–22, considers all these options and concludes that צעק usually refers to crying out for help by one in need of help. The usage of this verb in 14:31; 15:4,5,8; 26:17; and 30:19 always refers to a cry for help by people in a difficult situation.

[271] Goldingay and Payne, *Isaiah 40–55,* 1:217, conclude that this person will not cry out in anguish, while Westermann, *Isaiah 40–66,* 96, contrasts his cry to that of a new king who speaks to enact a new law or to make a public proclamation in the process of establishing justice and order in the land. Baltzer, *Deutero-Isaiah,* 128, compares this to a judge who does not shout or raise his voice when giving his final judgment.

[272] H. C. P. Kim, "An Intertextual Reading of 'A Crushed Reed' and 'A Dim Wick' in Isaiah 42.3," *JSOT* 83 (1999): 113–24, concludes that the servant will reach out and include even the hated Egyptians and Babylonians (the "wick" based on 43:17).

not destroy the lowly and weak people that others might reject as useless.[273] This attitude of not destroying oppressed and suffering people reveals the compassionate and true servant perspective of this individual. No one is unworthy of help; no one will be treated harshly or as unimportant and expendable. Instead, by faithfulness (*'emet* "dealing truthfully") to God's principles, the servant will cause God's rule of justice to be proclaimed and prosper. These methods contrast with the usual ways strong kings ruled their nations through the absolute display of military force and unchangeable commands that frequently showed little compassion for the weak and defenseless. Kings often cared more about the accomplishment of a task, like getting a road built, and were minimally concerned about those who suffered in the process of fulfilling the king's wishes. This verse demonstrates that God's tender care for the weak and oppressed (1:17; 40:11) will be exemplified in the servant's behavior.

42:4 The two roots[274] that describe the bruised reed as "bruised" and the smoldering wick as "dim" are applied to the servant in this verse. The servant will not break apart like a splintering reed or die out like a smoldering wick. Although expressed in a negative sense, this statement says something about the servant's determination to succeed and the strength of God's empowerment of the servant through the Spirit. The use of these verbs implies that the servant will suffer in ways that are somewhat similar to the suffering of those he was trying to help in v. 3; thus, in some ways he will identify with them and partake in their struggles. He will not be an aloof king who does not understand or sympathize with the despair of others. The nature of the troubles he will face is developed further in the later servant poems in 49:4,7; 50:6; 53:3–11, but not in these verses. In this verse God is assuring the audience that in spite of all these challenges the servant will maintain his divinely directed course of action until justice prevails. These characteristics and roles naturally exclude identifying the servant with a powerful and a violent king like Cyrus. Of course Cyrus did not establish justice for all the nations of the earth either; that is something that will be realized only when God sets up his own eternal kingdom of peace (2:1–4).

The servant's establishment of God's rule of justice will have an impact not just on the people of Israel but also on all the people on earth. This new reign of his instructions (*tôratô*, NIV "his law") will affect the establishment of justice even in the far islands of the sea (42:4b). These are the insignificant and faraway nations that are compared to fine dust in 40:15 and the people who tremble in fear in 41:5. They deserve only divine condemnation, but once these

---

[273] Baltzer, *Deutero-Isaiah*, 129, thinks that this refers to Moses functioning as a judge (Exod 18:13) who earlier did not ignore the plight of the weak and enslaved Israelites but defended a Hebrew against an Egyptian who was beating a Hebrew slave (Exod 2:11–14).

[274] The use of these same roots, כָּהָה "break" and רָצַץ "extinguish," identifies the circumstances of the weak servant with the people who were weak, thus directly connecting the life and destiny of the servant with the destiny of the audience he will serve.

people hear the divine revelation that the servant proclaims, these people will alter their thinking and their loyalty. Once the servant proclaims to them the laws of God, they will no longer be afraid, but they will wait in hope for their own salvation. J. L. Koole finds a similarity between this giving of the law in this verse and the establishment of the new covenant law in the hearts of God's people in Jer 31:31.[275] C. Seitz compares the nations waiting to hear God's "instructions" in 42:4 to the nations coming to Jerusalem to hear God teach his ways to the nations, a concept already mentioned in 2:1–4.[276] C. Westermann connects this teaching of the law to the announcement in 51:4–5 that God's "law will go out from me, my justice will become a light to the nations . . . my salvation is on the way, and my arm will bring justice to the nations." The act of "waiting, having hope"[277] in 42:4b is a sign of an enduring dependence on God and full acceptance of his theology of justice. In addition, their willingness to listen to what God has to say suggests that they have finally seen the uselessness of their impotent idols and have already rejected that theological worldview. These nations know that real justice will come to them as they join the millions who allowed the principles of God's kingdom to be established in their lives. Although the beginning of God's reign can be seen in the lives of people today when they allow God to rule their lives, God's people (both Jews and Gentiles) are still waiting in faith, looking forward to the hope of joining other believers from all over the world when God's glorious just rule is fully established throughout the whole earth.

GOD'S SERVANT WILL BE A COVENANT AND LIGHT (42:5–9)

⁵This is what God the LORD says—
he who created the heavens and stretched them out,
who spread out the earth and all that comes out of it,
who gives breath to its people,
and life to those who walk on it:
⁶"I, the LORD, have called you in righteousness;
I will take hold of your hand.
I will keep you and will make you
to be a covenant for the people
and a light for the Gentiles,
⁷to open eyes that are blind,
to free captives from prison
and to release from the dungeon those who sit in darkness.

---

[275] Koole, *Isaiah III, Volume 1, Isaiah 40–48*, 224, also sees the idea of giving a law as a royal function.

[276] Seitz, "Isaiah 40–66," 363, and Williamson, *Variations on a Theme: King, Messiah and Servant in the Book of Isaiah*, 137–38, argue that 42:1–4 is building on the ideas introduced in 2:1–4.

[277] The root יחל, "he waited" is a synonym with קוה "he hoped" in 51:5. This hope is based on the confident expectation that what God promised will be fulfilled.

⁸"I am the LORD; that is my name!
I will not give my glory to another
or my praise to idols.
⁹See, the former things have taken place,
and new things I declare;
before they spring into being
I announce them to you."

The second paragraph begins with a second pronouncement by God (42:5a), celebrating God's power in hymnic style (42:5). After the hymnic introduction, God makes two announcements, each beginning with "I am the LORD" (42:6,8)—a phrase that reveals the authority behind these words. The first message (42:6–7) directly addresses the "you" (v. 6), a pronoun that most naturally refers to the servant.[278] The second speech (42:8–9) addresses the audience, explaining how God's prophetic announcement of what will happen to the servant demonstrates his power to determine the future and consequently declares his glory to everyone. The structure of this paragraph is:

God the Creator speaks	42:5
The servant's mission	42:6–7
God's name is glorified	42:8–9

42:5   This new subparagraph begins with a messenger formula announcing that the following words are what Yahweh the Creator God speaks by identifying himself as the "true God Yahweh" (lit. "the God, Yhwh"; NIV "God the LORD"; cf. Ps 85:8 [Hb. 85:9]).[279] These introductory words assure the listener that this information is authoritative and not to be doubted or rejected. A second confirmatory characteristic of v. 5 is the use of traditional hymnic terminology (using participle forms[280]) that is common in Psalms (68:20; 77:15; 85:8; 104:2) and other oracles in the book of Isaiah (43:1,14; 44:2,6,24; 45:11,18). These participles, which describe God the speaker, are used as part of a self-introduction. Their function is to identify who is making the promises in 42:6–9. This enables the audience to decide if they want to believe what is said.

The audience should attribute great authority to what is said because the Creator of this world pronounced these statements (cf. Gen 1–2). The God who makes these promises is the one who "stretched out" (*nāṭâ*) the heavens

---

[278] Many commentators do not automatically assume that the "you" in 42:6 is the servant of 42:1–4 since the word servant is not found in this paragraph; nevertheless, Blenkinsopp, *Isaiah 40–55*, 209, is correct in putting these two paragraphs together because there are interconnections between the two subparagraphs. Others view 42:5–9 as an interpolation added by a later editor.

[279] The word "God" is not the usual אֱלֹהִים but הָאֵל "the God." The article is usually not connected to any name, so when it is prefixed to אֵל it means "the true God" (GKC §126e).

[280] Participles are common to the hymnic material in 40:22–23,26,28–29; Amos 4:13; 5:8–9; 9:5–6; and Ps 104.

and "spread out"[281] the earth (making a connection with 40:22 and Gen 1). Through his power he gave life and breath to all that went out[282] on the earth. It may appear that good agricultural practices will determine what crops grow or that people can control life through the use of birth control methods, but everything on this earth is here because it is God's will to bring it about. This message proclaims that there are no accidents and the world is not out of control. One of the ways God's controls everything that happens on the earth is by giving "breath" (*nĕšāmâ*) and a "spirit" (*rûaḥ*) to all living beings, gifts from God that determine who lives and who dies. All of these attributes demonstrate God's sovereign ability to rule this world with justice and sympathy for all people. Life on earth at this time was very different from what God originally created it to be, for the intrusion of sin brought death and destruction into this world. In order to restore the earth, God will someday send his servant to reintroduce the just rule of God into this sinful world.

42:6–7 The initial noun clause (it has no verb) in vv. 6,8 proclaims in authoritative terms (lit.), "I (am) Yahweh,"[283] giving yet another reason for the prophet's audience to confidently believe what will be said is true. In these verses God speaks directly to the servant, giving words of assurance first and then instructions that outline the servant's task. This person, as every other servant (41:9; 45:3) is assured that God called him, elected and chose him for a special purpose (similar to 42:1). This calling was in accord with God's righteous purposes of establishing justice in the earth. Some might be tempted to interpret these explanations of the servant's duties in 42:6a as unnecessary additions that repeat concepts about the servant from 42:1–4, but instead their repetition emphasizes their importance. Their presence here can be justified because now God is speaking directly to the servant (this was not the case in 42:1–4). In reference to the phrase "in righteousness," J. Oswalt states, "There is nothing incidental or underhanded in this call. It is at the right time, in the right place, and for the right purpose."[284] God "will strengthen"[285] (parallel to "uphold" in 42:1) the hand of this servant for whatever may happen in his life

---

[281] The verbal root רָקַע was also used in 40:19 to refer to the action of a craftsman who "beats out, spreads out" gold into a thin layer to cover the wood of an idol. The noun "firmament, expanse" רָקִיעַ (Gen 1:6) was the object that was formed when God "beat out, spread out" the heavens in Job 37:18; Isa 44:24.

[282] The noun צֶאֱצָאֶיהָ comes from the root יָצָא "he went out" so it refers to all that naturally goes out from something else (people, animals, or plants). It could be translated "descendents" when it refers to people or animals, but it also refers to the reproducing and spread of plants (Job 31:8).

[283] NIV translates אֲנִי יהוה as "I, the LORD," but as a noun clause the "to be" verb is implied (GKC §141), giving "I am the LORD."

[284] Oswalt, *Isaiah 40–66*, 117, but Watts, *Isaiah 34–66*, 11, translates the phrase "I have called you (sg) in salvation" which is the goal of the servant.

[285] The verb וְאַחְזֵק "and I will strengthen, strongly grasp," picks up the theme of God's strengthening from 40:29–30; 41:1,10 (these texts use a different root), for the same root is used in 41:6–7,9,13.

(just like every other servant in 41:10; 45:1) and providentially "keep"[286] this one protected from those who would like to destroy him. These promises suggest that every servant of God should not doubt God's commitment, empowerment, or purpose, though these promises do not preclude any of God's servants from suffering opposition. The life of Moses, Jeremiah, Job, and Daniel are clear examples of godly servants who did suffer greatly in spite of the fact that they were following God's instructions for their lives.

The description of the servant and his task in v. 6b contains some ambiguity so it is not easy to interpret it with precision. One must decide, who will be the audience this servant will influence? Although "people" (*'am*) often refers to the covenant people of God, it probably has a broader use in this verse because: (a) the use of "people" (*'am*) in v. 5 refers to all humanity; (b) the parallelism between "nations" (*gôyim*) and "people" (*'am*) in v. 6 suggests a broader meaning; (c) elsewhere God's rule is extended to all humanity (2:2–4; 19:18–25; 60:1–14); and (d) 42:1–4 expressly mentions that God will bring justice to the nations and distant islands, meaning nations other than just his chosen Hebrew people.

Next, one must decipher how to understand the phrases a "covenant of/for/ with the people"[287] and a "light of/to/for the nations." The second phrase uses images of light that are elsewhere connected to God as the light (Ps 27:1), to God's way as a light to guide one in the right path (42:16; 50:10; 51:4–5; Ps 119:105), or to God's righteous salvation as light (49:6; Ps 37:6; Mic 7:9). In 9:2 God's great work through the Messiah figure is connected to the coming of a great light, and in 60:1–3 the salvation of humanity is related to the appearance of God as a great light.[288] In this text the concept of the servant is connected to that same light and associated with the salvific light that comes from the Divine Light.[289] This light brings blessing, divine guidance, and salvation. The covenant terminology ("covenant of/for/with the people") could be narrowly connected to earlier theological statements about God's covenant

---

[286] The verb וְאֶצָּרְךָ could be interpreted as coming from יָצַר "he formed" or נָצַר "he kept," but if "form" was meant that should have been stated first. It is more logical for God to "keep" the servant as he strengthens him (cf. 49:8). North, *The Second Isaiah*, 110, takes these three first pers. verbs as jussives which express a wish or desire (GKC §109b), but jussives are second and third pers. verbs.

[287] D. R. Hillers, "*berit 'am*: 'Emancipation of the People," *JBL* 97 (1978): 175–82, disagrees with C. Torczyner, "Presidential Address," *JPOS* 16 (1936): 7, which take בְּרִית from בָּרָה "brightness, splendor" to match "light," but most readers would think of "covenant" when they find this word, not some other rare word.

[288] R. Clements, "A Light to the Nations," in Watts and House, *Forming Prophetic Literature*, 23–36, also explores the connection between אוֹר "light" in 42:6 and 9:2. Goldingay, *Message of Isaiah 40–55*, 165, finds a connection between the servant being a light in 42:6 and his behavior of not snuffing out a smoldering wick in 42:3.

[289] Hanson, *Isaiah 40–66*, 46–47, identifies Israel as the light, but in light of the blindness of Israel, it seems impossible to suggest that Israel is the servant who will be a light to the rest of the world.

with Abram, Moses, or David, but in this setting the phrase seems to be reminiscent of the promise that "all peoples on earth will be blessed through you" (Gen 12:3). One might even suggest that this terminology could also be related to the "new covenant" that will be written on the hearts of God's people (Jer 31:31–34) or with God's "everlasting covenant" with my servant David (55:3; 2 Sam 7:12–16; 23:5; Ezek 37:24–26), but these connections are not explicit in this text. The terminology here suggests that this servant is the personification or embodiment of the covenant;[290] thus, he becomes the vehicle through which the peoples of the earth will establish a covenant relationship with God (Mal 3:1). How this will exactly happen is somewhat of a mystery at this point, but later servant poems will explain more and more details about the ways this servant will make this covenant possible. It is important to understand everything the text says, but also to expect further revelation to fill in the blanks as new ideas occur in later texts. The reader must learn to accept a certain level of ambiguity in initial passages about this servant until more information is revealed.

The specific purposes of the servant (42:7) go far beyond anything that the sinful people of Israel or the pagan nations could do for themselves. Israel is repeatedly seen as sinful and blind (6:10; 29:18; 42:18; 43:8), and the idol worshippers among the nations need to have their eyes opened so that they will reject idolatry (44:18). In earlier messages Isaiah announced that God (35:5) or a righteous king (the Messiah) would accomplish the task of removing the blindness from the eyes of people so that they can see (35:3). Then they will see the light in all of its many meanings. It is not insignificant that the servant functions in this same role (suggesting a common identification), and it is not insignificant that this is a role that could not possibly be fulfilled by many of the candidates that commentators have identified as this servant (i.e., Moses, Isaiah, Cyrus, or the whole nation of Israel). One should not be quick to identify this servant who "frees captives from prison" with King Cyrus simply because he released the Israelites from the suffering of exile (42:22; 49:9),[291] for there is no indication that the Israelites were ever in prison during the Babylonian exile. Those who identify Cyrus here take a very literal interpretation of these words about "freeing captives,"[292] but Jeremiah's letter to the exiles

---

[290] Goldingay and Payne, *Isaiah 40–55*, 1:227, indicate that, "The person not only mediates but embodies the thing. Being a covenant with people implies embodying and expressing Yhwh's commitment to people." Westermann, *Isaiah 40–66*, 100, concludes that "the words, 'I make you as,' mean that the person addressed is destined to become a tool or means whereby God effects something on others."

[291] Watts, *Isaiah 34–66*, 119. Those who believe that Israel is the servant (Whybray, *Isaiah 40–66*) interpret this spiritually as releasing people from darkness or as the political liberation of people who are oppressed.

[292] Muilenburg, "Isaiah 40–66," 5:469, says "the release of the captives from prison is not to be taken as referring to liberation from exile but rather in a spiritual sense, a liberation of all the peoples from bondage."

(29:1–20), Ezekiel, Daniel, and Ezra do not portray the people in exile living in dungeons.[293] In addition, these promises of freedom and the opening of eyes do not apply just to Israel; they apply to all the nations and most of them were not in Babylonian exile. Therefore, the best approach is to interpret these phrases as metaphors of God's deliverance of people from the prison of spiritual darkness (blindness) and ignorance (9:2; 42:19–20; 43:8; 44:18–19) through the work of the servant. Another means of enlightening the nations will be through the teaching of God's word (42:4; 2:1–4).

42:8–9 The introduction to these verses is parallel to 42:6 ("I am the LORD"), but the words in these verses address the prophet's listening audience, not the servant as in 42:6–7. Now the author focuses attention on God's distinctive name, character, and the key principles that will guide his plans for the future. Possibly some people in Jerusalem were still confused about who God was and what God was doing. Now God provides another reminder that he, the covenant God named Yahweh, is the real power that controls the world and his covenant people (another answer to the question in 41:2). He assures them that they can be confident that everything the servant does will be accomplished through the direction and power of Yahweh; this is the name of Israel's God and the God who rules the world.

God's ultimate purpose in revealing himself and his name is to assure that his actions will bring glory (*kābôd*) to his name (41:16; 48:11) and not let people give credit to other supernatural beings who have not predicted the future or done anything that demonstrates their power. Baal prophets might make false claims about Baal's power or people like Rabshakeh might claim that the gods of his foreign army have given them victory in war (36:18–20), but the prophet has repeatedly announced that these gods are really nothing in comparison to God (40:15–26; 41:24). They cannot do anything good or bad (41:23); they cannot predict the future or show how the present is based on past predictions (41:22). God does all of these things; therefore, his name should be glorified for he truly is God Almighty. When the servant comes and enlightens the eyes of the blind people of the earth, then Israel and all the nations of the earth will finally understand who God is and honor him as they should.

42:9 One of the proofs that Yahweh is the only true God is his ability to predict the former things that have already happened, just as he said he would. This idea interlinks with the themes already expressed in the dispute in 41:21–29. Unfortunately, there is no hint in this text that would help identify exactly what these earlier events ("the former things") in Israelite or world history were. Consequently, this has led to speculation concerning what the prophet had in mind. This statement indicates that one of God's earlier prophecies has

---

[293] Of course if this message arose in the time of the Assyrian conquest by Sennacherib, he did claim to take 200,150 people as prisoners (*ANET,* 288).

already been fulfilled,[294] but that specific event is never identified. J. D. W. Watts suggests the "earlier things" refer to "the coming and victory of the Assyrians, the fall of Merodach-baladan's Babylon" which Isaiah predicted long ago, while R. N. Whybray attributes the former things "primarily to the events of Cyrus's career which preceded the composition of this passage."[295] Based on the setting assigned to these chapters in the introduction to 40:12–42:13, Watt's view seems more likely, but the main theological point of this claim can be understood without identifying any specific event.

The new events surrounding the coming of the servant of God are presented as another new way for God to demonstrate his divinity, for God states "I" (implying no one else) "am declaring"[296] to the people on the earth what will spring forth in the future. The idea of "springing up" (*ṣmḥ*) is used of plants growing (55:10), of people springing up like grass (44:4), the sudden appearance of righteousness/salvation in God's people (45:8; 58:8), and the surprising springing up of the praise from the nations (61:11). In each case the idea is associated with the sudden introduction of something new (43:19) that is connected to God's eschatological work of transforming humanity and nature. The use of "spring forth" in association with this servant's role suggests that his work is connected with these future events.[297] It may not be accidental that the noun form derived from this root (*ṣmḥ*) refers to the "Branch" of the Lord (4:2; Jer 23:5; 33:15; Zech 3:8), a messianic term for the Davidic Messiah. The "new things" refer to what God will do through his servant, but the ultimate purpose in sending this servant is not just to open people's eyes and free them from the darkness of their ignorance. The ultimate purpose is for these enlightened people to glorify God, for now they know for certain that he alone has the power to accomplish what he has foretold. These factors demonstrate to every reader that all praise and honor should be lifted up to honor this glorious God. He can open the eyes of the

---

[294] D. R. Jones, "The Tradition of the Oracles of Isaiah of Jerusalem," *ZAW* 67 (1955): 226–46, believes the former things refer to earlier prophecies in Isaiah's oracles that have already been fulfilled. C. R. North, "The 'Former Things' and 'New Things' in Deutero-Isaiah," *Studies in Old Testament Prophecy Presented to Prof. T. H. Robinson*, ed. H. H. Rowley (Edinburgh: T&T Clark, 1957), 111–26, understood that some earlier events might refer to Exodus events (43:16–19), but his primary conclusion is that the "former things" refer to the early conquests of Cyrus up to the fall of Sardis in 547 BC. The "new things" would relate to later conquests by Cyrus.

[295] Watts, *Isaiah 34–66*, 120; Whybray, *Isaiah 40–66*, 76, thinks "the former facts" הָרִאשֹׁנוֹת include the overthrow of Babylon and the release of the captives, meaning the Israelites in Babylonian captivity. Spykerboer, *Structure and Composition of Deutero-Isaiah*, 87, believes that "the rise of Cyrus belongs par excellence to the former things which have been declared and the return and restoration belong to the things to come."

[296] The participle מַגִּיד "causing to declare, announce" functions in the place of the verb in this sentence and probably should be given a present progressive or durative translation (GKC §116c,m-n).

[297] Young, *Isaiah*, III, 124, and J. A. Motyer, *The Prophecy of Isaiah* (Leicester: IVP, 1993), 322. The word צֶמַח יהוה "Branch of the Lord" in 4:2; Jer 23:5; Zech 3:8 refers to the Messiah.

blind to experience the reality of his power by transforming the hearts and minds of all people through the revelation and accomplishment of his words and through the work of his servant.

SING A HYMN OF PRAISE TO GLORIFY GOD (42:10–13)

> [10]Sing to the LORD a new song,
>> his praise from the ends of the earth,
> you who go down to the sea, and all that is in it,
>> you islands, and all who live in them.
> [11]Let the desert and its towns raise their voices;
>> let the settlements where Kedar lives rejoice.
> Let the people of Sela sing for joy;
>> let them shout from the mountaintops.
> [12]Let them give glory to the LORD
>> and proclaim his praise in the islands.
> [13]The LORD will march out like a mighty man,
>> like a warrior he will stir up his zeal;
> with a shout he will raise the battle cry
>> and will triumph over his enemies.

The end of this paragraph and the longer literary unit (40:12–42:13) is marked by this final hymn of praise,[298] a technique that is used to close other literary units elsewhere in the Book of Isaiah (12:1–6; 44:23; 49:13; 55:12–13). These calls to praise God have numerous parallels in the Psalms, but the prophet is not quoting verbatim from any known Psalm.[299] In this brief sub-paragraph the prophet is trying to persuade his audience to put behind them the pessimism of their present situation and all its problems (40:27; 41:11–12) and to be inspired by what God will do in the future. In the future God's covenant nation and people from the ends of the earth and the islands of the seas will sing God's glory when God sets up his kingdom.[300]

Some conclude that this paragraph should include 42:10–17,[301] but the connection between the hymn in vv. 10–13 and proclamation of salvation in

---

[298] These verses are not found in some Qumran scrolls (1QIs[b], 4QIs[b]) but are found in 1QIs[a] and other scrolls.

[299] One can find similarities with phrases in Pss 33:3; 96:1; 144:9; 149:1; Isa 24:14–16a.

[300] Muilenburg, "Isaiah 40–66," 5:470, calls this an "eschatological hymn," and the universal acceptance of God by the nations suggests that it is primarily talking about what will happen in the future. This orientation to the future does not exclude the prophet's audience from beginning to praise God now, for people today frequently praise God for what he will do in the future (especially at pessimistic events like funerals).

[301] McKenzie, *Second Isaiah*, 42–44, or P. E. Dion, "The Structure of Isaiah 42:10–17 as Approached Through Versification and Distribution of Poetic Devices," *JSOT* 49 (1991): 113–24, but even these authors conclude that 10–13 is a separate paragraph and v. 14 starts a new stanza. Dion finds a chiastic structure with v. 10 at the beginning being connected to v. 17 as an envelope at the end (but this *inclusio* is not convincing). He believes vv. 24–26 explain what the Warrior God of v. 13 will do. K. P. Darr, "Like Warrior, Like Women: Destruction and Deliverance in Isaiah

vv. 14–17 does not appear to be the main context for this hymn.[302] In 42:10–13 God is referred to in third person, and he is a warrior who is praised for his victories over his enemies, while in 14–17 God himself speaks with first person pronouns and omits any reference to himself as a Divine Warrior (though he does judge people in 42:15). Isaiah 43:10–12 are drawn together by the repeated use of imperative and jussive calls for people to praise God and repeated references to the "inhabitants" of places far away. And 42:13 stands by itself as a prediction of what God the Warrior will do in the future; therefore, it functions as the reason for praising God, a common factor in many hymns of praise (Ps 100:3,5 which give the reason for praising God). The structure is:

Call for people to sing God's praise	42:10–11
Reason for praising God	42:13

42:10–12   The text begins with an exhortation for[303] people throughout the world to sing praise to God. This will be a new song of joy, but the content of the new song is not much different from earlier hymns of praise. It is more likely that the people singing will be new, that the attitude of the singers will be new, and that the topic of praise refers to God's new works. The "new songs" in Ps 33:3 or 40:3 or in these verses do not seem to contain that many brand "new" ideas. This new singing of praise to God is a special celebration of God's new work in the lives of these singers. Once God acts to bring justice to all the earth through the work of his servant, there will be a new reason for these new believers to rejoice and sing God's praise.

Those who are encouraged to "sing" (*šîrû*) include people from the ends of the earth, implying the involvement of people from every place and the participation of all people. In order to emphasize the universality of this praise, the prophet calls on the sailors who go down to the sea in boats, those who live on distant islands (41:1,5; 42:4), nomadic desert dwellers, and people in isolated oasis villages in the desert to praise God. By picking out specific

---

42:10–17," *CBQ* 49 (1987): 560–71, reviews various ways people have outlined this material. She connects the woman giving birth (she is in anguish, fearful, crying, panic stricken) with God the Warrior by suggesting that they both give similar auditory shrieking sounds.

[302] Oswalt, *Isaiah 40–66*, 122, states that, "The hymn that begins 42:10 signals the end of the first section (41:1–42:9) . . . and the beginning of the second (42:14–44:2)." He connects 10–17 as a unit because: {a} psalms like 10–17 have a similar structure, (b) 14–17 continue the auditory images in 10–13, and (c) both 13 and 16 emphasize the sovereignty of God. Goldingay and Payne, *Isaiah 40–55*, 1:232–36, note that 10–13 end the section but maintain that 14–17 contain the cry that v. 13 refers to; therefore, they should be connected to the hymn. Spykerboer, *Structure and Composition of Deutero-Isaiah*, 92–93, makes a major literary break at 42:10, putting 42:10–44:5 together as a unit; nevertheless, he takes this hymn as a response to the new acts of God in 42:1–9 and does recognize that the hymn is a distinctive literary genre from the proclamation of salvation found in 42:14–17. None of these arguments for separating 10–13 from 1–9 are particularly strong.

[303] The imperative verb שִׁירוּ "sing" and the other imperatives in this section probably carry the sense of an admonition, an exhortation that expresses the desire of the speaker (GKC §110a).

groups, the prophet is not limiting God's praise to only these people identified; instead, these groups represent all people from all walks of life from all over the world.

Two specific unlikely places are identified (Kedar and Sela in 42:11), possibly to illustrate that this astonishing transformation will overtake even the Arab desert tribes (cf. 21:13–17) and the Edomites at Sela (those who dwell among the rocks) who hated the Hebrews at one time (Amos 1:11–12; Ezek 35–36; Obad 1:10–14). This was astonishing news, for few would have expected these foreign nations to praise the God of Israel. Surely a tremendous transformation would have to take place before these distant peoples would loudly proclaim God's praise. The songs of all these people will be filled with great joy (42:11). They will loudly sing from the mountaintops, implying that the singers will not be ashamed of what they are singing, but will want to let everyone around them know about God's greatness. The excited enthusiasm will overflow with rejoicing because these people now recognize who really is God (it has nothing to do with praising God for returning the exiles to their land). The purpose of this singing will be to proclaim God's praise (42:12) and establish his glory before all people, even those living in the far-off islands. This confirms the promise in 40:5 that in the eschatological[304] future, the glory of God will be revealed and that all humanity will see it; therefore, it is not surprising to read that all these people will glorify God for what he will do.

42:13   The final verse does not include any imperatives or jussives that call people to rejoice and praise God; thus the call to praise part of the psalm has ended. Verse 13 is comparable to the typical "reason for praise" that is found in many imperatival hymns of praise (Pss 96:4–6; 117:2; 135:4–18; 149:4). The imagery of God marching out "like a mighty man" or "like a warrior" (*kaggibbôr*) with a loud "battle cry" to defeat his enemies is thoroughly militaristic. This is consistent with God's role as a strong divine warrior in Exod 15:3–10,[305] and it fits the context of defeating the enemies of his people who are at war with them (41:11–16). Isaiah repeatedly pictures God as fighting for his causes (28:21; 29:2–3; 30:27–33; 31:4; 34:2–6) often in a theophanic appearance of his glory. The use of such imagery would be especially appropriate and comforting for Israelites who were presently in a military conflict. Using this same root (*gibbôr*), God is called the "Mighty God" in 10:21 or the "LORD mighty in battle" in Ps 24:8. His fighting will be fierce because he will "stir up, arouse" (from the root *ʿûr*, just like he "arouses/awakens" others to action—41:2,25; 50:4) within himself a zeal to win the victory over all his enemies. This zeal is like a fire (Deut 4:24) that ignites his fury so that he will be victorious over all his enemies. This zeal is outwardly compared to the

---

[304] Goldingay and Payne, *Isaiah 40–55*, 1:236, also view this as an eschatological hymn of praise.

[305] These images are also included in Judg 5:4–5 and Ps 18:7–15.

ferocious battle cry of troops as they madly charge into the swords of their enemy for hand-to-hand combat. Nothing will stop God's attack and nothing can prevent his victory. Such words of power and victory should arouse faith in those who hear these words.

THEOLOGICAL IMPLICATIONS. The Servant of the Lord sets an example and an ideal for every believer who desires to truly serve God. All of God's servants are his special chosen vessels who are filled with his Spirit so that he can use them to accomplish his will on earth. All are upheld by his power and kept through his providence (42:6). All should be concerned to not break or discourage the weak. All should be about the business of establishing God's righteous rule on earth, and none should falter or give up when opposition arises (42:3). Although every servant should be a light to others and should attempt to release people from the bondage of darkness that imprisons them, no one else can or has fulfilled this exact role like the special Servant described in 42:1–9. He is the only one who will successfully establish justice in the whole earth, and he alone will be a covenant to the nations. This Servant is not just a godly Hebrew or a super Christian; this Servant has royal responsibilities in some ways comparable to the Messiah and he will be very instrumental in bringing in the eschatological kingdom of God. All believers, and eventually people from all over the world, will rejoice in God's plan and sing God's praise for the transformation of this world through the ministry of his chosen Servant who is a light to all peoples.

Although the identity of this Servant in 42:1–13 is somewhat ambiguous, later writings such as the Aramaic Targum interpreted the Servant as the Messiah, and the New Testament saw Jesus as the fulfillment of this servant prophecy. He showed a servant spirit when he healed the sick, the bruised reeds of that day (Matt 12:15–21).[306] At his baptism he was the one God said that he was well pleased with (Matt 3:17; Mark 1:11; Luke 3:22), and at the transfiguration he was called the chosen one (Luke 9:35). His self-identified purpose was to serve others (Matt 20:28; Phil 2:7), and the new covenant was established through his blood (Luke 22:20). Jesus identified himself with the role of the one who would release those in prison and open the eyes of the blind (Luke 4:16–21), ideas that are found in Isa 42:7 and 61:1–2. Since Jesus was this Servant, he began the fulfillment of this prophecy during his life, but the complete fulfillment of Isaiah's prophecy awaits a future day when God will transform the hearts of all people on earth and cause everyone to give glory to God's name. In the meantime, all God's servants today need to follow the servant life exemplified in chap. 42. They should shout the good news of God from the mountaintops so that all people may understand who God is, what

---

[306] J. H. Neyrey, "The Thematic Use of Isaiah 42:1–4 in Matthew 12," *Bib* 63 (1982): 457–73. D. W. Pao and E. J. Schnabel, "Luke," in *CNTOT*, 280–81, discuss the distinctive Messianic interpretation of Isa 42:1–4 in Luke 3:22.

he has already done, and what he promises to do in the future. His mission to transform the world, so that all people will glorify God, should be the mission of all of God's servants.

3. God Will Deliver and Forgive the Sins of His Blind Servants (42:14– 44:23)

The next series of messages are loosely held together by a variety of common theological themes and the repetition of vocabulary. Israel is pictured as a blind servant that refused to serve God in 42:18–25; then in 43:8–15 God's blind servant is called to be a witness to God's work. Israel's disobedience is recounted as unwillingness to follow God's law in 42:21–24 and not honoring God with their sacrifices in 43:22–24. The prophet argues that idols are useless in 42:17; 43:8–13; and 44:6:20. The good news is that God has chosen Israel to be his people so they need not fear (43:1–7; 44:1–5); instead, they can be assured that God will forgive all their sins (43:25–26; 44:21–22).

SETTING.   This new series of messages are not dated to the reign of any king, so the historical and religious setting must be deduced from various hints within these oracles. Some of these small hints can be interpreted in alternative ways to fit different assumptions about the setting. For example, it is often not clear if one should interpret: (a) an idea literally or metaphorically; (b) a reference to Babylon as referring to the time of Nabopolassar, Nabonidus, Nebuchadnezzar, Merodach-baladan, or the reign of some other Babylonian king; (c) the time frame of a perfect verb could refer to a past event or be prophetic of the future; and (d) should one connect future events to the near future or to an eschatological period in the distant future. It seems appropriate to review two possible settings for these messages.

1. An Exilic Setting: Some commentators conclude that the Israelites being addressed were living in the Babylonian exile long after the time of the prophet Isaiah (around 540 BC). This thesis is based on the view that the long period when God seemed to be silent (42:14) was the Babylonian exile, but soon God will lay waste the mountains (42:15), that is, the Babylonian enemies of God's people.[307] This approach has the Babylonians plundering the people of Israel, leaving them in pits and the prison of exile because they did not listen to God (42:22,24). But there is still hope because God will redeem his people from exile by giving their enemies to other nations as a ransom (43:2–3).[308] This approach takes the defeat of Babylon (43:14) to refer to Cyrus's defeat of Nabonidus. J. D. W. Watts explains God's role

---

[307] Koole, *Isaiah III, Volume 1, Isaiah 40–48*, 254–56, assumes that the destruction applies to the defeat of Babylon, though the text never explains exactly what country will be devastated in 42:15.

[308] North, *Second Isaiah*, 120, took a more literal view and concluded that this refers to God giving these African territories to Cyrus in exchange for letting the Israelites return to their land.

as a warrior by pointing to God's support of Cyrus who defeated Babylon in 539 BC (42:13).[309] The condemnation of the people for not giving God proper worship in 43:23–24 is then related to the sins of the Israelite nation many years earlier before they went into exile. The announcement about God bringing disgrace to the temple and its officials is viewed as a past event (the fall of Jerusalem in 587 BC) on the basis of a textual emendation of a verb (43:28).[310] Finally, K. Baltzer interprets the prophet's mocking of the manufacturing of an idol in 44:9–20 as a dispute against Babylonian claims about their gods because "we must assume that, in the exilic situation especially, conflicts inevitably arose for the Jewish community through the side-by-side existence in professional life of different religions."[311] But is this assumption valid and is there enough evidence in the text to point to this interpretation of these historical events?

There are several problems with these conclusions that should be examined closely in order to determine if these interpretations of the evidence should be accepted. First, one should notice that only one passage mentions the future fall of Babylon (43:14) and none mention Cyrus by name, so the conclusion that this refers to Cyrus's defeat of Babylon is an interpretation that is very open to debate. Several questions need to be asked in order to decide what period in Babylonian history the prophet was referencing in 43:14. Was the exile the only time when God was silent for a time (42:14), or did this happen several times? Did Cyrus decimate the Babylonian kingdom of Nabonidus and create a group of Babylonian fugitives (42:15), or was this a fairly friendly conquest? Was the prophet referring to the conquest of Babylon in 704, 689, or 539 BC (43:14)? Was the making of idols out of trees (44:9–20) a common problem the Israelites had while they were living in Babylonian exile?

These issues become especially important when one realizes that some of these texts do not actually fit an exilic setting. For example, (a) C. Westermann, who generally accepts the exilic setting of these messages, had to conclude that the description of plundered people hiding in caves and pits in 42:22 does not fit what the exilic prophecies of Jeremiah, Ezekiel, and Daniel say about life in Babylonian exile.[312] (b) A second problem arises if one interprets 43:3 to be saying that God gave Egypt and Cush to Cyrus in exchange for the release

---

[309] Watts, *Isaiah 34–66*, 130, puts v. 13 with the following section and separates it from the hymnic context of 42:10–13.

[310] Blenkinsopp, *Isaiah 40–55*, 229, emends the imperfect verb (a future incomplete action) with a simple conjunction into a *waw* plus imperfect (completed action). Goldingay, *Message of Isaiah 40–55*, 226, recognizes that the verbs are imperfect but does not emend them. He simply claims that these verbs "both likely have a past reference."

[311] Baltzer, *Deutero-Isaiah*, 195, sets this in the context of other religious authorities that were mentioned in Dan 1–6.

[312] Westermann, *Isaiah 40–66*, 111–12, suggests these could be metaphorical terms picked up from laments to describe the plight of the oppressed.

of Israel from exile in 539 BC, for Cyrus did not defeat these nations.[313] (c) A third difficulty surrounds the suggestion that 43:14 describes Cyrus's defeat of Babylon in 539 BC, for this verse does not match Cyrus's joyful occupation of Babylon without a fight that is described in the Cyrus Cylinder.[314] (d) Fourthly, an understanding of the setting that does not require the textual emendation of 43:28 should be preferred. Although almost everyone agrees that the historical setting of these chapters can never be proven without a shadow of a doubt, a more probable historical situation might be reconstructed if these four problems can be avoided.

2. A Preexilic Setting: Four alternate explanations of the historical data mentioned above are possible, and these factors point to a likely setting around 701 BC when Sennacherib was attacking Judah during the reign of Hezekiah. (a) Sennacherib's devastating defeat of all of Palestine (Sennacherib refers to defeating 46 strong walled cities in Judah in the Taylor Prism), except Jerusalem, could explain how Judah was plundered, why some Hebrews were driven to hide in caves, and why there was no one to deliver the Hebrews from their enemy (42:22).[315] (b) Long ago the reformation exegete J. Calvin suggested that the Assyrian king Sennacherib's defeat and plunder of the Egyptian king Tirhakah (43:3, he was from Cush) shortly before 701 BC should be considered the ransom payment Sennacherib needed that caused him to spare Hezekiah and not destroy Jerusalem (36:6,9; 37:9).[316] (c) Isaiah 43:14 could coincide with Isaiah's earlier prophecy of the defeat of Babylon in chaps. 13–14 and 21:1–10, possibly a prophetic announcement that predicted Sennacherib's defeat of Babylon in 689 BC when the city was actually destroyed.[317] (d) If 43:28 comes from the time of Hezekiah, the polluting of the sanctuary in Jerusalem in 587 BC is still a future event, so there would be no need to emend the two imperfect verbs in this verse.

If Sennacherib's attack on Judah was the setting of 42:14–44:23, then the time when God was silent for a time (42:14) would refer to God not responding to Judah's cries for help as they suffered for months under the wrath of Sennacherib's army as he gradually defeated all of the major cities of Judah except Jerusalem. The condemnation of making idols out of Palestinian trees (44:9–20) fits this time period well because at that time Hezekiah tried to remove this kind of idolatry from Judah (2 Kgs 18:3–4). The useless offering of

---

[313] This account is described in Xenophon, *Cyropaedia*, vii., 6–20. Cyrus's son Cambyses did conquer them 17 years later in 522 BC.

[314] *ANET*, 315–16. Cyrus claims to have taken the city "without any battle . . . sparing Babylon any calamity." He claims to have "entered Babylon as a friend . . . and established the seat of government in the palace of the ruler under jubilation and rejoicing."

[315] The term בַּז "plunder, spoil" describes the taking of goods in war and a חוֹר "hole" was a place where people would hide themselves and their possessions (1 Sam 14:11).

[316] Calvin, "Isaiah," 321.

[317] S. Erlandsson, *The Burden of Babylon: A Study of Isaiah 13:2–14:23* (Lund: Gleerup, 1970), 91, quotes from Sennacherib's account of his total devastation of the city of Babylon.

sacrifices in 43:22–24 matches Isaiah's concerns in earlier oracles (1:10–15; 29:13), and the salvation oracles that encourage the people not to fear (44:1–5) would be an encouragement to trust God in this difficult time of Assyrian oppression. This setting for 42:14–44:23 would make it fit into the same general time frame as 40:12–42:13.

STRUCTURE. There is general agreement in identifying the many small paragraphs in 42:14–44:23, but it is more difficult to present a convincing case for the organization of these paragraphs into a series of logical or progressive literary units. The material is closed by a hymn in 44:23 (just like the last section was closed by the hymn in 42:10–13), and there are several repeated themes. Help in defining the divisions between the units in 42:14–44:23 is available by noting that this material has some parallels with the earlier sections in 40:12–42:13. It also included words of encouragement (40:28–31), a salvation oracle (41:8–20), and a hymn (42:10–13) that ends with a call to give glory to God (42:13); so it is not surprising to find some of these same characteristics in this new literary unit.

The first section, which encompasses 42:14–43:7, ends with a "do not fear" salvation oracle in 43:1–7 and concludes with a final call to give glory to God in 43:7. The second section includes 43:8–44:5 and it also ends with a similar "do not fear" oracle in 45:1–5. The third section in 44:6–23 is a unique taunt of idol worshippers that ends with a hymn (44:23) that proclaims the glory of God. This approach to the division of this literary unit supports the view that there are three main sections within this series of prophecies:

Fear not, God will deliver his blind servant	42:14–43:7
Fear not, the blind will be delivered and forgiven	43:8–44:5
Fear not idols, fear God and be forgiven	44:6–23

These sections are connected to each other and to what precedes them by common vocabulary.[318] In fact, some believe that 42:14–17 is so closely connected to 42:10–13 that they make 42:10–17 a literary unit.[319] Although this commentary disagrees with this analysis and concludes that hymns end each literary section, it is important to notice interrelated connections between these messages. An obvious inner connection between the three main messages identified above is the common "fear not" exhortation in 43:1,5; 44:2; 44:8.

(1) Fear Not, God Will Deliver His Sinful Blind Servants (42:14–43:7)

In this message Isaiah explains God's plans for the blind servant (42:18–19) who does not seem to understand God's actions (42:25b). This servant is the

---

[318] One example would be the reference to the "blind" in 42:16,19; 43:8; 44:18

[319] Both Oswalt, *Isaiah 40–66*, 122, and Spykerboer, *Structure and Composition of Deutero-Isaiah*, 93–95, find God as a warrior in both 42:13 and 14–15; so Spykerboer concludes that "10–12 (13) and (13) 14–17 are so interrelated that they cannot be separated from each other as two distinct passages."

nation of Israel, and it needs to realize that the present circumstances of the nation are directly connected to the sinful behavior of blindly ignoring God's covenantal instructions in the law (42:18–21,24). Therefore, God will allow these people to be plundered, so that they will once again listen to what he says (42:22–24). In spite of all their past problems, God assures his people of his love by reminding them that he has redeemed them; so they need not fear (43:1,5). In the future he will turn darkness into light and cause all his scattered people to return to their land (42:16; 43:5–6).

STRUCTURE.   The structure of this salvation oracle can be divided into three paragraphs based on their content (words of assurance in 42:14–17, explanations of Israel's punishment in 42:18–15, and a final encouragement not to fear in 43:1–7), grammatical characteristics (first person verbs dominate 42:14–17, but they are absent in 42:18–25), and differences in genre (43:1–7 is a salvation oracle).

The blind are not forsaken	42:14–17
The blind servant's sins result in punishment	42:18–24
Fear not, God will ransom and redeem his people	43:1–7

These messages are complex with a diversity of mixed literary genres; yet there are thematic connections that draw these paragraphs together. The "blind" in 42:16 can be connected to the "blind" in 42:19. Although God was silent for a short time during a time of great pain (42:14), and allowed his people to be punished (42:22), in the future God will summons his people by name (43:2,7) and deliver them from their punishment (43:3–6).

THE BLIND ARE NOT FORSAKEN (42:14–17)

14"For a long time I have kept silent,
   I have been quiet and held myself back.
But now, like a woman in childbirth,
   I cry out, I gasp and pant.
15I will lay waste the mountains and hills
   and dry up all their vegetation;
I will turn rivers into islands
   and dry up the pools.
16I will lead the blind by ways they have not known,
   along unfamiliar paths I will guide them;
I will turn the darkness into light before them
   and make the rough places smooth.
These are the things I will do;
   I will not forsake them.
17But those who trust in idols,
   who say to images, 'You are our gods,'
   will be turned back in utter shame.

C. Westermann classifies this oracle as a proclamation of salvation that traditionally follows a community lament, though this analysis is weakened by the fact that he must insert an implied reference to a previous community complaint.[320] Can one assume that this message was a response to a community complaint that God was silent too long and had forsaken his people (42:14a,16b), when the actual complaint is completely missing from this text? It may be better to view this as a salvation oracle even though it is missing the usual "fear not" formula. The purpose of this paragraph is to offer hope to the audience, but it was constructed a little different from other salvation oracles. The paragraph is filled with first person verbs concerning what "I," God, have or will do in 42:14–16, then 42:17 hints at God's plan to condemn anyone (in Judah or the nations) who might trust in idols. This paragraph refers to:

A time of divine silence	42:14
A time of destruction	42:15
A time of guidance and light	42:16
Shame for those who trust idols	42:17

42:14 This verse is usually translated to represent a contrast between God's past lack of intervention in 14a and the contrasting "but now" (NIV, cf. NASB, RSV) active involvement of God in the future in 14b, but there is no Hebrew particle that suggests or implies this "but now" contrasting interpretation. Since God repeatedly revealed his will and spoke to the people through the prophets, "I have kept silent" (*heḥĕšêtî*) relates more to a lack of God's action or an absence of his response to the prayers of his people as in 64:12. The two imperfect verbs indicate that God "repeatedly was still, acted deaf, was not answering"[321] and "was continually restraining myself" (*'et'appāq*) for a long time;[322] thus, the people did not experience God's intervening power or the grace of his compassion on their behalf.

In the second half of the verse God is compared to some aspects of a woman who is giving birth, for he is about to give birth to a new era in the future

---

[320] Westermann, *Isaiah 40–66*, 105, drew comparisons between 41:17–20 and 42:14–17, but these are quite different oracles. Melugin, *Formation of Isaiah 40–55*, 103, says "only here do we find Yahweh engaged in disputation; he argues against the complaint that he has been silent." Childs, *Isaiah*, 332, is one example of an approach that recognizes the dangers of an analysis that is based on what is not expressed in the paragraph and an approach that stretches form-critical analysis so much that one can hardly identify the form any longer.

[321] The root of this verb אַחֲרִישׁ "I was repeatedly silent" (GKC §107e refers to the repeated aspect of imperfect verbs) is also used in 36:21; 1 Sam 10:27; Mic 7:16.

[322] מֵעוֹלָם literally "from eternity" does not require one to say that God has done nothing from eternity past, for the central idea refers to a long undetermined period of time. It may seem like an eternity, but the period may be a relatively short period. E. Jenni, "עוֹלָם *'olām* eternity," *TLOT*, II: 852–62. Past continuous action seems to be a better way of interpreting the imperfect verb (GKC §107e) rather than suggesting a future translation that is more common for the imperfect.

(42:16; cf. 66:9–10). J. Oswalt limits the comparison of God to a woman giving birth strictly to the idea that both God and the woman cry out in agony,[323] while J. Muilenburg suggests that God was travailing with the distress of birth pangs at the terrible conditions on earth.[324] Both approaches focus on God's empathy and distress over the terrible situation of his people.

The final line could be interpreted in relationship to the woman in labor; thus NIV translates "I gasp and pant,"[325] but it is not clear what this implies about God.[326] If one notices the interlinking use of the idea of giving birth in earlier texts, it is twice associated with the agony the Israelites felt under the attack of Sennacherib (26:17; 37:3); so this verse may indicate that God was going through a sympathetic parallel agony similar to the birth pangs the Israelites were going through at the time of Sennacherib's attack on Jerusalem. God does these two things "together, at once" (*yāḥad*, absent in NIV; cf. NASB) to prove that he is not quiet any longer. God's action is then described in more detail in the next verse.

42:15 Two very different interpretations of this verse are possible because the text does not clearly indicate what land will be laid waste. The imperfect verbs may describe God's continuous past action[327] of drying up the land of Israel and thus function as a metaphor concerning God's defeat of Israel. If one follows this line of interpretation, v. 15 would describe God's judgment on the mountains and land of Judah, even though this caused God great agony in v. 14 (consistent with the plundering in 42:22,24–25). This interpretation seems unlikely in a salvation oracle.

A second interpretation is suggested if one translates these imperfect verbs with a future tense (as in the NIV, NASB, RSV). The severe judgment of God would then metaphorically[328] apply to the future destruction of Judah's

---

[323] Oswalt, *Isaiah 40–66*, 126, wants to stay away from thinking of God as a mother giving birth, although the prophet Isaiah claims that he was overcome with agony like a woman in childbirth because he identified with those suffering in 21:3.

[324] Muilenburg, "Isaiah 40–66," 5:473, thinks the imagery depicts the passion of God as he deals with the history of his people. Childs, *Isaiah*, 332–33, interprets this as God's refusal to end the exile of Israel. He then understands the judgment in 42:15 as God's defeat of Israel's oppressors. A problem with this approach is that it would be odd to indicate Babylon using the terms "mountains and hills," for the area around Babylon is a broad flat plain.

[325] I.e., if the root is נָשַׁם "he gasped" and one chooses the semantic field of "pant" for שָׁאַף.

[326] If on the other hand the last line were viewed as an interpretation of the metaphor of giving birth and the imperfect verbs were derived from different roots, this line would refer to "making desolate, devastating," while שָׁאַף will describe "crushing, devouring," and this would fit better with v. 15 (cf. Amos 2:7; 8:4). Goldingay, *Message of Isaiah 40–55*, 171, has "I will devastate and crush.

[327] Thus one might translate the imperfect אַחֲרִיב as "I repeatedly laid waste," thus representing the continuous, repeated, or incomplete action of the verb (GKC §107f-h).

[328] Baltzer, *Deutero-Isaiah*, 144, views the images in v. 15 as signs of a theophany descending to earth and destroying everything on earth (Mic 1:1–4). North, *Second Isaiah*, 113, changes אִיִּים "islands, coastland" to צִיִּים "deserts," but there is no reason why this word could not refer to "sandbar islands" that will appear in rivers that are drying up.

unidentified enemies[329] under images of laying waste the mountains and drying up their enemies, similar to 41:15.[330]

42:16 A distinctive change in God's relationship with the people of Jerusalem is envisioned in the future when God destroys these enemies. Violence and destruction will end; and God's tender guidance will begin to enlighten the eyes of God's people who are now spiritually blind, living in darkness, and unable to perceive the path they were supposed to follow (6:9–10; 29:9–10,18; 32:3–4; 35:5; 42:16–19). Although it might be tempting to associate this removal of blindness to the servant's role of opening the eyes of the blind (42:7), there is no way of identifying these two acts as the same events.[331] Instead of interpreting this as God literally leading the exiles on the "way" or "path" (*derek*) back from Babylon,[332] it is better to interpret these images as symbols (vv. 14–15 also should not be taken literally) of God: (a) his showing the people a spiritual way to walk that they presently do not understand, (b) his guiding them through the removal of their darkness and blindness, (c) his provision of the light to understand his truth; and (d) his smoothing out of the rough places in life. God will lift the cloud from the hardened hearts of those who cannot see or hear (6:9–10; 35:5) and do not believe.

The final promise of this verse assures the audience that God will do these things for them; he will not forget[333] or fail to keep his promises. This is God's stamp of divine approval, like an oath that will not change. No one should doubt his intentions or his ability to perform what he said he would do. People can trust God because he will not forsake his people; he will keep his promises.

42:17 The paragraph ends with a warning to those who trust in idols,[334] probably the enemies of Israel. Isaiah has already said that when God lays waste the land (42:15) he will defeat these forces, but here one learns that they will "retreat, return back, take flight" (the verb *sûg*) in great shame, terms that elsewhere describe the retreat of the Egyptian army (Jer 46:5) and the shame of idolaters who find that their gods are actually nothing (44:9,11). Earlier in

---

[329] Whybray, *Isaiah 40–66*, 78–79, concludes that the "turning of the fertile mountains and hills into arid deserts symbolizes the destruction of Israel's enemies."

[330] Schoors, *I Am God Your Savior*, 92, concludes that this "can only mean disaster for the enemies," though he assumes the Israelites were in exile at this time. If these verses are connected to the Assyrian crisis, it is possible that the destruction could metaphorically refer to the miraculous killing of 185,000 Assyrian soldiers by the angel of God in 37:36

[331] Motyer, *Isaiah*, 324–5; Oswalt, *Isaiah 40–66*, 126; and Seitz, "Isaiah 40–66," 369, make this connection. But if the servant's role fits into an eschatological setting, then his acts of opening eyes would be distinguished from the near future events when God acts on behalf of his people and opens their eyes in 42:14–17.

[332] Schoors, *I Am God Your Savior*, 92, understands this to be a new exodus of the people from exile.

[333] The verb עֲזַבְתִּים "I will not forsake/leave them" is a prophetic perfect (GKC §106n) which signals a change from God's past period of silence (42:14a).

[334] Goldingay and Payne, *Isaiah 40–55*, 1:249, say "Judeans tempted by images would once more need to see themselves addressed here."

41:11–12 God stated that Israel's enemies would became nothing and would suffer great "shame" (*bôš* in 41:11 and 42:17). This is the time when God will demonstrate his power as a "divine warrior" (42:13) who triumphs over his enemies (the Assyrian army left Jerusalem in defeat; cf. 42:11–13).

Since no foreigners likely heard this oracle of salvation, the desired effect of these words was to persuasively encourage the prophet's Israelite audience not to fear the foreign armies or their gods. Those who "trust" (*bāṭaḥ*—used frequently in chap. 36) in these false gods will fail and will be utterly put to shame. Victory will come to those who trust in God because God is going to act on behalf of his people by laying waste their enemy (42:15; 41:15–16a) and revealing to his people the light of his truth (42:16). Believers in every generation should never doubt God in their dark days when it feels like God has abandoned them, for in due time God will act on behalf of his people and shed his light and guidance on each situation.

THE BLIND SERVANT'S SINS RESULT IN PUNISHMENT (42:18–25)

18"Hear, you deaf;
  look, you blind, and see!
19Who is blind but my servant,
  and deaf like the messenger I send?
Who is blind like the one committed to me,
  blind like the servant of the LORD?
20You have seen many things, but have paid no attention;
  your ears are open, but you hear nothing."
21It pleased the LORD
  for the sake of his righteousness
  to make his law great and glorious.
22But this is a people plundered and looted,
  all of them trapped in pits
  or hidden away in prisons.
They have become plunder,
  with no one to rescue them;
they have been made loot,
  with no one to say, "Send them back."

23Which of you will listen to this
  or pay close attention in time to come?
24Who handed Jacob over to become loot,
  and Israel to the plunderers?
Was it not the LORD,
  against whom we have sinned?
For they would not follow his ways;
  they did not obey his law.
25So he poured out on them his burning anger,
  the violence of war.
It enveloped them in flames, yet they did not understand;
  it consumed them, but they did not take it to heart.

R. Melugin finds signs that God was involved with a dispute with his servant when he tried to explain to the Israelites why they were being punished in 42:18–25, but the first two subparagraphs look more like divine instruction that explain what God is doing, rather than a dialogue or disputational argument between two parties.[335] This paragraph continues the theme of blindness (42:18–19) from 42:16 and explains in much more detail the difficulties God's people faced (43:14) when God did not intervene on their behalf (42:22,24–25). It also adds new information that will help the audience understand how the people's rejection of God's instruction of the law resulted in their enemies plundering the nation of Israel. The paragraph can be divided into two parallel halves:

Who was the blind servant that was plundered?	42:18–22
Israel is my blind servant	18–20
God gave them his law	21
The people were plundered	22
Why did the servant receive God's anger?	42:23–25
Will anyone listen?	23
God plundered for not obeying his law	24
God sent war; Israel did not understand	25

The use of questions beginning with "who" (*mî*) and "hearing" (*šāmaᶜ*) vocabulary in 42:20 and 42:23–24 mark the beginning of these two subparagraphs. God's "law" (*tôrâ*) is set as a standard of conduct in vv. 21,24, while "plunder" (*bāzaz*) vocabulary appears in vv. 22,24. There is little that would suggest that this is a trial speech or a disputation, for as J. L. Koole noticed, there is a lack of forensic terminology that would be expected in a trial speech and a lack of discussion between opponents that might signal a disputation.[336] Instead, this paragraph should be viewed as a persuasive instructional speech, similar to 40:12–31, with similar paragraphs beginning with questions and ending with God's answers to these questions. The purpose of the paragraph is to persuade the Hebrew audience "to hear, look, and see" (42:18,23) the reasons for God's action against his people. Then hopefully they will take what God says to heart and alter their behavior (42:25b).

42:18–19 This new paragraph is addressed to the blind and deaf, terms that elsewhere refer to the Israelites who where unable to understand and unwilling to follow God's instruction (6:9–10; 29:18; 32:3; 42:7,16; 43:8; 44:18; 48:4). Two imperative verbs exhort them to "hear" and "look" so that they can

---

[335] Melugin, *Formation of Isaiah 40–55*, 104, saw similarities with the "who" questions in 42:19 and those in the dispute in 40:12,18,25, but Westermann, *Isaiah 40–66*, 109, compares this paragraph to a trial speech, especially 43:22–28.

[336] Hanson, *Isaiah 40–66*, 53, calls this another disputation, but Koole, *Isaiah III, Volume 1, Isaiah 40–48*, 264, rightly identifies the weakness of this literary comparison.

"perceive"[337] (NIV, "see") what God is doing. These words attract attention and suggest something important is going to be explained. The initial questions in 42:19 (marked by *mî* "who") are rhetorical questions. Is there any doubt about the identity of who is blind? But God has not given up on the blind (6:9–10),[338] for they are still his servant Israel. God speaks words of instruction so that his people can understand his ways, change their behavior, and function "as my messenger" (*kĕmalʾākî*; NIV, "like the messenger") who truly serves God. There is a certain level of absurdity in the situation. How can Israel serve God if she is blind and how can she be God's messenger to others if she cannot hear what God says? God's people must understand what their problem is (blindness and deafness) and must realize that God will lead them and heal their blindness (42:16) through the ministry of his faithful Servant (42:6–7).[339]

In addition to being "my servant" and "my messenger," in 42:19 Israel is called a "one committed" (NIV), "a dedicated one' (RSV), or "a covenant partner."[340] This descriptive title also presents something of a paradox. How can one be blind and still be God's servant or covenant partner? How can they be his covenant partners if they do not listen to and follow the instructions God gave them in the covenant documents? The audience did not respond positively to God's challenge as Isaiah did in 6:1–8 when God called him to serve and go as his messenger.

42:20 The nation's culpability is evident from the fact that she "was seeing"[341] much but did not pay attention to what she saw and heard. God provided enough information through his prophets, past revelation in the law, and through many life experiences in their own day so that these people would know what they should do. The "many things" (42:20) that they saw would

---

[337] The Hebrew infinitive construct (here לִרְאוֹת "to see, perceive, understand") frequently expresses purpose or results (GKC §114f-g).

[338] The pivotal role this text plays is discussed in C. A. Evans, *To See and Not Perceive: Isaiah 6:9–10 in Early Jewish and Christian Interpretation*, JSOTSup 64, 1989) and R. P. Carroll, "Blindsight and the Vision Thing," in *Writing and Reading the Scroll of Isaiah*, 80–93.

[339] P. Stern, "The 'Blind Servant' Imagery of Deutero-Isaiah," *Bib* 75 (1994): 224–32, believes the blind servant Israel in 42:19 is the same servant as the suffering servant in 53. Although both do suffer (Israel suffered for its own sins), it is impossible to suggest that Israel was innocent of sin like the suffering servant.

[340] מְשֻׁלָּם is a *pual* participle, but it is difficult to determine how to translate it. שָׁלַם has several meanings, but (a) "to be complete, perfect, fulfilled" (44:26) and (b) "have a covenant of peace, be dedicated" are possible meanings that fit here. The second root seems best. McKenzie, *Second Isaiah*, 45, emends the form to מְשֻׁלְחִי "my sent one" while the Old Greek derived the word from מָשַׁל "he rules" to render "rulers."

[341] NIV translates the first verb "you have seen," implying רָאִיתָ which agrees with the written tradition (Kethib) of the Masoretic text and 1QIsᵃ, but the oral tradition (the Qere) has an infinitive absolute form רָאוֹת "seeing" which is parallel to the parallel infinitive absolute פָּקוֹחַ "opening." Oswalt, *Isaiah 40–66*, 128, prefers the Kethib written Masoretic text while Koole, *Isaiah III, Volume 1, Isaiah 40–48*, 270, prefers the Qere spoken tradition. One can argue the scribal mistake going either way, and in the end the meaning is not changed significantly.

include God's great works of salvation when he redeemed them from Egypt (Exod 15), his defeat of the Canaanites and his giving of the land (the account of Joshua), and even recent times of punishment when the people did not trust God (7:1–25). Inexplicably, these lessons did not cause his people to learn what God was teaching them throughout their history because they did not "pay attention, keep, guard" (*tišmōr*) what they observed and refused to accept the implications of what they were seeing right before their eyes. "He"[342] (possibly "my servant" or "the one committed to me" from 42:19) did not internalize or appreciate what was happening. This fits the pattern predicted in 6:9–10.

42:21 The second basis for culpability was God's granting of explicit written instructions on how to maintain their covenant relationship. God did not withhold his wishes or hide what was involved in keeping the covenant relationship. It "pleased, was the desire of" (*ḥāpēṣ*) God to reveal his instructions[343] either "because of" or "for the sake of"[344] his righteousness (Ps 44:23,27). God's righteousness involves his faithful commitment to do what was right and true. This divine attribute resulted in the establishment of just principles to guide his relationship with his people so that everyone would know the just consequences of righteous and rebellious behavior. God did not hide these facts so that he could unfairly punish people for things they were unaware of, nor did he change the nature of the relationship without telling them. He graciously revealed these righteous guidelines for behavior through a series of written instructions known as his "instruction, law" (*tôrâ*), as well as God's instructions through prophets like Isaiah. His purpose was not to burden his people with a second-class set of legalistic rules or pedantic restrictive regulations. He viewed these divine instructions as a great and glorious revelation of his character, something that would set the wise Israelites apart from the other nations (Deut 4:6). Other nations would be amazed that they had such wisdom and insight into the will of their God and would marvel that Israel had a God that was so near that he could talk to them when they called on him for help (Deut 4:7). This revelation was a glorious gift of God. Pss 19:7–14 and 119 celebrate the blessedness of having God's revelation as a guide. The person who was walking in a close relationship to God exclaimed that they loved God's instructions (Ps 119:97).

---

[342] The verb in the first half of v. 20 is a second pers. sg. "you will guard, heed, observe" (תִּשְׁמֹר), but in the second half of the verse is a third masc. sg. "he will hear" (יִשְׁמָע). This variation does not seem to be significant and is found numerous times in the prophets and Psalms.

[343] In 55:11 the eschatological goal of God will be accomplished because when God's word goes forth it will accomplish what God desires or purposes. At that time they will hear and will fully understand.

[344] The preposition לְמַעַן frequently expresses (a) "for the sake of," (b) "in order that," and (c) sometimes "because, on account of."

42:22   Nevertheless, the people of Israel were not experiencing the joys of
a blessed life at this time, for the people "were being plundered and looted,"[345]
so the present circumstances of the Israelites were very discouraging. No reason is given for this condition, but one could assume that their present condition relates to the fact that the people were blind and did not follow the great
and glorious instructions from God. The terms "plundered and looted" come
from the context of losing a war (17:14; 2 Kgs 21:14). Once an army has defeated a city or a nation there is nothing that can prevent the victorious army
from taking whatever booty they desire from the helpless peasants. They could
take people as slaves, animals, grain, gold, and even ivory beds.[346] When a
nation is threatened, people in the countryside are often fearful of losing their
possessions and their lives so they often run into a fortified city or escape to a
desolate area where no one can find them. Some people will prefer to run into
the forested hills to hide in caves[347] in the ground (Josh 6:16; Judg 6:2; 1 Sam
13:6; 14:11; 1 Kgs 18:4). C. Westermann recognized that this verse could not
describe life in Babylonian exile, so he took these as metaphorical statements
from a lament, but there is no indication that this one verse is a lament.[348]

The absence of someone to rescue the people from the oppressor indicates the Israelite king and his army had no power to stop the one who was
plundering the land. This implies a military setting in which a war was being lost and is interlinked to common vocabulary used during the Assyrian
crisis (36:14–15,18–20; 37:11–12). The absence of a deliverer could have
theological implications (God did not rescue them), but the discussion is
focused on the helplessness of the people and the powerlessness of their king
at this point. The final clause indicates that no one is requiring the enemy to
"send these people back" (NIV). This questionable translation might imply
that people are in captivity, but there is no pronoun in Hebrew for the word
"them."[349] Thus this imperative exclamation does not imply the people are
in exile or that no one is strong enough to send these people back home from
Babylon. It merely indicates that no one is opposing the looters and requiring

---

[345] Both verbs are passive participles, which do not have tense but tend to describe "the un-
interrupted exercise of an activity" and express "simple duration" (GKC §116a,c). Consequently
passive participles (like בָּזוּז "being plundered" and שָׁסוּי "being looted") are often translated as
Latin gerunds (GKC §116e). Baltzer, *Deutero-Isaiah*, 152, says "verse 22 describes the present
distress."

[346] *ANET*, 287–88, indicates that Sennacherib took these kinds of things from Judah in 701 BC.

[347] בַּחוּרִים "in holes" (a preposition plus a pl. noun) was read by the translators of the Aramaic
Targum as the pl noun "young men," which is spelled in the same way.

[348] Westermann, *Isaiah 40–66*, 112, does not take these terms literally but sees them as part of
their memory in laments about the Babylonian defeat of Jerusalem in 587 BC. Muilenburg, "Isaiah
40–66," 5:478, goes out on a limb and imagines that the prophet seems to be describing Israel's
present condition under a figure of a caravan attacked by the Bedouin in the desert, plundered and
looted, and held prisoner in holes in the ground.

[349] The *hiphil* imperative הָשֵׁב "return!" has no object "them" and needs to be interpreted in
light of the looting in the beginning of the sentence.

them to "Restore!" (NRSV)[350] what they have taken. The context of taking spoil and looting happens when a nation is defeated in war, not when people have already been in exilic captivity almost 70 years. The historical event is not explicitly identified, but Sennacherib's desolation and looting of 46 cities in Judah fits this situation very well.

42:23   Some of the ideas in 43:18–22 are repeated again in 43:23–25 in a slightly different form in order to put more emphasis on the people's sinfulness (42:24b). A similar but slightly different question is asked in this context (using *mî* "who" as in v. 19). Instead of asking who is blind (42:19), this question asks if anyone in the audience will now listen to what God is saying?[351] Is anyone willing to be a listening servant rather than a deaf one (cf. the servant in 50:4)? This is a hopeful invitation that encourages people to pay attention to what is going to happen after this present time of being plundered. This might suggest that a change in their situation is possible. Since not hearing what God said led to their present disaster; hearing what God says now may bring about much better results in the future. Failure to listen is a sure path to ignorance and disaster; listening to what God says at least opens the possibility for a change in their present terrible situation.

42:24   What must they reconsider? The present plundered state of the nation is a well-known fact that everyone in the audience painfully recognized (42:22), but the question is why? Who gave Israel into the hand of those who looted and plundered them?[352] Was this just a freak accident, a political misjudgment that backfired, the wrong military strategy by some general, bad luck, poor timing, or did their covenant with God have something to do with this defeat (the curses of the covenant)? With a bold rhetorical question (*hălō᾽*) that implies a positive answer,[353] the prophet unflinchingly answered his question by affirming that God himself did this to them.[354]

But why would God do this? The prophet immediately confesses the nation's sins (similar to his reaction in 6:5), recognizing the reason for their punishment to be related to God "against whom[355] we have sinned." The

---

[350] Goldingay and Payne, *Isaiah 40–55*, 1:264, correctly translate this as "Give it back."

[351] The interrogative מִי "who" is used in clauses that indicate a desire or a wish for someone to do something (6:8; Ps 60:11[9]). They are to listen to "this" זֹאת, a probable reference to what is now being said or what will be said in the next verse.

[352] The Masoretic written tradition (Kethib) has לִמְשׁוּסֶה (with no vocalization associated with the ו) suggesting that the form is a pual participle, but the oral tradition (Qere) and 1QIsᵃ suggest we read the text as a noun לִמְשִׁסָה. The difference in meaning is minor, but it has a sg. form in the first half of the line "for a spoil" and then a pl. form at the end of the first line "to the robbers," though the line does make good sense as it is.

[353] The question marker with the negative הֲלֹא is used "in order to show it to be absolutely true" and is equivalent to "surely it is" (GKC §150e).

[354] In 41:4,27 God answers his own questions immediately after they are asked. This answering of questions is not that different from his answering of questions in 40:21–23,25–26,28.

[355] זוּ is used as a relative (instead of אֲשֶׁר) that is in the accusative "against whom" (GKC §138g) since the retrospective pronoun on לוֹ is the object of a pronoun (GKC §138b).

prophet makes no excuse for this sinful action; the people were just simply unwilling to "walk, follow"[356] in God's ways and stubbornly would not listen to his instruction in "his law" (*tôratô*). There was nothing unjust about the plundering of Judah; it was a forgone conclusion based on what God told them in the past (the curses in Lev 26; Deut 27–28 make this clear). If the people willingly choose to disobey God, there will eventually be a disastrous consequence because of God's curses. The prophet's hope is that some people in the audience will hear these words and confess their sins. In the final clauses the prophet turns to talk about what "they" did (no longer speaking of "we"). J. Calvin suggests that in the earlier "we" confession the prophet "included himself along with others, as being a member of that body, and confessed his guilt. . . . Because he was widely different from the great body of the people, he changes the person, and adds, '*They* would not'"[357] at the end of the verse. Thus on one level he identifies with his people's plight, but he was not one of those who were obstinate and among those who "were not willing" (*lō' 'ābû*) to listen to and obey the words that he received from God.

42:25 The paragraph ends with a dire reminder of what happens when the people are not willing to listen to God's *tôrâ*, do not confess their sins, and do not repent. God pours out his fierce anger[358] on his servant in the form of a violent war, though no specific war is mentioned in this verse. This suffering, plundering, and burning happened in Judah, not while the people were in exile in Babylon. Unfortunately the people did not seem to understand why they were consumed with the fire of God's wrath. The people did not "connect the dots" by recognizing that their sinfulness was the cause of their defeat.[359] God taught the lesson, but his Israelite students did not take the lesson to heart and learn anything from the experience. This lack of responsiveness explains why God viewed his servant Israel as a blind and deaf servant. As the New Testament illustrates (Matt 13:14–15), this spiritual blindness is not a trait that is limited to people in the distant past; it is present in some people in every generation.

---

[356] One normally expects to find an infinitive construct form here (1QIs[a] makes this an infinitive construct). Less frequently the infinitive absolute הָלוֹךְ "walking" functions as the object of a verb in place of the more usual infinitive construct (GKC §113d).

[357] Calvin, "Isaiah," *Calvin's Commentaries*, 313, believed Isaiah excluded himself because he was speaking of the "contempt and rejection of God, manifest by fiercely and haughtily shaking off his yoke."

[358] חֵמָה "wrath, anger" relates to God being "hot, burning" (44:15; 63:3; 66:15) while עֱזוּז emphasizes the "fierceness, violence" of the war that devastates the nation.

[359] McKenzie, *Second Isaiah*, 48, maintains that, "So insensible had Israel become that it could not even discern the presence of disaster." This seems unlikely, for when a nation is defeated in war, people notice. The problem was not that they did not notice the presence of disaster; the problem was that they did not connect this to God's punishment for their sins.

FEAR NOT, GOD WILL RANSOM AND REDEEM HIS PEOPLE (43:1–7)

¹But now, this is what the LORD says—
    he who created you, O Jacob,
    he who formed you, O Israel:
  "Fear not, for I have redeemed you;
    I have summoned you by name; you are mine.
²When you pass through the waters,
    I will be with you;
  and when you pass through the rivers,
    they will not sweep over you.
  When you walk through the fire,
    you will not be burned;
    the flames will not set you ablaze.
³For I am the LORD, your God,
    the Holy One of Israel, your Savior;
  I give Egypt for your ransom,
    Cush and Seba in your stead.
⁴Since you are precious and honored in my sight,
    and because I love you,
  I will give men in exchange for you,
    and people in exchange for your life.
⁵Do not be afraid, for I am with you;
    I will bring your children from the east
    and gather you from the west.
⁶I will say to the north, 'Give them up!'
    and to the south, 'Do not hold them back.'
  Bring my sons from afar
    and my daughters from the ends of the earth—
⁷everyone who is called by my name,
    whom I created for my glory,
    whom I formed and made."

The third paragraph in this section (43:1–7) follows the traditional "fear not" style of the salvation oracle (cf. 41:8–16) where God promises deliverance for his people. It is verbally connected to what precedes through the use of vocabulary about "burning" in 42:25 and 43:2. The beginning of the paragraph has a distinctive opening, "thus says the Lord," but the initial "but now" (wĕ'attâ) implies a reaction to the negative news in the preceding paragraph.[360] This paragraph can be divided into two sections by the (a) introductory "fear not . . . for I am with you" clauses that begin 43:1 and 5 or (b) into three sections based on the three promises of God (43:1,3,5).[361] Since 43:1 and 3–4 all

---

[360] Spykerboer, *Structure and Composition of Deutero-Isaiah*, 102, states "the word עתה is not simply an introduction to the salvation oracle . . . it illustrates the contextual coherence and functions as a linking phrase" to connect the thoughts of 42:18–25 with 43:1–7.

[361] This structure agrees with Westermann, *Isaiah 40–66*, 115, who finds in each paragraph a word of assurance, followed by a substantiation with a verb in the perfect tense, and a final

relate to God's redemption of his people, it seems appropriate to unite 43:1–4 into one paragraph; thus option (a) is preferable.[362] The divine assurances of comfort, based on divine promises in 43:1 and 7, form something of an *inclusio* that marks the beginning and end of this message. Both 43:1 and 7 have vocabulary explaining that God's plan is based on his past work of "creating, forming, and giving a name" to his people Israel.[363] The structural outline of this salvation oracle is:[364]

Fear not, for God will redeem you	43:1–4
Fear not, I created and redeemed you	1
I was with you through trials	2
Your Savior ransomed you	3–4
Fear not, for God will gather his people	43:5–7
Fear not, all children will return	5–6
The destiny of those who glorify God	7

The setting of the earlier salvation oracle in 41:8–16 was in a time of war where the "fear not" admonition of the salvation oracle was very fitting (41:10,13,14). The reference to various trials in 43:2 and the giving of Egypt, Cush, and Seba in 43:3 may be helpful in excluding certain settings. K. Baltzer connects the historical setting to Cyrus receiving booty from Egypt, Cush, and Seba in exchange for letting Israel go home from Babylonian exile.[365] But as C. Seitz says, "For this reading to work, it is necessary that the prophet Deutero-Isaiah be sufficiently ill informed about Cyrus's actual military

announcement about future salvation. Melugin, *Formation of Isaiah 40–55*, 104–105, argues for three divisions (1–3a; 3b–4; 5–7) based on the three promises by God. Childs, *Isaiah*, 334, finds three subparagraphs in 1b–2,3–4,5–7.

[362] Conrad, "The 'Fear Not' Oracles in Second Isaiah," 145–5, finds two subparagraphs: 43:1–4 and 43:5–7. He finds the structural organization of vv. 1–4 to include an: (a) introduction, (b) assurance, (c) basis of assurance, (d) results, (e) self-identification of the deity, and (f) promise. He distinguishes two sets of "fear not" oracles: (a) those based on a war oracle (41:8–13,14–16) and (b) those based on the form of patriarchal promises (43:1–4, 5–7; 44:1–5). The distinction in form is relatively small, though the latter group always has a self-identification of the deity.

[363] Repeated vocabulary include: בָּרָא "he created," יָצַר "he formed," and קָרָא בְשֵׁם "he called by a name."

[364] Goldingay and Payne, *Isaiah 40–55*, 1:271–72, find the following chiastic arrangement:
[1] Yhwh as one who creates, calls, shapes ("fear not")
[2] Yhwh's promise regarding a journey ("I am with you")
[3a] Yhwh in relationship with Israel
[3b] Yhwh as one who gave up people for Israel
[4a] Yhwh as Israel's lover
[4b] Yhwh as one who will give up people for Israel
[5a] Yhwh in relationship with Israel ("fear not, I am with you")
[5b-6] Yhwh's promise regarding a journey
[7] Yhwh as one who calls, creates, shapes

[365] Baltzer, *Deutero-Isaiah*, 159, but Herodotus, *History*, I. 153, and Xenophon, *Cyropaedia*, viii.6.20 both indicate that Egypt was not defeated until about 17 years later by King Cambyses, Cyrus's son.

activity"[366] that he would contradict what is later said in 45:13b (Cyrus took no reward). This is because Cyrus did not defeat these nations; their defeat took place 17 years later during the reign of Cambyses. Thus a setting in Cyrus's reign does not fit the content of this oracle. In the discussion of 43:2 the possibility of an Assyrian setting will be explored (similar to 41:8–16). J. M. Vincent suggests that it follows the pattern of a preexilic war oracle.[367]

43:1 This salvation oracle provides some positive hopes to counteract the negative news in 42:18–25. "But now"[368] (wĕʿattâ as in 44:1; 48:7; 49:5) alerts the reader to a major contrast between Israel's terrible judgment and the future care God will extend to his people. In order to persuade "you" (the audience) that this is not just "pie in the sky" empty optimism by someone who does not know what the future holds, this text assures the audience that these are the very promises that God himself has spoken (lit., "thus says the LORD").

Although it may have appeared to some that Israel's life and livelihood was heavily determined by the nation's relationships to its political allies and dreadful rivals (42:22,24), in reality a nation's past and future is primarily dependent on its relationship to God's acts of blessing or cursing. But being God's people does not mean that there will not be any evil people who will oppose them or that God will completely protect them from all the hard knocks of life. The appearance of Israel as a nation in Palestine was not due just to a series of political maneuvers that resulted in her creation as an independent group of tribes. God "formed, shaped"[369] Israel as a nation by a new divine act of creative power (participle from bārāʾ), just as astonishing and marvelous as the creation of the various aspects of nature (40:26,28; 42:5). In the Hebrew mentality creation was not just a one-time event that happened when the world began many thousands of years ago. Later oracles will speak of future acts of divine creation during the eschatological recreation of the new heavens and the earth (65:17; 66:22). God's creative process of making a nation that would be connected to his name started many years earlier with the choosing of Abram

---

[366] Seitz, "Isaiah 40–66," 376, also finds it odd that the prophet would pick out "relatively bit players in the world power game."

[367] Vincent, *Studien zur literarischen Eigenart und zur geistigen Heimat von Jesaja, Kap 40–55*, 147–61, connects this to a military crisis that is preexilic and compares this to Isaiah's "fear not" oracle to King Ahaz in 7:3–9 (or a similar oracle to Hezekiah in 37:6).

[368] וְעַתָּה "and now" is used repeatedly by Isaiah to mark a contrast. In 1:21 it contrasts the past righteous city with the present evil city; in 5:3,5 it introduces new phases in the development of the parable of the vineyard; in 16:14 it highlights the contrast between the past judgment of Moab with the future glory; in 36:8 it contrasts the useless hope in Egypt with the new possible hope through cooperation with the Assyrians; in 38:20 it marks the change from Israel's oppressed state to what God can do to deliver his people; in 44:1 it introduces another salvation oracle that contrasts with the judgment of the preceding oracle; and in 64:8 it contrasts past events of being laid waste with the future work of God the Potter.

[369] These participles from בָּרָא "he created" and יָצַר "he formed, shaped" could function as verbs, as relative clauses "the one created" and "the one who formed," or as nouns "Creator" and "Shaper" in apposition to "Lord" in the previous line.

in Ur, included the exodus from Egypt, the giving of the covenant, and eventually the possession of the land of Israel (Gen 12–Joshua). God was the one who created this group of people as his people when he redeemed them[370] from the bondage of Egypt (Exod 7–15) and entered into a covenant relationship with them (Exod 19:4–6). At that time God gave them a name[371] so that they would have an identity that would set them apart from all the other nations of this world (they were a "holy nation, a kingdom of priests"). This created the relationship in which God could say, "you are mine" (43:21; NIV, "for myself"), my prized possession (Exod 19:6).

The present circumstances of the nation were quite difficult (42:18–25), but these factors did not nullify God's committed covenant relationship to his special people. These creative, redemptive, and ownership words conveyed to the audience God's special commitment, protection, and kinship relationship to the members of his own family. What are the implications of these claims? God's past deeds and present relationship with Israel should motivate the prophet's audience to have no fear about the future, for God is fully committed to them. In times of trouble God's message to Abram (Gen 15:1), Isaac (Gen 26:24), and the Israelites (Exod 14:10,13) was to "fear not," for God would intervene on behalf of his people. If he faithfully did this in the past, is he not able to do it now and in the future?

43:2 How do the people know that God will redeem them? The prophet suggests that the nation's present problems with enemies who plunder them (42:22,24–25) must be put in the larger context of the basic relationship that the people of Israel have with their God. The two conditional clauses[372] could be temporal ("when") or hypothetical ("if") statements that connect God to their present trials and tribulations. Some suggest that the idea of going through waters is reminiscent of the people's passage through the Red Sea (Exod 14–15) or passing over the flooding Jordan River many years ago (Josh 3–4), but neither of those experiences were tribulations, they were both signs of God's miraculous ability to save. Instead if one looks for examples of this imagery in the writings of Isaiah, one finds that the destructive invasion by the Assyrians was compared to a great flood of water (8:7–8) that was about to drown them. The Assyrian defeat of Ephraim, the northern nation of Israel was compared to "a driving rain and a flooding downpour" (28:2). In addition the sound of many nations (the Assyrians) attacking Damascus was compared to "the raging

---

[370] גָּאַל "redeem" is used in the context of family kinship relationships and could refer to the general "deliverance" of the people from bondage or to the more specific redemption of the first-born (Exod 12–13; Num 8:14–18).

[371] In 40:26 God created the stars and gave each a name. Giving a name implies control, ownership, or parental authority over something that belongs to you.

[372] The initial כִּי is probably best understood as temporal "when" since the present war and plundering of Israel eliminates the "if" this might happen. It had happened already.

sea . . . the roaring of great waters" (17:12–13).[373] The imperfect verbs ("you pass through") in this sentence points to the many difficult events the nation is going through rather than one specific event.[374] God's word of encouragement is that he will be with them in the midst of these events (43:2a) and that these events will not totally destroy them. The references to fire and flames suggest a military conquest in which cities are burned. By using imagery comparable to past events where God miraculously delivered the people, God was encouraging his people to react with faith, for he had already proven his superiority over similar forces in the past.

43:3–4 God can make these kinds of promises to the people of Israel because he is (lit.) "Yahweh your God." He is the "Holy One of Israel" (6:3; 41:14,16,20) who is magnificently set apart from all the evil of this world, is gloriously transcendent, and is wholly other. This is the Holy God who has a covenant relationship with the people of Israel, so they need not fear Yahweh. In addition, he is "your Savior," a title that indicates that he has delivered them and will deliver them from physical danger (43:11; 45:15,17, 20, 22; 46:7; 47:13,15; 49:25).

Because God is powerful, totally other, holy, gracious, and related to his covenant people, he promises to give other nations as a ransom in order to redeem his people. A ransom[375] is a payment of money, goods, or people in exchange for the release of another person from a debt, imprisonment, or punishment. This financial transaction comes from the legal context of giving something as a satisfaction or payment for damages caused to an injured party (Exod 21:30; Num 35:31) as well as from the cultic context of ransoming people or animals that are dedicated to God (Exod 12:21–23; 13:11–16; Num 8:14–18). Seitz rightly observed that Cyrus did not defeat these three African nations; their defeat took place 17 years later during the reign of Cambyses.[376] Therefore one must conclude that the defeat of these nations in 43:3 had nothing to do with Cyrus allowing the Israelites to return from exile. In addition the perfect verb ("I gave") refers to a past event.[377] An alternative explanation of this verse might propose that the prophet was reminding his audience about how God

---

[373] Although Westermann, *Isaiah 40–66*, 118, connects v. 2 with "Israel's safe conduct on her journey" home from exile, both Motyer, *Isaiah*, 331, and Goldingay, *Message of Isaiah 40–55*, 190, properly observes that "the talk of water here is more suggestive of being taken into exile than of being taken back home."

[374] תַעֲבֹר is the imperfect "you are passing through/ you will pass through." North, *Second Isaiah*, 120, saw these as general dangers the people may face in the future (Ps 66:12) that may be reminiscent of the exodus. Westermann, *Isaiah 40–66*, 118, thought the prophet was promising a safe return from exile, but this is far too specific.

[375] The word כֹּפֶר relates to the idea of "making atonement, removing, taking away" sins in sacrificial texts, but in a legal context it refers to the price paid to ransom a life (Exod 21:30; Job 33:24; Prov 13:8). In Exod 30:12 it amounted to a half shekel given to God by every male above 20 years of age.

[376] Seitz, "Isaiah 40–66," 6:376.

[377] Usually the perfect verb refers to completed action in past time. It can refer to future events

defeated Egypt either: (a) in the past at the time of the exodus when God gave up Egypt to destruction in order to redeem his people from slavery (but there is no indication that this involved Cush and Seba) or more likely (b) how in recent days God gave the Assyrian king Sennacherib power over the Ethiopian army of Tirhakah when he confronted it in battle (30:1–7; 31:1–3; 37:9). If this later event is what this text is referring to, God would be suggesting that he delivered Israel from some of Sennacherib's wrath by allowing him to defeat the Egyptian army that included people from Egypt, Cush, and Seba.[378]

This past demonstration of God's sovereign power is something of a guarantee of God's future intentions to graciously intervene on behalf of his people (43:4). Rather than despising the people of Judah or completely giving up on them, God values his people, treating them as special and precious. All the positive terms in 43:4 ("you are precious and honored') would give the audience confidence that God would again do something great on their behalf. Because[379] God loves them[380] in spite of their failures and he wants the best for them in the future, he would even give[381] other people in exchange for them again if he needed to. What is significant is the depth of God's love and commitment to his people. In faith the audience can believe God's promise and put their trust in him.

43:5–6   The second half of this oracle of salvation goes back to the beginning issues in 43:1 and once again encourages the audience not to fear their present situation. As always, it is God's presence that can remove fear. "I am with you" (repeating 43:2a) means that they will never be alone, never be forgotten, and never be outside the reach of God's strong arm. Since God will be with them, he will understand their hurts and fears.

The specific promise God makes is that "I will bring" (speaking from the perspective of being in Judah) all the people back to the land—people in the east, west, north, south, and from the far corners of the globe (11:12). A. Schoors concluded that this was predicting the return from Babylonian captivity,[382] but Babylon was not to the west or south.[383] The emphasis is on everyone returning from every corner of the globe. This promise seems to build on the past

---

(the prophetic perfect, GKC §106m-n), but the contrast in these two verses is between past events in v. 3 which serve as the basis for confidence for future divine acts in v. 4.

[378] The text plainly states וּלְאֻמִּים תַּחַת נַפְשֶׁךָ "and nations instead of your soul," a clear indication of God's gracious deliverance of his people from a much worse destiny at the hands of Sennacherib's army.

[379] The מֵאֲשֶׁר that begins 43:4 is probably causal (GKC §158b).

[380] The phrase וַאֲנִי אֲהַבְתִּיךָ "and I myself love you" is an emphatic statement that emphasizes what God is doing.

[381] The interpretation of the verb is difficult. Although many (including NIV) read this as a prophetic promise about what God will do, it could be a subjunctive imperfect that explains what God "would, might, could" do, as Motyer, *Isaiah*, 332, suggests.

[382] Schoors, *I Am God Your Savior*, 75, simply states that "the mentioning of the four parts of the earth does not aim at geographical accuracy; it is but a circumscription of 'the whole world.' "

[383] It would be difficult to connect this return to the return from Babylon for only about 50,000

example of God's ability to return his people to the land of Israel after their deliverance from Egypt. If God had the power to do that in the past, then it is possible for him to do the same thing in the future. This promise probably goes beyond a simple political return of the people and is more of the flavor of 2:1–4; 60:1–10; or 66:18–21 with a strong eschatological nuance. J. Goldingay states that this promise "implies a horizon extending far beyond questions about a return from Babylon."[384]

43:7 Not everyone will return, just my sons and daughters, just those who are called by God's name (a slight distinction from 43:1). Nationalistic terminology and grandiose political aspirations are absent from these descriptions; the spiritual life of the people is the criterion that will ensure inclusion in this group of people. This promise relates only to the destiny of the faithful who have a covenant relationship with God, who are known as believers, and who bring glory to the name of God. God originally created the world and the nation of Israel to bring glory[385] to himself; so it is not surprising that in the end people will realize this goal and glorify God. This oracle says nothing about what will happen to those who do not fall within these tight requirements (their fate is explained in 34:1–15; 63:1–6; 66:24).

THEOLOGICAL IMPLICATIONS.   The difficult events of life sometime cause believers throughout history to wonder what God is doing and why he allows so many people to suffer (Jer 12:1–6; Hab 1:1–4). The fact is, sometimes God is not doing anything at all to intervene in the natural course of history (42:14) but is allowing the free will of evil men to accomplish their evil desires. If people fail to follow the laws of nature or of God, there are normal consequences that will naturally result. When God does not miraculously intervene to stop these normal consequences, people may feel abandoned or question if God really cares for them. These theological struggles with God's providential control of history only demonstrate how blind people are when it comes to understanding the ways of God. The fact is that God groans in agony and pain (42:14) as he watches his struggling people groan in agony and pain with the hard events in life. He will allow them to suffer, but he will not completely forsake them (42:16). Although it is nice to know that God empathizes with his people when they go through trials, some might ask: Why bother with God if he will not intervene in these situations or will not give full protection to his people? But this complaint completely misunderstands the positive purpose in God's discipline of his blind servants. When people sin against the Lord, he often allows the consequences of those sins to play out in ways that cause much

---

people actually came back at that time (Ezra 2:64–65). Many thousand instead chose to stay in Babylon where life was quite comfortable.

[384] Goldingay, *Message of Isaiah 40–55*, 195.

[385] The original purpose for creating people was לִכְבוֹדִי "for my glory"; thus it is not surprising that the Westminster Confession says that "the chief end of man is to glorify God and enjoy him forever."

pain (42:24–25; 2 Sam 12:10–14; 16:20–22). The experience of suffering the consequence of sin is a powerful reminder when temptation arises again.

God indicates that he treats people in different ways at different times of their lives. In a famine, a war, a natural disaster, or when fighting cancer, life may be traumatic and seemingly out of control without God's hand of compassion, but in God's own time there will be a day for human accountability and a divine response of grace or further judgment. Although no one can predict or second guess God's timing, it is possible to know how God frequently responds to people who have loved him and have responsibly carried out his will, as well as how he usually responds to those who do just the opposite. Rejecting God's instruction in his covenant (42:21,24) can bring on God's disciplinary wrath (42:15,17,22,24). But all hope is not lost when that first disciplinary action occurs, for God has the power to redeem the people he has created and loves (43:3–4). He has the power to open people's blind eyes to his truth; he has the ability to guide them through the trials of life and he has promised not to forsake those he has chosen (42:16). The believer can rest assured that eventually God will gather his people who are called by his name from all the corners of the earth (43:5–6) through his acts of redemption. This is not a universal promise of hope to all people or even all Hebrew people; it is a glorious expectation that will apply only to those who are called by his name. Then his people will fulfill their original purpose of glorifying God's name (43:7).

But people should not trust God simply because of the good things that may happen today or tomorrow. He should be loved and followed because he is the Almighty God who controls this world; he is holy, he is man's Redeemer, and he is trustworthy to do what he promises. God has chosen a people to be his own people; these are the people he loves and will redeem from their own blindness and sinfulness (43:1). He made them; he will be their Savior; he will gather them together; and he will fulfill his purposes through them. Through all these events God will bring great glory to himself (43:7). The need in the past and today is for everyone to remove the blindness from their eyes, to realize who this great God is, to recognize the need for his redemption, to understand his wonderful plan for humanity, and then to honor God by following his divine instructions and serving him. There is no need to fear the trials of this life when God is on your side, for his promises will be fulfilled.

(2) Fear Not, the Blind Will Be Delivered and Forgiven (43:8–44:5)

The paragraphs in this section are less dependent on each other, but they are held together by the common idea that God will intervene on behalf of his blind people to save them (43:8,10; 44:9,18). He is God, the Holy One, the Creator, the Redeemer, Israel's King, and the powerful one who will defeat Babylon (43:11,14–15). In spite of the fact that his own people are sinful blind servants (43:8,22–24), they can expect God to wipe out their transgressions, pour out his blessings, and give them his name (43:18–20,25; 44:3–5). This message picks up from the previous paragraphs' vocabulary of "blindness" (*ʿiwwēr* cf. 42:16,18–19 and 43:8), God's "servant" (42:19; 43:10), "I am God" (43:3,11,12,15), "gathering" (43:5,9), and "understanding" (*yādaʿ*, 42:16,25; 43:10), so the first paragraph in this next series of oracles fits the general contextual framework of the preceding speeches.

GENRE. The assembling of people to serve as witnesses (43:9–10,12) suggests that 43:8–15 may be imitating certain characteristics of a trial speech, though it is not as clearly presented as in 41:21–29. Nations are gathered together for this event and witnesses are called to testify; the aim of this interrogation is to determine who is right, and in the end a verdict is pronounced. Nevertheless, as H. C. Spykerboer properly maintains, "the main thrust in the passage is not a trial of the nations, but the self-revelation of Yahweh."[386] What is unique about this legal imagery is that both Israelite witnesses and people from the nations are summoned in order that they might come to know who God is.[387] Thus it is a stretch to suggest that the legal language and imagery actually depict a trial.

There is no agreement among commentators about how one should treat the brief reference to the fall of Babylon in 43:14–15. J. Blenkinsopp understands the defeat of Babylon as a message of hope for an Israelite audience (he includes it with the following paragraph), but K. Baltzer puts 43:14–15 with the first paragraph (43:8–15) because of the catchword connecting it to the preceding verses.[388] This appears to be the best solution to this difficult paragraph, for 43:15 repeats the same conception of God that is present in 43:10–13.

The proclamation of salvation in 43:16–21 includes a reminder of God's past deliverance of his people in the exodus events as a proof of his redeeming power, but its real aim is to point to a greater work of God when he will marvelously transform nature in the future. One must stretch the evidence to conclude that this is "a promise of a new exodus, i.e., the return from Babylon to the promised land,"[389] for there is no reference to people returning to the land of Israel. This text describes God's glorious transformation of nature in the eschatological era. These themes are verbally interlinked with similar eschatological

---

[386] Spykerboer, *Structure and Composition of Deutero-Isaiah*, 103–104, bases this on the fact that the nations do not speak. Only God speaks, and he is actually addressing Israel. Goldingay and Payne, *Isaiah 40–55*, 1:282 agree, stating that this section "as a whole is not a court scene but a manifold attempt at the conversion of Israel."

[387] Melugin, *Formation of Isaiah 40–55*, 110, makes this significant observation. This trial's purpose is to bring people to a place of faith where they believe (43:10).

[388] Seitz, "Isaiah 40–66," 376, and Baltzer, *Deutero-Isaiah*, 161, 168, rely on common words in both sections (redeem, Holy One of Israel, I am the Lord) and understand vv. 14–15 as the culmination of the trial, while Blenkinsopp, *Isaiah 40–55*, 226–27, finds a connection between the defeat of Babylon and God's victory over his enemies at the time of the exodus. Childs, *Isaiah*, 336, also puts vv. 14–15 with 43:14–21 because vv. 14–15 and 16–19 "offer two summarizing promises in the form of specific announcements." Melugin, *Formation of Isaiah 40–55*, 110, maintains that vv. 14–15 is in effect a salvation speech.

[389] Schoors, *I Am God Your Savior*, 94, takes this approach to interpreting these verses.

passages (35:1–2), so they should be interpreted similar to the way they were understood in 41:17–20. The lesson the Israelite audience should hear is that if God can completely make something new, like his eschatological transformation of nature, certainly God can be trusted to solve all of the people's present problems.

The third paragraph (43:22–28) is a mixture of accusations concerning Israel's sinfulness (43:22–24,27), plus a statement of judgment and forgiveness. Because of the exilic setting assumed by R. Melugin and A. Schoors and the legal terminology in 43:26, both commentators call this unit a "trial speech."[390] Although there is some legal vocabulary in 43:26, in light of the strong accusations against God's people, it seems better to hypothesize that this message is a judgment speech with a typical accusation of sin (43:22–24) and an announcement of punishment that includes an offer of forgiveness, if the people repent (43:26–28, somewhat similar to 1:18–20).

This long literary unit ends with a salvation oracle (44:1–5; similar to 43:1–7) that reassured the people of Israel that they need not fear, for they are God's chosen servants who belong to him and have his name. It has the typical: (a) self-identifications, (b) statements of assurance, (c) reason for assurance, and (d) promise.[391] In spite of the nation's sins, there is forgiveness and hope for those who belong to the Lord.

STRUCTURE. The structure of the whole literary unit is heavily dependent on the genre identifications made above, though the creativity of the prophet in revising and recreating these traditional forms of speech into new creations is evident at many points. These adjustments make it difficult to provide a traditional form-critical analysis of these messages. These problems have caused some confusion concerning the division between the first and second paragraph, since both 43:14,16 have introductory phrases announcing new words from God. The judgment imagery in 43:14–15 does not fit with the themes of God's deliverance and transformation of nature in 43:16–21, so it must fit with the preceding verses.[392] The reference to the "former things" in both paragraphs (43:9,18) draws these two paragraphs together,[393] and the defeat of Babylon primarily functions as a proof of the superiority of Judah's God over all other nations.

The accusations against Israel for inappropriate worship through sacrifices marks the beginning of a new paragraph in 43:22–28, and the end of this judgment

---

[390] Melugin, *Formation of Isaiah 40–55*, 115–16, and Schoors, *I Am God Your Savior*, 190–91, both assume the people are complaining against God and God is defending himself.

[391] Conrad, "The 'Fear not' Oracles in Second Isaiah," 143–51, outlines these as the key characteristics of the "fear not" salvation oracles.

[392] Westermann, *Isaiah 40–66*, 120, and Baltzer, *Deutero-Isaiah*, 161–62, include vv. 14–15 with what precedes, while Goldingay and Payne, *Isaiah 40–55*, 1:290–91, and Oswalt, *Isaiah 40–66*, 151–53, make vv. 14–15 the first part of 43:14–21.

[393] Melugin, *Formation of Isaiah 40–55*, 112, notes the double use of ראשׁנות plus the regular pattern of following trial speeches with salvation oracles in these chapters.

speech is marked by God's decision to punish his people for their sins. Isaiah 44:1 introduces the final salvation oracle with its contrastive "but now . . . this is what the LORD says," almost identical to the beginning of the salvation oracle in 43:1. The beginning of the following large literary unit in 44:6 is marked by an introductory clause announcing another new word from God. On the basis of this analysis the material within this unit can be structured into four paragraphs:

You are witnesses that there is no other God   43:8–15
God's deliverance transforms life   43:16–21
Burdensome worship brings judgment   43:22–28
Fear not, God's servants belong to him   44:1–5

YOU ARE WITNESSES THAT THERE IS NO OTHER GOD (43:8–15)

8Lead out those who have eyes but are blind,
    who have ears but are deaf.
9All the nations gather together
    and the peoples assemble.
Which of them foretold this
    and proclaimed to us the former things?
Let them bring in their witnesses to prove they were right,
    so that others may hear and say, "It is true."
10"You are my witnesses," declares the LORD,
    "and my servant whom I have chosen,
so that you may know and believe me
    and understand that I am he.
Before me no god was formed,
    nor will there be one after me.
11I, even I, am the LORD,
    and apart from me there is no savior.
12I have revealed and saved and proclaimed—
    I, and not some foreign god among you.
You are my witnesses," declares the LORD, "that I am God.
13Yes, and from ancient days I am he.
No one can deliver out of my hand.
    When I act, who can reverse it?"

14This is what the LORD says—
    your Redeemer, the Holy One of Israel:
"For your sake I will send to Babylon
    and bring down as fugitives all the Babylonians,
    in the ships in which they took pride.
15I am the LORD, your Holy One,
    Israel's Creator, your King."

The reference to God as a "Savior" (*môšî'a*) in 43:11 picks up the same theme from the previous paragraph (43:3), while the calling of the deaf and

blind in 43:8 continues the same themes in 42:16,18–19. Elsewhere the prophet uses legal language in speeches against the nations (41:1–7,21–24) or Israel
(50:1–3), but the legal language in this message is unusual in that it addresses
both Israel and indirectly the nations. This paragraph can be divided into four
parts.

An invitation for people to present their testimony	43:8–9
The appointment of "my servant" as God's witness	43:10a
The conclusion: "I act; I am God"	43:10b–13
God will act to destroy Babylon	43:14–15

43:8–9 Because of God's denunciation of other gods and his strong claims
to divinity, this paragraph is somewhat reminiscent of the legal language concerning the nations and their gods in 41:1–7. The main audience is Israel, God's
servant (the "you" in 43:10,12), but the action appears to involve the gathering
of both Israel and the nations to verify who really is the superior supernatural
power. When God calls for the blind to come forward,[394] he is calling for his
disobedient servant Israel (as in 42:16,18–19) to give their testimony. Although
the verb "lead out, bring out, come forward" (*hôṣî'*) is sometimes used in reference to bringing people out of bondage (42:6), there is nothing in the context
of this verse that would suggest or imply such a meaning here.[395] The problem
here is moral and theological blindness not captivity; so someone is exhorted
to bring out people from Israel to testify, parallel to the "gathering together" of
the nations in the next verse. The people of Israel who come to testify have eyes
and ears, but neither the eyes or the ears seems to be of any practical value,
for they do not enable this blind servant to understand God's true nature or to
believe in God (43:10; 6:10). Since they still have eyes and ears there is the
possibility of seeing, if they will only use their eyes and pay attention to what
they see and hear.

In 43:9 the second party gathered for these proceedings is "all the nations,"
similar to the nations that were participants in the proceedings in 41:1–7,21–
24. The dilemma that God puts before his audience should not be viewed as
an abstract hypothetical philosophical inquiry about ultimate reality or a hypothetical question about different theoretical ideas; instead, he was asking them
about the practical issues of life and the claims of the different supernatural
powers.

---

[394] The verb הוֹצִיא could be a *hiphil* perfect "he caused to go out," but based on the introductory use of imperatives to start the speeches in 42:1,21 the form is more likely an imperative "bring
forth." The Old Greek reads ἐξήγαγον, "I brought forth," and 1QIs^a has a first pers. sg. verb, so
these are witnesses to another textual tradition but without strong enough evidence to require a
change in the existing Hebrew text.
[395] North, *Second Isaiah*, 122, refers to bringing out "the captives whose sight has been im-
paired by long confinement in darkness (xlii., 18–22)."

In the question in 43:9b (beginning with "who" *mî;* NIV "which") God asks the participants to identify who can[396] foretell "this"[397] that now exists and who can describe how past events (the "former things" *ri'šōnôt*) explain the present things. This is essentially the same kind of question that was raised previously in 41:2–3,22–23,26. The "which of them (pl)" probably refers to the gods[398] (48:14) that the nations worship, though at this point they are not mentioned explicitly. The challenge is to bring forward competent witnesses that can testify so that[399] the claims of these gods can prove to everyone that they speak the truth and are reliable (*'emet,* "it is true").

Witnesses from among the foreign nations should stand up to inform "us," presumably God and his Israelite witnesses. As in 41:23, it appears that there is no one to witness on behalf of the other gods in this rhetorical debate. The absence of any witness should encourage the Israelite audience to look with great skepticism at the claims of those who bragged so much about the great power of their gods.

43:10a God does have witnesses that can testify to what he has said and done. Using the emphatic pronoun, God indicates in a verbless clause that "you, yourselves [*'atem*] are [implied] my witnesses," meaning the Israelites. Even though God's witnesses are ironically rather blind, their identity as divinely ordained witnesses is emphatically affirmed. They have heard what Moses and the prophets said would happen, and they know that these predictions did come true. God himself has appointed them to this task. They were chosen for this reason as Gen 12:3 suggests. Isaiah 42:19 indicates that God's blind servant is "the messenger I send," implying that they are to tell others about God.

Why were the Israelites chosen to be God's servants and witnesses? God answered that he chose them "so that[400] [they] may know and believe me," a response that focuses on Israel's own personal relationship with God as a fundamental goal of God's involvement with them. This included a personal recognition of God's divine sovereign power, plus a firm commitment to accept his will and to faithfully follow his guidance. This response of "belief"[401] was fundamentally based on understanding and accepting the idea that "I am he"

---

[396] The imperfect יַגִּיד probably is a modal subjunctive (GKC §107t, especially in questions) that addresses the ability to accomplish something; thus the translation is "who can tell."

[397] The antecedent of the word זֹאת "this" is not defined in the Hebrew text. Whybray, *Isaiah 40–66,* 84, thinks "this" refers to contemporary events, but then he specifically identifies "this" to mean the deeds of Cyrus, implying a postexilic setting. Baltzer, *Deutero-Isaiah,* 164, hypothesizes a dramatic situation in which the prophet is holding a prophetic scroll which is the "this" in the dialogue. It is impossible to specify what "this" refers to in this verse; possibly it means "something like this," that is, a former or future event.

[398] Koole, *Isaiah III, Volume 1, Isaiah 40–48,* 305, finds this theme of challenging "them" (בָּהֶם), the idol gods, to tell the future in the trial speech in 41:22–23,26 and 44:7.

[399] וְיִצְדְּקוּ probably introduces a final clause, "so that" (GKC §165a).

[400] לְמַעַן "in order that" introduces a purpose or final clause (GKC §165b) which often is translated in the subjunctive mood (GKC §107q-r).

[401] The verb וְתַאֲמִינוּ comes from אָמַן "he stood firm, sure" which will result in "confirming,

(*ănî hû'*) or "I am that one" who can be known and who is worthy of trust. Knowing about God or understanding something about God is not an end in itself. Instead, understanding God naturally leads to a personal acknowledgment of his presence and action, and this naturally leads to the creation of a firm personal relationship of trust.

43:10b–13 What then can one conclude based on the evidence of this inquiry? What is the verdict or conclusion one must come to? God presents a strong claim based on the logical fact that there were no divine beings that were formed by craftsmen before God.[402] It is also correct to say that no real gods will come to power after the God of Israel; thus none of the idols of the nations are equal or comparable with the God of Israel. This does not imply that God was formed like the wooden idols; it merely indicates that all the idol images that were formed by human craftsmen appeared on the scene long after God's creation and sovereign control of the universe was well established. God does not go on to classify these carved idols that claim to have supernatural powers, but the implication might be that they must be inconsequential and based on false mythology and tradition. If this is so, they cannot really be considered in the same class as Yahweh, Israel's God. Yahweh is unique among all the supernatural beings (a) because one can know that he lives based on his spoken prediction and the fulfillment of his prophecies, (b) because one can have a real relationship of trust with God, and (c) because no other gods have these qualities.

43:11 These facts naturally lead to the emphatic conclusion that God announces: "I, even I, am the LORD."[403] This announcement proclaims that the Israelites had such a difficult time seeing (they were blind) and believing (firmly holding). Yahweh is the Israelite covenant God; he alone is Israel's "deliverer, savior" from their enemies. This exclusive formula (44:6; 45:6,21) does not address the issue of whether other gods exist. It strongly denies the thought that there are any other powers that had done anything to influence Israel's history in a positive way. The implication in earlier passages was that the Egyptian gods cannot help them (31:1–5) and that the Assyrian gods cannot hurt them (36:18–20). Long ago the exodus events illustrated how God acted on behalf of his people and demonstrated his saving ability over enemy forces that were much stronger than the Israelites (Exod 14–15). If it was true then that Israel's

---

establishing" something that is sure. One who stands firm on what God says "believes" what God says. A firm stance also relates to the idea of being "sure, faithful" and not wavering.

[402] This apparently is an ironic reference to the idols being formed by woodworkers and goldsmiths.

[403] The parallelisms between vv. 11 and 12 are abundant. Both begin with אָנֹכִי "I," and the second clause in each verse begins with וְאֵין "and there is no." E. J. Revell, "The Two Forms of First Person Singular Pronoun in Biblical Hebrew," *JSS* 40 (1995): 199–217, suggests there is some rhythm or reason for the use of the longer or shorter form of the pronoun (in prose the shorter form is used by higher rank people), but there is no similar explanation for usage in poetry.

God was a Savior (*môšîă'* "savior, deliverer") in the past, is not his saving quality still available for Israel when they are facing new armies and their gods?

43:12 To drive this persuasive point home even further, God declared that he was the one who demonstrated his power and reliability by speaking (about the future) and then "saving" (*hôša'tî*, same root as in 43:3,11) his people as he promised he would. The degree to which the second line repeats or advances the argument is difficult to determine. "I proclaimed" (lit. "I caused to hear" *wĕhišma'tî*) may go beyond the earlier announcement of what would happen and may include God's explanation of the significance of his actions or his proclamation of his deeds to others. No pagan god did this;[404] in fact, God defeated the gods of Egypt (he was proven more powerful) in the process of delivering his people (Exod 12:12). Since Israel experienced these things and knows them from their earlier biblical traditions, they now are able to function in the role of being firsthand eyewitnesses to God's great acts of salvation history (43:12b; 43:10). The telling of their story will only confirm God's real divine qualities.

43:13 The final claim may argue that God has demonstrated his divine sovereignty "from ancient days"[405] when he created the heavens and the earth, but a more literal translation would be "even from today" (HCSB "also from today"; NRSV "henceforth") which focuses on the people's present problems, or "even from today onward" with a glance toward what will happen in the future.[406] If a previous time was in view, the text would probably read "before today" (48:7; Ezek 48:25). Verse 12 legitimates God's claim to be the one true God by means of past revelation and his great salvific deeds, which the Israelites have witnessed; so 43:13 is God's affirmation that he will continue to show his divine power at this time and into the future. "I am he" or "I am that one"[407] declares his status as the power that should be identified with these actions. No army (neither Egyptian, Babylonian, or Assyrian) and no other gods have in the past or can in the future save them. When God decides to do something, no one can reverse what he plans to do. When God acts, who can stop him? No nation or foreign god can interfere with the completion of the sovereign will of Israel's Almighty God. These claims were intended to create

---

[404] In this context the cryptic Hebrew phrase זָר בָּכֶם וְאֵין "and there was not among you a stranger" probably refers to a strange pagan god. L. A. Snijders, "The Meaning of זר in the Old Testament," *OTS* 10 (1954): 1–54, discusses the semantic range and different contexts in which this word is used.

[405] The Aramaic Targum translation points in this direction, reading עלמא "forever" and the Old Greek has ἔτι ἀπ' ἀρχῆς, "from the beginning." Oswalt, *Isaiah 40–66*, 144, accepts the translation "from the beginning."

[406] The phrase יוֹם מִ גַּם lit. "even/also from a day" is ambiguous. Watts, *Isaiah 34–66*, 124, translates it "also from today (on)," and Koole, *Isaiah III, Volume 1, Isaiah 40–48*, 314, provides a future, "and also henceforth." יוֹם לִפְנֵי would refer to what happened "before today."

[407] The short verbless clause הוּא אֲנִי "I (am) he/that one" is a self-identifying clause. The second word could be the personal pronoun "he" or the identical demonstrative pronoun "that."

faith in the power of God so that the Israelites would trust God to deliver them from their enemies.

43:14–15 The conclusion of this message is a fresh word from God, introduced with "This is what the LORD says." It is closely tied to what precedes, for God has already claimed that there was no other Deliverer or Savior other than God himself (43:3,11,12,13). He is their Redeemer (43:1,3,14) and the Holy One (43:3,14,15) who acts on behalf of his people. Thus 42:14a and 15 seem to repeat much of what was already said in 43:3a,11. These defining traits identify God as distinct from all other gods, and they explain what he has done and will do for his people.

The destruction of Babylon in 43:14b proves God's divine ability to predict the future, and it demonstrates his great power. This much is clear, but unfortunately, it is best to admit that the meaning of v. 14b is still quite mysterious and shrouded by many hypothetical reconstructions. Far too many have guessed at its meaning by emending various words in the text and by quickly assuming that this passage refers to Cyrus's defeat of Babylon in 539 BC. Consequently, there is much confusion and several different ways of looking at its meaning and historical setting.

Although this is the first reference to Babylon since 39:7, the destruction of Babylon was announced earlier in chaps. 13–14 and 21:1–10; so this news of the fall of Babylon should not have surprised those who knew Isaiah's past preaching. Commentators do not agree on three main issues: (a) Some believe 43:14–15 should be connected to 43:8–13, while others prefer to put these verses with 43:16–21.[408] (b) It is very difficult to interpret the Hebrew text itself, for it does not flow smoothly. This suggests that it may have to be emended slightly in order for it to make sense. (c) Commentators do not agree on the date of Babylon's destruction predicted in this prophecy. Was the prophet referring to an Assyrian or a Persian defeat of Babylon?

43:14 C. Westermann interpreted God's statement "I will send to Babylon" as a reference to God sending Cyrus the Persian king to defeat Babylon in 539 BC, which is further explained in 45:1–2, but J. Blenkinsopp noticed that this description of the violent fall of Babylon was inconsistent with Cyrus's own account of a peaceful occupation of the city of Babylon.[409] Taking a different tact, J. Smart did not find any connection between this verse and Cyrus's defeat of Babylon and the Jewish return from exile, but interpreted it as an eschatological prophecy of God's defeat of all Israel's enemies (not just

---

[408] See the introduction to 43:8–15 for a discussion of this issue.

[409] Westermann, *Isaiah 40–66*, 125, says, "This refers beyond question to Cyrus's capture of Babylon." Blenkinsopp, *Isaiah 40–55*, 227, explains this inconsistency as "deliberate suppression" of the truth about the fall of Babylon. In spite of this fact, Blenkinsopp still maintains that this was about the fall of Babylon. He calls this "a dangerous delusion, a typical 'fantasy of the oppressed' . . . Yet on reflection, a subjugated people can be forgiven for not taking a detached and objective view of events."

Babylon).[410] A third alternative that might better fit the setting of the destruction of Babylon would place this prophecy in the general context of Sennacherib's attack on Judah. Hezekiah foolishly entertained the envoy from the Babylonian ruler Merodach-baladan in his palace in Jerusalem in order to form an alliance with him (39:1). He was hoping that Judah and Babylon could resist the power of the Assyrian army together. Isaiah condemned this false trust in political alliances (39:6–7). In conjunction with these events, Isaiah also predicted the violent fall of Babylon (chaps. 13–14; 22:1–10) which was probably fulfilled when Sennacherib violently destroyed the city in 689 BC.[411] Of course the audience and the prophet himself did not know when in the future this destruction of Babylon might happen. Since 41:11–12 and other references in this literary unit (41:2–3,25; 42:14,17,22,25; 43:3–4) make sense in the context of Sennacherib's attack on Judah, this historical setting might help explain the general time period of 43:14–15. At least it relieves the conflict of suggesting that this was Cyrus's conquest, for it appears that Cyrus had a friendly reception when he came to Babylon.

This message about the fall of Babylon communicated the theological conclusion that a king of Judah, a foreign alliance with Babylon, and the foreign Assyrian gods do not control history. History was in the hands of the holy and totally transcendent God of Israel. He was the One who had the power to act as "your Redeemer" because he was the "Holy One of Israel" (43:14a). Babylon did not and will not save Judah. God himself will marvelously act as a kinsman who will redeem his people ("for your sake"). This redemption did not happen because the Israelites earned some special reward, nor did they deserve some special treatment. Their redemption was completely an act of divine grace. God's future plans for Babylon's destruction will enable the Israelites to understand and experience the reality of God's presence and allow them to come to know him as their real Redeemer. Babylon cannot help them.

God's action was to "send[412] to Babylon," but the prophetic message does not specify who or what nation was being sent. This is because the main focus of this prophetic message is always on what God does, not on the identity of the human instrument he uses. It appears that there will be a military force that will defeat Babylon and produce fugitives, but the identity of this attacking army is not revealed. Several textual emendations have resulted from wrestling with what God will cause to "go down, bring down" (*hôradtî*) in v. 14b.

---

[410] J. D. Smart, *History and Theology in Second Isaiah: A Commentary of Isaiah 35, 40–66* (Philadelphia: Westminster, 1965), 105, essentially takes "Babylon" as a symbol, just like many others view the name Babylon in chap. 13.

[411] D. D. Luckenbill, *The Annals of Sennacherib* (Chicago: Oriental Institute, 1924), 78–79.

[412] Although the verb שְׁלַחְתִּי is a perfect, which often expresses past completed action, the prefect also can be used prophetically of something that will happen in the future (GKC §106m-n).

The Hebrew could be communicating that (a) the gate "bars" will be brought down, referring to opening the gates of the city (45:2); (b) their prison gates will go down, implying freedom from Babylon's power, and (c) J. L. Koole prefers to follow the Old Greek "fugitives" (as in NIV), which is spelled almost identical to "bars" (NRSV "break down the bars").[413] Each interpretation indicates the divine overpowering of Babylon using another military power, but these images never mention anything about the returning of any Jewish exiles.[414] It is the Babylonians who will be fugitives when someone attacks their land.

The last line of the verse is equally enigmatic, for it literally appears to say: "and the Chaldeans (Babylonians) in ships of their joyful shouting." One might view these ships as great shipping vessels that the Chaldeans boarded in order to escape from their enemies or ships they were forced into after they were defeated. The Chaldeans lived south of Babylon near the Persian Sea, so it would be natural for them to run away from the fighting in hopes of traveling in the boats they loved to shout and brag about (NIV). K. Baltzer slightly changes the text to read "lamentations" instead of "ships," so that the line describes how their shouting will be turned into lamentation (RSV),[415] but this seems an unlikely proposal. All interpretations of this verse are difficult, but the general sense is evident; the Babylonians will suffer defeat. It is possible that the bringing down of Babylon may refer to what Sennacherib did when he defeated the city in 689 BC. As J. Blenkinsopp observed, this violent description of events does not match what happened when Cyrus peacefully entered the city in 539 BC. The theological message to the prophet's audience is that God is sovereignly in control of all the powerful nations on earth; therefore, they can trust him to be their Redeemer and their God.

43:15 To impress the truthfulness and reliability of this prophecy on the minds of the audience, the prophet once again declares that the One who was making these claims about the future was God himself. "I am the LORD," the Holy transcendent divine One, who created Israel as his people in the first place; he is the King who rules the world that he created. The audience should accept these words as truth for God has the power and authority to accomplish what he plans to do.

---

[413] "Bars" בְּרִיחִם versus "fugitives" בָּרִיחִים (from בָּרַח "he fled"; cf. LXX φεύγοντας). בָּרִיחַ, "fugitive" occurs elsewhere only in Isa 15:5; 27:1. מִבְרָח, "fugitive" occurs only in Ezek 17:21.

[414] Muilenburg, "Isaiah 40–66," 5:493, summarizes the verse by saying that God "will liberate his people from captivity."

[415] Baltzer, *Deutero-Isaiah*, 161, changes בָּאֳנִיּוֹת "in ships" to בַּאֲנִיּוֹת "with lamentations." Oswalt, *Isaiah 40–66*, 150, refers to their "waiting ships." W. E. Barnes, "The Masoretic Reading of Isaiah 43,14," *JTS* 29 (1927–28): 252–55, refers to other possible solutions to the problems in this verse.

GOD'S DELIVERANCE TRANSFORMS LIFE (43:16–21)

¹⁶This is what the LORD says—
  he who made a way through the sea,
  a path through the mighty waters,
¹⁷who drew out the chariots and horses,
  the army and reinforcements together,
 and they lay there, never to rise again,
  extinguished, snuffed out like a wick:
¹⁸"Forget the former things;
  do not dwell on the past.
¹⁹See, I am doing a new thing!
  Now it springs up; do you not perceive it?
 I am making a way in the desert
  and streams in the wasteland.
²⁰The wild animals honor me,
  the jackals and the owls,
 because I provide water in the desert
  and streams in the wasteland,
 to give drink to my people, my chosen,
²¹the people I formed for myself
  that they may proclaim my praise.

The proclamation of salvation in the second paragraph outlines a part of God's plan of action that no one can reverse or stop. His eschatological plan is believable because he successfully carried out his past plans. This oracle has two parts:

God delivered Israel at the exodus	43:16–17
God's deliverance of Israel	16
God's defeat of the army	17
God will transform nature	43:18–21
Forget the past	18
God's new things	19–21

The introductory phrase (lit.) "thus says Yahweh" in 43:16 marks the beginning of the first subparagraph, while the imperative exhortation in v. 18 ("forget") indicates the beginning of the final group of verses. First, God is introduced using a series of participles about his past activities (43:16–17), then his future acts are described (43:18–21). If God has the power to overcome the power of the sea and the horses and chariots of their past enemies, surely he can transform the future by reversing the curses of the past and bringing water and blessing to his land and his people (43:18–21). In an earlier proclamation of salvation (41:17–20) there were similar promises about the transformation of nature and the restoration of fertility to the earth. These future promises all appear to have eschatological significance, so they should not be directly connected to the fall of Babylon discussed in 43:16–17.

43:16–17 A new thought and genre of literature is introduced by another messenger formula, announcing that God himself spoke these words. The prophet introduces God by reminding the audience of God's mighty power, his guidance of his people through the Red Sea, and his defeat of the mighty armies of Egypt. God's role as Redeemer, Creator of Israel, and King is legitimated based on his past action. Using participles (*hannôtēn, lit.,* "the one who gives/makes" in 43:16; *hammôṣî*ʾ, "the one who causes to go out," in 43:17) that are frequently used in hymns,[416] the text focuses attention on who God is and what he has done. The verse celebrates God's miraculous deliverance of his people through the waters (43:16; 51:10; 63:11; Exod 14:21–22,29; 15:8) as well as his total defeat of the horses and soldiers of the Egyptian army (43:17; Exod 14:23–28; 15:4–5,10). God influenced the mind of Pharaoh to cause him to chase after the Israelites (Exod 13:1–4) in order to bring even greater honor to his name and cause the Egyptians to finally admit that he is God. As a result of chasing the Israelites into the sea, thousands of Egyptians died and no longer were a threat to the Israelites.[417] These brave soldiers will never rise again to threaten Israel for their life was snuffed out (43:17b). This marvelous event caused God's covenant people at the time of the exodus to fear God and believe what he said (Exod 14:31). Remembering these ancient events should also give the audience the courage to trust in God's power to rescue them from their present danger and defeat the enemies that threatened them. Indeed, God can work in amazing ways to accomplish his plan; so no human should ever set limits on what God can do.[418]

43:18–21 This short proclamation of salvation focuses on God's final eschatological transformation of nature.[419] It is appropriate for the audience to put their trust in God's past action like creation and the exodus, for these traditions and historical claims strongly support the prophet's theological position that God can be believed (43:10), for he does what he says he will do. These facts should never be ignored or set aside, for they provide assurances about God's character (46:9). But the prophet exhorts[420] his listeners not to allow just God's former

---

[416] Spykerboer, *The Structure and Composition of Deutero-Isaiah*, 107, concludes that the author was quoting a hymn.

[417] The verbs יִשְׁכְּבוּ and יָפֹמוּ are both imperfects which suggest a future translation, "they will lie down and they will not arise," but this is difficult because the prophet is describing a past event and because these two words are followed by two perfect verbs in the next clause which verify that the Egyptian army was extinguished. Apparently, the author was communicating the idea that the Egyptians "are continuing to lie down (present tense) and will not rise (future tense)" to emphasize the completeness of God's defeat of the enemies of Israel (GKC §106h for present tense usage).

[418] During the Assyrian crisis when Judah was hopelessly outnumbered and without any hope God surprised everyone by killing 185,000 Assyrian troops in one night, demonstrating that he still is Israel's Redeemer and still King over all the kings of this earth.

[419] Oswalt, *Isaiah 40–66*, 154, considers this a quotation reminding the audience of what he has already said.

[420] אַל תִּזְכְּרוּ "do not remember" is a mild request (GKC §109c) that expresses a wish; it is not a strong prohibition, for the prophet himself frequently refers to past events to support his teachings.

miraculous deeds[421] (the exodus in 43:16–17) to influence their faith decisions, for God is still alive and can be trusted to direct the future history of his people.

The future will involve God doing a new creative thing[422] that will far surpass anything accomplished in the past (43:19). The new thing is described as something that "springs up" (*tiṣmāḥ*) suddenly, just like the desert plants that surprisingly sprout in a completely barren area after a rain. Almost in astonishment the prophet rhetorically asks his audience, "do you not perceive it," implying that they should.[423]

This new thing that God will accomplish includes the transformation of dry deserts into areas that are blessed with water.[424] With a figurative poetic flare the prophet views all of nature praising and glorifying God for providing the water of life for the animals as well as the chosen people of Israel. In that new eschatological era (35:1–7; 41:18–20) God will care for his people by preparing the way before them (35:8),[425] just as he guided his people as they traveled through the desert after they left Egypt (Exod 13:21–22). This passage says nothing about "returning" to the "land of Israel" by "exiles," instead it emphasizes the reversal of the covenant curses on the land (Deut 27–28) and God's provision of life-giving water. God's transformation of life will include more than just a new physical environment; it will also have great spiritual significance. This water may appear simply to be physical water at first, but if the acceptance of God's provision of water has anything to do with the people praising God (43:21), then Koole suggests that the water of God may be a metaphorical reference to a source of spiritual renewal.[426] The paragraph

---

[421] In this context the "former things" רָאשֹׁנוֹת must refer to the exodus from Egypt. Whybray, *Isaiah 40–66*, 76, suggests in 42:9 that the former things refer to the earlier acts of Cyrus.

[422] הִנְנִי עֹשֶׂה "behold, I am doing" draws the subject of the participle "I" from the first pers. pronominal suffix on the word "behold" (GKC §147b). Watts, *Isaiah 34–66*, 135, relates these new things to the Persian power over Babylon and the return of the Israelites through the dry desert back to Judah. Although this was a great deed of divine deliverance, the text does not specify those events. It seems more appropriate to understand 43:18–21 as describing eschatological conditions in the distant future, not the return from exile in the near future.

[423] The imperfect verb (תֵדָעוּהָ) must have present significance rather than future, implying that they can now perceive through the eyes of faith what God will do in the future based on God's words to Isaiah. The rhetorical question introduced by הֲלֹא "do not?" implies "surely you do." The effect is to communicate that this is absolutely true (GKC §150e).

[424] For the phrase "streams in the wasteland" in 43:19b, 1QIsᵃ has "the desert into a path" to match the parallelism of the previous line "in the wilderness a way." These two words are not similar, so there is no minor confusion of letters in this case. Verse 20 has a similar reading, but "in the wilderness water, in the desert rivers" preserves good parallelism. North, *Second Isaiah*, 125, prefers the DSS reading.

[425] Koole, *Isaiah III, Volume 1, Isaiah 40–48*, 332, believes this refers to the road the exiles took as they returned from Babylon, but the interlinking vocabulary in 35:1–10 argue for the transformation of nature at the end of time. There is also no report in the postexilic books of Ezra, Nehemiah, or Haggai that God fulfilled this prophecy and transformed the deserts when the Israelites returned from Babylon.

[426] Ibid., 332, 336, believes "42:16 also talks about a spiritual renewal" and "that the 'water'

ends with the chosen people whom[427] God formed praising him (43:21b), just like the rest of nature. God originally formed nature and his people to honor him,[428] and now at last they will fulfill their original purpose as God miraculously brings about a new situation on earth. Based on verses like this, it is appropriate to conclude that one of the purposes for creating each person today is so that each one can honor and praise God.

BURDENSOME WORSHIP BRINGS JUDGMENT (43:22–28)

> [22]"Yet you have not called upon me, O Jacob,
>> you have not wearied yourselves for me, O Israel.
> [23]You have not brought me sheep for burnt offerings,
>> nor honored me with your sacrifices.
> I have not burdened you with grain offerings
>> nor wearied you with demands for incense.
> [24]You have not bought any fragrant calamus for me,
>> or lavished on me the fat of your sacrifices.
> But you have burdened me with your sins
>> and wearied me with your offenses.
>
> [25]"I, even I, am he who blots out
>> your transgressions, for my own sake,
>> and remembers your sins no more.
> [26]Review the past for me,
>> let us argue the matter together;
>> state the case for your innocence.
> [27]Your first father sinned;
>> your spokesmen rebelled against me.
> [28]So I will disgrace the dignitaries of your temple,
>> and I will consign Jacob to destruction
>> and Israel to scorn.

C. Westermann calls this a trial speech because of the legal language in 43:26, but most of the trial speeches are against the foreign nations and their gods; therefore, he concludes that 43:22–24 has the flavor of a disputation and the modified trial form only begins in 43:26.[429] This approach assumes or imagines that the prophet is speaking to an exilic audience that has a complaint against God. Westermann hypothesizes that the Israelites claim that they have faithfully served God (though this is never stated in the text), but God has

---

and the 'way' connote spiritual salvation." Thus the new order God will introduce is not the return of his people to the land; it is a return of the people to God.

[427] זוּ is used as a relative pronoun (instead of אֲשֶׁר) in the accusative "whom" (GKC §138g) since the retrospective pronoun on לִי is the object of a pronoun (GKC §138b).

[428] יְצַרְתִּי לִי "I formed for myself" indicates the special function his people had. They were created "for God" so that they might proclaim his praise.

[429] Westermann, *Isaiah 40–66*, 131, reads this dispute into the text, but it is not there on the surface of what was said. This makes his whole assessment of the oracle somewhat suspect.

destroyed his people by sending them into exile (43:28). If this is the situation, God is now defending his action by explaining that the nation's sinfulness caused him to bring judgment on them years earlier. This interpretation of these verses is necessary because, if the people are already in exile, it would be pointless for God to accuse them of not offering him sacrifices at that time, for the temple was already destroyed and sacrifices had stopped long ago.

Instead of hypothesizing a disputation beginning in 43:26 like Westermann or interjecting into the passage an unstated hypothetical complaint against God, it is better to view this message as a judgment oracle with a typical accusation of sin (43:22–24) and an announcement of punishment (43:26–28). The Israelites did not declare God's glory or praise him in their worship as God had wished (43:21); therefore, he "will profane, pollute" (*wa'ăhallēl*, "disgrace," NIV) their sanctuary at some point in the future. The frequent address to "you" (pl.) suggests that the prophet was speaking to an audience that was at present offering sacrifices, not about the failures of their fathers in a past generation.[430] If the present audience was sacrificing, then the prophet was speaking in preexilic times before the pollution of the sanctuary (43:28). These accusations and the call to enter into judgment sound somewhat similar to the accusations in 1:1–20. They are also similar to the accusation in 29:13 that the people were not truly honoring God. The ideal goal of this prophetic message would be for the people in this Israelite audience to admit their sin and for God to forgive them (43:25). If this would happen, peace could be established between the parties. If the audience would not be willing to confess their guilt, judgment will be necessary (43:28).

The structural organization of this paragraph has three aspects.

Accusation of worthless worship	43:22–24
Offer that God can forgive sins	43:25–26
Announcement of judgment	43:27–28

The paragraph begins and ends with references to Jacob/Israel and is held together by repeated terms ("wearied" from *yāga'* in 22,23,24; "burdened" from *'ābad* in 23,24) and a long series of negative clauses in vv. 22–24 (beginning with *lō'* "no, not") that contrast what "you" the people have not done, with what "I" God have not done.[431] A number of repeated terms also connect this oracle to the one before it.[432]

43:22–24 J. L. Koole follows the frequent interpretation that the modern interpreter must read into the text an unstated accusation against God by the Is-

---

[430] If he was talking about their fathers, he would have referred to "them," not you.

[431] B. L. Smith, "The Significance of Catchwords in Isaiah 43:22–28," *Colloquium* 15 (1982): 21–30, highlights the significant way the author uses words that apply to Judah and then uses them in a different way in the mouth of God. These interlinking verbal factors suggest that this is a carefully thought-out unified message.

[432] Isaiah 43:20 and 23 speak of honoring God; the former/first things are mentioned in 43:18 and 27; and remembering in 43:18,25,26.

raelites; thus, one is able to interpret 43:22 as God's refutation of the supposed Israelite complaint. Their perspective was that they merited God's protection and did not deserve exile because over the years they had consistently sacrificed to him.[433] It is always dangerous to interpret a text based on imaginary material that is not found in the text, so it seems much simpler to read this message as God making a straightforward accusation against his chosen people (not a defense against a false complaint) because they were not truly worshipping him. God is warning them of what will happen in the future if they do not change. Israel's sinfulness and blindness are repeatedly mentioned, so these prophetic accusations should be interpreted as part of an evangelistic appeal to convince the people in his audience that they need to confess their sins so that God can forgive them. This understanding of the judgment oracle, with its offer of forgiveness, is quite different from the more negative approach that finds God defending his actions to a group of complainers.

43:22 The initial accusation claims that (lit.) "not on me [emphasized by its position in the Hebrew sentence] did you call," suggesting that the praise and prayers of the people were not offered up to God (48:1).[434] They did not "seek the Lord while he may be found, call upon him while he is near" (55:6). Apparently they did what was technically required by the sacrificial system, even when it did not mean much to them. This is consistent with other passages dealing with their sacrifices in 1:10–11 and 29:13. Instead of restoring their relationship to God, they wearied him (NIV "you have not wearied yourselves for me"),[435] probably because of the countless rituals they repeated Sabbath after Sabbath and year after year. The whole idea of following all the instruction of covenantal law and the details of the sacrificial law probably seemed overwhelming and meticulous to some. By focusing on the ritual the people forgot about the freedom that God's forgiveness could bring to those who had a personal relationship with God. Apparently some people did not see these Levitical instructions as guidelines that they loved to do (Ps 119:105) or viewed them as exercises that brought

---

[433] Koole, *Isaiah III, Volume 1, Isaiah 40–48*, 336, as well as Schoors, *I Am God Your Savior*, 191, takes this approach. Goldingay and Payne, *Isaiah 40–55*, 1:306, hypothesize that the complaint of Israel was "we called on you and you have not responded."

[434] One could hypothesize that they called on the name of other gods, though that problem is not raised in this paragraph. This interpretation is rejected by Seitz, "Isaiah 40–66," 379, who suggests that the real problem was "improper, overloaded offerings," but this is probably being read in from 1:10–15. Another option is that they were using the name Yahweh when they sacrificed, but the sinfulness of their hearts prevented their prayers from coming to God (cf. 59:1–2). The formality of the ritual of the sacrificial system may have interfered with a real heart relationship with God.

[435] The preposition בִּי would usually be translated "with me," or "on account of me." NIV reads "for me" and NASB, HCSB, NRSV "of me," but usually the preposition בְּ does not express a genitive. NIV wrongly interprets the negative in the first clause as also serving the second clause (the Old Greek does have a negative in this clause, but it changes the meaning and makes God the subject of the verb in the second line). Since the negative לֹא was repeated in the second clause in both vv. 23–24, its absence here is significant.

them closer to God. Lacking a personal covenant relationship with God, their religious activities were merely formal activities of required obedience and not true expressions of a heart overflowing with love and joy.

43:23 This problem of not honoring God in worship exhibited itself in sacrificial activities at the temple. God's accusation that the people did not bring sacrifices cannot refer to the lack of sacrifices while the people were in Babylonian exile, for God allowed the temple to be destroyed and did not expect sacrifices to be offered if there was no temple.[436] The people did bring sheep to sacrifice in the preexilic period (1:11–13), but the burnt offerings that were supposed to be a pleasing aroma to God (Lev 1:9,13,17) did not bring any glory to God. This condemnation of their wearisome heartless worship is consistent with other preexilic prophetic announcements that God would not accept the sacrifices of sinful people (Amos 5:21–25; Hos 5:6; 6:6; Mic 6:6–8; Jer 7:22). These criticisms do not mean that God rejects all cultic worship at the temple. He commanded his people to worship him through the use of sacrifices (Lev 1–5). What God rejected was the sacrifices of people who did not turn from their sins. Their sacrifices were meaningless and a wearisome burden for him to bear (1:10–15).

The purpose of God's sacrificial instructions was not to enslave his people (43:23b), but to enable them to serve[437] him free from the guilt of their sins. It was an exalted position to be God's specially chosen servants; this was not intended to be a burden that wearied the people with heavy demands of incense offerings of frankincense. The prophet was not saying that God made no demands on his people or that he did not care how they worshipped him. God cared about their worship because the positive impact of the sacrificial system was tied to the symbolic nature of their understanding of the ritual. Their involvement with various rituals brought to mind key principles of salvation that were illustrated in the ritual.[438] The ritual was not an automatic mechanism for getting a reward from God but presented an opportunity to internalize and experience the theological principle illustrated in concrete action. When the

---

[436] Motyer, *Isaiah*, 338, argues that the people were always bringing sacrifices in the preexilic period and that God would not condemn them for not sacrificing during the exilic period when the temple was in ruins. He believes they became enslaved by their mindless repetitious acts and the wearisomeness of performing the same ritual. Thus the freedom of forgiven sins was not experienced, and the people did not enjoy the restoration of their relationship with God. In contrast, Goldingay, *Message of Isaiah 40–55*, 219–22, believes the problem is that the people did not bring God any sacrifices while they were in exile. But these accusations do not just say that the people brought nothing. Rather they did not honor God with what they brought and did not satisfy God's holy demands with what they brought. How could they weary God with sacrifices if they didn't bring any sacrifices?

[437] The verb עָבַד can mean anything from a positive idea of "serving" to a rather negative idea of "enslavement."

[438] An animal would have to die representing the principle that the wages of sin is death, that without the shedding of blood there is no remission of sin, and that a pure substitute could take one's place (e.g., Rom 6:23; Heb 9:22; 2 Cor 5:21).

real purpose and meaning of the ritual was ignored, the joyful service of worship could quickly turn into a dreadful performance of enslaving burdens. This perversion of the sacrificial system was not God's doing, but the result of the people twisting God's plan.

43:24 The essential relationship between God and his people did not revolve around the physical act of purchasing expensive fragrant cane[439] and giving God the best fatty portions that he desired (43:24a).[440] God's forgiveness was not based on how much a person could impress him with the size, value, or quantity of the sacrifices (Mic 6:6–8); God was primarily concerned about the heart attitude of the worshipper. Why were they coming? Did their action express a humble and contrite heart (Ps 51:17)? Was their focus on restoring their relationship with God and dedicating themselves to his service? True and acceptable worship must honor and glorify God; it dare not sink into self-service, manipulation, or an attempt to earn God's favor.

Instead of bringing what God wanted, the Israelites "enslaved" and "wearied, burdened, brought labor to" God (contrast the use of the same verbs in v. 23b) with their sinfulness. The weight of sin was not removed by these sacrificial gifts; the weight just continued to grow and grow. The sacrificial system was intended as a symbolic ceremony that would help the people think through the principles of atonement of sins so that they would be forgiven (43:25; Lev 5:10,13,16,18) and their sins would be removed as far as the east is from the west (Ps 103:12).

43:25 Suddenly the attention turns from the terrible failures of the Israelites to what God himself wants do about this situation. In bold contrast to what has preceded, God declares to his wayward children that it is not the sacrifice but he himself who wants to wipe out[441] their sins. The forgiveness of sin is a prerequisite for worship and fellowship with God (59:1–2). God freely offers atonement for sin for those who confess and turn from their sins. The sacrificial system was designed to encourage people to confess their sins and be forgiven. Only then would God not be burdened by their sins but could forget them and bury them in the deepest sea (Mic 7:18–19). Although it may not make much sense for God to blot out a person's sins and not hold him guilty for the evil done, such is the indescribable grace of God that is born out of his amazing love. He forgives because of who he is. He desires to be reconciled with his people so much that he makes the renewal of the God-man relationship possible. Being forgiven is not a thing that a person does; it is accomplished solely on account of God's merciful granting of complete freedom from guilt. In order to bring glory to God ("for my own sake" *lĕmaʿănî*), God will do what is not required, expected, or thought conceivable. He will completely blot out the

---

[439] There is a word play between "you bought" קָנִיתָ and "cane" קָנֶה.

[440] Isaiah 1:11 indicates that God had enough of the fat of their sacrifices.

[441] The verb is a participle מֹחֶה meaning God is the one who "blots out, dissolves, erases," like a disappearing mist (cf. 44:22). It reflects a situation that is the opposite of remembering sin.

problem of sin that separates himself from his people. Isaiah 52:13–53:12 will deal with this issue in more detail.

43:26 The problem with the people of Israel was that many had not confessed their sins and received forgiveness. Israel's past stubborn sinfulness and addiction to meaningless ritual interfered with their reception of God's offer to graciously forgive their sins. The question that remains is: Do these people want to reject their sinful past, to trust God completely, to receive God's forgiveness, and to serve God for the rest of their lives? Hypothetically, some Israelites might respond that they were innocent of any great sins and did not need God's help, but anyone who honestly examines their life must assess their past relationship with God and own up to the guilt of their sins. When the past is remembered (*hazkîrēnî*) and reviewed, the holiness of God will reveal the sin and convict the individual of his guilt (6:1–5). Both God and the sinner are involved in this reconciliation process "together" (*yāḥad*). But this coming together is not some sort of arguing or bargaining with God about one's guilt (cf. 1:18). God is not on trial, nor is there an open discussion of what can be defined as right or wrong. In the end, the sinner must declare where they stand in relationship to divine holiness. They must admit that they are sinners and confess their sins, so that they can enter a new relationship with God by being declared free of guilt.[442] The only other possibility is that they can choose to declare themselves innocent of sin and not willing to admit any wrong or guilt. But this will lead to God's holy judgment of them for their sins.

43:27–28 After this full explanation of the true source of forgiveness and this implied offer to completely blot out all their sin (43:25) so that they can stand in a just relationship with God (43:26), it is astonishing to read what happens next. There is no hint of repentance, no admission of guilt, and no acceptance of divine forgiveness. Instead, the nation's past sins are recalled, back to their ancient fathers (possibly Abram or Jacob) and the rebelliousness of past " arrogant spokesmen,"[443] a term that could refer to any important person (more likely a wicked priest, a false prophet, or evil king)[444] who led the people astray in their understanding of sin.

Since the people made no effort to turn from these evil ways, God announces in 43:28 that he "will profane/pollute"[445] (NIV "disgrace") the leaders of the holy place. This verb is an imperfect form, so it most likely refers to incomplete action that will happen in the future.[446] Therefore, one must conclude

---

[442] לְמַעַן תִּצְדָּק literally means "in order that you may be justified," which implies that the people will want to be justified before God and have their sins removed.

[443] The root לִיץ was connected to being a "big talker" by H. N. Richardson, "Some Notes on לִיץ and Its Derivatives," *VT* 5 (1955): 163–79. In the book of Proverbs this kind of person "boasts, mocks" (Prov 9:12), and this same idea is carried in Isa 28:22.

[444] Goldingay, *Message of Isaiah 40–55*, 225, claims that these "enigmatic 'mediators'" could include "Israel's leaders, kings, prophets and priests" who speak freely.

[445] The Aramaic Targum also treats this verb וַאֲחַלֵּל as a future imperfect.

[446] Oswalt, *Isaiah 40–66*, 157, maintains the Masoretic reading and translates the phrase "I will

that the temple was not polluted at the present time and that this message came before the exile of Judah. The leaders of the temple who will be profaned most likely refer to the high priest and other key officials (1 Chr 24:5), for they were responsible for the theological purity of what was taught in the temple and were mediators of God's forgiveness to the people. If the priests will be profaned and made unholy, they will no longer be able to offer sacrifices to a holy God (Lev 10:1–3). One can assume that the temple itself will also be desecrated and no longer fit for the worship of a holy God. This is implied in the final statement that indicates that God will inflict his chosen people with the curse of military destruction. Years earlier God set a holy war "ban" (*ḥ erem*, NIV "consign to destruction") on the Canaanites (Josh 6:17) that was to result in their utter extinction, but now God puts this ban of extinction on his own people. This appears to be a greater punishment than the plundering and looting described earlier in 42:22,24 and may point to the future destruction of the nation that took place when Nebuchadnezzar destroyed Jerusalem and its temple. These events will result in nations "scorning" (*giddûp*) and mocking of the Israelites and their God (Deut 28:37; 2 Kgs 9:7). This shame and national destruction was avoidable, if the people would only humble themselves and repent of their sins. Since they refused to come to God for forgiveness, the cost of their sin would be the death of their nation, the destruction of their holy place, and the defilement of their holy priests. The religious leaders were primarily responsible for failing to properly instruct their followers in God's ways, so the temple and its religious leaders will suffer greatly under the curse of a holy God.

This passage demonstrates that unacceptable worship and forgiveness are life and death issues. But the following paragraph assures the audience that God's plans for his people will not end with their punishment. God has future plans to save his people and transform them into those who truly are "my servants," those who gladly serve him and acknowledge their connection with the name of the Lord. Although everyone can rest assuredly that the future is securely in God's hands, the present destiny of every generation is partially in their own hands. Every reader of the prophet's words has the choice of responding to God's offer to forgive their sins. Although some may refuse to repent and consequently suffer under the curse of God's judgment, God's gracious offer of forgiveness is available for all who will confess their sins and determine to live a life that honors God.

---

profane." Baltzer, *Deutero-Isaiah*, 176, emends this verb and the next one from an imperfect with *waw* conjunctive to verbs with *waw* consecutives וָאֲחַלֵּל, thus giving a past tense meaning (the Old Greek translates these as past tense). Schoors, *I Am God Your Savior*, 196, drew the meaning of חָלַל from root II to mean "pierce, kill" because it provided a better parallel to having something under the ban and assigned to destruction. It would be far more acceptable for those who assume a past event to suggest that the imperfect verb could be used with a past significance than to change the text.

GOD'S SERVANTS BELONG TO HIM (44:1–5)

[1]"But now listen, O Jacob, my servant,
   Israel, whom I have chosen.
[2]This is what the LORD says—
   he who made you, who formed you in the womb,
   and who will help you:
 Do not be afraid, O Jacob, my servant,
   Jeshurun, whom I have chosen.
[3]For I will pour water on the thirsty land,
   and streams on the dry ground;
 I will pour out my Spirit on your offspring,
   and my blessing on your descendants.
[4]They will spring up like grass in a meadow,
   like poplar trees by flowing streams.
[5]One will say, 'I belong to the LORD';
   another will call himself by the name of Jacob;
 still another will write on his hand, 'The LORD's,'
   and will take the name Israel.

This oracle appears to combine features of the salvation oracle (44:1–2) and a proclamation of salvation in 44:3–5; thus it offers hope for God's chosen servants both in the near and far future.[447] It presents a stark contrast to the destruction announced in 43:22–28. The oracle begins and ends with references to God's people Jacob in 44:1 and 5. The paragraph starts with a call for the prophet's Israelite audience to pay attention (44:1) to a word of salvation from God so that the audience will not fear (44:2). Then 44:3–5 promises a new era of salvation based on the gift of God's Spirit. The results of God's blessing will be a transformation of nature so that a future generation of Hebrew children "will spring up" (44:4; 43:19 "springs up"). God's salvation is completely based on God's acts of choosing, helping, blessing, and naming.

This paragraph has the following structure:[448]

Identifications of God's chosen people	43:1
God's statements of assurance	43:2
Reasons for assurance	43:3
Results of God's transformation	43:4–5

44:1 The assurances of God's care for his people begin with an adversative "but now" (*wĕʿattâ* here and in 43:1), thus contrasting the present message of hope with the preceding curse of judgment (43:28). God reminds them that they are still "my servants." There is no hint of him completely relinquishing

---

[447] Goldingay and Payne, *Isaiah 40–55*, 1:320–21, also connect this oracle to the typical "fear not" oracle but find that its rationale in vv. 3–5 follows the pattern and content of the proclamation of salvation (as in 41:17–20).

[448] Conrad, "The 'Fear not' Oracles in Second Isaiah,"143–51, outlines the key characteristics of the "fear not" salvation oracles which come from a war setting.

his claims on the people of Jacob (as in 43:28). Israel is identified as God's nation by the fact that they were the people that God "chose" (*bāḥar*) to be a holy nation with which he would dwell (Exod 19:5–6). Their disobedience in 43:22–28 required discipline, but this does not mean that God has totally rejected them or wants to abandon his relationship with them.

44:2 Having identified his audience as "my servant" and "chosen one," God now explains (a) some of his other relationships to his people and (b) how this will make them change their identity. Repeating traditions that are found in 43:1,15; 51:13, the prophet reminds his audience that God formed this group of people as his own people from the very beginning (lit. "from the womb") when they first came out of Egypt. It is as if God is saying, you are my flesh and blood, my children, and my family. These claims identify the special status of the people (created and formed[449] by God). God has not forsaken his chosen servants, but he "will [repeatedly] help" them (41:10,13,14).[450] In light of these facts fear is unnecessary, for they are still God's chosen servants. These "upright"[451] people "Jeshurun" should trust in God.

44:3 "Surely, truly" (*kî*, NIV has "for") part of God's help is based on his future plan "to pour down" (*yāṣaq* as in 1 Kgs 18:34; 2 Kgs 3:11) so much water on their dry land that streams will flow where there used to be deserts. This parallels God's marvelous transformation of nature described in 41:17–20 and 43:19–21.[452] This will be a radical new day of restoration, new life, and divine blessing (it has nothing to do with a return from exile).[453] This is an eschatological renewal of the dead and thirsty land (30:18–26; 32:15; 35:1–10; Hos 2:21–23), a reversal of the destructive curse in 43:28. The people will be empowered by a special "pouring down" (using the same verb used of rain) of the Spirit of God. This is God's gift that abundantly fills and transforms everything it touches. The Spirit will give new life and refreshing blessings to

---

[449] These two concepts are expressed using two parallel participles יֹצֶרְךָ "the one who formed you" and עֹשֶׂךָ "the one who made you" to show God's power over their existence and his close relationship to them.

[450] 1QIsᵃ does not have an imperfect יַעְזְרֶךָ "he will help you" but has a participle "the one who helps you" (ועוזרכה) which matches the earlier participle "the one who formed you." There is no reason to choose this form above what is now in the Hebrew text. A participle would identify their status as the helped ones, but the imperfect verb marks their future as a time when he will continually or repeatedly help them (GKC §107i).

[451] The name "Jeshurun" יְשֻׁרוּן is also used in Deut 32:15; 33:5,26. It comes from the root יָשַׁר "to be upright"; so this implies that the nation will one day have a completely different moral character than it had in 43:22–28. M. J. Mulder, "יְשֻׁרוּן *yěšurûn*," *TDOT* 6: 472–77, gives a full discussion of this name. The Aramaic Targum has the more familiar "Israel" in place of "Jeshurun" and the Old Greek translated this as "beloved Israel," but this term of affection misses the central moral meaning of the Hebrew term.

[452] The imagery of the blessing of water and new life appears in the earlier positive messages in 12:3; 30:25; 32:2; 35:6.

[453] North, *Second Isaiah*, 132, states that the "pouring out of *water* and *copious rains* (ver. 3) does not refer to the transformation of the desert in preparation for a new Exodus."

a future generation of children (just like in 30:23–26; 35:1–2), like the water gives new life and brings fertility to the earth. The Spirit's role is not fully defined at this point, but the interlinking evidence in 32:15–18 connects the coming of the Spirit with a time of righteousness, peace, and divine blessing. This suggests that both physical and spiritual changes will be evident in this new era (Joel 2:28; Ezek 36:24–30). The Spirit's work is best identified by the transformation that comes from the Spirit's powerful presence.

44:4–5 As a result of the outpouring of the Spirit their descendents will sprout up among[454] the grass (not "like grass in a meadow" as in NIV, nor "like grass amid waters" RSV) and like trees by streams full of water (cf. Ps 1:3). In addition to the multiplication of people, a spiritual change will bring internal transformation to the people (44:5). The fact that the Spirit is to be poured out on "your descendants" (44:3) supports the view that this refers to changes in the Hebrew people. Nevertheless, the Hebrew text in 44:5 is somewhat ambiguous concerning the ethnic identity of these transformed people.[455] The individual identified as (lit.) "this one"[456] suggests either (a) one individual at a time rather than a mass movement or national revival, or (b) "this one" refers to the servant, a metaphor that describes the nation of Israel. R. N. Whybray concluded that these people who identify with God and Israel were foreign proselytes (56:3–8) who now take on a new name,[457] not Israelites who already had this name. The identity of these individuals cannot be easily resolved because rather general terminology is used to describe them. "This one" (*zeh*) would hypothetically allow anyone (both Hebrews and Gentiles) to make this choice to take on the name "I belong to the LORD." The contextual reference to the Spirit coming on future generations of "your offspring" (44:3) suggests these transformed people will include Hebrews; the fact that some will take the name "Israel" might suggest that some were not originally Israelites.

The important thing emphasized is not the ethnic or religious background of these people; the central issue is what these people choose to become. The Spirit's transforming power will make them want to be identified with God and his righteous people. The four lines in 44:5 present two basic means of iden-

---

[454] בְּבֵין means "in between, among" but the text is widely emended. The Old Greek has "[spring up as grass] between brooks" (ἀνὰ μέσον ὕδατος), while J. M. Allegro, "The Meaning of *byn* in Is 44:4," *ZAW* 64 (1951): 154–56, concluded that this word means "a green ban tree" based on Akkadian and Arabic documents that refer to a ban tree.

[455] Watts, *Isaiah 34–66*, 145, believes this refers to the revitalization of Jewish people in exile who were secularized and assimilated into the local culture where they lived. He believes that at some future time they will quit hiding their distinct identity and openly declare their loyalty to God. Since the pouring out of the Spirit is connected to an eschatological setting in 30:18–25, this should not be placed in an exilic setting.

[456] The first three clauses begin with זֶה "this one" which cannot be connected to any nationality. The context of 44:1–5 would favor a transformation of Hebrew people.

[457] Whybray, *Isaiah 40–66*, 95, finds this inclusion of foreigners similar to 56:3,6–8, but he admits that "this is not specifically stated." Hanson, *Isaiah 40–66*, 83, finds "universalistic tendencies . . . for the new era extended beyond the borders of the Jewish nation."

tification. The second and fourth parallel lines suggest that these transformed people will proudly and openly identify with the name of God's people, "Jacob" or "Israel." Both verbs are active imperfects, but K. Baltzer emends these verbs to make them passives or reflexives,[458] similar to the NIV, "will call himself." These emendations seem unnecessary, for it would not be surprising for these Spirit-filled people to identify themselves by using the title "Israel." Having the same Spirit unifying them together with other believers, they will gladly proclaim who they are.

A second sign of identification in lines 1 and 3 connects these people to God himself. In their conversations with others they will openly confess, "I belong to the LORD." This will not be something that they will be ashamed of or something they will hide from others. This phraseology ("belonging to the LORD") has parallelism with the writings on jars found in Palestine that claim that the content of certain clay pots "belong to the king."[459] In addition, it is known that some slaves had the name of their master on their skin.[460] The title these people will have on their hand will be[461] "belonging to the LORD." Although the exact custom is less than clear and the need for a literal interpretation of this practice is open to argument, the main point is that the Spirit's work in the hearts of these individuals will bring about a spiritual transformation that will cause them to identify themselves with God openly, boldly, and proudly.

THEOLOGICAL IMPLICATIONS. This section was designed to create hope in the midst of uncertainty by reminding the prophet's audience that (a) there is only one God; there is no other Savior, King, Creator, Holy One, or Redeemer that controls their past or future history (43:8–16); (b) God will defeat Babylon in the future, just like he defeated Egypt in the past, so it is inappropriate for the people to put their hope in Babylon instead of God (43:14–15); (c) in the future God will pollute his holy temple by allowing Judah to be destroyed because the people have polluted his temple by burdening God with their sins and useless sacrifices (43:22–28); but (d) at some point in the distant

---

[458] The *qal* imperfect יִקְרָא is active "he will call, give a name, identify" while the *piel* imperfect יְכַנֶּה is also active "he will entitle, bestow an honor." Baltzer, *Deutero-Isaiah*, 184, and many other commentators change these forms to a *niphal* reflexive (יִקָּרֵא) "he will call himself" and a *pual* passive (יְכֻנֶּה) "he will be honored" which only involves the changing of the vocalization of each form.

[459] Although לַיהוה אָנִי "belonging to Yahweh am I" is not exactly the same as the inscription לַמֶּלֶךְ "belonging to the king" that was found on numerous jar rims, both demonstrate possession or ownership by a certain party. Line 3 does have an exact parallel with לַיהוה.

[460] A. Guillaume, "Isa 44:5 in the Light of the Elephantine Papyri," *ExpTim* 32 (1920–21): 377–39; *ANET*, "Code of Hammurabi," #226–227 refer to the "slave-mark of a slave." Marks were put on the foreheads of the righteous in Ezek 9:4. It is true that Lev 19:28 forbids tattoos or branding a person; so this must be something else.

[461] There is no preposition before "hand," so some supply that the writing will be "on" (עַל) his hand (NIV) while Oswalt, *Isaiah*, 164, supplies the idea that he will write "with" (בְּ) his hand because Lev 19:28 prohibits tattoos.

future God will do a new thing by transforming nature and his people through the work of his Spirit (43:18–21; 44:1–5).

The prophet's message challenges all the traditional patterns of thinking with new alternatives. Do people really recognize that there is no other King, Savior, Holy One, and God, or do they sometimes put themselves, an alliance, or some other god in sovereign control of their present problems and their future hopes? Is there still some blindness (43:8), some reluctance to identify what is true (43:9), a bit of unwillingness to believe (43:10), or hesitance to serve as witnesses concerning the character and salvific works of God? God acted in the past in powerful ways to save his people and also predicts that he will do marvelous things for all his people (Hebrews and foreigners) in the future, but do his people really believe they can count on him to do this?

No one can stop or reverse what God determines to do (43:13), so why would anyone resist him and not trust him? Mighty nations were annihilated in the past (43:16–17), so there is every reason to believe that his predictions about the fall of other nations in the future will come true (43:14–15, 28). If he is God, he is able to accomplish his will. This text offers the encouraging hope that God is willing to forgive sinners (43:25), but it also warns that he will not accept useless sacrifices as a substitute for true repentance (43:22–24). He can miraculously transform this world and all the people in it (43:18–21; 44:1–5), but people must get serious about their relationship with God and be willing to confess openly that they belong to him. When people respond positively to God's grace, then they will fulfill their original purpose of bringing glory and honor to the name of God (43:7,20).

These factors present two starkly contrasting choices that will determine the destiny of every person: (a) people can resist God's call and his promises by refusing to confess their sins, by not honoring God with their worship, and by being paralyzed by fear of their enemies; or (b) people can believe God's promises, trust him for their redemption, be transformed by his Spirit, be his servants, and openly identify with God as they interact with others in this world. The first choice will lead to destruction and shame, while the second will result in forgiveness of sins, walking with God and his people, the removal of fear, and the blessings of the Spirit.

Every person in every age must answer several key questions about their identity. Are they spiritually blind, or do they fully understand their helpless state and their need to trust God? Do they identify themselves as God's chosen servants and do they function as his joyful witnesses, or are they weary of serving and worshipping God (43:22–24)? Are their sins forgiven and remembered no more (43:25), or are they in open rebellion against God? Are they fearful and silent, or do they openly proclaim that they belong to God? The prophet presents no option for a compromising middle ground when it comes to theological beliefs or personal commitment to God. God the Creator, Redeemer, King, and Holy One is the only hope that a helpless, spiritually blind person has. God's Spirit is the only One whose transforming power can bring true renewal for people in this hopeless world.

(3) Fear God, Not Idols, and Be Forgiven (44:6–23)

The final message of this long section (43:8–44:23) contains interlinking vocabulary that connects these words to earlier themes that God is King and Redeemer (43:14–15; 44:6), he is the first and the last (41:4; 44:6), and "there is no other God beside me" (43:10–11; 44:6). Questions of comparison with other gods are asked again (40:18,25; 44:7), people are told not to fear (43:1,5; 44:2,8), Israel is identified as God's witness (43:10,12; 44:8), Israel is called God's servant whom he formed (44:1–2,21), and God offers to forgive those who repent of their sins (43:25; 44:22). H. C. Spykerboer found several other catchwords that connect this quasipoetic text on the construction of idols with the context and the literary style of other passages in the scroll of Isaiah.[462] These examples show that the poetic framework around the quasipoetic satire on idols is consistent with the themes of the previous messages.

The internal unity of this message is complicated by the presence of a long satire against the idols that is in a quasipoetic style (44:9–20), placed between two short poetic pieces at the beginning and end of the satire about idols (44:6–8,21–23). The means of argumentation in the quasipoetic section does not follow the pattern developed in earlier references to the making of idols. Earlier discussions of the idol-gods (40:18,25; 41:1–5,21–29; 43:8–13) focus on comparisons between Israel's God and the idols of wood and stone, but 44:9–20 does not make any comparisons between God and the idols; so this treatment of this topic is somewhat unique, and there is no legal language here. The comparison between God and the idols are only in the introductory material in 44:6–8. In spite of these unusual factors, the prophet's description of how people manufactured their idols in 44:9–17 mentions factors that are commonly brought up in other messages about idols (40:19–20; 41:6; 46:5–7). The repetition of these issues suggests that the prophet has editorially put two distinct literary pieces (44:9–20 seems unique) together to form this message.[463] The origin of the narrative taunt is unknown (was it originally written by Isaiah, or is he quoting some other prophet?), though it now appears to be fully integrated into Isaianic language, for it uses vocabulary that is typical in

---

[462] Spykerboer, *Structure and Composition of Deutero-Isaiah*, 120–22, mentions words like כֻּלָּם "all of them," הֵן "behold, surely," and בַּל בִּלְתִּי "not" plus references to "witnesses" (44:8,9) and "form, shape" (44:2,9,10,12,21,24).

[463] Melugin, *Formation of Isaiah 40–55*, 120, considers the heaping of scorn on the idols in 44:9–20 as unique because: (a) there is a lack of legal terminology in vv. 9–20, so these verses are not related to the trial imagery in vv. 6–8; and (b) there are few thematic connections between vv. 6–8 and 9–20. These factors suggest that 44:9–20 were inserted here and do not smoothly flow out of vv. 6–8. Baltzer, *Deutero-Isaiah*, 192–93, has an extensive discussion of arguments for and against attributing this passage to Deutero-Isaiah. He claims that many of the themes in this passage are "intimately connected with the rest of the book . . . the same vocabulary is used here."

other messages that condemned the making of idols. Possibly the prophet is quoting a message he received at another time. W. R. Domeris maintains that the description of idol making fits a preexilic setting in Israel and not Babylonian idol building.[464]

The contrasts between these gods made of pieces of wood and metal and the God of Israel are not explicit in the central section of this oracle, but they are obvious to the listener/reader because the prophet uses vocabulary that was used elsewhere to contrast God and the idols. In spite of the unusual nature of this material, it is evident that the prophet was attempting to justify his conclusion that Israel's God is the nation's trustworthy divine Redeemer who will act on their behalf. He exhorts his audience to repent of their sins and shout for joy, for God has not forgotten his people (44:21–23).

GENRE.   The first few verses have some similarities to earlier imaginary trials where witnesses were called to declare what they know about God's divine power. They are able to witness that God has the power to reveal what will happen in the future and then control history in such a way that these things actually happen (44:6–8). Each of these speeches ends up concluding that the King of Israel, their Redeemer, and Lord Almighty is God, but the idol-gods have nothing to offer (40:18–20; 41:1–5,21–29; 43:8–13). Within this long speech are literary characteristics that include: (a) a "fear not" clause (44:8) that is more characteristic of a salvation oracle; (b) a long satire about building idols (44:9–20); (c) a few final exhortations that include a call to repentance (44:21–22); and (d) a call to praise God in the form of a hymn (44:23).[465] This amalgamation of diverse material demonstrates that this message has creatively combined several traditional forms of speech into a complex and unique prophetic presentation that was intended to convince the listeners to repent of their sins and trust in God.

STRUCTURE.   This message can be divided into four main paragraphs based on the literary style (poetic, quasipoetic, poetic, and hymn) and distinct content. Isaiah 44:23 closes the larger literary unit of 43:6–44:23 with a hymn of praise, similar to the closing hymn in 42:10–13.

God proclaims his uniqueness	44:6–8
Satire on trusting in useless idols	44:9–20
Admonition to remember and return to God	44:21–22
Concluding hymnic praise of God	44:23

J. Blenkinsopp has a different analysis because he maintains that 44:6–8 and 44:21–23 form one discourse, with the "remember" clause in 44:21 pointing back to v. 8, rather than to v. 20.[466] But 44:21–23 have few direct connec-

---

[464] W. R. Domeris, "Two Preexilic Passages in Isaiah 40–55," *OTE* 13 (1988): 29–41.

[465] Westermann, *Isaiah 40–66*, 139, also finds the description of God in 44:6 to be derived from a salvation oracle.

[466] Blenkinsopp, *Isaiah 40–66*, 235–36. Westermann, *Isaiah 40–66*, 139–42, believes 44:21

tions with the content of 44:6–8; therefore, it is probably wiser to hypothesize that 44:21–23 functions as a conclusion to everything ("these things" in 44:21) that the prophet said in this group of messages (42:14–44:23). The call to remember that the sons of Israel are God's servants and the call to return to God for forgiveness of sins summarize the prophet's purpose in this section.

GOD PROCLAIMS HIS UNIQUENESS (44:6–8)

> ⁶"This is what the LORD says—
>   Israel's King and Redeemer, the LORD Almighty:
> I am the first and I am the last;
>   apart from me there is no God.
> ⁷Who then is like me? Let him proclaim it.
>   Let him declare and lay out before me
> what has happened since I established my ancient people,
>   and what is yet to come—
>   yes, let him foretell what will come.
> ⁸Do not tremble, do not be afraid.
>   Did I not proclaim this and foretell it long ago?
> You are my witnesses. Is there any God besides me?
>   No, there is no other Rock; I know not one.'"

44:6 "This is what the LORD says" introduces this message as an authoritative revelation from God. In order to raise further the importance of these words, God identifies himself as the "King of Israel" (41:21; 43:15), a title that includes the roles of ruling over Israel, giving laws and customs for his people, insuring that justice is carried out, serving as the military commander-in-chief, protecting the nation from its enemies, and judging people.[467] Surely the audience should listen to the wisdom of their Divine King who controls the history of their nation. God is also their "Redeemer" (*gô'ēl*, as in 43:15) who has and will deliver his family members from danger and protect their freedom. This title reveals God's special connection to Israel based on the exodus events and their covenant relationship. He is also the "LORD Almighty," the Divine Warrior who will fight on behalf of his people. As a Divine Warrior he commands the hosts/armies of heaven. These titles describe God's special relationship to his people, and they remind the audience that his power is available to carry out his will on behalf of his people. Surely the audience should pay attention to someone who cares for them and will fight for them when they are attacked.

Finally, God announces that "I am the first and I am the last," a phrase that is not just a title but also a description of his unique sovereignty over all events.

---

is a substantiation of God's claims to deity in 44:6–8; thus the poetic material fits together as a complete trial speech.

[467] Smith, "The Concept of God/the gods as King in the Ancient Near East and the Bible," 18–38, illustrates how the roles of an earthly king are similar to God's roles.

He knows what happened in the past and has planned and revealed to his people some of the things that will happen in the future. This is not an abstract philosophical statement of his eternality but a reminder that his works span the whole scope of history from the beginning to the very end of time. This claim would give assurance to the audience that God knows all about their past problems and will be around to help them in the future. This point anticipates the argument that will be presented later in the narrative where a craftsman brings an idol-god into existence many years after he planted a seedling. When God claims to be the first (41:4; 48:12), it indicates that he preceded the first events of creation and will continue as the sovereign Ruler over creation until the very last events. C. Seitz suggests that these temporal categories of first and last are "inextricably related to the reliability of God's word through time."[468] These titles and descriptions of Israel's God set him apart from all other "gods" that might claim some supernatural power.

44:7 The comparative question "who [*mî*] then is like me?" reminds one of similar questions in other messages that deal with God's claim to sovereign divine power over all other gods (40:13,18,25; 41:2,4,26). The syntax of this verse is open to alternative approaches because there is no punctuation in Hebrew. The NIV has a short initial question and then three "let him" clauses. These three jussive verbs[469] encourage others to announce, if they can, what other gods can match God's sovereign and unique claims. J. L. Koole emends the text to read two somewhat parallel questions (lines 1 and 3) and two "let" clauses,[470] but it is always better not to emend the text if one can make sense of it as it is. In this case God is challenging anyone to make a comparison between God described in 44:6 and any other gods. They are advised to proclaim the facts and "lay it out in an orderly manner" (*ya'rĕkehā*) before "me" (that is before God). Specifically, God wants any other challenger to explain the events from the establishment[471] of the first people (possibly Adam, or the people of Israel) on the earth to the future things that will come. Can any other god declare "them, these things"?[472]

---

[468] Seitz, "Isaiah 40–66," 387; Williamson, "The First and the Last in Isaiah," 95–108, connects this title to God's past judgment and bringing of light in the future in 9:1 (8:23 in the Hebrew text), but there is no indication that a past negative and future positive idea is included in this title. This passage supports the theory that God worked in history in the past and will in the future, but this title does not carry any of the negative–positive connotations found in 9:1; thus it is questionable whether this title comes from that source.

[469] The jussive expresses a desire and can be translated with "let" ("let him proclaim it") or with modal like "may, might, should, would " ("he should proclaim it"). It communicates a wish or request (GKC §109b).

[470] Koole, *Isaiah II. Volume 1, Isaiah 40–48*, 370–72, emends the third line to read, "Who tells the ancient people the things to come?"

[471] The infinitive construct מִשּׂוּמִי contains the prefixed preposition מִן "from" before the construct form שׂוּם "setting, establishing." The suffix (ִ) on the construct form functions as the subject of the verbal form (GKC §115e). Thus this word can be translated "from my establishing" or "since I established" (NIV).

[472] The final word לָמוֹ may be an ancient pronominal suffix (GKC §91.l.3; 103f, fn 3) for

44:8 This initial challenge ends with words of encouragement to God's people. They do not need to tremble in fear or become dismayed (44:8).[473] There are no other gods that can exert their power or interfere with God's rule of this earth. It was God himself who proclaimed what would happen at a former time.[474] The prophet's audience knew about past prophecies from their traditions, and they were witnesses to the truth that God proclaimed. The absence of comparable claims by other gods and God's many true prophetic announcements push one to question: "Is there any other God besides me?" Can any of these other gods do what God does? The answer is unavoidable and expressed in a double negative (lit.): "There is no (other) Rock, I know not[475] (one)." The imagery of God as a rock creates images of a solid foundation that is an immovable source of protection and an impregnable solid foundation (Deut 32:4,15,18,30,37; 1 Sam 2:2; Ps 18:31). Rocks provide security, deliverance from attack, and a hiding place; rocks do not change. Since God does not know of any other being who has the stature, knowledge, power, temporal control over all history, and the leadership of the heavenly armies, the prophet's audience can be assured that their God is the only one who deserves their trust.

SATIRE ON TRUSTING IN USELESS IDOLS (44:9–20)

9All who make idols are nothing,
  and the things they treasure are worthless.
Those who would speak up for them are blind;
  they are ignorant, to their own shame.
10Who shapes a god and casts an idol,
  which can profit him nothing?

לָהֵמָּה "them, these things." Westermann, *Isaiah 40–66*, 138, follows the Aramaic Targum and Old Greek and emends the text to read לָנוּ "us" (also in RSV, NRSV).

[473] The verb "do not tremble in fear" is the jussive form אַל תִּפְחֲדוּ which describes a terrified fear that comes when God attacks (19:16; 33:14; Exod 15:16), not the usual אַל תִּירָא which is used in the context of not fearing because God will deliver his people (43:1,5; 44:2). The second verb in 44:8 (תִּרְהוּ) is found only here and must mean something parallel to the first verb. It is possible that ה was confused with א and that this is actually the frequently used verb יָרֵא "to fear," which is what 1QIs^a has. Blenkinsopp, *Isaiah 40–55*, 235, accepts the Qumran reading as the original, but Koole, *Isaiah II. Volume 1, Isaiah 40–48*, 374, rejects it as a simplification of a more difficult Masoretic reading.

[474] NIV "Did I not proclaim this and foretell it long ago?" could be more literally rendered "Did I not from then proclaim to you and tell?" The clause is a rhetorical question beginning with the negative interrogative הֲלֹא which expects a strong positive answer. The translation "surely" could communicate this absolute affirmation (GKC §150e). Schoors, *I Am God Your Savior*, 228, accepts this translation. According to *HALOT*, מֵאָז lit. "from then" can serve adverbially ("formerly, before, from of old"; cf. Isa 16:13) or conjunctively ("since"). Here it is an adverb, and its association with "since I established my ancient people" in v. 7 indicates that it refers to former times (as in 45:21; 48:5,7).

[475] בַּל is a form of the negative "no, not" used in some poetic texts. It is basically equivalent to the regular negative לֹא (GKC §152t).

¹¹He and his kind will be put to shame;
　　craftsmen are nothing but men.
　Let them all come together and take their stand;
　　they will be brought down to terror and infamy.

¹²The blacksmith takes a tool
　　and works with it in the coals;
　he shapes an idol with hammers,
　　he forges it with the might of his arm.
　He gets hungry and loses his strength;
　　he drinks no water and grows faint.
¹³The carpenter measures with a line
　　and makes an outline with a marker;
　he roughs it out with chisels
　　and marks it with compasses.
　He shapes it in the form of man,
　　of man in all his glory,
　　that it may dwell in a shrine.
¹⁴He cut down cedars,
　　or perhaps took a cypress or oak.
　He let it grow among the trees of the forest,
　　or planted a pine, and the rain made it grow.
¹⁵It is man's fuel for burning;
　　some of it he takes and warms himself,
　　he kindles a fire and bakes bread.
　But he also fashions a god and worships it;
　　he makes an idol and bows down to it.
¹⁶Half of the wood he burns in the fire;
　　over it he prepares his meal,
　　he roasts his meat and eats his fill.
　He also warms himself and says,
　　"Ah! I am warm; I see the fire."
¹⁷From the rest he makes a god, his idol;
　　he bows down to it and worships.
　He prays to it and says,
　　"Save me; you are my god."
¹⁸They know nothing, they understand nothing;
　　their eyes are plastered over so they cannot see,
　　and their minds closed so they cannot understand.
¹⁹No one stops to think,
　　no one has the knowledge or understanding to say,
　"Half of it I used for fuel;
　　I even baked bread over its coals,
　　I roasted meat and I ate.
　Shall I make a detestable thing from what is left?
　　Shall I bow down to a block of wood?"
²⁰He feeds on ashes, a deluded heart misleads him;
　　he cannot save himself, or say,
　　"Is not this thing in my right hand a lie?"

Some verses within this quasipoetic section exhibit many poetic parallelisms; thus the NIV arranges the whole section as if it were all poetry (NASB arranges these verses in a narrative format). Since there is no sharp distinction between rhythmic narrative and pure poetry, either way of presenting this text can be justified. It is important to notice parallelism when it occurs (44:9–11,18–20), but not to force it on a text when there is little parallelism present in other verses (44:12–17).

This paragraph is unusual in that it does not directly compare the idols to God ("the Rock" in 44:8) and does not directly address the prophet's audience (no second person verbs or second person suffixes). The prophet assumes that the audience can make the comparison between God and these idols without any help; so he focuses on satirizing the bizarre behavior of the craftsmen who construct useless idols in order to show how shameful it is for them to mislead the common people. The craftsmen who make the idols know full well how these images come into existence, but the uneducated peasant worshipper could be easily deceived by a well-carved and impressive gold-plated idol. These people have no understanding about the real nature of these idols. They are deluded and are mislead (44:18–20). Like 44:6–8, these verses (44:10,19,20) ask questions and then provide an answer. The structure of the paragraph is:[476]

Idol makers will be shamed	44:9–11
Construction of an idol	44:12–13
Idols come from a tree	44:14–17
Worshippers of idols know nothing	44:18–20

44:9 The first few verses condemn the carpenters who make idols. Although unstated explicitly as a contrast, this description of the process of making an idol-god should have set up an implied contrast in the mind of the audience between God who "forms, shapes" (*yāṣar*) humanity and the nation of Israel (44:2,21) and the craftsmen who "form, shape" (*yāṣar*) idols. All these who form idols are "worthless, empty" [477] (cf. Gen 1:2) because all their "desirable, valuable"[478] things (NIV "treasures," i.e., the idols of gold) ironically have no real value and bring no profit to anyone. Idols are a deception and they provide no benefits, even though some venerate them and treat them as if they had value. The experience of the idol makers put them in a situation where they are able to tell the truth (NIV "those who would speak up"; they are

---

[476] Goldingay and Payne, *Isaiah 40–55*, 1:336, suggest a chiastic arrangement of vv. 6–23 with v. 14 at the center. Although vv. 6–8 at the beginning balance with vv. 21–23 at the end, what happens in vv. 9–13 is not the same as what happens in vv. 15–20.

[477] תֹהוּ does not refer to "chaos" (Oswalt, *Isaiah 40–66*, 176, refers to it as "elemental chaos") but something that is empty and void of what is normally there. Since the idol makers do not tell the truth, they are mindless workers who are void of any wisdom; so anything they make is empty, void of value, and worthless. North, *Second Isaiah*, 140 translates this "empty-heads."

[478] חֲמוּדֵיהֶם is a *qal* passive participle from חָמַד which refers to something that has value, is desirable, is precious or dear.

"witnesses," *ʿēdēyhem* like Israel is a witness for God in 44:8) about the true origin and power of these wooden gods. The description "they[479] who do not see" (*bal-yirĕʾû*, NIV "[they] are blind; they are ignorant") could refer to the craftsmen who know and see the truth about these idols right before their eyes, or possibly to the worshippers who do not seem to recognize the insignificance and powerlessness of the objects they honor. It is unlikely that the idols are the subject of the verb.[480] The final verb "[they] will be put to shame" (*yēbôšû*, NIV "to their own shame") most naturally refers to the shame the craftsmen will experience (44:11). These makers of the idols will be judged ignorant and shameful when people finally discover the truth about these impotent objects of wood.[481]

44:10–11   Who are these people who form idol-gods from wood or cast metal images that provide no profit to anyone (44:10)? Who would dare to foist such an illusion on others? Who would be so audacious and heartless as to deceive the public with these worthless[482] pieces of wood when they know that the idols could not help the worshipper in any way? "Surely, behold" (44:11, often *hēn* will introduce a conclusion; cf. NASB; absent in NIV), judgment will fall on all the people and their associates who work in the idol-making business for "they will be put to shame" (*yēbōšû*). How dare these "mere men"[483] (NIV "nothing but men") imagine that they can create a divine being? K. Baltzer views v. 11b as an invitation for these builders of idols to stand up at court and answer for their deeds, but this is not a court setting.[484] On the other hand, C. Westermann (and NIV) interprets the final line as a negative verdict—"they will be brought down to terror and infamy."[485] Since all the verbs are identical grammatical forms, it is better to see them all as jussive challenges (lit.): "let all of them come together, let them stand up, let them tremble,[486] and let them become ashamed together." That is exactly what they deserve. The text makes no

---

[479] The word הֵמָּה has a dot above each letter. These are called *puncta extraordinaria* "extraordinary points" that may indicate a questionable or inauthentic text (GKC §5n). This word could be the pronoun "they" or the demonstrative pronoun "those." 1QIsᵃ omitted this word, then a later corrector added the word above the line. The Aramaic Targum translated this phrase "witnesses they are against themselves."

[480] Calvin, "Isaiah," 369, thought this refers to the idolaters, not the idols.

[481] Goldingay and Payne, *Isaiah 40–55*, 1:346, believe the shame will come because they will see that the idols do nothing. They will see nothing—the absence of action, power, and authority.

[482] The phrase לְבִלְתִּי הוֹעִיל "to not profit" uses the negative לְבִלְתִּי with an infinitive construct verb (GKC §114s) to express a final result, "so as to give no profit."

[483] Literally מֵאָדָם means "from man," but the partitive use of the preposition means "one from among mankind" (GKC §119w, fn 2), thus a "mere man." Another option would understand "from mankind" as meaning they were born from other humans.

[484] Baltzer, *Deutero-Isaiah*, 190, treats the verbs as jussives "let them be assembled . . . let them stand . . . let them be terrified."

[485] Westermann, *Isaiah 40–66*, 144. 1QIsᵃ has a *waw* introducing this clause, which would support this interpretation, but it is not in the MT text.

[486] In 44:8 Israel need not "fear" תִּפְחֲדוּ, but in 44:11 the builders of idols will fear יִפְחָדוּ.

direct comparison between the true God and these idols and their builder, but certainly the audience would have mentally noticed the dramatic differences.

44:12–17 This section describes the making of idols in greater detail, though there are questions about its chronological order (the cutting in v. 14a precedes the growing in v. 14b). It is possible to hypothesize that two different idols are being made, but it is more likely that this account describes the construction of one idol by both a metal worker (44:12) and a carpenter (44:13). At times it is difficult to translate the description of what these workers do because the grammar of some sentences is unusual and because several rare words are used.

44:12 Understanding the task of this skilled artisan is complicated by difficulties identifying what the verb is in the first line and the nature of the craftsman's work throughout the verse. If the "craftsman of wood" in v. 13 (NIV "carpenter") is seen as parallel to the "craftsman of iron" (NIV "blacksmith") in v. 12, then the first line in v. 12 is left without a verb. J. Muilenburg solves this problem by making the last word in the first line the verb "cuts" (*ʾāṣad*) instead of the noun "axe."[487] The NIV adds a verb ("takes") in the first line to solve this problem, and F. Delitzsch supplies the verb ("sharpens") assuming a haplography with the last word in 44:11 ("together").[488] This could be an unusual case of ellipsis where the verb in the second line is implied for the first line. The blacksmith "makes, works on" (implying *pāʿal*) a sharp instrument like an axe by "working on" (*pāʿal*) the unformed metal in the hot coals. Then he forms it by hammering on it with a great exertion of energy with his strong arms. It appears that he may be making a tool (an "axe") for the carpenter to use in making an idol (this would give greater continuity to the flow of the story), although this verse could be referring to the making of a metal idol. Either solution is possible, and the results would still be more or less the same. All this hard work leads to hunger and thirst, which causes a loss of strength and growing faintness. The satirical point is that God gives strength to the weak person (40:29–31), but the construction of the idol-gods brings weakness to the person who makes it.

44:13 The second worker appears to be the carpenter who works with wood, not a blacksmith. Once he has stretched out a "line" (*qāw*) to measure the wood, he will "draw, outline" (*yĕtāʾărēhû*) the shape he wants to cut, probably

---

[487] Muilenburg, "Isaiah 40–66," 5:512–13, bases his conclusion on the use of the word עצד "cuts" in the Gezer calendar.

[488] Delitzsch, "Prophecies of Isaiah," 208–9, follows the Old Greek in proposing this suggestion. Oswalt, *Isaiah 40–66*, 178, follows Delitzsch. This solution suggests that יחד at the end of v. 11 cause a scribe to skip over the original beginning of v. 12 (the error of haplography). This theory suggests that v. 12 actually began with the word יחד (a hiphil imperfect of the root חדד) which means "sharpen." This is a possible solution, but it would remove the parallelism between the beginning of vv. 12 and 13. If one ignores the parallelism between vv. 12 and 13, one could also take the first word (חרש) as a verb, giving "he fashions iron (with) a chisel."

with some sort of writing or cutting instrument.[489] To make the proper shape he will work the wood with a scrapping instrument, possibly a file, plane, or a chisel.[490] Many find the carpenter remarking or redrawing the object with the aid of a "compass" (NIV) because the root (*ḥûg*) refers to something "round," but K. Baltzer suggests that this is a "file" that enables the carpenter to draw out the rounded edges of the face and body that were originally drawn on the wood with some sort of marker.[491] The result of all this work is that the carpenter makes something that looks like the form of a human being, like a glorious man, the best that humans can imagine. This image then is put in a temple or shrine (lit. "house") for people to worship.

Although the author makes no comparisons with God, any Hebrew person in the audience would see the dramatic contrasts. In 40:12,22 God stretches out a line to mark off the breadth of the heavens, but in this text the idols are made by a man who stretches out a short line to make the outline of the idol. In addition, God is glorious and he displays his glory for all to see, but idols have no glory. Thus, the craftsmen make them to mirror the limited glory of humanity.

44:14–17 The topic changes in 44:14–17 from the details of constructing the idol to the initial process of getting the wood used to make an idol-god. This procedure will show how senseless it is to trust in objects of wood. How can one part of a tree be considered worthless and consequently burned to keep someone warm while another part of the tree is honored as a god? Parallel to the two men making the idols in 44:12–13 are two men (14–15,16–17) who cook food over a wood fire and then worship before a wooden idol. The action of these men will be evaluated in 44:18–20.

44:14 It appears that the first man cuts wood for an idol and then plants a tree to get some wood, a process that seems to be logically out of order. The solution to this problem is related to the grammatical use of the first verb. This verse begins with an infinitive construct verb that frequently introduces either a purpose or a temporal dependent clause,[492] not an independent clause ("he cut down cedars" NIV). The temporal use of the infinitive construct suggests the

---

[489] The word שֶׁרֶד means "plaited, braided" in the context of making the robes for the priests (Exod 31:10; 35:19; 39:1,41), but in this context this meaning hardly works. This must be a separate root referring to some sort of marking instrument. Since this word is used only here, it is difficult to define its meaning. Some guess it was a stylus, pencil, or a red ochre chalk that marked where to cut.

[490] The word מַקְצֻעוֹת is used only here so its meaning is implied from the root קָצַע "to scrape." This meaning is suggested from Lev 14:41 where this root is used to describe how one must "scrape" the wall of the house that has become unclean because of mildew.

[491] Baltzer, *Deutero-Isaiah*, 198–99, finds support for this suggestion in the Vulgate translation "the woodworker has worked with the file" and from Egyptian tomb art which depicts carvers using stone files to round legs of chairs.

[492] לִכְרָת could show purpose "in order to cut down" (GKC §114 e-g) as Oswalt, *Isaiah 40–66*, 178, or a temporal/attendant circumstances meaning "while he was cutting down" following Koole, *Isaiah II. Volume 1, Isaiah 40–48*, 391. Emending this verb by making it a finite verb

translation "while he was cutting down cedars for himself," or if it is a purpose use of the infinitive, "in order to cut down cedars for himself." The second phrase should probably be seen as an extension or explanation of the first dependent clause,[493] meaning "or in order to take a cypress[494] or an oak." This approach makes the first half of v. 14 a human thought or desire to find a tree so that he can make it into a god. The advantage of this approach to v. 14a is that it alleviates the temporal problem that is present in most translations because they have the man getting his wood before he plants the tree.

Once the man thought about his need for wood to make an idol, he then decided to plant some trees in v. 14b. The NIV translates the next clause "he let it grow among the trees," but he would have to plant the tree first before this meaning could make sense. Since the planting of the trees and letting the rain naturally cause it to grow come after this clause, the first clause must have some other meaning. C. R. North prefers "makes his choice" (way'ammeṣ)[495] which could suggest that this man first chose a sapling from the trees of the forest and then he plants it (the sapling)[496] somewhere else and lets the rain cause it to grow.

The types of trees mentioned in this verse have raised questions about the geographical location of the author. Although M. Dick believes the speaker has indebtedness to the wood/trees used in an orchard in Mesopotamia, S. J. Sherwin concludes that these kinds of trees, which were common in Palestine, were not native to Mesopotamia. Since images in Babylon were usually made of a wood core of tamarisk or mēsu wood, it appears that the writer of this information was a Westerner from Phoenicia or Palestine and was not writing about the way Babylonians build idols.[497]

(Muilenburg, "Isaiah 40–66," 5:513 and NIV) only creates a chronological problem with what happens in the second half of the verse.

[493] The verb וַיִּקַּח could be interpreted to be continuing the action of the preceding infinitive construct or as an epexegetical comment clarifying or explaining the first clause. Consult *IBHS*, 551, for the epexegetical usage.

[494] The word תִּרְזָה is a hapax legomenon, so its meaning is uncertain. Arabic *taraza* means "hard"; so it probably is a hard wood tree, possibly a cypress.

[495] The verb וַיְאַמֵּץ usually means "to strengthen, make strong," though North, *Second Isaiah*, 141, prefers another part of the semantic field—to strengthen in the sense of securing something for one's own advantage (cf. Ps 80:16). Oswalt, *Isaiah*, 179, also prefers "he secured it for himself."

[496] The word אֹרֶן is only found here; so it is difficult to determine the exact meaning. It must be some kind of tree. The Old Greek reading suggests that there may have been a textual error here (אֶרֶז "cedar"), or it is possible that the translators guessed at its meaning based on a similar sounding word. Akkadian has the similar *erēnu* "cedar."

[497] S. I. Sherwin, "In Search of Trees: Isaiah XLIV 14 and its Implications," *VT* 53 (2003): 514–29, allows for the possibility of this being a Westerner who was just recently exiled to Babylon and who was not acquainted with Babylonian image making, but this means the person was not describing Babylonian worship. This option seems unlikely. M. Dick, "Prophetic Parodies of Making the Cult Image," in *Born in Heaven Made on Earth*, ed. M. Dick (Winona Lake: Eisenbrauns, 1999), 43, connects these trees with the Babylonian rite of "the opening of the mouth" (*mis pî*).

44:15 The man uses the wood of the tree to serve two purposes.[498] He chooses to use one section of the tree for burning so he can keep warm and have a fire to bake some bread. In addition to this, he takes a different piece of wood and makes it into a god that he worships. He makes an idol then he bows down before it. Although the text makes no explicit conclusion at this point (it comes in 44:18–20), the listener cannot help but be astonished at such senseless activity. How can one part of a tree be honored as a powerful supernatural power and another part of the same tree be treated as an inanimate object that deserves no honor at all? Of course the question has to come up—how does one know which part of the tree is worthless and which part is a god? If one should accidentally choose the wrong part, one would be bowing down to something worthless and burning up a god!

44:16–17 Just in case the audience did not get the point, the author repeats his incredible description of the incomprehensible actions of another pagan man who follows the same process. It is as if the author is saying, "I'm not kidding; it is really true; I saw it." A man will burn half of the wood from a tree in a fire to roast meat so that he can eat, be satisfied, and keep himself warm from the heat of the fire. The man will say nothing about the value of the wood he is burning; he will only make a sigh of contentment and comment about what he sees (light) and how he feels (warm). In v. 17 the rest of the wood from that same tree is used to make an idol-god, then he will kneel down, worship, and pray. Now he says things quite different about the second piece of wood. His request, "Save me, for you are my god," implies that somehow this second piece of wood from the same tree has some supernatural power. The earlier narrative by Rabshakeh makes it evident that this was what ancient people thought the gods were supposed to do (36:14–20). This was normal practice of many ancient peoples, not anything unusual, but it made absolutely no sense to ask a piece of wood to do this. Ironically, people even today put very high value on some of the inanimate objects they own. They believe these objects can save them by giving them a high status in social situations, leverage in economic transactions, real security for the future, and importance in the eyes of others. They are not called "gods" today and they often are not made of wood, but they are objects of great desire.

44:18–20 The evaluation of the beliefs and behavior of these men forcefully illustrates the foolishness of worshipping idols. The idea that these men[499] can make a powerful divine being out of a lifeless random piece of

---

This was a ceremony intended to enliven the idol with the spirit of the god.

[498] The infinitive construct לְבָעֵר is often used to express purpose (GKC §114f).

[499] Some commentators struggle with the pl. verbs in 44:18. Koole, *Isaiah II. Volume 1, Isaiah 40–48*, 397, solves this problem by suggesting that the word "idolaters" in v. 9 is the subject of the verbs (he rejects the idea that the gods are the subject). Goldingay, *Message of Isaiah 40–55*, 243, connects the pl. back to the image-makers in 44:9–11. It is possible that these image-makers are included, but it seems that the two men in vv. 14–17 are the ones specifically referred to in v. 18.

wood makes no sense. These people do not know (*yādʿû*) and do not perceive (*yābînû*) the real significance of what they are doing (40:21; 43:10). Somehow their spiritual eyes are plastered over[500] so that they cannot differentiate (6:9–10) between a created thing (a piece of wood) and God who is the Creator of the world. The prophet does not attribute this blindness to any specific factor, but if these people were raised to believe these things by their parents and religious leaders, they would naturally be somewhat bound by that culture's false interpretation of reality ("their eyes are smeared/plastered over"). Some of them no doubt knew about other religious systems, but their hearts were closed to the option of choosing another way of understanding reality. This passage does not connect blindness to God's action or as a negative response to the preaching of the prophet (6:9–10; 29:10). It is always hard for people to see their own faults and the illogical thinking that goes into justifying their senseless beliefs and behavior patterns.

44:19 Part of the reason why the idol worshippers never figured out that these gods of wood were worthless is that they were blindly following accepted cultural patterns of behavior and did not spend the time to meditate or consider[501] the implications of what they were doing (44:19). They seem to have "no knowledge, no discernment" (*lôʾ daʿat wĕlôʾ tĕbûnâ*, as in v. 18) of the truth. If they would stop and think all this through, someone might make the observation that this does not make any sense. How can half of the tree be used for baking bread and roasting meat to eat (drawing from 44:15a,16) and half of the tree be used for making a god (drawing from 44:15b,17)? How does one know which half is the god? These idol makers should have wondered if it was really honest to claim that they had made a god from the same wood that they burned for cooking. From the prophet's point of view these idol makers were creating a "detestable thing" (or "abomination," *tôʿēbâ*) that was actually just a plain old "block of wood" (*bûl ʿēṣ*), not a god. In one sense these idol-gods were nothing but just a simple mass of carved wood fibers, but in another sense these idols were a powerful symbol of a detestable false god.

44:20 The conclusion is that the one who makes and worships an idol is "[one] who feeds on ashes." Animals feed (graze) on lush grass (11:7; 30:23), and people eat bread and meat (44:15–16); so the idea of feeding on dry dusty

---

[500] The word מֻח comes from the root טֻח and refers to the process of covering over something; for example, the plastering or whitewashing of a wall (Ezek 13:10,12).

[501] The Hebrew way of describing this kind of mental action was "he did not bring it back to his heart" (לֹא יָשִׁיב אֶל לִבּוֹ). In a similar manner, the prophet Haggai challenged the Israelites who were not rebuilding the temple to reconsider their ways (using שִׂים "place" rather than שׁוּב "return"; see "set it on their hearts," Hag 1:5,7; cf. Mal 2:2). Did it make any sense for them to rebuild their own houses and not build God's house? Did it make any sense to make the excuse that it was not the right time to build now? They needed to think about why they were suffering under a drought. Was this the result of God's blessing, or was it God's curse because they were not glorifying God?

bitter ashes presents a most distasteful image. Who would be dumb enough to want to eat ashes and who would continue to consume them? Certainly everyone would quickly come to their senses and stop immediately. By using this imagery the prophet is suggesting that the burnt wood that leaves ashes in 44:15–16 is identical to the idol the people worship. Since the idol-god and the firewood come from the same source, the idol-god is really no different from the ashes that are left after a fire has burnt out. Only a fool would look for nourishment from ashes and not realize how stupid he was. Only a person who had a heart that was totally deluded[502] would think that ashes were good or a god. The people who rely on idols are totally deluded into thinking that their theology and behavior is normal, beneficial, and true. But the truth is, the illusions of this person's heart have led him astray; "he has stretched" (*hiṭāhû* from *nāṭâ*; NIV "misleads") the truth so much that he ended up turning aside from God's way. The depth of human depravity caused by this deception makes it nearly impossible for the deceived one to deliver his soul from the grips of his own blindness.[503] Consequently, he will not confess that he was wrong or that the idol that he holds is a "deceptive falsehood" (*šeqer*, NIV "a lie"). The prophet does not underestimate the depth of the darkness and the strength of the grip that spiritual blindness creates on the heart of the idol maker. Those who accept sinful delusions have usually bought into the inner logic of that deceptive cultural frame of reference that blinds them from being able to see the deeper fallacies of what they believe.

ADMONITION TO REMEMBER AND RETURN TO GOD (44:21–22)

> [21]"Remember these things, O Jacob,
>   for you are my servant, O Israel.
> I have made you, you are my servant;
>   O Israel, I will not forget you.
> [22]I have swept away your offenses like a cloud,
>   your sins like the morning mist.
> Return to me,
>   for I have redeemed you."

44:21–22 Having inserted this reminder about the dangers and pitfalls of worshipping idols (44:9–20), the prophet now turns back to his Israelite audience with two exhortations (the imperatives in vv. 21a and 22b) and two assur-

---

[502] The *hophal* perfect verb (הוּתַל) is a passive that refers to completed action that was brought on the subject by something else. His heart, which was deluded, was lead astray by the false theological hopes he was taught. This word forms an asyndetic relative clause (a clause in which the relative pronoun is missing) GKC §155k; *IBHS*, 338. NIV treats the verb "deluded" as an adjective modifying heart.

[503] The imperfect verb יַצִּיל probably has the modal sense of "he *cannot* deliver" (GKC § 107 m-n,r).

ances (the "I will" promises in vv. 21b and 22a).[504] How should the Israelites think about their relationship with the divine Creator so that they do not fall into this erroneous thinking? They need to "remember,"[505] to think about the fact that they are God's servants (41:8–9; 43:10; 44:1), not the servants of these other gods of wood. They should remember that God formed them (43:1,21; 44:2); he was not formed out of the imagination of the Israelites like the idols (44:9,10,12). Because of this close social relationship between God and his servant ("you are my servants"), God makes a promise that he will dedicate himself to that special relationship and not forget Israel.[506] The challenge is for Israel to dedicate herself not to forget the nature of her privileged relationship with God. They need to beware lest they fall into the blinding trap of thinking that the idols that the nations worship have great power. The God of Israel is their Redeemer and King (44:8); he is the only real God who can determine their destiny.

The second exhortation (v. 22b) calls for the audience to repent and turn to God, not anyone else. God provides two rationales that should motivate the listeners to respond positively. First, God encourages his people to respond because he has wiped out their rebellion and forgiven them (43:25). Like a morning haze is swept away by a breeze,[507] so God will sweep away their sins so that they disappear from sight because he has forgiven them. This is a great example of God's grace extended toward the people he loves. Second, God calls for repentance because he has redeemed his people (v. 22b). In this context the idea of redemption refers to the redemption from sin rather than deliverance from some enemy. These two assurances demonstrate that God will remove the central problem (sin) that haunts the relationship between God and his people. God initiates the restoration of their relationship by graciously calling them, giving them faith, and providing for the removal of guilt; so now his servants need to initiate a response of repentance and turning to God.

CONCLUDING HYMNIC PRAISE OF GOD (44:23)

23Sing for joy, O heavens, for the LORD has done this;
    shout aloud, O earth beneath.

---

[504] O'Connell, *Concentricity and Continuity*, 182–83, also finds vv. 21–22 to be related to 44:6–8.

[505] זְכָר "remember" is an imperative that exhorts or admonishes the audience to act in a certain way (GKC §110a).

[506] North, *Second Isaiah*, 142, discusses various alternative approaches to תִנָּשֵׁנִי which is vocalized as a *niphal* imperfect. Some take it from root I, נָשָׁה "forget." North prefers root II, "deceive, play false with" while McKenzie, *Second Isaiah*, 70, makes this another imperative addressed to Israel, "do not forget me." NIV renders Hb. passive "you will not be forgotten by me" as an active "I will not forget you."

[507] Hos 13:1–3 has a similar comparison of the removal of idols and idol makers like the morning dew.

> Burst into song, you mountains,
>   you forests and all your trees,
> for the LORD has redeemed Jacob,
>   he displays his glory in Israel.

The long section 42:14–44:23 ends with a short hymn of praise to God, just like the conclusion of the preceding section (42:10–13).[508] In light of who God is, what he has done, and what he promises to do, all the inhabitants of the heavens and the earth should shout for joy and praise God. With grand poetic metaphors the prophet even pictures the transformed part of nature proclaiming God's glory (55:12–13). God's praise should come from the heaven above and the underparts of the earth. Mountains, trees, and forests should break forth with singing. Two reasons are given to summarize the motivation for praising God: (a) because God has acted (v. 23a) and (b) because he has redeemed his people (v. 23c). These two rationales sum up important aspects of God's sovereign grace displayed to his people. God is not a dead idol of wood that can do nothing; he is a living divine power who acts, creates, controls all of nature, and determines the history of humanity from the beginning of history until the final parts of his future plans are accomplished. Of course, among the greatest acts of God is his loving redemption of his people from sin. These divine deeds should cause people to praise God and glorify his name, for he alone is God. But God's glorification is not conditional or dependent on blind Israel's response; he will "glorify himself" (*yitpāʾār*, 44:23; cf. 49:3) in Israel. This issue is explained more fully in future chapters when God's glory comes to rest on and over his people (60:1–3). God will glorify his place (60:13), and people will glorify God with their gifts (60:9). God will be their glory (60:19), and then his people will be like a glorious crown in the Lord's right hand (62:3).

THEOLOGICAL IMPLICATIONS.   What are the key theological implications that develop out of this message about God and these man-made objects? Since a comparison between the idols and God was never stated explicitly in vv. 9–20, the commentary above focuses on what was said and only makes a few explicit references to an implied comparison. Nevertheless, at this point it is appropriate to identify many of the theological implications of the message. If people were aware of what the prophet had said earlier about God, the sensitive, spiritually minded person would immediately see how these factors contrast with what was said about the idols and the idol makers.

---

[508] Oswalt, *Isaiah 40–66*, 189–91, puts 44:23–28 together and sees the hymn as introductory to the longer section 44:23–47:15. He also did not see the hymn in 42:10–13 as the conclusion to the preceding section. This understanding of the hymn disagrees with how this study treats these structural markers as the conclusion to longer literary sections of the text (see "Structure" in the introduction to this commentary).

What was said?	What contrast was implied?
1. Men "form" idols (44:9)	God "forms" the world and his people
2. Idols do not help; give no profit (44:9)	God strengthens and helps his people
3. Their witness does not see, know (44:9)	God's witnesses see and know
4. Idol makers tremble in fear (44:11)	God's people need not fear
5. Idol makers will be ashamed (44:11)	God's people will not be ashamed
6. Idol makers get tired and weary (44:12)	God's strengthens so people are not weary
7. Idol makers measure on wood (44:13)	God measures out the heavens with his hand
8. Idols are images of humanity (44:13)	God made man in his image
9. Idols are wood and metal (44:14)	God made the wood and the metals
10. People worship what they make (44:15)	The Maker/Creator should be worshipped
11. People seek divine deliverance (44:17)	Only God can bring real deliverance
12. Idols blind people's eyes (44:18)	God opens people's eyes
13. Idols give no understanding (44:19)	God gives wisdom and understanding
14. Idolatry is a deceptive lie (44:20)	God reveals the truth
15. Idols lead people astray (44:20)	God calls people to turn from lies

These contrasts should have persuaded the prophet's audience to believe that the worldview of idolatry is based on deceptive lies that will not profit anyone. People who make an object of wood, stone, or metal and then bow before it are fooling themselves and setting themselves up for a shameful day of disillusionment. This world's various religions and philosophies may attempt to explain how things run in this world and these ideas may be widely held by millions of people, but any system of beliefs and practices that is not firmly based on what God says is a deception that will be of no profit.

God claims that people are sometimes blind and cannot see the truth (44:18–20). Left to their sinful ways, people know little about God and what he expects of them. Their eyes are frequently blinded by prejudice, traditional cultural customs, and false teachings. Too many people do not see the inconsistencies in their own beliefs and are easily misled by deceptive claims. Some may attempt to save themselves by good works, but relatively few come to the realization that these things will not save them. What they need is someone to tell them the truth about God (44:6–8) and the truth about their deceptions. They need to repent of their sins and accept God's forgiveness (44:21–22). There are only two ways to live: (a) a way of ignorance and shame that leads to no deliverance or (b) a way of understanding that leads to God's forgiveness and joy.

Confusion concerning the nature and will of God is present in every culture; it is not something limited to ancient cultures where idols were worshipped. Any religious person that elevates man-made things in this world (e.g., their possessions, status, role) to the status of being a source of strength, wisdom, or deliverance has bought into a deceptive cultural lie that will only bring fear and shame. Since every man-made source of meaning and security will result in failure and hopelessness, the only real solid hope for humanity is in God and his plans for this world.

4. God Will Restore Jerusalem but Offers Salvation to All (44:24–45:25)

This section contains two larger literary units (44:24–45:13 and 45:14–45:25) that focus on what will happen when God sends his people off to Babylon, as predicted in 39:6–7. The present and future generations need to know that Babylon (47:1–15) and its idols are really impotent (46:1–5) and that the strong ruler Koresh (NIV, Cyrus) will one day be involved in some way with the rebuilding of the temple in Jerusalem (44:26–28).

At this point the prophet addresses the many questions that his audience might raise about what will happen. Does this defeat mean that the Babylonian gods are more powerful than Israel's God? Is this conquest of God's people the beginning of the end of the nation of Judah, or will it arise to power once again? How will they be delivered from the power of Babylon? What are the theological implications if Judah is defeated? If these things happen, what does this imply about God's sovereign control of history?

To answer some of these questions the prophet presents a consistent portrayal of Israel's God as the Creator (44:24; 45:7,9,11,12,18) and the sovereign God who is in control of everything that will happen in the future.[509] His sovereign power and identity is hammered home in the repeated "I am the LORD" phrases (44:24; 45:3,5,6,7,8,18,19,21) that proclaim his name and what he will do. Among his many acts will be his empowerment of a king by the name of Koresh[510] to subdue many nations, thus setting the stage for the possibility of rebuilding Jerusalem (44:26,28; 45:1–4,13). This preannouncement of God's plans (emphasized in the repeated "says the LORD" phrase)[511] proves his sovereign control of history, and his plan should motivate his audience to trust

---

[509] Baltzer, *Deutero-Isaiah*, 209, rightly perceives that "the themes of the individual units are subordinated to the fundamental idea of God's sovereignty."

[510] Later history will call this king Cyrus, but if the goal of exegesis is to understand what the prophet said to his audience, it seems preferable to use the literal translation of the name of this unknown king because it better communicates what the audience first heard. Using the name Cyrus communicates to the modern reader much more information than what this text says because people today fully understand who this king was and what this king did.

[511] In order to emphasize this point the author repeatedly announces that כֹּה אָמַר יְהוָה "thus says Yahweh" (44:24; 45:1,11,14,18). God speaks to preannounce what he will do, demonstrating that he controls his people's history; therefore, they can trust him.

in his promises (44:26; 45:19,23). This knowledge about God should cause them to reject the baseless predictions of false prophets, wise men, and diviners (44:25; 45:16). Not only will God ensure that Jerusalem will be rebuilt, eventually people from many nations will gladly respond to God's power and salvation by bowing before him in praise (45:8,14–25). When people realize that God's great deeds of salvation are being accomplished, everyone will recognize that "I am the LORD and there is no other" god that is comparable to Yahweh (45:5,6,18,21).

SETTING.   When reading any prophetic message, the interpreter must be able to determine if the author is speaking about events that happened in the past (i.e., 7:1–2), describing a situation in his present setting (i.e., 7:3–6,10–12), or prophetically predicting things that will take place at some point in the future (i.e., 7:7–9). In the series of messages in 44:24–45:25 God speaks of past events when he created the earth and stretched out the heavens (44:25) plus a future day when Jerusalem will be rebuilt (44:26), but there is relatively little information that gives a hint about the present setting of the prophet and his audience in these oracles.

J. L. McKenzie concluded that the prophetic statements about Cyrus's conquests and the rebuilding of Jerusalem were made in a setting in Babylon between 550 and 540 BC after Cyrus had already gained great power and just a short time before the actual fulfillment of these events.[512] The problem with this conclusion is that it uses the date of the fulfillment of a prophecy as a guide to determine the date when the prophecy was given. But the prophet may have spoken about these things one, ten, fifty, or several hundred years (with eschatological prophecies) before the prophecy was fulfilled. An interpreter cannot assume that a prophecy always refers to something that will happen within a year or two; otherwise one would have to eliminate all eschatological prophecies from the Scriptures. C. C. Torrey tried to resolve this problem by eliminating the name of Cyrus (Hb. Koresh) as a later textual addition, while J. Smart reinterpreted the work of Koresh as the work of God's special Servant.[513] C. Westermann noted some similarities between the vocabulary used in the Cyrus Cylinder[514] and the account in 45:1–7, but the two accounts

---

[512] McKenzie, *Second Isaiah*, xviii, 78, 88, 97, concludes that this date would explain the reference to King Cyrus and it fits an audience in exile. But such a date almost eliminates the need for prophetic inspiration because almost anyone observing these events could have predicted that Cyrus would eventually attack Babylon.

[513] C. C. Torrey, *Second Isaiah: A New Interpretation* (New York: Scribner's, 1928), 41, considers the name "Cyrus" a later explanatory addition to 44:28 and 45:1 by a later hand, while Smart, *History and Theology in Second Isaiah*, 115–23, saw this passage as a creation of a fifth-century group in Jerusalem that were referring to the conquests of God's servant just before the beginning of his reign.

[514] *ANET,* 315–16, refers to Marduk, the chief Babylonian god, as "lord of the gods," a "righteous ruler," who "beheld Cyrus's good deeds and upright heart," and "took his (Cyrus's) hand." M. Smith, "II Isaiah and the Persians," *JAOS* 83 (1963): 415–21, noted numerous similarities

are not dependent on one another; so the Cyrus Cylinder cannot help date this message.[515]

A clue to the setting might be available in the woe oracle in 45:9–13. R. N. Whybray interprets these words as God's disputation against an Israelite audience that rejects God's plans to use a foreign king to restore the nation (compare this with a similar situation in Hab 1:12–17).[516] This approach to interpreting the setting of chaps. 44–45 is weakened by two factors: (a) There is no other passage that explicitly speaks of a similar Israelite rejection of the work of Cyrus. (b) In order to accept this approach one must assume that some Israelites have complained about the appropriateness of God using the pagan king Cyrus (Hb. Koresh) to accomplish his work (45:13). Since this king will be very gracious to the Hebrew people in exile and allow them to return to Jerusalem and rebuild the temple, it seems odd that any Hebrew would express an objection against one who was so kind to them. In contrast to Whybray's interpretation, J. L. Koole concludes that 45:9–10 is a citation of the people's own depressed statements that God responds to in 45:11–13.[517] In this approach the lamenting woes express the Israelites' discouraged response to God's plans because they realize they must accept whatever comes from their Maker. After hearing that God will restore Jerusalem, this is a surprising response, for one would certainly think that the prophet's audience would be extremely happy to hear about God's marvelous plans to restore Jerusalem through Cyrus in 44:24–45:8. While this general approach is on the right track, it would be better to call 45:9–10 a prophetic lamentation concerning what other Israelites were saying. They were complaining about some part of God's plans, so the prophet mourned about their unwillingness to accept what God the Potter will do in 44:9–10 (he does not quote what they say). But what negative part of God's plans for them would they likely reject?

One might suggest that the prophet's woeful lament reacts to the people's sorrow over the difficult situation they must go through (43:28; 39:6–7) before Cyrus's (Hb. Koresh) gracious work of rebuilding the city of Jerusalem. In response, God assures those who question his ways (45:11) that he will restore

---

between the first part of the Cyrus Cylinder and this section of Isaiah. He interpreted the Cyrus Cylinder as political propaganda. Since the city was peacefully captured, Smith concludes Isaiah's information came before the capture of Babylon and was inaccurate (a point that should have caused him to reevaluate his methodology and assumptions).

[515] Westermann, *Isaiah 40–66*, 156–57, notes that Marduk chose Cyrus, called him by his name, gave him success, took pleasure in him, and gave him world dominion, but he does not think that Isaiah's text was dependent on the Cyrus Cylinder.

[516] Whybray, *Isaiah 40–66*, 107–8, imagines two objections: (a) they question the likelihood that this prophecy will ever be fulfilled, and (b) they object to God's choice of a foreigner as an instrument for the salvation of his people. Muilenburg, "Isaiah 40–66," 5:526, generally agrees with this approach.

[517] Koole, *Isaiah III, Volume 1, Isaiah 40–48*, 450–51, supports this interpretation and believes the exiles are dejected and despondent (they are not objecting to the use of Cyrus).

Jerusalem (45:13), so they should not question what the potter is doing with the clay (45:9). Unfortunately, it is impossible to identify a specific historical setting when this issue arose. One might suggest that it arose immediately after 39:6–7 (701 BC) or after the fall of Jerusalem in 587 BC, but there is no way to prove either option. A somewhat related discussion of the role of the potter and the clay occurs in 29:16 in the context of the nation's attempt to hide its evil plans to save itself[518] during the Assyrian crisis, so one might imagine that there would be the same or a comparable crisis facing the audience in both settings.[519] Both speeches about a potter come at a time when the nation is facing the threat of divine punishment, so a lamenting woe because of a future divine discipline would make sense here. In the end one must be satisfied to point to an undefined setting sometime before the divine punishment of Judah and before the work of Cyrus (Hb. Koresh). Since the evidence for an exact date is not provided, no definitive setting can be assigned to these chapters.

STRUCTURE. The two messages in this unit reveal God's divine character to his own people and to all the nations of the world. He argues that he alone is God, the Creator and Redeemer, because he is able to predict, direct, empower, and assure his people that his plans will be accomplished (44:24–45:13). This material fits into two paragraphs:[520]

God will direct history through his shepherd Cyrus   44:24–45:13
One day, Israel and the nations will bow before God   45:14–25

These messages assure the listener that God is in charge of the future events related to the demise and revival of the nation as well as the eschatological work of providing everlasting salvation for people from all nations. In the distant future many will turn to God and be saved (45:14–23), then every knee will bow in worship before God and praise his holy name (45:24–25).

(1) God Will Direct History through His Shepherd Cyrus (44:24–45:13)

This section has several short paragraphs that begin with an announcement of a fresh word from God (44:24; 45:1). They are unified by their repeated portrayal of God as the Creator (44:24; 45:7,11,12), the one who alone is God (the "I am" statements in 44:24; 45:3,5,6,7,8).[521] Although it might be tempting to focus attention on the surprising naming of Cyrus (Hb. Koresh) as God's anointed and his shepherd, in actuality, God himself is firmly placed on the

[518] This is probably a reference to their alliance with Egypt (cf. 28:15; 30:1–5; 31:1–3).

[519] Williamson, *The Book Called Isaiah*, 59–63, states that the similarity between "29:16 and 45:9 may be regarded as a firm example of the literary influence of the earlier part of Isaiah on the later," but he draws no conclusion about the setting of 45:9 from this literary dependence.

[520] By contrast Spykerboer, *The Structure and Composition of Deutero-Isaiah*, 130, divides this material into three paragraphs: (a) 44:24–45:7; (b) 45:8; (c) 45:9–25. Below it will be argued that 45:9–13 continues the discussion of Cyrus; therefore, it should be part of the preceding unit.

[521] See comments on 41:2–4.

main stage throughout this speech. God's centrality is related to his past acts of creation, his redemption of his people, his present shaming of the wise men and diviners, his empowering of Cyrus to defeat many nations, and his future plans to rebuild Jerusalem (44:26,27; 45:1–4,13). If God can do all these things, the prophet's audience should trust his words (44:26) and reject any false teachings that others might propound (44:25). This explanation of God's future plans for his people is expressed in three paragraphs:

God directs the restoration of Jerusalem	44:24–28
God's direction of Cyrus proves he is God	45:1–8
God's sovereignty should remove all doubts	45:9–13

These literary units are held together by the common use of the phrase "I am the LORD" (44:24; 45:5,6) and by mentioning God's use of Cyrus (Hb. Koresh) to accomplish his purposes (44:28; 45:1,13). Cyrus is but one of the many instruments in God's hands as he sovereignly directs the past and future destiny of his people (10:5; Jer 50:1–3). Each person functions in his own time and way to accomplish the plans and purposes of God. The value of mentioning the name Cyrus in this rhetorical conversation is that the later fulfillment of this prophecy will provide one more proof that God controls history and functions as one who fulfills his plans. The audience needs to accept that he is God and trust him.

GOD DIRECTS THE RESTORATION OF JERUSALEM (44:24–28)

24"This is what the LORD says—
    your Redeemer, who formed you in the womb:

I am the LORD,
    who has made all things,
    who alone stretched out the heavens,
    who spread out the earth by myself,

25who foils the signs of false prophets
    and makes fools of diviners,
who overthrows the learning of the wise
    and turns it into nonsense,
26who carries out the words of his servants
    and fulfills the predictions of his messengers,

who says of Jerusalem, 'It shall be inhabited,'
    of the towns of Judah, 'They shall be built,'
    and of their ruins, 'I will restore them,'
27who says to the watery deep, 'Be dry,
    and I will dry up your streams,'
28who says of Cyrus, 'He is my shepherd
    and will accomplish all that I please;
he will say of Jerusalem, "Let it be rebuilt,"
    and of the temple, "Let its foundations be laid." '

R. F. Melugin finds in this paragraph a disputation promise arguing that God will restore Jerusalem.[522] But there is no one disputing what God claims in this paragraph; instead, this paragraph provides a message of hope and salvation that was heavily influenced by the use of participles (as in 40:22–23,28–29) and hymnic themes[523] that identify God's sovereign work.[524] K. Baltzer and J. P. Fokkelman note the repeated use of a series of three literary characteristics that gives structure to the material.[525] The paragraph can be divided into two parts:

A Claim: God does what he says he will do	44:24–26a
Yahweh is Creator and Redeemer	24
God will make fools of false prophets	25
God fulfills what his prophets proclaim	26a
A Proof: God will use Cyrus to rebuild Jerusalem	44:26b–28
God will restore Judah	26b
God has power over the deep	27
God will see that Jerusalem is rebuilt	28

These words were designed to assure the audience that they can trust God's promises of salvation. God will disgrace the temple and destroy Judah because of the people's sins (43:22–28), but this does not mean that God is powerless or that they should believe what some false prophets might say (44:25). All of God's plans will be fulfilled.

44:24–26a   The prophet had already informed his audience that it was part of God's plan to judge Judah through the Assyrians (22:1–13; 29:1–4) and the Babylonians (39:5–7). In earlier messages they had already heard words about the eventual restoration of his people at some point in the future (4:2–6; 9:1–7; 11:1–16; 14:1–3; 26:1–6; 29:22–24; 30:19–26; 32:1–8; 35:1–10), but they did

---

[522] Melugin, *Formation of Isaiah 40–55*, 38–39, 123, believes this unit uses the style of a hymn, because of all the participles, for the purpose of answering a disputation.

[523] C. Broyles, "The Citations of Yahweh in Isaiah 44:26–28," in *Writing and Reading the Scroll of Isaiah*, 399–421, finds similar themes in Psalms: (a) 44:24 in Ps 69:36; (b) 44:27 in Ps 74:15; (c) 44:28 in Pss 78:69–72; 132; and 77:16–21. He dates all these Psalms as exilic and concludes that the prophet was echoing these Psalms.

[524] H. Gressmann, "Die literarische Analyse Deuterojesajas," *ZAW* 34 (1914): 254–97, calls this a hymn, but God is speaking about himself; others are not praising him. Melugin, *Formation of Isaiah 40–55*, 122, believes the hymnic style of this paragraph functions as a disputational promise in which God argues against the claims of others that he will rebuild Jerusalem, but this gives far too much weight to false prophets and wise men in v. 25.

[525] Both J. P. Fokkelman, "The Cyrus Oracle (Isaiah 44,24–45,7) from the Perspective of Syntax, Versification, and Structure," *Studies in the Book of Isaiah: Festschrift Willem A.M. Beuken*, eds. J. Van Ruiten and M. Vervenne (Leuven: Peeters, 1997), 303–23, and Baltzer, *Deutero-Isaiah*, 211, find each of the new statements in vv. 24–28 beginning with a series of three participles (in 24 three *Qal* participles, in vv. 25–26a three *hiphil* participles beginning with מ, in vv. 26b,27,28 three participles with the article affixed, הָאֹמֵר). Long ago O. T. Allis, *The Unity of Isaiah* (Philadelphia: Presbyterian and Reformed, 1950), 64–70, noted these characteristics.

not know when this would happen or exactly how it would be accomplished. Those restoration messages that refer to the transformation of nature, the Gentiles worshipping God, and the coming of everlasting peace and justice should be considered eschatological, but this message appears to be a promise of restoration involving historical events well before the eschatological end of the age. God's plan to judge Judah was no doubt hard to accept, but his gracious promise to rebuild Jerusalem (44:28) was wonderful news. Since this plan involves judgment, God precedes this unusual promise with assuring words that were intended to convince the listeners that God has always accomplished everything that he has predicted. None of his promises have failed in the past, nor will they fail in the future.

Three substantiations were provided to motivate the audience to believe what God says: (a) God's past marvelous acts in the redemption of his people and the creation of the world demonstrate his authority and power to accomplish his will (44:24); (b) God's present plans will confound and demolish the skeptical wisdom of the false prophets and diviners (44:25); and (c) God will do what his prophets predicted he would do (44:26a).

44:24 Should the Israelites believe what God has promised? Should they trust God to restore the nation even though parts of it will be in ruins (43:28)? Yes, they should believe God because the one who is speaking to them is "your Redeemer [gō'ălekā], the one who formed you in the womb." God can be compared to a human redeemer because he fulfilled the responsibility of a family member by setting free or ransoming another family member who was in distress, in debt, or imprisoned.[526] The deliverance of the people of Israel from Egyptian bondage is the prime example of God's redemption of his people (Exod 14–15; Isa 51:10). The exodus experience of redemption was a time when God took a group of oppressed people and formed them into a nation. This divine title "Redeemer" describes characteristics of God that existed many years ago, but implicit within this title is the supposition that a God who goes by this name can still act in the same way in the future. The announcement that "I am the LORD" ('ānōkî yhwh) completes the dramatic introduction, but it only begins a long list of reminders about God's great deeds.

In hymnic style, using three participles, God announces that he was the one who "made, created" the world (44:23b); thus by implication, he can be trusted to handle any problems that arise in the world he made. He makes several assertions. (a) I am the one who made "all things" (kōl). Such a statement undermines the mythology of all other religious systems because it claims cre-

---

[526] H. Ringgren, "גָּאַל gā'al; גֹּאֵל gō'ēl; גְּאֻלָּה gᵉ'ullāh," TDOT, 2: 350–55, draws the meaning of this term from the legal and social life of people. Thus just as people freed or liberated people in their family from various perils, so God could act as the redeemer of people in his family. Sometimes a payment is made to redeem a person (Lev 25:47–54 in the case of redemption from slavery) or an animal (Lev 27:13–31 in the case of where it was dedicated to God), but the word also had a broader meaning of delivering people from oppression, an enemy, or death (Jer 31:11; Ps 107:2).

ative power for Israel's God over everything that exists. There are no exceptions; all other claims must be dismissed. (b) He is the one who "all alone" (*lĕbaddî*) stretched out (the second participle) the heavens like a tent cloth (40:22; 48:13). No other gods did this, and none helped him with this work. (c) He is the one who "beat out, spread out"[527] (the third participle) the vast distances of the earth. To express unique creative power, the verse ends in Hebrew with a rhetorical question, literally, "Who was with me?" NIV renders this paraphrastically "by myself."[528] C. Westermann views these statements as the self-glorification of a deity and believes "we can be certain that he adopted it from his Babylonian environment."[529] But there is good reason to doubt the certainty of this conclusion, for the style of using participles to glorify God by proclaiming what he has done was a common characteristic in Hebrew hymnic literature (Ps 103:3–5; Amos 4:13) and God makes similar claims elsewhere in Isaiah (40:22; 43:1,14a,15a; 44:2,6).

44:25–26a This portion is marked off by a group of three *hiphil* participles that begin each line and the three imperfect verbs at the end of each line. These participles express how God is sovereignly controlling this world at the present time.[530] God is the one "who foils, frustrates"[531] the interpretation of signs received by people who boast that they are able to explain what the gods mean by these signs.[532] J. L. McKenzie believes these people who deal with

---

[527] לקע can mean "to beat out, stamp out, stretch out" and describes the work of a goldsmith who hammers gold or silver into thin layers (40:19; Exod 39:3; Jer 10:9). N. C. Habel, "He Who Stretches out the Heavens," *CBQ* 34 (1972): 417–30, connects the second participle נׁטֶה "the one stretching out" with ideas related to God's tent (the heavens were his tent before the tabernacle was made), which in some ways corresponds to the world (Exod 25:9,40; 40:16–38).

[528] Goldingay, *The Message of Isaiah 40–55: A Literary-Theological Commentary* (London: T&T Clark, 2005), 255, says that the "overt polemic against the claims of and for other gods disappear—though such polemic may be covertly present, for other gods make parallel claims."

[529] Westermann, *Isaiah 40–66*, 156, also was aware of similar hymns used in Egypt. An example of a Babylonian hymn of this type is a hymn of Inanna: "I, the queen of heaven am I. Is there one god who can vie with me? I, a warrior am I. Is there one god who can vie with me?" T. Jacobsen, *The Treasures of Darkness: A History of Mesopotamian Religions* (New Haven: Yale, 1976, 138. But this theme of praising God as Creator and sovereign over history is common in Israelite hymns of praise, so there is no need to look for comparative examples outside of Israelite culture. Whybray, *Isaiah 40–66*, 103, rejects any connection to Mesopotamian literature because Mesopotamian examples come from a much earlier time and because Isaiah is here arguing against a polytheistic tradition.

[530] Baltzer, *Deutero-Isaiah*, 213, follows W. A. M. Beuken in interpreting the prophet "to express action that is going on now" or action that God is in the process of accomplishing (cf. GKC §116c,n for the use of the participle in present tense, expressing durative action).

[531] מֵפֵר comes from the root פָּרַר which means to "break, frustrate, annul, make ineffective." It is used when sinful Judah prays to God asking that he not "annul, break, make ineffective" the covenant he has with his people (Jer 14:21). In 2 Sam 15:34 David counsels Hushai to return to Jerusalem and eavesdrops on what Absalom was planning so that he could "annul, frustrate, make ineffective" these plans by informing David about these plans.

[532] These people are called בַּדִּים, which could come from בָּדַד, root I "to be separate, isolated"; root II, "a part, portion" (that is, a "limb" is part of a body in Job 18:13 or "bars" that are a

signs and omens are Babylonian *bārû* priests,[533] but the Babylonian officials by this name appeared hundreds of years before the time of Isaiah and it is not clear that these old methods of understanding the will of the gods were widely used in the later Neo-Assyrian period (680–612 BC).[534] Consequently, one should look at these religious people as either Israelite or foreign "idle talkers, liars," who claim to be able to explain various signs as revelations of the will of the gods. The text does not explain what kind of signs these were, but if their work was somewhat parallel to that of the "diviners" (*qōsĕmîm*; as in 3:2; Josh 13:22; 1 Sam 6:2; 28:8), these signs probably refer to attempts to explain the will of the gods through natural happenings (i.e., an eclipse, movement of the stars, a dream, a rainbow). God will "make[s] fools"[535] of those who attempt to explain the supernatural in this way, and consequently he will delegitimize these religious experts and bring into question the validity of their gods.

The second participle explains how God does the opposite of what is expected. He "turns back" (*mēšîb* "the one who turns, returns"; NIV "overthrows") the words of the wise men. These could be political advisors to a king or religious functionaries parallel to the diverse group of people who advised the kings of Egypt and Babylon (47:10; Exod 7:11; Dan 2:27). The result will be that God will make their knowledge foolishness.[536] These statements undermined the credibility of every source of trust except God himself. A person would have to be a fool to follow such unprofitable advice, for none of it would be reliable.

The third participle (44:26a) points to a dependable alternative. God is "the one who confirms, establishes, fulfills" (*mēqîm*; NIV "carries out") the statements made by his servant[537] and accomplishes the wise counsel provided

---

part of the gate of a city in Job 17:16); but more likely it comes from root III, "to talk idly, boast" (16:6; Jer 48:30; 50:36). In light of the parallelism with "diviners" and the "wise," these people might be religious officials, possibly priests at pagan places of worship, but this conclusion goes far beyond the evidence.

[533] McKenzie, *Second Isaiah*, 72, suggests that the Hebrew בַּדִּים was confused with בָּרִים, a simple confusion between ד and ר. With the find of *baddum* priests at the ancient city of Mari, this hypothesis is no longer needed.

[534] R. R. Wilson, *Prophecy and Society in Ancient Israel* (Philadelphia: Fortress, 1980), 89–124, describes the various religious functionaries in Old Babylon, Mari, and in the Neo-Assyrian period. In the later period, which is closest to the time of Isaiah, the *šabrû* apparently replaced the *bārû* priests (p. 112), but this spelling is not used in 44:25.

[535] There may be a play on words with the use of הָלַל "to be confused, blind, become a fool" (root III) and הָלַל "to praise" (root II). The diviners should bring praise to their gods, but when God interferes with their explanation of their signs, he shows these diviners to be very foolish and confused.

[536] The Hebrew word יְשַׂכֵּל means "to be wise, successful," which does not fit in this context. 1QIs[a] has יסכל and the Old Greek agrees with this reading. שׂ and ס are the same "s" sound. J. D. W. Watts, *Isaiah 34–66*, WBC (Waco: Word, 1987), 150, believes this "is a solid example of double meaning, or tongue in cheek sarcasm."

[537] NIV has "his servants" which follows the Aramaic Targum and a few Greek MSS to make it agree with "his messengers" in the second line. NASB and HCSB keep the sg. of the Masoretic

by his prophetic messengers. Thus God's words are reliable and trustworthy. J. Oswalt thinks "my servant" refers to the prophet himself while the second line expands the statement to include all the true prophets of God.[538] J. Muilenburg believes the servant is Israel, while J. Koole encourages more study into the possibility that this servant might be the "Servant of the Lord" mentioned in 42:1.[539] It is not very clear which of these possible interpretations to accept because of the ambiguity of the text. It seems to be saying that God's prophetic messengers (including Isaiah) are the authoritative ones people should listen to; they are not like the diviners, wise men, or idle boasters in 44:25. In God's eyes there is no debate or dispute about these issues; God is instructing his people concerning his past (creation and redemption), present (accomplishing his promises), and future (44:26b–28) plans, so that the audience will confidently follow him.

44:26b–28   The final subparagraph contains a series of three identical participles (lit., "the one who says" in 26b,27a,28a) that introduce what God will do sometime in the future. God is "the one who says" ($h\bar{a}'\bar{o}m\bar{e}r$)[540] to Jerusalem and to the cities of Judah three things: "It (Jerusalem) shall be inhabited . . . they [the cities of Judah] will be built. . . . I will restore them [the ruins]." If this prophecy was understood in the context of 43:28 or 39:6–7, then the audience would understand that people would once again dwell in the city of Jerusalem at some point after a period of time in Babylon. But no mention is made of Babylon in the immediate context, so one must be particularly careful not to read into this text more than what was evident to the audience. At the very least this promise expresses God's commitment to have people live in Jerusalem and the land of Judah after a war; he will not forsake his land or them.

In some ways 44:27 seems almost out of place, for its reference to the depths of the sea interrupts the discussion of rebuilding Jerusalem that continues in v. 28. There are numerous opinions about what "the watery deep" ($ṣ\hat{u}l\hat{a}$) means or symbolizes. Does it refer to the depths of the waters at creation (Gen 1:2), the depths of the ocean during Noah's flood (Gen 7:24), the depths of the Red Sea at the exodus from Egypt (Exod 15:4–5), a mythological reference to the god of the depths of the ocean, to the River Euphrates that was dried up during

---

and DSS texts. The Hebrew sg. reading is a harder reading, while the pl. would be a natural later adjustment that a scribe might make to make the two lines agree.

[538] Oswalt, *Isaiah 40–66*, 194, agrees with Young, *Isaiah*, 3:190, but Calvin, "Isaiah," 388, rejects this view.

[539] Muilenburg, "Isaiah 40–66," 5:518, says "the servant is prophetic Israel; to him Yahweh has revealed his word," but Koole, *Isaiah III, Volume 1, Isaiah 40–48*, 421, leaves room for this to refer to a Messianic approach because he is the one who will confirm and fulfill God's words and he was entrusted with the responsibility to proclaim God's words and establish God's justice.

[540] Waltke and O'Connor (*IBHS*, 621) discuss the translation of the participle as a relative clause, especially when it has the article (as in this case).

Cyrus's conquest of Babylon, or is the depths just a symbol?[541] If this passage is compared to other passages about waters or floods one realizes that: (a) Assyria was a destructive flood that attacked Israel and Judah (8:7–8; 17:12–13; 28:2; 30:28);[542] this would be a natural symbol of a future military attack in which God overcomes an enemy nation (43:2); (b) the deliverance of Israel through the waters of the Red Sea was a sign of God's miraculous deliverance (Exod 14–15; 43:2; 51:10). Thus water and flood imagery can function negatively or positively. Since 44:27 refers to the "drying up" of the waters (a positive point) instead of the coming of an overwhelming flood (a destructive image), one must interpret this passage as a positive act concerning God's deliverance of his people (comparable to the deliverance through the Red Sea on dry ground in Exod 14:21–22), not as a picture of some nation defeating God's people.[543]

Isaiah 44:28 returns to the themes in v. 26 and explains how God will accomplish this transformation of Jerusalem. For the third time the reader is informed that God is the One who says (*hā'ōmēr*) and accomplishes his will. He will speak to "Cyrus, my shepherd" (NIV, "who says of Cyrus, 'He is my shepherd'") to accomplish these things. As God's shepherd (a symbol of a king), Cyrus (Hb. Koresh) will be obedient and do everything God pleases. Specifically, he will give the instructions (*lē'mōr* "by saying") that Jerusalem and the temple should be rebuilt. The passive verbs ("let it be rebuilt" and "let its foundations be laid") indicate that Cyrus will not do the building but give permission so that others may do this work. This verse raises numerous interpretive problems.

Although it was concluded above that it is impossible to give a specific date for the proclamation of this prophecy, the reference to Koresh does raise numerous problems for interpreters. For those who date this prophecy to the

---

[541] Baltzer, *Deutero-Isaiah*, 218–19, discusses the possibility that the prophet was drawing his imagery from a mythical story about a conflict between Baal and Yam (the god of the sea) in Ugaritic mythology; thus, the enemies of God (the flood) are overcome just like in the mythology. Goldingay, *Message of Isaiah 40–55*, 259, says, "While it no doubt indicates that Babylon can be overcome, it would be prosaic to refer to Cyrus's famous alleged diverting of the Euphrates to facilitate his capture of Babylon, referred to by Herodotus (I, 191) and Xenophon (*Cyropaedia* 7)." D. M. Gunn, "Deutero-Isaiah and the Flood," *JBL* 94 (1975): 493–508, concludes that this passage fits with 50:2; 51:10; 54:9–10, and 55:10–13 to refer to Noah's flood. The Targum takes the depths to be imagery of Babylon.

[542] Isaiah 42:15 is a difficult verse to interpret. It appears after imagery of God's judgment in 42:13–14, but it uses "drying up" instead of "the coming overwhelming flood" imagery. Nevertheless, the context suggests that it has a negative meaning. Elsewhere, drought is a sign of God's judgment (Deut 28:22–24; 1 Kgs 17:1; Jer 14:1–9; Amos 4:7; Hag 1:9–11). If 44:27 is interpreted in light of 42:15, it would be possible to give the drying-up imagery a negative meaning. This approach might work if v. 27 were placed in the midst of 45:1–8 where Cyrus is defeating many nations, but that is not the context of 44:24–28.

[543] Childs, *Isaiah*, OTL (Louisville: Westminster John Knox, 2001), 353, concludes: "The address to the 'deep' resonates with the notes of the drying up of the floods at the Red Sea (Exod 15:5; Neh 9:11)."

time of Isaiah, it is odd to have such a specific prophecy that includes the name of an individual given about 160 years before the prophecy was fulfilled (assuming Koresh refers to Cyrus). Consequently, R. K. Harrison suggests that the name Koresh was probably a scribal gloss that was added to this text after the prophecy was actually fulfilled so that the reader would know what this prophecy was all about. Others defend the inclusion of this specific name so many years away from its fulfillment by pointing to another specific prophecy given over 160 years before Josiah fulfilled it by destroying an altar at Bethel (1 Kgs 13:2 was fulfilled in 2 Kgs 23:15–17).[544] Since 45:3 indicates that God "summons you by name," one might expect to find the name of this person somewhere within 44:28–45:8. Cyrus is probably a king because kings were often called shepherds,[545] but his origins, history, and the time of his decree concerning Jerusalem are left unstated. When a prophet would give a prophecy, he would not know whether it would be fulfilled in two years or one hundred years; so this prophecy would not have appeared unusual to the people hearing this message.

R. N. Whybray resolves this unusual reference to Cyrus by suggesting that a later prophet ("Deutero-Isaiah") wrote this section while living in Babylon during the time of the Persian king Cyrus (550–538 BC); thus it would not be odd to have a prophet predict these details in such a specific way, especially if he was already aware of Cyrus's growing power and past Persian policies toward exiled peoples.[546] Many critical commentators tend to have a perspective similar to Whybray and conservative studies generally disagree with him, so this controversy remains unresolved. Both groups accept this as a true prophecy,[547] but they disagree on the date when it was spoken because there is nothing in these verses that indicates the exact time when this prophecy was spoken.

The second problem relates to the identity of Koresh. From the point of view of the original readers and the meaning they understood (the main focus of any exegetical remark), the name Koresh[548] may have been totally unknown. In 45:1–8 the readers will learn that he will be a strong king who will defeat many nations and that he will not be a Hebrew king who knows God. He will be empowered by God to do these things so that everyone would know that there is

---

[544] R. K. Harrison, *Introduction to the Old Testament* (Grand Rapids: Eerdmans, 1969), 794–95. Torrey, *Second Isaiah*, 41, and Baltzer, *Deutero-Isaiah*, 223, also came to this conclusion. Of course this is always a hypothetical possibility, but without any evidence to support this idea, it remains unsubstantiated. Motyer, *Isaiah*, 355, rejects this approach because this section of the book of Isaiah is all about God being able to predict the future and accomplish what he says he will do.

[545] 2 Sam 5:2; Jer 3:15; 23:1; Ezek 34; Mic 5:5.

[546] Whybray, *Isaiah 40–66*, 20–23, 102–4.

[547] Commentators have sometimes been accused of not believing in prophecy, but the issue is more related to the time when the prophecy was given and fulfilled. Some critical commentators do not believe in prophecy that refers to events far in the future; instead, they claim that all prophecy referred to events in the prophets' context or in the near future.

[548] In Persian documents Cyrus is called *Kuru* or *Kuruš*.

no other God. But the text did not reveal to the original audience where Cyrus (Hb. Koresh) will come from, what nations he will defeat, or when he will arise to power. This text does not even say that he will defeat Babylon; so the prophecy about Cyrus is quite vague, except for the name. From the perspective of later years after the prophecy was fulfilled, Ezra 1:1–4 indicates that the Persian king Cyrus made a decree that allowed the Hebrews in exile to return to Jerusalem and rebuild the temple. This fulfillment information is important in order to understand how God fulfilled this promise, but if one is trying to understand what the prophet predicted and what the original hearers understood, one has to put aside our present knowledge of Cyrus's fulfillment and focus on God's encouraging promise to restore Jerusalem through this king sometime in the future. Their faith needed to be in God, not in this mysterious Koresh.

A third problem arises from the nature of the decree Cyrus will announce in 44:28b. Verse 28b is somewhat repetitious of the content of 44:26. J. Blenkinsopp omits v. 28b as a later addition. But repetition is a common characteristic of Hebrew poetry. The repetition here serves the purpose of clarifying and emphasizing the difficult and strange news that Cyrus (Hb. Koresh) is the one who will accomplish what God pleases.[549] Although the exact words in the two speeches are not identical (only "Jerusalem" and "build" are repeated), both express encouragement and a prediction that God will be responsible for the rebuilding of Jerusalem and the temple. Although Ezra 1:1–4 permits people to return and build the temple, it says nothing about rebuilding the city. One should not claim that this was a false prophecy because Cyrus did not complete the building of the temple or the city. Isaiah 44:28 indicates only that Koresh will encourage and give permission to accomplish the rebuilding of the temple. Cyrus permitted the laying of the foundations for the temple and Ezra's record indicates that did happen during his reign (Ezra 3:10). As events worked out over the years, opposition by local inhabitants led to delays and the stopping of construction (Ezra 4:1–5); so the temple was not completed until the sixth year of Darius (516 BC, Ezra 6:14), about twenty years after the original decree. The complete rebuilding of the cities of Judah and the city of Jerusalem was not completed under Cyrus, for Nehemiah was still working on this in 445 BC during the reign of Artaxerxes. Cyrus's decree in the Cyrus Cylinder (*ANET,* 315–16) indicates that he not only authorized the return of exiled people to their native lands, but also the building of their cities and sanctuaries.

GOD'S DIRECTION OF CYRUS PROVES HE IS GOD (45:1–8)

1"This is what the LORD says to his anointed,
**   to Cyrus, whose right hand I take hold of**
** to subdue nations before him**
**   and to strip kings of their armor,**

---

[549] J. Blenkinsopp, *Isaiah 40–55,* 244–48.

to open doors before him
  so that gates will not be shut:
²I will go before you
  and will level the mountains;
I will break down gates of bronze
  and cut through bars of iron.
³I will give you the treasures of darkness,
  riches stored in secret places,
so that you may know that I am the L ord,
  the God of Israel, who summons you by name.
⁴For the sake of Jacob my servant,
  of Israel my chosen,
I summon you by name
  and bestow on you a title of honor,
  though you do not acknowledge me.
⁵I am the L ord, and there is no other;
  apart from me there is no God.
I will strengthen you,
  though you have not acknowledged me,
⁶so that from the rising of the sun
  to the place of its setting
men may know there is none besides me.
  I am the L ord, and there is no other.
⁷I form the light and create darkness,
  I bring prosperity and create disaster;
  I, the L ord, do all these things.

⁸"You heavens above, rain down righteousness;
  let the clouds shower it down.
Let the earth open wide,
  let salvation spring up,
let righteousness grow with it;
  I, the L ord, have created it.

Part of the second literary unit appears to address Cyrus (he is the "you" in 45:2–5), but in reality the prophet is delivering this message to his Hebrew audience so that they will overhear what God is saying to and about this Cyrus (Hb. Koresh) figure who will play a key role in the rebuilding of Judah and its temple in Jerusalem. The reason God is doing this is explicitly explained in 45:6. God is telling them these things before they happen so that his Hebrew audience and all the people on earth will know that he is God. Thus God and the prophet are attempting to persuade the audience that they should trust God and praise him because of his marvelous deeds on their behalf.

The content of this paragraph is somewhat unique in Isaiah. C. Westermann calls 45:1–8 a royal oracle that draws on enthronement practices (comparing it to Pss 2; 110). and C. Seitz generally agrees, referring to this as God's commissioning of Cyrus.[550] Since there is no specific enthronement imagery, it is better to view these words as a revelation of what God plans for this king (but it was not a commissioning of Cyrus). These statements function like a message of hope and salvation for the Hebrew audience that overheard what God will do. The paragraph is connected to 44:24–28 by the repetition of the name Cyrus (44:28; 45:1) and the initial (44:24) and final (45:7) references to God as the Maker of everything. The structure of the oracle can be outlined as follows:

God plans to use Cyrus to defeat nations	45:1
God goes before and destroys all his opposition	45:2–3a
God did this for a reason	45:3b–4
God acts so that all people know he is God	45:5–7
God calls for a response of righteousness	45:8

The internal structure of 45:1–8 includes the repetition of phrases "I summon you by name" in vv. 3b and 4b, "though you do not acknowledge me" in vv. 4b and 5b, "I am the LORD and there is no other" in vv. 5a and 6b, and "so that" in vv. 3b,4a,6a. The conclusion to this paragraph is marked by a brief call for the heavens and God's people to respond to God's salvation by showering the earth with righteousness and justice in 45:8.

45:1   This oracle begins just like the previous one with an announcement that these are the words that the Lord has spoken, thus verifying their authenticity and authority. The following indirect statements picture Cyrus (Hb. Koresh) as "his anointed one" (*měšîḥô*).[551] The anointing did not happen in this verse, as might be expected if this were an enthronement ceremony; it has already happened. Those who were commonly anointed in Israelite life were the priests (Lev 4:3,5,16; 6:15) and kings (1 Sam 12:3,5; 16:12–13; 24:10; 2 Sam 1:14; 1 Kgs 1:32–40), and later this term will be used to describe the one who would bring peace and justice on the earth (61:1). Although it may seem a little surprising to have this term used of a foreign king, in 10:5 God used the Assyrian king as the rod in his hand to fulfill God's purposes. In 1 Kgs 19:15–16 Elisha anointed a Syrian king, and in Jer 25:9; 27:6 Nebuchadnezzar is called "my servant" because he accomplished God's will. The name or identity of this ruler is not the focus of these verses (it is mentioned only once); instead, the main emphasis of this paragraph is on God's sovereign work of accomplish-

---

[550] Westermann, *Isaiah 40–66*, 157, is followed by Melugin, *Formation of Isaiah 40–55*, 123, who also compares it to the commissioning of an Egyptian king (*ANET,* 449–450), but it is hard to overlook the absence of any reference to a crown, a throne, sitting at my right hand, or the name of a country this person is to rule over. Thus the commissioning is to a task, not the enthronement to be king.

[551] The Old Greek text reads χριστῷ μου "*my* anointed one," which would be comparable to "my shepherd" in 44:28, but there is no reason to presume that this is more original than the Hebrew text here.

ing his will through this king. God's taking hold of (lit. "strengthen," from the root *ḥāzaq*) his hand results in or has the purpose[552] of bringing nations into subjection before this king. God will unloose the sword and other instruments of war from the loins of the kings he fights,[553] making them defenseless before his advancing army. The next thing God will do is to open before him the "two doors" (Hebrew "dual" ending indicating two) and the gates of various undefined cities. In light of God's preparatory work, it is hardly possible to call this king a great conqueror; he merely cleans up the enemy after God defeats them.

45:2–3a Now God rhetorically addresses this king so that the prophet's Hebrew audience can overhear what God will do through him. Isaiah 45:2–5 appear as direct discourse to "you," but there is no indication that he was actually speaking to this king at this point.[554] Without hesitation God promises what he will do. (a) "I myself" (lit., *ʾănî*) will sovereignly go before you (repeating the same idea as in 45:1). (b) I will level the city walls.[555] (c) I will shatter bronze doors. (d) I will cut off iron bars on the gates. (e) I will give you treasures. Just as God defeated the enemies of Moses and the children of Israel many years earlier (Exod 13:21; 23:20–28; Deut 31:3), now God will direct a new person to accomplish his will. This long list of God's mighty acts emphasizes that God is in charge; he deserves the honor; he is behind everything that will happen. There is no identification of any specific city that this king will defeat because the text is primarily focusing on what God will do. Although many commentators try to connect these prophecies to specific fulfillments (the fall of Babylon and other nations Cyrus defeated),[556] the Hebrew audience would not know anything about the fulfillment until years later; thus none of that information would be part of the meaning the prophet conveyed or the meaning the original audience understood.

45:3b–4 Although one could connect the end of v. 3b to what precedes (as NIV), J. P. Fokkelman has effectively argued that the structure of these verses suggests that the two "in order that" (*lĕmaʿan*) clauses in vv. 3b and 4a should go together and modify the second part of v. 4. This puts the

---

[552] The use of the infinitive construct לְרַד could express either purpose or results (GKC §114f-h).

[553] NIV, HCSB, NASB, NRSV all translate this in parallel with the previous line and ignore that the verb in the second line (אֲפַתֵּחַ) is first pers. sg., referring to what God will do.

[554] Fokkelman, "The Cyrus Oracle (Isaiah 44,24–45,7) from the Perspective of Syntax, Versification, and Structure," 314, carefully distinguishes between the second degree discourse in v. 1 and third degree discourse in vv. 2–7.

[555] There is much confusion about the meaning of וַהֲדוּרִים. The Aramaic Targum has "walls." This may be based on Akkadian *duru* which means walls as smace C. H. Southwood, "The Problematic *hᵃhûrîm* of Isaiah XLV,2," *VT* 25 (1975): 801–2, proposes. 1QIsᵃ and the Old Greek have "mountains" implying וְהַרְרִים. This makes sense, but mountains is spelled וְהַרְרִים with one ר. The best solution is the "walls" of the Targum (and Akkadian *duru*).

[556] Whybray, *Isaiah 40–66*, 105–106, connects v. 2 to the conquest of Babylon and v. 3 to his conquest of Sardis in 546.

subordinate clause first before the main clause. So the thought process is: in order that this king might know[557] who is God and know who prophetically identified him by his name and in order that this king might know[558] that "Jacob is my servant and Israel is my chosen one," God gave him an honorable title (meaning God made Cyrus "my anointed one"). All this will happen even though this king does not know or will not acknowledge Israel's God. This suggests that God desired that this king would honor him and that he gave him every opportunity to recognize Israel's God and the Hebrew people as God's chosen ones, but somehow Koresh never did come to a full acknowledgment of Israel's God. Why was this? If this Koresh was Cyrus, a Persian king, he grew up accepting the Zoroastrian religion that honored Ahura-mazda as their good god and Angra-Mainyu as his great adversary. Cyrus also explicitly honored the Babylonian god Marduk in the Cyrus Cylinder (*ANET,* 315–16). It is not clear who he worshipped.[559] Some might try to make the case that Cyrus actually did acknowledge Israel's God based on Ezra 1:1–4, but since 45:3–5 says that Cyrus did not know God, one must conclude that Ezra 1:1–4 was either Ezra's Israelite theological slant on what Cyrus said or that the decree in Ezra was just a routine political document, much like many other documents that were composed by scribes for the numerous exiled peoples that Nebuchadnezzar had earlier settled in Babylon.[560] Surely there is hidden within these verses the implied admonitions that people need to recognize that (a) God is the one who directs the affairs of life; and (b) the victories of life do not come because a person deserves them; they come because a gracious God gives them.

45:5–7 Although God's revelation of himself and his wonderful deeds on behalf of Cyrus (Hb. Koresh) were not internalized by this king, God boldly claims that "I am the LORD," the one and only real supernatural power who controls history. The exclusivity of this claim is emphasized by the two additional short cryptic explanations: "there is no other" (*ʾēyn ʿôd* 44:6,14,18,21,22) and "apart from me there is no God." There were many other pretenders who claimed to be gods and many people who falsely believed that there were other deities with other names, but none of the other angels, seraphim, demons, or

---

[557] The use of the imperfect verb תֵּדַע "you will know" in a dependent final clause after לְמַעַן "in order that" expresses a modal subjective that is translated "you may/might know" (GKC §107q-r).

[558] It seems like the shortened second לְמַעַן "in order that" clause implies כִּי תֵּדַע from the first line, a frequent characteristic when synonymous incomplete poetry is used. Note the same thing appears in the first line of v. 3, where נָתַתִּי לְךָ "I have given you" is written in the first half of the first line but implied in the second half of that line.

[559] According to E. M. Yamauchi, *Persia and the Bible* (Grand Rapids: Baker, 1990), 419–24, he may have been a worshipper of Mithra. Clear evidence of Zoroastrianism does not appear in royal inscriptions until the reign of Darius at about 520 BC.

[560] The nature of this decree is discussed by H. G. M. Williamson, *Ezra, Nehemiah,* WBC (Nashville: Nelson, 1985), 6–14, and C. F. Fensham, *The Books of Ezra and Nehemiah,* NICOT (Grand Rapids: Eerdmans, 1982), 42–44.

other supernatural beings were Yahweh and they could not do what God could do. He is the one who will act on behalf of Cyrus by "girding" him for battle and at the same time "ungirding" his enemies (45:1b). Though this king will not acknowledge that it is God who is doing this, God will still accomplish his plan through him.

Verse 6 gives the broadest perspective of God's purposes in this plan. He will do this "in order that" (*lĕmaʿan*) the whole world from east ("the rising of the sun") to west ("its setting")[561] might know that there is no other God like Israel's God. To emphasize the point again, the prophet ends v. 6 with the same phrase that began v. 5. God claims "I am the LORD, there is no other." Other gods just cannot be compared to the God of Israel.

God acted for the benefit of his people Israel (44:4) but also to persuade people around the globe (44:6). This is a key theme that the prophet will address again in 45:20–25 when God invites the nations to repent and be saved, for eventually at the end of time "before me every knee will bow and by me every tongue will swear" (45:23). The worldwide impact of God's work of bringing his people back to their land is one of the greatest testimonies of God's divine character revealed to humanity. The exodus event was similarly designed in a marvelous way so that the "Egyptians would know that I am God" (Exod 7:5,17; 8:10,22; 9:14,29; 10:2; 14:4,18), but most of the Egyptians refused to recognize God's divine control of their lives. David's desire was that his defeat of Goliath would cause the entire world to know that there was a living and powerful God in Israel (2 Sam 17:46). Likewise, Hezekiah's prayer for deliverance from the Assyrian army of Sennacherib was motivated by the desire that all the nations would know by God's defeat of Sennacherib that Yahweh was God (2 Kgs 19:19). Although these great events made people aware of God's true power, in their arrogance and stubbornness, most people failed to submit themselves before God and acknowledge that he alone was God. Ironically God's work through this anointed king would reveal who God was to people around the world, but Cyrus (Hb. Koresh) himself would fail to accept God himself. All God's works testify that "I am the LORD; there is no other."

Isaiah 45:7 returns to the introductory themes of 44:24. The prophet not only states that God is the one "who formed [*yôṣēr*] you" (44:24) but he "forms [*yôṣēr*] the light" and creates the darkness (44:7). J. D. W. Watts suggests that this choice of contrasts interacts with the dualism of the Persian religion, but R. N. Whybray and most others doubt that this is a polemic against Zoroastrianism.[562] Since there is very limited knowledge of the development

---

[561] The final ה on the word וּמִמַּעֲרָבָה is a third fem. suffix without the *mappiq* (GKC §91e).

[562] Watts, *Isaiah 34–66*, 157, and Hanson, *Isaiah 40–66*, *Int* (Louisville: John Knox, 1995), 102, believe that the dualism of the day impacted the choice of words here, but Whybray, *Isaiah 40–66*, 106, and Muilenburg, "Isaiah 40–66," 5:524, object to this connection. It seems inappropriate for the prophet to introduce a Zoroastrian polemic in the conclusion of the oracle. Here he

of the Zoroastrian religion at this time, it is safer to interpret these affirmations without contrasting them with Zoroastrianism. Light and darkness can be interpreted to be phenomena in nature that God created (Gen 1), but there is no indication in the creation account that God created darkness. Therefore, it may be best to relate these two phenomena to the realm of history where God is understood as the Lord of what happens on each new day and every night.[563] The other comparative contrast is between the spheres of "peace" (*šālôm*, NIV "prosperity") and "disaster" (*rāʿ*, NASB "calamity"; KJV "evil"). These are not abstract philosophical statements but practical claims about God's control of everything that happens in history. The good times that bring peace, prosperity, and well-being are controlled by God and so are the terrible times when war, calamity, natural disasters, and death come upon people. God claims that he is the power and the director who "does, makes" all these things happen.

Verses 5–7 make general claims about God and are not descriptions of what God will do through Cyrus or any other person. Everything that happens in the world is connected to God's activity, whether it appears to be good or bad. It all works together to fulfill God's purposes, even if people do not understand or accept these things as the work of God.

45:8 These two paragraphs about God's work through Cyrus conclude with a final call for there to be a response to this news that God will bring his salvation to all the earth. R. Melugin calls this a hymn while others interpret it to be a prayer. Although the use of imperative verbs invites a comparison with similar forms in the hymn in 42:10–13, there is no call for people to sing or praise God in this verse. Instead, God is the speaker who is encouraging or commanding his creation to bring about the conditions of peace, righteousness, and salvation that will cause his salvation to arise in the future.[564] This verse is connected to what precedes by the "I am the LORD" clause (also in 44:5 and 6), the reference to creation (in 45:7), and the heaven and the earth (in 44:24).

God's desire and will[565] is that the heaven and the clouds should shower down righteousness on the earth like rain, that the earth should "open wide"[566]

---

is drawing conclusions, summarizing, challenging his listeners, and applying what he has said earlier.

[563] Westermann, *Isaiah 40–66*, 162, explains these terms in light of Gen 1, while Koole, *Isaiah III, Volume 1, Isaiah 40–48*, 441, says that it "talks about God's continuing, mighty, and reliable activity in the alternation of day and night."

[564] Melugin, *Formation of Isaiah 40–55*, 125, compares this to the hymns in 42:10–13 and 49:13 while Whybray, *Isaiah 40–66*, 106, calls this a fragmentary prayer inserted by a later disciple or editor to mark the end of a literary segment.

[565] The imperative verb הַרְעִיפוּ "rain, shower" is used as a command, exhortation, or a wish for the beginning of action to fulfill God's plan to bring salvation (GKC §110a-b). In place of this verb the Old Greek has εὐφρανθήτω "let it rejoice" and 1QIs^a has הרועו "shout" (cf. 44:23), but the imagery of the MT makes a more fitting parallel with the metaphors in the second line.

[566] The form תִּפְתַּח is probably a jussive which also expresses a command, desire, or wish of the speaker (GKC §109b). Baltzer, *Deutero-Isaiah*, 228, compares this imagery to fertility imagery

and produce salvation and righteousness (55:10). This metaphorical expression of God's desire was intended to encourage the prophet's audience to trust him. The audience not only knows some details about what God will do to establish his plans (44:24–45:7); they also know God's deep desires for this plan to be implemented. This fertility language reminds one of God's plans to bless the land (Deut 28:11–12), which happens when God removes his curse (Deut 28:23–24). But here God is not talking just about material blessing or even the deliverance from some enemy. The full extent of this promise will be seen when God one day establishes a period of salvation and justice on the earth for all humanity to enjoy (2:1–4; 42:1–4). As sure as "I am the LORD," that is how sure the audience can be that God's righteousness will invade the world of humanity and creatively transform it into a place of righteousness.

GOD'S SOVEREIGNTY SHOULD REMOVE ALL DOUBTS (45:9–13)

⁹"Woe to him who quarrels with his Maker,
      to him who is but a potsherd among the potsherds on the ground.
Does the clay say to the potter,
      'What are you making?'
Does your work say,
      'He has no hands'?
¹⁰Woe to him who says to his father,
      'What have you begotten?'
or to his mother,
      'What have you brought to birth?'

¹¹"This is what the LORD says—
      the Holy One of Israel, and its Maker:
Concerning things to come,
      do you question me about my children,
      or give me orders about the work of my hands?
¹²It is I who made the earth
      and created mankind upon it.
My own hands stretched out the heavens;
      I marshaled their starry hosts.
¹³I will raise up Cyrus in my righteousness:
      I will make all his ways straight.
He will rebuild my city
      and set my exiles free,
but not for a price or reward,
      says the LORD Almighty."

The third paragraph in this section is translated and interpreted in widely divergent ways; therefore, the translation and interpretation are somewhat

in the Baal myth, but it is more likely that the prophet was drawing on blessing and curse language from the covenant.

tentative. About all that is agreed on is that this paragraph is made up of two subparagraphs: 45:9–10 and 45:11–13.[567] The Aramaic Targum, Old Greek, 1QIs[a], and the Masoretic traditions do not agree on numerous words;[568] thus, most studies on this passage do not even agree on the basic translation of these verses. It is only possible to present a brief overview of two of the central issues in this debate. (a) The Hebrew Masoretic tradition appears to have two woe oracles in 45:9–10 and then a divine answer in 45:11–13. Since chaps. 40–55 do not have any other woe oracles, C. F. Whitley emends the text to eliminate the woes,[569] while others find a disputation (based on the use of the participle *rab* "strive, quarrel") between God and some irritated Israelites (or the foreign nations) who oppose God's choice of Cyrus (Hb. Koresh) as an instrument of their restoration.[570] (b) The text plainly states that someone "quarrels with his Maker," asking God, "What are you making?" (45:9), but the complaint is not presented in the first part of this paragraph. Therefore the complaint must be assumed from God's answer in 45:11–13. The three parts to God's answer are: Should people question God (45:11), if God is the Creator (45:12) and God stirs up someone to rebuild his city (presumably Koresh, 44:28)? Many commentators emend the text to "Will you ask me?"[571] (45:11) and conclude that the quarrel is about God's use of the foreigner Cyrus to build Jerusalem (45:13). This solution, though widely accepted, may not be the best interpretation, for why would any Hebrew quarrel about someone doing such a good thing as rebuilding Jerusalem?

J. L. Koole rejects these approaches, keeps the woes statements that are in the Hebrew text, and hypothesizes that 45:9–10 reflects the people's own de-

---

[567] B. D. Naidoff, "The Two-fold Structure of Isaiah XLV, 9–13," *VT* XXXI (1981): 180–85, finds two overlapping disputations, one about Israel's right to question God in vv. 9–11 and then a second disputation about either the appropriateness of God's choice of Cyrus or the dependability of Cyrus to accomplish this task in vv. 11–13. The conclusion in v. 13b states that Cyrus will accomplish God's purpose.

[568] Since the various texts are so diverse from the Masoretic Text and from one another, they are of little help in solving the textual problems. For example the Targum speaks against idolatry, "Woe to him who thinks to rise up against the words of his Creator and trusts that the images of the potter that are made from the dust of the ground will profit him."

[569] C. F. Whitley, "Textual Notes on Deutero-Isaiah," *VT* 11 (1961): 457–61, for רָב הוֹי "woe to him who quarrels" reads הֲיָרִיב "does one quarrel" (also BHS editor).

[570] C. R. Seitz, "The Book of Isaiah 40–66," *NIB* (Nashville: Abingdon, 2001), 399, says: "This is obviously a disputation speech." Blenkinsopp, *Isaiah 40–55*, 252, gives an interpretation based on the presence of rhetorical questions (in vv. 9–10 he finds five questions by turning the two "woe" statements into questions) followed by a divine response (vv. 11–13), which is similar to the structure of other disputations. Westermann, *Isaiah 40–66*, 165, believes that this oracle is spoken to answer "the nations, or the gods of the nations, who question Yahweh about his treatment of his sons." The reference to "my children" in 45:11 argues against this.

[571] Baltzer, *Deutero-Isaiah*, 232, changes שְׁאָלוּנִי הָאֹתִיּוֹת "ask me concerning the coming things" (NIV "Concerning things to come, do you question me?") into "Will you ask me . . .?" (הַאֹתִי תִּשְׁאָלוּנִי):

pressed statements that God responds to in 45:11–13.[572] The lamenting woes express the Israelite's discouraged attitude because they realize they must accept what their Maker has planned. Koole also believes that the people would be extremely happy to hear about God's marvelous plans to restore Jerusalem through Cyrus in 44:24–45:8, so it is more likely that their negativity is a result of giving up hope for the near future and passively accepting their fate. The main problem with this interpretation is that there is no hint that 45:9–10 is a quotation of what the Israelites were saying. Therefore, it seems better to view the woes as prophetic laments over the misguided Israelites. Some Hebrews in the prophet's audience were questioning God's plans for them (40:27; 41:10,14; 42:18–25; 43:26–28). The prophet lamented their inability to accept what God was doing in 45:9–10, then he legitimates God's works with reminders of who God is and what God will do in 45:11–13.

Since the Israelites were not happy with God's plans, one must assume that this prophetic lament reacts to the people's questioning of the difficulties they must go through. It is most likely that this difficult situation is not the gracious work of Cyrus who will rebuild the city of Jerusalem, but instead they are responding to (a) the same problem that was raised early in chaps. 40–44, or (b) to God's plans to defeat the nation and send them to Babylon (39:6–7). If their concern is about the first issue, then they were complaining that their situation is hidden from God and that he did not deal with them justly (40:27). They are fearful and dismayed because someone is waging war against them (41:10–12); they will be plundered because of their sinfulness (42:20–25). If it relates to a second issue, then they are fearful about the time when the temple will be polluted (43:28) and people will be taken to Babylon (39:6–7). The prophet promised that in the future God would strengthen and help them, but they were blind and paid no attention to God's promises (40:28–31; 41:10,13; 42:15–16; 43:2,5). The prophet responds by lamenting the people's unwillingness to accept the full picture (first destruction and then restoration) of what God will do in the future. God assures those who question his ways (45:11) that he will restore Jerusalem (45:13), so they should not question the difficult things the potter will be doing with the clay in the near future (45:9).

The structure of this paragraph is determined by the "thus says the Lord" clause in 45:11. Thus the two parts are:

Lamenting woes over those who question God	45:9–10
Woe, does clay question the potter?	9
Woe, do children question parents?	10
Do not question your Creator and Restorer	45:11–13
Should God's children question their Maker	11
God made the heavens, earth, man, and stars	12
God will raise up a restorer of Jerusalem	13

---

[572] Koole, *Isaiah III, Volume 1, Isaiah 40–48*, 450–51, supports this interpretation and believes the exiles are dejected and despondent (they are not objecting to the use of Cyrus).

These two parts of the paragraph are interconnected by the use of "his Maker" (*yôṣrô*) in 45:9,11, "work" (*pôʿēl*) in 45:9,11, "make" (*ʿāśâ*) in 45:9,12, and "hand" (*yād*) in 45:9,11,12. Of course the whole oracle is connected to the themes in the earlier messages about one who would come and restore Jerusalem (44:28; 45:13).

45:9   The prophet laments that his Israelite audience is unwilling to accept the plans that God has for his people. Instead of trusting God, they prefer to argue, quarrel, and complain about the God who formed them. Their complaint deals with their unhappiness about what God has planned for their future, but the specific content of their complaint is not quoted. Certainly, it does not seem that they would be complaining about the good things God would do through Cyrus (45:13). Their dissatisfaction must relate to negative experiences they must go through before those events. The prophet laments the inappropriateness of this negative response, for the Israelites can be compared to common "clay pots" (NIV "potsherd")[573] made by the master potter who formed them. Should the clay say[574] to the one who forms it, "What are you doing?" No, the clay is subject to the will of the potter and it does not determine what the potter's hands do with the clay. The clay is not the potter and does not have authority over the potter. Likewise people are God's servants and cannot take God's place and try to determine their own destiny. They must accept God's plan and do God's will, for the clay has only one purpose—to be formed and used according to the will of the potter.

The last phrase in v. 9 is obscure. It appears that in parallelism with the preceding line "your work" (the clay) says, "He has no hands."[575] This statement may suggest that the potter has no skill in using his hand while making the pot or that the potter's hands have no control over what happens to the clay. In either case, the one who says this appears to be questioning God's oversight or design of the pot.

45:10   The second lamenting woe is set in the social situation of the family. It would be lamentable and totally inappropriate for an impertinent child to question his mother and father about the birth of a baby. It is hypothetically possible that this child is asking about his own birth, but it is more likely that he is asking about a sibling. It would be unethical and absurd for a child to ask his parents why they are having more children or what kind of child they are

---

[573] חַרְשֵׂי אֲדָמָה the term "pots of the ground" can sometimes refer to the whole unbroken vessel (Lev 11:33; 15:12; Num 5:17), but at other times it refers to a sherd of broken pottery (30:14; Job 2:8; Ezek 23:54). Blenkinsopp, *Isaiah 40–55*, 250, prefers "sherd," but there is no indication that the word refers to a broken piece of pottery. Muilenburg, "Isaiah 40–66," 5:526, follows the RSV in emending חָרֶשׂ to חָרָשׁ "potter, manufacturer" while the Old Greek translated this term ὁ ἀροτριῶν "plough" from חָרַשׁ.

[574] When the imperfect form of the verb יֹאמַר is used in a question, it usually has a modal sense; thus, "should, can, ought" (GKC §107r,t).

[575] RSV has "handles" for יָדָיִם "two hands," which Watts, *Isaiah 34–66*, 151, follows. There are no other examples of such a usage, however, and it should be rejected.

having. So by analogy it is totally absurd for God's children to question their Creator or to try to determine what he does. Such statements are lamentable, for children should not criticize their parents for their family planning and God's children should not quarrel with God about his plans for his family.

45:11–13 Now that the prophet has lamented his audience's complaining as misguided and inappropriate for these simple objects of clay, God presents both a negative and a positive response ("thus says the Lord") to legitimate his own perspective on future events and reassure his people about his plans. The audience should not question the negative factors that loom so large in their minds; they should be comforted by God's repeated positive promise to restore the nation in the future. He is the master Potter who controls what happens to his pottery.

45:11 At first God addresses the complaining of the audience by reminding them who he is. He is Israel's "Maker" (*yōṣrô*) mentioned in 45:9; thus, he has the same role as the potter. He is Yahweh, the Holy One of Israel, and the One who formed Israel. These titles emphasize his identity, his unique name, and his unapproachable glorious transcendence that makes him separate from everything in this finite sinful world. He has the power to create and the ability to control all he has created. The glory of God is infinitely higher than his people, and his power is incomparably greater than anything on earth. Since this is so, it is astonishing that "my sons" (the Israelites) would dare to ask questions about God's plans for their future. Yes, it is incredible that "the work of my hands" (45:9), the Israelite people, would even think that they could command God to do something or not do something else.

The second half of 45:11 does not include the common Hebrew prefix marking a question (*hă*). G. R. Driver slightly emended the vocalization to turn the prefixed article *ha* into the interrogative marker, but this adjustment is not called for.[576] Two other possibilities are readily available. The imperative verb "ask me" (*šĕʾālûnî*, NIV "do you question me?") can be used ironically,[577] or the verb *tĕṣavvunî*, "give me orders," can almost be viewed as a senseless oxymoron that any reader would quickly understand.[578] Some Hebrew (and English) sentences do not begin with the sign of a question but can rely on intonation or

---

[576] G. R. Driver, "Studies in the Vocabulary of the Old Testament," *JTS* 34 (1933): 39, and A. Schoors, *I Am God Your Savior: A Form-critical Study of the Main Genres of Is XL–LV* (Leiden: Brill, 1973, 264, follows this emendation.

[577] C. R. North, *Second Isaiah: Introduction, Translation and Commentary to Chapters XL–LV* (Eugene: OR: Wipf and Stock, 2005), 153, rightly calls this an ironic use of the imperative; thus, it means just the opposite (GKC §110a). Amos's sarcastic imperative "enter Bethel and transgress" (Amos 4:4) was not a command to sin more; it meant just the opposite. One can leave the translation literal if people can pick up the sarcasm, or it could be put in a question form to make it clearer, "Should you enter Bethel to transgress?" or as a statement, "Do not enter Bethel and transgress." The same options are available here as ways to understand the imperative in v. 11.

[578] Koole, *Isaiah III, Volume 1, Isaiah 40–48*, 456–58, leaves the phrase as a statement and views it as an oxymoron that any reader would catch.

context to convey the idea that a question is being asked;[579] thus, it is possible to translate this short clause as a statement or a question. As a statement God would be encouraging the people to "ask me concerning the things to come for my sons," but it seems more likely that this is a question, "Should you ask me about the things to come for my sons?" The area of the people's concern relates to things that will happen in the future, presumably the hard and fearful times that are coming before the future rebuilding of the nation.

45:12 Having reprimanded the audience for its irreverent and inappropriate questioning, God reminds them that in the distant past "I myself" (NIV "It is I")[580] made the world and created man to live upon it. By implication he can handle the future of his people. Trust is partially based on past performance and the explicit power one can demonstrate in past situations. If God is powerful enough to stretch out the heavens with his hands (40:22; 44:24; 45:9b) and if he can command the stars to go to their place (40:26), there is good reason to trust that in the future he will do what he says he will do. People are in no position to command God to do anything (45:11b); he is the one who has the power to command others. If God is able to control, guide, keep track of, and care for the ten thousands of stars spread out over the immense heavens, surely he is able to deal with the important issues that his few people were facing on earth. There is also no need for anyone to quarrel with God's plans or question God's ability to do what he has promised.

45:13 This paragraph ends with one final reminder of God's plans for his people. Although his people may presently be facing a difficulty that causes them to question what God is doing, they can rest assured that "I myself [another emphatic use of the pronoun] will stir him up."[581] This verb is typically used of God's unusual moving of unexpected people to do his will. It is used of the stirring up of the dead (14:9), God's stirring up of the spirit of the Assyrian king Tiglath-pileser III (2 Chr 5:26), the stirring of Nebuchadnezzar and the Babylonians to attack Jerusalem (Jer 6:22; 25:32; 50:41; 51:1,11), and the stirring up of a strong man from the east who will conquer many nations (possibly Sennacherib, in 41:2,25). In this context the prophet is likely referring to God stirring up the

---

[579] In Gen 27:24 blind Isaac said to Jacob who was pretending to be Esau, "You are my son Esau?" In another context this would be a statement, but Isaac has heard the voice of Jacob; therefore, he questioned the truthfulness of Jacob's statement, "I am your son Esau" (GKC §150a gives other examples).

[580] The use of the subject pronoun אָנֹכִי "I myself" with a finite verb at the beginning of the verse and אֲנִי "I myself" with a finite verb at the beginning of the second line strongly emphasize God's role in this process (GKC §135a). These pronouns are not needed in Hebrew syntax because the subject pronoun is already present in the verb form; thus when it is added it is for purposes of emphasis.

[581] The perfect verb הַעִירֹתִהוּ "I will stir him" is a prophetic perfect of what God will do in the future (GKC §106m-n; NIV "I will raise up"), not a reference to what God has done (RSV "I have raised").

ruler Koresh (45:1).[582] The text makes it clear that his rise to power was not just a coincidence, a stroke of good luck, or something that he engineered through some savvy political maneuvering. The exact way in which righteousness relates to the stirring of this person is not clear, but it does not describe Cyrus's righteousness. This could refer to God's acting in righteous faithfulness to his preannounced plans to use Cyrus or to God's righteous ways of dealing with his people through Cyrus.[583] The main point is that God is the central actor stirring up this powerful ruler and providentially overseeing ("will level" in 45:2) his ways, so that it will be possible for him to build my city Jerusalem (44:28) and send out "my exiles" (*gālûtî*). The verse ends with a brief comment that gives one more proof of divine involvement in these activities. It would be normal to expect a great ruler to act out of selfish interest in order to achieve some financial gain in building Jerusalem. Since Cyrus will not do these things for any fiscal reward,[584] it is evident that the hand of God has directed his path.

THEOLOGICAL IMPLICATIONS.   Most people do not know what will happen in the future and have a very limited perspective on exactly how God will work out his plans in order to accomplish his will for them and this world. Frequently God's plans involve him bringing both spiritual and political transformations that impact many countries. During the Cold War between the United States and the former Soviet Union, many were wishing and praying for God to defeat Russia, but God chose to transform it from the inside by giving her new leaders who would initiate new perspectives that would radically change the tension within the world political system. In a similar manner, God impacted the world of Israel with tumultuous political changes that involved new leaders who caused a realignment of Assyrian, Babylonian, and Persian power. The common question that frequently comes to mind when we go through such times of instability and the emergence of new political powers is, "What is God doing, what will happen to us, and how will this all end?" (cf. Habakkuk's questions). In most instances believers have no way of answering these questions and must simply trust God for guidance and mercy, while praying for the political leaders involved to act wisely and patiently and to work for peaceful solutions.

---

[582] R. Albertz, "Darius in Place of Cyrus: The First Edition of Deutero-Isaiah (Isaiah 40.1–52.12) in 521 BCE," *JSOT* 27 (2003): 371–83, rejects the idea that these chapters were written in Babylon shortly before 539 BC. In order to avoid the idea that Isaiah's prophecy about the violent fall of Babylon failed and to place the prophecy near a time when Babylon was destroyed and Judah was restored, he hypothesizes (following Kratz) that the early redaction of the older Isaiah material took place in the time of Darius (520 BC); thus he identifies the person mentioned in 45:11–13 and 48:6–14 as Darius. This does not seem to be a valid conclusion since Darius did not do everything these verses talk about.

[583] C. F. Whitley, "Deutero-Isaiah's Interpretation of *ṣedeq*," *VT* 22 (1972): 469–75, believes that righteousness in this verse refers to the correctness of God's action.

[584] This passage argues against those who interpret 43:3 as God giving Cush and Seba to Cyrus as a reward.

In the negative political crisis facing God's people in Isaiah 44:24–45:13, there was a deep question about what God was doing (45:9–11), probably some fear about what certain diviners and wise men were prognosticating from their bully pulpits (44:25) and possibly a certain unwillingness to believe the generalizations about a future hope that Isaiah articulated (44:26a). How could these people believe that it would all work out in the end, that God would somehow make everything all right?

The three prophetic paragraphs in 44:24–45:13 provide a basis for hope in the providential plan of God. Although at times God's hand of direction is not always evident and the outline of his plan seems to be working itself out very slowly, those who trust God can be assured that he is quietly and subtly working through the circumstances of believers and unbelievers to accomplish his will. But some will always question why anyone should believe this when the hand of God directing these affairs is so difficult to identify and understand. One answer that any follower of the Lord can suggest (following the lead of what is said in this passage) is that past history and the future promises of God can only be explained on the basis of the idea that the sovereign hands of a potter has made this world, formed the clay people in it, and stretched out the heavens according to his plan (44:24; 45:9,12). He does not abandon what he created but sovereignly works each day to fulfill what he has promised in his plan (44:26). Part of God's will or plan is revealed in his words, and the accomplishment of his will is worked out through historical people who follow his plan. Thus God knows the future because he is the one who conceives what it will be, he chooses and anoints key people to fulfill the deeds he has planned (44:28; 45:1), and he guides these people by going before them to enable them to accomplish what they do (45:1–3a,13). This is all possible because "I am the LORD, and there is no other" (44:24; 45:5,6,7,8), "the Holy One of Israel," "your Redeemer," and "Maker" (44:24; 45:7,9,11,12). Both God's past deeds (such as creation) and his character (revealed by his names) serve as guarantees that his future plans will be accomplished.

Consequently, everyone should believe that it is true when God says that the ruler Cyrus will accomplish all that God pleases (44:28) and that God will fulfill his prophetic word about the restoration of Jerusalem through Cyrus (44:26–28). Even though Cyrus does not know God, he can use him in marvelous ways to accomplish his will for his people. Through all these things God will cause everyone else on the earth to know that he is God (45:3–6). The purposefulness of God's action indicates that these wars were not random acts of senseless violence that made no difference on the grand scheme of history. Every war, every political leader, and every person fits into the sovereign plan of God in some special way. Although people may at times wonder why certain things are happening, question how God could allow some tragedy to take place, or even rebel against what God has called for them to endure (45:9–11), his miraculous intervention will arrive in due time. In a time of crisis people must trust the Potter and believe that the Maker of all things knows what he is doing. His plans do involve the eventual restoration of his people, the appointment of a ruler who will accomplish a part of his plan, and the specific goals of sending away the exiles, the rebuilding of Jerusalem, and the laying of the foundations of the temple (44:26–28; 45:13). Eventually, God's salvation will fully arrive on earth, and the blessings of his righteousness will be evident to all people (45:8). This will be God's work and the fulfillment of his plan, so readers in every age can rest assured in God's promises because their faith in him is based on solid evidence about his past and future fulfillment of his plans.

(2) One Day, the Nations and Israel Will Bow before God (45:14–25)

The second part of this long literary unit (44:24–45:25) addresses the issue of the foreign nations coming to know God (45:6). Although it might not have made much sense to some Israelites to hear that their nation would one day suffer disgrace (43:28) and then later the people would be allowed to return to rebuild Jerusalem (44:28; 45:13), God has a purpose for all his ways. He was teaching his people and the nations about his hatred of sin, the uselessness of idols, and his true divinity based on his ability to predict and then accomplish his plans. In order to hold all these positive and negative factors together without losing hope and faith in God, the Israelites needed to understand that the ultimate goal of all of his interventions into history is his plan to save both Israel and many people from the foreign nations. This passage teaches that God's means of working with every nation throughout history will lead to the planned results of both Israel and the nations bowing before him and exulting in God their Savior.

This portion is connected to what precedes by its repetition of phrases about God like "there is no other" (45:5,6,14,18,22), but one should not conclude that God is speaking to Cyrus as J. D. W. Watts interprets this passage.[585] The two paragraphs in this section are each introduced with identical clauses that indicate that these are words of God (45:14,19) to his own people. R. Melugin classifies 45:14–17 as a unique type of salvation speech addressed to Israel, while 45:18–21 appears to have some characteristic of a trial speech (especially 45:20–21), and 45:22–25 is more of an exhortation to the nations that ends up functioning as a comforting promise to the prophet's Israelite audience.[586] In contrast to this approach it seems better to view the promise that "Israel will be saved" and "never be put to shame" (45:17) plus the declaration that "every knee will bow" before God (45:23) as parts of a proclamation of salvation. The universal consequence of God's plan indicates that this promise will not be

---

[585] Watts, *Isaiah 34–66*, 160–61, reconstructs a dialogue between God and Cyrus, showing that God and Cyrus's goals are identical. Baltzer, *Deutero-Isaiah*, 240, follows the same path by changing the fem. sg. pronominal suffixes "you" to masc. sg.

[586] Melugin, *Formation of Isaiah 40–55*, 126–31, treats these forms as flexible and believes the prophets were free to creatively modify typical parts of these forms.

fulfilled at the present time; it is an eschatological prediction parallel in some respects to themes treated in 2:1–4; 14:1–3; 19:18–25; and 60:1–14.

The messages in this section can be divided into two main paragraphs:

Some will be saved; some disgraced	45:14–17
Nations will turn to God and be saved	45:18–25

A connection between these two paragraphs is created by the repetition of several words: (a) "shame" (*bôš*) in 45:16,17 and 45:24; (b) "hide, be secret" (*sātar*) in 45:15 and 45:19; (c) "there is no other, there is no other" in 45:14, "there is no other" in 45:18, "there is no other God besides me" in 45:21, and "there is no other" (*'ēn 'ôd*) in 45:22; (d) "Savior" (*môšîa'*) in 45:15 and 45:21; and (e) "idols" (*ṣîr*, *pesel*) in 45:16,20. God's act of saving Israel and many people from the nations is a central theme that runs throughout this section. Those among the nations that continue to trust in idols and rage against God will eventually be put to shame (45:16–17,24b).

SOME WILL BE SAVED; SOME DISGRACED (45:14–17)

[14]This is what the LORD says:

> "The products of Egypt and the merchandise of Cush,
>> and those tall Sabeans—
> they will come over to you
>> and will be yours;
> they will trudge behind you,
>> coming over to you in chains.
> They will bow down before you
>> and plead with you, saying,
> 'Surely God is with you, and there is no other;
>> there is no other god.'"

[15]Truly you are a God who hides himself,
> O God and Savior of Israel.
[16]All the makers of idols will be put to shame and disgraced;
> they will go off into disgrace together.
[17]But Israel will be saved by the LORD
> with an everlasting salvation;
you will never be put to shame or disgraced,
> to ages everlasting.

The first paragraph raises many difficult issues of interpretation that commentators do not treat in the same way. For example: (a) should one interpret the chains and bowing of the foreign nations in 45:14 as the enslavement of foreigners by the Israelites, or are the foreigners voluntarily acknowledging the special role of Israel? (b) Is the statement about the hiddenness of God in 45:15 a confession by the prophet, Israel, or the foreign nations? (c) Are the people from the foreign nations in 45:14 Israelites who were scattered among the nations, or are these people actually foreigners? (d) Who is speaking in 45:16–17? These questions are answered as they arise in these verses. The structure of this paragraph can be divided into two parts:[587]

The submission and confession of the nations   45:14–15
    Nations will bring gifts and acknowledge God   14
    The hidden God is known as Savior   15
Idolaters will be disgraced; Israel saved   45:16–17
    All who trust idols will be shamed   16
    God will save Israel   17

Part of the reason why this passage is plagued with so many problems is because the speaker in each verse (except 45:14) is somewhat ambiguous. The Hebrew text indicates that God speaks in v. 14a and the nations are quoted in v. 14b. The second person pronominal suffixes "you" in both parts of 45:14 are feminine singular referring to Israel. Verse 15 addresses God with a confession of faith that refers to Israel, so this verse is probably a continuation of the foreign nation's new beliefs,[588] or a comment by the prophet.[589] Isaiah 45:16–17 are not spoken to God but to Israel ("you will never be put to shame"), so it is possible to view these words about being disgraced or not disgraced as a continuation of the words of the foreign peoples or of the prophet.[590] The conclusions one makes on these issues do not yield air-tight answers; they are probable conclusions, so it is wise to be humble about the certainty of any interpretation.

45:14–15   The message begins with another assurance to the Israelite audience that God has spoken, for some unusual information is proclaimed in these verses. God identifies people from three African nations (Egyptians, Cushites, and Sabeans) who will "come over, pass over" (*ya'ăbōrû*) to you (Israel) apparently out of their own free will. Although these nations are mentioned together in 43:3 as being given as a ransom in the place of Israel, this earlier reference has nothing to do with Cyrus's conquests[591] for he did not receive any bribe

---

[587] Spykerboer, *The Structure and Composition of Deutero-Isaiah*, 138, lists three arguments for maintaining the unity of this paragraph: (a) vv. 14–17 have the theme of Israel's salvation; (b) this passage is similar to themes in 45:20–25 where survivors of the nations recognize God; (c) vv. 14–15 have a similar confession to 45:24. This passage also shows similarities with 60:3–14.

[588] Koole, *Isaiah III, Volume 1, Isaiah 40–48*, 469, and Oswalt, *Isaiah 40–66*, 216, believe 14b–15 to be the confession by the nations to Israelites. Baltzer, *Deutero-Isaiah*, 242, maintains that vv. 14–15a are the prisoner's lament to Cyrus; thus 15b–17 are a statement of thanksgiving by Israel, for the nations would not know that the God of Israel was a Savior.

[589] Childs, *Isaiah*, 355, takes vv. 15–17 as "the prophet's reflection on the strange outcome" because "the salvation of Israel came in a totally unexpected manner." Blenkinsopp, *Isaiah 40–55*, 258, says that "v 15 is not the continuation of the v 14 confession of faith but a comment either by the author of 40–48, or by a later scribe."

[590] Goldingay, *Message of Isaiah 40–55*, 283, puts all of vv. 15–17 into the mouth of these foreign converts, but it is unknown if recent converts would have this kind of mature insight.

[591] Watts, *Isaiah 34–66*, 161, connects these events with the Persian defeat of Egypt in 525

or reward for helping the Israelites (45:13). One wonders if there is something special about these three nations or if these three nations are just representative examples of the many other distant nations that will come to Israel during the eschatological era. In fact, in earlier prophecies Isaiah has already stated that Egypt and Cush would turn to God and bring him gifts (18:7; 19:18–25). These nations will not come empty handed; they will bring with them possessions, gifts, and "tribute"[592] that they have toiled hard to acquire (18:7; 60:1–14). Their purpose in coming has nothing to do with restoring the losses of Israel when it was defeated;[593] these people come to honor the Israelites and especially the God of Israel. The imagery of these foreigners as coming in chains might be seen as some sort of enslavement, but this does not agree with the other images the text provides or with the overall emphasis made in the following verses (45:22–25). Out of respect for God and his Israelite people these foreigners will "follow you" (not be in front leading them) and in humility they will be yours, submitting themselves ("bow down") and pleading in prayers to God. In past eras the foreign nations were characterized by pride (chaps. 13–23), self-centeredness, violence, and materialism, but this will all disappear when they finally understand the truth about the God who the Israelites worship. The nation's behavior expresses their humble submission to the God of Israel and their deep respect for his Israelite people in cultural ways that made sense to them at that time. These people will show great appreciation and respect to the Israelites who understood the truth about God long ago.

The bold declarations about God in 45:14b–15 are probably the confession of faith made by the foreign people who will come to Jerusalem. Their four professions are that they emphatically[594] believe that: (a) God is with the Israelites; (b) there is no other God;[595] (c) God hides himself; and (d) the God of Israel is a Savior (45:21). The basis for these beliefs is unknown and unstated in this account (possibly through personal experience, talking to Israelites, a divine revelation, and the movement of the Spirit among them), but somehow

---

BC during the reign of Cambyses, and he connects these gifts to a ransom paid to Cyrus for the release of the Israelites in 43:3. This perspective contradicts 45:13, which means that 43:3 must be interpreted in some other way.

[592] Based on the usage of מִדָּה in Ezra 4:20; 6:8; Neh 5:4 one can translate this word "tribute" rather than "tall, stature" which would make it more parallel to "the products of Egypt. "The phrase could then be translated, "Sabean men bearing tribute" (NEB). A counter argument from 18:2,7 would be that the Cushites (not Sabeans) were known for their tall stature.

[593] Goldingay, *Message of Isaiah 40–55*, 284, makes these gifts after the time of exile parallel to the gifts the Israelites received when they came out of Egypt, but this passage refers to an eschatological time frame, not something that would happen after the exile ended.

[594] The initial ʾak "surely, truly" expresses the people's strong belief or certainty about what they are saying.

[595] The text distinguishes between אֵל "God" and the אֱלֹהִים "gods." This final clause אֱלֹהִים אָפֶס could also be translated "the gods (are) nothing" (cf. 40:17; 41:12,29).

these nations will understand truth about God that was partially hidden from them in earlier days.[596]

In what sense was the God of Israel hidden from the foreign nations? The *hithpa'al* participle could express a passive idea "the one who was hidden" or a reflexive meaning "the one who hid himself."[597] This is not a complaint against God for not helping people in trouble, which are so frequent in Psalms (10:1,11; 13:1; 27:9; 30:7; 55:1; 69:17; 88:14; 89:46; 102:2; 143:7), but a reflection on how God's action can sometimes be unusual, unexpected, and somewhat beyond the human understanding of the common person. Of course when the foreign nations worship idols and follow vain superstitions, this prevents them from understanding the works and the true nature of God. Even the Israelites needed a divine revelation that explained how several strange coincidences worked together to eventually accomplish the will of God. If there was no divine explanation of God's acts and plans, many of God's ways would still be hidden from human understanding (Rom 11:33; 1 Tim 6:16; the story of Esther). Having gained some understanding of God's hidden ways, the nations now can admire the skill and ironic results that God's action produces. Sometimes those events that initially appear to be unusual and have disastrous circumstances actually turn out to work perfectly together to accomplish his will. Apparently the nations that previously did not perceive the hand of God working in Israel will come to recognize that God truly dwells with this people. In the past the Egyptians came to recognize the hand of God fighting against them in the middle of the Red Sea when the wheels of their chariots came off (Exod 14:23–25), and the soldiers that were left of Sennacherib's army suddenly recognized the power of God's hand when the angel of God killed 185,000 soldiers in one night (37:36–38). In the eschatological period God will reveal himself in new and exciting ways that will cause many rebellious nations to turn to God (cf. 19:18–25). The reference to God as a "Savior" (*môšîaʿ*, as in 19:20) suggests that the nation's observation of the saving power of God will have a major impact on opening their eyes. At that point God's ways and his will for all humanity will no longer be hidden from their eyes and they will respond (cf. chaps. 60–62).

45:16–17 It is difficult to determine who is speaking in these verses. Hypothetically, the foreign nations could be reflecting on their decision to follow God in 45:16. Thus they could be confessing that disgrace and shame will fall

---

[596] Childs, *Isaiah*, 355, believes Cyrus's deliverance of the Hebrews and Africans from exile and Babylonian bondage may have caused these foreigners to acknowledge God. The nations acknowledged "Yahweh's sovereignty revealed above all in Israel's liberation . . . and the role of Israel in their liberation." This reasoning might be true if the prophecy was going to be fulfilled immediately after the return from exile, but if this was an eschatological prophecy, the return from exile would be an event that happened thousands of years earlier.

[597] The *hithpa'al* form can have either a reflexive, reciprocal, or passive meaning (GKC §54d-g). In 29:14 תִּסְתַּתָּר is translated "will vanish" NIV, "shall be hid" RSV; "shall be concealed" NASB, but most translations choose a reflexive sense of the participle מִסְתַּתֵּר in 45:15.

on those who continue to trust in idols. But 45:17 sounds more like a divine word of assurance to the Israelite audience, a promise that the nations could not make (no shame for Israel). Therefore, it seems better to view both 45:16 and 17 as divine promises intended to affirm the observations of the foreign nations and to encourage Israel to continue trusting in God, for he is the source of their eternal salvation.

The prophet draws a sharp contrast between the people in the foreign nations who confess their faith in God as the only God (45:15) and other people (possibly Hebrews or foreigners) who construct and worship "forms, idols"[598](44:9–20). All those people who worship these idolatrous forms will experience great shame and disgrace together. This coincides with what the prophet has said earlier about the shaming of those who follow idols (42:17; 44:9,11). In contrast to this group is the destiny of Israel (45:17), which will be saved by God with an "everlasting salvation."[599] The encouraging conclusion to this paragraph is that the Israelites will never suffer shame or disgrace throughout all eternity. The details of all these events are not spelled out. The reader is not told when the nation will turn to God, what will happen to cause the nations to change course and trust in God for their salvation, or exactly what this "everlasting salvation" involves. At this point God is more interested in communicating to his people only a few basic points about the future and the key choices every person and nation must make.

NATIONS WILL TURN TO GOD, BE SAVED, & EXPERIENCE JUSTICE (45:18–25)

^{18}For this is what the LORD says—
he who created the heavens,
  he is God;
he who fashioned and made the earth,
  he founded it;
he did not create it to be empty,
  but formed it to be inhabited—
he says:
"I am the LORD,
  and there is no other.
^{19}I have not spoken in secret,
  from somewhere in a land of darkness;
I have not said to Jacob's descendants,
  'Seek me in vain.'

---

[598] The term צִרִים is only found here in the Hebrew Bible, but since "craftsmen" were making idols in 44:9–20, this word must have a similar meaning. In BDB, 849–50, root I of צִיר means "envoy, messenger"; root II means "pivot, hinge"; and root III means "writhe, pangs of childbirth," but none of these fits the context in 45:16. Koole, *Isaiah III, Volume 1, Isaiah 40–48*, 471, draws this word from the root IV of צוּר "to form, fashion"; thus this pl. noun in 45:16 refers to "forms" (Exod 32:4) the craftsman makes.

[599] Paul says something similar in Romans 11:26a, just before he quotes from Isa 59:30–21.

I, the LORD, speak the truth;
  I declare what is right.

²⁰"Gather together and come;
  assemble, you fugitives from the nations.
Ignorant are those who carry about idols of wood,
  who pray to gods that cannot save.
²¹Declare what is to be, present it—
  let them take counsel together.
Who foretold this long ago,
  who declared it from the distant past?
Was it not I, the LORD?
  And there is no God apart from me,
a righteous God and a Savior;
  there is none but me.

²²"Turn to me and be saved,
  all you ends of the earth;
  for I am God, and there is no other.
²³By myself I have sworn,
  my mouth has uttered in all integrity
  a word that will not be revoked:
Before me every knee will bow;
  by me every tongue will swear.
²⁴They will say of me, 'In the LORD alone
  are righteousness and strength.'"
All who have raged against him
  will come to him and be put to shame.
²⁵But in the LORD all the descendants of Israel
  will be found righteous and will exult.

This paragraph expands on the information in 45:14–15 that people from several nations will respond positively to God. Since both the previous paragraph and this new paragraph deal with this same issue, they must be read together in order to understand the true nature of the worship of the nations (their respectful bowing to Israel in 45:14 and their worshipful bowing to God in 45:23) and to comprehend the full breadth of God's saving work in Israel (45:17) and the nations (45:14,22–23). God is not really hidden, for people can know him if they seek him. His acts of creating the heavens and the earth, plus his words that speak what is true and right (45:18–19), are solid evidence of his presence and his works. The nations should stop praying to idols that cannot save (45:20) and turn to a God who can save them (45:21–22). Eventually every nation will bow before God and recognize him as their only source of justice and salvation. At the end of this age all opposition to God will be defeated and all the righteous in Israel and the nations will praise God together (45:25).

Although some suggest that certain matters are under dispute in 45:18–21 (suggesting a trial speech or a disputation speech),[600] the purpose of the unit is not to argue out a case in court. This is a persuasive speech that proclaims that God alone is a saving God. It presents evidence to show that it would be foolish for those who follow idols to argue about who is God because God has all the evidence on his side. Such argumentation is useless because he alone speaks and predicts the future; therefore, the nations should perceive the uniqueness of God and turn to the one who can save them. The setting of this and the previous message is unknown, but the eschatological orientation of this proclamation of salvation in 45:22–25 should cause the reader to disconnect it from anything related to Cyrus.[601] This message about the future offers great comfort and encouragement to the prophet's Hebrew audience. God began to institute his plan long ago when he first created the heaven and the earth. He will successfully complete it on that final day when every knee shall bow before him. Comfort for every believer is available in knowing that God has planned the future and will accomplish it.

The following outline represents the structure of this paragraph:

God is Creator and Speaker; he is not hidden	45:18–19
Nations should know who is God and Savior	45:20–21
Nations should turn, be saved, and worship	45:22–23
Nations will praise God	45:24–25

This paragraph is held together by various ways of saying, "I am the LORD/God and there is no other" (45:18,21,22) and by God's concern to establish righteousness and justice for all people (45:19,21,23,24,25). All his deeds loudly declare that God alone is the Savior of humanity, and this will be one of the key reasons why so many people will exult and praise him (45:15,21,25).

---

[600] Whybray, *Isaiah 40–66*, 110, believes vv. 18–19 function as a disputation (though it does not have the precise form of one) and that vv. 20–25 is a trial speech. Melugin, *Formation of Isaiah 40–55*, 127–28, finds a trial speech in vv. 18–21 and an exhortation in vv. 22–25. Instead one should view the presentation of evidence for God's divinity as proofs (there is no trial) that will persuade the Israelites to believe that God's eschatological plan to save people from all nations will work. Thus, this is another unique message about God's great salvation.

[601] It is surprising that Goldingay, *Message of Isaiah 40–55*, 289–90, connects this message to the fall of Babylon and the person of Cyrus and believes that this "speech is a climax that resolves key questions raised by the prophet's understanding of Cyrus's significance in Yhwh's purpose." Even more baffling is Watts, *Isaiah 34–66*, 160–63, who believes God is having a dialogue with Cyrus and suggests that Cyrus is (a) calling Hebrews to gather together in v. 20a, (b) Cyrus calls for people to pay tribute in v. 22a, and (c) Cyrus proclaims that people should submit to God in vv. 23b–24a. Since Cyrus is not mentioned in this text and the message is about eschatological events, it is better to view this message as a defense and glorification of God rather than Cyrus. Childs, *Isaiah*, 355, says that "this section brings to a climax the theme of the unexpected salvation wrought by God through Cyrus," but there is no evidence that the Hebrews or all the nations praised God because of the work of Cyrus. God's reign of righteousness was not established by Cyrus's victories.

45:18–19 This new paragraph begins with another announcement that this is the authoritative word of God; therefore, one can count on its veracity (45:14a,18a). The paragraph begins with self-declarations about the God who is unique yet known from his revelation of himself. His identity as Creator and Speaker of truth functions as the firm foundation for understanding and believing everything he promises about the future.

The paragraph begins with "surely, truly" (*kî*; NIV "for"),[602] a particle that introduces this message as a reaffirmation of some of the things already said in the previous paragraphs. Verse 18 contains a series of Hebrew participles related to creation that attribute to God various actions that classify him as a unique being and explain how he can be known. God's identity as "the true God"[603] (v. 18; NIV "he is God") is supported by the claims that he is the "one who created" (*bōrēʾ*) the heavens, the "one who formed" (*yōṣēr*, NIV "fashioned") the earth, the "one who made it" (*ʿōśāh*), and the "one who established it" (*kônĕnāh*, NIV "founded"). J. Goldingay proposes that these "three images of shaping, making, and establishing . . . point to initial design and purposefulness, effective execution, and consequent firmness and security."[604] There is disagreement on what it means when God claims that he did not create the earth *tōhû* "empty" (NIV, HCSB), "a chaos" (NRSV), "a waste place" (NASB). Each of these translations is possible, but the context of the next line ("in order to be inhabited"[605]) suggests that "empty, uninhabited" is the best translation. Indeed, at creation God did not leave the world in its initial "empty" state (Gen 1:2) but filled it with stars, fish, birds, plants, animals, and people. These declarations demonstrate that he is God (there is no other God like him) and that he has a plan and a purpose for this world. Therefore the audience can trust him to carry out the rest of his purposes for this earth.

God's work with the world did not end at creation and the filling of the earth with inhabitants. Isaiah 45:19 indicates that God's commitment to what he created extended to speaking to the people he had created on the earth. Although God's glorious presence is not openly displayed on earth very frequently (6:1–13) and he does not speak to people in an audible voice every day, God did not completely hide himself from everyone (45:15). There are some aspects of God's person and his sovereign ways that are hidden from people, but the reason some think that God appears to be hidden is because they are blind

---

[602] Baltzer, *Deutero-Isaiah*, 245, understands the introductory כִּי in this way, though Oswalt, *Isaiah 40–66*, 217, argues for a causal connection and therefore makes 45:14–19 one message. The "thus says the Lord" clause appears to introduce a new message (thus כִּי it is probably not causal); therefore, it seems more appropriate to begin a new paragraph with v. 18.

[603] הָאֱלֹהִים is literally "the God," but since names and titles do not usually take a definite article, the addition of the article communicates that he is "the (real) God" (GKC §125f) or "this God" (GKC §126b).

[604] Goldingay, *Message of Isaiah 40–55*, 290.

[605] לָשֶׁבֶת is an infinitive construct from יָשַׁב "to sit, dwell, inhabit" which express God's purpose ("in order that") in creation (GKC §114f).

and stubbornly refuse to listen to what God did say (6:9–10; 29:9; 42:18–19). God did speak openly on Mount Sinai (Deut 5:23–29), but at other times he spoke in dark (secret) ways that were hard for people to understand. It goes beyond the evidence to conclude that the "place" (*māqôm*, NIV "land") refers to the grave,[606] that the "dark" (*ḥōšek*) land refers to Babylon,[607] or that this "speaking" contrasts with the dark and mysterious speaking in the occult practices of pagan religions. Something done in the darkness is simply something done "in secret, in hiding," for both refer to something that is not clear. God is saying that his communication of himself, his will, and his plans were not imperceptible, inaudible, unrecognizable, or impossible to understand. He spoke clearly to the Israelites through Moses and the prophets. God did not want his people to seek him and then go away having received "nothing" (NIV "vain") or to come up empty (it all be in vain).[608] God speaks what is "right, just" (*ṣedeq*);[609] he makes known the upright things that people should do.

45:20–21. Now the Israelite audience overhears God's imperative exhortation to "gather together";[610] a call that exhorts the survivors of the nations to come[611] to hear what God has to say. C. Westermann interprets this phrase in light of 45:1–7; therefore, he concludes that these are the Babylonian survivors left after the Persian defeat of Babylon.[612] Since 45:1–7 never mentions Babylon and 45:18–25 refers to what will happen to all nations in a later eschatological era, this option will not work. D. E. Hollenberg rejects the idea that God is addressing and offering salvation to the foreign nations in this pas-

---

[606] Schoors, *I Am God Your Savior*, 238, considers this option possible, but unproven and not that helpful. This view is supported by N. J. Tromp, *Primitive Conception of Death and the Nether World in the Old Testament* (Rome: Pontifical Biblical Institute, 1969), 96–97. Baltzer, *Deutero-Isaiah*, 246, connects this to Sheol based on similarities with 5:8–14

[607] Goldingay, *Message of Isaiah 40–55*, 291, bases his conclusion on 42:7 "and those who dwell in darkness from the prison" (which he thinks refers to the dark prison of Babylon) and 45:3 "I will give you the treasures of darkness" (which he thinks are the treasures of Babylon).

[608] Schoors, *I Am God Your Savior*, 233, prefers "in vain" for תֹהוּ; Muilenburg, "Isaiah 40–66," 5:535, believes the prophet is describing "vain idols," while Koole, *Isaiah III, Volume 1, Isaiah 40–48*, 480, says "God's promises do not signify chaos, lead by no means to nothingness."

[609] C. F. Whitley, "Deutero-Isaiah's Interpretation of *ṣedeq*," *VT* 22 (1972): 469–75, translates this clause "I Yahweh uttereth a divine decision (*ṣedeq*), I declareth what is destined (*mēšārîm*)." Schoors, *I Am God Your Savior*, 236, translates this and most other uses of *ṣedeq* with "salvation" or "victory."

[610] הִקָּבְצוּ is a *niphal* imperative. The *niphal* can express a reflexive idea (GKC §51c,), reciprocal, or mutual actions (GKC §51d), in addition to its more frequent passive meaning. The use of the imperative is likely an admonition or exhortation (GKC §110a).

[611] 1QIs^a has וָאֵהיוּ "and come, arrive" instead of יַחְדָּו "together," which creates a good parallel with וָבֹאוּ "and come" in the first half of the first line. Whybray, *Isaiah 40–66*, 112, accepts this reading as original. If "together" remains, it creates a parallel with "together" in v. 21.

[612] Westermann, *Isaiah 40–66*, 175, thinks that these survivors after the defeat of Babylon "stand, however, for the 'survivors of the nations' in general." Oswalt, *Isaiah 40–66*, 221, also connect v. 20 with the military conquests of Cyrus, but Cyrus and Babylon are not mentioned in 45:18–25 and these events were not fulfilled after the conquest of Cyrus; these are eschatological events (cf. 2:1–4; 60:1–14).

sage because he believes these survivors are "crypto-Israelites." These people are called "crypto-Israelites" because "Israel's lost sons and daughters have become so swallowed up within the nations that Second Isaiah can describe them as *foster children* (xlix, 22f.)."[613] They have disassociated themselves from Israel and have identified with the nations and their gods, so now God invites his foster children back. D. W. Van Winkle has examined this theory in relationship to the interpretation of 42:5–9; 49:22–23; 51:4–6 and properly concludes that *gôyîm* ("nations") does not refer to crypto-Israelites.[614] R. E. Clements also views this as an invitation to all the nations of the world to turn to God.[615]

Those who are rhetorically invited to assemble are those from among the foreign nations who have no understanding of God (44:18–19), for they still foolishly carry around their wooden idols on festival days and they continually pray to these objects (44:17) that cannot save them. Certainly anyone who is thinking critically about this issue would realize that these wooden idols are worthless gods, for they do not have the ability to save those who pray to them. J. Motyer stresses, "this inability is not a lapse but an inherent defect."[616]

In 45:21 the nations are challenged to consult together and present their evidence that can document which God or idol declared what would happen in the future. This is the same argument used in 41:21–26 to prove that idol-gods do not have the basic power to predict the future. The purpose for this collaborative research is to present the facts about which god/God has announced what would happen "from the distant past" (*miqqedem*) before it actually took place. But there is no need to imagine that there was a literal trial of the nations, for before any evidence can be found, organized, and presented by the nations, God provides the results of his own research into this issue by putting his answer in the form of a rhetorical question. "Was it not I, the LORD?" means, "Surely, it was I, the LORD."[617] The God of Israel announced what would happen before it happened (41:21–29), and this demonstrates that "there is no other God besides me" (43:11; 44:6,8; 45:6,14) who has the characteristics of Yahweh of Israel. God is not just another one of the many minor immoral gods

---

[613] D. E. Hollenberg, "Nationalism and 'the Nations' in Isaiah XL–LV," *VT* 19 (1969): 23–36; Whybray, *Isaiah 40–66*, 11–112; and N. H. Snaith, "The Servant of the Lord in Deutero-Isaiah," 187–200, also follow this interpretation.

[614] D. W. Van Winkle, "The Relationship of the Nations to Yahweh and to Israel in Isaiah XL–LV," *VT* 35 (1985): 446–58.

[615] R. E. Clements, "Isaiah 45:20–25," *Int* 40 (1986): 392–96, agrees but contrasts this recognition of God's offer of salvation with the Babylonian recognition of the god Marduk as king. When the prophet indicates that every knee will bow, the discussion seems to leave behind all contrast with any one local god and concerns itself with the ultimate and universal achievement of God's salvation among all nations.

[616] Motyer, *Isaiah*, 366, views Isaiah calling these idols "nonsalvific" gods.

[617] Sentences that begin with הֲלֹא "is it not" are used to show that something is absolutely true (GKC §150e).

of the ancient Near East. He is specifically "a righteous God and a Savior." As a righteous God he does what is right; he has the integrity to save those who are righteous. Thus the concepts of "righteousness" and "salvation" are intimately intertwined because his salvation confirms that he is reliable to do what is right for those who trust him. His righteousness confirms that his salvation is a just and victorious deliverance from those that might threaten to destroy the one who trusts God. These characteristics prove that God's just declarations about his salvation were not completely hidden from human knowledge (45:15), though the benefits of his gracious salvation were frequently not experienced by those who turned from God to worship idols of wood. These declarations by God should have encouraged the Israelite audience, for if their God functions as a righteous God who was a Savior in the past, then he is a reliable just God whom they can trust to bring about the salvation of Israel and all the nations in the future.

45:22–23   Verse 22 begins with another imperative verb that encourages the nations from the ends of the earth to "turn to me and be saved." The audience must respond by turning their face toward God, but they cannot save themselves. They must be saved (a *niphal* passive verb) by God. The use of one imperative after another imperative could be a coordinate relationship in which the addressees are encouraged to do two things ("turn and be saved"), or the first imperative can set down a condition and the second can describe the consequences if the conditions are met.[618] The second approach fits this context; therefore, the text communicates to the audience that when God calls, they should respond to the imperative encouragement to turn, because then God can respond to produce the consequence of salvation. Although God owes the nations nothing but judgment for their failure to follow him, he graciously invites these nations to join his people in experiencing God's salvation.[619] Since there is only one God like Yahweh, he is the only one who can offer the nations any hope for the future. This divine invitation is unlimited in its inclusive extension to all peoples and nations throughout the earth, but it excludes all who refuse to turn to God. This divine worldwide program of salvation reminds one of God's original purpose for choosing Abram in Gen 12:3. It was God's plan to work through the blessing of Abram and his seed to bring blessing on all the nations of the earth. The concept of God's positive plans for the nations was briefly addressed in earlier messages in 2:1–4; 11:10; 14:1–3; 19:18–25. In the commission of the Lord's servant, God gave him the important role of a light

---

[618] GKC §110f describes the syntactical relationships in which the second imperative gives the consequences.

[619] Watts, *Isaiah 34–66*, 162, misses the grand significance of this promise when he interprets this verse as a limited and meager promise by Cyrus. "Cyrus offers salvation to the borderlands of Palestine. The salvation he offers is restoration of a measure of political order and prosperity, protection from vandals and bandits, and a share in the imperial peace in exchange for fealty and tribute."

2

1

to the nations (42:6), and his ministry will result in people throughout the earth singing praise to God (42:10–13).

If there were any Hebrews who doubted God's intentions or his ability to accomplish this plan of saving many from the nations, 45:23 removes all doubts. Israel and the nations can rest assured that God will accomplish his plan because he has sworn an unalterable oath based on his own integrity. "By myself" (*bî*) indicates that the one who guarantees the outcome of this oath is no one other than the sovereign God who rules the whole world. The oath "ensures the reliability and irrevocability of his word of salvation."[620] What this means is that if Yahweh would fail to do what has gone forth from his own mouth, then one can assume that he is not God. Since Yahweh is God, it is totally impossible for his plans to fail (55:10–11). Since Yahweh is a God of "justice, integrity, truthfulness" (*ṣedeqâ*), he always does what he says. Therefore, no words that he speaks or plans that he makes will ever turn in a different direction or "return" (*yāšûb*, NIV "revoked") without fulfilling their intentions. If he can speak and create this world, certainly he can speak and bring salvation to the nations.

The sure word of God is that every knee will bow before him and every tongue will swear allegiance to him (45:23b). This includes Hebrews and non-Hebrews, all nations, all languages, and all people (cf. Dan 7:13–14). This ultimate triumph over sin and rebellious people who refuse to serve God demonstrates that in the end God's original plan to create the kingdom of God will be accomplished. The text does not say if this bowing before God is a coercive forcing of people to submit or a joyful and willing reverencing of God, but in light of 45:24 (compare with 63:1–8) it appears that some will bow because of the judgment they will receive and others will bow in gratitude and worship for the great salvation that God will pour out through his grace.[621] This indicates a universal appeal that ignores all distinctions of nationality, race, or ethnic background. There will be a worldwide response to God, but this prophecy that everyone will bow before God will not result in universal salvation for everyone. Later the apostle Paul will use this verse to legitimate proper behavior toward others (Rom 14:10–11) and to justify his call for God's servants to be humble (Phil 2:10–11).[622]

45:24–25 This paragraph ends with one more description of what will happen in that eschatological era of salvation. The first phrase (NIV "they will say of me") is unclear and somewhat awkward, plus the Old Greek, Qumran,

---

[620] Koole, *Isaiah III, Volume 1, Isaiah 40–48*, 487.

[621] Goldingay, *Message of Isaiah 40–55*, 297, and Oswalt, *Isaiah 40–66*, 224, refer to both groups of people who will ultimately bow before God's glorious presence.

[622] M. A. Seifrid, "Romans," in *CNTOT*, 684–85, shows that the central emphasis in this passage is God's/Christ's lordship that ensures the salvation of his servants and the defeat of his enemies. If one accepts this thesis, then ethical behavior is a humble submission to the will of God the Savior.

and the Masoretic Hebrew text do not agree.[623] If one does not emend the text, the natural flow of thought from 45:23 would suggest that one ("he will say to me") of those people bowing before God (or all of those bowing represented as one group)[624] will swear a commitment to God and give praise to God in the words contained in part or all of 45:24–25. This praise begins with the statement (lit.), "Only in Yahweh . . . [are] righteousness and strength." This confession of faith recognizes Yahweh as the one divine power who has these traits; so there is an exclusive character to this statement. This praise is based on God's past righteous deeds of directing the course of history (45:19,21,23). In order to control the events of history and accomplish his plans as he predicted, God demonstrated his "strength, power" ('ōz, 40:28; 42:25; 43:16) by showing that he has a mighty arm that is able to save all those who call on him.

Although this confession of praise could end in v. 24a (NIV; HCSB), some suggest that all of 45:24–25 includes words of praise (JPS) or just 24a and 25.[625] It seems best to limit the praise to 45:24a and view vv. 24b and 25 as describing the contrasting destinies of the wicked (45:24b) and the righteous (45:25). God's justice will be evident as it works itself out in the destiny of the people who "are incensed, angry" (ḥārâ, NIV "raged"), for they will come (45:24b)[626] before God and bow their knees. These are the people (both foreigners and Hebrews) who worshiped idols (42:17; 44:9,11; 45:16) and rejected God's ways. When they will come before God, they will be judged and will experience great shame, for at this point they will know the truth about this glorious righteous God they have rejected. On the other hand, all the descendents of Israel (implied "the righteous descendents" 45:25) and the believing foreigners (44:5; 45:22–23) will experience something totally different. "They will be right/righteous, made righteous, declared righteous" (yiṣdĕqû) and as a result they will praise God. This acclamation of joyous confidence in God was meant to encourage the Israelites to make wise choices in their daily lives be-

---

[623] The Old Greek has "saying," which implies a Hebrew text לֵאמֹר, while 1QIsᵃ has לְיָא יֵאמַר which may be a *niphal* passive verb: "to me let it be said." One could hypothesize that the MT has a scribal error of dropping one of the two *yod* letters in the Qumran tradition. Westermann, *Isaiah 40–66*, 174, follows the Old Greek reading "saying" (implying a Hebrew לְאמֹר). Schoors, *I Am God Your Savior*, 236, follows the Qumran imperfect reading and understands the לִי as an emphatic לְ; thus he translates the phrase "only in Yahwe, *it will be said*." Oswalt, *Isaiah 40–66*, 219, accepts the Qumran reading "let it be said."

[624] The perfect verb אָמַר is interpreted as prophetic perfect "he will say" (GKC §106n). HCSB unnecessarily turns the active verb into the passive "it will be said to Me," although this is a legitimate interpretation of an impersonal verb (GKC 121a).

[625] Koole, *Isaiah III, Volume 1, Isaiah 40–48*, 474, 490, takes all of vv. 24–25 as a quotation, Baltzer, *Deutero-Isaiah*, 248–51, makes vv. 24a and 25 quotations since both begin with בַּיהוה, and Whybray, *Isaiah 40–66*, 113, limits the quotation to v. 24a.

[626] North, *The Second Isaiah*, 156, is probably correct in viewing the sg. "he/one will come" יָבוֹא as a scribal error for יָבוֹאוּ which is found in 1QIsᵃ and 21 Hebrew MSS. This makes both "come" and "ashamed" pl. verbs. A possible reason for this error is that the next word after יָבוֹאוּ begins with a ו; thus the scribe wrote one ו but should have written two.

cause one choice will lead them to disappointment and shame while the other choice will result in times of great praise in the presence of God. This dramatic choice faces each person who lives on this earth today; so every person who hears of the righteous deeds of God must realize that their future depends on whether they are willing to turn to God and be saved (45:22).

THEOLOGICAL IMPLICATIONS.   These statements make it clear that if believers want others to turn to God, those who follow God must live in such a way that unbelievers understand that God is with his people (Israel then and the church today). God's deeds, his character, his name, and his honor should not be hidden from others but should be declared openly, even among people who do not know him, because many of them are now devoted to things that will not help them. If others knew that God is a Savior and that he can be their Savior, his ways will not be hidden anymore.

This message contains a blessed hope for all who trust in God, both for past and future generations of Hebrews and people from other nations. If one confesses that God is the Creator of the heavens and the earth (45:18), that he has spoken his plans and foretold the future before it happens (45:19a), that God speaks the truth and accomplishes his promises (45:19b,23), and that there is no other righteous God and Savior for humanity (45:21), then it is possible to turn to God and be saved (45:23). It does not matter who that person is, where that person is from, what their background is, or what they have thought or done in the past. A righteous God makes his salvation open to all, but he knows that not everyone will recognize his authority and trust in his words. Thus the prophet attempts to persuade his audience with a reasoned argument that lays out a series of criteria that his audience can either give assent to or deny. The one who hears these words knows that whoever will confess these truths and act upon them will be saved. The audience also knows that there will be a final accountability which will distinguish the final destiny of the righteous who praise God from the unbelievers who rage against God.

This passage served as a basis for the ministry of the apostle Paul. His goal was to reach the Gentiles by spreading the gospel to people who had never heard of Jesus' name. In Rom 14:7–12 he reminds his Gentile audience that there will be a final day of accountability before the judgment seat of God when every person will bow their knee before God and give account for their life. This knowledge has the practical implication of reminding every person that they do not live just for their own pleasures, but that they live before God. Therefore, people should not judge others or be a stumbling block to others but strive for peace and mutual edification (Rom 14:13–19). In Phil 2:3–8 Paul encourages his Gentile audience to follow the humble example of Jesus who became a man and died for all on the cross. One of the reasons people should follow Christ's example is that God will lift him up to an exalted place in the end. Paul then expands on Isa 44:23 and states that when God exalts Jesus every knee will bow before him and every tongue will confess that Jesus Christ is Lord. The message is clear to Hebrew and foreigners in both testaments. Everyone must make the important and practical decisions about God based on the knowledge that there will be a final day when every knee will bow before him.

5. Trust God Who Humbles Babylon and Offers Salvation to All (46:1–48:22)

These messages continue the prophet's attempt to persuade his hard-hearted Hebrew audience (not the Babylonians) that Yahweh, Israel's God, is the sovereign ruler who will accomplish all his plans to save his people. He is not like the silent and motionless images of Bel or Nebo that can do nothing (46:1–13). Part of God's plan is to destroy the proud city of Babylon to show that its gods and diviners are useless (47:1–15). Although the stubborn Israelites were often not attentive to God's words in the past and consequently suffered much, now they are challenged to hear God's new words and trust him for their future salvation (48:1–19). The overall unit ends with a hymn that calls the people to flee from the Babylonian ways and thought patterns and instead rejoice because God will redeem his people (48:20–21).

These chapters are somewhat unique within chaps. 40–55, for chaps. 46–47 might initially appear to belong among the oracles against the nations in chaps. 13–23. In fact, C. A. Franke has identified numerous interlinking connections between chaps. 14 and 47. (a) Both chaps. 14 and 47 are taunts that imitate a lament over the fall of Babylon. (b) 14:11,15,19 and 47:1,5 refer to "going down" to the underworld implying death. (c) 14:9,13 and 47:1 refer to "thrones" that kings sit on. (d) 14:6,17,29 and 47:6 describe the faults of Babylon and her king. (e) 14:8–10,13–14 and 47:7–8,10 refer to the pride of Babylon, including its claim that it has some sort of divine status.[627]

Each chapter within 40–55 has its own special emphasis, but chaps. 46, 47, and 48 are brought together by one central factor that is the focus of what God was trying to communicate. C. A. Franke believes that God makes the claim that "I am God, and there is no other" (46:9) in order to contrast himself with the idols of wood. This self-identification that God makes concerning his status is contradicted in 47:8,10 when Babylon proudly declares, "I am, and there is none besides me." This arrogant statement will be convincingly proven wrong once Babylon is defeated. Then Yahweh will be proven to be the only supernatural power who can legitimately make the claim that "I am he; I am the first and I am the last . . . I am the LORD your God" (48:12,17).[628] The idols did not

---

[627] C. A. Franke, "Reversals of Fortune in the Ancient Near East: A Study of the Babylon Oracle in the Book of Isaiah," in *New Visions of Isaiah*, ed. R. F. Melugin and M. A. Sweeney (Sheffield: Sheffield Academic Press, 1996), 104–23.

[628] C. A. Franke, "The Function of the Satiric Lament over Babylon in Second Isaiah (XLVII)," *VT* 41 (1991): 408–18, makes these comparisons on pp. 414–15.

predict the future, but God announced what would happen in the past and he will act to accomplish his plans in the future (48:3).

In addition, C. A. Franke and M. E. Biddle have shown how God's ways of dealing with the Virgin Daughter of Babylon and the Daughter of Zion are contrasted and reversed. Judah was weak and hopeless while Babylon was strong, but after the hopeless defeat of Babylon in chaps. 46–47, Zion will become strong and inhabited with many children in chaps. 49–55; 57.[629] These interlinking connections with key ideas in later chapters in the Book of Isaiah illustrate how important these chapters about Babylon's defeat are to the broader conceptual framework that is pursued in the rest of chaps. 49–55. The editorial placement of these chapters at this point in the book leads to new emphases in chaps. 49–55.

(1) Babylon and Her Gods Cannot Save Themselves (46:1–47:15)

These two chapters are thematically united because they both discuss the demise of Babylon, including the humiliation of her idols and the failures of her many religious practitioners. The central theological message develops around the contrast between Yahweh and the idols, Yahweh and Babylon, and the contrasting destinies of the nation that follows God and the nation that depends on idols and diviners. Helpless idols cannot save themselves or the people of Babylon (46:7b; 47:14,15), but Yahweh will save his people (46:4b,13). The gods have to be carried (46:1,7), but God will carry his people (46:4). Babylon proudly claims to be god (47:8,10), but Yahweh is a unique divine power and there is no other like him (46:9). This message ridicules the proud Babylonians and encourages the Israelites to trust in God's plan and rest assured in the knowledge that God fulfills all his purposes (46:10–11), for he is the true source of their salvation (46:12–13).

SETTING. A cursory reading of chaps. 46–47 gives the immediate impression that this prophecy was given sometime before the fall of Babylon. But clarity on a specific date vanishes when questions are raised about how long before the fall of Babylon this prophecy was uttered and exactly which defeat of Babylon is envisioned in this prophecy. There is a tendency for commentators to imply that this is referring to Babylon's defeat by the Persian king Cyrus. This focus on the fulfillment has lead to a tendency to subvert the ancient statement of what was at that time something of an ambiguous mystery. In its place some scholars have substituted a known fulfillment (the Persian defeat of Babylon) based on historical events.[630] Although everyone is interested

---

[629] Franke, "Reversals of Fortune in the Ancient Near East," 104–23, connects the contrast between Babylon and Zion in chaps. 48–55 while M. E. Biddle, "Lady Zion's Alter Egos: Isaiah 47.1–15 and 57.6–13 as Structural Counterparts," *New Visions of Isaiah*, 124–39, illustrates connections between eight passages which have fem. personifications of cities. Some of these comparisons will be dealt with as each of these personifications are examined in later chapters.

[630] The same authors who will argue strongly against reading a New Testament messianic

in the fulfillment of prophecy, one cannot read later fulfillment back into the prophecy without producing an enhanced meaning that is markedly different from what the prophet's original audience heard.

Hypothetically, the defeat of Babylon that the prophet announced could relate to: (a) the Assyrian king Tiglath-pileser III who defeated the Babylonian king Nabu-shuma-ukin around 729 BC; (b) Sargon II taking control of Babylon around 710 BC when Merodach-baladan ruled Babylon; (c) Sennacherib's defeat of Merodach-baladan around 703 BC and again in 689 BC when the city of Babylon was decimated; (d) Cyrus's taking control of Babylon in 539 BC; or (e) Xerxes' defeat of Babylon around 400 BC. Since Cyrus (Hb. Koresh) was mentioned in 44:28–45:1, many commentators believe this prophecy predicts this conquest of Babylon by Cyrus the Persian. This hypothesis is strengthened by the reference to God's summoning a bird of prey from the east to carry out his purposes in 46:11, but almost any of the foreign kings mentioned above could fit this broad descriptive metaphor (10:5; 41:2). Although every piece of information is helpful, two major problems have developed because many interpreters have read later fulfillments into these prophecies. These are the problems of (a) the historicization of the prophecy and (b) the falsification of the prophecy.

When a text is treated as fulfilled history, unidentified people are identified by name, general information about what will happen is applied to specific events, and the nontemporal generalities about the future are focused on a specific date. K. Baltzer's interpretation of 46:1–2 historicizes these verses into a solemn religious procession in Babylon where the idols of Bel and Nebo were paraded so that people could bow down to them. Then these gods collapse and are taken into captivity. But is this an appropriate interpretation? J. Goldingay notes that these pictures about the carrying of the gods could relate to: (a) the moving of gods from their rural temple into a main walled city in the event of war, (b) the moving of gods to a foreign country after a weaker nation (Babylon) was defeated, or (c) the religious New Year celebration where the gods were paraded (though this was actually stopped by Nabonidus for about ten years before the fall of Babylon).[631] Consequently Goldingay warns that a proper approach to understanding prophecies is to treat them "not so much a purportedly second-sight literal description of what will happen but an imaginative portrayal made on the basis of facts and traditions known to the author and audience."[632] By this he does not suggest that nothing is literal or that the interpreter should not use background information about Babylonian culture; he simply warns against treating a broad prophetic prediction as a completed

---

meaning back into an Old Testament text, will often think nothing of reading Cyrus's fulfillment of this text back into their exegesis.

[631] Baltzer, *Deutero-Isaiah*, 255, compares this to later Greek processions of the Dionysus cult. Goldingay, *Message of Isaiah 40–55*, 303–4.

[632] Goldingay, *Message of Isaiah 40–55*, 303.

historical account in which everything is spelled out in detail exactly as it happened. Interpreters should not turn prophecy into history.

A second problem arises when this prophecy is treated as an historical account of the fall of Babylon to Cyrus in 539 BC, for then the truthfulness of this prophecy is put in doubt. R. N. Whybray claims that "this is a further example of a prophecy which was not fulfilled; in the event Cyrus proclaimed himself a follower of Marduk and actively promoted the worship of Babylon's gods."[633] Thus this prophecy is false since Bel (Marduk) was not carried away into captivity in defeat but was embraced by the Persians. If Cyrus's account of his conquest of Babylon can be completely trusted (a legitimate question to ask of a piece of political propaganda), this conclusion seems almost inevitable, but a more judicious approach might look for other alternative explanations. Maybe (a) the Cyrus Cylinder does not tell the whole story (what happened to these gods a month later), (b) the contradictory nature of the evidence should point the reader to another conquest of the Babylonians and their gods and not the one by Cyrus, (c) the Babylonians are a metaphorical symbol of all of God's enemies (like Edom in chap. 34), or (d) the prophet is painting a picture of the eventual and ultimate defeat of the Babylonian gods without specifically implying that all of this will be fulfilled at one time in 539 BC. Without considering many other possible explanations of the prophecy, it would seem to be a little arrogant or premature to label this as a prophecy that was not fulfilled.

All that can be said is that this prophecy was given when the people of Israel were "stubborn-hearted" and "far from righteousness" (46:12) and before the fall of Babylon and the salvation of God's people (47:1–15). Its primary purpose was to assure the prophet's Hebrew audience that their God is greater than any idol and stronger than the power of the great Babylonian empire. When God defeats his Babylonian enemies and grants salvation to Zion (46:13), God will accomplish everything that he has planned (46:10).

GOD'S SUPERIORITY OVER IDOLS (46:1–13)

¹Bel bows down, Nebo stoops low;
   their idols are borne by beasts of burden.
The images that are carried about are burdensome,
   a burden for the weary.
²They stoop and bow down together;
   unable to rescue the burden,
   they themselves go off into captivity.

³"Listen to me, O house of Jacob,
   all you who remain of the house of Israel,
you whom I have upheld since you were conceived,
   and have carried since your birth.

---

[633] Whybray, *Isaiah 40–66*, 114, rejects the view that 46:1–2 "is a mocking allusion to the triumphant festival procession of the days of Babylon's glory."

[4]Even to your old age and gray hairs
    I am he, I am he who will sustain you.
I have made you and I will carry you;
    I will sustain you and I will rescue you.

[5]"To whom will you compare me or count me equal?
    To whom will you liken me that we may be compared?
[6]Some pour out gold from their bags
    and weigh out silver on the scales;
they hire a goldsmith to make it into a god,
    and they bow down and worship it.
[7]They lift it to their shoulders and carry it;
    they set it up in its place, and there it stands.
From that spot it cannot move.
Though one cries out to it, it does not answer;
    it cannot save him from his troubles.

[8]"Remember this, fix it in mind,
    take it to heart, you rebels.
[9]Remember the former things, those of long ago;
    I am God, and there is no other;
    I am God, and there is none like me.
[10]I make known the end from the beginning,
    from ancient times, what is still to come.
I say: My purpose will stand,
    and I will do all that I please.
[11]From the east I summon a bird of prey;
    from a far-off land, a man to fulfill my purpose.
What I have said, that will I bring about;
    what I have planned, that will I do.
[12]Listen to me, you stubborn-hearted,
    you who are far from righteousness.
[13]I am bringing my righteousness near,
    it is not far away;
    and my salvation will not be delayed.
I will grant salvation to Zion,
    my splendor to Israel.

The first chapter in this section focuses on God's divinity and superiority over idols, not on the fall of two key Babylonian gods. Bel and Nebo are mentioned only in the first half of 46:1–2, while the general practice of making idols is described in 46:6–7. But most of the chapter is about God, who speaks about himself and his purposes throughout 46:3–5,9–13. Since most of this chapter focuses on the good news of what God will do (which the idols cannot do), the genre of this passage functions as a word of salvation to the Hebrew people who heard these words.[634] The material can be outlined into two paragraphs that bring out these contrasts:[635]

Idols do not carry, but God carries and saves	46:1–7
Idols are carried, but God delivers	1–4
Idols are made, but cannot save	5–7
Trust God, he plans then accomplishes his purposes	46:8–13
God's deeds prove he is God	8–11
Respond to God's salvation	12–13

This message is connected to the previous chapter by the repetition of the idea of "carrying" (*nāśāʾ*) idols in 45:20 and 46:1,3,4,7 and the idea of "bowing" (*kāraʿ*) in 45:23 and 46:1,2,6. The persuasive nature of the message is communicated through the three imperative verbs that exhort the audience to "listen" (46:3), "remember" (46:8), and "listen" (46:12). The repetition of key words (especially "bear, lift up, carry" *nāśaʾ* in 46:1,3,4,7 and the synonyms "carry" *sābal* in 46:4a,4b,7 and "bear" *ʿāmas* in 46:1,3,4) help hold the paragraphs together and enable the prophet to contrast the idols with God.

46:1–2 The argument against all man-made idols that appeared repeatedly in past messages of the prophet (40:18–24; 41:5–10,21–24; 42:14–17; 44:6–20; 45:15–17) is now modified in order to contrast Yahweh, God of Israel, with two of the main Babylonian gods, Bel and Nebo. The name Bel means "lord," and it is similar to the Canaanite title Baal. Bel was a title attributed to Enlil in early Mesopotamian texts, but around 1,800 BC it became a title describing Marduk, the chief god of the city of Babylon. Marduk was the god who saved the younger gods of Mesopotamia from annihilation by defeating Tiamat in the Babylonian creation myth (the Enuma Elish), so Marduk was named the king of the gods (*ANET,* 60–72). Nabu[636] (Nebo) was the son of Marduk and the chief god of the city of Borsippa (seven miles southwest of Babylon). He was the god of wisdom, writing, and in charge of the "Tablets of Destiny," which described what would happen in the coming year. Ironically, in this message God announces that he himself will determine the destiny of these two gods.

---

[634] Koole, *Isaiah III, Volume 1, Isaiah 40–48,* 495, and Melugin, *Formation of Isaiah 40–55,* 131, find the major emphasis on God's salvation, though they see signs of a disputation speech in vv. 5–11. Whybray, *Isaiah 40–66,* 114–17, refers to vv. 3–4 as "a short promise of salvation," vv. 9–11 is called a "disputation . . . that resembles a trial speech," and vv. 12–13 is "a straightforward divine promise of immediate salvation."

[635] C. Franke, *Isaiah 46, 47, and 48: A New Literary-Critical Reading* (Winona Lake: Eisenbrauns, 1994), 72–99, provides an extended discussion of issues surrounding the structuring of the micro and macro factors that indicate the structure of this message. She finds within the structure a strong contrast between Yahweh and the gods of Babylon.

[636] The importance of Bel (בֵּל) is implied by the inclusion of his name in the Babylonian king Belshazzar, while the name Nebo (נְבוֹ) is part of the name of kings Nebuchadnezzar and Nabonidus.

The humiliation of these two gods is explained in an imaginative picture of the idols of these gods being carried away by animals. The scene does not appear to be the joyous annual New Year's procession of the gods through the streets of the city and probably does not describe the removal of the gods from minor cities into the great walled city of Babylon for protection just before a major war.[637] The reference to bowing and going into captivity (46:2) argues that the idols were defeated and will be war booty that will be taken away by a conquering army (1 Chr 14:12; 2 Chr 25:14; Jer 48:7; 49:3; 50:2; TANE, picture 145).[638] Although idols do not usually bow (except Dagan in 1 Sam 5:3,4), their submissive action coincides with the "bowing"[639] of those who carry idols of wood in 45:20–23. This text does not identify the person these idols will bow before (maybe the conquering general), so it is safer to interpret bowing as a sign of defeat and powerlessness. While purposely refraining from calling these objects gods, the passage describes how these "forms" (ʿṣb; NIV "idols") of wood or stone will be loaded on pack animals, and how these "things you carry" (nĕśuʾôtêkem, NIV "images") will become burdens that exhaust the strength of the animals moving them.[640]

The subject of the verbs in 46:2 is unclear. Initially it would appear that the idols are the subject, but this approach would make v. 2 repetitious of v. 1 and make the word "together" rather unnecessary. J. L. Koole suggests that it is the people of Babylon who will bow down "together" (yaḥdāw) with the idols.[641] The people of Babylon will not be able to save[642] the burden (the idols) that is on the pack animals because they (lit., "their soul" nāpšām) all will go into exile with these idols. Since Cyrus's was welcomed into Babylon and he restored the worship of Marduk (another term for Bel) and his feasts, this passage cannot be referring to his takeover of Babylon.

46:3–4 This divine exhortation encourages every Hebrew (those from Judah and Israel) to listen to what God has to say. In contrast to the powerless idols who have to be carried by pack animals and the people of Babylon (46:1–2),

---

[637] Baltzer, *Deutero-Isaiah*, 255, believes this is a parody of the New Year's festival, but the negative imagery makes this unlikely. S. A. Pallis, *The Babylonian Akitu Festival* (Copenhagen, n.p., 1926) discusses the Akitu procession. Seitz, "Isaiah 40–66," 406, and Motyer, *Isaiah*, 368, suggest that the idols are being removed from danger, based on Merodach-Baladan's action of removing the idols before Sennacherib attacked Babylon. This text is in E. Schrader, *The Cuneiform Inscriptions and the Old Testament* (London: Williams and Norgate, 1885–88), 2:36.

[638] Koole, *Isaiah III, Volume 1, Isaiah 40–48*, 498, supports the view that the idols are the spoils of war.

[639] The participle קֹרֵס is only used here, so it is difficult to give it a meaning. Presumably it has a meaning synonymous with כָּרַע "bow" which is used earlier in the verse.

[640] The God of Israel gives strength to the weary (40:28–31) while these gods take away strength and make animals weary.

[641] Koole, *Isaiah III, Volume 1, Isaiah 40–48*, 499.

[642] The verb מַלֵּט is a *piel* infinitive construct without the usual לְ prefix. It functions as the direct object of the preceding verb (GKC 114c§) to express the idea of permission of prohibition (GKC §1114l, "they will not be able").

God reminds his people that the Hebrews are "the ones who were carried, lifted up" ('ămusîm, a passive participle; NIV, "upheld") by God "from"[643] the time of their birth, a reference to the origin of the nation at the time of their exodus from Egypt (40:11; Exod 19:4; Deut 1:31; Hos 11:3). The contrast between God and these idols extends to the distant future as well, for when his people are old with gray hair, he will continue to care for them. In other words, God cares for his people from the cradle to the grave. The promise "I am he, I am he who will sustain you" (46:4) provides an emphatic 100 percent guarantee about God's power, his commitment, and his plan. Just in case this was not enough assurance for the Hebrew audience, God repeats his promise: "I [my-self] have made you and I [myself] will carry you" to make it 200 percent sure. Although at this point there should be no doubt about God's determined will, for the third and final time God shouts his promises, "I [myself] will sustain you and I [myself] will rescue you." The audience should be absolutely assured that his care will never end and that it will always be available. This presents an explicit contrast to the idols that were not able to rescue themselves or the people of Babylon (46:2a).

46:5–7   Having given such a stark contrast between himself and the chief gods of Babylon, God now asks the audience a rhetorical question, challenging them to identify some other divine being that "might be like"[644] (NIV, "com-pare") him (40:18; 41:7; 44:9). What characteristics are similar? In addition, God wants to know if anyone might be his equal?[645] The question could be as simple as, "Can anyone else carry people and save them?" or it may be as com-plex as, "Does anyone have the same status, reputation, abilities, qualities, or character as Yahweh, the God of Israel?" The obvious answer to that rhetorical question is that not one of these Babylonian gods is in any way comparable to Israel's God. This question is not part of a dispute[646] because there is nothing to dispute. These questions are part of another rhetorical argument that should cause the audience to respond positively and trust God (46:12–13).

In answer to this challenge, 46:6–7 list the impressive qualities of a hypo-thetical contender that some might try to compare with God. Of course this possibility is actually raised only to mock or show the ridiculousness of com-paring a man-made idol to the supreme God Yahweh. First, in order to make an idol someone must "pour out"[647] enough gold and weigh out enough silver

---

[643] The preposition מִנִּי is a poetic form of מִן which means "from," not "from me" (GKC §90,l).

[644] In questions the imperfect verbal form (תְדַמְיוּנִי) often functions as a modal or contingent action, expressed with helping words like "might, can, could, should, would" (GKC §107r,t).

[645] The verb תַשְׁווּ comes from the root שָׁוָה which means "to be level with, equivalent, like, comparable to, equal with" (BDB, 1000). NIV has "count . . . equal."

[646] Schoors, *I Am God Your Savior*, 274, suggests "the questions may introduce a disputation. And exactly as in xl 18–29, the answer consists of mockery of the idols."

[647] The meaning of the pl. participle הַזָּלִים is difficult to define. The Hebrew preposition זוּלָה means "except, only," so BDB, 266, hypothesizes a root II meaning "lavish" (found only once in

from their bag (people have to help make the god look impressive), then they must hire a goldsmith so that he can make a god (people must make the god), and finally they will "even" (*'ap*; NIV, "though") worship the idol. Once the idol exists it must be carried (as in 46:1) to a shrine where it rests (46:7). Once it is there, not much else happens. It just stands there in its place because "it cannot move"[648] from that place (the shrine where it was put). This immobility suggests a lack of life and an absence of power to reach out and help others. Nevertheless, some deluded people will cry out to the lifeless idol for help, but the cruel facts are that "it cannot answer" and "it cannot save"[649] no matter what a person's problems are.

These factors stand in strong contrast to Yahweh, the God of Israel. He has no form that limits him to one place; he is totally separate from earthly metals. In fact Yahweh made the gold and silver and was not made by people. God carries others and does not need to be carried; he moves to control everything that happens on earth. He hears when people cry out for help, and he is able to answer and to save. How could anyone be so foolish as to worship such useless idols of wood? The contrast between God and these idol-gods is overwhelming. How could people not trust Yahweh, the God who made and saves them?

46:8–11 Having highlighted the weakness and unresponsiveness of the idols, God now turns to declare his own glorious deeds. If people will just remember the past acts of Yahweh, they clearly demonstrate that he is an all-powerful God. The prediction of future events and the future fulfillment of God's plans prove that he can do whatever he purposes to do. R. N. Whybray's conclusion that this is a disputation that resembles a trial speech imagines that the Israelites have questioned God's decision to send Cyrus to deliver them, but there is no evidence in this passage that the Israelites question this issue at all.[650] The main point of this message is to prove that Yahweh, not the idols, is the real divine power who can be trusted. God's past acts prove that he is God (46:10), and promise (46:11) is only one of many reasons given for trusting in God for salvation. P. D. Hanson notes that "the principle underlying this inter-

---

this text), but this seems unacceptable for the Aramaic verb זוּל means "to be worthless, of little value." F. Delitzsch, "Prophecies of Isaiah," *Commentary on the Old Testament*, (Grand Rapids: Eerdmans, 1969), 234, proposes that the word comes from זָלַל "to shake, pour out" which makes better sense.

[648] The imperfect verb יָמִישׁ (from מוּשׁ) could be translated as a statement of fact "it will not move" or it could refer to willed action that expresses the subjunctive idea of "it cannot move" (GKC §107r-s). *IBHS*, 507, calls this the "non-perfective of capability" that describes what someone is or is not capable of doing.

[649] Since וְלֹא יַעֲנֶה and לֹא יוֹשִׁיעֶנּוּ are parallel to the verb "it cannot move," they also should express the subjunctive mood of "it cannot answer" and it cannot save him" (GKC §107r-s).

[650] Whybray, *Isaiah 40–66*, 116, implies from the promises God makes that the people of Israel doubted God's plan to send Cyrus. But one should not assume that every promise of hope originated in order to address some disputed point. In addition, Cyrus is not mentioned by name and v. 11 is just one piece of a much greater argument. Childs, *Isaiah*, 358, rejects this idea and refers to it as a "more speculative aspect of the form-critical approach."

pretation of history and enabling the prophet to discern a creative, redemptive pattern is theological. It revolves around faith in the divine promise, 'I have planned, and I will do it' (v. 11)."[651]

46:8 This paragraph begins with another imperative verb (also beginning 46:3,9,12) that exhorts the audience to "remember" (*zikrû*) and respond based on the statements God makes about his sovereign control of history. The "this" (*zōʾt*) that the people are to remember refers to claims made in the following verses. The second imperative (*hitʾōšāšû*, NIV "fix it in mind") is only found here, and it is difficult to determine its meaning.[652] One could hypothesize that its meaning should be parallel to the meaning of first imperative ("remember") or that there is a progression of ideas between the first ("remember") and the third ("return") imperative, with the second somewhere in between. No solution stands out as the obvious choice, and it is best to keep the Masoretic text and follow the suggested meaning of the Aramaic Targum ("take a firm stand"). The third imperative is parallel to remember in the first line, for it calls the audience to literally "cause it to return to your heart" (*hāšîbû ʿal lēb*) or to seriously consider what will be said. The audience God was speaking to was the "rebellious ones" (*pôšĕʿîm*; 43:25,27; 44:22; 48:8; 50:1), but there is no explanation of exactly how these people were being rebellious. Since no Israelite is accused of worshipping the idols in this passage,[653] their rebellion may be their fundamental unwillingness to trust in God to carry them, save them, and fulfill all his purposes in the future (46:4,10–11).

46:9 What specifically are these rebellious people to remember? Verse 9 charges them to remember the "former things" (*riʾšōnôt*) or past events from long ago. This could refer to God's creation of the world (40:21–22) or his great deeds of salvation in choosing and redeeming his people (41:9; 43:1,3,16–19), but in other cases the "former things" that will help increase their faith in God are all the things God has predicted before they happened (41:2–4,25–26; 42:9; 43:9; 44:7–8; 45:21).[654] C. Westermann rightly believes this "call to have faith

---

[651] Hanson, *Isaiah 40–66*, 115, believes that "the pattern of divine guidance in past and present provides the basis for a bold promise."

[652] The Targum connected this root to אָשַׁשׁ "to be firm, strong" which was accepted by Delitzsch, "Prophecies of Isaiah," 235; Blenkinsopp, *Isaiah 40–55*, 270–71, emends the texts to הִתְבּשֵׁשׁוּ "be ashamed" which is similar to the Vulgate; the Old Greek has "groan." H. Leene, "Isaiah 46:8—Summons to be Human?" *JSOT* 30 (1984): 111–21, draws the root from אֵשׁ "man," thus giving the meaning "show yourself as men" (as in KJV). The Syriac Peshitta has the equivalent of וְהִתְבּוֹנְנוּ from the root בִּין "to consider, understand" (RSV). C. Franke, *Isaiah 46, 47, and 48: A New Literary-Critical Reading*, 50–51, reviews 10 different approaches to interpreting this word and concludes that "stand firm" is best.

[653] Franke, *Isaiah 46, 47, and 48*, 54, believes the rebellious ones were exiles in Babylon who were tempted to forget God and worship idols sometime near the end of the exilic period.

[654] Goldingay, *Message of Isaiah 40–55*, 311, says "usage of the phrase 'former things' (see 41.22) suggests it denotes events that have happened in accordance with Yhwh's word," but he thinks that these events may include events that happened "only decades previously" based on 58:13 and 61:4. Some include Cyrus's conquest of Babylon as among the former things. C. R.

means bringing the nation's experience with God in history to bear upon the present."[655] When these people review the past acts of God, they should come to the faith conviction that "I am God, and there is no other; I am God, and there is none like me." In order to substantiate this unique, exclusive, and incomparable conclusion, God provides the audience with his interpretation of some of the key characteristics of his involvement in human history.

46:10 Rather than spelling out a long list of specific things God has done (as in 44:24–28), a general principle is explained that covers all his actions. In stark contrast to the idols that cannot even speak, much less tell the future (46:7), God is "the one who declares" (the participle *maggîd*; NIV, "make known") what has not yet happened, as well as what he will accomplish in the end. This refers to his revelation of future events to people. He is "the one who says" (the participle *'ōmēr*) something and it happens (Gen 1 illustrates this point). There should be no doubt about his future plans, for his purposes will be accomplished;[656] he does everything that he pleases. This correlation between his plans and what happens proves God's faithfulness and reliability.

In reality, people and nations are not the ones who determine the course of history; God is the one who plans and directs what will happen. The veracity of these plans is evident in the course of history, for some of the statements that God made in 14:24–27 have already been fulfilled. God stated that his plan and purpose was to crush Assyria, and he did that when his angel destroyed 185,000 Assyrian troops outside the walls of Jerusalem (37:36). His plans involved not just what will happen to the Israelites; he has plans for all the nations of the world, and nothing can stop him from accomplishing his will (10:5–6; 22:11; 30:1–5; 37:26). Although it may sometimes seem like this world is going to self-destruct because of the wars and terrible atrocities people inflict on one another, the world is not drifting aimlessly out of control toward a hopeless end. Kings and presidents may try to strategize and work together to direct the political affairs of the nations, but in reality it is the sovereign power of God's hand that will bring his plans (not ours) to fruition. Although there is evidence that the end will come with uncontrollable death and destruction

---

North, "The 'Former Things' and the 'New Things,'" *Studies in Old Testament Prophecy*, 111–26, uses 43:16–19 to prove that the former things refer to the exodus. N. Habel, "Appeal to Ancient Traditions as a Literary Form," *ZAW* 88 (1975): 253–72, concludes that the former things refer to the fulfilled words of God, such as creation and the exodus, but not recent events. H. G. M. Williamson, "First and Last in Isaiah," *Of Prophets' Visions and the Wisdom of Sages*, 95–108, believes that the use of this term in chaps. 40–55 is dependent on the use of the former and latter things in 8:23 (English 9:1).

[655] Westermann, *Isaiah 40–66*, 185, suggests that in "Deutero-Isaiah's view, there is no such thing as faith divorced from history . . . faith says 'yes' to the future, this is an affirmation that God can be depended on."

[656] J. Jensen, "Yahweh's Plan in Isaiah and the Rest of the Old Testament," 443–55, surveys this concept throughout the Old Testament. A wise counselor may present a plan of action that might work, but God has the ability to conceive of a perfect plan and also the power to carry out his wise plans in a successful manner.

(4:1–23; 34:1–15; Dan 7–8), afterward God will transform this world and its people in order to establish his holy kingdom for his people (2:1–5; 4:2–6; 25:1–26:6; 30:18–26; 35:1–10; 45:18–25). What he originally planned will appear; what pleases him will stand forever.

46:11 One of the specific things that God planned was to summons a "bird of prey" from a far-off land in the east. He would respond to God's instructions and thereby fulfill the purposes God formed long ago. The use of the participle ("the one who summons" *qōrēʾ*) helps connect v. 11 with the participles in v. 10. The final phrase "what I have planned that I will do it"[657] restates the principle in v. 10.

The identity of the "bird of prey" is kept secret,[658] but the imagery suggests that it represents a faraway unknown person in the east who will prey on someone else and accomplish God's purposes.[659] The Aramaic Targum connects this prediction to the call of Abram, a man from the east, and the gathering of the exiles. Drawing on the parallelism with Nebuchadnezzar being described as an eagle (Jer 49:22; Ezek 17:3), one might guess that this will be a powerful Assyrian, Babylonian, or Persian king. If one assumes that the readers could connect the hypothetical dots all the way back to 44:28–45:1,13, the ruler Koresh could be a candidate,[660] or if the hypothetical dots were connected back to 41:1–2, the Assyrian king Sennacherib might be intended—but these are only speculation. Since Cyrus did not treat the gods of Babylon according to the prophecy in 46:1–2, it is unlikely that he is the bird of prey in this passage. Since the bird of prey is not identified and his deeds are not described, it is impossible to identify the exact historical event mentioned with any degree of certainty. It is far more important to appreciate the importance of the general principle taught in these promises (God speaks and he establishes his plans), than to focus on an unidentified historical event. The threefold repetition of the particle *ʾap* "even, surely" (omitted in NIV) in the second half of this verse emphasizes that this promise is an unshakable truth that the listener can count on.[661]

46:12–13 This prophetic message ends with a call for the audience to "listen" (*šimĕʿû*) and respond. The audience is identified as those who are

---

[657] The third fem. pronominal suffix הָ "it" is attached to the end of אֲבִיאֶנָּה "I will bring it about." To the usual fem. הָ ending is added the *nun energicum* נ (frequently in pausal forms) which does not change the meaning of the word (GKC §58i-l).

[658] Baltzer, *Deutero-Isaiah,* 263, connects this word עַיִט with a bird that "screeches," and he connects it to the mythical Anzu bird that is associated with the sun and the ruler. He also notes that in the Egyptian culture the falcon was associated with the rising sun and the pharaoh.

[659] The Masoretic עֲצָתוֹ "his plan, his counsel" is written עֲצָתִי "my plan, my counsel" in the *Qere* and in 1QIsᵃ, which Oswalt, *Isaiah 40–66*, 233, and most others accept as the better reading.

[660] The use of the eagle as a symbol on the Persian royal ensign (Xenophon, *Cyropaedia* VII.1.4) could fit this imagery, but biblical writers often use another term (נֶשֶׁר in 40:31) for eagle.

[661] The particle אַף "even, surely" introduces an intensive clause (GKC §153; 154a, fn. 1).

"stubborn-hearted"[662] and those who are "far from righteousness." R. N. Whybray believes this refers to discouraged people who "questioned the prophet's
insistence that his intervention was imminent" and that the prophet is responding to these "skeptics."[663] But rebellion and sin, not discouragement, are the
problems. These people are the "rebels" in 46:8, but the exact nature of the
error of their way is somewhat ambiguous (there are additional descriptions
of these people in chap. 48). Hypothetically, one might propose that they were
not fully convinced that God was stronger than the idol gods or that they might
question God's complete control of history, but it is more likely that their error was a simple hard-hearted unwillingness to believe in God's ability to do
everything he planned. If they were not willing to believe God, they would not
be people who could demonstrate the righteousness of God in their lives by
acting in faith.

In contrast to the unbelief of the faithless audience, 46:13 declares that the
accomplishment of God's righteous acts of salvation are sure, are near, and will
not be delayed. One can be confident it will happen because God is not one
who is far away from his people. In fact, he is so near to them that it is possible
for him to care for them and act positively on their behalf. God's intention is to
establish his reign of justice, by giving the people of Zion his salvation in the
near future ("it will not be delayed") and by causing his splendorous grandeur
to be evident in his dealings with Israel. Although this does not refer to the return of God's "glory" (*kābôd*), the association of the temple with Zion and with
God's "splendour, glorious beauty" (*tip'artî*) causes J. Goldingay to associate
this promise with the restoration of the temple, the exaltation of Zion, and the
return of his physical presence to the temple.[664] Although these are aspects of
God's restoration of his people, this approach may be too focused on God's
presence in the temple. Elsewhere Samaria, Assyria, Babylon, and Egypt had
a "beauty, grandeur" (that often led to pride) that faded away because of God's
judgment (10:12; 13:19; 20:5; 28:1–4), but in the future God promises to restore the "glorious beauty" of Zion, will involve an eschatological transformation of nature and his people (4:4–6). This issue is explained more fully in future chapters when God's glory comes to rest on and over his people (60:1–2).
God will glorify his place (60:13), and his people will glorify God with their
gifts (60:9). God will be their glory (60:19), and then his people will be like
a glorious crown in the Lord's right hand (62:3). Thus the glory of God will

---

[662] McKenzie, *Second Isaiah*, 86–87, follows the Old Greek and translates this "you whose
heart despairs." He imagines that many people doubted the prophet's predictions of deliverance,
but Muilenburg, "Isaiah," 5:542, defends the appropriateness of the MT reading.

[663] Whybray, *Isaiah 40–66*, 117, also interprets these people to be discouraged (following the
Old Greek) rather than rebellious and stubborn.

[664] Goldingay, *Message of Isaiah 40–55*, 314, states that "this attractive physical return of
Yhwh symbolized by the restoring of the temple contrasts with the gloomy physical departure of
the gods."

be reflected in the glorious beauty of his creation of the new earth. But 46:13 seems to refer to an earlier time when God will display his glory among his people. Since this transformation is relatively near and not far off, it probably does not refer to an eschatological event.

This wonderful promise of hope is sometimes interpreted to be a significant "turning point in the book, since it is the first attempt at explaining the failure of Cyrus to live up to the expectations placed on him by the prophet's public."[665] Placing this material in a setting after Cyrus took over the Babylonian Empire and after the return of only a minority of Hebrews to Jerusalem, A. Labahn reconstructs a context for this passage as a time when: (a) Cyrus came to power but did not destroy Babylon and its gods as chaps. 46–47 suggests he would; (b) the grand new exodus of Hebrews back to Jerusalem did not happen (only a small group went back); and (c) the new times of salvation the people longed for did not arrive. This theory concludes that the people were discouraged and doubted the reliability of these optimistic prophecies of salvation found in the Book of Isaiah. This led to the need for a new explanation of these older prophecies in order to defend the validity of Isaiah's prophecies of salvation. Now salvation was said to be "near" but slightly delayed because of the sinfulness of the people.[666] B. Childs rightly objects to this redactional explanation as well as the over-historicization of the text that requires everything the prophet said to be fulfilled within the context of one defined historical context (the work of Cyrus).[667] When an interpretation causes one to conclude that God gave a false prophecy, one should always go back and rethink the basis for that interpretation. Consequently, this prophecy should not be viewed as a response to the discouraged Israelites who failed to see the fulfillment of God's earlier promises. This problem should be addressed in the light of interlinking themes in earlier chapters that address similar issues. The unwillingness of the audience to follow God is not new in 46:8,12. It was evident in the questioning of God in 40:27, in the people's fear in 41:10–14, in their blindness in 42:18–20, in their disobedient acts of not following God's laws in 42:24, in their unwillingness to worship God properly in 43:22–24, and in their sinful rebellion in 43:27. These earlier spiritual categorizations of the people help the reader to understand that the prophet is still speaking to a similar audience, if not the same audience he

---

[665] Blenkinsopp, *Isaiah 40–55*, 274, believes that 46:12–13 were added as "an explanatory comment a generation or two later than the bulk of chs. 40–48" since this theme is more at home in chaps. 56–66.

[666] A. Labahn, "The Delay of Salvation within Deutero-Isaiah," *JSOT* 85 (1999): 71–84, actually finds two delays of salvation, one in which the prophets explained as a short delay because they expected salvation to be near and a second later delay that was explained as a result of the people's sins (chaps. 56–59) due to the influence of Deuteronomistic teaching.

[667] Childs, *Isaiah*, 361–62, maintains concerning the redaction solution that "the very complexity of the argument raises initial suspicion" and concerning over-historicization he states that "prophecy is not simply a description of a coming historical event made in advance . . . rather Isaianic prophecy interprets the effects of God's entrance into human history."

addressed in chaps. 40–44. If that is the case then the near salvation of Zion, which will display the glorious beauty of God in 46:13, should be connected to God's deliverance of his people from the same military crisis the nation was facing earlier (41:11–12) when they were being plundered for their sins (42:22–25). In both situations God offers to bring deliverance.

NOTHING CAN SAVE PROUD BABYLON FROM HUMILIATION (47:1–15)

> [1]"Go down, sit in the dust,
> Virgin Daughter of Babylon;
> sit on the ground without a throne,
> Daughter of the Babylonians.
> No more will you be called
> tender or delicate.
> [2]Take millstones and grind flour;
> take off your veil.
> Lift up your skirts, bare your legs,
> and wade through the streams.
> [3]Your nakedness will be exposed
> and your shame uncovered.
> I will take vengeance;
> I will spare no one."
>
> [4]Our Redeemer—the LORD Almighty is his name—
> is the Holy One of Israel.
>
> [5]"Sit in silence, go into darkness,
> Daughter of the Babylonians;
> no more will you be called
> queen of kingdoms.
> [6]I was angry with my people
> and desecrated my inheritance;
> I gave them into your hand,
> and you showed them no mercy.
> Even on the aged
> you laid a very heavy yoke.
> [7]You said, 'I will continue forever—
> the eternal queen!'
> But you did not consider these things
> or reflect on what might happen.
>
> [8]"Now then, listen, you wanton creature,
> lounging in your security
> and saying to yourself,
> 'I am, and there is none besides me.
> I will never be a widow
> or suffer the loss of children.'
> [9]Both of these will overtake you
> in a moment, on a single day:

loss of children and widowhood.
They will come upon you in full measure,
  in spite of your many sorceries
  and all your potent spells.
[10]You have trusted in your wickedness
  and have said, 'No one sees me.'
Your wisdom and knowledge mislead you
  when you say to yourself,
  'I am, and there is none besides me.'
[11]Disaster will come upon you,
  and you will not know how to conjure it away.
A calamity will fall upon you
  that you cannot ward off with a ransom;
a catastrophe you cannot foresee
  will suddenly come upon you.

[12]"Keep on, then, with your magic spells
  and with your many sorceries,
  which you have labored at since childhood.
Perhaps you will succeed,
  perhaps you will cause terror.
[13]All the counsel you have received has only worn you out!
  Let your astrologers come forward,
those stargazers who make predictions month by month,
  let them save you from what is coming upon you.
[14]Surely they are like stubble;
  the fire will burn them up.
They cannot even save themselves
  from the power of the flame.
Here are no coals to warm anyone;
  here is no fire to sit by.
[15]That is all they can do for you—
  these you have labored with
  and trafficked with since childhood.
Each of them goes on in his error;
  there is not one that can save you.

After proving God's superiority over all idols by pointing to his ability to carry, deliver, save, declare what will happen, and accomplish what he plans, now the prophet illustrates the powerlessness of the mighty Babylonian Empire. While Zion looks forward to the time of God's salvation (46:13), Babylon will soon face the day of its destruction. This message is consistent with what Isaiah said earlier in chaps. 13–14. In arrogant pride the Babylonians may claim to be divine and undefeatable, but disaster will come when God takes vengeance on them, for no one will be able to deliver them from God's sovereign power.

J. Muilenburg views the chapter as a mocking taunt song against Babylon, but R. N. Whybray finds connections with other oracles against foreign nations (chaps. 13–23) and funeral songs over the dead.[668] Since the defeat of Babylon has positive implications for God's people, H. C. Spykerboer concludes that chap. 47 actually functions as an oracle of salvation for the Hebrew audience.[669] C. A. Franke identified numerous comparisons between this chapter and the language, form, and tone of the oracle against the king of Babylon in Isa 14.[670] She would call chap. 47 a lament or a parody of a lament because this unique prophetic creation utilizes some themes from laments to describe the humiliation of Babylon and her sorcerers.

The unified message of this chapter is structured into four paragraphs:[671]

God's vengeance brings the humiliation of Babylon	47:1–4
Babylon's control will end	1
Babylon will be humiliated	2–3a
The Holy God will execute his vengeance	3b–4
Reasons for God's anger against Babylon	47:5–7
Darkness will come, not honor	5
They had no compassion on my people	6
Thoughtless pride	7
Secure, evil, and proud Babylon will fall	47:8–11
Riches and sorcerers will not protect	8–9
Wisdom and blasphemy will bring disaster	10–11
Babylon's religious leaders cannot deliver Babylon	47:12–15
Can sorcerers and wise men save Babylon?	12–13
They cannot deliver or save anyone	14–15

The inner coherence of this chapter is enhanced by the repeated use of important words. For example: (a) "sit down" (*yāšab*) is used throughout the poem six times in 47:1a,1b,5,8a,8b,14. Babylon thinks that she "sits" securely (v. 8), but soon she will "sit" in the dust in darkness (vv. 1,5); (b) "come, go" (*bô*) is found in 47:5,9a,9b,11a,11b,13 to describe the many disasters that will come upon Babylon;[672] and (c) the negative particle *'ên,* "there is not," is found

---

[668] Muilenburg, "Isaiah," 5:543, 544; Whybray, *Isaiah 40–66*, 118, compares this chapter to the oracles against the nations in Isa 13–23; Jer 46–51; and Ezek 25–32, which also use mocking or taunt songs.

[669] Spykerboer, *The Structure and Composition of Deutero-Isaiah*, 154–56, bases this on the contrasts between Zion (46:13) and Babylon in this chapter.

[670] Franke, "Reversals of Fortune in the Ancient Near East," 110–23, lists three out of six features in chap. 47 that are typical of laments.

[671] Melugin, *Formation of Isaiah 40–55*, 135–36, divides the poem into vv. 1–4,5–7,8–9,10–11, and 12–15 based on form-critical and thematic criteria, but Franke, *Isaiah 46, 47, 48: A New literary-Critical Reading*, 156–57, argues that the repetition of themes of security, "you said in your heart" and "I am and there is no other" in both vv. 8–9 and vv. 10–11, tie them together.

[672] R. Lack, *La symbolique du livre d'Isaïe sur l'image littéraire comme élément de structura-*

in 47:1,10,14, and 15 to describe both what the Babylonians falsely claim ("I
am, and there is none besides me") as well as what will truly happen to them
("there is not one that can save you"). In addition, there are many words that
are repeated in close proximity to one another to make a point. For example: (a)
"daughter" (*bat*) appears twice in v. 1; (b) "take" (*lāqaḥ*) is in 47:2,3; (c) "uncover" (*gālâ*) is repeated in 47:2a,2b,3; (d) "say" (*ʾāmar*) is in 47:7,8,10; (e)
"know" (*yādaʿ*) appears in 47:8,10,11(2x); (f) "widow (hood)" (*ʾalmānâ*) in
used in vv. 8,9; (g) "to be able" (*yākal*) is in both vv. 11,12; and (h) "stand"
(*ʿāmad*) appears in 47:12,13. These repetitions illustrate the artistic skill of this
composition and strengthen the sense of unity within these subparagraphs.

Although the poem has many second person verbs and pronominal suffixes
(over 30) that refer to Babylon, there is no indication that the prophet was actually addressing a group of Babylonians. Like chap. 46, the prophet is addressing a Hebrew audience (notice "our Redeemer" in 47:4) to reveal to them God's
plans for Babylon. Since there is usually only an indirect address to a Hebrew
audience, the persuasive purpose for this message must be implied from the
content. It seems that the aim of the rhetoric goes deeper than just providing assurance that God will destroy Babylon (something already known from chaps.
13–14 and 21). J. Oswalt follows Alexander in suggesting that the "point of
these chapters is to teach the absolute power and unceasing grace of God"[673]
while C. Seitz concludes that the Daughter Babylon serves as a negative foil in
order to introduce the Hebrew audience to the positive salvation God will bring
to the daughter of Zion in the coming chapters.[674] J. Goldingay proposes that
the function of this message may "include that of indirectly warning the community not to be overly impressed by the enemy and of indirectly promising
the community's own deliverance by portraying the fall of its oppressor."[675]
The central contrasting themes that climax the end of chaps. 46 and 47 are
that God is able to save Zion (46:13), but Babylon, her gods, and her religious
leaders are powerless and not able to save Babylon (46:7; 47:13–15). The blasphemous divine claim of Babylon and her gods (47:8,10), that "I am, and there
is none besides me," are not true. Instead, the Hebrews must listen and respond
in faith to God's claims that "I am, and there is no other" (46:9,13).

The setting is unknown, but the interpreter should not quickly assume that
this refers to Cyrus's conquest of Babylon. At that time Babylon was not made

tion (Rome: Pontifical Biblical Institute, 1973), 85–86, believes the word "come, go" (*boʾ*) is a key
word throughout chaps. 40–55, for it announces how God's sovereign work in history is "coming"
to intervene in the lives of his people as well as all the nations of the earth.

[673] Oswalt, *Isaiah 40–66*, 241, uses this approach to argue that this is a general prediction that
illustrates God's work, rather than being a specific description of the fall of Babylon.

[674] Seitz, "Isaiah 40–66," 410, reads this chapter together with chap. 48 and interprets this to
refer to Cyrus's victory over Babylon, though nothing is said about Cyrus in chap. 47.

[675] Goldingay, *Message of Isaiah 40–66*, 316, follows Brueggemann in inferring that the
"prophet's task is thus to enable people to see Babylon differently, and thus not to define their own
position so hopelessly."

into a slave, and disaster did not come upon the city (47:11). J. Goldingay
admits, "It cannot be said that there is a close correspondence between the
events envisaged here and the actual events surrounding the fall of Babylon in
539 BC."[676]

47:1–4 What will happen to Babylon is described using the metaphorical
imagery of a personified daughter (47:1,5), virgin (47:1), queen (47:5), and
widow (47:8,9). The first subparagraph begins with imperative verbs addressed
to Babylon (compare the beginning of the following paragraphs in vv. 5,8,12)
and ends with the recital of the holiness and power of God's glorious name.
First comes the news of Babylon's decline and humiliation, then the reason is
given in 47:3.

47:1 The imperative verbs "go down" (*rĕdî*) and "sit" (*šĕbî*) picture the
queen's movement from the glorious throne in the luxurious royal court to the
filthy dust of the earth, a place where a highly privileged queen would never
sit. The act of going down is a sign of the humiliation of the Daughter of Babylon and the sitting represents the state where she will end up dwelling. Often
the person who sits in the dust is a person in mourning (3:26; 25:12; 26:5), but
the text never makes this connection explicit. C. R. North pushes this imagery
even further in order to connect the dust with the rubble of the destroyed city
of Babylon, while K. Baltzer extends the metaphor in another direction to include an allusion to death and the underworld, thus making this scene parallel
to the decent of the king of Babylon into the underworld in 14:3–22.[677] In
these cases, the interpreter must be careful not to read more into the text than
it actually says.

Part of the genius of this verse is its emphasis on the reversal of lady Babylon's destiny. The one who was once called "tender or delicate" will no longer
fit those descriptors because she will end up working like a servant or a slave
girl (47:1b). The title "Virgin Daughter of Babylon" and "Daughter of the Babylonians" (lit., "Daughter of the Chaldeans") are honorific titles which do not
refer to the young age of Babylon but draw on the image of a virgin as someone
who is beautiful, desirable, and unconquered. Babylon is an ideal woman who
is "tender, delicate" (*rākkâ*) and "having luxurious taste, dainty" (*ʿănuggâ*). All
this will dramatically change in the future, for the people around her will not
continue to call her[678] by these names or find these fine characteristics in her.

---

[676] Goldingay, *Message of Isaiah 40–55*, 317.

[677] North, *Second Isaiah*, 170, also finds this same meaning for "dust" (עָפָר) in 1 Kgs 20:10;
Ezek 26:4,12; Neh 4:10. Baltzer, *Deutero-Isaiah*, 271, finds a literal meaning and then a "second
level of the text, which depicts the underworld" though Sheol is never mentioned. He finds the
stripping of the daughter of Babylon to be similar to scenes in the Mesopotamian myth of the
"Decent of Ishtar into the Netherworld" (*ANET*, 106–109). Tromp, *Primitive Conception of Death
and the Nether World in the Old Testament*, 29, also interprets this phrase as going down to death
in the netherworld.

[678] The Hebrew clause כִּי לֹא תוֹסִיפִי יִקְרְאוּ לָךְ is a complicated syntactical construction explained in GKC §120c. When an incomplete verb ("you will continue") has a verbal complement

47:2–3a Next, the former great Daughter of Babylon is commanded to take "two millstones,"[679] probably a small set of millstones[680] that would be used in the kitchen, and then she is instructed to "grind" (another imperative) grain[681] (Exod 11:4; Num 11:8). Instead of enjoying the effortless life of having elaborate meals prepared and cooked for her when she was the queen, this woman will now suffer the humiliation of doing the menial and tiring work of making meals for others. As a hard-working woman she can no longer maintain the dignified look of an elite queen. Now she must adjust her behavior and looks so that she can accomplish her work. She can no longer stay inside or have servants shade her face from the sun like the privileged women of the day or show off the long fancy dresses the upper class women would wear. She is commanded to "take off your veil" (NIV, literally to "uncover your hair"), "strip off your long skirt,"[682] and "uncover the thigh" (NIV "bare your legs"), but the text does not say why. Does this prepare her for more hard labor in the field, is this the disrobing and sexual humiliation of a captive slave, or is this simply to prepare her to cross a stream? One thing is clear, she does not determine what she wants to do, and she is not able to act as a queen; instead, someone else commands and controls her behavior. The imagery could fit several settings, but the idea of crossing over rivers (47:4b) and being naked (in 47:3a) causes J. Motyer to conclude that this person representing Babylon is a captive going into exile.[683]

The acts of shaming the former beautiful Daughter of Babylon in v. 3a includes the uncovering of her nakedness and her shame being seen by others. This could refer to sexual violation by one of the victorious soldiers,[684] which was often a part of defeating an enemy city. This devastating disgrace and

---

("they will call") the latter is subordinate to the former. In such cases the subordinate ("they will call, proclaim") idea governs the former and the governing verb ("you will continue") expresses the manner of the action. Thus "they will call you" is modified by "continually." The unusual aspect of this construction is the use of an imperfect second pers. sg. verb תּוֹסִיפִי instead of a verb matching the number and person of the second verb (3 masc. pl.).

[679] The noun רֵחַיִם "two millstones" has a dual ending.

[680] A mill for grinding grain to flour has an upper stone that can be turned and a lower fixed stone that the upper stone turns on to grind the grain.

[681] Blenkinsopp, *Isaiah 40–55*, 280, finds a double entendre here and views the verb grind as "a euphemism for coercive sexual activity." He also concludes that the removing of the veil, lifting of the skirt, and nakedness "make it clear that the shaming of the woman involves rape." These interpretations go beyond what the texts actually say.

[682] The noun שֹׁבֶל is used only here in the Hebrew Bible so it is difficult to define, but 1QIs^a has שׁוּלַיִךְ "your skirt" (6:1; Nah 3:5), which makes good sense. A. F. L. Beeston, "Hebrew *šibbōlet* and *šōbel* (Is 47,2)," *JSS* 24 (1979): 175–77, suggests that it means "well" and is parallel to "streams" in the next phrase. The imperative verb חֶשְׂפִּי is translated "lift up" in NIV, but in 20:2; Jer 13:22 it refers "to stripping, tearing off" all the clothes in the context of going into captivity.

[683] Motyer, *Isaiah*, 372, interprets this as "a captive bound for exile."

[684] "Uncovering the nakedness" is a euphemism for sexual relationships in Lev 18:6–19.

revolting scorn will come on the city of Babylon, and there is nothing that she can do about it.

47:3b–4   Suddenly the text identifies the voice of God speaking about his plans for Babylon. These changes will not take place in a vacuum; God is the sovereign one who will bring all these things to pass on Babylon. He will "take vengeance" (*nāqam*), a Hebrew idea that does not carry the negative connotation of an irrational violent punitive reprisal that usually overreacts because of uncontrollable anger.[685] Instead, the Hebrew concept relates to the basic establishment of justice for one who has done wrong. This just divine punishment of Babylon will cause her to receive the right proportion of retribution based on the nature of her sins.

The last phrase in v. 3 is difficult because a straightforward translation would be "I will not meet a man." Such meetings can be for hostile purposes (Gen 3:8; Exod 5:20) or be related to a positive encounter (64:4[English 64:5]). Since God will not meet anyone after he executes his justice on Babylon, NIV translates the clause "I will spare no one." J. L. Koole prefers "I shall not attack like men" which inserts the comparative "like" but creates a good parallel with the preceding phrase. J. Blenkinsopp adopts "and no one will intervene" based on the translation of Symmachus, the Vulgate, and the third-person verbal reading of 4QIsd.[686] Most of the attempts to solve this problem end up expressing the same general point, which is that God will completely defeat Babylon.

Verse 4 explains who this God is who will execute justice against Babylon.[687] The prophet assures his Hebrew audience that God is "our Redeemer"; thus the establishment of justice against Babylon is carried out by the same God that defeated the Egyptians many years earlier. This is "our" God who will bring salvation to his people in the future (46:13). This God also has the title "Yahweh of Hosts" (NIV, "the LORD Almighty"), the Almighty Commander of the armies of heaven who fought and won holy wars against his enemies in the past and who will defeat all his enemies in the future (24:1–23; 34:1–15). He is the Holy One of Israel who sets himself apart from all ungodliness. These statements would give the Hebrew audience great confidence in God's ability to fulfill this prophecy against Babylon.

---

[685] G. E. Mendenhall, *The Tenth Generation: The Origins of the Biblical Tradition* (Baltimore: Johns Hopkins, 1973), 69–103, discusses the vengeance of God and cautions against interpreting this idea as a lawless blood revenge. It is used when judicial channels of bringing justice fail; then God uses his legitimate sovereign power to impose justice on evil powers.

[686] Koole, *Isaiah III, Volume 1, Isaiah 40–48*, 528–30, and Blenkinsopp, *Isaiah 40–55*, 277. C. Franke, *Isaiah 46, 47, and 48: A New Literary-Critical*, 118, prefers the translation "and I will not deal kindly with anyone."

[687] Some appeal to the Old Greek addition of "says" which could represent a scribal change of אדם "man" at the end of 47:3 to אמר "says" at the beginning of v. 4, but this emendation is not necessary. In addition the use of "our Redeemer" would have to be altered to "your Redeemer," and "his name" would have to be changed to "my name." So many changes make this option very unlikely.

47:5–7 This new paragraph briefly describes the consequences of God's vengeance on the Daughter of Babylon. After God granted this nation some power, it gradually became arrogant and misused the power God gave it; therefore, just like Assyria in 10:5–15, Babylon will one day lose its high status as the most important kingdom on the earth.

47:5 An imperative verb addressed to Babylon begins this verse. They are not just commanded to "sit down" (*šĕbî*) as in 47:1; now they are instructed to sit "in silence" and to "go into darkness." The lights, excitement, and noise of this busy capital city will end, but it is not clear that this symbolism should be carried even further to include aspects of imprisonment in a dark dungeon or consignment to death and the netherworld.[688] Since Babylon previously spoke about her glory and frequently dictated to other vassal states what they must do, this silence may simply mean that in her dreadful humiliated state Babylon will no longer have anything to brag about and that she will no longer tell others what to do.[689] Babylon will have no hope but will go through a dark time of her history. Her vassals will no longer respectfully give her adoring titles like "Honorable Queen (*gĕberet*)[690] of Kingdoms."[691]

47:6 God again speaks in first person verbs (cf. v. 3a) to explain why he will bring this humiliation on Babylon. First the Hebrew audience must understand that it is God who gives his covenant people into the hand of the Babylonians; thus, he will allow them to profane his precious possession Israel. This matches what was said in 43:27–28 about polluting the temple, and it fits in with earlier references to war against his blind and sinful servant Israel, for God was angry with her in 42:18–25. In the midst of these military conflicts it seems almost inevitable that the stronger nation will abuse and misuse its power in humiliating the weaker nation that is being defeated (cf. 10:5–11 for a similar Assyrian abuse of power). Cruelty toward the women, small innocent children, and the old in a time of war is a barometer of the morality of any strong nation.[692] Innocent and defenseless nonmilitary personnel could expect to receive at least a little bit of mercy and "compassion" (*raḥămîm*,

---

[688] North, *Second Isaiah*, 171, comes to this conclusion based on comparisons with 42:7 and 49:9, but Seitz, "Isaiah 40–66," 411, thinks this implies consignment to the underworld (cf. chap. 14).

[689] Muilenburg, "Isaiah 40–66," 5:547, refers to the situation when there will be "no more proud vaunting, the imperious commanding of subject peoples."

[690] The word used here does not literally mean "queen." גְּבֶרֶת refers to a person of honor, strength, wealth, responsibility, and position; so "honorable queen" is a good translation, though it does not express all the implications of this term.

[691] This imagery of Babylon in this chapter and Jer 51 had a strong influence on John when he described the Babylon of the future in Rev 18:4–8, although G. K. Beale and S. M. McDonough, "Revelations," *CNTOT* 1140–41, suggest that the prophecy against Tyre in Ezek 26–27 also had a significant impact.

[692] Westermann, *Isaiah 40–66*, 191, views this as the cruelty of the exilic experience in Babylon based on Lam 1:19; 2:21; 5:12, but these verses refer to what happened in Jerusalem, not in Babylonian exile. Later in the very next sentence Westermann admits that "the treatment meted out to the exiles in Babylon was not particularly cruel."

NIV "mercy") in such desperate situations, but none came in this situation. J. Motyer concludes that Babylon showed "pitilessness (*no mercy*, 6d), indiscriminateness (*even on the aged*, 6e), arrogance (*for ever . . . queen*, 7ab), and absence of moral sense (*consider . . . reflect*, 7cd)."[693]

47:7 The second reason why God will execute his justice against Babylon was based on her proud claims that "I will continue forever a Queen forever" (NIV, "the eternal Queen").[694] The Babylonian boast could refer to the somewhat natural thought that Babylon was a very strong nation and saw no opposing power that might threaten her hegemony; consequently she assumed her kingdom would continue indefinitely. C. A. Franke interprets the "I will be/continue" (*'ehyeh*) statement as a claim to divinity because this is the exact phrase used by God in Exod 3:14 ("I will be who I will be").[695] This status of being equal to the divine is clearly presented in the arrogant claims in 47:8, but the statement here in v. 7 only boasts of continuing power over her own fate and over other nations, a foolish supposition that is directly contradicted by God's statement in 47:3.

The second half of the verse accuses Babylon of not thinking through the past "things" (*'ēlleh*) she had done (v. 6) or considering the implications of what she was arrogantly boasting about. "You were not remembering" (*lō' zākartā*, NIV "you did not . . . reflect on") what might happen in the future. The NIV "what might happen" is literally "her/its end," but it is not clear what the suffix "her/its" refers to. The suffix could refer to: (a) the end of Israel (later God will bring it salvation); (b) the Babylonian people ("you") are not thinking about the end of Babylon (it will be destroyed), or (c) J. L. Koole proposes that Babylon was not remembering what God's prophetic words said he would do ("it" refers to those prophecies).

47:8–11 The third part of this poem contrasts Babylon's arrogant and self-confident view of reality with God's plan to turn this proud nation into a widow. These people thought that their wisdom and sorcerer's spells would protect them from disaster, but they will experience a catastrophe.

47:8 The beginning of this new subparagraph is marked with "and now" (*wĕʿattâ*, omitted by NIV) and another imperative verb that calls the Babylonians to "listen" to the accusations God makes against them. The Daughter of

---

[693] Motyer, *Isaiah*, 373, explains that while Babylon's action was formally within the will of God, it was an offense because of the manner in which they carried out God's will.

[694] The word עַד at the end of the first line has raised many questions and alternate solutions. 1QIsᵃ has עוֹד "still, yet," which McKenzie, *Second Isaiah*, 89, follows, and then he connects this word with the next phrase and translates it "still you paid no attention." Oswalt, *Isaiah 40–66*, 243, and the RSV interpret this word to introduce a result clause "so that," but D. N. Freedman, "A Note on Isaiah 47,7," *Bib* 51 (1970): 477–84, is correct in seeing this as a breaking up of a stereotypical phrase "forever and ever" into two parts by putting one part after "I will be" and the other part after "Queen."

[695] Franke, *Isaiah 46,47, and 48: A New Literary-Critical*, 124, concludes that "this is more than a declaration of political primacy. Babylon is making a claim to divinity."

Babylon is called a "prosperous, wealthy, luxury-lover, pampered" (*'ădînâ*, NIV "wanton creature") woman because she has all the wealth and booty of the nations she has conquered. Having every material thing that she could ever want, this queen sits in a very secure position and thinks privately in her heart (it does not say that she openly proclaimed this) that she has absolute power over everyone. Although the phrase "I am, and there is no one besides me" derives from an arrogant political feeling of being bigger, better, stronger, and in complete control of most of the civilized world, it recognizes no role for God's sovereign power in controlling history. Thus Babylon claims to have done away with the need for God ("there is no one besides me")[696] and has put herself in God's place. This is evident from the comparative statements by God in earlier messages, for God has claimed absolute authority for himself in saying, "I am, and there is no one besides me" (45:5,6,18,22; 46:9; Zeph 2:15). Babylon is claiming the same uniqueness that God claimed for himself, claiming the same sovereignty that only God has, and claiming such an absolute status that it leaves no room for God's role in this world. This is the height of foolish overconfidence, for any nation that claims to have absolute authority is sure to face the wrath of an angry God who will not share his glory with anyone else. Was it not God who raised up Babylon to power for this short time? She did not achieve this high status on her own. God knows her thoughts and will hold her accountable for proudly making herself into a godlike figure.

The second thought that Babylon has in her heart is the idealization that she will never sit alone as a widow without many children, never "know, experience" (*yāda'*)[697] the sorrow of bereavement. This refers to her false belief that her people and her vassal states will never be taken away from her by a stronger military power. Babylon depended on the taxation of her vassal states to fund her lavish lifestyle, just like an older woman would depend on her children to provide for her when she could no longer work. There is no need to identify exactly what people the author had in mind when using the husband or children metaphors,[698] but there is no linguistic reference back to the gods in chap. 46.

47:9 Having described the accusation against Babylon, now God explains the punishment he will bring on Babylon. God declares that the two things in

---

[696] This phrase ends with עוֹד אֶפְסִי which some translate "none other" (Blenkinsopp, *Isaiah 40–55*, 275, because the ending on אֶפֶס is considered an ancient genitive case ending (GKC §90,l). But it is possible to view this as a first pers. pronominal suffix "me"; one could get "none but/besides me." Even if this ending is considered an old case ending, if there is "no other," this automatically excludes God; thus the meaning is essentially the same with either interpretation of the Hebrew text.

[697] 1QIs[a] has probably misread the ד as a ר and the ע as a א; consequently it has אֵרְאָה "I will see" instead of אֵדַע "I will know." Although both readings make good sense in this sentence, the Masoretic is superior.

[698] A. Fitzgerald, "The Mythological Background for the Presentation of Jerusalem as Queen and False Worship in the Old Testament," *CBQ* 34 (1972): 403–16, tries to identify a god as the father and children as worshippers.

v. 8 that Babylon thought would never happen will happen "in a moment."[699]
The myth that Babylon is an almighty nation will collapse in one single day.
Widowhood and the loss of children will unexpectedly come on her, leaving
Babylon without material support and protection. To be childless was a great
shame in the ancient Near Eastern world and was a threat to a woman's status,
honor, and continued existence when she grew old. To have her citizens' taxes
sent elsewhere and her vassals' tribute contribute to the wealth of another king
meant that Babylon would be doomed.

The last part of the verse emphasizes that the nation's full destruction will
happen even though many sorcerers cast spells in order to stop it from happening. Babylon was known for its great interest in determining the future by
astrology and other religious practices. Archaeologists have found three books
that religious functionaries could use to interpret what the divine powers that
indwelt nature were communicating to people. The collection called *šumma
alu* included about 100 tablets of omens involving cities, animals, fire, houses,
and human relations. These would interpret what the gods were saying if an
animal died or if your house burned down. The *šumma izbu* helped these religious officials to understand the meaning of dreams and interpret the significance of deformed humans or animals. Some omens used the rising of smoke,
the pattern formed when oil was dropped on water, or the examination of the
internal organs of sacrificial animals to understand what the gods were saying.
The *enûma Anu Enlil* interpreted the movement of the sun, star, moon, planets,
an eclipse, plus meteorological events like thunderstorms, hail, rain, and even
cloud formations.[700] Some of the people who interpreted these handbooks and
cast spells were called *barû* diviners, the *āpilu* answerers, and the cultic priests
the *muḫḫu*. Isaiah indicates that these religious leaders, which Daniel calls magicians, diviners, Chaldeans, and enchanters (Dan 1:20; 2:2,27), will not have
any impact on God's plans. They may cast many spells to attempt to remove
dangers and use their broad knowledge of magic and charms to try to prevent
the fall of Babylon, but their efforts will be a waste of time, for God has de-
creed the future destiny of Babylon.

47:10   Other accusations include Babylon having a false sense of security or self-confidence (47:8) even while she was doing great evil,[701] for she

---

[699] The word רֶגַע can mean "in a moment, suddenly, quickly, in a short time," but it should not
be understood as in a short time from when the prophet spoke these words. Rather it suggests that
when the Babylonian Empire does collapse, it will happen quickly (Dan 5).

[700] Information about Babylonian religious texts and sorcerers can be found in A. L. Oppen-
heim, *The Interpretation of Dreams in the Ancient Near East* (Philadelphia: American Philosophical Society, 1956); A. L. Leichty, *The Omen Series šumma izbu* (Locust Valley, NY: Augustin,
1970); A. Goetze, *Old Babylonian Omen Texts* (New Haven: Yale University, 1947); E. Rainer,
Babylonian Planetary Omens (Malibu: Undena, 1975); R. C. Thompson, *The Reports of the Magicians and Astrologers of Nineveh and Babylon*, 2 vols. (London: Luzac, 1900); Wilson, *Prophecy
and Society in Ancient Israel*, 90–123.

[701] 1QIs[a] has בדעתך "on account of your knowledge" instead of the Masoretic בְּרָעָתֵךְ "on

thought, "no one sees me." It is not clear what kind of evil is described in this accusation. J. Oswalt points to trust in their magical arts, but J. L. Koole rejects this approach and suggests that this refers to the evil deeds already mentioned in 47:6–8.[702] Babylon thought she was divine (47:8, 10b) and acted like no one would see her or hold her accountable for her actions. She acted as if God did not exist and no one could judge her. Babylon was irresponsible, became a law to herself, and believed in the adage that "might makes right." Nevertheless, God knows what she has done and accuses her of allowing her great wisdom and knowledge to "turn them around" (from the root *šub*) from the right way of using all her vast resources. Instead, Babylon grew proud and acted as if she were God ("I am, and there is no one besides me," v. 10b).[703]

47:11 Having made numerous accusations, the prophet returns to provide more examples of God's punishment. God will execute his justice against Babylon by repaying "disaster, evil" (*rāʿâ*) in response to Babylon's "evil" (*rāʿâ* in 47:10). Although Babylon had great "knowledge" (*daʿat* in 47:10), she will not "know" (*yādaʿ*) how to deal with what God will bring on her. Those who were so secure (47:10) will not be able to atone for their sins or use some sorcerer's charm (cf. Isa 47:9) to ward off what God has planned.

This verse contains three clauses that tell what will happen to Babylon, and each of these punishment statements is followed by a clause that emphasizes that Babylon will not be able (each has the negative *lōʾ* plus an imperfect verb) to resist or prevent this disaster from falling on them. God's action in the initial clauses uses three parallel nouns to emphasize the enormity of the calamity, disaster, or sudden catastrophe that will come on Babylon. After each act the Babylonians would perform a futile act to counter what was happening, but these will only demonstrate the powerlessness of Babylon's religious officials. Their first act will be an attempt to "conjure it away" (NIV). The root *šaḥar* usually means "dawn, morning" which has a positive connotation of a better new day (8:20; 14:12). F. Delitzsch interpreted this to mean "from which you will experience no dawn,"[704] but it appears better to follow the lead of the Aramaic Targum ("to seek God") and interpret this as an infinitive construct (parallel to the two later infinitive construct verbs in this verse) from the root *šaḥar*

---

account of your wickedness," a simple confusion between ר and ד. Both make sense, but the Masoretic text is definitely the harder reading since "your knowledge" is found in the next line.

[702] Oswalt, *Isaiah 40–66*, 250, says, "Their mastery of the magical arts had led the Babylonians to believe that they understood the workings of the world so well that they were proof against any disaster." Koole, *Isaiah III, Volume 1, Isaiah 40–48*, 540, believes it refers to their arrogance and cruelty, since v. 10b quotes v. 8.

[703] Oswalt, *Isaiah 40–66*, 250, perceptively is reminded of all the greatness and wisdom in Nazi Germany. They, too, thought they could rule the world and believed that no one could hold them accountable for their action. Both nations seem to forget that they would be held ethically responsible for their actions.

[704] F. Delitzsch, "Prophecies of Isaiah," *Commentary on the Old Testament*, 242, believes there will be no dawn after a night of suffering through God's calamity.

"to seek" (Prov 11:27) or the Arabic root *sahara* "to charm."[705] In either case
the prophet is pointing to the Babylonians' inability to reach God (by prayers
or magical charms) so that they can somehow cause him to avert the disaster
he is bringing on them. This means that in spite of all their great knowledge
and wisdom (47:9), they do not know the most important thing: how to appease
God's anger.

The second reason why they will suffer divine justice is because they will
not be able "to atone" (*kāpar*) for their sins. This demonstrates that their religious philosophies of magic and sacrificing are not capable of bringing true
forgiveness of sin. They cannot buy God off with just another offering; God demands a complete confession of sin and true repentance before atonement can
be granted. Finally, the sudden catastrophe is unavoidable because they do not
know when it is coming (Dan 5), presumably because their eyes were blinded
concerning the possibility of this disaster happening to them.

47:12–15 The final section[706] of this persuasive poem continues the
theme that the nation's religious resources will be unable to save them from
God's justice. They can look to astrologers and their books of wisdom to determine the future, but the fact is that these religious leaders cannot even save
themselves. God will be victorious over them, and there is nothing they can do
to save the nation.

47:12–13 This section is introduced with an ironic imperative verb just
like the earlier ones (47:1,5,8). This imperative seems to mock or taunt[707] the
Babylonian effort to try to avert God's judgment. The nation's sorcerers are
challenged to "stand up" (*ʿimĕdî*), not in the sense of standing up for a trial, but
they are to keep working at the task of defending themselves and their country
from God's plan to execute his justice on them. With this encouragement to
use spells and sorceries (47:9), it appears "as though the prophet is saying,
'If you don't believe me, go ahead and put your trust in this foolishness.'"[708]
The Qumran scroll 1QIs[a] omits the last three lines of this verse (substituting
"until this day"), but in these two lines the prophet adds two important sarcastic
points. The Babylonians have worked hard; in fact, they have wearied themselves (40:28,30,31; 43:22,23,24; 46:2) with these useless spells ever since
the nation first began, so certainly one would expect that these wise sorcerers would have confidence in them now. Second, the prophet plays with their
psychology a little more by suggesting that just "perhaps" (*ʾûlay*) "you may be

---

[705] North, *Second Isaiah*, 172, also mentions other meanings such as "to tame, control," or if
the form is slightly emended *šaḥădāh* "to bribe it off."

[706] Westermann, *Isaiah 40–66*, 192, ignores the literary use of the imperative to introduce paragraphs and makes 47:10–12 a unit because they all deal with a similar topic. Franke, *Isaiah 46, 47,
and 48: A New Literary-Critical*, 102, 138, 156–57, supports the beginning of a new unit in v. 12.

[707] For the use of the imperative to taunt or mock someone, consult GKC §110a (as an "ironic
challenge"), or *IBHS*, 571, for the sarcastic use (cf. 1 Kgs 18:27; Amos 4:4).

[708] Oswalt, *Isaiah 40–66*, 253, takes this as a sarcastic challenge, especially 12b.

able to profit"[709] by these spells, perhaps you might cause someone to react in awe or terror. Of course the Hebrew reader knows that God knows that the idols are useless and of no profit (44:9,10; Jer 2:8) and that these spells cannot strike a fear like God does when he reveals the splendor of his majesty (2:19,21; 8:13).

Although there is no explicit sign that the first line of 47:13 is a question, a Hebrew interrogative sentence does not have to begin with the frequently used interrogative *hă*.[710] The initial clause makes much more sense as a question, instead of a statement of fact (as in NIV). If this is granted, then the rest of the verse becomes a second mocking encouragement for the Babylonian sorcerers to do something to save the Daughter of Babylon. With this approach J. L. Koole's conclusion that "there is no immediate connection between v. a and v. b" in 47:13 can be resolved.[711] In the first line God asks, "Are you [Daughter of Babylon] wearied with the multitude of your plans?" That is, he mockingly asks if they have not gotten weary trying to figure out which of the various options presented by their many religious advisors (spells, magical incantations, interpretations of the entrails of an animal, analyzing rising smoke, astrological signs, and other wise prognostication) is truly useful. Then the prophet returns to his challenge mentioned at the beginning of 47:12 to encourage the Daughter of Babylon to let her religious advisors "come forward . . . and save you."[712] Of course the Hebrew audience knows that only God is able to save people (43:3,11; 45:8,15,20). These religious advisors include the astrologers[713] who divided the sky according to the zodiac charts for each month and used this information to try to gain some control of the future. By observing the movement of the moon, stars, and planets they thought they could determine which days the gods would bring positive outcomes and which were negative days to avoid. For example, a Mesopotamian prophecy reads, "When Jupiter

---

[709] The construction הוֹעִיל תּוּכְלִי אוּלַי "perhaps you may be able to profit" expresses with the imperfect form a hypothetical possibility that may or may not be true; thus it should be rendered with a subjunctive modal verb expressing "might, may," rather than the indicative "will succeed" in NIV. This is another example (see my comments on Isa 46:5–7) of the "non-perfective of capability" that "denotes the subject's capability to perform the action" (*IBHS*, 507). See also the "contingent uses of the non-perfective . . . with particles expressing contingency" (Ibid., 210).

[710] GKC §150a refers to cases where the interrogative pronoun or adverb is not needed. As in English, Hebrew can change a statement into a question by intonation, changing word order, or when the context indicates the presence of a question.

[711] Koole, *Isaiah III, Volume 1, Isaiah 40–48*, 545.

[712] The verb יַעֲמְדוּ נָא is a jussive form which gives encouragement "let them stand up" (GKC §109a).

[713] The Hb. written tradition (*Kethib*) has *wrbh*, which may be read as a perfect pl. verb (הָבְרוּ). But the oral tradition (Qere) read *yrbh*, probably a pl. construct participle (הֹבְרֵי). The Qere is supported by 1QIs[a] (הוברי). The verb הבר occurs only here, but it is generally associated with a similar Arabic root רָאבַה that means "cut in pieces, divide." An Ugaritic verb רבה means "bow down, worship." The "dividers of the heavens" would be a reference to astrologers. Old Greek renders the phrase οἱ ἀστρολόγοι τοῦ οὐρανοῦ.

bccomes bright, the weapons of the king of Akkad will prevail over those of his foe."[714] Although the Babylonians may think that this kind of astrological wisdom might save them, they will find it is useless when Almighty God sends disaster on them.

47:14–15 The consequences of trusting in astrology and magical spells will result in these officials being like dry stubble that fire can quickly consume (5:24; 9:18–19; 33:11). It is difficult to know how far to carry this metaphor.[715] How can the astrologers be comparable to stubble, and is this metaphor suggesting that God is the flaming fire? Or is the point of the comparison simply to point out that these people will be quickly destroyed. In fact, God says that these religious officials will not even be able to deliver themselves, so why should the Babylonian people ever expect them to protect the rest of the nation from the destructive flames that God will send to devour them?

The second half of v. 14 refers back to images associated with the idol makers in 44:15–19, who use one part of a log to make an idol and another part to build a fire. At least a slow burning log can give consistent heat to keep people warm and can provide some light for several hours for those who sit and talk around the fire.[716] In contrast, the coals from stubble (the astrologers and magicians) are useless because the stubble quickly burns and the coals quickly die out. Taking a slightly different slant J. Goldingay suggests that this clause is saying, "The advisors with all their wisdom and knowledge are as useless as the images and as stupid as their makers and devotees, and will share the fate of both."[717]

Verse 15 concludes this message with the reminder that in spite of the Daughter of Babylon wearing herself out (47:11) by doing everything that these religious officials wanted her to do, there will be no deliverance (contrast 46:13). The usual translation of the second line presents a problem because it seems to refer to "traders, travelers" (*sōḥēr*) who have influenced the Daughter of Babylon "since childhood." It is odd to have a new group of people (the travelers) introduced in the conclusion of the poem when they have not been mentioned earlier. Verse 12 uses similar vocabulary to 47:15, but in v. 12 the prophet spoke about "your many sorceries, which you have labored at since childhood." In order to bring the thoughts in these two verses together, one could suggest that *sōḥēr* in 47:15 comes from the Akkadian root *sāhiru* "sorcerer," or one might hypothesize a scribal confusion in hearing the difference between the "s" and "sh" sounds of *šāḥar* "conjure" (47:11) and *sōḥēr* in this verse. Either approach would make this verse consistent with v. 12 and yield the meaning "your sorcerers from your childhood."[718]

---

[714] Thompson, *The Reports of the Magicians and Astrologers of Nineveh and Babylon*, lxvii.

[715] The Aramaic Targum says, "they have become weak like stubble."

[716] Both לַחְמָם "to warm" and לָשֶׁבֶת "to sit" are infinitive constructs (GKC §28b,67cc).

[717] Goldingay, *Message of Isaiah 40–55*, 336.

[718] Ibid., 337, accepts this change, while Oswalt, *Isaiah 40–66*, 253, 255, stays with the translation "traders."

The final point that illustrates the uselessness of the advise of the sorcerers and magicians is that each of them go off in their own direction, following a different theory with a different means of influencing the gods. Their wandering around for an answer only demonstrates their lack of knowledge of the real truth. One enchanter may recommend examining the liver of a chicken, another will advise watching the stars, and a third will want to interpret a dream, but none of these spiritual advisors will actually be able to offer any help in delivering the Daughter of Babylon from God's plan to execute his justice against this city. It is now abundantly obvious that Babylon's idols do not have the power to save her, her religious officials cannot find the right spell to counter God's decrees, and the Daughter of Babylon is doomed to destruction.

THEOLOGICAL IMPLICATIONS.   The persuasive conclusion that any honest person must come to after weighing the evidence in this message is that there are many theological paths that people have followed in order to identify a higher divine power, to understand his will, and to gain his approval, but not all paths lead to salvation. A rational evaluation of the evidence demonstrates that not everyone will see God's salvation. There are some who follow idols that craftsmen made from gold and silver, but these cannot help people on earth because they cannot move, speak, or save those who worship them (46:1–3,5–7). On the other hand, there is a God who can and has helped his people. He has plans, he announced the future ahead of time, and then he accomplished everything he plans in order to save his people (46:3–4,8–13). Thus from an apologetic point of view, not all paths lead to the same place in the afterworld. Therefore, people in every generation need to pay attention to the reality behind all religious claims so that they do not foolishly doubt or rebel against God's plans and end up trusting in a religious system that offers only false hopes. Since the chosen Israelites and the great empire of Babylon both suffered defeat under the hand of God, no one today should assume that they are immune from judgment, for God will do whatever it takes to establish a righteous people on this earth. No one and no nation can successfully oppose God's plans, for he will only save those people who trust him. The key question is: Who will trust him and be the people he saves?

Those who refuse to follow God's way will eventually end up like Babylon, sitting on the ground in shame instead of sitting on a royal throne (47:11). God's anger will fall on them when he executes his justice, just like he brought judgment on his own Israelite people (47:6a). Those who proudly think that they will rule forever (47:7), who oppress others (47:6b), who rest securely in the riches of their own false self-confidence (47:8), who trust in their own wisdom (47:10), and who allow false religious officials to lead them astray through magic, astrology, and spells, will suddenly suffer a great catastrophe from God. This disaster will finally demonstrate the futility of their religious beliefs, the impotence of their gods and religious officials, and the error of not recognizing God as the I am, the Redeemer, the Lord of Hosts, and the Holy

One (47:4). A world power in the future will follow the errors of Babylon, and God will destroy that Babylon too (Rev 18).

This knowledge of how God will deal with unbelievers is a warning that should keep all who desire to follow God from being led astray by the false philosophies in this world. In addition, God's words through the prophet provides an example of how one might communicate a warning to unbelievers who blindly follow the way that leads to destruction. In both cases one might ask: Has the divine power demonstrated that he has real power? Has this God foretold the future and then accomplished it? Does this divine power save the righteous and destroy the arrogant and wicked? Would this God be pleased with the behavior of people who are arrogant, oppressive, overconfident, claim special knowledge and wisdom, trust in magical spells, and pretend that they control their own destiny? These are some signs of a faith that is misdirected and displeasing to God Almighty. An honest self-appraisal is always a healthy step because it would be very sad to find people who call themselves believers displaying signs that they have not totally conquered the sins of arrogance, overconfidence, or the belief that they are the lord of their own destiny.

(2) Trust God Stubborn Israel; He Has and Will Fulfill His Word (48:1–22)

This chapter has attracted an unusual amount of controversy both in relationship to its content and unity. There are (a) apparent contradictions ("I have not spoken in secret" in 48:16 and "I will tell you of new things, of hidden things unknown to you" in 48:6), (b) unusual tensions between one verse that provides assurances of salvation and another verse that expresses strong condemnation, plus (c) clauses that appear to be unrelated to the context (48:16b). These have caused some commentators to doubt the integrity of the chapter. Long ago B. Duhm and more recently C. Westermann have attributed the negative verses of condemnation to a later exilic author, probably the author responsible for writing chaps. 56–66 (often called Trito-Isaiah),[719] but negative statements were already leveled against Israel in 42:18–25; 43:8,22–28; 45:9–13; and 46:8,12. There is no need to connect these thoughts to some other author. In contrast to this critical approach J. Muilenburg's rhetorical analysis of chap. 48 found it to be a homogeneous unit that summed up several of the arguments in earlier chapters.[720] C. A. Franke's study of chap. 48 found a unified

---

[719] Just within 48:1–11, B. Duhm, *Das Buch Jesaia*, 362, found that only vv. 1a,3,5ab,6–7b,8ab, and 11 were part of the original edition of this chapter; the rest was added by a later author. Westermann, *Isaiah 40–66*, 195–96, believes these expansions arose because someone was trying to give a new cultic application of the text to a postexilic community. Schoors, *I Am God Your Savior*, 285, provides a convenient chart of outlining which verses different scholars (Marti, Köhler, Mowinckel, Volz, Elliger, Begrich, and Westermann) identify as later additions to this chapter. In contrast Spykerboer, *The Structure and Composition of Deutero-Isaiah*, 156, states that "there is no need to eliminate, as is done by several scholars, the lines in which Israel is severely criticized . . . as later non-deutero-isaianic additions."

[720] Muilenburg, "Isaiah," 5:553, finds unity and structure in the poem based on the repeated

poem based on: (a) repeated key words, (b) a common tone of rebuke, (c) interconnected themes in the argument, (d) significant distribution of key words throughout the message, and (e) a balance between 48:1–11 and 48:12–22.[721] This appears to be a much more constructive prospective that will allow the interpreter to address some of the more problematic aspects of this chapter.

Chapter 48 has several verbal interlinking connections with chap. 47. For example, (a) the use of "suddenly" (*pit'ōm*) in both 47:11 and 48:3; (b) "the LORD Almighty is his name" in 47:4 and 48:2; and (c) Babylon proudly declares, "I am, and there is none besides me" in 47:8,10, and (d) God's declaration, "I am he, I am the first and the last" in 48:12. This arrogant statement by Babylon will be convincingly proven wrong because God is the only one who can legitimately say, "I am he; I am the first and I am the last . . . I am the LORD your God" (48:12,17).[722] Chapter 47 points out the failures of Babylon and chap. 48 addresses the failures of Israel, but both chapters recognize that Babylon will fall (47:1–3,11; 48:14).

The structure of this chapter is divided into two fairly equal paragraphs (with a hymnic conclusion at the end of the second). Each is introduced by an imperative call for the Hebrew audience to listen to what God is saying:

God condemns Israel's impiety, to defend his glory	48:1–11
If only Israel would listen to the words of God	48:12–22

Each of the two main paragraphs is marked by the opening call to "listen" (*šimĕʿû*, 48:1,12), and both paragraphs repeat this key word several times (48:1,3,5,6,7,8,12,13,16,20). The idea that God, not their wooden idols, is telling the people these things about the future is repeated in both paragraphs (48:5,14a). Each paragraph also contains several reasons for God's rebuke (48:4–5,7b–8,9–10,18–19,22), although there is more criticism of Israel in the first paragraph and more hope provided in the second paragraph. R. Melugin connects the form-critical background of 48:1–11 with a disputation, 48:12–15 with a trial speech, 48:17–19 with a divine word, and 48:20–21 with a hymn. Together these form a unique creative kerygmatic unit.[723] Although each of these sections has some general similarity to traditional patterns of prophetic

---

use of words like hear, call, speak, tell, and name. Blenkinsopp, *Isaiah 40–55*, 286–87, also notes that this is not the first time the Israelite audience has been criticized (cf. 42:18–25; 43:25–28; 46:8) and that the "shifts in mood and a sudden shift from reassurance to denunciation are not *in themselves* sufficient reason for postulating multiple authorship."

[721] Franke, *Isaiah 46,47, and 48: A New Literary-Critical*, 259, deals with issues of the macrostructure of the whole poem, though this argument is developed in greater detail within her discussion of the microstructure as well.

[722] Cf. C. A. Franke, "The Function of the Satiric Lament over Babylon in Second Isaiah (XLVII)," *VT* 41 (1991): 414–15.

[723] Melugin, *The Formation of Isaiah 40–55*, 139–42, believes this material was intended "to convince sinful Israel that Yahweh's plan is trustworthy . . . so that sinful Israel would not attribute his deeds to an idol . . . that his glory may not be given to another god (v.11)."

speech, the unique presentation of the material in this chapter causes these form-critical designations to have limited value. Greater attention must be given to the unique rhetorical formulation of this persuasive summary in order to catch the force of this prophetic confrontation and instruction in the light of the broader message. The audience has already heard of God's unhappiness with Babylon (chaps. 46–47), but now Israel is condemned; so in reality it is not that different from Babylon. It, too, will suffer if the people do not listen and respond to what God has said. In the light of all these many failures, if Israel has any real hope for the future, it is primarily due to the nature of her God, who ultimately does what he plans for his own glory and for his own name's sake (48:11).

GOD CONDEMNS ISRAEL'S IMPIETY TO DEFEND HIS GLORY (48:1–11)

> ¹"Listen to this, O house of Jacob,
>   you who are called by the name of Israel
>   and come from the line of Judah,
>   you who take oaths in the name of the LORD
>   and invoke the God of Israel—
>   but not in truth or righteousness—
> ²you who call yourselves citizens of the holy city
>   and rely on the God of Israel—
>   the LORD Almighty is his name:
> ³I foretold the former things long ago,
>   my mouth announced them and I made them known;
>   then suddenly I acted, and they came to pass.
> ⁴For I knew how stubborn you were;
>   the sinews of your neck were iron,
>   your forehead was bronze.
> ⁵Therefore I told you these things long ago;
>   before they happened I announced them to you
>   so that you could not say,
>   'My idols did them;
>   my wooden image and metal god ordained them.'
> ⁶You have heard these things; look at them all.
>   Will you not admit them?
>
>   "From now on I will tell you of new things,
>   of hidden things unknown to you.
> ⁷They are created now, and not long ago;
>   you have not heard of them before today.
>   So you cannot say,
>   'Yes, I knew of them.'
> ⁸You have neither heard nor understood;
>   from of old your ear has not been open.
>   Well do I know how treacherous you are;
>   you were called a rebel from birth.

⁹**For my own name's sake I delay my wrath;**
for the sake of my praise I hold it back from you,
so as not to cut you off.
¹⁰**See, I have refined you, though not as silver;**
I have tested you in the furnace of affliction.
¹¹**For my own sake, for my own sake, I do this.**
How can I let myself be defamed?
I will not yield my glory to another.

The first paragraph contains several words of confrontation. Its focus is to persuade that in spite of all the gracious things that God has done for Israel and said to them, they still do not honor God in their responses. They claim one thing but do another. They have been stubborn, and they have not opened their ears to understand what God has said and done. So how should God treat them? The blessings and curses in the covenant (Lev 26–27; Deut 27–28) prophetically lay out the principles of God's rule for his covenant partner as well as the detailed consequences that will fall on both those who love God and those who stubbornly reject his ways and rebel.

The structure of the first paragraph can be outlined into several parts:

Israel's actions do not match her rhetoric   48:1–2
Israel was stubborn even though God foretold the future   48:3–6a
Rebellious Israel did not listen when God spoke   48:6b–8
God deals with Israel in order to defend his glory   48:9–11

The first two verses are held together by their attention to the names (vv. 1a,1b,2b) that Israel and God are called. The second section (48:3–6a) reviews the former things God declared and did, while 48:6b–8 confronts the nation about their inability to "hear" what God says. Isaiah 48:9–11 repeatedly mention why ("for the sake of") God deals with Israel in this way. Together they present a forceful condemnation and by implication a call for the Israelites to act in new ways that please God.

48:1–2   This message begins with the imperative call for an Israelite audience to "hear" (*šimĕʿû*; 46:8; 48:6,12,16), that is, to listen to what the prophet is about to say. This method of introducing a message implies that something important is going to be said and that the audience needs to pay careful attention. Since this passage is addressed to "the ones who called themselves"[724] Israel, "the ones who swear an oath" (*hannišbāʿîm*) and "will remember, invoke"[725]

---

[724] The pl. *niphal* participle הַנִּקְרָאִים is interpreted as a passive by Koole, *Isaiah III, Volume 1, Isaiah 40–48,* 556 and in NIV, HCSB ("are called"), but Franke, *Isaiah 46, 47, and 48: A New Literary-Critical,* 170, argues for a reflexive meaning (cf. 44:5) since the "emphasis is on what Israel does to its discredit rather than what has been done to Israel."

[725] W. F. Smelik, "The Use of הַזְכִּיר בְּשֵׁם in Classical Hebrew: Josh 23:7; Isa 48:1; Amos 6:10; Ps 20:8; 4Q504 iii 4; 1QS 6:27," *JBL* 118 (1999): 321–32, rejects the views of M. Dahood ("male") and S. R. Driver ("boast") and follows M. Greenberg in attributing the meaning of "swear, take an oath," parallel to a similar clause in Josh 23:7. The verb יַזְכִּירוּ "they will remember" can be related

the name of the Israel's God, there is no doubt about who is being addressed. Although many individuals swore oaths throughout the history of the nation, the initial time when the nation swore its commitment to God was at Mount Gerizim and Ebal where they swore their allegiance to God by affirming the blessings and curses of the covenant (Lev 26–27; Deut 27–28; Josh 8:30–34). These documents told what would happen if they reject God.

This audience is "from the line of Judah" (NIV), a translation that was derived from the difficult *mimmê* which literally means "from the waters of" Judah. Four interpretive options are available: (a) One could hypothesize that this phrase is parallel to the "fountain of Jacob," a metaphor which refers to the semen/seed of Judah (Num 24:7; Deut 33:28; Ps 68:26; Prov 5:15). (b) Based on earlier usage in Isaiah "waters" could be a general metaphor for a destructive power (8:7; 43:2,16) or salvation (48:18,21).[726] (c) J. D. W. Watts[727] and others prefer to emend the text to *mimmēʿê* "from the bowels/loins" which more closely matches the metaphor in 48:19; Gen 15:4; 2 Sam 7:12; 16:11. (d) C. A. Franke views this word as a compound form of the preposition *min*, which is related to similar forms in 39:7 and 46:3.[728] In each interpretation of this metaphor the prophet is communicating that he is referring to the children of Judah. The inclusion of the names Jacob, Israel, and Judah unequivocally indicates that these words apply to a Hebrew audience.

All the fine things said about Israel and Judah in 48:1 are brought under suspicion by the final clause. The prophet accuses the audience of doing these things "not in truth or righteousness." Based on 10:20, J. Goldingay maintains that not doing things in truth indicates that there is no "match between words or appearance and reality . . . the people's oaths and invocations are words that lack a matching reality in life."[729] But J. L. Koole argues that these terms should not be interrelated only to the oaths and invocations that the people individually made; instead, at the broadest and deepest level these people do not deal with God with integrity and they do not walk before God in ways that are upright or truthful.[730] They do not follow the covenant stipulations as they promised when they entered into a covenant relationship with God. What these

---

either to (a) prayer in the name of God or (b) the use of God's name in making an oath.

[726] Koole, *Isaiah III, Volume 1, Isaiah 40–48*, 556, outlines numerous alternative options but ends up keeping the Masoretic "waters" and gives this metaphor a positive meaning that describes Judah before it was ruined and sent into exile.

[727] Both Watts, *Isaiah 34–66*, 175, and North, *Second Isaiah*, 174, prefer the emendation. In essence, if "water" refers to the seed and "bowels" is a euphemism for the sexual organ, both approaches are coming to the same meaning.

[728] Franke, *Isaiah 46, 47, and 48: A New Literary-Critical*, 170–71. GKC §103m discusses this compound form.

[729] Goldingay, *The Message of Isaiah 40–55*, 342, goes on to connect truth with "straightforwardness, transparency, and integrity."

[730] Koole, *Isaiah III, Volume 1, Isaiah 40–48*, 557, looks to parallel passages like Jer 4:2; 5:2; 1 Kgs 3:6.

wicked people actually do and what ought to be demonstrated in the righteous lives of these people are two completely different things. This accusation requires one to view the audience as people who had the right birthright, were part of the right social or ethnic group, and were associated with the right God, but unfortunately none of these right connections mattered because they did not have a profound impact on their lives (cf. 1:10–17). God has never been greatly impressed with good actors who can play their part, repeat all the right lines, or pretend that they know and deeply love him. His truth will unmask the fraud in every person's life.

Verse 2 describes several aspects that might otherwise point to the positive attributes of the community, but in light of v. 1b each of these must be pointing to additional meaningless aspects of their culture that did not have a positive transformational effect on their religious worldview. The initial *kî* is open to several interpretations, but it probably expresses the concessive idea "although"[731] (NIV does not translate this word). If this is the case, then this verse states that "although" the Israelites might claim external allegiance and religious identity with the holy city of Jerusalem, [732] just being a Hebrew or just living in a city where the Hebrew temple was built does not automatically make them holy. The same idea could be carried over to the second clause. "Although" (implied from the first line) these people might claim to lean, rely, or depend on the God of Israel, they need to realize that Yahweh of Hosts is his name. In other words, they flippantly speak of their dependence on Israel's God, but do they really trust in the all-powerful God of the armies of heaven? In light of v. 1b, v. 2 can hardly be a description of their true heart's devotion to God; instead, there is a masquerade of pious words that are not matched by a holy commitment to God.

There is a certain level of mystery about the setting of the Hebrew people addressed in this chapter, for in chaps. 40–48 the prophet seldom refers to his audience as the people of Judah, the citizens of the holy city. C. R. North maintains that the prophet is not addressing just the exiles but the whole nation throughout its history.[733] Yet in thinking about this approach one must ask: Was Judah always rebellious, and what does condemning every Israelite have to do with this specific audience? Since obstinate Israel is condemned elsewhere in chaps. 40–48, J. Goldingay concludes that this chapter is a response to a challenge by the people in exile who complained that God has not announced

---

[731] Long after completing my study of this verse it was pointed out to me that Seitz, "Isaiah 40–66," 417, also proposes to translate this כִּי as a concessive "though."

[732] McKenzie, *Second Isaiah*, 97, maintains that "the generation he addresses is the heir of Israel's past with its saving deeds and its sins. The contemporaries could scarcely have called themselves by the name of 'the holy city'." McKenzie points to a significant problem for those who maintain that the prophet was addressing sinful exiles in Babylon.

[733] North, *The Second Isaiah*, 175. This view is problematic for there were certain people, and even the nation at certain times, who were faithful to God. This would have to be a vast overgeneralization if it refers to everyone.

the present "new" events they are experiencing, as he announced the "former" events (47:3,6) before this.[734] Since there is no actual complaint in this chapter, this theory remains very hypothetical and is an unlikely solution.

The earlier analysis of chaps. 40–44 suggested that the prophet was not speaking to exiles but to people who were at war (42:11–12), who were blind servants (42:18–20), plundered and looted (42:22), who wearied God with their sacrifices that did not honor him (43:24–24), and who will have their sanctuary profaned (43:28). Possibly the prophet is now speaking more words of condemnation to this same group.

48:3–6a In the second accusation, God reminds the audience that he told the people about past and future events, caused words to go out from his mouth, and "was repeatedly causing people to hear" (NIV, "I made them known")[735] the "former things" long ago before they happened. The threefold reference to God speaking need not imply there was a dispute or charge against God that he had not spoken about the former things. Isaiah 41:21–22; 42:9; 43:9,16–21; 44:6–8; 45:20–21; and 46:9–11 refer to God's earlier announcement of "former things" that he would do; this announcement of the plan of God was known to individuals (Gen 12:1–3) as well as the nation when they confirmed their covenant with God and accepted the blessings and curses as his plan (Lev 26–27; Deut 27–28; Josh 8:30–34). In 41:21–22; 42:9; 45:20–21 the "former things" are not explicitly identified with any specific event,[736] but in 43:16–21 and 44:6–8 they are closely connected with exodus events. In the present passage God is pictured as acting suddenly. The two events that will happen "suddenly" (*pit'ōm*) in the book of Isaiah are the fall of Babylon in 539 BC (47:11) and the defeat of the Assyrians at Jerusalem in 701 BC (29:5). In previous speeches God defended his divinity to the foreign nations based on his ability to predict the future and then do it, but now God is bringing this same evidence to shame his own people who failed to trust God.

Verse 4 provides a logical basis ("because, for") for God's action in 48:5. God's motivation for acting was because of his knowledge[737] that the Israelite

---

[734] Goldingay, *Message of Isaiah, 40–55*, 345, claims that "The disputation presupposes the charge that YHWH had not spoken," but in light of all the similar passages which talk about God revealing the future, it is hard to imagine that this could have been the point of a dispute. The problem must lie elsewhere.

[735] The verb וָאַשְׁמִיעֵם is a *hiphil* imperfect; therefore, it should not have a past completed translation "I made them known" (NIV, RSV). Since the imperfect frequently expresses repeated or continual action, one of these types of action should be employed to emphasize that it did not happen once but happened repeatedly or continually (GKC §107e-f).

[736] Muilenburg, "Isaiah 40–66," 5:554, believes this reference to the former things also describes God's general acts of salvation, not one specific event. He doubts that "former things" could include Cyrus's early conquests as C. R. North proposed.

[737] The first word מִדַּעְתִּי is made up of the preposition מִן "from, because" plus the infinitive construct form of the verb יָדַע "he knew," plus the pronominal suffix "me." The suffix functions as the subject of the infinitive construct to produce the subordinate clause, "because I knew" (GKC §115e).

nation ("you" *'attâ* is singular) was "hard, stubborn" (*qāšeh*; as in Exod 32:9; 33:35; 34:9) and had a neck constructed of inflexible iron muscles that made it nearly impossible for it to turn to listen or change directions. Israel's forehead was so impenetrable that it metaphorically appeared like it was made of bronze (cf. Ezek 3:1–7). These metaphors of the nation's unresponsiveness were used again and again from Sinai to the exile. This is not some new or unusual characteristic of the nation.

Knowing these things about his people, God purposely decided to tell his people about his plans (48:5a) long before any of these things happened. A second reason why God did this (the first reason is given in v. 4) was that he did not want them to attribute his sovereignty to other gods or confuse his plans with the acts of various wooden images of some divine power (48:5b). In spite of what God told the Israelites about his plans and his ways, the nation consistently had problems with distinguishing the work of God from the work of idols. This problem existed at the time of the golden calf (Exod 32), when the people first came into the land of Canaan (Josh 24:14; Judg 2:10–13), when Solomon's kingdom was strong (1 Kgs 11), when the northern tribes within Israel were defeated (1 Kgs 17), all the way to the demise of Judah (2 Kgs 21; Ezek 8), and even a short time after the destruction of Jerusalem when some people fled to Egypt (Jer 43–44).

For the third time (48:3a,5a also use the root *šāma'* "hear") God reminds the stubborn listeners in 48:6a[738] that they have heard all these things he revealed to them in the past; consequently, they are held accountable for what they know. This suggests a somewhat confrontational tone (saying it three times). Also, the imperative command "look at them all" (*ḥăzēh kullāh*) sounds like an "in your face" demand. Finally, God asks why they would not "admit them" (lit. "Will you not declare?"), which gives the sense of confessing, acknowledging, or conceding that God was right in what he said. This also plays on the thought that the one who believes and knows what God has predicted would naturally want to announce it to others so that they will hear and believe.

48:6b–8 This new section contrasts the former things they have heard with the "new things" (*ḥădāšôt*) God is announcing "from this point on."[739] He has not totally given up on his people's ability to hear and is giving them another chance to listen and learn from his wisdom. These new things were "hidden" (*nāṣar*, "kept, guarded, preserved," a concept applied to the servant in 42:6; 49:8) and unknown.[740] The term "new things" was mentioned in 42:9 in

---

[738] Muilenburg, "Isaiah 40–66," 5:555, considers v. 6a a "superb transition" to the new thought in v. 6b, but Westermann, *Isaiah 40–66*, 197, believes "6a forms the conclusion of this section."

[739] מֵעַתָּה "from now, from this time forward" contrasts with "from long ago" מֵאָז in 48:3.

[740] At the end of the first clause in v. 6, what is new is referred to in a fem. sg. suffix כֻּלָּה "all of it." But before the end of the verse what is new is defined as the "new things" (חֲדָשׁוֹת) at the end of the verse the prophet says that "you did not know them," but here he uses a masc. pl. pronominal suffix. This kind of gender switch is found many times (GKC §144a).

the context of the new things God will do through the "Servant of the Lord." In each case the idea is associated with the sudden introduction of a new situation (43:19) that is connected to God's eschatological work of transforming people and nature. But R. N. Whybray suggests that the new things refer "probably to the entire chain of events which is expected to begin with Cyrus's conquest of Babylon."[741] Yet McKenzie recognizes "a slight inconsistency between the prophet's statements here that Israel has not heard these things and his repeated affirmations in the preceding poems."[742] To resolve this problem F. Delitzsch connects the "new things" with the redemption of Israel (physically and spiritually), the conversion of the Gentiles, and the creation of the new heavens and earth.[743] This solution seems unusually broad in this context (it does fit 43:19–21), but J. L. Koole narrows this down by using the literary context of chap. 48 and says, "The totally 'new' element will have to be sought in the full salvation (also that of Israel's return) which is made possible by the vicarious work of the Servant of Yahweh."[744] This is based on the "new things" used in the context of the Servant of the Lord in 42:9, the interpretation of 48:16 as a reference to the Servant of the Lord, and the new things said about the Servant's ministry in the very next chapter (49:1–13). This is a possible option, though it is difficult to provide a very precise definition of the new things from the limited information in 48:6. If this concept includes more than what is hinted at in 42:9 and 43:19, later messages will need to fill out the various "things" that should be viewed as new. Subtly implied by the comparison between the former and new things is the idea that God successfully accomplished the former things that he identified; thus, the present audience can be assured that God will bring about the new things at some point in the future.

48:7 These new things are new because they were created now, not a long time ago (*mēʾaz*). The sense in which these "were created" (*nibrěʾû*)[745] right now is puzzling. It is evident that God knew about these new things earlier, for

---

[741] Whybray, *Isaiah 40–66*, 128, gives a similar meaning to 42:9 and Childs, *Isaiah*, 375, maintains that "The entry of the new things was closely associated in 43:14ff with the coming of Cyrus. The Persian deliverer was the catalyst for the new age of redemption." My comments at 43:14 suggested that (a) it did not refer to the peaceful fall of Babylon by Cyrus, (b) Cyrus is not mentioned in this context at all, (c) a new paragraph begins at 43:16 that describes eschatological events of transformation, for there was no marvelous transformation of nature around 539 BC.

[742] McKenzie, *Second Isaiah*, 96–97, is not bothered by this "slight inconsistency," but surely the extensive announcement about Cyrus's name and purpose in 44:24–45:7 would seem to disqualify this as something was "new," "hidden," and "not known" to you (48:6b).

[743] Delitzsch, "Prophecies of Isaiah," 248, makes it refer to everything that will happen in the New Testament until the eschaton, but this seems to add more than is intended in this verse (though it is more fitting for the reference to new things in chap. 43).

[744] Koole, *Isaiah III, Volume 1, Isaiah 40–48*, 566, follows the interpretation of A. Condamin and W.A. M. Beuken.

[745] The perfect *niphal* verb נִבְרְאוּ is translated "They are being created" by Goldingay, *Message of Isaiah 40–55*, 347, but this expresses continual progressive action. The NIV "They are created" is a better translation.

he has kept/guarded them until now (48:6). They were a part of his plans for the world, so this information is not a new creation by God or something that he has just newly revised. It is a newly created message as far as the Israelites were concerned, for the contrasting statement claims that these are things they had not heard before this time. God's providential acts in the future are thus conveyed as a continuation of God's original creative work, for the events entailed in this new message are newly created or brought into existence as they happen.

Why did God not reveal these details much earlier? The text states that God did not want the people to say, "Yes I knew of them," but the meaning of this clause is unclear. J. Goldingay believes that Israel may have complained that God never said anything new; he just repeated the same old thing again and again. This newly created message and events would counter their complaints.[746] J. L. Koole who identifies the new things with the coming of the Servant, suggests that God did not want Israel to know about the Servant's new work earlier because they might then excuse their sins: "the mercy would have been too cheap."[747] J. Oswalt proposes that God did not want the people to know about these new future events because then the people would not have to live in a state of helplessness, needing God's help. If people knew what would happen, they would not have to live by faith, trusting God.[748] Another approach would be to look at the explanation that follows in the next verses.

48:8 The first half of this verse has three negative clauses, each introduced by "moreover, also" (*gam*; all three are omitted in NIV). This repetition heightens or intensifies the point being made.[749] The first negative statement repeats ideas in v. 7a that "moreover, you have not heard," but then the flow of thought is expanded. Not only did they not hear, "moreover" you did not know what they were all about (repeating the thought of v. 7b), and "moreover" for a long time your ear was not receptive[750] to hear what God was saying. Thus, God did not tell them about his new creation he had planned for the future because they would not listen (they were stubborn; 48:4; cf. 6:9–10; 42:20; 50:5). Having explained the Israelite ignorance and unwillingness to hear in v. 8, Isaiah develops God's view of their problem. NASB, NRSV, and numerous

---

[746] Goldingay, *Message of Isaiah 40–55*, 348, provides no evidence to support his suggestion that Israel made this kind of complaint.

[747] Koole, *Isaiah III, Volume 1, Isaiah 40–48*, 568, provides no evidence that this was a problem in Israel.

[748] Oswalt, *Isaiah 40–66*, 268, views this as God's way of fighting human attempts to be independent, all knowing, and in control of the future. By not telling the people this information, they had no security. They had to trust God.

[749] R. Alter, *The Art of Biblical Poetry* (New York: Basic Books, 1985), 43–44, 60, suggests that repetition is "a matter of insistence and emphasis" which heightens the importance of the point.

[750] The word פִּתְּחָה is a *piel* active "open," not a passive "has been opened" (NIV, RSV, NASB). North, *Second Isaiah*, 200, makes it a *niphal* passive verb, but the Old Greek had "I have not opened."

commentators interpret the introductory *kî* in v. 8b as causal ("for, because"), but it is unlikely the point that God caused the audience not to open its ears "because" he knew they were treacherous. NIV leaves the particle untranslated, presumably interpreting it correctly as emphatic ("truly, indeed"), thus making God's evaluation of the situation agree with what Israel did.[751] Although the people do not know much about God, God knows everything about them. He is aware that the people are "very treacherous"[752] (cf. 24:16; 33:1). This term often describes an unfaithful act of violating an agreement of loyalty (Hos 6:1; 8:1), a somewhat deceptive betrayal of a spouse, a political treaty with another nation, or a divine covenant partner (Jer 3:8,11,20). This behavior of treacherous unfaithfulness resulted in God calling them a "rebel" (*pešaʿ*) ever since the very beginning (metaphorically expressed as "from the womb"). This parallels Isaiah's statement in 1:2 and recalls the people complaining and rebelling against God during their wilderness journey (Exod 15:22–26; 16; Num 16; 20:1–13), their worship of the golden calf at Mt Sinai (Exod 32–34), and their refusal to go into the promised land from Kadesh-barnea (Num 13–14). Ezekiel 2–3; 16, and 23 also emphasize the nation's rebellious treachery from the very beginning. If Israel had this little receptivity and this much unfaithfulness toward God, one can understand why it would be a waste of time for God to reveal more about the new things in 48:7.

48:9–11 The last part of this paragraph is a conclusion that explains in positive terms why God does what he does and what his purposes are in dealing harshly with his people Israel. From the broadest perspective, the beginning phrase and the concluding phrase in this paragraph proclaim that all God's acts are designed to accomplish his primary goal of declaring his glory to all the people on the earth. With this end in mind God interacts with people in positive and negative ways, so that his people will honor him and so that other nations will see his works and praise him.

48:9 Having described the lack of integrity (v. 1), stubbornness (v. 4), closedness (v. 8a), and treacherous rebellion (v. 8b) in Israel, it would be natural to expect God to describe his determination to judge his people for their sins. But in the past and in the present situations God has repeatedly demonstrated that he was slow to anger (cf. Exod 34:6),[753] and he repeatedly held back[754]

---

[751] Franke, *Isaiah 46,47, and 48: A New Literary-Critical*, 198, translates this "yes."

[752] The Hebrew construction of an infinitive absolute plus a finite verb בָּגוֹד תִּבְגּוֹד expresses a heightening or strengthening of the idea, thus "treacherously you were treacherous" or "you were very treacherous" (GKC §113an).

[753] The imperfect verb אַאֲרִיךְ is not referring to a one-time past event (i.e., Exod 34), but the imperfect reflects God's repeated and continual longsuffering attitude of forbearance with his disobedient people (GKC §107e-f).

[754] The word אֶחֱטָם "I repeatedly held back" (an imperfect) is used only here; its meaning is uncertain and hypothesized based on the assumption that it is parallel to the preceding verb. BDB, 310, suggests that this word may be an Aramaic loan word. There is also a similar Akkadian verb that means "to curb, bridle," which fits the same semantic field.

his severe punishment so that his people would not be cut off.[755] Why does
he deal with them so mercifully? The two reasons this verse gives to explain
God's action are "for my own name's sake" and "for the sake of my praise."
God wants his people to praise him (12:1), to give thanks (12:3), to call on his
name (12:4), to make his name known among the nations (12:4), to sing and
shout about his deeds (12:5–6; 42:10–11), so that all people would give him
glory (42:10–12). The reputation of God's name is connected to the "oaths" he
has made in his name (48:1b) and to the destiny of the covenant people "who
are called by the name of Israel" (48:1a). His glory will be evident in his deeds
on their behalf (the exodus, conquest, and future promises), which other nations will observe; consequently, they, too, will desire to praise God (42:10–13;
45:20–25; 60:3–11; 66:18–23).

48:10   As if to prove the point, God illustrates his mercy by pointing to
an unidentified historic trial by fire in which "I smelted, refined you,"[756] but
this refining is qualified by distinguishing God's action toward Israel from the
somewhat parallel action of refining silver. This same kind of imagery may be
behind Jer 6:26–29 where the refining process has not produced something
"like"[757] pure silver but rejected silver.

The second half of the verse refers to the "furnace of affliction" which
could refer to any distant or recent severe trial, but J. Goldingay believes this
language specifically recalls the trials of slavery in the iron furnace of Egypt
(Exod 3:7,17; Deut 4:20; 1 Kgs 8:51; Jer 11:4). This conclusion is confirmed
if one accepts the textual reading "I chose you," for Israel's election is often
connected to this era of her history. These examples would prove God's long-
suffering patience with people who were not very pure. One problem with this
solution is that refining in the first clause and choosing in the second clause are
not very parallel. The reading in 1QIs[a] is derived from the root *bḥn* "to test"
which makes a good parallel to "refine,"[758] plus the root *bḥr* in Aramaic does
mean "melt, refine, try."[759] This translation is often preferred (NIV, NASB).

48:11   Although God does interact and respond to the sinful acts or repentance of people, in the final analysis God's actions are not determined by the

---

[755] The subordinate result clause לְבִלְתִּי הִכָּרִיתֶךָ "to not cut you off" is made up of a negative
plus an infinitive construct. The suffix on the infinitive construct functions as the object of the verb
(GKC §115b,c).

[756] Isa 1:25 refers to a future smelting of God's people and this statement, "I smelted you"
צְרַפְתִּיךָ which may refer to a recent severe trial like Sennacherib's near annihilation of the nation
or a past trial like their enslavement in Egypt.

[757] The product produced by this refining is לֹא בְכֶסֶף with the prefixed preposition בְּ functioning as what is called *bet essentiae* "like" (GKC §119i).

[758] In Hebrew the two words would look very similar: בְּחַרְתִּיךָ "I chose you" and בְּחַנְתִּיךָ "I
tested you" and could be explained as a simple scribal error.

[759] Delitzsch, "Prophecies of Isaiah," 250, and more recently in Z. Weisman, "The Nature and
Background of *bāḥur* in the Old Testament," *VT* 31 (1981): 447, who identifies Job 9:14; 29:25;
34:4 as other places where בָּחַר has the meaning of "try, test."

behavior of people. He will act for his own sake to accomplish his purposes and to carry out his plans. Although one would naturally expect from the covenant blessings and curses that sinful people would always receive the wrath of God, his love and forgiveness are always available (43:25; 44:22) and it is always possible for any nation to turn to God and be saved (45:22). In the end God will not allow his name to be profaned by sinful and rebellious people. They must either be judged or transformed through forgiveness. How can God allow his majestic glory to be diminished in any way? How could God ever allow people to give his praise and glory to another? These rhetorical questions indicate that the mere suggestion of such an idea is unthinkable. It will never happen because a holy God of immeasurable glory cannot go against his nature. He is holy and glorious; nothing will happen that might call into question his essence or impinge on his majestic reputation.

IF ONLY ISRAEL WOULD LISTEN TO THE WORDS OF GOD (48:12–22)

¹²"Listen to me, O Jacob,
  Israel, whom I have called:
 I am he;
  I am the first and I am the last.
¹³My own hand laid the foundations of the earth,
  and my right hand spread out the heavens;
 when I summon them,
  they all stand up together.

¹⁴"Come together, all of you, and listen:
  Which of [the idols] has foretold these things?
 The LORD's chosen ally
  will carry out his purpose against Babylon;
  his arm will be against the Babylonians.
¹⁵I, even I, have spoken;
  yes, I have called him.
 I will bring him,
  and he will succeed in his mission.

¹⁶"Come near me and listen to this:

 "From the first announcement I have not spoken in secret;
  at the time it happens, I am there."

 And now the Sovereign LORD has sent me,
  with his Spirit.

¹⁷This is what the LORD says—
  your Redeemer, the Holy One of Israel:
 "I am the LORD your God,
  who teaches you what is best for you,
  who directs you in the way you should go.

¹⁸If only you had paid attention to my commands,
  your peace would have been like a river,
  your righteousness like the waves of the sea.
¹⁹Your descendants would have been like the sand,
  your children like its numberless grains;
 their name would never be cut off
  nor destroyed from before me."

²⁰Leave Babylon,
  flee from the Babylonians!
 Announce this with shouts of joy
  and proclaim it.
 Send it out to the ends of the earth;
  say, "The LORD has redeemed his servant Jacob."
²¹They did not thirst when he led them through the deserts;
  he made water flow for them from the rock;
 he split the rock
  and water gushed out.

²²"There is no peace," says the LORD, "for the wicked."

The second paragraph exhorts the audience to listen (48:12,14,16; cf. v. 1) and respond to God. They should listen because he is the Creator who controls this world and because God will carry out his plans against Babylon (48:12–15). The Israelites should listen because God has called them to be his people (their election) and he will be their Redeemer. He wants to richly bless them, if they will only follow him (48:16–19). In the final verses God invites the audience to reject the Babylonian way, to flee from the Babylonian perception of reality, and to sing joyfully about God's redemption of his servant Jacob.

The material in this paragraph can be divided into three parts:

Listen, the sovereign God will carry out his plans	48:12–15
Listen to the Creator and eternal God	12–13
Listen, God's purposes will succeed	14–15
Listening would have brought blessing	48:16–19
Listen, God's Spirit has sent me	16
God's desire to teach and lead	17
Blessing available, if they had listened	18–19
Leave Babylon and shout for joy	48:20–22
Leave and shout, God's redemption has come	20–21
Judgment on the wicked	22

The form-critical approach of A. Schoors identifies 48:12–16 as a disputation, while R. Melugin believes it is closer to a trial speech because of the use of forensic terminology,[760] but the absence of any disputing voices[761] and the dominant use of the "listen" clauses (48:12,14,16) indicates that this is a unique instructional speech that persuasively calls for a response from the Hebrew audience. Some commentators make a break before v. 16, some after v. 16a, and some after v. 16, but the use of the commands to "listen" at the beginning of vv. 12 and 16 suggest that each call to listen introduces a new word from God.[762] The poem ends in vv. 20–21 with a hymnic response that the people are challenged to accept and repeat. At the end of this paragraph the editor who arranged chaps. 40–66 into three groups of nine chapters each (40–48; 49–57; 58–66) added the final warning in 48:22, which also appears in 57:21.

48:12–13 This paragraph starts by identifying God as the one who has "called" (the root *qārā'* in vv. 12a, 13b) his people into existence. The introductory call for Jacob and Israel to listen establishes a clear link with 48:1; thus one can conclude that this paragraph is connected to 48:1–11. In the verses following 48:1 Israel invokes the name of God, but questions are raised about Israel's worthiness to be called God's people. In v. 12 God still views Israel as "my called one" (48:1,12),[763] affirming his special relationship with his people. God identifies himself with a series of four "I" (*'ănî*) statements to remind the audience that they need to listen "to me." The verbless clause "I am he" distinguishes God from all other gods (42:8 has "I am the LORD"). "I am first; moreover [*'ap*, rendered "and"] I am last" is a unique claim that God makes to distinguish himself from all other objects that might claim to have a divine quality (cf. 41:4; 43:10; 44:6). J. Muilenburg believes this threefold assertion is "a characteristic triad, emphasizing the oneness, the uniqueness, and the eternity of God."[764] These claims are connected to the "I am" phrase that identify God's name in Exod 3:14 and with similar "I am" clauses in 45:6,18,22; 46:4,9; 47:10.[765] He is a God who controls things from the beginning to the

---

[760] Schoors, *I Am God Your Savior*, 279–82, considers vv. 12–13 the basis for the disputation. Melugin, *Formation of Isaiah 40–55*, 137, notes that in other trials there is a "summons to trial and arguments by means of a question introduced by *mî*" and finds similarities between this speech and 45:18–21.

[761] Whybray, *Isaiah 40–66*, 131, states that there is "a disputation in which Yahweh, as the speaker, seeks to overcome the exiles' doubts about the mission of Cyrus," but such a doubt is never expressed in this text but read into it based on what God is assumed to be confronting. These should be understood as words of instruction and encouragement, rather than part of a disputational argument.

[762] Childs, *Isaiah*, 376–77, and Koole, *Isaiah III, Volume 1, Isaiah 40–48*, 577, make a break after v. 16a, putting v. 16b with what follows. It is better to follow Muilenburg, "Isaiah 40–66," 5:559, and make a break before v. 16 based on the appearance of the imperatives that begin the literary piece in vv. 12–15,16–19, and 20–22.

[763] The participle מְקֹרָאִי is a *pual* participle, identifying the audience, which is periphrastically rendered in a relative clause in NIV and NASB.

[764] Muilenburg, "Isaiah 40–66," 5:559, finds these themes also emphasized in 43:10,13,25; 41:4; 46:4,6.

[765] See comments on 41:2–4.

end of time; nothing is outside his realm of influence. This includes everything, from his providential laying of the foundations of the earth (a construction metaphor; Pss 24:2; 102:25; Job 38:4–6), even to his act of spreading out the vast heaven (40:22; 45:12). He even summons the stars to stand in their place (40:22,26)[766] to demonstrate that he has the power to administer the inner workings of every part of the universe so that they all work synchronistically together as one unit. All these factors are intended to exalt God in the eyes of the Israelites. If the words of God's mouth are this powerful and his hands are this skilled, surely the Hebrew audience can listen to what he has to say.

48:14–15 A second imperative call summons a group of people to "assemble themselves"[767] together and listen to what God has to say to "all of you." The variation in pronouns from "all of you" (*kullĕkem*) to "among them" (*bāhem*) in the next phrase has created some confusion and a desire to make them consistent,[768] but this should be avoided, for this verse includes another challenge for the idols (the "them"), similar to what is found in earlier chapters (41:21–26; 45:21).[769] In this context Israel is rhetorically asked to identify any idol-god that has declared the things that God has revealed.

Verse 14b indicates what God has made known to his people. The statement that God "loves him/it" (*ʾăhēbō*) is unusual, though some relate it to God's love of a foreign ruler (possibly the Koresh of 45:1) who will come against Babylon. The Aramaic Targum adjusts the text to read "because he loves Israel," 1QIsᵃ has "my beloved" or "he loves me," and the Old Greek translation gives "loves you."[770] It is unclear whether these two Hebrew words should function as a separate clause ("God loves him"), or as is more likely, the subject of the verb "he will carry out, do" (*yaʿăśeh*). If "God-loves-him" (NIV "God's chosen ally") is treated as a compound name similar to the names in 7:3; 8:1–3,[771] it will naturally function as the subject of the verb. God will use the one he loves to accomplish his pleasure or purpose (44:28; 46:10) in regard to Babylon. The last phrase is misread in the Old Greek translation, "on the seed of Chaldeans," because the word for "seed" and "arm" look similar in an unpointed Hebrew

---

[766] Melugin, *Formation of Isaiah 40–66*, 137, uses this figure of speech and the questioning format in 48:14 to identify this as a trial, but there is no indication God is calling them to appear at court.

[767] The *niphal* imperative verb הִקָּבְצוּ could have a passive sense "be assembled" or a reflexive meaning "assemble yourselves." Although this term is associated with a trial in 43:9 and 45:20, people gather together to worship, makes decisions, go to war, celebrate a feast, and for a host of other reasons.

[768] North, *Second Isaiah*, 181, believes this message is spoken to "you" the nations about "them" the gods. 1QIsᵃ solves this problem by changing the second pronoun "all of you" (כֻּלְּכֶם) to "all of them" (כֹּלָם), thus making both pronouns third pl.

[769] Franke, *Isaiah 46,47, and 48: A New Literary-Critical*, 214–15, believes this kind of rhetorical question should have a negative answer. No other gods have revealed these things.

[770] Schoors, *I Am God Your Savior*, 280, uses the Qumran and Greek to come up with the unusual translation of "Yahwe is my friend."

[771] Muilenburg, "Isaiah 40–66," 5:559–60, takes this approach.

text.[772] This phrase indicates that it is God's arm that will accomplish his pleasure, even though an earthly ruler will accomplish God's will on earth.

To assure the Hebrew audience that this is totally God's work, 48:15 emphasizes "I, I" (*'ănî 'ănî*) will speak. "I" will call him to initiate this plan, then "I" will bring him, and the result will be that he will succeed in his path.[773] Since his path is directed by God and his success is empowered by God, his path is not his own and his success is not his own.

48:16　　Once again God calls the people to listen, suggesting that it is either the conclusion to vv. 12–16 (with the concluding call matching the call to listen in v. 12), or as seems more likely, 48:16 begins a new word from God in which a new speaker (the "me" in v. 16b) calls on the people to listen to what he has to say about a second important matter. J. L. Koole compares this imperative exhortation to "draw near [*qirĕbû*][774] to me" to the ideas of trusting God (1 Kgs 2:7; Zeph 3:2), to returning to God (44:22), and turning to God (45:22),[775] actions that would indicate the listener's acceptance of the persuasive arguments presented and a submissive attitude of trust in God. This acceptance would be based on their belief that from the very beginning God spoke to Israel about his pleasures and desires. In giving his law, the covenant blessings and curses, and prophetic announcements about the future, God made his will known; he did not keep his wishes "in secret" (*bassēter* in v. 16a). The people of Israel knew what God would do and what would be the consequences of their action. On the day that all these things actually do happen,[776] God was, is, and will be there. This affirms his providential care and oversight, insuring that his will is accomplished just as he has predicted it would.

After the call to listen (v. 16a) usually comes either the announcement of who is speaking, or the information the people are to listen to. In the second half of v. 16 there is a statement by an unknown person who claims to be sent by God. This appears to be the introduction of the speaker of a new message found in 48:16b–19. Although many commentators dismiss v. 16b as a later addition by a later author because it does not fit in this context,[777] it is always bet-

---

[772] The word "his arm" is spelled זְרֹעוֹ while "seed" is spelled זֶרַע, but without vowel points they appear almost identical. Cf. the issues involving הַזֶּרַע in Mal 2:3 (Clendenen, *Malachi*, 290).

[773] The Aramaic Targum and Old Greek texts use first person verbs throughout; thus, "I will give success" maintains a consistent glorification of God for his work. This is an easier reading, which is more pious; so it could easily appeal to a scribe, but it would be much harder to explain the Hebrew texts as a scribal error; therefore, it is undoubtedly the more original.

[774] קִרְבוּ "draw near" is an imperative verb that exhorts or admonishes the audience to act (GKC §110a).

[775] Koole, *Isaiah III, Volume 1, Isaiah 40–48*, 587, states "the point must be that God now invites his people to approach him in the sense that they should now seek his fellowship."

[776] The infinitive construct הֱיוֹתָהּ has a third fem suffix "it" functioning as the subject, "it happens/comes to pass."

[777] Whybray, *Isaiah 40–66*, 132, concludes that v. 16b does not fit in this context and must be a "fragmentary word spoken by the prophet about himself. It is reminiscent of 61:1." Westermann,

ter to attempt to explain what is in the text, even when it introduces unexpected material. J. L. McKenzie makes this "line the imagined response of Cyrus to the commission which has just been described."[778] Another solution is to suggest that this is the voice of the prophet speaking autobiographically.[779] But the prophet seldom refers to himself in chaps. 40–66, and most of the first person talk in these chapters occurs in the Servant poems. B. S. Childs goes to the old solution by F. Delitzsch and identifies this new messenger who was sent with the Spirit as the Servant who is more fully introduced in 49:1–6 (cf. 42:1). Yet at this point the speaker still remains anonymous, even while he quotes God and delivers the prophetic message in 48:17–19.[780] C. Seitz follows a similar approach, but in order to fit it into the context of the whole chapter, he interprets the first person testimony in v. 16b as a response to the question in v. 14 about who has revealed these things. "God did, and now he has sent 'me and his Spirit.'"[781] J. L. Koole, who also identifies this as the voice of the Servant, observes that in chap. 48 one finds the description of first things and then the announcement of the new things in 48:6a which begin with *mēʿattâ* (and *ʿattâ* in v. 7). This pattern is repeated in vv. 12–16 with the things that were already foretold in vv. 14–15; then there is the announcement of the Servant speaking 48:16b (probably the new things), which begins with *wĕʿattâ*.[782]

48:17 The ambiguous speaker in v. 16b (the Servant of 49:1–6) presents a divine revelation from Yahweh, their Redeemer (43:14; 44:6,24), the Holy One of Israel (41:14,16,29). These are somewhat familiar titles in Isaiah. They emphasize his covenantal identity with his people, his redemptive role on behalf of his people, and the sanctified character that sets him apart from all creation. This message of God (48:17) quoted by the Servant in this verse initially reminds the audience about two of God's roles as teacher and director. As the one who teaches his people, God taught them through revealing his will in the *Torah* as well as through the disciplinary and blessed experiences of life (cf. 54:13). By paying attention to these, the people were supposed to "learn to do right" (1:17), but instead during the time of Uzziah they rejected the law of

---

Isaiah 40–66, 203, maintains that the words in v. 16b "cannot possibly be explained in their present context . . . . They represent a fragment similar to 61.1. . . . Precisely the same sentiments are expressed in the Servant Song in 49.1–6, which suggests that the words may have been added in the margin at 49.1b (perhaps by Trito-Isaiah) . . . they may conceivably have formed part of 49.1–6."

[778] McKenzie, *Second Isaiah*, 99, rejects the view that it might be the Servant of the Lord or the prophet but finds these words not to be "a violent departure from the picture of Cyrus that emerges."

[779] Schoors, *I Am God Your Savior*, 281–82, says, "A Trito-Isaiah glossator, who made or knew lxi 1, has inserted vs 16c. probably because he had a damaged text and thought, in vs 16b the prophet is saying (sic) about himself." Oswalt, *Isaiah 40–48*, 278, says, "This is surely another case of the close identity between God and the prophet."

[780] Childs, *Isaiah*, 378.

[781] Seitz, "Isaiah 40–66," 419, believes vv. 14b–15 do not answer the question in v. 14a, ("Who among you has declared these things?") but v. 16b does.

[782] Koole, *Isaiah III, Volume 1, Isaiah 40–48*, 592, believes v. 16b refers ahead to 49:1–6.

God (5:24). They should have learned something about God's requirements of his covenant partners from the punishment God brought on their fathers (3:1–4:1; 7:1–25) when they brought disaster on themselves (4:9) and did not believe God's promises (7:9) or obey his laws (42:24). God's instructions were given for the purpose of teaching them "to be useful, successful" (NIV, "what is best").[783] This means that Israel had enough knowledge of what she was supposed to believe and do in order to fulfill the role God gave her and receive the blessings God had awaiting for her. In addition, Israel had God as a "director, leader" who graciously led her in the way that she should go. Initially this was manifest in God leading them out of Egypt, through the Red Sea, and through the wilderness (43:16; 48:21) and included God's promise to lead blind Israel in the future (42:19). This leading was not just a physical leading of the people from place to place, but included a spiritual leading through various worship songs, priestly instruction, wise proverbs, historical lessons, and new prophetic revelations. The point is abundantly clear; the Israelites had every opportunity to hear and follow the spiritual worldview that God had made known to them.

48:18–19   In spite of the availability of this knowledge, God laments that the Israelites did not pay attention to what he was teaching. "If only, oh that" (*lûa*)[784] expresses an unreal condition in the past that never happened (cf. Ps 81:14–17).[785] Although God tried again and again to communicate his will, the Israelites seldom ever listened to his commandments. God communicated to them the wonderful promises that the people could have received in order to enjoy God's blessing of peace and righteousness (key characteristics of God's rule), but they never did. This peace and righteousness is metaphorically compared to a river and the waves of the sea (cf. 66:12), but no further explanation is provided to identify the point of comparison. Was he thinking of the never-ending, constantly flowing nature of a river (41:18; cf. Amos 5:24), the breadth of the sea, or the never-ending coming ashore of wave, after wave, after wave?

The two additional things that God would have provided in 48:19 are much more specific. If they had paid attention to God's words, the Abrahamic promise of multiplying their seed like the sand would have come true (Gen 22:17;

---

[783] The infinitive construct לְהוֹעִיל "to be useful" expresses the purpose for God's instruction (GKC §114f-g).

[784] The conditional particle לוּא (usually spelled לוּ) expresses an optative wish that has not been fulfilled or that is not likely to happen (GKC §151e); thus it should be translated "Oh that you would have paid attention," and not as something that might be expected in the future. A. Rubinstein, "Conditional Constructions in the Isaiah Scroll," *VT* 6 (1956): 74–77, would change the readings of וַיְהִי to וְהָיָה in v. 18b based on the text of the DSS, but the Masoretic text has a normal and acceptable way of speaking about unfulfilled conditions in the past.

[785] Franke, *Isaiah 46,47, and 48: A New Literary-Critical*, 227–28, rightly criticizes North and others who translate this as a present hope for the future (the return from exile is still possible), rather than a past unrealized hope that is gone.

32:13). Yes, "your children" (NIV; lit. "what goes out")[786] from your loins/bowels have been like "the grains of it" (the sand of the sea).[787] The verse ends with a reminder of the suffering and trials that they could have avoided if they had only listened to God's instructions. God would have protected them and would not have allowed their name to be cut off or for them to be destroyed by their enemies. Isaiah 48:9 already mentioned God's gracious intervention of not allowing the people to be completely cut off for his own name's sake, but this did not prevent him from disciplining his people with great military trial that resulted in the death of thousands of people. God's desire was for them to avoid the heartache and misery of defeat, but once they rejected God, his presence could not go before them to defeat their enemies.

48:20–22   There seems to be a significant disjunction between the brief lament over missed opportunities in 48:16–19 and the sudden introduction of a message of hope in a joyful hymnic conclusion to this chapter in vv. 20–21. How can both statements be true for the same people? Since God is still speaking to "his servant Jacob," the only solution available is to imply that the message of hope applies to that believing community of Hebrews (his faithful servants) at some point in the future. C. Westermann believes this prophecy anticipates a future event because "there is no possibility of Israel's going forth, and as things are there is no sign of Yahweh's act of redemption. . . . It is an 'eschatological' hymn of praise."[788] Thus 48:20–22 are some of the new instructions that God is teaching his people. They should not reject the joyous hope that God provides for the future but believe God's promises, for they do not want to be among the wicked who will have no peace (48:22).

In light of past failures to listen, God offers another opportunity for his people to "come near me and listen" (48:16a), to pay attention to his words so that they can experience the peace that he promises (48:18a). The six imperative verbs in 48:20 exhort the people to believe God's message and to act on the basis of his promises. The first two imperatives ("go out," "flee") involve not just a hope of a life outside of Babylonian hegemony but a rejection of their worldview as described in chaps. 47–48. They must reject and leave behind

---

[786] The word וְצֶאֱצָאֵי comes from the verb יָצָא "he/it went out." In 34:1 and Job 31:8 this word refers to "plants" that "go out" of the earth; in Gen 1:24 it refers to "animals" that go out from the earth, but in 44:3 and 48:19 this term is parallel to the seed of mankind; so it must mean "descendents."

[787] The term כִּמְעֹתָיו has a comparative כ "like" and a third pers. suffix יו "it" which refers back to the sea. The remaining root מֵעֶה is used only here and probably means something like a small grain of sand. The Old Greek has "like the dust of the earth" which is obviously a paraphrase, but it fits the meaning perfectly.

[788] Westermann, *Isaiah 40–66*, 205; Childs, *Isaiah*, 378, also believes it is "eschatological since, according to the actual historical situation, Israel is still captive in Babylon." In contrast to this approach, Watts, *Isaiah 34–66*, 176, says vv. 16–20 are "depicting a expeditionary leader ready to begin a journey from Babylon to Jerusalem. . . . This position of the Vision should fit the role of Sheshbazzar."

Babylon's arrogant theological claims that she controlled the world and begin again to trust in God.[789] The concept of "fleeing" (*birḥû*) may be drawn from the earlier analogy of the exodus (Exod 14:5) as is the idea of "going out" (*ṣěʾû*, NIV "leave"; 11:8; 12:31; Jer 50:8; 51:45), but one should not read in the idea from Jeremiah that the people are fleeing because of a dangerous invading nation. J. Goldingay rightly concludes that "it is still not the case that Babylon has actually fallen and that the community is thus in a position actually to set out on a journey back to Palestine."[790]

The second pair of imperatives challenge the audience to openly announce their departure with shouts of joy and to confess with their mouths the things that God has promised. All four of these verbs ask for a response that demonstrates that the Israelites believe what God says and will boldly act on the basis of his promises. This joyous proclamation is not just a word of hope to their Hebrew friends and family. The last two imperatives challenge the audience to be willing to cause this message of hope to go out to the ends of the earth. They must declare that God has redeemed his servants (cf. 48:17). This does not speak of restoring the nation or building a temple but of God's gracious response to his servants who believe and trust him. Earlier this universal spreading of God's praise to the ends of the earth was found in a similar eschatological hymn of praise in 42:10–13 (cf. 40:9; 43:23; 52:9–11).

There are two contrasting ways to interpret 48:21: (a) as a continuation of the joyful confession of God's servants from v. 20[791] or (b) as a legitimation of the promise in v. 20 that will embolden the audience to believe God's words and shout for joy. Everyone agrees that it is an illustration drawn from the nation's exodus and wilderness tradition, but they differ on its relationship to present events (is it related to the experience of people in Babylon?). Once God redeemed his people from Egypt they did not thirst when they walked through the dry desert of Sinai (ignoring a brief time of thirst at Marah in Exod 15:22–25). God miraculously produced water from a rock to provide abundant water when there was no water in the vicinity. How did he do this? He split[792] the rock open to allow the water to gush out (Exod 17:6; Num 20:8,11; Deut 8:15; Pss 78:14–20; 105:41; 114:8).[793] J. Muilenburg interprets these words to be

---

[789] U. E. Simon, *A Theology of Salvation* (London: SPCK, 1953) approaches this dilemma as a spiritual challenge where the Israelites must leave this world's perspective (Babylon's) and attune their ears to God's way of thinking about what happens in this world.

[790] Goldingay, *Message of Isaiah 40–55*, 360, believes the prophet is actually seeking to hear a response of faith from the audience, not that they should pack up and start to move out on a trip. He differs from Franke, *Isaiah 46,47, and 48: A New Literary-Critical*, 235, who thinks that this envisions a solemn procession of Israelites.

[791] Koole, *Isaiah III, Volume 1, Isaiah 40–48*, 603, states, "It is therefore better, in my view to regard v. 21 as a continuation of v. 20 which is still spoken by the returning exiles themselves."

[792] North, *Second Isaiah*, 184, suggests the *waw* on וַיִּבְקַע is a *waw explicativum* explaining what happened in a previous verbal action (GKC §154a, note 1b).

[793] P. T. Willey, *Remember the Former Things: The Recollection of Previous Texts in Second*

saying that "As it was in the fateful days of the Exodus, so it will be in the new sojourn and return";[794] thus he views these as a literal prophecy of what would happen in the near future. C. Westermann wisely finds parallelism with the exodus experience, but does not see this as a prophecy of a literal repetition of these events. The main point is that God will give his "miraculous guidance and care" just like he did in the initial exodus experience.[795] They can trust God; he will provide for all their needs.

48:21 The final verse appears to be an editorial marker that divides chaps. 40–66 into three equal parts, each containing nine chapters (cf. 57:21). Although it may have come to have this function when the phrase was repeated in 57:21, the verse is quite fitting in its present context. It brings up the issue of God's positive offer of peace that was introduced in 48:18 and warns that it will not be available in the future for the same reason it was not available in the past. When people in the past did not pay attention to God's words, they missed the peace that God desires to offer and the same thing will happen to any future generation that fails to trust God. These wicked people will not be redeemed, will not sing for joy, and will not experience the peace of God. This shows the seriousness of the decision the nation has to make and the eternal consequences of their choice.

THEOLOGICAL IMPLICATIONS. The prophet closes out the first nine chapters with a rather strong rhetorical challenge that calls on his Israelite audience to listen and respond. God does not just disapprove of the beliefs and behavior of the Babylonians (chaps. 47–48); he is deeply disturbed by the Israelites' professions that appear to be orthodox but actually do not represent a true and faithful relationship with God (48:1–2). They may claim to be Israelites and identify themselves as the citizens of God's holy city (48:3), but they were stubborn, treacherous, and rebellious even though God revealed to them what would happen and then refined them when they were disobedient. In the final analysis, every person must come to understand that all of God's acts (positive and negative) are designed to bring glory to himself (48:11). Although all people are important in God's plans and he does care about his people, he is the Creator of this world, he controls all of history from the first events to the very last events, and he wants his people to trust him.

When people fall away from God, he will challenge them in various ways. In this case God calls for his people to listen to him, to hear him out, and respond accordingly. If they would just take into consideration who God is (the Creator, Lord of history, Redeemer, Holy One, Teacher, and Leader), then God would be able to pour out his blessing on his people. Unfortunately, many times people miss the blessings God has prepared for them (48:18–20) simply

---

Isaiah, SBLDS 161 (Atlanta: Scholars Press, 1997), 77–78, believes the Isaiah text is closest to Ps 78:15,20.
[794] Muilenburg, "Isaiah," 5:563.
[795] Westermann, *Isaiah 40–66*, 205.

because they do not listen and respond appropriately. So the challenge is: How will those who want to be his people and enjoy his miraculous care respond to his promises? Will they reject the ways of this world, will they shout for joy about God's redemption, and tell the whole world about his deeds? There is a clear choice with no middle ground. Respond to God's challenge and enjoy his redemption and peace or reject his promises and live without peace with the wicked. Just like these Israelites, every nation, family, and individual must hear the truth about their past sinfulness and be given the opportunity to respond to God's gracious invitation.

I. The Only True God Will Restore His People (40:1–55:13)
  6. God's Servant Will Bring Salvation to Israel and the Nations (49:1–13)
    (1) The Servant's Preparation and Responsibilities (49:1–6)
    (2) The Despised Servant's Role and Results (49:7–12)
    (3) Hymn of Praise (49:13)
  7. God Has Not Forsaken Zion (49:14–52:12)
    (1) Repopulation of Zion Will Prove God Has Not Forgotten (49:14–50:3)
      God Has Not Forgotten Zion (49:14–21)
      God Will Gather His Children, Save Them from Plunderers (49:22–26)
      God Will Ransom, Not Give Up on His People (50:1–3)
    (2) Follow the Example of God's Servant (50:4–11)
    (3) God's Past Salvation Encourages Faith for the Future (51:1–8)
    (4) God's Cup of Wrath Is Ended; Restoration Is Coming (51:9–52:12)
      God's Past Deeds Assure Future Intervention (51:9–16)
      The Fury of God's Wrath Is Over (51:17–23)
      Rejoice for God's Salvation Is Here (52:1–12)
  8. Exaltation and Joy Comes When Sin Is Taken Away (52:13–55:13)
    (1) The Exaltation of the Servant Who Takes Away Sin (52:13–53:12)
      Exaltation of the Servant (52:13–15)
      Report of the Servant's Suffering (53:1–9)
      Final Exaltation of the Servant (53:10–12)
    (2) God's Compassion Brings Children and a Covenant of Peace (54:1–17)
      Call for the Wife to Respond to God's Love (54:1–10)
      The Glorious Situation in Zion (54:11–17)
    (3) God's Grace and Covenant Bring Joy to the Repentant Sinners (55:1–13)
      Invitation to Participate in God's Provisions and Covenant (55:1–5)
      Invitation to Repent and See God's Word Fulfilled (55:6–13)

I. THE ONLY TRUE GOD WILL
RESTORE HIS PEOPLE
PART TWO (49:1–55:13)

6. God's Servant Will Bring Salvation to Israel and the Nations (49:1–13)

CONTINUITY AND DISCONTINUITY. It is possible to assume that the audience addressed in both chaps. 40–48 and 49–55 was (a) the same audience and (b) that they were facing the same general theological issues and (c) they were living in the same historical circumstances when they heard all these messages. Yet the topics in chaps. 49–55 do change somewhat, thus suggesting that these new messages in chaps. 49–55 may be addressing either a new audience or the same people in a new setting or people facing different threats or people confronting new theological issues. Although only a change in one of these factors could explain the thematic changes in these messages, it is difficult to identify which factor was the main area of change. Whatever is proposed must account for both a certain level of continuity with chaps. 40–48 as well as some level of discontinuity when one comes to 49–55. Another alternative that might explain this phenomenon is simply that the prophet editorially collected messages that were topically interrelated and placed them together in chaps. 40–48 and then placed another different group of topical messages together in 49–55.

One solution that attempted to account for these differences was to identify a difference location and time for each group of messages. Some have hypothesized that the location for the audience in all of chaps. 40–55 was the Babylonian exile. Later M. Haran proposed an Israelite setting for chaps. 49–66 because these chapters were primarily addressed to people living in the city of Jerusalem (49:14–26; 51:17–23; 54), contained descriptions of Jerusalem (49:18–22; 50:4–9; 51:1–3), rebuked people for sinfulness (50:10–11; 51:12–13; 55:2–3,6–7), and instructed people to "go out from there" (52:11) or "go out from Babylon" (48:20), which implies that the author was not "there in Babylon."[1] Although one might hypothesize that the change from exile in chaps. 40–48 to Jerusalem in 49–66 might account for the differences between chaps. 40–48 and 49–55, some commentators like C. Seitz suggest that Judah was the most likely provenance of the writer in all of chaps. 40–55, while M. Goulder believes the exilic references refer to what "Deutero-Isaiah of Jerusalem" said to people of Jerusalem.[2] These studies indicate that the evidence

---

[1] M. Haran, "The Literary Structure and Chronological Framework of the Prophecies in Is 40–48," *Congress Volume Bonn 1962*, VTSup (Leiden: Brill, 1963), 150–55.

[2] M. Goulder, "Deutero-Isaiah of Jerusalem," *JSOT* 28 (2004): 351–62, takes Zion and Jerusalem to refer to places in Israel rather than pointing to the exiles in Babylon.

for the location and date of the prophet is open to widely different interpretations, so it is difficult to attribute all these discontinuities in chaps. 40–55 to the audience being in a different location.[3]

Before one can propose an explanation for these differences, the first thing that has to be done is to identify what the common denominators are within each group of messages. Then one can compare these characteristics to the common factors in another group of chapters and identify the similarities and differences. The new messages that were collected together in chaps. 49–55 are set apart from chaps. 40–48 because of new theological emphases and because of the absence of previous topics. For example, the oracles in chaps. 49–55 are not about (a) the coming of a great conqueror of the nations, (b) the defeat of the Daughter of Babylon and her gods, (c) the uselessness of constructing and worshipping idols made of wood, (d) themes like the former things and the later things, or (e) descriptions of God as the first and the last; and (f) these messages are no longer addressed to the blind and sinful servant Jacob.[4] These were very important issues that were central to the message in 40–48, but chaps. 49–55 focus much more attention on the character, role, and difficult ministry of the Servant of the Lord (49:1–13; 50:4–11) and include a long discussion of the suffering and victory of this individual in 52:13–53:12. Alternating after each of these three Servant poems are proclamations of salvation that give new hope to the Daughter of Zion/Jerusalem (49:14–50:3; 51:1–52:10; 54:1–17). This creates the following pattern:

Servant poem	49:1–13
Salvation for Zion	49:14–50:3
Servant poem	50:4–11
Salvation for Zion	51:1–52:12
Servant poem	52:13–53:12
Salvation for Zion	54:1–17
Conclusion	55:1–13

---

[3] S. I. Sherwin, "In Search of Trees: Isaiah XLIV 14 and its Implications," *VT* 53 (2003): 514–29, concludes that the trees in 44:14 were not native Babylonian trees and that Babylonian images were not made of this kind of wood. C. Seitz, "The Divine Council: Temporal Transition and New Prophecy in the Book of Isaiah," 230. J. Smart, *History and Theology in Second Isaiah: A Commentary of Isaiah 35, 40–66* (Philadelphia: Westminster, 1965), 20–23, also found nothing that demands that the prophet wrote in Babylon; instead, it appears that he may be counteracting idol worship in Judah and looking forward to an eschatological restoration of people from the four corners of the earth. H. M. Barstad, "On the So-Called Babylonian Literary Influence in Second Isaiah," *JSOT* 2 (1987): 90–110, and his *The Babylonian Captivity of the Book of Isaiah: "Exilic" Judah and the Provenance of Isaiah 40–55* (Oslo: Novus, 1997), 64–65, concludes that there was little Akkadian linguistic influence on Isaiah's writing, and he found little evidence to support a Babylonian background for chaps. 40–55.

[4] See C. Stuhlmueller, "Deutero-Isaiah: Major Transitions in the Prophet's Theology and in Contemporary Scholarship," *CBQ* 42 (1980): 1–29, and specifically his chart of differences between 40–48 and 49–55 on pp. 5–9. P. Wilcox and Paton-Williams, "The Servant Songs in Deutero-Isaiah," *JSOT* 42 (1988): 79–102, lists some of these same characteristics from chaps. 40–48 that distinguish 49–55.

This positive hope for Zion and Jerusalem seems to replace the earlier discussion of the sinful rebellion and blindness of Jacob in chaps. 40–48. This Daughter of Zion should not be hopeless, for she will no longer suffer ruin, oppression, and widowhood because God's anger against her is past, her enemies will be defeated, and Mother Zion will have many children (49:17–25; 54:1–17). But it is difficult to know what caused this change in emphasis. It is not clear if these new messages are related to historical factors or if this is just a new literary section that addresses new issues. It would not be odd to have the author gathering similar material together in one place in chaps. 40–48 (this is true of chaps. 13–23) and then gather together another group of similar messages in chaps. 49–55 (a literary phenomenon). The first group talks about God's earlier treatment of his blind servant who rebelled against him (chaps. 40–48), then the second group of chapters focuses on what God will do in the future to restore his righteous people (chaps. 49–55).

Although chaps. 49–55 are different from 40–48, there are many interlinking connections that demonstrate a good deal of continuity with chaps. 49–55. One example of these interconnections is that the Servant who brings justice to all the nations in 42:1–13 reappears again in 49:1–13 as one who speaks God's message. The poem about the Servant in 49:1–13 is verbally interlinked with 42:1–13 at several points; thus, the author is telegraphing to the reader that both poems are about the same person.[5] In both texts: (a) the metaphor of a "servant" (*'ebed* in 42:1; 49:3,5,6,7) is used; (b) the Servant is a light to the nations (42:6; 49:6); (c) he is a covenant for the people (42:6; 49:8); (d) he will be involved with freeing captives (42:7; 49:9); (e) God will be glorified through his work (42:8; 49:3); and (f) each poem concludes with a hymn (42:10–13; 49:13).

But the two Servant poems are not exactly the same. In 42:1–13 God speaks about the Servant, while in 49:1–6 the Servant reports about his own life. The first poem focuses on the royal task of bringing justice to the nations, but the second poem spends more time on the human opposition to his work. The first poem involves more kingly roles while the second poem focuses more on the word from his mouth (possibly a prophetic role or the kingly role of giving a royal decree). None of this new information militates against identifying the Servant as the same figure, though the images of laboring in vain (49:4) and being abhorred by the nations (49:7) are not usually part of what one commonly

---

[5] In spite of these common characteristics Watts, *Isaiah 34–66*, WBC (Waco: Word, 1987), 119, identifies the Persian king Cyrus as the servant in 42:1–6, but Zerubbabel is the servant in 49:5–12 (p. 186). These identifications of the servant are not very likely. J. Goldingay, *The Message of Isaiah 40–55: A Literary-Theological Commentary* (London: T&T Clark, 2005), 152, says of 42:1–6 that "the servant is an antitype of Cyrus," and in 49:1–13 he believes the servant is the prophet (p. 367). H. G. M. Williamson, *Variations on a Theme: King, Messiah and Servant in the Book of Isaiah* (Carlisle: Paternoster, 1998), 149–51, believes that the role of servant is transferred to a new person who is designated as servant in 49:3.

attributes to a king who brings justice. Isaiah 42:2–4 has already introduced the reader to several unusual aspects of the Servant's ministry, including the idea that he will not falter in the face of opposition.[6] It is important to note that in both poems he will overcome and be victorious in spite of troubles.

Neither Servant oracle should be extracted from its literary setting and examined without paying attention to its continuity with other messages in its present literary context. Both poems are related to the surrounding context and communicate a message of hope to those who were concerned about how God would accomplish his plan of salvation for his people. The literary context of 49:1–13 derives from the last paragraph of chap. 48. The use of the first person statement in 48:16b, "the Sovereign LORD has sent me with his Spirit," can probably be identified as the words of the Servant in 49:1–13. If that is so, the notice that the people did not paying attention in 48:18 may partially explain the difficulty the Servant faced in accomplishing his task in 49:4. The assurances that the promises will be fulfilled in 49:7–12 will reverse what did not happen in 48:19. Since Babylon and its gods will one day be shamed as powerless (chaps. 46–47), they can offer no lasting hope to the people in this world. Since Israel is still stubborn and rebellious (48:4–8), the only hope for Israel and the nations is to look for God to establish his kingdom through the faithful Servant who will bring forth justice to all the earth (42:1–13). Many other interlinking connections that demonstrate some level of continuity will be examined in the coming chapters. The exegetical investigation of these themes in 49–55 will provide numerous hints about the level of continuity and discontinuity within these new messages.

INTRODUCTION.   The next series of chapters is introduced by another poem about the Servant mentioned in 42:1–13. News of his service is to be proclaimed to all the nations (49:1), and his role is not only to restore Jacob (49:5) but also to be a light to the nations so that God's salvation can extend to the ends of the earth (49:6). Although 42:4 hinted of some difficulty in completing the duties assigned to the Servant, here in 49:4 and 49:7 one learns that all his hard labor seems to be in vain and that some people despised and abhorred the Servant. Nevertheless, the Servant knew that God would give him his just reward (49:4) and that in the end those who abhorred him would change their minds and honor him by bowing down before him (49:7). This Servant will be glorified (49:5), and God will help him in his time of distress (49:8). Somehow this Servant will enable those in darkness to see the light that God provides (49:9), and then God will provide for all their needs (49:10). This is part of the great comfort that God will provide for his people.

GENRE AND STRUCTURE.   The form-critical evaluation of R. Melugin identifies 49:1–6 as a commissioning report that "used elements from a thanksgiving psalm" (49:5–6). He argues that 49:7 is an announcement of salvation,

---

[6] Consult the discussion of 42:2–4 for a fuller examination of these points.

that 49:8–12 is a freely formed prophetic speech imitating a salvation-assurance oracle, and that 49:13 is a hymn.[7] This analysis of 49:1–6 is not completely satisfactory,[8] for the first part of the poem contains an autobiographical report of the Servant's self-understanding and his memory of God's past commissioning (so this is not a new commissioning). There also seems to be a minimal connection to a thanksgiving psalm (the word "thanksgiving" is not used). The second paragraph (49:7–12) does contain some words that God speaks to assure the audience that in spite of many difficulties the Servant will accomplish his task of bringing salvation to Israel and the nations.[9] The final hymn (49:13) contains the call to praise God as well as the reason why one should do so. The structure of this Servant poem can be divided into three main paragraphs:

The Servant's preparation and responsibilities	49:1–6
The opposition to, the role, and results of the Servant	49:7–12
Hymn of praise	49:13

The information in this Servant poem does not suggest a date for its composition. The captives in 49:9 are not people in Babylonian exile, and the highway in 49:11 is not the road the exiles will take to get back to the land of Judah. This passage refers to an eschatological "day of salvation" (49:8) where people from many nations in the north, south, and west will come to God (49:12). As a consequence these people will have spiritual darkness removed from their eyes.

(1) The Servant's Preparation and Responsibilities (49:1–6)

[1]Listen to me, you islands;
  hear this, you distant nations:
 Before I was born the LORD called me;
  from my birth he has made mention of my name.
[2]He made my mouth like a sharpened sword,
  in the shadow of his hand he hid me;
 he made me into a polished arrow
  and concealed me in his quiver.
[3]He said to me, "You are my servant,
  Israel, in whom I will display my splendor."

---

[7] R. Melugin, *The Formation of Isaiah 40–55*, BZAW (Berlin: de Gruyter, 1976),69–70, 142–44, admits that vv. 1–7 are a creation of the prophet, plus vv. 8–12 are a "freely formed prophetic speech" indicating that he is not strictly following traditional forms.

[8] Many interpreters limit the servant poem to 49:1–6. J. W. Adams, *The Performative Nature and Function of Isaiah 40–55,* Library of Hebrew Bible/Old Testament Studies, 448 (London: T&T Clark, 2006), 142–45, limits the servant material in this way, though he admits that there is a similarity between 42:1–9 and 49:1–13

[9] There is no need to hypothesize that 49:1–6 and 49:7–13 are two totally separate poems that did not originally go together, as proposed by C. Giblin, "A Note on the Composition of Is 49,1–6 [9a]," *CBQ* 21 (1959): 210–12.

⁴But I said, "I have labored to no purpose;
    I have spent my strength in vain and for nothing.
Yet what is due me is in the LORD's hand,
    and my reward is with my God."

⁵And now the LORD says—
    he who formed me in the womb to be his servant
to bring Jacob back to him
    and gather Israel to himself,
for I am honored in the eyes of the LORD
    and my God has been my strength—
⁶he says:
"It is too small a thing for you to be my servant
    to restore the tribes of Jacob
    and bring back those of Israel I have kept.
I will also make you a light for the Gentiles,
    that you may bring my salvation to the ends of the earth."

The first paragraph recounts past events in a first person report by the Servant (49:1–2), including a quotation of what God said (49:3). Although these autobiographical comments seem to address the distant nations because the Servant's responsibilities will include his ministry to them (49:1a), in fact it is the Israelites in his audience who will actually hear what the prophet is saying.[10] In the midst of the Servant speech (49:4) is a quotation of what God said to the Servant (49:5–6). Verse 4 indicates that there was some negative reaction to his ministry, but God reaffirms his plan (49:6 is similar to 42:6) to have the Servant's role include both the restoration of Israel as well as a ministry to all the nations on earth. The flow of the presentation is observable in the repeated "I said/the LORD said" clauses that introduce each new part of the paragraph. This material falls into three subsections.[11]

Servant's relationship to God	49:1–2
God commissioned the Servant	49:3
Servant trusts God in spite of struggles	49:4
God's two-part commission for the Servant	49:5–6

49:1   The preceding chapters have just indicated that Babylon was not the answer to this world's problems (46–47; 48:20). Israel also failed to listen to God and receive his blessings (48:17–18), so what hope do God's people and the nations have? Their only hope is that God would graciously redeem Jacob

---

[10] This is somewhat similar to the situation in the oracles against the foreign nations in chaps. 13–23. Isaiah was talking about the foreign nations, but he was actually speaking to people in Judah.

[11] J. Goldingay and D. Payne, *Isaiah 40–55.* I. II. (ICC. London: T&T Clark, 2006), outlines the material into vv. 1–2 testimony, v. 3 Yhwh's word to the speaker, v. 4 testimony, and vv. 5–6 Yhwh's word to the speaker.

(48:20b) and that the nations would turn to God and be saved (45:22). But how will God accomplish this?

This paragraph begins with an imperative exhortation[12] by the Servant (rather than God) to the far-off nations, encouraging them to "listen" (*šimě'u*) to his own personal testimony about himself. This exhortation is somewhat parallel to God's earlier calls for the nations and Israel to listen to what God was saying (41:1; 44:1; 48:1,12,14,16). In this case the Servant does not challenge or condemn the nations; he simply tells the story of what God plans to accomplish through his life. For now, the distant small islands of the Mediterranean Sea (the "islands," *'iyyîm*) and all other faraway nations should "pay attention" (*wěhaqšîbû*, is another imperative) to the Servant so that they can understand God's plans for the world.

Having called the nations to attention, the Servant explains God's plans for his life (49:1b). The testimony of the Servant is that God's commissioning was authentic and was designed in detail before he was born. God took action and "called me" (*qěrā'ānî*) from the womb, and he "remembered/assigned my name" (*hizkîr šěmî*; lit "he cause my name to be remember"). These notions assure the listeners that this Servant was not a fraud and that he did not push himself forward to make his name great. The Servant was acting on God's behalf and under God's direction and authority. This Servant appears to be an individual[13] like Jeremiah (not the nation Israel), whose role was explicitly designed long ago (before his birth, as in Jer 1:5). This report of God's identification of the Servant and calling does not initially include any specification concerning the role or purpose of the Servant, though in later verses (49:5–6) God's purposes will become clear. The informed reader who can connect the dots back to the interlinking message in 42:1–13 already knows that the responsibilities of the Servant of the Lord involved the task of bringing justice to the nations. The Servant's role was to be a light to the people and a covenant to the nations (42:6–7; 49:6).

49:2   The preparation of the Servant for ministry to the nations involved God making the Servant's mouth a powerful instrument to declare God's messages. His mouth would be like a sharp sword. Sword imagery suggests the use of piercing-sharp speech, so it is possible for the Hebrew imagination to compare the sharp words that come from the lips (Ps 59:8 [Eng v. 7]; Prov 5:4), from the tongue (64:4 [Eng v. 3]), or from the teeth (Prov 30:14) to a cutting

---

[12] GKC §110a describes the use of the imperative in the sense of giving an admonition or exhortation.

[13] F. Delitzsch, "Prophecies of Isaiah," *Commentary on the Old Testament* (Grand Rapids: Eerdmans, 1969), 7:257, says, "What he affirms of himself is expressed in such terms of individuality, that they cannot be understood as employed in a collective sense, more especially when he speaks of his mother's womb." C. Westermann, *Isaiah 40–66*, OTL (Philadelphia: Westminster, 1977), 209, views this statement as an argument against the collective understanding of the servant.

sword. This indicates that the Servant will not accomplish the tasks described in this passage through military conquests (contrast 11:4)[14] but by speaking some strong words from God.[15] A second metaphor compares the Servant (probably also connected to his speech) to a pointed arrow[16] that can strike the enemy with a lethal blow from a distance. These images could be the offensive weapons of a kingly decree or a prophetic speech that can pierce the hearts of those who listen to God's words. These concepts broaden the audience's understanding of how the Servant's tools or abilities will enable him to establish justice (42:1–4). They suggest a somewhat aggressive role of confronting the thoughts and beliefs of his audience. Blenkinsopp interprets all these metaphors in terms from the political sphere of life, while J. Goldingay and D. Payne believe these metaphors were derived from a prophetic setting.[17]

The second and last lines of 49:2 mention God "hiding me" (*heḥbî'ānî*) in the shadow of his hand and in his quiver. This figure of speech might be comparable to being hidden under God's wings (Ps 17:8), an image of protection and care. No reason is given for this hiding, so it is unclear if this hiding involves protection from a powerful enemy or if God "hid him in secret until the time appointed for his service."[18] J. Oswalt suggests that these images imply that "the Servant is available for his master's use at any moment; the weapons are protected from the elements so that they can be most useful; they are out of sight until the right moment for them to be displayed."[19] On the other hand, part of this hiddenness may relate simply to the fact that the divine plan for the Servant was largely hidden until just the right time.

49:3 Now the Servant reassures his audience that God is the one who commissioned him to serve. He does this by quoting God's exact words, "you are my servant" (*'abdî 'āttâ*). This sounds like a choosing, an appointing, or a commissioning to a task on behalf of God. The remembrances of these words rang loud and clear in the Servant's ears, assuring him that whatever he did was God's work. These words reminded him that obedience to God's plan was his

---

[14] K. Baltzer, *Deutero-Isaiah* (Minneapolis: Fortress, 2001), 307, connects these images to the theme that "Yahweh is a Warrior" who destroys his enemies (Hab 3; Deut 32:39–43), but this does not appear to be the emphasis in this text.

[15] New Testament authors picked up similar images of the power of God's words to communicate a similar idea in Eph 6:17; Heb 4:12; Rev 1:16; 19:15.

[16] The word בָּרוּר is a passive participle that functions as an adjective (GKC §116e). Some have connected this root to בָּרַר "to purify, select" (BDB, 140) and view this pure arrow as one that is polished. J. L. Koole, *Isaiah III, Volume 2: Isaiah 49–55* (Leuven: Peeters, 1998), 9, suggests that it is more likely to hypothesize root II of ברר comparable to the Arabic *bārā*, which means "to sharpen."

[17] Goldingay and Payne, *Isaiah 40–55*, 2:157, find a great deal of attention to the mouth and speaking, while Blenkinsopp, *Isaiah 40–55*, AB (New York: Doubleday, 2000), 300, calls 49:1–6 a "political manifesto" with military imagery.

[18] Muilenburg, "Isaiah 40–66," *IB* 5:567.

[19] J. N. Oswalt, *Isaiah 40–66*, NICOT (Grand Rapids: Eerdmans, 1998), 290, indicates that this person "speaks of utility, preparedness, and effectiveness."

highest service. When hard times, opposition, or doubts arise, all those who truly serve God can gain great assurance and lasting hope by remembering when God originally called them to his service.

The last line indicates that God's purpose was in "glorying himself"[20] (NIV "display my splendor") through the Servant. This is consistent with God's earlier statement that his redemption of Jacob would display his glory in Israel (44:23). A major hermeneutical problem surrounds the interpretation of the word "Israel" in the second line, especially its relationship to the Servant. The word Israel has been dealt with in several ways: (a) C. Westermann and R. N. Whybray drop the word "Israel" from this verse because they believe it was added later by a redactor or scribe who was providing his interpretation of the Servant. None of the other Servant songs identifies this Servant by name so they believe that this poem should not identify the name of the Servant.[21] But a solution that alters the text should be a last resort and in most cases it should be followed only when there is good textual support or overwhelming logic in favor of a different reading.[22] (b) J. Muilenburg keeps the word "Israel" as an authentic part of the text and believes the Servant is the nation of Israel,[23] but if the Servant's role is to restore Israel (49:6) the Servant must be a righteous Israelite, for how is it possible for sinful Israel to restore sinful Israel? (c) Although P. Wilcox and D. Patton-Williams identify the servant in chap. 42 as Cyrus, in 49:3 and in the following servant poems they argue that the servant is the prophet himself. Since Israel failed to fulfill her role to bring salvation to the nation (chap. 40–48), now the prophet must do God's work and become the "true Israel."[24] The major problem with this approach is that there is no indica-

---

[20] The word אֶתְפָּאָר is a reflexive *hithpa'el* form "I will glorify myself." R. R. Ekblad, *Isaiah's Servant Poems According to the Septuagint: An Exegetical and Theological Study* (Leuven: Peeters, 1999), 85, indicates that the Old Greek translates this as a passive verb.

[21] Westermann, *Isaiah 40–66*, 209, lists four reasons for rejecting this as an authentic reading for this verse: (a) the word "Israel" is missing in one manuscript (but now it is known to be absent also from 4QIsd); (b) in this section of the book whenever there is a reference to Israel there is a reference to Jacob in the next line, and that does not happen here; (c) in the other servant songs the name of the servant is never given; and (d) the greatest problem is that v. 5 indicates that the servant's role is to bring back the people of Israel. In addition, the metaphors (coming from the womb of his mother) fit an individual, not the nation of Israel. Whybray, *Isaiah 40–66*, NCB (London: Marshall, Morgan, and Scott, 1975), 135–38, mentions some of the same reasons and considers the prophet Deutero-Isaiah as the servant.

[22] A. Gelston, "Isaiah 52:13–52:12: An Eclectic Text and a Supplemental Note on the Hebrew Manuscript Kennicott 96," *JSS* 35 (1990): 187–211, examined the Kennicott 96 manuscript and found numerous scribal errors; therefore, he gives little weight to the omission of "Israel" after the word servant.

[23] Muilenburg, "Isaiah 40–66," 5:565, says, "No solution can be more than tentative. The view here taken is that the identification with Israel raises the fewest obstacles." Williamson, *Variations on a Theme: King, Messiah and Servant in the Book of Isaiah* (Carlisle: Paternoster, 1998), 150–52, views the servant as an individual or a group within Israel, distinct from Israel/Jacob who is the blind servant.

[24] Wilcox and Paton-Williams, "The Servant Songs in Deutero-Isaiah," 79–102, keep the word

tion elsewhere that the prophet Isaiah ever functioned as a light or covenant to the nations (49:6), he did not bring justice to the nations (42:1–4), and his death did not bring atonement for the sins of all mankind (53:1–12). (d) G. P. Hugenberger concludes that the Servant is "a second Moses figure,"[25] while (f) the kingly role of establishing justice in 42:1–13 argues for a messianic interpretation of the Servant. The identification of the Servant's role as being a light to the nations (49:6)[26] connects this Servant to the messianic Servant in 42:6. This imagery also interrelates this Servant with God's great work through the Messiah figure described as a great light in 9:2. In 60:1–3 the salvation of mankind is related to the appearance of a great light that comes from the Divine Light, God himself.[27]

A major question regarding the interpretation of 49:3 arises concerning the syntactical relationship between the first and second line; specifically, the relationship of the word "servant" at the end of the first line to the word "Israel" at the beginning of the second line. One could hypothetically understand the two lines to flow together (ignoring the significance of the Hebrew *athnach* which marks a pause in the verse), with the word Israel standing in apposition to servant ("my servant Israel"), or it could function as a predicate ("you are Israel my servant").[28] Thus God will glorify himself through the servant nation Israel. In this approach Israel should have functioned as the servant but failed (48:19). The nation Israel should have become the ideal Israel who restores both unrepentant Israel and the nations, but it never happened that way. Another and better way of interpreting the syntactical relationships between the first and second line is to accept the full value of the pause in the verse (the Hebrew *athnach*), which comes after the word Servant (not after Israel). If this break is observed, one should then disconnect the word Israel from the

---

"Israel" but interpret it as the prophet because of a heightened individualism that begins with 49:1–6. Goldingay, *Message of Isaiah 40–66*, 151, proposes that Cyrus is the servant in chap. 42, but later (p. 367) in chap. 49 he identifies the servant as the prophet. Seitz, "Isaiah 40–66," 6:429, views the servant as Deutero-Isaiah and 49:3 as "a recommissioning in the light of developing circumstances" (the failure of Israel to fulfill its role).

[25] G. P. Hugenberger, "The Servant of the Lord in the 'Servant Songs' of Isaiah: A Second Moses Figure," in *The Lord's Anointed: Interpretation of Old Testament Messianic Texts*, ed. P. E. Satterthwaite, R. S. Hess, G. J. Wenham (Grand Rapids: Baker, 1995), 105–39, interprets Isaiah to have second exodus imagery, Cyrus to be the second Pharaoh, and the servant to be a second Moses. Baltzer, *Deutero-Isaiah*, 125, 306, 394, identifies Moses as the servant.

[26] Hanson, *Isaiah 40–66*, 46–47, identifies Israel as the light, but in light of the blindness of Israel, it seems impossible to suggest that Israel is the servant who will be a light to the rest of the world.

[27] R. Clements, "A Light to the Nations," in *Forming Prophetic Literature: Essays on Isaiah and the Twelve in Honor of John D. W. Watts*, ed. J. W. Watts and P. R. House (Sheffield: Sheffield Academic Press, 1996), 23–36, explores the connection between 42:6 and 49:6.

[28] Wilcox and Paton-Williams, "The Servant Songs in Deutero-Isaiah," 93, translate the verse, "You are my servant Israel, in whom I shall be glorified," an approach that completely ignores the Hebrew pause (the *athnach* marker) after the word servant ("Israel" should go with the second half of the verse).

clause that precedes ("you are my Servant") and connect it instead with what follows, giving an independent clause translated, "Israel in you I will glorify myself" (following the syntactical structure of Hos 14:4).[29] In this approach Israel would not be identified as the Servant or as the predicate of "you," but would refer to the place (the land of Israel) or the people (the people of Israel) where God will glorify himself through the work of his Servant, somewhat similar to 43:7. Both of these options could make sense and both could explain the meaning, though the second appears superior because it is more in keeping with what the prophet has already said in 44:23b and it takes seriously the punctuation within the verse.

49:4 In light of God's preparation, protection, and empowerment of the Servant, one would expect that there would now be a bright report of what was successfully accomplished by the Servant. Yet 42:4a hints instead at the difficulty of accomplishing the Servant's mission. Now the Servant reports his thinking[30] that he may have failed to accomplish his mission. His testimony is that "I exerted energy, became weary" (*yāga'tî*) and came up "empty" (*rîq*); "I completed, consumed" (*killēytî*) my strength and the results were "nothing, worthless" (*hebel*). These terms reflect his initial failure to accomplish his God assigned role, but there is no indication that this impacted his psychological state of mind. Thus these words do not express a sense of discouragement or frustration,[31] just an honest evaluation of the audience's unwillingness to listen to what the Servant had to say (cf. 6:9–11). It is also improper to read the first half of the verse without taking into consideration how this negative response was related by the Servant's strong confidence in 4b. But the later positive outcome should not erase or diminish the difficulty of having few people listen or follow him. The Servant confidently knew that God would help the Servant accomplish what he was asked to do; therefore, he would properly reward him. "Nevertheless, but" (*'āken*) is a strong disjunctive particle[32] that puts the first half of the verse in perspective. The Servant is assured that "my justice" (NIV "what is due me") is with God; "my work, action, reward for action" (*pĕ'ulātî*) is with God. This knowledge is not a fatalistic rationalization or a defense

---

[29] One might compare the syntax of Hos 14:4 where a similar final relative clause יָתוֹם יְרֻחָם אֲשֶׁר־בְּךָ is separated from what precedes by a semicolon or period (it comes after the *athnach*) and is translated (14:3 in English) "for in you the fatherless finds compassion" (in NASB it follows a semicolon), "for the fatherless receive compassion in you" (in HCSB it follows a period), and "in thee the orphan finds mercy" (in RSV it comes after a period). There is no textual reason to begin the NASB or NIV with the word "for." The "in you" (אֲשֶׁר־בְּךָ) in 49:3 is typically translated "in whom," which is connected to the servant, ignoring the "you." The "you" refers to Israel, not to the Servant.

[30] The verb אָמַרְתִּי "I said" can also mean "I thought" (Gen 20:11; 26:9; Num 24:11; Ruth 4:4). Sometimes to make this thought process crystal clear the author will write, "I thought in my heart" (Deut 8:17; 1 Kgs 12:26; Isa 14:13; 47:8,10; 49: 21).

[31] Blenkinsopp, *Isaiah 40–55*, 301, views this as an expression of his discouragement.

[32] F. J. Goldbaum, "Two Hebrew Quasi-Adverbs: לְכֵן and אָכֵן," *JNES* 23 (1964): 132–35, describes these particles as having an emphatic contrastive function.

mechanism that excuses the Servant's failures; it is an expression of confident trust that God will righteously analyze the activity of the servant and will take care of the final outcome in his own time and in his own way.[33]

49:5 Now the Servant reminds himself who God is and what God has promised to do for the Servant. God's promises and instructions are explained in 49:6, so v. 5 is a parenthetical introduction of the God who speaks these words—notice the "he says" in 49:6 after this introductory parenthetical introduction. "And now" (wĕ'attâ, 49:5) introduces this segment and points to something new, just as it introduces a change in the situation in other subparagraphs (43:1,19; 44:1; 47:8; 48:7,16b). The servant reminds everyone that it was God, Yahweh, who speaks, and he has authority over what the Servant does. God is not just a lifeless wooden idol formed by some craftsman; he is not just the one who called the Servant before he was born (49:1). God is the one who created the servant in the womb of his mother so that he could fulfill God's purpose of functioning as God's Servant. The Servant[34] was commissioned with the purpose "to bring back, return,"[35] the people of Israel "to him" (to God).[36] This indicates that the goal of the Servant's work is to cause the people of Israel to return spiritually or turn back to God. The nation's central problem that God was attempting to solve through the Servant was the people's personal relationship to God.

In the last part of 49:5 the Servant expresses his confidence in God. He realizes that any human evaluation of past failures or successes is not really that important. All that matters is that the Servant will eventually be honored in the eyes of God because of what he accomplishes for God. As he attempts to fulfill the purpose God gave to him in the midst of a good deal of fruitless toil (49:4), he can have confidence because God is "my strength" ('uzzî).

---

[33] Oswalt, *Isaiah 40–66*, 292, says, "Trust has ultimately to do with the final outcome, and of this the Servant is fully confident. . . . God, not the world, not even the Servant will make the final decision concerning the *work* [pĕ'ullâ, "'recompense for work'"; cf. 40:10]."

[34] Muilenburg, "Isaiah 40–66," 5:569, makes God, not the servant, the subject of this action. This alleviates the major problem for him of having the servant (the nation Israel) on a mission to Israel. Instead he has God on a mission to bring back Israel. This interpretation should be rejected.

[35] The *polel* infinitive construct לְשׁוֹבֵב comes from the verb שׁוּב "to return" and indicates God's goal or purpose (GKC §114f) for the servant. Blenkinsopp, *Isaiah 40–55*, 301, maintains that this bringing back of Israel includes "the idea of reintegration and return to the land (Jer 50:19; Ezek 39:27), physical restoration (Isa 58:12; Pss 23:3; 60:3), and moral regeneration."

[36] The MT has לֹא "no, not" but this does not make sense ("Israel will not be gathered"), so the *Qere* reading, 4QIsd, and the Old Greek read לוֹ "to him," which makes perfect sense and matches the previous parallel line. Baltzer, *Deutero-Isaiah*, 308–309, hypothesizes that if one keeps the "not" in the Masoretic text, this could mean that Israel will not be gathered into the underworld; thus she will not die, but in the end he accepts the reading of the *Qere*. Whybray, *Isaiah 40–66*, 139, accepts the meaning "sweep away" instead of "gather" for יֵאָסֵף but "return" and "gather" make a good synonymous parallel pair for these two lines. F. D. Lindsey, "Isaiah's Songs of the Servant, Part 2: The Commission of the Servant in Isaiah 49:1–13," *BSac* 139 (1982): 129–45, believes this is a spiritual return.

Remembering these comforting thoughts and being assured of God's desire to honor and strengthen him, the Servant is ready to face the challenge that God has assigned him.

49:6 Now God's spoken message to the Servant is revealed (the "LORD said" at the beginning of the parenthesis in 5a is now connected to the "he said" in 6a). Since it was God's desire to lift up and honor the Servant, God needed to give him an important responsibility. God indicates that the Servant's work would not receive great worldwide honor if he just took on the "smaller, lighter, easier"[37] task of restoring the tribes of Israel (a small percentage of the people on the earth). Therefore, God also gave him the task of reaching out to transform all the nations of the earth.[38] This should not be understood chronologically to suggest that the Servant got a revised job description at some point along the way, long after he received his first assignment. God's original plan always was to use the seed of Abram to bring his blessings on all the nations of the earth (Gen 12:3), and the earlier Servant poem already listed being a covenant to the nations as part of the Servant's purpose (42:6). Isaiah 2:1–5; 14:1–3; 19:18–25; and 45:18–25 already have confirmed that God desired to include the nations as eventual members of his kingdom, so this is not an adjustment in God's playbook to correct a defect in his strategic plan. God's desire was to greatly honor the Servant, so he gave him the tremendous responsibility of bringing God's salvation to the ends of the earth.

The two tasks that make up the mission of the Servant are introduced by infinitives that define the purposes[39] of his life. In the first role God appointed him "in order to raise up, establish" (*lĕhāqîm*) and "in order to restore, reestablish" (*lĕhāšîb*) Israel. No parameters are put on this restoration, so one might assume that the total restoration would include both spiritual and physical aspects. The means of accomplishing the second task in 6b was for the Servant to function as a light to the nations (49:6). The figure of light is connected in other passages where God is the light (Ps 27:1), God's law is a light that guides people (2:4–5; 42:16; 50:10; 51:4–5; Ps 119:105), and God's righteous salvation is a light (49:6; Ps 37:6; Mic 7:9). There is not much of an explanation of what the Servant would do so that he would serve as this light.[40] It is hypothetically possible to translate

---

[37] The word נָקֵל is a *niphal* perfect verb "to be small, easy, light" that is translated as a comparative because of the comparative use of the מִן (GKC §133a-c) that is prefixed to the next word מִהְיוֹתְךָ which is a *qal* infinitive construct with the second person suffix functioning as the subject of the verb. This gives the translation "than for you to be" (GKC §114e). Goldingay, *Message of Isaiah 40–55*, 372, translates the מִן with the causative sense of "because" but the comparative interpretation fits well here.

[38] Today one would not say it is dishonorable to have one person convert, but there is greater honor in having ten. So one should not imply that it was not an honor to bring back the tribes of Jacob. But it was a greater honor to bring God's salvation to the whole world.

[39] GKC §114f deals with the use of the infinitive construct to express purpose.

[40] E. Martens, "Impulses to Missions in Isaiah: An Intertextual Exploration," *BBR* 17 (2007): 215–39, follows Baltzer's interpretation that the role of the Servant is to be understood as an objec-

the last line in two distinct ways. If "my salvation" functions as the subject of the infinitive construct verb, the phrase would be describing the consequences of the Servant's light on the world ("so that my salvation may exist to the ends of the earth" NASB, NRSV, ESV). This translation affirms that the Servant's role as a light will allow God's salvation to have a worldwide influence. On the other hand, it is grammatically possible and actually preferable to view "my salvation" as the object of the infinitive, thus creating a translation parallel to what is found in the previous line. This approach would make the Servant be "a light to the nations and to be my salvation unto the ends of the earth." This translation indicates that the Servant is not just a means of getting God's salvation to the ends of the earth (45:20–24); somehow he himself will be God's salvation. Just how the Servant "will be" (not "bring" as in NIV) God's salvation will be explained in later oracles about the Servant (52:13–53:12).

(2) The Despised Servant's Role and Results (49:7–12)

⁷This is what the LORD says—

>the Redeemer and Holy One of Israel—
>to him who was despised and abhorred by the nation,
>>to the servant of rulers:
>"Kings will see you and rise up,
>>princes will see and bow down,
>because of the LORD, who is faithful,
>>the Holy One of Israel, who has chosen you."

⁸This is what the LORD says:

>"In the time of my favor I will answer you,
>>and in the day of salvation I will help you;
>I will keep you and will make you
>>to be a covenant for the people,
>to restore the land
>>and to reassign its desolate inheritances,
>⁹to say to the captives, 'Come out,'
>>and to those in darkness, 'Be free!'
>
>"They will feed beside the roads
>>and find pasture on every barren hill.
>¹⁰They will neither hunger nor thirst,
>>nor will the desert heat or the sun beat upon them.
>He who has compassion on them will guide them
>>and lead them beside springs of water.
>¹¹I will turn all my mountains into roads,
>>and my highways will be raised up.

---

tive genitive and translated "in order to bring light to the nations" and also "the one who brings the covenant to the nations."

^{12}See, they will come from afar—
some from the north, some from the west,
some from the region of Aswan."

In the second paragraph God speaks to give further information on the trials and roles of the Servant (in 49:1–6 the Servant was speaking), similar to the fuller expansion of 42:1–4 in 42:5–9. This paragraph briefly touches on the initial rejection and later acceptance of the Servant. God restates his commitment to help the Servant fulfill his mission, and then this paragraph ends with an extended discussion of God's help in bringing about the restoration of people from all over the world. After hearing about God's plans for his Servant, Israel, and the nations, the prophet's audience should have understood what God wanted them to do (return to God and trust his Servant). Their faith in God was undoubtedly strengthened with this information, but there was no doubt some confusion about the significance of the rejection of the Servant. Yet in spite of this, the Servant will extend God's salvation to all the people on the earth. These promises about what God will accomplish in the future do not relate simply to the physical return of a few thousand Hebrew people from Babylonian exile; these eschatological promises focus on God's final spiritual restoration of many people from every corner of the globe. The material can be outlined in three parts.

Nations despise, but God honors his Servant	49:7
The Servant will be a light and covenant	49:8–9a
Captives will be free and cared for	49:9b–12

The introductory "this is what the LORD says" is a fitting introduction to the second paragraph, although it is a little odd to find this same introductory clause repeated again so quickly in 49:8. J. L. Koole suggests that since 49:7 reports the negative ("abhorring") and positive ("pay homage") opinions of others, it is appropriate to begin 49:8 with a new introductory "thus says the LORD" to distinguish what God says from what others say, but this approach is not convincing.[41] The next part of the message extends from 8–9a, with the break after 9a being signaled by grammatical and topical changes.[42] Isaiah 49:8–9a describes what the Servant will do in a series of infinitive construct purpose clauses. Isaiah 49:9b begins a series of descriptive clauses pertaining to what "they" will do (using imperfect verbs) and what God will do for "them" (the peoples of the earth).

---

[41] Koole, *Isaiah III, Volume 2: Isaiah 49–55*, 37, makes some sense, but this argument is weakened by the fact that God himself speaks all of v. 7. It might be better to suggest that the effect of this repetition is an additional emphasis. The statements in vv. 7 and 8–12 are so different that the prophet wants to assure the reader that both are absolutely true divine pronouncements.

[42] A. Schoors, *I Am God Your Savior: A Form-critical Study of Is. XL–LV*, VTSup 24, (Leiden: Brill, 1973), 99, argues against H. E. von Waldow's idea of dividing 7–12 into vv. 8–10 and 11–12. Goldingay, *Message of Isaiah 40–55*, 376, makes 8–9a a separate subsection of this paragraph.

o

It is not necessary to rearrange the verses,[43] and it is dangerous to identify the form-critical nature of a literary production based simply on the use of certain vocabulary. Words can function in many literary settings, so it would be improper to suggest that the use of "despised" and "abhorred" terminology communicates to the reader that 49:7 is from a lament.[44] The text indicates that it is God who is speaking about the Servant's difficult situation in 49:7a, so the Servant himself is not lamenting his own situation. In addition, it must be noted that although v. 49:7a speaks about the despising of the Servant, 49:7b indicates that kings will later honor and bow down before the Servant. This does not sound like a typical lament.

49:7   The prophet begins this part of his speech by reminding his audience (the Servant and the Israelites who will hear/read these words) that in spite of some of the difficult words he will announce in the coming sentences, the one who is speaking to them is God, Israel's "Redeemer" (*gōʾēl*). He is a member of the covenant family who takes his family responsibility seriously enough to deliver his helpless family members when they are in trouble. They need to know that all he does is determined by "his holiness" (*qĕdōšô*), including his judgment of sinful unholy people, his saving of repentant people from their sins, and his plan to bring people from all over the world into fellowship with himself.

Verse 42:4a already hinted at the difficulties the Servant would face when it states that a certain portion of his work would produce no positive results. Now God reveals a little bit more about the depth of the problem the Servant will face in order to assure the audience that eventually the Servant will be honored. Thus the news in 49:7b is a message of hope about the exaltation of the Servant. Although he will initially be the despised one, "the abhorred one,"[45] the servant of kings, some day in the future all those people who formerly despised him will bow down before him. No reason is given that would justify why the Servant would be despised or abhorred so strongly by the nations, plus the

---

[43] Many (for example Westermann, *Isaiah 40–66*, 213–14) want to rearrange 7b after v. 12 because 7b appears to be the final positive ending, or they want to rearrange the verses (Muilenburg, "Isaiah 40–66," 5:575 puts v. 12 after v. 18) to make things fit a Western sense of logic. Nevertheless, it is better for interpreters not to impose their sense of order on the ancient writers. North, *Second Isaiah*, 191, suggests that 7b and the introduction of God speaking in 8a should just be deleted.

[44] Goldingay, *Message of Isaiah 40–55*, 375, connects "despised" (Ps 22:6[7]), the idea of being loathed (Ps 88:8[9]), and other similar terms to laments, but there is no indication that the servant is lamenting his situation in this verse.

[45] The second form לִמְתָעֵב is a preposition plus a *piel* participle "to the one abhorred." One would expect both verbs to be identical, but the first form לִבְזֹה is vocalized like a *qal* infinitive construct "to despise," which is an active form in the Masoretic text. 1QIsᵃ has לבזוי which is a *qal* passive participle "to the one despised." GKC §83a-c indicates that some infinitives and participles function as abstract nouns, which might be a logical explanation of the infinitive construct form in this situation. In the end there is some technical confusion about the exact way to understand this Hebrew form, but there is no confusion about what the prophet is saying about the Servant.

nations that will despise and abhor him are not named. Some of the mystery about these issues will be partially addressed in more detail in the servant poem in 53:1–12. Those who react to the Servant with such strong emotional rejection as loathing are the Gentile nations,[46] so at first it appears that the Servant's attempt to be a light to the nations (49:6) has backfired. The third descriptor of the Servant is not a participle, so the grammatical parallelism is broken and the meaning is unclear. In some odd way the Servant will be considered a "servant of rulers," but it is not clear how he will serve them. It is obvious that he will not rule over them by force but will work on their behalf. Possibly this refers to his work to bring justice to the nations (42:1) and be a light that will release them from the bondage of darkness (42:6; 49:6).

Having addressed the Servant in these three rather negative ways, in 7b God delivers to the Servant a hopeful message. The kings and princes in 7b probably represent the nations who were served by the Servant and the nations they lead are probably the nations that abhorred the Servant in 7a. Instead of continuing to loathe this Servant, eventually they will look at him and stand up, often a sign of respect (Job 29:8), and then falling prostrate they will bow down before him to honor him. Why do the kings do this? It must be something "they will see" (*yirĕ'u*), but that life-transforming observation remains a tantalizing mystery. Possibly their eyes will be opened, and they will finally understand that the Servant is actually a light to the nations and one who gives them hope (49:6). Isaiah 52:13–15 will address this theme as well, but at this point all the Israelite audience could possibly understand was that the rulers of the nations would completely change their perception and their response to this Servant. Instead of abhorring him, they will gladly honor him. This reversal should give the Servant confidence to accept a short period of loathing, for God is a faithful Redeemer who will ensure that the Servant accomplishes the tasks that God has given him. The Hebrew audience would also be warned by this reversal of opinions by the nations; they should be careful not to reject the Servant like the nations did at first.

The last line in v. 7 provides a key insight concerning why this royal change of attitude will take place. The heavenly reason why these kings and princes will change their evaluation of the Servant was "on account of, for the sake of" (*lema'an*) the faithful and Holy One, the God of Israel who chose the Servant. God's promises of faithfulness to support the Servant and uphold him could not be broken, and a holy God could not lie. A God who chose this special Servant had no intention of letting his plans fail, for the Servant was destined to be a light to the nations. Thus the human reason for the kings' change of attitude is unknown and a secondary issue. God's faithfulness and his firm determination to spread salvation to the ends of the earth is the ultimate factor that this Servant and every servant of God can depend on.

---

[46] At times unbelieving Israel is also given this title (Ezek 2:2), but this probably refers to the nations in 49:1 and 49:6.

49:8–9a The initial resumptive announcement indicates that what follows is another word from God. Then God broadens the audience's understanding of his plans for the Servant. A rather imprecise temporal marker ("a time of favor"—not 'my favor' as in NIV)[47] is set when God will respond positively to the Servant. That will be the beginning of God's "day of salvation" ($y\bar{o}m$ $y\check{e}\check{s}\hat{u}\cdot\hat{a}$, probably an extended period, not necessarily 24 hours). The temporal marker does not focus on the shortness of time or an exact date, just the absolute assurance that God will act positively at some point to bring his salvation. This is God's salvation for his people through the life of the Servant. At that appointed time God "will answer"[48] and "will help" the Servant, making it possible for him to function successfully (not "for nothing" as in 49:4) in the roles God assigned him. God will guard the Servant through the dark days and then in the time of salvation God will make him to be a "covenant of the people" (*běrît 'am*), as in 42:6. C. Seitz explains this statement by saying "He is the concrete means by which God's relationship with Israel is embodied and manifest."[49] Although "people" (*'am*) frequently refers to God's covenant people, the context of 42:6 argues for a more universal covenant for all people, including Israel. This Servant poem addresses God's plan for both Israel and the nations in 49:6, so it would be improper to limit this restoring of the land and release of the captives to the return of a few thousand Hebrews to Jerusalem from Babylonian exile.[50] Isaiah 49:6–7 and 12 (plus the Servant in chap. 42) relate the Servant's work to the eschatological plans of God for Israel and all the nations.[51]

Three results (expressed with three infinitives in 49:9a)[52] will come from the work of the Servant. His goal is: (a) "to restore the land," (b) "to reassign its

---

[47] The phrase רָצוֹן בְּעֵת "in a time of favor" is used in Ps 69:14 [Eng 13] of a time when God's love is seen and God answers the psalmist's prayer for salvation. In Isa 58:5 the inappropriate fasts that the Israelites practice are not ones that will be "acceptable to the Lord," nor are they "a favorable day to the Lord" in which he will bless them. Isa 61:2 refers to the "favorable year of the Lord" as a time when the Anointed One of God will preach good news, proclaim freedom, and provide comfort to all who mourn.

[48] The prefect verb עֲנִיתִיךָ should be translated in the future tense as a prophetic perfect (GKC §106n). It was not totally an accident that 1QIs[a] has both of the verbs in this line in the imperfect form.

[49] C. Seitz, "Book of Isaiah 40–66," *NIB*, 6:430, compares and contrasts the servant with Moses who cut a covenant, but this verse says something different, that "the servant is a covenant." One might ask, did Moses cut a covenant, or was it God who cut the covenant? Is the similarity as strong as Seitz suggests?

[50] Schoors, *I Am God Your Savior*, 101–102, believes "the verb *nḥl* is extremely frequent in the Hexateuch, indicating the occupation of the land by the Israelites. The deliverance of captives undoubtedly means the end of the exile."

[51] Goldingay, *Message of Isaiah 40–55*, 377, maintains, "In the context of vv. 1–7 the worldwide significance of being a 'covenant for the people' is more explicit here than was the case in ch. 42. Jacob-Israel's deliverance, the restoration of light to its own life, is designed to reach the nations to the ends of the earth."

[52] *IBHS*, 607, refers to the infinitive construct used to express results (also GKC §114f).

desolate inheritance," and (c) "to say to the captives, 'Come out.'" R. N. Why-bray interprets these literally, believing that "Yahweh promises to repopulate and restore the land of Palestine which has been left desolate as a result of the Exile,"[53] but it is doubtful that these words should point to this specific histori-cal event. The first act refers "to raising up, establishing" (*lĕhēqîm*) what was destroyed in the land (or the earth), the second act causes people "to inherit" their desolate family property, and the third requires the Servant " to speak" hopeful news to those in darkness and prison. These are all signs of restoration and repopulation of the land, which is an ideal of all Israelites. E. J. Hamlin views this as a reuse of Joshua traditions, while J. Oswalt finds the language of the Jubilee being employed (61:1–2).[54] The inclusion of freeing the pris-oner and those in darkness recalls 42:7 where the blindness that was covering people's eyes will be removed in the eschatological era when God establishes his kingdom. Israel is repeatedly seen as sinful and blind (6:10; 29:18; 42:18; 43:8), and the idol worshippers among the nations need to have their eyes opened so that they will reject idolatry (44:18). In earlier interlinking messages Isaiah announced that God (35:5) or a righteous king (the Messiah) would ac-complish the task of removing the spiritual blindness from the eyes of people so that they could see (35:3). It is not insignificant that the Servant functions in this same role. One should not be quick to identify this Servant who "frees captives" with the Persian king Cyrus simply because he released the Israelites from the suffering of exile (42:22),[55] for there is no indication that the Israel-ites were ever in prison during the Babylonian exile. Jeremiah's letter to the exiles (29:1–20), as well as Ezekiel, Daniel, and Ezra do not portray the people in exile living in dungeons. In addition, these promises of freedom and open eyes do not apply just to Israel; they apply to all the nations (49:12), and many of them were not in exile. Therefore, the best approach is to interpret these phrases as metaphors of God's deliverance of all people from the prison of spiritual darkness and ignorance (9:2; 42:19–20; 43:8; 44:18–19) through the work of the Servant. God is committed to using the Servant to ensure that all mankind will receive God's covenant blessing.

---

[53] Whybray, *Isaiah 40–66*, 141, attributes this to the work of God rather than the servant. Baltzer, *Deutero-Isaiah*, 316, rejects the view that this refers to exiles because they were not in chains; instead, he connects these prophecies to Neh 5 where people who have lost their land were enslaved by debt and are now freed. J. D. W. Watts, *Isaiah 34–66*, WBC (Waco: Word, 1987), 188, relates these words to Darius's political and legal reforms. Both of these potential fulfillments look for specific events in Israel's history that might possibly be related to some of Isaiah's statements, but it seems better to take this as an eschatological prophecy.

[54] E. J. Hamlin, "The Joshua Tradition Reinterpreted," *SEAJT* 23 (1982): 103–108; Oswalt, *Isaiah 40–66*, 298.

[55] Watts, *Isaiah 34–66*, 119. Those who believe that Israel is the servant (Whybray, *Isaiah 40–66*) interpret this spiritually as releasing people from darkness or the liberation of people who were oppressed.

49:9b–12 The final portion of this section refers to what "they" will do, the ones the Servant will set free. Using the imagery of sheep being cared for by a shepherd (cf. 40:9–11), the Servant promises these people that they will have plenty to eat (9b). They need not worry about food or drink or surviving in the hot sun (10a); "surely, truly" (*kî*, omitted in NIV) they can be certain that "the one who is compassionate to them"[56] (*mĕraḥămām*), God himself, will lead his sheep to fresh water (10b). To make travel easier, "my highway" will be raised up, and a path will be made through the rugged mountains (11). This imagery pertains to sheep so the interpreter needs to be careful not to interpret all these things that God will do as literal changes in the climate or the geographic features of the land. Elsewhere God does mention the transformation of the land into a place like Eden (51:3), but this message primarily communicates the idea that God will compassionately take care of all his people's needs.

They will be able to observe people coming from all directions: from the north, from across the sea (from islands in the Mediterranean), and from the land of "Sinim." This final location is sometimes identified as "Aswan" in southern Egypt, the land of the south in the Targum, or the far-off land of China,[57] but it probably refers to the city of Syene, near the island of Elephantine and Aswan (probably the *sîn* in Ezek 29:10; 30:15), on the southern border of Egypt. Although some who returned from Babylonian exile may have thought that their movement back to the land was a partial fulfillment of this prophecy, this prophecy points to a much greater event in the future when many people from all corners of the earth will experience God's compassion, provisions, and guidance when he provides his salvation. Interestingly, the text never says where these people will come to (there is no reference to Jerusalem). The text is only clear about whom they will come to, and that is really what is most important.

(3) Hymn of Praise (49:13)

> [13]Shout for joy, O heavens;
>   rejoice, O earth;
>   burst into song, O mountains!
> For the LORD comforts his people
>   and will have compassion on his afflicted ones.

Like the conclusion to the first Servant poem in 42:10–13, this message ends with a hymn of praise to God, giving a series of imperative verbs that encourage people to shout for joy. Neither Zion nor Israel is named as the group

---

[56] G. Rendsburg, "Hebrew *rḥm* = 'rain' [Is. 49,10]," *VT* 33 (1983): 357–62, suggests that "the one who gives rain" would be more fitting in this context, but the use of the same root in 49:13 argues against this proposal.

[57] Delitzsch, "Prophecies of Isaiah," 266–67.

of people who will shout God's praise or "burst"[58] into song. The phrase "his people" (*'ammô*) would probably refer to Israelites or to all the people in the nations that will come from all the corners of the earth (49:12). Here again with grand imagination the prophet sees the whole creation rejoicing and singing (44:23; 55:12–13; 65:17) because of God's great salvation. The reason for this wonderful hymn of praise is that God has comforted "his afflicted ones" (*'ăniyyāw*) who struggled in darkness (49:9a). These are the needy people who lived in spiritual darkness. God will have compassion on them, and consequently he will restore them to a covenant relationship with himself through the work of the Servant.

THEOLOGICAL IMPLICATIONS. There are many biographical details in this passage that are common to most of God's servants. Every servant of God has a calling from God, and each one has a mouth that can speak God's powerful words that can cut through the clutter of daily life and pierce the conscience of sinful men. God always is glorified when his servants faithfully serve him. Like this Servant, many of God's servants throughout the past centuries have labored hard and accomplished very little, particularly those ministering in virgin fields where the gospel has never been preached. In the midst of those trials, all those servants had the option of trusting in God for their strength and resting in his final heavenly reward, instead of any visible reward on earth.

Most of God's servants confine their ministry of service to one country or a few churches, but the worldwide ministry of this Servant identifies him as a very special servant. Who among God's servants would dare to claim that God has called them "to restore the tribes of Jacob and bring back those of Israel," plus the responsibility of being "a light to the Gentiles" so that God's salvation would reach to the ends of the earth (49:6)? Which of God's servants could say that their lives have included both a time of being "abhorred by the nations" and a time when "the kings see you and rise up, princes will see and bow down" (49:7)? Although this Servant has a role of declaring words (possibly a prophetic word or a kingly decree), this appears to be the same royal messianic Servant that was described in 42:1–13. The salvation that he will bring will transform this world into a completely different place. Those who receive God's compassionate gift of salvation will be people from all over the world. All who enjoy God's salvation should rejoice and shout about what God did through his faithful Servant.

The New Testament saw Jesus as the fulfillment of this Servant prophecy. He exemplified a servant spirit throughout his life (Matt 20:28; Phil 2:7), and the new covenant was established through his blood (Luke 22:20). Jesus identified himself with the role of the one who would release those in prison and

---

[58] The Hebrew text implies a jussive form (יִפְצְחוּ) "let them break forth," but the *qere* (oral tradition) and 1QIs[a] have an imperative verb (פִּצְחוּ) " break forth," which is parallel to the other imperatives in the verse. Either reading makes sense as recognized by A. Rubinstein, "Kethib-Qere Problems in the Light of the Isaiah Scroll," *JSS* 4 (1959): 127–33.

open the eyes of the blind (Luke 4:18–19), ideas that are found in Isa 42:7; 49:9, and 61:1–2. Jesus spoke words of compassion as well as sharp words of criticism (Matt 23). Certain rulers abhorred him (John 11:53; 15:19), but others believed in him (John 12:42). He was seen as a light to the nations (Matt 4:16; Luke 2:32) and the light of the world (John 1:9; 8:12; 12:35–36). Although Jesus fits the roles and experiences of this Servant, it is clear that the complete and final fulfillment of Isaiah's prophecy in 49:1–13 awaits a future day when God will transform nature and the hearts of people from the four corners of the earth. In the meantime, all God's servants today need to follow the Servant exemplified in chap. 49:1–13 and proclaim the good news that God will bring salvation to all who will listen.

7. God Has Not Forsaken Zion (49:14–52:12)

Chapters 49–52 are organized with alternating messages about God's Servant and the restoration of Zion. The Servant who was a light to the nations in 42:1–13 and 49:1–13 is described in 50:4–11 as a disciple who listens to God, suffers, but faithfully maintains his trust in God because he will vindicate the Servant's work. Zion is pictured as a place where there will be many children (49:14–50:3; 51:1–52:12), for God has not forgotten or divorced his people but is promising to restore them. He will send forth his salvation to his people. These themes are developed over several chapters, thus emphasizing again and again the prophet's message of comfort and hope.

The structure of these messages can be outlined as follows.

Repopulation of Zion proves God has not forgotten them	49:14–50:3
Follow the example of God's Servant	50:4–11
Pursue righteousness and see God's arm of salvation	51:1–8
God's cup of wrath is ended, restoration is coming	51:9–52:12

These messages are held together by a number of common themes that will be explained at the beginning of each paragraph. These proclamation oracles describe what God will do in Zion/Jerusalem and how this will impact the salvation of all the nations of the earth (49:22–26; 51:4–6; 52:7–10).

SETTING. The date when the prophet gave these oracles is unstated, but there are a few hints about the historical setting of the audience. The prophet refers to the nation as "ruined and made desolate and your land made waste" (49:19). The prophet predicts that God will "contend with those who contend with you" (49:24) and "will look with compassion on all your ruins" (51:3). God's people should not "fear mortal men" (51:12) because of "the wrath of the oppressor who is bent on destruction" (51:13), for the "cowering prisoners will soon be set free" (51:14). God will remove the "cup of his wrath," which his people have tasted, and "put it in the hands of your tormentors" (51:17,23). Jerusalem will be free of the "chains on your neck" (52:2), and the ruins will burst forth with songs of joy (52:9) when the Lord bares his arm in the sight of the nations (52:10). It is evident that Jerusalem was attacked; some people were taken captive, and oppressors laid waste parts of the land. Some verses present this oppression in a way that suggests that the audience is presently in the midst of a war, while others refer to ruins created in the past. Commentators have pointed to four quite different interpretations of the settings based on this information.

1. J. D. W. Watts identifies a setting during the reign of Darius, the Persian king, from 522–518 BC, about 200 years after the time of the prophet Isaiah.[59] He believes the geographical setting for these chapters is Israel during the time when the first exiles returned from Babylonian captivity, so Ezra 1–5 provides the historical backdrop for these events. The complaint in 49:14 was because Sheshbazzar accomplished little because Judah's enemies (Edom in Obad 5 and the people of the land in Ezra 4:1–4) were devastating the land (49:17). He believes the setting of 50:4–51:8 is in Jerusalem where the teacher Zerubbabel suffered (50:4–9), then Darius gave the people in Jerusalem comforting words in 51:1–4. Isaiah 52:8–12 refers to a second group of exiles that was preparing to return from Babylon.[60]

Few have followed this interpretation because there is very little basis for placing these words in the time of Darius. How could Darius be the servant that would be God's light to the nations, and what evidence is found in Ezra that suggests that Zerubbabel suffered like the Servant in 50:4–11? Since relatively few exiles initially returned to Jerusalem, why would they complain that there was not enough room for them in Jerusalem (49:20)? Two of the most interesting aspects of this interpretation are that Watts (a) locates the people in Israel and places them (b) in a time of conflict with enemies who oppose God's people. He interprets the setting fairly well, but his identification of this setting with the time of Darius is unconvincing.

2. R. N. Whybray interprets the setting in light of statements made in Lamentations (not Ezra 1–5) and places these events many years earlier than Watts. He believes the references to Zion oscillate "between Zion as the Jewish captives in exile and Zion as the actual city of Jerusalem," thus 49:14–23 relates to people living in the actual city of Jerusalem.[61] In contrast, 50:4–9 refers to the arrest of the prophet "by Babylonian authorities,"[62] and 51:1–8 is addressed to faithful exiles in Babylon "who are suffering some kind of humiliation at

---

[59] Watts, *Isaiah 34–66*, 180–81, 186, identifies the servant in 49:5–12 as Darius.

[60] Ibid., 189, 216–17, says "This exhortation to *depart* must be addressed to Babylonian Jews preparing another expedition to Jerusalem like the earlier one in 48:20."

[61] Whybray, *Isaiah 40–66*, 143, connects these people to "the Jews living in the vicinity of Jerusalem during the exilic period recorded in Lamentations, especially Lam 5:20–22." Goldingay, *Message of Isaiah 40–55*, 385, connects Zion to the city itself in 49:14–21, not the inhabitants, but he also connects these complaints to Lam 5:20. Seitz, "Isaiah 40–66," 6:431, maintains that, "the larger Isaiah discourse is an address to the situation described in Lamentations."

[62] Whybray, *Isaiah 40–66*, 151, compares 50:4–9 to Jeremiah's confessions.

he hands of the Babylonians, or perhaps even at the hand of fellow-Jews."[63]
In 51:17–20 the prophet addresses the complaints of the Babylonian exiles,
but in 51:19–23 he offers comfort to the actual city of Jerusalem (Lam 2:19;
4:21–22).[64] The section ends with the prophet predicting the defeat of Babylon
and the return of Babylonian Jews to Jerusalem (52:7–10).

Some have followed a similar perspective based on the general historical
setting provided by Lamentations, though they may disagree with Whybray on
the geographical setting (Babylon or Jerusalem). A significant problem with
this analysis is that it has difficulty: (a) identifying "those who laid you waste
depart from you" in 49:17; (b) explaining why the few people who returned
to Jerusalem (Ezra 2:64–65) find the space in Jerusalem too small (49:19–20);
(c) pointing to an actual time when the Gentiles carried Jews back to Jerusalem
and bowed before them (49:22–23); (d) recognizing that some prophecies are
about eschatological events and not the return from exile (51:1–8); and (e) fitting the wrath of the oppressor into this approach (51:13–14).

3. K. Baltzer connects the setting of chaps. 49–55 with events in the time of
Nehemiah in Jerusalem; thus he maintains that the problems and the people are
not related to exilic conditions or events. The problem is institutionalized slavery in Jerusalem for debts similar to what is discussed in Neh 5:1–13.[65] Thus, it
is not surprising to find that he identifies the opponents who devastate the land
as Sanballat, Tobiah, the Arabs, Ammonites, and Ashdodites (Neh 4:1,7). The
"place" that is too small refers specifically to the sanctuary in Jerusalem, and
God's redemption is the liberation of the people from the slavery of debts. God
will legally contend (*rîb*, 49:25b) with those who oppress the poor (51:13b) in
order to ransom his people from debt slavery (51:11–12). He will remove the
chains of debt (52:2–3), and their day of release will be celebrated (52:7–10)
with much rejoicing.

Baltzer locates the setting in the city of Jerusalem, but his interpretation of
the problem as the legal woes of those in debt slavery minimizes the nature of
the problem to a narrow class of people who have financial problems. The imagery of oppression is military, and taking captives as booty (49:25) refers to a
more serious military problem, rather than a poor person's inability to pay off
a debt. He wisely does not interpret these difficulties as problems of the exile,
but his alternative approach is hardly convincing.

4. A fourth avenue of interpretation takes seriously the oppression and war
terminology that describes what the people in Jerusalem were facing at the
time the prophet spoke. Since the Israelites did not experience military conflict
while they were in exile in Babylon, this must refer to some war before they

[63] Ibid., 157.

[64] In contrast to this opinion, Goldingay, *Message of Isaiah 40–55*, 418, concludes, "Whereas
earlier poems were rhetorically located in Babylon, 51:1–52:12 are rhetorically located in Jerusalem."

[65] Baltzer, *Deutero-Isaiah*, 30–31, 315, 324, 333, 368, 418, 461.

went into exile or immediately after they returned to Jerusalem. This military imagery about what happened at Jerusalem describes, "those who laid you waste" (49:17), "you were ruined and made desolate" (49:19), "can plunder be taken from warriors" (49:24), "the wrath of your oppressors" (51:13), "ruin and destruction, famine and sword" (51:19), and "my people have been taken away for nothing" (52:5). These phrases do not describe debt slavery, and they do not compare to anything known about Israel's experience while living in exile or shortly after the exile. The two most likely wars that might be reflected in these words are the Babylonian conquest of Judah from 605–587 BC or the Assyrian conquest of Jerusalem in 701 BC. In both cases Judah was devastated, captives were taken, booty was collected, and ruin, desolation, and famine encompassed the land. It is also important to note that "those who laid you waste depart from you" (49:17). The text indicates that "those who devoured you will be far off" (49:19). This does not describe the situation after the Babylonian conquest of the land, for the Babylonians were all around the exiles that lived in Babylon. An Assyrian setting matches this last point, for after God destroyed the 185,000 Assyrian troops, the rest of the Assyrian army did depart from Jerusalem. This fourth approach presents a stronger possibility for understanding the conflict that is represented in the setting of these chapters, though the setting of the audience is downplayed in some of these messages.

When using any one of the above approaches, the interpreter must distinguish between prophecies that deal with present issues (salvation oracles, disputations, and trial speeches) and prophecies where present problems will be resolved only in some future eschatological era (the proclamation of salvation). This last group of oracles may refer to or be set in a context of present-day problems (the context of the proclamation of salvation in 41:14–17 is probably set in context of 41:8–13), but the proclamation of salvation focuses on what God will do for his people in the distant future when he establishes his kingdom for his people and welcomes people from all the nations of the world to join them. The fulfillment of these prophecies does not fit any of the temporal periods identified above. This means that the historical setting of the present audience cannot be developed from what these speeches say about the future fulfillment of these prophecies.

(1) Repopulation of Zion Will Prove God Has Not Forgotten (49:14–50:3)

After hearing the great news about the Servant's task to restore God's people and be a light to the nations (49:6,8), one would expect a joyful response (49:13) because God's work will eventually lead to the establishment of his kingdom on earth. In light of this great hope, Zion's initial response in 49:14 seems somewhat incongruent, but it does express something about the difficult reality that the people were facing at the present time. They were not doing well, but this is exactly where the Servant found himself—"despised and abhorred" (49:7). Just as there was hope for the Servant because God would give him success in the end, so God's day of salvation awaits his people for God will have compassion on them (49:10,13,15). In continuity with 49:6–8, there will be a positive response by Gentiles and kings in 49:22–23, and both paragraphs mention the release of captives (49:9,24). Thus, both the negative and positive experiences of the Servant are interrelated to the experience of Israel in order to give the prophet's Israelite audience hope.

GENRE.   C. Westermann finds three proclamations of salvation in 49:14–26, each beginning with an issue that is disputed (49:14,21,26) and then a trial speech where there is a confrontation between God and Israel in 50:1–3.[66] A. Graffy divides the paragraphs differently and calls 49:14–26 a disputation with three answers (49:14–21,22–23,24–26),[67] R. Melugin creatively coins a new category, "the disputational pronouncements of salvation" to describe both aspects of these oracles.[68] But this approach seems to give too much attention to the questions raised. In reality, there is not much of a disputational quality to 22–23; there is no argument between different people in 24–26; plus in 50:1–2 God himself is the one asking the questions, not the Israelites.[69] Thus the main force of this message is to proclaim salvation in order to provide assurance and hope.

Earlier proclamations of salvation (41:17–20; 42:14–17; 43:16–21; 45:14–17,22–25) frequently contain eschatological information about God's ultimate salvation of his people and the nations in order to encourage people who were presently enduring some hardship. These future promises describe eschatological events and usually provide only a limited understanding of the audience's present situation.

It is significant that the Servant poem in 42:1–13 was followed by an eschatological proclamation of salvation in 42:14–17, and a similar pattern is followed here after the Servant poem in 49:1–13. This pattern of giving a proclamation of salvation after a Servant poem will be repeated again after the next two Servant poems in 50:4–11 and 52:13–53:12.

STRUCTURE.   This paragraph is marked by a change of the literary genre from a proclamation of salvation (49:14–50:3) to a servant oracle in 50:4–11,

---

[66] Westermann, *Isaiah 40–66*, 218–23, finds an assertion made by Israel in the form of a cultic lament in 49:14, but the main issues under discussion in the rest of the chapter do not appear to be issues usually put in a lament.

[67] A. Graffy, *A Prophet Confronts His People: The Disputation Speech in the Prophets*, AnBib 104 (Rome: Pontifical Biblical Institute, 1984), 91–98.

[68] Melugin, *Formation of Isaiah 40–55*, 148–51, does not believe this arises from a cultic lament and does not find three issues under dispute (vv. 22–23 merely offer more hope and are not an answer to another question in 21).

[69] B. S. Childs, *Isaiah*, OTL (Louisville: Westminster John Knox, 2001), 391, indicates that Westermann's identification of a dispute is "of little help in setting the context"; instead, he finds God refuting a complaint (49:14) rather than disputing over an issue.

so most conclude the present unit ends at 50:3.[70] This whole paragraph is about God's plans to repopulate Jerusalem with sons/children. This paragraph can be outlined into three parts.[71]

God has not forgotten Zion	49:14–21
God will gather his children, save them from plunderers	49:22–26
God will ransom, not give up on his people	50:1–3[72]

The beginning and end of the first subparagraph is marked with a quotation of Zion speaking (49:14,21). In the question in 49:14, Zion wonders what God is doing, but by the end of the paragraph God's assurances reveal that he has not forgotten her or her sons. God is intimately aware of her walls and her sons. Thus a Zion speech of amazement ends the first subparagraph, for she now understands that God will accomplish a marvelous thing in her midst. The second and third subparagraphs are marked with an introductory claim that a new word has come from God (49:22; 50:1). This section ends with the assurance that God has all power and that he is able to ransom his people from all their problems (50:1–3).

GOD HAS NOT FORGOTTEN ZION (49:14–21)

¹⁴But Zion said, "The LORD has forsaken me,
    the LORD has forgotten me."

¹⁵"Can a mother forget the baby at her breast
    and have no compassion on the child she has borne?

---

[70] Baltzer, *Deutero-Isaiah*, 329, puts a break after 50:1 and then makes 50:2–3 a separate unit. Muilenburg, "Isaiah 40–66," 5:578, puts 50:1–11 together, but he makes a subbreak after 50:1–3 and does not strongly interrelate the content of 50:1–3 to what follows.

[71] R. H. O'Connell, *Concentricity and Continuity: The Literary Structure of Isaiah* (Sheffield: Academic Press,1994), 195–96, develops a concentric chiastic diagram of 49:14–50:3 based on the protests in 49:14 and 24, with God's defense in 49:15–16 and 50:1–2, with reassuring words of consolation in 17–20, 22 and 25. This illustrates the repetition of themes, but the structural organization is disjointed and is not very convincing.

[72] Goldingay and Payne, *Isaiah 40–55*, 2:180, suggest that 49:14–50:3 covers the same idea found in 40:12–31, but in reverse order:

49:14–17 / 40:27–31	Plaint and response
49:18–21 / 40:25–26	Challenge to lift up eyes and look
49:22–23 / 40:21–24	Yhwh's sovereignty over kings
49:24–26 / 40:18–20	Yhwh's incomparable power
50:1–3 / 40:12–17	Yhwh's lordship over the created world

These comparisons are relatively minor in most cases. For example 49:22–23 mentions that kings will be foster parents and will bow down to the Hebrews, but 40:21–24 says nothing about these issues. Instead 40:21–22 talks about God's glorious throne in the heavens, while 40:23 refers to the rulers of this earth being nothing. Thus these comparisons are not very helpful to assist in understanding 49:14–50:3.

Though she may forget,
  I will not forget you!
[16]See, I have engraved you on the palms of my hands;
  your walls are ever before me.
[17]Your sons hasten back,
  and those who laid you waste depart from you.
[18]Lift up your eyes and look around;
  all your sons gather and come to you.
As surely as I live," declares the LORD,
  "you will wear them all as ornaments;
  you will put them on, like a bride.

[19]"Though you were ruined and made desolate
  and your land laid waste,
now you will be too small for your people,
  and those who devoured you will be far away.
[20]The children born during your bereavement
  will yet say in your hearing,
'This place is too small for us;
  give us more space to live in.'
[21]Then you will say in your heart,
  'Who bore me these?
I was bereaved and barren;
  I was exiled and rejected.
Who brought these up?
I was left all alone,
  but these—where have they come from?'"

The first part of this paragraph is developed around a question and God's answer to the question. God's answers provide assurance of his care for his people based on his promissory oath. This material can be outlined into four parts.

Zion questions God's care	49:14
God's first assurance	49:15–17
God's oath about many children	49:18–20
Zion recognizes her many children	49:21

The paragraph is centered around the imagery of a woman/mother who symbolizes Zion. The main issue is whether God has totally forsaken Zion and her children. God's response to his people proves that he has not forsaken them: (a) for in the future Zion will have many sons, (b) Zion is inscribed on the palm of his hand so he cannot forget them, and (c) their desolate places will one day be built and occupied by more people than can comfortably live in those places. These future promises should cause Zion to realize that God still cares for his people and will fulfill his promises to them.

49:14 The paragraph begins by quoting what the personified city of Zion says.[73] The city thinks that God has forsaken (*'āzab*) and forgotten (*šākaḥ*) her,[74] but the reason she feels this way is not stated. Is this just another example of petty complaining over some minimal discomfort, a deeply disturbing sorrowful lament, an example of rash unbelief in God's power, or a simple statement of the facts?[75] In earlier proclamations of salvation the people were fearful because God was silent for a while, had not yet defeated their enemies, and had not yet turned their darkness into light (42:14–16a), so in those paragraphs God promised to act on their behalf and not forsake them (42:16b). Later in another proclamation of salvation, it appears that God did hide for a while (45:15), but in response God assures his audience that he will fulfill his promises and save Israel (45:17). In light of these similar complaints, it is not that surprising to find more impatient statements that express some questions about God's lack of action on Israel's behalf. It is not necessarily a bad thing to want God's kingdom to be established on earth right away or for his servant to want God to restore Israel now (49:6), but unchecked impatience with the timing of God's plan can sometimes lead to doubt or even disillusionment. This proclamation of salvation addresses the concerns of the city of Zion by repeating some of God's past promises and assuring the people of Zion that God has not forgotten her.

49:15 The Lord answers this concern with a rhetorical question that everyone in his audience would naturally agree with; thus, it would have a strong persuasive quality. Is it possible that a nursing mother would forget (*šākaḥ*)[76] her infant child? The obvious answer would be no, this could never happen. A second example asks if a mother could live without having any loving compassion[77] for one of the children from her own womb? Most people

---

[73] Taking a different perspective E. J. Young, *The Book of Isaiah*. (Grand Rapids: Eerdmans, 1965–72), 3:284, claims that, *"Zion* rather designates the chosen people." Westermann, *Isaiah 40–66*, 219, believes this statement describes "the despondency and despair of the remnant of Israel." Since the city of Zion is distinguished from her sons (the people) in this passage, the place Zion cannot refer to the people in 49:14.

[74] P. T. Willey, *Remember the Former Things: The Recollection of Previous Texts in Second Isaiah*, SBLDS 161 (Atlanta: Scholars Press, 1997), 188–89, connects this abandonment with the same theme in Lam 5:20 and the fall of Jerusalem in 587 BC, but this is not the only time that God disciplined the nation and allowed them to be defeated by some natural or military force.

[75] Blenkinsopp, *Isaiah 40–55*, 310, claims that this complaint "carries undertones of marital desertion," but nothing like that is even hinted at so far in this paragraph. He is apparently reading the problem in 50:1–3 back into the initial phases of this paragraph, but vv. 14–26 do not use that comparative imagery. P. D. Hanson, *Isaiah 40–66*, Interpretation (Louisville: John Knox, 1995), 133, interprets these as Zion's "bitter complaints," but it is very difficult to read the emotional tone of these statements and to hypothesize the basis for the questions (all too often exegesis is subject to the lively imagination of the interpreter).

[76] GKC §107t indicates that imperfect verbs in interrogative questions are to be translated modally like a subjunctive; thus, "would a mother forget."

[77] The word מֵרַחֵם appears to be a *piel* infinitive construct with prefixed מִן. This could function as the verb of this clause and the מִן would be translated "without" (GKC §119w) because

who hear this question would say that it is almost unimaginable that such a thing could even happen. Having created a vivid picture of the ideal mother who does not forget her children, the second half of the verse compares God's lack of forgetfulness with a mother's lack of forgetfulness. "Even though"[78] "these"[79] two mothers might possibly forget (*šākaḥ*)[80] their children for a brief time (2 Kgs 6:24–30; Ps 27:10; Lam 4:10), God emphatically promises that "I myself" will never forget (*šākaḥ*) you, meaning Zion. This is a strong affirmation of his love and care for his people. It is unconditioned by any "if" clauses and absolute in its commitment. Elsewhere God's acts are compared to other activities of a woman (37:3; 42:14; 66:9,13).[81]

49:16 To reassure Zion and prove the point in an even stronger way, God opens his hand and challenges Zion to "observe, see" (*hēn*) an image that was permanently "engraved" (*ḥāqaq*) on the palm of God's hand. This is not a tattoo on the back of his hand, and it is not something written with weak ink that can fade or be erased; this is permanently carved into his metaphorical flesh. The object engraved on the palm of God's hand is a drawing of the walls of Jerusalem, but it is useless to speculate about which walls were engraved— were these partially broken down walls or the glorious walls of the future city (61:18; 65:17–19)?[82] When one has something engraved on his hand, it indicates an important relationship with someone who is very dear (44:5). No one engraves the name of an enemy or a casual friend on his hand. Having something like this on one's hands provides a constant reminder of the one who is loved because the engraving on the hands would be "continually before me" (Ps 16:8; 50:8).[83] This engraving was written on the powerful hands

---

someone who is in "separation from" a baby is "without" the baby. Another alternative which C. R. North, *Second Isaiah: Introduction, Translation and Commentary to Chapters XL–LV* (Eugene: OR: Wipf & Stock, 2005), 193, suggests is to imply the verb "forget" from the first clause and interpret this verbal form as a participle (requiring only a change of vocalization under the first letter) "the compassionate one" as the subject of the clause. This has the advantage of referring to two people, which seems required by אֵלֶּה "these" later in the verse. A second issue that arises is that the "woman" is the implied fem. subject of the participle מְרַחֵם (it functions as a verb), but it is masc. rather than fem..

[78] גַּם usually means "also, even, moreover," but GKC §160b suggests that it can have a concessive sense of "even though" which is the equivalent of גַּם כִּי. Since the כִּי is not in this text, this is a questionable solution, so it is preferable to simply translate this word "even."

[79] Koole, *Isaiah III, Volume 2: Isaiah 49–55*, 54, connects the pl. אֵלֶּה "these" to the two different children, but the forgetfulness issue is related to the mothers, not the children.

[80] The imperfect is used subjunctively "might, could, may" (GKC §107m,r).

[81] J. Schmitt, "The Motherhood of God and Zion as Mother," *RB* 92 (1985): 557–69, provides an extended discussion of these issues.

[82] I. Blythin, "A Note on Is xlix 16–17," *VT* 16 (1966): 229–30, considers the use of "walls" as a symbolization of the outer part of a person (Song 8:9–10), but it is better to view the walls simply as a representation of the city as a whole rather than one physical part of the city. Baltzer, *Deutero-Isaiah*, 326, connects these walls to the walls that Nehemiah rebuilt, but this is very unlikely.

[83] This might be compared to the wedding ring that is a constant reminder of the marriage relationship one has with the covenant partner that one loves.

that created the heavens and the earth (48:13), so it is very comforting for the audience to know that Jerusalem is carved on the almighty hands that can accomplish great things.

49:17   The subject of the verb is either "your sons" (*bānāyik*; accepted in NIV, KJV) or "your builders" (*bônyk*; accepted in NASB, NRSV, HCSB, ESV) which is found in the unvocalized manuscript of 1QIs^a. The difference between these two readings of the Hebrew text is dependent on which vowels are used. There is no agreement on which reading is more authentic, although there seems to be a preference for the word "builders" because it makes a better contrast with destroyers later in the verse. Nevertheless, the rest of this passage is mostly about what will happen to Zion's sons/children (49:15,18,20,22,25), and very little time is spent on issues related to building Jerusalem. J. Oswalt suggests that both ideas are meant and that the word was used as double entendre.[84]

The audience can be encouraged because at some point their sons/builders will hasten[85] to Judah, while those who tear down and lay waste[86] the nation of Judah will go out from it, presumably back to their own country. It is almost impossible to locate this event in history (the Assyrian or Babylonian conquest),[87] and one should avoid the temptation to connect these events with the building of the walls of Jerusalem by Nehemiah, for the general context of 49:14–26 foresees a much greater and magnificent return of people in the distant future.

49:18   Now comes God's oath of commitment to multiply the number of people in Zion far beyond anything that most of them could ever imagine. This will prove that God has not forgotten about Zion and that his promises to Jerusalem will be fulfilled. The audience (the city of Jerusalem) is exhorted in two imperative verbs[88] to notice what is happening around it. In the past the city was surrounded with flames in a time of war (42:25), with warriors and plunderers (45:25), but all that will change. All of her sons will gather together[89]

---

[84] Oswalt, *Isaiah 40–66*, 307, follows North, *Second Isaiah*, 193, who says that, "there is surely a *double entendre* here."

[85] The perfect verb מִהֲרוּ probably is a prophetic use of the perfect ("they will hasten"; NIV makes it present tense), referring to what will happen in the future (GKC §106n). Since the last verb יֵצֵאוּ "they will go out" is an imperfect form, it confirms that the first verb is a prophetic perfect pointing to a future setting.

[86] The sounds "*mhr*" are present in the verb "hasten," in the participle "over throwers" (*mhrs*), and in "destroyers" (*mhrb*) to make a nice series of word plays.

[87] If one were to guess based on a past setting (the second participle "those who laid you waste"), it would make more sense to interpret this as referring to the Assyrians leaving Jerusalem completely defeated, but this provides little evidence about the setting.

[88] The verbs שְׂאִי (from the root נָשָׂא "lift up") and וּרְאִי (from the verb רָאָה) are second person fem. imperatives that have the syntactical function of admonishing or exhorting the audience that hears this message (GKC §110a).

[89] The perfect *niphal* verb נִקְבְּצוּ "they will be gathered" or "they will gather themselves" must be referring to what will happen in the future (GKC §106n).

and come to Zion at some point in the future. Since many people in the prophet's audience at this time might find this statement to be rather unbelievable in light of their present situation, God swears an oath[90] (similar to 45:23), "as I live," and follows this with a typical "surely, it is indisputable" (*kî*, also used in 5:9 for emphasis) that would add persuasive qualities.[91] These people will come and will be viewed like precious jewels, like ornaments of gold or silver that might be fastened to the hand, neck, ears, ankles, or clothes of a beautiful woman (the city of Zion), like a bride who is dressed up for a wedding celebration. Although there was a minor gathering of a few thousand Israelites at the end of the Babylonian captivity,[92] this verse imagines something far more glorious with millions of people, not just several thousand.

49:19–20 The oath in v. 18 is continued into v. 19 by the two *kî* ("surely") clauses that contrast the present desolate state with the glorious future of the city. The interpretation of the first half of 47:19 is complicated by the absence of a verb to go with the three nouns ("your waste places, your desolate places, your devastated places") that describe the ruined situation in and around Jerusalem. NIV inappropriately follows an emendation of the text and turns these three nouns into verbal forms in order to make sense of these words. In addition it interprets 19a as a concessive clause beginning with "though." Instead, one should translate the initial *kî* as "surely" (it is a continuation of the oath in 18) and either: (a) assume a verb has fallen out in textual transmission; (b) treat this as an incomplete train of thought that is interrupted in 19b by a positive contrast; or (c) supply a "to be, to exist" verb that is frequently missing in normal Hebrew conversation. With choice (c) one might translate the clause, "Surely, your waste, your desolate, and your destroyed land exists." The second half of the verse contrasts this present state of affairs with the "surely, now you (Jerusalem) will be too[93] small/narrow for the inhabitants." The third part of the oath pictures a Jerusalem that is not desolate, destroyed, or uninhabited due to the past wars the nation has lost. The text does not say that their devourers will take them captive into exile; rather God gives his oath that these devourers will go far away.

---

[90] GKC §149 discusses oath formulas and notes that כִּי means "surely" following a curse or oath. GKC §159ee indicates that "the absolute certainty with which a result is to be expected is frequently emphasized by the insertion of כִּי."

[91] NIV mistranslates the intention of this word of assurance by placing it with the introductory formula rather than the oath. It puts the "surely" with "surely as I live," rather than with the oath, "surely, you will wear them as ornaments." The Hebrew כִּי כֻלָּם "surely all of them" places the emphasis on the totality of the restoration of everyone.

[92] Muilenburg, "Isaiah 40–66," 5:575, interprets these people as "the exiles returning from every direction, all of them bound for Zion," but Ezra and Nehemiah do not describe a glorious period of Jewish history when the nation was overrun with people. Muilenburg unnecessarily changes the order of the text by placing v. 12 after v. 18.

[93] The מִן which is prefixed to the participle יוֹשֵׁב "inhabitants" is probably a comparative use of the preposition (GKC §133c).

Verse 20 continues this theme, but in this verse the complaint about not having enough room[94] is placed in the mouths of all those people who will come to live in Jerusalem. These new people who come to Jerusalem are given the rather paradoxical title "sons/children of your bereavement," apparently an appellation that refers to sons of a woman who thought she had lost all her children. The thought of one person is that this place is too narrow and cramped for "me" (NIV for "us"), so this person exhorts another person saying, "draw near" (*gĕšâh* is an imperative verb from *nāgaš* "draw near")[95] so that there will be more room. This request is followed by a first-person cohortative verb that expresses the speaker's intention, "so that I can settle/dwell here."[96]

This is not describing postexilic Jerusalem,[97] for Jerusalem had so few people in it in the days of Nehemiah that he had to take extraordinary steps to force people to relocate in Jerusalem (Neh 11). The last part of v. 19 indicates that there were those who devoured Zion (*mĕballʿāyik* literally, "swallowed you up"), but it is difficult to determine if this refers to the military conquest of the Assyrians or Babylonians. The statements in 49:17b ("those who laid you waste depart from you") and 49:19 ("those who devoured you will be far away") sounds like the departure of the Assyrians after the angel of God destroyed the 185,000 Assyrian troops (37:36), but with so little information it is: hard to pinpoint any specific event. All this news makes one thing very certain; God has not forgotten about his people, and he does not plan to forsake them in their time of need. These promises also demonstrate that God will deal with Zion (giving her many children) just the opposite of the way he will deal with Babylon, for in chap. 47 Babylon will be destroyed and lose all her children.

49:21 The first paragraph ends with a positive evidence of God's care based on God's great promise of many children coming to Jerusalem. God's promises in 49:15–20 have demonstrated that God has not forgotten her. Zion responds with astonishment at all the people who will one day inhabit the city. Her astonishment is heightened because her wonderful situation will be so different from her past negative situations. Since Zion has experienced the loss of children (picked up from 49:19), barrenness, had some people exiled[98] and

---

[94] The perfect verb צַר "it is narrow, small" repeats the same root as the imperfect תֵּצַר־לִי found in v. 19.

[95] Goldingay and Payne, *Isaiah 40–55*, 2, 191, interpret this verb to mean "draw near [to somewhere else]" or movement away from the speaker; thus they translate the clause "move over." Unfortunately they provide no comparable examples where this sense is found in other passages.

[96] When an imperative verb is followed by a cohortative verb, the cohortative "expresses also a consequence which is expected with certainty . . . or an intention" (GKC §110g). This case seems to express an intention, but if one chooses to interpret the cohortative as expressing a consequence that was expected with certainty, the translations would be "for I will settle here."

[97] Whybray, *Isaiah 40–66*, 145, does not interpret these events as eschatological but claims that "the returning Israelites will include not only the descendents of the Babylonian exiles but the descendents of dispersed Israelites of all kinds." There is no hint that people from other nations returned with the exiles (Ezra 2).

[98] Koole, *Isaiah III, Volume 2: Isaiah 49–55*, 66–67, notes that these two words are not found

others who departed,[99] she felt left all alone. Thus it is somewhat natural to ask the question, "How did this happen?" Zion asks three questions in v. 21: (a) Who begat/gave birth to these for me? (b) Who raised these? (c) Where were these people? Based on 49:12, K. Baltzer identifies three groups of people represented by the three uses of "these" (ʾēlleh) in 49:21, but his identification of these groups is suspect, for the text seems to be referring to the same group of people throughout this verse.[100] J. Goldingay connects all these people with Jews in Babylonian exile,[101] yet 2:1–5; 11:11–12; 14:1–2; 19:18–25; 42:6,10–11; 43:6–7; 45:14–25 and 49:22–26; all indicate that Isaiah understood that the future inhabitants of Zion would include both Hebrews and people from all the nations of the earth. This explains why Zion is astonished and surprised at all "these" (ʾēlleh) people who now inhabit the land. Surely the abundance of the grace of God in the eschatological age will accomplish far more than anyone can possibly expect or even imagine (Eph 3:20).

GOD WILL GATHER HIS CHILDREN, SAVE THEM FROM PLUNDERERS (49:22–26)

[22]This is what the Sovereign LORD says:

"See, I will beckon to the Gentiles,
    I will lift up my banner to the peoples;
they will bring your sons in their arms
    and carry your daughters on their shoulders.
[23]Kings will be your foster fathers,
    and their queens your nursing mothers.
They will bow down before you with their faces to the ground;
    they will lick the dust at your feet.
Then you will know that I am the LORD;
    those who hope in me will not be disappointed."

[24]Can plunder be taken from warriors,
    or captives rescued from the fierce?

---

in the Old Greek translation; thus, he concludes that they were added later to explain the preceding words but are not part of the original text of this chapter. He also maintains that "DI does not use גלה elsewhere for 'go into exile,'" though he does recognize that this root (גְּלוֹת) is used in this sense in 45:13. Since most battles involved the exiling of people from the territory conquered, Judah had many experiences of people being exiled. During the Syro-Ephraimite war in 734–732 BC over 200,000 people from Judah were exiled for a brief time (2 Chr 28:8).

[99] These two verbs are problematic if they are applied to the city of Zion, for it was not exiled and it did not depart. One would be tempted to apply these verbs to the people of Jerusalem, but the "I" (וַאֲנִי) at the beginning of the clause clearly refers to Jerusalem.

[100] Baltzer, Deutero-Isaiah, 326–27, identifies the first group as exiles from Babylon, the second group as the remnant left in Jerusalem, and the third group as those enslaved by debt.

[101] Goldingay, Message of Isaiah 40–66, 390, states that the "reference is presumably to the offspring of Judeans who were born in exile."

²⁵But this is what the LORD says:

"Yes, captives will be taken from warriors,
    and plunder retrieved from the fierce;
I will contend with those who contend with you,
    and your children I will save.
²⁶I will make your oppressors eat their own flesh;
    they will be drunk on their own blood, as with wine.
Then all mankind will know
    that I, the LORD, am your Savior,
    your Redeemer, the Mighty One of Jacob."

This paragraph continues to focus on the theme of Zion's children by providing an answer to the questions asked in 49:21. This expanded explanation about how so many of her children will be brought back to Jerusalem provides further reasons for the audience to put their hope in God. God will cause foreign nations to bring Hebrew children to Zion, and then they will bow in deep respect (49:22–23); plus he will take captives away from former oppressors (49:24–25). The result will be that all the people on the earth will know that he is God (49:26b) and will put their hope in him (49:23b). As J. D. W. Watts says "Jerusalem's restoration is not an end in itself. It will serve to spread the knowledge of Yahweh."[102] This short paragraph can be divided into two parts:

People can hope in God for the nations will return children   49:22–23
All will know God when he saves them from oppression   49:24–26

The first part focuses more on what the nations will do to help restore Jerusalem, while the second concentrates more on what God will do to defeat evil nations so that additional people can return home.

49:22–23   The paragraph begins with a new introductory messenger formula that assures the reader that this truly is a divine word from God; this is not just the wishful thinking of a deluded prophet. The process of bringing these children back involves several steps. First, God will move the nations to action by: (a) lifting up his hand[103] and (b) raising up a "standard, banner" (nēs). God can lift up his hand or set up a standard in order to signal people to act according to his will by bringing judgment (5:26; 13:2), but in this case it is for the purpose of bringing salvation and hope (11:12; 62:10).[104] His beckoning goes

---

[102] Watts, *Isaiah 34–66*, 192, thinks this paragraph refers to the restoration of the Jewish people from Persia. This historicizes a future eschatological event and almost falsifies it, for 49:22–26 was not fulfilled in the postexilic era.

[103] Sometimes God lifts up his hand to swear an oath (Exod 6:8; Deut 32:40), which could hypothetically be connected with 49:18. Other times hands are raised to grant a blessing (Lev 9:22) or to signal someone into action (5:26).

[104] Oswalt, *Isaiah 40–66*, 310, concludes that the raising up of the standard "signals the destruction of Babylon," but there is no mention of Babylon and the signal appears to be a positive sign for the nation to move into action in an eschatological era. Westermann, *Isaiah 40–66*, 221,

out to unidentified "nations" (some are mentioned in 11:11; 60:3–12). This prophecy reports that the nations will respond positively to God's signal by bringing many children to Zion. This will reverse the terrible results of God's judgment that brought about the decimation and deportation of so many people in Israel. This fulfillment seems to be quite similar to the prophecy in 14:1–2, and it sounds similar to 66:20.

The earlier question about who raised these children (49:21) is addressed in v. 23. Kings and queens provided the tender royal care given to these children when they were raised in foreign lands. This implies a miraculous transformation of the foreign nations from enemies of God's people to sympathetic caretakers. They will come in peace to help God's people and to show respect by humbly bowing before them; thus, reversing a former situation in which the defeated children of Israel had to bow to foreign rulers. The bowing in this verse should not be read as an ugly revengeful domination of foreigners by Israelites. This figure of speech can be used in a domineering sense in a hostile context of defeated prisoners of war (45:14), but in this context Israel and the nations are not at war. Instead, people from both nations will know God, will come to serve him (2:2–5), will put their hope in him; and none of them "will be put to shame (*lô yēbŏšû*, NIV "disappointed," 49:23b). In other situations bowing down does not involve violent domination or any inkling of shame. For example, there was no shame when Ruth bowed to the ground when Boaz favored her with his blessing (Ruth 2:10), and there will be no shame when people meet the Lord and "bow before me" (45:28). Once the Jews observe these wonderful events happening, they will finally be convinced ("you will know" *wĕyada'at*) that this is God at work, for these people are "those who hope/wait for me" (*qōwāy*) and trust in God's promises. The hopeful person that patiently waits for God's salvation to arrive will not be disappointed when God acts to fulfill his promises (Ps 25:2–3; 27:13–14).

49:24–26 The initial issue addressed is a question that the prophet's audience may have raised concerning the promises made in 49:22–23. This question relates to the possibility of receiving back children from the stronger nation that plundered the people and took some captive. No enemy nation is mentioned, so it would be improper to limit this broad principle to the return of captives from any specific military defeat. The question is: Can the captured people and property be taken[105] away from those who took them captive? There is some uncertainty about who took these people because the term *gibbôr* is capable of being translated "mighty man, warrior," a term that could be used to refer

---

views the signal as a sign "to join battle . . . in a time of war," but there is no reference to fighting in vv. 22–23.

[105] When the passive imperfect verb יֻקַּח "will be taken" (from לְקַח) is used in a question, the verb should be translated as a modal, expressing the possibility of such action, "can it be taken" (GKC §107t).

to God (42:13) as well as strong humans.[106] The Qumran and Masoretic texts are not identical, so some would follow the harder Masoretic text.[107] But those who follow the Masoretic text have difficulty interpreting who the ṣaddîq is. B. S. Childs translates ṣaddîq as "victor" and makes it parallel to the "warrior, strong man" in the first line.[108] F. Delitzsch takes ṣaddîq as the "righteous," which refers to the "captive hosts of righteous" people.[109] A third view is that God is the "warrior" and "just one," so obviously no one can take people and plunder from him.[110] This approach is problematic because the answer (49:25) to the question (49:24) states that captives can be taken from this "warrior, mighty one," yet it is obvious that no one has the power to take things from God. Consequently, one is left to conclude that prophet is asking if valuables taken by a strong warrior or a prisoner of war held by a just person can be retrieved. Of course neither person would be very likely to give up what they now own, for they are very valuable to their new owners. The interpretation of this verse is complicated by some textual uncertainty about the parallel term ṣādîq "righteous one, victor," which is written 'rîṣ "fierce, awesome one, tyrant" in 1QIs^a.[111] The Qumran reading gives a better parallel term to "warrior" in the previous clause, and it is consistent with the parallelism between these two words in 49:25. Those who accept the Qumran reading find both 24 and 25 describing a strong foreign conqueror in both phrases.[112]

49:25   The prophet answers the hypothetical question in v. 24 in order to increase the faith of those who have heard his earlier promise in 49:17–18. With strong confidence he says "surely" (kî, NIV "but") God has promised that "even" (gam) those who will be taken as plunder by strong tyrants can be taken back from them; even the people the strong tyrants took can be rescued. How

---

[106] R. E. Watts, "Mark," *CNTOT* 146–47, believes 49:24 had some impact on the ideas behind what is said in Mark 3:27.

[107] Watts, *Isaiah 34–66*, 191; Baltzer, *Deutero-Isaiah*, 329, and Koole, *Isaiah III, Volume 2: Isaiah 49–55*, 77, are a few of those who prefer the Masoretic reading over the Qumran because it could have easily inserted the terms in v. 25 back into v. 24. Oswalt, *Isaiah 40–66*, 312, Whybray, *Isaiah 40–66*, 147, and North, *Second Isaiah*, 197, are some of those who prefer the reading in the Qumran text because it creates better parallelism.

[108] Childs, *Isaiah*, 388, 392, views this as a message of hope because "God will take on in battle the mighty, the warriors, the victors, tyrants, and adversaries." Baltzer, *Deutero-Isaiah*, 331, connects the "righteous one" to the Hebrews in Neh 5:1–13 who view themselves as righteous (an ironic usage) when they really are violent and force the poor people into slavery.

[109] Delitzsch, "Prophecies of Isaiah," 272, follows the view found in Aquila, the Targum, and early Rabbis like Rashi and Ibn Ezra.

[110] Goldingay, *Message of Isaiah 40–66*, 392–93, explores this option but decides against it.

[111] The Old Greek "unjust man" may not have had a similar text to that used in Qumran. They likely found "just" in the text but could not make any sense of it; therefore, they made a slight change to rectify the situation and wrote "unjust" to give a better parallel with the terms used in v. 25.

[112] Blenkinsopp, *Isaiah 40–55*, 315, says "the sense of ruthless and overwhelming power is expressed by describing Babylon as a warrior," but this reads into the text something not found anywhere in this chapter.

can this be accomplished? Who will do it? God emphatically says "I myself" (ʾānōkî) will "fight, contend" (ʾārîb) with those people who "fight, contend with you" (yĕrîbēk). This does not refer to legal contending in a court of law in this context but describes God's act of fighting for his right to have those individuals who belong to him. This is consistent with God's defense of his people in other texts (Ps 35:1; 43:1). They belong to him because they are his children. Therefore, God will be able to successfully take what belongs to him because he has the ability to "save, deliver" (ʾôšîaʿ) the sons of Israel. The shame of the past (49:23b) will be a thing of the past when God acts. What is humanly impossible and almost beyond human hope, God will do. There is no indication that this will be accomplished for God by some other nation; the force of the statement emphasizes only God's role in this marvelous act of deliverance.

49:26 This paragraph ends with concluding statements about what will happen to the strong tyrants God fights with in 49:25 and what will happen to the rest of humanity. The destiny of these enemies of God's people, called oppressors in 49:26 (picking up an idea already hinted at in v.17b), is graphically portrayed with metaphors of "eating, devouring" (the root ʾākal) the flesh and drinking the blood of others. These bloodthirsty tyrants who devoured others (not a literal cannibalistic eating)[113] will self-destruct and kill each other. This is exactly what happened earlier when Jehoshaphat opposed the Moabites, Edomites, and Ammonites (2 Chr 20:22–23) and when Gideon's 300 men surrounded the Midianites (Judg 7:22), for in both cases the enemy armies self-destructed because they turned on one another.

When the rest of humanity, including Jews and people from many other nations ("all flesh"), observes what God himself will do to these oppressors, they will come to know and will freely acknowledge that God is a real Savior, their Redeemer, and the Mighty One of Jacob. The power of seeing the truth will bring convincing evidence of the truthfulness of the character of God (40:5; 45:6,23). They will experience his acts of salvation and will be delivered from these negative experiences. They will realize that they are part of the family of God that he ransomed and redeemed from the clutches of other oppressive nations. Once these people experience God's grace they will know that Yahweh, the God of the Israelites is an Almighty God. These eschatological confessions of faith reveal the transformed nature of all humanity when God climactically enters the course of history, brings a violent end to the forces of evil, and establishes a redeemed people for himself. That will be a final world-changing event. The anticipation of that day should cause the prophet's audience and

---

[113] When nations besiege cities, the people inside the walls eventually run out of food, and in a few exceptional cases they turned to the cannibalistic act of eating their children (2 Kgs 6:24–31), but usually this is used in prophetic texts to refer to self-destruction by internal fighting against one another (9:19–20; Deut 28:53–57; Ezek 5:10). In Ps 27:2 the prayer complains that the enemies want to eat his flesh, but this is no doubt a metaphoric hyperbole meaning they want to kill him.

every reader of his words to be persuaded that even though some days may be very difficult, God will never forsake his people (49:14).

GOD WILL RANSOM, NOT GIVE UP ON HIS PEOPLE (50:1–3)

¹**This is what the LORD says:**

> **"Where is your mother's certificate of divorce**
> **with which I sent her away?**
> **Or to which of my creditors**
> **did I sell you?**
> **Because of your sins you were sold;**
> **because of your transgressions your mother was sent away.**
> ²**When I came, why was there no one?**
> **When I called, why was there no one to answer?**
> **Was my arm too short to ransom you?**
> **Do I lack the strength to rescue you?**
> **By a mere rebuke I dry up the sea,**
> **I turn rivers into a desert;**
> **their fish rot for lack of water**
> **and die of thirst.**
> ³**I clothe the sky with darkness**
> **and make sackcloth its covering."**

The last paragraph in this unit[114] also presents arguments and assurances that were designed to persuade the Israelites that God has not rejected them or forgotten about his promises to his beloved people. C. Westermann classifies 50:1–3 as a trial speech involving a confrontation between Israel and God, but it makes more sense to follow J. L. Koole who identifies it as a word of salvation, similar to 49:14–21 and 49:22–26.[115] R. N. Whybray assumes that God's response in 50:1 is an answer to an accusation that was part of a lament, but no lament or accusation is found in this text.[116] It seems better to conclude that God is responding to the question in 49:14 in a third way in order to help the people understand that God has not forgotten them. The paragraph can be outlined:

| Two questions about God's relationship to Israel | 50:1a |
| God's answer: Sin impacts their relationship | 50:1b |

---

[114] Seitz, "Isaiah 40–66," 6:435, separates 50:1–3 from 49:14–26 and understands 50:1–3 as part of 50:1–11 because 50:1–3 no longer addresses Zion as a mother. It refers to the audience as children, plus he believes the question in 50:2a is answered in 50:3–9. In contrast to this interpretation, these verses can be viewed as another answer to the question raised in 49:14.

[115] Westermann, *Isaiah 40–66*, 223, finds God as the defendant in this trial; Melugin, *Formation of Isaiah 40–55*, 51–52, calls 50:1–3 a disputation; while Koole, *Isaiah III, Volume 2: Isaiah 49–55*, 85,87, concludes that the main purpose of this short piece is to reassure the people with the good news that God has not forsaken them; he has the power to redeem them and take care of them.

[116] Whybray, *Isaiah*, 148, claims that God was accused of severing his ancient ties with his people "irrevocably and without sufficient cause."

Two questions about Israel's relationship to God	50:2a
God's answer: He has power over everything	50:2b–3

God's two answers are marked by introductory *hēn* "see, behold" clauses (omitted in NIV in vv. 1 and 2), while the questions are marked by the interrogatives "where" (*'ēy*), "who" (*mî*) in 50:1 and "why (*madûaʿ*), and the interrogative (*hă*) in 50:2.

50:1 This speech begins with another announcement that this, too, is the word that God has spoken to the prophet. God's questions are: (a) If God has forsaken and forgotten his covenant wife Israel (49:14), where is the certificate of divorce that needs to be granted to the wife? This refers to a literal "letter of cutting off" that a husband must give a wife that he "sends away, divorces" (the root *šālaḥ*). Although detailed information about the divorce process in Israel at this time is very incomplete, both Deut 24:1–4 and Jer 3:1,8 mention the practice of giving a written document to a wife that is divorced. One simple way to prove that God has not rejected the people of Judah is to point to the lack of a divorce document. Since no one could produce such a document, one must conclude that God's relationship with his people has not ended from God's point of view.

The second question delves into another possible explanation that one could hypothesize to explain the strained relationship between God and his people. If a man was in severe debt, he could sell his children, wife, or himself into slavery to a creditor (Exod 21:7; Lev 25:25; 2 Kgs 4:1; Neh 5:1–5). So the second question asks the audience concerning the hypothetical explanation that God sold his people to a creditor for some debt he owed. Can anyone identify God's debt, discover whom God was indebted to, or find out what the debt was for? These are rhetorical questions designed to prove just the opposite of what was intimated in the question. The problem in the relationship between God and Israel is not related to any negative thing that God has done.

This conclusion is mitigated by those who identify the Babylonian exile as a time when God divorced his people or those who suggest that the exilic period was an era when Israel was under subjection to Babylonian rule and therefore an indentured servant to the Babylonians.[117] This reading of the text denies the good news that this message is presenting. It would legitimate this complaint against God because he sent them into exile; therefore, he did divorce them or sold them. Yet the actual point of the passage is the positive message that God has not forsaken, forgotten, or sold them. Although there were a few earlier situations in the history of Israel when God did sell his people into the hands of

---

[117] Blenkinsopp, *Isaiah 40–55*, 315–16, and Whybray, *Isaiah 40–66*, 149, discuss these interpretations. The northern nation of Israel did receive a certificate of divorce (Jer 3:8), but there is no indication that that ever happened to Judah. Oswalt, *Isaiah 40–66*, 318, deals with the suggestion that "the people are saying that it is God's fault that they are in captivity."

other nations (Judg 2:14; 3:8; 4:2; 10:7; 1 Sam 12:9), this was not due to some divine misdeed (divorce or indebtedness) in order to get rid of them.

The real problem in the relationship between God and his people is found in God's answer in 1b. "See, behold" (*hēn*),[118] it was always because of their deliberate rebellious choices (*pāšaʿ*) and their iniquity that the people were sent away to endure times of trials. Israel's past tribulations were God's just discipline of his children; they were not intended to destroy the relationship he had with his people. God wanted to humble them and bring them back to himself.

50:2a Now God asks two additional probing questions that get to the heart of the problem in order to cause the audience to reflect more deeply on the real reason for past trials and difficulties. God asks why none of them answered him when he came and called them? This line of questioning lays the real blame at the feet of the people, for God was present ("I came") and God called, indicating at minimum a desire to have a relationship (or possibly he was calling them to repentance or for them to serve him). This suggests that God has long been ready to speak with them and work on their behalf, but "there was no one" (*ʾēn ʾîš*) who was willing to admit the people's sinfulness. They were not willing to come to talk to God about it in order to restore their relationship. The second question wonders why they did not answer. Was it because they thought God would not hear them or that his power (his hand) was too short to deliver them? If this was the case, it is evident that the people did not really know much about the true nature of God. Have they still not learned that God is "Yahweh, your Savior, your Redeemer, the Mighty One of Jacob" (49:26)?

50:2b–3 God's second answer begins like the first answer. "See, behold" (*hēn*, omitted in NIV), God has the power to simply speak a word of rebuke and the sea and rivers will dry up, then all the fish will die and begin to stink. God is also able to darken the heaven with his power. This confirms that God has the power to accomplish anything he decides to do. He does not lack in his ability to hear his people or save them.

God's negative power to destroy is illustrated by additional examples, but it is not very clear why these examples are provided. Is this drawing on positive tradition: (a) about God's past power to dry up the Red Sea so that the Israelites could be delivered from a past enemy; (b) from hymnic literature that praises God's sovereignty over nature; or (c) from traditions about God's ecological transformation (either renewal or degradation) of nature?[119] Since the source of these statements is unclear, one is only able to conclude that God is powerful enough to act in almost apocalyptic ways to demonstrate his power over everything in this world. No direct application to the prophet's audience is

---

[118] Koole, *Isaiah III, Volume 2: Isaiah 49–55*, 91, holds that הן "followed by the perf. form, draws attention to an evidently indisputable situation."

[119] Oswalt, *Isaiah 40–66*, 320, uses evidence of themes from Exod 7; 10; 15; Westermann, *Isaiah 40–66*, 225, suggests the use of declarative hymns of praise like 107:33; and Blenkinsopp, *Isaiah 40–55*, 317, makes a connection with statements of ecological renewal and degradation.

formulated, but it is very apparent that if God has this kind of power he is able to rescue his people from any situation (50:2), defeat any of their oppressors (49:25), and have compassion on his people (49:15). Does this sound like a God who has forsaken his people or one who is unable to rescue them?

THEOLOGICAL IMPLICATIONS. The oracles in this passage present assurances to people who feel like God has forgotten or forsaken them (49:14). Although a person's circumstances may seem rather difficult or hopeless at certain times, there are reasons to put one's hope in God. These proclamations of salvation argue that people can look at the future with hope because (a) God is less likely to forget his children than a mother is to forget her nursing child (49:15); (b) God cannot forget his people because the walls of Jerusalem are engraved on his hands (49:16); (c) God has not forgotten his people and will bring back a large multitude of Israelites to Jerusalem; in fact, there will be so many that there will not be enough room for them all (49:16–21); (d) the foreign nations will return children and then bow in respect, providing another reason for hope (49:22–24); (e) when God fights with and defeats their oppressors, everyone on earth will acknowledge who God is (49:24–26); and (f) God has not divorced his people but has the sovereign power to rescue them from any troubling situation (50:1–3).

Such promises give hope to the hopeless, cause the oppressed to realize that God's compassion is still available, and encourage the discouraged because God will fulfill his past promises. Although life may be difficult today, on some tomorrow God will bring about a new day when his enemies will be defeated and every person on earth will acknowledge and glorify the God of Israel. That future hope motivates every believer to not give up hope because of the trials and tribulations of this present age. Truly, God is the Savior, Redeemer, and the Mighty One of Jacob (49:26) who is worthy of complete trust.

(2) Follow the Example of God's Servant (50:4–11)

⁴The Sovereign LORD has given me an instructed tongue,
  to know the word that sustains the weary.
He wakens me morning by morning,
  wakens my ear to listen like one being taught.
⁵The Sovereign LORD has opened my ears,
  and I have not been rebellious;
I have not drawn back.
⁶I offered my back to those who beat me,
  my cheeks to those who pulled out my beard;
I did not hide my face
  from mocking and spitting.
⁷Because the Sovereign LORD helps me,
  I will not be disgraced.
Therefore have I set my face like flint,
  and I know I will not be put to shame.

> [8]He who vindicates me is near.
>   Who then will bring charges against me?
>   Let us face each other!
>   Who is my accuser?
>   Let him confront me!
> [9]It is the Sovereign LORD who helps me.
>   Who is he that will condemn me?
>   They will all wear out like a garment;
>   the moths will eat them up.
>
> [10]Who among you fears the LORD
>   and obeys the word of his servant?
>   Let him who walks in the dark,
>   who has no light,
>   trust in the name of the LORD
>   and rely on his God.
> [11]But now, all you who light fires
>   and provide yourselves with flaming torches,
>   go, walk in the light of your fires
>   and of the torches you have set ablaze.
>   This is what you shall receive from my hand:
>   You will lie down in torment.

After an abrupt end to the preceding oracle and without much of an introduction, suddenly the reader hears the voice of an obedient disciple of the Lord who is eventually identified as "his Servant" in 50:10. Most would identify this as the third Servant poem (similar to 42:1–13; 49:1–13) in which the Servant himself describes his experiences of remaining true to God's instructions (50:4–5) while he was undergoing undeserved suffering (50:6; as in 49:4,7). It would be difficult to identify this Servant as Israel for his ears are open to hear what God might say (50:4–5), and he has full confidence in God's vindication of his situation (50:8–9). Although R. N. Whybray hypothesizes that this refers to the mistreatment of the prophet who was arrested by Babylonian authorities and K. Baltzer suggests "that here a human being [Moses in his view] is talking to the assembled listeners after his death," neither of these approaches are very convincing.[120] This Servant is the same Servant described in 49:1–13 and whose suffering will be described in more detail in 53:1–12.[121]

---

[120] Whybray, *Isaiah 40–55*, 151–52, believes the Babylonians put the prophet on trial because of his predictions that Babylon would fall to the Persians. His confidence was based on his belief that God would send the Persians to defeat the Babylonians. Baltzer, *Deutero-Isaiah*, 339–41, believes the servant is Moses, and he relates these words to the Israelites mistreatment of Moses. Watts, *Isaiah 34–66*, 201–204, identifies the servant in 50:4–9 as Zerubbabel (the political leader of the Jerusalem exiles who returned shortly after Cyrus's decree in 538 BC) and the Persian king Darius in 50:10–11. Goldingay, *Message of Isaiah 40–55*, 402, proposes that the servant is the prophet who "claims to embody the attitude of the afflicted but trusting figure of Lam. 3. Walking in darkness (v. 10, cf. Lam 3.2), this figure nevertheless accepts whatever blows and insults that come."

[121] Consult the discussion of the servant in the introduction to 42:1–13.

This Servant passage is interlinked with material that comes before and after it. C. R. Seitz makes 50:1–11 all one unit (50:1–3 is not included in the previous paragraph) because a new audience (the children) is addressed in 50:1 and because in 50:4–9 the Servant answers the questions posed in 50:2.[122] K. Baltzer also makes a strong connection between the Servant poem and 50:1–3. He follows F. Delitzsch's suggestion that the person who asked the questions about why no one answered when he called in 50:2 was the Servant of the Lord who speaks in 50:4–9. This is parallel to the first person speech of the Servant in 48:16, just a few verses before the Servant song in 49:1–13.[123] A third method of connecting the Servant poem with what precedes is to notice the many contrasts between the disobedient people of Israel in 49:14–50:3 and the obedient Servant in 50:4–11.[124] The life of the Servant demonstrates the faithfulness of God to help his Servant when he is in trouble; thus the Israelites should not fear that God has forsaken them. From a more linguistic point of comparison R. Melugin noted the use of questions (*mî* "who") followed by answers (*hēn*, "see") in 50:1–2; 50:8–9; 50:10–11.[125]

C. Westermann properly rejected J. Begrich's view that this passage was an individual lament; instead, he proposed that this was "an individual psalm of confidence" that includes a confession of confidence and an expression of certainty that his requests were being answered. Although Westermann finds some connections with Jeremiah's laments, Jeremiah's laments often showed little confidence in God and sometimes included curses on his enemies (both missing in this poem).[126] The paragraph can be outlined into three parts:

The Servant listened and learned	50:4–5
The Servant endured suffering	50:6
The Servant confidently depended on God	50:7–9
Challenge to follow the Servant's example	50:10–11

---

[122] Seitz, "Isaiah 40–66," 6:435–36, presents the contrasting picture of a servant who listened to God and obeyed.

[123] Baltzer, *Deutero-Isaiah*, 335, maintains that "the Servant of God text (traditionally 50:4–11) begins already with v. 2." He outlines the passage into: his task and authority (50:4), what happened to him (50:5–8), and blessings and curses (50:9–11), which does not agree with the outline used below.

[124] J. A. Motyer, *The Prophecy of Isaiah* (Leicester: IVP, 1993), 398, makes the following contrasts: (a) No one in Israel listens and responds in Israel (50:2) but the servant of God listens (50:4). (b) Zion questions God's love, power, and help (49:14,22) while the servant is very confident in the Lord's help and nearness (50:7–9). (c) Zion suffers for its sins (49:1), but the servant suffers because he is obedient and innocent (50:5,8–9).

[125] Melugin, *Formation of Isaiah 40–55*, 152.

[126] Westermann, *Isaiah 40–66*, 226–228, compares Jeremiah's prayers which include a lament, a protestation of innocence, and an answer from God, which are somewhat comparable to the material in 50:4–11. Willey, *Remember the Former Things: The Recollection of Previous Texts in Second Isaiah*, 214–16, connects the imagery of this poem to the description of Jerusalem after its destruction in Lam 3:25–30.

The Servant is no longer giving biographical information in 50:10–11, so technically the Servant poem is over; nevertheless, the continuation of the question-(v. 10) and-answer format (v. 11) with the *mî . . . hēn* construction (parallel to 50:8–9) argues that these word of application were drawn from the life of the Servant and should be part of this paragraph.[127] B. S. Childs views 50:10–11 as "a commentary-like addition" to the Servant poem, similar to the extension of the Servant song (49:1–6) in 49:7.[128]

50:4–5 The one who introduces himself at the beginning of this poem is a disciple of the Lord. The Servant fully recognizes that his role of being instructed was a gift given to him from "the Sovereign LORD" who would help him endure and accomplish his task.[129] He was given a "disciples, instructed person's" (*limmûdîm*)[130] tongue (in 49:2 he is given a "mouth like a sharpened sword"), one that was well informed about what he should say and well equipped to say it persuasively. This divine equipping enabled him to know how to use his tongue compassionately "in order to sustain"[131] those who were weary with a good word from the Lord.[132] The people who are weary and the reason for their weariness are not defined in this verse, but in 40:29–31 weariness refers to those who are weak and stumble, who need God's strengthening.

---

[127] O'Connell, *Concentricity and Continuity*, 197–98, says that there is a concentric emphasis on obedience at the beginning (50:4) and the challenge for others to obey God's message at the end (50:10).

[128] Childs, *Isaiah*, 395, believes that these extensions "seek to draw out the implications" of the poem.

[129] The song uses the title יהוה אֲדֹנָי "my Lord Yahweh" four times (50:4,5,7,9) to make it extremely clear that God was involved with every aspect of his life and the reason why he is able to teach faithfully in spite of severe suffering (God is the Lord whom he serves). Oswalt, *Isaiah 40–66*, 323, states that, "its function is not only to impress on the reader the intimate association of the Servant with the Ruler of the universe, but also to emphasize both the seriousness of the calling and the certainty of the vindication."

[130] לִמּוּדִים is an adjective (BDB, 541), but it is not clear why a pl. adjective is modifying a sg. noun "tongue." This pl. form may be a pl. of abstraction ("discipling") intended to intensify the root idea (GKC §124d-e). Baltzer, *Deutero-Isaiah*, 340, views this as a strong contrast between God's servant Moses who was unwilling to speak and this new Moses servant. R. R. Ekblad, *Isaiah's Servant Poems According to the Septuagint: An Exegetical and Theological Study*, 129, 136, notes that the Old Greek translation has "chastened" in v. 4 and "chastening" in v. 5, indicating a slightly different understanding of this aspect.

[131] The infinitive construct לָעוּת gives the purpose of the prophet. The root עוּת is only used in this verse so its meaning is questionable. A similar Aramaic root עוּשׁ means to "help, sustain." It is not necessary to amend the text to לַעֲנוֹת "to answer" from the root עָנָה as Baltzer, *Deutero-Isaiah*, 338, suggests, for the servant is not answering someone's complaint or question in this oracle. Koole, *Isaiah III, Volume 2: Isaiah 49–55*, 106–107, has a long discussion of other suggested roots that various commentators have suggested as the root of this word. F. E. Greenspan, *Hapax Legomena in Biblical Hebrew*, SBLDS 74 (Chico: Scholars Press, 1984), 145–46, lists various guesses like עֵת "to teach" or לַעֲנֹת "to answer."

[132] This might suggest a prophetic role for the servant, but since this person is never called a prophet in this context, this definition may read more into the text than it implies. Certainly one does not have to be a prophet in order to instruct people by reading a fitting word from Scripture that will encourage a brother.

In the immediate context of 49:14–50:3 it appears that some Israelites were somewhat impatient for God to act and were becoming weary of waiting for him to act.

This ability to sustain the weary through his speech was enhanced because God "awakened"[133] the Servant to action "each morning";[134] specifically God awakened his ear so that it could hear what God was saying, just like a good disciple listens and internalizes what his master says. This does not mean that this person was one of Isaiah's disciples (8:16), for this Servant listens to God for his instruction. Back in 48:16–17 God called on his audience to listen to what he had spoken, for what he was teaching them was meant to direct them in the ways of God. Unfortunately, Israel failed to pay attention to what God said (48:18). In 50:5 the Servant's behavior is set in contrast to the rest of Israel, for he responded positively and listened to what God said. This is because God opened his ears so that he would hear, but the Israelites refused to hear because their ears were not open (48:8). Thus Israel rebelled (48:8), but the Servant of God did not rebel (50:5b). In other contexts the wicked close their ears to what is good (Ps 58:4–5) and the righteous close their ears to what is evil (33:15), but God is able to open the ears and reveal himself to his servants (1 Sam 9:15; 35:5). The prayer of all believers should be that God would open their ears to new ways of understanding and applying what God has communicated in his word. This Servant did not "turn his back" on God's plans for him but faithfully taught the weary what God said. He did not respond to this responsibility with excuses like Moses (Exod 3:11; 4:10–14) and Jeremiah (1:5–10). Although the message this Servant taught to his audience is not recorded in this oracle, the following verses record the audience's negative rejection of his message.

50:6 Earlier in 49:4 the Servant "labored to no purpose . . . spent my strength in vain for nothing" and in 49:7 he was "despised and abhorred by the nations," so the reader is already aware that there will be some difficulty in fulfilling the Servant's responsibilities. This verse gives additional information about the problems the Servant encountered when his audience rejected his ministry. The text does not specifically identify those who oppose him,[135]

---

[133] The root עוּר refers to God's act of enlivening, arousing, moving people to action. This root is found twice, once before "every morning" and once after it. This is the term used to describe God's arousing of a king in 41:1,25 and the Israelites in 51:9; 52:1 to action. The Masoretes marked this word with a *paseq* suggesting some uncertainty about it, so Whybray, *Isaiah 40–66*, 151, deletes it.

[134] The repetitious בַּבֹּקֶר בַּבֹּקֶר "in the morning in the morning" repeats the same phrase twice "to express entirety, or in a distributive sense" (GKC §123c), meaning "every morning."

[135] Goldingay, *Message of Isaiah 40–55*, 407, concludes that these were Babylonians who were attacking the prophet because he was saying the Cyrus the Persian king was to be their savior who would free the Israelites. None of these conclusions are drawn from this text, for the servant's message to his audience is not described, those who beat him are not identified, and the reason for beating him is not explained. In contrast, Blenkinsopp, *Isaiah 40–55*, 319, concludes that, "there is no indication that the speaker has been imprisoned by the Babylonian authorities and is awaiting trial." F. C. Holmgren, "The Servant: Responding to Violence (Isaiah 50:4–9),"

but someone was "smiting, beating" (from the root *nākâ*) him, "pulling out his beard" (from the root *māraṭ*), mocking, and spitting at him. Beating can be connected to the punishment one receives when arrested for a crime (Deut 25:2; Jer 20:2; 37:15), mocking and spitting are sign of disrespect (Num 12:14; Job 30:10), but the pulling out of the beard is rarely mentioned as a punishment. One example when this happened was when Nehemiah "rebuked them and called curses down on them. I beat some of the men and pulled out their hair" (Neh 13:25) because he was disturbed that the Hebrew people who intermarried with foreigners were not able to speak or read the Hebrew language. Here and in 2 Sam 10:4–5 the pulling out or shaving of the hair seems to be a means of humiliating a person. The text does not state why the Servant was receiving this kind of cruel and humiliating treatment. One might assume that he was mistreated because the audience opposed his preaching, just like the audiences of other prophets opposed their preaching (1 Kgs 19; 22; Jer 11:18–22; 15:10–18; 20:1–10; Amos 7; Mic 2:6), but this oracle says nothing about that issue. Some believers in the persecuted church today know of this kind of suffering, for from time to time they are forced to undergo similar beatings. Some have made the ultimate sacrifice and have been willing to give their life for their faith.[136]

The reaction of the Servant is amazing, for he voluntarily allowed himself (lit. "I gave" *nātattî*) to suffer this degrading abuse. In the midst of this abuse there appears to be no cries of innocence, no lamentation or weeping, and no calling for God to have vengeance on his persecutors (in contrast to Jeremiah). He accepts this mistreatment and does not hide[137] his face to avoid it or protect himself from such abuse. One should not agree with C. Westermann's view that "in that world's thought what the Servant here says of himself . . . means that he regarded the attacks, blows and insults as justified, and so concedes that God is on the side of his opponents."[138] There is no admission of wrongdoing or acceptance of guilt, no indication that the Servant believed he deserved this

---

CurTM 31 (2004): 352–58, argues "that the enemies assaulting the Servant consist of Jews who are rebelling against the teaching that the Servant embodies. . . . In their 'conversion' to the religion of the victor [the Babylonians], they doubtless became cynical of their earlier beliefs and stood in opposition to those who proclaimed them." It is better to follow J. W. Adams, *The Performative Nature and Function of Isaiah 40–55*, LHB/OTS 448 (London: T&T Clark, 2006), 167, and conclude that these opponents are only known as "those who resist the word of Yahweh and thus his messenger."

[136] J. Hefley and M. Hefley, *By Their Blood: Christian Martyrs of the Twentieth Century* (Grand Rapids: Baker, 1960) or K. A. Lawson, "The Suffering Church," *CT* 40 (July 15, 1996): 54–59, provides many examples of those who have suffered and died for what they believe.

[137] 1QIs\^a has הסירותי from the root סור "he turned" rather than הסתרתי "I hide" from the root סתר but the Masoretic reading makes good sense and does not need to be changed.

[138] Westermann, *Isaiah 40–66*, 230, seems confused in his interpretation of v. 7. He states that the "words say something that is strictly impossible—the Servant is certain that God is on his side, although his own conduct as expressed in v. 6 apparently indicated the reverse." These words of confidence would not seem so impossible, if the Servant's words in v. 6 were not misinterpreted.

treatment. The Servant's close relationship to God demonstrates that God was not opposing him. How "that world thought" (the original readers) about this picture of suffering is unknown and what his enemies thought or misunderstood about the Servant does not determine how God evaluates the Servant's suffering. The language clearly represents the willful submission of an innocent Servant of God to vile persecution.[139]

50:7 In spite of severe suffering the Servant expresses his confidence in God. The conjunction that begins the verse is probably expressing an adversative contrast "but" (NIV "because"). In contrast to the shaming and abuse of others, it is the "Sovereign God" (as in 50:4,5,9) who "will help me" (*yaʿăzār lî*), indicating the close trust relationship between God and the Servant. Since God has given him this role and gives him instruction daily, he is confident that God will assist him in the midst of his present trials. The nature of this help is not to be found in avoiding the persecution but in God's future vindication of the Servant (59:8). Two results will derive from this divine help. "Therefore, on account of this" (*ʿal-kēn*, omitted in NIV), the Servant will continue to carry out his work without a sense of shame or guilt; the humiliation intended to break his spirit (in 50:6) will not destroy his confidence in God. A second result ("therefore," *ʿal-kēn*) will be that the face that was not hidden from abuse in 50:6 will now be firmly set in a determined and unmovable direction to follow God's will. Persecution will not lead to fear that intimidates or weakens the will to act; instead, abuse will result in an unbreakable commitment (as strong as flint) to continue trusting God. This is a picture of absolute stubborn resistance to giving up his responsibilities (Jer 5:3; Ezek 3:8), a resolute determination to carry out the will of God. He absolutely knows for sure that the end results will not be "shame"[140] but vindication. God will uphold him and not deceive him; God will not bring on him the humiliation of trusting in a false hope. This stubborn commitment to God's way must be the perspective of all who truly trust and serve God, for in the end God never fails, even though persecution and tribulations may require a person to suffer severely for a while when they are innocent of any wrong.

50:8 Why does this Servant have such confidence? He knows God intimately. He knows that God is near his side. He knows that God is the one who will vindicate him. God is not some name given to the abstract unmoved mover of philosophy or the lifeless and powerless idols of the pagans. When God's Servants are in trouble, God is right there to "justify, declare just, acquit,

---

[139] Watts, "Mark," *CNTOT* 201–2, Jesus discusses his upcoming persecution and death with his disciple and alludes to 50:6 in Mark 10:34.

[140] M. S. Odell, "An Exploration Study of Shame and Dependence in the Bible and Selected Near Eastern Parallels," in *The Biblical Canon in Comparative Perspective*, ed. K. L. Younger, W. W. Hallo, B. F. Batto ANETS 11 (Lewiston: Mellen, 1982), 217–33, concludes that in biblical and Akkadian texts people experience shame as a result of a betrayal of trust. Divine abandonment brings about shame.

vindicate me" (*maṣdîqî*). This forensic term from the court describes what a judge declares with his verdict of "not guilty."[141] Since the Servant is so confident that God will view him as righteous, the Servant offers two parallel challenging questions. Who (*mî*) would[142] dare to contend with him in a lawsuit (Exod 18:13; Num 35:12)? If there should be someone, the servant presents the challenge "let us stand"[143] together (NIV "let us face one another") and present the evidence in court. The second parallel question begins with a question, "whoever" (*mî*) is "my accuser,"[144] plus a challenge in the cohortative "let us draw near" (NIV "let him confront me") to present the evidence. One might imagine that this might be a challenge to the persecutors in 50:6, but it appears that they have already abused the Servant without going to the bother of seeing if he is really guilty of any misdeed. Thus it is unclear whom the Servant is speaking to. Apparently he is challenging and denying the justice of what was done to him after this persecution. He still maintains his innocence.

50:9 The Servant's response to the two questions in 8b are supplied by an assertion almost identical to 50:7a: "see, behold" (*hēn*, omitted in NIV) the sovereign Lord will help me. In v. 7 this confession of faith in God assured the Servant that God would assist him during persecution, but in v. 9 this statement assures the Servant that God will assist him in being declared just in any trial. If this is the case, then the question in the second line asks, "who" (*mî*) is he that would dare to declare the Servant wicked; can anyone say that he is a guilty person? The obvious assumed answer is, no one. If God will declare him just (50:8), no one else can prove that he is guilty. Consequently, people should "see, behold" (*hēn*), that all those people who might try to condemn the Servant will end up looking like a moth-eaten garment. The significance of this metaphor is not very evident. It could point to the transience of such a garment (their life will soon be gone like an old moth-eaten garment), the imperceptible slow but sure destructive work of the moth (the unseen but sure erosion of their life), or just another image of the nothingness the wicked will become (41:24, there will be no substance to them or their claims—they are full of holes).

---

[141] Lindsey, "Isaiah's Songs of the Servant, Part 3: The Commission of the Servant in Isaiah 50:4–11," 216–29, expands the meaning of this vindication far beyond anything that can be explained from this passage by extensively drawing on New Testament interpretations.

[142] The imperfect verse following the interrogative מִי should be translated as a modal, expressing a contingency that "might, can, would" happen (GKC §107r,t).

[143] The cohortative נַעַמְדָה expresses a wish or desire (GKC §108c).

[144] The phrase בַּעַל מִשְׁפָּטִי is only found here and literally means "the lord of my judgment, the master of my cause." Motyer, *Isaiah*, 400, thinks this phrase refers to "the process of proving to be a master in a legal suit." In this context it must refer to the opponent rather than God. Although the terminology is different, Job 31:35 refers to a similar person who accuses him. Blenkinsopp, *Isaiah 40–55*, 322, thinks that this servant "anticipates being brought to trial by the Babylonian authorities for sedition," but this historicizes an eschatological text inappropriately.

50:10–11 The Servant's description of what happened to him ends with v. 9, but another voice (the prophet is speaking God's words)[145] reflects on what the Servant has said and challenges the Hebrew audience (the "you" in 50:10) to follow the example of the Servant of the Lord. While reflecting on the implications of these verses, the person suffering in 50:4–9 is identified as the "Servant of the Lord," but these verses offer no additional explanation concerning his exact identity.

Three problems need to be addressed concerning the translation and function of 50:10–11 and their relationship to 50:4–9. First, C. Westermann suspects that there was a disturbance in the arrangement of the text because there is no hymn at the end of the servant poem, like the hymn in 42:10–13 (after 42:1–9) and in 49:13 (after 49:1–12). Since 50:10–11 are not a part of a hymn, he rearranges the verses.[146] Although it is natural to expect an earlier pattern to continue, nothing requires that a hymn appear after every Servant poem. It appears that the hymns in 42:10–13 and 49:13 primarily function to close larger literary units, not just to mark the end of a Servant poem; therefore, the lack of a hymn is not problematic if this is not the end of a literary unit. Second, R. Melugin has difficulty understanding how these verses go together. He considers 50:10–11 a "sarcastic word of judgment in the mouth of Yahweh," thus he concludes that the Servant's statements of confidence in 50:4–9 are not designed "primarily to express trust; it is rather to lay the foundation for the condemnation of the unfaithful" in 50:10–11.[147] This interpretation places too much emphasis on the negative curse in v. 11 and not enough attention on the positive encouragement to trust God in v. 10 or the positive example the Servant sets for the audience. Third, it is difficult to know how to interpret the various clauses in 50:10. Is 10b about the Servant who fears God but sometimes has to walk in darkness (RSV, NRSV), making the whole verse one long question, or is 10b addressed to the audience (NIV, HCSB), meaning the verse has a question in 10a and an exhortation in 10b? The second approach seems superior.[148]

Thus the question asked in 50:10 is "who" (*mî*, as in 50:1,8) among those in the audience "reverences, stands in awe, fears" (*yĕrēʾ*) God and obeys the words of God like the Servant of God? This reverence refers to a pious respect and reverent conviction that moves the Servant to trust God. Part of the reason

---

[145] Muilenburg, "Isaiah 39–66," 5:587, believes God is speaking here.

[146] Westermann, *Isaiah 40–66*, 233, places 50:10–11 after 51:1a; thus he is able to identify "those who fear the Lord" in 50:11 with those "who pursue righteousness in 51:1a (both refer to a group of proselytes).

[147] Melugin, *Formation of Isaiah 40–55*, 152–53.

[148] Adams, *The Performative Nature and Function of Isaiah 40–55*, 160–61, has a long footnote discussing how to interpret מִי (better as an interrogative "who" than as an indefinite pronoun "whoever"), אֲשֶׁר (as dependent on 10a or beginning a new clause and dependent on 10b, plus the issue of who is the antecedent), and the meaning of the imperfect verbs in 10b (imperfect or jussive).

why the audience should follow God is because of the words (lit "voice") of his Servant. Since the Servant does not preach a message in 50:4–9 but only testifies about his life experience, one could conclude that the audience is being encouraged to: (a) listen and follow the message that the life of the Servant (50:4–9) communicates by example or (b) listen and follow the Servant's testimony in earlier poems. For example, people should respond to his declarations about his life and calling in 49:1–4 or about God's plans for him to be a covenant and a light to the nations in 49:6–12.

The second half of the verse appears to be an exhortation to those in the audience[149] who were walking in dark times similar to the oppression suffered by the Servant of the Lord. Even though there is presently not much of a sign of hope or light, "he should trust"[150] in the name of the Lord and "should rely, lean, depend" (*šāʿēn*) on his God. Walking in the light was urged earlier in 2:5 based on God's eschatological promises of his coming to Zion and establishing it as a place where all the nations will come to learn of God's law. Political and spiritual gloom and "darkness"[151] are pictured in 8:23–9:2 as the opposite of the great light that God will send to bring great joy and hope. Those who do not consult God and rely on mediums and spiritists will have no light (8:19–20), but those who go to the law and the testimony will know that the coming light of God's salvation is related to the establishment of his Davidic messianic ruler. Later 60:1–3 tells of a time when the light of the glory of God will descend on a world covered with darkness. All these passages consistently proclaim that the only hope for mankind and this world is the divine light of God. It provides a sure resource for people to depend on in a troubled and wicked world (similar to the world of the suffering Servant). This is the positive way that the audience should walk, but the emphasis given to the answer in 49:11 suggests that this application was also intended to address the many who were not among those trusting God.

50:11   This verse begins with an emphatic *hēn* "see, behold" (NIV "but"), which introduces the answer to a question in 10a, similar to the answer to the questions in 50:1b and 9. It begins with a strongly worded warning to those in his audience who "light their own fires," a metaphorical picture of those who create their own hope. They have rejected the light from God[152] and have cho-

---

[149] W. A. M. Beuken, "Jes 50:10–11: eine kultische Paränese zur dritten Ebed-prophetie," *ZAW* 85 (1973): 168–82, properly identifies the antecedent of אֲשֶׁר as מִי בָשֶׁם "who among you" in the audience.

[150] The imperfect verb יִבְטַח "he will trust" is probably a modal imperfect (GKC §107n) expressing what should be done. Koole, *Isaiah III, Volume 2: Isaiah 49–55*, 123, prefers an obligatory imperfect "he must trust" which is another viable option, while North, *Second Isaiah*, 205, and NIV translate this verb as a jussive "let him trust."

[151] The pl. "darkness" חֲשֵׁכִים may indicate an abstract pl. or a pl. of intensity (GKC §124d for abstract pl. or 124a for intensity).

[152] Watts, *Isaiah 34–66*, 204, believes the Persian king Darius is the servant of the Lord in v. 10 and that he is making this threatening warning, but surely it is God who is speaking in vv. 10–11.

sen to substitute their own hope (their light) for God's salvation. Ironically,[153] the prophet exhorts these wicked people to walk in their own light and destroy themselves. He does not actually want them to do this, but he states this absurd tongue-in-cheek encouragement in order to get them to see the error of their ways.[154] The last parts of the verse describe the destiny of those who refuse to listen to the warnings of the prophet and foolishly continue to follow their own light. They will receive from God's hand exactly what they deserve. They will end up lying down (possibly implying death) in a situation or place of "torment."[155] This is consistent with the picture of 66:24 where the dead bodies of the wicked will be in a place of torment where the worm does not die and the fire is not quenched.

(3) God's Past Salvation Encourages Faith for the Future (51:1–8)

> **[1]"Listen to me, you who pursue righteousness**
> **   and who seek the LORD:**
> **Look to the rock from which you were cut**
> **   and to the quarry from which you were hewn;**
> **[2]look to Abraham, your father,**
> **   and to Sarah, who gave you birth.**
> **When I called him he was but one,**
> **   and I blessed him and made him many.**
> **[3]The LORD will surely comfort Zion**
> **   and will look with compassion on all her ruins;**
> **he will make her deserts like Eden,**
> **   her wastelands like the garden of the LORD.**
> **Joy and gladness will be found in her,**
> **   thanksgiving and the sound of singing.**
>
> **[4]"Listen to me, my people;**
> **   hear me, my nation:**
> **The law will go out from me;**
> **   my justice will become a light to the nations.**
> **[5]My righteousness draws near speedily,**
> **   my salvation is on the way,**
> **   and my arm will bring justice to the nations.**

Goldingay, *Message of Isaiah 40–55*, 414–15, suggests that the prophet was addressing the Babylonian exiles, but there is no reference to any location in chap. 50. In the larger context Zion is mentioned in 49:14, and the children in 49:19–25 will be returning to Zion. In the following chapter Zion is comforted (51:3) because the ransomed will return to Zion (51:11).

[153] The use of the imperative לְכוּ is a sarcastic or ironic sense (GKC §110a), for the prophet really wants them to do the opposite and not walk in light of their own wisdom.

[154] Amos 4:4 is an ironic tongue-in-cheek encouragement for the audience to "go to Bethel and transgress." It is obvious that this is irony, for Amos was not in favor of the sinful worship of the golden calf at the Bethel temple.

[155] The word לְמַעֲצֵבָה is found only here in the Old Testament. This noun form comes from the root עָצַב "to grieve, distress, pain."

The islands will look to me
and wait in hope for my arm.
⁶Lift up your eyes to the heavens,
look at the earth beneath;
the heavens will vanish like smoke,
the earth will wear out like a garment
and its inhabitants die like flies.
But my salvation will last forever,
my righteousness will never fail.

⁷"Hear me, you who know what is right,
you people who have my law in your hearts:
Do not fear the reproach of men
or be terrified by their insults.
⁸For the moth will eat them up like a garment;
the worm will devour them like wool.
But my righteousness will last forever,
my salvation through all generations."

The organization of the material is this section of Isaiah is particularly difficult because all the surrounding paragraphs look forward to the coming of God's salvation. Although almost everyone agrees on where to make the paragraph breaks (after v. 8), few agree on how to put these paragraphs together to form a larger unit. A central decision relates to how one should deal with 51:1–8. Three proposed solutions are: (a) 51:1–52:12 is one long unit made up of several shorter paragraphs including 51:1–8.[156] One of the key linguistic characteristics that unify these paragraphs is the repeated use of double imperatives (51:9 "awake, awake"; 51:12 "I even I"; 51:17 "awake, awake"; 52:1 awake, awake."). In spite of including 51:1–8 within this longer segment, C. R. Seitz concludes that 51:1–8 "has a more immediate contextual relationship with the preceding chapter. . . . It serves to introduce the recapitulation and finale in 51:9–52:12."[157] J. A. Motyer also puts all of 51:1–52:12 within one long unit, but he does note a connection between those who pursue righteousness in 51:1,7 and those who fear God in 50:10. 51:1–52:12 are drawn together by the repeated use of vocabulary and similar patterns in the three oracles in this unit (51:1–8;9–16; 51:17–52:12).[158] (b) A second approach finds a close association between 51:1–8 and the material in chap. 50 (rather than with the

---

[156] Seitz, "Isaiah 40–66," 6:440–44, claims that "chaps 51–52 are not amenable to traditional or even modified, form-critical treatment, even of the sort employed throughout the commentary thus far" because there is an unusual amount of "creative freedom and sheer rhetorical brilliance." Seitz identifies a close connection between 40:1–11 and this unit.

[157] Ibid., 6:441. Goldingay, *Message of Isaiah 40–55*, 417, also makes 51:1–52:12 a unit, but he says little to defend this conclusion, though he does find a common rhetorical location in Jerusalem and a common portrayal of the people's experience of oppression (51:7,13–14,19; 52:5).

[158] Repeated words are "comfort" in 51:3,12; 52:9; "joy" in 51:3; 52:9; "the fury of the oppressor" in 51:13; 52:5, and others like the "arm of the Lord" in 51:5; 52:10.

speeches that follow). J. D. W. Watts identified a chiastic structure that covers 50:4–51:8 with Darius speaking from 50:10–51:8.[159] J. Oswalt connects 51:1–8 to the conclusion to chap. 50 because 50:10–51:8 is all about persuading people to heed the voice of the servant. Those who fear the Lord in 50:10 are the same people who pursue righteousness in 51:1, plus 50:9b and 51:8a have identical phrases about the moth devouring a garment. (c) A third approach makes an independent unit out of 51:1–16 and does not make it a part of the speeches before or after it. Although J. Muilenburg finds linguistic connections between 51:1–16 and chaps. 49–50, the dominant theme of God's comfort for Zion unites 51:1–16. The statement "Zion, you are my people" functions as a fitting conclusion to the paragraph in 51:16.[160] J. K. Kuntz identifies seven common factors that characterize this poem,[161] but many of them are not unique to 51:1–16.

Because of the following connecting and disconnecting factors, 51:1–8 will be treated as a separate paragraph. (a) There are many verbal connections between 51:1–8 and chap. 50; thus it appears that 51:1–8 should not be included with what follows in 51:9–52:12. (b) The use of double imperatives begins at 51:9 and not in 51:1–8, so this suggests that 51:1–8 should not be included with 51:9–52:12. (c) The regular internal structure of 51:1–8 is not comparable to what precedes or follows these verses; therefore, it seems that 51:1–8 is a short independent paragraph that is closely related to chap. 50.

The paragraph is structured around three imperative verbs that encourage listening to God (51:1,4,7), which are followed by three words of assurance and consolation:[162]

God will comfort Zion	51:1–3
God's law and salvation is for the nations	51:4–6
Your enemies will end; my salvation is forever	51:7–8

---

[159] The chiastic structure that Watts, *Isaiah 35–66*, 197, creates is not very convincing and ignores the fact that 50:4–9 are first-person speeches by the Servant, but there are no parallel first-person speeches in 51:7–8. This chiastic structure also ignores the identical phrases in 50:11 and 51:8, which seemingly should be connected to one another in some way in any chiastic structure.

[160] Muilenburg, "Isaiah 40–66," 5:589, only shows linguistic connections with the preceding chaps. and not with 51:17–52:12; although on p. 602–603 he does identify some linguistic connections between 51:17–52:12 and 51:1–16.

[161] J. K. Kuntz, "The Contribution of Rhetorical Criticism to Understanding Isaiah 51:1–16," in *Art and Meaning: Rhetoric in Biblical Literature*, JSOTSup 19 (Sheffield: JSOT Press, 1982), 140–71, identifies seven factors that enable this poem to communicate its central message: (a) Yahweh is presented in first-person terminology, (b) repeated divine imperatives, (c) the use of imagery, (d) the repetition of key words, (e) the use of contrast, (f) the employment of rhetorical questions, and (g) direct quotations. Nevertheless, many of these factors are common to numerous speeches in Isaiah (use of questions, imagery, repetition of key vocabulary, contrast, and imperatives), so unless these are not found in the chapter before and after, they do not present strong criteria to limit this unit to 51:1–16.

[162] O'Connell, *Concentricity and Continuity*, 199, outlines this passages into three calls (the imperatives) and three consolations.

R. Melugin found some disputational characteristics in 51:1–2, but the rest of the unit is primarily made up of assurances of God's salvation.[163] Those who agree with Melugin assume[164] that there were complaints (God had failed to fulfill his promises)[165] or doubts that caused a disputation concerning the coming of God's salvation. But no doubts are expressed; the only negative point is that there is some fear about the reproaches of their enemies in 51:7. Therefore, it seems more appropriate to consider these three short subparagraphs as eschatological proclamations of salvation[166] that were to function as words of assurance and encouragement. God reassures his faithful people that he will fulfill his promises and he will establish his rule over the whole world (the faithful do not doubt God).[167] The paragraph is held together by its common structure in the three subparagraphs (imperatives followed by a *kî* clause) and repeated vocabulary.[168]

51:1–3 An initial group of three imperatives (1a "listen," 1b "look," 2a "look") encourage an audience of believers based on who they are (51:1) and what God did in the past through Abraham and Sarah (50:2). These words function as a means of comforting people about what he will do for Zion in the future (50:3). This will involve a transformation of Zion into a paradise like the garden of Eden, which is an eschatological hope, not a description of the transformation of the area around Jerusalem after the people returned from exile.

51:1 God addresses an audience made up of a group of righteous Hebrews, "those who pursue righteousness"[169] and "those who seek Yahweh."

---

[163] Melugin, *Formation of Isaiah 40–55*, 156–57, follows Begrich's identification of 51:1–2 as a disputation.

[164] Whybray, *Isaiah 40–66*, 154, plainly admits that the "cause of their discouragement may be inferred from the reply which is given to them: they are concerned about the smallness of their numbers and fear, even if they are able to return to their homeland, they will be unequal to the task of restoration." This approach to interpretation is not a foolproof way of understanding a text. It would seem that some encouragements could derive simply from a desire to see greater faith. All encouragements are not a response to a negative problem of unbelief or discouragement.

[165] Oswalt, *Isaiah 40–66*, 333, claims that hardened unbelievers "will not be especially troubled by God's apparent failure to keep his promises . . . But for those that believe God, who are seeking him, hope deferred can be a trial." But where does the text say that there is some deferred hope?

[166] Muilenburg, "Isaiah 40–66," 5:589, call this "an eschatological oracle of comfort" that is based on "an appeal to the past and by a promise of future salvation."

[167] An alternative suggestion by P. D. Hanson hypothesizes that "50:4–9 introduces the Teacher and chap. 51 recites his lesson to the people." Hanson, *Isaiah 40–66*, 144, bases this on the close connection between the circumstances of the audience and the servant (both were weary, both were oppressed, both their enemies will be destroyed). Goldingay, *Message of Isaiah 40–55*, 417, accepts Hanson's perspective, and Baltzer, *Deutero-Isaiah*, 344–45, also believes the servant of 50:4–9 (he identifies the servant as Moses) is speaking in chap. 51.

[168] Koole, *Isaiah III, Volume 2: Isaiah 49–55*, 136, notes the repetition of צֶדֶק in vv. 1,5,7,8; הַבִּיטוּ in vv. 1,2,6; תּוֹרָה in vv. 4,7; and תֵּחַת at the end of vv. 6,7.

[169] The RSV translation "pursue deliverance" (רֹדְפֵי צֶדֶק) gives the term a exilic tone rather than a moral meaning. Muilenburg, "Isaiah 40–66," 5:590, agrees with this translation, but this weakens its parallelism with "seek the Lord," which definitely has a moral and the relational aspect

These are not sinners who have rebelled against God, so this may be the same group addressed as "the ones who fear God" in 50:10 or a group of future God-fearers.[170] Pursuing righteousness implies a desire to maintain a life characterized by that quality. Pursuing "righteousness" (*ṣedeq*) in Deut 16:20 is related to acting justly in a court of law, in Prov 21:21 pursuing righteousness is parallel to having a relationship of loving others, and in Zeph 2:3 the way to avoid God's judgment is to seek to be righteous and exhibit humility. God is one who acts with righteousness, so this pursuit of righteousness would involve endeavoring to act in ways consistent with the righteousness of God. The "seeking" (*mĕbaqšēy*) of God does not involve the activity of trying to find a God who is hidden in some faraway place; it is the activity of remaining in relationship with him at the sanctuary at a time of sacrifice (2 Chr 1:5) or through prayer (Gen 25:21–23; 1 Kgs 22:8). It involves earnest and concerted effort with singleness of heart (Jer 29:12–13; 2 Chr 15:2,12). The results of seeking God might involve his protection, his words of approval, or his presence with his righteous people. There is a connection between seeking God, pursuing righteousness and receiving the benefits (eschatological salvation) of having a relationship with God.[171]

In order to encourage this relationship with God this message instructs the audience to learn from past experience by looking to[172] the "rock" (*ṣûr*) and "quarry, pit" (*bôr*) from which they came. In some sense the present audience was "cut, hewn, dug" or "excavated, quarried"[173] from their parents. The imagery is odd, although one might find an analogical relationship between Sarah's dry womb and the "dry pit, hole, quarry" they were birthed from. F. Delitzsch suggests that this imagery was chosen because Abraham and Sarah were unfruitful, and getting children out of them was comparable to a divine miracle of bringing life out of a solid unfertile rock.[174]

---

of commitment. Schoors, *I Am God Your Savior*, 156, translates this term as "salvific judgment" (51:1) when God gains dominion over the world but translates it differently in v. 5. For a discussion of the different meanings of "righteousness," especially its use in chaps. 56–66 consult R. Rendtorff, "Isaiah 56:1 as a Key to the Formation of the Book of Isaiah," in *Canon and Theology* (Minneapolis: Fortress, 1993), 181–90.

[170] Most commentators connect the righteous people described in 51:1 with the same group referred to in 50:10, but the text is not very clear if this group in 51:1–8 is a later eschatological group of people who are righteous, or the righteous people in the time of Isaiah.

[171] Both Young, *The Book of Isaiah*, 3:307, and Koole, *Isaiah III, Volume 2: Isaiah 49–55*, 139, join these two aspects of "righteousness, salvation," though the moral relational aspect is the main point here.

[172] The Hebrew imperative הַבִּיטוּ "look, consider, take heed" functions as an exhortation, admonition, or word of encouragement to do something so that they can draw the right implications from it (GKC §110a).

[173] The word נֻקַּרְתֶּם is used in the Siloam inscription to describe the activity of the men who "dug, pierced through" Hezekiah's tunnel under the City of David in Jerusalem (*ANET*, 321).

[174] Delitzsch, "Prophecies of Isaiah," 282, says, "it was, as it were, out of hard stone that God raised up children."

51:2   This unusual imagery about the rock and quarry is explained as a reference to their ancient forefather and mother, Abraham and Sarah. The audience is encouraged a second time to "look, examine, notice" that Abraham was a man like them, who had to walk by faith in God's promises about the future. One of the reasons for bringing up the righteous man Abraham and his wife Sarah was to point out a comparison between the past history of the nation and what the future holds. Long ago God called one man[175] who did not have any children, so he was somewhat like Zion, which was "bereaved and barren" (49:21). When God called him from Ur many years earlier, it was "so that I might bless and multiply him" (Gen 12:1–3),[176] and this is still God's plan for the descendents of Abraham. Just as the children of Abraham increased through the ages, so God will act on behalf of his people in Zion to make them multiply.

51:3   Now the prophet reassures his audience (*kî*, "surely, it is indisputable," omitted in NIV) that these are God's words of comfort or compassion for the people of Zion because God is going to act on their behalf (40:1). God's intended transformation of Zion is compared to the radical transformation God will accomplish (*wĕyyāśem*, "he will establish, set up, make")[177] when he changes the deserts of earth into Eden, most likely the garden of God in Gen 2:8.[178] This will cause the people of God to rejoice, sing, and thank God.[179] This kind of imagery was employed earlier in numerous prophecies (41:17–20). In 35:1–2,6 God promised that the desert areas would rejoice and burst with blossoming plants, like the glory of Lebanon, because the glory of

---

[175] J. G. Janzen, "An Echo of the Shema in Isaiah 51:1–3," *JSOT* 43 (1989): 69–82, translates this "as one I called him," making the one refer to God in order to affirm "the central integrity of Yahweh" who as unchangeable has a unified will for his chosen people and is faithful to his plan (this contrasts with the gods who do not control history or have reliable unified plan).

[176] The past tense used in the NIV "I blessed him and made him many" implies a slight emendation of the *waw* that precedes the verb וַאֲבָרְכֵהוּ from a *waw* conjunctive in the Masoretic tradition (expressing repeated or continual incomplete action) to a *waw* consecutive. GKC §107b, note 2 makes the questionable suggestion that this is a place where the *waw* conjunctive "is no doubt a dogmatic emendation for וְ (*imperf. consec.*) in order to represent historical statements as promises." Muilenburg, "Isaiah 40–66," 5:591, and Goldingay, *Message of Isaiah 40–55*, 420, are two among many who reject the need to emend the Masoretic reading.

[177] The *waw* consecutive imperfect verb וַיָּשֶׂם should be translated with a incomplete future meaning, for the *waw* consecutive continues the meaning of the preceding prophetic perfect נָחַם (GKC §111w).

[178] Schoors, *I Am God Your Savior*, 163, doubts that these ideas come from Genesis 2 and claims that "the Genesis account is not the source of the other references to the Garden of God. . . . The conclusion then is obvious: Isa li,3 does not speak about a return to primeval paradise." This is just "a familiar popular tradition . . . The prophets only say with an impressive image: Zion, that now is in ruins, will be restored in all its splendor." In contrast Muilenburg, "Isaiah 40–66," 5:593, states, "The End will be like the beginning. Eschatological time will turn to primordial time." This would seem to be a more faithful reading of this prophetic tradition.

[179] J. G. Janzen, "Rivers in the Desert of Abraham and Sarah and Zion (Isaiah 51:1–3)," *HAR* 10 (1986): 139–51, supports connecting this prophecy to Eden traditions in Genesis.

the Lord will be there. Water, bubbling springs, and pools of water will transform the earth and bring rejoicing to the lame and blind, who will be healed of their troubles, because of the splendor of God's miraculous presence. In 32:15–16 the pouring out of God's Spirit will transform the deserts into fertile fields (43:19–20), and the earth will be filled with righteousness and peace. The prophet Ezekiel compares the former glories of the city of Tyre to the garden of Eden (Ezek 28:13) and the former splendor of Egypt to the trees in Eden (Ezek 31:16–18). In God's eschatological recreation of the earth (Ezek 36:24–36) Ezekiel describes how God will gather his people back to their land (36:24,31), cleanse the people of their sins (36:25,33), give them a new heart and his Spirit (36:26–27), and restore the fertility of their land like the garden of Eden (36:29–30,34–35). The joy and singing that will accompany this eschatological restoration of the land expresses a radical change in the attitude of the Hebrew people. These new conditions in Zion do not refer to the situation in Zion after the people return from Babylonian exile but something much greater and grander at the end of the ages.

This fertile and joyous time contrasts with the preeschatological conditions of Zion that the audience of the prophet was acquainted with. The condition of the earth before God miraculously acts to change this world is analogically compared to a ruins or a desert (the direct opposite of the garden of Eden).[180] In a comparative sense, the land around Jerusalem lacked abundant fertility and water; it suffered under the judgment of God. The people did not enjoy the fullness of God's gift of fertility to the land, and they were not filled with joy. These are formulaic descriptions of a general setting without God's blessings, so it is difficult to attribute it to any specific temporal period in Israelite history. Multiple wars year after year left portions of the fields and cities in ruins; repeatedly the land suffered from droughts and the existence of desert areas (the mountainous area just east of Jerusalem and large portions of the Sinai) were relatively unfertile. The prophet is communicating the assuring faith statement that this old world with all its problems and curses will be changed into a new world of joy and fertility.

51:4–6 The second subparagraph addresses what God intends to do for his righteous people, the other nations of the world, and the world as a whole. It announces both his plans to grant his salvation to his people as well as all the nations of the world. Because of these promises the audience can be confident that God's salvation is sure and will last forever. It is unclear who is speaking

---

[180] Westermann, *Isaiah 40–66*, 237, appears to take the "ruins" literally to refer to "Zion at present lying in ruins." Goldingay, *Message of Isaiah 40–55*, 422–23, chooses a more literal view when he states that "'its wastes' (see 44:27) makes it clear that 'Zion' denotes the physical city itself," but on the very next page he states "Literally, Zion has become a waste, Metaphorically it has become a wilderness or desert. Metaphorically it will become like Eden." If the concept of wilderness and Eden are metaphorical descriptions, it would be more logically consistent to say that "ruins, waste" is also metaphorical.

these words because God, or possibly the Servant of the Lord, could be proclaiming the good news in 51:4–5 (most of the actions conforms to the role of the Servant in chap. 42). It is probably best to interpret these as God's words, but it is clear that God and the Servant work side by side to accomplish the same goal of providing salvation and light to the nations.

51:4 Initially God calls a Hebrew audience ("my people," *ʾammî*)[181] with two imperative exhortations to "listen" and "hear"[182] what God has promised. They need to remember and pay attention to what he has said in earlier oracles "because" (*kî*, omitted in NIV) in an eschatological age God will cause: (a) the law, his teachings or instructions to go out; and (b) his justice to come quickly as a light to all the nations. The "instruction, law" (*tôrâ*)[183] that goes forth from Zion in 2:3 is a result of God teaching people from all the nations. Since the next line refers to God's justice influencing "the nations," one would assume that everyone will hear these divine teachings. The establishment of the justice of God throughout the earth will function as a light to the nations (42:6; 49:6); thus these nations will no longer walk in the darkness of their own understanding. These two characteristics are associated with the activity of the Servant of the Lord in 42:4, so the interlinking of the Servant's and God's activities is very evident. Presumably, both the Servant and God will declare his word to the nations, and at some point in time these nations will turn to God and be saved, bow their knees, and swear allegiance only to God (45:20–25; 49:26b). In 42:1–4 a key role of the Servant is to establish justice throughout the earth, and this passage assures the audiences that this responsibility will be accomplished in spite of opposition (50:6). While the Servant is the immediate person who will establish justice throughout the earth (42:1–4) and bring light to the nations (42:6), God's power will enable this justice "to rest" or "to come quickly"[184] when the Servant functions as a light to the nations.

---

[181] Westermann, *Isaiah 40–66*, 232, 235, reads "my people . . . my nation" as plurals "nations . . . peoples" and connect this admonition to the foreign nations, while Schoors, *I Am God Your Savior*, 154, changes only the second noun. The first "my people" clearly refers to the prophet's Hebrew audience who are the covenant people of God. The second term לְאוֹם frequently designates foreign nations, but in the sg. it does mean the people of God in Gen 25:23 and Zeph 2:9. Koole, *Isaiah III, Volume 2: Isaiah 49–55*, 148, rightly argues the case that these terms refer to Hebrew people.

[182] The repetition of two imperative exhortations could express some urgency, as well as the importance of these words. Muilenburg, "Isaiah 40–66," 5:593, maintains that this is a "strophe of remarkable intensity and power. . . . The imperatives are more urgent, the words of address more inward, the repetitions more impressive, and the imagery more vivid and sublime."

[183] Baltzer, *Deutero-Isaiah*, 351, approvingly quotes H. W. Wolff's statement (*Hosea*, Hermeneia [Minneapolis: Fortress, 1974], 176–77) that the "law, instructions" was "the entire disclosure of Yahweh's will, already fixed in writing." This assumes that God's instructions are in some written form, but even in 2:2–5 there is the assumption that God is orally teaching the nations that gather. This does not eliminate the possibility of a written account of God's will being in existence; it just focuses on the personal oral delivery of God's will to the nations.

[184] There is some confusion over the verb אַרְגִּיעַ which is also used in 49:19. Kuntz, "The Contribution of Rhetorical Criticism to Understanding Isaiah 51:1–16," 156, follows many other com-

51:5   The worldwide impact of God's work is summarized as it is implemented in the lives of people. The marvelous work of God that began in v. 4 will dramatically transform both Israel and the nations. In 51:4 God's "justice" came quickly as a light to the nations, while in 51:5 the impact of God's justice is evident because his arm "justly rules" the nations. In 51:4 the law "went out" to inform people of God's ways, but in 51:5 "my salvation goes out." The text does not say that these two concepts are identical terms or state a causal relationship between them, but one might legitimately conclude that the power (God's arm) of God's just rule will be the force that will implement God's salvation as a reality on earth. This universal revelation and sovereign application of divine wisdom and rule suggests that at some point God's distinctive and special treatment of Israel will end. Instead he will make himself known to all mankind, and people from all nations will respond positively to him (2:2–5; 14:1–2; 19:18–25; 45:20–25; 49:26; 60:1–16; 66:19–21).[185]

The second half of the verse describes the impact God's salvation will have on the foreign nations. The light and law of God (51:4) will result in the just rule of God (51:5), which will have a significant spiritual influence on people from many big nations as well as the far-flung somewhat insignificant small island nations[186] of the Mediterranean Sea. The NIV translation suggests that these nations "will look" to God. This verb communicates more than the observation of something with the eyes; it describes an eager looking with expectations, a looking that involves hopefully waiting for God to do something for them.[187] The second word expresses "hopeful waiting"[188] for the working of

---

mentators in putting this verb at the beginning of v. 5 and translating it "without delay, suddenly." This essentially follows the way the Old Greek text handled this problem. J. McKenzie, *Second Isaiah*, AB (Garden City: Doubleday, 1967), 118, puts this verb in v. 5 and translates it adverbially "in an instant." The verb רָגַע means either: root I "disturb" (used in 51:15) or root II "be at rest, repose" (BDB, 920–21), although G. R. Driver, "Linguistic and Textual Problems: Isaiah 40–66," *JTS* 36 (1935): 396–406, suggests the meaning "to flash forth" based on an Arabic cognate verb.

[185] No doubt this prophecy began to be fulfilled in Acts when Paul and other apostles began to preach the gospel to many Gentile nations, but surely this prophecy in Isaiah is looking toward the future for a much greater work of God at the end of time.

[186] The pl. noun אִיִּים can refer to the coastal regions around the Mediterranean (Philistia, Phoenicia, Greece, nations of North Africa, Caphtor, Crete, Tarshish, etc.) and include the small island nations as well. Hollenberg, "Nationalism and 'the Nations' in Isaiah XL–LV," *VT* 19 (1969): 23–36, claims that these nations are "crypto-Israelites" who live among the nations and have lost their identity; these are not foreigners. D. W. Van Winkle, "The Relationship of the Nations to Yahweh and to Israel in Isaiah XL–LV," *VT* 35 (1985): 446–458, properly rejects this approach. M. A. Grisanti, "Israel's Mission to the Nations in Isaiah 40–55: An Update," *TMSJ* 9 (1998): 39–61, gives a broad summary of the various contributions on both sides of this discussion and concludes that Israel has a place of priority over the nations, but Isaiah's message includes a strong universalism that extends God's salvation to all nations.

[187] The verb קָוָה is used in 5:2 of the farmer "looking for, waiting to see" good grapes grow; in 5:7 of God "looking, waiting to see" justice in Judah; in Job 7:2 this term describes a hired man who is "waiting for" his master to pay him his wages, while in Ps 25:20–21 the word refers to the "hopeful waiting" a person has that God will guard the one who walks uprightly.

[188] This verb is יַחֵל communicates the parallel idea of "waiting in hope." In 1 Sam 13:18 Saul

God's strong arm, a symbol of God's strong personal involvement in some activity.[189] The choice of these terms indicates that these foreign nations will put their trust in God. This universal concept of God's mission is consistent with the announcement in Gen 12:3 that through the seed of Abram all the nations would be blessed and consistent with the response of the nations in 45:22–25. Today's modern missionary movement works in concert with this worldwide plan of God, but sometime in the future God will miraculously consummate this plan when he intervenes in the course of history and draws many people to himself (19:18–25; 45:22–25; 60:1–11; 66:18–23).

51:6 The evidence that these events are eschatological and not related to the return from Babylonian captivity[190] is further confirmed by the divine announcement that at this time God will bring this evil world to an end. This verse begins with another imperative verb that exhorts the audience to "lift up"[191] their eyes to see what will happen in the heavens and a parallel admonition to "look, pay attention to" (*habbîṭû*, also used in 50:1b,2) to what will happen on the earth.

The picture drawn is related to the eschatological language of chap. 24 where the destruction of the heaven and earth are described in some detail.[192] The fading destiny of this world (the heaven and the earth) is contrasted with the permanent salvation God will provide his people in order to encourage the audience to maintain their faith in God. The description of what will happen to the heavens begins with a word of assurance, followed by three descriptions of this era. After an initial "surely, truly, it is indisputable" (*kî*, omitted in

---

anxiously "waited in hope" for Samuel to arrive to give the sacrifice so that the army could go to war; in Job 6:11 Job is questioning if he has the strength to continue "to hope, wait" for divine deliverance, and in Ps 130:7 the people of Israel are challenged to put their "hope" in the Lord's unfailing love.

[189] 1QIsᵃ reads this section "his arm will judge the peoples; the coastlands will wait for him, and in his arm they will hope," giving the second half of the verse a messianic interpretation.

[190] In contrast to this conclusion Goldingay, *Message of Isaiah 40–55*, 427, says that, "While the picture implies more than the mere down-to-earth victory of Cyrus over Babylon, it implies not less than that. . . .The prophet's picture is not mere eschatology. . . . It implies the exposure of Babylon's spiritual and intellectual resources, the downfall of the heavenly powers in which Babylon trusted." Nevertheless, since Babylon is not mentioned in this context and the end of the heavens and the earth are depicted, it seems that any attempt to tie these words to one local event (the fall of Babylon) is a misapplication of the universalistic language of the text. This does not appear to be a rhetorical flourish of hyperbolic language. McKenzie, *Second Isaiah*, 123, denies this verse is apocalyptic; instead, he translates "though the heavens be dispersed," suggesting that this might be some sort of hypothetical statement to drive home a point (כִּי can mean "though"). Koole, *Isaiah III, Volume 2: Isaiah 49–55*, 156, rejects this unreal or potential interpretation and concludes that this "verse refers to the end of the cosmos."

[191] The verb שְׂאוּ is an imperative form from נָשָׂא that functions as an admonition or exhortation for the audience to act in a certain way (GKC §110a).

[192] Westermann, *Isaiah 40–55*, 236, finds that "verse 6a and b use the language of apocalyptic, cf. the Isaiah apocalypse, chs 24–27, ch 24 in particular." Motyer, *Isaiah*, 406, believes this verse is describing the "transience of the created order . . . and its dramatic termination at the eschatological day (34:4)."

NIV, "for" RSV, NASB), he announces the signs of the end. First, the heavens "will fall apart" (NIV "will vanish"),[193] like a cloud of smoke falls apart and vanishes in the wind (Ps 37:20). Second, the rock solid and dependable earth is compared to an old garment that will wear out. The third description of the end times compares the death of the inhabitants of the earth to the death of "gnats."[194] This is very reminiscent of the ideas expressed in 24:1–3,18–23 where the very foundation of the earth shakes, the earth is split asunder, only a few people are left on earth, and God punishes all the powers in the heavens and on earth. This is a warning that people on earth should not assume that the things that are so important to their daily life and pleasures are permanent. One day God will cause all of this to disappear. In stark contrast to the temporal and unstable nature of this present world, God's salvation is a sure hope that will last forever (it will not pass away). The justice of God is dependable and will be permanently established, so every reader can confidently be assured that it will never "be shattered, be broken."[195] These promises give every believer a solid foundation for their faith in God; they can live in hope as they face the future even though the events of life may be difficult and appear quite hopeless. Assurances based on God's salvation are really the only worthwhile hope in this world.

51:7–8 The final subparagraph also begins with an imperative exhortation to "listen" (51:1,4) to another divine promise. This admonition is directed to "those who know what is right," indicating that this is most likely the same group of people addressed as "pursuers of righteousness" in 51:1. These are people who have put "my law in their hearts," a phrase that asserts the internalization of divine wisdom and truth, not just a mental awareness of its existence. They are not merely "seeking the Lord" (51:1), and they are not merely aware

---

[193] The root מָלַח appears to be a *niphal* perfect verb that has two possible meanings: I "to tear away, dissipate, fall apart" and II "to salt" (BDB, 571). Although the first meaning is rare, it fits the meaning here. The only real question is, does the word describe "tearing, falling apart," which fits the imagery of "rags, torn cloth" מְלָחִים (Jer 38:11), or does the idea have a broader connotation including "dissipate, vanish," which is hypothesizes from this passage in Isaiah? P. Katz, "Two Kindred Corruptions in the Septuagint," *VT* 1 (1951): 261–64, has an interesting explanation of how later misreading of an accurate Old Greek translation resulted in a later misunderstanding of this passage. H. G. M. Williamson, "Gnats, Glosses, and Eternity: Isaiah 51:6 Reconsidered," in *New Heaven and New Earth Prophecy and the Millennium: Essays in Honor of A. Gelston*, ed. P. J. Harland and C. T. R. Hayward, VTSup 77 (Leiden: Brill, 1999), 101–111, rejects Driver's suggestion that this word should follow the meaning of a similar Arabic root meaning "grow murky" which is accepted in the NEB.

[194] The word כֵן usually means "thus, so," but it probably is a sg. form related to the pl. כִנִּים "gnats" in Exod 8:12–14. 1QIs^a has כמוכן suggesting "like a locust." H. G. M. Williamson, "Gnats, Glosses, and Eternity: Isaiah 51:6 Reconsidered," 101–111, rejects the reading "gnats." Later in the article he suggests that "and they that dwell therein shall die in like manner" is a later gloss.

[195] The *niphal* passive verb תֵחָת comes from חָתַת "to shatter, brake, dismay." In this context what does not happen to God's salvation does happen to this world, so this last verb indicates that God's work will never be undone or without a solid foundation.

that the "law will go forth from me" (51:4); they have accepted the "instruction" (*tôrâ*) from God as their guide to personal behavior and moral beliefs.
But the *Torah* includes much more than just a set of laws; it is fundamentally a
revelation of God's power over creation and history, his promise that his presence with them will bring about the fulfillment of his plans, plus a theological
explanation of how to maintain a holy relationship with him. This means that
these people have rejected the worldview of their day and completely accepted
God's perspective on life and eternity. A heart acknowledgment of these ideas
implies an emotional commitment to God, not just an awareness of a set of
rules. That kind of devotion to God's way of thinking implies some sort of
personal relationship with God that is the basis for a continual knowledge of
his presence.

These righteous people are not to fear reproachful things that people will
say about them. Reproaches and insults[196] usually describe negative language
that defames the character and undermines the confidence of someone else, but
the text does not indicate what the content of these insulting words will be.[197]
The content of their statements will be designed to cause fear, so their ideas
will contradict the good things that God has promised and possibly threaten the
safety and welfare of these righteous people. Although one cannot suggest that
these righteous people will go through the exact same sufferings as the Servant
in 50:4–9, they, too, need to be prepared for a time of hardship and suffering because of their faith. They should not be "dismayed, terrified, shattered"
(*hātat*, also at the end of v. 6) by what they hear. They should not allow these
terrifying words to undermine their present belief system or their relationship
with God.

Verse 8 explains why the righteous people do not need to fear or be dismayed by the things people say. The truth is that these wicked people will
get their just punishment. The Servant of the Lord in 50:8–9 maintained his
confidence in God's vindication because he knew that God was just, knew that
God would help him, and knew that God will cause his accusers to be like a
moth-eaten garment (v. 9b). So, too, these righteous people should realize that
all those people who will try to condemn them with insulting words will end
up being destroyed just like a garment is destroyed when a moth eats it or a
wool cloth is destroyed when a "worm"[198] eats it (50:6). The significance of

---

[196] The idea of a "reproach" חֶרְפָּה and "insult" גִּדּוּפָה are generally synonymous terms that
are used in the context of "shame" and "humiliation" in 54:4, while Ezek 5:15 connects these terms
to "a taunt, a warning, and an object of horror." Zeph 2:8 describes Moab's words against Israel as
"insults," taunts, and threats while Ps 44:16 [MT 17] refers to "the taunts of those who reproach
and revile me."

[197] Whybray, *Isaiah 40–66*, 157, reads far too much into the context by suggesting that this
taunting was by a group of Babylonian people (or possibly fellow Jews) and was addressed to
people in exile. This comment is based on assumptions not found in this literary unit of the text.

[198] The word סָס is only used in this verse so its meaning is somewhat unknown. The cognate
term *sāsu* in Akkadian helps to define this as a worm/caterpillar that eats wool.

this metaphor points to the ultimate demise of those insulters who do not fear God or walk in his righteous ways. It is not clear if further implications should be drawn from these metaphors. That is, should one assume from this imagery that the decline of these people will be a gradual hidden deterioration like the slow process of a moth destroying a garment over several months, rather than a sudden downfall?[199]

A second reason for encouragement in the face of opposition (51:8b) is the undeniable truth that "my (God's) righteousness" and "my (God's) salvation" will last forever (as in 51:6b). God's plan will not be destroyed by any power in heaven and earth, so every person in every generation can count on his salvation. He will accomplish what he has promised, and once his final plan is enacted all opposition to God's glorious reign will cease to exist. This eternal perspective of divine salvation must be a central part of the hope that inspires all believers, especially those who must endure opposition and persecution. Although God's servants may experience some insults and abuses, the same God who dealt justly with his Servant in 50:9 will bring his justice and salvation to those who earnestly pursue righteousness and seek to have a committed relationship with God.

THEOLOGICAL IMPLICATIONS. The last two paragraphs (50:4–11 and 51:1–8) describe two situations in which a special Servant of God, plus other believers who emulate the Servant's commitment to God, face some level of opposition or persecution. Although the persecution is much severer in the case of the Servant of the Lord in 50:4–11, both passages contain some threats from others (51:7). The central theological hope for all those who find themselves in similar situations is found in the known character and promises of God. Those who listen to God's promises are disciples of God's words (50:4–5), have God's instructions in their hearts (50:10; 51:7), and know that God is a just God who will help his servants when troubles come (50:7–9; 51:7–8). God's fulfillment of his promises to Abraham and Sarah (51:2) prove that he is faithful to his past covenant promises; therefore, people in every age can trust and rely on him (50:10). Equally sure are his promises that he will bring great fertility to the earth (51:3), cause his justice to be a light that will attract people from all nations (51:4–5), destroy this old earth and its evil inhabitants (51:6,8), and bring in a time of eternal joy and gladness (51:3b,6b,8b). People in every age have to make a choice either: (a) to put their undying trust and confident hope in God's everlasting salvation and righteousness, which implies a commitment to a life of pursuing righteousness based on God's instructions in this *Torah*; or (b) to not accept God's instructions in the *Torah*, distrust his promises and help, reject his servant, and give up any hope of surviving God's future judgment.

---

[199] Goldingay, *Message of Isaiah 40–66*, 430, accepts these implications although he notes that "in Job 4:19–20 it denotes something speedy."

(4) God's Cup of Wrath Is Ended; Restoration Is Coming (51:9–52:12)

After a prayer for God to exert his power like he did at the time of the exodus (51:9–11), God promises to comfort his people and he exhorts them not to fear their oppressors (51:12–16). In the past God's wrath was poured out against his people, but in the future God will send his wrath against their enemies (51:17–23). God promises that the people of Zion will never again suffer like they did when they were oppressed by Egypt and Assyria (52:1–5); instead, they will shout for joy when God returns to Zion, exerts his power before the whole world, and redeems his people (52:6–10). In light of the sure fulfillment of God's redemption, the audience should transform their thinking, rejoice over God's coming victory, purify themselves, and put their trust in God (52:11–12). "Your God reigns" (52:7) is the glorious good news that marks the end of the struggles of this world and the full realization of the establishment of God's kingdom. Because of these strong promises, all believers can have a confident assurance that God's final salvation will happen. In spite of the tribulations of this present age, this great hope should motivate people to put their trust in God and purify their lives each day.

There is some difficulty in determining the limits of this literary unit. J. D. W. Watts divides these verses into two paragraphs (51:9–52:2 and 52:3–12), while C. Westermann divides these verses into 51:9–52:3, with 52:4–6 being an added "marginal gloss," 52:7–10 a hymn, and 52:11–12 a final short message to depart.[200] Since the parallel exhortations to "awaken" in 51:9,17 are followed by promises that substantiate the call to action with divine promises, J. L. Koole argues against making a paragraph break after 52:2.[201] The oracles in this section can be organized into three paragraphs:

God's past deeds assure future intervention	51:9–16
The fury of God's wrath is over	51:17–23
Rejoice for God's salvation is here	52:1–12

Each of these paragraphs is introduced by double imperatives (51:9,17; 52:1) from the same Hebrew root "awaken, arise" (*ʿûr*) that calls for action and a positive response. In the first paragraph there is a call for God's arm to "awak-

---

[200] Watts, *Isaiah 34–66*, 207–16, finds an initial "choral challenge to the Arm of Yahweh" in 51:9–11 matching a chiastically constructed concluding "choral challenge to Zion" in 52:1–2, but the development of the earlier imperative challenges 51:9,17 involved several verses, so it seems reasonable to expect the challenge in 52:1–2 to include several additional verses. The analysis of Westermann, *Isaiah 40–66*, 238–52, recognizes the hymnic character of 52:7–10 as the usual sign of the end of a major literary section (as in 42:10–13; 44:23), but his designation of 52:3–6 as a "marginal gloss in prose" prevents him from keeping all of 51:9–52:12 as one unit. O'Connell, *Concentricity and Continuity*, 200–204, links 51:9–52:2 and separates 52:3–12 as a separate message based on his chiastic arrangement of the text and the initial "thus says the LORD in 52:3.

[201] Koole, *Isaiah III, Volume 2: Isaiah 49–55*, 211, says "the promise [in vv. 1–2] is anchored in a simple rule of law, v. 3." Then "Verses 4–5 are open to various interpretations. In their turn they probably motivate v. 3."

en" and for him to act as a redeemer (51:9–11). In the second paragraph God responds that he will act on their behalf, so the people of Jerusalem should "awaken" and realize that their suffering is over (51:17–23). In the third paragraph the people of Zion are called to "awaken" to their new situation; they are the redeemed people of God. God now reigns as king; God's salvation has arrived; they can rejoice (52:1–10).

GOD'S PAST DEEDS ASSURE FUTURE INTERVENTION (51:9–16)

⁹Awake, awake! Clothe yourself with strength,
  O arm of the LORD;
 awake, as in days gone by,
  as in generations of old.
 Was it not you who cut Rahab to pieces,
  who pierced that monster through?
¹⁰Was it not you who dried up the sea,
  the waters of the great deep,
 who made a road in the depths of the sea
  so that the redeemed might cross over?
¹¹The ransomed of the LORD will return.
 They will enter Zion with singing;
  everlasting joy will crown their heads.
 Gladness and joy will overtake them,
  and sorrow and sighing will flee away.

¹²"I, even I, am he who comforts you.
 Who are you that you fear mortal men,
  the sons of men, who are but grass,
¹³that you forget the LORD your Maker,
  who stretched out the heavens
  and laid the foundations of the earth,
 that you live in constant terror every day
  because of the wrath of the oppressor,
  who is bent on destruction?
 For where is the wrath of the oppressor?
¹⁴The cowering prisoners will soon be set free;
 they will not die in their dungeon,
  nor will they lack bread.
¹⁵For I am the LORD your God,
  who churns up the sea so that its waves roar—
  the LORD Almighty is his name.
¹⁶I have put my words in your mouth
  and covered you with the shadow of my hand—
 I who set the heavens in place,
  who laid the foundations of the earth,
  and who say to Zion, 'You are my people.'"

This paragraph contains both a prayer to God (the "you" in 51:9–10) and an answer from God (the "I" in 51:12,15–16). R. Melugin classifies 51:9–11 as a call for help from a lament, but this interpretation is largely based on an assumed lament that is left unstated.[202] Since there is no complaint in the prayer in 51:9–10, it is somewhat precarious to identify this prayer as part of a lament. The one making the request does not justify this call for divine action on the basis of some act of oppression in 51:9–10 (signs of victory over opposition is present in vv. 12–13). It is not clear who makes this request, but it is probably either the righteous people in 50:10; 51:1,7 and/or the prophet himself. The one(s) interceding on behalf of the nation are not totally hopeless; instead, optimism is expressed based on God's past acts of redemption (51:9b–10) and God's past promises (51:11). God's answer in 51:12–14 promises that God will protect those who are fearful, feel the wrath of some oppressor, and need to be set free from prison. It is not clear who the oppressor is who is terrorizing the audience, but there is no indication in Ezekiel, Jeremiah, or Ezra that the people in exile were being terrorized or oppressed.

J. Motyer correctly views this prayer as a "proper response to divine promises" that was given in the preceding chapters.[203] These words are not just designed to encourage the one(s) praying but also to remind the people being prayed for that God will act on their behalf. In the conclusion, the prophet and the righteous people who trust God are given the promises that God will put his divine words of consolation "in your mouth" (51:16) and he will protect them with his hand.

The paragraph contains two parts:

Call for God to act as in the past	51:9–11
A call for Divine action	9a
Questions about God's past action	9b–10
Reminder of past promises	11
God's promise to intervene	51:12–16
Divine offer of comfort	12a
Questions about their fears	12b–13
God will intervene for his people	14–15
God's provisions for his servants	16

The first subparagraph begins with the double imperative "awake, awake" (51:9), and the second subparagraph begins with a double pronoun "I, even I" (51:12). After the initial double imperatives in v. 9a, 51:9b–10 contains a

---

[202] Melugin, *Formation of Isaiah 40–66*, 160, compares v. 9 to the "introductory cry for help" in Ps 80:3 (Eng, v. 2), while Childs, *Isaiah*, 403, states that v. 9 is, "much like the conventional community lament (Ps 44:24ff)." Hanson, *Isaiah 40–66*, 146, interprets the question "was it not you?" as a complaint, but that reads a great deal into this question. Such rhetorical questions assert what God did; they are not complaints.

[203] Motyer, *Isaiah*, 408, says that such promises, "betokens only the urgent longing that the blessed future should dawn at once."

series of three questions. Following the same pattern, after the initial double pronouns in 12a, 51:12b–13 contains a series of questions. Similar verbless clauses in 9,10,12, and 16 create a sense of continuity. The repeated references to God's marvelous acts of intervention in the past in 51:9b–11 and in 51:13,15,16 provide an added sense of unity.[204]

51:9a The speaker is unidentified, but B. Childs suggests that this is "the voice of the new people of God, who now bring forth a prayer for God finally to usher in the long-awaited eschatological period of joy and gladness."[205] One would assume that the prophet himself was among this group of people who trust God, seek the Lord, and have God's law in their hearts (50:10; 51:1,7). They request[206] that God's arm, the symbol of his personal involvement in history, should become active again.[207] This does not imply that God is asleep or that he has forgotten about his people; it is merely a call to action so that the people can experience the fulfillment of his promises. A second request is that his arm should "clothe itself with strength," an image drawn from the practice of soldiers putting a sheath on their arms to prepare for battle. This imagery may imply that those praying are asking God to defeat some enemy (this is very similar to Ps 89:10 [11]), but that enemy is not identified.[208] A third imperative calls for God's arm to rise into action, just like it did in the past (lit. "as in days of old, generations of long ago")[209] when God worked miracles on behalf of his people This reference to past events is imprecise, so it is impossible to know exactly what ancient events were in the author's mind until more specific information is mentioned.

51:9b–10 Now those praying ask God some rhetorical questions which imply a positive answer. "Was it not you?" (hălô ʾat hîʾ) means, "surely it was you." If God was the one who did great things in the past, surely he is able to do great things for his people now and in the future. A. Schoors concludes that

---

[204] In the questions הֲלוֹא־אַתְּ "was it not you" in 9b and 10, the verb has to be implied, and the same is true in the similar clause הוּא אָנֹכִי "I am he." Isaiah 51:16 has the verbless clause עַמִּי־אָתָּה "you are my people."

[205] Childs, *Isaiah*, 404. On the other hand McKenzie, *Second Isaiah*, 126, proposes that "the prophet now becomes the speaker; he addresses Yahweh in the name of Zion and calls upon him to act."

[206] When an inferior person addresses a superior person, the imperative verb has the sense of a request (GKC §110a), not a command or exhortation.

[207] The imperative verb is second fem. sg. עוּרִי because the word "arm" and most other parts of the body have a fem. gender. References to the activity of God's arm are found in 30:30; 40:10; 48:14; 51:5; 52:10; 53:1; 59:16; 62:8; 63:5,12.

[208] H. L. Ginsberg, " The Arm of the YHWH in Isaiah 51–63 and the Text of Isa 53.10–11," *JBL* 77 (1958): 152–56, makes this connection based on similar interlinking vocabulary (cf. 89:14,21).

[209] The pl. nouns דֹּרוֹת עוֹלָמִים "generations of eternities" are plurals of intensification to indicate that this was many years ago (GKC §124q). Hypothetically this phrase could refer to events as far back as creation, but usually it refers to some great deed in Israelite history (37:26; 45:21; 46:9–10; 62:9,11).

"two facts from primeval ages are viewed here: creation and deliverance from Egypt,"[210] in order to prove God's enormous power. Some view the mention of cutting up Rahab and the piercing of the monster as a reference to a victory over the chaos monster in Babylonian or Canaanite creation mythology.[211] Although the prophet may use the imagery of the surrounding culture, just as people today refer to Santa without believing in him, it is unlikely that the prophet was referring to the myth contained in the *Enuma elish* where the chief Babylonian god Marduk slew the dragon Tiamat (not Rahab) or the Canaanite myth where the god Baal slew Yam (not Rahab). Since (a) 51:10 refers to the exodus events (Ps 93:1–4); (b) it was the arm of the Lord that brought about the exodus (Exod 3:20; 6:6; 15:16; Deut 4:34; 5:15; 6:21; Pss 77:15–16; 136:12; Isa 50:2; 63:12); (c) Rahab is a title that often refers to Egypt (30:7; Ps 87:4); (d) at creation the sea was not made dry; and (e) in pagan mythology the sea monster was not "dried up" (from the root *ḥārab*),[212] 51:9b–10 must refer to the great deeds God did at the time of the exodus, not at the time of the creation of the world.[213] The slaying of the "monster, dragon" (*tannîn*) refers metaphorically to the defeat of Egypt (as in Ps 74:13–14; Ezek 29:3; 32:2).[214]

---

[210] Schoors, *I Am God Your Savior*, 122, believes that "the mythological picture of the fight and victory over Rahab, the sea monster" alludes to creation events, and Blenkinsopp, *Isaiah 40–55*, 332, agrees.

[211] Westermann, *Isaiah 40–66*, 241, says: "The language of vv. 9b and 10 describing God's act of creation in terms belonging to myth is directly taken over from myth and unsafeguarded. . . . And there can be no mistaking that v. 10b describes the victory over the chaos-dragon in exactly the same way as the Babylonian epic *Enuma elish*." Whybray, *Isaiah 40–66*, 158, rejects the Babylonian origin and argues that "the myth alluded to here probably comes from nearer home, from Canaan" because in the "Babylonian text such a battle was preliminary to the creation of heaven and earth by the god Marduk (*ANET*, p. 67)." J. M. Hutton, "Isaiah 51:9–11 and the Rhetorical Appropriation and Subversion of Hostile Theologies," *JBL* 126 (2007): 271–303, suggests that "mainstream Yahwism had subverted contemporary Canaanite literature through the reuse of a Canaanite hymn for a specific Yahwistic purpose. . . . Not only did Deutero-Isaiah appropriate and subvert a Canaanite hymn, but the prophet used the text in such a way to lampoon the Judahites who had previously appropriated the text for their own purposes." He connects 51:9–11 to Pss 74:13–15 and 89:10–11, which speak about crushing Rahab or Leviathan with your strong arm to argue that both creation and exodus imagery are used in this verse. These verses are then viewed as a deliberate allusion to the Ugaritic myth in *KTU* 1.3 III, 38–46, which he suggests comes from a hypothetical hymn of the goddess Anat.

[212] חָרַב describes what God did to the waters after Noah's flood (Gen 8:13), what God will do to the Nile River in the future (19:6), and what he did to the Red Sea (51:10; Ps 106:9), but it is not used in connection with creation events.

[213] Ps 89:9–10 refers to the crushing of Rahab, which is parallel to "your enemies," and is probably another reference to Egypt. The Aramaic Targum explicitly relates this imagery to destroying "Pharaoh and his army which were as strong as the dragon." Koole, *Isaiah III, Volume 2: Isaiah 49–55*, 170, also rejects the view that the prophet is referring to creation and limits the imagery only to exodus events. J. Oswalt, "The Myth of the Dragon and Old Testament Faith," *EvQ* 49 (1977): 163–72, limits the use of mythological imagery in the Old Testament while M. Wakeman, *God's Battle with the Monster: A Study of Biblical Imagery* (Leiden: Brill, 1973) finds extensive use of this mythological language in the Old Testament.

[214] Williamson, *The Book Called Isaiah*, 84–85, makes a direct connection between the refer-

Verse 10 eliminates any confusion concerning the imagery in 9b because it uses the phraseology connected with the crossing of the Red Sea during the exodus from Egypt. Technically, the verse is asking the question if God was not the one who dried up the road through the sea. Did he not make a path through the deep waters and redeem his people from the power of Egypt (Exod 14:16,21–22,29; Ps 106:9)? But the grammar actually suggests that this rhetorical question is more a statement of what God did; it is not an issue that these people are unsure of. These are images that remind everyone of God's power over nature and history, his ability to accomplish his purposes for his people in the most difficult of circumstances, and his ability to redeem his people.

51:11 At this point one might expect to hear a request or petition for divine assistance to redeem the people praying, but instead those praying quote an earlier promise made in 35:10. In the context of that eschatological proclamation of salvation, 35:10 concludes the glorious description of the restoration of the world with a prophecy of how the weak people will have strength, the lame will have the ability to walk, and the blind will see. At that future time the redeemed will return to Zion, the place where God is, and they will be filled with everlasting joy as they enter God's kingdom.

At first it might appear that 51:11 is God's positive answer to the preceding questions, but if this is so, how is one to understand the divine answer in 51:12–16?[215] J. Goldingay understands the nature of this problem, and he concludes that it is "more likely verse 11 continues the challenge"[216] introduced in 51:9–10 and that it functions as an additional argument for God to do what he has promised. This is a good approach to this verse, although the perspective of J. L. Koole that 51:11 is a prayerful wish for God to act in the future,[217] rather than a prophetic statement of what he will do, is equally possible. This quotation from 35:10 suggests that God should act now like he will in the final eschatological resolution of all the problems that sinful men have brought on

---

ence to Rahab in 51:9 and 30:7. In contrast to the many Rahab passages that refer to Egypt, it appears that Leviathan and the dragon in 27:1 refers to Assyria.

[215] H. C. Spykerboer, *The Structure and Composition of Deutero-Isaiah with Special Reference to the Polemics against Idolatry* (Meppel: Krips, 1976), 171, concludes that, "vs.11 must be taken as a later addition. If this is accepted, full emphasis falls upon Jerusalem and the restoration (and not upon the return of the exiles)."

[216] Goldingay, *Message of Isaiah 40–55*, 434, believes 51:11 supports the challenge in vv. 9–10, making the challenge more powerful because it reminds God of his past promise. Motyer, *Isaiah*, 410, says, "The exercise of prayer (51:9) arises out of faith (in the promises just made, 51:1–8) and begets strong faith that it will be so (51:11)." Melugin, *The Formation of Isaiah 40–55*, 160, refers to v. 11 as a "continuation of the *motivation* begun in v. 9c."

[217] Koole, *Isaiah III, Volume 2: Isaiah 49–55*, 178. As a subjunctive wish the one praying would be asking that God would cause the ransomed to return. As a quotation of a past promise, the prayer would be saying to God, you said you would do these things, with the implied demand that God act to fulfill his words. It is unlikely that the righteous would demand anything, though they might desire or request divine intervention.

this world. Those praying are not asking for anything as minor as the return of several thousand people from exile (Ezra 1–2);[218] they want to experience God's final restoration of the redeemed to Zion and participate in the everlasting joy that will fill the land at that time. An earlier reference to the exodus in 43:16–17 used this imagery to depict the future redemption of the world when God will do a "new thing" by transforming nature (43:19–20) and restoring his people into a nation that will praise God (43:21).[219] Just as the people rejoiced and sang God's praise in the Song of the Sea after the exodus (Exod 15), so God's people desire to sing his praise now and eventually when he redeems his people in the future. Another important eschatological change is the removal of all sorrow, mourning, and sighing (25:8; 30:19; 60:20; 61:3; 65:19; Jer 31:13), for at that time there will no longer be afflictions, fighting, and death. Those praying are looking forward to that day and interceding to encourage God to bring about that day in the near future.

51:12–13 God's answer to this prayer brings encouraging news of salvation. It begins with the emphatic double pronoun "I, even I, am he." This provides a strong affirmative answer to the rhetorical question "are you not he?" in 51:9b,10a. Yes, God identifies himself as the one who redeemed his people in the exodus (51:9b–10) and who promises to redeem them in the future (51:11), so it is correct to conceive of him as the "one who comforts you" (masc. pl.)[220] as 51:3 promised. The second half of the verse asks a series of rhetorical questions (similar to 9b–10). The audience was already encouraged not to "fear the reproaches of men" in 51:7b, so in this response God asks why anyone would still fear "men who will die"[221] (NIV "mortal men"), who are not much different from the grass that quickly dries up (cf. 40:6–8). If the Almighty God of the exodus is on their side, they have no need to fear the puny and transitory men of this world.

A second question inquires, "Have you forgotten Yahweh your Maker?" reversing the accusation of 49:14 where the people wonder if God has forgotten them. The problem is not with God's memory; the problem must be the poor memory of the people of Israel. If they would continually remember that their God was the Creator who "stretched out the heaven and laid the foundation of

---

[218] Westermann, *Isaiah 40–66*, 243, claims that "the 'redeemed' of v. 10b were taken to be Israel in the exile of Babylon" but Muilenburg, "Isaiah 40–66," 5:598, maintains that v. 11 forms "an eschatological climax."

[219] This is the same eschatological restoration of the world and his people mentioned in 11:10–16; 30:18–26; 32:15–20; 41:17–20; 43:16–23; 49:8–13.

[220] The masc. pl. pronominal suffix כֶם on the participle is a little surprising. The Old Greek translation has a sg. suffix which would more nicely agree with the second fem. subject pronoun אַתְּ in the next line. Apparently, "the one who comforts you (pl)" in line 1 refers to all the individual people who fear God, while the second fem. sg. "you" in line 2 refers to the sg. city of Jerusalem.

[221] Since poetry often omits the relative pronoun because of a tendency toward terseness, the imperfect verb יָמוּת "he will die" must be expressed in English as a relative clause (GKC §155h).

the earth," they would not live in constant fear of their oppressors who were trying to destroy them. Since these oppressors are not identified, it is difficult to connect this verse to any specific event.[222] The final line in 51:13 records God's reaction to this baseless human fear. Since God firmly holds the course of history in his hand and will carry it out according to his plans, there really is no reason to be afraid of any ranting tyrant or his army? The question, "Where is the wrath of the oppressor?" assumes that the oppressor will soon be nothing or is already nothing; thus the period of the audience has to be near the demise of the army/nation that was oppressing Judah. J. Motyer is correct in concluding that this passage cannot refer to people living in Babylonian exile,[223] for there is no sign of extensive oppression in Jeremiah's letters to the exiles (Jer 29), in the writings of Ezekiel, or Ezra. J. Goldingay connects these events to the fall of the Babylonian kingdom when King Nabonidus was ruling (Dan 5, at 539 BC),[224] but this has three problems: (a) There is no indication that the wrath of Nabonidus brought about the oppression of Hebrews in exile. (b) There is no indication in exilic books that the Hebrews feared Nabonidus. (c) There is no knowledge that Nabonidus oppressed people in Jerusalem.

Although it is not necessary to identify the exact date of this oppression to understand its message, another hypothetical setting that might at least be considered when interpreting these events is the concluding phases of the Assyrian conquest of Judah, when Sennacherib was oppressing Jerusalem with a large army. Isaiah 29:2,7 uses the same root ($\d{s}\^uq$) "oppressor" (51:13) to describe the Assyrians. In both chapters (29:16; 51:13) God wonders why the people are questioning or ignoring their "Maker." In the context of the oppression of chap. 29, Isaiah prophesied that, "the ruthless one will vanish . . . all who have an eye for evil will be cut off" (29:20), similar to the situation in 51:13b. When this actually happens, Isaiah predicts that people will wonder, "Where is that chief officer? Where is the one who took revenge? Where is the officer in charge of the towers? You will see those arrogant people no more"

---

[222] There is no indication that the Babylonians were trying to destroy the Hebrews that were taken into exile in Babylon in the other exilic or postexilic prophetic books. The oppression that is so strong that it threatens to destroy them must be a military conquest at some earlier period.

[223] Motyer, *Isaiah*, 412, notes that the exilic period was not a time of oppression. J. Morgenstern, "'Oppressor' of Isa 51:13—Who Was He?" *JBL* 81 (1962): 25–34, thought this oppressor was the Persian king Xerxes, the husband of Esther, but this happened much later. Koole, *Isaiah III, Volume 2: Isaiah 49–55*, 183, takes the more common view that Babylon is the oppressor, but Seitz, "Isaiah 40–66," 6:449, correctly concludes that this does not describe the period of Israelite captivity in Babylon. There is no evidence that the Babylonians were trying to destroy the Israelites while they were in Babylonian captivity; instead, Seitz believes this describes the ruin of Jerusalem in 587 BC (comparable to Lamentations and Jer 37–43).

[224] Goldingay, *Message of Isaiah 40–55*, 437, looks to a Babylonian king, while Blenkinsopp, *Isaiah 40–55*, 334, identifies the opponents as opposition within the Jewish community who reject the message of the servant, thus preparing the reader for the suffering of the servant in 52:13–53:12. Blenkinsopp rejects the view that this refers to oppression by the Babylonians during the exilic period.

(33:18–19). These questions about the sudden disappearance of the great Assyrian army around Jerusalem sound quite similar to the question at the end of 51:13b, "Where is the wrath of the oppressor?"[225] Another option that might be considered is that this oppression is referring to an eschatological enemy, just before God destroys them and establishes his kingdom.

51:14–15 As soon as the wrath of the oppressor has ended, there is the promise that God "will act quickly in order to bring freedom"[226] to his "cowering"[227] people (the word "prisoner" is a periphrastic addition in NIV) who were suffering under the hand of a stronger oppressor. This means that people of Jerusalem will not die and end up going down into the "pit" (*šaḥat*), a euphemism for the grave or Sheol. In addition, they will not starve to death because of a lack of bread due to a siege of the city (3:1; Jer 37:21). This deliverance does not fit what happened in 587 BC when the Babylonians successfully defeated Jerusalem, but in the midst of a siege of Jerusalem in 701 BC an angel from God killed 185,000 Assyrian troops that were around Jerusalem, thus freeing the city from the threat of famine, death, and the Assyrian siege (37:36). If an eschatological interpretation is preferred, this verse would describe the freeing of God's people after the defeat of God's enemies.

Why will these wonderful things happen? Did the people deserve this positive resolution of their situation or earn the pity of their oppressors? No, the profound reason for this change of destiny is wrapped up in the simple statement that "I am the LORD your God" . . . "the LORD Almighty is his name" (51:15). God's deeds on behalf of his people are compared to his sovereign power over the sea, but the meaning of the imagery is somewhat confusing. Does God rebuke and overpower the sea (common imagery to describe the Assyrian army in 8:7–8; 17:12–13), or is God's great destructive power over their enemies as great as the destructive power of the sea (30:28)? The solution is complicated by those who question the authenticity of the text,[228] view it as a later addition from Jer 31:35b, or derive the verb from a different root.[229] Each interpretation can express the metaphori-

---

[225] The defeat of Rahab is part of God's argument in 30:7 and 51:9. Although it is very difficult to define the historical setting of chap. 35:11, its present literary context in the midst of the Assyrian crisis may be another reason why it is quoted here in 51:11.

[226] The main verb "to hasten, be quick" (מִהַר) is modified by the infinitive construct "to free, open" (לְהִפָּתֵחַ), which explains the purpose of God's action.

[227] The active participle צֹעֶה is often connected to the Arabic *ṣaġa* "to bend."

[228] The Targum and Syriac have a word derived from גָּעַר "he rebuked" rather than רָגַע "he stirred," but 1QIs[a] agrees with the MT reading.

[229] Willey, *Remember the Former Things: The Recollection of Previous Texts in Second Isaiah*, 140, claims the Isaiah text echoes and depends on Jer 31:35 based on the assumption that Jeremiah is the earlier; nevertheless, she never wrestles with the textual evidence that might prove which author was the one quoting. Schoors, *I Am God Your Savior*, 127, regards v. 15 "as a quotation from Jer. xxxi 35, added by a glossator." Koole, *Isaiah III, Volume 2: Isaiah 49–55*, 188, wrestles with the options of deriving this verb from רגע (a) "to rest, calm down" (F. Delitzsch); (b) "to flash" (G. R. Driver); (c) "to split" (NEB); (d) "to stir, blow up" (NIV) and concludes that "to calm" is the best interpretation.

cal point that God's sovereignty can overpower their enemies. He is the one "who calms the sea when its waves roar" (he has power over their enemies) or he is the one "who stirs up the sea so that its waves roar" (he has more power than the sea), but the first is preferable because the imagery of roaring waves elsewhere metaphorically refers to the roar of the charging army, not to God's roaring (cf. 5:14; 14:11; 17:12; Jer 47:3; 50:42; Ps 89:10).

51:16 There is great confusion concerning who God is speaking to in this verse because the statements in 16a are nearly identical to statements made to the Servant of the Lord in 49:2 and 50:4 (cf. 59:21). Although one might initially be surprised by this direct address to the Servant, K. Baltzer believes these repeated words "establish a link, making clear that here too it is the Servant of God who is being talked about," while J. Goldingay finds no change of address and hypothesizes that God is here assigning to the people the task that was previously given to the servant.[230] B. Childs rejects the view that the Servant's role has been fused with that of obedient Israel; instead, "those who have followed in the servant's footsteps have been assigned a new prophetic task in now bringing the good news to Zion, which is an extension of the servant's tasks."[231] This dilemma is not easily resolved. The words in 51:16a are linked to the Servant of the Lord, but just as soon as he mysteriously appears, he disappears from the context of the conversation.

The solution may lie in viewing this verse as another means of assuring the audience (similar to the purpose of 51:15) that God will accomplish what he has promised his people and will answer their prayer in 51:9–11. Initially the prophet quotes God's past commissioning of the Servant (this is not a direct address to the Servant at this time) and his past promise to protect the Servant by hiding him in his hand (51:16a), thus assuring the audience that God's arm was already active in the past. What he called the Servant to do (49:2) will be accomplished; therefore the audience should trust God. If this is correct, then the final three infinitive constructs probably function in a similar way. NIV translates these verbs as participles ("who set," "who laid," "who say") and implies the first person "I" from 16a, but the infinitive construct normally depends on an earlier verb by modifying its action in some way. If God wanted to bring greater assurance to increase the faith of the audience, these infinitive constructs probably function to introduce a purpose or result clause[232] that

---

[230] Baltzer, *Deutero-Isaiah*, 364, interprets the servant as Moses who was the mediator of the covenant, which communicated good news that "you are my people" (51:16b). Calvin, "Commentary on the Book of the Prophet Isaiah," *Calvin's Commentaries* (Grand Rapids: Baker, 2003), 7:82, thought that this was assuring people that God was putting his words in the mouth of all the prophets, from Isaiah to Christ. Goldingay, *Message of Isaiah 40–55*, 439, believes the original failure of the people to be God's servants led to a calling of the servant (he views him as the prophet) to fulfill this role, but God still had the desire for his people to be his servant, so it is natural for God to now address the obedient people in the same way he earlier addressed the servant.

[231] Childs, *Isaiah*, 403–404.

[232] GKC §114f or *IBHS* §36.2.3 discuss this use of the infinitive construct. God put his words

refers to a future creation of the new earth[233] and the consummation of God's plans to restore his people to their covenant status of being "my people." With this approach, these words would demonstrate to the audience that God's arm was, is, and will be active. God's plan for the Servant of the Lord would lead to a new creation of the world for God will some day reestablish his relationship to his people, exactly what they were praying for in 51:11 and what God already promised in 51:3–6.

THE FURY OF GOD'S WRATH IS OVER (51:17–23)

> [17]Awake, awake!
>> Rise up, O Jerusalem,
> you who have drunk from the hand of the LORD
>> the cup of his wrath,
> you who have drained to its dregs
>> the goblet that makes men stagger.
> [18]Of all the sons she bore
>> there was none to guide her;
> of all the sons she reared
>> there was none to take her by the hand.
> [19]These double calamities have come upon you—
>> who can comfort you?—
> ruin and destruction, famine and sword—
>> who can console you?
> [20]Your sons have fainted;
>> they lie at the head of every street,
>> like antelope caught in a net.
> They are filled with the wrath of the LORD
>> and the rebuke of your God.
>
> [21]Therefore hear this, you afflicted one,
>> made drunk, but not with wine.
> [22]This is what your Sovereign LORD says,
>> your God, who defends his people:
> "See, I have taken out of your hand
>> the cup that made you stagger;
> from that cup, the goblet of my wrath,
>> you will never drink again.
> [23]I will put it into the hands of your tormentors,
>> who said to you,
>> 'Fall prostrate that we may walk over you.'
> And you made your back like the ground,
>> like a street to be walked over."

---

in the mouth of the Servant "in order to establish the heavens, to lay the foundations of the earth, and to say to Zion."

[233] Muilenburg, "Isaiah 40–66," 5:601, takes the creation as being the eschatological creation of the new heavens and the earth.

The second paragraph in this series begins with two imperatives just like the previous paragraph. It is another proclamation of salvation[234] that announces that the nation's past misery and divine punishment will end. The historical circumstances that brought God's wrath on the nation are not concretely connected with any specific historical event. J. Oswalt thinks that "the Babylonian captivity is in the background, providing the imagery, but it is never mentioned explicitly." J. Muilenburg believes the imagery depicts the fall of Jerusalem in 587 BC, and J. D. W. Watts connects this passage to events in Jerusalem during the reign of the Persian king Darius.[235] The location appears to be Jerusalem, and other interlinking references to "drunkenness" connect the state of the nation with a similar problem (drunkenness) that led to the military defeat of Egypt (19:14), the conquest of Samaria (28:1–4), and the people of Jerusalem during the Assyrian crisis (27:7–8; 29:9–12). Thus a military conquest somewhere in Jerusalem's history functions as a backdrop for explaining God's cup of wrath, but the specific war is left undefined.[236] The promise that God's people "will never drink again" from this cup of God's wrath (51:22b) suggests that God's salvation promises an end of war, relief from an enemy, and a reversal of fortunes (the enemy will drink of God's wrath). The paragraph can be divided into two parts:

God's cup of wrath on Judah	51:17–20
Jerusalem experienced God's wrath	17
She has no guide	18
She was devastated	19
Jerusalem is helpless	20
Removal of God's wrath	51:21–23
The cup of wrath is removed	21–22
Enemies will drink of God's wrath	23

References to the "cup, goblet" in 51:17,18,22 and being "drunk" in 51:17,21,22 tie the two parts of this paragraph together, while the "therefore" (*lākēn*) clause at 51:21 marks the change from God putting the cup of wrath into Jerusalem's

---

[234] Westermann, *Isaiah 40–66*, 245–46, connects 51:17–20 to the community laments in Lamentations which Isaiah quotes, then 21–23 is God's answer of salvation. Schoors, *I Am God Your Savior*, 128–29, has a similar analysis, but 17–20 merely indicates that God knew about Zion's difficult situation; it is not a lament. Blenkinsopp, *Isaiah 40–55*, 336, recognizes that this is not a lament, though it may have "incorporated the language of the traditional lament."

[235] Since Oswalt, *Isaiah 40–66*, 351, never finds an explicit reference to the captivity; it becomes an assumption based on the imagery. In contrast, Muilenburg, "Isaiah 40–66," 5:604, interprets the war imagery to be about the fall of Jerusalem while Watts, *Isaiah 34–66*, 210, connects these events to a much later period when the Persian king Darius reigned (520 BC).

[236] Willey, *Remember the Former Things: The Recollection of Previous Texts in Second Isaiah*, 159–64, believes the use of similar themes of children, cup of divine wrath, and being drunk in Lam 4:1–22 suggest that 51:17–23 is related to the fall of Jerusalem in 587 BC.

hand to the new situation in which the cup of wrath will be taken out of Jerusalem's hand and given to the enemies of Jerusalem (51:23).

51:17–20 The paragraph begins with two calls for the audience to "awaken yourself, awaken yourself" (from *ûr*), similar to the introductions to 51:9 and 52:1.[237] By calling lady Jerusalem to wake up and "stand up" (*qûmî*), God is indicating that the past period of being under the influence of God's judgment is coming to an end and a new era is about to begin. At the present time Jerusalem is metaphorically pictured as someone who is suffering under the effects of too much alcohol. The source of her staggering and dizziness comes from a cup of wrath that God handed to Jerusalem. In other contexts God's sovereign hand "laid the foundations of the earth" (48:13), protects his people in "the shadow of my hand" (49:16), and punishes people (50:11). This "cup of his wrath" symbolizes the portion or lot (Ps 16:5) that God uses to direct the destiny of people on earth.[238] As one drinks what is in the cup of destiny a specific measure of wrath is internalized; thus, the life of the one drinking is controlled by the content of the cup. Jerusalem drank and completely "drained"[239] this bowl of staggering, so she is fully experiencing the horrors of being under the wrath of God. The reason why Jerusalem suffered in this way is treated elsewhere; at this point Isaiah is interested in confirming that their suffering is not due just to the overwhelming strength of an enemy army; it is due to the sovereign plan of God. But if God has the power to give the cup to Jerusalem, he also has the power to remove the cup of his wrath and its horrible consequences.

51:18 When a person is incapacitated by drunkenness, the best thing that can happen is for a benevolent friend or caring relative to come along and rescue the person in need. Unfortunately, Jerusalem has no one to assist (lit "taking strong hold onto her hand") or guide her.[240] Those who should assist Jerusalem in the ways of godliness were her own children, specifically her priests, prophets, and kings. The text does not reveal why no one helped Jerusalem;[241] it only notes the loneliness, the helplessness, and the lack of concern by those

---

[237] In 51:9; 52:1 the *qal* imperative verb עוּרִי is used to exhort God (51:9) and Zion (52:1) to action, while in 51:17 the reflexive *hithpa'el* imperative verb exhorts Jerusalem to "awaken yourself."

[238] Jeremiah 25:15–27 makes extensive use of the cup-of-wrath imagery, and in Mark 14:36 Jesus prayed asking God to take this cup from me, referring to his approaching death on the cross.

[239] NIV says that Jerusalem "drained to its dregs" to translate two verbs שָׁתִית מָצִית "you drank and you drained."

[240] The two verbs "taking strong hold of" (מַחֲזִיק) and "guiding, leading" (מְנַהֵל) are participles that probably represent continuing action in present time (GKC §116a,c). 1QIsᵃ has confused the ה with a ח and has written מנחל "inheriting," which does not fit here.

[241] Goldingay, *Message of Isaiah 40–55*, 442, honestly admits that the interpretation "that the children are missing is presupposed," but why introduce something that is not necessary to understand this text? The misery of the situation is much greater if the children are there but just do not care to help.

who should have cared. Those with the family obligations to care for Mother Jerusalem totally failed to fulfill their responsibilities.[242]

51:19 The consequence of drinking the cup of God's wrath has caused "two things"[243] to happen to Jerusalem. Since four things are described in this verse, it is probably best to interpret these as two pairs. "Ruin and destruction" have a somewhat similar spelling in Hebrew, and both describe what happened to the land and cities of Judah, while "famine and sword" have a similar spelling in Hebrew and describe what happened to the people.[244] In the midst of this dire news God asks the question: "Who can shake/sympathize[245] with you?" and the more profound "How can I console you?"[246] Since Jerusalem was receiving the just consequence for her sins, there was nothing anyone could do to ease her pain. She had to endure it until it was complete, then God could comfort her (51:21–23).

51:20 The reasons why some of Jerusalem's children could not comfort her was because many of them were overcome, dazed, had fainted[247] in streets throughout the city. Being powerless to continue, they would lie down in the streets to await their inevitable fate, just like a helpless and exhausted antelope/

---

[242] Schoors, *I Am God Your Savior*, 130, interprets v. 18 to be describing the "depopulation of the city, presented under the image of childlessness," but it seems better to view the text to be speaking more about the irresponsible, unhelpful, and uncaring children who were there, which is a much greater tragedy.

[243] Literally "these two have happened to you." NIV adds the word "calamities." Although קֹרְאֹתַיִךְ looks like it comes from קָרָא "he called," sometimes the א takes the place of the ה (GKC §75rr), so this root is actually קָרָה "it happened."

[244] Muilenburg, "Isaiah 40–66," 5:604, believes this section "summarizes the disaster which befell Jerusalem in 586 BC," but there is nothing in this information that would enable one to specifically identify these general statements about the 587 conflict, in contrast to other military disasters on Judah.

[245] The imperfect verb יָנוּד means (BDB, 626): (a) to move to and fro, wander; (b) flutter (of birds); (c) show grief, lament, show sympathy; (d) wag the head. The verb refers to the common practice of moving the head back and forth while agreeing with and empathizing with another person's expression of sorrow (1 Kgs 14:15).

[246] The imperfect verb in questions can introduce a subjunctive idea of what can, would, should, or may happen (GKC §107r,t). The verb in the second question is a third person verb in 1QIs[a] (matching the first question), which is followed by Koole, *Isaiah III, Volume 2: Isaiah 49–55*, 202, and in the NIV, but this appears to be a much easier reading that smoothes out a problem. M. Dahood, "Isaiah 51,19 and Sefire III, 22" *Bib* 56 (1957): 404–19, emends the text to *m" 'ānaḥ mēk* "who will groan for you?" but this emendation is hardly needed to make sense of the passage. To protect God's reputation the Aramaic Targum has "there is none who will comfort you but I," thus turning a question into a positive promise.

[247] In Ezek 31:15; Amos 8:13; and in Jonah 4:8 the verb עֻלְפֶּה refers to the faintness brought on by not having water. Presumably, this word could be used in other contexts as well, although not having water is a common problem during a siege. Whybray, *Isaiah 40–66*, 163, hypothesizes that the second line in the verse is a "gloss introduced from Lam 2:19" and should be omitted because "these words hardly agree with the next line." Since the Aramaic Targum ("Your sons will be dashed to pieces, thrown at the head of all the streets"), the Old Greek ("Your sons are the perplexed ones, that sleep at the top of every street"), and Qumran text all testify to the presence of these words, one should not be quick to omit them.

oryx caught in a v-shaped trap or in a net.[248] They had no hope because God poured out the fullness of his wrath on them. Those who foolishly ignored God's holy standard were now realizing just how fearful it is to fall under the curse of God's wrath.

51:21–23 The initial "therefore" (lākēn) introduces the reversal of God's wrath on Jerusalem. Since God's people are hopelessly incapacitated in their present state (though not because of wine); at some point God will act on their behalf. Initially God draws attention to an announcement he will make by calling for his weak, faint, and oppressed people to listen to this new message he has for them. If they do not listen to the voice of God, some people might imagine that someone or something other than God has brought about their deliverance.

Verse 22 begins with an extended introduction of the divine speaker using four titles (possibly to counter-balance the four disasters in v. 19). God is introduced as "your Lord, Yahweh, your God, the One who will defend his people" in order to emphasize (a) his great power as master and lord who controls the whole earth, (b) his relationship to his people as Yahweh their covenant God, and (c) his function as a judge who is concerned that his people are treated with justice. This introduction signals to the audience that an important message is coming in 22b–23. This message begins with "see, behold" (hinnēh)[249] to introduce God's words of assurance so that the listeners would be awakened to the fact that something important is about to be revealed. The good news is that God has now taken away the cup of his wrath that caused his people so much drunkenness, trembling, and suffering. God promises that they will not have to drink any longer from this cup, but no explicit reason is given to explain why this change will take place. There is no hint that Jerusalem has earned God's grace or that they have repented of their sins in this verse. Many times the grace of God is just unexplainable.

The *waw* that begins 51:23 probably introduces a contrast[250] ("but," omitted in NIV) in God's future action. God's justice will move against "those who cause you to suffer,"[251] the enemy who was attacking Jerusalem in 51:13–14,19–20. But this text does not focus on God's revenge on Judah's enemies

---

[248] When an animal's legs get entangled in a net, it will initially jump and pull, trying its best to free itself from the net, but eventually it will wear itself out and lie down exhausted, having given up all hope of escaping. A. Terian, "The Hunting Imagery in Isaiah LI.20A," *VT* 41 (1991): 462–71, describes long v-shaped rock formations (like streets with rocks on both sides) found in semiarid areas which were used to trap wild animals in the small area at the point of the "v." Some suggest that these structures also may have been used as a corral for domesticated animals as well.

[249] הִנֵּה is used to draw attention to and introduce God's words in 3:1; 6:7; 7:14; 10:33; 17:1; 19:1; 24:1; 25:9; 30:27.

[250] The interpretation of the *waw* is very subjective, but when one action is strongly contrasted to another action, it is legitimate to interpret the *waw* as introducing an antithesis (GKC §154a; 163a)

[251] The *hiphil* causative participle מוֹגַיִךְ from יָגָה refers to those who cause suffering, pain, or grief, and it is used frequently in lamentations.

and does not describe what will happen to them when God puts this cup into their hands. One could assume that whoever the enemy is that will hold this cup of wrath will reap the severe consequences of God's wrath. Instead of focusing on the enemies' demise, the author draws attention to this enemy as a cruel conqueror who required people[252] to lie down on the ground so that they might humiliate God's people by walking on them. They surmised that killing people would be too merciful and it would bring too quick an end to their suffering. The enemy wanted to torture, humiliate, and shame the Israelites and exalt themselves as masters over them. Although the statement of what the enemy demanded may sound like an empty threat in the mouths of some, history records that Joshua illustrated his authority over his enemies by having his commanders put their feet on the necks of five Amorite kings (Josh 10:24), and ancient Near Eastern monuments from Egypt and Mesopotamia (*ANEP,* fig 249, 315, 524) actually depict the trampling of the bodies of the defeated. Some of these ways of inhumanly treating others were probably about as barbarous as some of the modern atrocities perpetrated by Hitler against the Jews in Europe, Pol Pot's genocide of people in Cambodia, the Serb's ethnic cleansing of Bosnia, and the genocide of Christians in Darfur.[253]

REJOICE FOR GOD'S SALVATION IS HERE (52:1–12)

¹Awake, awake, O Zion,
    clothe yourself with strength.
Put on your garments of splendor,
    O Jerusalem, the holy city.
The uncircumcised and defiled
    will not enter you again.
²Shake off your dust;
    rise up, sit enthroned, O Jerusalem.
Free yourself from the chains on your neck,
    O captive Daughter of Zion.

³For this is what the LORD says:

"You were sold for nothing,
    and without money you will be redeemed."

⁴For this is what the Sovereign LORD says:

"At first my people went down to Egypt to live;
    lately, Assyria has oppressed them.

---

[252] The enemy actually speaks "to your soul/neck" (לְנַפְשֵׁךְ). The noun נֶפֶשׁ is frequently translated "soul, living being, life," but often it is appropriately translated into English as a circumlocution for "you" (NIV). H. W. Wolff, *Anthropology of the Old Testament* (Philadelphia: Fortress, 1974), 14–15, lists this as one of several examples (1 Sam 28:9; Ps 105:18; Jer 4:10) where נֶפֶשׁ means "neck." Bowing down and making your back like a street for walking on means that one has put your neck on the ground.

[253] www.unitedhumanrights.org is one place where one can read about these atrocities.

⁵"And now what do I have here?" declares the LORD.

"For my people have been taken away for nothing,
    and those who rule them mock,"
                  declares the LORD.

"And all day long
    my name is constantly blasphemed.
⁶Therefore my people will know my name;
    therefore in that day they will know
that it is I who foretold it.
    Yes, it is I."

⁷How beautiful on the mountains
    are the feet of those who bring good news,
who proclaim peace,
    who bring good tidings,
    who proclaim salvation,
who say to Zion,
    "Your God reigns!"
⁸Listen! Your watchmen lift up their voices;
    together they shout for joy.
When the LORD returns to Zion,
    they will see it with their own eyes.
⁹Burst into songs of joy together,
    you ruins of Jerusalem,
for the LORD has comforted his people,
    he has redeemed Jerusalem.
¹⁰The LORD will lay bare his holy arm
    in the sight of all the nations,
and all the ends of the earth will see
    the salvation of our God.

¹¹Depart, depart, go out from there!
    Touch no unclean thing!
Come out from it and be pure,
    you who carry the vessels of the LORD.
¹²But you will not leave in haste
    or go in flight;
for the LORD will go before you,
    the God of Israel will be your rear guard.

The final section of this unit dramatically announces the good news of the eschatological coming of God's great salvation to the people of Zion. God's holy people will no longer be despised and humiliated by the Egyptians or the Assyrians (52:4), and God's name will no longer be blasphemed (52:5). This will be a time of peace and joyful singing of a song about God's redemption and salvation. They will sing before all the nations (52:9–10) when God comes to reign as King in Zion (52:7–8). The paragraph ends with admonitions to be separate from impurity (52:11), plus assurances of God's presence, guidance, and protection (52:12).

This material is sometimes divided into three somewhat separate paragraphs,[254] but to prevent undue fragmentation of the text and to draw attention to the final unified form of the canonical text, these three segments will be treated as subunits within one paragraph. This message can be outlined as:

Free and Holy Zion will not be sold again	52:1–6
Zion is strong, free, and holy	1–2
Oppression and blasphemy are over	3–6
Proclaim that God's salvation is here	52:7–10
Joyful news that God is King	7–8
Song of God's redemption	9–10
Be pure and trust in God's protection	52:11–12

These subparagraphs are interconnected by the positive news they present. The past history of the people contained times when Zion was taken captive and in bonds (52:2) in Egypt and Assyria (52:4), but the future will be a time of strength, holiness (52:1–2,11), freedom from oppression and redemption (52:2–5), knowing God (52:6,10), peace and salvation (52:7), joyful singing (52:8–9), and divine protection (52:12). At that future time God will reign as King, and the world will be transformed by his presence.

This paragraph is another proclamation of salvation with a hymn of praise (52:9–10) inserted just before the final verses. The insertion of a hymn marks the end of this literary unit, just like the hymns in 12:1–6; 42:10–13; 44:23; 48:20–21; 49:13 mark the end of other literary units. The most problematic feature for C. Westermann is what he calls "a marginal gloss in prose"[255] (52:4–6) that was editorial inserted into a poetic message. Nevertheless, (a) NIV, NJPS, and HCSB all understand 52:3–6 as having poetic qualities; (b) 52:1–6 has a structure similar to 51:17–23, including a call to action, plus divine promises that support the call; (c) the people of Zion in 52:1–2 are the same as "my people" in 52:3–6; (d) the troubles of Zion in 52:2 are related to the blasphemy of God's name in 53:5; and (e) Zion's future status as the holy city in 52:1

---

[254] Goldingay, *Message of Isaiah 40–55*, 446–58, has: (a) The Awakening of Jerusalem in 52:1–6; (b) Listening to the Lookouts in 52:7–10; and (c) Get Out from There in 52:11–12, which is the same structure used by K. Baltzer, *Deutero-Isaiah*, 365–91, and others. Blenkinsopp, *Isaiah 40–55*, 338, treats 52:1–12 as one paragraph.

[255] Westermann, *Isaiah 40–66*, 248, says, "5b and 6 are so corrupt that the original meaning cannot now be made out." Seitz, "Isaiah 40–66," 6:453, states that, "virtually all commentators regard the unit 52:3–6 as intrusive." Such judgments inappropriately impose modern conceptions of literary continuity, flow, and consistency on ancient texts that came from cultures that did not have similar standards. One may treat brief interruptions in the textual flow as parenthetical remarks, as background material that is necessary for one to get the full impact of what follows in the succeeding verses, or as integral points that need to be stressed in order to fill out the argument of the paragraph.

matches her new relationship to God in 52:6.[256] Thus the subparagraph demonstrates signs that it is a unified whole.

The historical setting is sometime after the nation spent time in Egypt and after some Assyrian oppression (52:4). There is no explicit reference to Babylon; although, J. Calvin inexplicably concluded that, "By 'Assyrian,' he means the Babylonians."[257] More recent interpreters suggest that the ambiguous phrase "and now, what do I have here" in 52:5 refers to the Babylonian captivity, but this approach is somewhat speculative because it inserts information that is not explicitly present in the text. The evaluation of this conclusion is developed in the analysis and interpretation of 52:5.

52:1–2 This oracle begins just like 51:9,17 with two imperative calls to "awaken, awaken" (*ʿûrî ʿûrî*). The people of Zion need to stir themselves to action based upon the call of God and his promises. This exhortation is addressed to Zion, just like 51:17, but this paragraph is not a repetition of 51:17–23. Earlier Zion was told to arise from her drunken stupor because God has taken his cup of wrath from her hand, but in this paragraph Zion is encouraged to "clothe/put on your strength" (similar to 51:9) and "clothe/put on your glorious garments." This suggests she will take on a new role and have a new status.[258] Earlier in the hymn of thanksgiving in 12:2 Isaiah tells how the people will one day confess, "the LORD is my strength," and at the end of time all nations will recognize that "in the LORD alone is righteousness and strength." God does promise to strengthen his failing servant Jacob (45:9), so Zion's strength is not something she can muster up on her own. This requires a trusting acceptance of God's strength and not depending on any other source of human strength.[259] The glorious and holy status of Zion is interlinked to earlier discussions of God's transformation of Jerusalem in 4:2–3. God states that he will grant Zion salvation and "my splendor/glory" (46:13), that she will be "a crown of splendor/glory on my right hand" (62:3), and like a royal bride (61:10). She will be a holy city (48:2) for God himself is holy (1:4; 5:16; 6:3; 10:17; 12:6; Lev 19:1). Thus it is true (*kî* "surely, truly" omitted in NIV), the uncircumcised foreigners will never defile the city again (cf. 35:8), a promise that has eschatological significance. J. Muilenburg believes the "uncircumcised" refers to both foreign oppressors (cf. Joel 4(3):17) and unclean Hebrews who have given in to syncretism and have worshipped other gods,[260] but the latter is a questionable ex-

---

[256] Koole, *Isaiah III, Volume 2: Isaiah 49–55*, 212, provides these and other arguments that illustrate the interconnectedness of these verses.

[257] Calvin, "Book of the Prophet Isaiah," 96.

[258] The new status and role of the high priest Joshua (Zech 3:1–6) was accompanied by new clothes, as was the new status of Joseph (Gen 41:41–43) and the promise to the one who could read the handwriting on the wall (Dan 5:7,16).

[259] K. Baltzer, *Deutero-Isaiah*, 370, observes that strength is not found in walls, armor, swords, or another nation.

[260] Muilenburg, "Isaiah 40–66," 5:607, bases this on the reference to this theme in 52:11. Seitz, "Isaiah 40–66," 6:454, believes this language is at odds with later references to many proselytes

tension of the meaning of this term, for the "uncircumcised" probably should be identified with the "oppressors" in 51:13 and the "tormentors" in 51:23.

Four imperative verbs in 52:2 exhort Zion to shake off the dust, arise, sit up,[261] and "loosen/open" (*pātaḥ*) the chains around the neck. Earlier in Isaiah the people had to endure physical oppression, plundering by their enemies, and life in prison with no one to rescue them (42:22; 51:14), but at other times the darkness of being oppressed seems to be more spiritual (49:9). If this passage is interpreted literally, based on the literal explanation of military defeat in 52:3–4, this historical setting may be the same problem addressed in 41:11–12; 42:22; and 51:14 (the Assyrian attack on Jerusalem). This might explain why these prophecies reflect some of the same terminology and promises that appear in chaps. 28–35.

52:3–6 Although many reject the authenticity of these verses, they have a legitimate function of quoting statements by God that should encourage the people of Zion to respond positively to God's admonitions in 52:1–2. These verses are unusual in that they include four messenger formulas identifying these statements as the words of God (51:3a,4a,5a,5b), plus a final declaration in v. 6 that assures the listener that "they will know that I foretold it." The theme of Zion being sold is not foreign to Isaiah's thinking (cf. 50:1), but the style of poetic parallelism (especially in v. 5) is difficult to understand. Nevertheless, as substantiations of the instructions in 51:1–2, these quoted statements function similar to (a) the quotation of 35:10 in 51:11; or (b) the quotation of God's promises in 51:22 (which substantiates 51:21), so they are not that unusual and there is little reason to attribute them to some later author.

52:3 Why should Zion respond positively to God's exhortation in 51:1–2? What would make the audience believe that they are free and that no foreign uncircumcised nations will come and destroy the city? First the people must understand the nature of past and present situations when they were under the power of foreign nations, so that they can understand what God will do in the future. The people of God can have hope for their future "because" (*kî* NIV "for" in 52:3) when God gives his people into the hands of their enemies, no compensation ("for nothing" *ḥinnām*) is paid. Therefore, there really is no formal sale or change of ownership; consequently, the people of Israel do not need to be redeemed with silver. J. L. Koole concludes that, "God's right to his people was not forfeited because no one bought them from him. Israel was and has always remained God's possession."[262] Thus, there is no external power that can prevent God from fulfilling his plan to redeem his people in the future.

---

joining themselves to the Lord in chap. 56 so he interprets chap. 56, as "a bold extension of the description found here" in 52:1.

[261] The RSV and NEB translate "O captive" by emending שְׁבִי "sit" to שְׁבִיָּה "captive," which is found in the last line of the verse. There is no need to make this emendation.

[262] Koole, *Isaiah III, Volume 2: Isaiah 49–55*, 220.

52:4 The basis for this conclusion in v. 3 is God's dealings with his people in past days. God reminds his listeners that past attempts by foreign nations to take God's people from him have never succeeded. God's people (they are still his possession) "in the beginning, at first, initially" (*bāri'šōnâ*) willingly went down to sojourn in Egypt for a while because there was a severe famine in the land of Canaan (Gen 45–47). The thought process almost seems broken off, since there is no reference to their time of oppression and redemption from Egypt. The point that the Egyptian experience illustrates is not explicitly clear, for the Israelites were not sold into Egyptian slavery. Since the argument of 52:3 mentions that the people will be redeemed, the Egyptian experience may serve as a past analogical example of God redeeming his people without needing to pay money. The second half of v. 4 refers to the people experiencing the oppression of the Assyrians. Here again the discussion seems cut off, for one does not know exactly what this example proves or if the author is referring to the oppression by Tiglath-pileser III (2 Kgs 15–16), Shalmaneser (2 Kgs 17), Sargon (Isa 20), Sennacherib (Isa 37–38), or someone else. In addition, this part of the verse says nothing about any deportation to Assyria (parallel to Israel living in Egypt) or God redeeming his people from Assyria without the payment of money (as in 52:4). A possible comparison might be derived from the use of the word *bě'epes*, which is sometimes translated "in the end" (NIV "lately"). But *bě'epes* is not used elsewhere in a temporal sense, so F. Delitzsch[263] and a host of others (NASB, HCSB) use the translation "without cause" (lit "for nothing"), thus making a connection with "for nothing" in 52:3.[264] In other situations in Isaiah where this word is used in relationship to nations, it indicates that Edom (and all the nations she represents) will be "nothing" (34:12), that God views all the nations as "nothing" (40:17), and that the enemy nation that is warring against God's people will be "nothing" (41:12). Thus this verse must be saying that the Assyrians oppressed his people and gained "nothing." When did the Assyrians oppress Jerusalem and gain nothing? The Assyrians fought valiantly and defeated many fortified cities around 701 BC, but in the end they were defeated when the angel of God killed 185,000 troops in one night (37:36). Thus all their effort was wasted for they gained nothing.

52:5 There is little agreement on how to interpret this verse or how it fits into the flow of the argumentation because many of the phrases are open to multiple interpretations. The question, "And now, what[265] do I have here?" could introduce (a) a conclusion that is drawn from the preceding examples or (b) a third example (in addition to the Egyptian and Assyrian situations in 52:4). Although the location of "here" is not defined in this verse, many com-

---

[263] Delitzsch, "Prophecies of Isaiah," 278.

[264] In Isaiah אֶפֶס usually refers to "nothing" (34:12; 40:17; 41:12) or that there is "none" (45:6; 46:9; 47:8) beside God who is comparable to his divine power.

[265] The oral textual reading in the *Qere* is מָה "what" instead of מִי "who, what," which is in the *Qere* spoken or oral tradition.

mentators believe "here" refers to a Babylonian location where the people were in exile.[266] The basis for this conclusion is not particularly strong because (a) there is no reference to Babylon in the immediate context and (b) in the preceding paragraphs the audience is identified with the location of "Zion/ Jerusalem" (49:14; 51:3,11,16,17; 52:1,2,9),[267] her walls are mentioned (49:16), she is oppressed by enemies (51:13,19,22–23), and the place of her future restoration in Zion will be too cramped (49:19–20). Thus it seems wiser to treat this question as an attempt to draw a logical conclusion from the preceding examples. This approach seems to be verified by the conclusion in the second line, which indicates that the statement in 52:3 is true. God's people were taken for nothing; God's people still belong to him. Therefore, they are free to follow the positive exhortations given in 52:1–2.

The second part of the verse seems to raise a second issue that may have bothered the audience and caused them to question God's statements about their freedom. That is, what is God planning to do about the uncircumcised rulers (52:1) who presently control the ancient Near Eastern world and blaspheme God's name. Even though the people of Zion were still God's people because the nations had paid nothing, God needed to take control of the foreign kings who ruled those nations. The interpretation of God's answer to this issue is difficult because of textual uncertainties.[268] Some commentators believe that the Jewish rulers in 52:5b were "wailing" (from the root *yalāl*) because of severe oppression, but others prefer to follow 1QIs[a] (and the Aramaic Targum) and conclude that foreign "rulers"[269] were "boasting, mocking" (from the root *halāl*).[270] Both interpretations can make sense; therefore, the textual decision must be based on the poetic parallelism within the last two parallel lines of the verse. Everyone recognizes that the final line refers to the blasphemous insults against the name of God by foreign rulers; consequently, the previous line that is parallel to it probably is saying that foreign rulers are "boasting, mocking" (following the Qumran text). The ideas of mocking and

---

[266] Muilenburg, "Isaiah 40–66," 5:609, states, "Yahweh is present among the exiles in Babylon and reflects upon the situation there in contrast to the situation in Egypt and in Assyria." This conclusion is hard to defend from this passage.

[267] Baltzer, *Deutero-Isaiah*, 373, maintains that, "according to the context, the *place* is clearly Zion/Jerusalem."

[268] K. R. Greenwood, "A Case of Metathesis in Isaiah LII 5B," *VT* 56 (2006): 138–41, addresses the textual and interpretive problems in this verse and concludes that there was a metathesis between the letters ׳ and ו at the end of the first word and the beginning of the second word; thus he reads מֹשְׁלָיו הֵילִילוּ "the rulers of it rejoiced," which means in his interpretation that the rulers of Babylon rejoiced.

[269] 1QIs[a] has the pl. form of the noun "its rulers" (מֹשְׁלָיו), which matches the following pl. verb.

[270] Watts, *Isaiah 34–66*, 215–16, believes Judah's rulers "boasted of their prowess"; Seitz, "Isaiah 40–66," 6:454, concludes that foreign rulers were boastfully mocking God, while Oswalt, *Isaiah 40–66*, 358, 363, interprets this phrase to be saying that Jewish leaders were wailing in anguish.

blaspheming[271] the name of God are textually interlinked in the book of Isaiah to the behavior of the Assyrian king in 10:12–15, the arrogant attitude of Sennacherib in Rabshakah's speeches in 36:4–20, the reproaches in Sennacherib's letter in 37:10–13, Hezekiah's description of Sennacherib's blasphemy against God in 37:4,17, and God's condemnation of Sennacherib's boasting in 37:21–29. Although this might hint at a setting for this passage, the main point the prophet is making in these and the next few verses is that God has power over any and every foreign uncircumcised king (52:1) that blasphemes his name. He reigns over Zion; these uncircumcised rulers are not in control.

52:6 "Therefore" (*lākēn*) in conclusion, in the future when God acts he will fully reveal who he is and his people will acknowledge his name and his glorious reputation. This implies that God is making a commitment to do certain things that will bring about this changed situation. If his name will be acknowledged as holy, as King, and as the covenant God Yahweh, he will need to (a) remove the foreign domination of his people by rulers who blaspheme his name, (b) restore his people as a redeemed holy nation, and (c) renew his covenant relationship between himself and his people. Because of God's revelation of himself and his acts on behalf of Zion, his people will experience his presence and power in such a vivid way that they will associate themselves with his name. A second thing that the people of Zion will know is that God has spoken and he has accomplished what he promised. "Behold, I am here" announces his real presence with them in Zion, his readiness to use his power to act, and his purpose to fulfill all that he has promised. His mysterious plans and hidden directions for human history will all be revealed as he brings to fruition this era and opens the door to his kingdom where God and man dwell together in unity and perfect harmony.

52:7–8 After calling Zion to action (52:1–2), assuring his people that their past cycles of oppression are over, and proclaiming that "I am here" (52:3–6), God now explains his plans to reign as King among his redeemed people in an era of peace and joy. This paragraph picks up several of the themes introduced earlier in 40:9–11, for in both oracles there are messengers who proclaim the good news (40:9) on the mountains of Jerusalem (40:9a) concerning God's coming eschatological rule on the earth (40:10).[272]

Initially a "messenger of good news" (*mĕbaśśēr*)[273] is introduced. The arrival of this person is a welcomed surprise and a "beautiful"[274] sight to behold,

---

[271] The word מִתְנָאֵץ is a *hithpa'el* participle form which has dropped the ה after the מ (GKC §55b).

[272] Willey, *Remember the Former Things: The Recollection of Previous Texts in Second Isaiah*, 117–18, believes that Isaiah is quoting from Nahum 2:1. There is no question that the two texts are interlinked by common vocabulary, but Willey assumes Nahum is the earlier text and never deals with the possibility that Nahum might be quoting from the book of Isaiah.

[273] In 40:9 Zion/Jerusalem is identified as the messenger of good news who speaks to the cities of Judah the amazing news that "your God is here" (52:6).

[274] The adjective נָאווּ probably comes from the *niphal* form of the root אוה "he desires," thus

for the people were anxiously waiting to hear what he would say. Although a messenger might be used to bring back news of a military victory (2 Sam 18:19–28),[275] this herald stresses the new era that God will establish rather than his victory over any enemy. The focus is primarily on the message this runner speaks; the identity of the messenger does not seem to be important. His message of good news proclaims four things in four separate proclamations. One should not ignore the repeated emphasis of the four participles[276] that depict the proclaiming of this good news. Human proclamation appears to be the means God has chosen to spread the news of his coming; thus every messenger of God's salvation plays a fundamental role in the spreading the good news that God reigns. When God comes to dwell among his people, the messenger's four proclamations announce that he will inaugurate a time of peace, goodness, salvation, and a period of Divine rule. "Peace" (šālōm) denotes an absence of hostility and conflict; the establishment of a period of unity, cooperation, and righteous relationships among mankind. A time of "goodness" (ṭôb) implies that the negative experiences of evil, hatred, sickness, and death will not be present any longer; instead, positive and helpful relationship will flourish for the benefit of all. "Salvation" (yĕšûʿâ) indicates that God will deliver people from anything that might harm, oppress, or attempt to overpower them. This will all be possible because God himself will reign as King over his kingdom.

God's reign as King over the world is a fundamental theological emphasis of both the Old and New Testaments. In the theocracy of Israel (a) God functioned as King because he was in sovereign control of history; (b) he was the lawmaker who instructed his people how to live; (c) he was the commander-in-chief of the armies of Israel and heaven; and (d) he functioned as the judge, protector, and savior of Israel.[277] L. Köhler claims that "God is the ruling Lord: that is the one fundamental statement in the theology of the Old Testament . . . .

---

the adjective means "desirable, lovely, fitting" (Ps 93:5; Song 1:10), GKC §75x. The interrogative particle "how" functions more as an interjection to express surprise and joy. מָה frequently means "what," but when it is used as an exclamation, it takes on the meaning of "O how . . ." (GKC §148a).

[275] David anxiously awaited the first sighting of a messenger from the battle with Absalom in 2 Sam 18:19–28, and the news of a coming runner brought great excitement. There is nothing special about the feet of this or any other runner; his swift feet are simply the means of getting the news quickly to the people who anxiously await his arrival. His feet are described as "beautiful" because the audience is happy to see him and expect him to deliver good news.

[276] These participles function verbally in this context (GKC §116m), communicating the action of speaking.

[277] G. V. Smith, "The Conception of God/the gods as King in the Ancient Near East and the Bible," *TJ* 3 (1982): 18–38, discusses the widespread use of kingship imagery to describe the functions of Israel's God, as well as the use of similar terminology in other nations to describe the limited kingship of minor gods over various aspects of nature (Baal as god of fertility and rain was king for a short time during the wet season of the year) or limited territorial rule (the god Asshur was the king of Assyria). M. Z. Brettler, *God Is King: Understanding an Israelite Metaphor* (Sheffield: Sheffield Academic Press, 1989) surveys the royal appellations, qualities, and trappings as they apply to God.

Everything else derives from it. Everything else leans upon it. Everything else
can be understood with reference to it and only it."[278] W. Eichrodt maintains
that the concept that unifies the Old and New Testaments "is the irruption of the
Kingship of God into this world and its establishment here."[279] God is repeatedly called "the Lord" or master who controls what is happening on the earth
(Gen 45:8; Ps 105:21), the "Lord of Hosts" who controls the armies of heaven
(Isa 6:5), the "King of all the earth" (Ps 47:2,8), the "King of Zion" (Ps 28:2),
and "my God and my King" (Pss 68:24; 84:3; 145:1). God is King because
he owns the earth that he created (Pss 24:1; 74:12–17; 95:3–5), he rules over
the nations of the earth (Pss 22:38; 47:2,7–8), and reigns supreme as King
(Pss 93:1; 96:10; 97:1; 99:1). Although God reigned as King in the past and
still today, not everyone recognizes his authority or bows before his throne; but
at some point in the future the King will come in person to reign over his kingdom, destroy all who oppose his rule, and establish his holy kingdom in Zion
(Isa 2:1–4; 4:2–6; 35:1–10; 40:9–11). This messenger reminds and reassures
Isaiah's audience that God's plan to reign as King over his kingdom will happen; thus they should respond positively to the call to action found in 52:1–2.
The "good news" (the gospel) that God reigns gives hope and courage to all
who hear this news.

This voice of good news is soon joined by a larger group of heralds who
quickly spread the good news (52:8). The people are not called to "listen"
(NIV);[280] they are merely informed about "the voices of the watchmen"[281]
who are raising their voices. This reflects the ancient cultural context where
watchmen on the walls of a city would be the first to see someone approaching
a city. The scene pictures them joyfully shouting in unison together about what
they see happening. God is returning to Zion. What a day that will be.

Unfortunately, some commentators have failed to perceive this prophecy as
an eschatological reference to the establishment of God's everlasting kingdom.
Instead they have interpreted these verses as a description of Israelite exiles
coming to Jerusalem. J. D. W. Watts believes the messengers are members of
an expedition of exiles traveling from Babylon to Jerusalem during the time of
the Persian king Darius. The message of v. 7 ("Your God reigns") means that
Darius, Yahweh's protégé, has firmly grasped the reins of power. Peace has
returned to the empire."[282] But Darius did not bring lasting peace, goodness,
and salvation to Jerusalem as Ezra 3–6 demonstrates. How could an Israelite

---

[278] L. Köhler, *Old Testament Theology* (Philadelphia: Westminster, 1957), 30.

[279] W. Eichrodt, *Theology of the Old Testament* (Philadelphia: Westminster, 1961), 26.

[280] The Hebrew קוֹל "voice, sound" is a noun, not an imperative verbal form (GKC §146b) that
functions as an interjection (as in the NIV, NASB, NRSV).

[281] The term "watchman" צֹפֶה sometimes refers to a prophet (Jer 6:17; Ezek 3:17; 33:2,7), but
in this case this character appears to be reflecting the cultural way news was commonly spread by
men high above the ancient city on its walls.

[282] Watts, *Isaiah 34–66*, 216–17, has the messengers in Jerusalem rejoicing over the return of
exiles from Babylon in 52:8, which he views as "hard evidence that Yahweh is returning to Zion."

prophet equate the coming of God to Zion with the rise of a Persian ruler? C. Westermann also confuses the interpretation of these verses by claiming that, "the exiles' coming back home and their restoration are one and the same as God's coming, his return."[283] He believes this is a message of hope to the people living in Babylonian exile, but J. L. Koole rightly limits 52:7–8 to the return of God alone, not to the restoration of the exiles.[284] Isaiah is speaking about an eschatological fulfillment similar to the initial prophecy in 40:1–11.[285] Faith in God's future establishment of his reign is a legitimate motivation for trust in God today or in the midst of any crisis.

52:9–10 Suddenly the text breaks into a hymn of praise (possibly borrowing from Ps 98:8 for v. 9 and 98:1–2 for v. 10) that contains (a) a call for people to praise God and (b) a reason for praising God.[286] This hymn marks the ending of this long literary unit (similar to the hymns in 12:1–6; 42:10–12; 44:23; 49:13; and 55:12–13). The prophet exhorts his audience with two imperatives, "Break forth, sing joyfully,"[287] for God is about to act to comfort and redeem them. The audience is identified as the "ruins of Jerusalem," but obviously ruins cannot sing, so a metaphorical understanding must be intended. This personification of Jerusalem cannot refer to exiles in Babylon[288] but must refer to those living in Jerusalem who complained of problems throughout this unit (49:14,19; 51:12–13; 52:1–5). This message of joy includes God's transformation of life by promising both physical and spiritual comfort and redemption (40:1–11; 49:13). The redemption of people will bring forgiveness of sin, restoration of a relationship with God, the removal of despair, the presence of God in their midst, as well as a new holy people, the fertility of the land, and the rebuilding of cities. If God can do this, there is good reason to rejoice.

But how is it possible for this transformation to take place? Verse 10 indicates that the same strong and holy arm of God that accomplished both

---

One should not confuse the return of Israelites after the exile with the personal return of God at the end of time.

[283] Westermann, *Isaiah 40–66*, 251.

[284] Koole, *Isaiah III, Volume 2: Isaiah 49–55*, 238, finds both motifs in Isaiah but argues that 52:7–8 refer only to God's return.

[285] Muilenburg, "Isaiah 40–66," 5:610, believes the prophet is referring to an eschatological event that "is more than the defeat of an historical enemy, more than the coming of Cyrus or any single nation. The theophany is universal, world wide in its range, and it comes at the end, fulfilling the whole of Israel's history and tradition (40:5)."

[286] C. Westermann, *Praise and Lament in the Psalms* (Atlanta: John Knox, 1981), 130–32, indicates that the typical imperatival hymn of praise contains a call to praise and a reason to praise.

[287] NIV "Burst into songs of joy" communicates the content of the exhortation (the translators may have followed 1QIs[a] which has a imperative followed by a noun, which is similar to the use of these two verbs together in 44:23; 49:13; 54:1; 55:12), but this misses the emphasis communicated by the double imperative verbs. This twofold structure is also present in 44:23 and 49:13.

[288] Westermann, *Isaiah 40–66*, 251, believes the "waste places stand for the suffering, bewildered and weary remnant of the nation in the exile and the Diaspora," but this picture is primarily based on his vivid imagination of the situation.

judgments (5:25; 9:11,16,20; 10:4; 30:30) as well as great victories (51:9) will unfurl God's strong arm into these affairs in order to accomplish these spectacular promises. There is no direct reference to the Divine Warrior defeating his enemies in this verse, although this thought might be behind the imagery. Through his powerful personal involvement he will perform his will for his people in the future in the sight of all the nations of the earth (Ps 98:1–2). What will impress the nations and draw them to him will be the marvelous "salvation of our God." This appears to be parallel to the earlier thought that "the glory of the LORD will be revealed and all flesh shall see it" (40:5; 62:2) because "the Sovereign LORD comes with power and his arm rules for him" (40:10; 59:19–20). Everyone from all the ends of the earth will observe his revelation of his power; thus his name and glory will be known throughout the world (Ezek 20:32–44). Elsewhere the prophet states that all mankind will know the Lord (49:26), and in 45:22–23 people from all the nations are invited to turn from their old ways and be saved. The eschatological promises in 60:1–11 and 66:19–21 indicate that many from the nations will respond to God's self-revelation and come to worship him.

52:11–12 This brief subparagraph after the hymn is unusual since the hymns usually end a section. Nevertheless, something similar happened after the hymn in 48:20–21, so it is possible that these verses were placed here when these sermons were edited and put into writing, just like 48:21. This exhortation includes five imperative verbs that encourage the people to "turn away from" (*sûrû*, twice) and "go out" (*ṣĕʾû*, twice), somewhat similar to 48:20. Some of the ideas expressed seem to be drawn from the past experience of the exodus from Egypt just as in 48:20–21. Since 52:11–12 do not indicate who or where the audience is and what exactly they were supposed to turn away from, these issues must be based on the context of 52:1–10. Isaiah 52:1–2,8–9 address Zion, the holy city of Jerusalem about what will happen in a future eschatological setting.[289] Her time of bondage and chains (Egypt and Assyria in 52:3–5) are past. In that future age she is going to be dressed with strength and splendor (52:1). In this new situation Zion is set apart from the uncircumcised and defiled foreigners who entered the city in the past (52:1), who mocked

---

[289] Delitzsch, "Prophecies of Isaiah," 301, interprets this to refer to going out of Babylon and relates the carrying of the holy vessels based on Cyrus's instructions that the exiles should take back to Jerusalem (Ezra 1:7–11) the gold and silver vessels Nebuchadnezzar took from the temple in Jerusalem. Whybray, *Isaiah 40–66*, 168, suggests that the author "sees Babylon already falling: the order is given to the exiles to leave the stricken city." This interpretation completely ignores the eschatological setting of 52:1–10, which provides the context for 52:11–12. He does admit though that "the defeat of Babylon, and the return home of the exiles which is implied in this passage" are implied factors that are not stated in this passage. Oswalt, *Isaiah 40–66*, 371, says "true throughout 49–55, the Babylonian exile is always in the background" though he does not limit what is said just to a Babylonian setting because this passage is talking about something greater than just physical bondage. Willey, *Remember the Former Things: The Recollection of Previous Texts in Second Isaiah*, 125–26, believes 52:11 depends on and is a reversal of Lam 4:15.

and blasphemed God's name (52:5). She will enter a time of peace, salvation, redemption, and God himself dwells in her midst (52:7–9). C. Westermann rejects the view that these verses describe the exiles leaving Babylon; instead, he finds the emphasis on the separation of God, the holy vessels of the temple, and the people from uncleanness.[290] C. Seitz properly connects the emphasis on preventing unclean and uncircumcised people from entering the holy city where Zion's holy God reigns as King (52:1,7), with turning away from uncleanness in 52:11.[291] If God is going to dwell among his people, the city must be holy (no unclean foreigners), the temple must be holy (no unclean vessels), and the people need to walk in holy ways (4:2–6). These exhortations appear to be addressed to the priests who would take care of the holy vessels of the temple. If God is to dwell in his holy temple, the priests need to separate themselves ("turn away from . . . go out from") from anything unclean and "purify themselves."[292] This suggests a spiritual commitment that rejects the sinful ways of the past and causes the priests to dedicate their lives to pure living so that they can minister at the temple where God will dwell.

This eschatological event will be different from past experience when God's presence dwelt among his people (52:12, at the time of the exodus from Egypt). This future separation from unclean foreigners will not be something that they have to do in haste because of some threat or fear, as at the time of the exodus (Exod 12:11,33; Deut 16:3). God will be there reigning as King in their midst in Jerusalem (52:6–7); he will protect them just as his presence in the pillar of fire protected the Israelites in the wilderness (Exod 13:21–22; Num 10:25). J. Motyer finds these images picturing a situation in which "there will be no unwelcome pressure in the situation and nothing to distract the mind from a calm commitment to walk with God in holiness."[293] This will be a time of peace without war with God dwelling with his people in Zion (2:2–4; 4:2–6).

THEOLOGICAL IMPLICATIONS.   This long literary unit (51:9–52:12) is an extended answer to the prayer in 51:9–11. It is evident throughout this section that the people of Jerusalem want God to act on their behalf (51:9) because they are fearful (51:12). They have suffered under the wrath of some oppressor (51:13–14) because God has poured out his wrath on them (51:17) and allowed them to experience destruction, famine, and the sword (51:19). Such is the destiny of believers throughout various periods of history, for sometimes difficulties come to test people's faith and at other times God tests people's unwillingness to repent by pouring out his wrath on those who justly deserve

---

[290] Westermann, *Isaiah 40–66*, 253, states that, "it would be wrong to regard its development in v. 11b as a literal description of the departure from Babylon.

[291] Seitz, "Isaiah 40–66," 6:455, claims that, "the charge is not, as is sometimes assumed, made from the perspective of exile itself. The priests are commanded to 'go forth from here.'"

[292] The word הִבָּרוּ is a *niphal* reflexive imperative from בָּרַר "to be clean, pure."

[293] Motyer, *Isaiah*, 422, interprets these images in 52:12 as pictures of God's care and the divine protection available for God's people.

his judgment. In the midst of suffering a believer should look to God for mercy and help.

Prayer is the means every believer has to come to God for wisdom to understand what is happening, for comfort in times of fear because of an oppressor, and for hope for deliverance from suffering. Believers can request that God act, beg him to use that power that slew the Egyptians and divided the sea (51:9–10) in order to ransom his people from trouble. One can even remind God of his past promise to bring peace, joy, and singing to the redeemed of the Lord (51:11). Although some may seek only human means to remove their suffering, in the end it is really God who controls what happens in every person's life and the life of every nation. Although people get impatient and want their time of suffering to end immediately, sometimes it will be severe and long lasting. Consequently it is not unusual for people to wonder, where this powerful God is. Does he know about the problems his people are enduring, and does he care enough about them to bring about relief? Why does he not act now to end such severe suffering?

In these prophecies God graciously responds to the prayers of his people. He explains that he knows about the difficult situations his people are in (51:12–14,19–21; 52:4–5) and that some of their problems happen because God himself brought judgment on them because of their sins (51:17–20). In spite of these problems, God assures those praying that he is the Creator of the heavens and earth (51:13,16b) and controls the seas (51:15), so there is no need to fear mere mortal men (51:12a). Soon God will remove the wrath of the oppressor (51:13b,23), cover his people with his protection (51:16a), and take away his cup of wrath (51:22). These comforting words remind the reader that suffering sometimes is deserved, that suffering is only for a limited time, and that God has the power to remove suffering. Of course, just because God chooses to remove the suffering of one person in one situation does not mean that he will act the same way in all other situations. His plans differ, his purposes for bringing suffering change, and his reasons for acting or not acting are often beyond human comprehension.

But one thing that is sure is that his past and future promises are true (40:1–11; 51:11). In the distant future he will come to dwell in Zion as King and bring peace and salvation to Jerusalem (52:7) and the rest of the world (2:2–5). The people of Zion must undergo a spiritual transformation so that she will become a holy city, removed from uncleanness, and free from oppression (52:1–2,11). It will happen some day; a messenger will shout on the mountains of Jerusalem that a time of peace and salvation has come to Zion because God reigns among his people (52:7–8). God will bare his arm just as the people requested (51:9; 52:10), and all nations will see his great salvation and protection (52:10,12). God's people need to wake up to God's plans, to cleanse themselves from uncleanness, and trust in God's promises. Life in this sinful earth is often very difficult, but God's reign will bring an end to these problems and usher the glorious era when he will rule as King. The suffering people go through on this earth will end someday soon. O Lord, may it come quickly!

8. Exaltation and Joy Comes When Sin Is Taken Away (52:13–55:13)

Although a majority of commentaries end this literary unit with chap. 55, F. Delitzsch and J. D. W. Watts extend this section from 49–57.[294] In contrast, R. H. O'Connell's analysis of the concentric literary design limits this section to chaps. 49–54; therefore, chap. 55 is put into the next unit because it fits with the strong appeal for the people to confess their sins and be reconciled to God.[295] M. Sweeney follows a similar conclusion, connecting the exhortations in chap. 55 to the instruction in chaps. 56–66 about how to constitute the new covenant community in Zion.[296] These alternative suggestions about the structure of this section have not gained widespread acceptance because there are linguistic signs that chap. 55 ends this section.

The reason why the majority of commentaries agree on making 55 the last chapter of this unit is because chap. 55:6–13 appears to be a final paragraph (some call it an epilogue), which matches several aspects of the introduction in 40:1–11 (some call it the prologue). C. Westermann claims that the "close connections with the prologue, especially 40:6ff, are obvious" while R. Melugin connects the theme of: (a) the return of the Lord in 55:6–7 to 40:1–2; (b) the promise of an exodus from captivity in 55:12–13 to 40:3–5, and (c) the reliability of God's word in 55:8–11 to 40:8.[297] Certainly the last point is the strongest. In addition the hymn in 55:12–13 appears to be the typical way of ending a literary unit in Isaiah 40–55.

The literary unit of Isa 52:13–55:10 is made up of another poem about the Servant of the Lord (52:13–53:12), another eschatological proclamation of

---

[294] Delitzsch, "Prophecies of Isaiah," 384, begins part III of chaps. 40–66 with chap. 58. Watts, *Isaiah 34–66*, 219, describes "Act X" (52:13–57:21) as "Restoration Pains in Jerusalem" and connects it to events in the reign of the Persian kings Darius and Xerxes (518–465 BC). He believes chap. 53 is about the death of the Hebrew governor of Judah, Zerubbabel, with chaps. 54–57 presenting the prophet's vision of the future in which God plans to use the Persian rulers to restore Jerusalem, reestablish proper worship, and open the temple to all people.

[295] O'Connell, *Concentricity and Continuity*, 150–52, describes the structure of 40–54, while pp. 215–19 make 55–57 a structural unit with the invitation to repent in chap. 55 matching the final ultimatum to renew the covenant in 65:2–66:24. Seitz, "Isaiah 40–66," 6:472, begins the third section of 40–66 with chap. 54 because of the many connections between 54–55 and 56–66, particularly the use of the pl. "servants" in 54:17 and Israel as married, common themes in 56–66.

[296] Sweeney, *Isaiah 1–39 with an Introduction to the Prophetic Literature*, FOTL (Grand Rapids: Eerdmans, 1996), 48, or his more detailed defense in *Isaiah 1–4 and the Postexilic Understanding of the Isaianic Traditions*, BZAW 171 (Berlin: de Gruyter, 1988), 87–95.

[297] Melugin, *Formation of Isaiah 40–55*, 87, or Muilenburg, "Isaiah 40–66," 5:642. L. J. Liebreich, "The Compilation of the Book of Isaiah," *JQR* 47 (1957): 122–24, divides 40–66 into two sections: chaps. 40–49 and 50–66. Chapters 50–66 are then divided into 50–55 and 56–66. The interlinking verbal connections between chap. 56 and 66 also argue for making chap. 56 the beginning of the next literary unit (Liebreich gives 6 examples on p. 124).

salvation about mother Zion having many children (54:1–17), and a final call for the people to come to God to repent of their sins (55:1–13). The arrangement of alternating Servant and Zion oracles is a consistent pattern throughout chaps. 49–55, so it is not surprising to find it employed in this unit. The strong interconnection between the suffering of the Servant in 49:4; 50:6–8 and 53:3–8 creates continuity within the subsections within chaps. 49–55. In addition, the prophecy that Zion will not be barren but have the hope of many children connects chap. 54:1–17 with 49:14–50:3 and 51:17–50:3. Chapter 55 concludes this larger literary unit (chaps. 40–55) with a call for the people to respond to the words of God in the preceding messages.

(1) The Exaltation of the Servant Who Takes Away Sin (52:13–53:12)

Those who identify the suffering servant with the nation of Israel suggest that the historical setting of this message reflects the suffering of the people of God in Babylonian exile and their deliverance from it.[298] In a variation of this approach, H. M. Orlinsky understands 52:13–15 to be about Israel who will be exalted after enduring the degrading conditions in exile, but he believes that the discussion in chap. 53 relates to "the prophet himself Second Isaiah."[299] Various authors have proposed similar scenarios that suggest that the servant was an individual who endured suffering (Second Isaiah, a Second Moses, Jehoiakim, or a leprous rabbi).[300] N. Gottwald and J. W. Miller hypothesize a political setting in which the prophet (the servant) was in Babylonian exile supporting the liberation of the exiles by the Persian king Cyrus. Since his political talk was not acceptable to the Babylonian leadership or the exiled Jews who were politically pro-Babylonian, the prophet (the servant) was arrested and imprisoned, then later freed.[301] Rejecting the individual and community interpretations, H. Gunkel proposed a completely different setting by suggesting that Isaiah 53 should be interpreted in terms of the Adonis-Tammuz cult, which featured a

---

[298] H. H. Rowley, *The Servant of the Lord* (Oxford: Blackwell, 1965), 35–40, reviews the perspective held by A. S. Peake, A. Lods, J. Lindblom, and others. Although P. D. Hanson, "The World of the Servant in the Lord in Isaiah 40–55," in *Jesus and the Suffering Servant: Isaiah 53 and Christian Origins* (Harrisburg: Trinity Press International, 1998), 9–22, does not identify the servant, the world of the servant in Isaiah 40–55 is that of the confused exiles of Judah who were trying to figure out God's plans in light of the failed Zion/David theologies of the past. He views the servant as God's new way of providing relief from their sins and infirmities (53:4) because the servant will remove them, thus giving God's people a new message to declare to the nations.

[299] H. M. Orlinsky, "The So-Called 'Suffering Servant' in Isaiah 53," in *Interpreting the Prophetic Tradition*, ed H. M. Orlinsky (New York: Ktav, 1969), 227–73. Whybray, *Isaiah 40–66*, 169, has a similar interpretation.

[300] Rowley, *The Servant of the Lord*, 3–25, reviews this perspective, which is held by S. Mowinckel (Second Isaiah), K. Baltzer, (Moses), E. Sellin (Jehoiakim), B. Duhm (a leprous rabbi).

[301] N. Gottwald, *The Hebrew Bible: A Socio-Literary Introduction* (Philadelphia: Fortress, 1985), 499–500, and J. W. Miller, "Prophetic Conflict in Second Isaiah: The Servant Songs in the Light of Their Context," in *Wort, Gebot, Glaube: Beiträge zur Theologie des Alten Testament*, ed. J. J. Stamm, E. Jenni, H. J. Stoebe; ATANT 59 (Zurich: Zwingli, 1970), 83–85.

dying and rising god.[302] K. Baltzer suggests that the servant (a second Moses figure) appears at a heavenly judicial court scene where his life is judged.[303] J. L. Koole concludes that these alternative theories about the Servant poem do not explain the evidence as clearly as the messianic interpretation.[304]

Most of these interpretations are not very convincing if one takes the view that all of these Servant poems are prophetic of a future figure in an eschatological setting when God will bring salvation to his people and the nations. As with most other future proclamations of salvation, the setting of the author and his audience is largely hidden and unknown. The undated future setting of the suffering Servant is primarily in focus. But this does not mean that the interpreter is totally in the dark about what this passage means. D. J. A. Clines is unduly pessimistic, finding a great deal of ambiguity in this passage. He identifies six unanswered questions: "Who is 'he'? What did he suffer? Did 'he' die? Who are 'we'? What led 'we' to change their minds about the Servant? Who are 'they'?"[305] The exposition of the text below will suggest that when these questions are dealt with in the context of the earlier poems about the Servant and the surrounding literary material, many of these mysteries and ambiguities begin to find answers.

When dealing with the identity of the Servant in 52:13–53:12 some reject the view that this poem is speaking about the messianic figure described earlier in 9:1–6; 11:1–5; or 32:1,15–20; 42:1–13. The final Servant poem assumes the reader knows what was said about the Messiah in these earlier chapters as well as the preceding prophecies about the Servant (49:1–13; 50:4–11).[306] The most important connection is that the earlier songs indicate that the Servant would have trouble with his ministry to Israel (49:4), would be abhorred and despised (49:7), and would even be beaten and mocked (50:6–7). Nevertheless, this Servant will not be discouraged or give up (42:4) but will bring forth justice and salvation to Israel and the nations by being a light and a covenant to them (42:4,6; 49:5–6,8). In the end God will vindicate and exalt the Servant (49:7; 50:8). The examination of these earlier poems led to the conclusion that

---

[302] Rowley, *The Servant of the Lord*, 26–27, reviews this perspective and rejects it because there is no atonement in this cult; moreover, it is very unlikely that a monotheistic prophet would adapt the ritual of a pagan cult.

[303] Baltzer, *Deutero-Isaiah*, 398, compares this to the heavenly dispute over the body of Moses in the *Assumption of Moses* or the trials of Joshua in Zech 4 or Job in Job 1–2.

[304] Koole, *Isaiah III, Volume 2: Isaiah 49–55*, 251, 259.

[305] D. J. A. Clines, *I, He, We, and They—A Literary Approach to Isaiah 53*, JSOTSup 1 (Sheffield: JSOT, 1976), 25–39. In contrast to the ambiguity of Clines, R. B. Chisholm, "The Christological Fulfillment of Isaiah's Servant Songs," *BSac* 163 (2006): 387–404, begins with the presupposition that this chapter is about Jesus in the New Testament, so there is very little ambiguity in his interpretation.

[306] The reader can review some of the possible identifications of the Servant or the conclusions drawn from the exegesis by referring back to those passages. Please consult the earlier analysis associated with the Servant poems in 42:1–13; 49:1–13; 50:4–11.

this Servant was a messianic royal figure[307] who would establish justice for all the nations but suffer opposition and physical abuse before his eventual vindication and exaltation. The present poem explains these issues in more detail and adds new information.

GENRE.   Although some have questioned the unity of this passage and its connection to its literary context,[308] according to the analysis of R. N. Whybray the form-critical background of 52:13–52:13 has the genre characteristics of a "song of thanksgiving for the deliverance of God's servant, Deutero-Isaiah"[309] from Babylonian prison. C. Westermann agrees with this approach but notes that the usual form of thanksgiving was significantly altered, for the narrator in 53:1–10 does not speak in first person singular terminology lamenting his own suffering as in other songs of thanksgiving. Instead, the "we" speakers are thankful because they are the ones who will receive the salvation accomplished by the one who suffers.[310] S. Mowinckel connected the negative statements about suffering to somewhat similar complaints of suffering in dirges or laments.[311] Because of the differences from the normal lament and thanksgiving song, R. Melugin suggests that it is misleading to find much influence from a psalm of thanksgiving; therefore, he identifies this as a new literary creation that uses two salvation speeches (52:13–15; 53:11–12) and a report by the nations concerning the suffering and triumph of the one who suffers.[312] The basic

---

[307] Williamson, *Variations on a Theme: King, Messiah and Servant in the Book of Isaiah*, 132, 153, states that "there is a considerable degree of agreement nowadays, but whatever else is to be said about the servant in Isaiah 42:1–4, he is presented to us in royal guise." Later he concludes, "that there are royal aspects to the person and work of the servant in 49:1–6." D. I. Block, "My Servant David: Ancient Israel's Vision of the Messiah," in *Israel's Messiah in the Bible and Dead Sea Scrolls*, ed R. S. Hess and M. D. Carroll (Grand Rapids: Baker, 2003), 17–56, rejects the view that the servant Messiah had prophetic and priestly roles; instead, he argues that he consistently is pictured as having a kingly role.

[308] B. Duhm, *Das Buch Jesaia* HKAT 3/1 (Göttingen: Vandenhoeck & Ruprecht, 1922), hypothesized that all the servant poems were inserted into their present literary context by a later redactor and that they are not connected to the literary context of the surrounding chapters. O. H. Steck, "Aspekte des Gottesknechts in Deuterojesajas 'Ebed-Jahwe-Liedern,'" in *Gottesknecht und Zion* (Tübingen: Mohr, 1992), 20–22, outlines the intra-Isaianic reception of this poem on five different levels that come from 539 to 270 BC. In the first level (539 BC) the prophet is God's servant, the second level (520 BC) is about Zion's vicarious suffering because of sin, the third level of redaction (the time of Neh) focuses on the returning exile servants, in the fourth (311–302 BC) the servant who suffers is no longer innocent, and in the fifth level of redaction (270 BC) the servant is the true people of God. This kind of subjective division and rereading of texts in redactional studies seems to have little value.

[309] Whybray, *Isaiah 40–66*, 169, 172, and *Thanksgiving for a Liberated Prophet: An Interpretation of Isaiah 53*, JSOTSup 4 (Sheffield: JSOT, 1978) compared this to passages like Ps 118.

[310] Westermann, *Isaiah 40–66*, 257, calls this "an individual psalm of thanksgiving (declarative psalm of praise) where the central portion is made up of . . . a report on the suffering and a report on the deliverance."

[311] S. Mowinckel, "The Servant of the Lord," *He that Cometh* (Nashville: Abingdon, 1954), 187–257, but this ignores that most laments are about the person's own oppression and hopelessness.

[312] Melugin, *Formation of Isaiah 40–66*, 74. Childs, *Isaiah*, 411, agrees with Melugin.

purpose of this message is to announce to Israel and the world that the Servant has provided salvation for "us" and "the many."

STRUCTURE. The structure of 52:13–53:12 fits into three paragraphs based on who is speaking and the topic under consideration (exaltation or humiliation). God speaks about the exaltation of "my Servant" (52:13; 53:11), while an unidentified group of people testify ("our message" in 53:1) about the Servant's suffering for "our transgressions" (53:5). This threefold outline connects the initial introductory paragraph with the final paragraph.

Exaltation of the Servant predicted	52:13–15
Report on the Servant's suffering	53:1–9[313]
The surprising, despised Servant	1–3
Vicarious suffering for our sins	4–6
Willing submission to death	7–9
Sacrifice leads to the exaltation of the Servant	53:10–12

These paragraphs are interconnected by the use of repeated vocabulary that draws these verses together.[314] J. Muilenburg refers to 14 different words that are repeated in this poem, but P. R. Raabe found 36 repeated words, with 19 key words repeated to highlight the contrast between the Servant's humiliation and exaltation as well as to contrast the difference between what people falsely believed to be true about the Servant and what really was true.[315] For example, the Servant will be "lifted up" and exalted in 52:13, but later in 53:12 one reads that he "lifts up" the sins of many. Another example is that the speakers esteemed him "stricken" and "afflicted" by God (53:4), but he was also "stricken" and "afflicted" for our transgressions. These contrasts and repeated terms illustrate the literary skill of the author and demonstrate the unity of this message.

Although this Servant poem is most closely related to the earlier Servant poems in 42:1–13; 49:1–13; and 50:4–11, it also has connections with its immediate contextual setting of chap. 52. Isaiah 52:1–10 refers to a future time in which Zion will be a holy city (52:1). This will happen because God will

---

[313] Childs, *Isaiah*, 411, and several other commentators divide the last two paragraphs based on the use of "we" speech in 53:1–11a and divine speech in 53:11b–12. Koole, *Isaiah III, Volume 2: Isaiah 49–55*, 262, divides the paragraphs into 53:2–3,4–5,6–7,8–9 while Goldingay, *Message of Isaiah 40–55*, 469, has a chiastic arrangement with 53:4–6 in the center and 11b–12 as the final section parallel to 52:13–15.

[314] A. R. Ceresko, "The Rhetorical Strategy of the Fourth Servant Song (Isaiah 52:13–53:12): Poetry and the Exodus-New Exodus Event," *CBQ* 56 (1994): 42–55, views the first rhetorical unit (52:13–15) and the last unit (53:11b–12) as matching sections that frame the rest of the poem because both refer to (a) the servant and (b) the many.

[315] P. R. Raabe, "The Effect of Repetition in the Suffering Servant Song," *JBL* 103 (1984): 77–84, presents a series of charts that illustrate these contrasts. M. L. Barré, "Textual and Rhetorical-critical Observations on the Last Servant Song (Isaiah 52:13–53:12)," *CBQ* 62 (2000): 1–27, finds seven word pairs being repeated (terms like "looks" and "appearance").

forgive their sins by washing away their filth and cleansing the blood stains from Jerusalem (4:3–4). In 53:4–6,8,11–12 the good news is that forgiveness is attained through the death of the Servant, thus explaining how the sins of the nations will be washed away. Isaiah 52:7 predicts a time to proclaim the good news of peace, salvation, and the reign of God as King in Jerusalem, and 53:1–10 refers to an almost unbelievable "message, report" of good news about a Servant who would bear the sins of many. Isaiah 52:10 refers to the Lord baring his arm in the sight of all the nations so that they can see the salvation of God. These ideas are consistent with and elaborated in 53:1 when the arm of the Lord reveals the Servant. Many nations and their kings will see, hear, and understand this message (52:15) just as 49:7; 51:4–5; 52:10 predict.[316] These interlinking connections suggest that this Servant poem in 52:13–53:12 is the climactic message that fills out the unanswered questions raised in these earlier oracles. It explains the personal action of God through the Servant that makes salvation possible to many, and it plays a fundamental role in convincing the nations to understand and accept the salvation that God offers.

EXALTATION OF THE SERVANT: 52:13–15

13See, my servant will act wisely;
   he will be raised and lifted up and highly exalted.
14Just as there were many who were appalled at him—
   his appearance was so disfigured beyond that of any man
   and his form marred beyond human likeness—
15so will he sprinkle many nations,
   and kings will shut their mouths because of him.
 For what they were not told, they will see,
   and what they have not heard, they will understand.

The Lord is the speaker in the first paragraph. His primary focus is to assure the reader that in spite of contrary appearances at times (50:4–11), the Servant will be exalted. Because this news of exaltation appears to run contrary to the utter humiliation and death of the Servant in 53:1–10, some have tried to reduce the tension by connecting 52:13–15 and 53:1–10 to different people (Israel in 52:13–15, the prophet in the 53:1–10) or by constructing a literary solution that attributes these different views of the Servant to different authors or redactors.[317] Such solutions are hard to sustain in light of the close verbal interrelationship between the paragraphs. Also, the exaltation speeches include

---

[316] Melugin, *Formation of Isaiah 40–55*, 168, develops these and other possible interlinking connections between this servant song and its preceding context. He views Isaiah 53 "as an extensive elaboration of 49,7."

[317] Orlinsky, "The So-Called 'Suffering Servant' in Isaiah 53," in *Interpreting the Prophetic Tradition*, 227–73, believes these two paragraphs are talking about different people while E. Haag, "Die Botschaft vom Gottesknecht," in *Gewalt und Gewaltlosigkeit im Alten Testament*, ed. E. Haag et al., QD 96 (Freiburg: Herder, 1983), 166–72, views the positive frame about the servant exaltation as secondary later addition.

hints of humiliation (52:14 and 53:12). These contrasting themes and paragraphs should not be removed or emasculated, for contrasts are built into the very fiber of this oracle. When a message explicitly reveals that something unheard of will be revealed in the Servant's life, that people's previous thoughts about the Servant will turn out to be totally mistaken, then one should expect to find conflicting perspectives presented within the paragraphs.

This brief paragraph includes three points:

An announcement of future exaltation	52:13
Many appalled at the Servant	52:14
The nations will be astonished	52:15

The interpretation of these verses are complicated by textual problems, the difficulty of interpreting some metaphors, problems with connecting the interrelated clauses, and the vagueness of terms like "the many," but these issues do not make it impossible to understand the main thrust of the message. The goal in interpreting these verses will be to try to understand what the original author was communicating to his audience at that time. After the exposition of 52:13–53:12, an excursus is added to consider how these ideas were later interpreted in Jewish and Christian circles.

52:13 Since this prophecy begins similar to 42:1; 50:9 ("Behold, my Servant"), this news about God's Servant ("my Servant," ʿabdî)[318] immediately connects this prophecy with what was already said in 42:1–13; 49:1–13; and 50:4–11. In light of the extreme suffering and humiliation of the Servant in 50:4–11, it is somewhat surprising for this explanation of the Servant's life to begin with his grand exaltation.[319] All the verbs used in this verse refer the Servant's extraordinary exalted position. NIV translates the first verb "will act wisely," (śākal)[320] which draws on the semantic meaning of this verb when it is found in wisdom contexts, but when this verb is used in nonwisdom contexts (which is the case here), this verb describes a person's "success"[321] because of their insight. In earlier poems about the servant it appeared that the servant's work might end up being "in vain" (49:4) and that his mistreatment might result in failure (50:6), but these threats will not prevent him from accomplishing his task with "success" (śākal). Later in Jer 23:5 the messianic Branch is described

---

[318] The Aramaic Targum on Isaiah adds the interpretive "the Messiah" after the reference to my Servant, but when the text turns to talk about suffering, the Targum does not apply this to the Messiah.

[319] Themes of the servant's exaltation in other poems came only toward the end of the story in 49:7b and 50:8–9.

[320] Barré, "Textual and Rhetorical-critical Observations on the Last Servant Song (Isaiah 52:13–53:12)," 9, translates "will be wise" and makes a connection with this term in Dan 12:3, plus he finds wisdom terminology in 52:15 "they will understand" and 53:11 "by his knowledge."

[321] The verb שָׂכַל means "success" when referring to Joshua (Josh 1:7,8), David (1 Sam 18:5,14), Solomon (1 Kgs 2:30), and Hezekiah (2 Kgs 18:7). This success is due to the wisdom and insight these people have in dealing with people in a wise manner.

as one who will be successful because he will establish justice and righteousness on the earth, which coincides with 42:1–4. Thus Jeremiah's commentary on these ideas indicates that he saw a similarity between the Branch and Servant and understood this person as a reference to a Davidic messianic figure.

Although 13b is not connected to 13a by a causal or result particle, one might at least suggest that the Servant's success will have something to do with his exaltation. His exaltation describes his glorification (cf. 49:5b) using three verbs: "he will be raised up; he will be lifted up; he will be high." The two passive verbs[322] indicate that someone else will raise him up, an idea that is consistent with God's promise to "give him a portion with the great/many" in 53:12. J. L. Koole suggests that these three acts of exaltation "correspond to the threefold humiliation of the servant in 53:4b,"[323] but no overt literary connection is made between these thoughts. These three verbs are sometimes used to describe the glory of God himself (cf. 2:11,17; 5:16; 6:1; 33:10; 57:15), but J. Goldingay probably reads too much into the text when he states that the Servant will "reach a position more like Yhwh's kingly status than a mere human being."[324] A very high position of honor is appropriate for one who successfully accomplishes what the Servant did. The highness of his exaltation does fit in with the royal imagery in 9:1–7 and 42:1–4.

52:14 Verses 14–15 are syntactically interconnected by the "as . . . so . . . so" syntactical formula of clauses, but it is not easy to understand this complicated syntactical construction. The interpretation of this verse is also made more difficult by the solid textual tradition of a second person reference to "you" (NIV; NRSV "him") in 14a, which is grammatically at odds with the third-person references ("him") throughout the rest of the verse.[325] The direct address to "you" in 14a could be explained as a typical prophetic switching between pronouns (GKC §144p), a textual error for "him," or a brief direct address to the Servant himself, which is followed by remarks that use the third-person pronouns.[326] The more difficult reading and probably the most original would be to accept the third option, which would indicate that the

---

[322] Goldingay and Payne, *Isaiah 40–55*, 2:288, interpret the *niphal* verb נִשָּׂא as a reflexive "exalt himself," but a passive seems more appropriate in light of the rest of the passage. Exalting oneself usually has the negative connotations of prideful exaltation, which God hates.

[323] Koole, *Isaiah III, Volume 2: Isaiah 49–55*, 265. One should not try to relate these terms to specific events in the life of the royal Messiah.

[324] Goldingay, *Message of Isaiah 40–55*, 472.

[325] The preposition and suffix in the Masoretic tradition is עָלֶיךָ "concerning you," but the Aramaic Targum, Syriac, and two Hebrew manuscripts have עָלָיו "concerning him." "Concerning you" is definitely the harder reading, and it is found in the Old Greek and Qumran texts, so it should be maintained. Muilenburg, "Isaiah 40–66," 5:616, and Blenkinsopp, *Isaiah 40–55*, 346, accept the emendation "concerning him," while Oswalt, *Isaiah 40–66*, 373, and North, *Second Isaiah*, 227, do not accept this emendation.

[326] Young, *Isaiah*, 3:336–37, and Westermann, *Isaiah 40–66*, 258, defend this parenthetical understanding.

Servant himself is hearing these words in 52:13–15 (though the first option is completely acceptable).

The subject of the verb in the first line of v. 14 is "the many," a reference to an unspecified group of people, possibly some of the same people mentioned later in 52:15 and 53:11–12. They appear to be the people who observe the Servant, but it is unclear if this term should be limited exclusively to the "many nations" of 52:15 (possibly the nations and coastlands of 42:1–4; 49:1), or if it also includes the people of Israel.[327] Since the Servant did not justify only the sins of the foreign nations (the "many" in 53:11) or bear the sins of just the foreign nations (the "many" in 53:12), it is apparent that the many[328] should encompass everyone, including Israel.

The "just as . . . so" construction in v. 14 is parallel to the contrasting "so" construction in v. 15.[329] These kinds of constructions may function as (a) a comparison that continues and explains things in more detail, or (b) as a contrast between the perspective of the "many" in v. 14 and the "many nations" in v. 15. If this refers to contrasting points of view, the "many" in v. 14 could be the perspective of the Israelites (they are the "we" in 53:1–6), with v. 15 expressing the perspective of the kings and nations.[330] Another contrasting option would be to find an initial response of horror by the many because of the suffering of the Servant (52:14), but a later positive response of astonishment at the end of the Servant's ministry because "the many" later understand that he suffered for their sins (52:15).

Why was the audience initially "astonished, horrified, appalled" (šāmĕmû)?[331] The reason for this horrified response depends on how the next line is translated. One could conclude that they were horrified because "the disfigurement (from the root šāḥat)[332] of his appearance was from man" (NIV,

---

[327] Those who hold that the servant is Israel naturally have to make the many refer to "the nations," but those who identify the servant with someone else can identify the many with either the nations or Israel. Blenkinsopp, *Isaiah 40–55*, 350, identifies the servant's disciples as "the many." B. Janowski, "He Bore Our Sins: Isaiah 53 and the Drama of Taking Another's Place," in *The Suffering Servant: Isaiah 53 in Jewish and Christian Sources*, ed B. Janowski and P. Stuhlmacher (Grand Rapids: Eerdmans, 2004), 48, believes that the many "refers to empirical Israel" as in many Psalms (3:2–3; 31:12–14).

[328] G. D. Kirchhevel, "Who's Who and What's What in Isaiah 53?" *TynBul* 13 (2003): 127–32 maintains that the "many" רַבִּים are the "rulers" based on Jer 39:13 and the Akkadian word *rab* "magnate, chief officer" in Babylon. The Babylonian military context of Jer 39:13 is not present in Isaiah 52–53 so this meaning is most unlikely.

[329] The article by P. J. Gentry, "The Atonement in Isaiah's Fourth Servant Song (Isaiah 52:13–53:12)," *SBJT* 11 (2007), 20–47, points out the importance of understanding this construction.

[330] Koole, *Isaiah III, Volume 2: Isaiah 49–55*, 266, and Delitzsch, "Prophecies of Isaiah," 306, create this kind of contrast between Israel and the nations. Equally defensible would be the response of the same group of many people at different times.

[331] The root שָׁמַם is often connected to acts of destruction, desolation, total obliterations, and the negative response of people when they realize the utter annihilation of what used to exist (49:8,19).

[332] To get this passive meaning it is possible to read this as a *hophal* participle, which is

"beyond that of any man") or "the anointing (from the root *māšaḥ*)[333] of his appearance from man." One must also decide if it makes more sense to speak of anointing (from the root *māšaḥ*)[334] the Servant's "appearance" and "form" more than other men or to speak of the disfigurement (from the root *šāḥat*) of his "appearance" and "form" from/because of man. The latter is in agreement with 53:2 where similar terms are employed; thus it seems best to reject the translations that refer to his anointing. In this approach the first "so" clause agrees with the "just as" clause (following the pattern in Josh 11:15; Isa 55:10–11).[335]

52:15 The "so" clause in this verse either adds a similar response of another group of people, or it gives a comparative contrast with the reaction of the same group at an earlier time and then at a later time. It is clear that kings will be quiet, shutting their mouths in astonishment and awe at the sight of what they observe in the servant's life (15b). The positive respectful reaction of "shutting their mouths" in 15 seems to contrast with the negative response of "horror" in 14, suggesting the "so" clause in 15 presents a contrasting clause (similar to the syntactical construction of Exod 1:12).[336] The respectful "shutting of the mouths" seems consistent with the idea that the kings of the nation

---

suggested by the Syriac Peshitta, or the Babylonian Hebrew pointing of the word. A. Guillaume, "Some Readings in the Dead Sea Scroll of Isaiah," *JBL* 76 (1957): 40–49, points to the Arabic *mašakhta* "ugly form, without comeliness" as a possible solution.

[333] The verb מִשְׁחַת is only found here, so there is some controversy about its root and meaning. If it comes from the root שָׁחַת then it means "ruined, disfigured," but Goldingay, *Message of Isaiah 40–55*, 490, takes the root to be מָשַׁח "anoint" based on his interpretation of 1QIs[a] מָשְׁחִי. Further discussion is available in A. Guillaume, "Some Readings in the Dead Sea Scrolls of Isaiah," 41–42, and W. Brownlee, "*Mshty* (Is 52:14 1QIs[a])," *BASOR* 132 (1953): 8–15. "Anointing" is possible (the Targum refers to this person as the anointed Messiah in 52:13), but the negative humiliation or the appalled response of the audience in the first phrase of 52:14 argues against the positive imagery of anointing. Also there seems to be no connection between anointing and good looks.

[334] Gentry, "The Atonement in Isaiah's Fourth Servant Song (Isaiah 52:13–53:12)," 20–47, accepts the translation "anoint" and compares this to the anointing of the high priest when he was installed into his office. He understands this anointed priestly person will sprinkle others for atonement and the forgiveness of sins, but this reads quite a bit into the simple statement of anointing. Baltzer, *Deutero-Isaiah*, 400, accepts "sprinkling" as the proper translation but rejects the view that this sprinkling is a "priestly purification." He understands this as a "gesture, similar to the greeting with rose water still encountered in the East today."

[335] The same syntactical construction appears in Josh 11:15 where both the first clause ("As the LORD commanded his servant Moses") and the second expanding clause ("so Moses commanded Joshua") are positive and not contrastive (cf. 55:10–11 for a similar clause). This would mean that the second clause would provide an explanation consistent with the first line, giving the translation "just as the many were appalled, so his disfigurement was from men." On the other hand some follow the syntactical pattern of Exod 1:12 where there is a similar construction ("just as . . . so . . . so"). Here one could have a negative idea in the first clause ("the more they were oppressed") and a contrasting positive clause in the second ("the more they multiplied"). This would give a contrastive comparison between "just as many were appalled at him" (a negative statement) "so his appearance was anointed" (a positive statement).

[336] This understanding of the "just as . . . so . . . so also" construction in vv. 14–15 results in the translation: "Just as there were many who were appalled at him, even so (a continuous comparison)

in 49:7 were rising and bowing before the servant, a sign of deep respect (cf. Job 29:9; 40:4). Their reaction to the exalted servant is consistent with the exaltation of the servant in 52:13.

This positive response at the end of 52:15b is complicated by a difficult verb that describes what the Servant will do to or for the many nations in 15a. The NIV, NASB, HCSB translations render this term "sprinkle," deriving the verb from *nāzâ*. This verb is frequently used in Leviticus of sprinkling blood on an altar (Lev 4:6; 5:9; 8:11,30; 13:7; 16:14,19).[337] E. J. Young interprets this as the Servant performing a purifying rite to cleanse the nations, suggesting that his disfigurement was not a punishment for his own sins as some thought (53:4), but instead his "sufferings are for the sake of an expiatory purification that produces a profound change in the attitude of those who behold him."[338] More recently J. Goldingay compares the Servant's sprinkling of many nations to the sprinkling of the Israelites in the Red Sea (Exod 15:14–16) and Moses' sprinkling of the people with blood when they were incorporated into the covenant (Exod 24:6–8).[339] Thus some of the people that earlier despised the suffering Servant were later brought into the covenant.

Some of these interpretations of sprinkling seem to read theological ideas into this text that are not explained in this context. At this point in the Servant poem it is quite unclear what this "sprinkling, splattering" is all about, but it is often thought that it introduces sacrificial or cleansing imagery. Since this verse does not explain what was sprinkled (blood or water), what this sprinkling did, or how it changed the perspective of the many nations, one must be careful not to overinterpret the imagery. There is a certain mystery to the work of the Servant that confused the people who observed the Servant's ministry. Many did not understand the mysterious work of the Servant until God revealed it to them (53:1); thus, what was happening spiritually needed divine interpretation.

This pivotal act of sprinkling appears to be one of the key factors that caused the kings and many nations to honor the Servant. This sprinkling is difficult to understand partly because no liquid is mentioned (as in Lev 4:17; 14:16) and

---

the disfigurement of his appearance was from man, but so also (a contrastive comparison) he will sprinkle many nations and kings will shut their mouths because of him."

[337] Root I of נָזָה is used 22 times in the Hebrew Scriptures and is normally associated with sprinkling blood, oil, or water. Usually when this verb is used the direct object of "sprinkle" is a liquid, which is not the case here, and usually the preposition "upon" (עַל) followed by the object comes immediately after the verb.

[338] Young, *Isaiah*, 3:338, views the servant fulfilling the priestly function with the work of the servant bringing purification to others. Muilenburg, "Isaiah 40–66," 5:618, follows Young and translates the verb "sprinkle" and connects it to the sacrificial ideas in 53:10. Ekblad, *Isaiah's Servant Poems According to the Septuagint: An Exegetical and Theological Study*, 187, suggests that the Old Greek translation "will be amazed" was based on their understanding of the root as חָזָה "seeing something amazing" or else they were just trying to match the next verb in the context.

[339] Goldingay, *Message of Isaiah 40–55*, 492–93, connects this Levitical imagery to similar imagery of the guilt offering in 53:10.

partly because the preposition ʿal "upon" does not follow the verb as it does in most Leviticus contexts. Consequently, some interpreters have looked for another possible meaning for this verb. They have proposed various emendations, though most follow root II of nāzâ, a root similar to the Arabic "to startle, cause to leap."[340] They then conclude that this startling effect coincides with the shutting of the mouths of kings, which is a sign of being astonished at what will happen to the Servant (cf. Job 21:5). The major problem with this alternative is that the Arabic root does not mean "to be startled" but "stand up, leap up."[341]

Thus it is best to conclude that the reason for the response of being horrified in 52:14 was the disfigurement of the servant by men, but the reason for the dramatic positive response of the kings in 15 appears to be this mysterious sprinkling of many nations (15a) which will result in a new understanding of the Servant (15b). When the Servant fulfills 53:1–12, the kings and nations will see, hear, and understand new things that they had never known before (49:7; Ps 72:11). J. Goldingay believes these kings will see the sovereign irruption of the reign of God among the nations described in 52:7–10,[342] but there is little in this paragraph that directly points to 52:7–10. J. Oswalt suggests that 52:14–15 contains a consistent theme by describing the humiliation of the Servant, an idea immediately picked up in the next verses of chap. 53, while C. Westermann believes that the startling thing these people will see and come to understand is the amazing unique exaltation and honoring of the Servant who was formerly disfigured, despised, and rejected.[343] If the report about the life of the Servant recorded in chap. 53 is what the nations will hear and will fully understand, it seems that these nations would hear about both the humiliation (in the first explaining "so" clause in 14b and 53:1–9) and the exaltation of the Servant (the contrasting second "so" clause in 15 and 53:10–12). They will hear the whole story from beginning to end, though there is inevitably more

---

[340] The Syriac has "purify," the Aramaic Targum "scatter," but the Old Greek has "cause to wonder." Westermann, *Isaiah 40–66*, 253, 259, suggests יִרְגְּזוּ "to leap, startle, agitate," but many follow root II of נזה that comes from the Arabic "startle, cause to leap." M. L. Barré, "Textual and Rhetorical-critical Observations on the Last Servant Song (Isaiah 52:13–53:12)," 10–11, proposes that this word comes from zhy "to shine, rejoice," which is used in post-biblical Hebrew, Aramaic, and Arabic.

[341] North, *Second Isaiah*, 228, recognizes that the translations startle "gives it an emotional content it never has in Arabic." Goldingay and Payne, *Isaiah 40–55*, 2:295 agree with North's assessment of this Arabic root and reject the meaning "startle" as a possible meaning for this Arabic word.

[342] Goldingay, *Message of Isaiah 40–55*, 494. In contrast Watts, *Isaiah 34–66*, 230, identifies what they were not told was the royal decree in Ezra 5:8–17, so these surrounding nations were surprised to see the temple go up. He places these events in the postexilic era, but this passage says nothing about the reconstruction of the temple in Jerusalem by Zerubbabel. Whybray, *Isaiah 40–66*, 170, who identifies the servant in 52:13–15 as the Israelites, believes the astonishing factor is the "sudden transformation of the status of the exiled Israelites."

[343] Westermann, *Isaiah 40–66*, 260; Oswalt, *Isaiah 40–66*, 380, admits that both interpretations are hypothetically possible but prefers the consistent emphasis on humiliation.

focus on the positive climax to the Servant's life. These people will be horrified and then humbled to hear of the suffering of an innocent Servant who will die in their place, but it will be even more astonishing to hear in the climax of the poem that God will raise this one to life, exalt him, and "give him a portion with the great/many" (52:12). In the end they will understand that the Servant will suffer for them, how his suffering will lead to his successful fulfillment of God's purposes, and why God will exalt him.

B. Childs follows W. A. M. Beuken's analysis of 52:15b that connects 52:15b to Israelites (not the kings or nations in 15a) who finally see and understand the life and purpose of the Servant. This association is based on the conviction that 53:1 is a report by believing Israelites who would naturally be the ones who would witness the life of the Servant, but J. L. Koole rightly rejects this approach because (a) there is no indication of a change of referent from the kings and many nations from 52:15a to Israelites in 15b, and (b) because the people in 52:15 have not heard or seen, but those in 53:1 have heard a message about the Servant that was revealed to them (42:1–13; 49:1–13; 50:4–11). Thus 52:15 describes the reaction of the nations while 53:1–10 is the report of what the believing Israelites saw when the arm of God was revealed to them.

REPORT OF THE SERVANT'S SUFFERING: 53:1–9

> [1]Who has believed our message
>   and to whom has the arm of the LORD been revealed?
> [2]He grew up before him like a tender shoot,
>   and like a root out of dry ground.
> He had no beauty or majesty to attract us to him,
>   nothing in his appearance that we should desire him.
> [3]He was despised and rejected by men,
>   a man of sorrows, and familiar with suffering.
> Like one from whom men hide their faces
>   he was despised, and we esteemed him not.
>
> [4]Surely he took up our infirmities
>   and carried our sorrows,
> yet we considered him stricken by God,
>   smitten by him, and afflicted.
> [5]But he was pierced for our transgressions,
>   he was crushed for our iniquities;
> the punishment that brought us peace was upon him,
>   and by his wounds we are healed.
> [6]We all, like sheep, have gone astray,
>   each of us has turned to his own way;
> and the LORD has laid on him
>   the iniquity of us all.

[7]He was oppressed and afflicted,
  yet he did not open his mouth;
 he was led like a lamb to the slaughter,
  and as a sheep before her shearers is silent,
  so he did not open his mouth.
[8]By oppression and judgment he was taken away.
  And who can speak of his descendants?
 For he was cut off from the land of the living;
  for the transgression of my people he was stricken.
[9]He was assigned a grave with the wicked,
  and with the rich in his death,
 though he had done no violence,
  nor was any deceit in his mouth.

These verses were spoken by an unidentified "we, us, our" group of people mentioned repeatedly in 53:1,4–6. Commentators have suggested three different groups may be speaking the "we" statements: (a) the nations mentioned in 52:14; (b) the prophet's disciples, or (c) the believing people of Israel. R. Melugin maintains that the "we" of this section refers to the nations who are confessing what they now understand (52:15) about the servant who suffered because of their sins.[344] This approach is partially necessitated by his identification of the servant as Israel, but there appears to be a contrast between a group that had not heard about the servant in 52:15 (the nations and kings) and another group who were told about him in 53:1. If on the other hand the servant is identified as the prophet as P. Wilcox and D. Paton-Williams suggest, the "we" who were writing about the prophetic servant would naturally be his disciples.[345] This proposal would seem to limit the work of the servant to the forgiveness of the sins of only a few righteous people and would suggest that the suffering of a sinful prophet might bring forgiveness of sins. Thus the "we" statements seem to best fit with the believing people of Israel. They are the ones who observed what God revealed to them. F. Delitzsch also notes that the "we" speeches in 16:6; 24:16a; 42:24; 64:5–6 all refer to Israelites.[346]

The structure of this paragraph is divided into three equal parts, centered around the vicarious suffering of the Servant for the sins of the world.

The surprising, despised servant	53:1–3
Questions about the report	1
His origin and appearance	2

---

[344] Melugin, *Formation of Isaiah 40–55*, 167, states that "the confession of the nations (53:1ff.) reveals their new understanding of the significance of the servant's suffering." Blenkinsopp, *Isaiah 40–55*, 351, rejects the view that the speaker is the nations because "the eulogist is an individual, almost certainly a disciple."

[345] Wilcox and Paton-Williams, "The Servant Songs in Deutero-Isaiah," 98. Whybray, *Isaiah 40–66*, 171, also identifies the servant as the prophet, but in his opinion the "we" refers to fellow exiles.

[346] Delitzsch, "Prophecies of Isaiah," 310, believes Israel is speaking in 53:1.

He was despised, not esteemed	3
Vicarious suffering for our sins	53:4–6
Misunderstandings of his affliction	4
He suffered; we benefited	5
We sinned, he bore our sins	6
Innocent Servant willingly dies for others	53:7–9
He submitted to death	7
He died for the sins of others	8
The innocent one was buried	9

Third-person singular verbs and pronouns ("he . . . him") dominate 53:1–3, third person singular and first-person plural verbs and first-person plural pronouns ("he/we" . . . "our/us") are concentrated in the second section in 53:4–6, then 53:7–9 returns to third-person singular verbs with third person pronouns ("he . . . him") like the first few verses. There is a natural flow in the account of the Servant's life from suffering, to death, to burial. These verses identify who he was, how he was treated, and why he suffered. Later, 53:10 refers to the Lord's purposes and promises about the Servant, so 53:10–12 is not part of the report by Israel. B. Childs and others make the literary unit 53:1–11a because the first-person divine reporting is not found in these verses (it is in 53:11b–12), but God's point of view pervades 53:10–12 even when he is not speaking in first person.[347]

53:1   This verse begins with two questions asked by a believing group of Israelites who have understood and accepted what the Lord revealed to them about the Servant. In earlier chapters Isaiah pointed out that many Israelites were deaf, blind, and failed to believe what God said (6:9–10; 7:9; 29:9–10; 42:18–19; 43:8; 48:4–8; 56:10), but the Lord promised that in the future he would remove their blindness and they would trust in him (also discussed in 29:18; 32:3–4; 35:5; 42:7,16). This is a report by those who now understand what God is doing. The first rhetorical questions are marked by the interrogative "who" (*mî*), but they also function somewhat like an astonished exclamation. If the verb is used modally,[348] then the first question is asking: "Who

---

[347] Childs, *Isaiah*, 411–13, depends too tightly on grammatical forms (first person) and ignores the fact that the human report ends in v. 9. Goldingay and Payne, *Isaiah 40–55*, 2:277, find a chiastic structure.

A–52:13–15 My servant will triumph despite his suffering.
  B–53:1 Who could have recognized YHWH's arm
    C–53:2–3 He was treated with contempt
      D–53:4–6 The reason was his suffering for us
    C'–53:7–9 He did not deserve his treatment
  B'–53:10–11aα By his hand YHWH's purpose will succeed
A'–53:11aβ-12 My servant will triumph because of his suffering"

[348] The verb should be translated as a subjunctive with "might, could, should, would" when it

would believe our report?" The question is not primarily asking how many people have believed what "we" have reported about the Servant; rather, it is communicating the fact that their report contains some astonishing factors that would be hard for anyone to believe. Belief and trust are always at the heart of every person's relationship to God, but sometimes God reveals things that are hard for people to accept.

The second question inquires about what group of people received God's revelation about the arm of the Lord. This question probably implies that most people have not heard about God's revelation and that some who have heard about the Servant have not understood the meaning of God's message. God revealed the "arm of the Lord,"[349] his miraculous saving power, to the "us" (the Israelites) who have believed what God has said. These are the ones who are now giving the report in 53:2–12. They are sharing what they understand in order to convince more people to believe what God has revealed to them about the Servant.

In earlier oracles the outstretched "arm of the Lord" brought deliverance to the Israelites at the time of the exodus from Egypt; it divided and overpowered the sea (51:9; Exod 6:6; 15:16). That same arm of divine power can act destructively to defeat the mighty nation of Babylon (48:14). In 40:10–11 and 52:7–10 God's powerful arm functions positively to rule the earth when he comes to reign. It will bring forth God's salvation to his people and to those living at the ends of the earth. J. Motyer suggests that the revelation of God's arm in 53:1 picks up the theme of the arm producing salvation in 52:10, indicating that the "arm of the Lord" is the Servant,[350] but most do not make this identification.

53:2 Now the report about the Servant begins by referring to his origins (2a) and his appearance (2b). He is compared to a young "shoot" (yônēq) and a "root" (šōreš) coming out of the ground, a metaphor that stands in sharp contrast to other metaphors that could be used (a stately grand oak). The use of this term suggests that the author may be attempting to interlink this servant with the messianic king in 11:1. There he is called a "shoot" (ḥōṭer)[351] from the stump of Jesse, and in 11:10 he is the "root" (šōreš) of Jesse, a kingly Da-

---

is "in a question indicating astonishment" (GKC §106p). Blenkinsopp, *Isaiah 40–55*, 345, accepts this modal interpretation while Childs, *Isaiah*, 413, rejects this approach.

[349] The arm of the Lord usually refers to the powerful providential work of God that accomplishes his will, as in 14:26–27; 30:30; 40:10; 51:9; 52:10; 63:12.

[350] Motyer, *Isaiah*, 427. This perspective is accepted by Oswalt, *Isaiah 40–66*, 375, and Williamson, *Variations on a Theme*, 164. Goldingay and Payne, *Isaiah 40–55*, 2:298, state that "Yhwh's arm is here virtually hypostatized . . . it is a revelation of a part of Yhwh in some sense representing Yhwh and distinguishable from Yhwh."

[351] Ekblad, *Isaiah's Servant Poems According to the Septuagint: An Exegetical and Theological Study*, 201–202, notes that the Old Greek has "as a little child/servant" and suggests that this was purposely done to create a link with the child in 9:6. Gentry, "The Atonement in Isaiah's Fourth Servant Song (Isaiah 52:13–53:12)," 32, also makes this identification.

vidic figure (cf. 4:2; Jer 23:5; Zech 3:8; 6:12).[352] This kind of plant imagery is also used of kings[353] in Ezek 17:31, Daniel 4, and in nonbiblical texts,[354] but this special shoot paradoxically came up from dry ground.[355] It is dangerous to read too much into each aspect of the symbolism, but certainly dry soil is not fertile ground and a person usually does not find lush plants growing in places where there is no water (contrast Ps 1:3). Such imagery might refer to the lowly background of his parents or the lowly state of the nation when he was born. At minimum, this kind of symbolism suggests that this person was not born in a palace of a world empire with all the luxuries that are usually afforded to persons of royalty. In spite of these lowly images, the Servant grew up "before him" (before God, referring back to 53:1),[356] which suggests a close relationship to God or at least God's careful attention to what was happening in his life.

In addition, three statements are made about his appearance, emphasizing three times that he did "not" (*lōʾ*) look like royalty. This person had no

[352] Consult the discussion of these two verses in Smith, *Isaiah 1–39*, 271 and 275. A. Millard, "Isaiah 53:2," *TynBul* 20 (1969): 491–92, suggests the translation "stock, stem" instead of "root" to give a better parallel to "shoot." J. Stromberg, "The 'Root of Jesse' in Isaiah 11:10: Postexilic Judah or Postexilic Davidic King?" *JBL* 127 (2008): 655–69, reviews the literature and rejects the idea that "root" refers to Jesse's ancestors based on biblical and nonbiblical texts that use "root, shoot" to refer to descendents. He also rejects the idea that the "root" refers to the community because the Davidic covenant concept underwent democratization in the exilic period. This democratizations concept was based on the statement in 55:3 that God will make "with you" לָכֶם an everlasting covenant. For this interpretation read O. Eissfeldt, "The Promises of Grace to David in Isaiah 55:1–5," in *Israel's Prophetic Heritage: Essays in Honor of J. Muilenburg*, ed. B. W. Anderson and W. Harrelson (New York: Harper and Brothers, 1962), 196–207, or M. Sweeney, "The Reconceptualization of the Davidic Covenant in Isaiah," in *Studies in the Book of Isaiah: Festschrift W. A. M. Beuken*, ed. J. van Ruiten and M. Vervenne (Leuven: Peeters, 1997), 41–61.

[353] About 70 years later Esarhaddon, the king of Assyria, was called "a precious branch of Baltil, and enduring shoot."

[354] In a Phoenician text, *Karatepe*, A. i, line 9–10, it says, "I kindly acted towards the root (*šrš*) of my lord and I set him on his father's throne." In Aramaic, *Sefire*, i. C, lines 24–25 in the curse "may his root (*šršh*) have no name," so both documents use the term "root" to refer to a descendent. The Old Greek understood "root" to refer to descendents in Isa 14:29,30; the Targum in Mal 4:1 [Heb 3:19] does the same thing; and Ben Sira 47:22 has a similar understanding. The Ugaritic "Tale of Aqhat," used *šrš* four times to mean "son, descendent," in lines 20–27, 41–43 "no son . . . nor scion (*šrš*) for him." See *The Ancient Near East: An Anthology of Texts and Pictures*, ed. J. B. Pritchard (Princeton: Princeton Univ. Press, 1958), 119.

[355] Whybray, *Isaiah 40–66*, 173, rightly rejects any connection between this phrase and the pagan fertility religion associated with the king-Tammuz cult, as suggested by I. Engnell, "The 'Ebed-Yahweh Songs' and the Suffering Servant," *BJRL* 31 (1948): 54–93.

[356] Many emend the pronoun to לְפָנֵינוּ "before us," meaning before the Israelites that are giving this report, but the unanimous textual evidence is for the harder reading "before him." Although one could hypothetically translate this reflexively "by itself," the preposition לְפָנָיו is not the usually way to express this. Taking another approach R. P. Gordon, "Isaiah LIII 2," *VT* 20 (1970): 491–92, suggests that this Hebrew clause "he will go up . . . before him" is an idiomatic equivalent to "he will go straight forward, straight up." L. C. Allen, "Isaiah LIII 2 Again," *VT* 21 (1971): 490, agrees and thinks this word in its "idiomatic sense fittingly serves to emphasize the limited, unfulfilled nature of his development."

impressive "form" (*tōʾar*, also used in 52:14); in fact, 52:14 indicates his form was disfigured in some way. He had no "majesty" (*hādār*), the glorious looks of earthly kings (Ps 21:5; 45:4) or the royal look that characterized the splendor of God himself (cf. 2:10,19,21). He also had no "appearance, look" (*mārʾeh*, also in 52:14) that would make him desirable to "us" (the Israelites). Earlier, King Saul's physical stature attracted people to him and caused them to want him to be their king (1 Sam 9:20). David was "ruddy, with a fine appearance and handsome features" (1 Sam 16:12), but these attractive external signs of a king were not something people could identify in this Servant. These physical features refer to the outward appearance which was not very impressive. In light of modern models of leadership and "Christian stardom" of some pastors and Christian television personalities one wonders if this Servant would have appeared as someone desirable according to modern leadership criteria. Would people recognize him for who he really was or would they ignore him or reject him? J. Oswalt suggests that "Deliverers are dominating, forceful, attractive people, who by their personal magnetism draw people to themselves. . . . People who refuse to follow that leadership frequently find themselves crushed and tossed away. This man does not fit that picture."[357]

53:3 Now this story about the life of the Servant tells how people treated him as a despicable person. Earlier in 49:4 it was mentioned that the ministry of the Servant did not go well; in fact, 49:7 indicates that he was despised by the nations. 50:6–8 refers to his mistreatment and suffering, but the present Servant poem goes far beyond both these earlier accounts. The initial participle probably should be translated adjectivally or verbally to agree with what follows.[358] Thus "despised" describes how contemptible, despicable, and revolting he was considered by some. The parallel NIV "rejected by men"[359] is an odd expression that literally means "ceased, stopped"[360] by men. Possibly it means that he "ceased to be among men" or was "shunned by men";[361] thus, in some way, the Servant was isolated from the community around him by his own people. No reason is given for this rejection and shunning, but such extreme measures suggest a major difference in their theological perspectives, not a minor difference of opinion.

---

[357] Oswalt, *Isaiah 40–66*, 382.

[358] The *niphal* participle often functions (*IBHS*, 385, 619) like an adjective or a stative verb ("despised"), rather than verbally ("he was despised").

[359] The word "men" אִישִׁים is an unusual form in place of the usual אֲנָשִׁים, but the significance of this unusual spelling is somewhat of a mystery. This form is also found in Ps 141:4 and Prov 8:4.

[360] The root חָדֵל means "cease, forbear, stop, desist." BDB, 293, provides some examples where the verb means "cease to be, come to an end" (Deut 15:11; Judg 5:6,7) or "be lacking, frail" (Job 19:14; Prov 10:19). Goldingay and Payne, *Isaiah 40–55*, 2:301–302, prefers "frail," meaning that his life is transient and frail, based on Ps 39:5. Clines, *I, He, We, and They—A Literary Approach to Isaiah 53*, 16, claims that the servant withdrew from society because he knew ugliness, but this text is talking about how other people responded to the servant, not what the servant did.

[361] Westermann, *Isaiah 40–66*, 262.

This Servant was also a man of "pains" and "suffering," expressions that suggest that he was mistreated physically or mentally (cf. 52:14). The author chose to use a passive participle[362] to communicate that the Servant "was known" (*yedûaʿ*) for his painful experiences. Although it may be easier to express this as an active idea ("he knew suffering"), the passive participle suggests that others connected his life and reputation to a time of great suffering. Suffering was not something that he was just peripherally acquainted with on the rare occasion; it was a pivotal factor in his life. When people mentioned this Servant, people would automatically connect him to this time of suffering.

In the last part of v. 3 someone is hiding his face. Is it the Servant, the Lord, the people, or someone else? The Aramaic Targum indicates that God has withdrawn his face and rejected him, but this interpretation contradicts the confident assurances of the Servant that God would vindicate him in 49:4,8; 50:7–9. There is also no indication that the Servant hid from the public or became a recluse,[363] so this phrase must be a comparative illustration ("as when people") depicting a scene in which people hide their faces from the Servant whom they reject or abhor because they do not want to see him or be reminded of this person. The last phrase in the verse returns to the initial observation that he was treated as a "despicable, despised" person, but now the text adds another factor that further explains how people treated him. The Israelite speakers giving this report (the "we") admit that we did not "think of him, esteem him" as one who should be highly valued or treated as important. The following verses will explain why he suffered and why people did not respect him.

53:4–6 The next section of the poem focuses on the servant's vicarious suffering for the sins of others, and it is set apart from what precedes by its "we" confessions. R. N. Whybray and H. M. Orlinsky find the servant "identifying" with those suffering but vigorously deny the idea that he suffered in the place of others. They claim that, "there is not found either here or elsewhere in the Bible any justification for the concept of vicarious suffering and atonement."[364] Although such a claim may depend on the definition given to

---

[362] 1QIsᵃ has the active participle יוֹדֵעַ "knowing" and the verb in Old Greek is also active, but these are easier readings of a difficult form. G. R. Driver, "Isaiah 52:13–53:12: The Servant of the Lord," in *In Memoriam Paul Kahle*, ed. M. Black and G. Fohrer, BZAW 103 (Berlin, de Gruyter, 1967), 90–10, and D. W. Thomas, "A Consideration of Isaiah LIII in the Light of Recent Textual and Philological Study, *ETL* 44 (1968): 79–86, suggested this is root II of יָדַע meaning "humble," thus "he was humbled with grief," but A. Gelston, "Knowledge, Humiliation or Suffering: A Lexical, Textual, and Exegetical Problem in Isaiah 53," in *Of Prophets' Visions and the Wisdom of Sages: Essays in Honor of R. N. Whybray on his Seventieth Birthday*, ed. H. A. McKay and D. J. A. Clines (Sheffield: JSOT, 1993), 126–41, properly rejects this approach.

[363] The Old Greek has "his face is turned away," but 50:5 indicates "I have not drawn back" and 50:6 "I did not hide my face from mocking and spiting." Lepers did cover their faces (Lev 13:45) but there is no indication this person was a leper.

[364] Orlinsky, "The So-Called 'Suffering Servant' in Isaiah 53," in *Interpreting the Prophetic Tradition*, 246. Whybray, *Isaiah 40–66*, 169, 175, has a similar interpretation and limits the servant's role to "identification with them in their suffering."

vicarious suffering, J. Scharbert's[365] study of the Mesopotamian substitute king ritual suggests that the idea of one person taking the place of another was not a foreign idea in the ancient Near Eastern world. A common person could take the place of the king and suffer the negative effects that would otherwise fall on the king. At the end of this ritual period of danger the substitute king would be killed. J. Walton finds interesting parallels between Isaiah 53 and the substitute king[366] but limits them to the conceptual level of substitution (denied by Orlinsky and Whybray) and sees no literary or religious connection between this pagan ritual and Isaiah 53. Biblical examples of substitution are illustrated in Moses' willingness to have his name struck from the book of life; that is, he would take someone else's punishment upon himself if God would not destroy Israel (Exod 32:32). Another early example would be the substitution of the blood of the dead lamb on the doorposts of the house so that the angel of God would pass over that Israelite house and not take the lives of the first-born child within (Exod 12:13;21–23).

One can find background for the substitutionary ideas in the sacrificial literature where: (a) the terminology of "bearing the sins" of another is used (53:4,6,12; Lev 10:17; 16:22) and (b) where the "guilt offering" is mentioned (53:10; Lev 5:14–6:7).[367] I. Kant rejected the whole concept of transferring guilt, concluding that guilt is "not a transmissible liability which can be made over to someone else, in the manner of a fiscal debt."[368] Yet the text of Isaiah repeatedly indicates that the Servant bore the sins of others. Leviticus 16:7–10, 20–22 describes the scapegoat bearing the sins of the people into the wilderness, which is a substitutionary bearing of sin (as in 53:4–6). Since this goat does not die and is not called a "guilt offering" (53:10), it is not a primary symbol used to construct the suffering servant imagery. The NIV translation of "guilt offering" (ʾāšām) connects the imagery of the servant in 53:10 to Lev 5:14–6:7, for in both the wiping out of guilt or the responsibility for the iniquity (Lev 5:1,17) is given to another to bear. Yet little of the rest of the sacrificial imagery of the "guilt offering" is explicitly employed in chap. 53. Thus one must carefully identify only the comparative links that the text points to, for there is a real danger of reading in much more of the sacrificial ideology from Leviticus than Isaiah 53 itself identifies. The ʾāšām is "the obligation to

---

[365] J. Scharbert, "Stellvertretendes Sühneleiden in den Ebed-Jahwe-Liedern und in altorientalischen Ritualtexten," *BZ* 2 (11958): 190–213, found similarities but did not believe this was the basis of Isaiah's idea because there was no atonement of guilt in this ritual.

[366] J. Walton, "The Imagery of the Substitute King Ritual in Isaiah's Fourth Servant Song," *JBL* 122 (2003): 734–43.

[367] W. Zimmerli, "Zur Vorgeschichte von Jes lxiii, *Congress Volume: Rome 1968*, VTSup 17 (1969): 236–44, searches for the prehistory of the language of "bearing iniquity" and found the bearing of the guilt of many the unique idea associated with the servant in Isaiah 53.

[368] I. Kant, "Religion within the Boundaries of Mere Reason," in *Religion and Rational Theology*, ed. A. W. Wood and G. Di Giovanni (Cambridge: Cambridge University Press, 1996), 113.

discharge guilt that arises for a situation of guilt"[369] and is a compensatory payment (Lev 5:16) because of guilt. It functions both in the context of legal and Levitical concepts because the two are essentially one integrated sphere of reality in ancient Israel. Thus chap. 53 does illustrate substitutionary action drawn from sacrificial concepts.[370]

53:4 The beginning of this short paragraph is marked with the particle *'āken* that can be translated adversatively "but" or emphatically "surely" to introduce a new thought. This verse continues the discussion of issues brought up in v. 3 ("sorrow, suffering, esteem"), but now the Servant's sorrows are related to "our sorrows." Three central statements are made. The first two in 53:4a represent the speakers' present understanding of the Servant while the third factor in 53:4b explains a former misunderstanding of the Servant's afflictions. First the speakers (the Israelites who are reporting about his life) admit that they had pain, sorrows, and suffering. There is no explanation of the source of these difficulties, though one would assume from other earlier stories in the Bible that either they suffered some punishment because of their own sins or they were innocent sufferers like Job. Second, the source of the Servant's suffering is connected to "our" suffering by claiming that he suffered because "he himself"[371] was the one who "carried, bore"[372] the consequences that belonged to "us." The act of "carrying, bearing" could suggest either participation with others by helping them carry their load (46:7; Exod 18:22; Num 11:17), or the verb could communicate the idea of "carrying" something for someone else by taking away the load that others were bearing (40:24; 41:16). The next two verses and 53:11–12 will make it clear that the Servant will take away the suffering that others were supposed to bear.

The third statement is actually a confession of the people's misunderstanding of the Servant's suffering. Picking up the negative evaluation of the Servant from 53:3b, the people admit in 53:4b why they did not esteem this person highly. Their confession is that "we ourselves" (*'ănāḥnû*) thought that the Servant "was being stricken" (passive participle), "was being smitten, beaten"

---

[369] R. Knierim, "אָשָׁם *'āšām* guilt," *TLOT*, 1:191–95.

[370] B. Janowski, "He Bore Our Sins: Isaiah 53 and the Drama of Taking Another's Place," in *The Suffering Servant: Isaiah 53 in Jewish and Christian Sources*, 48–74, accepts the influence of sacrificial terminology while H. Spieckermann, "The Conception and Prehistory of the Idea of Vicarious Suffering in the Old Testament" in *The Suffering Servant: Isaiah 53 in Jewish and Christian Sources*, 1–15, rejects a Levitical influence and points to prophetic influences where they suffered, bore the guilt, and intercede for Israel.

[371] The verb נָשָׂא "he carried" has within it the third-person pronoun "he," but to emphasize this amazing contrast between what he did and what we did, the text explicitly adds the pronoun הוּא "he" to the servant and "we" אֲנַחְנוּ in the next clause.

[372] The verbs נָשָׂא "to bear, carry" and סָבַל "to carry, shoulder" are synonyms that communicate the idea that "he carried" something that belonged to someone else. If he carried someone else's responsibility, one assumes based on the meaning of the word that he was successful in standing up under this additional burden (otherwise he would not have "carried" it).

(passive participle), and "was being afflicted"[373] (passive participle) by God himself. It is impossible from this verse alone to tie these verbs down to any specific consequences experienced by the Servant.[374] The speakers wrongly concluded that he was suffering afflictions that were justly sent by God for the sins he had committed. Their perspective was partially right and partially wrong, for God did smite him (cf. 53:10), but their understanding of why he was smitten was wrong (he was not being punished for his own sins).

53:5   This verse supplies specific answers to several questions and corrects some misunderstandings in 4b by clarifying the reason for the Servant's suffering. Four words (two passive verbs and two nouns) describe the specific kind of suffering endured by the Servant. The verb "he was pierced, slain"[375] is a verb that is used in the context of someone dying, often at the end of a sword (51:9; Job 26:13; Jer 14:18; Lam 4:9; Ezek 28:9). The second verb "was crushed" can refer either to general oppression (3:15) or to a fatal crushing that kills (Job 6:9). The noun "punishment" (*mûsār*) is a general term that refers to the "disciplining" of people (Prov 22:15; 23:13), but it can also refer to the punishment used to correct someone (Deut 11:2). "Wounds" sometimes refers to open bruises related to injuries during a battle (1:6; Gen 4:23). These terms graphically portray the depth of the suffering of the Servant, the seriousness of his pain, and the extent of God's smiting. These terms imply that the Servant was killed, a fact that later verses will clarify (53:8–9). The Aramaic Targum takes all of these verbs and applies them to God's destruction of the temple because of the sins of the nation and then it predicts its restoration, but this metaphorical interpretation of the Servant's suffering hardly fits the description of the Servant in this and the preceding Servant poems.

The first half of the verse indicates that the reason for this suffering was "because of our rebellion"[376] and "because of our iniquities." This forthright

---

[373] The *pual* participle מְעֻנֶּה comes from root II of עָנָה meaning "he humbled, afflicted, oppressed" and often refers to God's affliction of people for their sins. Koole, *Isaiah III, Volume 2: Isaiah 49–55*, 292, concludes that God is connected to the act of smiting, but the affliction is not directly connected to an act of God because human instruments usually are the ones who do the afflicting. This may overanalyze the language and attempt to derive too much from these statements. Motyer, *Isaiah*, 430, suggests that "smitten" and "afflicted" express the objective and subjective sides of his suffering.

[374] It is inappropriate to connect the passive participle נָגוּעַ "stricken" to refer to the idea that God struck this servant with leprosy just because this term is used repeatedly in Lev 13–14 to describe those who are struck with leprosy. This verb can be used in other contexts, and there is nothing specific in this context that points directly toward leprosy. Whybray, *Isaiah 40–66*, 175, believes the servant is the prophet Deutero-Isaiah and suggests that the people thought the prophet was suffering because he was a false prophet.

[375] Root II of הלל indicates that the dragon in 51:9 was killed, while in Ezek 28:9 this verb is parallel to the verb for "kill," and in Jer 14:18 and Lam 4:9 it describes what the sword does that results in death. Goldingay, *Message of Isaiah 40–55*, 502, translates this term "hurt," which is a very weak representation of its meaning.

[376] The word פֶּשַׁע refers to rebellious acts against the authority of God, not simply transgres-

confession of guilt plainly states that the Servant suffered the consequences for "our" (the Israelite speakers) sinful acts. This act was penal, for it involved a just punishment for rebellious acts. It was also substitutionary because the punishment that should have fallen on the Israelites who sinned were transferred instead to the Servant.

The second half of the verse addresses the consequent benefits that this transfer of punishment brought to "us." This punishment is specifically described in the last line as "his welts, wounds," possibly the consequence of being beaten (53:4). The phrase, "the punishment that brought our peace" (NIV), is an appropriate paraphrase of a construct relationship (lit "the punishment of our peace") that expresses a genitive of purpose.[377] This punishment was designed for the purpose of securing our peace, implying that peace was achieved with God because the just punishment he required was suffered by the Servant. The second benefit that accrued to the Israelite speakers was healing ($r\bar{a}p\bar{a}^{\circ}$) "on account of, by means of"[378] the Servant's suffering. The term "healing" is used in 19:22 to describe both the physical (from a plague) and spiritual restoration (they will turn to the Lord and he will respond) of a nation. Since the problems in 53:5 are rebellious acts and iniquities, it appears that the healing relates primarily to the healing of the people's spiritual relationship to God, though a more holistic eschatological interpretation would include both spiritual and physical healing.[379]

53:6 Instead of emphasizing or expanding on all the positive benefits of peace or healing from v. 5, the text reemphasizes the guilt of the speakers and

---

sions of God's laws. The preposition מִן "from" means that the consequence (suffering) "arose from, was derived from, was because of" our rebellion.

[377] GKC §128q refers to the wider use of the genitive to "include statements of the purpose for which something is intended." Thus the "cup of staggering" in 51:17 is a cup designed for the purpose of causing people who drink it to stagger.

[378] The preposition בְּ expresses the means by which something was accomplished (GKC §119o). North, *Second Isaiah*, 240, suggests this is a בְּ *preti* (of price) placed before the noun to express the price one pays to purchase something. Thus "at the cost of, in exchange for" would be the translation (GKC §119p).

[379] Numerous people have taken this verse to refer specifically to physical healing. Although this verse is dealing with spiritual problems, the Hebrews tended to think holistically, not creating a strong division between spiritual and physical healing because they were tied together. The clearest connection between these two types of healings is in eschatological texts that interrelate God's final salvation with both aspects of healing. Thus atonement through the forgiveness of sins will result in the eschatological healing of heart and body (25:7–8; 26:19; 30:17; 35:10; 51:11; 65:19). These two approaches to interpreting this theme can be found numerous resources. (a) In favor of including physical healing see J. Wilkerson, "Physical Healing and the Atonement," *EvQ* 63 (1991): 149–55, F. C. Darling, *Biblical Healing* (Boulder: Vista, 1989), D. E. Harrell, *All Things Are Possible: The Healing and Charismatic Revival in America* (Bloomington: Indiana, 1975), or M. G. Moriarty, *The New Charismatics* (Grand Rapids: Zondervan, 1992). Questioning these conclusions are R. L. Mayhue, "For What Did Christ Atone in Isa 53:4–5," *TMSJ* 6 (1995): 121–41, or W. K. Bokovay, "The Relationship of Physical Healing to the Atonement," *Didaskalia* 3 (1991): 26–35.

how the Servant took the condemnation for these sins on himself. The focus on his victory will come later (53:10–12). Right now it is time for the speakers to humble themselves and confess that "they went astray"[380] like wandering sheep that follow their own path. They deliberately "turned aside" (not accidentally) from the path that God their Shepherd provided for them. This admission of guilt is made by "all of us" (at the beginning and at the end of the verse), not some other group of people or a small portion of the people.

The second half of v. 6 introduces further understanding of God's involvement in the substitutionary transfer of punishment from the many Israelites ("we/us") to the singular ("he") Servant. Yahweh himself, the covenant God of Israel, "laid" (NIV) on him our iniquity. The verb (*pāgaʿ*) commonly means "to touch, meet, fall on, strike, encounter" and can be used in a peaceful setting or in a hostile context.[381] In 53:6 the iniquity of others "meet, struck, fell on" the servant, thus explaining the load he had to bear in 53:4. This imagery also supports a penal substitutionary role for the Servant.

53:7–9   The third section of the poem considers the consequence of having the punishment for the sins of "all of us" fall on the Servant. He did not just endure some mild affliction and minor suffering; he was killed even though he himself was innocent. These verses emphasize three points: (a) like a lamb the Servant was submissive to death without complaint; (b) the Servant was unjustly cut off because of other people's sins; and (c) the Servant died and was buried even though he was innocent.[382]

53:7   Initially, this verse affirms the Servant's humble submission to oppressive acts against him (in 7a), then the second half of the verse explains these factors by comparing the behavior of the Servant to a humble and helpless sheep (in 7b). This creates a vivid contrast between the many sinful sheep that were wandering astray in 53:6 and the single submissive sheep (the Servant) who was mistreated and killed.

The news about people despising and oppressing the Servant was announced in 49:7; 50:6–7; 52:14; and 53:3–5, so this information is not totally new. Isaiah 50:6–7 also indicates that the Servant did not fight his opponents to defend

---

[380] The verb תָּעָה "lead stray" is employed to describe how leaders "confuse, lead astray" people from the path of God (3:12; 9:15), how wise men "delude, lead astray" the leaders of Egypt (19:12–13). The use of sheep imagery and shepherding is common to the biblical way of life (2 Sam 5:2; Ps 78:70–72; Ezek 34:1–24). From early times God was viewed as their Shepherd (Gen 48:15; 49:24; Ps 23:1; 28:9 ; Isa 40:11; Jer 23:1; Ezek 34:11–16).

[381] In a traveling context this verb means "to arrive" at a certain place (Josh 16:7; 19:22), but in a military context it refers to "falling on, attacking" or killing an enemy (Judg 8:21; 15:12; 18:25), in legal context is, means "to execute, fall on, kill" a guilty party (1 Sam 22:18; 2 Sam 1:18; 1 Kgs 2:29), and in seven examples (including 53:12) it means "meet, entreat, intercede" (many of these are in the *hiphil*). The Targum understood both 53:6 and 12 in the sense of interceding but in v. 6 it makes no sense to say that Yahweh interceded. R. L. Hubbard, "The Root *PGʿ* as a Legal Term," *JETS* 27 (1984): 129–34, focuses on the meaning in legal cases.

[382] Motyer, *Isaiah*, 432, finds in v. 7 the procession where the servant is led out to die, v. 8a the execution, and v. 8b the burial.

himself; instead, he willingly "humbled himself"[383] by submitting to cruel acts against him. Although the text does not explain why he was willing to submit to such injustice and cruelty, the reader stands amazed at the willing sacrifice of the Servant. Up to this point the only motivation given was the Servant's confidence in God's vindication (50:8–9) and his determination (50:7) to accomplish the work God gave to him. The Servant accepted his role and did not even raise up his voice in protest. The imagery of the sheep led to the slaughter and the sheep brought before its shearer should be left to function merely as illustrations. The point the illustration makes is that the Servant was quiet just like a frightened sheep (cf. 42:2). One should not allegorically import the idea that the servant was scared like a sheep, was shaved of his hair like a sheep, or was slaughtered in the manner sheep are killed. At this point the sheep imagery is an appropriate illustration that fits in with the reality that v. 8 will announce. Since shearing and slaughter are not interpreted, one probably should not import into this verse sacrificial imagery of a lamb being sacrificed.[384]

53:8 The first half of this verse is somewhat ambiguous because one can legitimately attribute to the prepositions, nouns, and verbs several different meanings. The noun translated "oppression" in NIV could be more accurately translated as "restrained" (*'ōṣer*),[385] suggesting that he was arrested and imprisoned. The term "judgment" (*mišpāṭ*) could refer to: (a) the court, a place of judgment; (b) a sentence of judgment against a criminal; or (c) justice. The syntactical use of the preposition *min* is probably not partitive or comparative; instead, it has a separating or causal use ("from; because of") or a negative function "without."[386] R. N. Whybray suggests a temporal translation for the preposition: "after arrest and trial he was taken away."[387] It seems more reasonable to follow either J. Oswalt, who prefers the causal usage "because of the restraint of justice," or J. Muilenburg, who translates the clause "from imprisonment and from sentence [or judgment]."[388] One option implies that he was

---

[383] The *niphal* verb נַעֲנֶה probably is a reflexive "he humbled himself," though the *pu'al* participle of this same root was translated "oppressed" back in 53:4b. Oswalt, *Isaiah 40–66*, 391, translates this verb with a reflexive meaning.

[384] In Jer 11:19 the prophet pictures himself as a lamb led to the slaughter, but he is not suggesting that he is the fulfillment of Isa 53.

[385] The verb form of this root is used in 2 Kgs 17:4 referring to Shalmaneser "restraining, shutting up" וַיַּעַצְרֵהוּ Hoshea, which is parallel to his "imprisoning" him. In Jer 33:1 this verb refers to Jeremiah "being restrained, confined" עָצוּר (*qal* passive participle) in the courtyard of the guard (Jer 39:15; Judg 13:16).

[386] GKC §119w; 133a-c explains the partitive and comparative uses of מִן while GKC §119v-y discusses the causal usage.

[387] Whybray, *Isaiah 40–55*, 177, gives the preposition a temporal significance, but this is not the usual meaning of the preposition מִן.

[388] Oswalt, *Isaiah 40–66*, 393–94, focuses on the injustice of the trial proceeding (treating the two nouns as a hendiadys), while Muilenburg, "Isaiah 40–66," 5:626, tends to emphasize the verb; that is, from prison he was taken away to die.

taken from imprisonment and sentenced to death, while the other focuses on the lack of justice in the judicial process, which seems preferable.

The second clause asks a question about how the people who lived at that time (dôrô "his generation")[389] responded to his treatment. The verb (yĕśôḥ ēaḥ) questions if anyone "would pay attention"[390] to what was happening to the Servant or if anyone would think about what was going on long enough to comprehend its significance. J. Motyer prefers to translate the verb "pondered" because it "fits in better with Isaiah's insistence that throughout the Servant went unrecognized and his suffering aroused only misunderstanding."[391] C. Seitz concludes that the "important point is that the death of the servant required illumination from God"[392] if people were going to truly understand what it was all about. Although it appears that those who opposed and imprisoned the Servant had thought through their actions and knew exactly what they wanted to do to the Servant, the other people who observed these happenings did not seem to fathom the substitutionary role the Servant fulfilled by taking on himself the sins of many.

The second half of 53:8 indicates that the Servant died. R. N. Whybray admits that a literal interpretation of "he was cut off from the land of the living" would mean that the Servant died, but he rejects the literal meaning of these words and suggests that this passage should be interpreted like many Psalms which emphasize that the lamenter is near to death or as good as dead.[393] This interpretation is very hard to substantiate in light of the "piercing" in 53:5, being "cut off" in 53:8, and references to the "grave" and "death" in 53:9. This cannot refer just to being "cut off, chopped off" from other Israelites in the community, for such individuals would still be part of "the land of the living." Only dead people are cut off from the living. The LXX emphasizes this even more because the final clause is "he was led to death."[394]

---

[389] G. D. Kirchhevel, "Who's Who and What's What in Isaiah 53?" *BBR* 13 (2003): 127–31, translates this term "his fortune."

[390] The verb שׂיח means "to consider, meditate" (Ps 143:5) or "to talk, respond" about something (1 Chr 16:9; Job 12:8) and can relate to either a positive consideration (Ps 119:23) or more a negative connotation ("complain" in Job 7:11; "crying out" in distress in Ps 55:17 [18]). In questions, the imperfect verb often expresses a modal idea ("would," GKC §107t).

[391] Motyer, *Isaiah*, 434, believes they failed to ponder that the servant died for the rebellion of others.

[392] Seitz, "Isaiah 40–66," 6:466, believes that "Just being among the circle of witnesses did not enhance one's power of reception." This also explains the astonishment of the kings who finally understand what the servant has done (52:15)

[393] Whybray, *Isaiah 40–66*, 171–72, 177, says that "references to the Servant's vicarious suffering and death and resurrection are illusionary, partly due to a misunderstanding of the language of a particular kind of religious poetry and partly to the determination of Christian interpreters to find here a prefiguration of the suffering, death and resurrection of Christ."

[394] P. J. Gentry, "The Text of the Old Testament," *JETS* 52 (2009): 32, prefers the Old Greek reading that assumes a Hb. text of *nuggaʿ lammāwet*, "stricken to death," instead of the present reading of *lāmô*, "to him." See also J. de Waard, *A Handbook on Isaiah*, Textual Criticism and the Translator, vol. 1 (Winona Lake, IN: Eisenbrauns, 1997), 194–95. But since *lāmô* is a more dif-

Why did he die? The answer of the text fully agrees with earlier statements related to his suffering. Both his sorrows and death are directly connected to the sins of others. Although a verb is missing in 8b, one can easily understand that "a blow (was, came) on him because of the rebellious deeds of my people." It is odd to read "my people" in this verse since elsewhere in Isaiah this usually if found when God is speaking (40:1; 43:20; 47:6; 51:4; 52:4–6). Since 53:1–9 appears to be spoken by the Israelite followers of the Servant, 1QIs^a solves this problem by changing the pronoun suffix to third-person singular "his people," while C. Westermann emended the text to say "our people."[395] If the righteous Israelites are the "we" who are speaking 53:1–9, then "my people" means the people of Israel.[396]

53:9 This paragraph about the Servant ends with a notification about his burial (9a) and his innocence (9b). It was the common practice of people in this era for the relatives to bury all the family members in a large family tomb. The first verb in v. 9 describes the act of putting the Servant's body in a grave by using a third-person active verb ("he put, gave, made, assigned," *nātan*), not a passive verb ("he was assigned," NIV). Although it is possible to suggest that God ("he") put him in a certain grave, this verse seems to describe what humans did to the body of the dead Servant. 1QIs^a solves this problem by making the verb plural ("they assigned"), while the Old Greek has "I (God) will give"; but M. Dahood suggests that the subject is the singular collective term "my people," mentioned at the end of 53:8.[397] As an alternative, the subject could be an impersonal unidentified "one"[398] from among my people "gave, put, assigned" him a tomb with the wicked and the rich.[399] Since those who killed the Servant did not understand who he was, his death[400] and burial with

---

ficult reading and the next Hb. line ends with the word "in his death," *bĕmmōtāyw*, that is probably where the Greek translator derived his interpretation of *negaʾ lāmô* as ἤχθη εἰς θάνατον, "he was led to death."

[395] The Old Greek translation agrees with the MT, having "my people." Blenkinsopp, *Isaiah 40–55*, 348, accepts "his people" of the DSS, but Westermann, *Isaiah 40–66*, 254, prefers the first common pl. "our."

[396] Kirchhevel, "Who's Who and What's What?" 127–31, suggests that the readers "probably understood 53:8 to portray a king of Babylon as acknowledging the transgressions of his people." He believes this king is speaking to his magistrates because he takes the "many" to be "the great" (*rab*) based on several foreign names that have the prefix "Rab" (Jer 39:13). The servant is a slave they have mistreated and beaten, but he was later declared innocent. This interpretation is unlikely.

[397] M. Dahood, "Isaiah 53, 8–12 and Masoretic Misconstruction," *Bib* 63 (1982): 566–70. Oswalt, *Isaiah 40–66*, 390, makes "the grave" the subject but keeps a passive translation of the verb.

[398] GKC §144d indicates that the indefinite personal subject ("one") of some verbs is expressed with the third person sg.

[399] Goldingay and Payne, *Isaiah 40–55*, 31, 36, identify the wicked with the deported people in Babylon who are resistant to what the prophet speaks. He takes "the rich" to refer to wealthy Hebrews in Babylonian exile or as a description of Babylon and its king.

[400] Instead of "in his death" (בְּמֹתָיו) 1QIs^a has במותו "his tomb, burial mound," which is accepted as the better text in Goldingay and Payne, *Isaiah 40–55*, 2:315.

wicked criminals might be expected, but the connection to the rich is surprising. Consequently R. N. Whybray emended the text because he concludes "that the burial places of rich men and criminals should have been identical is highly improbable, and makes the line improbable."[401] Since the Old Greek and Targum both have "rich," the textual support for this reading is strong and it should not be changed. Since the rich are often represented as doing wicked things, these two words could refer to the same group of people. The significance of this point is not fully explained, but the burial of the Servant seems to have some quite unusual characteristics.[402]

The last part of 53:9 indicates that the Servant was innocent of any acts of violence or any deceitful words. Though some might have connected him with these kinds of ungodly acts because of his association with wicked people in his death and burial in 9a, 9b indicates that he did not commit any evil acts. Although this verse does not say he was totally innocent of all sins (only the ones listed), it indicates that the Servant did not die for stirring up rebellion against the authorities or by making deceitful claims about himself. This statement tends to disqualify the suggestion by some that the nation of Israel was the servant, for Isaiah repeatedly talks about the sins of the nation. One additional factor influencing the interpretation of 9b is the preposition 'al that introduces this part of the verse. This preposition often means "upon," but it can mean "because" or on a few occasions "although, even though, not withstanding."[403] "Because" gives a reason why he was buried with the rich and wicked, while "even though" creates a contrast, which makes more sense.

FINAL EXALTATION OF THE SERVANT (53:10–12)

[10]Yet it was the LORD's will to crush him and cause him to suffer,
and though the LORD makes his life a guilt offering,
he will see his offspring and prolong his days,
and the will of the LORD will prosper in his hand.
[11]After the suffering of his soul,
he will see the light [of life] and be satisfied;

---

[401] Whybray, *Isaiah 40–66*, 178, suggests that an emendation to "doers of evil" עֹשֵׂי־רָע or "demons" שְׂעִירִים are plausible, but prefers to take the unemended text by following the Arabic meaning of the word, "refuse, rabble." 1QIsᵃ has במותו which probably means "in his burial mound," but this word often refers to a "high place" of pagan worship in the Hebrew Bible, not "burial mound."

[402] Jesus' burial in the grave of the rich man Joseph of Arimathea (Matt 27:57) is sometimes associated with this prophecy, suggesting that the people intended to bury him with the wicked because they thought he was a criminal, but in actuality he was buried in the grave of a rich man. It is very difficult to derive this understanding from this verse.

[403] GKC §119aa-dd lists "upon, under, by, with, near, against," and 160a-c lists "although, in addition, notwithstanding."

by his knowledge my righteous servant will justify many,
   and he will bear their iniquities.
¹²Therefore I will give him a portion among the great,
   and he will divide the spoils with the strong,
because he poured out his life unto death,
   and was numbered with the transgressors.
For he bore the sin of many,
   and made intercession for the transgressors.

In the conclusion to this poem God reports his perspective on the Servant by returning to the theme of his final exaltation (as in 52:13–15). Although earlier verses indicated that men despised, pierced, and cut off the Servant, 53:6b indicates that behind the scenes it was God who caused the iniquities of us all to fall on him. In spite of this, God's plan was to exalt and prosper his righteous Servant because he was willing to bear the sins of many. These verses demonstrate that the death of the Servant was not a tragic mistake; his death will justify many and will bring the Servant honor. This positive ending to the story of the Servant can come to pass only if there is the possibility of some exaltation after death.

The structure of the final section is:

God's plan: taking guilt will bring success	53:10
God's Righteous One will justify many	53:11
God will exalt him who died for others	53:12

Using a third person reporting style about God, the prophet in 53:10 summarizes God's plan and his interpretation of the suffering and death of the Servant, as well as his desire to exalt the Servant in the future. In 53:11–12 God himself speaks in first person verbs, verifying these points and assuring the reader that God will exalt this one who died for the sins of others.

53:10   This new section starts with the Hebrew conjunction *waw* that contrasts ("but, yet, nevertheless") what the people saw and understood in the previous verses with what God planned, says, and will do in the future. The first and last lines refer to the two things that God willed, desired, or was pleased to do (the verb *ḥāpēṣ* and the noun *ḥēpeṣ*) because of what it would accomplish for the many sinners. God was pleased that the Servant's death would pay the price required for reparation so that guilt could be removed and a new relationship restored with sinners. God wants the reader to know that the rather strange things recorded in this tragic message about the Servant did not occur just as a regrettable accident or without some predetermined forethought. In fact, to the surprise of some, God's purposeful desires will be fulfilled through all these events. Thus the earlier hints about God's involvement in individual aspects of the life of the Servant (causing iniquity to fall on him in 53:6) applies also to the "crushing"[404] (53:5) and the "grief, sickness, suffering"[405] (53:3) of the Servant. God's punishment of sin, his love for others, and his plans to ultimately establish his worldwide kingdom required the removal of guilt to form a holy people (cf. 4:3–4).

The next line refers to the life of the Servant as a "guilt offering" ($'\bar{a}\check{s}\bar{a}m$), possibly picking up images of the lamb led to the slaughter in 53:7. The verbal meanings of this word relate "being guilty of something" or "suffering the consequence of guilt." These meanings influenced the semantic range of the noun that means "guilt" (Gen 26:10) or "compensation for guilt, restitution" (Lev 5:16; 1 Sam 6:3). This verse indicates that when the Servant gave up his life, he functioned as a compensation or restitution (similar to the reparation or guilt offering in Lev 5:14–6:7) to God for the damages done against him by those who sinned against him.[406] The rebellious deeds and iniquities of others (53:5a,6b,8b) led to the crushing of the Servant to pay the restitution for the guilt incurred by these sins. Although it is tempting to explain these concepts by importing all kinds of implied atonement imagery into this verse,[407] the term atonement is not used here, so the interpreter must be guided by the vocabulary used in this chapter. This concept of a person dying to provide restitution for the sins of everyone else is uniquely expressed in this passage, so it is important to recognize that this is a hard truth to understand. The legal and sacrificial imagery of giving a compensation/restitution sacrifice metaphorically hints at an interpretation of the Servant's death that only begins to unpack the revolutionary nature of what he did.

The second clause begins with $'im$, which the NIV translates as a concessive "though,"[408] while NRSV chooses "when." Most frequently $'im$ is translated

---

[404] The Aramaic Targum uses the Aramaic meaning of this word (דְּכָא) "cleanse, purify," but it should have the same meaning ("crush") it had in v. 5. Ekblad, *Isaiah's Servant Poems According to the Septuagint: An Exegetical and Theological Study,* 242, discusses the Old Greek translation "the Lord desired to cleanse him of the plague," which he feels was motivated by the translator's desire not to implicate God in the oppression of the servant.

[405] The word הֶחֱלִי is a *hiphil* form that comes from the root חָלָא ("to have grief, sickness"), and it appears that the final silent א has dropped or was assimilated (GKC §74k) because the following word begins with א (אִם). Westermann, *Isaiah,* 254, connects אִם to the preceding verb to get הֶחֱלִים "he healed" (from חָלַם "he grew strong") thus giving the translation "and [healed] the one who made his life and offering for sin." M. Dahood, "Textual Problems in Isaiah," *CBQ* 22 (1960), 406, tried to solve some of the אִם problems by connecting these two letters with the initial letter of the next word, thus giving him אָמֹה שׁם, "truly he made himself'" which is a clever solution, but it has no textual support.

[406] He seems to take the place of the sacrifice; this does not indicate a priestly role for the servant.

[407] Goldingay, *Message of Isaiah 40–55,* 511, makes a comparison to the scapegoat on the Day of Atonement (Lev 16:21–22) who carried away the guilt of the people, priesthood, and sanctuary, but this analogy is not brought up in 53:10.

[408] GKC §160a indicates this concessive use of אִם is found in 1:18 "though your sins be as scarlet, they shall be as white as snow."

"if,"[409] but an "if" clause tends to raise the question about whether the Servant will actually do this. Since the context indicates that the Servant has already died for the sins of others, the Servant's giving of his life is no longer a hypothetical "if" issue or an unfulfilled condition. The verb *tāśîm* could be second masc. singular ("you will make") with God as the subject (NIV) and "his soul" as the object of the verb.[410] A second approach is to interpret the verb to be a third fem. singular ("it/her soul will be/will be made") with "his/the servant's soul" (a fem. noun) functioning as the subject. The second option is preferable. It communicates that "his soul, his life" was made a restitution (usually it was a ram) for the life of the sinner in order to accomplish restitution for sins committed.

The second half of the temporal/concessive clause indicates that there will be positive consequences for the Servant who gave his soul as restitution for the guilt of others. The first positive result will be that the Servant will see his offspring (lit "seed"), a promise that implies that the Servant will live a long time in the future and see many spiritual children[411] as 54:13–14 confirms. These "seed, descendents" are the same group of people who are the "many" who are justified in 53:11. In earlier chapters the Servant's role was to bring back the sons of Jacob to God and to be a light to the Gentiles (49:5–6). Then in 45:22–25 God calls on people from all nations to turn and be saved and predicts that all the "descendents, seed" of Jacob will be righteous. Later chapters picture the nations coming to worship God in Zion (60:1–11) and the many descendents of Jacob functioning as "my servants" who will enjoy God's wonderful kingdom blessings (54:17; 65:8–16).

The second positive result will be that the Servant will "prolong his days," a phrase that encompasses the blessing of God (Deut 4:1,40; 5:16; 6:2; 11:8–9; 30:15–20). For these two factors to be possible the Servant must have had a long life after his death, although the prophet does not explain how this happens. R. N. Whybray eliminates this problem by claiming that the Servant never really died; thus this verse merely describes how the Servant will resume his normal happy life after his time of suffering.[412] Those who identify the Servant as the nation of Israel, find in these words the future restoration of the nation (similar to Ezek 37:1–14) envisioned in these words.[413] Others believe that the servant was the prophet Isaiah, so the extension of his life would simply refer

[409] GKC §159n-s gives several examples of אִם "if" with an imperfect verb to express conditions that may be fulfilled in the future.

[410] This results in the translations "though you (God) will make his soul a guilt offering," similar to the NIV translation.

[411] God refers to the Israelites as his spiritual children who are sinful (1:4), for from the beginning Israel was considered a firstborn son of God (Exod 4:21–22).

[412] Whybray, *Isaiah 40–66*, 177–80, believes this describes one who was near to death because of severe suffering.

[413] Muilenburg, "Isaiah 40–66," 5:629, rejects the idea of individual resurrection and views this as merely the future success and restoration of the nation.

to the continuation of his ministry by his disciples after his death.[414] None of these approaches are acceptable to those who view the Servant as an individual who actually died. This text does not explicitly address the issue of resurrection from the dead (26:19 does), but some dramatic change must have happened after the death of the Servant, if these positive consequences were achieved. The facts are known; the how is left unexplained. The Servant did have victory over the consequences of death; death did not end his ministry. The prophet's interest at this point was to speak to his audience about the benefits of the Servant's suffering, so an extended discussion of the resurrection would have pushed the conversation off the central focus. His goal was to persuade people to understand the positive consequences of the Servant bearing their sins so that they might enjoy the benefits he provides.

In light of these results one can rightly claim that the Servant successfully completed his task according to God's plan; thus God will be pleased with him (53:10c). This success connects the end of the Servant's ministry with the prophecy in 52:13 that foretold that the Servant would prosper and be exalted. Suffering great pain, being pierced and beaten, suffering for others' failures, and bearing the guilt that belongs to others may not sound like a successful life; but if this pleases God and it is his will, a true servant will lay down his life for others. Success in God's eyes does not relate to the money, praise, position, status, or worldly success that a person gains for himself.

53:11   This verse explains why the Servant (11a) and God (11b) will view the life of the Servant as successful. Unfortunately there are an unusually large number of disagreements on how to interpret many aspects of this verse, so it is necessary to discuss these one by one in order to discover what this verse is communicating. First, the interpreter must decide where to divide the first half of the verse from the second half. NIV and NASB follow those who break the verse after "be satisfied"[415] while NRSV and HCSB end the first half of the verse after "by his knowledge." The later approach divides the verse more evenly into two equal halves and should be followed.

Second, the first half of the verse describes two responses the Servant will have based on two verbs. The first line indicates that the Servant's response will be based on something he "will see," but no object is provided in the Masoretic text. Some assume he will see his offspring from 53:10, but the textual tradition in the Qumran Scrolls and the Old Greek add that he will see "the light,"[416] a reading that probably is original. The second line indicates

---

[414] Blenkinsopp, *Isaiah 40–55*, 355, finds in these words the continuation of the prophet's ministry, as described in 59:21 where God promises that the Spirit that inspired them will continue on in their descendents.

[415] Young, *Isaiah*, 2:357, and Delitzsch, *Isaiah*, 335, follow the Masoretic accentuation that puts בְּדַעְתּוֹ "with/by his knowledge" in the second half of the verse.

[416] The noun אוֹר is found in 1QIs[a], 1QIs[b], 4QIs[d], and the Old Greek and is widely supported in modern commentaries. I. Blythin, "A Consideration of Difficulties in the Hebrew Text of Isaiah

that the Servant "will be satisfied," indicating a positive evaluation based on ("because of," NIV has "after")[417] two factors: (a) his successful completion of the "work, travail, suffering" (*ʿāmāl*) he was given, and (b) "by his knowledge." The "work, travail, suffering" of his soul refers to the hard labor and suffering he endured in 53:3–9, but "his knowledge" is more ambiguous. D. W. Thomas suggested that this word may be derived from a parallel Arabic root *wadu'a* meaning "be quiet, humble," thus making the Servant satisfied with what he accomplished through his humiliation.[418] This provides good parallelism with "work, travail, suffering" in the preceding line, but there is little basis for this suggestion. If "by his knowledge" is kept as the best translation of this phrase, one must ask what knowledge might be intended. It appears that his knowledge that led to his satisfaction must be connected to the Servant "seeing the light" in the first line. If this "seeing the light" refers to his perception of how his travail and suffering led to "light, salvation" for others, one could understand that he would be "satisfied with his knowledge" of this wonderful benefit for others. His travail and suffering were not wasted; he satisfactorily accomplished what he was sent to do for the sake of others.

Third, the final lines describe in another way the accomplishments of "my Servant," who is also given the title the "Righteous One" (*ṣādîq*).[419] The interpreter should take "my Servant, the Righteous one" as the subject of the verb *yaṣ dîq* "he will justify, make righteous, bring into right relationship." A similar noun

---

53:11," *BT* 17 (1966): 27–31, discusses opinions for and against this reading, but in the end favors the Qumran reading. Goldingay and Payne, *Isaiah 40–55*, 323, suggest that the servant will see his offspring in v. 10; thus they reject the Qumran witness to the word "light." "By his knowledge" is then put with the next phrase. A Gelston, "Some Notes on Second Isaiah," *VT* 21 (1971): 517–21, rejects this Qumran reading as an explanatory gloss or dittography.

[417] The preposition מִ prefixed to the first word מֵעֲמַל is translated "after" in NIV. מִן frequently means separation "from," although GKC §119v-z also suggests: (a) causal "because of," (b) pregnant "without," or (c) partitive "some from, some of." Koole, *Isaiah III, Volume 2: Isaiah 49–55*, 329, indicates that the temporal usage "after" is usually only found in places where one is distinguishing between past and present events when a time factor is evident (see 53:8), so the causal fits better here as in 53:5.

[418] This issue is widely discussed. D. W. Thomas, "More Notes on the Root *yd'* in Hebrew," *JTS* 38 (1937): 404–405, accepts the translation "humbled"; J. A. Emerton, "A Consideration of Some Alleged Meanings of יָדֻע in Hebrew," *JSS* 15 (1970): 145–80, questioned although allowed this possibility. W. Johnstone, "*YD'* II, Be humbled, humiliated"? *VT* 41 (1991): 49–62, rejected this explanation of this verb in 20 cases (including Isa 53:3,11) but allowed it in 19 other examples. H. G. M. Williamson, "*DA'AT* in Isaiah LIII 11," *VT* 28 (1978): 118–22, suggested the translation "rest," but J. Day, "*DA'AT* 'Humiliation' in Isaiah LIII 11 in the Light of Isaiah LIII 3 and Daniel XII 4, and the Oldest Known Interpretation of the Suffering Servant," *VT* 30 (1980): 97–103, argued against this possibility. A. Gelston, "Knowledge, Humiliation or Suffering: A Lexical, Textual and Exegetical Problem in Isaiah 53," in McKay and Clines, *Of Prophets' Visions and the Wisdom of Sages: Essays in Honor of R. N. Whybray on his Seventieth Birthday,* 126–41, rejects the translation "humiliation."

[419] McKenzie, *Second Isaiah*, 131, drops this word because he thinks it is a dittography (צַדִּיק צַדִּיק are very similar in spelling), but there is no reason why this word could not be the subject of the verb.

and verb combination with these two roots in Deut 25:1–2; 1 Kgs 8:32 is translated "to declare the righteous innocent (righteous)" with the noun functioning as the object. But having already stated the innocence of the Servant in 53:9b, the last two parallel lines of this passage focus on what the Servant did for others and not on trying to prove the justness of the Servant once again.[420] The innocence of the Servant is already stated in the appositional relationship between the two nouns, "the Righteous One, my Servant." It is because the "Righteous One" is just that he is able to cause the "many" (functioning as the object)[421] to be right with God. The verb "will justify" has a forensic sense because the context of this chapter mentions bearing the guilt of others, punishment, and court proceedings (53:5,8,10), but it also has ethical implications as well (42:1–4) because his death has an impact on a person's relationship to God. This "declaration of the many as just" goes beyond any human act of weighing the evidence to decide if someone is innocent in a court of law (cf. Deut 25). Since the Servant bears the sins of the unjust and dies as a restitution offering to pay for the guilt of the sinner, the declaration of the "many" as just is possible because they now are without sin or guilt (it was carried away by the Servant). For some unknown reason the author chose not to use atonement or forgiveness terminology that is common in Leviticus, but the context of having "he" (*hû*), the Servant, bearing the sins and iniquities of the many argues not only for a substitutionary role of the Servant, but also the justness of those who now are no longer guilty of iniquity.

53:12   The poem begins the conclusion with "therefore" (*lākēn*), pointing to a strong connection between the suffering of the Servant and his exaltation in 52:13–15. Initially it appears that the first two lines are parallel to one another because both use the same imperfect verb "divide a portion, allot" (from *ḥālaq*), but the first verb explains what God does for the Servant while the Servant is the subject of the second verb. It is possible to translate the first line as God dividing to him (the Servant) a portion either "among the many" or "with the great" (*bārabbîm*). The parallelism with "the strong" in the next line would argue for "the great" in the first line, but in numerous examples "the many" and "the strong" are paired terms[422] plus this interpretation ("the many") would

---

[420] Goldingay and Payne, *Isaiah 40–55*, 2:325, translate this phrase "my servant will show many that he is righteous" (using an intransitive meaning) which puts the focus on the servant's vindication rather than the servant's justification of others. They view God justifying (acquitting) the just elsewhere in the Hebrew Bible but not the unjust. Muilenburg, "Isaiah 40–66," 5:630, follows a similar line of thinking and believes it is the servant who is being justified or proven to be in the right. Koole, *Isaiah III, Volume 2: Isaiah 49–55*, 333, argues that there is no intransitive use of the *hiphil* with this meaning, thus weakening the above argument.

[421] Usually the direct object is preceded by אֵת but here the text has לָרַבִּים, but at times the preposition לְ can function to introduce the direct object (GKC §117n) with the לְ expressing "in relations to." Motyer, *Isaiah*, 442, translates the לְ in this phrase to bring righteousness "to" the many.

[422] Goldingay, *Message of Isaiah 40–55*, 517, lists Exod 1:9 "the Israelites have become a much too numerous for us," which literally says "the sons of Israel (are) many more and stronger than us." Deuteronomy 26:5 refers to the Israelites becoming a "great nation, powerful and

match the reference to "the many" in 52:14 and the "strong" would match the "kings" in 52:15.[423] Two understandings are possible, based on the function and translation of *b* and *ʾēt*. If these are taken to be prepositions, God will divide "among the many" and "with the strong" (NIV takes this option). But this sharing with many others is not a very great exaltation of the servant and probably would not cause the kings to respond as 49:7; 52:15 suggest. But if the *ʾēt* is functioning as the sign of the direct object and not as a preposition,[424] this would mean that God will apportion to the Servant the "many" (probably the ones he has redeemed) and the Servant will apportion[425] the "mighty" kings as booty. This control over "the many" and the "mighty" kings indicates an exaltation fairly close to the exalted picture of 52:13.

There are four reasons for this exalted position of the Servant. (a) He was exalted "because" he poured out his life (lit "his soul") and died (53:8). His willingness to pay the ultimate penalty of suffering and death exemplifies a humiliation and sacrifice far above all others. (b) Although the Servant was not a sinful person (53:9), "he was numbered, listed, grouped; let himself be numbered" (*nimnâ*)[426] with the rebellious. Rather than remaining a high exalted one who was totally separated from sinners, the Servant allowed himself to be identified with the sorrows and sufferings of the rebellious people of his day. The people of that time despised and rejected him, wrongly assuming that God smote him because of his own sins (53:4). (c) He not only identified with the plight of sinful people, "he bore the sins of many" as 53:4,11 confirm. He accepted the load of their guilt so that he could make reparations for that guilt (53:11). The "many" refers back to the many he justified in 53:11, the many who were his portion in 53:12, the many Israelites who were appalled at his disfigured looks in 52:14, and the many kings who shut their mouths in 52:15. (d) He also "interceded for the transgressors." C. Westermann suggests that one should not conclude that this means that "he made prayers of intercession for them, but that with his life, his suffering and his death, he took their place."[427] The Servant's "intervention" would certainly refer to what he did in 53:1–11,

---

numerous," and 7:1 refers to other nations the Israelites must destroy as "nations larger (lit more numerous) and stronger than you." Isaiah 8:7 pictures the coming of the Assyrian as a "mighty floodwaters of the River" (lit "the strong and numerous waters of the River").

[423] Gentry, "The Atonement in Isaiah's Fourth Servant Song (Isaiah 52:13–53:12)," 41, prefers the translation "many" and "numerous." Compare also J. W. Olley, "'The Many': How is Isa 53,12a to Be Understood?" *Bib* 68 (1987): 330–56.

[424] Motyer, *Isaiah*, 442–43, and Muilenburg, "Isaiah 40–66," 5:631, take this approach. The בְ on בָּרַבִּים would not be viewed as a separate preposition but would naturally function to introduce the object of a transitive verb as GKC §119k suggests. Another approach would be to view this as a בְ *essentiae* GKC §119i which is often translated "as."

[425] Koole, *Isaiah III, Volume 2: Isaiah 49–55*, 339, understands the phrase "apportion the booty" in the sense of "to possess the booty" based on Gen 49:27; Exod 15:9; Judg 5:30; Isa 9:2–3.

[426] Motyer, *Isaiah*, 443, argues that this is a tolerative use of the *niphal* verb "he let himself be numbered."

[427] Westermann, *Isaiah 40–66*, 269, suggests that this word means "to intervene."

but since it is placed at the end of the message when the Servant is exalted, one might suggest that it refers to something done after his exaltation. This is especially implied by the change from perfect verbs (past completed action) to a final imperfect verb *yapgî'ă* "he will intervene, intercede." There is no expanded description of his future intervention on behalf of the many, but the future orientation of this activity implies that the Servant's work on behalf of the many will continue on into the future. This continued intervention/intercession might involve prayers for the many whose guilt he bore, or it might involve his intervention in the lives of many so that they will understand what he has done and accept the justification that he achieved when he bore their sins (53:11).

THEOLOGICAL IMPLICATIONS. It is difficult to enter the mystery of this poem about a suffering Servant without bringing the thoughts of hundreds of years of interpretation and application since the time of Isaiah. Today people in the Christian community are very much aware that the New Testament saw the death of Jesus as the fulfillment of this prophecy. People know about modern concepts of atonement and have little trouble believing in a glorified Servant who first suffered and died because the New Testament interprets it that way. But in the time of the prophets this was a rather unique and strange idea that earlier prophets had never spoken about. Some readers probably thought it was confusing and a little incoherent for a prophet to describe the great victorious kingly Messiah as a suffering Servant. Even today many Jewish people find it nearly impossible to connect the humiliation and death of the Servant with the role of the exalted royal Messiah. The newness of this thought, the wonder of this fascinating paradox, and the mysteriousness of a vicarious royal Messiah needs to reenter the picture anew if people today hope to struggle with the profoundness and the glory of the newness of the theological ideas proposed in this prophecy.

What could the Old Testament reader decipher about this Servant? The poem itself indicates that it will be hard for some people to believe this report (53:1) and that the kings who were told this were astonished at what they were told (52:15). Fortunately, this message is preceded by three other Servant passages, so the reader already has a good idea about who this Servant is, what he will do, and what he will endure. In each poem his identity is related to who he is and how he functions. His identification as a "tender shoot" and a "root" connects him to the Davidic figure in 11:1,10, a figure that is identical to the messianic son in 9:1–7. The exalted description of this Servant in 52:13 pictures him in a high royal role, having successfully accomplished his goals. The respect and awe of kings in 52:15 (cf. 49:7) also contributes to this messianic imagery. The role of sprinkling many nations remains quite obscure (52:15a).

This fairly consistent positive imagery is completely shattered by rather contradictory images of appalling disfigurement (52:14), the absence of the majestic look of a king (53:2), mistreatment and rejection, lack of respect, and suffering (53:3–4). The unusual theological explanation is that he suffered, was pierced, and was crushed for the sins of others (53:4–5). Although he was innocent (53:9b) and righteous (53:11), he did not object to this suffering (53:7b), so he died and was buried because of the sins of others (53:8–9). Even more astonishing, God himself caused the iniquities of others to fall on him so that peace and healing could come to many others (53:5b,6b). Surprisingly, it was God's will for him to pay for the restitution of others (53:10). On the one hand this looks like a terrible perversion of justice, but on the other hand it was part of God's unbelievable plan to transfer the guilt of many to this innocent Servant. He functioned as a substitute who took the penalty for others, and through this act he justified many (53:11). In spite of the unjust treatment of this Servant, this amazing story has a surprising and positive ending, for the Servant's substitutionary role caused the will of God to be accomplished (53:10). This suffering Servant will not only live again and see the light (53:11); he will be exalted again because he bore the sins of many (53:12).

This story does not speak explicitly of God's love for the world, the Servant's act of atonement, God's free grace, the imputation of righteousness, the promise of resurrection from the dead; and it does not specifically say what the many people need to do to gain the benefits of peace, healing, and justification. What this episode does reveal is that God has a plan to deal with the guilt of sin that separates people from himself. It is shocking to think that the righteous highly exalted royal Messiah was asked by God to intervene on behalf of terrible people all over the world by giving up his life to pay for the sins of others. The suffering and death involved in this plan demonstrates the heavy penalty for rebellion against God, but the peace, healing, and justification gained though these acts uncovers the tremendous accomplishments of this gracious plan. Where every person fails, the Servant gained the victory. God was able to turn the humiliating death of the Servant into the glorious exaltation of the Messiah because through death the penalty for sin was paid.

Excursus: The Early Interpreters of the Suffering Servant

The history of interpretation of this Servant began within the Old Testament itself. Sometimes this additional information is directly connected to this Servant, while at other times a passage may speak to the issues raised in this chapter (though it may not mention the Servant). One of the first places to look for additional information is in the immediate context of chaps. 54–55 and beyond. Here God tells of his plan to pour out his "everlasting kindness" and compassion on this people (54:8), promising that "my unfailing love for you will not be shaken, nor my covenant of peace be removed" (54:10), for "great will be your children's peace" (54:13). Although the Servant is not mentioned, the benefits of the work of the Servant in obtaining "peace" are evident (53:5). Why will things change so dramatically for Israel in the future in chap. 54? Why will the people enjoy God's love, compassion, and his covenant of peace? How can God restore "an everlasting covenant with you" (55:5)? It seems that the "steadfast mercies of David" refers to the faithful deeds of a David figure who is a "witness to the peoples, a leader and commander of the peoples" (55:5). This is the one who nations will hasten to, the one who God "has endowed with splendor" (55:5). This seems to refer to the Davidic Servant who will faithfully accomplish God's will through his suffering; thus making it possible for people (including the nations) to enjoy God's love, have peace, and an everlasting covenant.[428] Later in chap. 61:1–3 an Anointed One who has the Spirit of God on him (cf. 11:1–2; 42:1) will bring good tidings and justice to those who need it (cf. 11:4; 42:1–4,7; 49:9–10). This passage does not directly mention any suffering, but it adds to the overall picture of this Servant.

Although there is no detailed exposition of the "Suffering Servant" in either Jeremiah or Ezekiel, both pick up images from Isaiah and earlier texts. Jeremiah 23:5–6 connects this future Davidic king to the Branch (Isa 4:2), and speaks of his successful reign (cf. 52:13), and the bringing of justice, salvation, and peace to the earth (cf. 42:1–4). The prophet Ezekiel (34:23–31; 37:24–28) refers to the future messianic reign of "my servant David" and the establishment of an ever-lasting "covenant of peace" (cf. Isa 53:5; 55:3)[429] but makes no reference to the Servant's suffering. Three other possible references to Isaiah 53 are in Zechariah 11–13. In 11:8–14 the prophet uses the metaphor of a good shepherd to explain how a leader of the nation will be rejected; in 12:10 the prophet reports that the people of Israel will look on the one they pierced (cf. 53:5) and will mourn; plus 13:1,7–9 refers to cleansing from sin and a sword coming to strike "my Shepherd" (cf. 53:4b). The shepherd imagery in chap. 11 suggests that this was a king, but there is no statement that this shepherd died. In 12:10 there is the implication of death because the person is "pierced" (cf. 53:5), but the text does not say that this unidentified person died for the sins of the people. The reference to cleansing from sin in Zech 13:1 and the sword in 13:7–9 caused W. Rudolph to conclude that "the prophet is under the influence of Isaiah 53, where the verbs *ḥll* and *dkʾ* in 53:5 are synonymous with the verb *dqr*"[430] in Zech 12:10. In examining the visions of Daniel, J. Collins suggests that his reference to the wise (*maškîlîm*) "is taken from the 'suffering servant' of Isa 52:13" who justified the many (12:3).[431] Although there is some identical vocabulary between Isaiah and Daniel, Isaiah does not call the Servant "wise," but rather that he "prospers, is successful," and the Servant justifies many through his death. In Daniel the wise lead people to righteousness, but they do not bear the sins of others.[432] Thus later prophets after Isaiah seem to know about this mysterious Servant. They add very little that directly clarifies the identity and meaning of what would happen to the Suffering Servant in chap. 53, but Zechariah assures his readers that the Jewish people will one day respond positively to this one they pierced because the movement of God's Spirit in their lives will cause them to recognize their own guilt. This will

---

[428] Consult the later exegesis of 55:1–5 and P. J. Gentry, "Rethinking the 'Sure Mercies of David,'" *WTJ* 69 (2007): 279–304, for further discussion of these issues.

[429] For a discussion of Ezekiel's concept of the covenant of peace, consult D. I. Block, *The Book of Ezekiel 25–48*, NICOT (Grand Rapids: Eerdmans, 1998), 301–305; 419.

[430] W. Rudolph, *Haggai—Sacharja 1–8—Sacharja 9–14—Maleachi*, KAT 13/4 (Gütersloh: Gütersloher Verlagshaus, 1976), 223–24.

[431] J. Collins, *Daniel*, Her (Minneapolis: Fortress, 1993), 385, or H. L. Ginsberg, "The Oldest Interpretation of the Suffering Servant," *VT* 3 (1953): 400–404.

[432] J. A. Montgomery, *The Book of Daniel*, ICC (Edinburgh: T&T Clark, 1927), 472, believes the death of the wise (11:35) will justify many (12:3) and connects this idea to Isa 53:11.

result in the cleansing from sin because of their repentance and mourning.[433]

The first direct interpretation of Isaiah 53 was the Old Greek translation of this text. In general the Old Greek follows the Hebrew text, though the translators' unique choice of vocabulary and their attempt to resolve some of the difficult syntactical constructions sometimes led to different interpretations.[434] For example, at the very beginning of chap. 53, the Old Greek adds the vocative "O Lord," in 53:2 the Old Greek continues the thoughts of v. 1 by adding "we announced as a child before him," in 53:3 the Old Greek seems to carry over ideas from v. 2 when it adds "but his form was without honor and inferior to the sons of men," then in 53:4 the Old Greek indicates that this one bears "our sins" while the Hebrew has "surely, he bore our infirmities/griefs," plus the Old Greek omits the idea that he was smitten "by God." In the second half of the message in 53:8 the Hebrew "because of restraint, oppression" is translated in the Old Greek as "in his humiliation"; in 53:9 the Old Greek changes the Hebrew "he was assigned his grave with the wicked" to "I (God) will give the wicked for his grave." The Hebrew of 53:10 indicates that it was "God's will/God's desire" to bruise him, but the Old Greek says that the Lord desired "to cleanse him," plus the last line "and the will of the Lord will prosper in his hand" is varied and inserted into v. 11. The many difficulties in the Hebrew construction of 53:11 caused the Greek translators to struggle with its interpretation. The differences are so major both translations need to be compared side by side:

Hebrew	Greek
	The Lord also was pleased to take away
After the suffering of his soul, he will see	from the labor of his soul, he showed him
[the light] and he will be satisfied with	the light, and he will form [him] with
his knowledge; my righteous servant	understanding, to justify the just one who
will justify many, and he will bear their iniquities.	serves many well; and he will bear their iniquities.

D. A. Sapp concludes after his study of the differences between these texts that "at crucial points the LXX translators chose grammar, syntax, or vocabulary that reveal a divergent theological presupposition and consequently a different view of the fate of the Lord's servant."[435] These examples illustrate the difficulty of

---

[433] M. Hengel and Bailey, "The Effective History of Isaiah 53 in the Pre-Christian Period," in *The Suffering Servant: Isaiah 53 in Jewish and Christian Sources* (Grand Rapids: Eerdmans, 2004), 85–89, deals with the influence of Isaiah 53 on Zechariah and notes that the Targum does not interpret these Zechariah texts as having any relationship to Isaiah 53. He suggests that Daniel 11–12 may indicate that Daniel interpreted the servant in a collective sense (p. 98).

[434] R. R. Ekblad, *Isaiah's Servant Poems According to the Septuagint: An Exegetical and Theological Study,* studies each poem in detail and offers numerous suggestions that attempt to explain the Old Greek translation.

[435] D. A. Sapp, "The LXX, 1QIs^a, and MT Version of Isaiah 53 and the Christian Doctrine

understanding the vocabulary and grammar of this passage. It is always hard to know if variations are due to a periphrastic rendering of an odd Hebrew clause, if a change was based on a different textual base, or if translators are trying to give a new slant to the theological message. Whatever the cause of the variations, the results cause the reader of the Greek text to understand what was being predicted in a slightly different way. Numerous variations make no significant difference in what was communicated ("O Lord" in 53:1), but the announcement of a "child" in 53:1b may suggest an interpretive connection between this Servant with the "child" in 9:5. God's involvement in the Servant's suffering is somewhat changed in the Old Greek. God does not smite the Servant in 53:4, and in 53:10 the Lord "purges, cleanses" the servant and does not "crush him." In addition God's will in 53:11 is to "take away his suffering" and to "justify the just one," a conclusion that is quite different from "the Righteous One will justify many." M. Hengel concludes, "Although the motif of vicarious atoning suffering which effects salvation is weakened at a few points in the LXX over against the MT, it remains unambiguous."[436]

References to the Servant idea in Isaiah were picked up in the apocryphal Ben Sirach 48:10 (around 180 BC), which says that a future Elijah figure (48:1) will not only "turn the hearts of the father to the son" (cf. Mal 4:6 [MT 3:24]) but also "restore the tribes of Jacob" (Isa 49:6), but this does not pick up the suffering for sins of chap. 53. The apocalyptic Similitudes of Enoch (1 Enoch 37–71)[437] refers to the "son of man" from Dan 7:13 who is called "the Righteous One and Chosen One" (1 Enoch 53:6; Isa 53:11; 42:1). First Enoch 62:3–6 refers to kings and the mighty ones who will stand up and praise the Son of Man who will be sitting on a throne, possibly recalling the exaltation of the Servant in Isa 52:13–15 and Daniel 7:13–14. In other passages 1 Enoch takes up ideas from Isaiah 42 and 49.[438]

Two Aramaic documents from Qumran known as 4Q540 and 4Q541, which are also called 4QApocryphon of Levi[a-b], include 24 fragments (4Q541) and 3 additional ones (4Q540) which are dated to around 100 BC. 4Q541 refers to (in fragment 9, column i) someone who "will atone for all the children of his generation," but the people of that time "will utter many words against him . . . will

---

of the Atonement," in *Jesus and the Suffering Servant: Isaiah 53 and Christian Origins*, 170–92, believes these changes made the Old Greek less suitable for Christian quotation in the New Testament. Sapp claims that the servant in the LXX did not die, but v. 8 seems to clearly state this. The study of K. D. Litwak, "The Use of Quotations from Isaiah 52:13–53:12 in the New Testament," *JETS* 26 (1983): 385–94, notes several examples where the New Testament authors (Matt 8:17 quotes from Isa 53:4) appear to follow the Hebrew rather than the Old Greek text (Acts 8:32–33 is from the Greek text of Isa 53:7–8, and Rom 10:16 is from the Greek of Isa 53:1).

[436] Hengel and Bailey, "The Effective History of Isaiah 53 in the Pre-Christian Period," argues that this chapter repeatedly speaks of the Servant suffering for the sins of others.

[437] This is often dated somewhere between 50 BC and AD 50, sometime before the destruction of the temple by the Romans in AD 70. Historical events hinted at in 56:5–7 refer to an attack on Palestine by the Parthians and Medes around 40 BC. Some hypothesize a reference to Herod the Great bathing in warm springs to heal himself in 67:5–13, but this is unclear. Numerous fragments of 1 Enoch were found among the Qumran scrolls, but their date is uncertain.

[438] 1 Enoch 39:6 does refer to the many righteous ones which may reflect the "many" in 53:11–12; 1 Enoch 48:4 refers to the Son of Man as a "light to the nations" (Isa 42:6; 49:6). M. C. Reddish (ed.), *Apocalyptic Literature* (Nashville: Abingdon, 1990), 163–87, contains the text of the Similitudes of Enoch.

utter every kind of disparagement against him. His generation will be evil." Because of unclear letters and the fragmentary nature of fragment 24, column ii,
translations differ considerably. F. G. Martinez translates a key line "do not punish one weakened because of exhaustion and from being uncertain . . . do not
bring the nail near him,"[439] which sounds like it may be referring to Isaiah 53.
Nevertheless, the translation of M. Wise, M. Abegg, and E. Cook is completely
different: "But do not damage them by erasure or [we]ar . . . Do not touch the
priestly headplate."[440] Such differences do not produce great confidence in our
understanding of this text. 4Q540 does refer to suffering ("and distress will come
upon him") which some hypothesize refers to the persecution of the Messiah of
Levi,[441] though no redemptive impact is mentioned in this document.

The so called "Self-Glorification Hymn" (4Q491) found at Qumran is an Aramaic text that scholars used to assign to Michael the arch-angel, but because of
its content it may relate to the Suffering Servant of Isaiah 53.[442] Originally this
text was wrongly thought to be a part of the "War Scroll," but it describes one
who is given "an eternal, a mighty throne in the congregation of the angels. . . .
[There is no]ne comparable [to me in] my glory, no one shall be exalted besides
me. . . . [Wh]o has been considered contemptible like me? Who is comparable
to me in my glory? . . . And who like me [has refrain]ed from evil? Who shall
assault me when [I] ope[n my mouth?] . . . [Fo]r I am reck[oned] with the angels,
[and] my glory with the sons of kings."[443] The hymn never identifies the speaker
so there is considerable argument over whether this is the suffering Servant of
Isaiah 53 or if it expresses the hopes of the community of believers that they
will be glorified after their time of suffering. In any case no connection is made
between suffering and the bearing of the sins of others.[444]

The Qumran community did expect two Messiah figures in the future, one

[439] F. Garcia-Martinez, *The Dead Sea Scrolls Translated: The Qumran Texts in English*, trans
W. G. E. Watson (Leiden: Brill, 1994), 230. The key Aramaic word צצא is sometimes derived
from Syriac *ṣṣʾ* "nail," but in Exod 28:36; 39:30; Lev 8:9 Hebrew ציץ refers to the frontlet on the
head of the high priest.

[440] Wise, Abegg, Cook, *The Dead Sea Scrolls: A New Translation* (New York: Harper Collins,
1996), 314.

[441] Hengel and Bailey, "The Effective History of Isaiah 53 in the Pre-Christian Period," 106–
118, deals with the problems in these Qumran texts in detail.

[442] M. Smith, "Ascent to the Heavens and Deification in 4QMa," in *Archaeology and History
in the Dead Sea Scrolls*, JSPSup 8 (Sheffield: Sheffield Academic Press, 1990), 181–88, rejects the
view that these are Michael's the Archangel's words. Hengel and Bailey, "The Effective History
of Isaiah 53 in the Pre-Christian Period," 75–146, provides an extensive review of pre-Christian
Intertestamental references to Isa 53.

[443] M. Wise, M. Abegg, E. Cook, *The Dead Sea Scrolls: A New Translation*, 169.

[444] I. Knohl, *The Messiah before Jesus: The Suffering Servant of the Dead Sea Scrolls* (Berke-
ley: University of California, 2000), hypothesizes that an Essene leader Menahem, who claimed
to be the Messiah before the time of Christ, led a revolt against the Romans but was killed about
4 BC. Hengel and Bailey, "The Effective History of Isaiah 53 in the Pre-Christian Period," in *The
Suffering Servant: Isaiah 53 in Jewish and Christian Sources*, 143–44, highlights possible connections to the suffering servant as: (a) the person is exalted; (b) there is stress on the glory of
this person, as in Isaiah 53; (c) this person did suffer; (d) special wisdom is found in this person;
(e) he is sinless; (f) some lines reflect Isa 50:4,8–9; and (g) the vindication of God is near (50:8).
Unfortunately this person is never identified.

from the line of David (the Messiah of Israel) and one from the Levitical line (the Messiah of Aaron) and this idea is already imbedded in the "Testament of the Twelve Patriarchs."[445] This idea probably developed from passages like Jer 33:15–22; Ezekiel 44–46, Zech 4:14; 6:11–13, but neither Messiah is fully understood in the role of the suffering Servant of Isaiah 53. The Messiah of Israel is a political leader who is a warrior, while the Messiah of Aaron officiates at religious functions.[446] Of particular interest is the Messiah of Aaron who may function as a replacement for the wicked priests who ran the temple in Jerusalem during the Intertestamental era.

Copies of the Testament of Benjamin include the early Armenian translation (maybe as early as 50 BC) as well as, a later Greek version (possibly around AD 200) that was expanded by Christians. The contrast in 3:8 is significant (the later Christian additions are in italics). Jacob is speaking to Joseph: "In you will be fulfilled the heavenly prophecy *concerning the Lamb of God, the Savior of the world,* because the spotless one will be defiled (*betrayed*) by lawless men and the sinless one will die for the sake of impious men *by the blood of the covenant of Beliar and his servants.*" These italicized additions make the intent explicitly applied to Jesus the Lamb of God, but without these additions the spotless and sinless one must refer to the Servant of Isaiah 53.

The Wisdom of Solomon 2:12–5:23, especially 2:12–20 and 5:1–6, clearly draws information from Isaiah 53 and surrounding chapters. In 5:1–6 the righteous man will be afflicted (cf. 52:14; 53:3–6), people will be amazed at the salvation he brings (cf. 52:15), and people will repent, admitting that they spoke derisively about him (cf. 53:3). They thought he was without honor (cf. 53:3b,4b) and wondered why he was numbered among the sons of God (cf. 53:12). Thus in the end they will confess that they were the ones who went astray (cf. 53:6). In a somewhat similar account of the Servant of Isaiah, Wisdom of Solomon 2:12–20 "takes up the typical elements of the story of the persecution and exaltation of the righteous one: the conspiracy and its cause, the condemnation, the construal of death as an ordeal."[447] Largely missing from this account is the substitutionary atonement theme.

The Aramaic Targum of Isaiah is another document that testifies to the way people understood the Servant in Isaiah 53.[448] The use of Aramaic Targums may

---

[445] K. G. Kuhn, "The Two Messiahs of Aaron and Israel," in *The Scrolls and the New Testament,* ed. K. Stendahl (New York: Harper, 1957), 54–64. The two Messiahs are in Testament of Reuben 6:7–12, Testament of Simeon 7:2, Testament of Levi 18:2–4, etc.

[446] D. S. Russell, *The Method and Message of Jewish Apocalyptic* (Philadelphia: Westminster, 1964), 304–319, discusses the evidence and interpretation of these two messianic figures.

[447] G. W. E. Nickelsburg, *Jewish Literature between the Bible and Mishnah* (Minneapolis: Fortress, 2005), 206, explains how the ungodly misunderstood who the servant was, then he shows the falseness of their thinking. M. J. Suggs, "Wisdom of Solomon 2,10–25: A Homily Based on the Fourth Servant Song," *JBL* 76 (1957): 26–33, notes that Wisdom of Solomon uses the word "child, servant" in 2:13, similar to 53:1, relates this child to God his father and David in 2:16, and has the righteous man wronged and suffering a shameful death in 2:19–20. Wisdom of Solomon may have been interested in this person because the Old Greek refers to him as "my child shall achieve wisdom" (Isa 52:13). "Child, servant" is used within the Servant poems in 42:1; 49:6; 50:10; 52:13 and outside the Servant songs to refer to Israel in 41:9; 42:19; 43:10; 44:1,2,21,26; 45:4.

[448] Translations of the Aramaic Targum on Isaiah are available in J. F. Stenning, *The Targum of Isaiah, Edited with a Translation* (Oxford: Clarendon, 1949); B. D. Chilton, *The Targum of Isaiah:*

date back as far as the ministry of Ezra (Neh 8:1–8), but the Talmud (*b. Meg. 3a*) indicates that Jonathan ben Uzziel wrote the Targum on the prophets under the direction of Haggai, Zechariah, and Malachi. Although the present text of this Targum is dated to the fifth century AD, B. D. Chilton identifies references to historical events over a long period of time, suggesting an ongoing process of editing and expansion over several hundred years.[449] J. Ådna dates the Targum of Isaiah sometime shortly before the Bar-Kochba revolt against the Romans in AD 132–35.[450] The Targum interprets the triumphant verses to be about the exaltation of the Messiah, but those verses that speak about suffering and a shameful death are connected to what will happen to the Gentiles, wicked Israelites, and the temple. This has caused some to suggest that the Targum is an anti-Christian polemic in reaction to the interpretation of Isaiah 53 by early Christians. H. Hagermann has tried to discover what the Targum said in pre-Christian times, but this is a difficult reconstruction to defend objectively.[451] Although some changes in interpretation are simply due to the translator of the Targum connecting the meaning of a word to a different root, there are many others that are determined by his concept of who the Messiah is.[452] Since many verses having to do with suffering were not connected to the servant, what kind of messianic servant did the Targum end up with? In 52:13 it identifies "my servant, the anointed one (the Messiah)" as the person who is exalted. Through these changes all suffering is removed from the Messiah; instead, he is turned into a builder of the temple and a teacher of the law in 53:5: "He will build the sanctuary which is profaned for our sins, handed over for our iniquities, and by his teaching the peace will increase upon us, and when we attach ourselves to his words our sins will be forgiven." In addition, he takes on the role of intercessor for his people in 53:4: "Then he shall pray on behalf of our transgressions" (instead of "surely he took our infirmities"). In 53:7 "he was praying and he was answered" (instead of "he was oppressed and afflicted"), but 53:12

Introduction, Translation, Apparatus and Notes, in The Aramaic Bible, vol. 11 (Collegeville: Michael Glazier, 1987); A. Sperber, *The Bible in Aramaic, vol. III. The Later Prophets According to Targum Jonathan* (Leiden: Brill, 1962), or one can find a translation of Isaiah 53 in C. K. Barrett, *The New Testament Background* (San Francisco: Harper, 1989), 314–15.

[449] B. D. Chilton, *The Glory of Israel: The Theology and Provenience of the Isaiah Targum*, JSOTSup 23 (Sheffield: JSOT, 1982), 20–23, 109–10, identifies influences from first-century Palestine and fourth-century Babylon. For example, he suggests that the Targum on 28:1–4 presupposes that the Jerusalem temple in AD 70 is still standing while the Targum on 32:14 views it as a past event.

[450] J. Ådna, "The Servant of Isaiah 53 as Triumphant and Interceding Messiah," in Janowski and Stuhlmacher, *The Suffering Servant: Isaiah 53 in Jewish and Christian Sources*, 189–224.

[451] H. Hagermann, *Jesaja 53 in Hexapla, Targum, und Peshitta*, BFCT 56 (Gütersloh: Gütersloher Verlagshaus, 1954), 66–126, maintains that the Targum "combines a strict grounding in the original text with a method of translation that is in part highly artificial and tendentious, altering the sense." J. Jeremias, "παις θεου," *TDNT*, 5, 695, finds only two points where traces of a suffering Messiah still remain in Isaiah 53, and one of these is a questionable reading. He explains this reversal of the meaning of chap. 53 as an anti-Christian polemic against the Christological interpretation of the Early Church.

[452] In 53:7 the Hebrew נַעֲנֶה comes from עָנָה root III "be afflicted, bow down," but the Targum translator took the meaning from עָנָה root I "answer," which is a change not based on any theological understanding or presuppositions. But in 53:3 the straightforward "he was despised" gets unexplainably changed to "then shall all the kingdoms be despised."

has "he shall make intercession for many transgressions," which is consistent with the original Hebrew.[453] The Targum radically changes the meaning of Isaiah 53 by not applying any of the suffering to the Messiah.

Seen in this light, one can realize that Jesus' own teaching about his role as the Servant, plus his death and resurrection, enabled the New Testament authors to take a radically different theological interpretation of the suffering and death mentioned in Isaiah 53. To trace the uses of chap. 53 in the New Testament and beyond would take a separate book, a task on which others are already making good progress.[454] These works focus on the text used (Hebrew or Old Greek) in these allusions or quotations from Isaiah, the hermeneutical methodology employed, and the theological impact of Isaiah on the Gospels and Acts,[455] the Pauline letters,[456] the General Epistles, and Early Church commentators.[457]

---

[453] Ådna, "The Servant of Isaiah 53 as Triumphant and Interceding Messiah," in *The Suffering Servant: Isaiah 53 in Jewish and Christian Sources*, 207–22, describes three roles of the Messiah in detail.

[454] See especially the chapters by A. M. Leske (Matthew) and R. E. Watts (Mark) in Bellinger and Farmer, eds., *Jesus and the Suffering Servant: Isaiah 53 and Christian Origins*; the chapters by R. Beaton (Matthew), M. D. Hooker (Mark), B. J. Koet (Luke-Acts), J. R. Wagner (Romans and Galatians), F. Wilk (1, 2 Corinthians), J. C. McCullough (Hebrews), S. Moyise (1 Peter), and D. Mathewson (Revelation) in *Isaiah in the New Testament*, ed. S. Moyise and M. J. J. Menken (London: T&T Clark, 2005); C. L. Blomberg (Matthew), R. E. Watts (Mark), I. H. Marshall (Acts), and G. H. Guthrie (Hebrews) in *CNTOT*; P. Stuhlmacher (Gospels and Acts), O. Hofius (NT letters), and C. Markshies (Patristics) in *The Suffering Servant: Isaiah 53 in Jewish and Christian Sources*; and J. D. Cassel, "Patristic Interpretation of Isaiah," in *"As Those Who are Taught" The Interpretation of Isaiah from the LXX to the SBL*, ed. C. M. McGinnis and P. K. Tull, Symposium 27 (Atlanta: SBL, 2006), 145–69.

[455] M. J. J. Menken, "The Source of the Quotation from Isaiah 53:4 in Matthew 8:17," *NovT* 29 (1997): 313–27, discovers that Matthew does not use the exact form of the Old Greek translation of this verse or any of the versions (Symmachus, Aquila, or the Targum), so it appears that he may have made his own rendering by revising what other translations had. Also see S. E. Johnson, "The Biblical Quotations in Matthew," *HTR* 36 (1943): 135–41. R. H. Gundry, *The Use of the Old Testament in St Matthew's Gospel, with Special Reference to the Messianic Hope* (Leiden: Brill, 1975). H. van de Sandt, "The Quotations in Acts 13,32–52 as a Reflection of Luke's LXX Interpretation," *Bib* 75 (1994): 26–58, refers to quotes from Isa 49:6; 55:3; Hab 1:5, and Ps 2:7.

[456] See P. Dinter, "Paul and the Prophet Isaiah," *BTB* 13 (1983): 48–52; R. B. Hayes, *Echoes of Scripture in the Letters of Paul* (New haven: Yale, 1989); J. R. Wagner, *Heralds of the Good News: Paul and Isaiah "in Concert" in the Letter of Romans*, NovTSup 101 (Leiden: Brill, 2002); R. B. Hayes, "'Who Has Believed Our Message?' Paul's Reading of Isaiah," in *SBL 1998 Seminar Papers* 1 (Atlanta: Scholars Press, 1998), 205–25, treats the 31 quotations. He sets out seven criteria that can be used to identify echoes of Old Testament quotations in the New Testament. These works argue against the view of M. Hooker, *Jesus and the Servant: The Influence of the Servant Concept of Deutero-Isaiah in the New Testament* (London: SPCK, 1959), 127, that "in the writings of the theologians of the early church, we have found little evidence that the identification of Jesus with the Servant played any great part in the thinking of st Paul."

[457] B. S. Childs, *The Struggle to Understand Isaiah as Christian Scripture* (Grand Rapid: Eerdmans, 2004), 32–147, deals with the hermeneutical methods of interpreting Isaiah from Justin Martyr through Theodoret of Cyprus (AD 393–460) and does not focus on the understanding of Isaiah 53.

(2) God's Compassion Brings Children and a Covenant of Peace (54:1–17)

This prophecy is about the wife Zion who will have many children. The-matically, it is connected with similar themes in 49:14–50:3 and 51:17–52:12. In these earlier chapters Zion thought God had forgotten her and her children (49:14; 51:18,20) when she was left alone for a while (49:21b) and attacked (49:19; 51:19–22; 52:5), but God promised in the future she would have many children (49:17–21), and her enemies would be defeated (49:25–26; 51:23). Chapter 54 is parallel to these accounts, for once again Zion is barren (54:1) and was abandoned for a brief time (54:6–8), but God promised she would have many children (54:2–3) and be protected from attack (54:14– 15,17). This message in chap. 54 is connected to the servant poem in 52:13–53:12 by the repetition of several key words.[458] But as C. Westermann . . . states, "the subject of the promise is again not deliverance and restoration, but the new condition of salvation."[459] Thus the new spiritual condition of the nation with its promise of a new future era of salvation is the vision the prophet uses to encourage his audience to trust God.

The setting of the future promises of peace relates to some unknown escha-tological era (not a postexilic restoration),[460] but there are some hints about the nation's present troubles. R. N. Whybray connects the negative statements about their abandonment for a brief time to their exilic experience and the repopulation of Zion to the people's return from exile.[461] This approach is questionable, for the idea that "your sons will be taught by the Lord" (54:13) sounds very much like the eschatological description of things in 2:2–3 and the covenant of peace that is envisioned (54:10,13) should be connected to the eschatological Davidic covenant in 55:3 (cf. 9:6; 26:3,12; 53:5; 66:12).

The present setting of the audience is not clearly identified. If it fits the time of the similar oracles in 49:14–50:3 and 51:17–52:12, it would fit a time of war when the nation is being attacked, but God does not save them immediately. It appears that God has abandoned them (54:7; cf. 49:14). This could be connect-ed to the fall of Jerusalem in 587 BC or the attack of Sennacherib in 701 BC. Earlier it was suggested that Sennacherib's attack might fit chaps. 49–51 and the idea that God left them vulnerable to the enemies' attack "for a short time" in 26:20 (cf. 54:7–8) could be connected to the period when Sennacherib suc-

---

[458] "Many" is in 53:11–12 and 54:1; "seed, offspring" is in 53:10 and 54:3; "peace" is in 53:5 . . .

[459] Westermann, *Isaiah 40–66*, 277.

[460] Blenkinsopp, *Isaiah 40–55*, 360, says, "the poem moves to a consideration of the physical city with its walls, also anticipating Nehemiah's rebuilding program and his repopulation of Jeru-salem," but there is a serious problem with this interpretation for Nehemiah's effort never produced "battlements of rubies, hour gates of sparkling jewels" (54:12), and only about 50,000 people came back in the first return from exile (Ezra 2:64–66).

[461] Whybray, *Isaiah 40–66*, 185, says the "return from exile was to be the definitive fulfillment of Yahweh's promises," that her widowhood "clearly refers to the present, that is, to the Babylonian exile."

cessfully defeated 46 fortified cities of Judah. This would fit a time when the nation would feel desolate (54:1), a time when they would be afraid (54:4), a time when the city was afflicted (54:11), a time when the weapons of the enemy did not prevail against those in Jerusalem (54:17; cf. 37:35–37), but also a time when God could promise that they would not be humiliated by defeat (54:4) because he would send his angel to defeat 185,000 Assyrian troops. The time when they were abandoned for a short time (54:7) would not fit the fall of Jerusalem in 587 BC because they were completely abandoned to Nebuchadnezzar for 70 years, not just for a short time. These positive promises indicate that God still loves his people and that one day in the distant future he will establish his kingdom in all its glory. In other words, various things that happened in their present setting legitimated the idea that they should believe that God can do even greater things similar to these in the future.

W. A. M. Beuken argues for the unity of this chapter[462] which is made up of two main paragraphs:

| Call for the Wife to Respond to God's Love | 54:1–10 |
| The Glorious Situation in Zion | 54:11–17 |

Chapter 54 does not make an explicit direct logical connection between this new day for Zion and the work of the Servant dying for the sins of others (chap. 53). Although 54 does not discuss the exaltation of the Servant (52:13–15), the close association between these chapters naturally leads to the possibility that this call for Zion to respond has something to do with what happened in chap. 53. J. Oswalt suggests that "if 52:13–53:12 is understood as an expression of the means by which a restored relationship between God and his people is possible,"[463] it would explain what God has done through the Servant to make the marvelous promises in chap. 54 possible. Taking a different tack, J. F. A. Sawyer identifies several connections between chap. 53 and 54 by observing that both the Servant and the woman Zion are afflicted and humiliated, both are vindicated in the end, both will see offspring, and the nations (the "many") are affected by what happens to both (52:15; 53:11–12; 54:3).[464]

---

[462] W. A. M. Beuken, "Isaiah LIV," *OTS* 19 (1974): 29–70, argues for the unity of the chapter because (a) it is distinct from the chapter before and after and (b) there is a continuity of one person being addressed throughout chap. 54. He divides into two sections, 54:1–6 where the prophet is speaking and 54:7–17 where God is speaking. But the appearance of "says the Lord" at the end of 54:1 and at the end of 54:6 argues against this conclusion.

[463] Oswalt, *Isaiah 40–66*, 413, states that "further confirmations of the significance of 52:13–53:12 for chs. 54–55 is the continued emphasis throughout the two chapters on the issues of sin, righteousness, mercy, pardon, and relationship with God."

[464] J. F. A. Sawyer, "Daughter of Zion and Servant of the Lord in Isaiah: A Comparison," *JSOT* 44 (1989): 89–107, makes these and several other comparisons between the Servant and Zion.

CALL FOR THE WIFE TO RESPOND TO GOD'S LOVE (54:1–10)

[1]"Sing, O barren woman,
  you who never bore a child;
 burst into song, shout for joy,
  you who were never in labor;
 because more are the children of the desolate woman
  than of her who has a husband,"
                    says the LORD.
[2]"Enlarge the place of your tent,
  stretch your tent curtains wide,
  do not hold back;
 lengthen your cords,
  strengthen your stakes.
[3]For you will spread out to the right and to the left;
  your descendants will dispossess nations
  and settle in their desolate cities.

[4]"Do not be afraid; you will not suffer shame.
  Do not fear disgrace; you will not be humiliated.
 You will forget the shame of your youth
  and remember no more the reproach of your widowhood.
[5]For your Maker is your husband—
  the LORD Almighty is his name—
 the Holy One of Israel is your Redeemer;
  he is called the God of all the earth.
[6]The LORD will call you back
  as if you were a wife deserted and distressed in spirit—
 a wife who married young,
  only to be rejected," says your God.
[7]"For a brief moment I abandoned you,
  but with deep compassion I will bring you back.
[8]In a surge of anger
  I hid my face from you for a moment,
 but with everlasting kindness
  I will have compassion on you,"
 says the LORD your Redeemer.

[9]"To me this is like the days of Noah,
  when I swore that the waters of Noah would never again cover the earth.
 So now I have sworn not to be angry with you,
  never to rebuke you again.
[10]Though the mountains be shaken
  and the hills be removed,
 yet my unfailing love for you will not be shaken
  nor my covenant of peace be removed,"
 says the LORD, who has compassion on you.

C. Westermann concludes that the first paragraph includes a hymn of praise (54:1), a promise of salvation (54:4–5), and a proclamation of salvation (54:7–10), which together form a lament.[465] R. Melugin found: (a) a hymn (54:1), plus two substantiation clauses (54:2–3); (b) a salvation-assurance oracle (54:4) with two substantiation clauses (54:5–6); and (c) a disputation-like announcement of salvation (54:7–10).[466] This odd conglomeration of different genres does not provide much assistance in understanding this chapter. These formal characteristics are intermixed in chap. 54 and must be analyzed through the lenses of the content and rhetorical purpose of each part. The overall purpose of these words is to provide the people of Zion with assurances about the future so that Zion will be able to respond to God's offer of love and salvation based on solid reasoning. The seven imperatives in 54:1–2 and the negative exhortations in 54:4 express the need to respond, so the repeated substantiation clauses (introduced by kî "because") in 54:3,5,9,10 explain why this is a reasonable choice. Together these offer the needed assurances so that Zion, the metaphorical wife of God, can respond to God's promises and his future provision of salvation.

The structure of this paragraph is divided into three parts:

The once desolate woman should sing	54:1–3
Call to sing	1
Spread out because of many children	2–3
Do not fear embarrassment	54:4–5
Fear not shame	4
Because God is your Redeemer	5
God will love the one abandoned	54:6–10
God has not rejected her	6
She was abandoned only a moment	7–8
His covenant promise is as sure as Noah's	9–10

The imperative verbs call the woman to action, to sing and have no fear (54:1–2,4), for her metaphorical husband (God) has unfailing love for her. Although God did allow the nation to endure a brief time in the past when it faced his anger, now God offers this woman hope, compassion, peace, and an unshakable covenant (54:3,5,7–8).

54:1 The female figure who is the "barren one" (ʿăqārâ), whose husband is God, surely must refer to the city of Zion.[467] This fits the earlier pattern of

---

[465] Westermann, *Isaiah 40–66*, 271, suggests that these are "the three component parts of a lament," but 1–10 do not sound much like a lament.

[466] Melugin, *Formation of Isaiah 40–55*, 169–71; Schoors, *I Am God Your Savior,* 81, views 54:4–6 an oracle of salvation and on p. 131 he classifies 54:7–10 as a proclamation of salvation. Baltzer, *Deutero-Isaiah*, 429–30, finds a sacred marriage in chap. 54, but this pushes the imagery too far.

[467] Although the word "Zion" is not used in chap. 54, the woman who was the wife in the earli-

personifying Jerusalem as a woman (49:14–50:3; 51:17–52:12),[468] but it is odd
to find the text saying that "she did not bear" children, because in earlier texts
she had sons (49:17–18,20,22; 51:18,20). As far back as J. Calvin this was explained as a result of God's driving the nation into the banishment of exile,[469]
but losing children in war is different from not bearing children. B. Childs
resolves this dilemma by viewing the woman in the first part of the chap. 54 as
Sarah, then he connects the woman figure in 54:11–17 with Zion.[470] Although
Abraham and Sarah appear in 51:2, and Sarah (Gen 16:1), Rachel (Gen 29:31),
Manoah's wife (Judg 13:2), and Hannah (1 Sam 1:5–6) are examples of initial
barrenness, providing a basic understanding of this problem, nothing specific
in this passage identifies the woman in chap. 54 with any one of these barren
women. The simplest solution to this dilemma is to translate the perfect verbs
in a present or future tense (rather than past); thus she is not bearing children
now and is not now in labor (cf. similar images in 49:21).[471] Although she has
no expectation of having children at the present time because she was not in a
close relationship with God her husband, God predicts a change "because" (*kî*
introduces the substantiation) in the future the children of the woman who is
presently desolate and alone will number "many" (*rabbîm*) more than[472] the
children of the married woman.[473] These children are spiritual children in an

---

er chapters was Zion. The Aramaic Targum refers explicitly to Jerusalem five times in this chapter.
Oswalt, *Isaiah 40–66*, 415, states that the lack of this term "suggests that the prophet is consciously
resisting the limitation of the implications of God's forgiving grace," thus he believes it refers to all
Gentiles and Jews who will become the blessed people. Although God's offer of grace is universal
in other chapters (45:22–25), the use of the barren woman imagery whose husband is God (54:5) in
this chapter is consistent with its reference to Zion in earlier chapters. Sawyer, "Daughter of Zion
and Servant of the Lord in Isaiah: A Comparison," 89–107, carefully reviews passages where cities
(Tyre in chap. 23; Babylon in chap. 47; Zion in chaps. 49–99) are personified as cities and makes
a strong case for viewing chap. 54 as Zion.

[468] K. Jeppesen, "Mother Zion, Father Servant: A Reading of Isaiah 49–55," in McKay and
Clines, *Of Prophets' Visions and the Wisdom of Sages: Essays in Honor of R. N. Whybray on His
Seventieth Birthday*, 109–25, describes the image of Zion as a mother and wife.

[469] J. Calvin, "Book of the Prophet Isaiah," *Calvin's Commentaries*, 134–35. Muilenburg, "Isaiah 40–66," 5:633–34, views the destruction of Jerusalem as the divorce of God and his people,
with the exile as her time of barrenness. Motyer, *Isaiah*, 445, concludes the opposite saying that
"the contrast between the *desolate* and *her who has a husband* is not between Zion in exile and
preexilic Zion 'married' to the Lord."

[470] Childs, *Isaiah*, 427, is following the perspective of W. A. M. Beuken, "Isaiah LIV," *OTS* 19
(1974): 29–70, who finds two women, a barren one (Sarah in 1–3) and a forsaken one (Israel in
4–6). Koole, *Isaiah 40–55*, 350, refers to a patristic solution of referring to having no children as
having no converts from the Gentile world (2 Clement 2:3), but this is an unacceptable solution.

[471] The perfect verb can communicate action usually rendered in English by the present tense
(GKC §106g-l). The abrupt change from the initial second person vocative "sing" to the third
person "she was barren" is not unusual in prophetic texts (GKC §144p).

[472] The preposition מִן is a prefix on מִבְּנֵי that expresses the comparison "more are the sons
of . . . than" (GKC §133a-b).

[473] The text does not explain who this married woman is; thus it may be best to translate the
phrase as a general truth "more than anyone who is married." The Aramaic Targum interprets
this married one as "the children of inhabited Rome," leaving the possibility that they viewed the

eschatological era as 49:23; 52:6; 54:10,13–14 suggest, for at that time these people will acknowledge God and will be taught by God himself (cf. 2:1–5). If 49:22–23 are referring to something similar, the new children will include Hebrew believers but they will come back with the aid of foreign kings (cf. 60:1–14).

Consequently, with imperative verbs (54:1) God exhorts this woman in hymnic style to sing for joy, to shout with a resounding yell because a divine transformation of the woman's situation is going to happen in the future. This will be astonishing, a miraculous change, and a marvelous divine act. Now, even before the promise is fulfilled, the prophet encourages the woman to respond in faith and in anticipation of God's great love. She can rejoice because of what God will do. Since this is such a dramatic reversal of present reality, at the end of this verse God assures the audience that what is promised in this communication is indeed what God has said.

54:2–3 In order to picture this transformation in family terms that everyone in the ancient Near Eastern world would understand, God exhorts the woman with five more imperative verbs to broaden or enlarge the tent, and to stretch out[474] more curtains in their dwelling place. This was common practice when a family had more children or when a man added another wife. If a family wanted to expand their living space all the women had to do was to sew some more goatskins together to make the roof larger and then add a curtain or two for privacy. The initial imperatives encourage the listener to be optimistic in the expansion of the tent. "Make it wide" and "stretch it out" encourage the woman to not be shortsighted or pessimistic about how many children will be added and how much space will be needed. She is not to hold back her imagination in dreaming just how big the tent might need to be.[475] The final lines of v. 2 provide two further imperatives that describe the normal care one must give to any expanded tent. Additional stakes must be driven into the ground to hold up the new addition to the tent and since the tent is now broader the cords that are used to tie down the tent have to be a little stronger to withstand the additional wind pressure on the surface of the tent (cf. similar images in 33:20–21). These final instructions encourage people to believe that this needs to be a strong tent that will last and not be destroyed by any external force. This imagery should not be

---

destruction of Jerusalem in AD 70 as the desolate one. These two different women could refer to the same person (cities, nation) at different stages in her history (Muilenburg, "Isaiah 40–66," 5:633).

[474] The first verb is a second-person imperative exhortation "make wide," but the second verb is not an imperative (NIV "stretch out" turns it into an imperative). The imperfect verb could be viewed as a jussive "let your tent curtains be stretched out" (GKC §109b), or the verb could be some kind of modal imperfect (GKC §107m-r; *IBHS*, 31.4) to express obligation "the tent curtains must/should/ought to be stretched out."

[475] G. K. Beale, *The Temple and the Church's Mission: A Biblical Theology of the Dwelling Place of God* (Downers Grove: InterVarsity, 2004), 131, hypothesizes that the tent may in fact be the tabernacle of God, but there is relatively little that supports this view in 54:1–2.

allegorically interpreted (the pegs are the prophets and apostles); instead, the general imagery of expanding a tent should be broadly applied to the picture of preparing for a rapid expansion of additional people in Zion.

Verse 3 is probably a substantiation (it begins with *kî* "because," NIV "for")[476] of the exhortations in v. 2. It explains why the tent of Zion should be greatly enlarged. The tent metaphor is more broadly explained in this verse as a place for an increasing number of descendents to live. They will "spread out"[477] far and wide in all directions in fulfillment of God's ancient promise to the patriarchs in Gen 28:14. God told Jacob that his seed would spread out to the east, north, and south. The phrase "to the right and to the left" in 54:3 is a similar expression that means that the children (lit. "seed") of Israel will live in the greatly expanded city of Zion, which will explode "in all directions." There will be so many children that they will end up taking possession of property in other nations. Although this might suggest to some that there will be wars in which the Israelites will defeat and dispossess people living in other nations, there is no reference to war in this verse. Thus it is probably better to understand this passage to be describing the peaceful settlement of these additional believers in abandoned cities where no one lives. These images depict an explosive expansion of the people of God, thus assuring the prophet's audience that God cares for them. There is no claim that the Israelites will live in any other specific nation, but if Egyptians, Assyrians (19:18–25), and people from many other nations (2:2–4; 45:22–25) become believers when God sets up his kingdom, one can understand how the people of God will exponentially increase beyond anything that one can imagine. Barrenness and hopelessness will not be a problem, for there will be so many people that there will be no place to put them all.

54:4 Having already stated what the audience should initially do, the prophet now warns his audience about what they should not be tempted to do. The first half of the verse includes two parallel words of instructions. The imperative exhortation "do not fear" (cf. 41:10,13) suggests that the audience may have had some reasons not to believe or accept what God was promising. The fear of failure in the future, the fear that God might not respond right away, or the fear of believing what God said when others were not accepting these promises might have caused some to hesitate in their response. The second

---

[476] Koole, *Isaiah 40–55*, 355–56, translates the כִּי as "truly, surely," but in his discussion of the verse he states that "verse 3a may in fact be a motivation of v.2" suggesting that it is giving a reason, or the כִּי can be asseverative ("truly, surely").

[477] The verb תִּפְרֹצִי can have a rather violent connotation that involved breaking down something (5:5; 2 Chr 25:23), so Goldingay and Payne, *Isaiah 40–55*, 2:343, interpret it in this sense, which is somewhat consistent with the idea of dispossessing other nations in the next line. This is a possible interpretation, though it appears that the passage is not focused on war and the destruction of others; instead, it is explaining the exponential numerical growth; thus "spread out" is preferable.

exhortation, "you should not be ashamed"[478] implies that some people might have some subjective feelings of embarrassment about their past failures or their present condition that would prevent them from stepping out in faith and rejoicing at this point.

Both exhortations are followed by words of reassurance that are intended to help Zion overcome its fears and sense of shame. God promises that they will not feel shame again and will not be disgraced. K. Baltzer recognizes the seriousness of this fear, for shame and disgrace "call into question reputation, dignity, and honor . . . a person's social standing in a group." [479] Although this verse does not explicitly explain the reason for this shame, J. Oswalt provides two ideas that explain why the people might be having these feelings of shame and disgrace: (a) the childlessness of a woman, commonly viewed as reason for shame and humiliation (Gen 16:4; 1 Sam 1:6), and (b) God's failure to protect his people from defeat and exile. J. L. Koole suggests that in the context of chap. 53 one might conclude that "because of the Servant, Zion's guilt and shame are taken away,"[480] so these people do not have any need to feel shame.

The second half of 54:4 begins with another *kî*, "truly, surely (NIV omits it) to emphasize the truth of what is said in the first half of the verse. It relates the nation's shame to the past periods of her youth[481] and her widowhood. Since these are not connected to any specific identifiable events, commentators guess that the disgrace of her youth may refer to the time in Egyptian bondage (Whybray, Muilenburg), the period of the monarchy (Goldingay), or her pagan worship of Baal in the past (Baltzer), while her widowhood is usually connected to Babylonian exile. J. Motyer believes that these comments may just be another way of referring to "the common experience that would cover the whole adult life"[482] of the woman. Rather than focusing on the date or

[478] Both exhortations are mild prohibitions אַל־תִּכָּלְמִי "you should not be ashamed," and each exhortation is followed by a strong prohibition כִּי לֹא תַחְפִּירִי "because [NIV omits "because"] you will not be put to shame."

[479] Baltzer, *Deutero-Isaiah*, 438, believes shame involves a "diminution of quality of life." He connects this shame to false worship since Jeremiah and Ezekiel also connect idolatry as the reason for Israel's shame. J. Stiebert, "Shame and Isaiah," in *The Construction of Shame in the Hebrew Bible*, JSOTSup (Sheffield: Sheffield Academic Press, 2002), 87–109, views shame not in a legal context but "as a consequence of relational breakdown between humans and God because of a breakdown in moral conduct." He is not convinced that an anthropological model of defining shame is adequate because God is the one who gives honor or shame in order to bring about an examination of a person's life and encourage restoration and the removal of shame.

[480] Koole, *Isaiah 40–55*, 359, believes this conclusion is justified by the close connection between chaps. 53 and 54.

[481] A. Schoors, "Two Notes on Isaiah xl-lv," *VT* 21 (1971): 501–5, claims that עֲלוּמַיִךְ "your youth" is not a pejorative word, and that it should be interpreted as "bondage" based on a Ugaritic root.

[482] Motyer, *Isaiah*, 446, would make this as an expression referring to her whole life from youth to adulthood, though he also allows that it might refer specifically to Egyptian bondage and exile.

specific event the prophet might be alluding to, it seems wiser to pay attention to how forgetting these failures will help Zion face the future with optimism. If she continues to think about the sins that caused her husband to punish her in the past, she will feel ashamed, defeated, and worried that the same thing will happen again. By forgetting these past events, she will look at the present possibilities and the future potential more realistically, assuming that God will fulfill all his promises. She should be thinking about the glorious future of the nation that will be wonderful and so amazing and stop dwelling on those difficult days in the past.

54:5 A second reason to substantiate this lack of fear is "because" (*kî*, NIV "for") your Maker, meaning God the Creator, is "your Husband." These titles that define who God is are both plural participle forms. The plural does not refer to many Makers or several Husbands; instead, this is probably a "plural of majesty" (GKC §124k) similar to the plural form on the word "God" (*'elôhîm*). The word "Maker" (from *'āśâ*) refers to God as the one who "acts, does, makes" the world (cf. 43:7; 44:2; 51:13); thus he is all-powerful and can be trusted. God is also called the name "Husband" (from *ba'al*), a root that as a noun can mean "lord, husband" and as a verb can mean "to marry." This word was also used as the name of the Canaanite fertility god Baal,[483] but this god has nothing to do with what the prophet is talking about here. When God is designated as her Husband and Maker, these titles should assure the audience that God has not forgotten about his relationship with Zion. Being a husband also implies love toward his wife and an intimate relationship. Having a husband also creates the possibility of not being barren any longer.

God also has the name and reputation of being "the LORD Almighty," a title that indicates that he is the "Lord of Hosts," the commander of the armies of heaven, so there is no great earthly army that can prevent him from carrying out his will and protecting his own people. This Husband is the "Holy One of Israel" and "your Redeemer," titles that are often paired together (cf. 43:14; 48:17; 49:7). The name "Holy One of Israel" is a favorite one that probably rose to prominence in Isaiah's thinking because of his encounter with the majestic holiness of God sitting on a throne in chap. 6. This name emphasizes God's total otherness, his unapproachable glory, and his separation from sin. This God is totally different from all the man-made pagan gods, and he acts on behalf of his people Israel. As "your Redeemer" (*gō'ălēk*), he functions as a family member who is willing to restore a relative who is in need of redemptions because of some past debt or problem. Finally, the prophet assures his audience in Zion that this is the God who will one day be called the God of the whole earth. God will not be satisfied with ruling over a few thousand people,

---

[483] Goldingay and Payne, *Isaiah 40–55*, 2:346, say, "it would be appropriate enough for the prophet to declare that Yhwh will now finally take the place of Baal in Madam Zion's life."

or just one city or nation; he is the "Lord over all the earth"[484] (Josh 3:11), the
"King of all the earth" (Ps 47:8), for all the earth is his (Exod 19:5). One day all
the earth will see his glory (6:3; 40:5), and one day every knee will bow before
him (45:6,22–25; 49:26) and come to Zion to worship him (2:1–5). Surely, if
God is all this and will do all these things, this is a God the people can trust.

54:6 Now God calls to Zion with comforting words to assure the people
that he still loves them. The initial *kî* is probably not causal "because," but
either asseverative "surely"[485] or concessive "although" (NIV, "if"). In the
NIV Zion is addressed "as if you were a wife deserted and distressed in spirit,"
but this hypothetical interpretation seems unlikely. Because of sin God did
temporarily forsake them, but he did not divorce or permanently reject them
(50:1–3). God promised that he would not permanently forsake them (41:9,17;
42:16), but whenever the people faced a difficulty or a time of war, there were
those who wondered if God had forsaken them (49:14). They expected his
covenant blessings and protection at all times, so how else could they explain
the misfortune that they were enduring. In this situation of trouble, sadness,
and confusion God "will call you,"[486] proving that he has not forsaken Zion
his wife. This implies that he will intervene to help this woman with whom he
developed a covenant relationship when she was a "wife of youth, young wife."
This title would be a reminder of their early honeymoon days when everything
was going great and they were deeply in love. But the next statement about her
being rejected interrupts the positive imagery of the second half of the verse.
The connection between the "wife of youth" and being "rejected" is not clear
because the connector *kî* can be translated in many different ways. C. Westermann translates the imperfect verb as a past and the *kî* as a relative pronoun,
giving "like a wife of youth who has been rejected,"[487] but *kî* does not usually
replace the relative pronoun "who" and his translation of the imperfect verb
("has been rejected") is unlikely. The *kî* is sometimes given either a temporal
meaning "when" or a concessive meaning "although."[488]

---

[484] Watts, *Isaiah 34–66*, 235, takes כָּל־הָאָרֶץ "all the earth" to mean "all the land" of Israel,
but the eschatological nature of this message seems to have broader implications that are worldwide.

[485] GKC §159ee says "the absolute certainty with which a result is to be expected is frequently
emphasized by the insertion of כִּי."

[486] The verb קְרָאֵךְ is probably a perfect which refers to a future event promised by God,
sometimes called a perfect of certainty or a prophetic perfect (GKC §106n). This is probably not
the same root קָרָא "he named" used in v. 5. Goldingay and Payne, *Isaiah 40–55*, 2:347, take a
different approach understanding this to be a present perfect; thus, they view the calling as "happening right now; the verb is another instantaneous *qatal*."

[487] Westermann, *Isaiah 40–66*, 270, and Baltzer, *Deutero-Isaiah*, 432, both translate *kî* as
"who."

[488] Oswalt, *Isaiah 40–66*, 412, chooses "when she is rejected"; Goldingay, *Message of Isaiah
40–55*, 529, "when she has been abandoned"; while Whybray, *Isaiah 40–66*, 186, prefers "although" over when. The NIV gives a periphrastic translation "only to be rejected."

Since none of these options is particularly satisfying and almost all fail to translate the imperfect verb as "she will be rejected," A. Schoors suggests that the *kî* introduces an unreal question to express an absolute certainty, and this solution fits remarkably well in this situation.[489] This interpretation creates a strong contrast between the first saying of God in 6a, which hints at a more negative view of the relationship between God and Zion, and 6b, which describes a positive question by God. The translation of the question in 6b would be: "A wife of youth, would she be rejected?" taking the imperfect verb in a modal sense, which is common in interrogative sentences.[490] Thus the second half denies the supposition in 6a, since the implied answer to the question in 6b is, no she would not be rejected. This understanding of a positive and negative contrast in v. 6 fits the construction of 54:7–8, where vv. 7a and 8a refer to Zion being forsaken, while 7b and 8b refer to God's contrasting compassion and love.

54:7–8   The first half of vv. 7a and 8a admit that "for a brief moment"[491] (cf. Ps 30:5 [Hb. 6]) God forsook his people, an idea that is sometimes connected to the time the people spent in Babylonian exile.[492] This understanding of the 70-year length of the exile is somewhat problematic, for that is hardly "a brief moment," but an earlier interlinking use of this phrase "for a brief moment" in 26:20 suggests that the people need to hide themselves for a brief moment until God's anger was past. In 26:20 this phrase refers to that brief period when God allowed Sennacherib freedom to destroy Judah's 46 fortified cities. After that brief period of wrath was past, God promised that he would come forth and punish Zion's enemies (26:21–27:1), and he did just that in 37:36. It is impossible to determine what the "brief moment" of God's wrath is being referred to in this verse because of the limited amount of information in 54:7, but this earlier situation is a concrete example of the kind of thing the prophet was speaking about. This "brief moment" of "abandonment" in 7a is compared to a "flood/burst of anger"[493] when "I hid my face" in 8a (cf. 8:17). Isaiah 42:25 describes God's act of pouring out his wrath on the nation in similar terms as it suffers the violence of war while 8:7–8 (cf. 17:12–13; 28:2,17) describes the Assyrian occupation of Judah as an overflowing flood.

---

[489] Schoors, *I Am God Your Savior*, 81,84, translates this phrase "A wife of youth, will she ever be rejected?" Elsewhere this kind of question is introduced by אַף כִּי in Gen 3:1 or כִּי in Isa 36:19.

[490] GKC §107t describes the use of modal verbs in interrogative sentences.

[491] The Aramaic Targum has "with a little anger" to provide a more dramatic contrast to God's great compassion in the second half of the verse. The Targum's interpretation seems to be contradicted by v. 8a.

[492] Childs, *Isaiah*, 432, says this refers to the brief period of being forsaken in exile, while Watts, *Isaiah 34–66*, 237, views this as the destruction of Jerusalem. Isa 42:14 refers to the time when God kept silent and did not destroy their enemies as "a long time."

[493] The prophet's writing skill is displayed in the similar sounding בְּשֶׁצֶף קֶצֶף *bĕšeṣep qeṣep* at the beginning of v. 8.

This negative picture of the rocky past relationship between God and Zion is strongly contrasted with the positive future relations envisioned in 7b and 8b. The "small, brief" (qāṭôn) negative time is contrasted with the "greatnesses" (gĕdôlîm) of God's compassion. The root for the word "compassion" is related to the word "womb" (reḥem), so it expresses that maternal compassion a mother has for her child. This is the same term used in 49:13 for the compassion God has for his afflicted ones, and this term will also be used in 55:7 in relationship to God's compassionate forgiveness of those who turn from their sins. In this context God's compassion will motivate him to gather his people. This figure of speech should be interpreted as the reunion of the husband and wife.

A similar strong contrast is found in 8b where the brief moment of anger is set opposite the everlasting "steadfast covenant love" (ḥesed) with which God will "compassionately love" (a verb from rāḥam) Zion. His love will be unfailing, and he will act as their Redeemer (cf. v. 5) by rescuing them from their former situation. Zion does absolutely nothing to deserve or encourage God's act of love. In spite of Zion's past sinful failures, God's love will go far beyond any legal obligation God has to his people through the covenant; this is an eternal love that passionately expresses itself in deep motherly love for those he has chosen. God is their "Redeemer" (gôʾēl), a relative who cares about other members of his family who are in need of help.

54:9–10 This paragraph ends with an illustration that makes a few comparisons between God's present promises to Zion and his past promises back at the time of Noah and the flood. This presents another reason why the people should sing and shout for joy as 54:1 suggests. The initial verbless clause introduces the idea that "the waters[494] of Noah (are) this to me." The clausal comparison with "just as . . . so" (cf. 52:14–15) in 9b carries the essential point that God is trying to make, so the interpreter should be careful not to import extraneous parts of the flood narrative into this verse that are not a part the comparison.[495] This comparison is not about the land being punished by the flood but about God's everlasting promise after the flood. "Just as" (ʾăšer)[496] God swore a promise to Noah that he would never destroy the earth through another great flood in Gen 8:21; 9:11, "so" (kēn) now God has sworn (repeat-

---

[494] NIV has "like the days," which follows the reading of the Targum and 1QIsᵃ כִּימֵי "like the days of" while the MT has כִּי־מֵי "for the waters of" which agrees with the Old Greek. Oswalt, *Isaiah 40–66*, 412, follows the Qumran reading, while Koole, *Isaiah III, Volume 2: Isaiah 49–55*, 369, follows the text of the MT. There is not much difference in the meaning, although the reference to "waters" does remind the reader of God's punishment of the earth at that time.

[495] One should not suggest that the present generation has endured a universal flood, suggest that someone in the present time will play the role of Noah, or expect there to be a new rainbow. The text does not even compare the flood with any present judgment on the nation. Far too many commentators have let their imagination run wild by inserting all kinds of comparisons that are not mentioned in Isaiah.

[496] This use of אֲשֶׁר to mean "just as," which is equivalent to כַּאֲשֶׁר, is discussed in GKC §161b and BDB, 83.

ing the same verb as earlier) that there will come a time when he will not[497] be angry or rebuke[498] them ever again. When God says something, one can count on it because it is true. He will follow through to do what he has said he will do. When God swears or takes an oath about something, the reader can be certain that this will be achieved. In both of these instances sin brought divine judgment, but after the judgment God graciously gave his wonderful promise that describes his future compassionate dealings with his people. But when does this promise apply to Israel? Since the Romans later destroyed Judah and Jerusalem in AD 70 and AD 135 and the city has suffered many further wars in the years since then, this verse could not mean there would never again be war in Jerusalem after the time of the prophet Isaiah. This promise has to be understood in the eschatological context of the proclamation of salvation in chap. 54. When that time comes, God will transform this world and his people, establishing his kingdom of peace for all nations (cf. 2:3–4). The people will turn their spears into farm implements and never learn war again.

In order to further emphasize the absolute confidence the audience should have in God's promises, in 54:10 God compares his rock-solid covenant commitment to his promises to the permanence of immovable parts of nature. The initial *kî* could be translated as a concessive "though, although," though an asseverative meaning ("surely, indeed") is just as defensible.[499] In either case the sentence provides additional assurances that God will do what he says. In order to make this point another dramatic comparison is employed. The mountains and hills are as solid and unmovable as anything known on earth, but when a large earthquake hits, even the rock-solid mountains will shake or totter. Although some texts speak of God's solid control over the world and express this by saying that the earth "cannot be moved" (Ps 93:1; 96:10; 104:5), in other passages God's judgment of the world is so powerful and disruptive that the text pictures God shaking the land and mountains by earthquakes (Job 9:6; Pss 46:2–3; 82:5; Amos 8:8; Isa 13:13; 24:18–20). Thus the point of this text is not to argue whether or not the mountains can shake; it assumes that on very rare occasions God is so powerful that he can shake the seemingly stable mountains. Though this shaking[500] (the movement of the mountains) may seem almost unimaginable, it is far more unimaginable for anything to cause God's "steadfast loving-kindness" (*ḥesed*, as in vs. 8) to "depart, move" (using the same verb

---

[497] The sentence has no negative particle לֹא; instead, the preposition מִן functions as a negative (GKC §119y) as it does in 49:15. If one stops from being angry, one is not angry.

[498] The construct infinitives מִקְּצֹף "without anger" and מִגְּעָר "without rebuke" after "swearing" function as the object of the governing verb (GKC §114m).

[499] Oswalt, *Isaiah 40–66*, 412, translates כִּי as "for," but in his exegetical discussion of the verse he takes the כִּי as "if" in a condition contrary to fact sentence. Thus he translates the clause "If the mountains could depart [which of course, they cannot]" taking the verb as a subjunctive mood. Beuken, "Isaiah LIV," 50, prefers the concessive meaning.

[500] The verbs "move, depart" (from the root מוּשׁ) and "shake" (from the root מוֹט) are used in a modal sense of "may shake" (GKC §107m-r).

ISAIAH 54:10 **486**

used of the mountains above) from his people. Equally firm is God's absolute commitment to "my covenant of peace" which will not "shake, totter"[501] (using the same verb used of the hills above). This is a covenant that is even surer than Noah's everlasting covenant, but the full import of this covenant is not explained. J. Muilenburg suggests that this covenant of peace is related to the peace that the death of the servant mediates (53:5),[502] but chap. 53 does not mention a covenant and does not make an explicit connection with the covenant mentioned in 42:6.[503] Such a connection may be present, but one would feel much more confident about this connection if another verse addressed this issue more directly (cf. 55:3–4). Although the servant's bearing of people's sins will bring peace, the peace in 54:10 should probably be connected to the eschatological peace that will come with God's everlasting kingdom (cf. 52:7). The next paragraph refers to the peace that people will have when they are taught God's law, a peace that suggests that there is a union with God based on the setting described in 2:1–4. The covenant idea is also highlighted in the very next chapter (55:3) where it is connected to the everlasting covenant with David and this must be connected to the peace that the Messiah will bring (9:6–7; Ezek 34:25; 37:25).[504] Peace and salvation will be two of the great characteristics of the kingdom God has prepared for his people. In the last line of v. 10, God assures this audience that God's promise is based on the fact that he is the one "who has compassion on you." In this passage God's love and compassion are two of the prime motivations for his actions toward each person on the earth.

THE GLORIOUS SITUATION IN ZION (54:11–17)

¹¹"O afflicted city, lashed by storms and not comforted,
    I will build you with stones of turquoise,
    your foundations with sapphires.
¹²I will make your battlements of rubies,
    your gates of sparkling jewels,
    and all your walls of precious stones.
¹³All your sons will be taught by the LORD,

---

[501] The NIV translates both of these verbs as passives ("be shaken" and "be moved") throughout this verse, but they are active.

[502] Muilenburg, "Isaiah 40–66," *IB*, 5:638, says, "it is possible that the servant of the Lord was considered by the prophet to be the mediator of the covenant, as in the servant passages" (42:6; 49:8).

[503] Motyer, *Isaiah*, 449, connects covenants with sacrifices (Gen 8:20ff; 15:9–18; Exod 24:4–8; Ps 50.5) and suggests that the text "implies a peace resting on sacrifice—the death of the Servant," but this may read into this text more than one can assume.

[504] On the development of this theme in the ancient Near East, this text and other passages consult B. F. Batto, "The Covenant of Peace: A Neglected Ancient Near Eastern Motif," *CBQ* 49 (1987): 187–211, who connects this covenant with what the eschatological promises of restoration of idyllic conditions in Hos 2:18–25; Ezek 34:25; and 37:26 describe. He then tries to connect these motifs to primeval patterns of "planting peace" in ancient Near Eastern texts from Ugarit and the apocryphal book of 1 Enoch 6–11. D. I. Block, *The Book of Ezekiel 25–48*, 301–305, discusses these Ezekiel texts.

and great will be your children's peace.
¹⁴In righteousness you will be established:
Tyranny will be far from you;
   you will have nothing to fear.
Terror will be far removed;
   it will not come near you.
¹⁵If anyone does attack you, it will not be my doing;
   whoever attacks you will surrender to you.

¹⁶"See, it is I who created the blacksmith
   who fans the coals into flame
   and forges a weapon fit for its work.
And it is I who have created the destroyer to work havoc;
¹⁷no weapon forged against you will prevail,
   and you will refute every tongue that accuses you.
This is the heritage of the servants of the LORD,
   and this is their vindication from me,"
                    declares the LORD.

This paragraph is addressed to the same female figure as 54:1, but in this paragraph she is pictured as a city with gates and walls (54:11). After re-identifying the addressee, a new word from God is announced with "behold, I myself" (*hinnēh ʾānôkî*, 54:11b).[505] Isaiah 54:11–17 is linguistically interlinked with 54:1–10 by a common reference to "children, sons" (54:1,13), "no fear" (54:4,14), "peace" (54:10,13), and "create" (54:5,16). This new paragraph is a continuation of a proclamation of salvation[506] that describes eschatological events (not when the people return from exile). It explains the glories of the New Jerusalem in terms of its natural beauty, its internal spiritual dynamics, and its protection from all those who might attack it. The structure of this paragraph is:

The physical glory of Jerusalem	54:11–12
The addressee	11a
The ornamentation of the city	11b–12
The spiritual state of the city	54:13–14
Protection from oppression	54:15–17
Enemy attacks will fail	15
No weapon will prevail	16–17a
Conclusion	17b[507]

---

[505] Spykerboer, *Structure and Composition of Deutero-Isaiah*, 180, views the הִנֵּה in 54:11 "as a connecting particle with a demonstrative function," while Goldingay and Payne, *Isaiah 40–55*, 2:339, suggest that this term "reinforces the impression of resumptiveness," meaning the divine word that began in 54:1 is once again being resumed in 54:11.

[506] Schoors, *I Am God Your Savior*, 140, calls this passage a proclamation of salvation, but he recognizes that the structure is somewhat unusual.

[507] Watts, *Isaiah 34–66*, 241, puts v. 17b with 55:1–56:8, but it makes an excellent conclusion for chap. 54. Goldingay, *Message of Isaiah 40–55*, 543, does the same thing.

A unified theme plus a couple internal markers hold this paragraph together. Both 54:11b and 54:16 have new announcements by God starting with "behold, I myself," plus the emphasis on "righteousness" is repeated in 54:14 and 17. The paragraph ends with a concluding statement about what God's "servants" will inherit. As a whole this paragraph presents a great deal of hope about the future of Jerusalem and the people who will inhabit it. It will be glorious, it will be characterized by righteousness, and it will be secure from outside attack.

54:11a   The paragraph begins addressing the present people of Zion long before the glory of Jerusalem will be experienced as a reality. At this time they are "miserable, afflicted" (as in 49:13; 51:21) people, indicating that they are probably the same group of people addressed in 54:1. She is "storm tossed"[508] and has not yet experienced the comfort or compassion of God promised in earlier verses (40:1; 49:13; 51:3,12; 52:9).[509] From the limited nature of the evidence in 54:1 and 11, it is impossible to identify a specific setting or date for this message, but one should not assume that this has anything to do with the people in exile.[510] In fact, the references to people attacking Jerusalem in 54:14–17 might hint that this was a time of war when some strong tyrant was terrorizing them. Whatever the setting, God knows what the people are experiencing, but at this point he has not intervened to bring victory.

54:11b–12   Suddenly a positive promise is introduced with "behold, I myself" (*hinnēh ʾānōkî*). God is announcing his bold plans for the glorification of the city of Jerusalem. God is promising that he will step into the affairs of this miserable city and transform it with his power, creativity, and grace. W. A. M. Beuken notes that these verses have some similarity with Neo-Babylonian royal building inscriptions, though God and not a human king will build Zion.[511] In order to help these people visualize the extent of this change, God describes for his audience the external beauty of the eschatological walls of Jerusalem (not the walls Nehemiah built). First, he describes the foundation. God will set[512] your stones in "antimony" (*pûk*, NIV "turquoise"), a black

---

[508] The *qal* participle סֹעֲרָה is related to the noun סַעַר "storm, tempest, storm winds."

[509] Baltzer, *Deutero-Isaiah*, 448–50, has the strange idea that the three terms in 54:11a are actually three names of the goddess Anat of the Baal Epic; thus he makes 54:1–10 and this section a "dispute with the Baal-Anat Cult." He finds the name Anat hidden under the first term עֲנִיָּה *ʿāniyyâ*, but this whole approach seems very unlikely.

[510] Whybray, *Isaiah 40–55*, 188, believes that this "oracle of salvation take up the exiles' own complaints." Beuken, "Isaiah LIV," 55, believes the afflicted are the exiles in Babylon and those not comforted are the people who stayed in Jerusalem. "The woman represents the two groups of Israel's population."

[511] Ibid., 57. These building inscriptions often mention the kings name, then a description of how terrible the buildings were, a statement of how wonderfully he restored them, and a concluding prayer for the preservation of this building and the king's dynasty. He demonstrates that both this passage and ancient Near Eastern building inscriptions include (a) laying a firm foundation—v. 14; (b) no fear of enemies—v. 14; (c) weapons of enemies will be powerless—v. 17; (d) the well-being of their children—v. 17. He calls this a "foundation oracle" which promises God's blessing.

[512] The participle מַרְבִּיץ means "to stretch out, lie down" when it is used of cattle (Gen 29:2;

powder product that was used for mortar in setting stones in the construction of the original temple (1 Chr 29:2).[513] God himself promises, "I will set you" in "lapis lazuli, sapphires."[514] The next object decorated or made of rubies is difficult to interpret. The word is derived from the word "sun" (*šemeš*), but it is unclear what this refers to on the external walls of a city. Possibly this is something round that reflects the sun like a "shining shield"[515] on a wall or possibly this is the high "battlements, pinnacles" on the wall that the sun hits first when it rises in the morning? The gates will have sparking jewels imbedded in them and "your borders" (*gĕbûlēk*, NIV "walls") will have precious stones. This imagery is later picked up in Rev 21:18–21. This would be a glorious city, far beyond the wildest imagination of any Israelite.[516] G. K. Beale believes the whole city will become a temple; thus he understands the wonderful walls of precious stones in Rev and Isa 54:11–12 to be the walls of the temple.[517]

54:13–14 This transformation will also include a dramatic change in the spiritual atmosphere in Jerusalem. The statement that all "your sons"[518] will be taught by God reminds one of the picture of many foreign people coming to Zion to be taught by God in 2:3 and the Servant of the Lord who was instructed by God (50:4). This was one of the fundamental reasons for the nation's problems throughout the years. They were blind and would not listen to what God was saying (cf. 6:9–10; 29:9–10; 30:9). If they had only paid attention (48:17–18) to God's instruction, things would be quite different for the nation. A few earlier prophecies also told of a future day when the people's ears would be open and they would listen to God their teacher (29:18; 30:20–21; 32:3–4; 35:5; 42:17). This prophecy must relate to those events, and it is assumed that this learning will dramatically change the lives of these children. This assumption is verified because God's teaching will produce good results in the lives

---

Exod 23:5), wild beasts (Gen 49:9; Isa 11:6; 12:21), and of people who are like sheep (Ezek 34:14), so it is a little odd to have this term used of causing stones "to lie down to rest," as if they were living objects. Oswalt, *Isaiah 40–66*, 427, translates "*set . . . your stones* (lit 'couch your stones') probably means put them in a jeweler's setting."

[513] Second Kgs 9:30 indicates that this black powder was also used by women as an eyelid mascara.

[514] Some think this might refer to the famous blue *lapis lazuli* stones that were commonly used in ancient times in the design of artwork for royal palaces. G. A. Cooke, *A Critical and Exegetical Commentary of the Book of Ezekiel*, ICC (New York: Scribners, 1937), 21, maintains that sapphire "was almost unknown before the time of the Roman Empire."

[515] Koole, *Isaiah III, Volume 2: Isaiah 49–55*, 383, translates "your shields."

[516] North, *Second Isaiah*, 252, suggests this is a picture of God's bride, Zion, all dressed up like a beautiful woman.

[517] Beale, *Temple and the Church's Mission*, 132–33, 365–72.

[518] 1QIsᵃ has "your builders" בוניכי which is more connected to the content of 54:11–12, though there is no reason to question the text of MT "your sons" בָּנַיִךְ, which is repeated again at the end of v. 13. Westermann, *Isaiah 40–66*, 276, accepts the reading of the Qumran Scrolls as superior. Whybray, *Isaiah 40–66*, 189, takes the second reference to sons at the end of the verse as "your builders."

of his people. Instead of continuing in war, affliction, and no comfort like the present generation (54:11a), all their sons will have great peace. The dimensions of this peace are not explained in detail in this verse, but this peace probably is related to the "covenant of peace" (54:10) that God will make with his people when he has compassion on them. This peace likely relates to the peace in Zion (52:7) that will come when the good news of God's salvation is proclaimed and God reigns as King from Zion. Then there will be no fear, for the people will dwell in Zion together with God in perfect unity. The Servant's bearing of the sins of others also has to be a factor that enables there to be peace with God (53:5).

In 54:14 this new city will be founded[519] on "righteousness," a theological principle that the city will be named after in 1:26 ("City of Righteousness"). The coming of righteousness and justice is connected to the outpouring of the Spirit in 32:16–17 and the exaltation of the Lord in 33:5. It is only God who can bring salvation and righteousness to Zion (46:13). In many ways God's righteousness and his salvation are overlapping concepts (51:6b,13). When righteousness reigns in Zion, the world of oppression, tyranny, fear, destruction, and terror will be a thing of the past. This will be a new world without war and evil (cf. 2:4). This promises a level of security never known before, for God will be in this transformed city of Zion and his righteousness and peace will impact every area of life. This is an eschatological promise that embodies Israel's hope; it is not a promise of what life will be like in the time of Isaiah or after the exile.

54:15　　The final few verses deal with the hypothetical potential of being attacked by some outside military force. Since the previous verses promise peace and the absence of oppression, the *hēn* that begins v. 15 must be the conditional "if,"[520] not the more frequently used "behold." The hypothetically conditional part of the sentence assures the audience that if perchance one "actually made war"[521] against Zion, this will not be God's doing.[522] The point is not that God is no longer in charge of what happens on earth; God seems to be saying that he will no longer have any need to send enemies to judge his people since they are righteous. The second half of the verse explains what will happen to the person who might hypothetically attack or make trouble for Zion. "Whoever"

---

[519] The root כוּן is in the *hithpaʿal* form (the ת is assimilated; GKC §54c), which in this root can have a reflexive or passive meaning (GKC §54g).

[520] GKC §159w classifies הֵן meaning "if" as "a pure Aramaism . . . since the Aramaic word never had the meaning *behold*."

[521] The root גּוּר is not root I "to sojourn" (this is accepted by Delitzsch, "Prophecies of Isaiah," 351) but root II "to cause trouble, make war, attack." The syntactical formation of a finite verb with an infinitive absolute (גּוֹר יָגוּר) strengthens the verbal idea by either emphasizing the certainty, forcibleness, or completeness of the event (GKC §113n-o).

[522] The difficult אֶפֶס מֵאוֹתִי literally says "it is not from me" (cf. 5:8) or "nothing (is) from me."

($m\hat{\imath}$)[523] might[524] attack/make war with you (Zion), will fall "because of you"
or "fall, surrender to you." Since God has already promised that these violent
activities will not happen in 54:14, these hypothetical examples only provide
an additional sense of security and assurance that God will protect his people
from all danger.

54:16–17a The final two verses reemphasize God's omnipotence over
everything that happens (expanding on 14–15), thus providing one more assurance to the audience. This verse begins like 54:11 with "behold, I myself"
(*hinnēh 'ānōkî*), making it absolutely clear who created the "blacksmith, craftsman" (*ḥārāš*) who has the skill to make metal objects of war (1 Sam 13:19). He
makes these weapons of war by blowing on coals of fire to make it hot enough
to mold or shape an instrument (a spear or a sword) in accordance with his
handiwork. Presumably this is saying that God creates these skillful people
in Israel and in the foreign nations that might fight against God's people. Of
course God is also the one who has to create "the one who destroys, ravages"
things. So if there are going to be any vicious attacks in the future, God is going to have to create someone with the ability to make weapons and another
person who is going to know how to use those weapons to destroy others. One
way of stopping all this fighting then is for God not to create such persons. His
sovereign ability to create or not create enables him to have full control of the
future.

Verse 17a concludes this argument by giving the people of Zion an all-
inclusive assurance of God's sovereign control of every possible situation that
might arise. Specifically, what will God do about the weapons that already exist or the crude weapons that might be formed by someone who is not a skilled
blacksmith? Or what will God do with those destructive people that already
live on the earth? To answer these hypothetical problems God promises that
"all instruments" (there are no exception) that "might be formed"[525] (no matter who formed them in the past) for purpose of fighting against you, will not
succeed in accomplishing what they were made to do. God will intervene and
make these weapons ineffective in penetrating[526] what they were meant to destroy. In the same vein God promises that his people will be able to refute "every tongue" (every statement) that might hypothetically rise up against them

---

[523] The מִי is probably not functioning as an interrogative pronoun but as an indefinite pronoun
(GKC §137c).

[524] In order to make this sentence in some sense equivalent to the first hypothetical situation,
one can suggest that the subjunctive ("might, may, could") sense of the perfect is being used to
represent actions that are not real but hypothetically possible (GKC §106p).

[525] The imperfect יוּצַר is understood as a subjunctive expressing what "might" happen (GKC
§107m-r).

[526] Koole, *Isaiah III, Volume 2: Isaiah 49–55*, 396, claims that the concrete meaning of יִצְלָח
is "to penetrate," so if a weapon fails to penetrate what it is aimed at, it will not succeed in doing
any harm. Seldom does this word have this literal meaning; it usually means "success, prosper,
accomplish, finish."

to justify bringing judgment against the people of Zion. At this time there will be no slander, mockery, or false testimony against Zion. His care and protection are complete, so there is no reason for Zion to worry about God's future plans.

54:17b   The conclusion to this paragraph[527] and chapter is that the things mentioned in this message are the inalienable inheritance that the people of Zion will receive. Although this concept of an inheritance was traditionally connected to receiving the land of Palestine as their possession (Gen 15:7–8; 17:8; 28:4; Deut 4:1,21; Isa 49:8), now the heritage of the nation includes children (54:1), an enlarged tent to the left and right (54:2), promises of no shame (54:4), God's compassion (54:8), God's unfailing love and covenant of peace (54:10), a bejeweled city (54:11–12), sons taught by God (54:13), and divine protection (54:14–17a). These possessions are much more valuable than a small piece of real estate in the Middle East because they involve the unending implications of being recipients of God's compassion and love. But this is not all that God promises his people. The final line adds that "their righteousness" will come from God. The exact semantic meaning of the term "righteousness" is not agreed on; therefore, J. Calvin connects righteousness to "their right. . . . The Lord will defend his people,"[528] NIV, NASB, RSV use "vindication," and E. J. Young proposes "salvation."[529] The use of this same term in v. 14a and here refers to the restoration of a right relationship with God, which is made possible by God. It entails all that God has done to justify his people, including the removal of their sins through the death of the servant of the Lord (52:13–53:12). Each of the above translations touches on various aspects of what God did to bring his people into a right relationship with him, so a broad inclusive term like "salvation" seems most appropriate.

These blessings will be the inheritance of the "servants of the Lord" (this is the first time this term is used), a plural term that refers to a group of people who act like the singular "Servant of the Lord." They are the righteous in Zion who will enjoy God's coming kingdom. This term will be used repeatedly in the following chapters (56:6; 63:17; 65:8–15; 66:14) to distinguish the wicked from the righteous "servants of the Lord" who will follow God, serve him, worship him, and inherit the blessings of his kingdom.

---

[527] Goldingay and Payne, *Isaiah 40–55*, 2:363, puts 54:17b in with chap. 55:1–13; thus, 54:17b is the beginning of this new paragraph. They are following the section divisions marked in 1QIs[a]; thus, they reject the idea that 17b is a summary appraisal or conclusion to chap. 54.

[528] Calvin, "Book of the Prophet Isaiah," *Calvin's Commentaries*, 153, connects this word to God's "guardianship and protection."

[529] Young, *Book of Isaiah*, 3:373, says, "the servants of the Lord receive the wondrous salvation herein depicted as the free gift of God's grace."

(3) God's Grace and Covenant Bring Joy to the Repentant Sinners (55:1–13)

This chapter completes the long section of chaps. 40–55, as well as the shorter section of 53:13–55:13. Following a pattern somewhat similar to the promises and the imperative invitations to a feminine singular audience Zion in chap. 54, this chapter has additional divine promises and imperative exhortations to a masculine plural audience (to "everyone" in 55:1, which goes beyond "the servants of the Lord" in 54:17) to encourage them to respond to God's invitation to enjoy his abundant blessings. The connections between chaps. 54 and 55 are evident in the common reference to (a) joy and singing at the beginning (54:1) and at the end of these two chapters (55:12–13), (b) the coming of peace in 54:10,13; 55:12, (c) God's compassion on his people (54:7–8,10; 55:7), (d) God's love (54:10; 55:3), (e) God's covenant (54:10; 55:3), and (f) a new relationship with the nations (54:3; 55:4–5). The theological issues no longer focus on any of the present problems the nation was enduring; instead, attention is concentrated on the free food and water that are available, an everlasting covenant through a Davidic leader, forgiveness of sins, joy, and the fulfillment of all of God's promises. These seem to be eschatological promises that God will provide for the people living in the New Jerusalem where he will reign as king.[530] The structure of this chapter is divided into two paragraphs:

Invitation to participate in God's provisions and covenant	55:1–5
Invitation to repent and see God's words fulfilled	55:6–13

The repetition of a series of invitations at the beginning of both paragraphs suggests that there is some relationship between repentance (55:6–7) and the reception of God's blessings (55:1–3). There also seems to be a connection between the everlasting covenant (55:3b) and the everlasting sign (55:13b) at the end of each of these paragraphs.

The final paragraph (55:6–13) also functions as something of an epilogue, matching the prologue of 40:1–11 at the beginning of this long literary unit. The means by which God would offer comfort in chap. 40:1 is now clear. Now the people know how their sins will be paid for (40:2; 53:1–12; 55:6–7), now they understand that they do not need to fear the foreign nations, for they are nothing. In fact, many from the nations will come to acknowledge and worship God (40:6–7; 45:22–28; 52:15; 55:5). Now they know that God will do what he has said (40:8b; 55:11), and now they know that the glad tidings about the transformation of sinful Zion are truly something to shout about (40:9–11; 54:1; 55:12–13).[531] The final verses of chap. 55 are in the form of a hymn;

---

[530] H. C. Spykerboer, "Isaiah 55:1–5: The Climax of Deutero-Isaiah," in *The Book of Isaiah: Le Livre D'Isaïe*, ed. J. Vermeylen (Leuven: Peeters, 1989), 357–59, follows Eising's understanding that chap. 55 is referring to the transformation that will take place in the New Jerusalem.

[531] Goldingay, *Message of Isaiah 40–55*, 543, suggests that 55:6–9 form an *inclusio* with 40:6–8; 55:10–11 forms an *inclusio* with 40:3–5; and 55:12–13 is a paradoxical pairing with 40:1–2,

thus 55:12–13 mark the end of a literary unit, just as the hymns did in 12:1–6; 42:10–13; 44:23; 49:13; 52:9–10.

INVITATION TO PARTICIPATE IN GOD'S PROVISIONS AND COVENANT (55:1–5)

¹"Come, all you who are thirsty,
    come to the waters;
and you who have no money,
    come, buy and eat!
Come, buy wine and milk
    without money and without cost.
²Why spend money on what is not bread,
    and your labor on what does not satisfy?
Listen, listen to me, and eat what is good,
    and your soul will delight in the richest of fare.
³Give ear and come to me;
    hear me, that your soul may live.
I will make an everlasting covenant with you,
    my faithful love promised to David.
⁴See, I have made him a witness to the peoples,
    a leader and commander of the peoples.
⁵Surely you will summon nations you know not,
    and nations that do not know you will hasten to you,
because of the LORD your God,
    the Holy One of Israel,
    for he has endowed you with splendor."

Although chaps. 54 and 55 are closely interrelated, the sustenance and covenant mentioned in 55:1–5 are not offered to just people from Zion; they are available to everyone who comes to partake, including the nations (55:5). An initial cluster of twelve imperative or jussive verbs communicates a strong sense of encouragement and urgency in 55:1–3. God announces that he is freely giving the necessities of life and an everlasting covenant consistent with his promises to David (55:3b). Then in two "behold" (*hēn*) clauses (55:4–5) God explains how this everlasting covenant will impact the nation in terms reminiscent of the work of the Servant of the Lord in 42:1–6; 49:5–8. The structure of this paragraph is divided into two parts:[532]

| God's gracious invitation to freely eat | 55:1–3a |
| The impact of the everlasting covenant | 55:3b–5 |

Interpreters have suggested three possible backgrounds for the imagery of this paragraph: (a) the call of Lady Wisdom to those who pass by to enter her

---

but it seems better to focus on specific repetition of vocabulary or a theme and connect 55:10–11 with 40:8b.

[532] M. C. A. Korpel, "Metaphors in Isaiah LV," *VT* 46 (1996): 43–55, finds three sub-sections (1–5, 6–9,10–13), each having two sections.

house and eat of her truth (cf. Prov 9:1–8),[533] (b) the call of a water seller in the market place,[534] or (c) the invitation to a royal banquet (Davidic or a universal cultic feast).[535] Each of these settings has an appeal for people to come and partake of something, but the wisdom and market backgrounds do not furnish much insight into God's offering of a covenant to all nations (55:5). Thus an invitation to join a feast to celebrate the acceptance of a new covenant relationship seems the most fitting comparative analogy (cf. Exod 24). The Davidic background of this idea will be traced in the context of 55:3–5.[536] Thus the purpose of the message of 55:1–5 is to encourage people to accept God's invitation and to "listen to me . . . come to me" (55:2–3).

55:1–2a The person extending the invitation to come and eat is unknown until v. 3. It is God who is speaking in 3b, for he is the only one who could legitimately offer an everlasting covenant.[537] The plural verbs[538] indicate that God's invitation is to many different individuals, to "everyone" (*kôl*), or to the "servants of the Lord" in 54:17, not just to a singular group known as Zion or to a single individual. The first word "oh!" (*hôy*, omitted in NIV) is most frequently used in contexts where God is bringing judgment and people are lamenting their "woe" (*hôy*), but here it is just an interjection of surprise to gain people's attention.[539] Three times people are encouraged to "come" (*lĕkû*),

---

[533] J. Begrich, *Studien zu Deuterojesaja* (Munich: Chr. Kaiser Verlag, 1963), 59–61, makes the connection to Prov 9:1–12 and Sirach 24:19–21, but wisdom is usually not viewed positively in the rest of the book of Isaiah (cf. 47:10).

[534] P. Volz, *Jesaia II*, KAT 9 (Leipzig: Scholl, 1932), 138, first suggested the idea of a water seller. Westermann, *Isaiah 40–66*, 281–2, discusses the combining of these options.

[535] J. A. Sanders, "Isaiah 55:1–9," *Int* 32 (1978): 291–95, states that using "the traditional words of invitation to David's royal banquet, the prophet calls dispossessed Israel in Babylonian exile (around 540 BC) to a new role, a new identity, and a new mission." Verses 1–2 mimic the heralds of the king calling the people to the king's annual banquet of enthronement; they heard these words as "a new call from God to a new life." R. J. Clifford, "Isaiah 55: An Invitation to a Feast," *The Word of the Lord Shall Go Forth: Essays in Honor of D. N. Freedman in Celebration of His Sixtieth Birthday*, ed. C. L. Meyers and M. O'Conner (Winona Lake: Eisenbrauns, 1983), 27–35, finds parallels with a Ugaritic royal banquet and views 55:1–5 as a universal invitation to a cultic feast in the presence of God.

[536] W. Brueggemann, "Isaiah 55 and Deuteronomic Theology," *ZAW* 80 (1968): 191–203, interprets chap. 55 as a reaffirmation of his Davidic promises, taking up calls for people to seek God in Deut 4:29–31 and 1 Kings 8.

[537] S. Paganini, "Who Speaks in Isaiah 55.1? Notes on the Communication Structure of Isaiah 55," *JSOT* 30 (2005): 83–92, suggests that the Lady Zion is answering God, after being addressed in chap. 54. He bases this on what he interprets as a second fem. sg. pronominal suffix (ךְ‍ַ) in the last word in 55:5. This same Hebrew form can be interpreted as a second masc. pronominal suffix when it is in pause (GKC §58g), a preferable interpretation in this case. C. Baltzer, *Deutero-Isaiah*, 468, believes Lady Zion is beckoning the people to make a pilgrimage to Zion because Beuken noted that elsewhere God does not call people to "come to me."

[538] The imperatives לְכוּ, שִׁבְרוּ and אֱכֹלוּ are second masc. pl. imperatives used to exhort or admonish someone to act (GKC §110a).

[539] In Isa 1:4; 5:8,11,18,20,21,22; 10:1,5; 18:1; 28:1; 29:1,15; 30:1; 31:1; 33:1; 45:9,10 the word הוֹי means "woe" in a lament context relating to the judgment of someone, but in 1:24; 17:12; 55:1 הוֹי seems to be more of an exclamation (as in Zech 2:10,11; Jer 47:6).

twice they are encouraged to "buy grain" (*šibrû*), and once they are told to "eat" (*ʾĕkōlû*), but nothing much is known about their setting.[540] These products are the necessities of life that enable people to live, and 55:3a promises life to those who come. The water that God will provide might be connected to the water that will flow from eschatological Jerusalem (12:3; 33:20; Ps 46:4; Ezek 47:12; Joel 3:18; Zech 13:1; 14:8), to God himself who was a "fountain of life" (Ps 36:8–9), or to the "gently flowing waters of Shiloh" (a metaphor for God) that was rejected[541] (8:6; cf. Jer 2:13). Although this approach, which attempts to find a spiritual metaphorical equivalent makes sense with water,[542] it does not seem to work so well with the other commodities mentioned. Thus the abundant water, grain, wine, and milk appears to picture the blessings that God will pour out on the new jeweled city that was described in chap. 54. This is an amazing prophecy, consistent with the fertile world that Hos 2:21–23; Amos 9:13–14; Joel 2:19,23–24; and Ezek 34:25–31 describe in some detail.[543] The surprising factor in these exhortations is not the call to come and eat; it is the statement that "all" are invited and that all these things can be enjoyed for "no silver/money" (repeated three times). This is a complete reversal of their past experience, for previously it was commonly thought that God's blessings would fall only on the few who were his select chosen people and that every purchase would require a monetary (or moral) prerequisite. Now God indicates that he will freely supply all the needs of everyone, just as he offered his full salvation to all nations in 45:23–25.

In 2a the audience is encouraged not "to weigh out" clumps of silver (coined money was not invented until the Persian era) to pay for commodities that will not nourish a person. They were not to weary themselves[544] (NIV "labor") with what does not give true satisfaction. Why would anyone bother to do that? This admonition implies that some might be tempted to or already had looked for satisfaction in the wrong place. Since these verses are quite metaphorical,

---

[540] Muilenburg, "Isaiah 40–66," *IB*, 5:644, echoes thoughts similar to Whybray, *Isaiah 40–66*, 190, when he says that "Yahweh addresses his people, urging them to detach themselves from the involvement with the daily life in Babylon and to accept the promise he gives," but where is there any mention of the Babylonian way of life in these verses? Koole, *Isaiah III, Volume 2: Isaiah 49–55*, 405, refers to the "thirsty" as "the exiles are far from Zion in unsatisfactory conditions; they are in want," but where is their location found in these verses?

[541] Seitz, "Isaiah 40–66," *NIB*, 6:481, connects the water imagery specifically to 8:6 and sees it as the opposite of themes communicated in chaps. 6–8. The Aramaic Targum understands the "thirsty" to be those who want to learn and Ibn Ezra interprets the water as the Torah, while some of the Church Fathers saw this as an invitation to be baptized in water.

[542] In 44:3 the pouring out of water is compared to the pouring out of the Spirit. Other passages which use material things to communicate spiritual reality include Deut 8:3; Ps 42:1–2; 63:1; 143:6.

[543] Spykerboer, *Structure and Composition of Deutero-Isaiah*, 180–81, views this as a picture of the fertility of the new Zion.

[544] The verb יָגַע means "he wearied" in 40:28; 43:22, probably through excessive labor or stress; the noun refers to the work, or results of wearing oneself.

one might guess that this is a warning not to depend on laboring for material things for true spiritual satisfaction, not to weary themselves with worship that is just empty laborious ritual, or possibly not to try to find spiritual food for the soul from serving false gods.[545]

55:2b–3a Every person should "listen diligently"[546] to what God advises and eat the "good" things that he provides. Since what God offers is "good," what other sources offer must be bad or a least unsatisfactory and unfulfilling. The results of eating will not be a full stomach; instead, God promises that your soul "will delight"[547] in God's abundance and riches. At this point the imagery of eating food begins to fade away, and the spiritual reality of what the prophet was talking about begins to become clearer.

This subparagraph ends in 3a with a summarizing statement that fundamentally repeats 2b by emphasizing the call for a response. The audience will be able to partake of God's blessings only if they make the effort to listen to what God says and come to him. The old ways of being stubborn with closed ears and blind eyes (cf. 6:9–10) must be a thing of the past. If they want to be part of God's glorious kingdom "so that" they may live,[548] they must listen to God's offer and respond to God's gracious invitation to enjoy his feast. Thus this invitation has nothing to do with eating literal food, for God is prepared to impart his spiritual food that will completely transform their souls.

55:3b God also offers to cut an eternal covenant with "you" (pl.). The act of cutting reminds the reader of the tradition of "cutting up"[549] animals that accompanied the act of making a covenant (cf. Gen 15:9–21; Jer 34:18–20). This covenant is probably identical to the "covenant of peace" in 54:10, a covenant that promises to bring God's "unfailing love" and compassion. This is an everlasting covenant that extends unendingly into the future with no cut-off point. This means that the covenant is sure, lasting, and 100 percent dependable. In order to understand what this covenant is all about it is necessary to investigate

---

[545] Koole, *Isaiah III, Volume 2: Isaiah 49–55*, 408, and several other commentators believe that the background for understanding this oracle is the secularization of Israelites in Babylon who had assimilated Babylonian religion. There seems to be little in this oracle that suggests this background. This hypothetical understanding of the background appears to be the result of various assumptions or an overactive imagination.

[546] The Hebrew construction of an infinitive absolute after an imperative verb (שָׁמֹועַ שִׁמְעוּ) reinforces or strengthens the meaning of the verb (GKC §113n).

[547] The *hithpa'el* verb וְהִתְעַנַּג comes from עָנֵג "he refreshed, delighted," and it points to the need for people to spiritually delight themselves in all the wonderful riches that God provides.

[548] The imperfect verb with a *waw* וּתְחִי functions as a final clause (GKC §165b) to express purpose or results. GKC §111,i-l also discusses the use of the imperfect with *waw* consecutive "to express a logical or necessary consequence of that which immediately precedes" by employing the introductory "so that."

[549] What looks like an unusual imperfect verb form אֶכְרְתָה, because it has a final ה at the end, is a cohortative that shows emphatic determination or strong resolve to accomplish something (GKC §113n). Thus, one might translate 3b "I will surely make an everlasting covenant with you" or "I am determined to make an everlasting covenant with you."

how this covenant relates to other references to everlasting covenants as well
as its relationship to God's "everlasting salvation" (45:17; 51:6,8), "everlasting
joy" (51:11), and "everlasting kindness" (54:8). God's covenant with Noah is
mentioned in 54:9. God promised in Gen 8–9, "Never again will I curse the
ground because of man . . . never again will all life be cut off by the waters
of a flood." God promised "a covenant with all generations to come . . . the
everlasting covenant between God and all living creatures of every kind on the
earth" (Gen 8:21; 9:8–16). Nevertheless, that covenant seems to have no relationship with this everlasting covenant in 55:3. God also made an "everlasting
covenant" with Abram and his descendents in Gen 17:7,9–10,13 (cf. 51:1–2),
but there is not much overlapping vocabulary that would indicate that this covenant is directly connected to Abram's covenant. The one connection that does
exist with Abram's covenant is that both covenants involve God's blessing on
all nations through the seed of Abraham (55:4–5; Gen 12:3).

The reference to David in 55:3b naturally causes one to make a connection
with the Davidic covenant where God says, "I will establish the throne of his
kingdom forever . . . my love will never be taken away from him. . . . Your
house and your kingdom will endure forever before me; your throne will be
established forever" (2 Sam 7:13,15,16). Among the many promises to David
in Ps 89:28–29, God says that "I will maintain my love to him forever, and my
covenant with him will never fail. I will establish his line forever, his throne as
long as the heavens endure." Psalm 132:12 also states that "if your sons keep
my covenant and the statutes that I teach them, then their sons will sit on your
throne for ever and ever." In some passages that deal with the Davidic covenant,
there are requirements that the Davidic rulers must listen to and follow in order
for God's covenant promises to be fulfilled. Consequently there is considerable
discussion over whether one should translate the last line of 55:3b something
like "my faithful love promised to David" (NIV). This approach suggests that
the construct use of "David" is an objective genitive[550] ("to/for David") and
that it is God who gives "my faithful love promised to David" through his eternal covenant. But the word "my" in the phrase "my faithful love" is not in the
Hebrew text, and it is equally possible to view the construct use of "David" as
a subjective genitive which suggests that it is David's faithful acts of lovingkindness (his keeping of the covenant) that will enable the everlasting covenant
to be established by God. This does not mean that David earns this covenant
through his obedience and faithfulness; it just means that God is able to pour

---

[550] Those arguing for an objective genitive include H. G. M. Williamson, "'The Sure Mercies
of David': Subjective or Objective Genitive?" *JSS* 23 (1978): 31–49; W. C. Kaiser, "The Unfailing
Kindnesses Promised to David: Isaiah 55:3," *JSOT* 45 (1989): 91–98; H. Stoebe, "חֶסֶד *ḥesed*,"
TLOT, ed. E. Jenni and C. Westermann (Peabody: Hendrickson, 1997), 449–64. Those arguing for
a subjective genitive include A. Caquot, "Les 'Graces de David.' A Propos d'Isaïe 55/3b," *Semitica*
15 (1965): 45–59; W. A. M. Beuken, "Isa. 55,3–5: The Reinterpretation of David," *Bejdragen* 35
(1975): 49–64; P. J. Gentry, "Rethinking the 'Sure Mercies of David' in Isaiah 55:3," 279–304.

out his blessings and fulfill his promises only when a Davidic king faithfully follows God's instructions on how to live righteously and faithfully.

The choice between these two options (God's lovingkindness or David's faithful lovingkindness) in not an easy one. On the one hand, when the word "lovingkindness of" is in a construct relationship with another noun, that noun is usually the agent or subject of the action (the lovingkindness of God equals God's lovingkindness). Thus when the construct relationship in Ps 89:1 refers to the "LORD's great love," it is a good English translation of the literal "the lovingkindness of the LORD." This would be similar to translating Isa 55:3 as "the lovingkindness of David," a subjective genitive.[551] The text that is most parallel to Isa 55:3 is 2 Chr 6:42, but it has been used to support both interpretations of the genitive (the subjective genitive and the objective use of the genitive). A study of the grammar of this phrase argues for translating this phrase as a subjective genitive "the lovingkindness of David."[552] But this initial conclusion is complicated by the fact that we have many texts emphasizing God's acts of lovingkindness to David and only a few referring to David's lovingkindness (read Ps 89), so there is a natural tendency to think that this is referring to God's lovingkindness. Nevertheless, David and his sons were required to love and serve God as part of the Davidic covenant relationship or there would be divine correction (2 Sam 7:14; Ps 89:30–33). Thus there were both human and divine obligations of faithfulness in this covenant. Specifically, the human king must follow God's law and not violate God's decrees (Ps 89:30–33), which is consistent with God's instructions for the king in Deut 17:14–20.[553] Solomon knew that his father's faithfulness was a pivotal factor in God's blessings (1 Kgs 3:6,14; 9:4–5; 11:4,6; 2 Chr 6:14; Ps 132:12), and this factor plays a primary role in God's blessing or judgment of different rulers throughout the book of Kings. Thus, the theology of the Davidic covenant points to the importance of the Davidic ruler faithfully demonstrating steadfast covenant lovingkindness toward God by following God's covenant instructions in the law and ruling with justice as well as God's gracious lovingkindness to David.

---

[551] Williamson, "'The Sure Mercies of David': Subjective or Objective Genitive," 31–49, does find a few examples where an objective genitive might be or is likely to be intended. But Neh 13:14 hardly counts as an example because of the relative clause, and the use of the sg. "lovingkindness, mercy" in Ps 5:8 ("in your great mercy") and Ps 144:2 are not very convincing examples, plus the references in Ezra 7:28 ("who has extended his good favor to me"); 9:9 ("he has shown us lovingkindness"); Neh 13:22 ("show mercy unto me") all use prepositional phrases to express the object, so they are not exactly comparable to 55:3. Thus Jonah 2:9 appears to be the lone example of an objective genitive with the word "lovingkindness."

[552] Gentry, "Rethinking the 'Sure Mercies of David' in Isaiah 55:3," 279–304, examines the options thoroughly and lays out the options that need to be considered in making this decision, pointing the interpreter in the direction of accepting the subjective genitive interpretation.

[553] Ibid., 279–304, makes a strong point of this issue, following the interpretations of D. I. Block.

Another factor of prime importance that must be weighed is the question of which David figure is being spoken about: (a) the past Davidic king of Israel; (b) the community ("you" pl. *lākem*), which some view as now functioning as a king because the covenant has been democratized; or (c) the future Davidic messianic king. First, one must ask if this passage is speaking about the original David. Because of the reference to David it is logical to conclude that these words and their theological message derive from the author's memory or quotation of earlier traditions about God's promises to Israel's King David. Although the promise was originally given to the historical David (2 Sam 7:12–16), there is no way for the past David who is dead to impact the present or future status of the nation to fulfill this prophecy. Even though the language of the original Davidic covenant is the source from which the author draws this positive message (2 Sam 7:16), the fulfillment would come through David's ideal faithful son.

A second interpretative approach to these words connects the fulfillment of these promises to the plural "you" (*lekem*), the community of Israel that the prophet was speaking to in chap. 55:1–5. C. Westermann finds "a transfer of God's tokens of grace from the king (David) to the nation."[554] J. A. Sanders claims that "God is calling them to a new covenant, that is, a new self-understanding—an everlasting covenant like the one he made with David himself. . . . It is a royal covenant with all Israel the prophet is talking about. All Israel will be a king."[555] Williamson concludes that the making of a covenant with the nation is a "radical innovation" which involves "Israel's witness to the sovereignty of God among the nations."[556] Nevertheless he does not shy away from accepting this idea that Israel functions as a king. G. von Rad views this covenant "to have been made not with David but to the whole nation. It is, therefore, for all Israel that the promises made to David are to be realized: Israel is to become the 'sovereign ruler' of the peoples (55:4)."[557]

---

[554] Westermann, *Isaiah 40–66*, 283–85, is depending on the earlier interpretation of Volz ("The thing to be noticed here is . . . that the promise to David is transferred to the nation Israel.") and von Rad ("he understands them [the promises] to have been made not to David but to the whole nation. It is therefore, for all Israel that the promises made to David are to be realized.").

[555] Sanders, "Isaiah 55:1–9," 291–95. This approach of democratizing the covenant to all Israel is also supported by Korpel, "Metaphors in Isaiah LV," 43–55, who believes "the promises to the Davidic dynasty . . . are broadened to encompass all those who come to the teachings of the God of Israel." Eissfeldt, "The Promises of Grace to David in Isaiah 55:1–6," in Anderson and Harrelson, *Israel's Prophetic Heritage: Essays in Honor of J. Muilenburg*, 196–207, says "the fulfillment of the promises of grace to David lies not in the coming of a descendent of David . . . It means rather that the people who now languish in exile will achieve high honor." Williamson, " 'The Sure Mercies of David': Subjective or Objective Genitive," 31–49.

[556] Williamson, *Variations on a Theme: King, Messiah and Servant in the Book of Isaiah*, 117–19, finds this radical innovation is "that the covenant with David is here potentially transferred to the people as a whole."

[557] G. von Rad, *The Message of the Prophets* (New York: Harper, 1962), 208, calls this democratizing of the tradition as a "bold reshaping of the old Davidic tradition" an "extreme one," but the

R. J. Clifford suggests Israel will be a witness because "Israel's prosperity, visible to the nations especially in its new exodus-conquest, witnesses Yahweh's superiority and hence Israel's primary place among the nations."[558] But this interpretive approach is open to several objections. First, in Isaiah 1–39 (9:1–7; 11:1–4,10–12; 16:5) and later prophetic books (Jer 23:5; 30:9; 33:15,17,21; Ezek 34:23–24; 37:24–25; Hos 3:5) the covenant with David is not democratized to all Israel; instead, there is a strong hope for a messianic ruler from the house of David whose work will bring God's blessing on all Israel. This covenant through this ideal Israelite king will be for the benefit of Israel and the nations, but it is through the Davidic Messiah. Second, W. C. Kaiser[559] objects to democratization because the promises to David are "certain, unfailing" (2 Sam 7:15; Ps 89:37) and cannot be transferred to the people. Third, though all of God's covenants are with various great men of God, they have an impact on all the earth (the covenant with Noah in Gen 9), on Israel, and all the nations of the earth (the covenant with Abraham in Gen 12:1–3), on all mankind (the Davidic covenant brings blessing to Israel in Pss 89:15–18; 132:14–16 and involves a "charter for all mankind" in 2 Sam 7:19), and on God's sheep through the work of my Servant David (Ezek 34:23).[560] Fourth, J. Motyer argues that the phrase "make an everlasting covenant with you (pl.)" in 55:3b refers to the fact that the covenant is "for, in favor of" the plural recipients because God will bring them into the covenant blessings.[561] Fifth, the reference to the Servant as a "covenant to the nations" (42:6; 49:8) and the connection of this Servant with the line of David (the root of Jesse in 53:1) suggests a better alternative for understanding the Davidic nature of this promise that avoids the issue of democratization. Sixth, the attempt to democratize the Davidic ruler which was first brought up in 11:1 (the root from Jesse) was rejected at that point and it should be here for similar reasons.[562] The need for a Messianic Davidic figure

---

extremeness of this concept does not cause him to shy away from the idea. Taking a completely different track, Watts, *Isaiah 34–66*, 245–46, believes this is talking about God's establishment of the reign of the Persian king Darius who assisted in the restoration of Jerusalem.

[558] Clifford, "Isaiah 55: Invitation to a Feast," in Myers and O'Conner, *The Word of the Lord Shall Go Forth: Essays in Honor of D. N. Freedman in Celebration of His Sixtieth Birthday*, 27–35.

[559] W. C. Kaiser, "The Unfailing Kindnesses Promised to David: Isaiah 55:3," 91–98, keeps the promises to David intact but does not see this passage as messianic.

[560] Koole, *Isaiah III, Volume 2: Isaiah 49–55*, 412, recognizes that "the structure of a covenant calls for central figures as mediators." Ezekiel 34:23–24 refers to the placing of David as my Servant over the nation, but 34:25 refers to making a covenant with them (the people), so the two notions are not contradictory.

[561] Motyer, *Isaiah*, 454, views these blessings as David's worldwide rule and enduring rule. Young, *The Book of Isaiah*, 3:377, views the "for you" as an ethical dative of advantage "for your benefit," but this is questionable use of an ethical dative.

[562] Stromberg, "The 'Root of Jesse' Isaiah 11:10" Postexilic Judah or Postexilic Davidic King?" 655–69, argues convincingly against the democratization of the Davidic promise of a shoot and root from Jesse in 11:1.

cannot be removed simply by replacing this Davidic ruler with the community that benefits from his provision of the covenant. Finally, the concept of democratization if fully implemented should actually extend to everyone who might come to eat and listen (55:1–3a), not just to the community of Israel. Usually those who favor the democratization approach argue only for partial democratization to Israelites because full democratization would contradict the typical concept that Israel will be the means of spreading the benefits of the covenant to others and will rule over the nations (55:4–5).[563] Because of these problems, another interpretation is preferred.

The third approach to this Davidic covenant is to view it as a messianic promise. Although some references to David in Isaiah refer to the historical figure (29:1; 38:5), and some refer to his present descendents (7:2,13), others refer to a future messianic Davidic figure (9:7). The past Davidic covenant in 2 Sam 7 and Ps 89 are the sources of the promises that the Messiah will be the one who will ultimately reign eternally and finally bring peace and justice on the earth (9:1–7; 11:1–2). The context of Isaiah 54 refers to a future time when God will bring back to himself his covenant wife Zion with "everlasting kindness" and "unfailing love" in order to establish his "covenant of peace" (54:8, 10) in the glorious jeweled city of Zion (54:11–12). In this context God challenges people to "listen, come to me" (55:2–3) so that they can be part of the many who will enjoy the benefit of what God has promised his people. In this eschatological setting one would expect a reference to the future Davidic Messiah whose role was to establish justice (9:7; 42:1–4), bring back Israel to God (49:5), bring salvation to the ends of the earth (49:6), and bear the sins of many (53:4–5,10–12). Through his faithful acts of lovingkindness he himself will be a covenant to the people (42:6; 49:8). His faithfulness to the plan of God are extensively reviewed in the servant songs, and because of his faithful love Israelites and people from the nations will be declared just and many will enter a new relationship with God.[564]

55:4 Verses 4 and 5 begin with an exclamation (*hēn*, "surely, behold") that introduces two further aspects that might persuade the audience to listen and come to God. The audience needs to realize that this is the one ("him") God "appointed, gave" (the root *nātan*) to be a "witness to the peoples, a leader, and commander of the peoples." How is one to interpret these responsibilities? Although it is not hard to understand David himself as a leader (1 Sam 13:14;

---

[563] Seitz, "Isaiah 40–66," 6:482, rejects the view that the Davidic promises have now ceased and that these promises are now handed over to the people.

[564] In the New Testament the apostle Paul quotes from 55:3a as he was preaching to the people in Pisidian Antioch (Acts 13:34). In this setting, Paul quoted from Ps 2:7; Isa 55:3; and Ps 16:10 to prove that God fulfilled his promises by raising Jesus from the dead. Paul does not give a detailed explanation of his understanding of 55:3a, but he does apply it to Jesus, not the historical David or to the democratized people of Israel. A later New Testament interpretation does not prove how one should interpret this text, but this later interpretation does reveal how later readers understood the text.

25:30; 2 Sam 5:2; 6:21), he was not usually thought of as a commander of other peoples. W. A. M. Beuken proposes that David's praise of God (Ps 18:50) explains how he was a witness to others concerning God's great deeds.[565] Some of those who view the covenant as being given to the people of Israel in 55:3 also take 55:4 to refer to historical David (Ps 18:43) and suggest that David was a witness because "David's victories and conquests gave evidence of the God of Israel and of his espousing of his chosen people,"[566] though this is a rather innovative title to give to him.[567] Others believe this verse refers to the people who take over these roles from David (as in v. 3) and witness to other nations in the court proceedings to verify God's sovereignty (cf. 43:10; 44:8).[568]

Another way of understanding this terminology in the context of the book of Isaiah would be to relate these roles to God's plans for the life of the messianic Davidic person in 55:3. Some connect the idea of being a witness to the practice of making a mound of stones that would be a witness to future generations that a covenant was made at this place (Gen 31:44,48,52; Josh 24:25,27). But the texts describing the Servant do not contain any comparable physical features in the life of the Servant. Consequently, J. L. Koole suggests that it was God's plan that the Servant should witness to others about his life. The Servant trusted in the Lord's plan (his confident statement that God would vindicate him) even though it seemed at times like he was laboring in vain (49:4).[569] One might add that the Servant also witnessed to the islands and called the distant nations to hear what he had to say in 49:1–2, kings and many nations in 52:14–15 witnessed his suffering and glory, and 53:1–9 contains the report of his life that Israelites witnessed. In order for the Servant to function in the role of a light to the nations and a covenant to the people (42:6; 49:8), the nations would need to witness his life and hear of his life of suffering for their sins. P. J. Gentry concludes that the role of the biblical king was to read, follow, and teach *Torah* (cf. Deut 17:14–20) in order to institute justice and righteousness on the earth (cf. 9:1–7; 42:1–4); thus one of the chief ways the Davidic royal servant witnessed was by taking God's word to the nations as the four servant

[565] Beuken, "Isaiah 55,3–5: The Reinterpretation of David," 49–64, focuses much more on Ps 18 than Ps 89, but has an excellent discussion of the problems and key issues in interpreting 55:3–5. Gentry, "Rethinking the 'Sure Mercies of David' in Isaiah 55:3," 294–97, develops a strong case for understanding this passage to be about the Messiah's faithful deeds.

[566] Westermann, *Isaiah 40–66*, 285. J. Eaton, "The King as God's Witness," *ASTI* 7 (1970): 25–40, observes that David witnessed to the incomparable sovereignty of God, he exhorted and admonished others, and by his very existence he was an "evidential sign" to the nations of God's work.

[567] Williamson, *Variations on a Theme: King, Messiah and Servant in the Book of Isaiah*, 119–20, admits that this does not fit past royal traditions and "is a second element of innovation."

[568] Muilenburg, Isaiah 40–66, 5:646, rejects a messianic interpretation saying, "as David was a witness to the people, a ruler and a commander to the peoples, so Israel will perform the same functions in the world."

[569] Koole, *Isaiah III, Volume 2: Isaiah 49–55*, 416, considers the evidence for these words applying to the historical David but prefers an application to the Davidic Servant.

poems explain.[570] As "a covenant to the nations" (42:6) he was a witness and a light that enlightened their eyes.

The validity of this approach of applying this understanding is somewhat dependent on the possibility of applying the concept of a "leader, prince" (*nāgîd*) and "commander" (*mĕṣawwēh*) in 55:4b to the Servant. "Leader, prince" (*nāgîd*) was used of David in 1 Sam 13:14 (of Saul in 1 Sam 9:16; Solomon in 1 Kgs 1:35; Hezekiah in 2 Kgs 20:5) possibly to avoid some of the negative connotations of kingship in the ancient Near Eastern world.[571] Isaiah never calls this special Servant a "prince, leader" in any other passages,[572] but if a prince is a divinely appointed servant-ruler who receives the Spirit of God to empower him to rule justly and institute God's righteousness on earth, then this title fits the royal Servant figure (cf. 9:6–7; 11:1–5; 42:1–4). The third role that God planned for this individual was that he would be a "commander of the people." This is not a very clear role, but it may refer to the prince's function of speaking his thoughts to others or of his exercise of his authority over other people, much like David's political control over other nations (2 Sam 5:17–18). In light of the association with "prince, leader," the latter role should be favored. If this is still referring to the Servant, his exercise of authority over the nations must be connected to his royal responsibilities (cf. 9:1–7) when he judges and rules over them with righteousness (11:3–4,10–16; 16:5; 32:1,16–18; 42:1–4). Verse 5 probably explains at least one aspect of this prince's relationship with other nations.

55:5 The final *hēn* "behold, surely" begins a clause that points out how this Davidic figure will accomplish the plan of God described in 55:4. Directly addressing this prince and commander, God predicts that "you" (sg.) will call unknown "nation(s)"[573] who formerly did not have a relationship with this Davidic messianic Servant, but this text does not indicate exactly what will be said.[574] Presumably this will be a friendly call, an invitation to come, an offer to eat freely of God's spiritual food, and an exhortation to establish a relationship with God (55:1–2). Their running to him implies their acceptance of

---

[570] Gentry, "Rethinking the 'Sure Mercies of David," 279–304.

[571] D. F. Murray, *Divine Prerogative and Royal Pretension: Pragmatics, Poetics and Polemics in a Narrative Sequence about David (2 Samuel 5.17–7.29)*, JSOTSup 264 (Sheffield: Sheffield Academic Press, 1998), 288–90.

[572] Goldingay, *Message of Isaiah 40–66*, 549, translates this word "a leader," but in his discussion he relates this term to the verbal root נגד ("he announced"), concluding, "As a witness David was an announcer and a giver of Yhwh's commands." If the prophet were drawing this term from נגד, it seems that he would have used the *hiphil* participle מגיד; thus this suggested meaning seems inappropriate.

[573] The Old Greek has the pl. "nations," but the Hebrew might be considered a collective of "nations" in a sg. form.

[574] Concerning this verse Goldingay, *Message of Isaiah 40–55*, 549, states that, "the Judean community did not acknowledge Cyrus and this people (see esp. 45.9–13), but it will come to do so and will find that Cyrus's people respond to Israel's summons (45:14–25; 49:22–23)." This views the present Israelites in exile as the ones who would take over the role of the future David figure.

him and the establishment of a relationship, which agrees with the role of the servant in 49:1,6,8. These people may be the part of the "many" in 52:15 and 53:11–12 and those who come to Zion and to God in 2:2–3 and 60:1–12.[575]

The second half of the verse gives the reason these people will come running "to you." It will be "because of, for the sake of" (*lĕmaʿan*) your (sg.) God, the Holy One of Israel. What God has done is not explained here, but from 49:7 one learns that these nations will finally understand God's work through this royal messianic Servant and respond by bowing before him. In 52:14–15 the nations and their kings will be appalled and shut their mouths because they will finally understand what God did through the servant's suffering. Exaltation was accomplished because it was God's plan to glorify "you," the Davidic Servant. Earlier in 44:23 the prophetic hymn declared that through God's redemption of Israel he would display his glory in Israel, and in 49:3 he announced that his plan was to display his glory in Israel through the work of the Servant. Now in this verse God indicates that he will glorify the royal figure in 55:3–5. This is consistent with the announcement in 52:12 that this Servant would be "raised up, lifted up, and exalted." In spite of all that will happen to this person, people will one day understand God's purpose in all these things and glorify God and the Davidic royal Servant.

INVITATION TO REPENT AND SEE GOD'S WORD FULFILLED (55:6–13)

⁶Seek the LORD while he may be found;
  call on him while he is near.
⁷Let the wicked forsake his way
  and the evil man his thoughts.
Let him turn to the LORD, and he will have mercy on him,
  and to our God, for he will freely pardon.

⁸"For my thoughts are not your thoughts,
  neither are your ways my ways,"
                          declares the LORD.
⁹"As the heavens are higher than the earth,
  so are my ways higher than your ways
  and my thoughts than your thoughts.
¹⁰As the rain and the snow
  come down from heaven,
 and do not return to it
  without watering the earth
 and making it bud and flourish,
  so that it yields seed for the sower and bread for the eater,
¹¹so is my word that goes out from my mouth:
  It will not return to me empty,

---

[575] Martens, "Impulses to Missions in Isaiah: An Intertextual Exploration," 215–39, understands this as part of the grand missions emphasis in Isaiah which will be accomplished by the witness of this Davidic figure.

but will accomplish what I desire
  and achieve the purpose for which I sent it.
¹²You will go out in joy
  and be led forth in peace;
the mountains and hills
  will burst into song before you,
and all the trees of the field
  will clap their hands.
¹³Instead of the thornbush will grow the pine tree,
  and instead of briers the myrtle will grow.
This will be for the LORD's renown,
  for an everlasting sign,
  which will not be destroyed."

The last part of this chapter continues the call for people to respond to God's challenge so that they might enjoy the blessings promised in chap. 54 and be a part of the covenant community that will benefit from the everlasting covenant God will confirm through the faithful, sure, and loving deeds of the Davidic royal servant (55:3–5). If the people in the prophet's audience want to participate in everything that God has promised, they must first "listen to me . . . come to me" (55:2–3), "seek the Lord . . . turn to the Lord" (55:6–7), and repent of their sins. The blessings described in chaps. 54–55 are not false or deceitful hopes, silly dreams of grandeur, or just pious nationalistic rhetoric that will never be fulfilled. All that God promises will happen just as he said (55:9–10). Those who believe will sing (55:12–13) just as God encouraged them earlier in 54:1.

The structure of this final paragraph can be divided into three parts:[576]

Seek God for forgiveness	55:6–9
God's words are reliable and effective	55:10–11
Song of joy	55:12–13

This section functions as a call or admonition to repentance with various substantiations (introduced with *kî* "because" clauses in 55:8,10,12) to motivate the listeners to act based on what they have heard.[577] These verses serve as

---

[576] Korpel, "Metaphors in Isaiah LV," 43–55, links vv. 10–13 into one subparagraph, but the hymnic nature of 55:12–13 suggests that it should be a separate unit.

[577] Schoors, *I Am God Your Savior*, 293, views this as a disputation over whether God's words were entirely reliable. This hypothesis suggests that some people were denying the reliability of God's promises, but there is nothing in this chapter that suggests that idea. It is extremely dangerous to imagine settings that may have precipitated such prophetic speeches when there is little or no evidence that the prophet is responding to an objection. While it is legitimate to assume some need for this oracle, salvation oracles and calls to repentance may simply be offers of hope. In this case they come from an unknown setting. Whybray, *Isaiah 40–66*, 193, assumes there are doubters who question "God's power or the credentials of his prophet" because they do not believe in the "imminent appearance of Yahweh to save his people." Goldingay and Payne, *Isaiah 40–55*, 2:375, are clear about their assumption when they state, "The point is made as a general one, but of course

something of an epilogue that concludes chaps. 40–55. They pick up a few themes from the introduction in 40:1–11, but they do not really summarize everything that was communicated in chaps. 40–55. In 40:2 God announced that Zion's sin would be atoned, and 55:6–7 calls upon the nation to repent and restore their relationship with God for he will pardon their sins. These ideas are similar to the call to repent in 44:21, for God is the one who will blot out their transgressions (43:25), plus it is similar to the call for the nations to turn to God and be saved in 45:22. Because of 53:1–12 the audience now knows that the suffering servant will bear the guilt for the sins of many.

Although the people were told that God's words last forever and can be trusted (40:8) and the validity of God's promises are repeatedly substantiated by pointing to the fact that God is the Creator of the world, he controls the past and the future history of the nations, he is King and their Redeemer, the Holy One of Israel (40:22–23; 41:14,20; 43:3,14–15; 44:6; 45:11,21; 47:4; 48:17; 49:7; 51:13; 54:5). Once again in this epilogue God assures his people that his words are true and everything he says will happen (55:9–10). One day God's wonderful kingdom will be established (40:9–11), and then people will shout for joy and God will restore mankind and the earth (55:12–13, cf. 42:10–13; 49:13; 44:23). The everlasting sign of God's transformation of the world in 55:13 and the everlasting covenant that encompasses his new relationship with his people in 55:3 are two indications of God's gracious work among his people.

55:6–7 The first subunit begins with two imperative verbs that exhort the audience to action in order to prepare for the coming salvation of God, parallel to the calls for action in 55:1–3a. J. Motyer draws these two imperative exhortations together by suggesting, "There is a free entrance into life (1–5) through the moral and spiritual response of returning to God (6–11)."[578] The instructions to "seek" (*diršû*) God and "call" (*qĕrā'uhû*) are sometimes related to going to a temple to pray for God's help so that a person can live (Amos 5:4,6; Pss 22:26; 69:32). In 51:1 those who seek the Lord are people who listen to God, pursue righteousness, and look to God, while those who seek God in 58:5 are persistent in their search and are eager to know God's ways. In the book of Chronicles seeking God is a sign of a true follower who desires to know God's will and follow it. (2 Chr 12:14; 14:4,7; 15:2). Much earlier in Deut 4:29 God told the Israelites that if the people "seek the Lord your God, you will find him, if you look for him with all your heart" (cf. Jer 29:13). Seeking to get into

---

it implies that Second Isaiah's community can call on Yhwh in the particular circumstances of the 540s in Babylon and Jerusalem." This assumption does not seem to be justified from this text itself and the damage this assumption does is that it turns a pivotal call for a renewal of their spiritual relationships with God into a mere call for God to bring the people home from exile.

[578] Motyer, *Isaiah*, 456, links all three substantiations in vv. 8–13 into one paragraph. He makes a connection between "returning" to God in v. 8 and the "returning" word in v. 11, though the ideas associated with "returning" in each case are quite different.

contact with God involves calling on him, praying to him, and developing a relationship with him.

The time to seek and call is now, while God is available and near. The two clauses that express this temporal limitation of God's availability are made up of two infinitives of which the pronominal suffix ("him") functions as the subject.[579] These statements indicate that God is not always available to help, primarily because he hides himself from sinners for a short time when judgment is being enacted on a people (cf. 1:15; 45:15; 54:7–8; Deut 31:17; 32:20; Pss 13:1; 44:23–24). Although God is near to his people when they call on him (Deut 4:7; Ps 145:18; Isa 50:8; 51:5) and he is ever present as a refuge for those who are in trouble (Ps 46:1), he will not always appear and be near when people are suffering. These two limitations on God's availability argue that one should not let the opportunity to seek God and repent pass by without taking advantage of God's invitation because it soon may be too late and his judgment may come (cf. Ps 32:6).[580] Interestingly, Isa 65:1–2 indicates that God in grace often reveals himself to those who are not really seeking and who are not actively calling on him. They may be obstinate or uninterested in God, but God is interested in making himself known to them. This almost seems to be the case here, for God is freely offering hope to all those who "come to me" (55:1–3a), even before they have a chance to call on him (55:6–7). Those hearing this invitation from God now need to respond to his gracious offer and draw near to God.

Verse 7 says that one of the things that a wicked person must do when drawing near to God is to forsake their evil ways and evil "thoughts, plans." The verb "forsake" is traditionally translated as a continuation of God's invitation expressed in a jussive wish or desire[581] ("let the wicked forsake"). The act of forsaking past ways and thoughts involves the rejection of these behaviors and a decisive break from past beliefs, assumptions, priorities, and plans. Of course it is not always easy to separate instantly from past friends, past ways of doing things, or a past philosophy of life. The second verb encourages the audience to

---

[579] The word בְּהִמָּצְאוֹ is a *niphal* infinitive construct ("being found") with a temporal prefixed preposition and a third-person pronominal suffix "him" that functions as the subject. GKC §115e indicates that "the subject of the action represented by the infinitive is mostly placed immediately after it, either in the *genitive* or *nominative*." The *niphal* in this instance is "used to express actions which the subject allows to happen to himself" (GKC §51c), sometimes called a "tolerative" usage.

[580] The Aramaic Targum makes the limitations "as long as you are alive," thus avoiding the idea that God may not be available.

[581] In GKC §109b the jussive is used in "affirmative sentences to express a command, a wish (or a blessing), advice, or a request." Although the first verb יַעֲזֹב "forsake" could be an imperfect or a jussive, the second verb יָשֹׁב "return" is probably a jussive (the normal imperfect would be וְיָשׁוּב) though the accent has not retracted to the first syllable as in many jussives (GKC §48f-g, 72t). Goldingay, *Message of Isaiah 40–55*, 551, translates the verbs "must abandon" and "must turn," which suggests that he understands the verbs as modal imperfects communicating an obligation (GKC §107n).

"turn" to God after they have turned away from their past wicked life. This requires a transformation of the mind and heart by the Spirit of God. The plans of God may require his people to give up their dreams, change jobs, and move to live in another place, but the person who truly turns to God wants to serve him and eagerly desires to follow his direction. This request for a "turning, returning" in 55:7 is not referring to a geographical return but to a spiritual change of the will and a person's thinking. This is a turning to follow God.

The results of this forsaking of an old evil way of thinking and accepting a new godly perspective is that God will have compassion and will freely pardon those who respond. Although it is clear that God will have mercy on those who repent, it would be dangerous to draw the further theological conclusion that repentance is required before God can show mercy on anyone. That would almost suggest that certain works of faith automatically produce or earn for the believer a gracious divine response. Yet, many passages speak of God's love and compassion for sinful people, so it is clear that various aspects of God's mercy happen both before (cf. 65:1–2) and after repentance, though no human acts can earn God's grace. The "pardon" (*sālaḥ*) God offers is the forgiveness from the penalty for sins so that a new relationship with God is possible. The NIV translation "freely pardon" is not a very literal translation. The verb is "he will cause to multiply, increase," and the following infinitive construct means "to pardon." C. R. North translates this phrase as "he does much (*yarbēh*) in respect of forgiving," but the adverbial use of the verb in the phrase "he will abundantly pardon"[582] produces a better English understanding. The focus is not on this pardoning being free as in 55:1–2, but on how extensively God is able to forgive a multitude of many sins. In fact chap. 53 indicates that the servant will bear the sins of many people and that he will justify many (53:11–12).

55:8–9 The last two verses in this subparagraph pick up on the idea of the "ways" and "thoughts" of mankind from 55:7. In this brief first-person declaration from God ("declares the LORD"), he explains in two verbless clauses why it is necessary for people to reject and forsake their old ways of behavior and turn to accept the criteria set down by God. Put as plainly as possible the prophet says people do not act or think like God. The thoughts of an Almighty God who has created the world, controls the history of nations, and plans what will happen to each person have a world perspective that is beyond the realm of human comprehension. In addition, the gracious and compassionate ways of a God who is perfectly sinless yet willing to love, choose, help, uphold, and forgive very rebellious people is beyond anything any human being could ever imagine. His plans for the eschatological end of the world, the new heavens and the new earth, and the judgment of the nations are incredible. Of course,

---

[582] North, *Second Isaiah*, 260. GKC §114n, n. 2, indicates that in these kinds of constructions the principal idea is expressed in the infinitive while the main verb is rendered as a subordinate adverbial idea; thus one arrives at the translation "he will abundantly pardon." This is similar to the more usual adverbial use of the infinitive absolute (GKC §113h).

the news about the sending of his humble suffering servant to pay for the sins of many is an astonishing sacrifice of love.

Just how different are God's thoughts and ways from those of people on earth? In 55:9 the contrast between God and mankind is compared to the distance between the heavens and the earth. Such a comparison might make one wonder if there is anything that is similar between the thoughts of God and the common man. Surely there are few similarities between God and the wicked, but there are some similarities between the righteous believer who reads or hears about God's thoughts and ways and attempts to live a life consistent with God's instructions. Nevertheless, even with these few similarities with the righteous, it is not hard to accept the idea that God's plans and purposes are exceedingly higher than anything the smartest righteous person has ever thought or imagined. But is this text referring to all God's thoughts and plans or to a specific topic? Since nothing specific is mentioned, one could suggest that this is a broad principle that applies to all areas of life and thinking. Yet the contextual reference to God's compassion and forgiveness of sins in 55:6–7 indicates that the divine plan of redemption is the supreme example of God's higher thoughts and ways. Some people have a hard time being compassionate toward good people, and most find it hard to be merciful to extremely wicked people. Most people have difficulty truly forgiving those who wrong them, but God is willing to love the most unlovely and ungodly, even forgive those who do unforgivable evil against others and blaspheme the name of God. In fact, he planned to cause the suffering Servant to die so that many sinful people might live.

55:10–11 Now the prophet adds another related reason why people should seek God and repent of their sin. This reason is interrelated to the preceding point about the undeniable superiority of God's plans,[583] but now the prophet puts the focus on the absolute reliability of everything that God says or plans. Specifically, in the immediate context God is assuring the audience about the availability of forgiveness to all who come to him and repent (cf. 55:7). God's commitment that he will respond with compassion to all who seek him is a promise they can count on.

In order to make the point absolutely clear so that everyone can understand the point, the prophet develops a "just as [*ka'ăšer*] . . . so [*kēn*]" comparison between what happens in nature (v. 10) and what happens with God's words (v. 11).[584] Since the rain brings fertility to the ground and reliably comes every winter and spring, it serves as a good comparative analogy with God's words in 55:11. In addition rain can symbolize God's blessing (Deut 28:12; 1 Kgs 8:35–

---

[583] The author also makes a verbal connection in 55:10 by reusing the terms "heavens" and "earth" from v. 9. Of course the superiority and absolute reliability of God stand in sharp contrast to man who is like the grass that withers and dies (40:6–8).

[584] E. Lipinski, "On the Comparison in Isaiah 55:10," *VT* 23 (1773): 246–47, connects this comparison to Babylonian texts, but they do not mention snow.

36; Isa 30:23; Ezek 34:26; Joel 2:23), and Deut 32:2 compares rain to God's word (cf. Ps 147:15–18).[585] Although Israel has little snow,[586] both rain and snow represent precipitation and both come down from heaven just like God's word. Both rain and God's word are intended to have an impact on the earth and the people who live there. The rain causes the flowers to bud, crops to grow and produce fruit and seeds, but the ultimate purpose of all of this activity is to provide food for people to eat. So God's word has the function of producing fruit in people and feeding them on something that is more important than mere bread (cf. Deut 8:3). But the central comparison is that just as rain cannot fall on the earth without fulfilling the role God gave it, so God's words cannot fall from God's mouth in heaven without fulfilling the role God gave them on earth. God does not make impotent threats or empty promises; when he talks people should listen because what he predicts is exactly what will happen. When God swears something, it will certainly happen because he speaks with integrity and faithfulness. He does not take back his statements (45:23). When God speaks he externalizes who he is; his words represent his values, his will, and his existence. A divinity who has no will and does not reveal himself is a god that does not really exist. In contrast, God's words accomplish the plans and pleasures of God (55:11b). God's thoughts, words, and plans are powerful, for all he had to do was to speak and the worlds were created (Gen 1). This theme is emphasized throughout chaps. 40–55 because one of the most important reasons for trusting God is that he does what he says (cf. 46:11).

55:12–13   This paragraph (55:6–13), this literary unit (53:12–55:13), and this major section of the text (40:1–55:13) end with another hymnic refrain similar to 12:1–6; 42:10–13; 44:23; 49:13; 52:7–10. These words of joy and peace provide another reason that substantiates God's call for the people to "come to me" (55:2–3), to turn from their sins, and to be forgiven (55:6–7). If they respond appropriately to God's calling in 55:6–7, they will be able to enjoy the glory of the recreated earth. J. Muilenburg believes this "poem closes with the liberation from exile . . . He [the prophet] conceives of a new exodus and portrays it in all the glowing imagery of nature,"[587] but there is little that

---

[585] "Let my teaching fall like rain, and my words descend like dew, like showers on new grass, like abundant rain on tender grass."

[586] Although it is impossible to know just how much climate change has happened from the time of Isaiah until today, it appears that there never was a time when Israel had much snow. Mount Hermon on the northern border is the only mountain that gets a major amount of snow. At times snow can represent purity or cleansing (1:18; Ps 51:7), but nothing suggests that function in this verse.

[587] Muilenburg, "Isaiah 40–66," *IB*, 5:650. Whybray, *Isaiah 40–66*, 194, also views this as an exodus from Babylon, stating that, "Israel's return home will be 'Paradise Regained.'" He connects the growth of trees to "the miraculous fertility of the desert region through which the exiles are to travel." Childs, *Isaiah*, 438, says, "Israel will go forth from Babylon in peace, breaking forth into singing," but unfortunately there is no reference to Babylon in this verse. North, *Second Isaiah*, 262, asks "whether the Prophet intended this quite literally . . . If he did, he was quite mistaken" since this picture is nothing like the real return from Babylon.

indicates that this is talking about the people returning to Zion. J. L. Koole is right to suggest that "there are good reasons for assuming that this poetic description means more than just the return of the exiles."[588] The call of this chapter is to all who are thirsty; the desire is for everyone to reject wickedness and turn to the Lord. This passage is talking about events at the time when God transforms nature and restores its fertility. In some future eschatological age God will cause the deserts to bloom when the glory of the Lord is revealed (35:1–3); then the holy redeemed people of Zion will return to Zion with singing (35:8–10). This is the time when God will answer his people's prayers and cause rivers to flow from the barren heights, cause trees to grow in desert places (41:17–20). This is when the Spirit will be poured out (44:1–5), when God will reign in Zion and the redeemed will sing his praise (52:7–10), and when God's unfailing love will establish a new covenant of peace that will rest on the jeweled city of Zion (54:10–13). This is the time to which 40:9–11 was looking toward, when all flesh will see God and he will shepherd his people and gently lead them.

The hills singing and the trees clapping their hands is obviously not literal (55:12b; cf. 42:10–11; Ps 98:8) but expresses the joy that will fill the earth. The disappearance of the thornbush and brier mark the end of the old era of divine judgment and the curse; their replacements will be the beautiful cypress and the myrtle. This transformed world (cf. 65:17–19) will be "for the LORD's renown" (55:13); his name, his reputation, and his glory will be on display for all to see. This transformed new creation will never be cut off for this new world will be a sign of God's transforming power to redeem it and everyone in it. The hope of enjoying life with God when the eternal covenant and this new world are present is a great hope that motivates all people to turn from sin and seek a living relationship with God.

THEOLOGICAL IMPLICATIONS.   The overarching thrust of chaps. 54–55 is its repeated imperative call for people to sing (54:1), enlarge their tents (54:2), not fear (54:4), listen and come to the Lord (55:1–3), seek him, call upon him (55:6), and turn to him (55:7). These imperative exhortations are calling for a response of trust in God, so the reason they should trust God is repeatedly emphasized. They should respond to God because they will have many children (54:2–3); God is their Maker, the Almighty, the Holy One, and their Redeemer who has not deserted Zion (54:5–6). God will have compassion and everlasting kindness toward his people (54:7–8), unfailing love and a covenant of peace with them (54:10). He will rebuild Zion in great glory, protect it (54:11–17), and freely offer the people of Zion his benefits (55:1–3). The Davidic covenant will be renewed through the royal Davidic Servant, the Messiah who will be a prince and witness to the nations (55:3–5).

---

[588] Koole, *Isaiah III, Volume 2: Isaiah 49–55*, 445, indicates that "Babylon was no longer the starting point and in vv. 6f. the return was to Yahweh."

Whenever God's people are struggling in a difficult situation (54:4,7,15–17), there is hope for them because of who God is (our God, Almighty, Holy, and Redeemer), because of his unfailing love and compassion, and because of his promises to them. The fulfillment of all these eschatological promises will not fully be realized until a later date, but just knowing what God has prepared for those who love him makes today's trials seem less severe and very temporal. God's compassion, peace, love, and covenant will have a much greater everlasting impact on this world. If one can internalize these promises as real, then the thing to do today is to trust him, rejoice in his promises, and come to the Lord. Whenever sinful human beings seek to live in concert with God, one of the first things they must do is to confess their sins and get right with God (55:6–7), for he is anxious to forgive.

Although some will doubt God's promises or wonder about God's ability to produce such a wonderful future setting out of this sinful world, two primary factors can bring assurance that the future situation described in these verses is not just pie-in-the-sky dreams that will never be fulfilled. First, these things will be possible because God's royal Davidic Servant will be the one though whom God will make his everlasting covenant with all the peoples on earth. From the perspective of today, we know that this Prince and Witness to the nations has already accomplished the way for the many to be justified (53:10–13). God's compassion, his everlasting love, and his covenant of peace have already been revealed and accepted by millions of Hebrews and Gentiles. Second, many have already sought the Lord, confessed their sins, and been forgiven (55:6–7). They know for certain that God does have mercy and does forgive those who seek and trust him; thus, many of the statements in these prophecies have already begun to be fulfilled. Third, these promises are the words of God which are true and unfailing (55:10–11), so every reader can be confident that every aspect of these chapters will be fulfilled. All one has to do is respond to God's gracious call.

515

Creation of a New World of Joy and Abundance
(65:17–25)
God Honors the Humble Who Tremble (66:1–4)
God Will Give Zion Children and Joy (66:5–14)
(3) Gathering of All People to Worship God (66:15–24)

II. THE DESTINY OF GOD'S SERVANTS (56:1–66:24)

C. R. Seitz suggests that the final unit includes chaps. 54–66, while L. J. Liebreich grouped chaps. 50–66 together,[1] but most commentaries identify chaps. 56–66 as the final literary unit in the book of Isaiah. This new section begins with a word from God that challenges the people to act in just and righteous ways (56:1) and hold fast to God's covenant (56:4,6). They are not to be involved with pagan religious practices (57:2–13) because only the faithful and redeemed will enjoy the destiny of entering God's Holy Mountain in the final eschatological age. When people fast, it should be done in order to please God not themselves (58:3,5,13). They should reject injustice and confess their sins, for God is coming in righteousness to bring salvation, his covenant, and his Spirit to all the redeemed in Zion (59:1–21). At that time God's glory will shine over Zion, and people from many nations will come with their wealth to Jerusalem (60:1–16). This new eschatological city of righteous people will get a new name (60:18–23), a special Anointed One from God will announce good news of comfort (61:1–3), and God will establish his everlasting covenant with his people (61:4–9). The nations will see Zion's righteousness and many will come; Zion will receive more new names, promises of future blessing, and salvation (62:1–12). In addition, when God establishes this holy city, he will destroy all his enemies (63:1–6). Although God frequently acted in compassion toward his people in the past (63:7–14), the prayer of his people is that God would not hide his face any longer, would forgive their sins, and would not keep silent any longer (64:1–12). But before that can happen God must judge the wicked (65:1–7) and create the new heavens and the new earth. This new earth will contain a new city for his servants who tremble at his words (65:8–66:14). In the end, the wicked will be burned in fire (66:15–16,24), but the righteous among the nations will come to serve God in his Holy Mountain

---

[1] L. J. Liebreich, "The Compilation of the Book of Isaiah," *JQR* 46 (1956): 259–77, made chaps. 50–66 the final group of chapters in Isaiah based on the use of the terms עֶבֶד "servant" and רַחַם "compassion" as well as a group of twelve words that appear in chaps. 50 and 66. C. R. Seitz, "Book of Isaiah 40–66," *NIB*, 6:471–74, views this section to be dealing with the vindication of God's servants. Because of the close association of ideas in 55–56 (servants, banquets, persuasive form of speech), he includes chaps. 54–55 with 56–66.

(66:18–23). This is the final destiny of those who are called the humble "servants of God."

SETTING AND DATE. The various ways different commentators approach chaps. 56–66 and their relationship to chaps. 40–55 were already dealt with in the introduction under "Compositional Issues Related to 56–66," so the reader can consult that section for additional background on chaps. 56–66.[2] Since there are no references to specific Israelite or foreign kings in these chapters and only a few hints about the historical situation, it is impossible to provide anything close to an exact dating for each chapter or to identify which chapters were written first. There are many who suggest that the place where the audience is located is Jerusalem, but in most cases the Jerusalem mentioned in these chapters is actually the location of eschatological events when all God's servants (from Israel and the nations) will gather together in Jerusalem (60:1–63:6; 66:18–24). Therefore it is appropriate to question if this future setting has anything to do with the present location of the prophet and his audience.

R. N. Whybray believes the prophet is speaking to people in Jerusalem who have returned from Babylonian exile, while the temple is being built or has been completed (around 520–515 BC) and the community is dealing with a conflict over who should be admitted into this religious community.[3] Whybray cites several lines of evidence for connecting parts of chaps. 56–66 to events and issues during the time of Haggai and Zechariah: (a) Haggai has similar views of the future glory that God will pour out on Jerusalem (compare Hag 1:6–11; 2:7–9; Zech 7:15 with Isa 60:5,10,13); (b) the temple is still in ruins (Hag 1; Isa 63:18; 64:11) and worship is happening (56:6,7; 62:9; 66:6,20), although it lacks splendor (60:7,13; Hag 2:3); (c) Zechariah 7–8 and Isaiah 58 deal with the issue of fasting; and (d) Zech 7:8–10 and Isa 58:6–7 both express a need for just relationships between people. Nevertheless, the strong condemnation of leaders in 57:9–12, the persecution of the righteous in 57:1–2, and the gross pagan worship in 57:3–10 do not match anything mentioned in the preaching of Haggai, Zechariah, or Ezra 1–6.

Others have concluded that the conflicts mentioned in these chapters were tensions over land ownership between the exiles who have recently returned

---

[2] The recent study of B. C. Bradley, "The Postexilic Exile in Third Isaiah: Isaiah 61:1–3 in Light of Second Temple Hermeneutics," *JBL* 126 (2007): 475–96, begins with a survey of some of the main critical issues related to understanding chaps. 56–66, though he comes to quite different conclusions than this commentary.

[3] R. N. Whybray, *Isaiah 40–66*, NCB (London: Marshall, Morgan, and Scott, 1975), 196, concludes that one person did not write all these chapters. H. G. M. Williamson, "The Concept of Israel in Transition," in *The World of Ancient Israel*, ed. R. Clements (Cambridge: Cambridge University Press, 1989), 141–61, illustrates the difficulty of dating this material by showing that some conclude from 60:13 that the temple was already built, while others use the same verse to prove that it was not yet built. He believes that the purpose of chaps. 56–66 was to define who or what is Israel.

to Jerusalem from Babylon and those who remained in Jerusalem during the exile. Those who never went to Babylon confiscated the land of the people that were taken into exile (Ezek 11:14–21; 33:23–29), so after the people returned from exile, there was some question about which family rightfully owned the land. The main problem with this view is that Haggai does not mention any kind of conflict between these two groups over possession of the land; instead, he invites all the people of the land to work together and build the temple (Hag 2:4).[4] Taking a slightly different slant, M. Smith believes this conflict is between religiously syncretistic non-exiles and the upper class "Yahweh alone" party that returned from exile, but there is little indication that pinpoints this as a conflict between an upper class exilic religious group and the non-exiles.[5]

P. Hanson and A. Rofé hypothesized that there was a conflict between different postexilic priestly groups, but the positive words of hope are not addressed specifically just to priests, and relatively few of the negative words of judgment suggest that these troubles should be limited strictly to an inner priestly squabble.[6] J. Blenkinsopp connects the "tremblers at God's word" in 66:2,5 with the persecuted "tremblers at God's word" in Ezra 9:4; 10:3 who were excluded from holding land by the idolatrous temple priests who were in power in Jerusalem; thus, he places these events later in the time of Ezra (around 458 BC).[7] P. A. Smith follows the suggestions of L. Grabbe who reconstructs a conflict situation between those who believed that building the temple would hasten God's intervention (the TI group) and another group that focused on removing social injustices and religious syncretism (the TI2 group). If people wanted to see God intervene on their behalf, the TI2 group believed that dealing justly with others was a much more important issue to resolve than building the temple.[8] The evidence for the TI2 group has some basis because there are some oracles in Isaiah 56–66 that criticize social injustices (56:1; 57:1–2; 58:3–4,6;

---

[4] B. Schramm, *The Opponents of Third Isaiah*, JSOTSup 193 (Sheffield: Sheffield Academic Press, 1995), 62–63, claims that a conflict between the exiles and the people of the land is not present in Haggai or Zechariah 1–8.

[5] M. Smith, *Palestinian Parties and Politics that Shaped the Old Testament* (London: SCM, 1987), 75–95.

[6] P. D. Hanson, *The Dawn of Apocalyptic: The Historical and Sociological Roots of Jewish Apocalyptic Eschatology* (Philadelphia: Fortress, 1979), 209–27, believes there was a conflict between ruling Zadokite priests and a disenfranchised prophetic group of visionaries who had no power. A. Rofé, "Isaiah 66:1–4: Judean Sects in the Persian Period as Viewed by Trito-Isaiah," in *Biblical and Related Studies Presented to A. Iwry*, ed. A. Kort and S. Morschauer (Winona Lake, IN: Eisenbrauns, 1985), 205–17, identifies the priests as the group condemned in 66:1–4, but there is little evidence that would limit the problem to a group of priests.

[7] J. Blenkinsopp, *Isaiah 40–55*, AB (New York: Doubleday, 2000), 51–54, thinks Isaiah 56–66 and Ezra 9–10 address the same issues from different perspectives. In Ezra 9–10 the tremblers and Ezra are able to dictate policy while they were shunned either before or after Ezra's reform.

[8] P. A. Smith, *Rhetoric and Redaction in Trito-Isaiah: The Structure, Growth, and Authorship of Isaiah 56–66*, VTSup 62 (Leiden: Brill, 1995), 194–96, follows the recreation of L. Grabbe, *History of Judaism from Cyrus to Hadrian* (Minneapolis: Fortress, 1992), 89. Smith dates the four messages attributed to TI₂ (56:1–8; 56:9–57:21; 58:1–59:20; 65:1–66:17) to 515 BC because he

59:3–4,6–15), but it is hard to find arguments for and against the building of the temple in 55–66. This just does not seem to be the main topic (or even a minor topic) in most of these chapters.

From this small group of scholarly opinions, it is fairly clear that the historical data about the date and setting is difficult to pinpoint; otherwise there would not be so many competing understandings of the setting of chaps. 56–66. B. S. Childs is probably correct when he states that the information in these chapters does not "establish an absolute dating or an exact chronology."[9] G. I. Emmerson found that in 56–66 "there are no historical indicators here to enable us to date with any measure of precision even separate sections of the material, let alone the whole,"[10] though she later assumes a postexilic setting.

The following provisional conclusions about chaps. 56–66 will serve as the basis for the exegesis below: (a) The messages in 60:1–62:12 primarily refer to eschatological events; therefore, one cannot argue for a setting or date from verses which mention the building of the future walls of the city (60:10), an undefined past time of feeling forsaken (60:15; 62:4), the Lord's approaching return (57:15; 59:20; 62:10–12), or the existence of ruins (61:4), for these are rather general factors about past and future times. They do not say anything about the historical setting when this message was actually spoken. (b) The eschatological setting of the battle of the Divine Warrior in 63:1–6, the recreation of the new heavens and new earth in 65:17–25, and the end times promises to the righteous and the wicked in 66:7–24 are also eschatological issues which do not explain the setting or the date of the original audience when the prophet spoke. (c) Isaiah 56:1–8 indicates that those Hebrews and non-Hebrews who wish to worship in God's Holy Mountain in the temple (56:7), the eschatological temple in chap. 60, must act justly, please God, and hold fast to the covenant. Likewise, in 56:9–57:21 God reveals that sinful deeds will be judged, but God will guide his contrite and humble people to a time of eschatological restoration and peace on his Holy Mountain (57:14–21). Thus the prophet describes some things that holy people should always avoid (Baal and Molech worship in 57:3–9) and some things that God's servants should always do (be contrite and humble in 57:15) if they want to enjoy full salvation. The lament in 58:1–59:21 rejects action that does not please God and offers eschatological hope for the redeemed who confess their sins and receive God's everlasting covenant and his Spirit (59:20–21). (d) The lament in 63:7–64:12 questions the destiny of people who lament the loss of God's power, his zeal, his compassion,

---

interpreted 66:1–2 as a reference to rebuilding the temple in Jerusalem. He puts TI the author of 60:1–63:6 between 538 and 515 BC, with 66:18–24 added even later.

[9] B. S. Childs, *Isaiah*, OTL (Louisville: Westminster John Knox, 2001), 444, does not believe this information indicates that chaps. 56–66 can be assigned to "a separate historical person." G. I. Emmerson, *Isaiah 56–66* (New York: T&T Clark, 2004), 12, agrees.

[10] Emmerson, *Isaiah 56–66*, 12, thinks several authors from several uncertain periods of time are responsible for these chapters.

and his salvation (64:11,15; 64:5). The eschatologically oriented answer to this lament in 65:1–66:24 indicates that God has and always will reject those who offer pagan sacrifices (65:2–7,10–12; 66:3–4,15–17) but will allow his contrite and humble servants to enjoy the pleasures of his kingdom in the new heavens and the new earth (65:17–66:2,10–14b). Thus the whole unit of chaps. 56–66 is eschatologically oriented, so it is difficult to find any information in these messages that points to an identifiable historical date for the actual audience that first heard these messages. All these messages describe what people of all ages need to do if they want to enjoy the riches of God's glorious new kingdom and what they must avoid so they will not suffer under the wrath of God's judgment. This section identifies the destinies of those who will and will not enter God's glorious kingdom in the future.

STRUCTURE.   There are a wide variety of opinions concerning the extent of unity and the nature of the structure of chaps. 56–66. J. McKenzie finds "a collection of pieces from different authors [that] do not exhibit the unity that appears in Second Isaiah."[11] G. I. Emmerson explains the relationship between some chapters by pointing to a catchword in one paragraph that is repeated in the next (55:13; 56:5 or 59:19; 59:21).[12] In contrast, E. Charpentier understood the structure of chaps. 56–66 in the following symmetrical chiastic structure that demonstrates both planning and cohesion.

A–56:1–8—Conditions for the entrance to the People of God
    B–56:9–58:14—Reproaches to the wicked; promises to the faithful
        C–59:1–14—Two psalms and a confession of sin
            D–59:15–20—Divine vengeance
                E–60:1–22—The New Jerusalem, fiancé of God
                    F–61:1–11—The announcement of Messianic times
                E'–62:1–12—The New Jerusalem, fiancé of God
            D'–63:1–6—Divine vengeance
        C'–63:7–64:11—Two psalms and a confession of sins
    B'–65:1–66:17—Reproaches on the wicked, promises to the faithful
A'–66:18–24—Conditions for entrance to the people of God[13]

---

[11] J. McKenzie, *Second Isaiah,* AB (Garden City: Doubleday, 1967), lxvii, is even hesitant to speak of the "message" of these chapters; he does admit that this "collection is composed of more than scattered pieces assembled at random."

[12] Emmerson, *Isaiah 56–66,* 16–18, later indicates that she thinks the arrangement of the material is much deeper than mere catchwords since a logical consequence can be traced in the arrangement. She does see 60–62 as the central pivotal chapters in this unit and adopts something similar to Charpentier's chiastic structure.

[13] E. Charpentier, *Jeunesse du Vieux Testament* (Paris: Fayard, 1963), 79–80. This outline was updated and revised in E. Charpentier, *How to Read the Old Testament* (New York: Crossroad, 1981), 77, where both the B and B' segments are divided into two parts. J. Oswalt, "Isaiah 60–62," *CTJ* 40 (2005): 95–103 has a similar outline on p. 98, but he does recognize that not everything in chaps. 56–60 has a parallel part in chaps. 61–66 (61:1–3; 65:17–25; 66:5–16).

This analysis agrees with the widespread conclusion that the oracles of salvation in chaps. 60–62 form the nucleus or centerpiece of these messages,[14] but commentators have had a much greater problem agreeing on how the chapters before and after 60–62 fit in with this strong hope for the restoration of Zion. R. H. O'Connell also identifies a concentric chiastic design throughout these chapters, but his model includes chaps. 55–66 and his divisions of paragraphs do not always match those of Charpentier.[15] Several of the divisions between messages that are used in this commentary are similar to those of Charpentier, although the titles and overall organization are different (60:1–63:6 are made up of one larger unit divided into four paragraphs). There are some problems with Charpentier's outlining of these messages into smaller blocks, as well as difficulties interrelating the diverse messages into a united chiastic whole. Although a few similar themes are dealt with in both chaps. 56–59 and 63:7–66:17 (i.e., pleasing or not pleasing God in 58:3,13; 65:12; 66:4), the analysis below does not find the neat chiastic arrangement of Charpentier and O'Connell overly convincing. Sometimes there is relatively little similarity between the messages in the first half of this chiastic outline and those in the second half.[16]

It appears that these messages are organized into three longer segments (56–59; 60:1–63:6; 63:7–66:24) with 60:1–63:6 at the center.

1. The first unit (56–59) is centered around the need for people to act justly, do what is right (56:1; 58:8), and humble themselves (57:15; 58:5). They need to please God and hold fast to the covenant (56:2,4,6) so that they can enter God's holy mountain and worship him in the future (56:7; 57:13; 58:6; 59:20). Unfortunately God will find little evidence of justice on the earth (57:2,12; 58:2; 59:4,8,11,14,15).

2. The center unit (60:1–63:6) is focused on the coming of God, his people, the Gentiles, their wealth, and the Anointed One to enjoy the glorious kingdom of God at Zion. This will transform the city, the people, the joy, the presence of righteousness, the praise of God, and the name of the city (61:4–62:12). At that time everyone in Zion will be holy because God's wrath will destroy the wicked (63:1–6).

3. The third unit (63:7–66:24) is about the future destiny of God's Hebrew and Gentile servants who will inherit his kingdom (65:8–10,17–25; 66:5–14a,18–23) and the wicked who will not benefit from God's hand of salvation but will feel his fury and destruction (63:15–65:7; 65:11–15; 66:3–4,24).

[14] C. Westermann, *Isaiah 40–66*, OTL (Philadelphia: Westminster, 1977), 296.

[15] R. H. O'Connell, *Concentricity and Continuity: The Literary Structure of Isaiah* (Sheffield: Academic Press,1994), 219.

[16] Both section A and A' do refer to foreigners worshipping God, but one can hardly say that 66:18–24 is about the "conditions for entrance to the people of God."

Thus although each literary unit contrasts God's dealings with the righteous and the wicked, each major unit is unique with a sense of final fulfillment at the end. The general structure is:

The just will experience God's salvation	56:1–59:21
God will bring salvation to Zion	60:1–63:6
The destiny of servants and rebels	63:7–66:24

One might have expected the final eschatological kingdom in 60:1–63:6 to appear last, since it happens last in chronological order, but the present organization has the advantage of putting the description of God's glorious kingdom in the middle so that the dramatic concluding emphasis falls on the challenging question that every person must wrestle with: "What will be my destiny?" Do I want to be one of those rebels who will not experience the zeal, mighty power, tenderness, and compassion of God (63:15)? Do I want to endure his sword (65:12), fire (66:15–16), and eternal damnation (66:24)? Or do I want to be one of God's servants who will joyfully live in Zion in the new heavens and new earth with fellow worshippers from all over the world (65:17–15; 66:5–16, 18–23)? This is not a completely new question in Isaiah, but it is the most important one. Everyone's destiny hinges on how they answer this question.

This section of the book of Isaiah has a close relationship to the themes in other chapters. From beginning to end Isaiah has several hopeful messages about God's plans to establish his kingdom where righteous people from all over the world will dwell together with God in Zion (2:1–4; 4:2–6; 11:1–16; 33:17–24; 45:18–24; 52:1–12; 60:1–62:12; 66:27–24). Repeatedly, throughout Isaiah there are contrasts between the righteous kingdom of God and the unjust kingdom of man (2:1–5 versus 2:6–22; 3:1–4:1 versus 4:2–6; 9:1–7 versus 9:8–10:4; 24:1–23 versus 25:1–12; 34:1–17 versus 35:1–10). It is not surprising that chaps. 56–66 develop a contrast between God's holy world in Zion and the unjust kingdoms of man that God will judge (56:7–57:13; 59:15–20; 63:1–6; 65:1–16). Such contrast should motivate those who hear or read these messages to trust God and hold fast to the covenant so that they might enjoy the coming glorious kingdom of God (56:1–8; 57:14–21; 60:1–62:12; 66:18–24).[17]

1. The Just Will Experience God's Future Salvation (56:1–59:21)

Since chaps. 60:1–63:6 form a fairly clear literary unit in the center of these chapters, it would be natural to assume that 56:1–59:21 would be the first major section of chaps. 56–66. Relatively few studies work at defining the unity

---

[17] This picture of God's future kingdom is gradually developed and explained in more and more detail in 2:1–5; 4:2–6; 9:1–7; 11:1–16; 25:1–9; 26:1–7; 30:19–26; 32; 35; 40:1–11; 41:17–20; 42:1–13; 43:14–21; 45:20–25; 49:1–13; 51:1–6; 52:7–10; 54:1–17.

of these chapters because few treat these chapters as a literary unit. Instead, many commentaries address the individual paragraphs without commenting on how these paragraphs fit together. After noting that biblical writers sometimes begin and end a literary unit by repeating the same vocabulary, G. J. Polan recognized that the announcement of the nearness of the "coming" (*lābô*) of salvation at the beginning of the unit in 56:1 matches the idea that the Redeemer "will come" (*ûbā*) to Zion with salvation in 59:20 at the end of this unit. These two emphases on the coming of God to Zion provide a natural introduction to what happens in 60:1–3 when God's glory comes as a light to Zion and attracts people from many nations to come to the city of God.[18] The contrasting emphasis on the just who will and the unjust who will not experience God's coming salvation remains the focus throughout 56:1–59:21. These two emphases are seen in the back-and-forth counterpoints illustrated in the following chart of chaps. 56–59. This section ends in 59:15b–21 with a conclusion that emphasizes both themes.

Judgment comes on:	Salvation comes to:
	The just who keep the covenant (56:1–8)
Unjust leaders and idolaters (56:9–57:13)	The humble and contrite (57:14–21)
Unjust who fast (58:1–5)	Ones who please God in fasting (58:6–14)
Sinful, violent, and unjust (59:1–15a)	
God will come in wrath—and salvation (59:15b–21)	

Sin is the stumbling block that brings injustice, perverts the worship of God, and prevents people from enjoying God's kingdom; so it is not surprising to read that those who are sinners will eventually suffer under God's severe judgment. But the prophet does not focus just on past failures, for he repeatedly turns to the positive news that motivates people to faith so that they can experience God's salvation. God will overcome all the problems sin causes by taking vengeance on his enemies, forgiving humble people of their sins, and redeeming his people when he comes to Zion. In the end he will triumph over evil because his marvelous salvation is sure. Every reader of these promises can confidently walk joyfully by faith, knowing that their destiny is in God's hand and that he has already planned to reveal his glory to his servants in Zion someday in the future.

---

[18] G. J. Polan, *In the Ways of Justice toward Salvation: A Rhetorical Analysis of Isaiah 56–59* (Rome: Pontifical Biblical Institute, 1986), 19–22. The word "come" (בּוֹא) is used 11 times in chap. 60.

(1) All Who Keep the Covenant Will See God's Salvation (56:1–8)

[1]This is what the LORD says:

> "Maintain justice
>> and do what is right,
> for my salvation is close at hand
>> and my righteousness will soon be revealed.
> [2]Blessed is the man who does this,
>> the man who holds it fast,
> who keeps the Sabbath without desecrating it,
>> and keeps his hand from doing any evil."
> [3]Let no foreigner who has bound himself to the LORD say,
>> "The LORD will surely exclude me from his people."
> And let not any eunuch complain,
>> "I am only a dry tree."

[4]For this is what the LORD says:

> "To the eunuchs who keep my Sabbaths,
>> who choose what pleases me
>> and hold fast to my covenant—
> [5]to them I will give within my temple and its walls
>> a memorial and a name
>> better than sons and daughters;
> I will give them an everlasting name
>> that will not be cut off.
> [6]And foreigners who bind themselves to the LORD
>> to serve him,
> to love the name of the LORD,
>> and to worship him,
> all who keep the Sabbath without desecrating it
>> and who hold fast to my covenant—
> [7]these I will bring to my holy mountain
>> and give them joy in my house of prayer.
> Their burnt offerings and sacrifices
>> will be accepted on my altar;
> for my house will be called
>> a house of prayer for all nations."
> [8]The Sovereign LORD declares—
>> he who gathers the exiles of Israel:
> "I will gather still others to them
>> besides those already gathered."

This oracle joins together a series of admonitions and promises given to those who wish to maintain their covenant relationship with God (56:4,6). Central to this covenant relationship is the internal motivation and commitment to please God (59:4), to hold fast to the covenant (56:2,4,6), and to love God (56:6). This will produce behavioral actions that are consistent with God's

ways. The external demonstration of covenant life includes just relationships
with others (56:1), setting the Sabbath apart as a holy day dedicated to God
(56:2,4,6), serving God (56:6), and turning from evil (56:2). All those who do
these things will enjoy God's blessings (56:2), will experience God's salvation
(56:1), and God will accept their worship (56:7), even if they happen to be
foreigners or a eunuch (56:4–7).

This oracle seems to be dealing with a couple of questions raised by the
wide-open invitation for everyone to come to enjoy what God offers through
his everlasting covenant in chap. 55. Can just anyone come, enjoy this covenant
relationship, and worship at God's Holy Mountain (56:7; 60–62)? What are the
central things God requires of Gentiles who come and want to worship at this
temple? The answer impacts the Hebrew reader's understanding of what God
requires of all his people, as well as the Gentile's understanding of what God
expects of them. If Gentiles are to be included, the Israelites need to deal justly
with all righteous people from all backgrounds because God accepts worship
from all who keep their covenant relationship with him. Previous chapters have
talked about the eschatological inclusion of the Gentiles in 2:2–3; 11:10–12;
14:1–2; 18:7; 19:18–25; 42:6; 45:22–24; 49:6,22–23,26, and the invitation in
55:1 is open to anyone who wants to come. Isaiah 55:4 indicates that a leader
from the line of David will be a witness to the nations, so it is not surprising
to find a discussion of what is required of those Gentiles who want to worship
at God's temple. This positive message begins to prepare for the discussion of
the coming of people from all different nations in chaps. 60–62. This emphasis
on the inclusion of Gentiles at the beginning of this long group of chapters
(56–66) is somewhat parallel to a similar thematic emphasis at the end of this
unit in 66:18–23, but the discussions are not the same for there is no emphasis
on doing justice, holding fast to the covenant, pleasing God, or keeping the
Sabbath in 66:18–24.[19]

Although the mention of the Sabbath, the eunuch, and the foreigner creates
something of a disjunctive break with topics from earlier chapters, J. Muilenburg is correct in asserting that there is no "radical break with the past, but a
development"[20] of the theology of previous chapters. An immediate connection is made between (a) God giving these foreigners an "everlasting name
that will not be cut off" in 56:5 and the Lord's "everlasting name that will not
be cut off" in 55:13; (b) the open invitation for anyone (even foreigners) to
come, eat, and enjoy God's blessings in 55:1 and God's offer to bless all (even
foreigners) who hold fast to the covenant in 56:2; (c) God's word accomplishes
what "pleases" God in 55:11 and the eunuch does what "pleases" God in 56:4;

---

[19] Ibid., 80–88, investigates eight words that are found in both paragraphs and concludes that
these two passages form an internal inclusion marking the beginning and end of a literary unit.

[20] J. Muilenburg, "Isaiah 40–66," *IB*, 5:653, says, "The Poem in the whole is akin to Second
Isaiah." J. D. W. Watts, *Isaiah 34–66*, WBC (Waco: Word, 1987), 244–51, ties 56:1–8 so closely to
what precedes that he makes 54:17c–56:8 his literary unit.

(d) people are to seek God while he is "near" in 55:6 and God's salvation is "near" in 56:1; and (e) both chapters look forward to new people joining God's people when he establishes his eschatological kingdom (55:1,6–7; 56:3,6,8). In many ways chap. 56 is an expansion of the offer of salvation introduced in chap. 55,[21] specifying how two groups of people (and by implication all other non-Israelites) will be integrated into normal worship practices in the future.

The mention of Sabbath worship, sacrifices, the temple, prayer, and foreigners is sometimes associated with the controversial issues that arose in the time of Ezra and Nehemiah (Ezra 9:1–10:17; Neh 8:1–18; 9:14; 10:31; 13:15–22), for at that time there was a distinction between the Jews who returned from the exile and the non-Jews or part-Jews who made up the "people of the land" (Ezra 4:4–5; 6:19–22; 9:1–2; Neh 10:28). Thus some view 56:1–8 as either a reaction against Nehemiah's narrow exclusive attitudes, or possibly the more inclusive policy in 56:1–8 was what caused Nehemiah to tighten up criteria for membership in the postexilic community. But in contrast to this interpretation, G. I. Emmerson maintains that the postexilic background of Nehemiah does not fit 56:1–8 because, "The foreigners in question in Isaiah 56 are individual proselytes (cf. 44:5) threatened with exclusion from the community. . . . In contrast, those excluded in Nehemiah were not adherents of the Jewish faith."[22] Ezra and Nehemiah were not against proselytes to the Hebrew faith who were of foreign descent; they were against foreigners who rejected the Hebrew faith and refused to become proselytes. P. A. Smith suggests that the background of 56:1–8 is related to the many foreign proselytes who will come to Zion in chaps. 60–62. Thus, 56:1–8 indicates that they will not just be menial second-

---

[21] W. A. M. Beuken, "Isa 56:9–57:13: An Example of the Isaianic Legacy of Trito-Isaiah," in *Tradition and Reinterpretation in Jewish and Early Christian Literature: Festschrift für J. C. H. Lebram*, ed. J. W. van Henten et al. (Leiden: Brill, 1986), 48–64, suggests that Isa 56:1–57:13 is in fact a commentary on what was said in chap. 55. As a commentary on chap. 55, he concludes that 56:1–8 "elucidates further the place to which one goes, the categories of persons who are allowed in there, and the conditions on which they can enter." R. de Hoop, "The Interpretation of Isaiah 56:1–9: Comfort or Criticism?" *JBL* 127 (2008): 671–95, n. 50, lists numerous studies that have maintained the close connection between 56:1–8 and chaps. 54–55. Obviously those who do not accept the existence of a "Trito-Isaiah" also find a close relationship between these chapters.

[22] Emmerson, *Isaiah 56–66*, 62, counters the approach of Blenkinsopp, *Isaiah 56–66*, 51–54, who connects Isa 56–66 to Ezra 9–10 and Neh 13 based on the reference to "those who tremble at God's word" in Isa 66:2,5; Ezra 9:4; 10:3. The "servants" and the "tremblers" are members of the same persecuted eschatological-prophetic group who were opposed by a group of priests, the idolaters who delight in abominations. In Ezra 9–10 the servants and tremblers (Ezra was part of this group) were able to dictate a policy of separation, but in Isaiah 56 they were marginalized and persecuted. J. Vermeylen, *Du Prophète Isaïe à l'apocalyptique*, 458–57, also rejects the connection between Isa 56:1–8 and the background provided by Ezra–Nehemiah. Whybray, *Isaiah 40–66*, 197, is correct in rejecting a connection with the situation of Ezra–Nehemiah. N. H. Snaith, "Isaiah 40–66: A Study of the Teachings of Second Isaiah and Its Consequences," in *Studies in the Second Part of Isaiah*, ed. H. S. Orlinsky, VTSup 14 (Leiden: Brill, 1967), 135–264, views Isa 56:1–8 as a reaction against the strict limitations enforced by the Zadokite priests in Ezek 44:6–9, but 44:6–9 is against uncircumcised foreigners and does allow for foreign proselytes in 47:22–23.

class servants of the Hebrew people (60:7,10,14); they themselves will be able to fully participate with their Hebrew brothers as they serve and worship the Lord (56:6–7).[23] On this reading 56:1–8 refers to what should happen in that eschatological setting when God's salvation comes to Zion. The temple is a future temple, not the one mentioned in Ezra 6:15. There is nothing in 56:1–8 that allows one to identify the time when this message was originally spoken, for it relates to what will happen in a distant future setting.

J. Muilenburg classifies this oracle as "instruction or *torah*" by a prophet, while C. Westermann finds a proclamation of salvation in 56:1–2 and a lament in 56:3. Isaiah 56:4–7 substantiates a rejection of the complaint, and 56:8 is a promise.[24] Although all the texts in Isaiah that begin with an imperative verb instruct an audience on what they should do, this does not automatically turn all of them into the genre of *torah*. This oracle deals with future relationships between God, the Hebrew people, and foreigners (56:3), but the principles in this proclamation of salvation are not just applicable to the eschatological period. Underneath these exhortations concerning the future are principles that everyone should pay attention to, for God honors those who deal justly and hold fast to the covenant in every era of history.

The structure of this paragraph can be divided into three main parts:

Maintain behavior fitting a time of salvation	56:1–2
All who hold to the covenant will be accepted	56:3–7
Do not exclude anyone	3
Accept the eunuch	4–5
Accept the foreigner	6–7
God will gather many people	56:8[25]

---

[23] P. A. Smith, *Rhetoric and Redaction in Trito-Isaiah*, 59–60, rejects the view that the content of 56:1–8 implies that the temple has already been built, so he dates it between 538–515.

[24] Muilenburg, "Isaiah 40–66," *IB*, 5:652, and R. D. Wells, "'Isaiah as an Exponent of Torah: Isaiah 56:1–8," in *New Visions of Isaiah,* ed. R. F. Melugin and M. A. Sweeney, JSOTSup 214 (Sheffield: Sheffield Academic Press, 1996), 140–55, connect these verses to *torah* instruction, but it is very different from the book of Exodus or Deuteronomy, even though it deals with issues addressed in Deut 23. J. L. Koole, *Isaiah III, Volume 3: Isaiah 56–66* (Leuven: Peeters, 2001), 5, summarizes the various approaches and concludes that this is a proclamation of salvation regarding what will happen in the future.

[25] De Hoop, "The Interpretation of Isaiah 56:1–9," 671–95, includes v. 9 in this paragraph, viewing v. 9 as the conclusion to the first paragraph rather than the introduction to the next paragraph (pp. 673–78). This is based on the Masoretic division of the text (indicating a new paragraph) by an indentation of the line after v. 9 and not after v. 8 in several ancient manuscripts, including 1QIs[a] and 1QIs[b]. The implication of this change in paragraph breaks is that v. 9 would need to be given a positive interpretation rather than the usual negative interpretation. Thus this verse might be interpreted more like the positive invitation to a feast in Ezek 39:17 instead of the negative tone of Jer 12:9. De Hoop then connects this idea to God's final covenant with the beasts (Hos 2:18 [Heb 2:20]) and the peace between man and animals in Isa 11:6–8. In the end he views v. 9 to have a janus function of both concluding what precedes and opening what follows.

G. J. Polan recognized that "come" (*bô*ᵓ) in 56:1 and "assemble, gather" (*qābaṣ*) in 56:8 form a parallel inclusio that frames the description of God's salvation in this and several other literary units.[26] Isaiah 56:3–7 are naturally held together by the introduction of the complaint of the eunuch and foreigner in 56:3, followed by a separate treatment of the eunuch (56:4–5) and the foreigner (56:6–7). This paragraph demonstrates inner cohesiveness by the repetition of several vocabulary: "keep" (*šāmar* in 56:1,2a,2b,4,6), "do" (*ᶜāśâ* in 56:1,2a,2b), "assemble, gather" (*qābaṣ* in 56:8a,8b,8c), "hold fast, be strong" (*ḥāzaq* in 56:2,4,6), and "profane" (*ḥālal* in 56:2,6).[27]

56:1–2 The prophet's message begins with a divine messenger speech ("thus says the LORD"), assuring the reader that what follows has full authority and should guide the theology of the reader. J. Blenkinsopp hypothesizes that both 40:1 and 56:1 originally had their own full-blown superscriptions much like 1:1. These were used to set the following chapters apart as a unique and separate literary addition to Isaiah, but he believes these superscriptions were editorially removed during the last stages of editing the book.[28] Although this would clearly set chaps. 56–66 apart from 40–55, there is absolutely no textual evidence for this highly imaginative hypothesis. Thus this suggestion should be rejected.

The imperative exhortation[29] to "keep/maintain justice and do what is right"[30] encourages behavior that is characteristic of the acts of God and the Messiah (5:16; 9:7; 11:4; 16:5; 32:1,16–17; 33:5), so it is not surprising to hear that Isaiah earlier admonished his readers to "learn to do right and seek justice" (1:17). These were the behavior patterns that God expected his people to exhibit throughout their lives and especially in his glorious kingdom (1:21,26; 5:7; 26:9; 61:8). The lack of justice and righteousness periodically caused God to bring severe judgment on his people and other nations (10:2; 28:17; 29:21; 59:15b), so there is no question about the importance of these principles. B. Gosse reads 56:1–2 as a repetition of 55:6–7 because both reflect an ethical

---

[26] Polan, *In the Ways of Justice toward Salvation*, 51, finds this same function for these two terms in 60:1 and 4 (the terms are used parallel to one another in 43:5; 49:18; 66:18).

[27] Koole, *Isaiah III, Volume 3: Isaiah 56–66*, 3–4, and P. A. Smith, *Rhetoric and Redaction in Trito-Isaiah*, 50–53, discuss various attempts to break 56:1–8 into separate redactional units (often 1–2 and 3–8) as well as the assignment of several verses to later redactional layers. Childs, *Isaiah*, 455, concludes that this redactional approach "is not useful if it only succeeds in replacing the final form of the text with a historical process according to a highly subjective interpretive theory."

[28] Blenkinsopp, *Isaiah 56–66*, 29, 131.

[29] GKC §110a refers to the syntactical use of the imperative verb (both שִׁמְרוּ "keep, guard" and עֲשׂוּ "do") to express an admonition or exhortation.

[30] שִׁמְרוּ מִשְׁפָּט וַעֲשׂוּ צְדָקָה the phrase "maintain justice and do right" uses terminology that is very common in this literary section and earlier in Isaiah (see 1:27; 5:7,16; 9:6; 28:17; 32:16; 33:5; 58:2; 59:9,14), especially in a context concerning the behavior of judges and rulers, but in reality God expects similar behavior of every person. Although Deuteronomy might focus more on keeping the commandments and statutes, here God is more concerned with right relationships to others and God.

tone in relationship to the coming of God's salvation, but 55:6–7 focuses much
more on starting a just relationship with God though the confession of sins,
while 56:1a describes the just interpersonal relationships between people who
will enjoy God's coming deeds of salvation.[31] These are related issues, but the
behavior traits of righteousness and justice should not be seen as conditional
requirements placed on people who wish to enjoy God's salvation, for the message of 55:1–2 was that people could come freely and eat without paying any
price. It is not necessary to be righteous before a person can receive God's attention and salvation, for such a condition would exclude all mankind because
no one is truly righteous and no one deserves God's grace (64:6; 1 Kgs 8:46).
Instead, the prophet is encouraging people who are already a part of Israel's
covenant community to live in ways that are consistent with God's character in
light of the fact that God's salvation is near. Thus as J. Oswalt says, "obedience
is to be lived out as a response to salvation,"[32] not as a condition for receiving
God's gracious blessings.

The second half of the verse explains what God will do in the near future;
thus, it provides a persuasive theological rationale (*kî*, "because") that legitimates the idea that people should behave justly. The hope of enjoying God's
salvation ("my salvation" *yĕšûʿātî*) should motivate people to live according
to kingdom principles both now and in the future because in this new kingdom justice and "my righteousness" will reign and govern all behavior (9:7;
60:17). Several things should be noticed about God's salvation. First this offer
of salvation comes from God; it is God who brings it, and he is bringing it as
a reality to be experienced by his people. This salvation is not an imposition
of law and order by an outside force but refers to God's personal and visible
entrance[33] into human history to reign as King in Zion (52:7–10). He will draw
Israel and the nations to his light, transform the heaven and the earth (51:5–6;
60:1–3; 65:17), and institute all aspects of his plan of salvation. This will be the
time when God's victorious "righteous deeds" (*ṣĕdāqâ*)[34] will become evident,

---

[31] B. Gosse, "Sabbath, Identity and Universalism Go Together after the Return from Exile,"
JSOT 29 (2005): 359–70, connects these commands to the exhortations about justice and Sabbath
observance in Ezek 18 and 20. He quotes E. J. Kissane, *The Book of Isaiah* (Dublin: Brown and
Nolan, 1943), 2:208–9, who has a similar opinion of the relationship between 55:6–7 and 56:1.

[32] Oswalt, *Isaiah 40–66*, NICOT (Grand Rapids: Eerdmans, 1998), 455, claims that "the whole
structure of the book argues" against a conditional salvation dependent on righteous works.

[33] The idea of God's "coming, entering" is expressed with the infinitive construct לָבוֹא. The
infinitive construct could be functioning as a replacement of a finite verb (GKC §114d) since there
is no finite verb in this clause. Another option that may be better is to imply the "to be" verb and
then translate the clause "my salvation (is) near to coming," or "my salvations (is) coming soon."

[34] Righteous works relate to man's need to act righteously in his relationship with others (mostly in chaps. 1–39), while God's righteous acts relate to his deliverance and salvation (mainly discussed in chaps. 40–55). Studies on this concept are available in the work of J. Scullion, "SEDEQ-
SEDAQAH in Isaiah cc. 40–66 with special reference to the continuity in meaning between Second
and Third Isaiah," *UF* 3 (1971): 335–38; and J. N. Oswalt, "Righteousness in Isaiah: A Study of
the Function of Chapters 55–66 in the Present Structure of the Book," in *Writing and Reading the*

when he vindicates his people and faithfully fulfills his promises. Thus it is logical for the prophet to encourage the people of God who desire to be with God in that future kingdom to exhibit righteous behavior toward others now. God's past acts have already demonstrated his faithful and consistent pattern of righteous works of salvation toward all mankind, so it is appropriate for his people to mirror his righteousness.

Verse 2 functions as a blessing on the person (Hebrew or non-Hebrew) who responds to the exhortation in 1a. The "this" (zō't) that the blessed man does, often (but not always) refers to something new that is mentioned later, but the fact that "this" refers to something one "does" (connecting it to "does," ʿāśû, in 56:1a) suggests to some that "this" points back to the one who maintains justice and "does" what is right.[35] In either case one should not make a major distinction between the general moral actions encouraged in 1a and the specific cultic and ethical actions mentioned in 2b. There is not a great deal of difference between "keeping, maintaining" justice, "keeping, maintaining" the Sabbath, and "keeping, maintaining"[36] the hand from doing evil. These actions are further amplified by describing such action as "holding fast, holding strongly" (from a hiphil form of ḥāzaq "to cause to be strong"). These characteristics are all part of the righteous lifestyle of the blessed person. The "it" (bāh) that one should hold fast to is not identified, so one could argue from the context that a person is to hold on strongly to the promise of God's salvation (56:1b), to God himself (64:7[Hb. 64:6]), or to the covenant and its promises (56:4,6). In reality, those who hold on to any one of these naturally hold on to all the rest, so no essential distinction should be pressed.

Specific things that one should do and not do are briefly explained using a series of participles in 56:2b about "keeping." It is a little surprising to find a reference to keeping the Sabbath celebration because it is never mentioned elsewhere in chaps. 1–55 (except briefly in 1:13). Some authors connect this message to the discussion about Sabbath-keeping in the postexilic era in Neh 10:31 and 13:15. This is based on the belief that, after the destruction of the temple in 587 BC, Sabbath-keeping was one of the key ways of defining

---

Scroll of Isaiah: Studies of an Interpretive Tradition, ed. C. C. Broyles and C. A. Evans, VTSup 70 (Leiden: Brill, 1997), 177–91. Oswalt finds 12:1–6 to be using this term in a way similar to how it was used in chaps. 40–55 and 48:18; 51:1,7; 55:7, using the word similar to its usage (referring to right moral behavior) in chaps. 1–39. He believes that part of the purpose for writing chaps. 55–66 was written to unify the two perspectives on righteousness (p. 178). It appears that there is some level of unification already going on in all three sections of the book.

[35] GKC §136a points out that the demonstrative pronoun "this" זֶה "almost always points out a (new) person or thing, while הוּא . . . refers to a person or thing already mentioned or known." Yet he does give examples where this general principle is not followed. Whybray, *Isaiah 40–66*, 197, suggests that it has both a backward reference to 1a as well as a forward reference to 2b.

[36] Some form of the verb שָׁמַר is found once in v. 1 and twice in v. 2, while some form of עָשָׂה is used once in v. 1 and twice in v. 2.

the orthodox community of Israel.[37] But this approach is not overly convincing, for numerous passages (Amos 8:5; Isa 1:13; Jer 17:19–27; Ezek 20:13–26) indicate that Sabbath-keeping was already an important issue in preexilic Israel and a sign of the covenant from the beginning of the nation (Exod 31:12–17; Num 15:32–36). The discussion of the relationship between God and the person who holds fast to the covenant and keeps the Sabbath in 56:2 sets out some general principles that are later used to justify the inclusion of the foreigners and eunuchs who participate in Sabbath worship in 56:4–7.

First, the prophet must get his reader to accept the idea that all those who enjoy God's salvation (no matter who they are) should hold fast to the covenant, keep "from profaning" the Sabbath, and keep their hands "from doing"[38] evil. Since the Sabbath was the time when people joined together to worship God at the temple and 2:1–4; 18:7; 19:18–25; 45:22–23; 49:22–23; and 60:1–62:11 deal with both Israelites and non-Israelites coming to honor and offer gifts to God in the temple at Zion, certainly it is important for these same people (Israelites and non-Israelites in 56:1–8) to understand how they both will be guided by the same just behavior patterns and enjoy the same worship privileges in God's future kingdom. Neither group (Hebrews or people from the nations) should violate the holy nature of that day or defile the holy temple where they would come to worship. One should be careful not to interpret these instructions as legalistic requirements that set out to define a baseline of acceptable behavior. Instead, one should understand them as the natural, outward expressions of a heart that truly loves God.

56:3 The next subparagraph (56:3–7) assures all those who hold fast to the covenant that they will be fully accepted and included with all the other people who come to worship God at the temple. Two groups are mentioned, the son of a foreigner and the eunuch (60:3–10; 61:5). At that future time they will join themselves with the Israelites just like the proselyte Egyptians who came up out of Egypt with the Israelites in the exodus (Exod 12:38,48–49); Rahab, the harlot who lived in the Canaanite city of Jericho (Josh 2:8–13; 6:17,25); Ruth, the Moabite woman who married Boaz (Ruth 2:10); Uriah the Hittite (2 Sam 11:11), and a host of others in the past (1 Kgs 8:41) and the future (Isa 14:1; 60:3–11). Numbers 15:13–15 indicates that an alien who trusted God could offer sacrifices and that "you and the alien shall be the same before the Lord." Nevertheless, there were other aliens that were separate from the Israelites and

---

[37] Westermann, *Isaiah 40–66*, 310, views this as the new setting for this chapter. Although Sabbath-keeping was probably an important exilic marker that identified the Israelites in Babylon, there is no text that says this or describes Sabbath worship in Babylonian exile. Since the temple had already been built for almost 100 years at the time of Nehemiah 13 and the people were relatively free to worship as they pleased, it appears that Nehemiah found that Sabbath-keeping was not practiced by many Israelite people.

[38] The two "from" clauses מֵחַלְּלוֹ "from profaning it" (the suffix וֹ "it" refers to the Sabbath day") and מֵעֲשׂוֹת "from doing," are both infinitive construct forms that prefix the preposition מִן.

treated differently (Deut 14:21; 15:3). Possibly these included the heathen living among the Israelites who did not convert. Some commentators imagine that some Gentiles feared that they might be excluded from temple worship, but the tone of the rest of the book of Isaiah is very positive toward foreigners who turn to God, so this seems unlikely. While one might be able to hypothesize a possible reason why some foreigners might think the Israelites would exclude them from worship, it is hard to conceive of a reason for them to fear that the LORD himself "will surely exclude, separate"[39] them from being an integral part of his people.

J. Blenkinsopp hypothesizes that there was a wide division between "the 'servants of YHWH,' and the skeptics—those who, in anachronistic Hasidic terms, might be called the *mitnaggědîm*, 'the opponents' (50:11–12; 51:7–8). Isaiah 56–66 reflects the process by which the division widened into open schism."[40] He believes that the failure to see the fulfillment of the promises in chaps. 40–55 led to frustrations and a division in the community that redefined the criteria applied to those who would experience God's redemption. This involved ethnic, political, and religious criteria. He believes that in this situation the prophet in 56:3–7 is encouraging those who fear they might be excluded.[41] Blenkinsopp suggests that the group that was attempting to exclude the foreigners and eunuchs was "a more rigorist, integrationist, and ritualistic source within the community"[42] that accepted Ezekiel's exclusive ideas (Ezek 44:4–9 does not allow foreigners into the temple) and the Deuteronomic exclusion of certain foreigners and eunuchs (Deut 23:1–9). But this whole approach must be seriously questioned because it attempts to identify a human reason for rejecting certain disqualified people in the time of Nehemiah, rather than the divine reason (56:3) in a future eschatological era. More appropriately, P. A. Smith believes that the background for understanding 56:1–8 should be found in the description of the foreigners in chaps. 60–62; but his suggestion that "the portrayal of the role of the foreigners in humble and servile terms had provoked fear amongst the foreign proselytes in the community that they would be excluded from full membership"[43] is less convincing, for it is never voiced

---

[39] The Hb. expresses a strong statement by repeating the same root twice, one as an infinitive absolute and one as a finite verb (GKC §113n). Thus יַבְדִּילַנִי הַבְדֵּל "separating, he will separate me" means, "without a doubt, he will surely separate me."

[40] Blenkinsopp, *Isaiah 56–66*, 133, saw this as an inner Jewish conflict between those "who tremble at God's word" (66:5) and the "servants" group that was shunned by their fellow Jews.

[41] Ibid., 136.

[42] Ibid., 138. Hanson, *The Dawn of Apocalyptic*, finds within chaps. 56–66 a disenfranchised visionary group who followed "Second Isaiah" fighting against a powerful group of Zadokite priests who followed Ezekiel. This misunderstands the problems in Isaiah and Nehemiah, for both Isaiah and Nehemiah were against the inclusion of pagans (57:3–13; 65:1–7; Neh 9–10), and neither were against the inclusion of proselytes.

[43] P. A. Smith, *Rhetoric and Redaction in Trito-Isaiah*, 62. Koole, *Isaiah III, Volume 3: Isaiah 56–66*, 13, thinks that a more probable situation for this instruction might be the period when the

in any passage. A variation of this general approach might suggest that since the non-Israelites do not actually speak about any of their own fears, 56:1–8 is the prophet's proactive attempt to establish the status of the foreigners as being equal participants in the community of believers when they come to Zion in the future so that all those who read about them in chaps. 60–62 will not come to a false conclusion that they have an inferior status. Neither the foreigner nor any other Israelites should think that God would keep the converted foreigners or eunuchs in some special category that would exclude them from regular worship in Zion. Thus 56:3 would not be reporting an existing problem but aimed at heading off a potential misunderstanding in the future.

Although Deut 23:1–8 excluded certain foreigners, illegitimate children, and eunuchs from entering the temple up to the tenth generation, the tenth generation would be long past when God assembles his people and many Gentile nations in the future eschatological setting of chaps. 60–62. The "eunuch" (*sārîm*, possibly workers in the royal court of a king) is not given a national identity, so he may or may not be an Israelite. The initial concern of the eunuch is not explicitly related to God excluding him from temple worship but is connected to his status as "a dry tree" (*ʿēṣ yābēš*, 53:3b). It is possible to interpret this to mean that he can have no children just like a dry tree can have no fruit, but maybe the point goes even beyond this issue, for a dry tree is usually considered worthless, useless, and is consequently burnt up in a fire. Possibly the eunuchs felt worthless and despised by some members of Hebrew society. God's answer in the next verse responds to this potential feeling of worthlessness.

56:4–5 In order to alleviate any doubts about the status of the eunuch and foreigner, God announces a new authoritative word ("this is what the LORD says") to inform all future people in Zion about what he expects of them. If they are to keep their hands from evil (56:2b), they need to treat foreign people committed to the covenant with equality and respect. This instruction about the eunuchs includes (a) a description of their commitment to honor God (56:4) and (b) God's commitment to honor them (56:5).

The faithful eunuchs (56:4) are described in terms similar to the broad principles characteristic of every blessed man in 56:2. Keeping the Sabbath should not be interpreted merely as the formal compliance with a certain set of Hebrew ritual rules of behavior. Keeping the Sabbath has a much deeper spiritual meaning, for keeping the Sabbath implies both a covenant relationship with God and a desire to honor and glorify God's name. Setting aside the Sabbath day to the Lord indicates that this person recognizes the importance of weekly celebrating God's salvation and having a time of special dedication to the Lord (Exod 31:12–17). J. L. Koole rightly lays the emphasis "on

Israelites came back from exile, but Smith's view that it relates to the eschatological people joining with Israel in chaps. 60–62 seems like a better option.

the spiritual background of Sabbath observance, the acknowledgement of and fellowship with the creating and liberating God (Exod 20:11; Deut 5:15) who offers a prospect of the coming salvation."[44] This theological stance toward the Sabbath is coherent and consistent with the decision to "choose what pleases me,"[45] but the covenantal "choice" (*bāḥar*) to please God involves much more than just Sabbath activity. Because of his love, God first chose Israel as well as foreigners to be his covenant people (Deut 7:6–8). God's action of choosing them challenged the people to choose to walk in a way pleasing to God and to maintain a close covenant relationship with him.[46] God announced what would please him throughout the Pentateuch, and these statements focus not just on proper relationships with other people but, more importantly, on his people's love and fear of him (Deut 6:5,13,24; 10:12,19–20; 11:1,13,22; 30:6,16,19–20). "Holding firm, holding strong" (from *ḥāzaq*, as in v. 2) to the covenant relationship with God[47] means that people will submit their will to his will, be firm in their commitment to serve him, and consistently praise him. Holding on strongly indicates a firm conviction about continuing a relationship with God.

56:5 The future[48] blessings promised to the eunuchs who hold fast to the covenant are not recounted in full. Since these people will have no children, no continuing dynasty, and no pictures on the walls of future homes to remember them, God promises that there will be a future memory of their faithfulness within God's temple environment (within the temple walls of his house). The symbolic significance of the Hebrew phrase "a hand and a name" is less than obvious. Most often "hand" (*yad*) refers literally to a person's physical hand (Gen 48:17 "left hand") or metaphorically to human "power" (Isa 37:27) or God's "power" (Exod 13:3), but the translation "a place" (Deut 23:12) or a "monument" (1 Sam 15:12) fits the context much better. God's act of giving them a "name" (*šēm*) fits in with a "place, monument" since both provide a memory of the eunuchs for future generations. If this refers to erecting a stele, one would expect the verb "set up, establish" rather than "give," so possibly this describes an inscription in the honor of the eunuchs rather than setting up a stone stele. This memorial will be even better than having many children who may or may not remember the names of their forefathers. Picking up the phraseology from 55:13[49] (there it relates to God's "name, reputation"), God

---

[44] Koole, *Isaiah III, Volume 3: Isaiah 56–66*, 10,14. The reference to keeping "my Sabbaths" indicates that they belong to God and that there are many of them week after week.

[45] Literally they choose what "I desire" חָפָצְתִּי.

[46] In 65:12 and 66:4 one group of people chose not to do what pleased God.

[47] The last clause is an explanation of the previous two clauses. Thus the *waw* is probably a *waw* explicative (GKC §154a, n. b). Polan, *In the Ways of Justice toward Salvation*, 69–70, argues that the *waw* on this last item is a *waw explicative* which would "serve as a link to sum up what has been stated."

[48] The *waw* consecutive on the perfect verb וְנָתַתִּי (from נָתַן "give") expresses future action (GKC §112x, mm).

[49] J. Goldingay, *The Message of Isaiah 40–55: A Literary-Theological Commentary* (London:

promises that the remembrance of the eunuch's faithfulness will be eternal, one that will not be cut off (Ps 112:6).

56:6–7 The message to the foreigners is somewhat similar to what God said to the eunuch. First, God's desire is that the foreigners would commit themselves to bringing honor to God (56:6). Repeating familiar vocabulary from 56:3 and 4, these foreigners are identified as proselytes who have already joined themselves to God in order to[50] willingly love and serve God,[51] to keep the Sabbath, and to hold fast to the covenant. Being "joined to God" implies that they have forsaken all of their former gods and have chosen to bind themselves to God alone and worship (an act of "temple service"[52] as in 60:7; 61:6) only Israel's God. They do not just identify with God in some general cultural or external way; they love God's name and show this in their worship. Each of these characteristics expresses the depth of their devotion and the seriousness of these foreigners' commitment to honor God. These people could be a part of the group of servants mentioned in 54:17 or among the servants who reappear in 65:13–25.[53]

In 56:7 God promises to cause these foreign people to come into "my holy mountain," a promise that picks up earlier concepts of the nations coming to the temple in Zion (2:2b–3; 9:10–12; 14:1–2; 25:6; 45:20–25; 49:6,22) and later reference in this literary unit to the nations coming to Zion (57:13; 60:3–11; 66:18–21). When they come to worship, God will bring them joy as they spend time in "my house of prayer." Although one assumes that when people came to the temple they gave sacrifices, prayed for forgiveness of sins, thanked God for his blessings, sought guidance, lamented during difficult days, and made vows to God, many of the daily events going on in the temple are quite shrouded in silence. A few passages speak of the celebration and rejoicing that should accompany worship at the temple (Lev 23:39–40; Deut 12:7,12; 16:11,14 and various Psalms like 92:5; 95:1; 96:11; 97:8; 98:4; 100:1), and there are

---

T&T Clark, 2005), 317, believes the prophet is taking up the words in 55:13 that deal with the Lord's "name, renown."

[50] The acts of "serving, loving, and being" are three infinitive construct forms that express the purpose of joining God (GKC §114a).

[51] 1QIsᵃ omits this word (לשרתו) "to serve him." D. W. Van Winkle, "An Inclusive Authoritative Text in Exclusive Communities," in Broyles and Evans, *Writing and Reading the Scroll of Isaiah*, 423–40, believes this word was omitted because the "Qumran community had difficulty preserving Isa 56:6 since it implies that Gentiles are to be accepted as priests."

[52] "Servant" עֶבֶד, which overlaps with "minister, cultic official, servant," is a more general concept than שָׁרֵת, which is a more specific temple role. Isaiah 66:20–21 confirm that some foreigners will serve as ministers or priests in God's future temple.

[53] R. de Hoop, "The Interpretation of Isaiah 56:1–9: Comfort or Criticism?" 679, makes the point that openness to foreigners does not mean an open invitation for all to come, for there are clear limitations and requirements for any person who desires to worship in God's Holy Mountain. This same point is made by M. A. Sweeney, "The Reconceptualization of the Davidic Covenant in Isaiah," in *Studies in the Book of Isaiah: Festschrift für W. A. Beuken*, ed. J. van Ruiten and M. Vervenne, BETL 132 (Leuven: Peeters, 1997), 41–62.

a few examples of people praying at the tabernacle/temple (1 Sam 1:9–16; 1 Kgs 8:22–61; 2 Kgs 19:14–19), but there is no description of a typical Sabbath day at the temple. God views these two activities as the most important things that should go on in his temple. God assures all who hear or read this prophecy (both Israelites and foreigners) that he (will be) "pleased"[54] (NIV "accept"; cf. 60:7) with the sacrifices of the foreigners. Therefore, the Israelites should rejoice and welcome the foreigners who come to Zion in chaps. 60–62. This brief section ends with a strong concluding statement: "Surely, without a doubt" (kî),[55] in the eschatological era to come, God's temple will be called a house for all nations to come and pray.[56]

56:8 A final "word of the Lord" statement introduces the conclusion to this paragraph. P. A. Smith argues this verse fulfills two purposes. "First it justifies the statement made in v. 7b that God's temple would be a house of prayer for all nations. . . . Second, it reinforces the promise made to the foreigners of full participation in the worshipping community."[57] The means by which God will accomplish his plan will be through the "gathering" (qābaṣ used three times) of many people, for he is the one who gathers both the "outcasts"[58] of the people of Israel as well as other non-Israelites from the nations. This is a theme dealt with back in 2:2–3 and 11:10–12, where God promises that both Israelites and the nations will be gathered to Zion. This gathering process also involves a spiritual transformation of the hearts of people,[59] so that they will respond to God and naturally want to come to worship him in Zion. Later the prophet indicates that the nations will see the glory of God over his people and be drawn to him (60:1–3). They will also be moved by the message of freedom and comfort proclaimed by the "Anointed One" who has the Spirit of God on him (61:1–3).

---

[54] This verbless clause implies a "to be" verb in the future tense (i.e., "will be") to match the other future tense verbs in the verse. רָצוֹן is a noun that comes from the root רָצָה "to want, to be pleased with," so anything that pleases God is obviously acceptable to him. In 1:11–14 God was not pleased with the sacrifices that were being offered in Jerusalem.

[55] The כִּי is an asseverative expressing what is "absolutely certain" (GKC §159ee). The translations "for" in NIV, NASB, HCSB, RSV suggest instead a causal use of כִּי.

[56] When Jesus overturned the tables of the money changers in the temple (Matt 21:12–13; Mark 11:15–17; Luke 19:46), he quoted part of Isa 56:7 to justify his action. R. E. Watts, "Mark," CNTOT, 209–10, finds a parallelism between Jesus' condemnation of those in rebellion in his day and those in rebellion against God in Isa 56:9–57:13. Nevertheless, the issue of allowing foreigners and eunuchs into the temple in Isa 56:1–8 does not play into the context of Jesus' use of this verse.

[57] P. A. Smith, *Rhetoric and Redaction in Trito-Isaiah*, 65.

[58] The word נִדְחֵי can refer to those dispersed among the nations (in 11:12 this word is parallel to "the scattered"), but in the context of 56:1–8 the eunuch is the one who is in danger of being considered an "outcast" and not being allowed to enter into the temple.

[59] J. A. Motyer, *The Prophecy of Isaiah* (Leicester: IVP, 1993), 467, connects the outcasts "neither to the Babylonian exiles nor to geographic dispersal but to those scattered from the Lord. It seems better in light of the context of 1–7 to make this term refer to the eunuchs and the "others" to refer to those "from the nations."

THEOLOGICAL IMPLICATIONS. The principles explained in these verses inform the reader that every person in every nation has a choice to make about their relationship to God. God does not deal with people on the basis of their ethnicity or exclude people because they are a little different (the foreigner and the eunuch in 56:3–7); he deals with people according to (a) their willingness to hold fast to their covenant relationship with God, (b) their willingness to practice justice in all social relationships with other people, (c) their love and service to God, and (d) their joyful worship of God (57:6). God invites all people to pray, sing with joy, and worship him in his holy mountain (56:6–7) without regard to their race, country of origin, language, or former lifestyles. The key issues are (a) Whom do these people trust? (b) Who is the author of their salvation? (c) What is their commitment? (d) How do they maintain these commitments to God? and (e), Who do they pray to?

Daniel 7:13–14 refers to that future time when God, the "Ancient of Days," will give authority, glory, and power to the Son of Man who will reign over people from all nations and those who speak every language, for all are welcome in his kingdom. The racial divides, the ethnic prejudices, the denominational divisions, and the hatred of people who are different will have no place in God's future kingdom. Now if this principle is true and is an ideal that God will fully establish among his people in the future, is this principle not an ideal that his people should implement as they establish his kingdom among people today? If the kingdom of God has already been inaugurated by the coming of Christ, should not those who claim to be a part of his kingdom follow the kingdom principles God has laid down for his people? All should be welcome in God's temple to pray and worship. The question is not do they speak my language, do they dress like me, do they pray the same way I do, or do they sing the same kind of songs I sing? Acceptance into God's holy temple to worship is based on people's relationship to God, not their relationship to one cultural way of worship, one class, one race, one nation, or one denomination. If God welcomes everyone who holds fast to their covenant relationship to God, can those who call themselves the servants of God do anything less?

(2) God Rejects Evil Leaders and Idolatry; He Revives the Humble (56:9–57:21)

The mood of accusations, punishment, and revival in this oracle presents a significant change from the mood of assurance in 56:1–8. This message describes a past time when people were persecuted because their leaders did not care for the sheep under their charge (56:9–57:2). After a strong condemnation of the rebellious people who were involved with child sacrifice and the worship of idols (57:3–13), this message ends with an announcement that God will remove the obstacles that might trip up his contrite and humble people. He will guide them to a time of restoration and peace on his Holy Mountain (57:14–21). Thus 56:9–57:21 describes what will happen before God establishes his full salvation for his righteous people on his Holy Mountain in chaps. 55; 56:7, and 60–62. J. McKenzie concludes that there "is no obvious connection between this poem and lvi 1–8; in most of Third Isaiah the pieces are simply strung together,"[60] but W. A. M. Beuken rejects this approach and notes an interconnection with chap. 55, and both 56:7 and 57:13 relate these messages to what will eventually happen on God's Holy Mountain.[61]

C. Westermann thought that these accusations against these wicked leaders and pagan worshippers were characteristic of preexilic judgment speeches (Jer 6:17; Ezek 3:17; 34:1–10), so he concluded that there "can therefore be no shadow of doubt that 56.9–12 is an early preexilic oracle of judgment"[62] that was quoted, revised, and redirected toward a postexilic audience. This suggests that the wickedness of the postexilic era in Jerusalem was identical to what was going on in preexilic times, yet there is little independent evidence from any of the exilic books of the Bible to support this assumption about Israelite religious life after the exile. Haggai and Zechariah do not accuse the government leaders Zerubbabel or Nehemiah nor the prophets of that day of fleecing the flock, and they do not condemn rampant Canaanite worship in postexilic Israel. P. D. Hanson attempts to resolve this dilemma by not taking the description of pagan religious practices literally. Instead, he draws the very questionable conclusion that a visionary prophetic group is speaking these words, using traditional preexilic imagery, in order to condemn the defiled temple that the Zadokite priestly group was building in Jerusalem.[63] A third approach by B. S. Childs focuses on the theological function of 56:9–57:13 within chaps. 56–66 and the book as a whole. He believes this text identifies "the selfsame evils in the past with those of the present in spite of the eschatological hope of a new age of God's rule (65:25)."[64]

In spite of several attempts to find a specific historical setting for this message, it is impossible to point to an exact date. C. Westermann and J. Vermeylen properly identified these sins as preexilic sins similar to those mentioned elsewhere in Isaiah and several other preexilic prophets.[65] The point being made is

---

[60] McKenzie, *Second Isaiah*, 154, apparently found no logic or reason in the ordering of these chapters and not much of an interrelationship between them.

[61] Beuken, "Isa 56:9–57:13: An Example of the Isaianic Legacy of Trito-Isaiah,", 50. De Hoop, "The Interpretation of Isaiah 56:1–9," 683, also sees connections between 56:9–57:21 and chaps. 55 and 56:1–8.

[62] Westermann, *Isaiah 40–66*, 302, 319–25, views this author quoting earlier judgment oracles in 56:9–12; 57:3–6; and 57:7–13.

[63] Hanson, *The Dawn of Apocalyptic*, 198–99. This nonliteral approach seems difficult to justify from the words of the text but is required for his theoretical reconstruction. The more one reads into a text, the less convincing the interpretation and theory behind it is.

[64] Childs, *Isaiah*, 464.

[65] Westermann, *Isaiah 40–66*, 319; Vermeylen, *Du Prophète Isaïe à l'apocalyptique*, 458–64.

that on numerous occasions throughout the nation's history, poor political leaders and false prophets failed to serve the nation faithfully (56:9–12), so repeatedly the people ended up following false gods (57:3–9). The nation sought help from other nations instead of trusting only in God (57:9; cf. 30–31; 39) and consequently they had a deceptive relationship with God (57:8,11). On account of these sins, the only people who will have any hope will be those who walk humbly and contritely, trusting in God, the high and lofty One who has the ability to revive and heal the humble (57:15,19) as well as to punish the wicked (57:17, 20–21). This prophecy indicates that the same general patterns of the past will exist in the distant future just before God introduces his kingdom. God will extend his full salvation to the humble and contrite people on his Holy Mountain (57:13–21), but the blind, lazy, proud, and drunken leaders on the earth, and those who worship idols and involve themselves with all types of pagan worship, will suffer God's judgment and have no peace (57:17,20–21). If this was true in the past and will be true of the future, certainly these principles apply to all those who originally heard the words of the prophet and all who read it today.

This long message can be divided into three sections.

Failure in leadership	56:9–57:2[66]
Rejection of pagan worship	57:3–13
God will revive the lowly; judge others	57:14–21

These three paragraphs are held together by several structural factors: (a) The consequences of sinfulness described in 56:9–12 and 57:3–13 are not reported in these verses, so 57:14–21 is needed to complete the natural implications of what is announced in the first two paragraphs. (b) There is a repeated contrast between the life of the wicked and the righteous in each paragraph, which hold these paragraphs together.[67] (c) The repetition of vocabulary unifies these paragraphs, including references to the "way" (*derek* in 56:11; 57:10,14,17,18); "peace" (*šālôm*) for the righteous in 57:2 and no peace for the wicked in 57:19,21; "gain" (*beṣaʿ* in 56:11; 57:17); "they are not able" (*lôʾ yûkĕlû* in 56:10; 57:20); "renewal, revival" (*ḥāyâ* in 57:10,15), and "rest" (*nûaḥ*) in 57:2,20.[68]

---

[66] Motyer, *Isaiah*, 469, puts 57:1–21 together, rather than putting 57:1–2 with 56:9–12. He views 57:1–2 and 57:19b–21 acting as transition sections, framing what is in between because both speak of "peace." This ignores the strong connections between 56:9–12 and 57:1–2.

[67] See the contrast between the wicked in 56:9–12 and the righteous in 57:1–2, the wicked in 57:3–9 and the righteous in 57:13b, as well as the righteous in 57:15–19 and the wicked in 57:20–21.

[68] Polan, *In the Ways of Justice toward Salvation*, 29, provides a chart showing the frequency of eight words (judge, righteous, come, know, step/way, transgress, turn, and see) in these three paragraphs. Seven of these eight words are found in all three sections; "judge" is not found in 56:9–57:21. In addition one might add "set it on the heart" (NIV "ponder") in 57:1 and 11.

After God judges the wicked and revives the righteous, he will bring his people to his Holy Mountain (57:13); thus, the goal of his action in 56:9–57:21 fits in with the goal in 56:7–8; 60–62, and 66:18–24. The prophet is giving a persuasive warning to those who might be tempted to forsake God and worship pagan gods (which are the "you" in 57:3–13). They need to understand that their past leaders were incompetent (56:9–12), their past idolatrous ways did not save them (57:13), and that their only hope is in God, who will heal the lowly and contrite (57:15–16). If people want to dwell with God on his Holy Mountain in the future, all people in every era must remove those obstacles that would prevent this from happening (57:14), for in the future God will judge the wicked and bring salvation to his own people.

FAILURES IN LEADERSHIP (56:9–57:2)

[9]Come, all you beasts of the field,
   come and devour, all you beasts of the forest!
[10]Israel's watchmen are blind,
   they all lack knowledge;
 they are all mute dogs,
   they cannot bark;
 they lie around and dream,
   they love to sleep.
[11]They are dogs with mighty appetites;
   they never have enough.
 They are shepherds who lack understanding;
   they all turn to their own way,
   each seeks his own gain.
[12]"Come," each one cries, "let me get wine!
  Let us drink our fill of beer!
 And tomorrow will be like today,
   or even far better."

[1]The righteous perish,
   and no one ponders it in his heart;
 devout men are taken away,
   and no one understands
 that the righteous are taken away
   to be spared from evil.
[2]Those who walk uprightly
   enter into peace;
   they find rest as they lie in death.

The first paragraph in this literary unit describes the sins of past political and religious leaders of Israel. They were blind, self-absorbed, lazy, drunkards; people who were only interested in how they could get ahead. Because of these failures in leadership, none of them seemed to notice that the righteous people were perishing. C. Westermann views 56:9–12 as a judgment speech

and 57:1–2 as a lamenting complaint (like Ps 12).[69] Nevertheless, there is no
description of the punishment of the leaders in 56:9, so it would be best to
describe 56:9–12 as a series of accusations and 57:1–2 as another accusation
against those who do nothing while the righteous perish.

This paragraph can be outlined into two parts:

The leaders have no understanding	56:9–12
Call to destroy	9
Corrupt watchmen	10–11a
Corrupt shepherds	11b–12
Righteous perish; no one understands	57:1–2

The first subparagraph in 56:9–12 is interconnected to 57:1–2 by the repetition
of the idea that there is no understanding (*lô' yādĕ'û* or *'ên mēbîn*) in 56:10,11
and 57:1. The double invitation to "come" in 56:9 and the single call to "come"
in 56:12 (from *'ātâ*) are reminiscent of the double call to "come" (from *hālak*)
in 55:1, but different words for "come" are used and the reason for coming is
completely different. Another interlinking connection is that the wicked "lie
down" (*šōkbîm*) in ignorance (56:10) and because of this the righteous rest in
"their beds, places where one lies down" (*miškĕbôtām*) and die (57:2). From
the very early chapters of the book of Isaiah, poor leadership (1:10,23; 3:1–4:1;
7:1–12; 9:15–16; 10:12) caused God to hold the nation's leaders responsible
for many of the failures of his people, so it is not surprising to read that in the
future God will hold all these leaders accountable for their actions.

56:9   This paragraph begins with the unusual imagery of animals coming to eat. Unfortunately, the prophet never explains this negative metaphor
and his grammatical way of expressing his point is not very clear. The text
could be read to say that the beasts[70] of the field (the domesticated animals)
were coming to eat the beasts of the forest (the wild animals), but usually one
would expect just the opposite imagery since domesticated sheep do not eat
wild lions. Therefore it would seem more natural for one to interpret this statement to mean that both the animals (the nations) from the field and the forest
are coming to eat, but then there is no description of what they will eat. By
implication one might suppose that these beasts will eat the sheep the leaders were supposed to be protecting in 56:10. One also must decide if this is
a literal situation where animals are feeding on the dead bodies of troops (cf.
Ezek 39:17–18) or if these metaphorical animals are the enemy nations that are
destroying Israelites (probably not just the leaders).[71] In addition it is not clear
if God is exhorting (a common use of the imperative verb) some fierce nations

---

[69] Westermann, *Isaiah 40–66*, 319. Emmerson, *Isaiah 56–66*, 21, also calls this a judgment
speech, viewing 56:9 as a statement of judgment.

[70] The spelling of the construct form of "beasts of" (חַיְתוֹ) is unusual (GKC §90o) with the
1QIs[a] giving the more expected form חַיְתִי.

[71] Hanson, *Isaiah 40–66*, 197–9, interprets these images as "the princes of the earth, depicted

to "come"[72] or if the irresponsible blind leaders are by their irresponsible action allowing or permitting them (another use of the imperative)[73] to eat. With this later interpretation 56:9 becomes part of the accusation against the leaders of Israel. They allow both friendly (the domesticated animals, possibly through alliances or assimilation of foreign ideas) and unfriendly nations (the wild animals, possibly through war) to destroy the people. This was a common problem in Israel's past, and it will continue to exist throughout their history.

56:10–11a The word translated "watchman" (ṣōpeh) appears to be a verb in the written Hebrew text (ṣāpâ "heed, watch"), but the spoken *Qere* tradition and 1QIs[a] vocalize the word as a plural participle with a suffix ("his watchmen"),[74] a more likely alternative. The text emphasizes that "all of them" (kulām in vv. 10 and 11), all the prophetic watchmen (cf. Ezek 3:17), are spiritually blind. The phrase "all of them" emphasizes how terrible the spiritual situation is, for none of these prophets know what is really happening. This suggests that they are not listening to what God is saying, so they are not able to warn people about moral issues and the dire consequences of their sinfulness. These watchmen are compared to "dogs," a very strong derogatory condemnation (cf. 2 Sam 16:9) that evokes pictures of filthy mongrels, the scum of the earth that would eat anything. Usually dogs bark incessantly whenever they hear a strange noise or see something out of the ordinary, but these prophetic "dogs" are worthless because they are completely mute. Since they are not able or willing to bark, they provide no warning about the dangers that are coming. The text does not say why they are not able or are unwilling to bark, but if they have no relationship with God and have no prophetic visions from God, then they have nothing to say because they are cut off from God's revelation about future events.

The description of these dogs in 56:10b employs three participles. One could translate them as if they all function as verbs or suggest that some function as verbs and others as nouns.[75] Since the text is describing prophets who act like dogs, one would expect to find words that describe the behavior of

---

as domestic animals, fall prey to the wild beasts . . . a grim picture of divine judgment on those who exercise their governing power with wickedness and cruelty."

[72] The imperative Lamed–ה verbs usually do not have a ' replacing the dropped ה when a vocalic ending is added, but that is exactly what happens here (GKC §76d). It would be rather shocking if v. 9 was actually a sarcastic quotation of the essence of their prophecies.

[73] GKC §110a-c discusses the use of the imperative to exhort or admonish, give permission, and an ironic sarcastic use. Koole, *Isaiah III, Volume 3: Isaiah 56–66*, 33, supports a permissive sense.

[74] The difference between these two readings is the inclusion of a ' before the suffix in the Qumran text (צפיו). Hanson, *The Dawn of Apocalyptic*, 194–96, views these people as priests, but in all other biblical texts they are prophets. L. S. Tiemeyer, "The Watchman Metaphor in Isaiah LVI–LXVI," *VT* 55 (2005): 378–400, also prefers the *Qere* pl. reading of the Qumran text, which agrees with the use of pl. forms throughout the rest of the verse.

[75] GKC §116f,m describes the verbal function of the participle as the predicate of the sentence.

dogs that are parallel to the life of these prophets. The first participle presents textual problems because the word is otherwise unknown in Hebrew. If a scribe made a slight error in writing the initial letter of this word,[76] it would refer to "raving, seeing" (if used as a verb) or "a seer" (if used as a noun; NIV has "dream").[77] This may suggest that the prophets were raving about certain things just like mad raving dogs. The second and third participles pick up on the common practice of dogs spending their days sleeping, so these watchmen are also described as "sleeping, lying down" (šōkbîm). This indicates that they are not busy about God's work of warning people about their sins; instead, they enjoy a life of constant leisure. The third participle emphasizes their desire and dedication to "drowsy inactivity" (nûm); thus, these watchmen are "lovers of slumber."

The insatiable appetite of hungry dogs provides the final comparison in 57:11a. The statement that these watchmen have a great appetite[78] suggests that their focus was on gaining materialistic payment for their services (cf. Mic 3:5,11), rather than providing spiritual truth to those who were seeking God's wisdom. Like a dog that quickly gulps down his food and looks for more, these watchmen "did not know" (as in 56:10) what it meant to be "satisfied" (śāb'â) with their present material situation. They did not derive satisfaction from serving God faithfully, from meeting the needs of others, or from the earthly things that God providentially provided for them and their families. Instead, they were lazy, had lost their sense of calling to serve others, and were no longer interested in functioning as watchmen who warned God's people. These accusations serve as important warnings to those modern watchmen who are responsible to shepherd God's flock in the church today.

56:11b–12   Next the prophecy deals with irresponsible "shepherds," a term that frequently refers to the role of a king or prince (2 Sam 5:2; 7:7; Ps 78:72; Jer 3:15; 23:4–5; Isa 44:28; Ezek 34; 37:24). This royal person was given the responsibility to feed, guide, protect, and righteously care for the people in the nation (no specific nation is identified, but most assume they were Israelites). The book of Isaiah pays special attention to the arrogance and failures of political leaders in Israel and other nations (3:1–4:1; 10:5–15; 14:1–20; 37:21–29), but the leaders in this verse were totally inept at their job for they did not have any "understanding."[79] This theme interrelates the lack of knowledge of the watchmen in 56:10 with the lack of knowledge of the shepherds in 56:11 and

---

[76] The present word הֹזִים is unknown, but if the ה is a scribal error for ה then it refers to the prophetic role of being a "seer." Motyer, *Isaiah*, 468, prefers to keep the text as it is and interprets הֹזִים as a reference to the fact that dogs "lie around, pant."

[77] Hanson, *The Dawn of Apocalyptic*, 188, translates this "the seers are reclining," with the first participle functioning as a noun and the second as a verb.

[78] The Hebrew term נֶפֶשׁ usually is translated "soul," but here it must refer to the "appetite" of the throat (see a similar usage in 5:14).

[79] The object of the verb is the infinitive construct (GKC §114c,m) לְבִין from the root בִּין "he understood"; thus the literal translation is "they know no understanding."

the lack of knowledge concerning the perishing of the righteous in 57:1. This lack of understanding might refer to the spiritual ignorance of these leaders, but J. L. Koole also connects this ignorance to a consequent failure of these leaders to perform their practical duties wisely. Thus their irresponsibility led to the righteous perishing.[80] These leaders failed in two ways: (a) they turned to their own ways, and (b) each focused on his own profit. P. A. Smith draws attention to the repeated use of "way" (*derek*) throughout this message (56:11; 57:10,14,17,18) to condemn the sinful ways of the wicked and to highlight the contrasting righteous ways of God.[81] The "turning" (*pānû*) of the wicked was a turning away from God's way and to their own path of self-interests and profits. In a somewhat similar passage (33:14–15), Isaiah contrasts the sinners with the righteous who do what is right and reject action based on making profits through extortion and bribes. This verse ends with the somewhat obscure word *miqqāṣēhû*, which is not represented in the translation of the NIV. Literally one could translate the phrase "from its end"; thus, it makes the emphatic point that each day will be better "to the last one" (NASB) or "without exception."[82]

In order to more fully characterize the life of these irresponsible rulers, 56:12 quotes what they say to each other.[83] One individual calls to another and requests[84] that others "come," making a verbal connection with the call to "come" in 56:9. The second and third verbs are cohortatives that express this person's strong intention to take wine ("I will take wine") or to express self-encouragement ("let me take wine").[85] W. A. M. Beuken recognized that this situation in which evil leaders come and take from common people is set in sharp contrast to 55:1–3 where people "come" at God's invitation and have plenty to eat.[86] Thus he believes that 56:9–12 shows how the wicked are wasting the riches of God's salvation that God was providing his needy people in 55:1–3. The false assumptions of these wicked people is revealed in the final

---

[80] Koole, *Isaiah III, Volume 3: Isaiah 56–66*, 37, concludes that the interconnection between this phrase in the three verses suggests that they "particularly refer to the lack of responsibility in the downfall of the righteous."

[81] P. A. Smith, *Rhetoric and Redaction in Trito-Isaiah*, 70, finds the major contrast in 57:14 where God is able to provide the way of healing, peace, and life on his Holy Mountain. He believes this word "provides the fundamental antithesis" between the way of the righteous and wicked.

[82] Oswalt, *Isaiah 40–66*, 466, translates מִקָּצֵהוּ "without exception."

[83] Muilenburg, "Isaiah 40–66," 5:663; Hanson, *The Dawn of Apocalyptic*; 197, and Whybray, *Isaiah 40–66*, 201, all suggest that v. 12 is a drinking song similar to 22:13.

[84] The imperative verb from אָתָה "he came" is spelled like it is in v. 9 and functions as a request or admonition (GKC §110a).

[85] The verb אֶקְחָה from לְקַח is a cohortative (with the final ה) that functions to express "a consequence which is expected with certainty . . . or in fact an intention." Beuken, "Isa 56:9–57:13—An Example of the Isaianic Legacy of Trito-Isaiah," 58, concludes that this "taking" is a taking away from others because one is stronger than the weaker person. He compares what is done here to the excessive drinking in Isa 5:11–12,22 and 22:13.

[86] Beuken, "Isa 56:9–57:13—An Example of the Isaianic Legacy of Trito-Isaiah," 59, notes that both passages have words like (a) come, (b) satisfied, (c) wine, and (d) eating.

two lines of 56:12 where one leader assures the others that their life of pleasure and wine will not end soon (cf. 22:13). This deluded optimism is also present in the exaggeration that tomorrow "will be great beyond measure." This paragraph will later conclude that a day of accountability will be coming in the future (57:17–21).

57:1–2   The final two verses in this paragraph describe the terrible things that were happening to the righteous[87] or devout people because the blind and self-centered leaders were failing to lead the nation in righteous ways. These verses function as another accusation against these wicked leaders. It is somewhat puzzling why the term "righteous" at the beginning of the verse is singular, while the term "devout men" is plural, and then the "righteous" at the end of the verse is singular again.[88] The interpreter might hypothesize that a single individual "righteous one" is identified (some suggest Isaiah, Hezekiah, or the Servant in chap. 53), but it seems best to conclude that the singular "righteous" is used in a collective sense concerning a group of righteous people (see Gen 18:23,25; Pss 7:10; 12:1; 31:18; 37:16; Ezek 13:22; 33:12; Mic 7:2; Mal 3:18). Since this passage picks up several words used in the final Servant poem in 52:13–53:12,[89] it is possible to suggest that the righteous in this passage are the "seed" of the Servant and consequently they share the same fate as the righteous Servant who died. Both are taken away and both end up in the grave.

Righteous persons[90] (probably a collective) are lost and perish (see Mic 7:1–2), but no one (*ʾên*) seems to pay any attention (lit. "no man sets it upon the heart") or investigate what is happening. The leaders fail to perceive the injustice going on; no one (*bʾên*) seems to understand the significance their inaction will have on society. In light of the context in 57:2, the gathering/taking away of the "men of covenant faithfulness" (*ʾanšê ḥesed*) probably refers to the righteous men being gathered to their fathers in the grave (see Gen 25:8; Num 20:26; Jer 8:2). The final clause of the verse begins with a *kî* that could introduce an object clause that explains what the people do not understand

---

[87] This verse begins and ends with the word "the righteous one" (הַצַּדִּיק), drawing attention to its importance to this verse.

[88] The Aramaic Targum eases this problem by making all the nouns plural (NRSV and NEB follow the same pattern).

[89] Both passages refer to the "righteous" (צַדִּיק, 53:11 and 57:1), "peace" (שָׁלוֹם, 53:5 and 57:2), and "healing" (רָפָא, 53:5 and 57:18–19); and both righteous ones die. J. Blenkinsopp, "Who is the Ṣaddiq of Isaiah 57:1–2," in *Studies in the Hebrew Bible, Qumran, and the Septuagint Presented to E. Ulrich,* ed. P. W. Flint, E. Tov, J. C. Vanderkam, VTSup 101 (Leiden: Brill, 2006), 109–20, adds additional connections, like both were taken away or gathered (53:8; 57:1), all turned to their own way (53:6; 56:11), no one gave a thought about what was happening to either righteous one (53:8; 57:1), and the servant and his seed in 53:11 is comparable to the righteous one and the devout men in 57:1. Of course Blenkinsopp views the servant in 53 as the righteous in Israel. He also notes that the Qumran people later used 57:1–2 to interpret the death of the Teacher of Righteousness in the *Damascus Document,* 20:14–22.

[90] Some Church Fathers thought this referred to Christ while others thought it might be Isaiah himself.

(translating *kî* as "that," as in NIV),[91] or it could introduce an independent emphatic clause, "surely, indeed." There is little agreement on the meaning of the final part of this verse. Some conclude that it is saying that God will take the righteous out of this world "because" (*mippnê*) God is about to pour out "calamity" (*hārā'â*) on the wicked, while others interpret the verse to say that "on account of, because of" (*mippnê*) the "evil" (*hārā'â*) in society, the corrupt leaders take away the righteous (kill them).[92] The first option tends to read too much into the simple statement that "away from evil the righteous one is gathered/taken away," for the passive verb does not have a subject (God) and the place where he is gathered is not identified. But a similar problem exists for the second option, for it reads in the idea that the corrupt leaders are the ones who are taking these people away. If the "gathering/taking away" in 57:1c refers to the same "gathering" (to their beds in the grave) in 2b, then it is appropriate to conclude that the righteous people go to the grave away from the evil in this world. Isaiah 57:1 does not explain if this is a divine act of sparing people or if it is an evil act of persecution by wicked humans.

57:2   There are three lines in this verse, but NIV changes the order by putting line c first, then it gives line a and b. In Hebrew the verse is constructed somewhat similarly to 57:1, for it has a mysterious singular verb "he" (probably the righteous) who enters into a future peaceful situation (a euphemism for death); but the second clause has a plural verb "they rest" in their beds, and the final clause has a singular participle that refers to one who walks uprightly (the righteous one). The second clause is the problematic one. Does it refer to the plural devout men from 57:1 who peacefully rest in their "beds" (*miškĕbôtām*, a euphemism for "death" in NIV) in the grave, making 57:2 all about the righteous? Or does the second clause refer to the wicked who just lie around, sleeping and ignoring the fact that the righteous are perishing (as in 56:10)? In light of the absence of any other reference to the wicked leaders in 57:1–2 and any explicit reference in 2c to those who walk uprightly, it is best to refer all three lines to the righteous. There is a reason why these things are happening to the righteous. The blind political leaders and the drunken prophets were so self-centered that they did not understand that their failures in leadership were having a negative impact on the preservation of a righteous seed on the earth.

REJECTION OF DECEITFUL WORSHIP AND POLITICS (57:3–13)

3"But you—come here, you sons of a sorceress,
   you offspring of adulterers and prostitutes!

---

[91] The כִּי can introduce the object of the verb "understand" (GKC §157a).
[92] Oswalt, *Isaiah 40–66*, 470, prefers the first option.

⁴Whom are you mocking?
  At whom do you sneer
  and stick out your tongue?
 Are you not a brood of rebels,
  the offspring of liars?
⁵You burn with lust among the oaks
  and under every spreading tree;
 you sacrifice your children in the ravines
  and under the overhanging crags.
⁶[The idols] among the smooth stones of the ravines are your portion;
  they, they are your lot.
 Yes, to them you have poured out drink offerings
  and offered grain offerings.
 In the light of these things, should I relent?
⁷You have made your bed on a high and lofty hill;
  there you went up to offer your sacrifices.
⁸Behind your doors and your doorposts
  you have put your pagan symbols.
 Forsaking me, you uncovered your bed,
  you climbed into it and opened it wide;
 you made a pact with those whose beds you love,
  and you looked on their nakedness.
⁹You went to Molech with olive oil
  and increased your perfumes.
 You sent your ambassadors far away;
  you descended to the grave itself!
¹⁰You were wearied by all your ways,
  but you would not say, 'It is hopeless.'
 You found renewal of your strength,
  and so you did not faint.

¹¹"Whom have you so dreaded and feared
  that you have been false to me,
 and have neither remembered me
  nor pondered this in your hearts?
 Is it not because I have long been silent
  that you do not fear me?
¹²I will expose your righteousness and your works,
  and they will not benefit you.
¹³When you cry out for help,
  let your collection [of idols] save you!
 The wind will carry all of them off,
  a mere breath will blow them away.
 But the man who makes me his refuge
  will inherit the land
  and possess my holy mountain."

Suddenly the reader is introduced to a long list of accusations that an un-identified group of people are involved with aspects of pagan worship that were common in the preexilic era but are unknown in other postexilic writings.[93] These included sorcery, prostitution, rebellion, lying, the sacrifice of children, idolatry, pagan sacrifices and symbols, Molech worship, and numerous other sinful activities (57:3–9). By doing these wicked things, these people, and any-one else who follows this way of life in the future, demonstrate their depen-dence on useless things that cannot help them. These acts reveal that these people have forsaken the true God (57:11–12). At some point God will expose their evil deeds and will refuse to intervene to save them when they are in trouble. In contrast to this destiny for sinners, God will care for those who take refuge in him (57:13b). The promise that the righteous will some day live on God's Holy Mountain connects the promise in 56:13b to a similar eschatologi-cal promise in 57:7. If people wish to enjoy God's glorious future kingdom described in chaps. 60–62, they must reject this kind of wicked behavior.

There is not much agreement on the outline of this paragraph.[94] Although C. Westermann understands 57:3–6 and 7–13a as two judgment speeches, they function primarily as a long series of accusations (57:3–10) with a threat of judgment for the wicked and a promise for the righteous in 57:11–13.[95] The second masculine plural pronouns "you" seem to be necessitated by the imag-ery of "sons" in 57:3–5, while the second feminine singular pronouns "you" are demanded by the use of imagery of an adulterous woman in 57:6–10; but they both fit together to describe unrighteous leaders and people. The parts of this paragraph are drawn together by similar questions in 56:4 and 11 and a series of common accusations. The structure of this paragraph is:

The wicked seed of an adulteress	57:3–5
The prostitution of the nation	57:6–10
God's threats and promises	57:11–13

---

[93] The common explanation that this author is describing postexilic sins in traditional terms commonly used in preexilic times seems a precarious argument. P. A. Smith, *Rhetoric and Re-daction in Trito-Isaiah*, 81, defends this position by arguing about historically unproven "pos-sibilities," or things one might "suppose": (a) "It is quite possible that the poet used elements of traditional language and style . . . to portray present day offenders as descendants of their apostate forefathers of the preexilic and exilic periods." (b) "We may suppose that those who remained in Palestine during the Babylonian exile continued in their own ways, and that their postexilic descendants still continued to do so for some time." (c) "The poet appears to alter elements of traditional language, such as the Deuteronomistic expression 'under every green tree.'" This kind of reasoning is not particularly convincing.

[94] Oswalt, *Isaiah 40–66*, 475, concludes that "verses 3–4 are an announcement of divine judgment against such people. Then vv. 5–10 describe their behavior." Polan, *In the Ways of Justice Toward Salvation*, 124–45, divides this chapter into (a) 57:3–5; (b) 57:6; (c) 57:7–10; and (d) 57:11–13.

[95] Westermann, *Isaiah 40–66*, 321; P. A. Smith, *Rhetoric and Redaction in Trito-Isaiah*, 82–83. Blenkinsopp, *Isaiah 56–66*, 156, suggest this is a trial speech ("draw near" in 57:3), but very little trial language is used, and 57:6 does not appear to be a punishment statement as Westermann suggests.

This paragraph is connected to the preceding paragraph (56:9–57:2) by several verbal connections: (a) "set it upon the heart" in 57:1 and 11; (b) plays on the root *šākab* "bed, sleep" in 56:10, 57:2,7–8; (c) "love" (*'āhab*) in 56:10; 57:8; and (d) "ways" (*derek*) in 56:11; 57:10,17–18. Although this paragraph moves well beyond the picture of failed and impotent leadership in 56:9–12, it supplements the picture of these bad leaders by describing how their blind inattention to religious life allowed pagan perversions to flourish. In certain ways this passage is reminiscent of the adulterous imagery in Hos 1–3; Ezek 16 and 23, and it presents a very strong contrast with images of the people of God as the wife who will be restored to her husband (49:14–50:3; 54:1–10). M. E. Biddle identified verbal connections between the images of fallen Babylon in chap. 47 and the sinful alter ego of Zion in 57:6–13 in order to show that postexilic Jerusalem followed the sins of preexilic Jerusalem (and Babylon), so it must first be removed before the glorious New Jerusalem can appear.[96] Since the sinful deeds in 57:3–10 do not mention Zion specifically, it is better to view these sins as representative of the common sins that wicked people (including Israelites) have committed in the past and will continue to commit up to the time God finally judges the wicked (57:17,20–21). Then God will judge the wicked and call the righteous to join him at his Holy Mountain (57:13b,18–19).

57:3 The initial statement "but you" (plural, *vattem*) refers to a new group of people, not the righteous in 57:1–2 (cf. 65:11). The imperative exhortation to "come near, draw near" is naturally used when one person wants to gain someone's attention in order to communicate an important message.[97] The new people in the audience are addressed as the "sons of a sorceress"; that is, they are the children of one who practices the pagan art of divination, magic, or soothsaying. Being children should be understood metaphorically as followers committed to the same ideology. They have taken on the syncretistic tendency of depending on the manipulation of objects to determine the will of the gods so that they can know how to interpret their circumstance and understand what they need to do in the future to appease the gods (cf. 2:6). Divination and sorcery are usually mentioned together and both were forbidden in the *Torah* (Lev 19:26; Deut 18:10,14), but they were practiced during the reigns of Saul (1 Sam 28:7), Ahaz (Isa 8:19), Manasseh (2 Kgs 21:6), and Zedekiah (Jer 27:9). These people are also called the "seed" (*zera'*), not of Abraham or

---

[96] M. E. Biddle, "Lady Zion's Alter Egos: Isaiah 47.1–15 and 57.6–13 as Structural Counterparts," in *New Visions of Isaiah,* ed. R. F. Melugin and M. A. Sweeney (Sheffield: Sheffield Academic Press, 1966), 124–39, concludes that Zion was essentially replaced with the New Jerusalem and not restored. He does not adequately defend his position that these sins were actually committed by the people of postexilic Jerusalem. In fact he finds the sins mentioned here to be closest to those described by the prophet Jeremiah and Ezekiel in preexilic times.

[97] Although קְרָבוּ "draw near" may be used in a courtroom context as in 41:1, in that context the text explicitly indicates that the drawing near is "for judgment," but this additional modifier is missing in 57:3. In 34:1 the drawing near is to hear God's words of judgment for the nations, but there is no trial, and in 48:16 people are to come to hear words of hope.

the Servant but of prostitutes and those who commit adultery.[98] This is similar to preexilic terminology associated with the sexual perversity rampant at the Baal temples (cf. Hos 4; Ezek 16) as well as the terminology that describes the nation's spiritual and political unfaithfulness to God.

57:4 According to the NIV translation, the second accusation relates to the arrogant and contemptible attitude of sneering, mocking, or jeering. Several commentators believe these wicked people sneer and laugh at the righteous in 57:1–2,[99] but in all other examples the root *ʿānag* has the positive meaning of "delight" (55:2; 58:14; 66:11; Job 22:26; 27:10). Thus the question posed is: "Concerning whom do you delight?"[100] In other words which god/God do you enjoy following and serving? Where does your sense of satisfaction come from? This question prepares the way for later questions about their worship of pagan gods in 57:4–9.

The second and third questions relate to the use of the mouth and tongue, but the meaning of these gestures is far from certain. The imagery of "making the mouth wide" can refer to (a) people figuratively opening their mouths so that God can fill it (Ps 81:10[11]), (b) wicked people speaking evil things (Ps 35:21), or (c) the ground/grave figuratively swallowing someone (Isa 5:14). Its meaning must coincide with the meaning of the phrase "making the tongue/language long" in the last line, but this gesture is an equally ambiguous cultural expression. Since the rest of 57:3–13 deals with pagan worship and not with the oppression of the righteous, it seems best to follow J. L. Koole, who does not connect 57:4 to the persecution of the righteous in 57:1–2. He connects all of 57:3–5 to practices of pagan worship, suggesting that the two images of speaking with a wide mouth and a long tongue are symbolic ways of inquiring about the grand speeches, long prayers, and many words of appreciation they give to another god.[101]

The implied answer to these questions is partially provided in the rhetorical question in 57:4b (beginning with *hălôʾ*).[102] This rhetorical question is not really inquiring into this matter in order to gain information; it is actually making a statement about what is well known by using a question format. Is not their delight and are not their words of appreciation based on the fact that they

---

[98] Both "sorceress" and "adulterer" are participles translated as nouns, but the final term is an imperfect verb "and she commits fornication" וַתִּזְנֶה which is hidden behind the NIV noun "prostitute."

[99] Oswalt, *Isaiah 40–66*, 476; Whybray, *Isaiah 40–66*, 203, thinks this refers to rude gestures and contempt toward the righteous in 57:1–2.

[100] Koole, *Isaiah III, Volume 3: Isaiah 56–66*, 54–55, argues that עָנַג has a positive meaning and does not mean "make fun of" in a negative sense.

[101] Koole compares this to the long time the prophets of Baal called on their god in 1 Kgs 18:26–28 (Ibid., 55).

[102] When a question begins with הֲלֹא "is it not," it shows that the matter under consideration "is absolutely true" (GKC §150e). Thus one could translate this question as having the impact of a statement, for it "is equivalent to *surely it is*."

are the children of "rebellion" (*pešaʿ*) and the "seed" (*zeraʿ*) of deceivers? The prophet is accusing them of these things; he is not really asking if this might be true. Rebellion against God and the acceptance of deceitful theological beliefs are associated with lying words and false statements about pagan gods elsewhere (44:20; 59:3,13; Jer 3:10,23; 5:2,31; 6:13; 7:4), so in light of the contextual reference to idolatry in 57:5–9, it is natural to conclude that the intent is similar in this verse.

57:5 The prophet now describes specific acts of rebellion where the people have accepted deceitful falsehoods. He appears to be describing Canaanite fertility cults and possibly worship associated with the pagan god Molech. The people who go to these places of worship are "hot, burn,"[103] a term that describes both the heat of a fire (44:15) and animals in sexual heat at conception (Gen 30:38). This terminology probably refers to sexual passion associated with the sacred prostitution carried on as a part of fertility religions. This activity sometimes took place at open-air Baal temples "under every green tree"[104] or by a large fertile oak tree (cf. 1:29; 1 Kgs 14:23; 2 Kgs 16:4; Hos 4:13; Jer 3:6; Ezek 20:28). Those who practiced these fertility rituals believed that divine blessing and fertility would come not from keeping the covenant with Israel's God but from imitating the sexual prowess of the Canaanite god Baal.

The second half of 57:5 mentions the sacrifice of children (lit "slaughtered" from *šāḥaṭ*), a practice that is sometimes associated with the worship of the god Molech. The Hebrews were aware of these sinful sacrifices as far back as Lev 18:21, and this kind of worship seems to be practiced alongside Baalism without any conflict (Jer 32:35; Zeph 1:4–5); in fact, sometimes children were sacrificed to Baal (Jer 19:5).[105] According to this verse these rituals were practiced in valleys and under rocky ledges, even in the rocky Valley of Hinnom on the south side of the city of Jerusalem (cf. Jer 7:31; 19:2; 32:35). This kind

---

[103] This word probably comes from חָמַם and is a pl. *niphal* participle with a prefixed article (GKC §67u, dd).

[104] P. A. Smith, *Rhetoric and Redaction in Trito-Isaiah*, 129, connects the worship "under every green tree" to the worship of the goddess Asherah based on 1 Kgs 14:23; 2 Kgs 17:10, and Jer 17:2, but in other texts this activity is not connected to Asherah (Deut 12:2; 2 Kgs 16:4; Jer 2:20; 3:6).

[105] K. Spronk, *Beatific Afterlife in Ancient Israel* (Neukirchener: Neukirchener Verlag, 1986), and J. Day, *Moloch: A God of Human Sacrifice in the Old Testament* (Cambridge: Cambridge University Press, 1990), deal with the evidence for and history of Molech worship. K. van der Toon, "Prostitution," *ABD* 5:510–13, has raised some questions about the connection between sacred prostitution and Baalism because this aspect is not emphasized in the Ugaritic myths, but the Bible repeatedly makes this connection. A fuller discussion of Canaanite religion is found in S. Ackermann, *Under Every Green Tree: Popular Religion in Sixth-Century Judah*, HSM 46 (Atlanta: Scholars Press, 1992). M. Weinfield, "The Worship of Molech and of the Queen of Heaven and Its Background," *UF* 4 (1972): 133–54, argues that the Molech ritual was one of initiation and dedication to a god, not the burning of babies, but near a temple in Carthage archaeologists found numerous burned skeletons of infants. T. J. Lewis, *Cults of the Dead in Ancient Israel and Ugarit*, HSM 39 (Atlanta: Scholar's Press, 1989) 143–58, connects these verses to a mortuary cult.

of worship existed in Judah during the time of Ahaz (2 Kgs 16:3–4) and Manasseh (2 Kgs 21:1–7), and before the fall of Judah (Ezek 16:20), but here is no mention of people practicing rituals related to either of these pagan religions after the exile. These practices are mentioned as examples of the sinfulness of the wicked and may be connected to what was happening at the tombs in 65:4.[106]

57:6 Using the imagery of a prostitute, 57:6–10 describe the prostitution of the nation (religious and political prostitution) by referring to her with second feminine singular pronouns ("you").[107] The NIV adds "the idols" at the beginning of this verse to identify the use of the smooth stones in various valleys, but the text actually refers only to things that are "smooth, slippery" (ḥālaq) in the valley. This could refer to "smooth stones" which were smoothed off by the rapid flow of water over them, but there is nothing in the description that would argue that these smooth things were identical to the idolatrous standing stones found at some pagan cultic sites in Israel. W. H. Irwin emends the text so that the "smooth" things refers to a grave for the dead,[108] but J. Blenkinsopp and J. L. Koole make the attractive connection between this word and a Semitic root found in Ugaritic and Akkadian that means "to die, destroy, perish."[109] Thus one can translate "with the dead of the valley is your portion/inheritance." The concepts of "inheritance" and "lot"[110] are connected with the idea of Joshua granting a portion of God's land to each Israelite tribe based on the casting of lots (Num 26:55; Josh 15:1). This interpretation indicates that these people will receive their inheritance not from their gracious and compassionate covenant God but from the dead and the pagan gods of the underworld.

In 57:6b these people even pour out drink and cereal offerings as a meal for the dead and their gods to eat. They have perverted a legitimate way of giving thanks to God with a drink offering (Exod 29:40–41; Lev 23:13) and a gift of grain (1:13; 66:3; Lev 2:1) into something that is sinful. Seeing all this perversity, God asks the rhetorical question: "Should I have compassion/be appeased by these things?" Obviously God will not be pleased with what the

---

[106] Muilenburg, "Isaiah 40–66," 5:665, has the opinion that there "is no coercive reason for believing that the attraction of the Canaanite and other nature cults ceased after the fall of Jerusalem," but he offers no evidence to support his suggestion that it did continue in Israel.

[107] Polan, *In the Ways of Justice*, 135, noted the repetition of גַּם in both vv. 6 and 7, and both verses contain a form of עָלָה "bring up, go up," thus drawing these two verses together. In contrast, Westermann, *Isaiah 40–66*, 322, puts v. 6 with what precedes and interprets it as a punishment statement.

[108] W. H. Irwin, "The Smooth Stones of the Wadi: Isaiah 57.6," *CBQ* 29 (1967): 31–40, connects בְּחַלְּקֵי to a grave for the dead.

[109] Koole, *Isaiah III, Volume 3: Isaiah 56–66*, 60, indicates that Ugaritic has this word parallel to the word "death" (ḥlq // mt) and that Akkadian has ḥalāqu "to be destroyed."

[110] The unusual הֵם הֵם initially appears to be a dittography, but the repetition could be for emphasis ("they, they"), or the second הֵם may function as a substitute for the "to be" verb (GKC §141g–h).

wicked are doing, and their pagan offerings will only increase his anger. Everyone in the prophet's audience could figure out that God would not respond positively to these deceitful pagan activities. The same principle is still true, for going through the approved rituals of the faith (or some that are not found in Scripture) never has gained God's approval unless the people involved have truly had a change of heart and have turned from their sinful ways.

57:7 Now the description of pagan worship turns from what was happening in the valleys to what was going on at cultic sites on the tops of mountains, a typical place to construct a illegitimate place of pagan worship (Hos 4:13; Jer 2:20–25; Ezek 16:25). Some believe this is describing pagan worship on Mt Zion itself, which might fit with the time of Manasseh (2 Kgs 21),[111] but it could refer more generally to any false worship on any mountaintop. Earlier Isaiah had emphasized that God's place of dwelling would be above all the other mountains (2:2) and that everything else that was high and lifted up would be humbled and brought low (2:11,12,14,17), for God alone is high and lifted up upon his throne (6:1; 33:10). By using this same terminology, which rightly belongs only to God, the prophet has emphasized the fact that these places of worship are a blatant rejection of God's high-and-lifted-up status.[112] Instead of lifting up the Lord, these people put their beds at various high places,[113] suggesting that these were places of sexual prostitution (Jer 2:20; Hos 4:13; Ezek 16:15). Part of the purpose[114] of going up to these high places was also to offer sacrifices that might appease the gods at that shrine.

57:8 The text does not clearly indicate whether the door mentioned in this verse refers to a door into an individual's home or if this was inside the door to a public temple (this fits the context better).[115] Because the "bed" in 57:7 is mentioned again in 57:8, both verses probably refer to what was happening in

---

[111] Hanson, *The Dawn of Apocalyptic*, 199. P. A. Smith, *Rhetoric and Redaction in Trito-Isaiah*, 85, says "the most likely referent of v. 7a is Mount Zion (cf. 40:9), to which illicit cults have apparently spread." He interprets this whole section as describing a mortuary cult, so the "bed" in v. 7 refers to the place in the grave where the dead person lays. Beuken, "Isa 56:9–57:13: An Example of the Isaianic Legacy of Trito-Isaiah," 53, believes that the "woman addressed, the adulterous Zion, does not climb the mountain as a herald of good tidings to announce God's arrival (40:9), but she climbs the holy mountain of YHWH in order to bring her lovers, the gods, offerings in adultery (59:7)."

[112] Childs, *Isaiah*, 467, emphasizes the intentional contrast created by this reuse of earlier terminology.

[113] P. A. Smith, *Rhetoric and Redaction in Trito-Isaiah*, 85, is one among many who think this high place refers to Mount Zion. Although this mountain could be Mount Zion, this is never stated, so it seems better to view the prophet as describing pagan worship by the wicked on a much broader scale.

[114] The infinitive construct (לִזְבֹּחַ "to sacrifice") is frequently used to express purpose (GKC §114f).

[115] Whybray, *Isaiah 40–66*, 204, calls this "idolatrous worship practiced privately at home" while Koole, *Isaiah III, Volume 3: Isaiah 56–66*, 66, says that "the door and doorpost here are those of the sanctuary." F. Delitzsch, "Prophecies of Isaiah," *Commentary on the Old Testament* (Grand Rapids: Eerdmans, 1969), 7:374, takes this to be a private home where the occupants have

public places of worship on some high mountain. Since some places of worship did not even have doors, behind the door or the doorpost of a pagan place of worship may simply mean inside the temple area.[116] The "memorial, remembrance" (*zikrôn*) or "monument" (NIV "pagan symbols") in this temple is left unexplained, so it is almost impossible to know the full theological significance of this pagan object. Nevertheless, imaginative and speculative guesses suggest everything from (a) a phallic symbol that symbolized the sexual nature of the Baal fertility religion, (b) a simple sign that indicates that this was a place of prostitution, (c) a memorial sacrifice left behind (Lev 2:2), (d) a list of names of the people who contributed to the construction of the temple (cf. Neh 2:20), or (e) a memorial that helped people remember the dead.[117] It is impossible to prove if any of these proposals fit the "memorial, remembrance" mentioned in this verse. Instead of remembering God, they were making objects that memorialized their pagan beliefs. The next line refers to people turning from God (lit. "from me"), uncovering themselves (*gillît*), and going up to the beds provided at the temple. The phrase "you made your bed wide" may literally mean the temple prostitute opened her bed to many lovers, or it may be a metaphorical reference to people being open to the worship of many gods.

The second half of 57:8 is equally difficult to understand. Often interpreters associate the "you cut, cut off" (*kārat*) with cutting a covenant, but the word covenant is not found in this text and the prepositional phrase "from them" (*mēhem*) is used instead of the more usual phraseology of making a covenant "with them" ('*imhem*). There appears to be a textual problem with the second masculine singular verb (all the other verbs are feminine singular), so many commentators prefer the reading in 1QIs^a which is based on the root *kārâ* "he bought, bargained."[118] If the prepositional phrase "from them" was used in a partitive sense,[119] one might translate this phrase "you made an agreement for yourselves with some of them." The final charge accuses these people of loving their beds, the places where the immoral sexual activities took place. If there is any doubt about what these people loved to do or what was going on in these

---

removed the "Shema" that was posted on the doorpost and instead put it behind the door so that they would not see it.

[116] Koole, *Isaiah III, Volume 3: Isaiah 56–66*, 66–67, suggests this statement was given from the point of view of a person inside the temple where the bed was; thus what is behind the door is outside the temple building. Motyer, *Isaiah*, 473, suggests that if this "memorial" was something written on the doorpost, this would be a direct contrast to earlier commands to write God's law on their doorposts (Deut 6:9).

[117] It is possible that the prophet may be referring to pagan activities similar to those described in Ezek 8:5–18 or 16:15–34. Muilenburg, "Isaiah 40–66," 5:667, makes the unlikely connection with the phallic symbol based on the association of the well-known word זִכְרוֹן "remembrance, memorial" with the word זָכָר "male."

[118] Whybray, *Isaiah 40–66*, 205.

[119] If the preposition מִן on מֵהֶם is understood as a partitive, this phrase would be translated "some from among them" (GKC §119w, n. 2).

beds at their temple, the final two words at the end of the verse clarify that the person involved in this bed was looking at a naked person.[120]

57:9 The discussion changes somewhat in 57:9–10, but there are two distinctly different ways of understanding the level of discontinuity these verses have with 57:6–8. Some interpret 57:9–10 as a continuation of the condemnation of pagan worship but with a more specific focus on the Molech cult of the dead. Others believe that 57:9–10 do not continue to describe the pagan worship in 57:6–8; instead, the prophet is now condemning unfaithful political action by comparing these actions to an act of unfaithfulness toward God.[121] Thus both their religious action (57:6–8) and their political action (57:9–10) were acts of prostituting their loyalty to other things than God.

Those who propose a ritual connection in 57:9 interpret the oil as a drink offering (57:9) given to foreign deities, either to the Canaanite god Melek, the Amonnite god Milcom (1 Kgs 11:5), or the Moabite god Molech[122] (accepted in NIV). In the Hebrew Bible Molech is related to the god who accepts the sacrifice of children (Lev 18:21; 2 Kgs 21:6), and T. J. Lewis has connected these verses specifically to a mortuary cult for the dead.[123] This approach is based on ancient Near Eastern texts that refer to one of their gods by the name *mlk/maliku*,[124] but H. P. Müller presents strong evidence to suggest that the term "molech" refers to a child sacrifice to a pagan god, and thus it is not the name of a god.[125] Consequently there is some confusion about what those texts about "molech" are actually referring to. Since "sacrificing children" was

---

[120] The text literally refers to a "hand" יָד, a euphemism for the male genitalia as many, such as Oswalt, *Isaiah 40–66*, 480, suggest. "Hand" is often a symbol of strength so it is not surprising that it also relates to sexual strength. In contrast, Koole, *Isaiah III, Volume 3: Isaiah 56–66*, 71, prefers to interpret this as the depiction of the hands of a dead person on a monument.

[121] Blenkinsopp, *Isaiah 56–66*, 160–61, accepts the Molech interpretation, while Motyer, *Isaiah*, 474, interprets 57:9–10 as political unfaithfulness by a king.

[122] It is hypothesized that the different pronunciation מֹלֶךְ "Molech" was a Hebrew invention because they took the vowels from בֹּשֶׁת "shame" and substituted them in place of the usual מֶלֶךְ "Melek."

[123] T. J. Lewis, *Cults of the Dead in Ancient Israel and Ugarit*, HSM 39 (Atlanta: Scholar's Press, 1989) 143–58. Cf. M. H. Pope, "The Cult of the Dead at Ugarit," in *Ugarit in Retrospect: Fifty Years of Ugarit and Ugaritic*, ed. G. W. Young (Winona Lake, IN: Eisenbrauns, 1981), 159–79, also relates this verse to necromancy. G. C. Heider, *The Cult of Molek: A Reassessment*, JSOTSup 43 (Sheffield: Sheffield Academic Press, 1985); id., "Molech," *ABD* (New York: Doubleday, 1992), 4:895–97.

[124] These texts go back to the third millennium BC at Ebla, later texts from Mari, Punic texts from Carthage in North Africa, and Phoenician texts.

[125] The study of H. P. Müller, "מֹלֶךְ *mōlek*," *TDOT*, 8:375–88, finds the *mōlek* pronunciation already present in Phoenician and Punic documents and traces the meaning back to "offering," not the common suggestion of "king." It appears to be a child sacrifice/offering that (a) fulfills a vow and expects the gods to provide future blessings because the one sacrificing has faithfully carried out such an extraordinary sacrifice or (b) was given in a time of great distress (see 2 Kgs 3:27). He questions if this was truly the name of a pagan god; instead, he associates this term with a sacrificial offering.

mentioned in 57:5, one can understand why many interpret 57:9 to be another reference to "molech" cult practices.

Nevertheless, the Hebrew text actually has the word "king" (*melek*) not "Molech" (*mōlek*) in 57:9; thus, the most straightforward understanding of the verse would point to political acts of unfaithfulness which involved traveling to other nations to present expensive gifts (olive oil and perfumes; cf. Ezek 23:36–41) to their kings as a means of maintaining or achieving political stability through friendly relationships or a treaty. Possibly the prophet was reminding his audience of an earlier situation during the Syro-Ephraimite War in 734–732 BC when the wicked king Ahaz worshiped Baal, passed his son through the fire, and sent envoys with rich presents to the Assyrian king Tiglath-pileser III, rather than trusting God to deliver the nation as Isaiah had prophesied (7:1–10; 2 Kgs 16:1–20; 2 Chr 28:1–4,16–27). This failure to trust God was also a problem for Hezekiah when his "ambassadors, envoys" went far away to Egypt (1:1–9; 30:1–7; cf. Ezek 23:16) and also when he accepted envoys from Babylon that were interested in forming a political coalition against Assyria (39:1–6).[126] This idea of comparing political dependence on other nations to prostitution was already used by Hosea, and later Ezekiel will also use this kind of imagery in the description of Judah's apostasy (Ezek 23). At the end of 57:9 there is a reference to descending to the "grave" or "Sheol," an idea that Isaiah earlier connected to Judah's "covenant with death" with Egypt in 28:15.[127] Past generations prostituted themselves by trusting in other nations rather than trusting God, but this kind of unfaithfulness will only seal their demise and quicken their descent into Sheol.

57:10 The paragraph draws to a close with a summarization and interim conclusion concerning what these people have accomplished. All these perverted ways (political and religious) of trying to find help from different human and religious sources of strength led to a certain level of "weariness" (*yāgāʿ*). These searchers for hope worked hard to find their way and expended much effort (compare the labors of Babylon in 47:12,15) and never said "despair, give up, (it is) hopeless" (from *yāʾaš*, cf. Jer 2:25). The second half of the verse explains that somehow through "your own strength" (lit. "your hand") you found life or the renewal of life. Presumably this means that through the use of pagan gods and ritual and the use of political treaties these people maintained their life and gained enough strength to continue on; therefore, they did not become

---

[126] The reference to "envoys, ambassadors" causes one to give a political interpretation to this verse, for kings sent envoys to other nations. It would be odd to have an envoy sent to a Molech temple.

[127] The discussion of this topic in G. V. Smith, *Isaiah 1–39*, 1:486 where the "covenant with death" and "vision of Sheol" are connected with the leader's false hope in their alliance with Egypt. They thought that this alliance would bring them deliverance and salvation from the Assyrians, but in reality God said it actually would bring them death. J. Day, *Molech*, 62–64, connects 28:15 to Molech worship, but this seems very unlikely in light of the plain discussion about the Egyptian alliance in chaps. 30–31.

"sick, faint, powerless" (*ḥālâ*). Although people throughout the ages have tried these and various other means to get through times of conflict and trouble, God is not impressed with human efforts; instead, he wants people to humbly trust him in their times of distress.

57:11 At this point the conversation turns from a series of accusations about pagan religious practices and political unfaithfulness to question (similarly to 57:4) the people about their relationship to God. God, the questioner, asks, "Whom[128] do you fear?" But it is not clear if this is asking whether they act out of fear of other nations, or if they act out of fear of some gods.[129] Since 57:6–8 refers to their worship of other gods and 57:9–10 describes their alliances with other nations, the broad question in 57:11 is about more than just the names of the gods and nations they feared. This question inquires more deeply about the reasonableness (the why question) of their reaction to such impotent nations and gods (cf. 40:15–21). The unreasonableness of their fearful response is underlined by their need to "continually lie, deceive" (*kāzab*)[130] themselves and others about the power of these nations and idols in order to make their fears seem reasonable. Because they deceived people and caused them to fear pagan gods, it was natural for them not to fear the true God of Israel, so gradually God became less and less important and in time was essentially forgotten. The Hebrew language expresses this by reversing the word order for emphasis: "Me, you did not remember."[131] Since these people were able to control the nation through religious and political manipulation, they thought they did not need God (cf. 57:1)[132] and failed to reflect on the consequences of their action. God was so remote from their frame of reference (their worldview) that they gave no attention to how he might respond to their action.

In the second half of 57:11, God questions why these people ignored their relationship to him. Could it possibly be that these people ignored God because

---

[128] The question uses the interrogative pronoun מִי preceded with the sign of the direct object אֵת in order to indicate that the interrogative pronoun functions as the object; thus the translation of it should be "whom."

[129] Delitzsch, *Isaiah*, 376, believes "It was of men—only mortal men, with no real power (ch. li.12)—that Israel was so needlessly afraid." Muilenburg, "Isaiah 40–66," 5:668, interprets this to be asking about what gods they fear.

[130] The imperfect verb תְּכַזֵּבִי is improperly translated as a passive in past tense "you have been false" (NIV), but the imperfect usually refers to continual or repeated action and the *pi'el* form is not passive. GKC §109u suggests that after a question, the imperfect often has a modal sense, so one might translate the clause "that you should deceive." NIV adds "to me" (it is missing from the Hebrew text), which either follows the Old Greek text or was added to create a parallel for the next line ("remember me").

[131] The usual order of verb plus object is reversed and the object "and me" (וְאוֹתִי) appears first in the clause.

[132] Literally the text claims that these people "did not set it on their heart" to consider the positive or negative implications of their choices, specifically, how God might punish them for this rejection of him.

he "was being silent and hiding?"[133] In the future eschatological period when God establishes his kingdom at Zion, he will no longer be silent (62:1), and when he punishes the wicked, he will not be silent (65:6). Thus God's silence refers to a time when he did not speak or act in a favorable way (42:14; 62:1; 65:6). One might think that this could hardly refer to the times of the prophets, when God repeatedly spoke messages through numerous prophets and repeatedly delivered and brought judgment on nations. God's hiding or silence could apply to any short period of time when God did not immediately answer the prayers of his people (8:17; 59:2; 64:7; Deut 31:17; Mic 3:4; Ezek 39:23–24). For example, the lament of the people who were suffering under the attacks of Sennacherib complained that they were waiting for God to act (26:8), and they did not see his hand of judgment on their enemies (26:11) because God was hiding his face for a moment (40:27; 54:7–8). Since God did not immediately answer the people's prayers but allowed them to suffer defeat for many days, it appeared to them that he was silent and not interested in them. This perverse pragmatic response that requires instant gratification concerning what they want done, without first considering why God might be putting them through this kind of experience, demonstrates the shallowness of their relationship with God. If he does not quickly satisfy all their needs and grant their every request, they quickly turn away and ignore him. Maybe this is not that different from the consumer mentality that has infiltrated some modern churches. Is the biblical worldview all about how God can make me feel good? This verse suggests that part of what gives people a sense of the real presence of God in their lives (the opposite of God being silent) are their own acts of fearing, remembering, and thinking about him.

57:12 God cannot be ignored, and forgetting about him does not mean that he will forget about the things people have said or done. At some point in the future God will reveal everything they have done; that is, at some future point he will be silent no longer (in contrast to 57:11). This is expressed by the repetitious use of the personal pronoun "I" (*'ănî*), giving the emphatic emphasis "I myself will declare."[134] The promise to expose "your righteousness" implies that God has a record of everything these people have done and knows just how righteous or unrighteous they really are (cf. 58:1; Dan 7:10). God's records will show that their lives were not characterized by godliness, for 57:3–11 primarily describe a life that is devoid of righteousness. It is possible

---

[133] The *hiphil* participle from חָשָׁה "silent" tends to express durative action in past, present, or future time. After the word "was being silent" the Heb text has וּמֵעֹלָם "and from eternity," which is hard to understand. In what sense could it ever be claimed or imagined that God had not acted "forever, from eternity?" The "and" is also unusual and unnecessary with this reading. A better explanation based on the Old Greek tradition suggests that this word is a participle from עָלַם "he hid." Thus the text would claim that God "was being silent and hiding."

[134] The verb אַגִּיד means "I will declare," so the addition of אֲנִי "I" is repetitious and creates an emphatic emphasis that could be translated "I, I will declare" or "I myself will declare."

that these pagan practices were intermixed with some worship at the temple in Jerusalem (cf. 58:1–14), which they thought God would honor. When the facts are revealed and the motivations of their hearts are exposed, God will show that many of their so-called righteous deeds look more like filthy rags (64:6). In the second half of the verse,[135] God warns that all their righteous deeds and works, which they were counting on, will not profit them at all. This verse strongly argues against the popular beliefs of cultural Christians who naively think that God will be impressed with all their good works and that these will get them into heaven.

57:13 Consequently, God mockingly suggests to this audience, "let your collection of idols save you"[136] when you cry out for help.[137] Your "collection"[138] (lit "the things gathered together") is not defined in this verse, so T. J. Lewis suggests it refers to a collection of dead ancestors,[139] but most commentators believe this refers to a collection of the pagan gods mentioned in the discussion within 57:3–11. Obviously, these gods will be of no help to these sinful people. The statement that "all of them" will be carried off by the wind could refer to the useless idols in their collection or to the people who worship these idols.[140] They have no more substance to them than the rulers of this world who are blown away by God and will be scattered like chaff by the breath[141] from his mouth (17:13; 29:5; 40:25; 41:15–16).

After this series of accusations in 57:3–13a comes a bold contrasting offer of hope to the one who takes refuge in God (cf. 4:6; 14:32; 25:4; Pss 5:11–12;

---

[135] The NIV translation has God exposing both righteousness and works, but the grammatical structure is odd. Some put "righteousness" with the first verb and then connect "works, deeds" with the second verb in the sentence because וְאֶת־מַעֲשַׂיִךְ "and your works" has the sign of the direct object, while צִדְקָתֵךְ "your righteousness" does not have the sign of the direct object before it; thus, it appears that they are not written as a pair "your righteousness and your works" but as two separate items (Westermann, *Isaiah 40–66*, 323). The problem is that one is left with the translation "and your works, they will not profit you," with "your works" as the subject of the sentence. This contradicts the grammatical function of the sign of the direct object which precedes "your works."

[136] The imperfect verb יַצִּילֵךְ "they will save you" probably functions as a jussive to express a desire, wish, or request (GKC §109a–b); thus the translation could be "let the collection save you" or "the collection should save you."

[137] The initial clause uses a temporal infinitive construct construction בְּזַעֲקֵךְ in which the object pronoun ךְ "you" functions as the subject of the verb (GKC §115e).

[138] Westermann, *Isaiah 40–66*, 323, emends קִבּוּצַיִךְ "your collection" to שִׁקּוּצַיִךְ "your abominations."

[139] Lewis, *The Cult of the Dead*, 151–52.

[140] Oswalt, *Isaiah 40–66*, 483, pictures the collection of idols as "a chimera, a vapor, an imagination of human minds that have rejected the truth," While Beuken, "Isa 56:6–57:13—An Example of the Isaianic Legacy of Trito-Isaiah," 53, thinks that a better contrast between 13a and 13b would be created by a contrast between the godless and the pious people. Thus "all of them" refers back to the "sons of a sorceress" in 57:3 and the harlot in 57:6.

[141] There may be something of a pun in the choice of חֶבֶל to express this idea, for חֶבֶל means "breath" as well as "nothing." Both ideas express how weak and unsubstantial the false gods are. In contrast, God is described by the opposite pun כָּבוֹד which means "heavy" and "glorious."

17:7; 31:19–20). As a refuge God can protect people from bad weather, disease, death, false accusations, and the attack of an enemy army. God promises that those who trust him for protection and for their needs have the great assurance that they will inherit the land, for God owns it (Exod 9:29; 19:5; Lev 25:23; Ps 24:1) and will give it to them. They will take possession of the sacred mountain of Zion, just as 56:7 indicates. This reconfirms God's commitment to give to Abram and his seed the land (Gen 12:1–3; 13:14–17; 15:18–21; 22:15–18) and reminds this audience of similar promises by God throughout the book of Isaiah (2:2–4; 14:1; 56:7; 60:21; 65:9). God has not forsaken his people or his promises. This Holy Mountain is the place where God will dwell among his people (cf. 57:15). There is no suggestion in these verses that this refers to the people returning to the land from exile; this is the eschatological fulfillment of God's promises sometime in the distant future.

GOD WILL REVIVE THE LOWLY; JUDGE OTHERS (57:14–21)

⁴And it will be said:

> "Build up, build up, prepare the road!
>   Remove the obstacles out of the way of my people."
> ¹⁵For this is what the high and lofty One says—
>   he who lives forever, whose name is holy:
> "I live in a high and holy place,
>   but also with him who is contrite and lowly in spirit,
> to revive the spirit of the lowly
>   and to revive the heart of the contrite.
> ¹⁶I will not accuse forever,
>   nor will I always be angry,
> for then the spirit of man would grow faint before me—
>   the breath of man that I have created.
> ¹⁷I was enraged by his sinful greed;
>   I punished him, and hid my face in anger,
>   yet he kept on in his willful ways.
> ¹⁸I have seen his ways, but I will heal him;
>   I will guide him and restore comfort to him,
> ¹⁹creating praise on the lips of the mourners in Israel.
>   Peace, peace, to those far and near,"
>   says the LORD. "And I will heal them."
> ²⁰But the wicked are like the tossing sea,
>   which cannot rest,
>   whose waves cast up mire and mud.
> ²¹"There is no peace," says my God, "for the wicked."

The final paragraph in the long section 56:9–57:21 functions as a proclamation of salvation about what will happen in the future when God sits upon his high and holy royal throne to rule the earth. These verses explain what will happen to those who trust God in 57:13b. These are "my people" (*'ammî*) who will enter into God's future kingdom because God will revive the hearts of the contrite and lowly (57:15). This new situation will be possible because the stumbling blocks of sin and the wicked people who oppress the righteous will be removed (57:1–2,17,20). All suffering will be over and God will bring healing, comfort, and peace to his people (57:18–19). The oracle ends with a brief contrasting explanation of what God will do to the wicked (57:20–21).[142]

This paragraph is organized into three parts.

Call to prepare the way	57:14
Divine salvation for the humble	57:15–19
God's promise of revival	15
God's anger will end	16–17
God's healing and peace	18–19
Punishment of the wicked	57:20–21

P. A. Smith has summarized some of the redactional attempts to reconstruct the growth of this oracle (by "Trito-Isaiah" and other redactors) but wisely concludes that the interlinking terms within this oracle and its interconnections with earlier and later oracles in Isaiah argue more for a unified literary product.[143] The repetition of earlier themes from chaps. 1–55, some of which will appear again in chaps. 60–62, enables the interpreter to place these promises in their proper eschatological context. For example, the building up of a road in 57:14 has a connection with the preparation of a road in 40:3; 52:1; and 62:10, and the end of God's anger in 57:16 is related to the same theme in 51:22; 54:9. Within this paragraph itself one finds the repetition of words like the "way" *derek* (57:14,17,18), "anger" *kāṣap* (57:16,17), "heal" *rāpāʾ* (57:18,19), and "wicked" *rāšāʿ* (57:20–21). This paragraph contrasts the destiny of the righteous and the wicked, similar to the contrasts in both 56:9–57:2 and 57:3–13; thus, all three paragraphs within this section follow a somewhat similar pattern.

The theology of this proclamation of salvation centers everything that will happen around God's holy presence (57:15). His plans are to revive the lowly and contrite, to heal them, and to give them peace and joy. This will be possible once his anger punishes the wicked and his wrath has completed its work. The audience is encouraged, therefore, to prepare for the coming of the Lord and to

---

[142] This brief contrasting reference to the wicked in 57:20–21 is parallel to the brief contrasting reference to the righteous in 57:13b.

[143] P. A. Smith, *Rhetoric and Redaction in Trito-Isaiah*, 88–89, reviews the works of Westermann, Sekine, Koenen, and Vermeylen, who attribute parts of these verses to "Trito-Isaiah" (Westermann connects 14–19 to "Trito-Isaiah" and 20–21 to a later redactor, but Sekine has a redactor adding 15b,18b–19a, and 20–21) and parts to other later redactors. Smith argues against these conclusions and suggests that this paragraph was not written by "Trito-Isaiah" and that vv. 20–21 should not be separated from this unit. An earlier study by Muilenburg, "Isaiah 40–66," 5:670, claims that "in style, language, and thought it is closely allied with Second Isaiah."

trust his promises. They must turn from their wickedness so that they will not suffer under the punishment of his anger.

57:14 The message begins with an ambiguous "one will say"[144] (NIV "it will be said"), which is similar to the ambiguous voices that called out in 40:3–6. Although the one who speaks is not identified by name, the later reference to "my people" makes it clear that the one talking is speaking the words of God. B. S. Childs concludes that this is a quotation formula informing the reader that this is a citation of 40:3.[145] When one compares 57:14 with 40:3, the two texts show some similarities and some differences. "Build up, build up" is repeated later in 62:10 (referring to a highway), but it is not found in 40:3, though 40:4 does refer to the building of roads. "Prepare the way" is found in 40:3; 57:14 and 62:10, but in 40:3 it refers to preparing a way for God, while in 57:14 and 62:10 the way is being prepared for people. The phrase "remove the obstacles out of the way of my people" might also function as a summary of 40:4, while 62:10 refers to "raising up a banner for the nations." Thus the vocabulary used has some similarity with 40:3, but 40:3 calls for preparation for the coming of God, 57:14 calls for the preparation for the coming of my people, and 62:10 calls for preparation for the coming of the nations. Thus it is questionable if one can call this a quotation. It seems more like a periphrastic allusion or re-molding of 40:3. J. Blenkinsopp views this as a later contemporizing of the earlier messages in chaps. 40–55 because (a) the people are in a different situation after the exile, (b) the Persian king Cyrus has failed to do everything that chaps. 40–55 have expected him to do, and (c) the people's sins have kept the great expectations of chaps. 40–55 from being fulfilled.[146] This approach relies on W. Zimmerli's conclusion that the author of chaps. 56–66 is reinterpreting ideas in 40–55 by spiritualizing them.[147] C. Seitz, B. S. Childs, and J. Oswalt do not accept this approach because of several difficulties. (a) Many of the prophecies in chaps. 40–55 are about an ideal future and have nothing to do with what Cyrus was supposed to do for the Israelites. (b) This interpretation implies that God's promises are conditionally dependent on the moral behavior of his people, implying that they are earned, not graciously given by God according to his foreordained plan. (c) The so-called spiritualizing approach is dependent on viewing 40:3 as a literal return of the people from exile and 57:14 as a spiritual return to God, but the exegesis of 40:3 above[148] suggests that 40:3

---

[144] The *qal* perfect verb with *waw* prefix is active, not passive as in the translation of the NIV. The perfect verb is usually understood as a future prophetic perfect in this verse (GKC §106n), though Childs translates it as a regular perfect verb in the past tense.

[145] Childs, *Isaiah*, 469–70, prefers simply "he said" and treats this as an introduction to a quotation which cites 40:3.

[146] Blenkinsopp, *Isaiah 56–66*, 169.

[147] W. Zimmerli, "Zur Sprache Tritojesajas," *Schweizerische theologische Umschau* 20 (1950): 110–122, interprets the author of chaps. 56–66 to be giving an ethical or spiritual interpretation to the earlier texts he alludes to or quotes.

[148] Read the conclusion on 40:3 in the exegetic discussion of that verse.

is not talking about the literal return of the exiles. It is an encouragement for the prophet's audience to spiritually prepare themselves for the eschatological coming of God so they might enjoy the future kingdom with him.

The repeated encouragement for people to "build up"[149] calls for action that would metaphorically prepare the way for the people to dwell in the presence of the holy and exalted God who will dwell with his people (57:15).[150] This spiritual preparation involves the reorientation of their political, social, and theological way of life (their worldview) by removing "obstacles, stumbling blocks" (*mikšôl*) that were causing God to hide himself and his blessings from them. Later in Ezekiel, the evil stumbling blocks of that time are defined as their money (Ezek 7:19), idols (Ezek 14:3), and evil people (44:12),[151] but 57:14 only suggests that it is something that keeps one from following God's ways. Certainly the sinfulness mentioned in 56:9–12 and 57:3–13a identify some of the evil stumbling blocks that would keep people from enjoying God's presence. In every era sin is the obstacle that prevents people from enjoying the revival of a person's discouraged spirit and a sense of God's presence (cf. 59:1–2).

57:15 God now gives new words of promise and exhortation that describe his coming to dwell with his people (57:15b–21). Initially God introduces himself in 15a. The one who will speak the following words is the "high and lofty One,"[152] expressed with participles that identify God's exalted existence, similar to what was experienced by Isaiah in a vision when he saw the king high and lifted up (6:1–5). God "dwells" (NIV "he lives") forever without beginning or end and is uniquely defined by his holy name (his holy reputation). These introductory self-identifiers legitimate the authority behind the following words, and they distinguish God from everything that goes on at the pagan high-and-lifted-up places of worship in 57:7. When God speaks (15b), he refers to himself as an exalted holy God who is transcendent, but not totally unapproachable, for he will dwell with the contrite and humble.[153] One of God's central

---

[149] The imperative verbs סֹלּוּ סֹלּוּ "build up, build up" encourage people to action (GKC §110a) by figuratively repairing or reconstructing a new way of life.

[150] P. A. Smith, *Rhetoric and Redaction in Trito-Isaiah*, 91, and Childs, *Isaiah*, 470, believe the command to build up and prepare are directed to heavenly beings, based on 40:1–3, not to men on earth. The text of 57:14 does not identify exactly who the audience is.

[151] D. I. Block, *The Book of Ezekiel Chapters 1–24*, NICOT (Grand Rapids: Eerdmans, 1997), 146–47.

[152] The two participles רָם "the high one" and נִשָּׂא "the lifted up one" are synonyms that are used to describe God in 6:1; 33:10. They emphasize God's transcendence over the entire world and his exalted status in comparison to human beings. In 40:15,17 the nations are nothing and in 40:22 the people of the earth are like grasshoppers.

[153] S. W. Flynn, "Where is YHWH in Isaiah 57,14–15?" *Bib* 87 (2006): 358–70, reviews the various ways the versions struggle with the transcendence and imminence of God (does he dwell in heaven or on earth?). He concludes that the LXX, the Targum Pseudo-Jonathan, and the Peshitta emphasize his transcendence more, as do most commentators, but Flynn argues for a balanced understanding because other passages refer to God coming and dwelling in an earthly temple.

purposes on earth is stated in unambiguous terms. His will and desire is "to revive"[154] the contrite, those who have their spirits crushed by someone stronger. Earlier God's will was to revive the life of the servant who was crushed for our iniquities in 53:5. Isaiah 2:1–4; 4:2–6; 32; 35; 40:1–11; and 52:1–10 have already addressed some of the aspects of God's coming to earth to reign over his people, and chaps. 60–62 will add more information about those events. One thing is already clear: the wicked will be punished with death (57:3–13a), while the humble will be given a glorious new life with God.

57:16–17 These verses assure (the *kî* is "surely, truly"; NIV omits it)[155] the righteous that they will only have to live a little longer in this sinful and oppressive world until the period of God's wrath will end the struggle between the righteous and wickedness. God has been patient with many people, waiting for them to respond positively to him for a long time (57:11), but he will not "contend, bring charges against"[156] people by being angry at their sins forever. It is a just act for God to convict people of their sins and to discipline them for their sins, but this fight against human sinfulness and oppression (cf. 57:1–2) will continue only for so long. Why will it last only for a limited period? Because if God would continue to express his anger and would justly judge sinful people for too long, soon all of them "would faint away"[157] and all the living souls which God created would perish (as in the flood of Gen 6–8). If God was not so longsuffering, but instantly required justice and punished each of us as we deserve, the death of Ananias and Sapphira in Acts 5:1–10 would not seem unusual at all.

God's desire is not to destroy mankind (cf. Ezek 18:32) but to transform them through love and discipline. The reason why God disciplined these people was (a) because he was angry over their sinful desires for "gain" and (b) because discipline can teach people to do what is right and reject what is wrong. The exact parameters of what the word "gain" (*beṣaʿ*) means is unclear. It could be strictly limited to include unjust oppression of the weak for financial gain, but this seems too narrow of a focus. A "gain" in any area of life produces positive results, pleasure and security; thus, the leaders in 56:9–12 enjoyed the good life by laying around and "seeking their own gain," for they thought they were

---

[154] Purpose or goal is expressed with the *hiphil* infinitive construct לְהַחֲיוֹת "in order to give life, revive." The ungodly in 57:13 are blown away by the "wind" (רוּחַ) in 57:13a, but the lowly are revived by God's Spirit (רוּחַ) in 57:15. The "humble" (שְׁפַל) in 57:15 are revived by God, but the wicked are "humbled, go down" (וַתַּשְׁפִּילִי) to the grave and death.

[155] The asseverative כִּי "truly, surely" indicates that something is absolutely certain (GKC §159ee).

[156] The verb אָרִיב "I will contend" comes from רִיב, a verb that refers to being in conflict, making argumentation against, or taking someone to court.

[157] There are questions about the meaning of the verb יַעֲטוֹף "grow faint" in NIV, NASB, NRSV, "proceeds" in RSV, and NEB based on the Old Greek. "Grow faint" fits the context of this word in Pss 61:1 (Hb 61:3); 77:3 (Hb 77:4), and in the superscription to Ps 102 (Hb 102:1). The imperfect verb can have a subjunctive translation "would grow faint" (GKC §107x).

gaining by causing the righteous to perish in 57:1–2. The sons of sorcerers and ungodly worshippers of idols who were involved with sexual perversions and political intrigue in 57:3–10 thought their religious devotion and political maneuvers would "gain" them the favor of the gods and their neighbors. Anyone who tries to gain security and happiness, life and fulfillment, merely through human effort is doomed to failure. God is the only source of real security and gain. Because of misdirected human attempts to gain security and pleasure, people have turned from God to other things, so it is necessary for God to discipline them to bring them back to himself. He allows difficult times to fall on them (his curses; cf. Lev 26), but sadly many people continue on with their evil ways and do not stop to learn from God's discipline.

This concept of divine hiding or abandoning[158] people is a human way of expressing man's sense of separation from God because of sinfulness and suffering, as well as God's refusal to respond to human requests for his intervention. The psalmist knew that because God was gracious, compassionate, and abounding in love, he would judge sin. But he believed that his anger would not last forever (Ps 103:8–9). Indeed there were times when the sinfulness of man caused God's anger to bring very severe judgment on the earth (the flood, the fall of Sodom, and the defeat of Jerusalem). For a while he abandoned his sinful people and allowed them to be judged (2:6), just as God predicted he would in Deut 31:17. At times this is described as God being hidden (1:15; 40:27; 59:2) or silent (42:14) or God abandoning (54:7–8) his people to allow them to learn about the consequences of their sinful ways. Unfortunately, it appears that at this time few people learned from these lessons because, in spite of their punishment, many continued to turn away from God.[159] Since many people seem to be hopelessly controlled by these evil desires, God will one day call a halt to his attempts to transform mankind. On that day he will rescue the righteous and bring final judgment on the wicked.

57:18–19 God's gracious deeds to comfort the righteous are described first, then in 57:20–21 the prophet summarizes what will happen to the wicked. God's dealings with mankind are partially based on what he knows people are doing (57:18a); thus, he is a personal God who interacts with people by giving an appropriate blessing or curse. The text does not say if God has observed evil ways of behavior or righteous living in 57:18a; thus, it is impossible to

---

[158] The Hb expresses this with the infinitive absolute הַסְתֵּר which functions adverbially to expresses the manner or attendant circumstances under which this action took place. Thus the action of the main verb "I smote him" is modified and explained by the infinitive absolute "by hiding" ("my face" is not in the Hb text). Elsewhere God hides his face and allows people to be punished (8:17; 54:8; 64:6). The concept suggests that God withdraws or hides his love and compassion so he does not intervene to save or respond to people's prayers. Sin breaks a person's relationship to God (59:1–2).

[159] The word שׁוֹבָב frequently has a positive meaning referring to the "turning, returning, repentance" of people back to God, but in this example it means "turning away" from God (cf. Jer 3:14,22).

say if his response is a gracious forgiving of sinful people ("but I will heal" as in 19:22) or the giving of a gracious gift to righteous people ("so I will heal"). The second suggestion makes the most sense since 57:18–20 deals with how God will deal with the wicked.

God declares, "I will heal him," a concept that coincides with God's earlier promise to "revive" the lowly and contrite in 57:15. Healing can literally refer to healing from a disease or wounds (30:26), but a broader ethical meaning includes healing the heart of its defects (as in 53:5; Ps 103:3) and disappointments (Pss 34:18; 147:3).[160] Healing is only the beginning of God's work, for he will also "guide, lead"[161] them in the future so that they will not be left alone without divine assistance. The third divine act will be for God to "repay" (NIV "restore") comfort to him (the righteous) and to those who mourn because of the way they were mistreated in the past (cf. 54:7–8; 57:1–2; 61:2–3).[162] Everything that caused heartache, pain, violence, oppression, and loss in the past will be removed so that God's healing power might transform this evil world and create a new world based on his grace. This is all the work of God. Thanks be to God!

Verse 19 continues the marvelous description of what God will do for the righteous. When he comforts those who mourn, God will give his people the ability to create[163] new words on their lips because at that time they will experience his fresh healing, his comfort, and his presence. These words will be words of praise to God (cf. 12:1–6; 25:1–4,9–12; 26:1–6; 42:10–13; 44:23; 49:13), so it would be somewhat natural to suggest that the words "peace, peace to those far and near" are the words that God creates on the lips of those who formerly mourned.[164] His peace is announced to all people in the world (a merism),[165] not specifically to those far off in exile and those near in Jerusalem.[166] This probably coincides with his creation of a new heaven and a new earth (65:17).

---

[160] Westermann, *Isaiah 40–66*, 330, believes this word of hope is directed to the people who are still in exile.

[161] The verb אֶנְחֵהוּ could hypothetically come from the root נוּחַ "he rested" or נָחָה "he guided, led." The second is preferable in light of the repeated references to the "way" people go.

[162] Whybray, *Isaiah 40–66*, 211, and Koole, *Isaiah III, Volume 3: Isaiah 56–66*, 107–108, puts "to his mourners" with v. 19.

[163] The active participle בּוֹרֵא sometimes does not have an expressed subject (GKC §116s). In such cases a subject can be supplied from context, or one can translate the participle as a gerund (NIV "creating") that modifies the preceding verbal idea.

[164] E. J. Young, *The Book of Isaiah*. (Grand Rapids: Eerdmans, 1965–72), 3:413, seems to take all of the second half of v. 19 as the people quoting what God said; thus, "says the Lord" is parenthetical, indicating who originally said this.

[165] Polan, *In the Ways of Justice toward Salvation*, 158, argues that this is simply a merism that identifies the whole by explicating its parts.

[166] Whybray, *Isaiah 40–66*, 211, believes it specifically refers to "the Jews in Jerusalem and the Jews scattered throughout the world." Young, *Isaiah*, 3:413, thinks those near are the people who belong to the covenant and those far are the Gentiles.

57:20–21 After dealing with God's grace to the righteous, the paragraph ends with a brief contrasting comparison about what God will do with the wicked. This is parallel to the structure of 57:3–13, which predominantly deals with the wicked and ends with a brief comparative contrast about what God will do for the righteous. The wicked leaders fail to take care of God's flock (cf. 56:9–12), persecute the righteous (57:1–2), and worship pagan gods (57:3–10). These people have forsaken God (57:8), wearied God (57:10), and have dealt deceitfully with God (57:11), so now God will expose their evil (57:12). In 57:20 the wicked enemies of God are compared to the raging sea, reminding the reader of earlier comparisons of the Assyrian army to the raging sound of the sea (5:30; 17:12–13). Such wicked forces, no matter how strong or how many, will not prevail, for they themselves are in utter turmoil and without any peace. They are not able to rest,[167] and all they can accomplish with all their violence and furor is compared to stirring up muck and mire. They sound frightening, and they cause a great disturbance, but in the end all one can say is that there will be "no peace"[168] for the wicked people who follow this path. This presents a strong contrast with the wonderful promise of "peace, peace" (57:19) for the righteous.

THEOLOGICAL IMPLICATIONS. This complicated message divides mankind into two groups: the righteous and the wicked (especially wicked leaders). Although in this present life the righteous may suffer and die (57:1–2), in the end the righteous will be revived, healed, comforted, and given eternal peace (57:18–19) in the presence of God at his Holy Mountain (56:7; 57:13). In contrast, the life of the wicked leaders and those who follow them is characterized as irresponsible and uncaring (56:9–12), oppressive (57:1–2), cut off from God (57:8), and dedicated to the worship of pagan gods (57:3–10). Their destiny is divine judgment (57:12–13a), no rest, and no peace (57:20–21). They will miss all the wonderful things God has prepared for his humble and contrite people.

Since some leaders are blind to the things of God and lack knowledge of God, people need to choose their leaders extremely carefully. If their leaders are mute and do not warn people about sin, if they love to dream and take life easy, if they are motivated by money, possessions, material gain, and if they persecute righteous people who do not agree with them, then one should not be enticed by their words and pious claims. Equally dangerous are those who lust

---

[167] One usually expects to find an infinitive construct after לֹא יוּכַל "he will not be able," but in this case the text has an infinitive absolute (הַשְׁקֵט) before the finite verb. Here it functions as the object of the verb (GKC §113d).

[168] This phrase is appended to 48:22 as well. It appears to generally fit the context of 57:20–21 and 48:22. It appears to be a somewhat mechanical editorial means of marking of the division of chaps. 40–66 into three equal parts of nine chapters each (40–48, 49–57, 58–66). Although 48:22 does mark the end of a literary unit (chaps. 40–48), 57:22 does not mark the end of a major literary unit.

after and eventually follow sexual immorality, who accept the lifestyle of the pagans, and who forsake the ways of God. Although these people may sometimes talk and act like religious people, the real question is, do they fear God (57:11)? In the end every person's works will be exposed for what they really are (57:12), but then it will be too late for these evil people to cry out to God for mercy, and their judgment will be severe (57:13a,16–17,20–21).

There will always be some people in this world who choose to serve themselves, develop their own ways of gaining security in this world, forget God, and worship other gods (money, fame, prestige). This evil path may seem easier, more popular, more fun, and it certainly avoids the perils of persecution, but is it the way of divine peace, healing, comfort, and revival? This prophecy calls on people to carefully make their choices and to be ready to accept the consequences of those choices.

(3) God Accepts Those Who Please Him (58:1–59:21)

Although earlier chapters have already distinguished in various ways between the lifestyle and destiny of the righteous and the wicked, these two chapters address the impact of sinful attitudes and behaviors on God's relationship with those who claim to be the people of God. It may appear that some are eager to please God (58:2), yet in reality they are far more interested in pleasing themselves (58:3). They need to be far more concerned about righteous living if they want to experience God's blessing. A deeper analysis of these people's behavior demonstrates that they lie, shed innocent blood, act unjustly, and have evil thoughts that separate them from God (59:1–8). If they would finally agree to confess their sins (59:9–15a), then God would be pleased and his strong arm would work to bring them salvation (59:15b–21).

Chapters 58–59 go together because they have a "consistency of subject matter, approach, and tone that sets them apart as a distinct section."[169] The complaint in 58:3 seems to govern everything that is discussed in these two chapters (there is no new complaint in chap. 59) since, as J. A. Motyer claims, "59:1–13 elaborates and applies chapter 58."[170] C. R. Seitz notes that 58:1 begins with the sentinel announcing "to the house of Jacob their sins," and this section ends with an inclusio about "those in Jacob who repent of their sins" in 59:20.[171] G. Polan emphasizes the clear connection between the justice dis-

---

[169] Blenkinsopp, *Isaiah 56–66*, 176. Later, on p. 185, he claims that there is a "clear association of style, mood, and substance" between the chapters.

[170] Motyer, *Isaiah*, 484, but he connects 59:14–21 with the warrior hymn in 63:1–6, thus making 59:14–63:6 the central literary unit in chaps. 56–66. M. J. Lynch, "Zion's Warrior and the Nations: Isaiah 59:15b–63:6 in Isaiah's Zion Traditions," 244–63, also connects 59:15b–21 with 63:1–6, seeing them as an *inclusio* around the tradition about Zion's restoration in 60–62.

[171] Seitz, "Isaiah 40–66," 498. It should be noted that 58:14 also contains a concluding reference to Jacob.

cussed in 56:1 and the development of that theme in chaps. 58–59.[172] O. H. Steck maintains that chaps. 58 and 59 are not two independent speeches but are closely connected and quite parallel to the structure of 56:9–57:21.[173] Finally, P. A. Smith identifies interlinking vocabulary, the repeated use of body imagery (finger, fist, hand, tongue, lips), and a repeated emphasis on different roots defining "turning" (*sûr* in 58:9; 59:15; *šûb* in 58:13; 59:20; *sûg* in 59:13,14) and "justice" (*ṣedek/ṣĕdāqâ* in 58:2,8; 59:4,9,14,17) that draw chaps. 58 and 59 together.[174]

The structure of this material is:

Doing as you please is unacceptable	58:1–14
God accepts those who confess their sins	59:1–15a
God will bring salvation and justice	59:15b–21

The setting of chaps. 58–59 is left unidentified and thus is the subject of a good deal of speculation. Since there is no reference to sacrifices or the temple (an argument from silence), C. Westermann presumes that chap. 58 was uttered before the reconstruction of the postexilic temple in Jerusalem in 516 BC.[175] J. D. W. Watts places these events much later at the beginning of the reign of the Persian king Artaxerxes (465–458 BC), while P. D. Hanson proposes a setting parallel to Zechariah 7–8 because both deal with the issue of fasting (between 537–520 BC).[176] Since hypocritical worship, various aspects of social injustice, evil thoughts, and inappropriate fasting are present in some people in nearly every generation, it is impossible to assign a specific date to this sermon.[177]

This message appears to be communicating a series of general principles that everyone should avoid (actions that do not please God) because God is

---

[172] Polan, *In the Ways of Justice toward Salvation*, 175–77, also finds a chiastic structure within chap. 58 and seven uses of the words fast, day, and Yahweh in chap. 58.

[173] O. H. Steck, "Beobachtungen zu Jesaja 56–59," *Studien zu Tritojesaja*, BZAW 203 (Berlin: de Gruyter, 1991), 169–86. Oswalt, *Isaiah 40–66*, 493, finds the same three-part structure in 56:9–57:21 operating again in 58:1–59:21. Each begins with a statement about true religion (56:1–8; 58:1–14), each demonstrates that the people fail to live up to God's requirements (56:9–57:13; 59:1–15a), and each section ends with God's action on behalf of his people (57:14–21; 59:15b–21).

[174] P. A. Smith, *Rhetoric and Redaction in Trito-Isaiah*, 99–101, includes the repetition of (a) אָוֶן "wickedness" in 58:9; 59:4,6,7; (b) נְתִיבוֹת "streets"; (c) דָּבַר (infinitive absolute) "speaking" in 58:9,13; 59:4,13, (d) בָּקַע "break forth" in 58:8; 59:5; and (e) הֵן "behold" in 58:3,4; 59:1.

[175] Westermann, *Isaiah 40–66*, 335. Hanson, *The Dawn of Apocalyptic*, 104, also places this chapter before the temple was built (circa 530 BC). Although Hanson finds evidence of a conflict between two groups in Jerusalem (pp. 108–113), this is God's criticism of the whole community, not one specific group.

[176] Watts, *Isaiah 34–66*, 265–67, outlines the events going on in the Persian Empire at this time. Hanson, *The Dawn of Apocalyptic*, 104, has his own reconstruction.

[177] Fasting is a repeated response to trials in Josh 7:6; Judg 20:26–27; 1 Sam 7:6; 2 Sam 12:16; Jer 36:9; Lamentations; Joel 1:12–13; Zechariah 7–8.

just (58:2) and is against injustice (58:6). In the end God will break forth his light (58:8); he will unfold his righteous deeds of salvation (59:15b,16b–17) to the redeemed. In the distant future God will establish justice (59:21) through his own work of salvation, and the redeemed will come to Zion to enjoy his wonderful kingdom forever (59:20–21).

DOING AS YOU PLEASE IS UNACCEPTABLE (58:1–14)

[1]"Shout it aloud, do not hold back.
  Raise your voice like a trumpet.
 Declare to my people their rebellion
  and to the house of Jacob their sins.
[2]For day after day they seek me out;
  they seem eager to know my ways,
 as if they were a nation that does what is right
  and has not forsaken the commands of its God.
 They ask me for just decisions
  and seem eager for God to come near them.
[3]'Why have we fasted,' they say,
  'and you have not seen it?
 Why have we humbled ourselves,
  and you have not noticed?'

 "Yet on the day of your fasting, you do as you please
  and exploit all your workers.
[4]Your fasting ends in quarreling and strife,
  and in striking each other with wicked fists.
 You cannot fast as you do today
  and expect your voice to be heard on high.
[5]Is this the kind of fast I have chosen,
  only a day for a man to humble himself?
 Is it only for bowing one's head like a reed
  and for lying on sackcloth and ashes?
 Is that what you call a fast,
  a day acceptable to the LORD?

[6]"Is not this the kind of fasting I have chosen:
 to loose the chains of injustice
  and untie the cords of the yoke,
 to set the oppressed free
  and break every yoke?
[7]Is it not to share your food with the hungry
  and to provide the poor wanderer with shelter—
 when you see the naked, to clothe him,
  and not to turn away from your own flesh and blood?
[8]Then your light will break forth like the dawn,
  and your healing will quickly appear;
 then your righteousness will go before you,
  and the glory of the LORD will be your rear guard.

⁹Then you will call, and the LORD will answer;
  you will cry for help, and he will say: Here am I.

"If you do away with the yoke of oppression,
  with the pointing finger and malicious talk,
¹⁰and if you spend yourselves in behalf of the hungry
  and satisfy the needs of the oppressed,
then your light will rise in the darkness,
  and your night will become like the noonday.
¹¹The LORD will guide you always;
  he will satisfy your needs in a sun-scorched land
  and will strengthen your frame.
You will be like a well-watered garden,
  like a spring whose waters never fail.
¹²Your people will rebuild the ancient ruins
  and will raise up the age-old foundations;
you will be called Repairer of Broken Walls,
  Restorer of Streets with Dwellings.

¹³"If you keep your feet from breaking the Sabbath
  and from doing as you please on my holy day,
if you call the Sabbath a delight
  and the LORD's holy day honorable,
and if you honor it by not going your own way
  and not doing as you please or speaking idle words,
¹⁴then you will find your joy in the LORD,
  and I will cause you to ride on the heights of the land
  and to feast on the inheritance of your father Jacob."
                              The mouth of the LORD has spoken.

These verses wrestle with a misunderstanding about what God was doing or not doing among his people. Some people believed that they were faithfully worshipping God but were not being appropriately rewarded for all their pious efforts (58:3). In response God instructs the prophet to remind these religious Israelites that a special divine blessing does not naturally flow forth from God to people who do not desire to please God in all area of their lives. The well-being of the whole community is interrelated to the righteous behavior of each individual person within the community. If the people keep fasts and the Sabbath in the way God has directed them and do not focus on their own pleasures (58:6-7, 9-10a,13-14), then God will respond by revealing his presence, their light will shine, healing and righteousness will be present, and God will guide them into his wonderful kingdom (58:8-9,10b-12,14). This message involves a correction of those who have misunderstood God's just ways of dealing with them.

This chapter can be divided into two paragraphs:

A fast that does not please God   58:1–5
Results of a fast that pleases God   58:6–14

These two paragraphs are held together by their common discussion of fasting (*ṣûm* and cognates in 58:3[2x],4,5[2x],6), terminology about "pleasing, delight" (*ḥāpaṣ* and cognates in 58:2[2x],3,13[2x]), "call" (*qārā'* in 58:1,5,9,12,13), and what is "righteous" (*ṣedeq* in 58:2[2x],8), as well as a question-and-answer style. Nevertheless, the structural makeup of each paragraph is quite different because 58:6–14 contains a series of "if you do this . . . then [this is what will happen]." This is not the style of 58:1–5.

A FAST THAT DOES NOT PLEASE GOD (58:1–5).   The paragraph begins with God's plan to make known to the people their sins. Their pious behavior is contrasted with the reality that they have forsaken the covenant and that just behavior is required of followers of the covenant (cf. 56:1–8). Thus G. J. Polan states that "56:1 is the skeletal message of the relationship between right and just actions and salvation," [178] which chaps. 58–59 explain in greater detail. The importance of this relationship is illustrated by the prophet's answer to the negative complaining in 58:3a. If these people are fasting in real humility that brings them closer to God, then this should naturally impact their relationships with others (58:5). Since God saw that this was not happening, what the people were doing was not acceptable to God. The prophet is not saying that God rejects all acts of fasting; instead, he is rejecting the fast that has no impact on a person's relationship to God and others. This paragraph contains:

Instructions to make Jacob's sins known	58:1
Outward signs of pleasing God	58:2
Question: Why fast if no reward?	58:3a
Response: Does this fast please God?	58:3b–5

58:1   This new paragraph begins like many others, with an imperative instruction for someone (probably the prophet; cf. 40:3,6) to cry out literally "from the throat," an expression that might be interpreted as a loud cry (NIV). This parallels the instructions, "do not spare" (the voice) which encourages this person not to spare his throat when he yells, but to speak everything loudly and clearly so that everyone knows about God's perspective on justice.[179] The exhortation to "raise your voice like a trumpet" has a similar meaning, but may additionally suggest that these words are a sharp or a dire warning that people should pay attention to, just like they would respond to the blowing of a trumpet on a city wall in a time of war. The prophet is supposed to declare loudly and clearly that the house of Jacob is committing sinful deeds (*ḥāṭā'*, "missing the mark") and acts of rebellion (*pešaʿ*, "treason, rebellion"). The choice of the name Jacob, along with the more common "my people" may have reminded the audience of the patriarch's sinful rebellion against God (cf.

---

[178] Polan, *In the Ways of Justice toward Salvation*, 315.

[179] It is less likely that this phrase means that this person was not to be timid or fearful about what he says. This approach would suggest that he should not spare any of the ugly or embarrassing details that a refined people would prefer not to hear.

2:6; 8:17; 43:27; 46:3; 48:1; 59:20; Gen 27; 32–33). This introduction suggests that a judgment speech will follow, but the format that follows is very different from the normal judgment speech. Verse 1 provides the reason for the prophet's speech (God told him to cry out) and legitimates the idea that these criticisms come from God.

58:2 Initially it appears that this verse presents information that is contradictory when compared to v. 1. In spite of this[180] negative assessment of the Israelites in 58:1b, God was aware that among the various aspects of daily life (lit. "day by day," as in Gen 39:10), many pious people "were repeatedly seeking"[181] God, and many "were repeatedly delighting in" (*ḥāpēṣ*) knowledge (a noun, not a verb) about the ways of God. It is normal for a Hebrew sentence to begin with a verb, the subject, and then the object of the verb, but in this sentence the object "me" is written first to emphasize the idea that it is "me" they seek. One would think that people who seek God and want to understand his ways are doing the right thing and have the right priorities. One might limit God's "ways" to the ways he directs the history of the world and each person's life (cf. 40:3), or the ways of God could be referring to God's instructions in the law (2:3), but these two are closely interrelated because God's ways of dealing with people in history reveal the principles encoded in the law and vise versa. In light of the complaint in 58:3, J. L. Koole concludes that God's ways refer to the ways God responds or does not respond to people's pious actions.[182]

One would think that these acts of repeatedly seeking God were the devoted acts of a righteous person who loves God and keeps his commandments. For example, Deut 4:29 presents the ideal of seeking God with the sure promise that you will find him; David encourages people to seek God in 1 Chr 16:10–11; 22:19; 28:9, and God himself calls on his people to seek him in 55:6; 2 Chr 7:14. The evil kings throughout Israel's history are those who did not seek God (2 Chr 12:14; 16:12), and the good kings are those who did seek God (2 Chr 14:4; 15:2; 19:3; 20:3–4; 26:5; 30:19; 34:3). The Psalms encourage people to delight in the Lord and his laws (Pss 1:3; 37:4; 119:16,24,35,70,77,143,174) because this will lead to life and God's blessing. Nevertheless, it is the sinful people of 58:1b who are acting very piously and talking like true followers of God.

---

[180] This verse begins with a *waw*, but it is difficult to know how to translate it. If one has already read the rest of the message, it is possible to look back and suggest it has the value of a strong adversative ("but, yet") or concessive meaning ("although").

[181] The imperfect verb יִדְרֹשׁוּן describes continued or repeated actions (GKC §107f,g). The ending ןו with the *paragogic nun* appears over 300 times in the OT. This final ן may appear for euphonic reasons or be due to the influence from Aramaic where this ending is normally used (GKC §47m-o).

[182] Koole, *Isaiah III, Volume 3: Isaiah 56–66*, 125, specifically believes this should "be taken to mean God's action in delivering people from the extremity in which they still find themselves."

The second half of v. 2 compares (they are "like") the people of Jacob to a "nation, country" (not a "people")[183] that acts in righteous ways and has not forsaken the judicial decisions of God. But why are they described as only being "like" some ideal nation that does these things? Does this not suggest that they look like the people of God but are not actually a righteous nation? The likeness is seen in the fact that the people "were repeatedly asking"[184] God for righteous decisions and "were repeatedly delighting in" the nearness to God. This last phrase could refer to the people delighting in their own coming to the temple to worship when they draw near to God, or it could refer to their delighting when God draws near to them and brings them salvation. Either approach can make sense in this context, but the first is preferred. What this verse is revealing is that people can look, act, talk, and delight in the things of God, yet still not be the people of God (cf. Matt 7:21–23). A good, moral, cultural Israelite knows how to act, talk, and behave in religious circles, but knowing the cultural expectations of an Israelite is not the same as knowing God.

58:3a Now the prophet quotes the disturbing question that these pious people (the "we" in 3a) have asked of God. Why does God not take notice of our fasting? Why does God not seem to know that "we humbled"[185] ourselves before him? The fast mentioned is not identified, but one annual fast when people were supposed to humble themselves was the Day of Atonement (cf. Lev 16:29) when all the people in the nation gathered at the temple to confess their sins. Of course, this question could have arisen because of no outward response from God to an occasional fast that was called because of a drought, an attacking enemy, or some other special problem (1 Sam 7:6; 2 Sam 12:16; 1 Kgs 21:27; Neh 9:1). A fast might include denying oneself of the pleasures of eating or drinking so that time could be spent praying, seeking wisdom and comfort from God. Sometimes when people fasted they also put on sackcloth, put ashes on the head, wept, tore their clothes, and cried out to God for his mercy with prayers of intercession (Job 1–2; Neh 1:4; Dan 9:3). The hope was that God would notice the pain and sorrow the people were expressing, the self-denial they endured, and their repentance. After seeing the sincerity of the people's fast and their humility, it was expected that God would intervene in their lives and resolve the problems they were facing. But this was not happening even though the people were fasting. The attitude of the people questioning God in 58:3a is hard to perceive, yet it is central to any effort to understand their questions. Are they asking why God has not acted yet (an issue of timing) and not really accusing God of some injustice, are they bitterly complaining about his apparent abandonment of them in a time when they were facing a

---

[183] It is surprising and a little disconcerting that God does not call his people עַם "people" instead of גּוֹי "a nation," a term that usually refers to a pagan nation.

[184] The imperfect verb יִשְׁאָלוּנִי describes continued or repeated actions (GKC §107f,g).

[185] The word עִנִּינוּ "we humbled" is a *pi'el* form from the root עָנָה "he humbled," and not the more frequent root meaning "he answered."

difficult problem, or are they just expressing some disappointment that some earlier positive prophecies have not yet been fulfilled?[186] B. Schramm believes that this "passage introduces us to the fundamental theological question dealt with in Third Isaiah: the attempt to come to terms with the failure of YHWH's promises, as uttered by Second Isaiah, to materialize."[187] This reconstruction reads a great deal into 58:3 and is not accepted in the exegetical discussion below. This is because there is no accusation that God's "promises" have failed, and there is no reference in this context to a specific "promise in chaps. 40–55" that did not come true. If such a complaint were intended, the people would probably have quoted a promise stated in an earlier message within chaps. 40–55. The lament and confession in 59:9–15a indicate that they were looking for justice, righteousness, light, and deliverance (59:9,11b,14), but God could not establish a place of justice when their lives were so corrupt. They thought they could earn God's favor and blessing, but a little ritual fasting does not establish justice and righteousness in the community. They do not seem to really be that much interested in justice (59:4,8,11), so how can God's just kingdom be established among them? The problem being explained is not so much the failure of God's promises, but the failure of the people to understand how they must live if they want to participate in a just and righteous kingdom.

58:3b–5 The prophetic response to these questions delivers God's analysis of the situation. It begins with *hēn* "behold, indeed" (NIV "yet") that calls people to pay attention to what God will say. God accuses them of finding "pleasure, delight"[188] (probably their own pleasures) on their day of fasting instead of focusing on what "delights" God. This phrase probably does not mean that they accidentally find pleasure in something, but that they find pleasure in certain things because they are purposely trying to satisfy themselves. In vv. 3b and 4 God is not condemning fasting[189] but the fact that "you oppress all your workers"[190] on a fast day. God cannot accept their worship as true devotion

---

[186] Whybray, *Isaiah 40–66*, 213, states that the "people's lamentation here reflects their disappointment with the incompleteness of their restoration . . . the fullness of the expected blessing had not been realized."

[187] Schramm, *The Opponents in Third Isaiah*, 133, properly rejects Hanson's analysis of the situation. Hanson believes this refers to the conflict between one group that fasts (the Zadokite priests) and another group who are focused on social justice (the visionaries).

[188] Koole, *Isaiah III, Volume 3: Isaiah 56–66*, 130, identifies the semantic range of meaning for the word חֵפֶץ in 58:3,13 to be similar to the use of this word in Eccl 3:1,17; 5:7; 8:6 as "matter, affair" and in light of the context of the next line suggests "business affairs." Thus their fasting has lost its focus on God, and, instead, they continue to think about making more money. This is a possible interpretation, but it seems unnecessary to limit their distraction only to business affairs. The broader meaning of "pleasure, delight" would encompass a large variety of attractive distractions (including business) which might occupy people's thinking.

[189] M. L. Barré, "Fasting in Isaiah 58:1–12: A Reexamination," *BTB* 15 (1985): 94–97, maintains that fasting is not rejected, but if it is not "accompanied by love of neighbor it is empty ritual."

[190] The Aramaic Targum interprets this clause to say, "you draw near to your idols." The root

to godly ideals when they oppress others. Can God have compassion on them when they have no compassion on their workers? Exactly what this means is not fully explained. J. Oswalt finds heavy irony here because "they are not actually fasting so as to practice oppression, but the prophet says that this is what the outcome is."[191] Nevertheless, if these people fasted during the day for several hours and did not give their servants the day off to fast, is this not somewhat oppressive? One could also imagine that the master might be very upset if the worker did not get as much done as they usually did when he was around to supervise them. This scenario fits in with 58:4, for it pictures the fast day ending with the boss angry with the servants over what has or has not been accomplished. In fact, at times this led to the physical mistreatment of others. These charges indicate that some of these pious worshippers saw no connection between their beliefs about God, his forgiveness, and his justice and the way they related to other people at their place of work. They briefly humbled themselves before God and sought his compassion, but then they went off and arrogantly maintained oppressive control over their workers without any compassion. They asked God to forgive them for their wrongs but then immediately went out and did not forgive their workers for their failures.

The conclusion to this initial evaluation of fasting practices is stated in 58:4b. The prophet indicates that the people "should not/cannot fast"[192] like they did on that day of fasting and expect God to respond positively to their fasting (cf. 58:3a). If their goal is "to cause their voice to be heard on high"[193] and have God respond positively to their humiliation and fasting, then they must integrate their faith professions of humility and their desire to serve God into their daily relationships with other people. If a person's confession of delight in God is not real, if it is not connected to a changed attitude, if fasting does not lead one to act differently, does that pious confession of delighting in God mean anything?

Verse 5 asks a series of three questions marked by the *hă* interrogative. Initially God asks if a fast that "I would choose"[194] would have these kinds of

---

נָגַשׂ means "he approached, drew near" in most usages, but there appears to be another root meaning "he oppressed, exacted," which is used here (BDB, 620). The noun used is also easily confused with עָצָב root I. "idol," but root II. means "pain, grief, hurt" (accepted by Watts, *Isaiah 34–66*, 268, "you suppress all your pains") and root III. "toilers, workers" (BDB, 780, a meaning hypothesized for only this passage).

[191] Oswalt, *Isaiah 40–66*, 498, concludes that "their religious exercises are for themselves, primarily to serve those covetous instincts."

[192] The negated imperfect verb לֹא תָצוּמוּ must have a subjunctive mood of "should not fast, cannot fast" (GKC §107n,w).

[193] The infinitive construct verb לְהַשְׁמִיעַ "to cause to hear" may communicate a purpose or a result (GKC §114f).

[194] The verb אֶבְחָרֵהוּ "I will choose it" should have a subjunctive translation ("I would choose") in this question, as GKC §107t suggests.

oppressive actions in it (58:2–4) or would it be a day for a man "to humble"[195] his soul? One might expect that the implied answer to the first half of the question is no, but the second half of the question about humility sounds like a good thing. But one should not jump too quickly to answer the question.[196] The first question merely raises the neutral question, Was this a fast that God would choose and delight in? The second half of the question presents a means by which the audience can evaluate whether this fast was or was not a delight to God. Was there a true humbling of the soul? The second question continues to ask about the purpose and practices of a true fast that God would choose to delight in. Would one of the purposes for fasting be to bow down one's head like a reed and lie down in ashes and sackcloth? Both of these were regularly practiced (1 Sam 12:16; 1 Kgs 21:27; Jer 6:26), so there is nothing inherently wrong with either of these acts. Finally, at the end of 58:5 God asks in a third question: is this the kind of fast that he would find pleasurable or pleasing? J. Muilenburg concludes from this verse that "the mere motions connected to the fast are meaningless."[197] In this verse there is no direct criticism of these traditional signs of fasting, just an inquiry into the audience's evaluation of what they were doing. The following verses will suggest that if one just goes through the motions of an appropriate fast, it will not be the kind of fast that will delight God.

RESULTS OF A FAST THAT PLEASES GOD (58:6–14). There is no major break between these two paragraphs, for both fasting and doing what pleases God are central to the whole chapter. This paragraph is built around three somewhat parallel subparagraphs (58:6–9a,9b–12,13–14), which contain a series of conditions and results. The conditions outline the activity that pleases God in questions (*hălô* in 58:6,7) or "if" clauses (*ʾim* in 58:9b,13a) and the "then" clauses (*ʾaz* in 58:8,9,14) that explain the positive consequences that will result from actions that delight God. Those who claim to delight in knowing God's ways and want to ask for his just decisions (58:2) will now hear about God's ways and how people can walk in justice and righteousness.

P. A. Smith connects these requirements to the person described in 61:1–4 because several ideals are mentioned in both passages (caring for the poor and loosing the bonds of the captives in 58:6–7 and 61:1). In addition, the positive results overlap since both sections refer to the coming of righteousness (58:8; 60:21; 61:3), the coming of the glory of the Lord (58:8; 60:1), and the coming

---

[195] The infinitive construct עַנּוֹת without the usual לְ prefix expresses the purpose (GKC §114f) one should have when they come to the fast.

[196] NIV adds the word "only" in two phrases in v. 5 to make the statement a criticism of their fasting, but "only" is not in the Hb. text.

[197] Muilenburg, "Isaiah 40–66," 5:680, believes this verse contains "biting satire" about the external aspects of worship, which may not express what is in the heart. Childs, *Isaiah*, 478, claims that "the prophet satirizes with utter disdain the pious bowing of the head like a weed," but this satirical interpretation is less than obvious.

of a great light (58:8; 61:1–3).[198] This connection would be realized when the reader comes to 61:1–3, but at this point the reader does not yet know the content of this later chapter. At this point the reader would be prone to connect the ideas in 58:6–14 to ideals established in earlier chapters of Isaiah. For example, B. S. Childs believes God's function as a rearguard in 58:8 was drawn from the same phrase in 52:12.[199] The coming of a great light was part of the messianic imagery in 9:2 and the servant who was a light to the nations in 42:6; 49:6. The coming of God's glory was predicted earlier in 4:5; 6:3; 24:16; 35:2; 40:5. It is not necessary to hypothesize that chap. 58 is drawing on ideas in later chapters (61:1–3), but certainly chaps. 60–62 legitimate a common perspective within the larger literary unit.

The structure of the paragraph is:

Caring for the oppressed will bring dramatic changes	58:6–9a
What one should do	6–7
The results	8–9a
Removing oppression will bring transformation	58:9b–12
What one should do	9b–10a
The results	10b–12
Not doing as you please on the Sabbath will bring joy	58:13–14
What one should do	13
The results	14

This paragraph is held together by the parallel structure of the three subparagraphs, each identifying ways to act that please God as well as the natural consequences of such action.[200] These promises look forward to that eschatological day when God's glory will come to earth; he will transform nature, establish justice and righteousness between people, and cause mankind to delight in God. This does not suggest that people today can create some sort of heaven on earth through proper social relationships, helping the poor, and stopping oppression. Nevertheless, if these are the ideals that delight God, then people who want to follow God's ways will attempt to implement within this fallen world as many of God's ideals as possible.

58:6–7 The first set of ideals illustrate some of the practical behavioral implications of a fast that God would honor. The introductory question marker, "is it not" (*hălôʾ*), expects a positive answer; thus, one could almost translate

---

[198] P. A. Smith, *Rhetoric and Redaction in Trito-Isaiah*, 111, hypothesizes that the chap. 58 is drawing on themes from chap. 61, but if one is reading this text in the order it was written, they would not be aware of any connection with chap. 61.

[199] Childs, *Isaiah*, 478, follows the analysis of Zimmerli in this example.

[200] Goldingay, *Isaiah*, 325–26, understands the first paragraph to be 58:1–9a and the second to be 58:9b–14, but the three subparagraphs above are so similar that they must be put together into one paragraph.

this "surely it is."[201] What kind of actions is it that God "would choose" (NIV "have chosen")[202] for a person who wants to please God and demonstrate authentic evidence of a humble heart? God's fast does not remove or disparage appropriate ritual expressions of worship, but it integrates the attitudes of fasting with the behavior of a person before and after the fast. When one fasts and prays for divine intervention from an oppressive force (a drought, an enemy, a wicked neighbor), the ideal answer is for God to remove all oppression and give people freedom from injustice. If the people praying want or expect God to respond and bring them freedom from oppression, the people praying should do everything in their power to assist the hand of God in bringing freedom from oppression to everyone in that community.[203] Thus God is interested in behaviors consistent with his character as follows.[204] (a) "Opening up, loosing" (pth)[205] the bonds of wickedness implies that one would help people get free from wicked people or wicked habits that entrap them. (b) Tearing away the ropes of a yoke suggests people should help others get free from unjust agreements that bind them, possibly working agreements that enslave people, foreign alliances that impose heavy tribute, or a personal enslavement that a person cannot escape. (c) Sending out the oppressed to a new situation of freedom implies that people who were broken or crushed by the weight of abuse should be set free from the one oppressing them (possibly abuse from slavery, the courts, or an abusive spouse). Finally, (d) the prophet summarizes it all by encouraging the people fasting that "you should break"[206] every yoke that binds people. It is difficult to know if this is a literal call for freeing people from slavery, a call for the humane treatment of the abused workers in 58:3b–4, or if this is just a metaphorical call for the removal of the sinful deeds that bind and enslave people. The practical acts of mercy toward people in need in 58:7 suggest that 58:6 should also be interpreted to be addressing practical relationships between people and should not be interpreted just as a broad metaphorical exhortation. These instructions on interpersonal relationships are not new

---

[201] The question marker prefixed to the negative (הֲלֹא) "is it not" is used "in order to show it to be absolutely true" (GKC §150e).

[202] The imperfect verb אֶבְחָרֵהוּ should not be translated as a past perfect "have chosen it." In interrogative questions the imperfect verb is often subjunctive expressing what "might, should, can" happen (GKC §107t).

[203] Whybray, *Isaiah 40–66*, 215, states that the prophet is "saying that God does not primarily want fasting but something else altogether." This fails to see that there is a connection between what the one fasting wants (freedom, rescue from danger, release from oppression) and what God wants the fasting person to do for others.

[204] The word זֶה "this" at the beginning of the verse is epexegetically explained by the four verbal clauses that follow (GKC §113b).

[205] The infinitive absolute פַּתֵּחַ "open, loose" could be functioning as an imperative (GKC §113bb) or as a substitute for a finite verb (GKC §113y).

[206] The final verb is a second-person finite imperfect תְּנַתֵּקוּ "you should break" that is modal expressing what people ought to do (GKC §107n).

ideals, for the law and the prophets repeatedly address the proper treatment of others and condemn the abuse of the weak by the powerful.

Verse 7 deals with ways to help poor people with the practical necessities of life. These instructions also begin with "is it not" (*hălô'*, similar to 58:6), implying that the audience already knew that a fast included sharing[207] food with the hungry (Deut 14:28–29; 15:7–11; Esth 9:20–22; Job 22:7; Prov 22:9; Ezek 18:7,16). J. L. Koole suggests that maybe "somebody organizes a meal on a fast-day itself, acts as host, but does not eat any food personally, and thus makes his fast-day a feast for others."[208] In addition to giving food to the hungry, "you should bring"[209] the homeless into a place of shelter from the cold and rain, and "when, if" (*kî*) you see someone without proper clothing, "then you should cover him."[210] Especially when there is some need in a person's own family (lit. "flesh"), one should not hide himself and ignore the problem. Even though jealousy, misunderstandings, or hatred can sometimes develop between brothers (Cain and Abel; Jacob and Esau, Joseph and his brothers), people should be quick to help family members in their time of need. These examples indicate that people have responsibilities to watch out for the well-being of all those who live around them. Each person can be part of the process of answering the prayers of others who fast and pray for God to provide for their needs.

58:8–9a The results of observing the kind of fast that God would choose are grouped under two "then" (*'az*, 8a,9a) result clauses. The transformational blessings that will naturally follow people who practice a spiritual fast that pleases God and helps others are (a) your light will break through like the dawn and (b) healing. God is the light that judges evil in 10:17; the Messiah is the light that brings joy, peace, and justice in 9:2ff; the Suffering Servant is a light to the nations that brings salvation to the ends of the earth in 42:6; 49:6. God's law and justice also shine God's light and salvation to the nations in 8:20; 51:4–5. Thus "your light" breaking forth refers to people reflecting the light of God among his people (cf. 60:1–3). To a limited degree this is possible when God's people follow God's ways, but these conditions will be fully experienced on earth only in the eschatological time of God's healing (30:26; Ps 103:3) as 57:18,19 have already proclaimed. The verbs describe action in which salvation breaks forth or quickly "sprouts" (*tiṣmāḥ*, cf. 42:9; 43:19), suggesting a sudden appearance of God's work of salvation.

---

[207] The verb פָרֹם is an infinitive absolute which can function as a substitute for the finite verb (GKC §113y) in hurried or excited style. This verb means to break or divide food; thus, "share" is an acceptable translation.

[208] Koole, *Isaiah III, Volume 3: Isaiah 56–66*, 138, recognizes that the sharing does not have to be limited to the fast day. On other days a person could share a meal with a poor person.

[209] Probably the subjunctive expressing what one ought to do (GKC §107n).

[210] The *waw* consecutive perfect verb וְכִסִּיתוֹ can introduce a command or wish (GKC §112aa) when it is the apodosis of a conditional sentence (GKC §112ff).

The second half of 58:8 appears to allude to what the prophet has already said in 52:12b, where it promises that God will go before and after his people, gathering[211] them up in one place so that he can deliver the children of Israel from Pharaoh's great army at the Red Sea (Exod 14:19–20). This is a metaphor of his guidance before them and safety, protection, and security behind them. C. Westermann believes the prophet has taken this earlier promise of a return from exile in 52:12 and spiritually reinterpreted it here, but B. S. Childs rejects this approach and views this quotation as a confirmation of the truth of this earlier word from God, though he does find some reorientation due to the new circumstances in chap. 58.[212] Nevertheless, chap. 52 envisions an eschatological time when Jerusalem is a holy city where the Lord reigns (52:7) and brings his salvation to the whole earth (52:10). It appears that both 52:12 and 58:8 refer to God's eschatological protection of his people. God's "righteous presence" (*ṣedeq*) and glory will surround these people.

The second "then" (*ʾaz*) clause describes the transformation in the relationship between God and his people when they follow the fast that God would choose (58:9a). Previously in 58:3a the people complained that God did not respond to the people's pious activity, but in this verse God promises that in the future he will answer them when they call because it will be a true fast that God will accept. He will assure them with words of comfort when he speaks to them, "here I am." His presence ("here am I") will not leave them, for at that time he will reign in their midst (cf. 52:7–10).

58:9b–10a   The structural pattern of the previous paragraph (58:6–9a) is repeated (as explained in the outline above) with a description of the natural results (58:10b–12) that will happen, "if, when" (*ʾim*, 58:9b) the people implement a more holistic conception of fasting. These verses describe what will happen if the people remove the oppression that exists on their fast days (58:3b–4). Three interrelated negative acts are forbidden: (a) a yoke of oppression, (b) pointing the finger and (c) wicked talk. The yoke (cf. 58:6) that oppresses should be removed so that there will be no legal or social obligation on people who are unjust or oppressive (slavery, financial, or social obligations). "By pointing"[213] the finger at someone (cf. Prov 6:13; Isa 57:4) or "speaking evil" in everyday life or in a courtroom setting, one can threaten or mock someone else and put them in a difficult oppressive situation. In v. 10a two

---

[211] The verb יַאַסְפֶךָ comes from אָסַף "he gathered, assembled" so a literal translation is "he will gather you together." It seems somewhat periphrastic to translate this verb as a noun "your rear guard," although this idea is not totally off base. One who gathers people who are panicked into a safe place functions to guard them from danger.

[212] Westermann, *Isaiah 40–66*, 338, follows W. Zimmerli's views on this reinterpretation of 52:12 while, Childs, *Isaiah*, 478, rejects Zimmerli's explanation that this is an ethical reinterpretation.

[213] The verb שְׁלֹחַ "sending out, stretching out" is an infinitive construct that could be resolved into a finite verb (GKC §114d) or could express attendant circumstances (GKC §114o) such as "by stretching out, pointing."

interrelated positive acts are encouraged, (a) the "pouring out"[214] of your soul for the hungry and (b) the satisfying of the soul of the poor, afflicted person. Although one might expect, based on the admonition to give food to the hungry in v. 7a, that there would be similar instructions in this verse, instead God now expects them to give themselves (lit "your soul") to the hungry, implying a much deeper commitment of the heart and a much broader access than just a loaf of bread. The measure of success is when the "soul"[215] of the afflicted person is satisfied; thus, as 58:7b suggests, one is not to hide or ignore physical needs.

58:10b–12   The result clauses in vv. 10b,11,12 are surprisingly not introduced with "then" (*'az*) but the *waw* conjunction ("and, then, therefore"), which can function to introduce the apodosis of a conditional sentence. The consequent divine blessings that one can expect to follow are an elaboration of what was already said in 58:8. The shining of your light will be as bright as the high-noon sun, so it will remove all the darkness and gloom from this wicked world. God is the source of all light, and his light brings salvation to all his people (cf. 2:5; 8:20; 9:2; 10:17; 42:6.) Thus the rising of "your light" refers to how people will reflect the light of God's salvation to others (cf. 60:1–3). Verse 11 explains how God will guide his people (cf. 57:18) at all times (just as he did in the past during the wilderness journey in Deut 32:12; Ps 23:3) and will satisfy their souls in "dry places"[216] (just as he did in their wilderness journey). He will strengthen their bones, and they will be like a well-watered metaphorical garden or a spring that never stops.[217] These are pictures of life, vitality, and blessings. This picture implies not only the blessing of God on his people, but the ability of his people to impart blessings to others who come to this garden or spring.

The final consequences in 58:12 should also be interpreted metaphorically to refer to the people. Just as the references to the people in 58:11 as a garden or spring should not be taken literally, so the reference to ruins, foundations, and walls should not literally refer to the city of Jerusalem.[218] In fact, there

---

[214] The verb וְתָפֵק is from the root פוק "pour out," which is a *hiphil* jussive form which is commonly used in the protasis of a conditional sentence. Thus the *waw* before the verb should function to introduce another "if" clause, continuing the syntactical structure that precedes it (GKC §109h) in v. 9b.

[215] The word "soul" (נֶפֶשׁ) can mean "throat" or "appetite, desire," which would tend to limit the obligation to the afflicted to food that satisfies the desires of the throat, yet "soul" in the first half of the verse cannot be translated in this manner, so this approach seems a unlikely interpretation.

[216] The word בְּצַחְצָחוֹת is found only here, but it is probably related to the word צָחֶה "dried out, sun scorched."

[217] Literally, the spring never "will deceive" יְכַזֵּבוּ, that is, it will never stop giving water.

[218] Muilenburg, "Isaiah 40–66," 5:684, suddenly takes a more literal approach in v. 12 and imagines that this refers to the rebuilding of Jerusalem caused by the Babylonian captivity in 587 BC. Whybray, *Isaiah 40–66*, 217, refers to the "exaggerated, or vague, language of poetry" in this verse but still insists that it is talking about the "rebuilding activity, repairing the ravages caused

is no mention of Jerusalem in this context, so what is being built is a people, described as a metaphorical city. A subject for the verb "they will build" appears to be missing, but if the prepositional phrase "from you" is understood as a partitive use of the preposition, then "some from among you"[219] could serve to identify the "they" who will build the everlasting ruins, the foundations for many generations. Just as the new city of Jerusalem will have a new name in 1:26 and 60:14, so the people of God will have new names (cf. 61:12) based on who they are or what they do. This passage celebrates those people who are called "Repairer of the Breeches," "Restorer of the Paths for Dwelling." These images are not easy to understand. At minimum, God is indicating that his new kingdom (not the postexilic reconstruction) will involve the everlasting restoration of something analogically comparable to the normal world that they presently know. God's people will be involved in some way in making their eternal place of habitation (cf. 60–62). It will last forever, and the old negative reputations and old negative titles will be replaced by new positive titles that portray the conditions in God's new realm.

58:13–14 These final verses concerning Sabbath observance build on the same kind of conditions (*'im,* "if" in v. 13) and results (*'āz,* "then" in v. 14) patterns that are exhibited in the two previous subparagraphs. By repeating several words used in earlier paragraphs, these verses are strongly interlinked with the rest of the chapter[220] even though there is a change of topic to discuss how people should observe the Sabbath. Thus the prophet wants his audience to know that these basic theological principles apply to all their worship activities. C. Seitz connects the Sabbath discussion here with 56:1–8 because both chapters emphasize acting justly (56:1; 58:2,6), pleasing God (56:4; 58:2,3,13), and express a hope for future joy (56:7; 58:14).[221] The people's action on the Sabbath can become unacceptable ritual (just like the fast) that is rejected by God, or their worship can become something that is his and their delight. The first clause warns about what they need to avoid, the second explains what they should do, and the third includes both what they should do ("honor it") and should not do ("do as you please").

---

many years ago by Nebuchadnezzar's troops and by subsequent neglect." J. Oswalt, *Isaiah 40–66,* 507, thinks that the ruins "may be specifically those of Jerusalem after the destruction of 587 BC., but they need not be limited to those." He generalizes the comment saying that the ruins "speak eloquently of human failures and loss."

[219] If the prepositional phrase מִמְּךָ "from you" is a partitive use of מִן then the translation could be "some from among you" (GKC §119, n. 2).

[220] Westermann, *Isaiah 40–66,* 340–41, believes these verses were added by a later redactor, but Polan, *In the Ways of Justice toward Salvation,* 225–27, presents evidence to demonstrate that the lexical interconnections show that these verses are an integral part of the chapter because they repeat words like "delight," "way," "call," "find," "speaking," "if . . . then," and "Jacob," which are used in earlier verses.

[221] Seitz, "Isaiah 40–66," 499–500, also finds a connection with themes of righteousness, Zion, land, and inheritance between chaps. 54 and 58.

If the people want to experience the joy of the Lord (58:14), they need to be sure that they do not turn their foot from proper Sabbath practices "in order to do"[222] what delights or gives them pleasure on God's holy day. Verses 3b–4 suggest that some people were doing what pleased themselves and had their workers laboring in the field on a fast day, so they were not really setting that day apart as a holy day. By not setting the day apart as completely holy, people were showing that they did not think God could supply all their physical needs if they did not work on a fast or Sabbath day. Thus they were not trusting God to meet their needs. Since the Sabbath is God's day, it will only be holy and set apart to him if people do what delights God. What they need to do is to call the Sabbath a "delight, pleasure," a holy day that honors God. People make something holy and honorable not just by their words but by their actions. In v. 13b the prophet concludes that people honor God and the Sabbath by not[223] (a) doing things their own ways, (b) "finding"[224] their own pleasures, or (c) speaking a word. J. L. Koole relates the "ways" in the first clause to "business journeys," the "finding" in the second clause to "finding your business,"[225] and the speaking in the third clause to making business agreements, but there seems to be little indication that these factors should be focused so narrowly just on issues of business activities. The last phrase about "speaking a word" does not mean that a person must be silent and not talk at all. Most commentators and translations suggest that it refers to "idle words," though the Old Greek translators thought it referred to speaking a word in anger based on 58:3–4.

The "then" (ʾāz) clause in 58:14 indicates that people who make the Sabbath holy will naturally find that "you will delight yourself"[226] in the Lord (contrast 57:4). God's response will be to cause his devoted people to ride "on/over" the heights, just like he promised the children of Israel back in Deut 32:13.[227] Deut 32:11 compares God's guidance and protection to the care an eagle has for its young (cf. Exod 19:4), and 32:13b connects the results of God's care to his abundant provision of fruits, honey, oil, milk, wheat, and animals. In a similar manner, in 40:31 God promises to cause his people to soar on the wings of an eagle. These positive images of flight above the heights where God rides among the clouds (19:1; Deut 33:26; Hab 3:8) present thoughts of victory and

---

[222] The infinitive construct עֲשׂוֹת "to do" is used to express their purpose (GKC §114f).

[223] The preposition מִן often means "from," but it can have a negative force, so sometimes it should be translated as "without, no" as in describing people being "from strength," or "without strength," which means that they have "no strength" (GKC §119w-y).

[224] The verb is an infinitive construct from מָצָא "he found" (NIV has "doing").

[225] Koole, *Isaiah III, Volume 3: Isaiah 56–66*, 155, 157.

[226] The *hithpaʾel* verb is reflexive; thus, the translation "delight yourself" is appropriate (GKC §54d).

[227] E. H. Merrill, *Deuteronomy*, NAC (B&H, 1994), 415, interprets this metaphor to be referring to Israel's dominion over the land and ideas of strength and triumph. J. L. Crenshaw, "*Wĕdōrēk ʿal-bāmôtê ʾāreṣ*," *CBQ* 34 (1972): 39–53, takes the unlikely view that this image comes from foreign mythology.

power, so God is here offering to share the benefits of his sovereignty with his holy people. This will involve their possession of the land that their fore-father Jacob inherited from God and the blessing of abundant produce from this fertile land (cf. 30:23; Amos 9:13–15; Hos 2:21–22; Ezek 34:14,26–27). Although these are marvelous promises, how can one know for certain that all these positive promises will actually come to pass? God's persuasive proof of authenticity is: "truly, it is absolutely certain"[228] that what the mouth of the Lord has spoken will happen.

NOT DOING JUSTICE IS UNACCEPTABLE (59:1–21)

The second part of the long section that makes up 58:1–59:21 is unified with what precedes it, since both chapters (and all of chaps. 56–59) deal with questions related to human justice and righteousness in relationship to God's coming salvation. The whole unit is initiated in 56:1 with a call for people to maintain justice because God's salvation is close at hand. God will expose the righteous deeds of all men (57:12) because he is a God of just decisions (58:2) and is against injustice (58:6), but his righteous salvation will bring healing to the righteous (58:8). In chap. 59 God is disturbed because there is no justice (59:4,8); thus, it is not surprising that people would lament in 59:9,11,14 be-cause there is no justice. In response to this situation, God will act in justice with righteous deeds of salvation (59:15b,16b–17) to redeem mankind. God's desire for covenant loyalty (56:4,6) undergirds his relationship with mankind, and this loyal relationship with God will finally be established (59:21) through his own work of salvation.

God's desire is for people to act justly, please God, love and serve God, and maintain their covenant relationship with him (58:4,6), but many people were characterized by wickedness and injustice (58:3–5,9–12; 59:3–13a), thus cutting themselves off from a close relationship with God (57:8,16–17; 58:3; 59:1–2,11–13). Nevertheless, in the end God will answer those who call on him (58:9a), heal, and bring salvation to his people. Then all God's people will worship him with joy (56:7; 57:18–19; 58:8,14; 59:19–21).

In spite of this generally consistent flow of thought in these chapters, R. N. Whybray views 59:4–8 and 21 as later interpolations and finds little that links 59:1–15a with the final paragraph in 59:15b–21.[229] But G. Emmerson has just the opposite opinion.[230] Certainly the Lord's statement that there is

---

[228] The יִכ that precedes this final phrase is an asseverative *kî* that precedes a statement that is absolutely certain (GKC §159ee).

[229] M. J. Lynch, "Zion's Warrior and the Nations: Isaiah 59:15b–63:6 in Isaiah's Zion Tradi-tions," 245, finds numerous "semantic links" of repeated vocabulary between 59:15b–21, chaps. 60–62, and 63:1–6.

[230] Whybray, *Isaiah 40–66*, 219–20, does not think 59:1–21 displays unity. Goldingay, *Isaiah*, 328–36, identifies 56:9–59:8; 59:9–15a; and 59:15b–20 as separate paragraphs, thus destroying the unity within 59:1–21. Emmerson, *Isaiah 56–66*, 29, notes the connections between no justice in 59:9,11,15 and the salvation that was far off (59:11) and is not near (59:18–21).

"no justice" (*mišpāt*) in 59:15b is directly related to almost identical statements in 59:4,8,9,11,14, and the theme of "righteousness" (*ṣedeq*) is found in 59:4,9,14,16,17. In fact, the comment that God's hand is not too short to save people in 59:1 almost demands that there be a fuller discussion that describes how God's powerful hand will save the covenant people who repent of their sins (as in 59:15b–21). Since 59:20 ends with "declares the LORD" and 59:21 is in narrative format with two additional "says the LORD" clauses, it is legitimate to view this verse as a separate additional comment. J. L. Koole argues that it functions both to sum up the work of God in chaps. 58–59 and to provide a smooth transition to the new salvation of Zion described in chaps. 60–62.[231]

The chapter is organized into three paragraphs:

God rejects the prayers of the unjust	59:1–8
Confession of sins of injustice	59:9–15a
God will bring salvation and justice	59:15b–21

There is nothing in these verses that points to the date of this message. The sins appear to be very similar to preexilic sins condemned by earlier prophets, but the violence, injustice, lies, evil thoughts, and turning away from God could probably fit almost any historical setting.[232] Injustice pervades the state of humanity, so the only hope is for God to establish his justice and salvation. How will this happen? God will always judge unjust people, so their only hope is to confess their sins (59:9–15a). In spite of any human attempts to establish a world of justice, it will not happen; therefore, God will personally enter the picture in his eschatological coming to earth, put on righteousness, repay his enemies, and redeem those who repent of their sins (59:15b–21).

God Rejects the Prayers of the Unjust (59:1–8).

¹Surely the arm of the LORD is not too short to save,
    nor his ear too dull to hear.
²But your iniquities have separated
    you from your God;
  your sins have hidden his face from you,
    so that he will not hear.
³For your hands are stained with blood,
    your fingers with guilt.
  Your lips have spoken lies,
    and your tongue mutters wicked things.
⁴No one calls for justice;
    no one pleads his case with integrity.

---

[231] Koole, *Isaiah III, Volume 3: Isaiah 56–66*, 168.

[232] Westermann, *Isaiah 40–66*, 345, claims that "59.1ff were spoken after the return had taken place" but provides no evidence to support this position; thus, one must presume that this is an assumption he is making. In fact, Westermann also says, "The words here used could be those of a charge made by a prophet of preexilic days (to some extent they are this, word for word)."

They rely on empty arguments and speak lies;
   they conceive trouble and give birth to evil.
⁵They hatch the eggs of vipers
   and spin a spider's web.
Whoever eats their eggs will die,
   and when one is broken, an adder is hatched.
⁶Their cobwebs are useless for clothing;
   they cannot cover themselves with what they make.
Their deeds are evil deeds,
   and acts of violence are in their hands.
⁷Their feet rush into sin;
   they are swift to shed innocent blood.
Their thoughts are evil thoughts;
   ruin and destruction mark their ways.
⁸The way of peace they do not know;
   there is no justice in their paths.
They have turned them into crooked roads;
   no one who walks in them will know peace.

This paragraph contains a series of accusations of sinfulness. These accusations reinforce and expand similar claims already made in 56:9–12; 57:3–13a; and 58:2–5. J. Motyer does not find a major break in the presentation between chaps. 58 and 59, but claims that "59:1–13 elaborates and applies chapter 58."[233] This connection with chap. 58 is enhanced by the use of similar introductory particles like "behold" (*hēn*) in 58:3b,4 and 59:1. The problem of God not hearing was raised in 58:3a,4b, and the answer is addressed in 58:1–2 and then again in 59:9. Although there is a connection between these two chapters, the discussion in 59:1 is a much broader and a more fundamental prophetic response that goes far beyond the specific question of fasting in 58:3a.[234] B. S. Childs maintains that "chapter 59 addresses the ontological question of the nature of evil,"[235] but Hebrew thought focuses much more on sinful practices than on ontological issues.

One should not read into this passage a major new dispute between God and his people or imply that there is hidden behind 59:1 an assumed new major community lament that complains about God.[236] The questions that were raised back in 58:3–4 were already partially answered in two ways. First, in 58:8–9a,10b–12,14 God promised that he would hear and save his righteous people who please him (thus he will act). Second, God explained in 58:4 that people cannot expect their voice to be heard on high if they are only concerned

---

[233] Motyer, *Isaiah*, 484, believes that "verses 1–2 find their background in 58:3–4."

[234] There is also very little that would suggest that this prophetic response addresses why the promises of chaps. 60–62 have not arrived.

[235] Childs, *Isaiah*, 486.

[236] Westermann, *Isaiah 40–66*, 344–45, assumes a community lament and finds an acute conflict between God and the people, but this is mostly read into the text.

with pleasing themselves and continue to act unjustly. Chapter 59 provides additional broad support for the logic of the points already made in chap. 58; it is not a rebuttal of some new unstated complaint or accusation against God.

This paragraph addresses these issues by claiming that:

Sins separate people from God	59:1–4
God can hear and save	1
Sin separates people from God	2
Sins of the hands and mouth	3–4
The results of a sinful life	59:5–8
Animal analogies of sin	5–6
Sins of the feet and thoughts	7
They have no justice or peace	8

These verses are held together by their description of the many different kinds of sins the people are committing. There are an unusually large number of images using parts of the body (hand in 59:1,3,6; ear in 59:1; face in 59:2; fingers in 59:3; lips in 59:3, tongue in 59:3; feet in 59:7), and the use of animal images draws 59:5–6 together. The final verses in each subparagraph deal with issues of no justice (59:4,8).

59:1 The introductory "behold" (*hēn*, NIV "surely") draws attention to a new literary segment in the argumentation against the idea that God has not responded to the people. As the prophet has affirmed earlier in 50:2, God has the power[237] to save his people, and he will fulfill the promises made in 58:8–9a,10b–12,14. He is the one who created this world, and he controls the destiny of every nation. In fact the nations of this earth are like a speck of dust when compared to God, and the man-made gods of this world are nothing (cf. 40:12–31). God's hand is not short and unable to reach out to help his people. If the truth were known, his salvation is actually close at hand (56:1). His ears are always open to the prayers of his righteous people (cf. Ps 34:6 [Hb. 7]), just like he already claimed in 58:9. God is ready and anxious to hear the prayers of the humble sinners who are seeking forgiveness, guidance, and hope.[238] Can anything keep God "from saving" his righteous people or "from hearing"[239] what they are saying? Surely the answer is no. But on the other hand, not everyone who prays is one of God's righteous people.

---

[237] The word יָד refers to the "hand, power" of God, not his "arm" as in NIV.

[238] The problem that many commentators find (e.g., P. A. Smith, *Rhetoric and Redaction in Trito-Isaiah*, 114–15; J. Oswalt, *Isaiah 40–66*, 513; Muilenburg, "Isaiah 40–66," 5:687) relates to God's delay in providing his people salvation, but there is no reference to any delay in fulfilling any of God's promises. The point is that when religious people sin, their sin has, does, and always will keep God from hearing and saving some people.

[239] The infinitive construct מֵהוֹשִׁיעַ "from saving" and מִשְּׁמוֹעַ "from hearing" have the מִן "from" prefixed preposition, with the infinitive construct translated as a gerund (GKC §114o).

59:2 Since the assurance of v. 1 champions God's power to hear and save, the problem must lie elsewhere. The introductory "instead, but"[240] in 59:2 blames human sinfulness, which "causes a separation"[241] between God and the sinner. Since Almighty God is holy (57:15), dwells in his Holy Mountain (56:7; 57:13), and is set apart from all sinfulness, sin can interfere with a person's relationship with God. This means that, when God relates to people, (a) he will not accept worship of sinners who do not please or honor him (58:3,5,13) but (b) will answer, help, and be with the righteous who do please him (58:7–9,13–14). Sin will exclude some people from direct access to God, but physical characteristics, nationality, or ethnicity (56:2–3) will have no impact. God relates to people on the basis of their heart's condition. The behaviors of keeping or not keeping the covenant, pleasing or not pleasing God, and acting justly or unjustly are part of what determine a person's relationship with God (56:4,6). When sin controls the life of people, sin hides "the face"[242] of God and makes communication impossible. Sin is like a solid brick wall or a giant chasm that separates people from God, and the only thing that can penetrate that wall is a confession of sin. In other passages God himself "hides" (from the root *sātar*) his face when ungodly people offer unworthy sacrifices (1:15) or do not trust him (8:17; cf. 54:8; 64:7 [Hb. 6]), so it is possible to describe this separation as either an act of God (Deut 31:17–18; 32:20; Ps 102:2; Isa 45:15; Jer 33:5; Ezek 39:24) or something sin causes (59:2). The results are always the same; sin hides the face of God "from hearing"[243] what the sinner says.

59:3–4 What sins have caused this separation from God? The sins identified in this paragraph are connected to the different parts of the body that commit these sins. In the first pair of acts, the "palms, hands"[244] that shed blood "are defiled"[245] with the blood of those they have killed. Parallel to this idea are the fingers of these sinners that "are defiled" (this verb is implied from the

---

[240] The conjunction כִּי־אִם "but, nevertheless" expresses an adversative idea that is the antithesis of what preceded (GKC §163a). Sometimes these two words could even be translated "no, on the contrary, nevertheless."

[241] The *hiphil* participle מַבְדִּלִים is causative, pointing to what causes the separation between God and some of his people.

[242] The Aramaic Targum has "it hid his face," but פָּנִים "face" is a pl. noun that refers to the many faces one can exhibit (sad, happy, concerned, doubting). In this case "sin" is the subject of the verb, not God, and "Face" is a circumlocution for God himself. There is no need to emend this text to "his face" as in NIV, NSRV, NASB.

[243] Both at the end of v. 1 and at the end of v. 2, the same infinitive construct מִשְּׁמוֹעַ "from hearing" is used. The preposition מִן "from" is prefixed before the infinitive construct, which is translated as a gerund "from hearing" (GKC §114o).

[244] The word כַּפֵּיכֶם means "your palm," using the exact same word employed in 1:15. The "palm" refers to something that is open to receive something and is also commonly used to express something that one is in control of. What a person does leaves a telltale sign on the hands of the person doing it.

[245] The *niphal* verb נְגֹאֲלוּ comes from root II, meaning "defile, pollute," which could give the reflexive translation "your palms defiled themselves with blood" or the passive "your palms were defiled with blood."

preceding line) with "iniquity, guilt" (*ʿāwōn*). This imagery could represent actual involvement in violent crimes against another person, or it could refer to people who facilitated the demise of others (indirect involvement). In either case, these people are guilty in God's eyes.

The second pair of sinful acts relates to what people have said with their lips and tongues (59:3b). God was looking for words of praise on their lips (57:19), but instead they spoke "lies, falsehoods, deceptions" (*šeqer*, 57:4; 59:13). They "mutter, mumble, moan" (from *hāgâ*, cf. 59:11) unintelligible wicked sounds instead of "meditating on, mumbling" (from *hāgâ*) God's word (Ps 1:2). Their thinking and speech betrays what their heart truly desires. How can God have a personal relationship with people who defile themselves with such wickedness? How can God pour out his wonderful blessings on people whose minds produce such evil? Can God believe anything they say?

Next in 59:4 are the legal perversions that encompassed their social relationships. The NIV indicates that absolutely no one "calls for justice," but this translation could lead to a misunderstanding of what the prophet is actually saying. This verse is not saying that the unjust people never take other people to court to resolve an important legal matter. Observing the parallel ideas in the second line assists in the interpretation of the first line. The last word in each line indicates that people do not speak "with faithfulness" (*ʾemûnâ*, NIV "with integrity"), so a parallel thought in line 1 is that they do not speak "with justice." The two verb forms refer to "summoning, calling" people to court (cf. Job 9:16; 13:22) and the way people were "being judged"[246] while at court; thus, there were problems both with people bringing unjust suits against others as well as unjust decisions being made when these lawsuits were dealt with in court. The next four infinitive absolute verbs[247] tell how (the manner) the wicked manipulated the legal system to achieve their unjust results. These people practice injustice "by trusting in empty claims,"[248] by speaking "lies, nothing," by conceiving trouble in their thoughts, and by giving birth[249] to iniquity. These four methods of perverting justice demonstrate that some people are working very hard to gain an advantage over others by initiating frivolous lawsuits (making empty claims), by testifying falsely about what actually happened, by thinking up schemes that will enrich themselves, and by carrying out these schemes. This is reminiscent of the empty claims that were brought against the righteous man Naboth at the instigation of Jezebel (1 Kgs 21:7–14).

---

[246] The first is an active participle קֹרֵא "is calling, summoning," while the second verbal form is a passive participle נִשְׁפָּט "is being judged."

[247] The infinitive absolute can "describe more particularly the manner or attendant circumstance . . . under which an action or state has taken place" (GKC §113h).

[248] The word תֹּהוּ refers to something that is empty (without any people or animals); for example, it is used of the situation when God first created the world (Gen 1:2).

[249] The infinitive absolute הוֹלֵיד comes from the root that means "to bear, give birth."

It is not surprising to hear that people like this have no communion with God, for such sins prevent God from acting on their behalf.

59:5–6 Now the prophet uses a series of animal analogies to characterize the wickedness of these sinners. The exact kind of reptile named in v. 5a is unknown. Based on other animals mentioned in similar passages (11:8; 14:29 and Ps 58:4[Hb. 5]), one would assume this refers to a dangerous snake that lays eggs (not all snakes lay eggs). In some ways these sinful people are comparable to the snake that hatches its eggs and the spider that weaves its web. How are they similar? In the first case, the eggs of a snake are eaten, and that person dies from the poison found within the egg. In the second example, a person is holding a cracked egg that is almost ready to hatch a snake. Then suddenly out comes a poisonous baby snake that can kill a person. Both actions lead to deadly consequences, just like the evil consequences that come from the wickedness of these sinners. Truly, the consequences of sin are death.

Verse 6 explains how the works of these sinners are like the works of the spider that spins an intricate cobweb. Although a spider web may appear to be beautiful in its symmetry and design, in reality the threads of the cobweb of a spider "will not be" (NIV "is useless") sufficient to function as clothing to hide someone from the sun. So sinful people "cannot cover themselves"[250] with their sinful cobweb of evil deeds to hide what they have done. Just as the spider's web brings "violence" (*ḥāmās*) and death to the insect that flies into it, so the evil deeds of sinful people who spin their webs of violence will bring great harm to those who get caught by their evil schemes.

59:7 Now the prophet leaves his animal comparisons and directly addresses the ways of violence and injustice practiced by these evil people. These people are not pictured as those who try to do the right thing or who want to live in peace with others or who think the best of others. They do not hesitate for a moment when the opportunity comes to take advantage of others. These people cannot make the excuse that the devil made me do it. Their feet will eagerly run toward evil (cf. Prov 1:16; 6:18), instead of running away from evil. They will quickly hurry "in order to shed"[251] the blood of innocent people; they do not hesitate or think twice about what they are doing. This must refer to the violent taking of the life of another person who has done nothing wrong (they are innocent). Cain's killing of Abel is an example of shedding innocent blood on the ground (Gen 4:8–10), and Jezebel's plot to falsely accuse Naboth of treason in order to take his vineyard is another famous example of killing the innocent for personal gain (1 Kgs 21). This behavior is exactly the opposite of the righteousness and justice God desires in 56:1, and this kind of action

---

[250] The *hithpa'el* verb יִתְכַּסּוּ "they will cover themselves" expresses a reflexive idea (GKC §54d). In this case the imperfect verb is probably used modally to express the subjunctive idea of what "can, should, might, or would" be accomplished (GKC §107m-n).

[251] The infinitive construct לִשְׁפֹּךְ "in order to shed" expresses their purpose (GKC §114f).

explains why the prophet repeatedly emphasizes that no justice was found among these people (59:8,11,14,15).

The source of such violent wickedness comes from the perverse thought life of these wicked people. There are no verbs in the second half of this verse, so one must imply the "to be" verb. Their thoughts are thoughts about how they can do iniquity. Evil thoughts played a primary role as a precursor to evil deeds in many narrative stories. Joseph's brothers plotted and thought to do him harm (Gen 37:12–28; 45:4–8; 50:20), but God turned their evil thoughts into something very good. Micah expresses God's anguish over the powerful people in Jerusalem who thought up plots to take property from the poor in the evening and then carried out their plans the next morning (Mic 2:1–2). Because of Haman's anger at Mordecai, Haman thought about or plotted how he could execute Mordecai and all the Hebrew people (Esth 3:1–6; 8:3), but Queen Esther revealed the evil thoughts he had devised in his mind (Esth 7:3–6; 9:24–25), and Haman was executed. In all these examples, sinful deeds first developed in the thought life of the individual, and then these people acted upon the evil imagination of their minds. The consistent results are that people bring violence and destruction into the lives of others. This may happen on a desolate highway, where others might not see the perpetrator, or in almost any other place that one might imagine. Later v. 8 will refer to the "ways" and "paths" where people "walk," so this "highway" (from *měsilâ*) is just another way of saying that these evil acts are done wherever people carry out their normal business of life. This highway of violence contrasts with God's holy highway where the righteous will walk in 35:8–10. That highway will not have any wicked people on it, and there will be no dangers for the redeemed people who walk there. They will rejoice and sing the praises of God.

When the apostle Paul wanted to talk about the depraved sinfulness of mankind, he collected several descriptions of Israel's sinfulness together in Rom 3:10–18 (most were from Psalms). Included in this group of quotes is Isa 56:7–8a, which appears in Rom 3:15–17. Thus Paul did not see a great deal of difference between the evil confronted by the prophets and the manifestations of evil behavior in his day. Sinful people tend to act in the same way, no matter when they live or what culture they are a part of. All are guilty before God.

59:8   Earlier, in 57:18–19 God promised to guide, restore, heal, and bring peace to his righteous people (cf. 26:3,12; 32:17–18), and in 57:20-21 he promised to give no peace to the wicked. This is because the wicked do not know anything about the way of life that is characterized by peace or justice. The point is not that they do not know about the concept or requirements of a just life (cf. 42:16; 56:1); it is that they are blinded by their evil thoughts and are unwilling to accept the just ways of God. Consequently, they do not act justly toward other people and ignore the instructions of God about acting justly (56:1; 59:8,11,15). So it is not surprising that they do not "know, experience" peace and justice in their daily life. Their paths are "twisted"[252] instead of being straight; they do not display integrity. If a person acts in these ways, it is impossible for that person to have a life blessed by God's peace.

Confession of Sins (59:9–15a)

⁹So justice is far from us,
     and righteousness does not reach us.
We look for light, but all is darkness;
     for brightness, but we walk in deep shadows.
¹⁰Like the blind we grope along the wall,
     feeling our way like men without eyes.
At midday we stumble as if it were twilight;
     among the strong, we are like the dead.
¹¹We all growl like bears;
     we moan mournfully like doves.
We look for justice, but find none;
     for deliverance, but it is far away.

¹²For our offenses are many in your sight,
     and our sins testify against us.
Our offenses are ever with us,
     and we acknowledge our iniquities:
¹³rebellion and treachery against the LORD,
     turning our backs on our God,
fomenting oppression and revolt,
     uttering lies our hearts have conceived.
¹⁴So justice is driven back,
     and righteousness stands at a distance;
truth has stumbled in the streets,
     honesty cannot enter.
¹⁵Truth is nowhere to be found,
     and whoever shuns evil becomes a prey.

All of a sudden the verbs and pronouns change to first-person plural ("we, us") in these verses, signaling the beginning of a new paragraph. In addition, the tone turns from a series of accusations of sinfulness and injustice to a humble confession of sins that one might expect to find in a community lament.[253] J. Muilenburg views 59:9–11 as a community lament and 59:12–15b as a confession of sin, but since there is no appeal to God for deliverance, it is not a

---

[252] Their paths "are twisted, made crooked" עִקְּשׁוּ because they are corrupt people, which is opposite the path of the man of integrity who walks on a secure path (Prov 10:9).

[253] Blenkinsopp, *Isaiah 56–66*, 191, claims that this "is certainly not a community lament" since there is no appeal for divine assistance or assurance of a positive outcome, while Whybray, *Isaiah 40–66*, 223, maintains that it "contains two characteristic elements of the corporate lament found in the Psalms and Lamentations," though other characteristics are missing.

typical community lament. It seems better to follow C. Seitz, who concludes that this is probably a prophetic prayer of intercession on behalf of the community, somewhat similar to the great intercessory prayers found in Ezra 9:6–14; Neh 9:5–37; and Dan 9:4–19.[254]

These verses can be divided into three parts:

The misery of no light	59: 9–11a
Confession of sin	59:11b–13
Summary: There is no justice	59:14–15a

This paragraph is connected to what precedes and follows by repeated references to the main themes of "justice" (*mišpāt* in 59:4,8,9,11,14,15b)[255] and "righteousness" *ṣedek* (59:4,9,14,16,17). First, the people were accused of telling lies in 59:3,4 and now there is a confession that they have told lies in 59:13. They are accused of not being honest in 59:4, and now there is a confession in 59:14,15a that they have not told the truth. In addition, the light-and-darkness contrasts in 59:9–10 pick up these same themes from 58:8,11. In general, the confession of sinfulness matches the earlier accusations, for their iniquities have rebounded on them.[256]

59:9–11a The new paragraph is marked by the introductory "therefore" (*ʿal kēn*), which makes a causal link between the presence of the sins in 59:1–8 and the following confession. The prophet identifies with his audience's distress ("we, us") just like Ezra, Nehemiah, and Daniel identified with the sinful people they were praying for. Thus, the prophet included himself within the group that finds justice far away. God's salvation, his light, and his presence are hidden because sin has separated God from mankind and sin has hidden his face (59:2). The absence of God's presence and salvation produces darkness and gloom instead of the salvation many people were longing for. Thus what "we hope for" (*nĕqawweh*) was not happening; instead, only darkness prevailed. Evidently this hope was some sort of wish or a natural human desire for better times in which they would experience God's justice and salvation. This unfulfilled human desire might be compared to their inadequate seeking for God and their inauthentic attempts to draw near to God in 58:2. People can wish for many things, but usually hopes are fulfilled through responsible planning, careful discipline, and wise choices, not by walking directly contrary to the just and righteous ways that God desires to establish. Authentic hope is willing to wait, trust in God's timing, and follow God's just ways because trust is securely founded in the person of God who sovereignly planned the future

---

[254] Muilenburg, "Isaiah 40–66," 5:690; Motyer, *Isaiah*, 486; and Childs, *Isaiah*, 488, believe some in the community speak these words. For those who think this is the prayer of the prophet, see Seitz, "Isaiah 40–66," 501; Oswalt, *Isaiah 40–66*, 519; and Goldingay, *Isaiah*, 331–32.

[255] D. Kendall, "The Use of *mišpat* in Isaiah 59," *ZAW* 96 (1984): 391–405, distinguishes between human acts of righteousness and God's salvific righteous deeds.

[256] Polan, *In the Ways of Justice toward Salvation*, 282.

and has all the power necessary to accomplish what he has planned (8:17; 14:26–27). Although these people wanted to experience God's blessing, they now admit that they failed to experience what they hoped for. Something went wrong somewhere.

Verse 10 points to the blindness and failures of the group the prophet is interceding for. He is confessing their confusion and their failures. Blindness is a metaphor that is often used to explain sinful people's lack of understanding of God's ways and their failure to follow God's instructions (other descriptions of the blind are found in 6:9–10; 29:9; 42:18–19; 43:8; 56:10). The prophet compares these people, who have not experienced God's justice and salvation, to confused blind people who grope around in darkness looking for a wall. This blindness was predicted in the covenant curse in Deut 28:28–29, and now it has happened to these sinful people. The three cohortative verbs used here could express mutual encouragement ("let us grope like the blind")[257] if this phrase was introduced as a quotation of what these people were saying, but that is not the case. Thus the verbal forms are somewhat of a mystery, and they probably do not function as cohortatives.[258] Nevertheless, there is no doubt about what the verse is talking about. The prophet confesses that (a) we have no spiritual eyes to see; (b) we metaphorically stumble around in the middle of the day like a normal person would at twilight, and (c) we look like dead people among the healthy.[259] At minimum, this admission reveals how futile and frustrating their spiritual blindness is. God's future promise to remove the nation's blindness is a repeated theme in the book of Isaiah (29:18; 32:3; 35:5; 42:18–19; 43:8).

The unhappiness and misery of these people is compared to the woeful sounds of a groaning bear or the moaning sound of a dove. These appear to be expressions of disappointment, sorrow, pain, and misery based on the usages of this metaphor in other passages about the moaning of doves. In 38:14 Hezekiah cries and moans like a dove because Isaiah told him that he will soon die, and in Ezek 7:16 the survivors of the sword, famine, and plague that fall on Jerusalem moan in agony like doves. There is no indication that this intense moaning[260] is an expression of their repentance for their sins. But it does appear that the prophet is communicating how these sinful people are finally honestly facing the reality of the terrible situation they are experiencing (59:2–8) and their great sense of sadness and frustration (59:9).

---

[257] The cohortative verb נְגַשְׁשָׁה with final ה either expresses (a) self-encouragement or (b) self-determination (GKC §108b), but neither of these seem appropriate in this case, unless this is a mocking of these people.

[258] This may be an exceptional form that does not carry a cohortative sense (GKC §108g).

[259] This word is only used here, so its meaning is difficult to discern. Westermann, *Isaiah 40–66*, 343, emends the text and translates "sit in darkness," but it seems better to derive it from the root שָׁמֵן "to be fat, well fed, healthy" and explain the initial א as a prefixed prosthetic א (GKC §85b) which was added for euphonic reasons.

[260] The intensity of the mourning is suggested by the use of the infinitive absolute verb with an imperfect (הָגֹה נֶהְגֶּה), giving the meaning "moaning, we will moan."

59:11b–13 Now the prophet returns to the issue of the people's "continual hope"[261] for "justice," which was mentioned in 59:9. But as before, there is still no justice, and the salvation they hoped for is still "far away" (*rāḥaq*, as in 59:9) "because" (*kî*, 59:12) sin is still present in their lives. Since the people have not yet fully confessed, repented, and turned away from their sins, these many rebellious deeds still separate the people from God (59:12 agrees with 59:2). But in 59:12 the prophet names, owns, and confesses these sins on behalf of the people. He admits that it is true; many rebellious deeds, sins, and acts of iniquity were done. These were things "we" did, so "we" are responsible for them, and they testify against "us." At this point their failures are not ignored, denied, or blamed on other people. Sin can only be dealt with when people face it directly and decide to reject a sinful way of life. The prophet confesses "we acknowledge that we have sinned against you." The prophet is no doubt hoping that his frank admission will encourage others to confess the sins that they have committed. His remorse and his willingness to take responsibility should encourage others to boldly renounce their evil ways (cf. Ezra 9–10).[262] This courageous and godly confession presents a powerful practical example for all leaders who wish to lead their people in a time of revival and rededication.

Following the syntactical pattern already established in 59:4b (the use of infinitive absolutes), the prophet enumerates how these people sinned by using a series of six infinitive absolute verbs to identify more specific ways the people have rebelled against God (59:13).[263] He acknowledges that they have sinned (a) by rebelling, (b) by being hypocritical toward God, (c) by turning from following God, (d) by speaking oppressive words, and (e) by both conceiving and (f) uttering lying words. Rebellion is a rejection of the authority of the one in power (in politics it refers to treason), while hypocrisy[264] involves making positive statements about something but doing something very contradictory. The ideal was for people to walk after God, but these people turned back to their sinful ways and did not follow God's instructions. The last two sins relate to "imagining"[265] evil thoughts and speaking deceptive words, but a specific example of this is not included. All of these sins destroy the possibility of having a relationship with God, so these sins must be confessed and

---

[261] Both 59:9 and 59:11b use the *pi'el* imperfect verb נְקַוֶּה to express continued or repeated action, "we were hoping, we continually hoped" (GKC §107b,e).

[262] When Ezra heard about the detestable behavior of the priests and Levites who defiled the holy seed of God by marrying unbelievers (Ezra 9:1–2), he was so emotionally devastated that he tore his garments, pulled out some of his hair, sat appalled, and prayed a long confessional prayer. In the middle of his prayer, people gathered to hear Ezra's prayer and they, too, confessed their behavior (10:1–2).

[263] GKC §113d,h indicates that the infinitive absolute can be used "to describe more particularly the manner or attendant circumstances . . . under which an action or state has taken place."

[264] The root כָּחַשׁ refers to acting deceptively, swearing falsely, failing to do what was said.

[265] The word הֹרוֹ infinitive comes from הָרָה "he conceived" and הֹגוֹ comes from הָגָה "he uttered." The unusual infinitive absolute form is explained in GKC §75n.

forsaken. Some of these sins, such as rebellion and lying, may have impacted relationships with other people as well as their relationship with God. These sins originate in the wicked hearts of evil people, so there is a need for both forgiveness and a radical transformation of these people. God can transform how people think as well as how they act. Every sinner knows how hard it can be to reject certain sins, but every saint knows that victory is possible through God's grace.

59:14–15a The last part of this paragraph drops the first-person plural confessional tone and outlines the consequences of all this sinfulness on the larger community. What is now present is a situation where justice and righteousness do not thrive (thus this verse summarizes the disappointment of earlier verses). Instead justice is "far away" (*rāḥôq* in 59:14, which picks up 59:9,11). Justice was to be instituted within all aspects of life and should be an integral part of all business and social relationships, but now it "is customarily turned back"[266] and excluded from having any part in these relationships. This agrees with the statement that the consequence for the future is that righteousness "continually stands off"[267] and is not embraced. When "trustworthiness, truth" (*'ĕmet*) stumbles in the streets where people interact and do business, truly upright people are excluded from doing business. Although this text may primarily reflect what was happening with human aspects of justice, righteousness, and truth, in another sense the same thing could be said of God's attempts to infiltrate society with justice and truth. God would like to see these ideals present in Israel, but, because of their sinfulness, God's just hand was pushed away and his salvation stands and waits to come at another time. In essence, this confession of sin is explaining and justifying the argument found in 59:1–2. The prophet agrees with God's analysis of the problem so he steps forward in order to begin the process of repentance so that sin will no longer prevent God from answering their prayers.

In v. 15a the prophet comes to the central problem of the people's lack of faithfulness and the total absence of truthfulness in their dealings with God. Truthfulness in relationships between these people and God has not just momentarily stumbled for a brief second; truthfulness and faithfulness are nowhere to be found in this community. In fact, they are totally and completely lacking in everything these people say and do. This has the consequence of making righteous people into the enemies of those who are trying to carry out their evil schemes. In effect, the righteous end up "making themselves spoil, plunder"[268] because they are hated, and the wicked take advantage of them.

---

[266] The perfect verb וְהֻסַּג is used "to express facts which have formerly taken place, and are still of constant recurrence, and hence are matters of common experience (the Greek *gnomic aorist*)" as suggested in GKC §106k.

[267] The imperfect verb תַּעֲמֹד probably has a present tense rendering (GKC §107g-h) if it describes an action that repeatedly or customarily happens in the present time.

[268] The reflexive *Hithpa'el* participle מִשְׁתּוֹלֵל comes from שָׁלַל "he plundered, spoiled" with

Things are in such an impossible mess that God needs to intervene and set things right.

God Will Bring Salvation and Justice (59:15b–21).

> The LORD looked and was displeased
>> that there was no justice.
> 16He saw that there was no one,
>> he was appalled that there was no one to intervene;
> so his own arm worked salvation for him,
>> and his own righteousness sustained him.
> 17He put on righteousness as his breastplate,
>> and the helmet of salvation on his head;
> he put on the garments of vengeance
>> and wrapped himself in zeal as in a cloak.
> 18According to what they have done,
>> so will he repay
> wrath to his enemies
>> and retribution to his foes;
> he will repay the islands their due.
> 19From the west, men will fear the name of the LORD,
>> and from the rising of the sun, they will revere his glory.
> For he will come like a pent-up flood
>> that the breath of the LORD drives along.
>
> 20"The Redeemer will come to Zion,
>> to those in Jacob who repent of their sins,"
>> > declares the LORD.

21"As for me, this is my covenant with them," says the LORD. "My Spirit, who is on you, and my words that I have put in your mouth will not depart from your mouth, or from the mouths of your children, or from the mouths of their descendants from this time on and forever," says the LORD.

The final paragraph describes God's direct intervention in affairs on earth to establish his justice. This will resolve the problem of having no justice on earth in 58:1–59:15a. The news of God's future coming to Zion appears to be God's direct response to the preceding prayer.[269] God's promised plan of action in 59:15b–21 will happen at some unknown eschatological date, and his powerful coming to establish justice will impact both the wicked sinners (59:18) and the righteous (59:19–20). Since justice and righteousness did not prevail on the earth because of human sin (59:4,8,11,14,15b), God will use his own righteousness to inaugurate a new era of divine rule through his Spirit (59:21;

---

metathesis of the שׂ and the ח (GKC §54b).

[269] Muilenburg, "Isaiah 40–66," 5:694, and Blenkinsopp, *Isaiah 56–66*, 195, understand 59:15b–20 as a response to 59:9–15a, while Whybray, *Isaiah 40–66*, 226, does not regard these verses as an answer to 59:9–15a.

60:1–62:12). With this triumphant conclusion, 58:1–59:21 can close[270] so that
the next phase of God's plan (60:1–63:6) can be explained.

P. D. Hanson identifies 59:15b–21 and 63:1–6 as Divine Warrior hymns which
carry on the traditional image of God defeating his enemies, similar to passages
like Exodus 15 or Psalm 48.[271] Although there is some resemblance between
these two Isaiah passages (59:15b–20; 63:1–6),[272] the Divine Warrior imagery
is much more explicit and graphic in 63:1–6; thus, 63:1–6 seems to be more
related to the similar oracle against Edom in 34:1–15 than the broad perspective
of 59:15b–21. Isaiah 63:1–6 has a much clearer description of a theophany that
annihilates evil, while 59:15b–21 is more descriptive of how the righteous hand
of the Lord will save the righteous and destroy his enemies. Isaiah 59:15b–21
predicts both divine wrath as well as God's salvation, while 63:1–6 only speaks
of God's wrath. Isaiah 59:15b–21 prophetically refers to what will happen, but
in 63:1–6 one actually observes God accomplishing his victory on the Day of
the Lord. Thus 59:15b–21 functions effectively as a conclusion to chaps 56–59
because it proclaims that in the end God will establish justice on the earth.

This paragraph can be divided into three parts

What God saw	59:15b–17
What God will do	59:18–20
God's covenant promises	59:21

This outline is based on the use of several *waw* consecutive imperfect verbs
that explain what God saw and what he did to prepare himself to address the

---

[270] Motyer, *Isaiah*, 489, groups 59:14–63:6 as one literary unit about the Anointed Conqueror.
He finds four paragraphs in this unit: (a) 59:14–60:22; (b) 61:1–9; (c) 61:10–62:12; and (d) 63:1–6,
with each paragraph initially introducing information about the Anointed One. E. Charpentier,
Jeunesse du Vieux Testament (Paris: Fayard, 1963), 79–80, also saw a parallelism between the two
warrior hymns, but his outline is quite different from that of Motyer (see the introduction to chaps.
56–66). This outline was updated and revised in E. Charpentier, *How to Read the Old Testament*
(New York: Crossroad, 1981), 77, where both the B and B' segments are divided into two parts.

[271] Hanson, *The Dawn of Apocalyptic*, 124–27, 203–205, interprets this hymn as God's vindication of a weak, persecuted priestly sect against a powerful group that was corrupting temple
worship. M. J. Lynch, "Zion's Warrior and the Nations: Isaiah 59:15b–63:6 in Isaiah's Zion Traditions," 244–63, identifies an a-b-a pattern with the two warrior panels (59:15b–21 and 63:1–6)
surrounding the central panel in chaps. 60–62. The main verbal connections are in 59:16 and 63:5,
although both paragraphs do speak of "garments" and "vengeance" (59:17; 63:1,4).

[272] Blenkinsopp, *Isaiah 56–66*, 196, lists five connections between 59:15b–20 and 63:1–6:
(a) God is a Redeemer who "comes" to Zion (59:20) and who will "come" from Edom (63:1);
(b) God dons military attire in 59:17 and blood-stained clothes in 63:1–2; (c) God is a vindicator
in 59:16–17, and God announces triumph in 63:1; (d) there was no one to help in 59:16 and in
63:3; and (e) God's action will bring redemption (59:20; 63:1) and vengeance (59:17; 63:4). Point
(a) only indicates that both "come," a coincidental comparison that carries no significance. Point
(b) is weak because the "garments" in 63:1,2,3 are never identified as the breastplate and helmet
or any kind of military armament. Overall one might conclude that 63:1–6 borrows from some of
the ideas in 59:15b–20, which describes in detail the battle that is only hinted at in chap. 59. The
strongest connection is between 59:16 and 63:5.

evil situation on earth (59:15b–17). In the following verses, the verbs change to imperfects that describe what God will do to resolve the problems he observes on earth (59:18–20). The final verse is set off by its narrative style and both an initial and concluding "says the LORD" messenger formula. Isaiah 59:21 functions as a transitional statement that connects the righteous who repent in 59:19–20 with those who will dwell in Zion when the light of God's glory shines over the earth and God fulfills his covenant with his people (59:21; 61:8).[273]

59:15b–17   The paragraph begins by assuring the listeners/readers that God has seen the lack of justice that exists on the earth (15b,16a). This is consistent with past accounts in Gen 6:5 when God "saw" (from *rā'â*) that the wickedness of man had become very great, his recognition that the sins of Sodom and Gomorrah were great in Gen 18:20–21, or his observation of the great sin of worshipping the golden calf at Mount Sinai in Exod 32:9. In every situation, when God observes injustice, "it is evil" (from *rā'a'*) in his eyes, so it is not surprising to find God responding negatively to the lack of justice described in chaps. 58–59. God is patient and long-suffering with sinful people, but eventually he will justly deal with the problem of sin and sinful people.

A second thing that God "saw" (from *rā'â*, 59:16) was that there was not one person who could or would address this serious situation of rebellion and sinfulness among mankind. Possibly God was looking for someone to "intervene"[274] and crush these evil people, or maybe he was looking for someone like the righteous Abram figure who interceded on behalf of Sodom (Gen 18:22–33) or someone like Moses who intervened for the Israelites at Mount Sinai when they worshipped the golden calf (Exod 32:11–14) or someone like the Servant in 53:12 who would intervene for the rebellious sinners. Intervention implies that one is willing to meet with someone concerning an important issue and to deal with that person in order to resolve the issue. Intervention may require strict enforcement of a principle or law or physical force against an accused person (a negative intervention that brings about justice), or one may entreat someone on behalf of the accused (a positive intervention that resolves a false accusation). Since no one stepped forward, this left an appalling situation in which nothing was being done to confront and defeat the evil that dominated the world and nothing was being done on behalf of the righteous. God's reaction to these circumstances in v. 16b was to employ his arm, a symbol of his power, to do his work of salvation (from *yāša'*). Parallel to God's almighty power are "his righteous deeds" (*ṣidqātô*), an idea that is parallel to God's salvation in the preceding line. Righteousness is that moral quality of

---

[273] Koole, *Isaiah III, Volume 3: Isaiah 56–66*, 168, believes "v. 21 offers a transition to the description of Zion's new salvation in chap. 60."

[274] The *hiphil* participle מַפְגִּיעַ comes from פָּגַע which in the *qal* means one "is encountering, meeting" and, in a negative context, refers to "striking or falling on" someone. In the *hiphil* it refers to "causing one to encounter, to entreat" or, in a negative context, "causing to attack."

acting justly and faithfully that directs God's hand to accomplish his righteous deeds of salvation and judgment. Thus God's power and uprightness will direct all that he does.

Additional means of righteous empowerment are spelled out in 59:17. God is anthropomorphically pictured as being clothed with divine qualities, as if they were parts of the armor of a soldier. Elsewhere God is described as being clothed with majesty, glory, and light (Job 40:9–10; Pss 93:1; 104:1) or being robed with righteousness and justice (Job 29:14). God is sometimes explicitly pictured as a Divine Warrior fighting his enemies (42:13; 52:10; 63:1–6; Exod 14:14; 15:3) with his metaphorical sword and arrows (34:5,6; Deut 32:41–42), but it is more common to just hear about God's defeating his enemies (Deut 7:1–2,23–24; 9:3–4). In this context the explicit warrior imagery is quite limited, hinted at only in 59:17a, and his military costume of a breastplate and helmet are actually figures of comparison (*kĕ*, "like").[275] One might imagine that the breastplate and helmet are protective gear to stop the arrows of the enemy, but God hardly needs protection in a fight. His fighting also needs no offensive weapons like a sword or spear, for his powerful arm will implement his righteous rule over both the righteous and the wicked. The focus should be on what God brings and not on the comparative analogies. It is not very significant that salvation is connected to the helmet rather than the breastplate. When God appears, righteousness, salvation, vengeance, and zeal will be evident to all who encounter him. The first two attributes will bring hope to the righteous, while the last two will bring destruction to the wicked. The presence of these characteristics communicates that in God's interaction with mankind he will use his righteousness and salvation as well as vengeance and zeal because they are part and parcel of how he responds to the just and the wicked. The clothing identifies who God is and what God will do. God does not give his clothing (the helmet of salvation) to anyone, but his possession of salvation signals to the audience his ability to work in these ways. The imagery of God's "clothing" (from *lābaš*; NIV "put on") metaphorically identifies God, just as people identify a king by what he wears. Some might object that a God of love should not be characterized by "vengeance," but *nāqām* simply refers to God's establishment of his justice. God's total commitment to accomplish these things is communicated by referring to his zeal (9:6; 26:11; 37:12). It describes God's determined effort to faithfully accomplish his goals with unstoppable power.

59:18–20 Now that God is fully prepared to intervene in this situation, the imperfect verbs in these verses describe what God will do in the future to bring

---

[275] In the New Testament Paul uses similar terminology in Eph 6:13–17 to describe the armor Christians should wear as they fight against the forces of evil. He was probably influenced by the imagery in this text. F. S. Thielman, "Ephesians," in *CNTOT*, ed. G. K. Beale and D. A. Carson, 831–32, suggests that Paul was depending on Isaiah 59 as well as other OT passages that describe the imagery of war.

about justice. In both the first and the second part of this verse it is stated that God "will repay"[276] people according to "the recompense" (gĕmûl) that each deserves. Although there is no pronoun on "the recompense," one interpretive possibility is to assume that the first usage refers to the deeds of recompense that the wicked have wrongly inflicted upon others. If this is the case, then it makes sense for God to repay his enemies with wrath as a fitting recompense for the sinful ways that they have dealt with others. This is how God's justice always works; it is fair, proportionate, and balanced, with a punishment that appropriately fits the crime. The adversaries or enemies of God are not fully identified in this verse, but in the context of chaps. 56–59 they would be the blind watchmen in 56:10, those who lie, worship other gods, and forsake God in 57:3–10, those who do not please God in their fasting in 58:1–5, and the sinners who do not act justly in 59:3–8. The final reference to God repaying the evil deeds of the people in the distant islands indicates that God plans to institute his justice throughout the earth, over both the Hebrew people in Israel and the distant nations living in the far corners of civilization. In earlier messages Isaiah described how the people in the distant islands of the sea were taught about God's sovereign control over the great kings of history (41:1–4) so that they would know and fear Israel's God. God determined through the work of the Servant to bring justice to these islands and all other parts of this world (42:4; 51:4) so these people could sing for joy (42:10,12). If these people refuse to respond and trust God, he will hold them accountable and justly repay them (59:18).

This divine judgment will cause people all over the world (from the setting of the sun to the rising of the sun) to fear the name and glory of God (59:19). At that time when the Lord brings forth his judgment on the wicked, he will also cause his glory to fill the earth (6:3; 40:5, and Ps 72:19) and bring his salvation to all people. The wicked will fear God's name because of his wrath, but the righteous will revere God's name because they will see the glory of the Holy One (6:3; 57:15). God's holy arm will powerfully reveal God's power to the nations, and through it he will bring both judgment and salvation to all the earth (52:10). When these nations see God's glory, many will respond positively by loving God, serving him, and binding themselves to the Lord (56:6). The Name and the Glory are representations of God that reveal his identity and divine character to others. God's glory will appear in Zion when he establishes his kingdom (4:2–5), and his splendor will strike terror into unbelievers and humble them (2:10,21). Earlier texts indicated that this extension of God's kingdom will include representatives from all nations (2:2–4; 14:1–3; 18:7; 19:19–25; 42:6; 45:22–23; 49:26; 51:5), and this idea will be further amplified in chaps. 60–62 and 66:18–24.

---

[276] The use of the same verb יְשַׁלֵּם, "he will repay" twice emphasizes God's determination to hold everyone accountable for their deeds.

This small subparagraph ends by summarizing the two effects (negative in v. 19b and positive in v. 20) of God's coming. God's coming in 59:19b is compared to a flood of water (somewhat similar to 30:27–28), but it is possible to understand the words in this verse in quite different ways. The problem revolves around how one translates the words *ṣār* and *nōssâ* and how one understands their grammatical functions within the sentence. *ṣār* appears in the immediate context (59:18) to mean "adversary, enemy" and *nōssâ* as "standard, banner" (*nēs*); thus, KJV translates this part of the verse, "When the enemy shall come in like a flood, the Spirit of the LORD shall lift up a standard against him."[277] This pictures God fighting and overcoming the forces of evil that attempt to engulf the world. This fits the context and maintains the connection between the "enemy, adversary" in 59:18 and 19. It offers assurance that God will be victorious over his enemies.

Others reject this interpretation because (a) the verb "he will come" most naturally refers to the coming of the glory of God in 19a; (b) the word *ṣār* is placed after "like a stream," so it functions as an adjective modifying stream; and (c) *nōssâ* appears to be a verb from *nûs* "he fled, drives."[278] Various emendations of this text have been proposed to alleviate some of these problems, but it is always best to struggle with the present Hebrew text.[279] If *ṣār* "oppressive" is an adjective modifying "the river,"[280] then God's coming is compared to the irresistible force of a large oppressive stream of water flowing down a steep ravine. This is an image that would be easily understood in a country where a dry wadi can quickly become a major stream in a few seconds (in a downpour almost all the water quickly washes down the hills and immediately becomes a fast-flowing torrent as it roars down the wadi). The last phrase describes the "wind, breath" of God "driving" (a participle from *ṣar*) this flood of water on. Just as the "wind, breath" of God could cause a great storm for the boat that Jonah was in (Jonah 1:4), so God's wind can increase the oppressive or destructive power of the water flowing down this wadi.

The positive effect of God's coming in 59:20 will be that he will function as the Redeemer (using the participle *gōʾēl*) who will come to Zion. This divine

---

[277] Young, *The Book of Isaiah*, 440, and Motyer, *Isaiah*, 492, follow this interpretation. A Rofé, "Isaiah 59:19 and Trito-Isaiah's Vision of Redemption," in *The Book of Isaiah: Le Livre D'Isaïe*, ed. J. Vermeylen (Leuven: University Press, 1989), 407, n. 1, notes that this interpretation is consistent with the understanding of this verse by the Jewish commentators Rashi, Ibn-Ezra, and Radak.

[278] Oswalt, *Isaiah 40–66*, 526, and Koole, *Isaiah III, Volume 3: Isaiah 56–66*, 206–208, discuss these options and favor a translation similar to what is found in NIV, NASB, NRSV, HCSB.

[279] Rofé, "Isaiah 59:19 and Trito-Isaiah's Vision of Redemption," in Vermeglen, *The Book of Isaiah*, 407–10, reviews several alternative emendations and suggests some new ones of his own (he changes צָר to צִיר "envoy"), but none are particularly convincing.

[280] The main stumbling block to accepting this interpretation is that the adjective usually agrees in gender, number, and definiteness with the noun it modifies. This is not true in כְּנָהָר צָר since there is no article on the adjective. GKC §126z recognizes that there are numerous examples where this usual grammatical principle is not followed.

role gives the weak strength in a time of trouble (41:14; 43:14) and is often used in association with other titles like King, Holy One, Almighty, First and Last (44:6; 47:4; 48:17; 49:7; 54:5). The Redeemer title is connected to God's formation of the nation when it came out of Egypt, their deliverance from their enemies (44:24; 47:4; 54:5) and their salvation (49:26; 60:16; 62:11–12). Elsewhere the righteous are called the "redeemed" (35:9); in addition the prophet mentions God's past and his future acts of "redeeming" his people (43:1; 48:20; 52:9; 63:9). Only in 44:22 and 59:20 is redemption connected to the removal of sin. J. L. Koole argues that this act of redemption forms an inclusio with God's ability to save in 59:1.[281]

God's coming to function as a Redeemer applies specifically in this passage to those in Zion[282] and all those who turn from their rebellious deeds (the nations are included in God's people in 59:19; see also 2:2–4; 19:19–25; 45:22–23; 60:1–62:12; 66:18–21). This indicates that people from Zion will confess their sins, turn from them, and be forgiven (4:2–4). These are the formerly rebellious people of Jacob (58:1) who will now turn in a new direction and be counted among those who enjoy the benefits of God's redemptive work. Although no explicit connection is made with the Servant poem in 52:13–53:12, where the problem of sin is dealt with through the death of the suffering Servant, one should not forget that the reader had already read this explanation, so they understood how God would forgive these sins. The oracle ends with "says the LORD" to signal the limits of this message.

59:21   The final verse in narrative style introduces an additional word from the Lord ("says the LORD" is used twice) that the prophetic editor added at this point to help transition the present discussion in chap. 59 to the establishment of God's kingdom in chaps. 60–62.[283] In spite of the introduction of new themes like the covenant, M. J. Lynch has argued that 59:21 fits the general pattern of royal Zion traditions used elsewhere, for in this context and in the exodus context God the Divine Warrior defeats his enemies, makes a

---

[281] Koole, *Isaiah III, Volume 3: Isaiah 56–66*, 209. He also connects redemption with covenant in the next verse, a connection already suggested in 49:7–8 in the Servant poem and in the eschatological promises in 54:8–10.

[282] In the NT this verse is quoted (Rom 11:26) by Paul from the loose Old Greek translation which refers to those "from Zion." The second half of the verse in Romans is even more interpretive because it translates "he will turn godlessness away from Jacob." In both clauses the ל, which usually means "to, for," is interpreted "from," the usual translation of מן. C. R. Bruno, "The Deliverer from Zion: The Source(s) and Function of Paul's Citation in Romans 11:26–27," *TynBul* 59 (2008): 119–34, believes Paul drew this quotation from Isa 59:20; 27:9a, and 2:3. Since the Babylonian Talmud (*Sanh. 98a)* found a messianic meaning here, it is not surprising that Paul did too.

[283] Westermann, *Isaiah 40–66*, 352, concludes that 59:21 does not fit into the style and content of 59:1–20 and fits better with 66:22ff. Blenkinsopp, *Isaiah 56–66*, 200–201, believes the verse can "be best explained as a prose colophon to chs. 56–59, serving not only as an authentication of what has been written as genuine prophetic discourse but also as the signature of the prophetic author of the discourse."

covenant with his people, and then invites them to come and worship at his temple (chaps 60–62).[284]

The interpretation of this verse is complicated because God appears to be speaking to two different audiences. First, God makes a covenant with "them" (third masculine plural) in 21a, the people who revere God's name and repent of their sins (59:10–20). Then he puts his Spirit on "you" (second masculine singular) and his words in "your" (second masculine singular) mouth. The "them" would naturally refer to those in Zion (59:20) and the Gentiles from the east to the west (59:19) who repent of their sins, but references to "my Spirit" being on an individual ("you") reminds one of statements about "the Spirit of the LORD" resting on the Messianic "shoot" and "Branch" from Jesse in 11:2, God's promise to "put his Spirit" on the Servant who brings justice to the nations in 42:1, the person who is sent by God "with his Spirit" in 48:16, and the figure in 61:1 who will have the Spirit on him. In contrast, R. N. Whybray interprets this in light of Joel 2:28–29 and concludes that this refers to God's outpouring of his Spirit on all flesh (63:14).[285] Nevertheless, the repeated reference to the Spirit and word of God coming to the Messiah and the Servant suggests that this masculine "you" is distinct from the "they" in 59:21a.

The verse begins with the subject pronoun "I," which seems to be somewhat detached from the following verbless clause. Many translate this pronoun "as for me" (similarly to Gen 17:4 where God is making a covenant),[286] but elsewhere the subject pronoun functions to emphasize that it was "I myself" (45:12; 48:15; 50:5; 51:12) or to emphasize the pronominal suffix of the same person on a following noun ("my covenant").[287] This would result in a translation, "It is mine; this is my covenant with them," which emphasizes that this is God's covenant that he grants to others. It is not promoted by any person, is not guaranteed by human effort, and is freely granted to all people who repent and come to God (49:19–20). In the broader context of the Servant being a covenant to the nations in 42:2; 49:8, the everlasting covenant in 55:3, and the everlasting covenant in 61:8, this covenant must refer to the eschatological covenant that God will establish with his people in the future (Jer 31:31–34;

---

[284] M. J. Lynch, "Zion's Warrior and the Nations: Isaiah 59:15b–63:6 in Isaiah's Zion Traditions," 254–55, finds God defending justice, providing a place of refuge (Zion) for the disenfranchised, and welcoming all people to worship at his temple.

[285] Whybray, *Isaiah 40–66*, 229, interprets the two phrases (v. 21a and v. 21b) together and ignores the contrasting pronouns. Muilenburg, "Isaiah 40–66," 5:696, has a similar approach. Emmerson, *Isaiah 56–66*, 74, thinks this refers to the prophet and distinguishes him from the "them" in v. 21a. Watts, *Isaiah 34–66*, 287, maintains that this refers to God giving the Persian king Artaxerxes the spirit of rulership and service, while the words refer to positive decrees he would make concerning the Jews (Ezra 7:11–26; Neh 2:7–9), an unlikely interpretation.

[286] GKC §143a gives this as an example of a subject followed by an independent noun-clause that form a compound sentence.

[287] GKC §135d describes the situation in which the pronoun "serves to give strong emphasis to a suffix of the same person," but often the suffixed word is found before the subject pronoun, though in 135f he gives examples where the pronoun precedes the noun with the suffix.

Ezek 34:23–25; 37:24–28), which is also connected to the fulfillment of the Davidic covenant in 2 Sam 7:14–16.[288]

The second promise is not with "them" but with "you." This one will be recognized by a special gift of "my Spirit." There is no doubt about how dramatically the transformational power of the Spirit and the coming of the glory of God will impact all aspects of life and all people who live in God's kingdom (32:15–20; 35:1–10; 44:1–5; Ezek 34:22–31), but this verse focuses on that special gift of the Spirit that God will pour out on one person, probably the Davidic Servant Messiah. This verse does not explain how this gift will impact the Servant (cf. 9:1–2; 61:1–3) unless the presence of God's word is dependent on the gift of the Spirit. God is the one who will put words in the mouth of this Servant; he will not speak lies, deceptions, sneering statement, or mockery (59:3–4,13–15). The statement that the words God will give to him will never leave the mouth of this divine ambassador emphasizes the completeness of his internalization of God's thoughts. The results of his faithful ministry and the results of the transformation of mankind will cause the "offspring, seed, children" (from *zera*ʿ) of this Servant to speak the same words as the Servant. The "seed, offspring" would refer to those who follow the spiritual advice of the Servant (53:10), not the offspring of sinners who were rebellious (57:3; 58:1). These are the people who have confessed their sins, repented, and turned from iniquity (59:20). These are the "many" from Israel and the nations who were justified when the Servant suffered for their sins (53:11). These covenant followers are the people who will enjoy the kingdom of God described in chaps. 60–62.

THEOLOGICAL IMPLICATIONS.   The message of chaps. 58–59 clearly distinguishes between the lifestyle, religious behavior, and the faith of two different groups of people. Although they are all somewhat religious, one group fasts in order to achieve some personal gain (58:1–3), but their hearts are not focused on the things of God or on how to practice a godly life of justice in relationship with others. They have their own desires that they delight in, so they do not please God (58:3,13). These people wondered why God did not answer their prayers (59:1–3), but it is clear that their sinful lies, blood-stained hands, lack of integrity, acts of violence, and evil thoughts separated them from God (59:1–8). The prophetic rebuke of these people is a clear warning to all hearers of his words to truly seek to practice justice and to confess all sins so that God is not separated far from those who worship him. Self-serving prayers and rituals are useless; therefore, people should not pray in order to satisfy personal pleasures but to delight and honor the Lord (58:13–14). Prayers, feasts, fasts, and Sabbath worship should come from a heart of joy and generosity to others, then the answers to prayer, the light, the hope, and the healing that people

---

[288] Motyer, *Isaiah*, 492–93, and Koole, *Isaiah III, Volume 3: Isaiah 56–66*, 212–13, have a similar understanding of the covenant and the "you" mentioned in this verse.

desire will richly overwhelm them because God will be with them (58:8–9,14).
God can and will save those who call on him (58:13), but sinfulness cuts off a
person's relationship with God and the possibility of a positive divine intervention (59:1–3).

The only hope for those who follow a lifestyle of sin (59:1–8) is for them to
confess their sins and pray for mercy, or for them to have some godly person
intercede on their behalf (59:9–15a). In this case, the prophet's intercession
precedes any acts of confession, but the chapter ends with the indication that
there were some in Jacob who did repent of their sins (59:20). Unfortunately,
to God's amazement, there are far too few who seem to love the lost and carry
on a vibrant life of intercession (59:16). The practice of intervention by intercession is hard because it requires a selfless and endless dedication that is
not discouraged by the failures and disappointments of people who stubbornly
refuse to acknowledge their rebellion against God (59:10–13). Intercession requires that the intercessor identify with the failures of the wicked and love
them in spite of their treachery and lies. In the end, only God can change these
lives, and his power and grace are the only hope there is for them, but God can
choose to respond to dedicated intercession. God is the Redeemer who comes
to his people and offers a new relationship based on repentance (59:20). He is
righteous and just, so the ungodly need to fear him lest they miss out on the
salvation that he offers. People from Judah and around the world will fear him
and enjoy the blessings of his covenant relationship, so it is incumbent on all
who hear these words to respond so that they can enjoy the eternal kingdom
that has been made possible through God's special, Spirit-endowed Servant
who declares the word of the Lord (59:20).

2. God Will Bring Salvation, Transform Zion, Destroy the Wicked (60:1–63:6)

The themes in 60:1–63:6 continue and expand ideas already introduced in
1–59,[289] creating continuity with and the expansion of earlier visions of the eschatological situation in Zion. Some of the earlier themes that are picked up in
this section include (a) the gathering of the sons of Israel in 60:4 is connected
to the same idea in 11:11–12; 43:5–6; 49:18,22; 54:7b; (b) the gates being open
and never shut is found in both 60:11 and 45:1; (c) the knowledge that God is
Savior, Redeemer, the Mighty One of Jacob is used in 60:16 and 41:14; 48:17;
49:7,26; (d) the work of the Anointed One in 61:1–3 is similar to the work of
the Servant in 49:8–9; (f) the preparation of the way in 62:10 appears to be
based on imagery similar to what was used in 40:3; (g) God's coming with his

---

[289] Blenkinsopp, *Isaiah 56–66*, 57, compares the repatriation in 60:4 with 49:18,22; the sub-
jugation of foreigners in 60:14–16 to 49:23; opening the gates of Jerusalem in 60:11 to 45:1; the
nations bringing goods in 60:9 to 51:5; the multiplication of many trees in 60:13 to 41:19; knowing
God as savior in 60:16 to 49:26; God coming with his rewards for Zion in 62:11 to 40:10.

recompense with him is found in 62:11 and 40:10; 59:18; and (h) God's wrath is poured out on the evil nations in 63:1–6 and 34:1–15; 59:15–18.[290]

There are also several close connections between chaps. 59 and 60. Both 59:19 and 60:2 refer to the "glory" (*kābôd*) of God which will come to Zion; 59:21 and 60:16 describe God as a "Redeemer" (*gōʾēl*); 59:9,11,14,16,17 and 60:17,21 repeatedly refer to "righteousness" (*ṣidāqâ*), and the key term "light" (*ʾôr*) is found in 59:9 and 60:1,3,20. Of course, the central concept of God's covenant in 59:21 must be related to the everlasting covenant in 61:8, and the giving of God's Spirit in 59:21 could easily be related to the work of the Spirit in 61:1. Thus the final message at the end of chaps. 56–59 does not appear to be randomly thrown together without thought to its relationship to chap. 60. Isaiah 59:15b–21 appears to be purposely integrated into several themes within 60–62 by the repetition of several identical theological concerns.

Many redactional approaches apportion several verses within chaps. 60:1–63:6 to later stages of rereading the message of earlier passages in the book of Isaiah (from chaps. 2–39 as well as 40–55) in the light of a new situation.[291] They believe these messages are quite distinct from chaps. 56–59 because salvation is conditioned on righteousness and justice in chaps. 56–59, while there is no conditionality in 60:1–63:6.[292] P. A. Smith has identified significant weaknesses in these redactional studies that attempt to find several later additions or reinterpretations within these chapters.[293] Those who find contradictions between chaps. 56–59 and 60:1–63:6 related to the issues of the conditionality of salvation and the divisions between different groups tend to ignore the following: (a) Chapter 60 describes a time of salvation after the destruction of the wicked in 63:1–6; therefore, divisions among people (the righteous and the wicked) are a thing of the past in chap 60. Salvation has already arrived, so the time for conditions is now past. (b) Isaiah 59:15b–21; 60:10,12,15; 61:1,4,7; 62:8 refer to past times when conditionality was a key factor deter-

---

[290] Many other passages could be added, such as 61:1 compared to 11:1 and 48:16; 61:1 similar to 42:7 and 49:9; 61:8 compared to 55:3. Also see previous note.

[291] M. Fishbane, "Revelation and Tradition: Aspects of Inner-Biblical Exegesis," *JBL* 99 (1980): 343–61, notes the connection with 1–39; for example, the light in 60:1–2,17–18 with 9:1–3; 60:1,5,9,14,17 with 2:3,5,7,10; and 62:10–12 with 11:9. Oswalt, *Isaiah 40–66*, 10–11, believes that chaps. 56–66 pull together ideas from 1–39 and 40–55 into one unified presentation. J. Oswalt, "Isaiah 60–62," *CTJ* 40 (2005): 95–103 makes this same point on p. 97.

[292] Westermann, *Isaiah 40–66*, 298, also points out that chaps. 56–59 describe a division between the righteous and the wicked, while there is no similar division in chaps. 60–62.

[293] P. A. Smith, *Rhetoric and Redaction in Trito-Isaiah*, 26–38, describes the redactional approaches of J. Vermeylen, O. H. Steck, and K. Koenen, who assign several verses to another author who was a disciple of Isaiah. For example, Vermeylen assigns 60:14–18,21 to a later author who focuses on the Jewish community in Jerusalem, who overpower their enemies because these themes are different from the cosmic perspective of Zion as the glorious dwelling place of God in vv. 1–13. Thus he views 60:14–18,21 as a rereading and reinterpretation of 60:1–13. Smith evaluates the basis and logic of these conclusions and rejects these conclusions; instead, he argues persuasively for the unity of chaps. 60–62, although he extends this literary unit from 60:1–63:6.

mining God's punishment for the wicked and his salvation for the righteous, so this concept is not foreign to the thinking or message of these chapters. (c) Various chapters within chaps. 40–55, which 60:1–63:6 are closely connected to, also distinguish between the wicked and righteous, and they recognize conditionality to salvation (48:1–22). Therefore, this study will proceed on the conclusion that there is a literary unity and general coherence between chaps. 60:1–63:6 and a similarity between the theology in it and chaps. 40–59. All these chapters present a picture of God's salvific plans for Jerusalem and all other people (Hebrews and Gentiles) who have come to glorify God. The theology of chap. 60 is not fundamentally inconsistent with the eschatological passages already found in chaps. 2–55 or with the situation in 56–59; it simply describes a time after chaps. 56–59 and after 61:1–63:6 when God's kingdom has already been established.

R. N. Whybray connects the date and setting of the messages in chaps. 60–62 to the time of Haggai and Zechariah. Many Jews "have returned to Palestine but have subsequently awaited in vain for the fulfillment of Deutero-Isaiah's other prophecies. The city is still in ruins and the people, far from prosperous, regard themselves as still forsaken by God."[294] It seems unlikely that this kind of specific dating can be derived from the information provided within chaps. 60:1–63:6, for these messages describe what God will do in an eschatological period in the distant future, not what was happening in the time of Isaiah or any other prophet. References to the past devastation of the land (62:4) are so general that it is impossible to connect them to any one political situation, for the land was devastated by Shishak King of Egypt in the time of Rehoboam (1 Kings 14:25–28), during the Syro-Ephraimite War in the reign of Ahaz (2 Kings 16; Isa 7), during Sennacherib's conquest in the time of Hezekiah (2 Kings 18–19), and at the fall of Jerusalem (2 Kings 25). It is hypothetically possible that these words came from almost any period of the prophet's ministry and were editorially placed here because they address the issues being discussed in chaps. 56–66. But the practice of referencing several earlier themes through allusions and quotations suggests that these messages

---

[294] Whybray, *Isaiah 40–66*, 229, is not sure if the temple is being built or is already finished. Watts, *Isaiah 34–66*, 294, connects these events to Artaxerxes' decree that allowed Ezra in 458 BC to lead a group of pilgrims back to Jerusalem. Nevertheless, the coming of the wealth of the Persian Empire hardly matches the glorious picture that is found in chaps. 60–62. Hanson, *The Dawn of Apocalyptic*, 59–76, believes chaps. 60–62 presents the vision of a prophetic visionary group that opposed the exclusive priestly program of restoration found in Ezek 40–48. Blenkinsopp, *Isaiah 56–66*, 247, rejects Hanson's analysis and reconstruction. R. E. Clements, "'Arise, Shine; For Your Light has Come': A Basic Theme of the Isaianic Tradition," in Broyles and Evans, *Writing and Reading the Scroll of Isaiah*, 441–54, at first admits that "we do not know the author's identity or circumstances," but later he suggests that "the situation surrounding the rebuilding of the Jewish temple in Jerusalem in the years 520–516 BC provides a plausible, but by no means exclusive, period setting for such a message." Later he admits that there is a "lack of any clear indication of historical background" and that there "is nothing at all within it that offers a more precise indication of its time of origin other than its contextual setting in the book."

of salvation came later than the messages quoted from chaps. 2–59; thus, they should be dated toward the end of the prophet's ministry.

The vision of the future presented in these chapters expects God to appear in all his glory in Jerusalem (60:1–3). Both Hebrews and Gentiles will come to Zion to present their wealth and worship to God (60:4–22). But before the kingdom of God will be established in Jerusalem, the Spirit of God will come on his anointed messenger of good news who will announce the coming of a new era of freedom and joy (61:1–3). This glorious period will involve the rebuilding of Zion, the making of an everlasting covenant, and the acknowledgment of God as Lord by all people (61:4–9). This will result in great joy and the singing of praise to God (61:10–12). God will give Zion a new name (62:1–5), and a watchman will announce the good news to Zion (62:6–9). Since God will accomplish all these wonderful things, people need to prepare themselves for the day when the Savior of Zion comes (62:10–12). It will happen as soon as God judges the evil nations of this earth (63:1–6).

These prophetic messages describe God's plans to display his glory through the proclamation of his good news, his righteous people, his holy city, and his Anointed One. This will be possible once God has judged the evil peoples remaining on the earth (63:1–6). These oracles can be organized into four messages.

God's glory will come to Zion	60:1–22
The Anointed One announces God's favor	61:1–11
The transformation of Zion	62:1–12
Divine justice will bring wrath on the wicked	63:1–6

These chapters are united by common references to the themes of (a) the gathering of Israel and her children in 60:4,9; 62:10; (b) the glorification of God in 60:16,21; 61:3; (c) the glorification of Zion in 60:7,13; 62:2–3,7; (d) the renaming of Jerusalem in 60:14,18; 61:3b; 62:4,12; and (e) God's judgment of the wicked on the day of his vengeance in 60:12; 61:2; 63:4–6. These promises about this eschatological time include the transformation of the city of Zion, the coming of many righteous people, and the judgment of the wicked. Knowledge of these factors should cause the prophet's audience to trust God and glorify him for what he will do for his people.

(1) God's Glory Will Come to Zion (60:1–22)

The first message of salvation describes how God's glorious coming as a light to Zion (60:1–3) will glorify God and the city of Zion where he will dwell. His coming will attract Hebrews and Gentiles from around the world. They will come with gifts of gold, sacrifices, and praise to God (60:4–9). Although in past times Judah was judged (60:10,15,18), in the future all who oppose God will perish (60:12) and all those who love God will come to the holy city of the Lord. Then Hebrews and Gentiles will experience the presence of their Savior and Lord (60:16) and the transformation of Zion. In that day God's light will be brighter than the sun (60:19), and everyone there will be righteous and bring glory to God (60:21).

The structure of this message is organized in three parts.

God's glory will attract nations to honor him	60:1–9
Times have changed: Foreigners will help glorify Zion	60:10–16
The transformation of the new city of Zion	60:17–22

This chapter is held together as a literary unit by repeated references to (a) the "coming, bringing" (from *bô'* in 60:1,4a,4b,5,6,9,11,13,17a,17b,20) of the Lord, people, and wealth to Zion; (b) ideas related to "glorifying" (from *pā'ar* in 60:7,9,13,19,21) God and Zion, and (c) the coming of the "light" (*'ôr* in 60:1–3,19–20).[295] This presents a picture that is similar to the eschatological coming of God predicted in 40:5, described in 4:4–6; 52:1–2, and hinted at in 58:8,10. The purpose for God's coming will be to glorify himself and Zion.

GOD'S GLORY WILL ATTRACT NATIONS TO HONOR HIM (60:1–9)

¹"Arise, shine, for your light has come,
 and the glory of the LORD rises upon you.
²See, darkness covers the earth
 and thick darkness is over the peoples,
 but the LORD rises upon you
 and his glory appears over you.
³Nations will come to your light,
 and kings to the brightness of your dawn.

⁴"Lift up your eyes and look about you:
 All assemble and come to you;
 your sons come from afar,
 and your daughters are carried on the arm.
⁵Then you will look and be radiant,
 your heart will throb and swell with joy;
 the wealth on the seas will be brought to you,
 to you the riches of the nations will come.
⁶Herds of camels will cover your land,
 young camels of Midian and Ephah.
And all from Sheba will come,
 bearing gold and incense
 and proclaiming the praise of the LORD.

---

⁷All Kedar's flocks will be gathered to you,
　　the rams of Nebaioth will serve you;
　　they will be accepted as offerings on my altar,
　　and I will adorn my glorious temple.

⁸"Who are these that fly along like clouds,
　　like doves to their nests?
⁹Surely the islands look to me;
　　in the lead are the ships of Tarshish,
　　bringing your sons from afar,
　　with their silver and gold,
　　to the honor of the LORD your God,
　　the Holy One of Israel,
　　for he has endowed you with splendor.

The end of the previous paragraph predicted a time when God would put on righteousness and salvation (59:17), judge the wicked (59:18), come to Zion as Redeemer (59:20), and establish his covenant relationship with his people through that special one who would have God's Spirit (59:21). This new message in 60:1–9 is directly connected to 59:15b–21, and it alludes to numerous ideas expressed in chaps. 2–59. Announcements about God's plan to come to Zion and transform this world are first found in 2:1–4 and 4:2–6, so it is not surprising to find another explanation of this wonderful promise about the nations coming to Zion in chap. 60. Isaiah has provided many additional hints about this kingdom, including 9:1–7 and 11:1–16, which introduce the Davidic Messiah and the gathering of Hebrews and Gentiles to Jerusalem. In 14:1–2; 18:7, and 19:19–25 the prophet identifies people from the nations who will be a part of God's righteous people, and in 30:18–26; 32:1–8,15–20; and 35:1–10 he mentions the coming of the Spirit, the transformation of nature, the coming of the glory of the Lord, and God ruling as King in Zion. The eschatological proclamations of salvation in chaps. 40–55 also deal with many of these same themes (40:9–11; 41:17–20; 43:1–7; 44:1–5; 51:1–8; 52:1–10; 54:1–17). Thus chap. 60 has thematic contacts with many earlier prophetic speeches, but it also has its own unique emphasis.

The progression of thought in 60:1–9 is:

Light will come	60:1–3
Call to arise, shine	1
Light removes darkness	2
People will come to the light	3
Nations will come	60:4–9
Nations return your people	4–5a
Wealth comes; people praise	5b–9

These descriptions of eschatological Zion are about the "coming"[296] of God's light, the nations, Israel's sons, and Israel's joy, so that his people may enhance the beauty of God's temple and honor God himself, who will appear in all his splendor. This message provides encouragement and hope for all the righteous people on earth who continually pray that this glorious era will come very soon.

60:1 The "glory" (*qābôd*) of God refers to the majestic, physical presentation of God's holiness that is visible to human sight (cf. 6:1–8). The glory of God appeared to Moses in the fire within a bush in Exod 3:2–6; the glory of God at Mount Sinai was connected to a great cloud and fire (Exod 24:15–17; Deut 5:4–5,23–27); the awesome appearance of God's glory in the call of Ezekiel involved "an immense cloud with flashing lightning surrounded by brilliant light" and "the center of the fire looked like glowing metal" (Ezek 1:4,27). The bright light that is connected to the appearance of God's glory (58:8; 59:19–20; 60:1) is also a symbol of God's salvation (9:1–2; 58:8; 59:9; Ps 27:1). The light of the glory of God is called "your (second feminine singular) light" (also in 58:8,10) because this divine appearance of God is for the benefit of the righteous people of Zion. Isaiah 40:3–5,10–11 also predicted the coming of the glory of God with power, ruling the earth, and tenderly caring for his sheep. This will be the time when God reigns and restores Jerusalem (cf. 52:7–9).

The instructions of God in 60:1 exhort his people in Zion (based on 59:20–21) to action, encouraging Zion to "arise" (similar to 51:17; 52:1; Ps 72:19), for a new day is dawning. Those in Zion do not need to grope as if they were walking in some dark gloom (59:9),[297] for in this revelation the prophet observes that the light provided by God's holy presence is now here on earth, displayed in its full splendor. But God's coming is not just to benefit Zion alone. God's people in Zion are to "shine, produce light" (*'ôrî*) by reflecting God's "light" (*'ôr*) to others. Just as Moses' face reflected the glory of God after he spent forty days on Mount Sinai in the very presence of God (Exod 34:29–35), so the people of Zion will shine by reflecting his glory to all who see them. The two motivations for shining are "because" (*kî*, NIV "for") your light "has/will come" [298] and because the glory of God "has/will brilliantly rise" over you.

---

[296] The verb בּוֹא is used in 60:1,4[2x],5,6,9,11,13,17[2x] and its meaning extends from "come, enter" to "cause to enter, bring" in the *hiphil*.

[297] These images that contrast light and darkness were earlier used as early as 9:1–2 [Hb. 8:23–9:1].

[298] The perfect verb בָּא is translated "has come" in NIV. This is a very acceptable interpretation in most cases, but in this instance questions are raised about the relationship between this past tense translation in 60:1 and the future tense in 60:2. One might suggest that in light of the imperfect verbs in 60:2 (יְכַסֶּה "it will cover" and יִזְרַח "it will brilliantly rise") that it is better to interpret this perfect verb in v. 1 as prophetic perfects that refer to the future (GKC §106n), thus making them both look to a future event. Muilenburg, "Isaiah 40–66," 5:698, interprets these perfect verbs as prophetic perfects.

The verb "he brilliantly arose/will arise" (*zāraḥ*) is commonly used to describe the rising of the bright sun in the morning, but it also functions to describe the brilliant appearance of the theophany of God in Deut 33:2 and the brilliant arising of the "sun of righteousness" in Mal 3:20.[299] It is a fitting metaphor, for just as the bright rays of the rising sun are reflected off buildings in blinding brilliance, so God's glory will be brilliantly reflected off the lives and hearts of his people in Zion. This exhortation is an encouragement for all believers not to let the darkness of this world snuff out the brilliance of God's light that every believer should reflect toward others who need some hope (cf. Matt 5:14–16).

60:2 Another motivation for shining is "because" (*kî*) there is a great need in this world for light and for the impact of God's salvation. At the time of God's brilliant appearing, the earth and all the people in it will be covered with darkness, doom, and hopelessness (cf. 9:1). It would be somewhat dangerous to read into this reference to "darkness covering the earth" any specific historical event,[300] for the author is speaking of undefined circumstances in a distant eschatological era. The severity of that dark time is emphasized by its grip on the whole earth. If something like a blanket covers an object, it completely envelops it, casting a dark cloud of hopelessness over it because those under the covering cannot see the light. This negative characterization of darkness is contrasted with the glorious light that "will brilliantly rise"[301] over Zion. The appearance of God's glory will remove the cloak of blindness that covers the earth because his glory will be seen in its full brilliance. The relationship of God's glory to Zion is described as being "upon you" or "over you," which seems to identify God's location, his presence, and the people he will reign over. This statement affirms the same promise that the seraphim spoke in 6:3 and fills out the prediction that all flesh will see the glory of the Lord when it is revealed (40:5). The final phrase begins the transition to the next verse, for it indicates that God's glory "will be seen" (a passive verb) by others. This is no doubt related to the time when the nations will see Zion's righteousness (62:2) and may be the same events described in 66:18–19.

60:3 Verse 2 does not identify exactly which people will see God's glory over Zion, but 60:3 answers that question. It is somewhat unclear what it means when the text says that the nations and their kings who are in darkness will come to "your light." "Your light" could legitimately refer to the light reflected

---

[299] Clements, "'Arise, Shine; For Your Light has Come': A Basic Theme of the Isaianic Tradition," 441–54, indicates that some connect this tradition with the light from the star that the Magi followed in Matt 2:1–12.

[300] Westermann, *Isaiah 40–66*, 357, says that the prophet "finds himself unable to point in advance to a definite historical event" and that he does not associate this darkness with the people living in exile.

[301] The future reference of the imperfect verbs (יִזְרָח "it will brilliantly arise") suggests that the perfect verbs in 60:1 are prophetic perfects referring to a future event, just like the perfect verbs in 60:3.

by the people of Zion or refer to God himself, the light of Zion.[302] However, this distinction may be a splitting of hairs, for throughout this section God is closely identified with Zion, so its light and glorification are the light and glory from God reflected by his people. It is also significant to note that both the Servant of God in 42:6 and 49:6 as well as the Davidic Messiah in 9:1–2 were also identified as a light to the nations. The following verses will identify some of the nations (66:19–21 names additional nations) that will be attracted by this bright shining light.

60:4–5a This imperative exhortation is for Zion to "lift up" its eyes and "see,"[303] similar to the exhortation in 49:18a. Zion is to look all around in order to observe how people are coming to Zion from every direction. They will bring "your sons" and "your daughters" (as in 49:12) as well as their wealth (60:5b–9). This does not refer to the rather small population of Hebrews that returned to Jerusalem after the exile, but to what will happen at the time when God establishes his eternal kingdom.[304] Although 2:2–5 refers to the eschatological coming of the nations to Zion for worship, it does not indicate that they will bring back Hebrews who were living in foreign nations. Isaiah 11:10–16 does prophesy a gathering of the Hebrews from the nations, and 14:1–2 mentions the nations helping Israelites and bringing them back to their land. Isaiah 49:17–18,22–23 also mentions the nations bringing back Hebrews to Zion. The effect is that both Israelites and foreigners will end up in Jerusalem in order to worship God at his temple. This act of bringing people back to Jerusalem could be interpreted as simply an act of kindness, but 56:8 suggests that God is the guiding force who will gather his people back to Zion from far and near. The imagery related to the return of the daughters at the end of this verse is complicated by a broad range of meanings associated with the word *ʾāman* (NIV "are carried").[305] Although J. L. Koole believes the daughters were "being nursed" by foreigners based on 66:12, the idea of "carrying" small children on the hip or in a side sling of cloth seems a better parallel with the "coming" of the sons in the preceding line. Earlier in 49:22 the young daughters were carried on the shoulders of others, and in 66:20 people are carried on horses,

---

[302] The suffix "your" is second person sg., but it is unclear if it is masc. or fem. Usually the fem. form is ךְ and the masc. form is ךָ. Since the suffix is ךְ, one could conclude that "your light" refers to the fem. figure Zion. Nevertheless, when the masc. suffix ךָ is in pause because an *athnach* or *silluq* accent is under it, it changes to ךְ (GKC §29n); thus, from a grammatical point of view either interpretation is possible.

[303] The verb שְׂאִי is an imperative from נָשָׂא "he lifted up," while וּרְאִי is from רָאָה "he saw." Both are second fem. sg., so they exhort Zion to notice what will happen.

[304] Westermann, *Isaiah 40–66*, 358, says, "in Trito-Isaiah's time the return of the exiles was still a matter of expectation. By far the greatest number, then, must not have come back," but this noneschatological interpretation just does not fit the glorious description of chaps. 60–62. Did God's glory appear in Zion in all its splendor and attract people from all nations at that time?

[305] אָמַן can mean (a) to be firm, stand firmly; (b) to believe, be faithful, trust; (c) to nurse, or (d) to support.

chariots and wagons, on mules, and on camels. The point of this verse is not to explain how these children ate or to suggest that these children were orphans without Hebrew parents; rather, God is assuring the audience that he will make certain that no one will be left behind, not even the helpless children who are not yet able to walk.

As a result ("then" *ʾāz*, v. 5a) of observing God's amazing presence in their midst and his astonishing work in bringing foreigners and their children to Zion, the people of Zion will (a) be radiant, radiate joy,[306] (b) fear or tremble with excitement (*pāḥad*, NIV "throb"),[307] and (c) have a broad or enlarged heart. This transformation of Zion's attitude describes their joyfulness, and their amazement at the miraculous things God will do. The people in Zion will be so excited that they will shake because they cannot contain themselves. The reference to a broad or enlarged heart[308] is a puzzling metaphor that may refer to Zion's joyous acceptance of all the foreigners that come.

60:5b–9 A slightly different topic is introduced with "surely, it is true" (*kî*, omitted in NIV) in the middle of v. 5. This introductory term assures the audience that all that the prophet says will happen. The nations (mentioned already in 60:3) will not only transport people back to Jerusalem; they will also bring gifts to Zion so that they can be presented to God. The amazing gifts they will bring to God include things from all over the world. 60:5b refers to the "wealth" (NIV) from the sea and the "riches" (NIV) of the nations, but the terms that describe these gifts are unusual. The first term usually refers to the "roaring sound, noise, tumult" of large waves in the sea, of people talking, or of God's roaring (13:4; 17:12; 31:4; 33:3; 51:15),[309] but in some contexts the semantic range of this term is extended to include the idea of the "multitude of people" who are making this roaring sound as they arrive (5:13; 16:14; 29:5,7,8). Thus this verse must refer to the multitude of people that will come from far distant nations to Zion on ships of the sea. The second term can refer to the (a) great physical strength of a person or God (2 Chr 26:13; Hab 3:19), (b) the strength or valor of a warrior, (c) an army (1 Sam 16:18), (d) the moral strength or worth of a person (Ruth 3:11), or (e) the wealth of a person (Gen 34:29). Verse 5b is thus an introductory summary statement that broadly categorizes the things ("riches, wealth") and many people ("the multitudes") that will come to Zion.

---

[306] Root I of the verb נָהַר refers to the "streaming, flowing" of the nations, which is used in 2:2, but root II of נָהַר refers to "being radiant" here and in Ps 34:6.

[307] פָּחַד usually is translated "he feared" with a negative connotation, but at times this root is in a positive context (cf. Jer 33:9) with the possible meaning of "he trembled with excitement."

[308] Today people talk about welcoming others with open arms, but people also refer to those who care for foreign immigrants who have nothing as having a big heart.

[309] Koole, *Isaiah III, Volume 3: Isaiah 56–66*, 228–29, accepts this meaning and pictures the "roaring waves of the sea" bringing riches in ships to Zion. BDB, 242, maps out the various meanings this term may convey.

60:6–7 A vast number of camels laden with gold and incense will cover the land. They will arrive from Midian, a Bedouin tribe to the south[310] and from Sheba (cf. Ps 72:10,15), another Bedouin tribal group that lived in the Arabian desert area to the southeast of Israel.[311] These foreigners will freely offer their valuable gifts to God and lift up their voices to praise God. Presumably, the gold would be used to beautify the temple where God would dwell, and the incense would be offered on the altar of incense. The content of the people's praise is hinted at by the use of the verb *bāśar* "proclaim good news."

Other Bedouin tribes will come from the northern Arabian Desert area of Kedar (21:16–17; 42:11) and Nebaioth. Both of these rather insignificant desert tribes were the offspring of Abram's son Ishmael (Gen 25:13). These traders who roamed the area around Tema and Dedan will gather all their animals[312] together so that they can serve the needs of the people in Zion. Some of the animals from this group (the clean animals) will be offered up on the altar and will be a pleasing and favorable sacrifice to the Lord. Through all these gifts and activities, God will be glorified, and he will make his temple in Jerusalem a glorious place.

60:8–9 Although these verses continue to refer to the nations coming to Zion, new groups of people from the west (the area of the Mediterranean Sea) are observed approaching. Initially, a question is posed about the identity of this strange new phenomenon on the distant horizon to the west. Who are these people (*mî 'ēlleh*, similar to 63:1), and what is this movement of objects flying back and forth like distant clouds in the sky? It may be that the billowing sails of ships looked like clouds in the distance and that the movement of these boats back and forth in the wind reminded the observer of doves darting around at an opening into a nesting area. Who is coming on these boats/ships, and why are they coming?

The answer to these questions in 60:9 identifies these as people from distant coastlands of the Mediterranean Sea who "trustfully wait for, eagerly looking for"[313] God (lit. "for me"). At the front of this flotilla of boats are people riding on large and fast ships from Tarshish (cf. Ps 72:10, many hypothesize from Spain). These ships are bringing children and silver and gold from faraway

---

[310] Midianites came from Midian, a son of Abram and Keturah (Gen 15:2). Jethro was from Midian (Exod 3:1). Later they attacked Israel in the time of Gideon (Judg 6:1). Ephah was the son of Midian (Gen 25:4), so these two groups probably come together.

[311] Sheba also comes from Abram (Gen 25:3) and may be the group of traders mentioned in Ezek 27:22 who sell the finest spices, precious stones, and gold.

[312] Oswalt, *Isaiah 40–66*, 542, interprets the flocks figuratively as the leaders of Nabaioth. Later he takes a metaphorical interpretation of God's house as a reference to God's people and the beautification of the house as the joining of the nations. This approach should be avoided unless there is a clear indication of a metaphorical meaning within the text itself.

[313] Root I of the verb קָוָה means "he waited, longed for, hoped for," while root II of קָוָה means "he gathered." Either can make sense in this context. Isaiah 51:5 uses similar vocabulary to create a similar image.

nations to Zion. Why do they come, and what will they do with their gold? They are coming and bringing these people and gold "on account of" ($l\check{e}$)[314] the glorious reputation connected to the name of God throughout the world and on account of the holiness of God. These people will know about this great God because he will reveal himself to the world (cf. 19:19–25; 66:18–23) by saving his people and glorifying Zion by his glorious presence there. When God establishes his kingdom, he will draw all mankind to worship and glorify his name.

TIMES HAVE CHANGED: FOREIGNERS WILL HELP GLORIFY ZION (60:10–16)

[10]"Foreigners will rebuild your walls,
    and their kings will serve you.
  Though in anger I struck you,
    in favor I will show you compassion.
[11]Your gates will always stand open,
    they will never be shut, day or night,
  so that men may bring you the wealth of the nations—
    their kings led in triumphal procession.
[12]For the nation or kingdom that will not serve you will perish;
    it will be utterly ruined.

[13]"The glory of Lebanon will come to you,
    the pine, the fir and the cypress together,
  to adorn the place of my sanctuary;
    and I will glorify the place of my feet.
[14]The sons of your oppressors will come bowing before you;
    all who despise you will bow down at your feet
  and will call you the City of the LORD,
    Zion of the Holy One of Israel.

[15]"Although you have been forsaken and hated,
    with no one traveling through,
  I will make you the everlasting pride
    and the joy of all generations.
[16]You will drink the milk of nations
    and be nursed at royal breasts.
  Then you will know that I, the LORD, am your Savior,
    your Redeemer, the Mighty One of Jacob.

The next paragraph in this oracle of salvation describes what the foreigners will do after they come to Zion. In the past foreigners came with their armies to destroy Jerusalem, but now they will be involved in building the city and temple with cypress wood and gold. Any rebellious nation will perish (60:12), former enemies will humbly serve God and his people (60:14), and everyone

---

[314] Koole, *Isaiah III, Volume 3: Isaiah 56–66*, 237, argues for interpreting the preposition ל as "on account of" rather than the more usual locative "to" ("to bring your sons . . . to the name of God").

will call Zion the "City of the LORD" (60:14). Israel's days of troubles and oppression will be over, for God will make his dwelling place glorious and use the nations to meet the needs of his people. Then all people will realize that the Holy One is their Savior, Redeemer, and Protector (60:16).

The paragraph is divided into two parts.

Nations will build, not tear down the City of God	60:10–14
Foreigners enter and build	10–11
Some foreigners will be destroyed	12
The glorification of Zion	13–14
The hated will be cared for and know the Lord	60:15–16
Rejected will be exalted	15
You will know your Savior	16

This new era when foreigners will assist in the glorification of Zion is set in contrast with Israel's past time of divine wrath and foreign oppression (60:10,14,15). Old relationships will change, for in the future foreigners will come to assist and serve the Israelites, not tear down Jerusalem and kill its citizens.[315] This is because God will no longer act in wrath to punish Israel for its sins. These transformed foreign nations will not only come to minister to the people in Zion, but they will also bring glory to the Lord, the Mighty God who dwells in Zion.

60:10–11 God will transform the foreign nations as well as his ways of dealing with his own people. In the past God used the foreign nations as instruments of his wrath to bring judgment on his people (10:5–6; 54:7–8; 60:10b), but in the future God's relationship with his own people will change and he will have compassion[316] on them and deal with them and the foreign nations in a completely new way. This will happen because God will transform the hearts of his people and the hearts of the people in the foreign nations so that they will want to honor, praise, and glorify God (60:6,9,13). God will send them healing and light (58:8); they will repent of their sins (59:20). God will send his Spirit, give them a new covenant (59:21; 61:8), and in righteousness he will bring salvation to the ends of the world (59:16–17; 66:18–23). After his glory appears in Zion, the Hebrews and the foreign nations will see God's glory and come to worship him. When the foreigners come to Zion with all their gold and silver, they will give it to God to honor him and glorify his dwelling place in Zion (60:6,9,13). Isaiah 60:7b refers to the beautification of the temple where God dwells, but 60:10a mentions the building of walls and v. 11a mentions the reconstructed gates of the city. This agrees with other traditions about this

---

[315] J. Oswalt, "Isaiah 60–62," *CTJ* 40 (2005): 95–103, makes the point (p. 101) that some foreigners will join Israel, others will serve, and those who refuse will be destroyed.

[316] The perfect verb רִחַמְתִּיךְ "I had motherly love, compassion" functions as a prophetic perfect ("I will have motherly love, compassion") describing what God will do in the future (GKC §106n).

theme (44:26; 49:8; 58:12; 61:4), for at that time the foreigners will not only glorify God, they will also assist the Hebrew people in any way they can.

The notification that the gates of Jerusalem will be open "night and day" in 60:11 means all the time, but 60:19 indicates that there will be no night in the future. The open gates may indicate that there is such security at this time that there will be no need to close the "gates, places of entry" (60:18 raises questions about the need for literal gates). Although there may be no need for gates, the reason given for not shutting the gates in v. 11 is that there are so many people coming into Zion with so many gifts that it is necessary to keep the entrances to the city open 24 hours a day "in order that, so that"[317] all the people who march through the gates in procession after procession will have the time to bring their gifts to God.[318] One might compare this to the marching of the nations into an Olympic stadium, except this marching of the nations will go on all day and night for unending days.

60:12   C. Westermann considers this verse to be a prose gloss that was added at a later time by another author.[319] In sharp contrast, J. L. Koole believes the "arguments adduced against the authenticity of 60:12 are not convincing."[320] The words "nation and kingdom" and "they will perish" are found in the first line of this verse, and these are parallel to the words "nations" and "they will lie in utter ruin" in the second line, so there is a good level of poetic parallelism within 60:12. Furthermore, the idea that God would judge a nation that does not serve him is consistent with God's past dealings with Israel in 60:10b,15a and the way that God said he would deal with the rebellious foreign nations in 11:14. The point that 60:10–12 is making is that people (Israel and the nations) may choose to reject God and suffer his punishment (10b,12,15a) or they may choose to serve and glorify God (10a,11,14,15b).

Initially the prophet refers to a single unnamed nation or kingdom that might refuse to honor God with gifts for Zion or might not praise and honor God. That nation's rebellious attitude will mean that "they will perish"[321] under God's divine judgment. No one and no nation will be able to oppose God's establishment of his final glorious kingdom. All people in all nations must bow

---

[317] The infinitive construct לְהָבִיא serves to express either the purpose or the result of their coming (GKC §114f).

[318] Westermann, *Isaiah 40–66*, 360, thinks the gates are open to accommodate all the people, while Whybray, *Isaiah 40–66*, 234, points out that the security of the situation made it unnecessary for them to close the gates.

[319] Westermann, *Isaiah 40–66*, 360, says its subject matter and prose form indicate that v. 12 is a marginal expansion by a later editor. Blenkinsopp, *Isaiah 56–66*, 215, also calls this verse a "prose gloss." Muilenburg, "Isaiah 40–66," 5:703, considers v. 12 "a prosaic addition by a writer who misunderstood and misinterpreted the poet's mood and thought."

[320] Koole, *Isaiah III, Volume 3: Isaiah 56–66*, 221, 241–42. He notices a similar statement about those who fail to serve Nebuchadnezzar in Jer 27:8.

[321] There is a nice wordplay between the similar sounding verbs "they will not serve you" (לֹא־יַעַבְדוּךְ) and "they will perish" (יֹאבֵדוּ).

and worship God or else "they will lie in utter ruins."[322] This verbal construction strongly emphasizes the assurance that God will truly protect his people from their earlier oppressors.

60:13–14 There will be no opposition to God's plans; instead, the glorious things found in Lebanon will come to Zion to beautify it. Earlier the "glory" referred to the glory of God (60:1,2,9), but here it refers to the glorious trees (the pine, fir, and cypress; similar to 10:18; 35:2) that will grow to great heights. This could suggest that they will bring giant logs from these trees to construct God's temple, although the implications of similar language in 35:2 and 41:19 suggest that these glorious trees will be transplanted and will grow in the temple courts.[323] Their purpose is to show the splendor[324] of the place of "my sanctuary, my holy place" (*miqdāšî*), the place where God dwells. God is determined to glorify the place of his royal throne, the place where the metaphorical feet of the transcendent Holy God rest on the earth (66:1; Pss 99:1,5; 132:7).

Although 60:12 describes the elimination of all negative opposition to God, 60:14 pictures those transformed nations that formerly oppressed and despised God's people as traveling to the city of Zion on bended knees,[325] bowing themselves down[326] (cf. Ps 72:9,11) to honor Zion, the City of Yahweh. The former oppressors who will humble themselves are not identified by name, but now they express their great submission to God's authority and give due honor to the place where God dwells. This unforced humility should not be twisted into any kind of Jewish nationalistic oppression of foreigners or an embarrassing enslavement that takes revenge on the enemies of Judah. What these foreign nations will do is no different from what every person must do when they appear before God. All people must humble themselves completely, forsake all temptations of pride and self-worth, and confess their total dependence on the majestic Holy One who rules this world. Ultimately, these nations bow because they have seen the glory of God (60:1–3) and they believe in the Holy God who dwells in Zion. This radical transformation will turn former enemies into fellow worshippers; angry despisers of God will turn into those who honor God and his people. At this time Zion will be holy—its people will be holy and its

---

[322] The use of the infinitive absolute verb חָרֹב "ruining" with the imperfect verb יֶחֱרָבוּ "they will ruin" provides a strong assurance that what is said will happen with absolute certainty (GKC §113n).

[323] Delitzsch, *Isaiah*, 418, takes this position. Childs, *Isaiah*, 498, also finds this to refer to a new paradise with great trees, not an inventory of lumber for temple construction.

[324] The infinitive construct לְפָאֵר "to glorify, beautify," expresses the purpose of the trees" that will grow in the temple courts (GKC §114f).

[325] The infinitive construct can be translated as a gerund when it expresses the attendant circumstances surrounding some action. Thus שְׁחוֹחַ "while bending low" describes how "they will come" (GKC §114o).

[326] The *hithpa'el* verb הִשְׁתַּחֲווּ is a *hištaphel* form of חָוָה with a reflexive meaning of "they will bow themselves down."

visitors will be holy; therefore, it will be honored as a holy city of God and Zion will exist as the city of the great King (48:2; 52:1; Pss 46:5; 48:2,9).

60:15–16 This radical divine transformation of mankind will impact Zion and the Hebrews living there as well. In the past, the sinful city was in the state of being hated and forsaken[327] (compare similar statements in 2:6; 27:10; 49:14,21; 54:6) when God struck it in his anger (60:10b), but no specific war or time of divine punishment is identified. The history of the nation is filled with enemies that hated Israel (Egyptians, Philistines, Edomites, Syrians, Ammonites, Moabites, Assyrians, and Babylonians), but there were only a handful of times when war was so severe that travel was suspended (34:10). This verse declares that in the future these dire circumstances will not ever exist again; "instead" (*taḥat*) God promises that "I will make you, transform you" (from the root *śîm*) into something that is the total opposite of your past experiences. Zion will be eternally "exalted, majestic, glorious" (*gě'ôn*, NIV "pride"),[328] a source of joy for all the generations of people who live in it. This joy and exalted status characterizes the marvelous way God will transform his people and his holy city.

Verse 16 explains a second change involving God's gracious care of Zion. Zion is metaphorically compared to a child being nursed in the royal household or to a child drinking the milk of the nations (similar to 49:23). In the modern world this figure of speech makes little sense and its nonliteral meaning is obvious since real babies do not nurse from the breasts of kings (males). Nursing is a symbol of someone providing physical and emotional satisfaction, tender-loving care, and giving healthy nourishment, so the promise of being nursed in the king's palace or by the foreign nations implies that the child (Zion) will have absolutely the very best care possible with all its needs met. The nations will not suck Israel dry through heavy taxation, forcing the people into slavery or heavy labor; instead, Zion will be filled with the riches of other nations.

When this happens the people of Zion will once again recognize, accept, and acknowledge that Yahweh their God is truly their Savior. The creator of the heavens and the earth, the Holy One of Israel, and the Almighty God of Jacob will have once again demonstrated that he is their Redeemer. When God acts and reveals his redemptive power, people cannot help but realize that he truly is God (43:10; 45:3,6; 49:23b,26b). His glorious and mighty deeds of salvation on behalf of his people will prove beyond a shadow of a doubt that Yahweh is God.

---

[327] The words "hated" שְׂנוּאָה and "forsaken" עֲזוּבָה are both passive participles. The passive participle "indicates the person or thing in a state which has been brought about by external actions" (GKC §116a).

[328] The word גָּאוֹן can describe (a) something "high, majestic, exalted," (b) God's "exalted majesty," and (c) negatively, man's "exalted pride." NIV chose "pride," apparently implying a good kind of pride (4:2), but pride usually has a negative connotation, so "glorious, majestic, exalted" seems a better translation.

THE TRANSFORMATION OF THE NEW CITY OF ZION (60:17–22)

¹⁷Instead of bronze I will bring you gold,
  and silver in place of iron.
Instead of wood I will bring you bronze,
  and iron in place of stones.
I will make peace your governor
  and righteousness your ruler.
¹⁸No longer will violence be heard in your land,
  nor ruin or destruction within your borders,
but you will call your walls Salvation
  and your gates Praise.
¹⁹The sun will no more be your light by day,
  nor will the brightness of the moon shine on you,
for the LORD will be your everlasting light,
  and your God will be your glory.
²⁰Your sun will never set again,
  and your moon will wane no more;
the LORD will be your everlasting light,
  and your days of sorrow will end.
²¹Then will all your people be righteous
  and they will possess the land forever.
They are the shoot I have planted,
  the work of my hands,
  for the display of my splendor.
²²The least of you will become a thousand,
  the smallest a mighty nation.
I am the LORD;
  in its time I will do this swiftly."

The last paragraph in chap. 60 continues the theme of divine transformation mentioned in 60:15 using contrasting "instead of" (*taḥat*) clauses. Four more precious or stronger metals will be used "instead of" weaker metals (60:17a-b), but more significant will be the change in the hearts of their rulers (60:17c) and the end of violence and destruction (60:18). The transformative influence of the light of God's presence will even make the sun and moon redundant (60:19–20). Finally, the prophet points out the transformation of mankind. They will now act only in righteous ways that glorify God (60:21). This paragraph can be divided into three segments.

Changes in looks and behavior	17–18
God's light, not the sun's	19–20
The righteous display God's glory	21–22

In this paragraph there is no mention of the contributions of the nations; instead, the focus is on how "I," God, will give Zion a transformational makeover with superior materials, superior spiritual leaders, a superior state of peace without war, superior spiritual names, the superior light of God's presence, and superior spiritual people who are righteous. God's presence and his promise to transform this world will change everything. He is God, and he will do all these things when he establishes his eschatological kingdom.

60:17–18 This paragraph begins with contrasts between good building materials (copper, iron, wood, and stone) and the best building material (gold, silver, copper, and iron) that could be used to build the new city of Jerusalem. Although King Solomon used much gold in constructing the original temple (1 Kgs 6:19–29; 10:21), through the years foreign kings demanded expensive tribute; consequently, gold and other metals were taken from the temple (1 Kgs 14:25–27; 15:16; 2 Kgs 18:14–15; 24:13; 25:13–17). The walls of the city were of stone; its gates were made of wood covered with bronze (45:2); and the common homes of the average citizen were, of course, not normally built of silver or gold. In the future eschatological kingdom, "instead of" (*tah at*) the common building materials that were usually used in Israel, God will replace them with the best and richest possible metals to glorify every part of the city of Jerusalem and beautify God's dwelling place in the temple. Although there is a danger of being overly literal in conceiving of this New Jerusalem, one should not abandon all literal meanings and completely substitute a spiritual immaterial sense. Usually, the literal and the spiritual are interrelated and work together; thus, it would make little sense to speak about a spiritually superior setting that was dark, drab, and common. The reality of a new spiritual era would naturally include the transformation of the material setting because the two are so naturally interconnected in biblical theology.[329]

The second change (60:17c) will involve the spiritual transformation of the nation's political principles of leadership. Previously the nation had experienced some good and godly leaders like Hezekiah who trusted God like no other king (2 Kgs 18:1–6), but they also had wicked leaders like Ahaz who failed to trust God (7:1–10). In the future the principle of "peace" will be a key governing factor[330] that will guard and direct the nation's relationships. In a real sense there will actually be no need for walls to protect people because peace will reign in that future era (cf. Zech 2:2–4). Righteousness will be the second principle that will serve as "rulers, officials" (*nōgĕśîm*) to guide the nation. In reality the nation will not need rulers, judges, and government officials to keep people in line if everyone follows the principles of righteousness and peace. Selfishness, pride, anger, deceit, covetousness, and every other sort of evil will no longer rule the hearts of mankind. God will transform people's

---

[329] The material and spiritual aspects are combined in the perfect setting in the garden of Eden in Genesis 2–3, but sin caused the cursing of the ground, interpersonal relationships, and the people's spiritual relationship to God. In addition, the blessings and curses in Deut 27–28 demonstrate the direct interconnectedness of the material and spiritual state of the nation.

[330] The word פְּקֻדָּה comes from פָּקַד "he visited, he appointed, he judged." The noun form refers to a government official who watches over, supervises, and judges what is happening.

hearts so that new desires, new godly values, and new motivations will direct their thoughts and actions. C. Westermann observes that there are no messianic expectations in these verses and that this "era of salvation has no king,"[331] but this is a weak argument from silence. Just because the Messiah is not mentioned in this verse does not mean that this part of the scroll disagrees with or contradicts other portions of the prophet's vision of the future. It only takes a brief examination of other messianic (9:6–7; 11:3–4; 16:5; 32:1,15–18) and servant (42:1–4) passages to realize that this royal figure will have a central role in establishing God's righteousness on earth. At this point the text's focus is on how God will transform Zion and instill a new principle (righteousness and peace) that will guide the nation.

Verse 18 describes the third change that will transform the political and social life in Zion. The past life of the nation was characterized by political violence and destruction as nations, tribes, ethnic groups, individuals, political opponents, and enemies struggled to gain more and more power and influence. Since peace and righteousness (60:17; 2:1–4) will guide the behavior of every person within the borders of Zion, television reports and world news will no longer be filled[332] with stories about murders, rapes, muggings, home invasions, stabbings, wars, or any other violent crimes (59:6–7). Instead the people of Zion (the "you" in 18b) will "call, give a name to" (from *qārā'*) your walls "Salvation" and to your gates "Praise." J. Muilenburg concludes that there will be no walls around Jerusalem in that day (also stated in 26:1; Zech 2:2–3); instead, "Salvation" is personified as a wall of God's protection around them.[333] This approach contrasts with what one might conclude from reading 60:10–11 and 54:11–12, but these two different ways of looking at the walls simply express, in physical terms, similar concerns about security and the peaceful state of the New Jerusalem. The reason for calling the gates "Praise" is left unstated. Possibly this name was chosen because all those who enter the city gates will be praising the Lord (60:6b,11) and because the gates are connected with praise in earlier Israelite hymnic traditions (26:1–3; Pss 24:7–10; 100:4; 118:19–20).

---

[331] Westermann, *Isaiah 40–66*, 363. One could look at hundreds of verses in Isaiah and find nothing about the Messiah, but the absence of any reference to the Messiah in these verses does not prove anything because his writings do include other nearby verses that do mention this messianic ideal. If the poem in 61:1–3 is connected to the earlier "servant poem" in 49:8–9 and the anointing of the Spirit to 11:1 and 42:1, then chaps. 60–62 do not completely ignore this important theme.

[332] Literally, "it will not be heard again" לֹא יִשָּׁמַע עוֹד points to the absence of crimes and the results of crimes of violence. עוֹד "again, any longer" is repeated in 18, 19, and 20 to point out the changes God will bring to Zion at this time.

[333] Muilenburg, "Isaiah 40–66," 5:705, and Koole, *Isaiah III, Volume 3: Isaiah 56–66*, 253, view this as describing an eschatological setting when there really would be no walls and gates. Blenkinsopp, *Isaiah 56–66*, 217, compares these new names to the symbolic names given at the dedication of the walls of Jerusalem by Nehemiah (Neh 12:27–43).

60:19–20   The text now returns to the theme of God's glory as the light that will remove all darkness. This moves the topic back to the initial theme in 60:1–3, creating something of an inclusio in this chapter. The glory of God's presence will be so bright that the sun and moon will not be needed "again, any longer" ('ôd).[334] God established the role of the sun and moon at creation to rule over the day and the night[335] in Gen 1:14–18, but once the brightness of God's glory comes to dwell in Zion, that old era will be past and new conditions will prevail. Isaiah 60:19 does not say that God will destroy or remove the sun and moon, just that they will be redundant and rather unnecessary in light of the wonderful light that proceeds from the glory of God. The sun can remove some aspects of darkness, but the real transformation of this world will happen when the light of God's glory removes the blindness and darkness of sin and evil from this world. God's light will be "unending, eternal" ('ôlām), not a temporary light that lasts only twelve hours like the sun (cf. Ps 72:5,17). The concept that God himself will be "your glory" indicates that God's people will be changed by the presence of his glory, will identify with his glory, and will reflect his glory.

Since God's light will replace the sun and moon, their new sun (God himself) and their new moon (God himself) will never set or grow dim ('ôd) "again, any longer" (60:20).[336] The eternality of God's light as a source of light is much greater than the sun and moon, the endurance of his light is much longer, and the confidence one can put in this light gives one much more security. This is because God's glorious light will shine brightly forever, without end. The presence of God's glory is not just a source of light; his glory is a source of complete salvation.

The transforming power of God's salvation will impact every aspect of human existence. One area that God's glorious salvation will transform is the sorrow and mourning that is caused by sickness, violence, and death. The history of Israel and the world as a whole is a story of continuous sinfulness, where one person crushes, destroys, kills, or oppresses another. God's salvation will end the rule of sin and the consequent sorrow that it brings on the oppressed. This theme continues what Isaiah said earlier about the end[337] of all sorrow and tears (30:19; 35:10; 51:11; 61:3) and even the end of death itself (25:8).

---

[334] Childs, *Isaiah*, 499, suggests that the text has now entered the realm of apocalyptic thinking. Because these verses are apocalyptic and have left the realm of this world and its history, Westermann, *Isaiah 40–66*, 364, concludes that vv. 19–20 are a later addition to this text. Yet a similar concept of the future era of God's kingdom is found in 13:10; 24:23; 30:26, so it was not unknown to Isaiah. Zechariah 14:7 picks up this idea, and it also appears again in *1 En.* 18:11–19:3 and Rev 21:23; 22:5, so it does have close connections to apocalyptic literature.

[335] The Old Greek text and 1QIs[a] add "by the night" in connection with the moon, thus giving parallelism with "by day" in the first line. This is probably an addition and not original. If God was shining so brightly that one does not need the sun, then night will cease to exist.

[336] Rev 21:5 describes this same experience when John saw the New Jerusalem coming down out of heaven.

[337] שָׁלְמוּ "they will complete, end" refers to the completion of an earlier era and assumes the

60:21–22 This paragraph ends with a description of the transformed people who will live in Zion. These new conditions of no sinfulness or sorrow are due to the fact that all of the Hebrews and foreigners from the nations "will be"[338] righteous and holy (4:3–4). C. Westermann follows Volz in understanding the "righteous" as merely those who partake in God's salvation, for he does not accept the notion that this chapter "envisages a spiritual change in the nation."[339] J. L. Koole rightly questions this conclusion and argues that the title "righteous" (here and in 56:1–8; 57:1–2) refers to someone who is pious, who walks uprightly (keeps God's ethical norms), acts according to God's will, and is one of God's disciples just like the Servant.[340] Chapter 60 describes a future eschatological era when all of God's sinful enemies are already judged (60:12), so these chapters refer to a future time when this world and all the people in it will undergo a great spiritual transformation. All will be forgiven and all will be holy (4:2–6; 33:24). Justice and righteousness are consistent characteristics of God's future kingdom (9:6–7; 11:4–5; 32:1) and part of what he requires of all those who wish to please him (56:1–2).

At this time the promise to Abram that his descendants will possess the land (Gen 15:7,18–21; 17:7–8) will finally and completely be fulfilled. Earlier when the prophet was describing the glory of Zion in chap. 54, the text specifically states that the descendants of the Hebrews would possess the land, and this is not the only reference to this idea (58:14; 61:7; 65:9). Those who live there are described as "the shoot of my planting"[341] and "the work of my hands." J. D. W. Watts translates the first phrase "Yahweh is the Guardian of his planting"[342] so this verse seems to refer to the righteous people as "my planting," parallel to the vines planted in 5:1–7; 27:2–6 and in 61:3 in the immediate context. Earlier

---

inauguration of a new era, the fulfillment of God's promises. This may well be the end of the era spoken of in 40:2 and the beginning of the era of the coming of the good news in 40:9–11.

[338] The text has a verbless noun clause, "your people, all of them, righteous," that needs to have a "to be" verb supplied (GKC §141f). The tense of the supplied verb must be deduced from the context. In this case a future translation seems most appropriate since the verbs just before and after this noun clause are imperfects.

[339] Westermann, *Isaiah 40–66*, 363, also finds a strong contrast between this unconditional statement that all will be righteous and other statements in chaps. 56–66 that only one group of people in the nation will enjoy the blessings of God. In contrast, Blenkinsopp, *Isaiah 56–66*, 217–18, says that "The promise is not unconditional, and those to whom the promise is addressed in this section of the book are the servant and elect of YHWH (65:9). Possession of 'my holy mountain' is not promised to all, only to those who take refuge in the God of Israel (57:13)."

[340] Koole, *Isaiah III, Volume 3: Isaiah 56–66*, 258, believes צֶדֶק in 1:26; 51:7 and צְדָקָה in 32:16; 33:15; and 54:14 have ethical connotations and cannot be translated "salvation."

[341] The written Heb. text has "his planting" מַטָּעוֹ, while the spoken Heb. *Qere* has "my planting" מַטָּעִי, which matches the first person suffix on "my hands" in the next line.

[342] Watts, *Isaiah 35–66*, 292–94, follows 1QIs^a and inserts יהוה "Yahweh" after this clause and derives the meaning of the noun נֵצֶר from root I, "keeper, guardian" rather than root II, "shoot, sprout." This is a solution first suggested by I. F. M. Brayley, "Yahweh Is the Guardian of His Plantation: A Note on Is 60,21," *Bib* 41 (1960): 275–86. Blenkinsopp, *Isaiah 56–66*, 205, 207, prefers "the shoot that I myself planted."

in 11:1 the "sprout" (*nēṣer*) referred to the Messiah and in 14:19 to the rejected proud king of Babylon, so it may refer to royalty here also. W. A. M. Beuken believes this "sprout" (*nēṣer*) should be identified with the messianic sprout in 11:1.[343] Although the Messiah will be an important part of God's eschatological kingdom, it is not necessary to identify the Messiah as the "sprout" in this verse to prove that point. This verse seems to be talking about God's righteous people, not just one righteous person. The use of the sprout imagery may be saying something about the royal status of all the righteous people in God's future kingdom (or at least hint at a connection between the righteous sprouts and the messianic sprout?). Less problematic is the claim that these people are the work of God's hands, a statement that shows God's shaping of them (43:7) and his identification with them. God's purpose for planting these shoots, working with them, and fulfilling his promise of the land is "to bring glory to myself, to display my splendor" (as in 43:7; 44:23; 60:7,9,13).[344]

The promise to Abram was that God would make of him a great nation and that his children would become as numerous as the stars in the heavens or the dust of the earth (Gen 12:2; 13:15–16; 15:5; 16:10; 22:17). Now God repeats the promise that the most insignificant or powerless person or tribe will greatly multiply and become a thousand strong; the least among the nations will become a mighty and powerful nation. This promise of divine blessing, multiplication, and strengthening can only be explained as the marvelous work of God. The noun clause "I am Yahweh" confirms who will do these things and is an oath-like assurance that promises a sure fulfillment. The audience should not doubt or wonder about these wonderful promises, for when the right time comes and everything is ready, God will quickly act and accomplish what he has promised. This assurance to every believer is an encouragement to faithfully persevere each day, but it also provides hope that soon God will come for his righteous people and end the misery that is associated with this sinful world.

(2) The Anointed One Announces God's Favor (61:1–11)

Although God speaks in chap. 60, the one anointed by God is the dominant speaker in chap. 61. This passage describes how God has anointed him with the Spirit and has tasked him with several responsibilities (61:1–3) that are similar to some of the duties of the Servant in chaps. 42 and 49. His work will benefit the broken-hearted, involve the rebuilding of ruined cities, cause the nations to bring their riches, and result in a double blessing (61:4–7). This will happen because God hates injustice and will reward his people with an everlasting covenant (61:8–9). God's great salvation will bring a great outpouring of joy and praise from his people (61:10–11).

---

[343] Koole, *Isaiah III, Volume 3: Isaiah 56–66*, 259, refers to the conclusions of Beuken.

[344] The *hithpa'el* infinitive construct verb לְהִתְפָּאָר is reflexive and used to show purpose, "in order to glorify myself" (GKC §114f).

This message of salvation explains how God will accomplish the great salvation already announced in chap. 60. Before God appears in all his glory, he will offer salvation to all people through the work of the Anointed One, through God's faithfulness to the eternal covenant, and through a double divine blessing. God will transform his people, their situation, his city, and the nations who observe God's blessings on his people. This transformation will bring good news, freedom, God's favor, comfort, gladness, the splendor of the Lord, rebuilding, wealth, a double portion of blessing, and an everlasting covenant. Then people who acknowledge God will rejoice, be saved, and praise God. What a wonderful, marvelous, and glorious time this will be!

The structure of this news of God's salvation is organized into three paragraphs.

God's Anointed One preaches good news	61:1–7
God's faithfulness and covenant with his people	61:8–9
A joyous response to God's blessings	61:10–11

Chapter 61 is closely interconnected to its context. The figure in 59:21 who has God's Spirit on him and God's words in his mouth can probably be connected to the figure in 61:1–3 who has received God's Spirit. The everlasting covenant that he will make in 61:8 can be connected to the covenant God's provides in 55:3 and 59:21. The reversal of conditions through God's transformative power in 60:15–21 is paralleled with additional reversals in 61:3–7. Both chapters mention the "righteous" (60:21; 61:3) as the "plantings of the Lord" (60:21; 61:3), plus both describe the riches of the nations that will come to Zion (60:5–9; 61:6), but it is obvious that chap. 61 is placed in a temporal setting sometime before chap. 60. In chap. 60 the glory of the Lord has already appeared and the righteous are living in Zion glorifying God, but in chap. 61 the people are still broken-hearted and in need of freedom (61:2), grieving and mourning (61:3), and still looking forward to that time when God will pour out his double blessing (61:7). Isaiah 61:9 looks forward to a day when the nation will observe what God has done for his people and acknowledge God themselves, but in 60:3–16 the nations are already coming to Zion to worship and glorify God.

GOD'S ANOINTED ONE PREACHES GOOD NEWS (61:1–7)

¹The Spirit of the Sovereign LORD is on me,
   because the LORD has anointed me
   to preach good news to the poor.
He has sent me to bind up the brokenhearted,
   to proclaim freedom for the captives
   and release from darkness for the prisoners,
²to proclaim the year of the LORD's favor
   and the day of vengeance of our God,
to comfort all who mourn,

³and provide for those who grieve in Zion—
  to bestow on them a crown of beauty
    instead of ashes,
  the oil of gladness
    instead of mourning,
  and a garment of praise
    instead of a spirit of despair.
  They will be called oaks of righteousness,
    a planting of the LORD
    for the display of his splendor.

⁴They will rebuild the ancient ruins
  and restore the places long devastated;
  they will renew the ruined cities
    that have been devastated for generations.
⁵Aliens will shepherd your flocks;
  foreigners will work your fields and vineyards.
⁶And you will be called priests of the LORD,
  you will be named ministers of our God.
  You will feed on the wealth of nations,
    and in their riches you will boast.

⁷Instead of their shame
  my people will receive a double portion,
  and instead of disgrace
    they will rejoice in their inheritance;
  and so they will inherit a double portion in their land,
    and everlasting joy will be theirs.

A central interpretive issue in this paragraph is the identity of the person God anoints and sends out to share the good news in 61:1–3. The Aramaic Targum and many commentators today identify this person as the prophet Isaiah,³⁴⁵

---

³⁴⁵ Westermann, *Isaiah 40–66*, 366; Whybray, *Isaiah 40–66*, 239–40; Muilenburg, "Isaiah 40–66," 5:709–10; and P. A. Smith, *Rhetoric and Redaction in Trito-Isaiah*, 34, believe 61:1–3 refer to the "a prophetic figure." The view of Watts, *Isaiah 34–66*, 302, that this anointed one is the Persian king Artaxerxes should be rejected, and Hanson's *The Dawn of Apocalyptic*, 60–67, conclusion that this refers to the collective voice of the Levitical-visionary minority group that opposed the Zadokite-led hierocratic group seems most unlikely. Seitz, "Isaiah 40–66," 504–505, concludes that the first person voice in chap. 61 is the prophet "Trito-Isaiah," but he views him "as a servant follower of the martyred servant of 52:13–53:12." This is similar to the opinion of W. A. M. Beuken, "Servant and Herald of Good News: Isaiah 61 as an Interpretation of Isaiah 40–55," in Vermeglen, *The Book of Isaiah: Le Livre D'Isaïe*, 411–42, who concludes that the servant figure is a fluid figure, so the person in chap. 61 is presented as a manifestation of the servant, but actually he is one of the offspring of the Servant and not the Servant himself. This is heavily based on 44:2–3 where the text indicates that God will pour out his Spirit on "your offspring" (this person in chap. 61 is that offspring). Blenkinsopp, *Isaiah 56–66*, 221, maintains that "the mission to utter spirit-inspired prophecy will be carried on into the future by the disciples of the seer who is here addressed . . . the voice we are hearing in 61:1–3 is that of a disciple of the Servant and therefore one of the 'Servants of YHWH' mentioned in chs. 65–66." R. Heskett, *Messianism within*

but this understanding does not pay enough attention to the many interlinking connections between this passage and earlier statements in the book of Isaiah. Consequently, it is not surprising to find that 1QMelchizedek in the Qumran literature and the New Testament (Luke 4:18–19) connected this person to the Messiah and the ministry of Jesus. Since the prophet operated within Israelite history and the figure in 61:1–3 functions within the eschatological era described in chaps. 60–62, this person cannot refer to the prophet Isaiah, "Trito-Isaiah," or some ruler (Artaxerxes) in the past.[346] The role and responsibilities of this person allude to roles similar to that of the Servant in chaps. 42; 49; 50; and 53. In 42:1; 48:16; and 61:1, both figures are endowed with God's Spirit, a gifting that also applied to the Messiah in 11:2.[347] Although some different roles are emphasized for each figure, there are overlapping characteristics that suggest that these figures may be the same individual.[348] The expectation that someone would come and proclaim "good news" was hinted at earlier in 40:9; 41:27; and 52:7. In 40:9 the people of Zion are those who proclaim this good news to the cities of Judah, and it is assumed that God was the one who announced this good news to these heralds. In 41:27 God indicates that he will give Jerusalem a "messenger of good news," and 52:7 refers to "the messenger

---

the Scriptural Scrolls of Isaiah (London: T&T Clark, 2007), 225–38, reviews the various opinions of over 50 authors.

[346] Heskett, Messianism within the Scriptural Scrolls of Isaiah, 260, uses this line of reasoning to exclude an Old Testament prophet.

[347] J. Collins, The Scepter and the Star: The Messiahs of the Dead Sea Scrolls and Other Ancient Literature (New York: Doubleday, 1995), 118, 205, believes that because this person "claims to be anointed, and so he is מָשִׁיחַ, or "the anointed one," the Messiah. S. Mowinckel, He that Cometh (Oxford: Blackwell, 1956), 226, 255, connects the speaker in 61:1–3 to the servant in 42; 49; 50; 52–53, but that servant is identified with "Second-Isaiah." W. Brueggemann, Isaiah 40–66, WBC (Louisville: Westminster John Knox, 1998), 213, connects the anointing and the coming of the Spirit with what happened to David; thus he understands the person in chap. 61 to be a royal figure, though he does not call him the Messiah. W. Kaiser, The Messiah in the Old Testament (Grand Rapids: Zondervan, 1995), 183, claims that "Isaiah displays a Messianic figure." B. Webb, The Message of Isaiah, BST (Downers Grove: InterVarsity, 1997), 233–34, connects this person in chap. 61 to "both the Servant of chapters 40–66 and the Messiah of chapters 1–35."

[348] The gifting by the Spirit in 11:2 is for the royal duties that require wisdom, understanding, counsel, power, knowledge, and fear of the Lord, which all allow one to judge with righteousness and care for the poor and needy. The gifting of the Spirit in 42:1 also is for the royal duties of bringing justice to the nations, but it also involves his care for the bruised reed and the smoldering wick. Later in 49:1–13; 50:4–11; 52:13–53:12, additional roles are assigned to the Servant. The gifting of the Spirit in 61:1–3 includes prophetic responsibilities of preaching and caring for the poor, using terms almost identical to 42:7 and 49:9. In 45:1 Cyrus is anointed, but there is no reference to the Spirit in this case. Williamson, Variations on a Theme: King, Messiah and Servant in the Book of Isaiah, 178, concludes that "the most plausible point of association for the reference to anointing is to Cyrus, in the sense that this figure is consciously taking over part of his unfinished work." Nevertheless, the anointed person in chap. 61 does not (as in chap. 45) "subdue nations" and "break down gates of bronze and cut through bars of iron," nor is the person in chap. 61 promised the "treasures of darkness." Even when there is some similarity of thought (the bringing of freedom to captives), it is God who opens doors and breaks down gates, not Cyrus, so in reality the comparison is more between God's work and the work of the Anointed One.

of good news" of peace and salvation. The Servant is never called a "messenger of good news"; thus, the description of these individuals is not completely synonymous, for in each new discussion different emphases are developed. The Servant passages tend to describe the work of the Servant, while 61:1–3 focus more on the proclamation of the good news. A central point to remember is that the Servant's work did bring salvation (49:6b,8), the central aspect of God's good news. The three verbs ("to proclaim the good news, to call out, and to comfort"[349]), which are used to describe the work of the Anointed One in 61:1–2, are not used in earlier Servant poems to describe the role of the Servant, but 49:13 does indicate that his work will bring comfort. Several other terms in 61:1–3 do appear in the paragraphs about the Servant. (a) Verse one refers to bringing good news to the "poor, afflicted ones" (*ʿănāwîm*), while 49:13 announces comfort for "his afflicted ones" (*ʿănîyāw*).[350] (b) Verse 1 also mentions a coming release of "those bound" (*ʾăsûrîm*), while 42:7 predicts the release of the "prisoner, bound ones" (*ʾassîr*) and 49:9 describes God's work on behalf of "those bound" (*ʾăsûrîm*). (c) Verse 1 refers to "opening" (*pĕqaḥ*) the prison, while 42:7 mentions "opening" (*lipqōaḥ*) eyes that were blind. (d) The "year of favor" in verse 2 appears to be equivalent to the "time of favor" in 49:8. (e) The word "faint" (*kēhâ*) appears in both 61:3 and in 42:3. Thus, some of the good news proclaimed by the Anointed One in chap. 61 appears to be an expanded proclamation about the work of the Servant.[351] The overall function of both the "Anointed One" in 61:1–3 and the "Servant" in chaps. 42 and 49 is to bring God's salvation to his people so that the nations will see God's marvelous work and turn to him.

The material in 61:1–7 is grouped into two parts.

The work of the Anointed One	61:1–3
Proclaiming the good news	1
Announcing God's favor and wrath	2
Gladness instead of despair	3
God's blessings on Zion	61:4–7
Renewal of devastation	4
Help from foreigners	5
Wealth for God's ministers	6
Blessing instead of shame	7

The first subparagraph (61:1–3) is all about what the Anointed One will say and do for the people who are in despair. Once the Anointed One is introduced, his

---

[349] The root for "comfort" (נחם) is used in 40:1; 49:13; 51:3,12,19; 52:9; 54:11; 61:2.

[350] The messianic figure in 11:4 also will bring just judgment for the afflicted.

[351] M. Sweeney, "Reconceptualization of the Davidic Covenant in Isaiah," 41–62, points out numerous literary connections between 61:1–3 and earlier messages in Isaiah. Similar connections are identified by R. B. Chisholm, "The Christological Fulfillment of Isaiah's Servant Songs," *BSac* 163 (2006): 387–404.

responsibilities are described using a series of six infinitive construct verbs that will bring hope "instead of" (*taḥat*) hopelessness. The second subparagraph (61:4–7) describes how God will use various groups of people to bring special blessings on Zion "instead of" (*taḥat*) shame.

61:1 The coming of the Spirit is repeatedly connected to significant changes on the earth and God's establishment of his Kingdom (11:2; 32:15; 42:1; 44:3; 48:16; 59:21), but the "me" who receives the Spirit in this verse is not immediately identified by name. God's anointing of a person is often connected to the reception of the Spirit (1 Sam 10:1,9–10; 16:13; 2 Sam 23:1–2; 1 Kgs 19:16), but the key factor to be noted is that it is God who empowers and directs this person through the Spirit. Thus the Anointed One is doing tasks assigned by God (he was sent by God), and the power of the Spirit will guarantee that he will successfully accomplish the will of God. Although this paragraph is not structured like other call narratives (Isaiah 6; Jeremiah 1; Ezekiel 1–3),[352] it does give a detailed description of the tasks God has assigned to this Anointed One. Essentially, his responsibilities overlap with and echo several of the tasks assigned to the Servant (42:7; 49:9–10; 50:4), although the emphasis in this paragraph is focused much more on the proclamation and comfort provided through words rather than through acts of bringing forth justice (42:1–4) or restoring Israel and the nations (42:6; 49:6,8–9).

The general assignment is to preach the good news. The content of the good news is a message of hope proclaimed to people in Zion (61:3a) who are presently "afflicted, poor," "broken-hearted," "captives," or "prisoners" (61:1). Isaiah 61:3 indicates that some in the audience "mourn" or "grieve," but these negative characteristics are so general that it is very difficult to tie them down to any specific historical setting. C. Westermann does not believe these terms refer to the deliverance of people in exile but relates this condition to the need for relief from the economic debts mentioned in 58:6.[353] Nevertheless, none of these clauses ever reveal why the audience is presently in this difficult condition, and they do not appear to describe the people who returned to Jerusalem after the exile. Therefore, it is just as possible for one to suggest that these

---

[352] Seitz, "Isaiah 40–66," 514, concludes that this is not a call narrative, but "in some sense it offers a clarification of a call already underway"; thus in some ways this clarification is similar to Isaiah 6, for in that situation God redirected or clarified the call of Isaiah because the prophet was entering a new era when people would not listen to what God said and when God was planning to harden the hearts of many and bring judgment on the nation.

[353] So Westermann, *Isaiah 40–66*, 366, but this may misconceive the setting since 61:1–3 does not say that economic indebtedness was the reason why people were broken-hearted, captives, or in prison. Childs, *Isaiah*, 506, also believes this refers to "release from economic slavery within the land." Bradley, "The Postexilic Exile in Third Isaiah: Isaiah 61:1–3 in Light of Second Temple Hermeneutics," 488, believes the author is describing a release of people from exile even after many people have already returned from exile because the author has made the hermeneutical move of regarding the exile as an ongoing theological state of the people (rather than an historical reality at that time), partially based on the view of the exile in the prayers in Neh 9:32,36–37 and Ezra 9:7.

heartbroken people who are mistreated refers to the same righteous group of people who were mistreated in 57:1–2 and the contrite and lowly people of 57:15.[354] This would indicate that the author makes a clear distinction between the righteous who suffer and the oppressors who afflict the righteous.[355]

The audience is made up of the "afflicted" (*ʿănāwîm*), a term that can refer to anyone who is oppressed by others or humble before God.[356] The broken-hearted are despondent in spirit and discouraged, probably the people in 57:15 that God will revive. The reason why they are broken-hearted is unknown, but physical, social, or spiritual problems might cause this condition. "Captives" (from *šĕbî*) could refer to those taken as prisoners in a time of war or those bound for economic or spiritual reasons. "Those bound" (*ʾăsûrîm*, NIV "prisoners") could hypothetically relate to the "release" (*dĕrôr*) of slaves in the Sabbatical year or the year of Jubilee (Lev 25:10; Deut 15:12; Jer 34:8,15,17), but this is questionable for there is limited evidence that the Hebrews followed this practice throughout their history. The picture of these individuals in 61:1–3 is quite imprecise and their condition does not point to a specific identifiable situation in the history of the nation. The overall content of chap. 61 suggests that it refers to a time shortly before the establishment of the kingdom of God.

The specific tasks assigned to this Anointed One who was sent by God are outlined in a series of infinitive construct clauses. First, this Anointed One is "to proclaim good news" (the infinitive construct *lĕbaśśēr*)[357] by telling people that their past situations will change and that a new period of history is about to begin. This idea of sharing the "good news" of what God will do is found at several points in the book of Isaiah. In the eschatological setting of 40:9, God encourages "those who bring good news" (*mebaśśeret*) from Jerusalem to lift up their voices and proclaim that God is here and graciously reigns over his people with peace and salvation (41:27; 52:7; 60:6). If one can connect the proclamation of good news in 61:1 with the good news in 40:9 and 52:7, then the essential point of this good news is that "God reigns" and his eschatologi-

---

[354] Seitz, "Isaiah 40–66," 514, takes this option and connects this righteous group of people with those afflicted in 51:21 and the afflicted in 54:11. Bradley, "The Postexilic Exile in Third Isaiah: Isaiah 61:1–3 in Light of Second Temple Hermeneutics," 483–84 makes the case that this was socioeconomic oppression by those who controlled the temple.

[355] There is a tendency on the part of some commentators to distinguish the author of chaps. 60–62 from the author of the rest of chaps. 56–66 based on the conclusion that the author of chaps. 60–62 does not distinguish between the righteous and wicked chaps. 56–59 and chaps. 63–66 do distinguish between these groups), but 61:1–3 appears to identify two groups (the righteous and the oppressors) in Jerusalem before the coming of God's kingdom.

[356] Root II of עָנָה speaks of being powerless and thus vulnerable to being taken advantage of by those with greater power. This term may describe those "oppressed" by a strong military, those who are "needy, poor" for financial reasons, or those who are "weak" or "afflicted" by the wealthy and powerful. This term can also be used in a positive sense of the "humble, meek, lowly" (66:2; Num 12:3; Prov 3:34; 16:19), who out of a righteous heart and a great fear of God walk humbly and with a contrite spirit in this world.

[357] The infinitive construct expresses God's purpose in sending this person (GKC §114f).

cal kingdom is going to begin. This means that the problems associated with righteous people living in a sinful world will end when God's reign is fully established.

Second, this person was sent by God "to bind up"[358] or heal (Ps 147:3) the hurts of his people. This seems to be related to 30:18–26, which describes God's salvation as arriving and transforming this world. There will be no more adversity when the righteous see God with their own eyes, for he will defeat their enemies, bless their land, "bind up" the bruises, and heal the wounds that he inflicted on them. It is unclear how this will happen. Will spoken words miraculously bring this healing and bind up these wounds, or will there be some other method of accomplishing this task? Third, this Anointed One is "to proclaim" (*liqrōʾ*) liberty,[359] a term that is used in Jer 34:8,15,17 to refer to the release of slaves, which should happen every six years (Exod 21:2–3; Lev 25:12; Deut 15:12–15). It would be somewhat dangerous to read all this background of releasing slaves into the use of this term in 61:1 and thereby limit the use of this term solely to the release of slaves from bondage. At minimum, this could involve the proclamation of a metaphorical release from any past social or spiritual enslavement the people were under. In addition, one wonders if this task only involves proclaiming something to be so, or whether this person will do something to accomplish this release.

61:2 The fourth task is also "to proclaim" (*liqrōʾ*), but now the one speaking declares that the "favorable year of the Lord" and the "day of vengeance" of our God has arrived. In 34:8 and 63:5 the day of God's vengeance refers to the time when God will pour out his wrath and bring just judgment on the wicked. Earlier in 49:8 (also 60:10) the "year of God's favor" is associated with the "day of salvation" when God has compassion on his people. It is that time when God enacts his eternal covenant to restore his people and restore their land. These events appear to describe what will happen on the Day of the Lord when "our God" begins to reign in power in his new kingdom.

The fifth role for this person is to comfort all those who were mourning and sorrowing. Isaiah 60:20 suggests that all mourning will end in God's everlasting kingdom. Isaiah 57:18–19 provides more detail about God's comforting of these mourners when it describes this comforting as healing the lowly and contrite, guiding them, bringing peace, and causing them to praise God. This will bring healing and peace to all. Again one wonders if this "Anointed One" will only proclaim what God will do, which is as far as this verse goes, or if he

---

[358] This infinitive construct לַחֲבֹשׁ "to bind up" conveys the purpose of restoration to physical or spiritual health.

[359] Koole, *Isaiah III, Volume 3: Isaiah 56–66*, 272, connects this root דְּרוֹר to the Akkadian *durārun* "to be exempt from tax," thus it refers to release or freedom, similar to the freedom gained on the sabbatical year or Jubilee year (Leviticus 25). R. B. Chisholm, "The Christological Fulfillment of Isaiah's Servant Songs," 402, n. 39, also refers to early decrees form Isin, Larsa, Eshnunna, and Babylon that remit debts and provide freedom for people sold into slavery.

will play a central part by doing something (as in the Servant passages) in order to make this day of comfort possible.

61:3 The sixth responsibility of this "Anointed One" is "to provide" (*lāśûm*, NIV "and provide") for those grieving in Zion "by giving"[360] them something new and "beautiful, glorious" (*pĕ'ēr*)[361] for their head. This will replace their past use of "ashes" (*'ēper*, a word play on *pĕ'ēr*), a sign of mourning. In addition, in order to emphasize the stark contrast with the past, the author compares this transformation of life to having oil (Pss 23:5; 45:8, which contrasts with the times of mourning), a festive headdress (3:20; Ezek 44:18), or an opulent garment that is worn in a time of praise instead of ashes at a time of fainting and mourning. This metaphorical way of describing the outward transformation of a person's clothes and behavior betrays a deep transformation of this person's situation as well as their psychological reaction (by their "spirit" *rûaḥ*) to the changes God will introduce at this time (60:20, "the days of mourning will be completed"). The point is that mourning, which was so often a part of the nation's history, will end and praise will begin. The head ornament (a positive symbol) will be used "instead of" the ashes (a negative symbol) because a new era of salvation has arrived.

The final part of 61:3 identifies the new people of Zion, after the "Anointed One" accomplishes all his work, as "oaks of righteousness" and as the "plantings of the LORD." The second metaphorical designation is connected to this same imagery in 60:21b. These "plantings" (his people) are God's vines planted in his vineyard (5:1–7; 27:2–6), and at this time they will produce the fruit of righteousness instead of bad fruit. The symbolism of being like oaks may communicate how strong, well-rooted, and glorious these righteous people will be. These are the people that God planted "to bring glory to himself" (60:21b)[362] for all the marvelous things that he has done. This purpose clause indicates that one of the main goals of mankind will be to fulfill this joyful responsibility of glorifying God forever. Those who receive God's good news, freedom, comfort, and experience this transformation will have many reasons to loudly praise and glorify God's name.

61:4 The next paragraph (61:4–7) no longer refers to the purposes or goals of the "Anointed One"; instead, it focuses on how God will bless the city

---

[360] The first infinitive construct לָשׂוּם "to provide" is used to show purpose (GKC §114f), but the second infinitive construct לָתֵת (from נָתַן) is used to express attendant circumstances or manner "by giving" (GKC §114o, although NIV renders it "to bestow"). Many commentators omit the phrase, "to provide for the mourners of Zion" (NIV "for those who grieve in Zion"; McKenzie, Whybray), although others emend the text by changing the verb or adding words that may have been lost in transmission (Westermann), but the text can make sense as it presently stands.

[361] The word פְּאֵר is derived from the verbal root פָּאַר "to be beautiful, glorify," which appeared frequently in chap. 60. This noun probably denotes a glorious crown, in some ways comparable to the glorious headpiece of a bride (61:10) or a priest (Exod 39:28; Ezek 44:13).

[362] The *hithpa'el* infinitive construct verb לְהִתְפָּאֵר is reflexive and is used to show purpose "in order to glorify himself" (GKC §114f).

and all the people in it. These changes might be called the subsidiary consequences that arise out of the marvelous, transformative work of God and his
Anointed One. These announcements confirm that the work of this "Anointed
One" will be successful and bring about dramatic changes for Zion and for the
people who dwell in Zion. One of the ways these people will bring glory to
God will be through the rebuilding of Zion. This repeats what was said earlier
in 58:12 (and hinted at in 49:8 and 54:3), using the common vocabulary of
"building" and "raising up" what various enemies destroyed in earlier days.
The ruins of these devastated cities are not connected to any specific war in
this text; rather, they encompass the destruction caused by all the wars of their
forefathers over the past, many generations.[363] Isaiah 61:4 expands the earlier
picture of rebuilding (49:19; 60:10,18) by adding the thought that "they will
renew" (ḥiddĕšû) the ruined cities. It is possible that this new day and these
new things may well be connected to the renewal of the heaven and the earth
(65:17; 66:22) that seem to go along with the new name for Zion (60:14; 62:2).
The coming of these new conditions could also be connected to the coming of
the servant in 42:9–10, the new spirit in Ezek 11:19; 36:26, and the new covenant in Jer 31:31; Ezek 37:26. These conditions imply a new era of history, a
return to a wonderful life in the land and an expanding population of righteous
Hebrews and foreigners.

61:5 This renewed city will have both Hebrews and non-Hebrews from
many foreign nations in it. Isaiah 60:3–16 describe some of the foreigners who
will come with gifts and sacrifices to give to God. Once these people have
arrived and have worshipped the Lord (56:3–7; 60:70), not all of them will
immediately return to their homelands (66:18–20), but some will assist the
Hebrews by shepherding their sheep, plowing their fields, and dressing their
vineyards. This describes a reversal of roles in the past. Earlier the Israelites
had worked their land and cared for their flocks in order to pay the heavy taxes
that foreign nations demanded of them, but in the future these foreigners "will
stand" (ʿāmdû)[364] before the Israelites, waiting and ready to help them in any
way they can. There is no indication that this involves any kind of forced labor
or revenge against the nation; rather, one should assume that this service will
be done out of gratitude, thankfulness, and cooperation.

61:6 Now the message directly addresses ("you," ʾattem), the future righteous Hebrew audience in Zion. In this new kingdom they will not be kings,

---

[363] Literally, וָדוֹר דּוֹר means "generation and generation," but it functions to express the idea
of "many generations." The same construction is found in 58:12 and is similar to the slightly varied
construction "from generation to generation" in 34:10,17 and 13:20; 51:8. "Many generations"
refers to what happened "in the past, formerly" רִאשֹׁנִים and what happened in "ancient, eternity
past" עוֹלָם; thus, these terms should not be limited to or related to the deeds of Nebuchadnezzar
or Cyrus.

[364] The perfect verb וְעָדְמוּ should be interpreted as perfect with *waw* consecutive, indicating
a future event (GKC §112x).

taskmasters, or judges of the nations; instead, they will focus their attention on serving God and others by functioning as "priests of Yahweh" and "ministers, servants of our God." This does not mean that all Levitical tribal responsibilities will be abolished or democratized[365] (though this priestly group will be expanded according to 66:19–21); it just means that all the Israelites will now function in the role God originally designed for them in Exod 19:6. They will have a spiritual role of ministering to the nations; thus, the nations will recognize[366] the special status of those who were used by God to bring knowledge of the truth to these nations. As priests the Israelites mediate the riches of God's blessings to the nations, so it is not surprising that the nations will joyfully share their riches to supply the material needs (the food to eat) of those who minister to them. In the past the Israelites supplied food for the priest, but now the foreign nations will provide food for the Israelites who will then be considered priests of God.

The final phrase is difficult because of textual variants, numerous hypothetical emendations, and some confusion concerning the root that this verb comes from. If the emendations that change the text are set to one side, one needs to choose between three main options. (a) The verb comes from the root *yāmar* or *mûr* "to exchange," and the people are taking the glorious riches of the nations in exchange for their service as priests. (b) The verb comes from the root *yāmar* or *mûr* "to exchange," and the people are exchanging their clothes for glorious priestly garments.[367] (c) The verb comes from root II of *'āmar,* "speak proudly, boast, glory" (following 1QIs[a]), so the Israelites are "boasting, glorying" in these riches. None of these options are overly convincing, so any solution must be tentative. The third suggestion is followed in several translations (NIV "boasts"), but since elsewhere in these immediate chapters people are pictured as glorifying God (60:6,9,19) and riches are given to glorify God's dwelling place, it seems rather unusual, if not inappropriate, for the Israelites to boast or glory in the riches of these nations. There is no obvious solution to this problem, but option (b) may make the best sense. Since these people are now called priests or ministers of the Lord, it would be natural for them to be fed and be clothed in the glorious things brought by the nations.[368]

---

[365] Hanson, *The Dawn of Apocalyptic*, 68, believes that this refers to an "astonishing democratization of the formerly exclusive sacerdotal office," but Blenkinsopp, *Isaiah 56–66*, 226, rightly rejects this hypothesis, concluding that the Gentiles will support the Israelites, just like the laity formerly supported the priests. Schramm, *Opponents of Third Isaiah*, 145, does not accept the view that the priesthood will be abolished at this time and everything will be democratized.

[366] This recognition of the Israelites' status is signified by how the nations will refer to them, using two *niphal* passive verbs ("they will be called" תִּקָּרֵא; "it will be said" יֵאָמֵר). This naming is a confession or a statement of the beliefs of the nations concerning the new spiritual role of Israel. This is comparable to the similar naming in 60:18; 61:3; 62:2–4. Each represents the new reality of life in God's kingdom.

[367] Koole, *Isaiah III, Volume 3: Isaiah 56–66*, 284, summarizes these and other options but prefers option (b).

[368] The literal translation might be "you yourselves will change (garments) into their glorious things"; the garments mentioned in 61:3 are implied (cf. 52:1; Exod 28:2,40).

61:7 This paragraph ends with additional "instead of" (*taḥat*) statements similar to those in 60:17 and 61:3. The text is somewhat cryptic, so a verb needs to be supplied in the first line ("there will be");[369] in the second line one must supply a second, parallel, "instead of" prepositional contrast.[370] Israel's old way of life involved sin, rebellion, divine judgment, and the emotional feelings of shame, but God promises that their new life in God's kingdom will substitute a "double"[371] portion (cf. 40:2) instead of shame. The content of the "double" portion is not defined, but the parallelism with the next line implies that the double portion must be something extraordinarily good. The second implied "instead of" clause contrasts the nation's many past periods of dishonor with the future promise that the people will rejoice in the new apportionment of land that God will give them (implying a great honor). The last two lines do not add more "instead of" contrasts but explain the resulting changes ("therefore," *lākēn*; NIV "and so") that the first half of the verse describes. The "double"[372] refers to a double portion of land the people will possess when God brings about these changes, while the "rejoicing" refers to an "everlasting joy" that they will have. The theological perspective that underlies these actions is that God, the owner of the land, has graciously given possession of it to his people (Lev 25:23). He does not view it as sold permanently to any foreigner or debtor; therefore, he directs that the land should come back to the original family that received it as an everlasting possession (Lev 25:8–28). In 61:7 the Israelites will receive back double, not only their original possession of land, but also the wealth of the nations. Surely this will be a cause for great joy.

GOD'S FAITHFULNESS AND COVENANT WITH HIS PEOPLE (61:8–9)

8"For I, the LORD, love justice;
   I hate robbery and iniquity.
In my faithfulness I will reward them
   and make an everlasting covenant with them.

---

[369] The NIV adds the verb "they will receive," but usually in a verbless noun clause one should supply a "to be" verb (GKC §141b); thus, one might translate the clause "instead of your shame, (there will be) a double portion."

[370] Frequently, synonymous lines of parallel poetry may have one member in the second line missing (in this case the preposition "instead of"). In such cases the missing member of the second line can be supplied in the second line when the two lines show close parallelism.

[371] J. M. Lindenberger, "How Much for a Hebrew Slave? The Meaning of *Mišneh* in Deut 15:18," *JBL* 110 (1991): 479–82, rejects M. Tsevat's translation of מִשְׁנֶה as "equivalent" based on the use of the word *mištannu* in an Akkadian text from Alalakh. He concludes that this Akkadian word means "to pay," not double or equivalent, so it has nothing to do with the meaning of מִשְׁנֶה in Deut 15:18 or this text in Isaiah.

[372] One wonders if this thought may have some connection to a similar idea in 40:3 where God announces the comforting news that when his kingdom comes and all flesh see the glory of God (40:5), Zion will receive double (using a different root [כִּפְלַיִם] than what is found here) for all her sins. Double blessings would be a comforting word, while double punishment would be a discouraging word.

⁹**Their descendants will be known among the nations**
 and their offspring among the peoples.
All who see them will acknowledge
 that they are a people the LORD has blessed."

The flow of thought is briefly interrupted by a divine speech that affirms (a) the theological principles that characterize the actions of a covenanting God and (b) the results that this action will have on all the nations of the world that observe what God will do for his covenant people. This statement by God reaffirms or confirms the truthfulness of some of the promises already made by the "Anointed One" in 61:1–7.[373]

61:8 The initial *kî* "surely, truly" assures the reader that the speaker "I, Yahweh" is a God who "loves"[374] actions characterized by justice. Love is a choice of the will that God makes; it is his choice to be emotionally involved by displaying his deep commitment to his people and to show his approval of a specific kind of favored action. God's choice to love just action is evident in all his behavior; it is central to his command that the Israelites should "maintain justice" (56:1) and his advice to avoid injustice (58:6; 59:4,8,14,15). When "justice and salvation/righteousness" are used of God's activity, justice can take on the meaning of "saving justice" or God's "just saving deeds" (59:11,14), but when it refers to human acts of justice, it refers to moral behavior that treats other people with equity and fairness. In order to emphasize the point, God states that he hates (the opposite of loves) human actions that involve unjust taking of things that belong to others as well as all other acts of "iniquity."[375]

Those who are fully committed to God's moral standards of justice will receive from God an appropriate "response, compensation." Elsewhere God promises to bring his "recompense, reward, what is due" (40:10; 49:4; 62:11) with him when he comes to earth, although it is never fully described. God can be counted on to do this because he acts in "faithfulness, truthfulness" (*'emet*) with those he loves. The essence of what God is talking about is a covenant agreement that he has with his righteous followers. This will be an eternal covenant relationship with his people, probably the same covenant spoken about in 54:10; 55:3; 59:21. God is here guaranteeing the everlasting Davidic cov-

---

[373] Childs, *Isaiah*, 506, believes that in these words God "confirms the word of the servant figure" in 61:1–7.

[374] The verbal component is a *qal* participle (אֹהֵב) that is functioning verbally (GKC §116f) to express a durative action (GKC §116c).

[375] The word בְּעוֹלָה appears to be the preposition "with, in" plus the noun "burnt offering"; Hanson, *The Dawn of Apocalyptic*, 58, and Motyer, *Isaiah*, 503, accept this understanding and connect it to other prophetic criticisms of sacrificial offerings that God rejects (Amos 5:21–22; Isa 1:10–15). But a reference to a sacrificial offering does not really fit the context well, so some suggest that this word is the result of a scribal error for עַוְלָה "injustice, iniquity." Another option that does not require a scribal error is to derive this word from the same root that is found in Job 5:16 (עֹלָתָה); Pss 58:3; 64:7 (עוֹלָה), meaning "iniquity." This is the way the Old Greek translation understood this word (ἀδικίας) "injustice."

enant relationship described in 55:3, probably the same covenant relationship that the "Anointed One" who has the Spirit will implement (59:21; 61:1–3).[376] J. L. Koole also finds affinity between these statements and some of the claims in the Servant poems (42:1–4,6; 49:8), for that Servant will be a key factor in establishing a covenant relationship with the nations.[377]

61:9 Now God describes how the implications of this covenant will impact the life and reputation of the "seed, offspring" (*zeraʿ*) of the Israelites, a consequence already promised to those who repent in 59:20–21. C. R. Seitz connects the enhanced reputation of the righteous offspring to the work of the Servant, for he, like them, will also be lifted up and be highly exalted (52:13).[378] An even stronger connection exists between the impact of the Anointed One who has the Spirit (59:21) and the repentant seed (59:20–21). God will make his covenant with these people (59:21–22); God's presence will be with them (60:1–3); the Anointed One will work on their behalf (61:1–3); and God's blessing on them (61:6–8) will mark these people as unique. The other nations will recognize this unique relationship God will have with his people.[379]

The second half of the verse reemphasizes the special relationship between the Israelites and God. It will be seen, recognized, and acknowledged as a direct result of the blessing of God. Two points are implied by these facts. First, God's marvelous work among the righteous, holy, and repentant Israelites will serve as a witness to other peoples. Second, the eyes of the blind nations that formerly despised and attacked the Israelites will be opened so that they can appreciate the great work of God among his people. J. Oswalt finds in these factors the fulfillment of the Abrahamic blessing in Gen 12:3, for at this time through Abraham's "seed" all the nations of the earth will be blessed.[380] The idea of the inclusion of the Gentiles was introduced in 2:1–4 and has appeared again and again throughout the book of Isaiah (14:1–2; 18:7; 19:18–25; 45:20–25; 49:22–26; 60:1–14), but in this verse the presence of the nations is specifically connected and limited to their recognizing God's blessing on the covenant seed. One might imply from this verse that the nations would not just observe God's grace on Israel based on other passages like 60:1–11, but the

---

[376] Other later references to this new everlasting covenant are in Jer 31:31–34; 32:40; Ezek 16:60; 37:26. Some of these texts connect this covenant with "my servant David" and God's eschatological work, which will transform this world.

[377] Koole, *Isaiah III, Volume 3: Isaiah 56–66*, 290, concludes that "In him the 'covenant' (בְּרִית) is also personified, 42:6f; 49:8f."

[378] Seitz, "Isaiah 40–66," 515, also makes a connection between the offspring of the servant in 53:10 and the offspring in 61:9. Both the servant and the offspring are lifted up, but the lifting up of the offspring is connected to their repentance (59:20–21), their just behavior, and the gracious work of God (61:9).

[379] Note the special way the nations treat the Israelites and their children in 60:3–14; 61:4–6.

[380] Oswalt, *Isaiah 40–66*, 573.

focus of this verse is primarily on nations' new ability to identify God's people as a very blessed people.

JOYOUS RESPONSE FOR GOD'S BLESSINGS (61:10–11)

¹⁰I delight greatly in the LORD;
my soul rejoices in my God.
For he has clothed me with garments of salvation
and arrayed me in a robe of righteousness,
as a bridegroom adorns his head like a priest,
and as a bride adorns herself with her jewels.
¹¹For as the soil makes the sprout come up
and a garden causes seeds to grow,
so the Sovereign LORD will make righteousness and praise
spring up before all nations.

The "I" person speaking in these verses is no longer God but probably the Anointed One, based on similarities with 61:3[381] (not the community of Zion).[382] This person is "clothed with the garments of salvation," a concept that would only be applicable to Zion if its salvation were already accomplished. Yet 61:11 looks forward to that future time when righteousness and praise will spring up, and 62:7 clearly pictures Zion sometime before God's glorious transformation of it. Their Savior does not come until 62:11–12.[383] These two verses are a hymn in which the Anointed One rejoices (a) over what God has done to prepare him (not Israel) for his work of bringing salvation (61:10) and (b) over what God will accomplish through his work (61:11).

61:10   The speaker emphatically declares his intention to rejoice ("rejoicing, I will rejoice")[384] and then reemphasizes the point by describing how his soul will exult in "my God," a term of endearment that indicates a close relationship. The reason for this joyful response is "because" (*kî*) of what God has done. Since God is the one who "has caused me to be clothed"[385] with salvation, God deserves all the credit for preparing this Anointed One to bring the

---

[381] Linguistic connections with the surrounding material are evident in שׂושׂ "rejoice" in 61:3,10; 62:5; the root עָטָה in 61:3,10; פְּאֵר "crown of beauty, garland" in 61:3,10; and תְּהִלָּה "praise" in 61:3,11. C. Seitz, "Isaiah 40–66," 514–15, identifies the same speaker in 61:1–3 and 61:10–11. He believes these both refer to the prophet.

[382] Muilenburg, "Isaiah 40–66," 5:714, thinks that "the prophet is speaking as a representative of Zion; her words are his words" even though he recognizes that the "language, literary forms, imagery, and literary parallels are messianic." Westermann, *Isaiah 40–66*, 371, also views this hymn of praise as "the communities' responsory of acceptance of the message of salvation." Oswalt, *Isaiah 40–66*, 474, has a similar view.

[383] Motyer, *Isaiah*, 504, attributes these words to the Anointed One while Seitz, "Isaiah 40–66," 515, believes the first-person speaker is one speaking in 61:1–3, the prophetic servant.

[384] The use of a finite verb with an infinitive absolute שׂושׂ אָשׂישׂ "rejoicing, I will rejoice" emphasizes "either the certainty (especially in the case of threats) or the forcibleness and completeness of the occurrence." Thus one might translate "I will exuberantly rejoice."

[385] The verb הִלְבִּישַׁנִי is a *hiphil*, which expresses a causative relationship.

gift of salvation to others. The garments of salvation and robe of righteousness are metaphors (similar to the "clothes of vengeance" in 59:17) that describe how God has empowered the person wearing the clothes to accomplish the task (61:1–3) of establishing salvation. Having the character and the ability to grant salvation and righteousness will enable the possessor of these qualities to deliver people from their former unrighteous state and will prepare them to enter into God's glorious kingdom.

The second half of the verse expands the clothing metaphor by comparing the accessories worn by the Anointed One with wedding finery. The text identifies a fine turban (similar to what a priest might wear)[386] that would be worn by a bridegroom and the expensive jewelry that a bride might wear, but the two participants in the wedding are left unidentified. The interpreter might guess that the author is using the same analogy found a few verses earlier in 61:3, where the Anointed One replaces Zion's ashes of mourning with a crown of beauty, or one could follow the imagery later in 62:5 where God is the bridegroom and Zion is the bride. Since the people involved in the wedding ceremony are not identified and are merely present to provide a comparative analogy, the safest approach would be to focus on the accessories instead of the people. Thus the second half of the verse is comparing God's preparation of the Anointed One to putting on the finest, richest, and most beautiful finery that people would wear at a wedding. Since the turban and jewels are not interpreted, it is probably best not to guess what these fine accessories symbolize. Possibly one should take a few steps back from the wedding imagery and simply note that God has fully and magnificently prepared the Anointed One.

61:11 The response of joy ends with a second reason (*kî*, "because)" that explains why the Anointed One rejoices. This reason is expressed by making a comparison (*kā . . . kēn*; "as . . . so") between the earth's ability to cause plants to spring up and the Lord's ability to cause righteousness to spring up. Every reader in an agricultural economy would know that when the rain falls on the soil, shoots will spring up out of the dormant roots of grass; seeds that were sown in a garden or field will start to grow. These undeniable facts of nature are compared to what the Lord will do to cause his seeds of righteousness and praise to spring up. It is a great joy to know that God has the power to produce these unstoppable results. The comparison presents a guarantee or promise that the Spirit's empowerment of the Anointed One is sure to bring about the results of salvation and righteousness. The exuberant praise that will spring up from Zion will be the people's joyful response to God's great gift of salvation. The final comment in this hymn is that this human praise of God will be heard by

---

[386] The verb יְכַהֵן comes from the root idea "he will act priestly, be a priest," but it is difficult to fit this into the grammar of the sentence. The general idea communicated is that the bridegroom has a fancy turban on, similar to one worn by a priest.

all the nations. This partially explains why the nations will come to Zion and will join in this praise of God (52:10; 60:6,9; 66:18).

(3) The Coming Transformation of Zion (62:1–12)

This section describes the changes that will take place in Zion as God works toward establishing his kingdom. Righteousness will shine forth (62:1), and Zion will receive a new name (62:2–4,12), and it will be filled with joy and praise (62:5,7,9). In many ways chap. 62 continues the discussion in 61:11, but now the focus is on the transformed results in the city of Zion instead of on how God will bring about this transformation. In addition, in 62:1,6–7,10–11 there is a new emphasis on urging God to establish his kingdom and a new urging of people to prepare themselves for its arrival. It is not necessary to suggest that this urging of God arises because of some disappointment or a divine failure to act; it could simply flow out of a deep desire to experience the fulfillment of past assurances, oaths, and divine proclamations about the future (62:2–4, 8–9,11–12). If God has promised something wonderful, it is natural for God's people to want to see him fully transform their situation on earth so they can be a part of it.

There is no identification of the one speaking in this chapter, except the divine speeches in 62:8–9,11. It is entirely possible that even these divine speeches are quotations of what God has promised in the past, rather than direct speeches. R. N. Whybray identifies God as the speaker (using first person speech) in 62:1,6a,8–9, with the rest being either a prophetic commentary (62:2–5,6b–7) or a series of quotations from earlier passages in Isaiah (62:10–12).[387] C. Westermann and many others believe the prophet "Trito-Isaiah" (the one described in 61:1–3) is the first person voice in 62:1,6 and that he quotes the words of God to substantiate his outlook for the future.[388] A third option is similar but identifies the speaker as the Anointed One of 61:1–3, rather than the prophet "Trito-Isaiah."[389] This appears to be the best option.

The structure of this message of salvation is united together by a strong expectation of the coming transformation of Zion. The Anointed One will speak on Zion's behalf until her salvation is visible to all people, until her new names are reality, until God rejoices over her (62:1–5). Intercessors will also call on

---

[387] Whybray, *Isaiah 40–66*, 246–51, largely depends on the interpretation of D. Michel. Delitzsch, *Isaiah*, 434, also views God as the speaker in vv. 1 and 6.

[388] Westermann, *Isaiah 40–66*, 373–79, rejects vv. 8–9 as later additions and derives his basic understanding of this passage by comparing it to a community lament. It seems odd to have such a wonderful and hopeful passage built off of a lament. Blenkinsopp, *Isaiah 56–66*, 233, 238, also believes the prophet is speaking in vv. 1 and 6, but Muilenburg, "Isaiah 40–66," 5:717, 720, identifies the prophet as the speaker in v. 1 but God as the speaker in v. 6.

[389] Childs, *Isaiah*, 510, views chap. 62 as a continuation of the words of the servant figure in 61:1–9. Motyer, *Isaiah*, 505, has the same perspective.

the Lord until God fulfills his sworn oath concerning Jerusalem (62:6–9). God has said that the coming of Zion's Savior is near, so the people must prepare for that glorious day (62:10–12). The message in this chapter fits into three paragraphs.

Proclaim a new name for Zion   62:1–5
Assurances about the establishment of Zion   62:6–9
Prepare for the coming of the Savior   62:10–12

The first and second paragraphs are interconnected by similar structures in 62:1 and 62:6–7. Both paragraphs begin by referring to someone who should "not be silent . . . until" God has accomplished his work. The conclusion in 62:10–12 announces the coming of God's salvation in fulfillment of the intercessory prayers offered earlier in the chapter. The presentation of new names to God's people after the coming of Zion's Savior in 62:11–12 fulfills the hopes of those who longed for new names in 62:2,4. The chapter is held together by a common expectation of the renaming of Zion.

PROCLAIM A NEW NAME FOR ZION (62:1–5)

¹For Zion's sake I will not keep silent,
   for Jerusalem's sake I will not remain quiet,
 till her righteousness shines out like the dawn,
   her salvation like a blazing torch.
²The nations will see your righteousness,
   and all kings your glory;
 you will be called by a new name
   that the mouth of the LORD will bestow.
³You will be a crown of splendor in the LORD's hand,
   a royal diadem in the hand of your God.
⁴No longer will they call you Deserted,
   or name your land Desolate.
 But you will be called Hephzibah,
   and your land Beulah;
 for the LORD will take delight in you,
   and your land will be married.
⁵As a young man marries a maiden,
   so will your sons marry you;
 as a bridegroom rejoices over his bride,
   so will your God rejoice over you.

This paragraph looks forward to changes in Zion when salvation will arrive, when nations will observe its glory, when the city will have a new name, and when God will rejoice over his people. Everything will be transformed; salvation will replace silence, and the name "My-Delight" will replace "Desolation." This point is made in both segments of this paragraph.

62:1 God is promising not to be "silent" (from the root *ḥāšâ*) or "quiet" (from *šāqaṭ*) as he was in the past (42:14; 57:11; 64:12; 65:6); thus, he will intervene and act on behalf of his people. Although this is a possible interpretation, why would God later set up "watchmen" to remind him of what he has already determined and still desires to do (62:6)?[390] One solution to this problem is to suggest that the Anointed One, who speaks throughout 61:4–7,10–11, continues to speak in chap. 62. If this person is identified with the Servant who was commissioned to restore Israel and bring salvation to Jacob and the nations (49:6), to bring justice and salvation to all people (42:1–4; 62:1b), and to intercede on behalf of sinners (53:12), then one could view the statement in chap. 62 as part of his fulfillment of his commission.

The anointed speaker commits himself to the urgency of seeing the fulfillment of God's plan to bring salvation to Zion. The means of accomplishing this goal will be to speak out, but the text does not say to whom he will speak or who needs to hear his words of encouragement. One might assume that he would "preach the good news" and "proclaim the year of the Lord's favor" and "comfort all who mourn" (61:1–3) so that Zion would repent of her sins and receive God's Spirit and covenant (59:20–21). In addition, 62:6 suggests that one could intercede for God to act favorably on behalf of his people. C. Westermann compares this intercession to the Angel of the Lord interceding for the sake of Jerusalem in Zech 1:12.[391] The impact of this commitment not to be silent is that it provides assurance to the reader that absolutely everything is being done to hasten Zion's day of salvation.

The goal of these prayers to God and the preaching of the good news to Jerusalem was to bring about the fulfillment of God's promise of salvation. This will be the day that righteousness, victory, and vindication will be evident as the brightness of the sun or a burning torch. These figures of speech (the rising sun and a bright light in 62:1) were earlier connected with the coming of the glory of the Lord (60:1–2,19). A burning torch was also connected with God's glorious presence in earlier traditions (Gen 15:17; Exod 3:2; Deut 4:11). Thus these figures of speech could refer to the coming of God who brings justice and salvation, or it could simply be comparing the brightness of God's day of sal-

---

[390] Isaiah 62:2–5 also refers to God as if another person is speaking about him. If God were speaking, the first-person language would probably carry on throughout this material.

[391] Westermann, *Isaiah 40–66*, 374–75.

vation to the brightness of the new sunlight in the morning, which thoroughly removes all darkness.

62:2 Speaking directly to Zion (second person "your"), the speaker describes the results of the victorious salvation of Zion that will come like a blazing torch (62:1). The nations of the earth will see the marvelous transformation that will happen to Zion; their rulers will observe the glory of God that rises over and rests upon his people (40:5; 58:8; 60:1–3). When these foreigners observe these changes and see how God has honored Zion with great splendor (60:9), they will refer to Zion with a new name (60:14,18; 61:3,6), which God will give to Zion (Jer 3:17; 33:16; Ezek 48:35). The giving of a new name is usually associated with a new status, a radically new situation, or a new characteristic or association. This is not a name that the foreigners will invent, nor will the people of Zion do some self-promotion by putting out a new sign at the city gate. God is the one who will identify some new characteristic, such as "City of the LORD" (60:14), and will designate[392] a new name based on some unique feature. T. D. Andersen connects this new name with the wedding imagery in 62:5,[393] but, if that were the case, these two verses would be connected more closely.

62:3 Before any name is mentioned, the new conditions, character, and association of Zion are expressed by comparing the city to some expensive and precious royal jewelry. This does not refer to a crown that Zion or God will wear; it is merely an analogy of something extremely expensive and unique, something guarded and precious, something having great dignity and royal prestige. In contrast, Samaria's royal wreath in 28:1 faded because of pride and drunkenness, but Zion itself is pictured as a royal crown that will have great "splendor."[394] Earlier in 60:19 God said that he himself would be Zion's "splendor, beauty, glory" (*tĕperet*).

The significance of God carrying this royal crown in his "palm" (*kap*) is left unexplained, but certainly when God holds something so special in his hand, it belongs to him and is protected from all harm. This imagery would also convey that what was being held is very precious, and others would recognize God's love for this very precious jewel. J. L. Koole prefers the interpretation that "God himself delights in the observation of his splendid crown Zion, which he

---

[392] The verb יִקֳּבֶנּוּ is from the root נָקַב which can mean (a) "he pierced, bore through," (b) "he designated, distinguished, named." The form is a *qal* imperfect with a third masc. sg. suffix (GKC §58j for the suffix form). This may go back to the practice of piercing the ear of a person or animal to distinguish it from those owned by other people. In a sense these piercings were like brands of the names of the owner. The other possibility might come from boring or engraving a name on an object to identify the owner. This name could have been carved on the crown in 62:3, just like the names of each tribe were carved on the stones on the priest's breastplate (Exod 28), but the text never says this.

[393] T. D. Andersen, "Renaming and Wedding Imagery in Isaiah 62," *Bib* 67 (1986): 75–80.

[394] The word תִּפְאָרֶת refers to something of "beauty, luster, splendor." A crown or head ornament was worn at weddings (Song 3:11) by the high priest (Zech 6:11), and by kings.

holds before Him in His hand";[395] thus, one might imagine the constant gaze
and constant attention God gives to his people. What a change from the days
when God had to turn away from his people because of their sinfulness.

62:4 Now Zion's old names are rejected and new names are introduced.
The reason why "it will no longer be said"[396] is that there will be a total transformation of Zion from what it used to be. When an enemy army defeated
God's people it would be natural to assume that this happened because God
had "forsaken" (Azubah)[397] their land (60:15). Earlier in 54:1–8, God recalled
the former days when the nation was without children (v. 1), ashamed and
humiliated (v. 4), deserted and rejected (v. 6), and abandoned (v. 7), so it is not
surprising that someone might use derogatory nicknames like "the one who is
abandoned"[398] or "desolation" to describe the land of Israel.[399]

The change of names begins with an adversative *kî* "but, nevertheless"[400] to
assure the audience that it will be called Hephzibah, which means "my delight
is in her," a clear affirmation of the pleasure God has with the people he loves.
The formerly desolate land will also get the new name Beulah, which means
"married, possessed" (from the root *bāʿal*), a metaphor that aptly describes the
covenant relationship. These new names are not just perfunctory or meaningless new labels carelessly thrown about; they accurately describe the new state
of the nation in the future when God has marvelously transformed his people
and their land. The old way of life will be over, and this new reality will involve
a complete transformation of God's people.

62:5 To hammer this point home even further, the Anointed One promises to Zion that "surely, it is indisputable" (*kî*) that "just as"[401] an unmarried young man "marries, possesses" (from the root *bāʿal*) an unmarried young

---

[395] Koole, *Isaiah III, Volume 3: Isaiah 56–66*, 306, compares this to God's observation of the
engraving of Zion on his hand in 49:16.

[396] The negated passive לֹא־יֵאָמֵר "it will not be said" indicates that the change will be so
dramatic that those who used to give Zion bad names will never (עוֹד "again, any longer") dream
up a derogatory name again.

[397] Young, *Isaiah*, 3:469, notes that Azubah was the mother of Jehoshaphat (1 Kgs 22:42) and
Hephzibah was the mother of Manasseh (2 Kgs 21:1), but no association is made in Isaiah with
these real people.

[398] The *qal* passive participle עֲזוּבָה is used substantively: "the abandoned one."

[399] Although (a) "Abandoned" (Azubah) is the name of Jehoshaphat's mother (1 Kgs 22:42;
2 Chr 20:31)—possibly because her mother died at childbirth—and also the wife of Caleb
(1 Chr 2:18–19), and (b) "My delight is in her" (Hephzibah) was the name of Manasseh's mother
(2 Kgs 21:1), these facts do not suggest that the author used a list of the mothers of Judah's preexilic kings and Jer 3:14; 4:27–29 to create puns on these names, as suggested by B. Halpern, "The
New Names of Isaiah 62:4: Jeremiah's Reception in the Restoration and the Politics of 'Third Isaiah'," *JBL* 117 (1998): 623–43. Williamson, "Isaiah 62:4 and the Problem of Inner-biblical Allusions," *JBL* 119 (2000): 734–39, correctly observes that it is more likely that Isaiah was depending
on his own use of these ideas in 6:11–12 and 54:5.

[400] According to GKC §163a, "The antithesis (*but*) is introduced by כִּי אִם, e.g. 1 S 8[19] *and
they said, Nay, but we will have a king over us*; Ps 1[2] &c.; frequently also by *kî* alone."

[401] 1QIsᵃ adds the preposition כְּ "just as" before the verb, thus showing that this is a com-

girl, so your sons will "marry, possess" (from the root *bāʿal*) you (Zion). This means that there will be a permanent mutual love relationship between God, the people, and Zion in this covenant relationship. The joy and excitement of newlyweds will surround this event, for God himself will rejoice in finally accomplishing the plan that he set out so many years ago. In the end God's miraculous transformation of the people will bring back the joy and delight that should have always characterized the relationship between God and his chosen people.

ASSURANCES ABOUT THE ESTABLISHMENT OF ZION (62:6–9)

⁶I have posted watchmen on your walls, O Jerusalem;
    they will never be silent day or night.
You who call on the LORD,
    give yourselves no rest,
⁷and give him no rest till he establishes Jerusalem
    and makes her the praise of the earth.

⁸The LORD has sworn by his right hand
    and by his mighty arm:
"Never again will I give your grain
    as food for your enemies,
and never again will foreigners drink the new wine
    for which you have toiled;
⁹but those who harvest it will eat it
    and praise the LORD,
and those who gather the grapes will drink it
    in the courts of my sanctuary."

There are two main problems that face the interpreter of these verses: (a) Who is speaking? (b) Who are the "watchmen" and "those who cause to remember"? Earlier in the introduction to chap. 62, it was concluded that the Anointed One from 61:1–3 continues to speak in chap. 62, so he is the "I" who is responsible for instructing these watchmen about their responsibilities. The "watchmen, guards" (*šōmrîm*) and "those who cause to remember" (*hammizkirîm*) appear to be two roles assigned to the same individuals. Prophets are sometimes given the role of a watchman (Ezek 3:17–21; Jer 6:17), and 56:10 seems to use this metaphor to describe the blind prophets who were not warning the nation of Israel of dangers because they were mute and sleeping.⁴⁰² In 52:8 watchmen have the positive role of announcing to the nation the coming of the Lord. This seems a better solution to this problem than Whybray's conclusion that these

---

parison. Even without the preposition it would be obvious to any reader that this is a comparative metaphor.

⁴⁰² L. S. Tiemeyer, "The Watchman Metaphor in Isaiah LVI–LXVI," *VT* 55 (2005): 387–89, finds watchmen referred to in 57:14 based on the use of "obstacles" (idolatry) here and Ezek 3:20–21. She suggests the imagery of blowing the trumpet in 58:1 also connects this action to the role of a watchman.

are heavenly angelic beings (as in Zech 1:12).[403] These prophets remind God of his promised oath to never give his people into the hands of foreigners. When God responds and causes his people to enjoy the fruits of their work, this will cause them to praise him. These prayers and the reminders of God's oath reassure the audience that God will work on their behalf just as he has promised. This short paragraph is divided into two points.

Watchmen provide assurance of divine action   62:6–7
God's oath gives assurance of God's plans   62:8–9

Both words of assurance appeal to God as the ultimate source of all hope for the future, and both divine acts will result in the people praising God for what he will do in Jerusalem (62:7b,9a). There is no doubt about what God will do, and there is no doubt about how people will respond to God's great deeds.

62:6   It is not always easy to provide words of assurance that will completely convince an audience that what is being said is really true. In order to increase the audience's level of confidence beyond what was already provided in 62:1, new words of bold assurance are added in this paragraph.[404] Rather than just bluntly restating an abstract principle or simply repeating what was already said earlier, it is sometimes more effective to draw word pictures that portray aspects of security and evidence about the nation's hope. The imagery in this verse, which was meant to communicate a strong sense of confidence in what God would do, draws from the common practice of having a watchman placed on a city wall to warn the city about dangers. Just as watchmen provide security to a city because they are able to announce to people what is happening outside the gate, so several prophetic watchmen are being stationed to watch over the city of Jerusalem and to announce the good news of God's coming (40:9; 52:8). All day and all night they will never be silent. J. Muilenburg primarily views this as the work of intercessors "who pray unremittingly for the fulfillment of the divine promises."[405] The difficulty with this interpretation is that the watchmen analogy does not suggest this function and the royal court official who "remembers"[406] was not known as an intercessor. The "one who remembers" was an official recorder of information (1 Sam 18:6; 1 Kgs 4:3; Isa 36:3) who kept track of what the king said and wanted done. In this case this person, who was presumably a recorder of divine words and plans, is also to have no rest. Thus the watchman/recorders are constantly and vigilantly

---

[403] Whybray, *Isaiah 40–66*, 249. Emmerson, *Isaiah 56–66*, 78, accepts the angelic interpretation (also the view of the Aramaic Targum) as does J. Oswalt, *Isaiah 40–66*, 584.

[404] Both words of assurance include the phrase "I/they will not be silent" (אֶחֱשֶׁה לֹא in 62:1 and יֶחֱשׁוּ לֹא in 62:6).

[405] Muilenburg, "Isaiah 40–66," 5:720.

[406] The term הַמַּזְכִּרִים is a *hiphil* pl. participle that comes from זָכַר "he remembered." In Isa 36:3 it refers to a court official who records what was said so that it can be remembered. There is no indication that this is a court recorded action that the king advocated on behalf of certain individuals.

doing the work of God by causing everything God has said to be recorded and published abroad (52:8). Lest one take all this too literally, the reference to the court recorder is simply a graphic way of asserting that God never forgets his promises (they are all recorded).

62:7 The watchman/recorders, who are not to be silent (62:6), are instructed not to give God rest from his task of fulfilling all his plans for Jerusalem. This does not suggest that God might forget some aspect of his promises; it simply expresses to the audience that urgent communication, coordination, and action are taking place within the royal, divine throne room. Therefore, they can be assured that God will establish his kingdom in Zion. But the goal is not just to inaugurate his kingdom on earth at Jerusalem; he has the further goal of transforming[407] Zion into a place of praise in the earth. This suggests that the nations will see the marvelous things that God will do in Jerusalem and will come to join them in praising God (60:6,9,18; 61:10–11). God's purpose in all of this is to bring glory to himself (60:9,19; 61:10).

62:8–9 What are some of these promises that are included in God's plans for his people? It is unnecessary to recite them all, but the prophet appears to quote some of God's promises in order to remind the audience that God has not forgotten what he swore that he would do for them. The swearing of an oath presents an irrefutable and unchangeable promise that God must keep as a faithful and truthful God (cf. 45:23). When people swear an oath, they invoke the name of God to assure the listener that God will hold them accountable if they fail to keep their oath. Likewise, God swears by himself and his holiness (45:23; Jer 51:14; Amos 4:2; 6:8) because there is no higher authority to swear by. Not only does God's oath provide full assurance that God's promises will come true; confidence is created because God's mighty arm (41:10; 51:9; Exod 4:34; 5:15; Ps 44:4) has unlimited power and will accomplish all that God has planned.

The content of God's oath relates to earlier conditional covenant promises made in Deut 28:30–33. God promised that if the people did not listen to what he said and carefully follow his commands, then God would give their property and grain to their enemies (similar to Lev 26:16; Amos 5:11). But if these people love God and faithfully serve him, God will bless them with great crops, and their enemies will not be able to take any of these things away from them (Lev 26:3–5; Deut 28:3–11). The oath itself begins with 'im, "if," which is a conditional particle that expresses contingency, but after an oath formula this word usually means "not."[408] God promises "not" to give their grain as food or their wine as drink to their enemies. Since this promise relates to

---

[407] The verb עָשָׂה means "to make," but frequently God's action of making actually involves the remaking or transformation of something that already exists.

[408] As BDB, 50, explains, "After an oath (expressed, or merely implied) אִם (the formula of imprecations being omitted) becomes an emph. negative," translated "not." GKC §149a-c translates אִם "certainly not" when it is used to introduce promises or threats. The explanation of this

eschatological events, one should not identify these "enemies" or "foreigners" as the Babylonians, Persians, Samaritans, or Edomites.[409] The ultimate destiny of God's enemies is further described in 63:1–6.

Verse 9 provides positive words of assurance that would bring comfort to the prophet's audience. The initial *kî* could be translated adversatively as "but, nevertheless" or asseveratively "surely, it is indisputable."[410] God promises that those who sow, cultivate, and reap the grain and wine will have the pleasure of eating it in the future. Isaiah 59:18 and 60:12,18 indicate that one of the reasons for this is that God will eventually completely destroy their enemies. These wonderful harvests will lead to joyful times of great praise to God in his temple courts. This situation implies that at that time the people will fully recognize that these are the gracious gifts of God. Joy, eating, and drinking were a fundamental part of worship at the temple (Lev 7:15–17; 1 Sam 1:9) and especially at festival times (Deut 16:7,13–15; 2 Chr 30:22–24). In spite of all this eating, in the future the real reason for gathering together at the temple will be to worship God, rejoice, and praise him for all his gracious gifts (Deut 16:11; 2 Chr 30:21–22). This is the kind of worship that actually does happen in 60:6,9.

PREPARE FOR THE COMING OF THE SAVIOR (62:10–12)

[10]Pass through, pass through the gates!
   Prepare the way for the people.
Build up, build up the highway!
   Remove the stones.
Raise a banner for the nations.

[11]The LORD has made proclamation
   to the ends of the earth:
"Say to the Daughter of Zion,
   'See, your Savior comes!
See, his reward is with him,
   and his recompense accompanies him.'"
[12]They will be called the Holy People,
   the Redeemed of the LORD;
and you will be called Sought After,
   the City No Longer Deserted.

Chapters 60–62 end with a call to action similar to 40:3 and 57:14 because Israel's salvation is coming to Zion. The reason why people are to make the preparation described here is that their action will in some way be a catalyst

phenomenon assumes the suppression of part of the oath. Thus the self-imprecation, "may the Lord do to me even more, if (אִם) I do it" means "certainly I will not do it."

[409] Muilenburg, "Isaiah 40–66," 5:722, makes these suggestions.

[410] GKC §159ee describes the asseverative use as expressing what is an "absolute certainty," thus one might give the translation "surely, it is indisputable." GKC §163a deals with the adversative use which means "but, nevertheless."

that will enable the foreigners in 60:3–14 to come to worship God in Jerusalem. Once the Anointed One in 61:1–3 completes his work and renews God's covenant with his righteous people (61:8,11), then Jerusalem will get a new name (62:1–5) and God's promises will be fulfilled (62:8–9). This will leave Zion in the position where she is ready to receive God's salvation (62:11) and her holy redeemed people are able to reflect the light of God's glory. This will attract the nations (62:10,12) and inaugurate the wonderful events described in chap. 60. This paragraph emphasizes three main points.

Prepare the way for the nations	62:10
Salvation is coming	62:11
The redeemed are holy	62:12

62:10 Assuming that the preceding statements and the divine oath given in 62:1–9 have provided strong assurance that God will fulfill his promises, God instructs someone with imperative verbs[411] to prepare the way for the arrival of many people from all the nations of the world. These instructions could apply to all the righteous people in Jerusalem (the most likely conclusion) or specifically to the watchmen and the recorders mentioned in 62:6. They are encouraged to pass outside the gates of Jerusalem and make all necessary road repairs by building up low places and clearing unwanted stones. In addition, a banner is to be raised (11:12; 49:22) over the nations, an act that identifies them with God and the people in Jerusalem.

Although similar terminology about preparing a symbolic highway is used in several situations, it is important to recognize the distinctions between the various settings and not confuse all references to a highway as descriptive of the same event. Although there is an exhortation to prepare a highway in 40:3, this highway is for the coming of God to Jerusalem and is not related to the instructions in 62:10. The prophet also describes an eschatological highway (11:16; 35:8; 49:11) that God's holy people will use to return to Jerusalem, but 19:23 and 62:10 refer specifically to a highway used by Gentiles from the nations.[412] This road that the people in Zion are to prepare is a spiritual way of life that smoothes the relationship between God and man. By paying close attention to the way one walks, a person's relationship with God is built up and all offensive stumbling stones are removed. This suggests that the believers in Jerusalem will have a significant role to play in reaching the nations. They have a responsibility to live in a way that makes it possible for the nations to see the light of God reflected in their walk (60:1–3), a responsibility that every

---

[411] The verbs עִבְרוּ "pass through," פַּנּוּ "prepare," סֹלּוּ "build up," סַקְּלוּ "clear stones," and הָרִימוּ "lift up" are all imperatives that exhort people to action.

[412] Whybray, *Isaiah 40–66*, 251, correctly rejects the idea that this is a highway used by Babylonian exiles as they return to Jerusalem. Westermann, *Isaiah 40–66*, 379, believes they are preparing the way for Jewish exiles to return to the city of Jerusalem, but הָעַמִּים "the peoples" refers to Gentiles.

believer must accept so that they can be an effective witness to the work of God in their lives.

62:11 A second reason for drawing the nations to Zion will be the coming of her salvation. This verse is divided into three parts by the three interjections "behold, see" (*hinnēh*). The first third of the verse announces that God has made a declaration that is addressed to all people on the earth. Thus in addition to preparing the way for the nations and lifting a banner over the nations (62:10), God himself will deliver an important message to all the nations of the earth. The second "behold" clause reveals what the nations heard. They will hear someone[413] making an announcement about Zion that states, "Behold, your salvation has come." If the reader were to understand this in light of the similar statement in 40:10 and 60:1, then this refers to the inauguration of God's kingdom on earth. This process is described in more detail in chap. 60, for once the nations see the light of God's glory shining in Zion, they will then know that salvation has come to Zion (60:1–3,9,14). The third "behold" repeats 40:10b, announcing that when God brings salvation to the earth, he will also bring his marvelous salvific accomplishments (his recompense) with him. What this verse communicates is that God's work of salvation is not limited to his work in Zion with his covenant people; his salvation is a world-transforming power that will impact the lives of all the people from every nation in the world (cf. 45:22–25). Although J. Oswalt finds messianic imprints within this verse, the verbal connections and quotation appear to be more closely connected to God's work in chaps. 40 and 60 rather than the work of the Messiah in chap. 9, the Anointed One in chap. 61, or the Servant in chaps. 42, 49, or 53.

62:12 The people in the nation will call the people in Zion new names, similar to the new names in 62:2,4. The identification of Zion with the name the "Holy People" will finally fulfill the great calling God originally designed for his people back in Exod 19:6 and commanded in Lev 19:2. This does not indicate that they will be totally separate from the other righteous nations who will come to Zion, but this name is a witness of the total transformation of these sinful people and their complete dedication to the Holy God of Israel. The second name, the "Redeemed of Yahweh," reminds everyone that these peoples' existence is due to God's redemptive acts[414] of paying the debts of a family member and freeing them from their former bondage. The third and fourth names "Sought out" and "City not Forsaken" go together and reemphasize the reversal of the names back in 62:4. Some had called her "Deserted" or "Desolate," but that will not be true any longer. Thousands upon thousands will seek out a place to dwell in this New Jerusalem so that they can be among

---

[413] Koole, *Isaiah III, Volume 3: Isaiah 56–66*, 324–25, believes that the inhabitants of the nations will say these words when they recognize the glory of God's light upon her (60:1–14), but the text seems to suggest that God is the one saying these words.

[414] God is the Redeemer (גֹּאֵל) who redeems his people in 35:9; 43:1,14; 44:6; 51:10; 59:20; 60:16.

those who lift up praise to God. When the nations come to God at his temple (60:5–11), all glory will go to God for his marvelous salvation.

(4) Divine Justice Will Bring Wrath on the Wicked (63:1–6)

¹Who is this coming from Edom,
from Bozrah, with his garments stained crimson?
Who is this, robed in splendor,
striding forward in the greatness of his strength?

"It is I, speaking in righteousness,
mighty to save."

²Why are your garments red,
like those of one treading the winepress?

³"I have trodden the winepress alone;
from the nations no one was with me.
I trampled them in my anger
and trod them down in my wrath;
their blood spattered my garments,
and I stained all my clothing.
⁴For the day of vengeance was in my heart,
and the year of my redemption has come.
⁵I looked, but there was no one to help,
I was appalled that no one gave support;
so my own arm worked salvation for me,
and my own wrath sustained me.
⁶I trampled the nations in my anger;
in my wrath I made them drunk
and poured their blood on the ground."

This paragraph introduces the final annihilation of the nation of Edom, a picture of God treading out the grapes in a wine press, and God's wrathful judging all nations. These images are in sharp contrast with the positive images of joy, blessing, worship, and the welcoming of the foreign nations in chaps. 60–62. O. H. Steck claims that the redactor responsible for chaps. 60–62 did not write these verses, while Whybray states that these verses "are unrelated to their immediate context."[415] Nevertheless, this new emphasis is not entirely unexpected or totally unrelated to God's positive plans for Zion,

---

[415] O. H. Steck, "Tritojesaja in Jesajabuch," in Vermeylen, *The Book of Isaiah: Le Livre D'Isaïe*, 390–94, connects this paragraph with a fourth-century BC redaction that condemned foreign nations and unfaithful Israelites. Whybray, *Isaiah 40–66*, 252, in spite of this view, goes on to say that there "is an undeniable literary relationship between them and 59:15b–20 and they have in common with 61:2 the theme of the day of vengeance (verse 4)." Blenkinsopp, *Isaiah 56–66*, 247–48 also finds 63:1–6 "clearly discontinuous with and from a different source than ch. 60–62," but he then tries to connect the questions and answers in 63:1–3 with the watchman who asks questions in 21:6–9,11–12, but this hardly seems like a similar situation (there is no indication in this text that the watchman in 62:8 is asking these questions).

for hidden within the wonderful news of the establishment of the kingdom of God in chaps. 60–62 are hints about God's plan to judge those who refuse to serve him (60:12) and his plan to remove all enemies who formerly took the grain and wine that the Israelites worked so hard to produce (62:8–9).[416] This eschatological Day of the Lord was already explained in great detail in 2:6–22, 24:1–23, and 34:1–15, so the message of judgment on the wicked is not new, nor contradictory to what was said elsewhere in Isaiah. In fact, in each of these similar messages there are similar contrasting message of salvation and judgment (2:1–5; 25:1–12; 35:1–10 describe God's salvation, while 2:6–22; 24:1–23; 34:1–15 explain his judgment). Even within 63:1b, the purpose of God's righteous action of judgment is connected to his plan to save others. This day of vengeance on the nation will also be a day of redemption for his people (63:4), so God's powerful arm will not only destroy, but it will also bring salvation (63:5b). The interconnection between these two aspects of God's plan is also evident by the fact that the Anointed One will proclaim both the "year of favor" and the "day of vengeance" (61:2). J. A. Motyer believes the Anointed Conqueror in 61:1–3 is the one who will finally vindicate God's justice and destroy the wicked in 63:1–6.[417]

The interlinking connection 63:1–6 has with 34:1–15 serves as a guide to its interpretation. As in chap. 34, Edom serves as a symbol of all the rebellious and unjust nations that oppose God.[418] Although the initial attack may appear to be on the small nation of Edom in 63:1, both 63:3 and 6 mention God trampling "the nations," not just Edom. God plans to vindicate himself on his "day of vengeance" (34:8; 63:4) and rid the world of evil nations, but what was once prophesied long ago in chap. 34 and briefly hinted at in 59:17–18, is now actually happening in chap. 63. The literary context of chaps. 40–66 (and especially 60–62) makes it abundantly clear that not everyone in all the foreign

---

[416] P. A. Smith, *Rhetoric and Redaction in Trito-Isaiah*, 43–44, found 63:1–6 so closely connected to chaps. 60–62 that his division of the material is 60:1–63:6. Motyer, *Isaiah*, 489, finds a close interrelationship between all of 59:14–63:6, for he puts all of these messages into one literary unit about the Anointed Conqueror. Childs, *Isaiah*, 516, maintains that "there are a host of phrases from chapter 62 that resonate in chapter 63, and indicate clearly that the latter oracle is most certainly not just a loose fragment or independent oracle, but one that has been carefully positioned."

[417] Motyer, *Isaiah*, 489–90, 509–11, equates the "King in chapters 1–37, the Servant in chapters 38–55, and the Anointed Conqueror in 59:14–63:3." The Early Church Fathers (Tertullian and Origen) applied these verses to Christ. Oswalt, *Isaiah 40–66*, 595–96, has a similar view and understands Edom to be a symbol of rebelliousness and all that prevents people from being the Holy People they should be.

[418] B. Diou, *Edom, Israel's Brother and Antagonist: The Role of Edom in Biblical Prophecy* JSOTSup 169 (Sheffield: Academic Press, 1994) explains why there was such strong resentment between Israel and Edom before the exile, but he strongly emphasizes Edom's vengeful action after the fall of Jerusalem in 587 BC and their taking of Israel's land (Ezekiel 35–36; Obad). Strangely, he goes on to state that he does not believe this passage relates to the destruction of Edom. But if Edom is merely a symbol of the nations, then there are no historical markers that can help date this message to any historical events in the history of the nation of Edom.

nations will experience the wrath of God. Isaiah 45:20–25; 59:19; 60:3–11; and 62:2,10 indicate that people from the nations to the east and the west will come to Zion because they fear the name of the Lord. Thus 63:1–6 assures the Hebrew reader that God is all-powerful and his plans to institute his glorious rule in Zion have already begun; in fact, all those nations that did not fear God and did not come to worship him in Zion have now been destroyed. This paragraph expands and explains the destruction of the wicked nations in 60:12.

This paragraph is made of two parts.

Questions about what is happening	63:1–3
Who is coming?	1
Why are the garments red?	2–3
Explanation of God's vengeance	63:4–6

The first part of the paragraph involves two questions and God's answers in first-person responses). F. Holmgren[419] identified two chiastic structures in 63:1–6, ABA´ (vv. 1–2) and ABA´ (vv. 3–6), although the answer in v. 3 appears to go logically with the question in v. 2. The repetition of vocabulary, a common theme, and plays on words draw these verses together as a literary unit. P. D. Hanson calls this a proto-apocalyptic utopian "Divine Warrior Hymn," but most hymns do not contain a dialogue of questions and answers.[420]

63:1 This oracle begins with the question "Who is this?" This question alerts people and draws their attention to the unusual and sudden appearance of a strong person in glorious crimson robes coming from Bozrah, a major city in the territory of Edom. C. Seitz hypothesizes that the one asking this question is the sentinel in 62:6, but there is nothing in 63:1 that confirms this interpretation.[421] This person is coming from Edom, a nation located to the south of Jerusalem. Edom was the nation chosen to symbolize all the hostile nations because (a) it was a nation that epitomized what it meant to be an enemy of God's people (34:1–6; Amos 9:12); (b) its name (ʾĕdôm) "Edom" is spelled like "mankind" (ʾādām) and thus becomes a convenient symbol for all nations;[422] and (c) its name (ʾĕdôm) also allows for a wordplay on the word

---

[419] F. Holmgren, "Yahweh the Avenger: Isaiah 63:1–6," in *Rhetorical Criticism: Essays in Honor of J. Muilenburg,* ed. J. Jackson and M. Kessler (Pittsburgh: Pickwick, 1974), 133–48. The first ABA' in 63:1–2 makes some sense based on the repeated words "red garments" and "robed" in both A sections (Holmgren lists five repeated items, but only two are valid), but this division seems unlikely because it separates the second question in 63:2 from its answer in 63:3 ("tread" דָּרַךְ and "garments" בֶּגֶד are in both verses). Holmgren has insightfully drawn attention to the extensive repetition in these verses.

[420] Hanson, *The Dawn of Apocalyptic,* 203–208. Blenkinsopp, *Isaiah 56–66,* 247, notes that "the question and answer format is not antiphonal in the manner of Ps 24 . . . and is not comparable to the dialogue in the Cantiles."

[421] Seitz, "Isaiah 40–66," 518. Nevertheless, the role of watchmen in 62:6 seems to be that of (a) assuring the people of Zion based on God's oath and (b) reminding God of his promises.

[422] In the unvocalized early Hebrew text, these two words would look the same. In fact, the Old

"red" (*ʾādōm*) in 63:2 (cf. Gen 25:25). In other texts God also comes from the south, the Edomite area (Deut 33:2; Judg 5:4; Hab 3:3), so this is not an unusual location.

What is noteworthy about this person is his clothes and his walk. The clothes distinguish him from the common traveler because they are crimson-colored[423] garments. Based on 63:3b,6, it appears that his garments were not this color originally but that this crimson color was caused by stains from the blood of his enemies, which turned his garments a different color.[424] This person was also "glorious, splendid, majestic"[425] in his dress, which is either a sign of his royalty or that he had just won a great victory. The walk of this person is "stooping, bending over,"[426] a term that must be used to describe the appearance of a person walking uphill in a slightly bent-over position. This walk is not a sign of weakness, but an indication of the "greatness of his strength" as he charges forward.

In 63:1b this person coming from Edom responds to the initial question. The approaching figure does not give his name;[427] instead he gradually reveals who he is by describing his purpose and characteristics. This use of a first-person pronoun with a descriptive participle is somewhat similar to other places where God identifies himself.[428] The one answering "speaks with righteousness," that is, he speaks truthfully in accordance with the standards of justice. The audience can be assured that what he will say is, in fact, true. The final clause "mighty to save" is not firmly connected to the grammar of what precedes.[429] This problem could be solved by assuming these final words are in opposition to what precedes; thus, he is not only speaking in righteous ways, but he will also act mightily to save. Another equally viable alternative is to make the participle "who is speaking in righteousness" a subordinate clause, with "I am mighty to save" being the main clause. These identifying markers suggest that it is God who is approaching Zion (46:13; 51:5; 57:7–10; 62:11).

Greek translator of Amos 9:12 thought the word אֱדֹם "Edom" was actually אָדָם "mankind." See G. V. Smith, *Amos* (Fearn: Christian Focus, 1998), 372, 380, for a discussion of this passage.

[423] This is the only time חֲמוּץ appears in the Hebrew Bible. The versions interpret this to mean "red"; the word may be related to חֹמֶץ "sour red wine, vinegar."

[424] Rev 19:13–16 also refers to one whose robe is stained with blood as he tramples out the winepress in God's anger. He will be the King of kings and Lord of lords.

[425] The word הָדוּר may be a passive participle from הָדַר "to be honored, have majesty, dignity" (assuming a scribal error of reading the ר as a ד, a fairly common mistake in Hebrew transcription).

[426] The participle צֹעֶה refers to the "bent over, cowering" prisoner in 51:14. Blenkinsopp, *Isaiah 56–66*, 245–46, prefers to emend the word to צֹעֵד "marching."

[427] Based on earlier similar battle reports in 34:1–15, one can assume that this is God himself.

[428] In 41:4b,13,17b; 43:3,11,15; 44:24 it is typical to have אֲנִי plus a participle in a divine self-identification verbless clause.

[429] Blenkinsopp, *Isaiah 56–66*, 245–46, changes רַב "mighty, many" to רִיב "to contend" and thus translates the last line "who contends in order to save," but this emendation is unnecessary.

63:2 A second question asks for an explanation of the unusual red garments this person wears. The second part of this question suggests a possible explanation for how one might get these red stains while working in the farming culture of that day. Were these clothes stained because this person was treading out grapes in a winepress? Such an explanation makes sense in an agricultural setting, but for some reason the questioner wants to confirm that this is the reason for these red stains.

63:3 The one coming from Edom (God himself) answers this question affirmatively, but in doing so he gives a somewhat semiallegorical interpretation of his treading of the grapes. The first word (*pûrâ*) is used only here and in Hag 2:16, but in Hag 2:16 it appears to refer to a container that would hold a measure of wine. Most assume that this word means something parallel to the wine vat in 6:2, but since it is a different word than wine vat, it must refer to another specific part of the winepress. This imagery of treading on the grapes is employed elsewhere in judgment contexts (Lam 1:15; Joel 4:13 [Eng 3:13]), so the symbolism is not unusual.

The Lord indicates that he did this work alone; no other nations were employed to carry out his destructive plans. Earlier God used the nation of Assyria as the rod of his punishment to judge Judah in 10:5, but this time he did not use another nation. This may express some disappointment that some righteous nation (possibly the people of God in Zion) did not side with God against these evil nations or just be a statement of fact that he alone is the only one who is truly able to destroy evil from this world. This report should have given the audience confidence that they can trust God to remove all evil nations.

There is some difficulty knowing exactly how to translate the two imperfect verbs concerning "trampling" these grapes (the nations) in wrath. J. Oswalt resolves this dilemma by identifying these imperfect verbs as "contemporaneous past" imperfects,[430] but it would also make good sense to view this trampling as continuous or repeated action in the past (GKC §107b). In fact, the repetition of the verbal idea of trampling suggests that he trampled them again and again. The second term for "trampling" (*rāmas*) is not usually used for crushing grapes but is found when one describes the destruction of people (16:4; 26:6; 28:3; 2 Kgs 1:17,20). As God trampled down these grapes (the nations), the "juice" (*nēṣaḥ*, NIV "blood") from the fruit splattered[431] on the garment of the one doing the treading. As a result of this vigorous activity, "I stained,

---

[430] The two imperfect verbs with *waw* conjunctive וְאֶרְמְסֵם and וְאֶדְרְכֵם are often translated in past, present, or future time to express repeated or continual action (GKC §107a-i). Blenkinsopp, *Isaiah 56–66*, 246, believes this is "probably for more vivid narrative style," while Whybray, *Isaiah 40–66*, 254, prefers to repoint these verbs to be *waw* consecutives. GKC §107h discusses actions "which although, strictly speaking, are already finished, are regarded as still lasting on into the present time, or continue to operate in it."

[431] The verb יֵז comes from the root נזה "sprinkle." The נ drops in the *Qal* imperfect form, and when the final ה drops, the *dagesh forte* in the ז drops out. GKC §76c discusses doubly weak verbs like this one, and GKC §20, 1 mentions the drop of a *dagesh forte* at the end of a word.

defiled"[432] my garments. This reply answers the second question, but there is more to explain about these events.

63:4 In the second half of this message (63:4–6) God explains the imagery of 63:1–3 and reveals why he will do these things. The motivation for God acting this way was because a "day of vengeance, vindication" was in his heart. The word "vengeance" (*nāqām*) is somewhat hard to translate because for many English readers this word often carries connotations of senseless madness, bitter revenge, and a selfish paying back that will even the score. These concepts are not part of God's vengeance or his day of vengeance (34:8; 61:2). Vengeance involves the establishment of justice, a paying of a recompense for what was done in the past (59:18). That day will be the time when people will be held accountable for their past action; it will be that time when God humbles the proud (2:11–17) and when God himself will be exalted (2:11–12,17).[433]

As in 2:1–22; 34–35; 61:2, the negative and positive aspects of the great final Day of the Lord are present here in 63:4. Thus it is not surprising to read that the second thing that was in God's heart was to cause the year of redemption to come. This "year of my redemption" would refer to the positive redemption of God's people.[434] At that time the Anointed One of 61:1–3 will proclaim freedom and release, comfort all who mourn and grieve, and bring about the transformation that is described in chaps. 60–62. In effect, God is confirming the truthfulness of 61:2 and assuring the reader that God has carried out what he said he would do. Of course this raises the question, Is it God or the Anointed One of 61:1–3 who is acting in 63:1–6? Although one hesitates to make a big distinction between the "day" of vengeance and the "year" of redemption, the author could have used "day" in both phrases, so the distinc-

---

[432] The verb גָּאַל often means "redeem" (root I), but here it has the opposite meaning of "defile" (root II). This verb אֶגְאָלְתִּי is an obvious scribal error for it has both the first person imperfect prefix א as well as the first person perfect suffix תִּי, an impossible form. GKC §53p suggests this may be an Aramaic influence, although C. H. Gordon and E. J. Young, "אֶגְאָלְתִּי (Isaiah 63:3)," *WTJ* 14 (1951): 54, observe that there are similar forms in the early Amarna Letters, and M. Dahood, "Some Aphel Causatives in Ugaritic," *Bib* 38 (1957): 62–73, found similar forms in Ugaritic.

[433] H. G. L. Peels, *The Vengeance of God: The Meaning of the Root NQM and the Function of the NQM Texts in the Context of Divine Revelation in the Old Testament* OTS 31 (Leiden: Brill, 1995), 164–70. G. E. Mendenhall, "The Vengeance of God," in *The Tenth Generation: The Origins of the Biblical Tradition* (Baltimore: John Hopkins, 1973), 69–104, states that "in Isaiah 61:1–4, the 'day of vengeance' has nothing to do with violent punitive actions against an enemy," probably because of the positive context of the work of the Anointed One in 61:1–3. Nevertheless, the "year of the Lord's favor" and the "day of vengeance" are probably two sides of the same day. For God's people there will be favor on the Day of the Lord, but for the rebellious there will be God's wrath; thus, it seems appropriate to connect the "day of vengeance" in 61:2 with the negative judgment of the nations in 63:1–6.

[434] Koole, *Isaiah III, Volume 3: Isaiah 56–66*, 340, correctly opposes those who understand this redemption in terms of the negative work of a redeemer who is an "avenger of blood" (Num 5:16–34). Although the context is negative, 61:2 has already shown that it is appropriate to provide a balanced presentation of both the negative and positive sides of the Day of the Lord.

tion does suggest that the results of God's redemption will be longer lasting, but certainly it will last much longer than a year.

63:5 This verse appears to expand on the ideas in 63:3 (and it parallels 59:16) in order to emphasize again that God alone executed his judgment on these evil nations. In both 59:16 and 65:5 God observes what is happening in the world, and in an anthropomorphic response he is appalled[435] that there was no "helper,"[436] or "supporter, upholder," who would oppose the evil that runs wild in this world. This statement illustrates the astonishing path that a totally depraved world can follow and the human inability to right the wrongs or even stand up for what is right. Therefore, it is evident that the hope of mankind will not come through gentle diplomacy, compromise with evil nations, or an idealistic hope that some human organization of nations will right the wrongs and control evil nations. God's strong arm is the only source of real strength and true salvation against the forces of evil in this world. This powerful arm not only will bring salvation to his people but also will deliver the full force of his wrath on those who reject God. Interestingly, in 59:16b it is God's faithfulness to the principle of righteousness that supports his work, but in 63:5 it is God's wrath or his hatred of sinfulness that supports his work of punishing evil nations.[437] These two verses are not contradictory; instead, they illustrate how God's justice results in the utter condemnation of sinners, if righteousness is not present. It is not an oxymoron to say that God righteously loves the whole world but that he must justly and ultimately reject all those who stubbornly follow the path of sinfulness.

63:6 This brief message ends with a climactic announcement that God "continually, repeatedly"[438] trampled the nations in his anger. This uses common warfare imagery of overpowering and treading under foot the defeated enemy (14:19,25). There was no letting up, no getting tired, no mercy, and no one who escaped his punishment. In a second symbol the prophet picks up the imagery of causing someone "to continually be drunk"[439] because they were drinking the cup of God's wrath (29:9; 51:17–22). The picture is somewhat astonishing for in their stupor of drunkenness and self-deception, these people are caused to drink more and more wrath, bringing greater and greater destruction on themselves. The result will be that their sins will cause them to self-destruct as God causes their "juices, blood" (note the wordplay with v. 3) to

---

[435] The verb אֶשְׁתּוֹמֵם "I myself was appalled" from the root שָׁמַם is a *hithpolel* (GKC §55b; this is identical to the *hithpa'el* in meaning) that undergoes a metathesis in which the שׁ and ת change places because the prefix אֶת is before an "s" sound (GKC §54b).

[436] The NIV "to help" translates the *qal* active participle "helper" (functioning as a noun) as if it were an infinitive construct.

[437] Whybray, "Word-Substitution in Isaiah 63,5 and 59,16," *JSS* 8 (1963): 52–55, discusses the relationship between these verses.

[438] The use of the imperfect is either to represent continual or repeated action (GKC §107b).

[439] This is another imperfect (וַאֲשַׁכְּרֵם) with *waw* conjunctive that must express continual or repeated action in the past (GKC §107b).

go down to the ground. An equally permissible translation would suggest that the final word of the sentence should be derived from *nēṣaḥ* (root II), meaning "glory";[440] thus, God caused their glory to go down to the earth.

THEOLOGICAL IMPLICATIONS. Hearing the good news about the coming of God's kingdom is always an encouragement to believers who live in a corrupt and sinful world that has little respect for God. Although many believers are overly concerned about the date of the second coming when God's kingdom will come to earth in full force, the really important thing to know and be fully convinced of is that God has the power to accomplish what he has promised. God knows what must happen if he is going to dwell among his people (61:1–3), and he has a plan that will rid the world of sinners (60:12; 63:1–6). He does intend to transform Zion and give it a new name (61:4–62:12), changing its character forever. He will accomplish all this through his powerful arm, through the Spirit (59:21), through his everlasting covenant (61:8), and through the Anointed One who will declare the good news of God's coming (61:1–3). In the midst of this process, many foreigners in many nations will see the light of God's glory over Zion and the righteousness of God's holy people, and they will bring their wealth to Zion to worship and glorify God (60:3–14). This glorious news gives a brief glimpse at those eschatological events that (a) will precede the Day of the Lord, (b) an explanation of what will happen on the Day of the Lord when he tramples the nations, and (c) a preview of what Zion will be like after the Day of the Lord when God comes to dwell with his Hebrew people and many believers from the foreign nations.

These eschatological promises give assurance to all believers and provide a motivation for the people of God to proclaim the good news to the nations today. The people in the nations of the world will either see the light of God's glory through the lives of his holy people, or they will perish without hope because they are blinded by the darkness of their own sins. Many will joyfully come proclaiming God's praise (60:6) and honoring God with their wealth (60:9), but those who will not serve God will perish (60:12). After the judgment on the Day of the Lord, all people will know God as their Savior, Redeemer, and the Mighty One (60:16). Zion and the nations that come to it will be known as the City of God, Zion of the Holy One (60:14), the holy people, and the redeemed (62:12). God will bring about a great spiritual and physical transformation of Zion, his Hebrew people, and the nations. These glorious changes are heavily dependent on the work of an Anointed One (61:1–3), a person whose roles seem to overlap with that of the Servant in earlier chapters. This is the person who seems to be the key individual that will enable God to accomplish and complete his plans. He is the one who can turn mourning into

---

[440] Watts, *Isaiah 34–66*, 316, translates it "eminence," while Koole, *Isaiah III, Volume 3: Isaiah 56–66*, 343, prefers "glory."

gladness and despair into praise. He is the key to the fulfillment of prophecy and the introduction of God's kingdom among men.

If this Anointed One is the Servant, one can understand how the New Testament writers and Jesus himself (Luke 4:18–19) could connect Jesus' ministry to the poor and despairing people mentioned in this prophecy (Matt 11:5). Jesus was seen as the light of the world (Matt 4:16; Luke 2:32; John 8:12), but not all of these prophecies were fulfilled in his lifetime. Rev 21:10–21 describes the New Jerusalem coming down from heaven in terms similar to the glorious picture provided in chaps. 60–62. That will be the time when God's light will replace that of the sun and moon (60:19; Rev 21:23; 22:5), the nations will come with their wealth to Zion (60:3,5; Rev 21:24,26), the gates of the city will never be closed (60:11; Rev 21:25), all the people left will be holy (60:21; 61:6; 62:12; Rev 21:27), all sorrow will be a thing of the past (60:20; Rev 7:17), and God will bring his rewards with him (62:11; Rev 22:12). But before this can happen God must trample the sinful nations that reject him in the winepress of his wrath (63:1–6; Rev 14:18–20; 19:15).[441] Although the book of Revelation has much more to say about the severe persecution that will precede the establishment of God's kingdom, Isaiah has much to say about the coming of the nation to worship and glorify God. From the time of Isaiah to the time of Revelation, God's plans have not changed. God's plans are sure, so it is vitally important that each person is ready for that glorious day. God will be vindicated in the end; his original plan of creating a holy people who glorify him will be accomplished. Why would anyone not want to be a part of the glorious celebrations that will happen when the light of God's glory fills the earth?

3. Lament and Response: the Destiny of Servants and Rebels (63:7–66:24)

The final group of chapters includes what appears to be a community lament (63:7–64:11) that includes praise to God for his past compassion, questions about why life in this world is so difficult, a confession of the sins of the people, and a call for God to show his power to save his people. This prayer begins by celebrating God's many past merciful deeds when he became their Savior, and how he used Moses and his Spirit to guide his people through the Red Sea (63:7–14). But the people lament that at the present time they are no longer seeing God's mighty hand and compassionate work on their behalf (63:15–19). They request that God would work on their behalf and do awesome things (64:1–5a). The problem was that the people were sinful and cut

---

[441] These and other references to Isaiah are discussed by G. K. Beale and S. M. McDonough, "Revelation," in *CNTOT*, ed. G. K. Beale and D. A. Carson (Grand Rapids: Baker, 2008), 1,151–54. There are some differences between these accounts, for Isaiah and Ezekiel 40–48 have an eschatological temple, but John saw no temple (Rev 21:22).

off from God's mercy; therefore, they confessed their sins and called for God to remove his anger and afflict them no more (64:5b–12).

After this lamenting prayer, God answers them in 65:1–66:24 with an announcement of his plans both to destroy all those who sacrifice in pagan gardens and eat the meat of pigs (65:1–7) and to graciously act on behalf of his faithful servants (65:8–16). God will create for them a new eschatological world and a New Jerusalem filled with joy, abundant crops, children, and peace that will be enjoyed by people from all over the world (65:13–66:15).

This long section contains three main literary units.

Lament over God's dealings with Israel [63:7–64:11][442]	63:7–64:12
God's answers: Some receive wrath, others salvation	65:1–66:14
The gathering of all people to worship God	66:15–24

These messages have numerous connections with themes used earlier in Isaiah 1–62:[443] (a) 65:25 alludes to or quotes from the wonderful promises about peace between man and the animals in 11:6a,9a; (b) the pagan offerings in gardens in 65:3 and 66:17 remind one of similar pagan practices in 1:29–30, and (c) 63:11–14 refers to the exodus events that are repeatedly mentioned in earlier chapters (11:15; 51:10). Although this lament provides a strong break from the description of the glories of God's future kingdom in chaps. 60–62, both do refer to Jerusalem as being forsaken (62:4; 64:10) as well as Jerusalem being the glorious place (60:7; 64:10) where earlier generations praised God (62:9; 64:11).[444] Both refer to a time of God's anger (60:10; 64:4,8), mention the former ruins of Jerusalem (61:4; 64:9–10), and use illustrations from the harvesting of grapes (63:1–6; 65:8).

---

[442] The Hebrew numbering for chap. 64 is different from the English because 63:19, a long verse in Hebrew, is divided in English into 63:19 and 64:1; thus the English numbering system in chap. 64 is always one number higher than the Hebrew. The English numbering system will be used in this commentary, although in chapter outlines the Hebrew versification will be inserted in brackets.

[443] A. J. Tomasino, "Isaiah 1.1–2.4 and 63–66, and the Composition of the Isaianic Corpus," *JSOT* 57 (1993): 81–98, argues that similar vocabulary, themes, and structural organization connect these two sections of Isaiah. He notes the repetition of (a) "the heavens and the earth" at the beginning of the first and last units in the book (1:2 and 66:1); (b) the father–son metaphor in 1:2–4 and 63:8–10,16; (c) animal comparisons in 1:3 and 63:13–14; (d) the desolation of the land in 1:7; 54:9–10; (e) illegitimate sacrifices in 1:11–13 and 66:3; (f) appeal for repentance in 1:16–20 and an explanation of the consequences of not repenting in 66:4; and a similar organization of topics in individual paragraphs like 1:10–20 and 66:1–6 as well as the whole section. He concludes that the author of chaps. 63–66 used chap. 1 to give the book a sense of unity and cohesion, though he actually proposes a double redaction of 63–66 to explain all the evidence.

[444] P. A. Smith, *Rhetoric and Redaction in Trito-Isaiah*, 44–46, provides an extensive list of interconnections.

Although Whybray[445] does not find a close relationship between the lament in 63:7–64:12 and chaps. 65–66, many would appropriately view 65:1–66:24 as God's answer to the lament. The lament claims that God has "hidden his face" (64:7), but God's answer in the response is that he has revealed himself to those who truly seek him (65:1). The truth is that he called, but they did not answer him (65:12; 66:4). God refers to a time in the future when he will not keep silent (62:1, 64:12; 65:6) but will answer people before they finish calling (65:24). To those who questioned, "Where is God?" (63:11), comes the answer, "Here am I" (65:1). The problem is that some of these people are "rebellious" and "obstinate" (63:10; 65:2), so the solution is that God will judge those who are wicked (63:1–6; 66:15–16).

(1) Lament Over God's Dealings with Israel (63:7–64:12 [Hb 64:11])

Although J. D. W. Watts compares this message to the Deuteronomic sermon /prayers in Deuteronomy and Chronicles, with a lament in the center,[446] P. D. Hanson concludes that it is closest to a communal lament (Pss 36; 44; 74; 77; 79; Lamentations) with an introduction (63:7–14) that recites the great deeds of God.[447] H. G. M. Williamson's comparison of this lament with other examples in Psalms led him to conclude that Psalm 106 and Nehemiah 9 are the closest to this passage.[448]

One group of commentators place the author in Jerusalem, but there is still a difference of opinion about the setting. Some have suggested that this lament reflects (a) the attitudes of people shortly after the destruction of the temple in 587 BC, (b) the attitudes of people in the period of Haggai and Zechariah, or (c) the frustrations of people in the time of Nehemiah.[449] P. D. Hanson

---

[445] Whybray, *Isaiah 40–66*, 266, argues that "Although at first sight verse 1 might suggest that this chapter contains Yahweh's answer to the preceding lamentation, there is no connection between these two passages." In contrast, Hanson, *The Dawn of Apocalyptic*, 80–81, maintains that the lament "is tightly bound to chapter 65," which furnishes the answer to the query in 64:12.

[446] Watts, *Isaiah 34–66*, 329–30. He also compares it to parallel passages that use Israelite history (Psalms 44; 74; 79; 106; Exodus 15; Deuteronomy 32) and prayers in 1–2 Kings, 1–2 Chronicles, Ezra 9:6–15; Neh 1:4–11; 9:5–37; Dan 9:4–19).

[447] Hanson, *The Dawn of Apocalyptic*, 81. C. Westermann, *Praise and Lament in the Psalms* (Atlanta: John Knox, 1981), 213, believes the common preexilic biblical lament gradually developed into a penitential prayer in the postexilic period, but in *Isaiah 40–66*, 386, he calls 63:7–64:11 a community lament that was written shortly after 587 BC. L. A. Flesher, "Isaiah 63:7–64:11(12) as Post-Destruction God Lament: Socio-Rhetorical Development of Remnant Theology in Third Isaiah," Unpublished paper read at SBL (2006), compares 63:7–64:11 with both penitential prayers and laments and finds it closer to the lament. Blenkinsopp, *Isaiah 56–66*, 258, also concludes that, "this lament should therefore be distinguished from the penitential psalms, in which the confession of sin, personal or communal, is more clearly in evidence."

[448] H. G. M. Williamson, "Isaiah 63,7–64,11: Exilic Lament or Post-Exilic Protest?" *ZAW* 102 (1990): 48–58 rejects (a) Psalm 44 because the writer protests his innocence and does not confess his sins; (b) Psalm 74, 77, 78 because they lack a confession of sins, and (c) Psalm 79 because it lacks an historical review.

[449] P. V. Niskanen, "Yahweh as Father, Redeemer, and Potter in Isaiah 63:7–64:12," *CBQ* 68

connects this lament to people living in Israel shortly after its Babylonian conquest in 587 BC. He believes this lament was spoken by a sectarian group of Levitical visionaries who were disappointed because God was delaying the coming of his glorious kingdom (chaps. 60–62). The reference to Abraham and Israel in 63:16, who do not know "us" is interpreted by Hanson to be a negative reference to the Zadokite priests who led the exiles back to Jerusalem. They have rejected the Levitical visionaries (the "us" group) who stayed in the land, and it is these Levites who are lamenting in 63:7–64:11. In 63:17 these rejected Levites who follow the ideals in chaps. 60–62 call themselves God's faithful servants, the remnant of true Israel. They want God to act miraculously on their behalf like he did in the past (63:15,19; 64:1) and remove their enemies, the Zadokite priests who defile the temple (63:18).[450] This hypothetical, reconstructed conflict between different priestly groups is most unlikely, and there is very little that would suggest that this lament is based on an internal conflict for power between competing priestly groups.[451] The problem that this lamenter is addressing is that God has not mercifully intervened on behalf of his people. The solution is for the people to confess their sins and for God to once again rule over his people with power (63:18).

Since there does not seem to be any clear historical setting hinted at in this lament, it seems best to follow B. S. Childs, who states that the information in these chapters does not "establish an absolute dating nor an exact chronology."[452] Thus a synchronic reading of the lament in 63:7–64:12, in the literary context of the preceding hope that God would establish his glorious kingdom (60:1–63:6), seems to offer the best solution to this problem. When people hear about this wonderful eschatological kingdom in chaps. 60–62, they will want to be a part of it and not suffer the destiny of God's enemies who will experience his wrath (60:12; 63:1–6). They know that those who will be in his kingdom are those who reflect the glory of God (60:2–3), who proclaim the praises of God (60:6), and honor him (60:9). They will be righteous people (60:21), priests of the Lord (61:6), and those who receive new names (62:4,12). Since this is not the state of the world in the time of Isaiah or today, what can people do to ensure that they can enter God's kingdom and do not experience his vengeance? The eschatologically oriented answer to this lament in 65:1–66:14 explains God's future plans for all people from every era of history. It indicates that God has and always will reject those who offer pagan sacrifices

(2006): 397–407, dates this lament to the sixth century BCE but the final form of the text did not appear until the postexilic era.

[450] Hanson, *The Dawn of Apocalyptic*, 92–99.

[451] Williamson, "Isaiah 63:7–64:11. Exilic Lament or Post Exilic Protect?" 48–58, properly rejects this hypothesis because there is no evidence that a group of Zadokite priests who returned from exile called themselves Abraham and Israel. Childs, *Isaiah*, 525, and Oswalt, *Isaiah 40–66*, 616–17, also reject Hanson's reconstruction.

[452] Childs, *Isaiah*, 444, concludes that it is impossible to date these messages and does not believe this information indicates that chaps. 56–66 can be assigned to "a separate historical person."

(65:2–7,10–12; 66:3–4,15–17) but will allow his contrite and humble servants to enjoy the pleasures of his kingdom in the new heavens and the new earth (65:17–66:2,10–14b). Thus the whole section (63:7–66:24) is eschatologically oriented, describing what people of all ages need to do if they want to enjoy the riches of God's glorious new kingdom. In addition, it reveals what people must avoid in order not to suffer under the wrath of God's judgment.

The structure of this lament is divided into two main parts:

A history of compassion and failure	63:7–14
Request for divine intervention and confession	63:15–64:12
	[63:15–64:11][453]

There is some repetition of vocabulary between these two unique sections, but since each paragraph is a different part of the lament, there is not that much overlap. E. C. Webster notes the use of "everlasting" (*ôlām*) in 63:9,11,16; 64:4; "save/savior" (*yāša*) in 63:8; 64:5; "our Father" (*'ābînû*) in 63:16; 64:8; and "glorious" (*tip'eret*) in 63:12,14,15; 64:10.[454] The unity of this prayer is partially based on its similarity to other laments that include a historical recital of history, such as Psalm 106 and Neh 9:5–37.[455]

A HISTORY OF COMPASSION, WITH FAILURES (63:7–14)

⁷I will tell of the kindnesses of the LORD,
  the deeds for which he is to be praised,
  according to all the LORD has done for us—
yes, the many good things he has done
  for the house of Israel,
  according to his compassion and many kindnesses.
⁸He said, "Surely they are my people,
  sons who will not be false to me";
  and so he became their Savior.
⁹In all their distress he too was distressed,
  and the angel of his presence saved them.
In his love and mercy he redeemed them;
  he lifted them up and carried them
  all the days of old.
¹⁰Yet they rebelled
  and grieved his Holy Spirit.

---

[453] The division between chaps. 63 and 64 differs in Hebrew and English. D. M. Carr, "Reading Isaiah from Beginning (Isaiah 1) to End (Isaiah 65–66): Multiple Modern Possibilities," in Melugin an Sweeney, *New Visions of Isaiah*, 188–218, has a similar outline of this material and the subpoints under 63:15–64:11.

[454] E. C. Webster, "The Rhetoric of Isaiah 63–65," *JSOTSup* 47 (1990): 89–102.

[455] Blenkinsopp, *Isaiah 56–66*, 257, properly questions the value of those who hypothesize various redactional layers in the history of the composition of this lament, including Pauritsch and Sekine who find four different redactional layers. Blenkinsopp does view 63:11 and 64:1–2 as later glosses.

So he turned and became their enemy
and he himself fought against them.

[11]Then his people recalled the days of old,
the days of Moses and his people—
where is he who brought them through the sea,
with the shepherd of his flock?
Where is he who set
his Holy Spirit among them,
[12]who sent his glorious arm of power
to be at Moses' right hand,
who divided the waters before them,
to gain for himself everlasting renown,
[13]who led them through the depths?
Like a horse in open country,
they did not stumble;
[14]like cattle that go down to the plain,
they were given rest by the Spirit of the LORD.
This is how you guided your people
to make for yourself a glorious name.

This community lament presents a typical response that any group of people might have when they compare their own difficult situations with how God graciously led and marvelously cared for his people in the past. Honest reflection inevitably will cause people to lament about the depravity of this sinful world, confess their sins, and call out to God for compassion so that they can enjoy the blessings of the glorious eschatological kingdom described in chaps. 60–62. This lament begins with a brief hymnic historical review (similar to Psalm 106) of earlier times when God dealt compassionately with his people and saved them when they were in trouble (63:7–9). In spite of God's love and mercy, the people rebelled against God, so eventually God became their enemy (63:10). This time of grace and mercy was especially evident in the period of the exodus from Egypt when God's strong arm brought his people miraculously through the Red Sea by dividing the waters to make a path through the sea (63:11–14). This brought great glory to God's name.

This historical review is centered around God's steadfast love and goodness over the past centuries. God's past ways were seen as something of a predictor of his expected behavior in the future; thus, this prayer requests divine favor in the future in spite of human sinfulness. In the future, people want to see signs of divine love poured out in their lives so that they can be assured that they will experience the glories of God's future kingdom. Since some religious people will not see God's sovereign work on their behalf, they will begin to question why God is not showing his gracious compassion on them (63:15). Then they will make requests for divine intervention (63:17).

The structure of this message is divided into two subparagraphs.

God was compassionate, but Israel rebelled	63:7–10
God's deeds of compassion	7–9
Israel rebelled and became an enemy	10
Where is the powerful God who led his people?	63:11–14

The repeated references to God's steadfast love (63:7a,7b), saving (63:8,9), the Holy Spirit (63:10,11), days of old (63:9,11), glorious (63:12,14), our Father (63:16a,16b), and name (63:12,14,16,19) draw these verses together. All these verses remember the past, but the next paragraph in 63:15–64:5a introduces a series of imperative verbs that ask God for future deliverance comparable to what he did in the past.

63:7 The paragraph begins by introducing the theme of God's steadfast covenant love[456] and compassion; then in the following verses this theme is illustrated from events in the history of Israel. When one "remembers, recounts"[457] to others the steadfast loving acts of God, he is retelling a story of God's love and thereby praising God. The speaker does remember these events, but by telling others about his memories, he causes them to remember and join in his praise of God. The opening is similar to the hymn of praise in Ps 106:1–2, "Give thanks to the Lord, for he is good; his love endures forever. Who can proclaim the mighty acts of the Lord or fully declare his praise?" In each case the one speaking is inviting others to remember with him what God has graciously done.

What is memorable and deserving of great praise? The great things God did, especially the many good things he mercifully did to save his people. The audience is to call to mind not just this general principle but to remember his many acts of steadfast covenant love "according to all" (*kĕ'al kōl*) that was accomplished. This suggests that they are to remember the details about each specific situation, what problems were encountered, how God provided for "us," and what the results of his gracious intervention were. This might include even some mundane things like God providing daily food for the family, or it might include marvelous miracles like causing the walls of Jericho to fall when the people shouted and the priests blew their trumpets (Joshua 6). These great deeds could include God's goodness and compassion to people in the distant past, like his covenant with Abram (Genesis 15), his sovereign care over Joseph when he was in prison (Gen 39:19–23), his protection of Moses when he was a baby in the Nile River (Exodus 2), Gideon's great victory over Midian

---

[456] R. J. Bautch, "An Appraisal of Abraham's Role in Postexilic Covenants," *CBQ* 71 (2009): 42–63, views the reference to God compassion (חֶסֶד) as "the foremost in a series of technical terms that have been linked to the concept of covenant." This refers to the Mosaic covenant relationship that those lamenting wish to restore.

[457] The *hiphil* verb אַזְכִּיר means "I will cause to remember" God's great deeds, which naturally brings praise to him.

(Judges 8), David's victory over Goliath (1 Samuel 17), and the destruction of 185,000 Assyrian troops that surrounded Jerusalem in the time of Hezekiah (37:36). Of course, it could have included incidents in their own lives that had happened only recently too. Why repeat all these stories? It is always uplifting and encouraging for people to retell the stories of God's love to his people; thus, believers in every era of history should be encouraged to remember and tell others about what God has mercifully done for them and his people over the past centuries. Since emphasis is placed on God's "steadfast covenant love" (*ḥesed*), by beginning and ending this verse with this thought, the goal of the speaker is to cause all those listening to think about the good things in the past and not to focus just on the difficulties they have right now. If they still are God's covenant people, is it not possible for God to be compassionate to them again?

The "I" figure that speaks is left unidentified, but one might assume that this could be some religious official, a priest, a prophet, or an elder in Israel, but in fact the text is completely silent on this point. In the rest of the lament, the pronouns "we, us, our" (63:7,15–19; 64:3,5–12) are used repeatedly, suggesting that these words were voiced in the context of a community gathering. The "us" in 63:7 refers to the house of Israel in the next parallel line, so it is possible that these words were spoken at a public Sabbath service or on a feast day that focused on God's past goodness.

63:8 God's own words are remembered first and foremost in order to illustrate God's goodness and steadfast covenant love to Israel. The basis for God's compassion to Israel was the covenant relationship in which God took Israel to be "my people." This refers back to Exod 6:2–7 when God remembered his covenant with Abraham and promised to bring his children into the land of Canaan. Having heard the cries of the Israelites in Egyptian slavery, God promised to deliver them out of Egypt. He said, "I will take you as my own people, and I will be your God" (Exod 6:7).[458] This relationship of love had stipulations that regulated the behavior of the parties in the relationship so that they could maintain their relationship without offending one another. God voluntarily committed himself to do certain things for his people (the blessings and curses of Deuteronomy 27–28), and his people voluntarily committed themselves to love, fear, serve, worship, and obey God (Deut 6:5; 10:12; 30:16,19–20). God had no intentions of breaking his side of the covenant relationship, so he thought, based on this love commitment, that "surely, truly" (*ʾak*) his people would not "deal falsely, violate" (the root *šāqar*) their covenant agreement. Consequently, God became their Savior (59:1; 60:16; 63:1) by delivering and setting them free. This great act brought them up from the land of Egypt, from slavery, from the Egyptian army, and from the nation's trapped position before the Red Sea (Exod 13:31–42; 14:1–31).

---

[458] This covenant formula is reiterated in Lev 26:12; Deut 29:13; Jer 7:23; Ezek 11:20.

63:9   There are several textual problems that require attention before one
can arrive at the meaning of this verse. The Masoretic written tradition of the
Hebrew text says, "in all their affliction, he did not (*lōʾ*) afflict," while the spoken or oral Hebrew *qere* tradition has "in all their affliction, there was affliction
to him (*lô*)."[459] Although both could make sense, it seems best to reject the Old
Greek translation that changes "affliction" (*ṣār*) to "messenger, envoy" (*ṣîr*)
and keeps the negative clause "he did not afflict."[460] Additional problems with
this Old Greek translation are that (a) Exod 23:20–23; 32:34; 33:2; Num 20:16
all indicate that Israel was guided by God's angel as well as God's "face, presence" (*pānîm*, Exod 33:14–15; Deut 4:37); thus the Old Greek translation creates a false contrast; and (b) it contradicts the fact that God did afflict the Israelites when they rebelled against him.

Although the time of affliction is not specifically identified, the phraseology
indicates that it happened "in days of old" (NIV) before he redeemed them,
took them up, and carried them, all imagery that suggests this refers to the nation's affliction in Egypt. It appears that this verse is communicating the idea
that God suffers or is distressed ("he was afflicted") when his people suffer affliction. This concept is known from Judg 10:15–16, which states that initially
God rejected the Israelites' cry to be saved from their oppressors, but after they
confessed their sins and got rid of their foreign gods, God "could bear Israel's
misery no longer," so he saved them. Surely God's emotional involvement with
people who are unfaithful affects him with grief (63:10; Gen 6:6; Ps 78:40;
Hos 6:6; 11:8–9), and he delights and gains pleasure from those who honor
him (1 Sam 15:22; Ps 149:4; Isa 42:1; 62:4).

The angel of his presence who saved the Israelites must refer to the angel of
God that traveled before the nation when they came out of Egypt (Exod 14:19;
33:2–20). This angel is the same manifestation of God himself that appeared
to Moses at the burning bush (Exod 3:2–6) and was revealed in the pillar of
fire and cloud that guarded and guided the nation (Exod 23:20; 32:33). This
example justifies the belief that God revealed himself in a visible way to work
for the deliverance of his people from the affliction of Egypt. These great deeds

---

[459] There are 15 places in the Hebrew Bible where the *kĕtîb* (written Hebrew text) and the *qĕrê*
(spoken Hebrew text) do not agree and the *qere* substitutes the word (לֹו "to him") for (לֹא "not") in
the *kethib*. The Old Greek translation took this word as a negative and understood צָר "affliction"
as צִיר "messenger," giving the translation "not a messenger, not an angel, but the Lord himself
saved them." Watts, *Isaiah 34–66*, 324, keeps the negative ("he did not afflict"), which follows the
Targum, but clearly God did afflict the nation with many just judgments against the Israelites while
they were in the wilderness, particularly for the worship of the golden calf in Exodus 32, for refusing to take the land in Numbers 13–14, and for the sin at Baal-Peor in Numbers 25. Muilenburg,
"Isaiah 40–66," 5:731, and Westermann, *Isaiah 40–66*, 385, prefer the Old Greek understanding of
this text. The Old Greek makes a different verse division between v. 8 and v. 9, implies two negatives, changes the meaning of "affliction," and adds a contrasting conjunction "but," all signs that
the translator was doing the best he could in paraphrasing a difficult verse.

[460] If "he did not afflict" were meant, it would be most natural for there to be a pronoun אַתָּה
"you" after this verb, but this is not found.

demonstrate his deep love for his people, for God redeemed them out of their merciless situation. God's love was evident through his merciful acts of sparing his people further pain and by carrying them through the Sinai Wilderness for 40 years (Exod 19:4; Deut 1:31; Isa 46:4; Hos 11:3). The time frame seems to relate to the wandering years, but the NIV phrase "the days of old" is literally "all the days of eternity," a hyperbolic way of referring to the almost unending days spent in the wilderness.[461]

63:10 Instead of continuing to talk about what God did, the discussion moves to what "they" did, presumably the people of Israel, the same "they" mentioned in 63:8. God did not expect his people to deal falsely with him (63:8) after he saved, loved, and carried them for so long. But they did "rebel, resist,"[462] a common theme appearing in the book of Numbers (Num 10:22 refers to rebelling 10 times) when they complained about their food (Numbers 11), Moses' leadership (Numbers 12, 16), and their inability to enter the land because of the giants (Numbers 13–14). This rebellion "grieved, injured" the Holy Spirit, an anthropomorphic way of explaining that God was afflicted and saddened when his people sinned and did not trust him to give them the land. Elsewhere God metaphorically "regrets" (Gen 6:6), "is grieved" (1 Sam 15:35), is "saddened, has pity" (Jonah 4:10), and "weeps" (Jer 9:10), so it should not be surprising that God is negatively impacted by the rebelliousness of his people.

It is stated here that the rebellion was against "his Holy Spirit,"[463] terminology that is seldom found in the Hebrew Bible (63:10–11). In Ps 51:11 David asks God not to take "your Holy Spirit from me," as God had removed his Spirit from Saul when he sinned (1 Sam 16:14) and disqualified himself for further leadership. The poetic parallelism in Ps 139:7 connects the Spirit with the presence of God. Nehemiah 9:20 refers to God who gave "your good Spirit to instruct" the people while they were in the wilderness, and in Neh 9:30 the Spirit of God was employed to admonish people through the ministry of the prophets. Numbers 11:16–26 refers to God's Spirit on Moses being distributed to the 70 elders of Israel in order that they might be able to help Moses with the heavy task of leading the nation. B. S. Childs views the Holy Spirit as "the holy presence of Yahweh," while Oswalt believes that the concept of the Holy Spirit "is close to the fully developed NT concept of the third person of the Trinity,"[464] J. L. Koole calls this a personification of God himself, while

---

[461] If anyone spent 40 years, which equals 14,600 days, with nothing to do in a hot and dry wilderness, they would understandably be prone to call it an eternity.

[462] When this verb מָרָה is used in 1:20, the additional explanation is that they willfully "refused" to do what God desired. In 30:9 "rebelling" is parallel to the act of "lying, deceitfulness."

[463] 1QIsᵃ has רוּחַ קוּדשׁיו "the spirit of his holy ones," apparently thinking of angelic beings (Ps 89:6,8).

[464] Childs, *Isaiah*, 524. Oswalt, *Isaiah 40–66*, 608, believes "most commentators" have this same opinion, but there are relatively few who would speak of the Trinity based on this verse.

J. Muilenburg classifies this reference to the Holy Spirit as "a personification which moves in the direction of an hypostasis."[465]

Since God the Spirit is holy, the rebellion of the people led to God "changing, turning" (*hāpak*)[466] from being a Savior (63:8) to being an enemy (cf. Deut 32:23; Jer 30:14). Thus, instead of having steadfast covenant love, compassion, and goodness toward Israel, he fought against them. Part of the covenant agreement was that if the nation did not worship God alone, did not love and serve him, and did not follow his stipulations, God would send a curse on them. This agrees with the theology of the introduction to the book of Isaiah, for in 1:20 God warned his people that "if you resist and rebel, you will be devoured by the sword." Thus the mighty Divine Warrior (Exod 15:3; 42:13,24; Isa 63:1–6; Jer 21:5) brought war and his sword against his own people because they rejected him. A similar explanation could be given for the outcome of the Syro-Ephraimite War in 7:1–10, for Ahaz was told, "If you do not believe, you will not last."

63:11 In the second part of this paragraph, a second act of remembering is mentioned ("and he remembered"), but at first it appears to refer to God himself remembering. Nevertheless, it is clear from 63:11b–14 that these are remembrances about what God did. C. Westermann emends the text to make it a plural "they remembered," but Israel is often treated as a single individual body.[467] The Israelite community is remembering key spiritual things about Moses and his people that happened innumerable days ago (lit. "forever" *ʿôlām*).

The first question is about the whereabouts of God—the one who brought them up[468] from the sea. The reference "with the shepherd(s) of his flock" must be talking about Moses and the other leaders of the tribes.[469] This question suggests that some people were wondering if the God who did great miracles for the people long ago is now no longer in the business of doing such marvelous things for his people. Somehow God does not seem to be as present in such a visible way to shine his love and compassion on his people. The second question is also about God's whereabouts—the one who put in their/his midst his Holy Spirit. It is logically possible to interpret his Holy Spirit as being put in the midst of "it," meaning "his flock," or on "him," meaning Moses (and the

---

[465] Koole, *Isaiah III, Volume 3: Isaiah 56–66*, 359. Muilenburg, "Isaiah 40–66, 5:732.

[466] The transformation envisioned in הָפַךְ is illustrated in Saul's life in 1 Sam 10:6; here it says that when the Spirit came over Saul, he was changed into a different person.

[467] Westermann, *Isaiah 40–66*, 385, prefers וַיִּזְכֹּר "and he remembered." Schramm, *Opponents of Third Isaiah*, 151, argues that וְאַזְכִּיר "and I will cause to remember" should be read parallel to 63:7. Delitzsch, *Isaiah*, 454, makes "his people" the subject.

[468] "The one who brought them up" is a *hiphil* participle from עָלָה with a third masc. pl. pronominal suffix. The *hiphil* gives a causative emphasis, indicating that God was the reason they were able to come up out of the Red Sea alive, while the Egyptian soldiers drowned.

[469] NIV has "shepherd" in the sg. following the Targum and Old Greek, which makes good sense, while the Hb. has a pl. "shepherds." The pl. of shepherds could possibly refer to all the different leaders (the 70 elders) of the tribes of Israel.

other leaders). Either textual record could fit Num 11:16–25, for in that context God did give his Spirit first to Moses and then later to the 70 elders of Israel.

63:12–14a The third thing remembered is that God is "the one who caused to go"[470] his "glorious, awesome, miraculous"[471] arm. This is the arm that is powerful enough to rule his future kingdom (40:10), bring salvation (52:10; 59:16; 63:5), gently care for his sheep (40:11), defeat his enemies (30:30; 48:14; 51:9), bring justice to the nations (51:5), and make eternal promises that he will keep (62:9). This is the arm that empowered Moses' right arm so that he was able to do almost unbelievable miracles (the plagues in Exodus 7–11) while in Egypt. Although the starting and the stopping of the ten plagues could have been listed to illustrate the power of God's arm through Moses, at this point only the dividing of the waters of the sea is mentioned (Exod 14:16,21–22).[472] The result was that God's "name/reputation" (šēm) became famous from that time until forever. The song of praise to God in Exodus 15 began that process of making God's name famous throughout the nations. Rahab the harlot in Jericho and all the Canaanites (Josh 2:9–11) knew about God's awesome power over the Egyptians and his ability to divide the Red Sea. Years later when the Israelites fought the Philistines, the Philistine army feared the God of Israel because they also had heard the stories about God defeating the Egyptians (1 Sam 4:7–8; 6:6). Of course, the Hebrew people themselves were the main ones who remembered the marvelous power of God year after year through their feasts. In their singing of praise to God, they spread the news of his reputation far and wide; thus, it is not surprising to hear people frequently mention God's power over Egypt and the sea in their hymns (Pss 66:5–6; 106:8–9; 136:12–13).

Verse 13 continues to recount God's glorious deeds. He was the one who led them[473] through the "depths"[474] of water in the Red Sea on dry ground, implying that this crossing of the Red Sea was not at the shallow end of that sea where the water was just a few feet deep; this happened at a place that was very deep. Of course, one would expect the bottom of a sea to be very rugged and muddy, but did the Israelites have trouble crossing on the rough floor of the sea? This verse compares the people's passage through the sea to a horse effortlessly walking in a wilderness without a struggle or a stumble. This comparative illustration is saying that the Israelites' crossing through the sea miraculously went smoothly.

---

[470] The third participle describing God's activity is מוֹלִיךְ, "the one who caused to go," another *hiphil* coming from הָלַךְ.

[471] The word תִּפְאָרֶת relates to "awesome wonders, glorious things, impossible things."

[472] Motyer, *Isaiah*, 515, attributes this statement to the dividing of Jordan (Joshua 3), but Moses was dead (Deuteronomy 34) before the people ever crossed the Jordan.

[473] Parallel to the *hiphil* participle מוֹלִיךְ, lit. "the one who caused to go," at the beginning of v. 12 is the same *hiphil* participle מוֹלִיכָם with a suffix, lit. "the one who caused them to go."

[474] תְּהֹם "deep, ocean depths" is the same word used in Gen 1:2, but in Exod 15:5,8 and Isa 51:10 it refers to the depths of the Red Sea.

The comparison of the Israelites to cattle (probably sheep and goats) going down into a valley in v. 14a is difficult to understand because it is not clear if this still relates to the people crossing the Red Sea or if this refers to their later settlement in the valleys of Canaan when they inherited the land. The second line compares the "rest" (from *nûaḥ*) God's Spirit gave the people to cattle resting in a lush valley. The picture is not fully drawn, but one might imagine sheep resting in a valley after a long day of walking through step hillsides in search of grass to eat. But how does this relate to the past experiences of the Israelites? Since (a) "rest" is often associated with the end of the conquest of Israel and the people's peaceful settlement in the land (Deut 3:20; 12:10; Josh 1:13; 22:4), and (b) it seems unlikely that rest could refer to the people "resting" while they crossed the Red Sea, J. Muilenburg follows the versions and slightly emends "rest" to read "led" (from *nāḥâ*).[475] Although this makes good sense, and one can understand why the Aramaic and Greek translators might have chosen this option, there is no textual reason for choosing it. J. Oswalt maintains the text as it is and relates v. 14a to rest in the land after the conquest,[476] but the contextual evidence of 63:11–13 argues that the historical context of this rest was during the exodus. Therefore, contextually one must conclude that God's Spirit gave the Israelites the faith, peace, and rest in God so that they were gladly willing to walk down into the Red Sea, just like cattle gladly entering a peaceful valley without fear.[477]

63:14b   This paragraph ends with a concluding summary statement. The initial "so, thus" (*kēn*, NIV "This is how") refers back to what was just said and introduces this conclusion. In all these and many other incidents that could be listed, God sovereignly guided/led his people in miraculous ways that demonstrated his compassion and steadfast covenant love to them (63:7). The good things that God accomplished demonstrated just how great God is. Because of these saving deeds, God gained a glorious reputation (63:12b) among the Israelites and the nations, a name that is above all other names, and a fame that causes his followers to both praise and trust in him for the future. These words of praise to God give the one lamenting in the following verses hope that this same God will graciously act once again on behalf of his people.

REQUEST FOR DIVINE INTERVENTION AND CONFESSION (63:15–64:12)

**15Look down from heaven and see
from your lofty throne, holy and glorious.**

---

[475] Muilenburg, "Isaiah 40–66," 5:735, follows the Aramaic Targum and Old Greek translations that refer to the Spirit "leading" them, which would more naturally fit the context of leading people in 63:12–13 and the setting of crossing the Read Sea.

[476] Oswalt, *Isaiah 40–66*, 609, and Whybray, *Isaiah 40–66*, 259, prefer the context of rest for the Israelites when they took possession of the land.

[477] Koole, *Isaiah III, Volume 3: Isaiah 56–66*, 368, has a similar interpretation.

Where are your zeal and your might?
     Your tenderness and compassion are withheld from us.
¹⁶But you are our Father,
     though Abraham does not know us
     or Israel acknowledge us;
   you, O Lord, are our Father,
     our Redeemer from of old is your name.
¹⁷Why, O Lord, do you make us wander from your ways
     and harden our hearts so we do not revere you?
   Return for the sake of your servants,
     the tribes that are your inheritance.
¹⁸For a little while your people possessed your holy place,
     but now our enemies have trampled down your sanctuary.
¹⁹We are yours from of old;
     but you have not ruled over them,
     they have not been called by your name.

¹Oh, that you would rend the heavens and come down,
     that the mountains would tremble before you!
²As when fire sets twigs ablaze
     and causes water to boil,
   come down to make your name known to your enemies
     and cause the nations to quake before you!
³For when you did awesome things that we did not expect,
     you came down, and the mountains trembled before you.
⁴Since ancient times no one has heard,
     no ear has perceived,
   no eye has seen any God besides you,
     who acts on behalf of those who wait for him.
⁵You come to the help of those who gladly do right,
     who remember your ways.
   But when we continued to sin against them,
     you were angry.
     How then can we be saved?
⁶All of us have become like one who is unclean,
     and all our righteous acts are like filthy rags;
   we all shrivel up like a leaf,
     and like the wind our sins sweep us away.
⁷No one calls on your name
     or strives to lay hold of you;
   for you have hidden your face from us
     and made us waste away because of our sins.

⁸Yet, O Lord, you are our Father.
     We are the clay, you are the potter;
     we are all the work of your hand.
⁹Do not be angry beyond measure, O Lord;
     do not remember our sins forever.

Oh, look upon us, we pray,
   for we are all your people.
¹⁰Your sacred cities have become a desert;
   even Zion is a desert, Jerusalem a desolation.
¹¹Our holy and glorious temple, where our fathers praised you,
   has been burned with fire,
   and all that we treasured lies in ruins.
¹²After all this, O LORD, will you hold yourself back?
   Will you keep silent and punish us beyond measure?

The introduction of first-person plural pronouns ("we, our, us") signals the beginning of a new paragraph and the start of the lament portion of the prayer. This community lament has many of the common characteristics of other community laments in Psalms, but it also has a few significant differences. For example, Psalm 44 begins with remembering God's great deeds of the past (44:1–8), laments God's rejection and their enemies' scorn (44:9–16), but then the lamenters claim to be innocent of any sin, to have not forgotten God (44:17–22), and they end up requesting for God to awake, rise up, and help his people (44:23–26). The central difference is that the lamenter(s) in Isa 63:15–64:12 confess the people's sins and admit that the people were not calling on God (64:5b–7); they do not claim that they are innocent.

P. Hanson understands this lament to be the complaints of an oppressed visionary group of Levites against the Zadokite priests who were in power. This approach is rejected here because it imaginatively reads into the text much of Hanson's own preunderstanding of the situation.⁴⁷⁸ Instead, it appears that the problem is made up of three aspects: (a) God is not doing what some Hebrews want him to do for his people (63:15–17,19); (b) because of some enemy, which is not named by country, ethnicity, or location, some sacred cities and sanctuaries in Judah are defiled and trampled (63:18; 64:10–11); and (c) the lamenter(s) admit that "we" have sinned and made God angry (64:5b–7).

Interestingly, there is an absence of military terminology that might be expected if the enemy was involved in a siege in which the city was destroyed and many people in Judah were killed. Three possible interpretations should be evaluated as possible settings for this lament and the response to it in chaps. 65–66. First, this section could refer to problems shortly after the destruction of Jerusalem and the temple in Zion in 587 BC since the city was destroyed and the temple burnt (64:10–11).⁴⁷⁹ There are two significant problems with

---

⁴⁷⁸ Hanson, *The Dawn of Apocalyptic*, 79–100, lays out his sociological analysis of the lamenters and those who were their enemies. Schramm, *Opponents of Third Isaiah*, 152–4, rejects Hanson's analysis because the "issue in the lament is not exclusion from the cult but rather the destruction of the cult."

⁴⁷⁹ Blenkinsopp, *Isaiah 56–66*, 259, rejects the view that this refers to "a Samaritans or Proto-Samaritans' complaint against the *gôlâ* Jews" of Ezra 4:1–5 or of the situation of Jerusalem at the time of Nehemiah (Neh 1:3). So one is left with a possibility that this was spoken shortly after the fall of Jerusalem in 587 BC (Muilenburg) or a few years later (Williamson).

this proposal: (a) there is nothing in this text to indicate that the setting is a military attack by an enemy; and (b) there is a question as to how a lament from 587 BC would fit in with material that most date to the postexilic period. Many commentators would put most of chaps. 56–66 long after the return from exile (after 516 BC since the temple is rebuilt). The natural question that arises is, Why would an editor put a lament from 587 BC in the midst of postexilic material from after 516 BC? Because of these problems, Blenkinsopp considers this proposal only "plausible if unproven."[480]

A second option would be to simply take the perfect verbs in 64:10 as prophetic of what God would do in the future if the people did not confess their sins and God's anger was not removed.[481] The lament in 63:15–64:12 would be the prophet's prayer of intercession for God to have compassion on his people. This also is a plausible theory but one favored by very few.

A third alternative favored by J. Blenkinsopp suggests that since this lament has a "close connection with the passage that follows [the answer to the lament appears in chaps. 65–66], one could with equal plausibility favor the hypothesis of a purely literary work that imitates the language and themes of the psalms of lamentation."[482] Although he believes that 64:10–11 refers to the fall of Jerusalem and that they present a tone similar to Lamentations,[483] it must be remembered that this is a "literary creation" that sets out a pattern for penitential prayers for the future. This literary proposal, which is not fully developed, might suggest that since the answer to this lament is found in 65:1–66:24, then a case could be made that these enemies who defile and trample the temple are actually the obstinate people in 64:5b–7 who also provoke God with their pagan sacrifices, sit at graves, and eat pig's flesh (65:2–4; 66:3,17). These people behave similarly to the group of people who were earlier condemned as a brood of evildoers who forsake the Lord (1:4), who trample down the courts of the temple (1:11–12; 63:18), and who worship at sacred oaks and gardens (1:29). People from other nations are not pictured in these verses as warriors who oppress and kill; instead, the foreigners are presented as followers of God who will one day come to Zion, experience the coming of God's glory, and proclaim God's coming to others (66:18–21). Since the answer to the lament presents an eschatological solution to the problems presented in the lament, it is possible that the lament is a literary creation of what will be happening in the

---

[480] Blenkinsopp, *Isaiah 56–66*, 259, also rejects the view that this could refer to the occupation of the Ptolemy I in 302 because the temple was not burned down.

[481] Motyer, *Isaiah*, 521, rejects a postexilic setting for this lament because 64:12 could not have been spoken by people in that setting, for "the problem of the immediate postexilic days was not divine inaction but human failure as the returnees lapsed into carelessness and left the house unbuilt." Thus he prefers to view this lament as an Isaianic meditation arising from revelation that God gave to him about the eventual destruction of Jerusalem. Thus he takes the verbs as "perfects of certainty" and translates the phrase "your cities are to become. . . ."

[482] Blenkinsopp, *Isaiah 56–66*, 259.

[483] Ibid., 266.

last days just before the Divine Warrior treads upon evil in his wrath (63:1–8) and creates a new heavens and a new earth (65:17). The prophet would be lamenting the evil that will fill the earth during those last days, so he intercedes for God to have compassion on behalf of his people. This option will be employed in interpreting this literary unit.

The message in this lament is structured into four paragraphs.

Lament over a lack of God's presence	63:15–19
Call for God to powerfully intervene	64:1–5a
Confession of sins	64:5b–7
Call for God to answer this prayer	64:8–12

These four paragraphs are interconnected to one another because they all fit into the plan of a lament and use first-person plural pronouns. This section uses several imperative verbs calling on God to look (63:15), return (63:17), not be angry (64:9a), look upon us (64:9b); it also uses numerous questions (63:15,17; 64:5,12). There is some repetition of vocabulary between this paragraph and the first part of the lament (63:7–14), but since each paragraph is a different part of the lament, there is not that much overlap. E. C. Webster notes the repeated use of the words "everlasting, old" (*ʿôlām*) in 63:9,11,16; 64:4; "save/savior" (*yāšaʿ*) in 63:8; 64:5; "our Father" (*ʾābînû*) in 63:16; 64:8; and "glorious" (*tipʾeret*) in 63:12,14,15; 64:10.[484] The unity of this overall prayer is partially based on its similarity to other laments that include an historical recital of history, followed by a lament, such as Psalm 106 and Neh 9:5–37.[485]

LAMENT OVER A LACK OF GOD'S PRESENCE (63:15–19) [63:15–19a].   The change in tone from the praises of God in 63:7–14 to the lament in these verses is dramatic. Instead of celebrating God's love and compassion, the lamenter questions where God is and why he has not been compassionate to his servants. Instead of remembering God's many past acts of compassion on behalf of his people, now the one praying asks for God to act once again for the benefit of his people. In some ways this lament almost seems to blame God for part of the nation's problems, but later in 64:5b–7 the lamenter admits that the people's rebellion and sin are the major reason for God's inaction.

This part of the lament is organized in two parts.

Where are God's zeal, might, and love?	63:15–16
Complaint	15
Rebuttal	16

---

[484] E. C. Webster, "The Rhetoric of Isaiah 63–65," 89–102.

[485] Blenkinsopp, *Isaiah 56–66*, 257, properly questions the value of those who hypothesize various redactional layers in the history of the composition of this lament, including Pauritsch and Sekine who find four different redactional layers. Blenkinsopp does view 63:11 and 64:1–2 as later glosses.

Why does God not rule over us?	63:17–19
Complaint	17a
Request	17b–18
Conclusion	19

If a people have experienced the compassion of God's intervention on their behalf in the past, it is disconcerting when they no longer experience God's presence and grace. Consequently, it is natural for people to ask questions about this change in God's involvement with them. Where are the zeal, power, and compassion of God that they used to experience? Where is this God who acted as their Father and Redeemer? Why does it appear that God is not actively ruling over his people anymore?

63:15–16 The initial complaint is against God. The lamenter does not accuse God of some wrong but simply calls for God to "look, take notice"[486] from his distant heavenly abode (as in Ps 80:1–2) in order to find out what is really happening on earth. The preceding hymnic praise of God in 63:7–14 recognizes the nearness of God to his people in the past because of the "angel of his presence" and his acts of redemption as well as his love, mercy, powerful arm, leading, and his setting of the Holy Spirit among them; nevertheless, at this time the Lord seems far away in his glorious, exalted place in heaven. Thus the one praying does not doubt God's existence, his holiness, or his sovereignty; he just wants to see God act on behalf of his people now. Later it will become evident that sin (64:51–7) has caused a separation (cf. 59:1–2) between a holy God and his sinful people; thus, God cannot act on behalf of his people.

The lamenter questions where God's zeal and might have gone? Where are the "deep rumblings of your innards"[487] and compassion "unto me" (ʾēlay, NIV, "from us")[488] that are withheld. Zeal refers to God's strong determination, his absolute commitment to accomplish what he has promised (9:7; 59:17). Might is simply God's power, often military might, to bring to pass his plans for his people. Inward emotional convictions and compassionate love are two of the central internal motivations that move God to action. These are the characteristic ways of God, the heart of God that the lamenter has failed to observe. J. Oswalt envisions this as a time when the people have returned from

---

[486] The initial verb הַבֵּט is a *hiphil* imperative from נָבַט "he looked, noticed." Since people do not command God to do anything, the imperative verbs must function as a request (GKC §110a).

[487] The phrase הֲמוֹן מֵעֶיךָ (NIV "your tenderness") literally refers to the "noise of your bowels," a metaphor for the deepest emotions and convictions that drive behavior. In English people have a "gut feeling" about something, but in Hebrew thinking, this is not an intuition or feeling; it is a driving passion based on convictions.

[488] The text and 1QIsᵃ have אֵלַי "unto me," not "from us," which would be מִמֶּנּוּ. The Old Greek and Aramaic Targum have the pl., which NIV follows. "From us" is obviously the easier reading, which is not original. Muilenburg, "Isaiah 40–66," 5:736, freely emends the text to "do not restrain yourself," אַל־תִּתְאַפָּק.

exile and are rather helpless when their enemies confront them, not seeing God do many miracles on their behalf.[489] Yet if the people had recently witnessed God's act of defeating Babylon, stirring up Cyrus to send them home to Jerusalem, giving them safety as they traveled back home, and allowing them to complete the temple, then it hardly seems likely that they could say that they had not seen God's might, compassion, and zeal for his people. It is impossible to identify the specific situation from the little amount of information that is provided here; in fact, based on the eschatological answer from God in chaps. 65–66, it may be most appropriate to find the setting for these troubles in an eschatological context.

Having expressed that the people feel somewhat alienated from God, the rebuttal in 63:16 explains why this situation seems so contradictory to the way things should be. The one making this complaint makes the strong assertion that "'surely, truly' [*kî*] God is our Father," and then at the end of the verse God is again called "Father" and "Redeemer from eternity past." "Father" is not a frequent name or title given to God in the Hebrew Bible, possibly because people wanted to avoid any fertility connotation of sexual fatherhood. The Israelites are often called "sons, children" (Exod 4:22; Isa 1:2,4; Hos 11:1–4), and early on God is called both "Creator" and "Father" (Deut 32:8,18; Ps 103:13). A similar idea is found in Isa 45:9–12 where God is both the Potter as well as Father. It is difficult to know what this title implies in this limited context. Is it an attempt to impose some familial responsibility on God, or is it meant to make an emotional connection to a hurting member of the family? At minimum, this title proclaims that there is a close, personal ("our"), spiritual relationship to God, but it could even include the associated idea that God elected them to be his children. In the context of 63:15, this part of the prayer expresses some confusion or at least some disappointment that their Father and Redeemer has not acted more forcefully on behalf of his children.

Within 63:16 is a contrast between their spiritual Father, who is God, and their physical father, Abraham. The Israelites claim God as their Father "though" (*kî*)[490] there seems to be some question if their famous forefathers Abraham and Israel (Jacob) would know or acknowledge these suffering people as their children. What this implies is unclear.[491] Is this saying that Abraham and Israel are dead and can no longer help them, so they are depending on God their spiritual Father? Is this a formula that implies that the patriarchs would reject them

---

[489] Oswalt, *Isaiah 40–66*, 611.

[490] The concessive use of כִּי, "though," makes good sense in this situation (*IBHS*, §38.2).

[491] Bautch, "Abraham's Role in Postexilic Covenants," 42–63, suggests that these lamenters are saying that "their covenant relationship with God does not extend through Abraham to the people; their covenant is to be made directly with God because Abraham does not know them." This is based on an interplay with Gen 18:19 and Deut 33:9. This seems to be an odd interpretation because elsewhere Abram is used in a positive light.

because they have strayed from the faith of their fathers?[492] It appears that this phrase could be saying that because of the people's difficult situation and the lack of divine action on their behalf, the patriarchs would not recognize them as the Hebrew people they knew in the past. These people can only appeal to the compassion and deliverance of their heavenly Father and Redeemer.

63:17–19 A second complaint to God relates to the way he rules over the earth. The questions are (a) "Why Yahweh, would you cause us to wander[493] from your ways?" and (b) "Why would you harden our heart from fearing you?" These statements seem to come very close to blaming God for the nation's present problems. Since God is sovereignly in control of everything that happens on the earth, it is logical to conclude that God has caused or at least allowed Israel to fall into sin and is partially responsible for their present situation. God could have intervened at any time and prevented this situation from happening by removing the temptation to sin or by making them strong enough to stand against evil. Since he did not do this, they appear to suggest that God has some direct or indirect responsibility for their situation. There is some theoretical basis for this complaint, for in 6:9–10 God encouraged Isaiah to preach and "make the heart of this people calloused; make their ears dull." But in order to understand the whole picture about hardening, one must recognize that God's hardening of people like Pharaoh (Exod 7:3,13; 9:12; 10:1,20,27; 11:10) took place only after Pharaoh hardened his own heart (Exod 7:22; 8:15,19,32). Elsewhere people are warned not to harden their hearts but to be generous (Deut 15:7) and not to harden their hearts like the Israelites did in their wilderness journeys (Ps 95:8), so it appears that there are two sides to hardening. This prayer could either be (a) wrongly blaming God because those praying do not want to accept full responsibility for their own sinful situation, or (b) complaining that God did not supernaturally act to remove the temptations of life so that they would stop wandering and avoid hardening their own hearts.

In spite of this failure to fully confess their own failing at this point (later this will happen in 64:5b–7), the lamenter requests that God should "return, turn"[494] from his present course of action (allowing the hardening of their hearts) and turn to look favorably on his people as he did in the past (63:7–14). If God is the sovereign ruler of this world, he can change the course of history by being compassionate and merciful "for the sake of" (*lĕmaʿan*) his servants and his inheritance. This appeal to God's own interests should bring about a

---

[492] Whybray, *Isaiah 40–66*, 260–61, prefers the first interpretation. Hanson, *The Dawn of Apocalyptic*, 93, has the unlikely view that this refers to the group of people who returned from exile (here called Abraham and Israel) who did not recognize those people who stayed in the land.

[493] The imperfect verb in questions frequently expresses a modal sense; thus, a subjunctive mood for this verb should be translated "would, should, might" (GKC §107t). The verb תָּעָה means "he wandered, strayed," and refers to wandering off the path and going off on their own way.

[494] The verb שׁוּב "return, turn" is an imperative that either requests or exhorts God (GKC §110a).

divine response of intervention because these people are his family and his followers. This hope is based on the idea that God is their Father and Redeemer who delivered his people from Egypt and chose them to be his sons. They have a covenant relationship with God in which they have agreed to serve him and consequently inherit the land. They not only inherit God's land, but they themselves are the heritage of God, his possession. Surely in light of these factors God will do something for his own family.

63:18   The reason why God needs to listen to this request and turn with compassion and steadfast covenant love toward his servants is because of some of the negative consequences that have fallen on them. Unfortunately, the verse is not very clear and innumerable emendations are offered to attempt to resolve these problems. Widely accepted is the emended reading, parallel to the second line, "Why have the reprobates made light of your holy place?"[495] Following this interpretation, the complaint refers to reprobates defiling the temple and the destruction of the temple. These acts are often related to the desecration and burning of the temple in Jerusalem in 587 BC. But before one accepts this option too quickly, he should try to solve the text's problems without emending the text, if that is possible.

The problems are semantic, grammatical, and historical. First, the semantic meaning of the initial noun "for a little while" (*miṣʿār*) is questionable because (a) in the other four uses of this word (Gen 19:20a,20b; Job 8:7; 2 Chr 24:24) it does not have a temporal meaning, and (b) the Israelites in 587 BC did not lose possession of the temple for a short time (it was about 70 years). Second, the root *yāraš* can mean (a) "to possess" or (b) "to dispossess." Third, "the people of your holiness" (*ʿam qādšekā*) could refer to (a) your holy people, (b) the people of your holy place, or (c) the people of your holy land. Fourth, the word "enemies" (*ṣārēnû*) can be used of political or religious enemies. Fifth, it is unclear if "the people of your holiness" is the subject or the object of the verb. Finally, there is the difficulty in connecting what this says to any events in the past or future history of Israel.

If all emendations are set aside, one can argue that (a) the word "possess, dispossess" needs a direct object,[496] (b) there is no contrast ("but now," NIV) between line 1 and 2, and (c) *ʿam qādšekā* must refer to "your holy people" who are the servants and heritage of God in 63:17. Thus the first line (minus the first word) should read, "they dispossessed your holy people." The first word always refers to something that is few in number, so hypothetically it could be employed to describe a few days or years, a short period of time. Although many quickly define this historical event as the time when the Babylonians

---

[495] This emended translation is accepted by Blenkinsopp, *Isaiah 56–66*, 255, and Whybray, *Isaiah 40–66*, 262, suggests a similar, "Why have the wicked treated thy sanctuary with contempt?"

[496] Delitzsch, *Isaiah*, 462, makes "your holy people" the subject, but then he supplies an object "your holy land."

(the "enemies") took "holy people" from Jerusalem as captives and "trampled" the holy temple (see 64:10–11), the seventy years period of exile was hardly a "little while." Since there is no war or killing mentioned in this context and the problem is primarily the spiritual rebellion of the Israelites (63:10,16–17), an alternative to this understanding might suggest that the text is referring to a defilement of the temple by unfaithful Hebrews (cf. 1:11–15) and a loss of control of what was going on in the temple area for a short time. This happened in the past during the reigns of ungodly Israelite kings (for example during the reign of Ahaz in 2 Chr 28 or Manasseh in 2 Chr 33), and it will happen in the future (Dan 8:23–25; 9:25–27; 11:31–37). The problem is that many people have sinned and hardened their hearts against God (63:17), and this has led to the desecration of the temple area by ungodly leaders and their followers (56:9–57:13; 58:1–5; 59:1–15a; 64:4b–6b; 65:1–7; 66:3–4,17). Thus the spiritual problem is that the people do not honor God as their King and the Lord of the nation; consequently, God does not powerfully rule over them by providing his protective hand of mercy and miraculous acts of salvation. It is impossible to pinpoint a definitive date from the small amount of information in this problematic text. This verse merely describes the nation and the temple in a terrible situation. These factors alone should motivate God to restore his honor and act on behalf of his people.

63:19 [63:19a]   The lament section ends with what might be called a summary of the situation. The first line appears to be missing a word after "we are/ we have become." NIV adds the word "yours," while NRSV and NASB add "like" to smooth out the flow of thought, but neither addition is demanded. Furthermore, the retrospective pronoun "over them" (*bām*) implies that a relative pronoun is implied earlier in the verse.[497] This leaves the translations, "we are/ have become those whom you did not rule over for innumerable days," which again points back to the idea that they have not seen God's zeal, might, and compassion in action (63:16) as one would expect were God acting powerfully on their behalf as their Father and Redeemer. In the second line, the lamenting Israelites make a somewhat parallel claim that they are/have become "those upon whom your name was not called." These statements reveal how much these people feel separated from God and how far their sinfulness has carried them away from God. They do not see his strong arm ruling over them; instead, it appears as though God treats them no differently than the pagans whom God never called to be his people. The one praying believes that the people who are called the "people of Yahweh" should receive special attention and divine intervention from their God. The problem, of course, is that God cannot deal with them compassionately as long as they continue in their sins and do not confess them or turn from them.

---

[497] GKC §159m translates this phrase "we have become as they over whom (בָּם not בָּנוּ) thou no longer bearest rule."

CALL FOR GOD TO POWERFULLY INTERVENE (64:1–5a). [Hb. 63:19b–64:4a]   The Hebrew chapter division is unfortunate and inappropriate, for the change from the complaint in 63:15–19 to the petition occurs in the middle of 63:19. Thus the English chapter division, which takes place in the middle of Hebrew text of 63:19, represents a superior understanding of the change of thought in v. 19. The lamenter now offers his petition that requests that God should have acted by intervening on behalf of his people. In fact, God's inactivity should have ended long ago. He should have revealed his full power just like he did in the past at Sinai and on so many other earlier occasions. The two terms that tie these verses together are the verb "to act, do" (ʿāśâ) in 64:3,4,5a and the prepositional phrase "before you" (mippānêkā) in 64:1,2,3. The paragraph is organized around two points:

Call for a theophany   64:1–3 (Hb 63:19b–64:2)
Call for God's help   64:4–5a (Hb 64:3–4a)

64:1 [63:19b]   Earlier the lament has raised the problem of God's seeming absence or inaction (63:15), so this petition calls for God to respond by becoming actively involved with his people once again. The first wish has a perfect verb "you split" (qāraʿtā). It refers to something that the speaker wishes God had done in the past.[498] Thus the future-oriented NIV translation, "Oh that you would rend the heavens," should actually relate to the past, "Would that God had already split the heavens." The petitioner wishes that God had left his heavenly home long ago, had split open that solid curtain in the sky that hides him from human view, had come down to earth in his full glory, and had caused all of nature to "quake"[499] (Judg 5:4–5; Pss 18:7; 97:1–4). The prayer wishes for a divine theophany of the full glory of God similar to examples of his divine appearances in the past (cf. Deut 5:22–29; 32:22; Ps 18:8–16; Mic 1:3–4; Nah 1:3–6; Hab 3:3–15). In these situations God not only revealed his glory, but he also spoke his words to people, confronted evil, demonstrated his power, and brought salvation. The lamenter wants the glorious light of God's help (cf. 60:1–3) and the wrath of God's vengeance on his enemies to be seen by all men (63:1–6). In fact, his wish is that people had seen God in action long ago.

64:2 [64:1]   One might expect that this verse would give additional examples of situations in the past when God's great and glorious presence intervened in the affairs of mankind, but initially the picture is not all that clear. This verse uses a comparison related to the way fire kindles "stubble, brushwood"

---

[498] The particles לוּ or לוּא introduce the mood of something that is unfulfilled but still possible. When it comes before a perfect verb, as in 63:19b, it communicates "a wish that something might have happened in the past" (GKC §151e). If the verb is imperfect, then the wish relates to the future.

[499] The verb נָזֹלּוּ could hypothetically come from נָזַל "it flows, melts" but more likely from זָלַל "it shakes," since double-ע verbs usually double the ע radical with a dagesh forte (לּ) when the verb has a consonantal or vocalic ending (GKC §67c).

hămāsîm, an unknown term that is only found here in the Hebrew Bible (cf. Mal 4:1).[500] The second comparison comments on how fire makes water boil, but it is not connected with the rest of the verse very well.[501] These two references to fire must be comparisons that help the reader to understand the brilliance and hotness of the fire that is associated with the appearance of God's glory (60:1–3; Exod 3:2; 19:18; Ezek 1:4,27). In the past when God caused the brilliant fire of his glorious presence to be seen, he did this for a purpose. This happened "in order to make known"[502] God's name to his adversaries so that the nations would tremble because of God's presence. One thing is certain: if God had only appeared in all his glory and power as he had in the past, things would be totally different now.

64:3 [64:2]   Now comes a reference to past examples of the power of God's theophany when he appeared in all his brilliant glory. The specific situation is not all that clear, but it is at least possible that he was remembering the time of the giving of the law at Sinai when God's glory appeared on the top of the mountain. That was the time when he did "awesome things," fearful things that revealed God's power and glory. The common person was frightened and amazed at the extent of God's power when his glory was revealed over Mount Sinai (Deut 5:22–29). They would immediately realize their total inability to protect or defend themselves. This awesome revelation of his glory was far beyond anything anyone could imagine.[503]

The second half of the verse ("you came down and the mountains quaked at your presence") is identical to 63:19b, but this does not seem to have any structural, chiastic, or concluding significance; it just provides a repeated emphasis on a central point in the petition. In 63:19b there is a wish that God had done this earlier, while in 64:3 there is a recognition that God had indeed done this many years ago, as the initial hymn records (63:7–14). The petitioner who is aware of what happened in the distant past wishes that similar things had happened again. His only hope is that God will show his power and glory on behalf of his people.

64:4 [64:3]   C. Westermann calls this verse a "final piece of praise"[504] because it records the great things that God has done, his uniqueness, and the

---

[500] Koole, *Isaiah III, Volume 3: Isaiah 56–66*, 386, connects this word to a similar Arabic term that means "stubble" and notes that 1QIs[a] has the spelling עמסים, which A. Guillaume, "Some Readings in the Dead Sea Scrolls of Isaiah," *JBL* 76 (1957): 40–43, relates to the Arabic *ghamis*, which means brushwood.

[501] NIV adds "come down" from 64:1 to help integrate these first two lines with what follows.

[502] The infinitive construct לְהוֹדִיעַ communicates the purpose that God had in mind (GKC §114f).

[503] The imperfect verb נָקוּה could be a modal form expressing the possibility of what people might or could hope to see (GKC §107r).

[504] Westermann, *Isaiah 40–66*, 396. In addition, his translation of v. 4a adds לֹ at the beginning of the sentence (p. 391), thus turning this into a wish, "O that thou wouldst meet." Whybray, *Isaiah 40–66*, 263, heavily emends this verse by suggesting several changes—omitting words, changing

miraculous appearance of his glory in various theophanies. Although it could function effectively in a praise hymn, this paragraph is not praising God in this literary context. In light of the petitionary context of these verses, it is better to interpret 64:4–5a as support for the call that God act on behalf of his people in 64:1a. This call for action was based on the claim that from innumerable days in the past no one in any nation has ever heard of a God like Israel's God, and no eye has ever seen anything comparable to the God of Israel. This is not a theoretical argument or an inquiry about what people believe from their religious upbringing. He is arguing on the basis of real-life experiences in which God said or did something that was undeniably miraculous. He is attempting to define what is real and true based on human observation of things that happened to them. Because God came down in a cloud and a pillar of fire on top of Mount Sinai and spoke with an audible voice (Deut 5:22–27), there is absolute proof from experience that he exists, is a fearful and terrifying God, is powerful enough to shake Mount Sinai, wants to have a covenant relationship with his people, and can speak and communicate to mankind. In all these things God is unique. Although other religions may claim that their gods spoke and acted powerfully in their ancient mythological eras, has anyone actually seen them say or do anything in their lifetime? The implied answer is a resounding "No!"

When God revealed himself through the plagues in Egypt and by dividing the Red Sea, his action also proved that he can be trusted to assist his people. Thus, from experience the Israelites know that God is one who acts on behalf of those who trustingly wait for him. They did not get out of Egypt immediately (they had to wait until the 10 plagues were completed); they did not always have enough water to drink in the wilderness; they did not destroy Jericho in one day. In each case the Israelites can look back at their experiences with God and remember how they cried out again and again. Although they had to wait many years before God actually delivered them (Exodus 1–14), in each case God did act. Finally, when Moses came and told them that God planned to deliver them, the Israelites believed what God said (Exod 4:29–31). In a similar manner, Jericho was not conquered by the brilliant strategy of Israel's elite army. They had to wait and believe that God would defeat the city in his own way, so they marched around it day after day. But, finally, after six days of marching and waiting, God did destroy the walls of Jericho (Joshua 6). These and hundreds of other experiences taught them that if they were obedient, trusted God, and waited for his timing, he would eventually act on their behalf. Earlier in the book of Isaiah, Ahaz was challenged to trust God during the Syro-Ephraimite War (7:1–9), but he failed to do so. Instead, he sent messengers to the Assyrians and trusted them to help him (2 Chronicles 28), so God did not deliver him from his enemies. These past experiences justify

the number and person of verbs, and following a text closer to the Old Greek and Paul's quotation of this verse in 1 Cor 2:9. None of these appear to be required to make sense of this verse.

calling upon God to do something because the one praying knows that God "will act"[505] on behalf those who wait for him.

64:5a [64:4a] A corollary of waiting for and trusting God is obeying him and following his paths of righteousness. J. Muilenburg inserts the particle *lû* to make this another request for God to help them, similar to 64:1, but this amounts to a major change in the meaning of this phrase.[506] Since the previous verse ended with an imperfect verb which describes what God will do, it would not be odd to have the perfect verb in v. 5a be a prophetic perfect ("you will meet the ones who rejoice"), continuing this confident train of thinking that expects God to act in response to these petitions. God's covenant relationship with his people required that they do what God had commanded them to do in order to maintain their covenant relationship with him and receive his blessings. God will "meet, encounter, interact" (the root *pāgaʿ*) with (a) those who rejoice,[507] (b) those who act righteously, and (c) those who will remember God and his ways of doing things. One must assume that the interaction at this "meeting" will be positive (NIV paraphrases "come to help"), rather than neutral or negative ("fall on, attack" in Judg 8:21). Thus the emphasis is just on the privilege of meeting or encountering God (as in previous theophanies), not on all the positive blessings he might pour out on those who joyfully follow him.

The first requirement is to "rejoice," a word that describes the joy of those who are in a right relationship to God. Elsewhere, rejoicing is the glad response of nature (35:1) when God transforms the parched wilderness into blossoming flowers. People will also rejoice in the Lord in Jerusalem (61:10; 66:10) when he establishes his everlasting covenant with his people. They will rejoice because at that time he will establish the new heavens and the new earth (65:17). Even God will rejoice as he welcomes his people into his kingdom (62:5; 65:19). Of course rejoicing is not just something that people will do only in a later eschatological era; people should experience a deep-seated joy in the Lord in every era of history because of the marvelous work of God. But this is just the opposite of the attitude of the people in the complaint in 63:15–19.

The second requirement involves "doing righteousness, acting justly." Eventually believers will be clothed with a robe of righteousness (61:10) and be called "oaks of righteousness" (61:3), so all human relationships will depict God's righteous ways of acting. In the meantime God's people should

---

[505] The verb יַעֲשֶׂה is an imperfect verb that probably refers to the future "he will act" (NIV "who acts").

[506] Muilenburg, "Isaiah 40–66," 5:741, adds לִ֫, which he thinks dropped out because of haplography, for the previous sentence ends with לוֹ "to him." This gives the translation "O that thou wouldst meet him who repents and does righteousness." This textual change is a rational possibility, but it needs some linguistic clue to make it probable.

[507] The word שָׂשׂ is a participle from שׂוּשׂ, "the one who rejoices," which functions as a direct object (it follows the sign of the direct object marker אֵת), not as the adverb "joyfully" as in NIV.

"maintain justice and do what is right" (56:1; 58:2,8) when dealing with other people. Part of God's present work on earth is to enable his people to shine forth God's righteousness and his salvation so that unbelievers will come to know him (62:1–2). The confession of sin in 64:5b–7 indicates that this kind of behavior was not characteristic of the people at this time.

The third aspect is expressed in a more awkward way. The text does not have another participle parallel to the preceding two participles but instead literally reads "they will remember you in your ways." The one praying this petition has remembered God and some of God's ways throughout this prayer, especially in 63:7–14 and 64:1–4. Of course, the memory of God's ways is not an end in itself; God's ways are an example to follow "so that" (a good interpretation of the *waw* before the verb) they will act like God acts. These are high requirements that the Israelites do not meet, so one wonders why they are mentioned at this point in the petition. It is possible that this lamenter is suggesting that he is rejoicing in God's ways (63:7–14), confessing the nation's sins and getting right with God (64:5b–7), and remembering God's ways (64:1–5a). Thus, he is waiting hopefully (64:4b) so that God will act on behalf of himself and his community.

CONFESSION OF SINS (64:5b–7) [64:4b–6]. The beginning of this new paragraph is marked in 64:5b by the introductory interjection "behold" (*hēn*, NIV "But") and the movement to the new topic of confessing sins. The first-person plural pronouns ("we, us"), are used and the lamenter(s) talk of God's anger instead of his awesome theophanic acts. The sinfulness of the nation is so endemic and deeply ingrained in the people's ways of acting that there is a question about the possibility of being saved from these sins. This text pictures the deep depravity of these sinful people and the terrible impact sin has had on the lives and future of that nation. The good thing is that the one praying is admitting and confessing these sins, though it is surprising that there is no explicit call for God to be gracious and forgive these sins, and there is no promise to turn from these sins. This paragraph can be divided into two parts.

Terrible sin led to anger	64:5b–6
Failure to call on God led to God hiding	64:7

64:5b [64:4b] The first half of 64:5 spoke of the ideal of God meeting people who do right and follow him, but suddenly in v. 5b the lamenter(s) recognizes that in the near past "you yourself were angry"[508] with your people. God's anger is actually mentioned before the admission that "we sinned" (NIV reverses the order and puts God's anger after the people's sin), but the connection between these two acts is not spelled out explicitly."[509] Although a

---

[508] The presence of the personal subject pronoun אַתָּה "you" is unnecessary since the person and number of the verse is found embedded in the prefixes and suffixes on the root; thus, when the subject pronoun is used it creates an emphasis "you yourself" (GKC §135a).

[509] NIV makes a temporal connection between the two and puts the reference to sin first, but

causal ("because") or temporal ("when") connection is possible, F. Delitzsch proposes a better alternative translation, "and we stood as sinners," which fits in better with a confession of guilt. This translation also allows one to keep the Hebrew sentence order.[510]

The last clause is particularly difficult and is often emended to make sense out of it.[511] Literally the text reads "in them for innumerable days and we shall be saved," but what does this mean? NIV omits the first clause and makes the second clause into a question. Since the first half of the line does not have a verb (there are two verbs in the preceding line), it is normal in Hebrew to assume the "to be" verb as implied in a verbless noun clause.[512] Adding this implied verb, one would get the translation "we were in them [i.e., in sins] for innumerable days." The final clause could be a question that expresses pessimism that there is any hope,[513] as in NIV (though there is no question marker in this phrase in the Hebrew), but in a confession of sin it seems more likely that the clause would be a more positive statement that expresses optimism, "yet we can be saved."[514]

64:6 [64:5] The confession of sin continues with the honest admission that uncleanness has infected everyone in the community; no one is righteous, not even one (cf. 1 Kgs 8:46). This shows that the problem being faced by this community was not some outside military force or a problem related to their material circumstances. The central difficulty was the people's personal inability to avoid what was sinful. Sin had so pervaded their lives that even the things that most people would usually regard as righteous deeds were in fact more like filthy menstruation rags. This is an honest appraisal of the filthiness of sin, which is relatively rare in the past or today. Too often sin is deemed a slight mistake, a small or relatively minor infraction that is not really significant enough to confess. It is all too easy to overlook sin, forget it, or excuse it, assuming that it will not have a major impact on anyone's relationship to God. Instead, the sinner should follow the example of the person confessing sins in this passage. Sin is a dark and destructive act that makes a person an enemy of God. The sinner is more repulsive than a vile and rancid menstrual cloth. This

---

God's anger comes first in the Hebrew text. Childs, *Isaiah*, 527, argues for a causal connection with וַנֶּחֱטָא, "because you were angry, we have sinned." S. Blank, "'And All Our Virtues'—An Interpretation of Isaiah 64:4b–5a," *JBL* 71 (1952): 149–54, blames God for making the people sin.

[510] Delitzsch, *Isaiah*, 468, finds a parallel to this rendering of this word in Gen 43:9. Another alternative is to translate the verb וַנֶּחֱטָא as "and we continually/repeatedly sinned."

[511] The NRSV translation, "because you hid yourself we transgressed," reflects extensive emendation, while the Old Greek "therefore we error" is not of much help.

[512] The verbless noun clause usually "represents something *fixed, a state*" and is often made up of two nouns, but in this case there is a prepositional phrase and a noun (GKC §140e, 141f).

[513] Delitzsch, *Isaiah*, 468, suggests that this is a question: "and shall we be saved?"

[514] This understands the last verb וְנִוָּשֵׁעַ as a *niphal* imperfect that has a modal sense that expresses a wish or a possibility (GKC §107m-r). HCSB gives a positive meaning to this phrase rather than making it a question that is pessimistic.

graphically repulsive imagery is a stark contrast to the clothing of salvation and righteousness that believers will wear in God's future kingdom (61:10).

The second half of the verse compares sinners to a withered fading leaf on a tree. Elsewhere Isaiah refers to people under God's judgment as dying plants or withering leaves (1:30; 28:1,4; 40:7) instead of a living, vibrant plant that is bearing fruit. What happens when leaves fade and dry up? Soon the wind blows, and the useless leaves are carried away. So it is with these people. The person confessing these sins recognizes that "our iniquities, like the wind, carry us away."[515] The interpretation of this imagery could move in several directions. Is it saying that people are literally dead and sin carries them away to Sheol, or is this symbolism a reference to living an unproductive life in which they are carried away into the paths of evil by their iniquity? At minimum one can say that dried-up leaves are of no use to the tree or anyone else. When a leaf is living and productive, it is securely connected to the branch and the wind does not affect it; but when a leaf dies and loses its connection to the tree, the winds can easily blow it away. It loses control of its fate and all hope for the future.

64:7 [64:6] The situation has become so bad that no people "call"[516] on God's name to confess their sins or to pray for those who were swept away by their iniquities. No one bothers to "stir himself, arouse himself"[517] in order to seize or grasp onto God for help. People either are too busy with their own affairs, do not recognize the problem that sin has caused in the community, just simply do not care, or do not want to get involved. Possibly some do not know what to do or where to go for help, while others may not think it is any of their business, while a few others may not realize that God could help them if they called. This statement could be viewed either as the petitioner's accusation against the community, or as seems more likely, a frank admission of the utter failure of the people to even look to God for deliverance. They have moved far from their past traditions where God was intimately involved with every aspect of life (63:7–14) and have so seldom gone to God for help that many no longer even think to enlist his powerful arm to help them. Even today far too many people try everything else that might possibly resolve their problems and only go to God for help when everything else has utterly failed.

Part of the reason why some people do not go to God for help is that it appears to them that God has hidden his "face" from them and their community.

---

[515] The verb יְשָׂאֻנוּ from נָשָׂא is third masc. pl. "they carried us away," which appears to have a sg. subject ("our iniquity"). As a sg. noun with a suffix, וַעֲוֹנֵנוּ spells "our iniquity," while one would expect וַעֲוֹנֹתֵינוּ "our iniquities" if it were pl. This word should be interpreted as a pl., based on the pl. form of the verb, so one should conclude that this is either a defective form or a scribal error in which the י was omitted before the suffix (GKC §91k).

[516] The *qal* participle קוֹרֵא "one who calls" and the *hithpa'el* participle מִתְעוֹרֵר "the one who stirs himself" refer to durative action.

[517] The *hithpolel* participle מִתְעוֹרֵר is a reflexive form, "one waking himself up" (GKC §54.d, 67.l).

In the earlier words of praise, past times were remembered when God was not hidden; instead, he intervened and was compassionate toward his people (63:7). The angel of God's presence saved them when they were afflicted (63:9), and the Holy Spirit was among them (63:11). At other times, God's powerful arm was stretched out on their behalf (63:12). Nevertheless, in the petitionary section of this prayer, the lamenter admitted that these great acts of salvation were no longer happening, so there is the wish that "you would have come down from heaven and the mountains would have shook because of your presence" (64:1; cf. 60:1–3). The evidence that God has hidden his face[518] is based on the fact that God allowed his people to melt "in the hands of our iniquities" (not our enemies). Melting means that the people have no power to withstand and fight against these wicked ways; instead, they succumb to temptations and are defeated by iniquity. It is only by the power of God that anyone is able to reject sinfulness and not be defeated by it. God has already explained that he has hidden and will hide his face because of the people's sinfulness (59:1–2), so it is not surprising to read that he did not answer them. In effect, he was hiding his face from them and not looking on them with favor (57:17) because sin has separated them from God (59:1–2).

CALL FOR GOD TO ANSWER THIS PRAYER (64:8–12) [64:7–11]. The beginning of this paragraph is marked by the introductory "and now" (wĕʿattâ), an end to the confession of sins (64:5b–7), and the use of negative requests ("do not be angry') that call for God not to continue his negative relationship with his people but to act on their behalf.

The material is organized into two parts.

You made us, so do not be angry	64:8–9
We suffer, so do not afflict us more	64:10–12

The rhetorical questions in these verses express the deep desires of people who desperately want God to intervene on their behalf. The logic is: if you are our Father who made us and if you care anything about your children, how can you keep silent and not act on our behalf? Although such logic may not always move God to act immediately, it is always good for believers to recognize their complete and utter dependence on God's grace and cry out for his help. No one knows if the future years will hold good or bad times, but history indicates that God will allow people to suffer for various reasons. Whether the suffering is a just judgment for sins or a test of faith, it is always wise for people to lay out their problem before God and plead for his mercy and intervention.

64:8 [64:7] Initially the one praying returns to the theme of God's fatherhood, which was addressed in the lament in 63:16. "And now" (wĕʿattâ) God's

---

[518] Earlier in 1:15 God states that he will hide his face and not pay any attention to the sacrifices of the people because they are presenting abominations and their hands were full of blood. Isaiah 59:1–2 indicates that the people's sins have caused God to hide his face from them and not pay attention to their prayers.

fatherhood functions as a reason why he should act to rescue his people. Since he is the head of their family and their partner in the covenant, it is logical to expect that he would respond to the pleas of his covenant people. The second related image of God pictures him as the master potter (cf. 29:16; 45:9) and Israel as the clay that he works with to form his people. This is not a negative characterization of the people (i.e., that they are "dirt"); it is simply a metaphor of God's sovereignty over the nation. Since God formed this clay into Israel, his covenant nation (43:1,7,21; 44:21), he must value it and show some love for what he made. Can he just ignore what is his, or should he work with his clay to make it something that will bring glory and honor to his name?

64:9 [64:8] The two rationales for action in the previous verse suggest that God should not be angry with his people in an excessive manner (*ʿad mĕʾōd*) or to an excessive extent of time (*ʾal lāʿad*). If God's anger were extremely and ongoingly harsh, the nation of Israel would eventually be extinguished from the face of the earth. This prayer does not say that all suffering should stop immediately or that God was unfair to punish them for their sins, but it does ask for relief and compassion from severe persecution or oppression. In some ways this is something of an admission that God's anger was deserved, but it is also a request that it should not go on much longer. Possibly the one praying is suggesting that the punishment that they have endured so far has had its intended purpose. It has brought them back to God.

A key to any changed relationship with God is for the people to confess their sins and turn from their evil ways. In the preceding verses the people have recognized where they failed (64:5a-7), have confessed their sins, and now desire to return to a positive relationship with God. Their desire is that God would not remember their sins forever. This is consistent with the hymnic statements in 63:7 that God is a God of compassion and steadfast covenant love. Ps 103:8–12 indicates that God does not treat sinners as severely as they deserve because of his great love for them, that he does not maintain his anger forever (103:8–9), and that he does not remember their sins because he removes their transgressions as far as the east is from the west (103:12). Similarly, Mic 7:18–20 refers to God's forgiveness of transgressions, his plan not to stay angry forever, and his casting of forgiven sins into the depth of the sea. Earlier in 43:25 God refers to himself as a God who "blots out your transgressions" and "remembers your sin no more." Hezekiah's prayer in 38:17 also thanked God that "you have put all my sins behind your back."

Assuming that God will not be angry forever and will not remember their sins forever, a final request asks that God once again "should look, should take notice"[519] (63:15) of the condition of his people instead of turning his

---

[519] The imperative verb הַבֶּט־נָא functions to present a request to God (GKC §110a). The addition of נָא after the imperative verb is frequently added "to soften a command or make a request more courteous."

face away from them (64:7). This request is not on behalf of any one group of people within Israel; it is a request that applies to "all of us"[520] who are his people.

64:10–11 [64:9–10]   The second part of this request (64:10–12) relates to God's treatment of those who suffer in what some might consider "extreme"[521] ways. The temporal relationship between these events and the one praying is hard to determine,[522] but it is difficult to fit this into a time after the return of the people from exile, for at that time the people could not blame God for turning his back on them, for he had just defeated Babylon and safely brought them back from exile.[523] Ezekiel's vision of the glory of God in Babylon (Ezekiel 1–3) indicates that God did not completely turn his back on the captives when they were in Babylonian exile either. Jeremiah also believed that a remnant of good figs was to come from the group of people in exile (Jer 24:1–10). So what setting might this passage fit? If one looks ahead at the response of God to these complaints and requests, it is clear that (a) God will be available (65:1–2a), (b) God will punish the sinners because of their sinfulness (65:2b–7), and (c) and God will bring his righteous servants to inherit his land and worship at his Holy Mountain (65:7–16). Thus it appears that these laments are related to the eschatological fulfillment of God's plans for his servants. The audience needs to know that, before that final Day of the Lord, people will suffer, and extreme judgments will fall on the wicked, but none of these can prevent God from creating the new heavens and the new earth (65:17), where he will dwell with his people and bring them peace. Daniel 7 also speaks about a future time of great persecution before God destroys the evil beast and the horn, but in the end the source of evil will be cursed, and God will bring his saints into his eternal kingdom.

Isaiah 64:10–11 contain three examples of what almost anyone would consider extreme examples of God's punishment: (a) the desolation of the holy cities throughout the land, (b) the desolation of the city of Jerusalem; and (c) the destruction of the temple. As for the first example, "holy cities" are sometimes related to Zion and Jerusalem (the Upper and Lower cities), but this term is more likely a reference to "all the cities" (a rather extreme number) in the land of Judah because all the land is God's holy land. A punishment of a few cities

---

[520] The use of כֻּלָּנוּ "all of us" in 64:8 and 9 indicates that this is a prayer on behalf of the community, not one priestly group as opposed to another priestly group as Hanson suggests.

[521] Isaiah 64:8 brought up the question of extreme punishment and 64:12 ends with this same concern.

[522] Blenkinsopp, *Isaiah 56–66*, 253, 265, argues for a present relationship "Your holy cities are a wilderness" and connects this to some of the laments in Lamentations, immediately after the fall of Jerusalem in 587 BC. NRSV has a past interpretation "your holy cities have become a wilderness," which is grammatically unlikely, while J. Motyer, *Isaiah*, 521, suggests the possibility that these perfect verbs could be perfects of certainty, "Your cities are to become a wilderness."

[523] Often chaps. 56–66 are placed in a postexilic setting, but this prayer does not fit that period.

might seem appropriate and justified, but the desolation of all the land seems to be an extreme response. Secondly, the desolation of Jerusalem, the most important political and religious city in the nation, seems to manifest an extreme amount of anger on God's part. The third and most extreme example (64:11) of God's anger is the destruction of the holy and glorious temple (1 Kings 6) where all the past generations worshipped God. It is odd to hear this temple called "our holy and glorious house" instead of the more usual "your house" (56:5,7; 60:7; 62:9), though it is possible that "our" could include "God and his people's" temple. On the other hand, "our temple" shows how dear it was to the Hebrew people, that it was the temple that their parents worshipped in and was very deeply missed.[524] The destruction of the temple is extreme, for it was burned with fire. Daniel 7:25; 8:11–14; 9:26–27; 11:30–31 refer to similar future trials for God's people, including the trampling and desecration of the temple. The last thing mentioned is the ruin of "all our precious things," a nebulous phrase. Although this could refer to personal possessions, J. Muilenburg believes this refers to the precious gold and silver objects in and around the temple precinct.[525]

64:12 [64:11] This paragraph and the lament end with a final plea for God's mercy in the form of a twofold question that should probably be translated "would/could/can you restrain yourself concerning these things?"[526] The NIV provides a temporal interpretation in the phrase "after these things," but the clause would be better translated "concerning these things," that is, those things mentioned either in the whole lament or specifically those mentioned in 64:9–11. This asks if it would not be possible for God to restrain himself from his carrying out these and further acts of anger. Will he continue to restrain his compassion and not be merciful to his people?

The second half of the verse asks a similar question: "Would God continue to be silent and would he oppress us excessively?" This prayer provides no assurance about what God will do in the future, but the question suggests that this severe judgment is not the way of a God of compassion. There is a deep desire to see his steadfast love, to see him turn toward them very soon. These questions in v. 12 have no answer, yet they appear to suggest that it was just for God to judge their sin. They imply that God is not the kind of God who will be silent forever. He is not one who exacts extreme punishments on his people for a long time. This prayer may be partially based on his past practices mentioned

---

[524] Whybray, *Isaiah 40–66*, 266, minimizes the significance of this change by saying, "There is probably no significance in the fact that the temple, called 'thy sanctuary' in 63:18, is now called 'our . . . house: this is merely a slight change of mood in the expression of grief."

[525] Muilenburg, "Isaiah 40–66," 5:744. On the other hand, this could also refer to pleasant/precious places, possibly the personal homes and farms of the people.

[526] The *hithpa'al* תִּתְאַפָּק (also used at the end of 63:15) is an imperfect in an interrogative sentence that expresses possible action that might take place. The verb is usually translated with "would, could, should, can, or might" (GKC §107t).

in 42:14, but the reader will soon find out in 65:6 that he will not continue to
be silent. He will answer his people.

THEOLOGICAL IMPLICATIONS. Does this prayer have any significance for modern believers? Does this lament create an example that people
today should pray? If it does, why do people seldom hear their pastors or fellow believers praying to God like this? Is praying to God mainly just a series
of requests for physical healing, or is there more to it? Is praying just about me
and my relationship to God, or is there still a valid reason for offering prayers
of intercession that bring the needs of the community to God? Although the
"pastoral prayer" used to play a significant role in many church services in
the past, fewer and fewer churches are including it in the upbeat consumer-
oriented programs of today.

Nevertheless, this community lament offers a paradigm that has many attractive features for people in a congregation who have real needs. This community
lament illustrates a balance between praise (63:7–14), confession (64:5b–7),
and petition (63:15–19). It includes an emotional remembrance of the good old
days of the past as well as the needs of the people. It praises God for his past
compassion, questions why life in this world is so difficult, offers a confession
of the sins of the people, and calls for God to show his power to save them. The
central request is a deep longing to see God's mighty hand and compassionate love at work on their behalf in the future (63:15–19). This prayer squarely
faces the problem that sin cuts people off from God's mercy and argues for the
necessity of humbly confessing sins (64:1–5a). In a modern world where there
are so many problems, there are a host of people in most congregations who
are asking for help and wondering "how can we be delivered" (64:5b) from
these difficulties? All too often people have forgotten to call on God for help
(64:7). The wise leader should teach his people to pray for a renewed sense of
God's presence and a new demonstration of his zeal and power (63:15). God
hears these kinds of prayers, and 65:1–66:14 demonstrates that he answers
them too.

(2) God's Answer: Wicked Get Wrath; Humble Get Salvation (65:1–66:14)

Numerous authors have suggested that chaps. 65–66 function as a conclusion to the book of Isaiah because these chapters are connected to the themes
and vocabulary of chap. 1.[527] After identifying the repetition of the same words
in chap. 1 and chaps. 65–66, L. J. Liebreich proposed that these chapters function as an *inclusio* that unite the whole book of Isaiah.[528] Later R. Lack and M.
Sweeney expanded these observations, noting that the strongest connection is

---

[527] G. V. Smith, *Isaiah 1–39*, NAC (Nashville: B&H, 2007), 96, for a list of several key vocabulary connections.

[528] L. J. Liebreich, " The Composition of the Book of Isaiah," 276–77.

between 1:29–31 and chaps. 65–66.[529] W. A. M. Beuken found three conclusions in chaps. 65–66, with 65:1–66:14 being the conclusion to Trito-Isaiah, 66:15–20a being the conclusion to both Deutero and Trito-Isaiah, and 66:20b–24 being the conclusion to the whole book.[530] A. J. Tomasino provides numerous arguments for connecting 1:1–2:4 with 63:7–66:24, not only on the basis of vocabulary but also because of common themes and the overall structure of both sections.[531] D. M. Carr focused on some of the differences in conceptualizing God's relationship to the nation of Israel (they should repent in 1:2–28) and God's different ways of dealing with different groups within Israel (he will save the righteous and judge the wicked in 1:29–31; 65–66). But he maintains that ancient readers and oral hearers did not have a conscious literary preoccupation with literary coherence like modern readers do and that "a construal of these two texts as parts of an overarching literary whole does not represent the reconstructable intent of the editors."[532] M. A. Sweeney's most recent study of chaps. 65–66 argues that these chapters cite texts from throughout Isaiah (chaps. 2–4; 5; 6; 11; 13; 37:3,30–32), and thus they function as a conclusion to the whole book of Isaiah.[533] All these studies suggest that chaps. 65–66 have a double function; they not only answer the lament in 63:7–64:11, but they also bring many earlier themes in this book to a conclusion by raising some of the same issues found in chap. 1.

In this answer[534] to the lament, God presents his response to some of the issues raised in 63:7–64:12. God will judge those who ignore him and worship in pagan gardens (65:1–7). He will give the land and his blessing to his chosen servants but will bring his sword against those who have forsaken him

---

[529] R. Lack, *La symbolique du livre d'Isaïe: Essai sur l'image littéraire comme élément de structuration,* AnBib 59 (Rome: Pontifical Biblical Institute, 1973), 139–41. M. Sweeney, *Isaiah 1–4 and the Postexilic Understanding of the Isaiah Tradition,* BZAW 171 (Berlin, de Gruyter, 1988), 21–24.

[530] W. A. M. Beuken, "Isaiah Chapter LXV–LXVI: Trito-Isaiah and the Closure of the Book of Isaiah," in *The Congress Volume: Leuven 1989,* ed. J. A. Emerton, VTSup 43 (Leiden: Brill, 1991), 204–21. O. H Steck, *Studien zu Tritojesaja,* BZAW 203 (Berlin: de Gruyter, 1991), 217–28, 263–65, rejects Beuken's threefold conclusion theory and suggests that chap. 1 should be compared to the conclusion in 63:7–66:24 since both laments (1:5–9; 63:7–64:11) are answered in 65–66.

[531] A. J. Tomasino, "Isaiah 1.1–2.4 and 63–66," 81–98, believes these interconnections imply that "the final chapters of Isaiah were composed based on the pattern of the first oracle of Proto-Isaiah," through a double redaction of chaps. 65–66.

[532] D. M. Carr, "Reading Isaiah from Beginning (Isaiah 1) to End (Isaiah 65–66): Multiple Modern Possibilities," in *New Visions of Isaiah,* ed. R. F. Melugin and M. A. Sweeney, JSOTSup 214 (Sheffield: Sheffield Academic Press, 1996), 188–218, but he does believe that 1:29–31 were possibly added to chap. 1 by the editor of chaps. 65–66, since these verses represent the theology of 65–66.

[533] M. A. Sweeney, "Prophetic Exegesis in Isaiah 65–66," in Broyles and Evans, *Writing and Reading the Scroll of Isaiah,* 455–73.

[534] Schramm, *The Opponents of Third Isaiah,* 155, argues that the "primary function of 65:1–25 is to attack the fundamental presupposition of the speaker of the lament, the assertion that כלנו עמך ('we are all your people'). To this assertion 65:1–25 responds by saying 'No, you are not!'"

(65:8–16). God will create the new heavens and the new earth that will be full of rejoicing, long life, security, the enjoyment of the fruits of hard labor, and peace (65:17–25). God will honor the humble and contrite but will bring harsh times on those who do not respond to God's call and continue with their involvement in pagan practices (66:1–4). But Zion will give birth to many children who will rejoice, have peace, and receive God's comfort (66:5–14). In the end God will bring people from all nations into his glorious kingdom but will judge the wicked with his fire and sword (66:15–24).

Many have questioned the literary unity of this answer to the lament. C. Westermann attributes various segments within this answer to four different layers of redaction, based on form-critical divisions.[535] B. S. Childs rightly questions the results of the redactional reconstructions of these chapters and supports those studies that argue for some level of unity within this section.[536] J. Muilenburg finds unity because God speaks all of chap. 65 while 65:1–2,12 and 24 draw the whole together by their common emphasis on God's answering those who call on him.[537] A detailed analysis by E. C. Webster has identified a strong sense of unity within chap. 65 because of repeated references to God's "calling" (65:1,12,24), the "former" ways (65:7,16,17), and a reference to iniquities, contrasts, and blessings in each of the following paragraphs (65:1–7,8–16,17–25).[538] P. A. Smith also argues for the unity of the whole unit 65:1–66:17.[539] This section starts out condemning false worship (65:2–4) and ends with a similar condemnation (66:17).

Although Whybray[540] does not find a close relationship between the lament in 63:7–64:12 and chaps. 65–66, many would view 65:1–66:14 as God's answer to the lament. The lament claims that God has "hidden his face" (64:7), but the response indicates that God has revealed himself to those who truly seek him (65:1). He called, but they did not answer him (65:12; 66:4), and in

---

[535] Westermann, *Isaiah 40–66*, 307, ties (a) 65:16b–25; 66:6–16 to the first strand of information, (b) 65:1–16a; 66:3–5,17 to a second redaction, (c) 65:17,25; 66:6,15–17,20,22,25 to a third layer of redaction, and (d) 66:18–19,21 to a fourth redactor who is open to the inclusion of the Gentiles. Vermeylen, *Du Prophète Isaïe à l'apocalyptique*, 492–503, attempts to identify seven different redactional layers of additional material that was gradually included in chaps. 65–66.

[536] Childs, *Isaiah*, 533, notes the positive contributions of P. A. Smith, E. C. Webster, and W. A. M. Beuken, who all argue for unity.

[537] Muilenburg, "Isaiah 40–66," 5:745, 758, connects chaps. 65–66 because of their similar eschatological point of view, similar imagery and mood, and the same division of the nation between the apostates and the faithful.

[538] Webster, "The Rhetoric of Isaiah 63–65," 89–102; see especially the summary that lays out the whole chapter on p. 101.

[539] Smith, *Rhetoric and Redaction in Trito-Isaiah*, 129–32, points to the importance of 66:17, which closes this section. He divides this material into two subsections: (a) 65:1–66:4, which is addressed primarily to the apostates, and (b) 66:5–17, which is primarily addressed to the faithful.

[540] According to Whybray, *Isaiah 40–66*, 266, "Although at first sight verse 1 might suggest that this chapter contains Yahweh's answer to the preceding lamentation, there is no connection between these two passages." In contrast, Hanson, *The Dawn of Apocalyptic*, 80–81, maintains that the lament is "tightly bound" to chap. 65," which furnishes the answer to the query in 64:12.

the future he will not keep silent (62:1; 64:12; 65:6) but will answer before
they finish calling (65:24). To those who questioned "Where is God?" (63:11)
comes the answer "Here am I" (65:1). The problem is that some of these people
are rebellious, obstinate (63:10; 65:2), and involved with pagan worship (65:3–
5; 66:3), but the solution is that God will judge the wicked (65:6–7,12; 66:4–6)
and have compassion on his humble and contrite servants (66:2; cf. 57:15).
The organization of this literary unit is divided into five paragraphs.[541]

Wrath if you ignore God and use pagan ritual	65:1–7
Contrasting destinies: Destruction and blessings	65:8–16
Creation of a new world of joy and abundance	65:17–25
God honors the humble, judges those who go their own way	66:1–4
God will give Zion children and joy	66:5–14

The internal unity of these paragraphs is signaled by their repetition of common
vocabulary,[542] while the overall theme of all the paragraphs is the stark contrast between God's dealings with (a) the rebellious, who worship like pagans,
and (b) his faithful servants who humbly follow him. Each group of people will
receive its appropriate reward when God finally destroys the wicked and brings
his servants into his glorious new heavens and new earth.

WRATH IF YOU IGNORE GOD AND USE PAGAN RITUALS (65:1–7)

¹"I revealed myself to those who did not ask for me;
  I was found by those who did not seek me.
To a nation that did not call on my name,
  I said, 'Here am I, here am I.'
²All day long I have held out my hands
  to an obstinate people,
who walk in ways not good,
  pursuing their own imaginations—
³a people who continually provoke me
  to my very face,
offering sacrifices in gardens
  and burning incense on altars of brick;
⁴who sit among the graves
  and spend their nights keeping secret vigil;
who eat the flesh of pigs,
  and whose pots hold broth of unclean meat;
⁵who say, 'Keep away; don't come near me,
  for I am too sacred for you!'
Such people are smoke in my nostrils,
  a fire that keeps burning all day.

---

[541] Motyer, *Isaiah*, 522–23, organizes these two chapters (all of 65–66) into a chiastic structure
centered around the great promises about the future in 65:13–25. Nevertheless, 65:1 and 66:18–21
are hardly parallel members of this chiastic structure.

[542] Webster, "The Rhetoric of Isaiah 63–65," 89–102, deals with these issues in chap. 65.

> 6"See, it stands written before me:
>   I will not keep silent but will pay back in full;
>   I will pay it back into their laps—
> 7both your sins and the sins of your fathers,"
>   says the LORD.
> "Because they burned sacrifices on the mountains
>   and defied me on the hills,
> I will measure into their laps
>   the full payment for their former deeds."

God's answer to the preceding lament is that he was not completely silent in the past and will not be silent in the future. He did reveal himself to his people (65:1–2a), but they were stubborn and repeatedly offered pagan sacrifices, ate pork, and were involved with cults of the dead (65:2b–5). Because of these sinful ways, God will not keep silent any longer but will judge these people according to the nature of their sins (65:6–7). This traditional judgment speech is structured with an accusation of sinfulness followed by a divine punishment. This answer disputes the previous claim that God was silent (63:11).

Accusations against sinners	65:1–5
They did not seek me	1–2a
Their pagan practices	2b–5
God will intervene in judgment	65:6–7

God's initial answer states what he has done in four first-person perfect verbs as well as two interjections with first-person pronominal suffixes (*hinnî*, "behold me; here am I"). This repeated emphasis on what God ("I") has graciously done to make himself known (1–2a) creates a strong contrast with what the obstinate people in the nation (described using a series of participles) did that provoked God (2b–5). The conclusion in 65:6–7 returns to the first person "I" statements that explain how God will intervene in their lives in the future. He will not keep silent but will punish them.

65:1–2a The repeated emphasis on God's calling and answering his people in 65:1,12,24; 66:4 demonstrates that there is a direct relationship between the earlier complaints in 63:7–64:12 where some lamented that they had not seen God's zeal (63:15) because he hid his face (64:7) and was silent (64:12). Now God bluntly presents page 2, the rest of the story about his relationship to his people. The real facts are that God was not hidden in some dark faraway place where no one could find him, as some supposed (64:12). If the first two verbs can be understood as tolerative *niphal* verbs,[543] then God is defending himself against the false accusations that he does not care about or respond to those who worship him. God does allow people to seek him, and

---

[543] *IBHS* §23.4f-g and GKC §51c view the tolerative as expressing what "the subject allows to happen to himself or to have an effect on himself."

he does allow himself to be found,[544] but no one answers (or calls 64:7) as 50:2 has already stated.[545] His willingness to answer and help the righteous was promised in 58:9 and will be emphasized again at the end of this chapter (65:24). God's theological claim that he answers prayers can be defended from historical experience, for when the Israelites cried out to God in Egypt (Exod 3:7–8), in the period of the Judges (Judg 3:9,15; 6:7–14), during the reign of Asa (1 Chr 15:2,4), or when Sennacherib attacked Hezekiah in Jerusalem (37:1,4,14–21), he always heard and responded to his people. The rebellious people who lamented in 63:7–64:12 may have said a few prayers in the past, but did they truly seek and trust in God alone (65:3–5)?

God's statement goes far beyond the idea that he has answered those who called. It argues that, on at least some occasions, God graciously answered and compassionately appeared to those who were not even seeking or asking for him. This could be referring to examples like God's appearance to Moses in the burning bush, even though there is no indication that Moses was seeking a divine encounter with God (Exod 3:3–6). God appeared to Isaiah in chaps. 6 and 20 to commission him for his service, but there is no indication that Isaiah was seeking God on either occasion. Many of the prophecies in the book of Isaiah could serve as examples of situations where God revealed himself and his instruction to his people, frequently without them ever seeking advice from God (30:2).[546]

To this sinful Israelite "nation" (gôy), a derogatory term for foreign nations that is used instead of the covenant term "people" ('am), God says, "Here I am; here I am!" This repetition could indicate something of God's frustration with this obstinate[547] nation that did not call[548] and the urgent need for them to wake up and turn to him. One can almost imagine in modern terminology, God waving his hand and screaming out this exclamation, "Wake up, over here, I'm right beside you!" The failure to call on the name of God indicates just how far these people are from God. If people then or today do not call on God, it is not surprising that they feel distant from God.

In v. 2a God claims that he even spread out his hands to them, offering to help and to care for them; he did not hide his face as they claim in 64:7. This did not happen just once but "all day long," an expression that describes both

[544] P. A. Smith, *Rhetoric and Redaction in Trito-Isaiah*, 135, observes the close connection between the vocabulary in 65:1 and 55:6–9 ("seek," "find," "call").

[545] Apparently they are seeking guidance from pagan cults, as 65:3–5; 66:3,17 indicate.

[546] Paul in Rom 10:20 quotes this verse, seeing the principle that God reveals himself to those who do not seek God applying broadly to both sinful Gentiles as well as Hebrews. M. A. Seifrid, "Romans," *CNTOT*, 665–66.

[547] 1QIsᵃ has the less likely סורר "disobedient," but the MT סורר "stubborn, obstinate" is preferable.

[548] The *pu'al* passive verb קֹרָא would be translated "they were not called by my name," but the versions (Qumran could support several grammatical interpretations) argue for an active voice interpretation.

God's patience, his devotion, and his persistent attempt to reach out to these "people" (*'am*). At this point he uses the more personal term "people" instead of "nation" (65:1), but he does not use "my people" (*'ammî*), for they are an obstinate and rebellious people. This picture of a gracious God who wants to speak with his people presents a stark contrast from what these rebellious people said about God in their lament (63:7–64:12).

65:2b–3a   The reason why these people have not truly sought God and have not responded to his stretched-out arms is spelled out in detail in the following verses. Initially, the blame is related to general factors concerning their ways (2b) and how their action affects their relationship to God (3a). Isaiah 65:3b–5 will spell out specific ways in which these people have rejected God. The first of seven participles describes those who walk[549] in evil ways, follow after evil thoughts, and reject God (cf. 59:1–2).[550] The basis for their perverse theological understanding is "their own thoughts," not the divine revelation in the *torah* or the preaching of the prophets. Earlier in 55:7 there was a call for the wicked to seek God and forsake their evil ways and thoughts, but obviously these people have not repented and forsaken their old ways and thought processes. These are people who are provoking God (v. 3a) by their evil ways and their perverse thinking. This happens continually, indicating that their offensive behavior is widespread among this group and has become a part of their accepted norm. The fact that this is done "before me, to my face" (*'al pānay*) suggests that these things are done openly where God can see them, in God's holy presence, or in the temple area itself (64:1,6). Since God's presence is not exclusively limited just to the temple precincts, these offences should not be limited just to the activities in his holy courts.

65:3b–5a   Because of a general lack of information about various pagan religious practices throughout the history of Israel, there is a good deal of confusion on how to understand the pagan worship described in these verses.[551] These offensive acts are part of the worship ritual practiced by a group of Hebrews, not by pagans from other nations. The first two rituals in 65:3b are described in two participle phrases as (a) those who are sacrificing in gardens and (b) those who are burning incense on bricks.[552] These sins may be connected to the pagan worship described in 57:3–8; 66:3,17, as well as the worship among the sacred oaks and gardens in 1:29–30. J. Motyer connects these practices to preexilic Canaanite cultic practices, but others assume that

---

[549] The participle הַהֹלְכִים "the ones who are walking" has the article, suggesting that it is used as a noun or a relative clause (GKC §116g,o).

[550] In 63:17 they blame God for their evil ways, a sign of just how their perverse thoughts and theological understandings had twisted their own sense of personal responsibility.

[551] Hanson, *The Dawn of Apocalyptic*, 147, understands the charges in 65:3–5 as symbolic and hyperbolic, not literal. He treats these as "symbols of illegitimate practices in the central cult" by the religious, elite Zadokites, who are claiming exclusive rights to the temple in 65:5.

[552] The Old Greek translation apparently did not know this word, so it translated "to demons."

these practices continued to exist into the postexilic era. W. Houston's study of unclean animals comes to the very tentative conclusion that "although the evidence is scattered and difficult to interpret there is some indication that in Syria-Palestine, as well as in neighboring countries, that the pig, and possibly other animals, while not normally used in public cults, was employed as a victim, and eaten, in obscure and perhaps secret cults offered to the dead or deities of the underworld."[553] Such limited archaeological and literary knowledge of these secret cults argues against the possibility of drawing any firm conclusions about the origin or nature of the pagan worship in this verse.

Verse 4 describes four more practices: (a) sitting among the graves, (b) spending the night in hidden places and (c) eating the flesh of pigs, and (d) eating unclean meat. T. J. Lewis connects all these practices to the cult of worshipping the dead and Molech worship,[554] but one must be careful in interpreting these actions, for this verse does not say what these people were actually doing in these tombs and hidden places.[555] There is no explicit reference to ancestor worship or necromancy[556] (cf. 8:19) or Molech worship in this passage, so this could simply be an accusation that they were eating unclean food (Num 19:16). J. L. Koole states that pigs "hardly played any role as a source of meat in Canaan and the surrounding countries,"[557] so this appears to be a ritual setting that purposely rejects earlier eating prohibitions (Lev 11:7; Deut 14:8), even allowing people to drink things that were abominable.

Finally in 65:5a these condemned people are quoted, claiming that they view themselves as holy; thus, they do not want others to come near them to defile them. The imperative command "draw near to yourself"[558] must mean something like "keep to yourself," being parallel to the second mild prohibition "do not touch me." The rationale for this instruction is that they are holy. Since this is usually an intransitive verb, it usually does not take an object, but there is a suffix ("you") after this verb in this sentence. The Old Greek solves this problem by omitting the object, while J. Blenkinsopp, who interprets this as the cult of Asherah, interprets the suffix as an indirect object "I have been set

---

[553] W. Houston, *Purity and Monotheism: Clean and Unclean Animals in Biblical Law* (JSOTS 140; Sheffield: Academic Press, 1993), 168.

[554] T. J. Lewis, *Cults of the Dead in Ancient Israel and Ugarit,* 158–60, 389–91, who also finds signs of Molech worship and necromancy in 8:16–20; 19:3; 28:15,18; 29:4, and 57:9.

[555] "And in hidden places" וּבַנְּצוּרִים is divided into two words, בֵּין צוּרִים "between rocks," by M. Dahood, "Textual Problems in Isaiah," *CBQ* 22 (1960): 408–9. This change is not needed because the text makes sense as it is.

[556] Westermann, *Isaiah 40–66,* 401, believes that their presence in the tombs "was for the purpose of obtaining oracles from the dead," but this is never said in this text. Schramm, *The Opponents of Third Isaiah,* 146, relates this verse either to "consulting or caring for the dead."

[557] Koole, *Isaiah III, Volume 3: Isaiah 56–66,* 416.

[558] The imperative verb in the phrase קְרַב אֵלֶיךָ could be translated as an exhortation or command, "draw near to yourself," but it is impossible to draw near to yourself; thus, this must be an idiomatic way of saying something like "keep to yourself," similar to the next statement "do not touch me."

apart from you,"[559] which might better be translated simply as "I am holy to you/with reference to you." This appears to be a rather ironic twist to the real facts because these pagan worshippers are anything but holy. God is holy and everything they were doing looks like it belongs to some brand of pagan practices that defiles them. This blasphemous (or arrogant) claim of being holy was probably made by priestly individuals who officiated at these hidden places, but these statements could also have applied more broadly to the "rebellious people/group" that followed these practices.

65:5b Smoke and fire are often associated with God's anger (Deut 29:20; 32:22), but in this context these terms appear to be a very anthropomorphic description of God's negative reaction to the vile acts of these people. He responds to them just like people would react when smoke from a fire is blown into their face and up their noses. Israel's worship and the burning of sacrifices and incense were supposed to be a sweet-smelling aroma to God (Lev 1:9,17; 2:2,9,12), and God wanted the fire on the altar to be perpetually burning all day long (Lev 6:13). But these pagan people and their practices were[560] more like the smoke that makes the eyes burn, irritates the nose and lungs, and causes a person to cough and turn away. This offensive irritation was not a mild or temporary discomfort; it went on every day, all day long (matching "all day long" in v. 2a).

65:6–7 The punishment at the end of this judgment speech begins with an interjection "behold" (*hinnēh*) to capture the audience's attention and reinforce the certainty of what God will do. God refers to something that "is written"[561] before him, but it is not clear if this is a written judgment decree (8:1; 30:8; Jer 22:30; 25:13; Job 13:26), a book containing the names of the living (Exod 32:32–33), a reference to an earlier part of the book of Isaiah, or a scroll that records the evil deeds of these sinners (Dan 7:10; Mal 3:16). The last option perhaps makes the most sense.

Although the earlier lament claimed that God was silent (64:12) and has not intervened on their behalf (63:15,19), God now announces that they will soon see him in action for he will no longer be silent. The next clause begins

---

[559] Blenkinsopp, *Isaiah 56–66*, 267–8, based on GKC §116x gives examples where the remoter indirect object is connected to the verb in the direct object slot. J. A. Emerton, "Notes on the Text and Translation of Isaiah 22:8–11 and 65:5," *VT* 30 (1980): 437–51. Whybray, *Isaiah 40–66*, 270, prefers to change the vocalization of the word into a *pi'el* form, which can take the object: "for (otherwise) I should communicate holiness to you." Finally, the Aramaic Targum gives a comparative understanding of the clause by translating "I am holier than you" (cf. NRSV). L. S. Tiemeyer, "The Haughtiness of the Priesthood: 65,5," *VT* 85 (2004): 237–44, reviews the versions and various options in great detail and prefers the comparative translation. She views both these priests and those offering the sacrifices in 63:3 as haughty YHWH priests working at the temple.

[560] This verbless noun clause אֵלֶּה עָשָׁן, (lit.) must have a verb supplied: "These [are] smoke in my nostrils."

[561] The fem. passive participle כְּתוּבָה "is written" is used verbally as the predicate in this sentence (GKC §116f,m), and it refers to something that was already recorded. Muilenburg, "Isaiah 40–66," 5:748, believes this writing refers to God's sentence of the sinners, but he also compares this to a heavenly accounting system similar to the Babylonian book of destinies.

with a conjunction creating a contrast between what he will not do and what he will do.[562] Although a contrastive translation like "but" is appropriate in other grammatical contexts, "except, until, unless" is a better translation in this context.[563] This restrictive sense indicates that God will not keep silent about their sins "until, unless" he has exacted a just recompense. In order to emphasize God's holy plans to judge these sinful people, he again states, "Indeed, I will justly recompense, repay" (a prophetic perfect). The final prepositional phrase "into their laps, bosom" is unclear. J. Oswalt suggests that this is a double entendre, referring both to the bosom which is the area of the heart, the essence of a person, as well as the place where people would hold things that they had collected in the folds of their outer garment (Ruth 3:15).[564] Although these people were probably looking for God to judge their enemies and not to have compassion on them, God's plans were quite different from what these so-called "holy" people thought.

Verse 7a makes a parenthetical statement about the breadth of God's judgment as well as a direct accusation using second-person pronouns ("your"), shifting from the third-person pronoun "their" in v. 6. It presents a broad perspective about how God will deal with all sins. This text does not focus on any particular type of sin, but, in light of the context of 65:2b–5, this statement may be directed at all examples of pagan worship that existed in Israel. God holds every past generation and the then-present one responsible for their own iniquities; they both have sinned in similar ways by accepting certain pagan practices. One will not be punished instead of the other, and the present generation cannot blame their parents for all their problems (cf. Ezek 18:1–4).

It is strange to have "declares the Lord" in the middle of the verse instead of at the end of the verse where it might be more expected.[565] It is possible that the final clause is an afterthought that was added to clarify and emphasize what has already been said, for it tends to repeat or continue the statements already made in 65:6. The final portion of 65:7 contains a brief reason for God's judgment and a repeated emphasis on God's determination to require full accountability for all their sins. There are two possible ways to connect this final clause to what goes before it. This could be a final sentence giving the reason ("because" *ʾăšer* as in NIV) for God's judgment by pointing to sins of pagan sacrifices on hilltops, a phrase that is often associated in Kings and

---

[562] NIV, NASB, NRSV, HCSB all translate אִם כִּי as "but," though Whybray, *Isaiah 40–66*, 271, indicates "until" would be a better translation.

[563] GKC §163c indicates that when אִם כִּי is followed by a perfect verb, which is the case in 65:6, it introduces an exceptive clause similar to 55:10. The versions understand this as "but"; also, J. L. Koole, *Isaiah III, Volume 3: Isaiah 56–66*, 420, defends "but" by taking the perfect verb as a prophetic perfect "will repay"; nevertheless, the syntax argues against this understanding of the clause.

[564] Oswalt, *Isaiah 40–66*, 640–41, believes this repayment "will go to the very center of life."

[565] This unexpected location has produced a multitude of critical reconstructions of this verse.

the prophetic books with the worship of Baal (57:7; 1 Kgs 14:22–24; 16:4; 17:10; Jer 3:6; 17:2; Ezek 6:13; 20:27–28; Hos 4:13). Another more natural approach would not view this as a causal phrase but as a relative clause ("who" *ʾăšer*) modifying "your fathers"; thus, it is a continuation of the first half of the sentence.[566] This might identify a distinguishing factor between the worship of the fathers (on the hilltops) and the sons (in gardens), though 57:7 tends to raise questions about such a distinction. Thus the point may be that all types of pagan worship (in the gardens and in the hills) "provoke, taunt, revile" (from *ḥārap*) the holiness, righteousness, and glory of God. Therefore, just as v. 6 said, God will require a just recompense that is proportionally measured out into their laps according to the vileness of their sinful deeds. They will suffer the consequences that they deserve, but it will not be the response that they were expecting from God.

CONTRASTING DESTINIES: DESTRUCTION AND BLESSINGS (65:8–16)

⁸This is what the LORD says:

"As when juice is still found in a cluster of grapes
    and men say, 'Don't destroy it,
    there is yet some good in it,'
so will I do in behalf of my servants;
    I will not destroy them all.
⁹I will bring forth descendants from Jacob,
    and from Judah those who will possess my mountains;
my chosen people will inherit them,
    and there will my servants live.
¹⁰Sharon will become a pasture for flocks,
    and the Valley of Achor a resting place for herds,
    for my people who seek me.

¹¹"But as for you who forsake the LORD
    and forget my holy mountain,
who spread a table for Fortune
    and fill bowls of mixed wine for Destiny,
¹²I will destine you for the sword,
    and you will all bend down for the slaughter;
for I called but you did not answer,
    I spoke but you did not listen.
You did evil in my sight
    and chose what displeases me."

¹³Therefore this is what the Sovereign LORD says:

---

[566] The word אֲשֶׁר most frequently functions as a relative pronoun introducing a subordinate clause that modifies a noun (GKC §155), but it can function circumstantially to introduce a causal clause (GKC §158b). J. Oswalt, *Isaiah 40–66*, 634, and J. L. Koole, *Isaiah III, Volume 3: Isaiah 56–66*, 422, interpret this as a relative, while most translations prefer the causal interpretation.

> "My servants will eat,
>   but you will go hungry;
> my servants will drink,
>   but you will go thirsty;
> my servants will rejoice,
>   but you will be put to shame.
> ¹⁴My servants will sing
>   out of the joy of their hearts,
> but you will cry out
>   from anguish of heart
>   and wail in brokenness of spirit.
> ¹⁵You will leave your name
>   to my chosen ones as a curse;
> the Sovereign LORD will put you to death,
>   but to his servants he will give another name.
> ¹⁶Whoever invokes a blessing in the land
>   will do so by the God of truth;
> he who takes an oath in the land
>   will swear by the God of truth.
> For the past troubles will be forgotten
>   and hidden from my eyes.

This paragraph is a continuation of God's answer that is directed primarily to "you" (65:11–15), the sinful people God will judge. The prophet explains in bold contrasts how God will distinguish between his servants and those who reject God. His servants who seek him will inherit the land, never be hungry, rejoice, and have a new name, but those who forsake and do not listen to what he says will have nothing to eat, suffer shame, be slaughtered, and receive God's curse.

Although it is not surprising to read about a curse on those who forsake God, commentators have noted that there is a major break between God's dealing with "all Israel" as one entity in past messages and the development of an extensive contrast between the apostates in Israel and "my servants" (65:13–15). While it is true that God did wonderful things for all his people during the time of Moses (63:7–13), the main clue to the resolution of this lament is the recognition that God has always acted on behalf of those who trust in him and do justice (64:4b–5a) and has always been angry with those who sin (64:5b). This contrast was already evident in the discussion of those who will enter God's kingdom in chaps. 61–62 and those who will suffer God's wrath in 60:12; 63:1–6. It was also evident in the contrasting destiny of those who forsake God in 57:3–13a and the contrite and lowly who take refuge in God (57:13b–15). As early as 1:18–19,24–28; 10:20–23; 22:15–24, it was abundantly clear that God would distinguish between the righteous and the wicked in Israel, so one should not view this distinction as a new theological development that is first introduced at this point.

The followers of God in this paragraph are identified as the "seed" of Jacob (65:9) and "my servants" (65:9–15) who will inherit God's kingdom (60–62). W. A. M. Beuken identified these plural "servants," who first appeared in 54:17, as the spiritual seed (45:25; 48:18; 53:10) of the "Servant of the Lord" (52:13–53:12).[567] God will fulfill all his glorious promises to these servants but will bring his curse on those Israelites who are involved with pagan worship in 65:1–7,11–12. The structure of this paragraph is divided in two sections.

Destiny of the servants and those who forsake God	65:8–10
God's treatment of good grapes	8
Blessings for his servants	9–10
Destruction for others	11–12
Contrasting destinies	65:13–16
God's contrasting plans	13–14
God's blessing and curse	14–16

The messenger formulas that introduce these two new divine revelations in 65:8 and 65:13 help define the overall structure of this material, while the change of topics in 65:17 marks the introduction of a new paragraph in 65:17.[568] Another linguistic marker that helps define 65:8–16 is the reference to God's "blessing" (65:8, NIV "good") at the beginning of the paragraph and another reference to God's blessing in 65:16 at the end of the paragraph. One connection between this paragraph and the preceding one is the contrast between those who "seek me" in 65:10b and those who "do not seek me" in 65:1. God will not destroy all the seed of Jacob (65:8b) but will bring forth from the nation his special chosen servants who will seek him (65:9–11). The earlier lament called for God to act in compassion and salvation, and this answer indicates that God will do just that for his servants, but not for all Israel. His judgment will fall on those who forsake him.

65:8 The paragraph begins with another announcement that this is what God says. Although it may seem unnecessary to say this again and again, the persuasive abilities of the prophet are heavily dependent on the authoritative source of his message. People need to know that the message he delivers is not a biased political agenda or just his own private opinion, especially when he is dealing with a somewhat controversial topic.

The first answer to the lament in 65:1–7 sounds very severe, and it provides no hope to those in the nation who did not call on God's name (65:1). Some

---

[567] Beuken, "The Main Theme of Trito-Isaiah: 'The Servants of the Lord,' " *JSOT* 47 (1990): 67–87, struggles to make this the main theme since the word "servants" does not occur until 63:17 and then not again until chaps. 65–66. Nevertheless, even when the "servants" are not identified by this title, most of chaps. 56–66 do talk about those who please, honor, follow, praise, and honor God, even though the term servant is not used.

[568] Westermann, *Isaiah 40–66*, 406, extends this unit from vv. 8–16b, putting v. 16b with the following paragraph.

view this as a major theological change from the earlier belief that all Israel would be saved.[569] Nevertheless, earlier messages have talked about a righteous remnant, and numerous earlier messages make a distinction between the wicked and the righteous in Israel (1:26–27; 4:2–3; 6:13; 10:20–23; 17:4–6; 50:10–11; 57:3–13a, and 57:13b–15),[570] so it was well known that God did not plan to destroy or to save everyone within Israel. This verse communicates similar information by comparing what a farmer does with grapes at harvest time (God had his own vineyard in 5:1–7; 27:2–5). The verse is built around an "as (the farmer) . . . so (God)"[571] syntactical construction that draws on the common practice of grape harvesters. Late in the grape season the grape pickers trim the vines (18:5), but as they do this they will find some clusters that are dried up and sour as well as a few clusters that still have a few grapes with juice in them. The common thing that most vineyard owners would tell their workers is, "Do not destroy the whole cluster ('it')." The reason for sparing the cluster from destruction is that there is still a "blessing" (*bĕrākâ* NIV "good") in it. The blessing refers to the positive gift of vitality and joy that the juice can provide to the one eating the grapes. The last part of the verse indicates that God will act just like (*kēn* "so, thus") the grape pickers. Responding to the lament's request for God to do something "for the sake of your servants" (63:17), God now responds that he will not destroy all of Israel "for the sake of my servants." Some will be spared.

65:9–10   God's commitment to his servants goes much beyond not destroying them.[572] Although there is not much juice left in the cluster of grapes, implying that his servants are few in number, God will cause to go out from both Jacob and Judah (i.e., from all the tribes) "seeds, descendants" (*zeraʿ*) just as he has promised in earlier prophecies. Sometime in the future these

---

[569] Schramm, *The Opponents of Third Isaiah*, 158, states "we are witnessing here a major change in the theology of the Hebrew Bible. Salvation is no longer conceived purely in national terms."

[570] G. Hasel, *The Remnant: The History and Theology of the Remnant Idea from Genesis to Isaiah* (AUM 5; Berrien Springs: Andrews University, 1980), treats the long history of this idea, before and within Isaiah. Whybray, *Isaiah 40–66*, 272, believes this concept in 65:8 is different from the remnant concept and that a more individual understanding of faith did not arise until after the exile; nevertheless, individual responsibility was present as early as Cain (Genesis 4), Levi, and Simeon (Gen 49:5–7; Exod 32:25; Num 25:9,14), and the whole law requires individuals to be accountable for their actions. Jeremiah's contrast between the good and bad grapes (Jeremiah 24) is a late preexilic example of this distinction that God will make between people in Israel.

[571] The initial כַּאֲשֶׁר could be translated "when" but the appearance of כֵּן "so" implies that it should be translated "as" to complete the comparison (see GKC §161b for the comparative use and 164d for the temporal use).

[572] P. A. Smith, *Rhetoric and Redaction in Trito-Isaiah*, 140–42, rightly rejects the view that 65:9–10 does not fit into its present context because it does not present information applicable to those who forsake God, the prophet's audience at this point (the view of Westermann). Isaiah 65:9–10 is linguistically integrated within the context (see "seek" in 65:1,10), expanding on the treatment of the good grapes in 65:8 and agreeing with the strong distinction between the righteous and the wicked.

offspring will arrive from other faraway countries (43:5–6; 60:4–5) with great singing (51:11), and there will be so many that there will not be enough room for them (54:2–3). These are the people who will inherit the land of Israel ("my mountains"). This is a reference to the hill country of Judah and Israel, the place that God will restore to his people (49:8; 54:3; 57:13b; 60:21; 61:7), but these mountains probably represent the whole land of Israel. There is no specific mention of the coming of the Gentiles (60:3–9) because in these verses God is talking specifically about what he will do for his servants within Israel. At this point the promise that they will live in the land refers only to the righteous within Israel, not to the whole nation. This verse describes God's future plans for "my chosen ones" and "my servants" from Israel in order to assure them that God has not forgotten them or changed his plans about what he promised them in the past. These assurances reaffirm the promises to Abram that God would give the land to his seed as an eternal inheritance (Gen 13:14–15; 15:18–21; 17:8; 26:3; 28:13; 35:12). Since these words are spoken primarily to those who forsake God, they function as a persuasive argument for all people to change their ways if they want to experience the rich blessings and fulfilled promises that God's "servants" will enjoy.

Verse 10 refers to specific areas in the land of Israel where people will live. The Sharon Plain in the western part of the country is a relatively flat, fertile pastureland (35:1–2; 1 Chr 5:16; 27:29) that runs north and south between the coastal plains along the sea and the mountainous hill country, extending south from the Carmel Ridge. The valley of Achor on the eastern side of the country is the narrow infertile valley that leads up from the Jordan River to the hill country of Israel. It is most famous for the sin committed by Achan in Joshua 7. Both of these locations will be lush areas for people to pasture their herds in the future. People and fertility probably should not be limited to just these two locations; these two places represent what will happen to the whole land. Hosea 2:15 also refers to a future time when God will transform the valley of Achor into a place of hope. These lands will be transformed for the enjoyment of "my people" who "seek me" (55:6, but contrast 65:1). "My people" are those who commit themselves to God and follow him; they belong to God and respond to God when he calls. Those who seek God are those who know that they cannot make it on their own; they recognize that their only source of guidance, assistance, and salvation must be God. This promise of land does not refer to God giving back the land to the exiles who came back from the Babylonian captivity after Cyrus defeated Babylon (Ezra 1:1–4);[573]

---

[573] Westermann, *Isaiah 40–66*, 405, considers this as "a prophecy spoken during the exile, promising the descendants of those living in foreign countries that they will eventually repossess the land." This reference to the postexilic situation seems to contradict what is promised in 65:17–25. This view of the fulfillment would also mean that this was a false prophecy, for all these wonderful things did not happen after the people returned from Babylon to the land of Judah.

instead, it refers to what God will do in the future eschatological era spoken of in chaps. 60–62 and 65:17–25.

65:11–12 Having reiterated all the great things that God will do for his chosen people, the prophet now turns back to address his audience ("you"), the people who have forsaken God. These verses present the antithetical way God will deal with "you" ('*attem*), the people who are not his servants, thus creating a strong contrast with 65:8–10. In some ways these words reiterate and add to what was already said about these obstinate people in 65:1–7. Earlier God reached out to these people by revealing himself to them, but they did not seek God (65:1). Instead they "were forsakers of"[574] God (65:11), a term that implies that they left behind someone who they had a close relationship with at some earlier time, as 63:7–14 suggests. The results of forsaking involve the ending of past relationships, no talking to a former friend, and probably an involvement with someone else. Forsaking God also involved abandoning the worship of God at the temple in Jerusalem.

In the second half of 65:11, these people substituted pagan worship (57:3–13; 65:3–7) for the worship of the God of Israel, providing proof that they have forsaken God. The identity of the gods "Fortune" and "Destiny" is often connected to the Syrian and Phoenician *Gad* and the Arabian *Meni*. These are gods who were responsible for a person's fortune in the future.[575] Tables were arranged before these gods with a ritual meal of food and drink in order to appease them. This might suggest that the Hebrew people were very concerned about their future at this time and were not willing to trust God for their future salvation. It is difficult to know how closely these activities are related to the pagan worship described in 57:3–13a; 65:3–4. It is not completely clear if all these passages are describing the same group of people or if the prophet is referring to practices of different groups.

God's response to this pagan worship in 65:12 is that God himself "will determine the destiny" (a word play)[576] of these people, not the pagan gods of destiny. His plan is to deliver these people to the sword so that all of them will

---

[574] The masc. pl. construct participle עֹזְבֵי "forsakers of" probably functions verbally, while the second pl. participle הַשְּׁכֵחִים with the article prefixed probably should be translated as a relative clause "the ones who forgot."

[575] The reference to גָּדַד "to cut, apportion" explains the connection with the idea "fortune." This name could possibly be found within the names of the Canaanite towns Baal-gad (Josh 11:17) and Migdal-gad (Josh 15:37). This seems similar to מְנִי "destiny" (from מָנָה "to count, give a portion), which may be the goddess of fate that was worshipped by Arab tribes under the name "Manat" just before the appearance of Mohammed. The Old Greek translated the first term as "demon" and the second as "good fortune," thus Oswalt, *Isaiah 40–66*, 648, hypothesizes that these were the gods of good and bad fortune. Blenkinsopp, *Isaiah 56–66*, 278, indicates that, "As late as the fifth century C. E., the Syriac ecclesiastical writer Jacob of Sarug reports that people were preparing meals (corresponding to the Latin *lectisternia*) for Gad." He also states that this name is attested much earlier in Ugaritic, Amorite, Phoenician, and Punic texts.

[576] Both the name מְנִי "Meni" and the verb מָנִיתִי come from the same root מָנָה "he apportioned, determined the destiny."

be slaughtered. This indicates that there will be a military conquest in which their gods will not be able to control or prevent their destiny of death. J. L. Koole notices the irony that, "Those who kneel for these gods must kneel under the judgment"[577] of God's heavy hand. An additional reason that justifies this response is that God called them (55:6–7; 58:1) and spoke to them through the prophets, but in their stubbornness they did not listen or respond to anything these prophets said (65:1,24; 66:4). These factors demonstrate that God graciously tried to include them within his servants; therefore, they are fully accountable for their choice to reject his warnings and ignore his grace. Their error was not only related to what they did not do but also to what they did do. The final sentence accuses them of purposely acting in ways that would arouse God's anger. They chose to do what was evil, things which did not please God (58:3,13; 66:4). When people know what is right and what will honor and glorify God yet purposely choose to defy God's authority and test his patience, they should not be too surprised when God reacts strongly to their defiance. From the descriptions in 64:5–7; 65:1–7 and now in 65:11–12, it is fairly easy to understand why these people did not experience God's intervention on their behalf.

65:13–14 The introduction of a new word from God marks the beginning of the second subparagraph in 65:13–16. The reception of this new message demonstrates to the audience that God is not silent, that he does answer prayers, and that he can be found by those who call on him (65:1). After receiving God's answer, they need to listen carefully to what he has said and then respond with their answer (65:12).

Based on the preceding principles, God, "therefore" (*lākēn*) will treat his own faithful servants differently from those who have forsaken him. Every other line in this verse contrasts (a) God's destiny for "my servants" and (b) those who forsake God (*'attem* "you"); thus, this is an oracle of judgment with news about the salvation of others included.[578] Although these destinies are not initially classified as God's blessings and curses, the reference to "a blessing" in 65:16 suggests that these antithetical destinies may have their origin in the covenant blessings and curses described in Leviticus 26 and Deuteronomy 27–28.[579] Three contrasts are enumerated in 65:13, each beginning with

---

[577] Koole, *Isaiah III, Volume 3: Isaiah 56–66*, 437, finds כָּרַע "he knelt" refers to the positive worship of God in 45:23 as well as the negative falling down before an idol in 46:1.

[578] Emmerson, *Isaiah 56–66*, 31–32, finds a symmetrical structure in this chapter. It begins by describing God's judgment on the apostates (65:1–7), then contrasts the fate of the apostates with his servants (65:8–16a), and concludes with his blessings for his servants.

[579] P. A. Smith, *Rhetoric and Redaction in Trito-Isaiah*, 143, correctly draws the background to these destinies from the blessings and curses. Blenkinsopp, *Isaiah 56–66*, 281, finds the background in the eschatological banquet found in the *Enuma Elish*, III, 139–38, the Ugaritic Baal text 51.IV,35–39, and the later texts of *1 Enoch* 34:4–35:7; 60:24; *4 Ezra* 6:52; and *Baba Batra* 74b where people will feast on the flesh of Leviathan. Strangely, he does not mention the eschatological banquet in 25:6–8 or the offer of plenty to eat in 55:1–2.

"behold, pay attention" (*hinnēh*, omitted by NIV) to set them apart from one another. The first contrast is between God's servants who will have food to eat (Lev 26:5,10) and those who will be hungry (Lev 26:26; Deut 28:48). The second contrast is between those who drink and those who will be thirsty, while the third contrast is between those who will rejoice and those who will suffer shame. A future time of joy is frequently listed as a characteristic of those who receive God's blessings, especially the joy of being in God's eschatological kingdom (12:3,6; 25:9; 30:29; 35:1–2,10; 51:3,11; 52:8–9; 54:1; 55:12; 58:14; 60:15; 61:7; 65:18; 66:5a), but shame will come upon those who do not trust in God, especially those who worship idols (26:11; 42:17; 44:11; 45:16–17,24; 66:5b). The contrast between these two destinies is stark, uncompromising, and final, for there will be no middle destiny for those who tried to do good or who were not that bad. A person is either a dedicated servant of God who seeks after God and pleases him, or one is a rebel who forsakes God and trusts in other things. Based on one's choice, the destiny of people is either glorious and wonderful or extremely terrible. There is no equivocation or doubt about what will happen; it is spelled out very clearly in plain and simple language that everyone can understand.

This contrast continues in 65:14 with a fourth "behold" (*hinnēh*). In this contrast, "my servants" will joyfully sing with jubilation, while "you" will cry out for help, wail, and moan. The one will respond from the "goodness" (*ṭôb* NIV "joy") of the heart, and the other will respond out of a painful heart and a broken spirit. All the hopes and dreams of God's servants will be wonderfully fulfilled as they experience the presence of God and the glorious kingdom he has prepared for his people (chaps. 60–62). Those who forsake God will be painfully aware of their utterly hopeless condition without God. All along God desired that all of his people would have a humble and contrite spirit (57:15; 58:5), but some people will refuse to honor God and humble themselves. When they are finally punished for their sins, their pride and selfish spirit will finally be broken, but then it will be too late to change their destiny. All they can do at that point is to regretfully cry out in anguish because they will fully realize the desperate consequences of their foolish choices.

65:15–16 Verse 15 makes a transition from these contrasting destinies in order to arrive at a conclusion. It continues the contrast of vv. 13–14, but now (a) in a different form, (b) without "behold" at the beginning of the sentence, and (c) by mentioning "you" first and "his servants" second. The legacy that these two groups leave for posterity will be a curse (65:15) and a blessing (65:16). The name of those who forsake God ("you" in v. 15a) will be used in an oath of cursing when "my chosen ones" (*bĕḥîray*) are casting a curse on some evil person. For example, in Jer 29:20–23 the prophet Jeremiah tells about the sins of Ahab, the son of Kolaiah, and Zedekiah, the son of Maaseiah, who prophesied deceptions, committed adultery, and did outrageous things. Because of these evil deeds God handed them over to Nebuchadnezzar, the

Babylonian king so that he could put them to death. In 29:22 Jeremiah refers to a future curse in which people will say, "May the LORD treat you like Zedekiah and Ahab whom the king of Babylon burned in the fire." In Isaiah 65:15 the name of this group of people is not provided, but the destiny of that group and anyone cursed using their name will be death. 1QIs[a] has a shorter text here, and there is some confusion over the pronouns,[580] but these factors should not cause one to omit this phrase.[581] J. L. Koole keeps the text as it is and rejects the views that line 2 is a quotation of what one of God's chosen ones might say when they would curse someone; instead, he interprets this as a statement of what God will do.[582]

This contrasts with the different name that God will give to his servants (65:15b). They will not have a name associated with a curse, for when God transforms a person's life and directs them on a new path, he often gives them a new name that points to their new destiny. As a sign of God's future plans for each person, Abram received the new name Abraham (Gen 17:5), Sarai got the new name Sarah (Gen 17:15), and Jacob became Israel (Gen 32:28). In the description of God's glorious kingdom in chaps. 60–62, Jerusalem will have the name "City of the LORD" (60:14), "Hephzibah" and "Beulah" (62:4); her walls will be called "Salvation" and her gates "Praise" (60:18), and the people will be called "priests" and "ministers of the LORD" (61:6) and "Holy People, Redeemed, Sought After, and City no Longer Deserted" (62:12). These new names say something about the character or nature of the new entity God will create.

The result[583] of all this is that, when God transforms his people in that future kingdom, people will confidently invoke a blessing using the name of the "God of truth"[584] because they trust him completely. His faithfulness to the truth assures the one speaking that God will be sure to accomplish what he has said he would do, for his character does not change. The same thing applies to any one of God's servants who makes an oath. He will swear in the name of the God of truth, for at that time he will see with his own eyes the glory of God

---

[580] 1QIs[a] drops 65:15b–16a, but this would destroy the contrast between the blessing and the curse. The pronoun in the word שְׁמְכֶם "your (pl.) name" does not agree with וֶהֱמִיתְךָ "and he will cause you (sg.) to die." The Old Greek makes both pronouns pl., though the second could be a collective.

[581] Westermann, *Isaiah 40–66*, 403, follows others who simply drop the second line because the pronoun does not agree with the first line.

[582] Koole, *Isaiah III, Volume 3: Isaiah 56–66*, 441, rejects the view of the Jewish exegete Rashi because the verb וֶהֱמִיתְךָ is perfect rather than a jussive and because there is no comparative particle at the beginning of the clause.

[583] Isaiah 65:16 begins with the relative pronoun אֲשֶׁר which NIV translates "whoever," but it is more likely that this usage introduces a result clause "so that" (GKC §165b, *IBHS* §38.3).

[584] Deuteronomy 29:16–21 (Hb. 29:15–20) seems to be part of the background for this statement, for it warns an Israelite not to invoke a blessing on himself while he is worshiping other gods because this will bring a disaster on the land. The big difference, of course, is that 65:16 refers to a time after the establishment of God's kingdom.

and know that he truly is a God who does not deceive or disappoint those who serve him (Gad and Meni of 65:11 are nothing).

P. A. Smith and several others begin the next paragraph in 65:16b, but it appears that this sentence ends the preceding paragraph and functions as a transition to the next paragraph.[585] Isaiah 65:16b begins with *kî*, which could introduce a causal phrase ("because, for" NIV), thus strongly connecting it to what precedes. But it is probably better to interpret it as introducing a concluding and emphatic ("truly, it is indisputable") final sentence that ends this paragraph. At the time when God's servants and Jerusalem get new names and everyone takes an oath by the name of God, people will be living in a new era of history. Existence in the kingdom of God where God alone is honored and glorified will cause a change of perspective and a new orientation to life. At that time in God's kingdom, when everything is transformed, the past troubles of life will be forgotten[586] and hidden from memory. Although one could easily understand how God's servants who are living in God's presence in this new world would quickly forget about all the terrible events of the past, this verse seems to state that God himself will put the events of the former sinful world behind him and concentrate on life in the new world he will create for his saints. This does not comment on what people will remember about the trouble of this present world, but if there will be no sorrow in that realm and God forgets about the past, one would assume that people also would forget about all their past failures as well (cf. 65:17).

CREATION OF A NEW WORLD OF JOY AND ABUNDANCE (65:17–25)

[17]"Behold, I will create
  new heavens and a new earth.
 The former things will not be remembered,
  nor will they come to mind.
[18]But be glad and rejoice forever
  in what I will create,
 for I will create Jerusalem to be a delight
  and its people a joy.
[19]I will rejoice over Jerusalem
  and take delight in my people;
 the sound of weeping and of crying
  will be heard in it no more.

---

[585] P. A. Smith, *Rhetoric and Redaction in Trito-Isaiah*, 143, 149, finds 65:16b has a "strong anticipation and certainty of the new age and Yahweh's imminent intervention, offers the basis for the promises made to the servants in the preceding verses, and forms a transition to the announcement of God's new creative activity in vv. 17–18." This agrees with the analysis above, showing the subjectivity of making some of the paragraph breaks. This commentary would make the break at v. 17 because it begins with "behold," introduces a bold new theme, and looks to the future (v. 16b looks to the past).

[586] The *niphal* perfect verb expresses a passive idea in past time. NIV "will be forgotten" probably takes the verb as a perfect of certainty.

²⁰"Never again will there be in it
an infant who lives but a few days,
or an old man who does not live out his years;
he who dies at a hundred
will be thought a mere youth;
he who fails to reach a hundred
will be considered accursed.
²¹They will build houses and dwell in them;
they will plant vineyards and eat their fruit.
²²No longer will they build houses and others live in them,
or plant and others eat.
For as the days of a tree,
so will be the days of my people;
my chosen ones will long enjoy
the works of their hands.
²³They will not toil in vain
or bear children doomed to misfortune;
for they will be a people blessed by the LORD,
they and their descendants with them.
²⁴Before they call I will answer;
while they are still speaking I will hear.
²⁵The wolf and the lamb will feed together,
and the lion will eat straw like the ox,
but dust will be the serpent's food.
They will neither harm nor destroy
on all my holy mountain,"
says the LORD.

Now God repeats many of the earlier promises (chaps. 25; 35; 60–62) he made to all those who choose to be his servants. This new situation and these new things are part of what are now called a "new heavens and a new earth" (65:17). This way of describing God's glorious kingdom emphasizes the radical transformation that will take place when God establishes his kingdom. Indeed, the past world will not only be forgotten (65:17b); it will pass away and be replaced. This new creation will engender feelings of joy and gladness, the end of sorrow; people will live long, there will be peace among men, and there will be clear communion between God and his people and a period of peace among the animals. This sounds almost like a return to the paradise of the garden of Eden before sin entered the world.

C. Westermann has suggested that this paragraph about the new world God will create for his future kingdom was dislocated from its original position with chaps. 60–62,[587] but there is no textual evidence showing that 65:17–25 was

---

[587] Westermann, *Isaiah 40–66*, 296–99, 307, believes that Trito-Isaiah was not the author of this paragraph because it harks back to the thinking of Deutero-Isaiah. He believes these promises are to all Israel and without conditions. Also, the theme of people eating what they work for in 65:21–23 is similar to what is found in 62:8–9. This is true, but the statement in 62:8–9 promises

ever directly attached to chaps. 60–62. Both messages talk about the glories of God's future kingdom, but this topic is discussed in numerous unconnected chapters scattered throughout chaps. 1–62. P. A. Smith correctly notes that if one does not assume some dislocation, then contextually this promise of a new heavens and a new earth should relate only to the people called "my servants" in 65:8–16;[588] thus, it has a somewhat unique thrust when compared to chaps. 60–62. These are "my people" (65:19,22) and "my chosen ones" (65:22), a people blessed by God (65:23), terms that are contextually defined as God's servants in 65:8–16. The new heavens and earth where these servants will live could be connected to the "new things" in 42:9; 43:19; 48:6 or the "things to come" in 41:22 (described in 41:17–20). R. N. Whybray believes that this paragraph is about the immediate renewal of Jerusalem (except 65:17 which is a later eschatological addition),[589] but the themes of a new creation, great rejoicing, no weeping, long life, and peace among the animals were firmly connected to eschatological events in earlier chapters of Isaiah (4:2–6; 11:6–9; 25:8; 30:19; 35:10), and these did not take place after the Hebrew people returned from their exile in Babylon. These eschatological promises function in the larger literary context of 65:1–66:14 as a persuasive argument that should motivate those who were forsaking God to reconsider their choices and also function as an encouragement for God's servants because God will vindicate their trust in him.

This paragraph is organized into four parts.

God's new creation	65:17
Rejoicing and long life	65:18–20
God's blessing	65:21–23
Harmony and peace	65:24–25

The breaks in these subparagraphs are not as clearly marked as in many other paragraphs; thus, there is some diversity in the way commentaries divide up these promises. Although 65:18–19 focuses on joy, v. 18 is also closely connected to the creation theme in 65:17. Second, it is unclear if 65:20 should be by itself or if it should be connected to what precedes or follows. Thus the

---

protection against foreigners, which is not the case in 65:21–23. If both passages are about the same topic, it is natural that there would be some overlap (both talk about joy, peace, and Jerusalem). It seems impossible to limit an author's ability to talk about a theme only in one passage, especially when he speaks about that same theme in a new contextual setting. The new and different themes connected to God's glorious kingdom in 65:17–25 (the creation in 65:17–18 and peace among the animals are not found in chaps. 60–62) argue for this paragraph being a separate new discussion.

[588] P. A. Smith, *Rhetoric and Redaction in Trito-Isaiah*, 145, connects the "my people" in 65:19,22 with the "my people" in 65:10 in the previous paragraph.

[589] Whybray, *Isaiah 40–66*, 275, takes 65:17 as a later partial duplication of the theme of creation from 65:18. Since the postexilic era was not characterized by these kinds of conditions, it hardly makes sense to suggest that this is a false prophecy about the postexilic era.

subdivisions are very intertwined with a good deal of overlapping and inter-mixing of ideas. What is clear is that this paragraph is strongly connected to 65:8–16 by terminology related to "my people" ('ammî, 65:10,19,22), "my chosen ones" (bĕḥîray, 65:15,22), and my "seed" (zeraʿ, 65:9,23). This para-graph is not constructed like 65:8–16, for there is no contrast between God's servants and those who forsake God in this proclamation of salvation.

65:17 The new paragraph begins with a solemn announcement of God's great work, introduced with "behold, I" (hinnî) to emphasize the amazing fact that God "will create"[590] a new heavens and a new earth. Although the king-dom God will establish was not described in these terms earlier, the reference to the shaking of the foundations of the whole earth, it being split asunder (24:18–19), and the vanishing of the heavens (51:6), hints at the need for a new creation.[591] The idea of "newness" (ḥădāšâ) correlates closely with the concept of creation, for creating is a unique new act of God that is set in con-trast with the present conditions. This transformation into something new was already implied in the "new things" mentioned in 42:9, the presence of the glory of God in Zion in 60:1, and giving the city and the people new names in 62:2,4,12. Other prophets refer to this eschatological time as the period when God will give a new covenant (Jer 31:31; cf. Isa 55:3) and the people will have a new heart and spirit (Ezek 11:19; 18:31; 36:26). All these references indicate that the efforts of mankind will never fully transform this world into a better place; it will require the miraculous work of God to bring about the real change that people long for. God's work of salvation is a marvelous creative effort in which he recreates the world and his chosen people into a new, totally unimagi-nable, and glorious kingdom where God dwells among mankind. Although the sinfulness of mankind has not defiled the heavens (though sinful angels have), this sounds like a complete redoing of Gen 1:1 after the destruction of this present sinful world (cf. 34:4). This new world with its transformed people will be so completely different that God's servants will not remember the "former world"[592] (48:13) of sin, suffering, hunger, death, and destruction. In fact, this new world will be so different that even the more positive aspects of the former things will probably fade from memory.[593]

---

[590] The participle בּוֹרֵא is frequently translated as a present tense verb, but here it should be translated with a future tense because it comes after הִנְנִי (GKC §116p).

[591] Second Peter 3:5–13 and Rev 21:1 communicate a similar situation. Westermann, *Isaiah 40–66*, 408, thinks this new heavens and earth refers to a "miraculous transformation" and "do not apply that the heavens and the earth are to be destroyed" because that is a theme of apocalyptic (Rev 21:1), not prophecy. Muilenburg, "Isaiah 40–66," 5:755, holds that the "meaning is not that the present world will be destroyed . . . but rather that the present world will be completely trans-formed." Nevertheless, since 24:1–23 already envisions the destruction of the heavens and earth, this concept is already a part of Isaiah's prophetic understanding of the end times.

[592] The word הָרִאשֹׁנוֹת "the former things" serves as a sort of catchword that connects the previous paragraph (65:16b) with this present paragraph (65:17b).

[593] In 65:11 the sinful people forgot God, but in the future God and all his servants will forget

65:18 In reaction to the things that will not happen in 65:17b, this verse describes the positive things that will happen. The initial particles *kî ʾim*[594] in 65:18 usually introduce a contrast or the opposite of what was just mentioned. Singing and rejoicing will abound from that time on because of God's new creation. These two verbs are imperatives that could be interpreted as offering words of assurance, but it seems better to view these as imperative verbs that exhort the people to rejoice (NIV, HCSB, NRSV, "be glad and rejoice")[595] in what God will create. In order to emphasize the wonderful significance of this new creation of Jerusalem, using almost the same terminology as 65:17, 65:18 states, "Behold, I will create Jerusalem,"[596] which C. Westermann interprets as an explanation of what it means to create the new heavens and the new earth. Thus, he believes that the statement in 65:17 about the new heavens and the new earth is a grand exaggeration of what is actually described in 65:18.[597] J. D. Levenson also views these verses as synonymous statements and questions if the recreation in 65:17 is universal because "The reconstruction of the temple-city was not only a recovery of national honor, but also a renewal of the cosmos, of which the temple was a miniature."[598] Although the temple was the center where God's presence dwelt and the place from which he impacted the world, the temple and the world are not synonymous locations or theological terms. Such harmonization should be avoided, for three things are described in these two verses: (a) the creation of the new heavens and the earth, (b) the creation of a new Jerusalem, and (c) the joy of the people. Jerusalem and its people are not the only entities on earth that need revitalization through God's creative efforts; the whole world has been impacted negatively by the presence of evil, destruction, sorrow, and the curse (51:6). But, of course, the Hebrew audience is most interested in what God will do in Jerusalem, the place where God dwells and the center of their world. Earlier Isaiah described many new things that will happen in Jerusalem. People from all nations will come to learn from God at Jerusalem, and war will end (2:2–4; 14:1–2; 19:18–25); the holy survivors of Israel will come to a newly created Jerusalem (4:2–6); there will be peace between the animals and people (11:6–9), praise of God and

---

about this past world of idolatry and pagan worship (65:16–17). These past things will not even "come up" תַעֲלֶינָה into the mind of these people.

[594] כִּי־אִם functions to introduce an adversative clause (GKC §163a) that expresses the antithesis ("but, nevertheless") of what was stated earlier.

[595] The imperative verb can express an admonition or exhortation to do something (GKC §110a) "be glad," but it can also offer an assurance or promise (GKC §110c) that "you will have gladness."

[596] Both 65:17 and 65:18b begin with כִּי־הִנְנִי בוֹרֵא "for behold, I will create." This similarity raises the question, Are these two verses describing two similar acts or the same act?

[597] Westermann, *Isaiah 40–66*, 408, says "v. 18b follows directly on v. 17, and this makes it clearer that the reference in v. 17a is to the change to be wrought in Jerusalem and its population."

[598] J. D. Levenson, *Creation and the Persistence of Evil* (San Francisco: Harper & Row, 1988), 89–90, finds only one act in these two verses, the reconstruction of the temple.

banqueting (25:1–26:6), the end of sorrows, a time of great prosperity, a new light (30:18–26), an outpouring of the Spirit and justice and peace (32:15–20), and the transformation of nature (35:1–10). This new world will involve the coming of the glory of the Lord to Mount Zion where he will rule and care for his people (40:5–11; 60:1–3). Additionally, this new world will mean the transformation of nature and many other new things (41:17–20; 43:16–21; 44:3–5; 48:9–11; 50:1–3), the salvation of people from all nations (45:18–25; 49:22–26; 60:3–11), the repopulation of Zion with people and joy (49:14–21; 51:9–11; 54:1–10), the appearance of God's salvation when the heavens and earth vanish (51:4–6), the enthronement of God in Zion (52:1–10), the giving of a new everlasting covenant (55:3), the transformation of Zion into something glorious (60:15; 62:7), and the appearing of the Anointed One (61:1–3). God's new creation will include nature, the nations, the Israelites, Jerusalem, and the temple. Thus God's new work will not be limited to the narrow sphere of Israelite interest in one small location (the temple). When God creates, he does not just patch up a few things so that everything looks relatively nice on the outside; he starts all over again from the beginning and creates everything brand new from top to bottom. His grand creative work will be worldwide, including all of the heavens and every part of the earth, all peoples, all nations, all aspects of nature, all places, and all relationships that God has with the things that he creates.

65:19 The theme of rejoicing dominates both v. 18 and v.19. People are exhorted to be glad and rejoice because of what God will do in v. 18a. Then God says that he will create a New Jerusalem to cause people to rejoice in v. 18b. This will cause God to rejoice over Jerusalem and its people in v. 19a. Although it is somewhat natural to expect that people will rejoice in this wonderful, new world that God will create, a more significant point is that God himself will take pleasure in what he creates. One would expect that God would be happy about everything in this new creation, but two of the things that will give him the greatest pleasure will be this wonderful new city of Jerusalem and his new holy people. Jeremiah 31:41 also refers to God rejoicing over all the good things he will do for his people, and Zeph 3:17 talks about God rejoicing over his people with singing. Both of these acts will fulfill what he promised he would do in Deut 30:9.

The prophet expresses the idea that there will be great joy, both by making this positive statement and also by making the negative comment that there will be no more tears (65:19b; Rev 7:17). This was already promised back in 25:8 when God said that death would end when his kingdom arrives; thus, there will be no weeping for the dead. Isaiah 30:19 places the end of weeping in the context of an era when God will have compassion on his people, give them new teachers, rain and prosperity, and a change in the sun and moon. In 61:2–3 the Anointed One will comfort those who mourn, but he will also turn mourning into praise. Isaiah 65:19 puts this promise in the context of the establishment of the new heavens and the new earth. At that time, all sickness, pain, disappointment, loneliness, rejection, military defeat, financial loss, and every other possible source of crying will cease to exist. These will be things of the past that people will quickly forget as they enjoy the wonderful presence of God in his kingdom.

65:20 Continuing the contrasts between the past world of sin, suffering, and death, the message now moves to talk about concrete examples that illustrate the radical changes that will exist in this new world that God will create. In most ancient Near Eastern societies, the medical profession was able to offer only very limited assistance when people were sick or injured. If there was any trouble in giving childbirth, there was little that could be done to save a premature child. Once born, many children still died of diseases that today are easily cured by basic modern medicines. But at that time an infected wound, a bowel blockage, diarrhea, pneumonia, cold, appendicitis, or a broken bone could lead to death. In order to illustrate the absence of these diseases and the long life that people will live, two comparative illustrations provide an emphasis on long life. There shall never be "from there"[599] (NIV "in it") an infant who will die in the first few days of his life, a quite common event in ancient Israel. A second change is that there will never be in that place an old man who will not fulfill his appointed years. No age limit is placed on the old man, but when someone 100 years old is still considered a young man, you know he is going to live a very long time.

The reference to death and a curse on the sinner presents some problems, for one would not expect these to be present in the new heavens and the new earth (cf. 26:6–9).[600] Muilenburg resolves the problem about "sinners" being present in this kingdom by translating this definite participle as, "the one who comes short"[601] (i.e., of 100 years) will be under a curse. Although it is impossible to make this description of God's final kingdom exactly identical to 26:6–9,[602] these examples (the infant and the old man) should be interpreted primarily as illustrations of the unusual positive conditions that will be present

---

[599] עוֹד מִשָּׁם is difficult, but the words mean "from there," that is, there will not be an infant "from there, that place" who will עוֹד "any longer" exist for just יָמִים "days."

[600] A. Gardner, "Isaiah 65,20: Centenarians or Millenarians?" *Bib* 86 (2005): 88–96, suggests that people in God's new kingdom will make bad choices and sin. Isaiah 65:22 compares the length of life to a tree, and Gardner suggests that an oak can live to be up to 1,600 years old, while cedars and some olive trees can live to be 2,000 years old.

[601] Muilenburg, "Isaiah 40–66," 5:756. The participle הַחוֹטֶא is usually interpreted as a noun ("the sinner") or resolved into a relative clause ("the one who misses the mark, the one who sins"). NASB has "the one who does not reach" and HCSB "the one who misses." חָטָא is used in a non-moral sense of missing or failing to do something (Judg 20:16; Job 5:24; Prov 8:26).

[602] Motyer, *Isaiah*, 530, denies that these examples imply that there will be death in God's kingdom. He takes this as a hypothetical situation ("if a sinner"), but that puts an awful lot of weight on the *waw* that precedes the participle "the sinner, the one who misses, the one who does not reach." Delitzsch, *Isaiah*, 490, believes 26:8 is about the ultimate end of death, while 65:20 is about the limitation of the power of death.

at that time. Since there will be no sinners in God's final kingdom and all the people will be holy (62:12) and righteous (60:21), it appears that the last illustration of someone being cursed by God is more of a hypothetical situation drawn from life in this sinful world. It was used merely to illustrate the point that people will live a very long time. Thus, if one lived only 100 years, people would think that person was under some curse. Of course, people will not live to be just 100 years old and people will not be under a curse in God's newly created world.

65:21–22 The material situation described in these promises implies the end of all wars in which enemy nations invade, destroy property, and steal the fruit of a farmer's labor. In addition, they imply the end of oppression of the poor by the wealthy landowners who legally and illegally take property from the oppressed because the poor cannot pay their debts. In order for these conditions to exist, the land will have to experience a time of security from the invasion of foreign troops who are prone to destroy or steal whatever they can get their hands on. Since other people (foreigners or Israelites) will not take by force what a person has worked for and built, the possibility exists for people to experience great prosperity, contentment, and enjoyment of a prolonged life. At that time people will be able to enjoy the rewards of their hard work. This verse does not specifically say that God will reward them, but this can probably be assumed since God is the one who will create these new conditions when he establishes this new world. This glorious era will be the time when all the covenant blessings will be experienced in their fullness (Lev 26:5), and there will be no covenant curses (Deut 28:30; Amos 5:11; Mic 6:15; Zeph 1:13). Isaiah 65:22a says the same thing in negative statements, confirming what will not happen.

Verse 22b goes back to briefly touch on the issue of long life from v. 20 in order to integrate it with the theme of enjoying what one has worked for. First, the days of "my people" are compared to the days of a tree, a metaphor that produces images of longevity, strength, and fertility. Elsewhere the cut tree is a symbol of death and destruction (10:18–19,33–34), while the vibrant producing tree is a sign of strength, stability, and fertility (29:17; 32:15; 35:2; 60:13).[603] God's people are even called "oaks of righteousness" (61:3) that will display God's splendor. The final comment connects the hard work of building houses, developing vineyards, and sowing and harvesting crops in 65:21 to the pleasure of being able to make full use of everything that one grows. This produces a sense of satisfaction because a person is able to provide sufficient food for his family and is able to "consume, use"[604] all of it. "Enjoy" in the NIV translation

---

[603] K. Nielsen, *There Is Hope for a Tree* (Sheffield: JSOT, 1989), deals with all the various uses and images of the tree.

[604] The verb בָּלָה often relates to something being old and worn out (garments in Deut 8:4; 29:5) or the earth (50:9), but it can also describe something that is "consumed, fully used" (Job 21:12). Here it describes the full use of all that the people have worked on in 65:21–22.

is implied from being able to make full use of these products; it is not part of the meaning of this verb. These are the benefits that God will grant solely to "my people" and "my chosen ones," not to any other group.

65:23   The final description of God's blessings on these people contrasts what will not happen (v. 23a) with what will happen (v. 23b). Verse 23a summarizes what has already been said in 65:21–22; people will be rewarded for their work because all their efforts will not be wasted or come to naught. Others will not take what they have worked so hard to accomplish. Isaiah 65:23b summarizes what was already said in 65:23a about children. The family that has a child can be assured that that their infant is not going to die or cause people to be "dismayed, terrified."[605] These two assurances are founded on God's promises. God assures his servants that they and their children are destined to receive his blessing, not his curse. The fact that the children will also experience these blessings implies that this period will last for many generations. In this new earth, nothing one does will be a waste of time or a source of frustration and futility, for God's plan is to protect his people from misery and appropriately reward his servants with many blessings. C. R. Seitz believes these statements indicate that the curse of Genesis 3 will be removed because there will be no premature death, no thorns to make human labor ineffective, and no pain in childbirth.[606] This issue will be further addressed in 65:25.

65:24   The next blessing promises God's care and close personal attention to the needs of his people. Previously, people complained that they were not seeing God's zeal, might, tenderness, and compassion (63:15). It seemed that God had hidden himself (64:7) or at least was not miraculously acting on behalf of his people like he used to (63:15; 64:1–3). Earlier God asserted that he was available and that he had called to them, but they did not answer because of their sinfulness (65:1,12). But when the new heavens and the new earth are created for God's servants, God will be attentive to his people: "I myself will answer"[607] them before they actually call. His second promise is that "I myself will hear" while they are still speaking. These assurances indicate that God (a) will know everything that people will be thinking about, (b) will pay attention to everything people say, and (c) will instantaneously provide a answer. This suggests a very close personal relationship with God and the total absence of the sins that formerly separated God from mankind (59:1–2).

---

[605] The noun בֶּהָלָה refers to "terror, dismay," while the verbal form refers to being disturbed, dismayed, terrified (Ps 78:33), or being stricken by a wasting disease (Lev 26:16); it is a synonym of the "anguish" of mothers being attacked in war (Jer 15:8). Koole, *Isaiah III, Volume 3: Isaiah 56–66*, 461, suggests that this may refer to the reversal of the curse on giving childbirth in Gen 3:16.

[606] Seitz, "Isaiah 40–66," 544 connects all this to the curse on the serpent in 65:25 (Gen 3:14).

[607] The inclusion of the personal subject pronoun with the verb is unnecessary because the person is included within the verb form. Thus when the subject pronoun is included (in this case אֲנִי) it creates an emphasis on the subject (GKC §135a).

65:25   The conclusion to this paragraph summarizes in a condensed form
the eschatological picture of the relationship between the wild and domesticated animals in 11:6–9.[608] Although this was promised earlier in the context
of the coming messianic shoot from the stump of Jesse (11:1), this emphasis
on the Messiah is missing in the context of 65:25. Yet B. S. Childs properly
asks the question if the readers would not have known the earlier contextual
use of this verse and made that connection even though it is not explicit in
chap. 65.[609] Although one cannot know exactly what different readers thought
when they examined this passage, it is safe to assume that at least some readers
would have made the connection between 11:6–9 and 65:15. Silence about an
issue (the Messiah) does not imply that a person does not believe something or
that this passage contradicts another passage; it merely indicates that the focus
of this passage is centered around other issues (God's blessings).

God explains this new setting by describing a state of complete harmony
and oneness among animals that formerly were enemies. In the future, the
wild meat-eating wolf (the predator) and the defenseless little lamb (the prey)
will graze "together"[610] in peace and unity. In addition, the ferocious lion (the
predator) will eat straw with the ox (the prey). Although animals can sometimes represent people,[611] there is no indication that these animals are symbolic of anything other than animal life. Leviticus 26:22 mentions the curse of
being killed by wild animals, but Hos 2:18; Ezek 34:25,28 (see also Isa 11:6–9;
35:9) refer to a future time when there will be peace between man and animals.
This almost sounds like a return to the paradise of the garden of Eden before
God's curse fell on people. God's new work will impact all parts of the natural
world.

The mentioning of the snake that will eat dust is completely different from
what 11:8 says about snakes, and it does not describe a state of peace between
the snake and another animal. If this refers back to the curse on the snake in
Gen 3:14, it appears that the curse on the snake is not lifted. The snake will not
be allowed to eat normal food but will suffer the humiliation of eating dirt just
like some of God's other enemies did (49:23; Ps 72:9). There is no indication
that the snake was identified with Satan in this verse. In the second half of the
verse, God promises that these animals will do no harm or destroy anything on
God's Holy Mountain in Zion. This connects these promises with the earlier

---

[608] J. T. van Ruiten, "The Intertextual Relationship between Isaiah 65.25 and 11.6–9," in *The Scriptures and the Scrolls: Fs A. S. van der Woude*, ed. F. G. Martinez et al., VTSup 49 (Leiden: Brill, 1992), 31–42, compares these two texts and concludes that the shorter version in 65:25 is based on the longer version in 11:6–9.

[609] Childs, *Isaiah*, 538–39, suggests that one can look for the author's explicit meaning from its immediate context, but he differentiates this from the possible meaning that a reader might derive from a broader understanding of the earlier use of this theme in 11:6–9.

[610] This is expressed with כְּאֶחָד "as one."

[611] In Ezek 22:25 "her princes within her are like a roaring lion tearing her prey" and 22:27 "her officials within her are like wolves."

comments about what was going to happen on God's Holy Mountain (56:7; 57:13; 60–62; 66:20) when he establishes his glorious kingdom on the new earth. These promises end with a final phrase "says the LORD," a concluding reminder that assures the audience that all these things are the authoritative promises of God.

GOD HONORS THE HUMBLE WHO TREMBLE (66:1–4)

¹This is what the LORD says:

> "Heaven is my throne,
>   and the earth is my footstool.
> Where is the house you will build for me?
>   Where will my resting place be?
> ²Has not my hand made all these things,
>   and so they came into being?"
>   declares the LORD.

> "This is the one I esteem:
>   he who is humble and contrite in spirit,
>   and trembles at my word.
> ³But whoever sacrifices a bull
>   is like one who kills a man,
> and whoever offers a lamb,
>   like one who breaks a dog's neck;
> whoever makes a grain offering
>   is like one who presents pig's blood,
> and whoever burns memorial incense,
>   like one who worships an idol.
> They have chosen their own ways,
>   and their souls delight in their abominations;
> ⁴so I also will choose harsh treatment for them
>   and will bring upon them what they dread.
> For when I called, no one answered,
>   when I spoke, no one listened.
> They did evil in my sight
>   and chose what displeases me."

The literary makeup of the whole unit (65:1–66:24) suggests that chap. 66 is a continuation of the response to the lament in 63:7–64:11 as well as a conscious attempt to reuse vocabulary from chap. 1[612] in order to create some sense of unity for chaps. 1–66. Both chap. 1 and chaps. 65–66 recognize serious theological and practical problems within the nation and two distinct destinies for the righteous and the wicked. These theological similarities provide some cohesiveness between chap. 1 and chaps. 65–66, summarizing the

---

[612] L. J. Liebreich, "The Compilation of the Book of Isaiah," *JQR* 46 (1956): 276–77, and Schramm, *The Opponents of Third Isaiah*, 161–62, list 21 terms that are used in chap. 1 and chaps. 65–66.

destinies of these two conflicting worldviews and encouraging the audience to live in a way that will produce the best destiny for themselves. W. A. M. Beuken also believes specific paragraphs within chap. 66 were written to conclude Third-Isaiah, Second Isaiah, and the entire book.[613]

This paragraph continues to develop the contrast between the contrite or humble followers of God mentioned in 57:15 and those who will receive God's harsh treatment because of their pagan worship (57:3–13a; 59:1–15; 64:1–7; 65:1–7). The false worship of idols and the eating of pigs will result in God's wrath coming on one group (66:3–4), but God will highly esteem the humble who tremble at God's word (66:2b,5). This continues the discussion of the contrasting destinies of the obstinate people who forsake God (65:2,11) and "my servants" who will inherit the future kingdom of God (65:8–15).[614]

Commentators have offered a variety of interpretations of the temple in 66:1. P. Hanson views 66:1–4 as "an indictment and sentence against an allegedly defiled group which is building the temple"[615] around 520 BC. C. Westermann takes this as a general statement that does not oppose the building of any specific temple; it opposes statements like Hag 2:19 that suggest that salvation is dependent on building a temple.[616] Some have thought that this is a rejection of the Samaritan temple built on Mount Gerizim around 400 BC, or that this verse is arguing for a total rejection of all ritual ceremonies and advocating purely spiritual worship.[617] In light of the condemnations in 66:3–4, it appears that there are two problems being addressed: (a) inappropriate trust in the temple building and (b) opposition to the pagan syncretistic ritual that

---

[613] Beuken, "Isaiah Chapter LXV–LXVI: Trito-Isaiah and the Closure of the Book of Isaiah," 204–21, concludes that (a) 65:1–66:14 is the conclusion to Trito-Isaiah, (b) 66:15–20a serves as the conclusion to both Deutero and Trito-Isaiah, and (c) 66:20b–24 is the conclusion to the whole book. Although this approach makes some interesting connections with earlier material, this complex redactional composition of chap. 66 into separate conclusions is not very obvious, for material that is dealt with in one section is found in the wrong conclusion. For example, Seitz, "Isaiah 40–66," 545, notes that the vindication of the servants in Trito-Isaiah is found in 66:22, which is supposed to be the conclusion to the whole book. Also false worship in chap. 1 is found in 66:1–6, which was supposed to be the conclusion to Trito-Isaiah. Chapter 66 is primarily a continuation of chap. 65 and a conclusion to the whole book based on its relationship to chap. 1.

[614] Seitz, "Isaiah 40–66," 545, states that "chap. 65 and chap. 66 should be read together. . . Chapter 66 is a logical, direct, sustained continuation of the argument of chap. 65."

[615] Hanson, *The Dawn of Apocalyptic*, 163, later interprets this as a struggle between a hierocratic group of Zadokite priests who were controlling the temple and an oppressed Levitical/prophetic group of priests who followed Second Isaiah, had no power, and were accusing the Zadokites of defiling the temple. He places all this around 520 BC when Haggai was encouraging these Zadokites to rebuild the temple. Rofé, "Isaiah 66:1–4: Judean Sects in the Persian Period as Viewed by Trito-Isaiah," 205–17, concludes that this is primarily an attack on the syncretistic practices of the priests.

[616] Westermann, *Isaiah 40–66*, 413, derives this verse from the Psalms (50; 113:5–6), but its use in this context must determine its meaning, not its use in the Psalms.

[617] Muilenburg, "Isaiah 40–66," 5:758–59, surveys these and other options that commentators have suggested, and then he critiques each.

some people (not just priests) were practicing. Having a temple building will not save anyone. Having a temple building where syncretistic ritual is carried out will only condemn people.

The beginning of the paragraph is clearly marked by an introductory messenger formula in 66:1 ("This is what the LORD says"), and the paragraph appears to extend through 66:4 because 66:5 begins with another messenger formula. In contrast to this assessment, E. C. Webster argues that the first paragraph includes 66:1–6 based on the repetition of *Leitworte* and the purposeful arrangement of this material into a concentric chiastic structure.[618] P. A. Smith has properly noted the weakness of some of these arguments and rejects this division of the paragraph; instead, he gives greater emphasis to the change of address to the righteous ("you who tremble at his word" in 66:5) and the messenger formula that mark the next message in 66:5.[619] The structure of this paragraph is:

What does God want—a temple or humble people?   66:1–2
What does God not want?   66:3–4
    Accusations of abominations   3a
    Judgments for abominations   3b–4a
    Accusations of not listening   4b

The reference to God calling out to his people and the reprobates not answering in 66:4 connects this paragraph closely with the same theme in 65:1,12,24 and the complaints against God in the lament in 63:7–64:11. The accusations of false worship in 66:3 are closely connected to similar problems in 65:2–4, and the false "ways" (*derek*) in 66:3 are connected to the "ways" of an obstinate people in 65:2. These interconnections indicate that 66:1–4 is a continuation of God's answer to the lament in 63:7–64:11. The sinfulness of the nation reminds one of the terrible abominations in the time of Manasseh (2 Kings 21; 2 Chronicles 33) and the sins mentioned in 1:29–31, although there is no way of dating this material to any era of Israel's history.

66:1 The reference to God's throne and house is somewhat confusing. This appears to be a quotation or a reference to a previous statement that God's presence cannot be limited to Solomon's temple in 1 Kgs 8:27–30, but it is not very clear what this statement is supporting or condemning in this context. Was

---

[618] E. C. Webster, "A Rhetorical Study of Isaiah 66," *JSOT* 34 (1986): 93–108, divides the paragraphs into 66:1–6,7–14,15–24; Beuken, "Does Trito-Isaiah Reject the Temple? An Intertextual Inquiry into Isa. 66:1–6," in *Intertextuality in Biblical Writings: Essays in Honor of Bas van Iersel,* ed. S. Draisma (Kampen: Kok Pharos, 1989), 53–66, and Oswalt, *Isaiah 40–66,* 665, identify the first paragraph as 66:1–6.

[619] After a close examination of Webster's approach, P. A. Smith, *Rhetoric and Redaction in Trito-Isaiah,* 153–4, observes that some "complementary terms" in Webster's chiastic structure are not identical ("house" בַּיִת in 66:1 is not an exact complement to "palace, temple" הֵיכָל in 66:6). Some subsequent repetition of words is quite normal in this section of Isaiah, but that does not necessarily require one to create a chiastic structure of the paragraph.

this meant to (a) discourage people from rebuilding the postexilic temple in Jerusalem, (b) serve as an indication that God rejects all ritual worship in favor of a right inner spiritual relationship to God, or (c) be an attempt to recognize God's worldwide influence, presence, and interests far beyond this one specific location. The positive statements about God's future temple on his Holy Mountain in 56:7; 60:7,13; 62:9; 66:6,20–21 argue against the position that God is against temple-making and wants only nonritual worship of the heart. The positive statements in favor of building the postexilic temple in Haggai 1–2 and Zech 1:16; 4:6–10 argue that this is not a condemnation of those who want to build the postexilic temple.

This paragraph must be read in the context of the earlier lament and God's initial answers in chap. 65. It reiterates and begins to conclude the issues related to the people that God will "esteem, look on"[620] (66:2b). The earlier lament questioned if God would not "look on, consider" (63:15; 64:8) his people who are not seeing his salvation. Those who have forsaken God have wondered where God's zeal and might was (63:15; 64:7–8) and sought the favor of other gods through pagan sacrifices (65:2–5,7; 66:3). The truth, of course, is that God was always right there by them, was always available, wanted to have a relationship with them (65:1–2), and was not and will not be silent (65:12; 66:4).

So where is God and what is he doing? Why was he not helping these people? The answer to these questions relates first to who God is, where God is, and what God "esteem[s]" (v. 2b). God is one who is sovereignly present, reigning over the whole heavens and the whole earth (66:1). This imagery presents God as a King on a throne, ruling over all the kingdoms of the earth;[621] he is not limited to any temple made by some king (1 Kgs 8:27–30) or to any one group of people. The idea that God is a king who is enthroned in heaven is a theme found in the preaching of the prophets (6:1–6; 29:11; 37:16; 40:22; 63:15; Jer 10:10–11; Dan 4:17,25,32,37; 5:21; 6:26; 7:9), the narrative stories in the historical literature (Exod 15:18; 1 Kgs 8:23,30,34,36,39,43,45; 22:19), and in the nation's songs of praise (Pss 2:4, 11:4; 29:10; 47:2,7–9; 93:3; 95:3–5; 97:1,9; 99:1–4).[622] This concept demonstrates his great glory and his majestic authority, as well as his extensive power over everything that exists in this world. He is not just interested in one small temple building, one small people group, or things on one small planet (Earth) in the vast heavens. Although people in the past and today may think God is completely focused just on them and their concerns, his interests and control extends beyond the vast scope of space and time.

---

[620] The root נבט means to "look at" something (Exod 3:6) with the eyes, "to consider, show regard to, pay attention to" (22:8; 51:1–2) with the mind.

[621] Stephen quotes Isa 66:1–2a in Acts 7:49–50.

[622] G.V. Smith, "The Concept of God/the gods as King in the Ancient Near East and the Bible," *TJ* 3 (1982): 18–38, traces various references and images to God as a king in the Bible.

When Isaiah saw the Lord as the high-and-lifted-up King in chap. 6, he recognized his own unholiness as he stood in the presence of the awesome holy Lord of Hosts. He experienced the cleansing power of God's forgiveness (6:6–7), and he also heard God's call to go and speak God's message to the unclean people who lived in Judah. The experience of seeing a vision of God in his heavenly temple caused him to realize that one day the glory of God would fill the whole earth (6:3), not just the small city of Jerusalem or just the state of Judah. Throughout the book of Isaiah, God reveals his plans for the destruction of all nations of the earth (chaps. 13–23) as well as the salvation of people from all nations (2:1–5; 11:10–16; 14:1–2; 19:18–25; 45:22–25; 60–62; 66:18–23). His plans as King of the heavens and the earth are to transform this world by creating a new heaven, a new earth, a new people, a new Jerusalem, and a new situation without death or the curse (65:17–25). Yes, he is King over the whole heavens and earth.

The two rhetorical questions about the location of God hint at a misunderstanding by the people, who felt somewhat forsaken by God. On the basis of what 66:1 claims, the answer to the hypothetical questions, "Where (*'ê zeh*) would you build"[623] a house for me?" and "Where (would you build)[624] a place for my rest?" is that it is impossible for any people to build a temple that is adequate for such a universal King who rules the heavens and the earth. People cannot corral God in a building, limit his work or presence to one location, or create a time of rest for God by human efforts. This does not mean that God rejects temples and the ritual worship people offer there; it means that God's future work among all peoples of the earth will be a universal work not limited by his confinement to one temple building in one location.[625] This means that the main issue God "looks at, considers, values" is his relationship with people. His presence is related to his dwelling in the midst of his holy people, and his rest relates to ending the struggle with sinful people who defile the earth and become his enemies. The new heavens and new earth will be the place where God will rest (60:21; 65:17–25; 66:22); this will be the New Jerusalem where God dwells among his holy people from all nations (60:1–11).

66:2a   The third rhetorical question is part of God's answer to these questions. In it God explains why a temple is not the main thing God considers when evaluating his relationship to people. In this question God could be asking who made the temple stones, wood, gold, and sacrifices, but in light of 66:1 it is best to broaden out the question to include "all these things," a phrase

---

[623] In interrogative questions the imperfect verb expresses a modal sense (GKC §107r,t) of "should, would, could, might."

[624] There is no verb in the final clause, a common characteristic of synonymous incomplete parallelism. In such cases it is appropriate to supply the missing piece from the first line ("would you build") to the second line.

[625] Schramm, *The Opponents of Third Isaiah*, 164, rightly rejects the idea that this is an anti-temple polemic.

which must encompass everything in the heavens and the earth. Since he is the Creator of everything, God's hands caused all these things to exist. This means that giving back to God some neatly stacked stones that form a temple and giving him a few sacrificial animals that he made is like a child giving a father a gift that was found lying in his father's closet. The key things of importance are the thoughts and intentions of the child, not where the child found the gift. So with God, the temple and its sacrifices are not the key things that God considers (he made and owns all these things) but the worshipful thoughts and reverent intentions of his loving children.

66:2b   What does God "esteem" (or "look for, consider," from *nābaṭ*)? Three terms describe the kind of people (not the place and all that goes on there) that God looks for so that he might have a relationship with his people. The first trait is that they are "humble"[626] and dependent on God. The second term describes a person with a "contrite spirit,"[627] a term that does not refer to being despondent but lowly and dependent on divine help (57:15). The third characteristic of the people God wants to have a relationship with is that they "tremble" at God's word (cf. Ezra 9:4; 10:3). People like this stand in awe before the King of kings who made the heavens and the earth. They deeply respect what God has said, take it very seriously, internalize it and make it part of their worldview, and then they implement it in their daily walk and thinking.

66:3a   Now there is a description of what God does not look for and what he does not want to find in any people on the earth. These vile people are described using seven participles that are arranged either in a list or in comparative pairs if the word "as" or "like" is implied (NIV, NRSV, KJV, NASB).[628] If the latter, the condemnation is saying that those who offer a legitimate sacrifice (an ox or lamb) are like or no better than those who offer illegitimate sacrifices (a dog or pig). An alternative and better approach is not to add any connectors ("like, as")[629] between these participles; thus, rather than comparing one evil act to another, the statement is suggesting that the same person does all of these things.[630] The main criticism is that people sacrifice both legitimate and ille-

---

[626] The word עָנִי "humble, poor, afflicted" often refers to an "oppressed" person (60:14) because of social, material, or political powerlessness. The metaphorical meaning would refer to those who are not proud or arrogant in spirit but realize that they are deeply dependent on God, unworthy to come into his presence, and owe everything they have to God. The humble exalt God while the proud exalt themselves (cf. 2:11,17).

[627] The adjective נָכֵה is used only three times (here and in 1 Sam 4:4; 9:3 "crippled of feet"), but the root נָכָה means "he smote," which most frequently appears in the context of fighting and war. If a person's spirit is "crippled," this person knows that he cannot make it on his own but needs help.

[628] The Old Greek creates a comparative relationship between these participles; 1QIsᵃ has a comparative כ "as, like" in the first line but not in the rest. Watts, *Isaiah 34–66*, 350, supplies the "is just like" comparative in each clause.

[629] J. L. Koole, *Isaiah III, Volume 3: Isaiah 56–66*, 477, is one who does not add the "like, as" comparative particle to these verses.

[630] HCSB translates the clauses as a series, and some commentaries prefer this solution.

gitimate sacrifices because they have accepted the syncretistic religious rituals of Judah as well as pagan practices (57:3–13; 65:2–7).[631] Thus the main goal is not to condemn legitimate sacrifices or sacrificial ritual in general, just the foolish acts of an impure person who does not distinguish between legitimate and illegitimate sacrifices.

Their sacrifice of an ox, a lamb, grain, and a memorial offering are fully acceptable ways of worshipping God by a repentant sinner (Leviticus 1–5). There are numerous questions about the nature of the sacrifices that are illegitimate. What is implied by the act of the "one who kills (lit. "strikes)"[632] a man? J. Muilenburg concludes that the "one who kills" a man must refer to human sacrifice, not just murder.[633] In light of the sacrificial context of this list of activities, killing appears to be implied (not just striking) since all of the other objects are offered as a sacrifice. This may refer to human sacrifice similar to that mentioned in Jer 7:31 or 19:2–6 where sons and daughters were sacrificed in the valley of Ben Hinnom as an offering to Baal (Ezek 23:37–39). The breaking of the neck of the dog was also probably part of a sacrificial offering. J. M. Sasson has collected examples of the Hurrian and Mari text where canines were used in sacrifices, and a Hittite archive refers to the making of a treaty in which "a man, a kid, a puppy-dog, and a suckling pig are cut in half" as part of the covenant-making ritual.[634] Verse 3 does not reveal what this ritual ceremony was for, but it is clearly outside the normally accepted practices prescribed in Leviticus. The offering of the blood of an unclean pig (64:3; 66:17) would have been considered most vile.[635] But it is not clear what exactly was done with the pig's blood because there is no participle connected with this act to describe how it was used. In such cases,

---

[631] J. S. Sasson, "Isaiah LXVI 3–4a," *VT* 26 (1976): 199–207, offers the suggestion of translating these clauses as contrasts, "He who (once) slaughtered an ox (would now) slay a man." This contrasts the good acts they used to do in the past with the negative acts they are now doing. This could work for the first four comparisons, but the last two acts in 66:3 list two negatives that do not present a contrast. In addition, it seems that if the prophet was trying to express a distinction between what happened in the past and present, he would not have used participles to represent both actions. Rofé, "Isaiah 66:1–4: Judean Sects in the Persian Period as Viewed by Trito-Isaiah," 205–17, takes the first participle as the subject and the second as a verb. This causes him to conclude that the ones being condemned are the priests who are currently serving in the temple (not all priests), possibly those opposed by Ezra and Nehemiah. Blenkinsopp, *Isaiah 56–66*, 51–54, 296, agrees with this understanding and identifies those who tremble at God's words in 66:2,5 as the same people as those in Ezra 9:4; 10:3. Oswalt, *Isaiah 40–66*, 669–70, also uses Haggai, Zechariah, Ezra, Nehemiah, and Malachi to help identify these groups.

[632] The participle מַכֵּה comes from נָכָה "he struck, smote," which can refer to a lethal or non-lethal blow. This verb might describe two men in a wrestling fight or a person being killed with a sword in war.

[633] Muilenburg, "Isaiah 40–66," 5:762. Hansen, *The Dawn of Apocalyptic*, 180, calls this murder.

[634] Sasson, "Isaiah LXVI 3–4a," 199–207. Though these examples are probably unrelated to this Isaiah text, they do indicate that the pagan religions in other nations did use these kinds of animals and even people in their sacrifices. He suggests that 66:3 may represent preexilic practices.

[635] Sasson (Ibid.) mentions that the Greeks used swine's blood in ritual purification ceremonies

most interpreters supply the participle from the preceding line ("one who presents"), so that this act relates both to the presenting of a grain offering and the offering of pig's blood. On the other hand, it may be that a word has dropped out of this text since blood is usually poured out or sprinkled (Exod 24:6; Lev 1:5; 5:9). Of course, if this is a pagan ritual, they may have dealt with the blood in ways quite different from traditional Hebrew ritual. The last pagan practice was the "one who worships an idol" (NIV). The Hebrew literally refers to this practice as "one who blesses wickedness," but the semantic field of meaning for the word "wickedness" includes its use as a pun for the city of "Bethel" (the house of God), which was called "Beth-Aven" (the "house of an idol/wickedness" in Hos 4:15; 10:5). This name was given because of the golden calf that Jeroboam I put there (1 Kgs 12:26–30). God's people were to bless and praise the Lord, but these people were now giving their praise to a pagan idol.

66:3b–4a In the last two lines of 66:3, the long series of participles is broken, and two finite verbs identify additional abominable acts of worship. Both 66:3b and 66:4a begin with a reference to the act of "choosing," with *gam*, a word that means "so, also, even, moreover" preceding both verbs. This use of *gam* indicates some correspondence or correlation between what "they" (*hēmmâ*) did and what "I" (*ʾănî*) will do.[636] This could be expressed by "even as, just as they chose . . . so I also will choose." This construction enables the author to create a clear relationship between the crimes that they committed and the punishment that God will choose to bring on these people. The statement "they [themselves] have chosen"[637] pins responsibility on their free decision to act "according to their own ways" (65:2) by doing things that are not circumscribed or informed by God's ways. Their ways are explained as the abominations in which their soul delights. Earlier God identified his own people as those "who choose to please, delight in me" (56:4), but these people purposely "choose what does not please" (65:12) God. Their participation is not just a routine ritualistic performance of meaningless rote words and actions that are meaningless ritualistic routine; these are pagan activities that they completely enjoy, for "their soul delights" in doing them. How perverse and twisted are their values? The fact that they love these things and are pleased to be involved with these disgusting and deplorable abominations shows just how spiritually depraved these people really are.

The only appropriate and possible response to these abominable and ungodly choices is for God himself to choose to bring on these people a just punishment (66:4a). Yes, this is God's free choice, for he could react in patience

---

[636] GKC §154a, n. 1; BDB, 169, גַּם, section 4.

[637] The construction הֵמָּה בָּחֲרוּ "they themselves chose" unnecessarily includes the subject pronoun הֵמָּה to emphasize the subject's responsibility in the action. The subject of a verb is already expressed in the verb form, so a separate pronoun is normally omitted except in cases where one wishes to emphasize the subject (GKC §135a).

and be long-suffering for a little longer, or he could forgive their sins and choose to love them in spite of their sins, or he could choose to bring a brief period of discipline to draw them back to himself. In this case, God chooses "their actions, their deeds"[638] (NIV "harsh treatment"), but this seems an odd thing for God to choose. A periphrastic rendition of this that makes more sense in English might be, "I will choose to address their deeds"; thus, God is not going to permit them to continue doing what they have been doing any longer; rather, he will appropriately respond. The way he will respond will be to bring on them what they dread. They thought they were protecting themselves from future calamity by worshipping these pagan gods, but this was a foolish act of placing their security in the wrong place. What they dreaded is not defined here, but the positive destiny they were fervently hoping for will not happen (65:11); instead, God will intervene and destroy them as he promised earlier (65:11–12).

66:4b   The ultimate reason for all this evil behavior, false worship, and pagan syncretism goes back to the fundamental fact that these stubborn people have forsaken God and refused to respond when God called to direct them in the right path. This is the repeated emphasis in this answer to the lament (cf. 65:1). The wicked people God will judge were totally unwilling to listen when God was speaking to them (65:12); consequently, they sealed their own destiny because they excluded the possibility of having a positive relationship with God. This was an affront to God; it revealed a deep disrespect because they even refused to speak with him or listen to anything he had to say. If this was their attitude, it seems that God cannot reach them with words; thus, he must respond with severe actions.

The final clause in 66:4c reconfirms what they chose in 66:4b and pinpoints the responsibility on those who willfully made the wrong decision. Instead of listening to God and choosing to follow his instructions, they did what was evil in God's eyes. They no doubt had some knowledge of what God wanted from their knowledge of Hebrew traditions in the *Torah*, but doing these things did not please them. Their souls gained delight and pleasure in doing what did not please God. This reminds one of the key issues discussed in relationship to fasting in chap. 58. Those people participated in the fast, but they did what gave them "delight, pleasure" (58:3,13; 65:12) instead of doing what pleased and delighted God. Such clear statements about the nature of these bad choices and the consequences of them are a clear warning to all who read these words.

---

[638] The noun תַּעֲלֻלֵיהֶם "their actions, deeds" comes from the root עָלַל "he did, worked," so it seems to refer to "their evil deeds" described in the previous verses. Koole, *Isaiah III, Volume 3: Isaiah 56–66*, 481, take the suffix as a subjective genitive and translates "they did wrong." In other words, God is choosing to focus on what they did wrong in order to bring on them what they feared, that is, their punishment.

GOD WILL GIVE ZION CHILDREN AND JOY (66:5–14)

[5]Hear the word of the LORD,
    you who tremble at his word:
  "Your brothers who hate you,
    and exclude you because of my name, have said,
  'Let the LORD be glorified,
    that we may see your joy!'
  Yet they will be put to shame.
[6]Hear that uproar from the city,
    hear that noise from the temple!
  It is the sound of the LORD
    repaying his enemies all they deserve.

[7]"Before she goes into labor,
    she gives birth;
  before the pains come upon her,
    she delivers a son.
[8]Who has ever heard of such a thing?
    Who has ever seen such things?
  Can a country be born in a day
    or a nation be brought forth in a moment?
  Yet no sooner is Zion in labor
    than she gives birth to her children.
[9]Do I bring to the moment of birth
    and not give delivery?" says the LORD.
  "Do I close up the womb
    when I bring to delivery?" says your God.
[10]"Rejoice with Jerusalem and be glad for her,
    all you who love her;
  rejoice greatly with her,
    all you who mourn over her.
[11]For you will nurse and be satisfied
    at her comforting breasts;
  you will drink deeply
    and delight in her overflowing abundance."

[12]For this is what the LORD says:

  "I will extend peace to her like a river,
    and the wealth of nations like a flooding stream;
  you will nurse and be carried on her arm
    and dandled on her knees.
[13]As a mother comforts her child,
    so will I comfort you;
    and you will be comforted over Jerusalem."

[14]When you see this, your heart will rejoice
    and you will flourish like grass;
  the hand of the LORD will be made known to his servants,
    but his fury will be shown to his foes.

Once again, two groups of Hebrews are distinguished. This new paragraph is addressed to "you who tremble at his word," the humble and contrite of 66:2. They are opposed by another group of Hebrews (*'ăḥêkem*, "your brothers") who hate them (66:5). The makeup of these two groups continues to be an issue that is surrounded by much speculation and imaginative guesswork.[639] The identification of the two groups who are opposing one another is often heavily dependent on implications drawn from hints provided in these verses as well as insights drawn from other texts outside of Isaiah. This issue will be more fully addressed in the exegesis of 66:5. This paragraph is organized into four parts.

Shaming of God's enemies	66:5–6
Birth of many in Zion	66:7–9
Joy and comfort for Jerusalem	66:10–11
Peace, prosperity, and comfort	66:12–14

The first subparagraph refers to God's judgment on his enemies while the last three describe God's blessing for those who tremble at his words. These verses are connected to their context because (a) the wealth of the nations coming to Zion in 66:12 is consistent with what was already stated in 60:5–11; 61:6; (b) the joy and rejoicing in 66:10–14 is closely related to that same theme in 65:18–19; and (c) the judgment of God's enemies in 66:5b–6 agrees with 60:12; 63:1–6; 65:6–7,15. The contrast between the destiny of God's enemies and those who tremble at his word should have brought some sense of assurance and hope to those who were faithful to God. One wonders if there are not some lessons hidden within this chapter that could be helpful for churches that are being torn apart by competing factions that hate one another. It is sad but true that in the midst of many of these conflicts, it is somewhat difficult to identify the humble and contrite person (66:2b) that God would esteem.

66:5 This new paragraph is introduced as another authoritative word from God addressed to "you," the people who tremble when hearing God's word. These are the humble and contrite people described in 66:2, who are esteemed by God. They do not offer legal and illegal sacrifices like their apostate Hebrew brothers (66:3). Many conclude that one group is made up of the wealthy and politically powerful people of that time based on the rendering of *měnaddêkem*, those "who exclude [or "push out"] you," but this is not a necessary conclusion. Any group of people (strong or weak) can exclude others from their special circle of friends based on age, sex, ethnicity, social status, political party, economic status, religious affiliation, theological position, or for a host of other reasons. C. Westermann compares this "pushing out" to the much later use of this term in the Talmud where it describes the excommunication of people from the synagogue, but this illegitimately imposes on 66:5 a

---

[639] These are discussed in the introduction to chaps. 56–66 under the heading "Setting and Date."

foreign setting from many centuries later.[640] J. Oswalt's conclusion that those "who are doing the casting out are the wealthy, the priests, and the nobles,"[641] reads far too much into this controversy and imposes on this text a setting from outside Isaiah (i.e., from Ezra, Nehemiah). J. Muilenburg does not find a strong difference in social status between these two groups but believes the conflict is over one faithful group that is dependent on the theological teaching in the law and the prophets and another group that "relies on the efficacy of a material temple and a syncretistic sacrificial system."[642] All of these attempts to specify a particular group should be avoided, for all one needs to say from 66:5a is that one group hates the other and quite naturally excludes them from participating in some of their activities. More can be concluded based on issues raised in this and later verses.

There are two hints about this conflict, and neither seems to have anything to do with building a temple. The first issue is presented in the statement that one group excludes the other "because of my name." But there are two ways of understanding this claim. Either (a) the syncretistic brethren who hate those who fear God's word exclude these humble and contrite brethren "on account of, because" the humble give exclusive honor to God's name, or (b) the brethren who hate those who fear God's name exclude those who fear God's word from their group in order that they might protect the name of God. The preposition *lĕma'an* can express "in order that, for the sake of, on account of."[643] The second option would create an extremely ironic situation since the practices described in 65:3–5,7; 66:3,17 suggest that those who offer syncretistic offerings are not truly devoted completely to the name of God. Thus the first option appears to fit the situation much better.

The second hint at what is going on in this context is found in the quotation of what the hateful brothers say to the people who tremble at God's word. Unfortunately, it is not all that clear who is being quoted, so there are two very different interpretations of this saying. First, the majority of commentators conclude that the syncretistic worshippers are quoting what the humble and contrite say in order to mock them. Since the statement is directed to a higher power (God himself), it is fair to assume that the imperfect verb ("to glorify,

---

[640] Westermann, *Isaiah 40–66*, 416. Whybray, *Isaiah 40–66*, 282, rightly criticizes those who imply that the verb cast out "had already acquired the later technical sense of 'excommunicate.'"

[641] Oswalt, *Isaiah 40–66*, 670, concludes that the "major concern is their own aggrandizement." This claim seems to be unsubstantiated in Isaiah 65–66, for in this immediate context there is no condemnation of these people for their pride, desire for wealth, or social status.

[642] Muilenburg, "Isaiah 40–66," 5:764, understands the conflict as theological rather than a social conflict between the wealthy and the poor.

[643] The preposition לְמַעַן can be translated " for the sake of, in order that, on account of." P. A. Smith, *Rhetoric and Redaction in Trito-Isaiah*, 163, prefers "in order that" and believes the syncretistic worshippers who wanted to build the temple ironically thought they were honoring God's name.

honor") functions as a jussive wish or request,[644] but it does not function as a passive verb ("be glorified").[645] In this interpretation the humble look forward to the eschatological coming of God in all his glory so that they can enjoy with God his glorious kingdom described in chaps 60–62; 65:17–25. The syncretistic worshippers quote these idealistic eschatological hopes of the humble in order to ridicule their piety and their delusional dreaming about this idealistic future era (chaps. 60–62).[646]

A minority view explained by P. A. Smith takes the quotation to be expressing the valid perspective of the syncretistic worshippers who want to build the temple so that they can see God's glorious appearance and enjoy his presence among them once again.[647] Although grammatically possible, this approach suggests that the syncretistic worshippers were really interested in seeing God's glorious presence and his name glorified, yet the passages about their syncretistic worship do not give this impression at all (57:3–13; 64:5–7; 65:2–7; 66:17). This interpretation also assumes a very strong bond with the temple building and God's glory, but other passages about this syncretistic group talk much more about their worship among the oaks, in the valleys and hills, by graves (57:5–9), and in the gardens (66:3; 66:17) instead of in the presence of God at the temple. Thus this interpretation is not preferred.

These two hints suggest that two of the major differences (and there were undoubtedly many others) between these two groups were that those who trembled at God's word (a) gave exclusive worship and glory to God's name and totally rejected all syncretistic worship, and (b) they put their trust in the eschatological promises of the coming kingdom of God when God will come to earth and reveal his glory to all people (chaps. 60–62). Two other differences already mentioned in 66:1–2 were that those who trembled at God's word (c) put their hope in their relationship to God rather than temple building and (d) lived a humble life and did not offer both legitimate and illegitimate sacrifices.

This verse ends with a word of hope for those who trembled at God's word. They can be encouraged, for one day in the future God will shame those who offer these pagan offerings and mock the theological beliefs of the humble. Although life may have trials and tribulations that are very trying for God's people, those who follow God and are fully committed to him know that in the end God will be on their side and they will enjoy the future with God. For

---

[644] The jussive form is often spelled exactly like the imperfect; thus, it is distinguished only by context (GKC §48f). The jussive is used to express a wish, desire, or request (GKC §109a-b).

[645] Most translations have "let God be glorified" as if the verb was the passive יְכֻבַּד. Instead the verb is active יְכַבֵּד "may God become glorious."

[646] Koole, *Isaiah III, Volume 3: Isaiah 56–66*, 485–7, views this quotation as a taunt by the hostile brethren who oppose the humble.

[647] P. A. Smith, *Rhetoric and Redaction in Trito-Isaiah*, 164, appears to make much more of the need or desire to rebuild the temple than is implied in 66:1–5. He believes an editor moved this verse from vv. 15–16 and placed it here to give the whole a quasiapocalyptic flavor.

a short time the syncretistic brethren have tried to shame those who trembled at God's word, but in the end they will suffer a much worse destiny when God shames them.

66:6   R. N. Whybray takes this verse as "a prophecy of divine judgment against the nations,"[648] which functions in this context as God's judgment against those who hate the people who tremble at God's word. In reality, the judgment seems more focused on the Hebrew people who offered syncretistic offerings when God brings his final judgment of all mankind (cf. 24:1–23; 34:1–15; 63:1–6).

This future judgment is pictured in this verse as a time characterized by three great "voices, sounds, thundering noises" (*qôl*), a noun that NIV translates as if it were the imperative verb "hear." The first noise is the "sound of tumult from the city." This "tumultuous sound" was earlier used in reference to the masses of revelers who will enter Sheol (5:14) as well as the "uproar" of many warriors that make a noise similar to the roaring of the seas (17:12–13). The direction where this "sound" is coming from is then specified as the temple area, the place where God dwells. B. S. Childs believes this sound comes from God's heavenly "temple, palace" (*hêkāl*, not *bêt* "house"), not from an earthly building in Jerusalem (66:1).[649] Finally, the third "sound" pinpoints this noise to be the voice, or sound of an angry God. Earlier in 30:30 the majestic voice of God came in raging anger accompanied by fire, cloudburst, thunder, and hail to shatter the Assyrian army. Amos 1:2; 3:8 compares the Lord's voice of warning to thunder and the roaring of a lion, while Joel 2:11; 3:16 (Hb. 4:16) compares God's voice to thunder and roaring when he comes to judge the earth. If God's mighty voice can speak so that the whole world is created (Genesis 1), just imagine how destructive his thundering voice will be when he speaks and his judgment instantly happens. This must be referring to events on the final Day of the Lord because that is the time when God will finally establish his justice on the earth by repaying his enemies their just rewards. Knowing this, all the humble and contrite can rest assured that eventually God will justly deal with those who hate them and repay all those who are involved with syncretistic worship.

66:7–9   Suddenly in the next three subparagraphs (66:7–9,10–11,12–14) God addresses his faithful followers with images of hope and joy in a proclamation of salvation. The message in 66:7–9 is centered around the themes of "having labor" (*ḥîl* is used three times) and "giving birth" (*yālad* is used five times). The key stylistic feature in 66:8–9 is the posing of several odd ques-

---

[648] Whybray, *Isaiah 40–66*, 283, partially bases this on the reference to "all men" in 66:15–16. Isaiah 66:5–6 and 66:15–16 form a judgment envelope around the positive themes in 66:7–14.

[649] Childs, *Isaiah*, 541, makes a connection between this passage and 6:1–13. Westermann, *Isaiah 40–66*, 419, suggests that this assumes that the earthly temple has already been built, but Koole, *Isaiah III, Volume 3: Isaiah 56–66*, 488, correctly points out that this is all happening in the distant future, not in the Old Testament era.

tions. These questions invite the audience to think about what normally happens and notice how God will act in unexpected and exceptional ways. E. C. Webster classifies these questions as riddles (comparable to Samson's riddle in Judg 14:14,18) since they express ideas that are so unusual.[650]

Verse 7 sets up this unusual situation in which an unnamed woman "gave birth"[651] before "she begins labor"[652] and the parallel circumstance where a woman delivered a son[653] before pain begins to come over her. This event is unusual both with respect to the speed of the delivery and the total absence of any pain. This reports a phenomenon so unexpected that one suspects this must be a miraculous act. In v. 8 the prophet challenges the listeners to explain this phenomenon (like one would explain a riddle). Obviously, no one has ever heard or seen anything like this.[654] Consequently, the prophet provides the following rhetorical questions in v. 8b in order to begin to unfold the explanation of this unusual birth. First, the reader is lead to understand something about who was born. The question, "Is a nation given birth to[655] at one time?" reveals that this riddle is talking about a nation of people. But the riddle is still somewhat puzzling, for the population of a nation normally grows gradually over many years as mothers give birth to new children year after year. The final two lines of v. 8 provide some more answers to these questions. "Surely" (or "truly," *kî*; NIV "yet") the mother that gives birth is Zion, and the children that are born are the many people who dwell in Israel. This is expressed by verbs that view these events from an eschatological perspective in which all these things have already happened.[656] This prediction about the future is similar to the earlier promises of many children in 49:16–26; 54:1–8; 60:4.

Verse 9 adds additional rhetorical questions that have the effect of assuring anyone who might question or still have doubts about what God is planning to do. Some might wonder whether God can do what seems to be a total impossibility, while others might question if this multiplication of people will happen that quickly. The question (lit.) "Would I myself[657] cause to break forth [i.e., the birth process] and not cause [anything] to be born?" (NIV "Do I bring to

---

[650] Webster, "The Rhetoric of Isaiah 63–65," 89–102, connects this with the theme of the barren one producing many children in 54:1.

[651] The perfect verb יָלְדָה "she gave birth" refers to completed action (GKC §106a).

[652] The imperfect verb תָּחִיל "she begins labor" probably communicates an incipient action that is just beginning.

[653] The Aramaic Targum gives a periphrastic interpretation of this "male child" זָכָר by interpreting this as a reference to "her king," which presumably has messianic implications.

[654] The sg. and pl. demonstrative pronouns זֹאת "this" and אֵלֶּה "these" refer back to the surprising things mentioned in 66:7.

[655] The verbs יוּחַל is a passive *hophal* "given birth through labor," not an active verb as in NIV, and יֻלַּד "given birth to" is also a passive *niphal*.

[656] The verbs are in the perfect. The NIV "no sooner is Zion in labor" is quite periphrastic for the literal "Truly, Zion labored."

[657] The pronoun "I" is already in the imperfect verb אַשְׁבִּיר, so when the personal pronoun אֲנִי "I" is added, it produces an emphasis "I myself" (GKC §135a).

the moment of birth and not give delivery?") expresses how illogical these doubts are. A woman does not go into labor, and the amniotic fluid in the birth chamber does not break, if there is no child in the womb. So also God does not begin to fulfill his promises about the rebirth of his people without causing that new nation of people to be born. The audience can be sure that the one process leads inevitably to the other.

The second question also expresses a virtual impossibility. God asks if "I myself," being the one who causes births,[658] would shut up the womb from being fertile? (NIV reverses the Hebrew clauses and renders, "Do I close up the womb when I bring to delivery?") J. Blenkinsopp connects these promises to the concerns of people in Jerusalem in the postexilic period, but J. Muilenburg properly interprets this as an eschatological promise.[659] These questions indicate that God, who has the power to give birth to a new heavens and a new earth and to fulfill his eschatological plans, will not stop in the middle of it so that he does not finish what he promised. God is faithful to do what he says, and his sovereignty is so great that he is able to accomplish what he plans to do. This would comfort all who heard these statements, for they could be assured that these things would happen because God is the one who spoke these promises. Zion will not accomplish these things out of her own determination or willpower; these unusual events will be fulfilled because no one and nothing can stop God from fulfilling his promises.

66:10–11   Since all these wonderful things will happen, God encourages his people to rejoice and be glad[660] in the promise that he has given them about the tremendous increase in population. Joy and gladness typically are associated with the future fulfillment of God's promises (49:13; 51:11; 54:1; 60:5; 61:10–11; 65:13,18–19; 66:5b). Those who should rejoice are those who "love"[661] Zion and all who previously mourned for her. Although one might assume that those who love and previously mourned over Zion would be Hebrew people, the Gentile nations that will come to Zion in 60:1–11 will also love the place where God will reveal his glory, and they, too, will rejoice with those who are rejoicing in Jerusalem.

Verse 11 is connected to the preceding call to rejoice with a conjunctive particle usually expressing result or purpose (*lĕmaʿan*, technically a preposi-

---

[658] The participle with the prefixed article הַמּוֹלִיד usually is interpreted as a substantival relative clause "the one who causes to be born" (GKC §116o).

[659] Blenkinsopp, *Isaiah 56–66*, 305, believes that this promise indicates God is the one who will bring people back to Judah; they should not put their faith in Cyrus or Darius. According to Muilenburg, "Isaiah 40–66," 5:765, "The thought is eschatological throughout."

[660] The three imperative verbs שִׂמְחוּ, גִּילוּ, and שִׂישׂוּ could function as words of encouragement or "to express a distinct promise" (GKC §110a-b).

[661] The participle from the verb אָהֵב is used to express the idea of passionate love that is not based on obligation, covenants, or requirements. God's election love motivated him to act on behalf of undeserving people, and people have the choice to express their love for Zion and the God who dwells in it.

tion that can also mean "for the sake of, on account of"). One could suggest the people should rejoice (v. 10) "in order that, so that" they will be satisfied and comforted with all that Zion will provide (HCSB, "so that you may nurse and be satisfied from her comforting breast"), or one could conclude that the people should rejoice "on account of, because" (NIV, "For you will nurse . . . ") Zion will provide all that they need to satisfy and comfort them. Although both interpretations are acceptable, it is preferable to interpret this verse as expressing the result of the rejoicing: they will have satisfaction and be comforted by all that God will do for them.

God's salvation was earlier symbolized using the metaphor of a mother providing milk for her children (49:23; 60:16), but in those contexts it was the foreign nations that were providing for the needs (the milk) that the Hebrew people would have. This passage pictures Zion as the source of all that a sucking child would ever need. As a nursing mother provides for the nourishment of her child, so Zion's breast will provide both satisfaction for nourishment as well as emotional comfort and security (v. 13). To emphasize the enormity of these provisions, the second half of v. 11 expands this picture to imagine a child who "drains out"[662] his mother's breasts and who delights because of her glorious "breast, nipple."[663] Although Zion is said to be the source of these provisions, both 49:23 and 60:4–16 suggest that the foreign nations will provide an enormous amount of wealth to Zion, and ultimately it is God who provides comfort, protection, and provisions for all the needs of his people (40:1,10–11; 41:17–20; 49:13–18; 51:3–5,11–12; 53:7–10, 66:12–13).

66:12–14 This short subparagraph is introduced with a new messenger formula that assures the reader that this, too, is part of what God has said. If this *kî* is causal ("because"), the following words provide a substantiation of the promises in 66:7–11, but if the *kî* is asseverative ("surely, truly"), it is adding another sure promise from God.[664] In this case, the causal meaning is best, for the following words justify the preceding claims by stating that in actuality it is God who guarantees all these promises.

The audience can have faith in the truthfulness of these promises in vv. 7–11 because it is actually God who "will extend"[665] the peace that the people in Zion will enjoy. The abundance of God's peace (57:18; 60:17) is compared to the enormous amount of water in a river (48:18), and the overwhelming abundance of the "glory, wealth" of the nations (60:4–11) is compared to a flooding

---

[662] The verb תָּמֹצּוּ probably comes from מָצָה/מָצַץ "he drained out," referring to getting the last drop of milk out (51:17). In Ugaritic the meaning is "he slurped."

[663] The word זִיז is found here and in Ps 50:11. In means "nipple, breast" in other Semitic languages.

[664] GKC §159ee deals with the asseverative use of כִּי, and §158b treats the causal usage.

[665] The verb is the participle נֹטֶה, which functions as a verb in this sentence. Many verbal participles express durative action in present time, but when a participle is preceded by הִנֵּה, as it is in this case, the action is future (GKC §116a,c,p).

stream. Peace is an immaterial feeling of well-being in a person's relationship to the world, others, and God, while the wealth of the nations is a material blessing comparable to the promises of abundant milk in 66:11. Thus, it is not surprising that this imagery from v. 11 is picked up again in v. 12b. In this case the people are not metaphorically sucking at the breasts of Zion; instead, the nations are assisting God's people in Zion in three ways. The nations will nurse them (49:23), carry them (49:22; 60:4), and play with them.[666] This presents a picture of a future time when all the needs of God's people will be abundantly supplied.

While v. 12 explains the role that the nations will fulfill in providing for the needs of Zion, v. 13 focuses on God's role. Using an "as . . . so" (*kĕ . . . kēn*) syntactical construction, God compares himself to the mother with her child. In this verse God does not nurse his children, but he comforts them with his love and cares for them like a mother comforts her children. What God does is emphasized by adding the personal pronoun (*'ănōkî*, "I myself") and by describing the action twice, once from God's perspective ("I myself will comfort you") and once from Jerusalem's perspective ("you will be comforted"). This analogy is used to express the depth of God's strong love and his personal care for his beloved people. This imagery is fitting because God has a personal covenant relationship with his people. He saved them from Egyptian slavery, led them by the hand through the wilderness, gave them an inheritance in his land, and protected them from their enemies. His firm commitment to bring his people into his glorious kingdom (chaps. 60–62) and the new heaven and the new earth (65:17–25) are proof of how much he loves his people. Hearing these promises, the prophet's audience should be moved to rejoice and take great comfort in God's assuring words. He has not forgotten those who tremble at his words (66:2,5). His eschatological kingdom is designed just for them.

Verse 14a concludes these three positive subparagraphs with a final word of comfort for God's servants and a contrasting word of warning to God's enemies in v. 14b. The fullness of comfort will come when God's people will see and actually experience all the results of God's marvelous deeds on their behalf. Once this happens, their emotions will be uncontrollable, for their hearts will rejoice with unstoppable gladness that will surely be mixed with praise. The imagery of their bones "flourishing"[667] like grass is peculiar because one does not usually think of bones "sprouting, flourishing." Apparently "bones" represents the physical side of people (Ps 6:2 [Hb. 6:3]; Prov 15:30) that God

---

[666] Since the text does not say who will do this, Blenkinsopp, *Isaiah 56–66*, 306–307, interprets this as the activity of the nations, while Koole, *Isaiah III, Volume 3: Isaiah 56–66*, 501, believes it is Zion who will nurse, carry, and play with her children.

[667] The root פָּרַח means "he sprouted, budded out, flourished" when speaking of plants and, metaphorically, of a nation. Early Church Fathers saw this as a reference to the resurrection (the restoration of the dry bones of Ezekiel 37) but this seems unlikely.

will restore, while the heart in the previous line represents the emotional side of people.

The final two lines contrast God's plan for his servants and his enemies. The hand of the Lord refers both to his personal touch and presence as well as the power of his might that accomplishes his will. This presence and power "will be made known, will be revealed"[668] because God will no longer need to hide himself because of human sinfulness (59:1–2). Instead, he can freely reveal his glory and the glories of his future kingdom so that people can fully experience his presence and his blessings. The NIV translation interprets God's hand as being known "to his servants," but the preposition ʾet does not mean "to," but "with," or it is a sign of the direct object. Since the passive verb "known" does not take a direct object, ʾet must be the preposition "with." The grammar thus suggests the translation "the hand of the Lord with his servants will be known" (cf. NRSV). This reflects the situation in 60:1–5, where God's glorious presence in Zion with his people is made known to the nations all around the world because God's people will reflect his glory to others. In contrast to this wonderful situation, God will be furious with his enemies. This final comment functions as a transitional statement that moves the discussion to God's severe punishment of the wicked in 66:15–17.

(3) Gathering of All People to Worship God (66:15–24)

¹⁵See, the LORD is coming with fire,
     and his chariots are like a whirlwind;
he will bring down his anger with fury,
     and his rebuke with flames of fire.
¹⁶For with fire and with his sword
     the LORD will execute judgment upon all men,
     and many will be those slain by the LORD.

¹⁷"Those who consecrate and purify themselves to go into the gardens, following the one in the midst of those who eat the flesh of pigs and rats and other abominable things—they will meet their end together," declares the LORD.

¹⁸"And I, because of their actions and their imaginations, am about to come and gather all nations and tongues, and they will come and see my glory.

¹⁹"I will set a sign among them, and I will send some of those who survive to the nations—to Tarshish, to the Libyans and Lydians (famous as archers), to Tubal and Greece, and to the distant islands that have not heard of my fame or seen my glory. They will proclaim my glory among the nations. ²⁰And they will bring all your brothers, from all the nations, to my holy mountain in Jerusalem as an offering to the LORD—on horses, in chariots and wagons, and on mules and camels," says the LORD. "They will bring them, as the Israelites bring their grain offerings,

---

[668] The passive verb נוֹדְעָה "it will be known, revealed" indicates that whoever knows these things does not understand or experience these things because of their active discovery of them or their innate wisdom. God will make these things known to them.

to the temple of the LORD in ceremonially clean vessels. ²¹And I will select some of them also to be priests and Levites," says the LORD.

²²"As the new heavens and the new earth that I make will endure before me," declares the LORD, "so will your name and descendants endure. ²³From one New Moon to another and from one Sabbath to another, all mankind will come and bow down before me," says the LORD. ²⁴"And they will go out and look upon the dead bodies of those who rebelled against me; their worm will not die, nor will their fire be quenched, and they will be loathsome to all mankind."

The final paragraph begins with a description of the glorious coming of God in a theophany, accompanied by fire, his sword, and his chariot (66:15–16). He will come in wrath to bring destruction on all those who worship pagan gods, including any Hebrews who are involved with syncretistic worship (66:17). It is at this time that God will reveal the majesty of his presence on earth so that all people, even the foreign nations around the world who have not known him, will see his glory (66:18; 60:1–3). Then people will go to these nations, tell them of God's glory, and bring many back to the Holy Mountain in Zion to worship God (66:19–20). Some will even serve as priests in God's temple as people from every nation gather in Zion to bow down before God (66:21–23). In contrast, the wicked will go to a terrible loathsome place of eternal fire and the undying worms (66:24).

There is not much agreement on the division of this last paragraph. P. A. Smith views 66:18–24 as the last paragraph, but 66:18 provides a weak introduction to a paragraph and it refers back to what was happening in 66:15–17.[669] C. Westermann believes 66:7–14 are "set in the framework (vv. 6 and 15f.) of an epiphany in which God comes to judge the world."[670] On the other hand, it seems more likely that the paragraph begins at 66:15 because (a) "see, behold" (*hinnēh*) provides a better introduction to a new paragraph or a new part of a message; (b) "fire" and "all flesh" terminology begin and end this paragraph (66:15–16,23–24); (c) 66:15 introduces the theophany appearance of God which is assumed in 66:18; and (d) this division would mean that there is a discussion of the destiny of both the wicked and the righteous in the final paragraph of this book (which is common in these chapters). The structure of this paragraph divides it into two parts.

---

[669] P. A. Smith, *Rhetoric and Redaction in Trito-Isaiah*, 159, identifies vv. 5–17 as a unit, with the negative judgment in vv. 5–6 at the beginning connected to a similar theme in vv. 15–17, while Westermann, *Isaiah 40–66*, 417–24, puts vv. 6–16 together, identifying v. 17 as an independent unit that is a later expansion that has no connection to what comes before it or after it, and identifying vv. 18–24 as another late addition. Schramm, *The Opponents of Third Isaiah*, 171, rejects Westermann's conclusion about v. 17

[670] Westermann, *Isaiah 40–66*, 418, finds this same pattern in other texts (Deut 33) and before and after chaps. 60–62, but Blenkinsopp, *Isaiah 56–66*, 304, concludes that v. 6 and vv. 15–16 have little in common, so he finds a stronger connection between the fire in vv. 15–16 and vv. 22–24.

God comes in fire to judge	66:15–17
God's fire executes judgment	15–16
Syncretistic worship will end	17
God's glory will attract all nations	66:18–24
Bringing all nations to worship	18–21
Two contrasting destinies	22–24

There is a great diversity of opinions about these final verses. J. Blenkin-sopp believes 66:15–16 have nothing in common with 66:17 and that 66:18–21 have nothing in common with what precedes in 66:17.[671] In stark contrast, E. C. Webster has illustrated the numerous repetitions of vocabulary that demonstrate the concentric unity of each part of 66:15–24.[672] As the conclu-sion to the book of Isaiah, it is evident that there are some connections with the introductory themes in 1:29–31 and some connections with 56:1–8. W. A. M. Beuken believes 66:15–24 functions as a conclusion to Trito-Isaiah, Deutero-Isaiah, and the book as a whole based on its connection with 1:1–31; 40:1–11; and 56:1–8,[673] but the connection with 1:29–31 is probably the clearest.

66:15–16 This paragraph begins with *kî hinnēh*, literally, "Surely behold" (NIV "See"; cf. ESV "For behold"), which marks the introduction of some-thing that the reader should pay particular attention to. These verses expand on the transitional phrase in v. 14b, which predicts the coming of God's fury. A theophanic appearance of God "will come,"[674] accompanied by fire, a storm-like wind, and a chariot. The fire is typically observed whenever people are permitted to see a glimpse of God's glory (Exod 3:2; 14:24; 19:18; 24:17; Deut 5:22–25; Isa 29:6; 30:30; Ezek 1:27–28). The storm depicts the swirling thick clouds that are associated with God's appearance on earth (Exod 19:16; Deut 5:22; 33:26; Pss 18:9; 68:4; Isa 19:1; 29:6; 30:30), and the chariot is likely the vehicle that God rides on (19:1; Pss 18:12; 104:3; Jer 4:13; Ezek 1; Hab 3:8).

In v. 15b the purpose of God's glorious coming is explained. He will appear "in order to turn, return"[675] (NIV "bring down") his anger and his rebuke on

---

[671] Blenkinsopp, *Isaiah 56–66*, 307, 312. Sweeney, "Prophetic Exegesis in Isaiah 65–66," 455–73, makes 66:5–24 the last literary unit in Isaiah, but 66:15–24 is the last paragraph. Watts, *Isaiah 34–66*, 362, has 66:6–24 as the last unit.

[672] Webster, "The Rhetoric of Isaiah 63–65," 89–102, finds the repetition of "fire" in vv. 15–16, "all flesh/all nations" in vv. 16,18, "my glory" in vv. 18–19, "bring" in vv. 20–21, "new" and "be-fore me" in vv. 22–23, and "all flesh" in vv. 23–24.

[673] Beuken, "Isaiah Chapter LXV–LXVI: Trito-Isaiah and the Closure of the Book of Isaiah," 204–21, convincingly demonstrates that the theophany of God in 66:15–16 introduces this final paragraph.

[674] The imperfect verb יָבוֹא refers to incomplete action either (a) in the present, which is "con-tinued for a shorter or longer time," resulting in the translation "is coming" (NIV, GKC §107f), or (b) in the future "will come" (RSV, NASB, HCSB, GKC §107i).

[675] The use of the infinitive construct verb (לְהָשִׁיב) often introduces a purpose clause (GKC §107f).

those who deserve it. In Ps 78:38 the return of God's anger involved the restraining or withdrawing of his wrath, but in this context he will "repay, return, give back" what these sinful people deserve (Exod 31:34; Isa 59:18). In other passages God's strong arm (63:5) or feet (63:3) deliver God's wrath on others, but here his fury will reveal his anger and flames of fire will make known his rebuke (cf. 30:27–30).

In order to reemphasize the terrible fury of God's wrath, the prophet once again in v. 16 states that "surely, truly" (*kî*, NIV and others, "for") the fire that characterizes the outward presence of God's purifying holiness and his sword will execute his judgment on all flesh. Earlier Isaiah predicted that fire would destroy those who rejected the law of God (5:24), will destroy both the pomp of the proud Assyrian (10:16–17; 30:27–31) and the proud people of Babylon (47:14), and will consume all God's sinful enemies (26:11; 33:14). The power of God's sword will destroy those who resist and rebel (1:20), Leviathan (27:1), Assyria (31:8), all nations (34:5–6), and those who forsake the Lord and worship pagan gods (65:12). The reference to "all flesh" suggests that this message is describing a climactic final universal eschatological judgment. This is not just a punishment of one foreign nation that does not follow God. The exact meaning of "all flesh" is explained in the following discussion as every person (including Israelites) who has rebelled against God (66:17). "All flesh" does not include the millions from the nations and from Israel who will proclaim God's glory and come to his holy mountain to bow down before him (66:18–23). This must be referring to the Day of the Lord or the Day of God's Vengeance (2:6–22; 13:1–16; 24:1–23; 34:1–15; 63:1–6).

66:17 This divine judgment will not fall just on the distant pagan nations on the other side of the world. God's wrath will come on all idolaters who are involved in abominable ritual practices.[676] These practices are connected to activities of the Hebrew people that were condemned in 1:29; 65:35; 66:3, and it is possible that this is the same group that was described in 57:3–13a and 59:3–8. These practices do not follow the Hebrew traditions prescribed in Leviticus 11, so it is not surprising that God would call these things horrible abominations. God's evaluation of these pagan practices makes it very clear that these Hebrew people will be among the "all flesh" that God's sword and fire will annihilate.[677]

The people condemned are "those who sanctify themselves" and "those who purify themselves,"[678] a comment that reminds one of 65:3–5 where those

---

[676] Westermann, *Isaiah 40–66*, 422, claims that 66:17 "has no natural connection with what comes before or after," so he takes it as a later expansion of 65:3b–5,7. But certainly this verse fits with v. 16, for it defines which people in "all the earth" will suffer under God's judgment.

[677] P. A. Smith, *Rhetoric and Redaction in Trito-Isaiah*, 166, rightly views the purpose of these verses to be to put "God's judgment of his own people within the framework of a universal act of judgment. As has already been pointed out, 25:1–7 espouses the same ideology."

[678] Throughout this section participles have been used to describe these wicked people. These

worshipping in gardens and eating pigs flesh claimed that they were so holy that other people had to keep their distance. In one sense only God can make one holy (59:16–17,20–21), but on the other hand there were times when God called for the people to "sanctify themselves, consecrate themselves" in the sense of preparing themselves to meet God. In Exod 19:10–11,14–15,22 God required three days of purification and consecration so that the people would be ready to meet God at Mount Sinai. Similarly, God required a consecration of the people before they crossed the Jordan River with Joshua (Josh 3:2,5), and the prophet Samuel asked Jesse and his sons to consecrate themselves when he went to anoint the next king of Israel (1 Sam 16:5). Women also performed purification rituals after childbirth (Lev 12:1–7) as well as people with skin diseases (Lev 13:1–46) and mildew on their clothing (Lev 13:47–59). Everything and everyone had to be clean before they were prepared to reenter the temple grounds to worship God. Thus 66:17 is probably describing a consecration or purification ritual that took place at (or at the entrance to) pagan gardens where there were sacred altars and trees (1:29; 65:3).

Those involved with this ritual appear to be following "one"[679] in their midst (at the center was their leader). Numerous commentators have wondered if these practices have some connection to the detestable pagan worship under the temple in Ezek 8:6–18. This Ezekiel text describes the idolatrous carvings of unclean animals on the walls and the 70 elders of Israel involved in pagan worship with Jaazaniah in their midst. In addition, some women were mourning for the dead god Tammuz, and others were worshipping the sun.[680] There may be a limited connection between what the elders of Israel did under the temple and what the people did in their sacred gardens; at least both accounts identify Hebrews as being involved with abominable pagan worship in Israel. The ceremonies in these gardens and graves (65:3–4) involved the eating of pigs, rats, and other abominable foods (65:4b). These were outlawed as unclean in Lev 11:7,29, so this worship is a direct assault on everything that was sacred to God. Consequently, when God comes in the fire of his wrath, he

---

two participles (הַמִּתְקַדְּשִׁים and הַמִּטַּהֲרִים) function as part of the compound subject of the verb "will come." With the article prefix (GKC §116g,o), they can be translated as nouns or more likely as relative clauses ("those who purify themselves"). Both are *hithpa'el* reflexive verbs.

[679] The Hb. has אֶחָד "one," which is masc., but the oral tradition of the Qere and 1QIsᵃ have the fem. אַחַת "one," suggesting a female goddess (Asherah) or a priestess of Asherah. Many try to emend the text to clarify what it says, but since there is so much diversity among the versions, it is impossible to discover which reading is more original. For example J. A. Emerton, "Notes on Two Verses in Isaiah (26:16 and 66:17)," in *Prophecy: Festschrift für G. Fohrer,* ed. J. A. Emerton, BZAW 150 (Berlin: de Gruyter, 1980), 12–25, suggests that there was a partial error of vertical dittography from the line above.

[680] Blenkinsopp, *Isaiah 56–66,* 311–12, believes these two passages relate to similar worship, but he dates the practices in 66:17 to the Hellenistic period, not to a setting before the fall of Jerusalem in 587 BC, which was the sixth year of Ezekiel's exile (Ezek 8:1).

will stop all these practices and end the lives of these rebellious people.[681] To prevent any doubt about the authoritative nature of this prediction, the prophet adds the final trump card, "this is what the LORD says."

66:18–21 This new subparagraph drops the discussion of God's dealings with the wicked who worship pagan gods in order to address what will happen to those who proclaim God's glory and worship him. In some ways this raises a subject somewhat similar to 56:1–8, where God approved the authentic worship of foreigners and eunuchs who act justly and maintain their covenant relationship with God. Verse 18 begins this transition by announcing that God will appear in all his glory before the nations of this world. The following verses indicate that many nations that did not know about God will suddenly respond positively at this time.

The first half of v. 18a is difficult to interpret because "their actions and their thoughts" (*maḥĕšābâ*, NIV "imaginations") are not grammatically integrated into the rest of the sentence. The initial "I" (*ʾānōkî*) subject pronoun is often followed by a verb or participle, but in this case it is followed by "their actions and their thoughts"; thus a verb needs to be supplied. J. Blenkinsopp resolves this problem by transferring the phrase "their actions and their thoughts" to v. 17; thus, these two factors are added to the list of things that God will end.[682] The Old Greek translation solved this problem by adding the verb *epistamai*, "I know," producing "I know their deeds and their thoughts," while the Aramaic Targum refers to "their deeds being revealed before me." F. Delitzsch explains the elliptical phrase as "I (will punish) their deeds and their thoughts" and takes the participle "is coming" as an ellipsis for "the time is come."[683] But this makes v. 18 a negative continuation of v. 17, an unlikely resolution.

There is no obvious solution to these grammatical problems, but since v. 17 ends the negative pronouncements against the wicked with "says the LORD," it seems best to connect v. 18a to what follows and not to v. 17. Because of the elliptical nature of the grammar, a verb like "I know" or "I will reveal" needs to be supplied, but this should not be taken as a word of condemnation. Rather, it is God's knowledge of the hearts of the foreign nations (concerning their openness to responding to him) that partially explains why he will act at this time. A second elliptical comment reveals that "(the time) has come" for

---

[681] The word "together" (יַחְדָּו) must mean that both the pagan sacrifices and those offering pagan sacrifices will both come to an end.

[682] Blenkinsopp, *Isaiah 56–66*, 309–10, follows Duhm and concludes that these two words were misplaced and that they actually belong in 66:17. This leaves v. 18 as a simple straightforward positive statement: "I am coming to gather all the nations." A second problem is that the participle בָּאָה "am coming" is a fem. sg., indicating that "I" God is not the subject (NIV makes God the subject).

[683] Delitzsch, *Isaiah*, 508, rejects the idea of supplying "I know." By inserting "I will punish," v. 18 continues the thought of 66:15–17. This is thought to be the final battle against the nations mentioned in Zech 14. Koole, *Isaiah III, Volume 3: Isaiah 56–66*, 517, supplies אַגִּיד "I will reveal" based on the same construction in 57:12.

God to gather people from all nations and many different languages. The goal of God's new revelation of himself will be to cause all these foreign people to come to Zion and see God's glory (as in 60:2). This is not a new idea, for Gen 12:3 indicates that one of the results of calling Abram and his family was that through him all the nations of the earth would be blessed. Earlier traditions in Isaiah also refer to a day when many nations will stream to Zion to hear God teach (2:1–4); people from many nations will come to the Root of Jesse (11:10) and become servants of God's people (14:1–2). Egypt and Assyria will worship God (19:18–25). The Servant will be a light to the nations (42:6; 49:6). People from the ends of the earth will turn to God and be saved (45:22–25), and people from many foreign nations will bring their wealth to glorify Zion (60–62).

66:19 A partial explanation of how this will happen is provided in the next verses. The exact nature of God's "sign" (*'ôt*) is not explained, so it could be anything from something as simple as a rainbow in the sky (Gen 9:12) or a banner or standard to signal to the nations (11:12; 49:22; 62:10) or spectacular miracles like those performed when the Israelites came up out of Egypt (Exodus 7–11). It might be the miraculous defeat of Gog and Magog (Ezek 38:18–23; Joel 3:9–16), God's personal appearance on the Mount of Olives to save his people with a great earthquake (Zech 14:1–5) or some completely new divine act unparalleled in previous history.

God will send some of the "survivors"[684] within the nations to the remaining nations on the earth as witnesses to what has happened. They will declare "my glory" among the nations that have not heard about God (including the sign in v. 19a). This involves what might rightly be called the final worldwide missionary movement that will assure that all people on earth have heard and have had a chance to repent and worship God. One should assume that this list of nations represented a group of future nations; thus, this list should not be viewed as an exhaustive or definitive list. Some people will go to Tarshish in the west, and 60:9 indicates that ships from Tarshish will bring people and gold to Zion to honor God. The second name (*pûl*) is unknown, but several translations have *pûṭ*[685] (Gen 10:6; Jer 46:9; Ezek 27:10; 30:5; Nah 3:9), which is often identified as Libya (as in NIV). This is probably not Put (Libya) but may be the unknown future country of Pul. The third country of Lud (Gen 10:13,22; Jer 46:9; Ezek 30:5), which was famous for its archers, may refer to the Asia Minor country of Lydia.[686] The fourth country is Tubal

---

[684] The word פְּלֵיטִים "survivors, remnant, those who escape" often refers to Hebrew survivors of some destruction (4:2; 10:20), but here it refers to non-Israelites. Watts, *Isaiah 34–66*, 362, 365, leans toward the view that these are Hebrew believers in the Diaspora.

[685] The Old Greek has Φουδ, which probably represents a Hb. פוד, but the Aramaic Targum and 1QIsᵃ agree with the Masoretic tradition. Before one too quickly jumps to this well-known name, it should be remembered that usually when the Hb. פוט is found in Isaiah, the Old Greek translates it Λιβυες. Since it did not translate this word as Λιβυες, it is possible that they did not have the Hb. פוט in their text.

[686] First Kings 22:34 and Jer 46:9 also mention the archers of Lud (Lydia).

(Gen 10:2; Ezek 32:26; 38:2–3; 39:1) in Asia Minor, and the last country named is Javan (Gen 10:4; Zech 9:13; Dan 8:21; 10:20; 11:2), a reference to the early population of Greece. People will also spread the good news to unnamed areas in faraway islands and coastlands (probably outside the Mediterranean Sea). This list of nations may be a purposeful reference to the dividing of the nations in Genesis 10 (the sons of Ham, Shem, and Japheth) in order to suggest a reversing of the division of people into one people in this eschatological age. The goal is "to proclaim, reveal, announce" (from *nāgad*) the glory of God to these people who have not heard "a report of me"[687] and who have not seen God's glory demonstrated by his marvelous deeds. This may indicate that some will not see the sign that demonstrates God's glory in v. 19a. This evangelistic effort of proclaiming the good news will be undertaken in order to give all peoples an opportunity to respond and in order to accomplish God's plan to have people in his kingdom worshipping him from every tribe and every nation (Dan 7:14).

66:20–21 Because of these missionary efforts, "all nations will stream" (2:2) to God in Zion. Those who go out to the distant foreign nations will return to Jerusalem, bringing with them many people from all over the world (cf. 60:3–11). These foreign people, who will become fellow "brothers"[688] in the faith, are described as an "offering to Yahweh," a gift to God. This does not refer to the things these people will bring as their offering to God (60:5–9). These people themselves are gifts to God, fit for his use and enjoyment. This is somewhat parallel to the Israelite giving the Levites as a wave offering (Num 8:11,13,15; 18:11,13,15) and a gift to God.[689] These people will be brought to Jerusalem on every imaginable form of transportation (horses, chariots, wagons, mules, and camels).[690]

In v. 20b the bringing of foreign converts as a gift offering to God is compared to the Israelites bringing a gift offering in a clean vessel to the temple. The point of this comparison is not completely apparent. It seems somewhat odd for there to be a comparison between the clean vessels that the Israelites used to carry their offerings and the animals and wagons that will carry these foreigners. Therefore, it is more likely that the survivors who go to these foreign nations will bring the foreign converts and will offer these holy people to

---

[687] The word שִׁמְעִי "my hearing, my report" is a noun drawn from the root שָׁמַע "he heard." The NIV translates "my fame," which would be the content of the "report of me."

[688] אֲחֵיכֶם "your brothers" could be identified as Hebrews living among these foreign nations as Oswalt, *Isaiah 40–66*, 689 suggests, based on 11:10–16 and 60:1–22. So C. R. Seitz, "Isaiah 40–66," 549. Young, *Isaiah*, 3:534, believe this text is "speaking of the Gentile converts as *your brethren*."

[689] G. V. Smith, "Paul's Use of Ps 68:18 in Ephesians 4:8," *JETS* 18 (1975): 181–90, develops the analogy between the Levites in the book of Numbers and the "pastors/teachers," etc., who were seen as God's gift to the New Testament church.

[690] The fem. pl. noun כִּרְכָּרוֹת is found only in this passage, so its meaning is problematic and tenuous.

God just like the Israelites brought their offering of the Levites in Num 8.[691] Thus, these believing foreigners will no longer be considered unclean as 56:1–8 indicates, but they will be able to fully participate in the worship in God's holy temple. This indicates that the former Levitical distinction between clean and unclean will one day be removed because everyone and everything will be holy when God establishes his eschatological kingdom in Zion (60:21; 62:12; Zech 14:20–21).

66:21 At that time God will take some of these foreign people for himself so that they can serve as priests and Levites, just like he did originally when he took the Levites for himself in Numbers 8.[692] The main question in the interpretation of this thought is, To whom does "some of them" (mēhem)[693] refer? P. A. Smith concludes that these people who function as Levites and priests are taken from the Gentile nations, which seems a better interpretation than A. Rofé's view that these people are Hebrews from the Diaspora.[694] This act implies the total elimination of a distinction between Israelite and non-Israelite believers and the full participation of Gentile believers in God's new kingdom and the worship that will go on there. This was partially fulfilled with the acceptance of Gentiles as full-fledged believers in the New Testament era, but a fuller unity and oneness will be seen in the future. In many ways, the denominational, ethnic, and racial division within the church today should be an uncomfortable sign of just how far the modern church is from the ideals God has designed for his people.

66:22–24 The issues discussed in these verses are based on God's earlier promise to create a new heavens and a new earth in 65:17–24. These new words of assurance in v. 22 state that God is giving promises that are "truly, surely" (omitted in NIV) just as dependable as the "continued existence"[695] of the new heavens and the new earth. The promises in v. 22b are that "your name" and "your descendants" will continue to exist and serve God just as long as the new heavens and the new earth stand. The difficulty in interpreting this

---

[691] Emmerson, *Isaiah 56–66*, 106, rightly rejects Westermann's opposition to the interpretation of these verses as a missionary movement and concludes that Gentile nations are described as clean vessels.

[692] This connection may have been used by Paul in Eph 4:7–12 when he compared God's taking the Levites captive for himself and then giving them back as gifts to Israel (Num 8:18; Ps 68:18). This is analogous to what God did with the pastors, evangelists, and others who were God's gifts to the NT church. They, like the Levites and these people in Isa 66:21, became God's possessions and then were given back to serve God's people. G. V. Smith, "Paul's Use of Ps 68:18 in Ephesians 4:8," 181–90.

[693] This appears to be a partitive use of the preposition מִן and could be translated "some from among them" (GKC §119, n. 2).

[694] P. A. Smith, *Rhetoric and Redaction in Trito-Isaiah*, 168, believes these were Gentiles, while Rofé, "Isaiah 66:1–4: Judean Sects in the Persian Period as Viewed by Trito-Isaiah," 205–17, believes they were Jews.

[695] The participle עֹמְדִים "standing" refers to something that continues to stand, endures, or continues to exist.

promise is related to defining "your descendants." B. Schramm views this as a promise of reassurance to the Diaspora Israelites who may wonder about their place because of the influx of so many foreigners. Here God promises that they will not be ignored, forgotten, or replaced but will have an eternal place before God.[696] One could equally make the point that "your descendants" could refer to the descendants of the foreigners who come to Jerusalem, but this either-or approach seems very inappropriate and somewhat out of place at this time in God's kingdom. If the Israelites and foreigners are one people and individuals from both groups will serve as Levites, the wall of distinction between them has already been removed (65:17). Thus "your descendants" are more likely to be the spiritual descendants of both the Hebrews and these foreigners. These are the spiritual descendants of the Servant (53:10; 54:17), the ones who are repeatedly called "my servants" (65:8,9,13–15).

66:23   The unity and universality of this new people of God will be boldly displayed in their worship, for at this time the wicked will already be judged (66:15–17). The people who will come to worship and bow down before God will include millions upon millions (45:23–24; 60:3–11), absolutely everyone ("all flesh") that is alive on the earth at that time. Their worship will continue from New Moon to New Moon, from Sabbath to Sabbath (56:1–7), from feast to feast. The point is that these people will continually and repeatedly come before God to worship him with joy. This is why they are in God's kingdom; they will not forget to honor and glorify God as their forefathers sometimes were prone to do. Faithfulness, devotion, and honor will rise up as an offering of praise from the hearts of all God's servants. It is clear that the wall of sin that separated God from mankind is completely removed at this time and a wonderful mutual relationship of fellowship and worship has sprouted to solidify God's connection to his people.

66:24   The final verse contrasts the wonderful destiny of God's servants with the terrible destiny of those sinners who failed to trust God (66:15–17). Unfortunately, not all people on earth will enter into the kingdom God has prepared for those who love him. "Those who rebel"[697] against God and do abominable things (66:3,17) will face the sword and fire of God's judgment (66:15–16). It was clearly stated as early as 1:19–20 that people can choose to be obedient or they can choose to resist and rebel against God. The sword will devour those who refuse to love God. This fate may be the destiny of those who forsake God in any time period, but it will definitely be the eternal destiny of those who are unwilling to repent and turn to God before they die.

Verse 24 describes the horrible sight of decaying carcasses of the people whom God has judged in 66:15–16. This gruesome picture might have devel-

---

[696] Schramm, *Opponents of Third Isaiah*, 172–73, also takes your brothers in 66:19 to refer to Diaspora Israelites.

[697] The definite participle הַפֹּשְׁעִים "the ones who rebel" functions as an adjective that modifies men. It refers to someone who rejects the authority of another person.

oped out of the actual sight of the decomposing carcasses of the 185,000 Assyrian troops that were left to rot in the fields around Jerusalem when God defeated the army of Sennacherib (37:36). Later the prophet Jeremiah (7:30–33; 31:40) draws a similar scene, but this time it is associated with the decomposing dead bodies in the valley of Slaughter, where detestable human sacrifices were conducted in the Hinnom Valley. In both cases there were thousands of rebellious people who died and rotted in the field because they refused to trust God. Because there were so many bodies (185,000 Assyrian troops), the birds and the worms could feast on those that were unburied, so the only solution was to burn these bodies to remove the stench and prevent an outbreak of diseases. Such incidents, which the people saw and experienced, seem to provide some of the cultural backdrop for the idea that there is an eternal place of fire and decaying flesh for those who rebel against God.[698]

The servants of God will know "what has happened" to the wicked, but there is no morbid fascination with those who suffer God's severe judgment. The text does not say that the righteous will repeatedly watch these people suffer or laugh and mock them. Neither would the righteous Israelite of Isaiah's day go down to look at or mock the dead bodies of the children sacrificed to the pagan gods Baal or Molech in the valley of Ben-Hinnom, but they knew what had happened to those who rebelled against God and followed these pagan practices. Even today many churches have cemeteries beside them which function as a silent reminder that every individual needs to make the right choices before their end comes.

This final verse has the rhetorical effect of causing the readers, who may be enthralled with the glorious thoughts of being in the new earth where God will dwell among his servants, to focus their attention on the diametrically opposite destinies that God has prepared for the evil people on this earth. Every reader must decide what destiny is most desired: (a) the joy of living in the wonderful kingdom of God before the very presence of his glory or (b) enduring the sword, fire, and worm of God's judgment. The first choice comes with life-changing challenges and requires a complete commitment to trust God. Only those who love and serve God are able to enter his kingdom.

THEOLOGICAL IMPLICATIONS. The answer of God in chaps. 65–66 responds to the laments of those who were confused about the ways of God, and it addresses issues raised by people even today. Although some may wonder if God exists, he is not hiding or ignorant about what is happening on this earth. He is here and available to everyone (65:1), but he will not listen to the laments of the obstinate sinners who provoke God by living a life of rebellion against God (65:3–5; 66:3,17). But one day God will respond to these

---

[698] These ideas are used in Matt 25:41 and Mark 9:46,48 to describe the place where those who reject God will end up. It is the opposite of the kingdom of God. Watts, "Mark," *CNTOT*, 192–94, notes that this imagery of hell (gehenna) is common in Qumranic texts, Jewish apocalyptic texts, and rabbinic writings.

people in wrath and justly judge them for their sins (65:6–7; 66:15–25). Thus, it is essential for every person on earth to understand that God will not treat everyone the same; not everyone will end up in heaven for eternity. There will be a dramatic distinction between the destiny of God's servants (65:8–15) and those who forsake God and refuse to be God's servants (65:11–15). The reason is that God has reached out and called for all people to come to him, but some will foolishly not respond to God's call (65:12) and will choose to go their own way (66:3). They will not be humble and contrite and will not tremble at God's words, so God will not esteem them or treat them as his children (66:2). Their destiny is to face the sword and fire of God's judgment (66:15–16) and miss the glories of God's wonderful kingdom.

What will they miss? Isaiah 65:17–25 indicates that they will not be able to enjoy the new heavens and the new earth nor participate in the joyous celebrations there. They will not be blessed by God to enjoy the fruits of their labor or live in a place where all violence between people is gone (65:23–25). They will not delight in the abundance God will provide from all the nations of the world. They will also miss the great gathering of millions of people from all the nations that will come to worship God together in Jerusalem (66:18–23). They will miss the experience of dwelling in the presence of a loving Almighty God. Instead, their destiny will be far away from God and his people in a horrible place that can only be compared to that place where the fire and worm rule supreme forever and ever (66:24).

Bibliography

Achtemeier, E. *The Community and Message of Isaiah 56–66: A Theological Commentary*. Minneapolis: Augsburg, 1982.

Alexander, J. A. *The Prophecies of Isaiah*. Grand Rapids: Zondervan, 1953.

Allis, O. T. *The Unity of Isaiah*. Philadelphia: P&R, 1950.

Baltzer, K. *Deutero-Isaiah: A Commentary on Isaiah 40–55*. Minneapolis: Fortress, 2001.

———. "Liberation from Debt Slavery After the Exile in Second Isaiah and Nehemiah." Pages 477–84 in *Ancient Israelite Religion*. Edited by P. D. Miller Jr. et al. Philadelphia: Fortress, 1987.

Barré, M. L. "Textual and Rhetorical-Critical Observations on the Last Servant Song (Isaiah 52:13–53:12)." *CBQ* 62 (2000): 1–27.

———. "Fasting in Isa 58:1–12: A Reexamination." *BTB* 15 (1985): 94–97.

Barstad, H. M. "The Future of the 'Servant Songs': Some Reflections on the Relationship of Biblical Scholarship to Its Own Tradition." Pages 261–70 in *Language, Theology, and the Bible*. Edited by S. E. Balentine and J. Barton. Oxford: Clarendon Press, 1994.

———. "On the So-called Babylonian Literary Influence in Second Isaiah." *SJOT* 2 (1987): 90–110.

Beuken, W. A. M. *Jesaja, Deel II, III*. POT. Nijkerk: Callenbach, 1979, 1983.

———. "The Unity of the Book of Isaiah: Another Attempt at Bridging the Gorge Between Its Two Main Parts." Pages 50–62 in *Reading from Right to Left*. Edited by J. C. Exum and H. G. M. Williamson. JSOTSup 373. Sheffield: Sheffield Academic Press, 2003.

———. "Isaiah Chapters LXV-LXVI: Trito-Isaiah and the Closure of the Book of Isaiah." Pages 204–21 in *Congress Volume Leuven 1989*. Edited by J. Emerton. VTSup 43; Leiden: Brill, 1991.

———. "The Main Theme of Trito-Isaiah." *JSOT* 47 (1990): 67–87.

———. "Isa. 55,3–5: The Reinterpretation of David." *Bijdragen* 35 (1974): 49–64.

Blenkinsopp J. *Isaiah 40–55*. AB. New York: Doubleday, 2002.

———. *Isaiah 56–66*. AB. New York: Doubleday, 2003.

Brettler, M. Z. "Incompatible Metaphors for YHWH in Isaiah 40–66." *JSOT* 78 (1998): 97–120.

Broyles, C. C., and C. A. Evans, eds. *Writing and Reading the Scroll of Isaiah*. 2 vols. Leiden: Brill, 1997.

Brueggemann, W. *Isaiah 40–66*. WBComp. Louisville: Westminster John Knox, 1998.

———. "Unity and Dynamics in the Isaiah Tradition." *JSOT* 29 (1984): 89–107.

———. "Isaiah 55 and Deuteronomic Theology." *ZAW* 80 (1968): 191–203.

Carr, D. "Isaiah 40:1–11 in the Context of the Macrostructure of Second Isaiah." Pages 51–73 in *Discourse Analysis of Biblical Literature*. Edited by W. Bodine. Atlanta: Scholars Press, 1995.

———. "Reaching for Unity in Isaiah." *JSOT* 57 (1993): 61–80.

Carroll, R. P. *When Prophecy Failed: Reactions and Responses to Failure in the Old Testament Prophetic Tradition*. London: SCM, 1979.

———. "Blindness and the Vision Thing: Blindness and Insight in the Book of Isaiah." Pages 79–93 in *Writing and Reading the Scroll of Isaiah*. Edited by C. C. Boyles and C. A. Evans. Leiden: Brill, 1997.

Ceresko, A. R. "The Rhetorical Strategy of the Fourth Servant Song." *CBQ* 56 (1994): 42–55.

Childs, B. S. *Isaiah*. OTL. Louisville: Westminster/John Knox, 2001.

————. *The Struggle to Understand Isaiah as Christian Scripture*. Grand Rapids: Eerdmans, 2004.

Clements, R. E. "A Light to the Nations: A Central Theme of the Book of Isaiah." Pages 57–69 in *Forming Prophetic Literature*. Edited by J. W. Watts and P. R. House. JSOTSup 235. Sheffield: Sheffield Academic Press, 1996.

————. "The Unity of the Book of Isaiah." *Int* 36 (1982): 117–29.

Clifford, R. J. "Narrative and Lament in Isaiah 63:7–64:11." Pages 93–102 in *To Touch the Text*. Edited by M. P. Horgan and P. J. Kobelski. New York: Crossroad, 1989.

____. *Fair Spoken and Persuading. An Interpretation of Second Isaiah*. New York: Paulist, 1984.

————. "The Function of Idol Passages in Second Isaiah." *CBQ* 42 (1980): 450–64.

Clines, D. J. A. *I, He, We, and They: A Literary Approach to Isaiah 53*. JSOTSup 1. Sheffield: University of Sheffield, 1976.

Coggins, R. J. "Do We Still Need Deutero-Isaiah?" *JSOT* 81 (1998): 77–92.

Conrad, E. W. *Reading Isaiah*. Minneapolis: Fortress, 1991.

————. "The Community as King in Second Isaiah." Pages 99–111 in *Understanding the Word*. Edited by J. T. Butler et al. JSOTSup 37. Sheffield: JSOT Press, 1985.

————. "The 'Fear Not' Oracles in Second Isaiah." *VT* 34 (1984): 129–152.

Cross, F. M. "The Council of Yahweh in Second Isaiah." *JNES* 12 (1953): 274–78.

Davies, G. I. "The Destiny of the Nations in the Book of Isaiah." Pages 93–120 in *The Book of Isaiah: Le Livre D'Isaïe*, ed J. Vermeylen. Leuven: Peeters, 1989.

Delitzsch, F. *Commentary on the Old Testament, VII: Isaiah*. Translated by J. Martin. Grand Rapids: Eerdmans, 1973.

Duhm, B. *Das Buch Jesaja*. Göttingen: Vandenhoeck & Ruprecht, 1892.

Dumbrell, W. J. "The Role of the Servant in Isaiah 40–55." *RTR* 48 (1989): 105–13.

————. "The Purpose of the Book of Isaiah." *TynBul* 36 (1985): 111–28.

Elliger, K. *Die Einheit des Tritojesaja*. BWANT III/9. Stuttgart: Kohlhammer, 1928.

Emmerson, G. I. *Isaiah 56–66*. OTG. Sheiffield: JSOT, 1992.

Franke, C. "The Function of the Satiric Lament Over Babylon in Second Isaiah (XLVII)." *VT* 41 (1991): 408–18.

————. "The Function of the Oracles against Babylon in Isaiah 14 and 47." *SBL Seminar Papers* 32 (1993): 250–59.

Gelston, A. "The Missionary Method of Second Isaiah." *SJT* 18 (1965): 308–318.

————. "Knowledge, Humiliation or Suffering: A Lexical, Textual and Exegetical Problem in Isaiah 53." Pages 126–41 in *Of Prophets' Visions and the Wisdom of Sages*. Edited by H. A. McKay and D. Clines. Sheffield: Sheffield Academic, 1993.

Gitay, Y. *Prophecy and Persuasion: A Study of Isaiah 40–48*. FLT. Bonn: Linguistica Biblica, 1981.

Goldingay, J. *Isaiah*. NIBC. Peabody: Hendrickson, 2001.

————. *The Message of Isaiah 40–55: A Literary–Theological Commentary*. London: T&T Clark, 2005.

Goldingay, J., and D. Payne, *Isaiah 40–55*. I. II. ICC. London: T&T Clark, 2006.

Habel, N. "'He Who Stretches Out the Heavens.'" *CBQ* 34 (1972): 417–30.

Hanson, P. *The Dawn of Apocalyptic: The Historical and Sociological Roots of Jewish Apocalyptic Eschatology*. Philadelphia: Fortress, 1979.

Haran, M. "The Literary Structure and Chronological Framework of the Prophecies in Is. XL-XLVIII." Pages 127–55 in *Congress Volume: Bonn, 1962*. VTSSup 9. Leiden: Brill, 1963.

Jeppesen, K. "Mother Zion, Father Servant: A Reading of Isaiah 49–55." Pages 109–125 in *Of Prophets' Visions and the Wisdom of Sages*. Edited by H. A. McKay and D. Clines. Sheffield: Sheffield Academic Press, 1993.

Kaiser, W. C., Jr. "The Unfailing Kindness Promised to David: Isaiah 55.3." *JSOT* 45 (1989): 91–98.

Kaufmann, Y. *The Babylonian Captivity and Deutero-Isaiah*. New York: Union of American Hebrew Congregations, 1970.

Koole, J. L. *Isaiah III, Volume 1, Isaiah 40–48*. Netherlands: Pharos, 1997.

———. *Isaiah III, Volume 2, Isaiah 49–55*. Leuven: Peeters, 1998.

———. *Isaiah III, Volume 3, Isaiah 56–66*. Leuven: Peeters, 2001.

Laato, A. "The Composition of Isaiah 40–55." *JBL* 109 (1990): 207–28.

Liebriech, L. "The Composition of the Book of Isaiah." *JQR* 47 (1956–57): 126–27.

McKenzie, J. L. *Second Isaiah*. AB 20. Garden City: Doubleday, 1968.

Merrill, E. H. "The Literary Character of Isaiah 40–55: Survey of a Century of Studies on Isaiah 40–55," *BSac* 144 (1987): 24–43.

Melugin, R. F. "Israel and the Nations in Isaiah 40–55." Pages 249–64 in *Problems in Biblical Theology*. Edited by H. T. C. Sun and K. L. Eades. Grand Rapids: Eerdmans, 1997.

———. "The Servant, God's Call, and the Structure of Isaiah 40–48." *SBL Seminar Papers* (1991): 21–30.

———. *The Formation of Isaiah 40–55*. BZAW 141. Berlin: de Gruyter, 1976.

Mettinger, T. N. D. *A Farewell to the Servant Songs: A Critical Examination of an Exegetical Axiom*. Lund: Gleerup, 1983.

Miscall, P. D. *Reading Isaiah: Poetry and Vision*. Louisville: Westminster, 2001.

Motyer, J. A. *The Prophecy of Isaiah*. Leicester: IVP, 1993.

Muilenburg, J. "The Book of Isaiah: Chapters 40–66." Pages 381–773 in *IB*. Vol V. Nashville: Abingdon, 1956.

Murtonen, A. "Third Isaiah: Yes or No?" *Abr-Nahrain* 19 (1980–81): 20–42.

North, C. R. *The Suffering Servant in Deutero-Isaiah*. Oxford: Oxford University Press, 1948.

O'Connell, R. H. *Concentricity and Continuity: The Literary Structure of Isaiah*. Sheffield: Academic Press, 1994.

Oswalt, J. *The Book of Isaiah 40–66*. NICOT. Grand Rapids: Eerdmans, 1998.

Polan, G. J. *In the Way of Justice toward Salvation*. New York: Lang, 1986.

Raabe, P. R. "The Effect of Repetition in the Suffering Servant Song." *JBL* 103 (1984): 77–81.

Rendtorff, R. "The Book of Isaiah: A Complex Unity. Synchronic and Diachronic Reading." *SBL Seminar Papers* 30 (1991): 8–20.

Rofé, A. "Isaiah 66:1–4: Judean Sects in the Persian Period as Viewed by Trito-Isaiah." Pages 205–218 in *Biblical and Related Studies Presented to Samuel Iwry*, Edited by A. Kort and S. Morschauser. Winona Lake: Eisenbrauns, 1985.

Rowley, H. H. *The Servant of the Lord and Other Essays on the Old Testament*. Oxford: Basil Blackwell, 1965.

Schoors, A. *I Am God Your Savior: A Form-Critical Study of the Main Genres in Is XL–LV*. VTSup 24. Leiden: Brill, 1973.

Schramm, B. *The Opponents of Third Isaiah: Reconstructing the Cultic History of the Restoration*. Sheffield: Sheffield Academic Press, 1995.

Seitz, C. "How Is the Prophet Isaiah Present in the Latter Half of the Book? The Logic of Chapters 40–66." *JBL* 115 (1996): 219–40.

———. "Isaiah 40–66," *NIB*: 6. Nashville: Abingdon, 2001.

———. "The Divine Council: Temporal Transition and New Prophecy in the Book of Isaiah." *JBL* 109 (1990): 229–47.

———. "Isaiah 1–66: Making Sense of the Whole." Pages 105–26 in *Reading and Preaching the Book of Isaiah*. Edited by C. Seitz. Philadelphia: Fortress, 1988.

Smart, J. D. *History and Theology in Second Isaiah*. Philadelphia: Westminster, 1965.

Smith, G. V. *An Introduction to the Hebrew Prophets: The Prophets as Preachers*. Nashville: Broadman and Holman, 1994.

———. *Isaiah 1–39*. NAC. Nashville: B&H, 2007.

———. "The Concept of God/the gods as King in the Ancient Near East and the Bible." *TJ*3 (1982): 18–38.

Spykerboer, H. C. *The Structure and Composition of Deutero-Isaiah with Special Reference to the Polemic Against Idolatry*. Meppel: Krips, 1976.

Sweeney, M. "The Book of Isaiah in Recent Research." *Currents in Research: Biblical Studies* 1 (1993): 141–62.

Torrey, C. C. *The Second Isaiah: A New Interpretation*. New York: Scribner's, 1928.

Van Ruiten, J. T. "The Intertextual Relationship between Isaiah 65.25 and Isaiah 11.6–9." Pages 31–42 in *The Scriptures and the Scrolls: Fs A. S. van der Woude*. Edited by F. G. Martinez, et al. VTSup 49. Leiden: Brill,1992.

Van Winkle, D. W. "The Relationship of the Nations to Yahweh and Israel in Isaiah XL–LV." *VT* 35 (1985): 446–58.

Vermeylen, J. "L'unité du livre d'Isaïe." Pages 11–53 in *The Book of Isaiah: Le Livre D'Isaïe*. Edited by J. Vermeylen. Leuven: University Press, 1989.

Watts, J. D. W. *Isaiah 34–66*. WBC. Waco: Word, 1987.

Webster, E. C. "The Rhetoric of Isaiah 63–65." *JSOT* 47 (1990): 89–102.

———. A Rhetorical Study of Isaiah 66," *JSOT* 34 (1986): 93–108.

Westermann, C. *Isaiah 40–66*. OTL. Philadelphia: Westminster, 1969.

Whybray, R. N. *Second Isaiah*. OTG. Sheffield: Sheffield Academic Press, 1983.

———. *Thanksgiving for a Liberated Prophet: An Interpretation of Isaiah 53*. JSOTSup 4. Sheffield: JSOT, 1978.

Wilcox, P., and D. Paton-Williams. "The Servant Songs in Deutero-Isaiah." *JSOT* 42 (1988): 79–102.

Williamson, W. A. M. *The Book Called Isaiah: Deutero-Isaiah's Role in Composition and Redaction*. Oxford: Clarendon Press, 1994.

———. "First and Last Isaiah." Pages 95–108 in *Of Prophets' Visions and the Wisdom of Sages*. Edited by H. A. McKay and D. J. A. Clines. JSOTSup 162; Sheffield: Sheffield Academic Press, 1993.

Young, E. J. *The Book of Isaiah*. 3 vols. Grand Rapids: Eerdmans, 1965–72.

Selected Subject Index

Person Index

Selected Scripture Index